THE ANNALS
OF
AMERICA

THE ANNALS OF AMERICA

Volume 21
1977–1986

Opportunities and Problems
At Home and Abroad

ENCYCLOPÆDIA BRITANNICA, INC.

Chicago London New Delhi Paris Sydney Taipei Tokyo Seoul

The editors wish to express their gratitude for permission to reprint material from the following sources:

America Press, Inc., for Selection 102B. Reprinted with permission of America Press, Inc., 106 West 56th Street, New York NY 10019. © 1984. All rights reserved.

The American Bar Association for Selection 40. Reprinted from the Tort and Insurance Practice Section of the American Bar Association's *Forum,* Fall 1981. Copyright 1981 by the American Bar Assocation. Reprinted by permission.

American Enterprise Institute for Selection 46. Copyright American Enterprise Institute. Reprinted by permission.

American Heritage for Selection 14. © 1978 American Heritage Publishing Co., Inc., *Horizon,* January 1978. Reprinted by permission.

The American Legion Magazine for Selection 11. Reprinted by permission, The American Legion Magazine, Copyright 1978.

The American Psychological Association for Selection 23. REPRINTED WITH PERMISSION FROM PSYCHOLOGY TODAY MAGAZINE. Copyright © 1978 American Psychological Association. Also for Selections 110 and 117. REPRINTED WITH PERMISSION FROM PSYCHOLOGY TODAY MAGAZINE. Copyright © 1985 American Psychological Association.

American Scientist for Selection 38. Reprinted by permission.

The American Society for Public Administration for Selection 17A. Reprinted with permission from *Public Administration Review* © 1978 by The American Society for Public Administration, 1120 G Street, N.W., Suite 500, Washington, D.C. All rights reserved.

Mr. David C. Anderson for Selection 65. Reprinted by permission.

Mr. Orville Bach for Selection 32. Copyright 1980 by Times Mirror Magazines, Inc. Reprinted by permission.

Bantam Books, Inc., for Selection 29. Reprinted from IACOCCA: AN AUTOBIOGRAPHY, by Lee Iacocca and William Novak. Copyright © 1984 by Lee Iacocca. By permission of Bantam Books, Inc. All rights reserved.

Basic Books, Inc., for Selection 50. Adapted from WEALTH AND POVERTY by George Gilder. Copyright © 1980 by George Gilder. Reprinted by permission of Basic Books, Inc., Publishers.

Mr. Daniel J. Boorstin for Selection 106. "Myths of a Scientific Society," in *Science Digest,* December 1984. Copyright 1984 by Daniel J. Boorstin, author of *The Discoverers.*

Bulletin of the Atomic Scientists for Selection 67. Reprinted by permission of the BULLETIN OF THE ATOMIC SCIENTISTS, a magazine of science and world affairs. Copyright © 1982 by the Educational Foundation for Nuclear Science, Chicago, IL 60637.

Dr. Arthur F. Burns for Selection 18A. Reprinted by permission.

Business Week for Selection 37. Reprinted from Feb. 11, 1980, issue of *BusinessWeek* by special permission. © 1980 by McGraw-Hill, Inc.

The Center for the Study of Democratic Institutions for Selection 17B. Excerpted from "Proposition 13—The California Model of the Taxpayers' Revolt: The Constitutional Attack." Reprinted with permission of *The Center Magazine,* a publication of the Center for the Study of Democratic Institutions.

Christianity and Crisis for Selection 79. Reprinted with permission, copyright *Christianity and Crisis* May 2, 1983. 537 West 121st Street, New York, NY 10027.

City News Publishing Co. for Selection 26A. Reprinted by permission of *Vital Speeches of the Day,* Vol. XLVI No. 3, Nov. 15, 1979, p. 83. Also for Selection 27A. Reprinted by permission of *Vital Speeches of the Day,* Vol. XLV No. 10, March 1, 1979, p. 326. Also for Selection

Contents

1979–1981

1980

1985

OPPORTUNITIES AND PROBLEMS AT HOME AND ABROAD

In Pictures

Introduction

Jimmy Carter of Georgia, the first Southerner to be elected President since the Civil War, was sworn in as the 39th President of the United States on January 20, 1977. The occasion was auspicious: the divisive Nixon years, together with the Ford epilogue, had passed, and the country could now look forward to a new era. When Jimmy Carter stepped down from the podium, took his wife Rosalynn's hand, and started to walk up Pennsylvania Avenue toward the White House, there was a real sense of newness and, perhaps, of hope. Unfortunately, however, a large portion of the public deemed Carter's inaugural speech uninspiring. It was the first of many disappointments in a presidency that saw an intelligent, humane man ground down by events and by his own bad luck, which was compounded of an uncertain sense of timing and perhaps a lack of confidence in his own ability to lead. He shared his deepest concerns with his fellow citizens and spoke, in a famous speech, of a "miasma" at the heart of the nation. Maybe it was there, but surely it was in his own heart, and so in the eyes of many he failed to lead the nation, and his presidency ended up a broken one, like those of Kennedy, Johnson, Nixon, and Ford before him.

Carter was not without triumphs. The Israeli-Egyptian peace treaty was one; the initiation of diplomatic relations with China was another; the signing of SALT II after a meeting with Brezhnev in Vienna was a third. But even during those early years he could not handle the national economy. He never found a way to deal with inflation, nor could he solve the energy problem. It was a foreign debacle that will be the longest-remembered episode of his presidency. On November 4, 1979, radical students in Tehran, Iran—demanding the extradition of the deposed shah of Iran, who was being treated at a U.S. hospital—took more than 50 Americans hostage at the U.S. embassy. For the remaining 442 days of his term of office Carter did hardly anything else but try to free them. He finally succeeded, after many humiliations, on the very day his successor was inaugurated.

The man who replaced him in the White House could not have been more different. Smooth, a great communicator, a former actor and superb salesman, Ronald Reagan may have had a less complicated mind than Jimmy Carter's but had vastly greater confidence in the rightness of what he believed. His confidence was catching; by Election Day of 1980 his coattails were long enough to sweep a Republican majority into the Senate for the first time in a generation, and even in the House, where the Democrats retained control, Reagan had a majority on many issues.

His program for the country had four main aims. He wanted to reduce taxes. He wanted to make America's defenses strong again. He wanted to decentralize government as well as reduce its impact on the lives of citizens. And he wanted to bring about a social and moral revolution in thinking by reversing a long-term trend, as he conceived it, toward libertinism, irreligion, and a failure of patriotism. He did reduce taxes and control inflation, but these achievements did not produce a surge in the economy. As a consequence, the large increase in defense expenditures brought about the most massive deficits in the country's history. His plan for a "new federalism" never got off the ground, but he was successful in bringing about a new emphasis on patriotism and a sexual counterrevolution after the openness of the 1960s and '70s.

Reagan's record in foreign affairs was also a compound of successes and failures. He seemed to view the world in a bifurcated way, with "good guys" on one side and "bad guys" on the other. This left him little room for compromise and negotiation, for example, with the Soviet Union, which he persisted in calling an "Evil Empire" throughout his first term. At the end of six years in office the Communist world probably feared the United States more than it had in 1980, and perhaps respected it more, as well. Reagan's refusal to give an inch on such matters as his Star Wars initiative at Reykjavik in October 1986 was seen by the Soviets, and most of the nonaligned nations of the earth, as fundamentally destabilizing. Though a few years later, his hard-nosed stance would be cited as a major factor in the demise of the Soviet Union and the end of the Cold War.

The left-leaning Sandinista government of Nicaragua was another of Reagan's bad guys, and he admitted more than once that he would consider himself justified in removing it, even if by force. Though he was a vocal proponent of the anti-Sandinista rebel group known as the Contras, the Boland Amendment of 1984 restricted him from providing U.S. military aid to the Contras. When it came to light in late 1986, however, that government officials had violated this very law, Reagan's style of government came under severe criticism. The secret sale of U.S. arms to Iran and the covert diversion of these proceeds to fund the Contras became known as the Iran-Contra Affair, and it bedeviled Reagan during the closing years of his two-term administration.

Chronology: 1977–1986

1977

January. Bitter cold temperatures plus raging blizzard deplete nation's supply of natural gas.

Jan. 1. Having officially sanctioned ordination of women in 1976, Episcopal Church ordains first woman priest in Indianapolis.

Jan. 4. Congress convenes and Senate chooses new leaders: Robert C. Byrd of W. Va. as majority leader and Howard H. Baker, Jr., of Tenn. as minority leader.

Pres.-elect Carter announces new conflict-of-interest guidelines.

Jan. 9. Oakland Raiders beat Minnesota Vikings 32–14 in Super Bowl XI.

Jan. 12. Pres. Ford delivers final State of the Union address, warns that "constant buildup" of Soviet military might is a threat to U.S.

Jan. 17. Convicted murderer Gary Mark Gilmore is executed by firing squad at Utah State Prison; he is first person to be executed in U.S. in nearly 10 years.

Theodore C. Sorensen, ex-Kennedy aide, withdraws name from consideration as head of CIA in face of growing congressional opposition.

Jan. 18. Centers for Disease Control in Atlanta announces discovery of cause of Legionnaire's Disease.

Jan. 19. In one of his last official acts, Pres. Ford pardons Iva Toguri D'Aquino, known during World War II as "Tokyo Rose."

Jan. 20. Jimmy Carter is sworn in as 39th President of U.S.

Jan. 26. U.S. publicly rebukes Czechoslovakia on human rights violations of 1975 Helsinki accords.

Jan. 27. Pres. Carter reasserts intention to press issue of human rights worldwide. **Feb. 24.** U.S. announces it will reduce foreign aid to countries guilty of human rights violations.

Feb. 1. NBC announces it will broadcast 1980 Olympic Games from Moscow. Agreement involves more than $100 million.

Feb. 7. Citizens of West Berlin send

$225,000 in aid for cold-stricken towns in U.S. Gesture is in memory of help given by Americans in time of need.

Feb. 9. Figures indicate Alex Haley's *Roots* is most-watched TV show in history; 130,000,000 saw program, aired Jan. 23–30.

Mar. 2. House votes stringent code of ethics for itself. **Apr. 1.** Senate does likewise.

Mar. 5. In unprecedented two-hour radio broadcast Pres. Carter accepts telephone calls from and discusses concerns with 42 callers in 26 states.

Mar. 9. Food and Drug Admin. announces ban on saccharin.

Members of Hanafi Muslim sect seize control of B'nai B'rith headquarters and two other buildings in Washington, DC; one person is killed and a score are injured. **Mar. 11.** Twelve gunmen give up and release 134 hostages.

Mar. 17. Pres. Carter addresses UN, calls on all nations to advance cause of human rights.

Apr. 7. Andrew Young, U.S. ambassador to UN, apologizes to British for having called them "a little chicken" on racial matters during Apr. 5 TV interview.

Apr. 9. U.S. seizes Soviet trawler for fishing violations. Vessel's owners and captain are heavily fined.

Apr. 20. Pres. Carter presents new energy plan for U.S. to Congress.

Apr. 28. HEW Sec. Joseph Califano

signs regulations outlawing discrimination against handicapped.

May 4. Former Pres. Richard M. Nixon, interviewed on TV, admits he "let the American people down."

May 6. Labor Dept. announces that unemployment has dropped to 7 percent, lowest figure since Dec. 1974.

May 11. Government agencies announce ban on spray cans using chlorofluorocarbons, to take effect in two years; chemical is said to destroy ozone layer.

May 16. Pan Am helicoptor crashes on top of Pan Am building at height of evening rush hour in New York City; five die.

June 5. Government scandal involving influence peddling by South Korean agents and businessmen is revealed in Washington, DC.

June 6. Supreme Court rules that states may not make death penalty mandatory for convicted killers of police officers without taking into account mitigating circumstances.

June 12. First lady Rosalynn Carter concludes successful two-week diplomatic tour of Latin America.

June 20. First oil from Alaska's North Slope begins flowing into trans-Alaska pipeline. **July 29.** Oil reaches tankers at Valdez, is shipped to refineries.

June 26. Gays march to protest discrimination in many U.S. cities.

June 30. Dept. of Transportation mandates air bags or automatic lap and shoulder belts in all cars by 1984. Order is later rescinded.

Pres. Carter drops program to produce B-1 strategic bomber.

July 13. Massive power failures plunge Westchester County and New York City into total darkness at 9:34 PM; losses from looting and vandalism are estimated at $1 billion.

July 20. Mind-control experiments by CIA during 1950s and '60s are revealed; controversy ensues.

Aug. 4. Pres. Carter signs into being new Cabinet-level Department of Energy.

Carter urges action on illegal aliens in U.S.

Aug. 10. Negotiators announce agreement in principle on accord to turn over control of Panama Canal to Panama; political battle begins in U.S.

Sept. 7. Wisconsin judge is ousted by irate voters who refuse to accept his notion that rape is "normal male" response to provocative female dress.

Sept. 16. Dissident Episcopalians, in protest against ordination of women priests, announce formation of independent body to be named Anglican Church in North America.

Sept. 21. Carter budget director Bert Lance, a long-time friend and supporter, resigns after controversy about his personal finances.

Sept. 23. Landings of supersonic Concorde planes allowed at selected U.S. airports.

Oct. 18. New York Yankees beat Los Angeles Dodgers to win World Series four games to two; Reggie Jackson hits three consecutive home runs, each on first pitch, in last game.

Nov. 1. U.S. formally cancels membership in International Labor Organization.

Pres. Carter signs law raising minimum wage from $2.30 to $2.65 an hour starting Jan. 1, 1978.

Nov. 15. Pres. Carter welcomes Shah of Iran at White House; demonstrators for and against Shah clash nearby.

Nov. 21. National Women's Conference convenes in Houston.

Dec. 10. Farmers drive trucks and tractors into Washington, DC, and 30 state capitals to focus attention on financial troubles.

Dec. 20. Pres. Carter signs new Social Security tax bill that, it is hoped, will put program on sound financial basis for next 50 years. Contributions will rise markedly over the years.

Dec. 28. Pres. Carter names G. William Miller new head of Federal Reserve Board, replacing Arthur F. Burns.

1978

Jan. 4. U.S. announces plan to shore up dollar, weakened by high trade deficit. Similar efforts continue throughout year, but without success.

Jan. 6. U.S. returns to Hungary jeweled crown of St. Stephen, symbol of Hungarian nationhood. Gesture is indication of improved relations between U.S. and Hungary.

Jan. 15. Dallas Cowboys win Super Bowl XII, beating Denver Broncos, 27–10.

Jan. 24. Pieces of Cosmos 954, a Soviet satellite, land in northwestern Canada; some fragments are found to be highly radioactive.

Feb. 6–7. Worst snowstorm since 1948 batters northeast; Boston has 27 inches, most in its history.

Feb. 18. Ireland's prime minister, John Lynch, urges "Irish people abroad, especially in the U.S.," to stop supporting terrorist organizations in Northern Ireland.

Mar. 15. Coal strike involving 160,000 miners ends on 100th day.

Mar. 16. Senate by narrow margin approves first Panama Canal treaty; second treaty is approved Apr. 18.

Mar. 17. Worst oil spill in history occurs when U.S.-owned *Amoco Cadiz* breaks in half off coast of Brittany.

Mar. 22. Berkey Photo wins record $112.8 million judgment from Eastman Kodak, which is said to have monopolized amateur photo business.

Mar. 27. Pres. Carter proposes massive urban aid program; it is criticized by several mayors for being inadequate.

Apr. 6. Pres. Carter signs into law bill raising mandatory retirement age from 65 to 70. This provision of the law will take effect on Jan. 1, 1979.

Apr. 7. Pres. Carter defers production of controversial neutron bomb for later decision.

Apr. 10. Three former high officials of FBI are indicted for approving illegal break-ins and searches aimed against Weathermen radicals in 1972–73.

Apr. 13–26. Nearly 432,000,000 shares are traded on N.Y. Stock Exchange over ten-day period; 63.5 million are traded on Apr. 17, an all-time record. Dow Jones average rises 62 points to 810.12.

Apr. 24. Carter approval rating drops to 39 percent, nine points down from March; analysts credit change to dissatisfaction with Carter's handling of economy.

Apr. 27. Scaffolding inside utility company cooling tower in W. Va. collapses, hurling 51 workers 170 feet to their death.

May 15. Senate approves sale of jet fighters to Saudi Arabia and Egypt after Pres. Carter demands that sales be made to balance sales to Israel.

May 20. FBI agents arrest two Soviet citizens in N.Y. as spies. **Oct. 30.** The purported UN employees are sentenced to 50 years in prison.

May 26. Legalized casino gambling begins in Atlantic City, NJ.

June 6. California voters overwhelmingly endorse state constitutional amendment (Proposition 13) to reduce property taxes by half.

June 22. House votes to cut off aid to South Korea until it cooperates with investigation of influence-peddling scandal.

U.S. Nazi party calls off march in Skokie, predominantly Jewish suburb of Chicago where many survivors of death camps reside.

June 28. Supreme Court ruling in Bakke *v.* California requires U. of California to admit Bakke to medical school but upholds principle of affirmative action.

Two U.S. reporters in Moscow are summoned to court and accused of publishing "slanderous information" about the Soviet Union. USSR closes case after withdrawing demands on Aug. 18.

July 10. U.S. court of appeals in Denver upholds right of terminally ill cancer patients to use controversial drug Laetrile.

July 13. Congress approves massive financial aid program for New York City.

July 28. Bureau of Labor Statistics reveals that inflation was at 11.4 percent level for second quarter.

Aug. 1. Washington, DC, grand jury indicts seven for auto-bombing murder of former Chilean foreign minister Orlando Letelier, an outspoken critic of Chilean dictator Pinochet.

Congress approves end of four-year-old Turkish arms embargo.

Aug. 15. Grand jury in Washington, DC, indicts high officials of Church of Scientology, charging conspiracy to steal government documents.

Aug. 17. Three Americans complete first successful balloon flight over Atlantic in Double Eagle II.

Sept. 17. Camp David meeting ends in triumphant success for Pres. Carter, who worked with Israeli Prime Minister Begin and Egyptian Pres. Sadat to bring about peace in Middle East.

Sept. 25. Total of 150 persons are killed when two planes collide over San Diego.

Sept. 29. First indictments are handed down in far-ranging investigation of corrupt practices involving General Services Admin.

U.S. and Colombia agree to cooperate to combat drug trading.

Oct. 6. Senate extends deadline for ratification of Equal Rights Amendment from Mar. 22, 1979, to June 30, 1982.

Oct. 17. New York Yankees win fourth game in a row after losing first two to defeat Los Angeles Dodgers in World Series.

Oct. 20. Wall Street ends worst week in its history with 59-point drop in Dow Jones average. **Oct. 24.** Pres. Carter proposes anti-inflation measures in TV speech. Market rebounds in following days.

Nov. 6. New York newspaper strike ends after 88 days.

Nov. 18. Murder of Congressman Leo J. Ryan in Guyana triggers mass suicides and murders at Jonestown.

Dec. 15. U.S. and China simultaneously

announce establishment of full diplomatic relations to start Jan. 1, 1979.

Dec. 17. OPEC announces increase in benchmark oil price from $12.70 to $14.54 a barrel.

Dec. 27–30. Revolutionary crisis in Iran reaches acute stage; analysts conclude that Shah will probably not be able to retain control of country.

Dec. 31. Investigation of John Wayne Gacy, suspected mass murderer of teenaged boys, continues when 26 bodies are found buried beneath his house. **Mar. 12. 1980.** Gacy is found guilty of killing 33.

1979

Jan. 1. People's Republic of China and U.S. formally establish full diplomatic relations; U.S. simultaneously severs relations with Chinese Nationalist government in Taiwan.

Jan. 16. Faced with revolutionary turmoil, Shah of Iran flees to Egypt.

Jan. 17. Vernon E. Jordan, Jr., head of National Urban League, announces that African Americans are "on verge of disaster" owing to a predicted U.S. recession.

Jan. 19. John Mitchell, former Attorney General, is last Watergate prisoner to leave prison; 25 men served prison terms in affair.

Jan. 21. Pittsburgh Steelers win Super Bowl XIII (their third championship), beating Dallas Cowboys 35–31.

Jan. 24. Bureau of Labor Statistics reports inflation rate of 9 percent for 1978. **Jan. 30.** Record trade deficit for year of $28.5 billion is announced by Dept. of Commerce.

Jan. 28. Chinese leader Deng Xiao-ping is warmly received in Washington, DC, at start of nine-day visit.

Jan. 30. Embattled Prime Minister Bakhtiar of Iran agrees to permit Ayatollah Khomeini to return from exile; it is common knowledge that Khomeini has been directing revolution from abroad. **Feb. 11.** Khomeini supporters oust Bakhtiar who flees country.

Feb. 8. Carter administration announces withdrawal of support for Nicaraguan dictator Somoza in hope that he will be forced to negotiate with Sandinista rebels.

Feb. 14. Adolph Dubs, U.S. ambassador to Afghanistan, is shot and killed after being kidnapped by Muslim extremists in Kabul.

Mar. 5. Voyager 1 spacecraft comes within 175,000 mi. of Jupiter and relays information about planet and its moons.

Mar. 26. Egyptian Pres. Sadat and Israeli Prime Minister Begin sign formal peace treaty on White House lawn, ending 30 years of intermittent warfare.

Mar. 28. Major nuclear accident occurs at Three Mile Island nuclear power plant near Harrisburg, PA. **Mar. 30.** Nuclear Regulatory Commission warns that meltdown of reactor core is a possibility.

Apr. 5. Pres. Carter announces he will decontrol domestic oil prices in two stages, 80% on June 1 and the other 20% one year later.

Apr. 10. House subcommittee makes public documents showing that seepage of toxic chemicals at Love Canal region in Niagara Falls, NY, has been secretly known since 1958.

Apr. 18. Actor Lee Marvin is required by Los Angeles court to pay $104,000 "palimony" to woman with whom he has lived for six years.

Apr. 27. U.S. exchanges two Soviet spies convicted Oct. 1978 for five leading Soviet dissidents.

May 6. Over 65,000 persons march in Washington, DC, to protest against nuclear power.

May 9. U.S. announces that, after seven years of negotiations, new draft treaty limiting strategic arms (SALT II) has been signed by U.S. and Soviet representatives. **June 18.** SALT II is signed by Pres. Carter and Soviet Pres. Brezhnev at Vienna ceremony; treaty is subject to ratification by U.S. Senate.

May 21. 5,000 gays protest voluntary manslaughter verdict for killer of San Francisco Mayor George Moscone and Supervisor Harvey Milk on Nov. 17, 1978.

May 25. In worst air disaster in U.S. history 274 persons are killed in crash of DC-10 on takeoff from Chicago's O'Hare Airport. **May 29.** FAA grounds all DC-10s; ban is lifted on July 13.

June 7. Pres. Carter approves development of new mobile intercontinental (MX) missile.

June 12. English Channel is crossed for first time by man-powered flying machine, a device pedaled by American Bryan Allen; flight covers 25 mi.

June 26. House passes first bill funding large-scale production of synthetic fuels.

June 28. Pres. Carter announces that U.S. will accept 14,000 Indochinese refugees a month for 12 months, twice current quota.

June 29. OPEC raises oil price to $18–$23.50 a barrel; Western nations meeting in Tokyo agree to try to limit oil imports.

July 10. Senate defeats proposed constitutional amendment to end Electoral College and allow direct election of President.

July 11. U.S. space station Skylab enters atmosphere and disintegrates over Australia and Indian ocean during its 34,981st orbit since it was launched in 1973.

July 15. Pres. Carter announces new energy plan in TV speech.

July 17. Pres. Somoza of Nicaragua resigns and flees country; leftist Sandinistas take over.

July 20. Pres. Carter ends planned withdrawal of U.S. troops from South Korea; 32,000 troops will remain for at least two years to combat "steady growth" of Soviet military power.

Aug. 15. Andrew Young resigns post as ambassador to UN after latest in long list of controversial statements and actions.

Aug. 23. Aleksandr Gudonov, principal dancer wtih Bolshoi Ballet, defects to U.S. during Bolshoi's New York engagement; his wife elects to return to Soviet Union.

Sept. 1. Unmanned spacecraft Pioneer 11 transmits photos of rings of Saturn in flyby of planet.

Sept. 8. Actress Jean Seberg commits suicide. **Sept. 14.** FBI admits it slandered Seberg in 1970 for political reasons, causing deep depression.

Sept. 12. House votes down resolution that would have required all 18-year-olds to register for a possible draft.

Oct. 3. Dept. of Agriculture announces that USSR will be allowed to buy record quantities of U.S. grain during next year.

Oct. 7. Pope John Paul II completes visit to U.S. with vast outdoor mass in Washington, DC.

Oct. 10. Rockefeller University announces successful genetic repair in a defective cell.

Oct. 12. During first visit to U.S. in 19 years, Cuban president Fidel Castro addresses UN, castigates U.S. as chief cause of many world problems.

Oct. 17. Pittsburgh Pirates triumph in World Series by beating Baltimore Orioles, four games to three; Pirates win last three games.

Oct. 22. Deposed Shah of Iran arrives in U.S. for medical tests.

Oct. 26. South Korean Pres. Park Chung Hee is assassinated by head of Korean CIA.

Nov. 1. U.S. announces $1.5 billion federal loan guarantee plan for ailing Chrysler Corp.

Nov. 4. Iranian militants seize U.S. embassy in Teheran, take some 90 persons hostage.

Nov. 24. Pentagon admits that thousands of U.S. troops in Vietnam were sprayed with Agent Orange, a carcinogenic herbicide.

Dec. 3. Eleven youths are killed in stampede at rock concert in Cincinnati.

Puerto Rican terrorists assault U.S. Navy bus near San Juan; two are killed and 10 injured.

Dec. 4. UN Security Council unanimously demands release of hostages in Iran; Iran refuses.

Dec. 15. World Court condemns Iran for holding of hostages. Deposed Shah leaves U.S. for Panama.

Dec. 27. Soviet Union invades Afghanistan; president is executed.

1980

Jan. 4. Pres. Carter announces embargo of grain sales to USSR; he cites Soviet attack on Afghanistan.

Jan. 14. Surgeon General announces that lung cancer among women is increasing dramatically due to their increased cigarette smoking.

Jan. 20. Pittsburgh Steelers win Super Bowl XIV by beating Los Angeles Rams, 31–19.

Jan. 23. In his State of the Union address Pres. Carter warns USSR that any attempt to gain control of Persian Gulf area will be resisted; declaration extends Monroe Doctrine to region.

Jan. 25. Labor Dept. reports 1979 inflation of 13.3 percent; highest level in 33 years.

Jan. 28. Canadian diplomats in Teheran help six U.S. diplomats to escape; Canada then closes its Iran embassy.

Feb. 2. First news of so-called ABSCAM investigation by FBI is announced on NBC.

Feb. 4. Census Bureau estimates that some six million illegal aliens are in U.S. Number, though large, is one half previous estimates.

Feb. 28. Dept. of Transportation announces that all 1979 foreign and most domestic cars have failed stringent safety crash tests.

Mar. 1. U.S. casts first vote ever against Israel in Security Council. **Mar. 3.** Pres. Carter admits that vote was cast in error.

Mar. 5. Pakistan refuses U.S. offer of aid, complaining that aid package of "only" $400 million is too small.

Mar. 13. Ford Motor Co. is acquitted by jury in Winamac, IN, in case involving death of three girls in a Ford Pinto.

Mar. 17. Pres. Carter signs 1980 Refugee Act, which extends definition of refugees to include persons from every part of the world.

Mar. 27. Mt. St. Helens, in southwestern Washington, erupts for first time since 1857. **May 18.** Violent new eruption kills at least 34 persons.

Price of silver plummets, threatening financial empire of wealthy Hunt family of Texas.

Apr. 2. Most banks increase prime lending rate to record 20 percent.

Apr. 4. Police in Evanston, IL, arrest 11 members of FALN, terrorist group advocating independence of Puerto Rico. Indictments later charge them with score of bombings.

Apr. 7. U.S. severs diplomatic relations with Iran, which is still holding 53 Americans as hostages.

Apr. 13. Four small boats carrying 326 Haitians arrive in Florida, largest total for a day yet recorded. 30,000 Haitians are estimated to have arrived in past two years.

Apr. 17. Pres. Carter concedes that a "short recession" has probably begun. Some analysts are more gloomy.

Apr. 22. U.S. Olympic Committee backs ban on U.S. participation in upcoming Moscow Olympics.

Apr. 25. Carter administration issues bulletin conceding that attempt to rescue Iranian hostages has failed with loss of lives of eight servicemen. **Apr. 28.** Secretary of State Cyrus R. Vance resigns in protest.

May 5. Rep. Robert Drinan, D.-Mass., the only priest in Congress, is forbidden to seek reelection, reportedly by papal order.

Flow of Cuban refugees increases when Pres. Carter states that U.S. will accept all "with open arms." By June 3 number of arrivals exceeds 100,000; violence erupts in holding camps.

May 8. Benigno Aquino, noted Marcos opponent, is released from Philippine prison and allowed to fly to U.S. for heart operation; he says he expects to return in three weeks.

May 17. Racial riots erupt in Miami after all-white jury acquits four policemen of murder in fatal beating of young black insurance executive.

June 3. Series of seven tornadoes strike Grand Island, NE, killing three, injuring 200.

June 30. Supreme Court, in 5–4 decision, limits use of Medicaid funds for abortion except in cases of rape or incest or where life of woman is threatened.

July 11. Iran releases Richard I. Queen, one of hostages, for medical reasons, found later to be multiple sclerosis.

July 14. Pres. Carter's brother Billy registers as foreign agent of Libya, admits receiving large loan from Libyan sources.

July 14–17. Ronald Reagan and George Bush nominated for President and Vice-President in Republican convention in Detroit. **Aug. 11–14.** Democrats renominate Jimmy Carter and Walter Mondale in New York City.

July 16. Pres. Carter orders $7 million in relief for areas of south-central U.S. hit by weeks of above-100° temperatures.

July 19. Summer Olympic Games open in Moscow; 65 nations, including U.S., do not attend.

July 24. American Petroleum Inst. announces 14 percent drop in oil imports.

Aug. 2. Two-week period in which all males born in 1960–61 must register for draft ends with 93 percent compliance, according to Selective Service System; antidraft groups dispute claim, citing wide noncompliance.

Aug. 20. U.S. reveals that it is developing so-called Stealth aircraft, designed to be invisible to radar.

Aug. 31. Rep. Michael O. Meyers, D.-Penn., and three co-defendants become first persons to be convicted in ABSCAM investigation.

Sept. 4. Saudi Arabia nationalizes remaining 40 percent of Aramco, vast oil company originally owned by four U.S. oil companies.

Sept. 17. Leaders of Poland's new independent labor unions meet to form national federation, which registers under name Solidarity. **Oct. 24.** Group gains legal status.

Sept. 19. Fuel explosion at underground Titan 2 nuclear missile silo in Arkansas kills one, injures 21, and hurls nuclear warhead 750 feet. Reports say there is no other damage.

Sept. 30. U.S. sends four radar command planes to Saudi Arabia to protect against Iranian attacks.

Oct. 17. Economic reports indicate that recession is over.

Oct. 21. Philadelphia Phillies win World Series, defeating Kansas City Royals, four games to two.

Oct. 23. U.S. screen and TV actors end 94-day strike.

Nov. 4. Reagan swamps Carter in U.S. presidential election; Republicans take Senate for first time since 1956, but Democrats retain control of House.

Nov. 12. Congress approves measure converting 104 million acres of Alaska to national parks and conservation areas.

Voyager I flies past Saturn, sends back much information and dramatic photos of Saturn's rings.

Dec. 2. U.S., EEC, and NATO all warn USSR against invasion of Poland.

Dec. 8. John Lennon shot down by Mark David Chapman, former mental patient, outside New York City home.

Dec. 19. Most banks raise their prime rate to 21.5 percent, the all-time high.

Dec. 31. Census Bureau announces first figures on 1980 census, indicating total population of 226,504,825—11.4 percent over 1970 figure.

1981

Jan. 7. Figures published by auto in-dustry show that 1980 car sales fell 20 percent below 1979, making 1980 worst year since 1961. Major U.S. auto companies lost more than $4 billion in year; 300,000 workers were laid off.

Jan. 8. National Centers for Disease Control announces that outbreaks of in-fluenza are found all over the country, with epidemics in several areas.

Jan. 20. Ronald Reagan is sworn in as 40th President. At 69, he is the oldest person ever to assume the office.

After 444 days of captivity, 52 U.S. hostages are allowed to leave Iran on Algerian plane. They are flown to Wiesbaden, W. Germany, for debriefing, and arrive in New York Jan. 25.

Jan. 23. Bureau of Labor Statistics re-veals that 1980 inflation was 12.4 percent, for second consecutive year of double-digit rate.

Jan. 25. Oakland Raiders win Super Bowl XV, defeating Philadelphia Eagles 27–10.

Jan. 26. Supreme Court rules that states may permit TV coverage of criminal trials.

Feb. 2. Secretary of Education T.H. Bell rescinds proposed plan to require public schools to teach foreign-speaking pupils in their native language.

Feb. 5. Pres. Reagan, in first televised address from White House, calls for support of his new economic program.

Jury of Marine Corps officers convicts Pfc. Robert R. Garwood of collaborat-ing with the enemy and assaulting a fellow soldier while he was prisoner of war in Vietnam.

Feb. 17. Reagan administration proposes aid to anti-leftist forces in El Salvador.

Feb. 18. Reagan administration announces that it will "faithfully implement" agreements leading to release of Iran hostages. **July 2.** Supreme Court holds that Presidents Carter and Reagan had legal authority for agreements.

Mar. 1. British Prime Minister Margaret Thatcher ends visit to U.S. She says she is "impressed with striking similarity" between her policies and those of Reagan administration.

Mar. 5. Atlanta receives nearly $1 million in federal funds to help counter terror caused by series of child murders over past 19 months.

Mar. 16. Los Angeles Board of Education votes to end mandatory busing intended to achieve racial integration.

Mar. 19. Reports show that drug use among high school students has peaked but that one-third of students are problem drinkers.

Mar. 22. Cost of postage for first-class letter advances from 15 to 18 cents.

Mar. 30. Pres. Reagan is shot in chest by lone gunman outside Washington, DC, hotel; others are also wounded. John W. Hinckley, Jr., is immediately apprehended and identified as assailant.

Apr. 7. Justice Dept. announces that one-third of nation's households were victimized by crime in 1980.

Apr. 12. U.S. launches first space shuttle, *Columbia*, from Cape Canaveral, FL. Construction of *Columbia* took three years longer than expected and cost $9.9 billion.

Apr. 20. U.S. accepts full responsibility and agrees to indemnify Japan for accidental sinking of *Nissho Maru* by U.S. submarine.

Apr. 24. Pres. Reagan lifts embargo on grain sales to USSR.

May 1. Japan offers to limit auto exports to U.S. during next three years; proposal is made in response to threat of import quotas.

May 6. U.S. orders Libya to close its diplomatic mission in Washington, DC, citing "general pattern of unacceptable conduct."

May 13. Pope John Paul II is shot and seriously injured as he rides in open car through St. Peter's Square in Rome. Lone gunman is immediately seized.

June 12. U.S. baseball players strike, halting major league season.

June 16. U.S. announces that it is now willing to sell certain weapons to People's Republic of China.

June 21. Wayne B. Williams is arrested in Atlanta and charged with latest in series of murders of children and young adults that have terrorized city.

June 25. Supreme Court rules that armed forces may draft only males.

June 29. UMW coal strike is settled after a three-month dispute that cost miners about $710 million in lost wages.

July 10. Secretary of Agriculture warns California farmers that their produce may be quarantined if their efforts to control devastating infestation of Mediterranean fruit fly are not more effective.

July 16. House subcommittee announces its opposition to UNESCO plan for a "new world information order" that would include the licensing of journalists.

Aug. 3. Professional Air Traffic Controllers Organization (PATCO) goes on strike across U.S. Administration fires all controllers who do not return to work and controls air traffic with substitutes and supervisory personnel.

Aug. 10. Secretary of Defense announces that U.S. is producing neutron bombs.

Aug. 19. U.S. fighters shoot down two Libyan planes that attacked U.S. aircraft 60 mi. from Libyan coastline.

Aug. 25. Voyager 2 transmits more spectacular information about and photos of Saturn in flyby.

Sept. 15. Pakistan officially accepts six-year, $3.2 billion U.S. aid package that includes both economic assistance and military credits.

Sept. 19. Estimated 250,000 persons attend union-supported rally in Washington, DC, to protest government cutbacks in social programs.

Sept. 25. Sandra Day O'Connor is sworn in as first woman member of Supreme

Court. Senate has unanimously approved her appointment.

Sept. 29. U.S. federal debt ceiling is raised to above $1 trillion.

Oct. 6. Egyptian Pres. Sadat is assassinated during military parade in Cairo.

Oct. 22. PATCO union is decertified by National Labor Board.

Oct. 28. Senate gives Pres. Reagan major foreign policy victory in approving sales of AWACS surveillance planes to Saudi Arabia.

Los Angeles Dodgers defeat New York Yankees in World Series, four games to two.

Nov. 10. U.S. claims USSR used chemical warfare in Asia; holds that reported "yellow rain" was in fact toxic chemicals.

Nov. 14. Space shuttle *Columbia* completes shortened second flight.

Dec. 2. White House reports that Libyan-trained assassination squads have arrived in U.S.

Dec. 4. Pres. Reagan signs executive order broadening power of CIA to investigate Americans.

Dec. 7. Reagan administration reveals that federal deficit will climb to $109 billion in 1982, $152 billion in 1983 and $162 billion in 1984 because of deepening recession.

Dec. 29. Pres. Reagan announces sanctions against USSR because "it bears a heavy and direct responsibility for the repression in Poland."

1982

Jan. 7. Pres. Reagan issues statement reversing his preelection opposition to registration of 18-year-olds for possible future draft.

Jan. 8. American Telephone & Telegraph Co. agrees to give up 22 Bell System companies in order to settle antitrust suit brought against it by Justice Dept. AT&T would no longer provide local service but could expand into data processing, computers, etc.

Jan. 13. Plane crashes into 14th St. bridge on takeoff from Washington National Airport at height of rush hour and in snow storm; 78 die.

Jan. 22. Labor Dept. announces that inflation for 1981 was 8.9 percent, lowest level since 1977.

Jan. 24. San Francisco 49ers win Super Bowl XVI, defeating Cincinnati Bengals 26–21.

Jan. 28. U.S. Brig. Gen. James L. Dozier, abducted in Italy previous Dec. 17, is rescued from Red Brigade kidnappers by Italian antiterrorist forces in carefully planned raid.

Jan. 29. U.S. notifies nine commercial banks that it will cover $71 million of debts, guaranteed by U.S. government, that Poland cannot pay.

Feb. 19. De Lorean Motor Co., of Belfast, founded by former U.S. auto maker, goes into receivership despite intensive efforts by Northern Ireland government to keep it afloat.

Feb. 24. Pres. Reagan warns that "new Cubas will arise from the ruins of today's conflicts" if nothing is done to prevent it.

Feb. 27. Wayne B. Williams is convicted in Atlanta of murdering two of 28 black children and young adults killed over two-year period; he is sentenced to two life terms.

Mar. 2. Senate passes bill that virtually ends school busing for racial integration.

Great Britain announces decrease in oil price to $31 per barrel; price had reached height of $38 a year before.

Mar. 10. U.S. places embargo on import of Libyan oil.

Mar. 11. Sen. Harrison Williams, D-N.J., resigns after ABSCAM conviction when Senate threatens expulsion.

Mar. 23. Pres. Reagan announces plan to revitalize urban areas by encouraging investment in "enterprise zones."

Apr. 26. Immigration and Naturalization Service begins roundup of illegal aliens in many U.S. cities. Several groups protest action because, they say, it appears to be racist.

Apr. 30. Law of the Sea treaty discussions end; most nations approve treaty, but U.S. is one of four that refuses to sign.

May 4. Washington trial of John Hinckley, Jr., for shooting Pres. Reagan in 1981 starts. **June 21.** Jury finds Hinckley not guilty by reason of insanity; verdict occasions wide controversy.

May 13. Braniff becomes first major

U.S. airline to file for reorganization under Ch. 11 of federal Bankruptcy Act.

June 1. Supreme Court rules that police may search closed containers in autos without warrants; ruling expands 1925 decision.

June 3. Congress passes bill prohibiting identification of current U.S. intelligence agents.

June 12. Massive parade and peace rally numbering as many as 1,000,000 persons is held in New York City.

June 15. Supreme Court rules in 5–4 vote that illegal aliens must have access to free education.

June 18. Congress extends 1965 Voting Rights Act for additional 25 years.

June 22. Dept. of Justice charges 18 Japanese with conspiring to steal industrial secrets from IBM.

June 25. Alexander Haig resigns as secretary of state; he is replaced by George P. Shultz.

June 30. Efforts to pass Equal Rights Amendment end in failure when only 35 states approve it. ERA is reintroduced in Congress in July.

July 2. Supreme Court, 9–0, upholds ban on use of children in pornographic pictures. Court also upholds, 8–0, right of organizations to boycott businesses to promote equal rights.

July 5. Penn Square Bank of Oklahoma fails because of huge losses on bad oil loans, amid warnings that other banks will be in serious trouble.

July 16. Sun Myung Moon, founder of Unification Church, is sentenced to 18 months in prison for tax fraud.

Aug. 9. White House confirms that Reagan administration will not submit "new federalism plan" to Congress until 1983 owing to opposition from many state governors.

Aug. 19. Congress passes $98 billion increase in tax revenues that Pres. Reagan calls "80% tax reform" rather than largest tax increase in history.

Sept. 9. Congress overrides Reagan veto of $14.1 billion supplemental appropriations bill that President had called "budget-buster."

Sept. 15. Philippine Pres. Ferdinand Marcos arrives in U.S. for official state visit, despite protests because of bad human rights record.

Sept. 21. National Football League players go on strike, halting NFL season. **Nov. 16.** Strike is settled.

Oct. 2. Seventh victim of Extra-Strength Tylenol capsules filled with cyanide dies in Chicago area; epidemic of such poisonings continues during month. **Nov. 4.** U.S. regulations requiring tamper-proof packaging of over-the-counter drugs are announced.

Oct. 7. New York Stock Exchange sets one-day record when 147,070,000 shares are traded; analysts cite lower interest rates. **Oct. 8.** Discount rate is lowered to 9.5 percent, lowest level since 1978.

Oct. 20. St. Louis Cardinals narrowly defeat Milwaukee Brewers in World Series by a score of four games to three.

Nov. 2. Republicans retain 54–46 majority in Senate but suffer moderate loss of 26 seats to Democrats in House in mid-term elections; Democrats also increase governorships to 34.

Nov. 5. Labor Dept. announces that unemployment has reached 10.4 percent, highest rate since 1940, indicating deep recession.

Nov. 10. Soviet leader Leonid Brezhnev dies of heart attack; he is replaced by Yuri V. Andropov, ex-head of KGB.

Nov. 13. Monument dedicated to memory of 57,939 killed or missing in Vietnam War is dedicated in Washington, DC; memorial contains names of all those killed.

Pres. Reagan lifts controversial ban on use of U.S. technology in Soviet Siberian-European pipeline.

Nov. 16. After four test missions shuttle *Columbia* completes first operational flight with crew of four men.

Dec. 2. Barney B. Clark, retired dentist, receives world's first permanent artificial heart in surgery in Salt Lake City.

Dec. 7. In major setback for Pres. Reagan, House rejects request for $988 million to build and deploy first five MX missiles.

1983

January. Government economic figures confirm weakness of economy in previous year.

Jan. 13. After week of unsuccessful negotiations U.S. announces freeze on textile exports from China. Amid angry responses, China retaliates with comparable decreases in U.S. exports.

Jan. 23. Washington Redskins take Super Bowl XVII, beating Miami Dolphins, 27–17.

Feb. 2. Soviet and U.S. negotiators resume strategic arms reduction talks (START) in Geneva.

Feb. 8. Hitachi, Ltd., leading Japanese electronics firm, pleads guilty to conspiracy to obtain classified IBM computer information.

Feb. 18. Edwin P. Wilson, ex-CIA agent, is sentenced to prison and heavily fined for illegally exporting explosives to Libya.

Feb. 22. U.S. offers to buy all homes and businesses in Times Beach, MO, because of high level of dioxin in soil; cost is estimated at $33 million.

Mar. 9. Anne M. Burford resigns as head of Environmental Protection Agency after series of conflicts with Congress.

Mar. 21. Barney Clark, first recipient of artificial heart, dies after 112 days.

Mar. 23. Pres. Reagan delivers TV address to nation in which he proposes construction of a U.S. strategic defensive system based on concept of an impervious defense against nuclear attack. Project is soon dubbed "Star Wars." Analysts note that it would replace doctrine of mutual and assured destruction (MAD) with one of mutual and assured survival (MAS). However, many scientists question whether such a system is technically possible.

Mar. 25. Pres. Reagan signs legislation designed to provide about 350,000 new jobs as a recession continues.

Mar. 31. Roy L. Williams, president of International Brotherhood of Teamsters, is sentenced to 55 years in prison for fraud and conspiracy.

Apr. 4. China is angered when U.S. gives political asylum to top Chinese tennis player, Hu Na.

Apr. 9. Space shuttle *Challenger* lands in California at end of successful maiden voyage.

Apr. 12. Chicago elects Harold Washington as first black mayor in election marked by racism.

Apr. 18. U.S. embassy in Beirut is destroyed by car bomb; among 63 fatalities 17 are Americans.

Apr. 20. Pres. Reagan signs Social Security reform bill that increases Social Security taxes and trims benefits. Measure is designed to insure long term solvency of program.

Apr. 27. In address to joint session of Congress Pres. Reagan calls for more aid to Central America to avert crisis there.

May 2. Senate gives MX missile tentative approval in return for promise by Pres. Reagan that he will be more flexible in arms negotiations.

May 4. House approves watered-down endorsement of a "mutual and verifi-

able freeze and reductions in nuclear weapons."

May 9. U.S. cuts Nicaraguan sugar quota to put economic pressure on Sandinista government.

May 24. Supreme Court holds that Internal Revenue Service can deny tax exemption to private schools that practice racial discrimination.

U.S. government declares that lethal disease acquired immune deficiency syndrome (AIDS) is the nation's top medical priority.

June 13. Unmanned spacecraft Pioneer 10 crosses orbit of Neptune and thus becomes first man-made vehicle to leave solar system.

June 15. Supreme Court issues three decisions that limit power of state and local governments to restrict access to legal abortions. **June 28.** Senate votes down anti-abortion amendment to Constitution.

June 16. U.S. agrees to pay $20,000 each to surviving Japanese-Americans detained in camps during World War II, as "act of national apology."

June 18. Pres. Reagan reappoints Paul Volcker chairman of Federal Reserve Board.

June 23. Supreme Court overturns so-called legislative veto in far-reaching decision.

June 24. Shuttle Challenger lands in California after near perfect mission; crew includes Sally K. Ride, first U.S. woman in space.

July 15. Despite widespread protests in Greece U.S. negotiates extension of its Greek military facilities for five years.

August. Statistics show that August is hottest month ever for U.S. as a whole, with major crop losses in Middle West. **December.** Cold wave sweeps across U.S. for two weeks starting Dec. 17, with many records broken.

Aug. 11. Series of computer raids throughout U.S. is traced to group of young men in Milwaukee.

Aug. 16. U.S. admits that it protected Klaus Barbie, notorious head of Nazi Gestapo unit during World War II, as paid spy beginning in 1947. U.S. sends formal apology to France for having interfered with capture of "Butcher of Lyons."

Aug. 21. Benigno Aquino, outspoken critic of Marcos regime, is shot and killed minutes after returning to Manila following three-year U.S. exile.

Aug. 27. Crowd of more than 250,-000 gathers in Washington, DC, to commemorate 1963 march climaxed by memorable "I Have a Dream" speech by Rev. Martin Luther King, Jr.

Sept. 1. Soviets shoot down unarmed South Korean airliner that has strayed off course and breached Soviet airspace. All 269 persons aboard are killed, including 61 Americans.

Sept. 29. Pres. Reagan cancels scheduled trip to Manila in wake of Aquino assassination, which it is felt may have been organized by Marcos regime.

Oct. 16. Baltimore Orioles defeat Philadelphia Phillies in World Series, four games to one.

Oct. 19. Senate votes to honor slain black civil rights leader Dr. Martin Luther King, Jr., with annual federal holiday on his birthday, Jan. 15, 1929. Holiday will first be celebrated on the third Monday in January, 1986.

Oct. 22. An estimated two million persons demonstrate across Europe to protest planned deployment of U.S. Pershing II and cruise missiles.

Oct. 23. Car bombs kill hundreds of U.S. and French servicemen in military installations in Beirut. **Dec. 28.** Defense Dept. releases report stating that attack was "preventable." Pres. Reagan accepts responsibility.

Oct. 25. Seven-nation assault force headed by U.S. Marines and Army Rangers begins predawn invasion of Caribbean nation of Grenada. **Oct. 27.** Pres. Reagan says that invasion took place just in time to prevent Grenada from becoming "Soviet-Cuban colony."

Dec. 15. Reagan administration decides that friendly nations in need of U.S. arms may procure them in the future "without draining their reserves"—that is, without payment.

Dec. 22. Joint General Motors and Toyota auto manufacturing plant in California is approved by Federal Trade Commission.

Dec. 29. U.S. announces that it will terminate membership in UNESCO by end of 1984; statement emphasizes that dissatisfaction does not extend to UN itself.

1984

January. Government figures released during month show strong resurgence of economy during 1983; forecasts for 1984 are hopeful.

Jan. 1. Divestiture of AT&T takes effect as company is broken up along lines decided by federal judge.

Jan. 3. Syria releases captured U.S. Navy pilot after personal appeal by Rev. Jesse Jackson to Syrian president.

Jan. 12. Panel headed by J.P. Grace, chairman of W.R. Grace & Co., reports that imposition of more "businesslike" government operations could save $425 billion over three years. Many proposals would be politically unacceptable, however.

Jan. 19. U.S. lifts some sanctions on Poland, noting "general improvement in conditions."

Jan. 22. Los Angeles Raiders win Superbowl XVIII, beating Washington Redskins 38-9.

Feb. 1. Pres. Reagan submits budget to Congress including huge increase in military spending and $180 billion deficit. Major debate ensues.

Feb. 7. Lebanese army is routed in West Beirut by Shi'ite and Druze militiamen. Pres. Reagan announces redeployment offshore of U.S. troops.

Feb. 9. Yuri Andropov dies in Moscow; he is replaced Feb. 13 by 72-year-old Konstantin U. Chernenko.

Mar. 5. Supreme Court rules that public financing of a Nativity scene does not in itself violate First Amendment separation of Church and State.

Mar. 20. Soviet tanker hits mine off Puerto Sandino, Nicaragua. USSR charges U.S. with complicity in mining harbor; CIA concedes this in April. **Apr. 10.** Congress repudiates U.S. role in mining ports.

Apr. 7. Japan agrees to increase U.S. imports of beef and citrus products.

Apr. 10. Crew of space shuttle *Challenger* repairs orbiting satellite in complex maneuver.

Apr. 19. Federal judge in Chicago rules that Standard Oil Co. (Indiana) is totally responsible for damage caused by breakup of *Amoco Cadiz* off France in 1978.

May 1. Pres. Reagan concludes six-day visit to China during which TV broadcasts of his speeches omit remarks extolling personal freedom, capitalism, and religious faith.

May 8. USSR announces it will not compete in 1984 Los Angeles Olympic Games, claiming that U.S. does not plan adequate security.

May 10. Rumors of financial difficulties start run on assets of Continental Illinois Bank, one of nation's 10 largest. **May 17.** Federal aid package of $1.5 billion is announced. **July 26.** U.S. bank regulators say U.S. will buy most of bank's "problem" loans for total aid of $4.5 billion.

World Court rules that U.S. should cease from mining Nicaraguan ports.

May 24. El Salvador jury finds five former members of country's National Guard guilty of murdering three U.S. nuns and a female lay assistant.

House votes $62 million in emergency aid for El Salvador but turns down aid for Nicaraguan contras.

May 28. Eleven years after end of Vietnam War, unidentified U.S. casualty from war is buried at Tomb of Unknown Soldier in Arlington National Cemetery.

June 2. Pres. Reagan, during trip to Ireland, visits ancestral family home at Ballyporeen.

June 12. Supreme Court rules that lower courts may not set aside bona fide seniority systems to preserve jobs of minority workers hired under affirmative action programs.

June 27. After intercession by Rev. Jesse Jackson, Cuba releases 22 American prisoners held on drug charges. Action is step toward normalization of relations between Cuba and U.S.

July 16. Democratic Convention opens in San Francisco, nominates Walter Mondale for President and for Vice-President, Geraldine Ferraro, first woman nominated for post.

July 18. Deranged gunman kills 21 persons in and near McDonald's restaurant in San Ysidro, CA, before being shot by police.

July 28. Olympic Games open in Los Angeles. In absence of Soviet Union and other Eastern bloc countries U.S. dominates games, winning 83 gold medals.

Games turn out to be financial success also as crowds throng stadiums, millions watch on TV.

Aug. 3. Record Wall Street week closes with highest volume of trading ever— 236,570,000 shares on Friday alone— and rise of 87 points on Dow Jones index.

U.S. responds to political amnesty announced July 21 in Poland by lifting more of sanctions it had imposed when Solidarity leaders were arrested in December 1981.

Aug. 16. Former automaker John De Lorean is acquitted in Los Angeles on drug charges.

Aug. 22. Ronald Reagan and George Bush renominated by Republicans in Dallas. **Aug. 23.** Reagan injects religion as issue into campaign in talk at prayer breakfast.

Sept. 7. Mexico announces that, after six weeks of negotiations, its major creditor banks (all U.S. institutions) have agreed to reschedule debts amounting to $48.5 billion.

Sept. 10. House approves compromise legislation providing for stronger health warnings on cigarette packages. Senate approves bill Sept. 26.

Sept. 20. Car loaded with 385 lb of TNT is driven through hail of bullets and explodes in front of U.S. embassy annex in East Beirut. Fourteen persons are killed in third car-bomb attack on a U.S. compound in 17 months.

Sept. 28. Pres. Reagan and Soviet Foreign Minister Andrei Gromyko engage in "forceful and direct" discussions in White House.

Sept. 29. In joint U.S.-Italian investigation, hundreds of Mafia suspects are arrested in two countries.

Oct. 2. For first time in history FBI agent is arrested and charged with espionage. Richard W. Miller admits in questioning turning over documents to Soviet agents.

Oct. 17. Democratic Congressmen reveal they are investigating controversial CIA manual distributed to anti-Sandinista contras in Nicaragua. Manual seems to authorize political kidnappings and assassinations. **Nov. 10.** White House admits "lapses in judgment" but denies violation of laws.

Oct. 20. Detroit Tigers complete World Series rout of San Diego Padres, four games to one.

Oct. 26. In historic operation at Loma Linda Medical Center in California, "Baby Fae" (otherwise not identified) is given baboon heart. **Nov. 15.** Baby Fae dies after rejecting heart.

Nov. 2. Margie Barfield, convicted murderer, is executed in Raleigh, NC. She is first woman to be executed in 22 years.

Nov. 6. Reagan swamps Mondale in national election with record 525 electoral votes; Mondale takes only his own state, Minnesota, and District of Columbia. Republicans retain Senate.

Nov. 28. Sen. Robert Dole of Kansas is elected new majority leader of Senate, replacing retiring Howard Baker of Tennessee.

Dec. 3. Toxic fumes from Union Carbide chemical plant in Bhopal, India, are reported to kill more than 2,000 persons.

Dec. 7. Bishop Desmond Tutu, recipient of 1984 Nobel Peace Prize, visits Pres. Reagan at White House and charges U.S. with aiding and abetting apartheid by not exerting sufficient pressure on South Africa.

Dec. 10. Cuba agrees to take back some 2,500 "excludable" immigrants who had entered U.S. in 1980.

Dec. 22. Manhattanite Bernhard Goetz shoots and wounds four teenagers who had asked him for money in New York subway train. His claim of self-defense is widely believed, but he is indicted for attempted murder Mar. 27, 1985.

1985

Jan. 2. Japan and U.S. discuss huge Japanese trade surplus as Congress presses President to impose trade curbs.

Jan. 3. California Institute of Technology announces it will build world's largest telescope on ridge of Mt. Mauna Kea, on the island of Hawaii.

Jan. 5. Colombia turns over four persons to U.S. for prosecution on federal charges of drug trafficking and money laundering.

Jan. 14. U.S. announces indictments of 16 persons accused of smuggling Central American aliens into U.S. or giving them refuge after arrival. Government contends that most of those given sanctuary were merely escaping poverty, not persecution, and thus were not qualified to seek asylum.

Jan. 18. U.S. defies World Court in suit charging it with illegal attacks against Nicaragua.

Jan. 20. San Francisco 49ers defeat Miami Dolphins in Super Bowl XIX, 38–16.

Jan. 21. Ronald Reagan takes oath of office and delivers inaugural address but inaugural parade is cancelled owing to strong winds and bitter cold.

Jan. 24. Space Shuttle *Discovery* begins top secret military mission.

Manhattan jury finds *Time* magazine guilty of false and defamatory writing in suit brought by Ariel Sharon, Israel's former defense minister, but denies article was published with "reckless disregard for truth"; thus Sharon is unable to collect damages.

Feb. 4. ANZUS naval exercises scheduled for March are cancelled when New Zealand premier refuses to allow U.S. nuclear ships in ports.

Feb. 14. Big Three U.S. automakers report total 1984 profits of $9.81 billion, 50 percent higher than 1983.

Feb. 18. Gen. W.C. Westmoreland drops $120 million libel suit against CBS in negotiated settlement that includes statement by CBS that it never meant to impugn Westmoreland's patriotism or loyalty.

Feb. 20. Prime Minister Margaret Thatcher becomes first British leader since Winston Churchill to address U.S. Congress. She expresses strong support for Star Wars plan.

Mar. 12. U.S.-Soviet arms talks convene in Geneva despite death of Soviet leader Chernenko two days before; Chernenko is replaced by Mikhail Gorbachev.

Mar. 17. Pres. Reagan meets in Quebec with Canadian Prime Minister Brian Mulroney, who announces an agreement between the two countries to try to control acid rain.

Mar. 18. ABC is sold to Capital Cities Communications Inc. for $3.5 billion, largest business acquisition to date outside of oil industry.

Apr. 8. India sues Union Carbide Corp. in Manhattan Federal Court, charging it with responsibility in Bhopal gas leak that killed 1,700 and injured 200,000 in December 1984.

Apr. 9. In nationally televised address Prime Minister Nakasone urges Japanese to buy foreign and especially U.S. products, even if doing so will harm native industries.

May 1. U.S. announces end to all trade with Nicaragua, asserting that Nicaragua's actions threaten U.S. security.

May 2. E.F. Hutton Co. pleads guilty to thousands of federal charges regarding manipulation of accounts. Investigation of company continues in subsequent months.

May 5. Pres. Reagan, faithful to his promise to West German Chancellor Helmut Kohl, a staunch ally, lays wreath at Bitburg Cemetery, which contains graves of slain Nazi SS troops.

May 20. John A. Walker, retired Navy warrant officer, is arrested and charged with spying for the Soviet Union. Walker's son, Michael, a yeoman third class, and his brother, Walter, a retired naval officer, are also arrested later in month.

May 21. A 30-year-old teacher who has taken fertility drugs gives birth to septuplets in California.

May 28. In televised address Pres. Reagan proposes new tax system that would be "clear, simple, and fair." Individuals would pay less, corporations more, in reform of tax code.

June 11. Karen Ann Quinlan dies after 10 years in coma, at age 31.

June 14. Shi'ite gunmen hijack TWA plane between Athens and Rome, kill one passenger, a U.S. Navy diver, and hold others hostage for up to 17 days.

July 9. David Stockman, controversial director of Office of Management and Budget, announces he will resign Aug. 1.

July 10. Coca-Cola announces it will bring back original Coke under name of "Coca-Cola Classic" after widespread protests against taste of new, substitute product.

July 13. Pres. Reagan undergoes surgery for intestinal polyp, which is found to be malignant, but prognosis, doctors say, is good.

"Live Aid" 17-hour rock concert held in London and Philadelphia raises $70 million for aid to starving peoples in Africa.

Aug. 5. Five members of Puerto Rican terrorist organization FALN are convicted of seditious conspiracy in Chicago.

Major league baseball strike begins, ends after two days.

Aug. 14. Hanoi returns remains of 26 Americans killed during Vietnam war; an additional 2,464 MIAs are still not accounted for.

Aug. 27. Crocker National Bank of San Francisco is fined for failing to report some $3.9 billion in cash transactions over four years.

Sept. 1. Team of U.S. and French marine explorers find wreck of luxury liner *Titanic,* which sank off coast of Newfoundland in 1912.

Sept. 6. Labor Dept. reports that unemployment rate is lowest in five years.

Sept. 19. First of two massive earthquakes strikes Mexico City; later reports estimate 20,000 dead and vast damage.

Oct. 7. Four Palestinian terrorists seize Italian cruise ship *Achille Lauro,* kill 69-year-old American man, and dump his body and wheelchair into the sea.

Oct. 11. Boston-based International Physicians for the Prevention of Nuclear War is given 1985 Nobel Peace Prize.

Oct. 16. Sen. Paul Laxalt visits Pres. Marcos of Philippines in Manila, conveys message from Pres. Reagan expressing "grave concern" over Marcos policies.

Oct. 24. UN celebrates 40th anniversary in New York City without being able to agree on a declaration to mark the occasion. Observers call the atmosphere "testy."

Oct. 27. Kansas City Royals complete dramatic comeback to defeat St. Louis Cardinals in all-Missouri World Series, four games to three; Royals win last three games.

Nov. 9. Soviet seaman Miroslav Medved returns to USSR after convincing U.S. officials he has changed his mind about defecting to U.S.

Nov. 19. U.S.-Soviet summit begins in Geneva with unanticipated two-hour closed-door meeting between Pres. Reagan and Secretary Gorbachev. Two men agree to meet again in 1986 and 1987.

Dec. 8. World oil price structure collapses as OPEC meeting in Geneva ends in disarray.

Dec. 12. Some 248 U.S. soldiers returning home for Christmas from peacekeeping duty in Sinai are killed in crash of chartered plane in Newfoundland.

Dec. 23. Pres. Reagan signs into law two agricultural bills that together constitute most fundamental change in U.S. government farm policy in half a century.

1986

Jan. 6. U.S. delegation arrives in Hanoi for talks aimed at resolving issue of 1,797 Americans still unaccounted for some 10 years after end of Vietnam war.

Jan. 8. Pres. Reagan signs executive order freezing all Libyan government assets in U.S. in retaliation for Libya's presumed support for terrorism.

Canada and U.S. issue joint report on acid rain, urging U.S. government to financially assist industry to develop methods of burning coal more cleanly.

Jan. 21. Five organized crime figures are convicted in Kansas City, MO, of skimming proceeds from casinos in Las Vegas. Similar trials are conducted in New York and Boston.

Jan. 24. Voyager 2 spacecraft speeds by Uranus, transmitting data it will take years to analyze.

Jan. 26. After season during which they dominated NFL, Chicago Bears rout New England Patriots in Super Bowl XX, 46–10.

Jan. 28. U.S. space shuttle *Challenger* explodes 74 seconds after launch from Cape Canaveral, FL. All seven persons aboard are killed.

Feb. 4. Crude oil prices fall to $15 a barrel after OPEC meeting fails to curb production. Price was $30 a barrel as recently as November 1985.

Feb. 7. Haitian Pres. Jean-Claude Duvalier is overthrown and forced to flee.

Philippine election creates chaos amid widespread charges of massive fraud by Marcos backers. Corazon Aquino refuses to concede defeat when independent count confirms her election. **Feb. 22.** Military supporters desert Marcos, who flees country three days later; Aquino is declared legally elected president.

Feb. 19. Senate approves UN Convention stigmatizing genocide as an international crime; action had been stalled in the Senate since 1949.

Mar. 4. U.S.-Soviet arms control talks in Geneva are recessed with no sign of significant progress having been made.

Mar. 7. U.S. orders large cuts in Soviet missions to UN; cuts are related to alleged espionage activities.

Mar. 17. Japanese yen reaches highest level against U.S. dollar since end of World War II, trading at 175.50. Decline of dollar was planned to help ease U.S. trade deficit.

Mar. 24. U.S. aircraft deliberately enter airspace over Gulf of Sidra that Libyan leader Qaddafi has declared off limits; shots are fired by both sides, and two Libyan patrol boats are damaged.

Apr. 2. Bomb explodes aboard TWA jet bound from Athens to Rome; four persons, one an infant, are swept out of gaping hole in fuselage and plunge to death below. **Apr. 5.** Bomb explodes in West Berlin discotheque, killing two and wounding many.

Apr. 14. U.S. planes based in Britain bomb five sites in Libya in retaliation, according to Pres. Reagan, for Libyan-supported terrorist acts such as bombing of West Berlin discotheque. Strike is itself called act of international terrorism by Arab and East-Bloc countries.

Apr. 28. Worst nuclear accident in history hits Chernobyl power plant 80 miles north of Kiev, capital of the Ukraine. Poisonous cloud hovers over Western Europe for weeks and many thousands are evacuated from Kiev region.

May 1. Several members of so-called Sanctuary Movement are convicted in Tucson, AR, of conspiring to smuggle Salvadorans and Guatemalans into U.S.

May 4. Economic summit meeting in Tokyo pleases U.S. delegation by issuing strong statement condemning persons or governments that support international terrorism.

June 9. U.S. presidential commission issues report detailing cause of *Challenger* explosion. Report also lists long series of engineering and managerial mistakes that virtually assured that a tragedy would happen sooner or later.

June 27. During meeting in Manila Secretary of State George Shultz informs New Zealand's prime minister that U.S. no longer feels bound by 35-year-old ANZUS Pact owing to New Zealand's reluctance to allow visits by nuclear-armed U.S. vessels.

June 30. Supreme Court rules 5–4 that Georgia law prohibiting sodomy does not violate constitutional right to privacy. **July 2.** Court backs minority hiring quotas in certain circumstances; civil rights leaders hail decisions as landmark victories for affirmative action.

July 14. Richard Miller, first FBI agent ever to be convicted of espionage, is sentenced to two life terms and 50 years in prison, all to be served concurrently, for spying for Soviets.

July 17. Senate, by 87–10 vote, approves extradition treaty with Great Britain that would facilitate deportation of accused I.R.A. terrorists who had sought refuge in U.S., claiming their crimes were expressions of political dissent.

July 25. Farm experts estimate that severe drought and searing temperatures in Southeast will cause losses of over $2 billion in crops and livestock.

July 29. Jury finds that NFL's de facto monopoly of professional football has damaged rival USFL but awards only $1 to USFL on grounds that NFL had not acted illegally or improperly.

Aug. 14. Outcry follows report that U.S. narcotics agent has been kidnapped and tortured by Jalisco State police in Mexico. Relations with Mexico are strained.

Aug. 23. U.S. seizes Soviet diplomat G. F. Zakharov as spy. **Aug. 30.** In apparent reprisal, Soviets arrrest Nicholas Daniloff, Moscow correspondent for *U.S. News and World Report*, and charge him with spying.

Sept. 16. William H. Rehnquist is sworn in as 16th chief justice of Supreme Court. His Senate confirmation by vote of 65–33 followed lengthy and divisive hearings on his suitability for post.

Sept. 18. Philippine Pres. Corazon Aquino addresses Congress, asks for aid and defends her low-key approach to problem of Communist insurgents.

Sept. 27. Senate passes broadest changes in tax laws in 40 years; changes will produce major revisions in U.S. investment strategies.

Sept. 29. U.S. reporter Daniloff is released by Soviets and allowed to return home as U.S. releases G.F. Zakharov.

Oct. 6. American Eugene Hasenfus is shot down by Nicaraguans while cargoing military supplies to Contras; action reveals wide network of supply efforts in and out of U.S. government.

Oct. 11–12. President Reagan and Soviet leader Gorbachev meet in Reykjavik, Iceland, in summit that comes close to agreement on deep arms cuts, but meeting ends in failure when Reagan refuses to yield on Star Wars plan.

Oct. 17. Congress approves landmark immigration bill that bars hiring illegal aliens but gives amnesty to millions who have resided in U.S. since Jan. 1, 1982.

Oct. 27. New York Mets beat Boston Red Sox in seventh game of World Series marked by dramatic comebacks by both clubs.

Nov. 4. In mid-term elections Democrats regain Senate by 55–45 margin, increase margin in House slightly.

Nov. 12. Pres. Reagan confirms that Iran has received arms in secret deals that counter stated U.S. policy; he says action was taken in hopes of freeing hostages. Major controversy ensues.

Nov. 14. Big arbitrage trader Ivan F. Boesky is fined $100 million for illegal insider trading in Wall Street; stock market plummets but revives next day.

Nov. 26. Pres. Reagan, in surprise announcement, says that money earned by arms sales to Iran was diverted to Contras through secret Swiss account; two key members of National Security Council staff are released.

Nov. 28. In what Moscow calls "a major mistake" U.S. exceeds SALT II limits on deployment of nuclear arms.

Dec. 2. Attorney General Meese asks for special prosecutor to investigate Iran arms sales question.

1977

1.

MARLENE W. LEHTINEN and GERALD W. SMITH:
Debate on Capital Punishment

The debate about the merits of capital punishment continued during the ten years before the execution, on January 17, 1977, of Gary Gilmore, even though during nearly all of this decade no one was executed in the United States. But the tide of public sentiment seemed to be turning in favor of this ultimate punishment, and the death of Gilmore, opponents feared, was likely to initiate a series of executions. Arguments against the death penalty were often published, but reasoned arguments for it were rarely heard, despite the apparent fact that large numbers of persons approved of it. The following carefully thought out and painstakingly documented debate on the subject, which appeared six months after Gilmore's death, is almost unique in the public record. It is reprinted here only in part, and without the extensive notes that accompanied the original. The two authors were both professors in the department of sociology at the University of Utah.

Source: *Crime & Delinquency,* July 1977.

A: MARLENE W. LEHTINEN
AN ARGUMENT FOR THE DEATH PENALTY

SINCE JUNE 2, 1967, only one person has been executed in the United States, despite the fact that forty-one states have statutory authority to invoke the death penalty for a variety of crimes from murder to armed robbery. From 1930 to June 2, 1967, 3,859 persons were executed under civil jurisdiction, 3,826 by state authorities, and 33 by the federal government—an average of 103 a year for the entire period. During the last ten years of that 37-year span, the average annual number of executions was less than forty.

The death penalty has been limited to the most serious offenses and its application, in this country as in the rest of the world, has been severely limited. On June 29, 1972, the U.S. Supreme Court ruled, in *Furman v. Georgia,* that the death penalty, as imposed up to that time, amounted to "cruel and unusual punishment" in violation of the

Eighth Amendment to the Constitution. Subsequently, thirty-six states revised their death penalty statutes to satisfy the Court's objections. In July 1976, the Supreme Court held that the death penalty is a constitutionally permissible punishment for certain categories of murder when the sentencing authority is permitted to exercise a certain degree of discretion. Although the new laws have been subjected to numerous court challenges—up till January 17, 1977, none of the more than 500 persons on death row in thirty states had been executed under a post-*Furman* statute—it is likely that the July '76 ruling will soon clear the way to resuming application of the death penalty. Our general reluctance to execute, along with the mandated discretionary restructuring, will probably keep the number of executions relatively low.

More frequent and systematic utilization of the death penalty, I contend, will result in a net saving of lives. Critics of the death penalty argue that its use in the past shows no evidence of greater general deterrence. This argument is false. As will be shown below, there is no evidence that proves the death penalty is not a unique deterrent. Recent study, in fact, suggests that use of the death penalty would deter potential homicide offenders. I maintain that the death penalty is important for the protection of society. Under appropriate circumstances, society has the moral right and obligation to take the life of one of its members to ensure the protection of all.

GENERAL DETERRENCE

Rational men fear death more than anything else. The use of the death penalty, therefore, has a potentially greater general deterrent effect than any other punishment. The individual or special deterrent effect of the death penalty goes without saying, since it is absolute.

A number of scholars have questioned the superior deterrent effectiveness of the death penalty. The most frequent form of attack is based on statistical arguments like the following:

1. There is no discernible statistical association between the existence of the death penalty and the willful homicide rate.

2. States that have abolished the death penalty have not shown a statistically significant increase in their willful homicide rates.

3. States that once abolished the death penalty and then reintroduced it show no statistically significant decrease in their willful homicide rates.

4. Comparisons of contiguous states, one state with and the other without the death penalty, show no variation in the willful homicide rates that can be attributed to the existence of the death penalty.

Statistical arguments, like the above, however, are of limited value: they say only that the death penalty's general deterrence superiority compared with alternative punishments has not been demonstrated statistically. It has yet to be shown, however, that the death penalty is not more effective than other punishments. Failure to prove an effect does not mean there is no effect.

To begin with, the statistical data on homicide do not distinguish cases in which the death penalty can be imposed from those in which it cannot.

A more serious objection is the lack of sensitivity of the statistics themselves. General crime rates are not accurate indicators of the amount of crime in society. According to victimization studies, from two to ten times more crime occurs than is accounted for in the *UCR*, which includes only crimes known to the police. . . . This could seriously affect statistical data and conclusions about the possible superior general deterrent effectiveness of the death penalty.

Another serious objection to statistical arguments based on per-100,000-population crime rates is the inherent insensitivity of such rates to small but significant variations in capital offense rates that can easily mask any superior deterrent effectiveness of the death penalty. . . .

The correct and appropriate conclusion is that, while the statistical data do not demonstrate the death penalty's superior general deterrence, they do not thereby demonstrate the reverse. The data fail to show that the death penalty is *not* a superior deterrent. Variation within capital crime rates can easily mask the superior general deterrent effectiveness of the death penalty. In the example above, even a minor variation of 30 lives a year would be significant, although not statistically significant. If only 5 persons a year in each state maintaining the death penalty—about 200 individuals nationally—were deterred from committing homicide because of the existence of the death penalty, the saving of innocent lives in and of itself would be significant even though it would not significantly affect the willful homicide rate statistically.

Scope of Deterrence

Deterrence is too narrowly defined when it includes the assumption that the threat of punishment produces fear in the populace and that it is this fear that reduces the number of criminal viola-

tions. Deterrence is the result of more than fear alone. Law, said Durkheim many years ago, encourages law-abiding behavior by justifying conformity; the conforming majority are the most significant clients of the criminal justice system. The sanctioning provisions provide demonstrable proof of the value of conformity. More than any other penalty, the death penalty reinforces the value of conformity to law, whose ultimate authority is diffused into the subconscious of the citizenry. Criminals do not simply examine types of crime and then rationally choose those that present the smallest risks of apprehension and the lowest levels of punishment. Much human behavior is based more on emotion than on ratiocination. The punishment structure of law may exert its strongest effects morally and pedagogically, in which case the consequences of changes in punishments would not be expected to appear within a single generation. The death penalty is a case in point.

Not all the effects of the death penalty can be examined directly. The moral, pedagogical effects of the death penalty reinforce conformity to all law, not just the law of capital crimes. A broader theory of deterrence, therefore, would examine general conformity to law and the manner in which the death penalty might be a unique deterrent. . . .

Reverse Deterrence

There is some support for the argument that the death penalty has operated as an incentive to murder, a fusion that has come to be known as "the homicide-suicide phenomenon," meaning that persons who wish to commit suicide commit murder in order to have the state do for them what they cannot do themselves. Some of them may be

UPI/Bettmann

Condemned murderer Gary Gilmore after hearing the date set for his execution by firing squad.

this form of self-destruction. How large this group is and, given rigorous and systematic use of the death penalty, how large it would become are open to question. The NAACP Capital Punishment Project suggests that this group makes up a large proportion of persons who have been executed. Given the capricious and arbitrary manner in which the death penalty has operated, this is a biased sample. But, since widespread and systematic application of the death penalty might increase the number of persons eager to be executed and willing to murder to achieve this aim, the state should take steps to mitigate the effects of this phenomenon.

One way to do so would be to eliminate the glamor and melodrama of murder trials and executions. The state should present its case in a dignified manner and the court should curtail any opportunities for sensationalism. Media coverage of trials and executions should be limited to a professional reporting of facts.

The execution itself has always fascinated both the media and the public, partly because of the manner in which it is carried out. All of the methods used so far—hanging, shooting, gas, and electrocution—are primitive, guaranteed to raise the public's emotional temperature, and totally unnecessary. We have not taken advantage of the means provided by medical technology—sedatives administered by physicians in hospitals—to produce death in a quiet, painless, and dignified manner. The hospital setting would also make possible the excision of organs for transplant purposes; thus, the administration of the death penalty can be likened to eradication of a diseased entity, the murderer, that has infected otherwise healthy tissue, society.

categorized as persons with weak self-concepts and strong needs for the publicity of a public trial and execution; among others in this group are religious fanatics who regard suicide as a sin but not murder absolved by execution. If this phenomenon characterizes a substantial proportion of people who have been executed, the total elimination of the death penalty as an alternative might save the victims of those bent on this form of suicide.

There is no simple rebuttal of this argument against the death penalty. Probably we will always have among us a number of deranged persons bent on

DISCRIMINATORY APPLICATION OF THE DEATH PENALTY

Historically, the death penalty has been applied discriminatorily against men and blacks. Between 1930 and 1967, only 32 women were put to death—less than 1 per cent of the total of 3,859 persons executed in the United States. During that period, 55 per cent of those executed were blacks, who constitute only 10 per cent of the population. Executions for rape show even greater discrimination against blacks: in that period, 89 per cent of the 455 men executed for rape were black. Excluding seven executions in Missouri, all executions of blacks for rape occurred in the South. Blacks accounted for 76 per cent of those executed for robbery and 100 of those executed for burglary.

Some have argued that this record of discrimination is reason enough to abolish the death penalty. But discrimination need not—and, with proper safeguards, would not—occur in the future. Thirty-six states and the federal government revised their death penalty statutes post-*Furman* to reduce or eliminate possible discriminatory application. The majority in the recent Supreme Court decision held that procedural safeguards can be designed to provide fair and nondiscriminatory application of the death penalty.

The system has operated to execute men, blacks, the ignorant, and the poor. A system designed to apply the death penalty nondiscriminatorily would probably execute a far greater number of such persons, simply because the crimes that call for execution are most frequently committed by them.

EXECUTION OF THE INNOCENT

What of the possibility that innocent persons will be executed? Bedau cites 74 cases "occurring in the United States since 1893 [to 1962], in which a wrongful conviction of criminal homicide has been alleged and, in most cases, proven beyond doubt"—a wrongful-conviction average of about one a year. In 43 of these cases, the defendant was sentenced to a life term or to a term of years. Of the 31 defendants sentenced to death, 23 were not executed. Thus, in only 8 of the 74 cases in 70 years was the innocent defendant executed—an average of less than one every nine years. The execution of an innocent person is not insignificant, and the number of innocent persons convicted and innocent persons executed may actually have been larger than 74 and 8, respectively. But the risk of wrongful conviction and wrongful execution is extremely low.

Since that risk is negligible, society should not be unduly concerned about the possibility of fatal error, given the present competency of our courts. Concern about the loss of innocent lives must be restrained; it must not be—and, indeed, is not—the overriding consideration. The state is constantly making decisions that jeopardize the lives of innocent people. For example, its decision to impose a speed limit as high as 55 miles an hour is at least partially responsible for the 46,200 lives lost each year on our nation's highways: many innocent lives could be saved if the state imposed a speed limit of 10 miles an hour and designed highways and regulated automobile manufacture to make exceeding this limit impossible. Decisions such as these are founded on compromise—the need for efficient and rapid transportation justifies the cost in innocent lives. Similar decisions are seen in committing troops to battle in the national interest; establishing safety, health, and environmental protection regulations in industry; and setting medical research priorities that condemn some to a premature and often painful death so that others may live. It is evident that the state must constantly set priorities and standards to achieve given goals. Merely setting state standards and priorities frequently means the sacrifice of innocent lives, an inherent cost of governing and decision-making. The possible loss of innocent lives as a result of the implementation of the death penalty, under these circumstances, should be a minor consideration. Its cost should be weighed against the possible benefits to be achieved for society with the rigorous and systematic employment of the death penalty. . . .

CONCLUDING ARGUMENTS FOR THE DEATH PENALTY

The systematic and widespread application of the death penalty would preserve life. Its deterrent effect would be greater than that of any other punishment. By sparing the life of a murderer, we sacrifice the lives of the innocent.

Punishment has a legitimate place in the criminal justice system. The principle of punishment places a limit on society's intervention in an individual's life and on the kind and amount of criminal deviance that will be tolerated. The death penalty provides an upper limit that reinforces not only society's strongest taboos but other norms as well. Failure to execute an offender when execution is deserved undermines not only the norm violated but all of our other social norms.

The state has a duty to protect all of its citizens. It assumed that duty when individuals gave up their right to private justice through personal revenge in exchange for protection by the state.

The state's duty, therefore, is to extract an appropriate level of retribution for the victim. Failure to do so undermines public confidence in the system. By failing to punish appropriately, the criminal justice system loses the support and respect of its most important clients, the law-abiding populace; the result is a higher crime rate generally and the brutalization of society. The state's use of the death penalty provides citizens with added protection while increasing the public's general respect for law.

In exercising its duty to protect its citizens, the state will always be forced to sacrifice some for the good of all. Government priorities and goals require political decisions that have negative, even deadly, consequences for some. This cost must be borne for the common good. The captain of a ship in a storm may need to sacrifice the crewman who was washed overboard in order to ensure the safety of the ship, its remaining crew, and passengers. The state is in the same position with the death penalty. The lives of some must be sacrificed so that others may live.

The state's failure to use the death penalty, when appropriate, stems from the unwarranted assumption that all life is equally valuable. All life is not equally worthy. Life in a living, breathing human body is not in and of itself of value. What is valuable and in need of preserving is a good life rather than a bad or dishonorable life. To preserve the good life and to raise the quality of life, we should retain and impose the death penalty.

B: GERALD W. SMITH
ARGUMENTS AGAINST THE DEATH PENALTY

THERE IS A VERY GOOD REASON why few scholars have written favorably about the death penalty: the arguments in favor of it are insupportable. Professor Marlene W. Lehtinen's effort to present a reasonable and logical justification for the death penalty, while interesting and in some ways clever, fails to make a convincing case. It fails, I believe, simply because no case can be made. The use, especially *extensive* use, of the death penalty in modern civilized nations not only is unnecessary but is harmful to the social order.

DETERRENCE

Current statistical data do not indicate that the death penalty as a deterrent is superior to available alternatives. Since the existence of the death penalty has no discernible effect on the willful homicide rate, some scholars have concluded that it is not a superior deterrent. This conclusion, says Professor Lehtinen, is erroneous because "Failure to prove an effect statistically does not mean there is no effect." She argues that the statistical data are too "insensitive" to show the death penalty's superior deterrent effectiveness and that they could, therefore, mask significant variations in willful homicide rates. She presents a hypothetical case: if the existence of the death penalty deterred five persons a year from committing homicide in each death penalty state, the saving in innocent lives would be significant, even though the statistical indicators of homicide rates would not change significantly.

Professor Lehtinen's reasoning contains several basic flaws. To begin with, while it is true that not proving an effect does not mean there is no effect, not proving an effect also does not mean that there is an effect. Her assumption, in regard to the death penalty's possible superior deterrent effectiveness, is that the effect (imagined, not demonstrated) exists but is not picked up by the insensitive crime statistics. The opposite conclusion, however, could just as reasonably be conjectured: if, because of the existence of the death penalty, five persons were encouraged to commit a capital crime, the loss of innocent lives would be the same as in Lehtinen's hypothetical case, and the crime statistics would, similarly, not be affected by this degree of variation. Thus a simple revision of the example gives the opposite consequence: the existence of the death penalty results in a loss of innocent lives. That something (i.e., superior deterrent effectiveness of the death penalty) is possible is not a sound basis for believing it exists. Hypothetical cases merely illustrate possibility; they are not proof. In this instance two possibilities—that the death penalty is a superior deterrent and that it is not—can be conjectured. Examination of the data from abolition states and death penalty states, during a period when capital offenders were being executed, reveals consistently lower homicide rates in the abolition states.

A similar pattern emerges when we examine homicide rates in contiguous death penalty states and abolition states during a comparable period: death penalty states generally have higher homicide rates than their neighboring abolition states. Examination of actual homicide rates shows that any hidden or masked effects of the death penalty are the opposite of what Lehtinen conjectures—the existence of the death penalty is associated with the greater loss of innocent lives. It is just as reasonable and, given the data, more plausible to believe that the statistical data mask the superior protection of an abolitionist policy.

Risk of Execution

Lehtinen argues that in modern times the risk of execution has always been so low that the difference in actual penalties imposed in death penalty states and abolition states is negligible. She underestimates the actual risks. Her data show that, from 1945 to 1954, 775 persons were executed for murder, an average of 77 a year. She then concludes that, "Given . . . an estimate of 7,268 incidences of murder and non-negligent manslaughter annually, the chance of execution was less than 1 in 100." She is stacking the deck because only a small proportion, perhaps 10 per cent, of the 7,268 incidences of willful homicide would qualify for the death penalty under the statutes. The data include willful homicide from abolition states where the death penalty is not possible, as well as multiple killings by one individual. If we could reduce the 7,268 incidences of willful homicide to individual killers who would qualify for execution, we would probably find that about one-tenth of the possible candidates were actually executed. A 10 per cent chance of execution is not a negligible risk. The absence of statistically significant variations in contiguous death penalty and abolition states may mean, as Lehtinen conjectures, that the risk of execution was not high enough to make a difference and that raising the risk of execution might make a difference; on the other hand, it may mean that the deterrent effects of the death penalty are no different from those of alternative punishments available. Lehtinen consistently conjectures a favorable deterrent effect when a different outcome is equally plausible.

To raise the conditional probability of execution, Lehtinen proposes that we execute, at a minimum, all first-degree murderers—about 3,000 persons a year, or 15 per cent of the approximately 20,000 willful homicide offenders. Doing this, she believes, will increase the deterrent effectiveness of the death penalty and reinforce the taboo on killing. The opposite result seems to me more likely. By taking so many lives, the state expands the acceptability of killing, undermines the value of life in general, and sets a poor example for its citizens. Intentional killing is an odd way to reinforce the taboo on murder. The diminution of morality to a *quid pro quo* ethic encourages vindictiveness and hostility. Acceptance of Lehtinen's proposal would reduce our civilization to a barbaric level where life is short, cheap, and brutal.

Though Lehtinen insists that the law-abiding masses are the most important clients of the conformity-encouraging criminal justice system, her proposal gives them the basest example to emulate. A system of just and appropriate punishment based on due process, equal protection, and fundamental fairness is important to achieve adequate social protection, but conducting blood sacrifices to appease an appetite for justice is unnecessary and destructive. The degree of punishment should be the minimum necessary to achieve the goal of social protection. Although deterrent considerations are important, some compromises are possible with reform and rehabilitation considerations. Some research concludes that it is not the amount but the fact of punishment that most deters. We ought to be able to harmonize the crime prevention goals of deterrence with programs designed to prevent recidivism in offender populations, without significant loss and with a net gain. Compromise of the goals of punishment with considerations of mercy, love, and reform sets a far better model for the community than a proposal that fosters anger, hostility, and vindictiveness. I want to live in a community that cherishes principles of justice based on love, mercy, and reform. I seriously doubt that even Professor Lehtinen would want to live in the kind of community her proposal would create. . . .

Reverse Deterrence

The homicide-suicide phenomenon is an established fact: some persons commit murder in order to be executed by the state; for them, the existence of the death penalty is an incentive to murder. Estimates of the extent of the phenomenon differ; however, there is general agreement that it is not negligible. Lehtinen's suggestion for lessening this effect of the death penalty by reducing the pomp and sensationalism of trial and execution is unrealistic. Cases involving the death penalty have a high degree of public interest, and it is unreasonable to expect the media to reduce their coverage of these cases. Similarly unrealistic is her suggestion that executions be conducted in hospitals by physicians. Physicians are not likely to abdicate their responsibility to save life. They are not likely to accept the role of state executioner and, even if they did, would not thereby significantly reduce the homicide-suicide phenomenon. A good deal of pomp and sensationalism would probably surround executions carried out precisely as she suggests. On the other hand, executions disposed of secretly and easily, without appropriate ceremonial trappings and the fundamental safeguard of public accountability, depreciate life in general.

Each method carries the seed and substance of totalitarianism.

Increasing the number of executions, advocated by Lehtinen, can be expected to intensify the homicide-suicide phenomenon. With extensive and systematic use of the death penalty, we increase the incentive for committing suicide in this manner and, thereby, expand the loss of innocent lives.

DISCRIMINATION

In the past, application of the death penalty has been discriminatory, resulting in the execution of a disproportionate number of men, blacks and other racial and ethnic minorities, and the socially and economically disadvantaged. Juries tend to be more lenient to defendants from their own socio-economic classes. I do not share Lehtinen's belief that "procedural safeguards can be designed to provide fair and nondiscriminatory application of the death penalty," a belief held also by the U.S. Supreme Court justices who announced recently that some kind of controlled discretion by the sentencing authority could prevent discrimination. The controlled discretion model will not end the discriminatory application of the death penalty. We will continue to impose the death penalty on the poor and socially and economically disadvantaged classes because they are least capable of defending themselves before middle- and lower-middle-class juries. Given the realities of our system of justice and continuation of the death penalty, I do not believe that discriminatory application of the penalty can be eliminated. In a few years we can analyze cases resulting in execution and determine whether the new guidelines work. Of course, if we find that controlled discretion has failed to eliminate discriminatory application of the death penalty, the discovery will have come too late for those executed.

EXECUTION OF THE INNOCENT

Lehtinen maintains that the risk of executing the innocent has been fairly negligible. I agree. However, her proposal of a 4,000 per cent annual increase in executions means that we would be executing a significant number of innocent people. Nothing that she or anyone else has said can justify that possibility. An execution is irreversible; other sentencing alternatives are not. . . .

CONCLUSION

The state has a duty to protect its citizens from crime. It should carry out this protective responsibility with a minimum of intervention in individual lives and the lowest net loss in human suffering. The use of the death penalty is inconsistent with this goal.

There is no evidence to indicate that the death penalty provides better protection for society than the available alternatives afford. The deterrent, educational, and moralizing functions of punishment are largely independent of the nature of the penalties employed.

The death penalty adds nothing to these functions of punishment; it subtracts much. The taking of a human life is an evil in itself and should be endured only for a greater good. It is incumbent on the advocates of the death penalty to prove that positive social effects will result from its use. Failure to demonstrate such effects should compel us to avoid use of an irrevocable penalty.

The use of the death penalty does not increase respect for law and the system of criminal justice—it undermines it. The death penalty places a low value on human life and sets a poor model for the community; in so doing, it undercuts the taboo on killing and increases the future probability of killing. Beccaria made the same argument in 1764:

> The death penalty cannot be useful, because of the example of barbarity it gives men. If the passions or the necessities of war have taught the shedding of human blood, the laws, moderators of the conduct of men, should not extend the beastly example, which becomes more pernicious since the inflicting of legal death is attended with much study and formality. It seems to me absurd that the laws, which are an expression of the public will, which detest and punish homicide, should themselves commit it.

Let's do it!

GARY MARK GILMORE, last words prior to his execution
by firing squad, Point of the Mountains, Utah,
January 17, 1977

Egyptian President Anwar Sadat, left, President Carter, and Israeli Prime Minister Menachem Begin clasp hands to symbolize their mutual pleasure upon signing the Middle East Peace Treaty in 1979.

TROUBLES ABROAD PART I

The presidency of Jimmy Carter began on a happy note and ended on a sad one. When he moved into the White House in January 1977, the Watergate scandal was over, and the Vietnam era had passed. Carter came to Washington as an outsider, promising integrity and new approaches to problems, both domestic and foreign. During three years of his presidency there were some striking successes in foreign policy. In December 1978 Carter announced that full diplomatic relations with China would resume the next January 1. Cementing ties with China was hailed as a significant step toward world peace. In June 1979 Carter and Soviet leader Leonid Brezhnev met for three days in Vienna and ended their talks by signing an updated version of SALT II, a treaty limiting the deployment of nuclear weapons that was heeded by both sides—although it was not approved by the Sen-

ate until November 1986, when Ronald Reagan breached the treaty's limits. Jimmy Carter's greatest triumph came in March 1979. The previous September he had brought together at Camp David, the presidential retreat near Washington, D.C., Menachem Begin, the Prime Minister of Israel, and Anwar Sadat, the President of Egypt, for talks that would lead, Carter hoped, to a peace treaty between the two countries that might promote wider peace efforts in the Middle East. The three men negotiated for a week, emerging exhausted with a tentative agreement. But there was still much to be done, including some arm-twisting by Carter and a trip to Jerusalem and Cairo early in March 1979. On March 26 the treaty was signed in Washington. Their hopes that it would inaugurate an era of peace in the Middle East were not to be realized, however.

While Jimmy Carter was hosting China's Deng and meeting with Brezhnev in Vienna, the deep troubles that would undermine his presidency were brewing in the Middle East. The government of the Shah of Iran fell in January 1979, and the cruel though charismatic Ayatollah Khomeini returned to his native land from exile to establish an Islamic state. In February the American ambassador to Afghanistan was murdered in Kabul. These two political tremors heralded much more serious events that would soon imperil Carter's foreign policies and cause people to forget his earlier successes. The U.S. embassy in Teheran was attacked by leftist guerrillas on February 14. Then on November 4 Iranian students, with the tacit approval of the new government, attacked the embassy again, subdued its small guard, and took some 60 persons hostage. There ensued one of the most unnerving and humiliating episodes in U.S. history. President Carter did everything he could to free all of the hostages—most of the women and the blacks in the group were released after a few days—alternating between pleas and threats over a period of 444 days. But his options were severely limited by distance and by his commitment to ensuring that all the hostages be released unhurt, as in fact they finally were. In December 1979 his troubles were compounded when the Soviet Union invaded Afghanistan, murdered its president, and installed a puppet government. The Afghans resisted bravely, and Carter wanted to help, but again his options were few.

(Opposite top) China's Vice Premier Deng Xiaopeng and President Carter applaud after signing agreements at the White House; (bottom) President Carter and Soviet leader Leonid Brezhnev have just signed the SALT II treaty in Vienna. (Top) Pro-Khomeini women of Iran demonstrate their loyalty by wearing the chador, a traditional garment favored by Khomeini; (bottom) Iranian demonstrators burn the American flag shortly after their takeover of the U.S. Embassy.

UPI/Bettmann

AP/Wide World

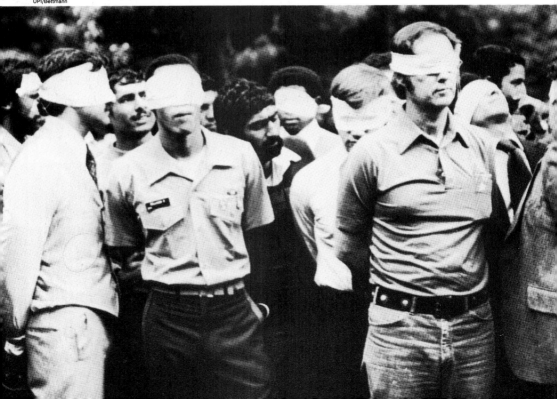

In the United States, indignation mounted as photos were released of blindfolded American hostages being paraded before their captors in the streets of Teheran. Everything the Iranians could think of to humiliate Carter and his country they did, with full television coverage daily. On April 24, 1980, an attempt was made to rescue the hostages with an armed force of transports and combat helicopters, but it ended in bitter failure when three of the helicopters crashed and a transport was severely damaged in a collision in the Iranian desert. Eight Americans were killed, and Khomeini crowed that it was "a stupid act that had no chance of success." The President disagreed, and added: "There is a deeper failure than that of incomplete success. That is the failure to attempt a worthy effort—a failure to try." In America that morning glum crowds nodded their heads and agreed, as one New Yorker put it, "That man don't have no luck." Jimmy Carter's lack of luck dogged him until he gave up the presidency in January 1981, after his resounding defeat by Ronald Reagan in the November election. The hostages were freed as Reagan was being inaugurated. Carter flew to Wiesbaden, West Germany, as a private citizen to meet the newly freed hostages.

Photos by UPI/Bettmann

(Opposite top) Iranian students stand guard outside the gates of the U.S. embassy in Teheran, where the embassy staff is being held hostage; (bottom) this photo, brought to the U.S. by an Iranian, shows the hostages being paraded before the public by their captors. (Top) About three months after their capture, the hostages read accumulated mail; (center) all that is left of a mission to rescue the hostages is charred bodies and the wreckage of aircraft; (bottom) the hostages finally come home; here, they are on their way to the White House.

Central America was beginning to emerge as a focal point of American foreign policy in the last year of Carter's term. On December 4, 1980, the bodies of four U.S. churchwomen were found in an unmarked grave near San Salvador; right-wing extremists took responsibility for their murders. The newly installed civilian president of El Salvador promised that the murderers would be brought to justice, a promise he found difficult to keep. This was only the first in a series of troubles that pre-occupied President Reagan during his tenure. Terrorism was another one. On December 17, 1981, the Red Brigades, an Italian leftist terrorist group, kidnapped Brig. Gen. James L. Dozier, a U.S. army officer, from his Verona apartment. He was sequestered for 42 days in a small room without windows. He was finally rescued on Jan. 28, 1982, in a dramatic raid on an apartment in Padua by Italy's elite antiterrorist commando unit.

(Top) Three American nuns pray over the bodies of three nuns and a lay sister, who were murdered by right-wing terrorists and buried in an unmarked grave in El Salvador; (bottom) Brig. Gen. James L. Dozier after his release from a "people's prison" where he had been held for 42 days by the Red Brigades in Padua, Italy.

2.

Gerald R. Ford: State of the Union Address

The American Constitutional system requires that an outgoing President remain in office for nearly three months while his elected successor, be he political friend or foe, gathers his powers, forms his Cabinet and staff, and readies himself for the tasks he will face upon his inauguration. The "lame duck" President is also required, as almost his last official act, to deliver an address to the Congress giving them his sense of the State of the Union as he leaves it to his successor. Such final addresses have often taken on the character of emotional farewells. This was the case with President Ford's last State of the Union address, delivered January 12, 1977, and reprinted here in part. In it he described the troubled times in which he had inherited the presidency, commented on the strength of the institutions that had allowed him to rule unchallenged, and, at the end of the speech, recalled with tears in his eyes the many years he had spent in the Capitol.

Source: *Congressional Quarterly: Historical Documents of 1977,* January 1977.

To the Congress of the United States:

In accordance with the Constitution, I come before you once again to report on the State of the Union.

This report will be my last, maybe.

But for the Union, it is only the first of such reports in our Third Century of Independence, the close of which none of us will ever see. We can be confident, however, that 100 years from now a freely elected President will come before a freely elected Congress chosen to renew our great Republic's pledge to Government of the people, by the people, and for the people.

For my part, I pray the Third Century we are beginning will bring to all Americans, our children and their children's children, a greater measure of individual equality, opportunity and justice, a greater abundance of spiritual and material blessings, and a higher quality of life, liberty and the pursuit of happiness.

The State of the Union is a measurement of the many elements of which it is composed—a political union of diverse states, an economic union of varying interests, an intellectual union of common convictions and a moral union of immutable ideals.

Taken in sum, I can report that the State of the Union is good. There is room for improvement as always, but today we have a more perfect union than when my stewardship began.

As a people, we discovered that our Bicentennial was much more than a celebration of the past; it became a joyous reaffirmation of all that it means to be Americans, a confirmation before all the world of the vitality and durability of our free institutions.

I am proud to have been privileged to preside over the affairs of our Federal Government during these eventful years when we proved, as I said in my first words upon assuming office, that "our Constitution works; our Great Republic is a Government of laws and not of men; here, the people rule."

The people have spoken; they have chosen a new President and a new Congress to work their will; I congratulate you—particularly the new members—as sincerely as I did President-elect Carter. In a few days, it will be his duty to outline for you his priorities and legislative recommendations. Tonight, I will not infringe on that responsibility, but rather wish him the very best in all that is good for our country.

During the period of my own service in this Capitol and in the White House I can recall many orderly transitions of governmental responsibility—of problems as well as of position, of burdens as well as of power. The genius of the American system is that we do this so naturally and so normally; there are no soldiers marching in the streets except in the Inaugural Parade; no public demonstrations except for some of the dancers at the Inaugural Ball; the opposition party doesn't go underground but goes on functioning vigorously in the Congress and the country; and our vigilant press goes right on probing and publishing our faults and our follies, confirming the wisdom of the framers of the First Amendment.

Because the transfer of authority in our form of government affects the state of the union, and of the world, I am happy to report to you that the current transition is proceeding very well. I was determined that it should; I wanted the new President to get off to an easier start than I had.

When I became President on August 9, 1974, our Nation was deeply divided and tormented. In rapid succession, the Vice President and the President had resigned in disgrace. We were still struggling with the after-effects of a long, unpopular and bloody war in Southeast Asia. The economy was unstable and racing toward the worst recession in 40 years. People were losing jobs. The cost of living was soaring. The Congress and the Chief Executive were at loggerheads. The integrity of our Constitutional process and of other institutions was being questioned.

For more than 15 years, domestic spending had soared as Federal programs multiplied and the expense escalated annually. During the same period, our national security needs were steadily shortchanged.

In the grave situation which prevailed in August 1974, our will to maintain our international leadership was in doubt.

I asked for your prayers, and went to work.

In January 1975, I reported to the Congress that the state of the union was not good. I proposed urgent action to improve the economy and to achieve energy independence in ten years. I reassured America's allies and sought to reduce the danger of confrontation with potential adversaries. I pledged a new direction for America.

Nineteen seventy-five was a year of difficult decisions, but Americans responded with realism, common sense and self-discipline.

By January 1976, we were headed in a new direction, which I hold to be the right direction for a free society. I was guided by the belief that successful problem-solving requires more than Federal action alone; that it involves a full partnership among all branches

UPI/Bettmann

President Ford accepting applause before his State of the Union address.

tinued progress possible, synchronizing the skills of three independent branches of government, reserving fundamental sovereignty to the people of this great land.

It is only as the temporary representatives and servants of the people that we meet here—we bring no hereditary status or gift of infallibility and none follows us from this place. Like President Washington, like the more fortunate of his successors, I look forward to the status of private citizen with gladness and gratitude. To me, being a citizen of the United States of America is the greatest honor and privilege in this world.

From the opportunities which fate and my fellow citizens have given me, as a member of the House, as Vice President and President of the Senate, and as President of all the people, I have come to understand and to place the highest value on the checks and balances which our founders imposed on government through the separation of powers, among co-equal Legislative, Executive and Judicial Branches.

This often results in difficulty and delay, as I well know, but it also places a supreme authority under God, beyond any one person, any one branch, any majority great or small, or any one party. The Constitution is the bedrock of all our freedoms; guard and cherish it; keep honor and order in your own house; and the Republic will endure.

It is not easy to end these remarks; in this chamber, along with some of you, I have experienced many, many of the highlights of my life. It was here that I stood 28 years ago with my freshman colleagues as Speaker Sam Rayburn administered the oath—I see some of you now, Charlie Bennett, Dick Bolling, Carl Perkins, Pete Rodino, Harley Staggers, Tom Steed, Sid Yates and Clem

and levels of government, and public policies which nurture and promote the creative energies of private enterprises, institutions and individual citizens.

A year ago, I reported that the state of the union was better—in many ways a lot better—but still not good enough.

Common sense told me to stick to the steady course we were on, to continue to restrain the inflationary growth of government, to reduce taxes as well as spending, to return local decisions to local officials, to provide for long-range sufficiency in energy and national security needs. I resisted the immense pressures of an election year to open the floodgates of Federal money and the temptation to promise more than I could deliver. I told it as it was to the American people and demonstrated to the world that, in our spirited political competition, as in this chamber, Americans can disagree without being disagreeable. . . .

This gathering symbolizes the Constitutional foundation which makes con-

Zablocki, and I remember those who have gone to their rest.

It was here we waged many, many a lively battle, won some, lost some, but always remaining friends. It was here surrounded by such friends, that the distinguished Chief Justice swore me in as Vice President on December 6, 1973. It was here I returned eight months later as your President to ask you not for a honeymoon, but for a good marriage.

I will always treasure those memories and the many, many kindnesses. I thank you for them.

My fellow Americans, I once asked for your prayers, and now I give you mine: May God guide this wonderful country, its people, and those they have chosen to lead them. May our third century be illuminated by liberty and blessed with brotherhood, so that we and all who come after us may be the humble servants of thy peace. Amen.

Good night and God bless you.

3.

JIMMY CARTER: Inaugural Address

Jimmy Carter was sworn in as the thirty-ninth President of the United States on January 20, 1977. His inaugural address was one of the shortest on record— only fourteen minutes—and extremely low-key. The New York Times *applauded editorially "a welcome theme of simplicity, which consciously moved away from the grandiose." The* Times's *commentator, William Safire, was more critical, calling the speech "pedestrian." Be that as it may, the address clearly stated the concerns of the President in a nonrhetorical manner that would mark most of his public utterances over the next four years. If the speech was undistinguished, it was followed by a precedent-shattering event. After concluding his remarks and accepting the less-than-tumultuous applause of the large crowd, President Carter took his wife's arm, stepped down from the podium, and walked rather than rode the mile-and-a-half down Pennsylvania Avenue from Capitol Hill to the White House. It was a memorable moment in presidential history.*

Source: *Congressional Quarterly: Historical Documents of 1977,* January 1977.

FOR MYSELF and for our nation, I want to thank my predecessor for all he has done to heal our land.

In this outward and physical ceremony we attest once again to the inner and spiritual strength of our nation.

As my high school teacher, Miss Julia Coleman, used to say, "We must adjust to changing times and still hold to unchanging principles."

Here before me is the Bible used in the inauguration of our first President in 1789, and I have just taken the oath of office on the Bible my mother gave me just a few years ago, opened to a timeless admonition from the ancient prophet Micah:

"He hath showed thee, o man,

President and Mrs. Carter walking down Pennsylvania Avenue in the inaugural parade.

what is good; and what does the Lord require of thee, but to do justly, and to love mercy, and to walk humbly with thy God." (Micah 6:8)

This inauguration ceremony marks a new beginning, a new dedication within our government, and a new spirit among us all. A President may sense and proclaim that new spirit, but only a people can provide it.

Two centuries ago our nation's birth was a milestone in the long quest for freedom, but the bold and brilliant dream which excited the founders of this nation still awaits its consummation. I have no new dream to set forth today, but rather urge a fresh faith in the old dream.

Ours was the first society openly to define itself in terms of both spiri-

tuality and human liberty. It is that unique self-definition which has given us an exceptional appeal—but it also imposes on us a special obligation—to take on those moral duties which, when assumed, seem invariably to be in our own best interests.

You have given me a great responsibility—to stay close to you, to be worthy of you, and to exemplify what you are. Let us create together a new national spirit of unity and trust. Your strength can compensate for my weakness, and your wisdom can help to minimize my mistakes.

Let us learn together and laugh together and work together and pray together, confident that in the end we will triumph together in the right.

The American dream endures. We must once again have full faith in our country—and in one another. I believe America can be better. We can be even stronger than before.

Let our recent mistakes bring a resurgent commitment to the basic principles of our nation, for we know that if we despise our own government we have no future. We recall in special times when we have stood briefly, but magnificently, united; in those times no prize was beyond our grasp.

But we cannot dwell upon remembered glory. We cannot afford to drift. We reject the prospect of failure or mediocrity or an inferior quality of life for any person.

Our government must at the same time be both competent and compassionate.

We have already found a high degree of personal liberty, and we are now struggling to enhance equality of opportunity. Our commitment to human rights must be absolute, our laws fair, our natural beauty preserved; the powerful must not persecute the weak, and human dignity must be enhanced.

We have learned that "more" is not necessarily "better," that even our great nation has its recognized limits, and that we can neither answer all questions nor solve all problems. We cannot afford to do everything, nor can we afford to lack boldness as we meet the future. So together, in a spirit of individual sacrifice for the common good, we must simply do our best.

Our nation can be strong abroad only if it is strong at home, and we know that the best way to enhance freedom in other lands is to demonstrate here that our democratic system is worthy of emulation.

To be true to ourselves, we must be true to others. We will not behave in foreign places so as to violate our rules and standards here at home, for we know that the trust which our nation earns is essential to our strength.

The world itself is now dominated by a new spirit. Peoples more numerous and more politically aware are craving and now demanding their place in the sun—not just for the benefit of their own physical condition, but for basic human rights.

The passion for freedom is on the rise. Tapping this new spirit, there can be no nobler nor more ambitious task for America to undertake on this day of a new beginning than to help shape a just and peaceful world that is truly humane.

We are a strong nation and we will maintain strength so sufficient that it need not be proven in combat—a quiet strength based not merely on the size of an arsenal, but on the nobility of ideas.

We will be ever vigilant and never vulnerable, and we will fight our wars against poverty, ignorance and injustice,

for those are the enemies against which our forces can be honorably marshalled.

We are a proudly idealistic nation, but let no one confuse our idealism with weakness.

Because we are free we can never be indifferent to the fate of freedom elsewhere. Our moral sense dictates a clearcut preference for those societies which share with us an abiding respect for individual human rights. We do not seek to intimidate, but it is clear that a world which others can dominate with impunity would be inhospitable to decency and a threat to the well-being of all people.

The world is still engaged in a massive armaments race designed to insure continuing equivalent strength among potential adversaries. We pledge perseverance and wisdom in our efforts to limit the world's armaments to those necessary for each nation's own domestic safety. And we will move this year a step toward our ultimate goal—the elimination of all nuclear weapons from this earth. We urge all other people to join us, for success can mean life instead of death.

Within us, the people of the United States, there is evident a serious and purposeful rekindling of confidence, and I join in the hope that when my time as your President has ended, people might say this about our nation:

That we had remembered the words of Micah and renewed our search for humility, mercy and justice;

That we had torn down the barriers that separated those of different race and region and religion, and where there had been mistrust, built unity, with a respect for diversity;

That we had found productive work for those able to perform it;

That we had strengthened the American family, which is the basis of our society;

That we had ensured respect for the law, and equal treatment under the law, for the weak and the powerful, for the rich and the poor;

And that we had enabled our people to be proud of their own government once again.

I would hope that the nations of the world might say that we had built a lasting peace, based not on weapons of war but on international policies which reflect our own most precious values.

These are not just my goals. And they will not be my accomplishments, but the affirmation of our nation's continuing moral strength and our belief in an undiminished, ever-expanding American dream.

4.

JIMMY CARTER: Letter to Andrei Sakharov

Around the time of President Carter's inauguration, in January 1977, Andrei Sakharov wrote him a letter, in Russian, describing conditions in the U.S.S.R. and in other countries of the Soviet bloc, and pleading for Carter's aid in making known to the world the plight of dissidents in the Soviet system. Sakharov himself was already one of the best known of the dissidents; a nonviolent man and a famous nuclear scientist, he had been and was to be punished, sequestered, and exiled for his rebellious beliefs in free speech and human dignity. Sakharov's letter was translated by his wife into broken but effective English. "It's very important," it began, "to defend those who suffer because of their unviolent struggle, for openness, for justice for destroyed rights of the other people. Our and your duty are to fight for them. I think that a lot depends from this struggle—trust between the people, trust to the high promises and in the final result—international security." The handwritten letter, signed by Sakharov, arrived at the State Department on January 21, 1977. Carter's reply was made public on February 5. It occasioned worldwide press coverage—which was one of the aims, at least, of Sakharov's initiative.

Source: National Archives: Carter Presidential Materials.

THE WHITE HOUSE
WASHINGTON
February 5, 1977

Dear Professor Sakharov:

I received your letter of January 21, and I want to express my appreciation to you for bringing your thoughts to my personal attention.

Human rights is a central concern of my Administration. In my inaugural address I stated: "Because we are free, we can never be indifferent to the fate of freedom elsewhere." You may rest assured that the American people and our government will continue our firm commitment to promote respect for human rights not only in our own country but also abroad.

We shall use our good offices to seek the release of prisoners of conscience, and we will continue our efforts to shape a world responsive to human aspirations in which nations of differing cultures and histories can live side by side in peace and justice.

I am always glad to hear from you, and I wish you well.

Sincerely,

Jimmy Carter

Professor Andrei Sakharov
Moscow, USSR

5.

GEORGE F. KENNAN: "Democracy" as a World Cause

President Carter's letter to Andrei Sakharov (see Selection 4) was only one in a long series of initiatives by his administration in the area of human rights. Early in January 1977 a manifesto had been signed by prominent intellectuals in Czechoslovakia demanding human rights as spelled out in the Helsinki agreement of 1975 (signed by Czechoslovakia among other countries); as Czech police began rounding up the signatories, the U.S. government protested officially, although vainly. In February Carter denounced Idi Amin, the dictator of Uganda; in March he addressed the United Nations, calling upon them to work with both friends and foes to advance the cause of human rights. But not all citizens approved the President's moral approach to foreign policy. Some, even those— for example, in Amnesty International—who worked hardest to secure the rights of oppressed people everywhere, feared the official stance concerning human rights would tend to "politicize" the issue, making it harder to achieve real progress against brutal crimes committed against individuals. Others, like the political pundit George F. Kennan, felt that it was inappropriate, as well as ineffective, for the government to inject ethical judgments into its foreign policy decisions. In a 1977 book, Kennan expressed a view that has often been expressed throughout America's history.

Source: *The Cloud of Danger*, II:5.

WE CONTINUE TO HEAR it said or suggested in a thousand ways and from a thousand sources that a major concern of American diplomacy, worldwide, should be the advancement of self-government by other people. Our government is criticized for allegedly supporting Latin American "dictators." It is criticized for failing to support (as the critics see it) "majority rule" in Southern Africa. It is urged to make the repressive actions of the Soviet government towards dissident intellectuals an issue in Soviet-American relations. In a host of ways the thought finds expression in the American media that America has a duty to encourage and support the growth of democratic institutions, or at least the assurance of human rights, across the world, and that this should constitute a major, and even overriding objective of American policy on a global scale.

There are a number of reflections which cause me, for one, to have deep misgivings about this thesis.

First of all, I know of no evidence that "democracy," or what we picture to ourselves under that word, is the natural state of most of mankind. It seems rather to be a form of government (and a difficult one, with many drawbacks, at that) which evolved in the eighteenth and nineteenth centuries in northwestern Europe, primarily among those countries that border on the English Channel and the North Sea (but with a certain extension into Central Europe), and which was then carried into other parts of the world, including North America, where peoples from that northwestern European area appeared as original settlers, or as colonialists, and had laid down the prevailing patterns of civil government. Democracy has, in other words, a relatively narrow base both in time and in space; and the evidence has yet to be produced that it is the natural form of rule for peoples outside those narrow perimeters.

All distinctions in forms of political authority, including that which people try to draw between "democracy" and "dictatorship," are of course relative, not absolute. There is a bit of conspiracy, and of authoritarianism, in every democracy; and a bit of democracy in every dictatorship. Besides, people influence each other. Political fashions and pretenses have a way of spreading. The urge to play at being "democratic," in the sense of setting up institutions the names of which suggest self-government, has affected most of the world. Few governments fail to support some pretense of this nature; even the names they often choose for themselves ("People's," "Democratic," "Republic," etc.) are designed to convey this suggestion. Possibly, this has some significance for the future. It seems to have very little for the present. Some of the nastiest and most brutal tyrannies now masquerade under titles of this nature. Even if "democracy" were the wave of the future (and the longer span of history affords no grounds for supposing that it is), the future in question would not be the immediate one; and whoever made it his objective to realize the dream of a democratically governed world in any short space of time, to the sacrifice of more pressing needs of the international community, would be behaving very quixotically indeed.

Secondly, I know of no reason to suppose that the attempt to develop and employ democratic institutions would necessarily be the best course for many of these peoples. The record of attempts of this nature has not been all that good. Time and time again, authoritarian regimes have been able to introduce reforms and to improve the lot of masses of people, where more diffuse forms of political authority had failed. As examples one has only to think of Portugal under Salazar, of China under Mao, even of Cuba under Castro, because, distasteful as the Castro regime may be to many people (myself, I may say, included), we have to accept the testimony of dispassionate witnesses that it

Cuban President Fidel Castro with sugarcane workers in Jamaica.

has introduced many useful reforms and done much for the common people. If the question be asked whether the great popular masses of this world, as distinct from restless intellectuals, prefer democratic institutions to prosperity and economic security, it would be a brave man who would undertake to answer that affirmatively in the light of the historical record. Those Americans who profess to know with such certainty what other people want and what is good for them in the way of political institutions would do well to ask themselves whether they are not actually attempting to impose their own values, traditions, and habits of thought on peoples for whom these things have no validity and no usefulness.

Finally, I think we should note that if America were to try to become, as John Quincy Adams put it disapprovingly, the "guarantors" instead of the "friends" of the liberties of half the world, there is no reason to suppose that we would make a very good job of it. One notes that even among those Americans who profess the most passionate attachment to this cause, the actual application of the enthusiasm is highly selective. They seem, in fact— these advocates of efforts to assure the liberties of other peoples—to fall into two categories: those (the Greeks, the Jews, the Cubans, the blacks, etc.) whose interest is largely confined to the political fortunes of people of their own ethnic origin; and those others, the professional liberals, whose concern for the cause of democracy elsewhere purports to rest on general principles but seems to confine itself in actuality to the brutalities of right-wing authoritarianism, as in Chile or Greece, or to those of white European authoritarianism wherever the latter affects people of different racial identity. These preoccupations lead to heavy pressures on the United States government to intercede on behalf of Jewish dissidents in Russia, of Castro's opponents in Cuba, of Chilean oppositionists, and of various African resistance leaders striving for the removal of white power in Southern Africa in favor of the establishment of their own. They show no comparable concern for the nameless and numberless Chinese who may have fallen victim to the rigid intellectual and physical discipline of the Chinese Communist regime; for the several tens of thousands of Africans slaughtered just in the course of recent years by other black Africans who had the power to slaughter them; for the Indians abruptly and brutally expelled from Kenya and Uganda; for the thousands of Angolan blacks forced to flee across the border into Southwest Africa and to seek the protection of the South African authorities; nor indeed, in the case of the Soviet Union, for the hundreds of thousands of non-Jewish people (Crimean Tartars, Volga Germans, and what you will) who are still suffering from the measures taken against them in the Stalin period. These and other such peoples simply do not fit into the highly selective limits to which the enthusiasm of various Americans for other people's liberties is normally confined.

There is every reason to suppose, therefore, that even if the United States government were to accept a solemn commitment to devote itself to the cause of the promotion of democracy in other parts of the world, the ensuing measures of policy would not be apt to reflect any very fair and principled devotion to this cause. What would be more likely to happen would be that the commitment would be instantaneously seized upon by factions within the American citizenry interested in achieving certain objectives relating to those who were their particular *bêtes noires* among other governing groups or those who were the particular objects of their sympathy among those out of power. The other victims, or subjects, of authoritarianism—those who had no constituency among the members of these American pressure groups—would continue to be ignored, as they are today.

Nor is there any reason for confidence that the results of such American efforts to interfere in the internal affairs of other countries would invariably lead to any great improvement in the respective governmental conditions, even if the efforts in question were nominally successful in achieving the overthrow of the regimes against which they were directed. There is a tendency among Americans to assume that anyone who finds himself victimized by, or in opposition to, a given dictatorship or authoritarian regime is ipso facto a fighter for freedom, devoted to the principles of liberal democracy, and certain, if helped to political success, to adopt these principles and to carry them into practice. American diplomatic history affords one example after another of this naïve assumption. Things are, unfortunately, seldom just this simple. Too often, the highest hope of political dissidents in an authoritarian society is the dream of someday treating their tormentors as their tormentors have treated them—an objective not likely to have anything to do with the principles of democracy. By and large, successive governments in a given society tend to resemble each other in methodology if not in professed ideology. Particularly in a society accustomed to brutal or authoritarian rule, it is hard for anyone to govern, however lofty his original intentions, by methods strikingly different from those to which people have become accustomed by long experience and tradition.

For all these reasons it is difficult to see any promise in an American policy which sets out to correct and improve the political habits of large parts of the world's population. Misgovernment, in the sense of the rise to power of the most determined, decisive, and often brutal natures, has been the common condition of most of mankind for centuries and millennia in the past. It is going to remain that condition for long into the future, no matter how valiantly Americans insist on tilting against the windmills. American policy-makers would do better to concentrate on those areas of international relations where the dangers and challenges are greatest and where America has the greatest possibilities for useful and effective action. These, as it happens, are ones that have little relation to the cause of democracy as such. And they are quite enough to absorb all the energies and resources we can devote to them.

6.

Jimmy Carter: The Moral Equivalent of War

Even before he was inaugurated, Jimmy Carter and his closest advisors had decided that the growing use and declining supplies of energy was one of the most pressing problems the administration would face during the next four years. With his accustomed rhetoric of commitment, Carter therefore went before the nation in a televised speech on April 18, 1977, declaring that his proposed energy program would be "the moral equivalent of war." He repeated the phrase—owed to philosopher William James—in an address to a joint session of Congress on April 20, in which he spelled out the details of his program. Carter's initiative was not at first successful. There was immediate negative reaction to his proposal of a "gas guzzler tax" on large automobiles and to some other elements of the program. By the end of 1977, with the administration apparently not behind it with much enthusiasm, legislation was still not forthcoming to enforce it. But the American people were responding, nevertheless, to Carter's pleas for conservation. They bought smaller cars, turned down their thermostats, used less electricity. Less than a decade after Carter's impassioned plea, it was largely owing to their efforts that there was a worldwide "energy glut" and prices of energy were falling. Carter's April 18 speech is reprinted here.

Source: *Congressional Quarterly: Historic Documents of 1977,* April.

TONIGHT I WANT TO HAVE an unpleasant talk with you about a problem unprecedented in our history. With the exception of preventing war, this is the greatest challenge our country will face during our lifetimes. The energy crisis has not yet overwhelmed us, but it will if we do not act quickly.

It's a problem we will not solve in the next few years, and it is likely to get progressively worse through the rest of this century.

We must not be selfish or timid if we hope to have a decent world for our children and grandchildren. We simply must balance our demand for energy with our rapidly shrinking resources. By acting now we can control our future instead of letting the future control us.

Two days from now, I will present to the Congress my energy proposals. Its members will be my partners and they have already given me a great deal of valuable advice.

Many of these proposals will be unpopular. Some will cause you to put up with inconveniences and to make sacrifices. The most important thing about these proposals is that the alternative may be a national catastrophe. Further delay can affect our strength and our power as a nation.

Our decision about energy will test the character of the American people and the ability of the President and the Congress to govern this nation. This difficult effort will be the "moral equivalent of war"—except that we will be uniting our efforts to build and not to destroy.

I know that some of you may doubt that we face real energy shortages. The 1973 gas lines are gone, and with the springtime weather our homes are warm again.

But our energy problem is worse tonight than it was in 1973 or a few weeks ago in the dead of winter. It is worse because more waste has occurred, and more time has passed by without our planning for the future. And it will get worse every day until we act.

The oil and natural gas we rely on for 75 per cent of our energy are simply running out. In spite of increased effort, domestic production has been dropping steadily at about 6 per cent a year. Imports have doubled in the last five years. And our nation's independence of economic and political action is becoming increasingly constrained. Unless profound changes are made to lower oil consumption, we now believe that early in the 1980s the world will be demanding more oil than it can produce.

The world now uses about 60 million barrels of oil a day, and demand increases each year about 5 per cent. This means that just to stay even we need the production of a new Texas every year, an Alaskan North Slope every nine months, or a new Saudi Arabia every three years. Obviously this cannot continue.

We must look back into history to understand our energy problem. Twice in the last several hundred years there has been a transition in the way people use energy. The first was about 200 years ago, when we changed away from wood—which had provided about 90 per cent of all fuel—to coal, which was more efficient. This change became the basis of the Industrial Revolution.

The second change took place in this century, with the growing use of oil and natural gas. They were more convenient and cheaper than coal, and the supply seemed to be almost without limit. They made possible the age of automobile and airplane travel. Nearly everyone who is alive today grew up during this age and we have never known anything different.

Because we are now running out of gas and oil, we must prepare quickly for a third change, to strict conservation and to the renewed use of coal and permanent renewable energy sources, like solar power.

The world has not prepared for the future. During the 1950s, people used twice as much oil as during the 1940s. During the 1960s, we used twice as much as during the 1950s. And in each of those decades, more oil was consumed than in all of mankind's previous history combined.

World consumption of oil is still going up. If it were possible to keep it rising during the 1970s and 1980s by 5 per cent a year as it has in the past, we could use up all the proven reserves of oil in the entire world by the end of the next decade.

I know that many of you have suspected that some supplies of oil and gas are being withheld. You may be right, but suspicions about the oil companies cannot change the fact that we are running out of petroleum. All of us have heard about the large oil fields on Alaska's North Slope. In a few years when the North Slope is producing fully, its total output will be just about equal to two years' increase in our own nation's energy demand.

Each new inventory of world oil reserves has been more disturbing than the last. World oil production can probably keep going up for another six or eight years. But sometime in the 1980s it can't go up any more.

Demand will overtake production. We have no choice about that. But we do have a choice about how we will spend the next few years. Each American uses the energy equivalent of 60 barrels of oil per person each year. Ours is the most wasteful nation on earth. We waste more energy than we import. With about the same standard of living, we use twice as much energy per person as do other countries like Germany, Japan and Sweden.

One choice is to continue doing what we have been doing before. We can drift along for a few more years. Our consumption of oil would keep going up every year. Our cars would continue to be too large and inefficient. Three-quarters of them would carry only one person—the driver—while our public transportation system continues to decline. We can delay insulating our houses, and they will continue to lose about 50 per cent of their heat in waste.

We can continue using scarce oil and natural gas to generate electricity, and continue wasting two-thirds of their fuel value in the process. If we do not act, then by 1985 we will be using 33 per cent more energy than we do today.

We can't substantially increase our domestic production, so we would need to import twice as much oil as we do now. Supplies will be uncertain. The cost will keep going up. Six years ago, we paid $3.7-billion for imported oil. Last year we spent $36-billion—nearly ten times as much—and this year we may spend $45-billion.

Unless we act, we will spend more than $550-billion for imported oil by 1985—more than $2,500 for every man, woman, and child in America. Along with that money—that we transport overseas—we will continue losing American jobs and becoming increasingly vulnerable to supply interruptions.

Now we have a choice. But if we wait, we will live in fear of embargoes. We could endanger our freedom as a sovereign nation to act in foreign affairs. Within ten years we would not be able to import enough oil—from any country, at any acceptable price.

If we wait, and do not act, then our factories will not be able to keep our people on the job with reduced supplies of fuel. Too few of our utilities will have switched to coal, which is our most abundant energy source. We will not be ready to keep our transportation system running with smaller, more efficient cars and a better network of buses, trains, and public transportation.

We will feel mounting pressure to plunder the environment. We would have a crash program to build more nuclear plants, strip-mine and burn more coal, and drill more off-shore wells than if we begin to conserve now. Inflation will soar, production will go down, people will lose their jobs. Intense competition for oil will build up among nations, and among the different regions within our own country. If we fail to act soon, we will face an economic, social and political crisis that will threaten our free institutions.

But we still have another choice. We can begin to prepare right now. We can decide to act while there is still time. That is the concept of the energy policy we will present on Wednesday.

Our national energy plan is based on ten fundamental principles.

—The first principle is that we can have an effective and comprehensive energy policy only if the government takes responsibility for it and if the people understand the seriousness of the challenge and are willing to make sacrifices.

—The second principle is that healthy economic growth must continue. Only by saving energy can we maintain our standard of living and keep our people at work. An effective conservation program will create hundreds of thousands of new jobs.

—The third principle is that we must protect the environment. Our energy problems have the same cause as our environmental problems—wasteful use of resources. Conservation helps us solve both problems at once.

—The fourth principle is that we must reduce our vulnerability to potentially devastating embargoes. We can protect ourselves from uncertain supplies by reducing our demand for oil, making the most of our abundant resources such as coal, and by developing a strategic petroleum reserve.

—The fifth principle is that we must be fair. Our solutions must ask equal sacrifices from every region, every class of people, and every interest group. Industry will have to do its part to conserve, just as consumers will. The energy producers deserve fair treatment, but we will not let the oil companies profiteer.

—The sixth principle, and the cornerstone of our policy, is to reduce demand through conservation. Our emphasis on conservation is a clear difference between this plan and others which merely encouraged crash production efforts. Conservation is the quickest, cheapest, most practical source of energy. Conservation is the only way we can buy a barrel of oil for a few dollars, for about $2. It costs about $13 to waste it.

—The seventh principle is that prices should generally reflect the true replacement cost of energy. We are only cheating ourselves if we make energy artifically cheap and use more than we can really afford.

—The eighth principle is that government policies must be predictable and certain. Both consumers and producers need policies they can count on so they can plan ahead. This is one reason I am working with the Congress to create a new Department of Energy, to replace more than 50 different agencies that now have some control over energy.

—The ninth principle is that we must conserve the fuels that are scarcest and make the most of those that are plentiful. We can't continue to use oil and gas for 75 per cent of our consumption as we do now when they make up only 7 per cent of our domestic reserves.

We need to shift to plentiful coal while taking care to protect the environment, and to apply stricter safety standards to nuclear energy.

—The tenth and last principle is that we must start now to develop the new, unconventional sources of energy that we will rely on in the next century.

Now, these ten principles have guided the development of the policy I will describe to you and the Congress on Wednesday night.

Our energy plan will also include a number of specific goals, to measure our progress toward a stable energy system. These are the goals that we set for 1985:

• To reduce the annual growth rate in our energy demand to less than 2 per cent.

• To reduce gasoline consumption by 10 per cent below its current level.

• To cut in half the portion of U.S. oil which is imported—from a potential level of 16 million barrels to 6 million barrels a day.

• To establish a strategic petroleum reserve of one billion barrels, more than a six-month supply.

• To increase our coal production by about two-thirds to more than 1 billion tons a year.

• To insulate 90 per cent of American homes and all new buildings.

• To use solar energy in more than two and one-half million houses.

We will monitor our progress toward these goals year by year. Our plan will call for strict conservation measures if we fall behind.

I can't tell you that these measures will be easy, nor will they be popular. But I think most of you realize that a policy which does not ask for changes or

sacrifices would not be an effective policy at this late date. This plan is essential to protect our jobs, our environment, our standard of living, and our future.

Whether this plan truly makes a difference will not be decided now here in Washington, but in every town and every factory, in every home and on every highway and every farm.

I believe this can be a positive challenge. There is something especially American in the kinds of changes that we have to make. We have been proud, through our history, of being efficient people.

We have been proud of our ingenuity, our skill at answering questions. We need efficiency and ingenuity more than ever. We have been proud of our leadership in the world. And now we have a chance again to give the world a positive example.

And we've always been proud of our vision of the future. We have always wanted to give our children and grandchildren a world richer in possibilities than we've had. They are the ones we must provide for now. They are the ones who will suffer most if we don't act.

I've given you some of the principles of the plan.

I am sure each of you will find something you don't like about the specifics of our proposal. It will demand that we make sacrifices and changes in every life. To some degree the sacrifices will be painful—but so is any meaningful sacrifice. It will lead to some higher costs, and to some greater inconveniences for everyone.

But the sacrifices can be gradual, realistic, and they are necessary. Above all, they will be fair. No one will gain an unfair advantage through this plan. No one will be asked to bear an unfair burden. We will monitor the accuracy of data from the oil and natural gas companies for the first time, so that we will know their true production, supplies, reserves, and profits.

Those citizens who insist on driving large, unnecessarily powerful cars must expect to pay more for that luxury.

We can be sure that all the special interest groups in the country will attack the part of this plan that affects them directly. They will say that sacrifice is fine, as long as other people do it, but that their sacrifice is unreasonable, or unfair, or harmful to the country. If they succeed with this approach, then the burden on the ordinary citizen, who is not organized into an interest group, would be crushing.

There should be only one test for this program—whether it will help our country. Other generations of Americans have faced and mastered great challenges. I have faith that meeting this challenge will make our own lives even richer. If you will join me so that we can work together with patriotism and courage, we will again prove that our great nation can lead the world into an age of peace, independence, and freedom. Thank you very much and good night.

7.

Anita Bryant and Brian McNaught: Gay Rights

In January 1977 the Miami Metro Commission passed an ordinance barring discrimination against homosexuals in employment, housing, and public accommodations. The vote on the question was highly confrontational: a group calling itself Dade County Coalition for the Humanistic Rights of Gays tried to shout down, but was shouted down by, another group called Save Our Children, founded by pop singer Anita Bryant and her husband Bob Green. Save Our Children continued to agitate against the ordinance, and in a city-wide referendum on June 7 it was voted down by a two-to-one margin. Nationally, large numbers of gays responded by marching in protest in many cities on June 26, and on other occasions thereafter. Miss Bryant also continued her campaign. Reprinted here are, first, a chapter from Miss Bryant's book, The Anita Bryant Story, *in which she describes the events leading up to the January vote; and, second, a "response to Anita Bryant" by a leading Roman Catholic gay journalist, Brian McNaught.*

Sources: *The Anita Bryant Story,* Chapter 2, 1977.

The Humanist, October 1977.

A: ANITA BRYANT
THE BATTLE FOR MIAMI

THE BATTLE LINES were drawn in Miami on that memorable cold January morning. The foot soldiers were housewives and mothers, religious and civic leaders in opposition to a well-organized, highly financed, and politically militant group of homosexual activists.

We emerged at the scene of the controversy as an unorganized but deeply concerned and committed group of parents and citizens upon whom had been foisted an ordinance which was against everything we believed in and stood for. We had neither marshaled our defenses, nor had we developed a strategy as the leaders of the militant homosexual movement had obviously done. We had done our homework: We did know why we were there, but there was nothing political or militant in our motives. Most of us had never seen each other before, and our first introductions were at the courthouse.

As the nation was to see in succeeding weeks, our stand brought death threats, harassment, heartache, distortions of statements by the media, tremendous pressures, disruption of our private lives, and a host of problems we had not envisioned when we took our stand. For me, in addition to all of the above, it brought job discrimination and the loss of a lifelong dream of having a television show of my own. We were cast as bigots, haters, discriminators, and deniers of basic human rights. And all of this happened because we were sincerely concerned for our children and our community.

I felt strong, confident, and at peace. I had carefully studied the wording of the amendment. I knew the Scriptures. My own personal preparation for the confrontation was complete. People were praying. We had prayed, and even while we were in that hearing, the Lord was reading my heart and hearing the cries welling up from deep within me. I knew God's hand was upon us.

The local "gay" activists were there with those who had joined them in their defense of the ordinance. Under the banner of the Dade County Coalition for the Humanistic Rights of Gays, they flexed their political muscles. While much of the media and sympathizers to the homosexuals were shouting about discrimination, the spokesman for the local group admitted at the hearing that homosexuals as individuals *are* able to obtain housing, employment, and education without discrimination in Dade County. "We are there now and what we want to do is tell you where we're at," their avowed leader said.

"If there is no discrimination, then there is no need for this ordinance," said Mayor Steve Clark.

We outnumbered the opposition by eight to one at the hearing, even though they brought in some speakers from out of state. Homosexuals in Dade County had made a discovery during the local elections the preceding year—they discovered they had political clout. Dade County became another testing ground for them in their continuing nationwide efforts to gain so-called rights and lifestyle approval. This was to be proved in the months ahead as political organizers from around the country joined them in launching a full-fledged crusade.

Proponents of the ordinance framed the issue as civil rights versus bigotry. Nothing could have been further from the truth. At the hearing, the leaders of the homosexual movement had their say first. When it came time for those of us who opposed the ordinance to speak, some very articulate religious and civic leaders in the community presented views which we felt validated our stand and would compel the Metro Commission to reverse its original vote.

Reverend Charles Couey from South Dade Baptist Church was the first man called on to speak for our side. There was an immediately noticeable hush throughout the room as this man of God

AP/Wide World

Anita Bryant speaking against a gay rights ordinance in Miami, Florida.

stood with only the Word of God in his hands and, without expounding or explaining the Scripture in any way, read from the first chapter of Romans. . . .

The Roman Catholic Church, through its attorney, prominent Miamian Joseph Fitzgerald, said the ordinance would permit known practicing homosexuals to teach in private church schools and to act as role models for their pupils, showing that homosexuality is an acceptable and respectable alternative to the life-style of the children's parents. This, he said, would be directly counter to teachings of the Catholic Church. Later, Archbishop Coleman Carroll, prestigious leader of South Florida's heavy Catholic population and its fifty-six schools, said the Church would refuse to obey the law and would oppose it vigorously in the courts. . . .

Robert M. Brake, a Coral Gables city commissioner and a former Metro Com-

missioner, said the ordinance was a bad law and maintained that homosexuals were already granted all rights against discrimination under existing federal laws. This effort, he said was a carefully disguised attempt to break down further the moral fabric of society. He said the law would give these people special privileges that would only be to the detriment of society in general and children in particular. . . .

When it was my turn to speak, I addressed the mayor and members of the commission with these words:

I come here today with no prejudice in my heart, no hate, no anger, or judgment against my fellowman. But I do come with a deep burden for my country, my community, and my children's well-being.

The commissioners have already received my letter and know full well my stand as Christian, and I make no apologies for that.

I'm speaking to you today not as an entertainer who has worked with homosexuals all my life—and I have never discriminated against them; I have a policy of live and let live as long as they do not discriminate against me. But I am a wife and a mother, and I especially address you today as a mother. I have a God-given right to be jealous of the moral environment for my children.

I remind you that the God who made us could have made us like the sea turtle who comes in the dark of night and buries her eggs in the sand and never cares about her children again. But God created us so our children would be dependent upon us as their parents for their lives. And I, for one, will do everything I can as a citizen, as a Christian, and especially as a mother to insure that they have the right to a healthy and morally good life.

The cry of work discrimination has been the key that has unlocked the door of freedom to *legitimate* minority groups; now, it is time to recognize the rights of the overwhelming majority of Dade County who are being discriminated against because they have the right to say no. Just when did the word *discrimination* start meaning "I can't say no"? The people of Dade County can't say no now in the areas of housing, employment, and education. But I can, and I do say no to a very serious moral issue that would violate my rights and the rights of all decent and morally upstanding citizens, regardless of their race or religion.

We urge the Dade County Commissioners to act responsibly for the vast majority of their constituents. . . .

Because we were not organized, Orthodox Rabbi Phineas Weberman did not get to speak, but he did present his statement to the commissioners afterwards. He said his five-thousand-year-old religion had always condemned homosexuality as unnatural, unproductive, sinful, and a flagrant violation of God's laws and the laws of the vast majority of mankind in all ages.

And there were others who spoke out against the ordinance that day. We all agreed that we were opposed to their demands for what they considered a basic "right" and the affirmation by society that what they were doing was right. But our voices were united in protest. It was not solely a religious issue, as our opponents kept insisting; it was a moral issue on which society has a right to make its own contrary judgment.

Of course we were naive enough to think our presence and testimony were going to sway the commissioners. Had it been an actual court trial, the case would have been thrown out because the only reason for proposing the amendment was to show discrimination where there was none.

Immediately after hearing arguments from both sides, the commission voted. The measure was passed by a five-to-three vote, setting up what had to be an inevitable future confrontation. The fight was not over. . . .

I was visibly stunned, as were all others. I couldn't believe it. I was devastated. I sat there, and I heard the result of the vote, and I thought. *This is a free country, and if we present our case and we're right and if it's proven, then we should win it.*

That's what shocked me so badly—to think we live in a country where freedom and right are supposed to reign, a country that boasts "In God we trust" and has such a rich spiritual heritage; yet where internal decadence is all too evident, where the Word of God and the voice of the majority is sometimes not heeded at all. Has it come to this: that we are a society that in fact does glorify aberrant behavior and oppresses the rights of the majority on a moral issue? I was not the only one in the room that day who was throroughly disillusioned. . . .

As we stood outside the courtroom chambers, we knew we had to face this moral crisis. Later on I knew, from information that had been sent to me, that in California this same kind of battle had been fought and all but lost due to the apathy of the public. With the help of our local religious and civic leaders, I sensed that we as wives and mothers had to march out of our living rooms and fight for the repeal of this ordinance. I joined with Judi Wilson and others who emphasized, "This is not a hate campaign. We're motivated because we love our children, our nation, and our country. And we have love and concern for homosexuals, too."

B: BRIAN McNAUGHT

WHY BOTHER WITH GAY RIGHTS?

"HYPOCRITES," stated Matthew Henry, "do the devil's drudgery in Christ's livery."

"Patriotism," insisted Samuel Johnson, "is the last refuge of a scoundrel."

Once again, misuse of the hyphenated proper noun *God-and-Country* has been employed to express fear and hatred and has succeeded in undermining basic human rights. Immediately prior to the June 7, 1977, defeat of a civil-rights ordinace for homosexuals in Dade County, Florida, Anita Bryant Green, spokesperson for the Florida Citrus Commission and Save Our Children from Homosexuality, Inc., told her followers: "[I dare to speak out] as a mother—as an American—as a Christian. I urgently need you to join with me and my family in a national crusade against this attack on God and His laws. It's really God's battle, not mine!"

According to most national press reports, many of the 202,319 Dade County residents who voted to repeal the Human Rights Ordinance saw the issue as a religious question. While much of our media intelligentsia found Ms. Bryant comical, she succeeded in convincing her public that gay civil rights were anti-God and anti-American, playing upon their fear that Miami would become "Sodom by the Sea."

There was little education disseminated in the Florida fight. Save Our Children perpetuated every known myth about homosexuals and created a couple of new ones. Homosexuals, insisted Ms. Bryant, are condemned by God. They seek to wear women's clothing, if they are men. They are sexually interested in children. Even those who aren't should not be allowed to be around children, who might be persuaded to become gay because of the influence of the positive role model. Homosexual acts, she said, are hideous because men eat each other's sperm, which is the essence of life. The Dade County ordinance would promote bestiality. Californians, she concluded, suffered a major drought because of God's wrath over the state's protection of gay civil rights. Ms. Bryant, who announced that many of her friends were homosexuals, insisted there would be no problem if gays would only stay in the closet.

If arguments for or against civil rights must be based upon the Bible, homosexuals should have nothing to fear. While the traditional position has been that selections of the Old and New Testaments (Genesis 19, Leviticus 18; Paul's letters to Romans, Corinthians, and Timothy) indicate God's abhorrence of homosexuality, a growing number of Scripture scholars from every major Christian denomination are now insisting those passages have been taken out of context and actually have nothing to do with what we know as "constitutional homosexuality." These arguments have been most recently supported by the controversial report on human sexuality by the Catholic Theological Society's Committee on Sexuality.

Wearing the clothing of the opposite gender is known as transvestism, which according to every available study is generally engaged in by heterosexuals. Ms. Bryant televised film clips from a San Francisco Gay Pride parade, in which several persons in "drag" participated. While there are certainly a number of gay men who parade in dresses, the number is small and their participation is more tolerated than encouraged.

Pederasts, or those persons who are sexually interested in children, again generally come from the heterosexual community. Police records indicate that the majority of such crimes involve fathers with their young daughters. Dr. Mary Calderone, director of the Sex Information and Educational Council of the U.S., writes: "The statistics are that it's heterosexuals who do most of the raping and the seducing."

Nevertheless, Save Our Children frightened voters with their "reminder" that an Orange County high-school band instructor was recently charged with ten counts of sexual relations with boys under eighteen years of age. They also could have recalled the twenty-seven young boys murdered in Houston by thirty-three-year-old bachelor Dean Allen Corll; and had time been on their side, the current charges against Los Angeles homosexuals Patrick Kearney and David Hill for killing forty men, the largest mass murder in this country's history.

This scare tactic prompts several questions. Does anyone presume that gay men and women are not as upset by seduction and murder as nongay persons? Why does the sexual orientation of a homosexual murderer or seducer make headlines when a case involving a heterosexual is never portrayed as a "straight" murder? Did Jack the Ripper, the Boston Strangler, the Dallas sniper, or Richard Speck represent the sickness of all heterosexuals? Despite the statistics that heterosexuals are more prone to rape and seduce, wouldn't it be absurd to characterize all heterosexuals as rapers and seducers of children and therefore unfit for teaching positions?

Furthermore, what kind of society provides victims for this country's Dean Corlls and Patrick Kearneys? Corll's victims were gay runaways who were rejected by their families. Kearney and Hill preyed upon individuals who were forced onto the street to find sexual liaisons. Who saved these children? . . .

In discussing homosexual lovemaking, the former Miss Oklahoma not only threw medical science back to the time when we believed that sperm was life in itself and the womb only a receptacle, but also suggested that *all* homosexuals engage in the *same* forms of sexual expression. Furthermore, there was the implication that *only* homosexuals were covered by sodomy laws. Surveys among the gay population clearly indicate that there is no one thing everyone engages in, be it anal intercourse, fellatio, or even kissing.

Ignoring the comment about the California drought, Save Our Children's desire to have homosexuals stay in the closet is perhaps the most troublesome attitude of even rational and sympathetic observers. "Your mother and I don't broadcast what we do in the bedroom," my father once said, "Why must you?" "Because," I replied, "you are not oppressed for what you do or don't do in the bedroom."

Battling myths and generalizations of "sick and sinful" labels by the psychiatric and religious professionals, homosexual women and men are incredibly concerned about public image and the mental health that results from self-acceptance and public acceptance.

"Coming out" as homosexual to self, to loved ones, and to working associates not only eliminates the need to dodge questions, dinner invitations, and anti-gay humor, but also enables the individual to produce more effectively and love more genuinely. An article in the Washington *Law Quarterly* by Irving Kovarsky entitled "Fair Employment for the Homosexual" states: "Thus the homosexual employee who is aware of his employer's policy toward homosexuals lives in fear, knowing that he will lose his job and will be unable to find other employment if discovered. A reasonable assumption is that the 'closet' homosexual performs less efficiently because of inner torment. . . . The employer, maximizing profit, should be interested in the mental well-being of the unknown (and known) homosexual employee."

For many persons, the Dade County vote was a test of "I'm OK, you're OK." More than a question of civil rights, it was a battle for public and self-acceptance. The eleven o'clock news on June 7 was felt by homosexuals across the world to be saying: "We're OK, you stink."

Gays in Dade County likened Anita Bryant to Adolf Hitler. Several columnists criticized that rhetoric as a sensationalized appealed to Miami Jews. But how sensationalized was it? Germany was wrought with unemployment, a "swinging" upper class, crime, and discontent. Hitler was seen as a harmless fool whose following was large enough to ensure him a place in the public eye, but too small to be seen as a threat. Gay rights had attracted the attention of a variety of noted scholars and personalities. Legislation pended in the Reichstag to repeal a repressive Paragraph 175. Once Hitler's bandwagon began to roll, he expanded his purist preaching and with the consent of what was imagined to be the majority, began actualizing his dreams by burning books and enacting laws that limited the freedom of those persons outside his vision. Two hundred twenty thousand homosexuals were herded into concentration camps, forced to wear the pink triangle, and exterminated.

Anita Bryant arrived on the scene during a similar climate, made more dangerous by what pollster George Gallup refers to as "a profound religious revival." Six out of ten persons today, he reports, see "born-again Christian" as "devout, God-fearing persons." Having already established a Pat Boone reputation for wholesomeness by her role as spokesperson for America's favorite breakfast drink, the former Miss America runner-up and mother of four entered the gay-rights struggle with the announcement that God had singled her out to fight His fight. When confronted with scientific studies that challenged her position, Ms. Bryant would either quote Leviticus 18 or break into a rousing rendition of the "Battle Hymn of the Republic."

Once the sweet taste of victory was anticipated, Anita expanded her saccharine rhetoric and God's crusade to include husbands and wives who engage in fellatio and/or cunnilingus. Save Our Children also announced the intention to carry their campaign across the country, with special emphasis placed on the defeat of H.R. 2998, a bill currently before the House of Representatives that would amend the Civil Rights Act to include sexual orientation as grounds upon which no one can be arbitrarily discriminated against.

Ms. Bryant failed in her attempt to drive gay men and women back into the closet. According to *Time* magazine, the 350,000 homosexuals who marched during Gay Pride Week in late June composed the largest single street demonstration since the antiwar rallies of the 1960s. She did succeed in Dade County, however, in eliminating protections for homosexuals against discrimination in housing, employment, and public accommodations. She also succeeded, though I know it wasn't her intent, in escalating violence against homosexuals. Bumper stickers in Florida proclaimed "Kill a Queer for Christ!" Since June 7, there have been a rash of gay-victim murders. In San Francisco, a man was stabbed by four men who proclaimed, "This one's from Anita."

Murder and defeat of civil rights under the banner of God-and-Country should be a familiar scenario to Americans who have studied the struggle for human rights in this country. The Bible and the "Battle Hymn of the Republic" have been used as a one-two punch against Jews, atheists, blacks, women, sex educators, and those who advocate separation of church and state. This dynamic duo was even immortalized in the film *Inherit the Wind,* in which antievolutionist Matthew Brady (William Jennings Bryan) announced he was more concerned with the "Rock of Ages" than he was with the age of rocks, and his followers paraded through town with Bible, flag and familiar choruses of that old faithful "Battle Hymn," promising to hang the Darwinian schoolteacher from the old apple tree.

What makes the current scene most threatening to the entire American population is the possible meaning of Anita Bryant's "normal majority" and her Dade County victory chant, "Enough, enough, enough!"

Gay political activists have identified a strange coalition at work against homosexual civil rights. Prior to Save Our Children, the Roman Catholic Church has been seen as the principal foe. With the emergence of popular media figure Anita Bryant, other groups have begun to stick their heads out of the quagmire and identify themselves as anti-gay. These include the John Birch Society, the Ku Klux Klan, Catholics United for the Faith, and the Right-to-Lifers.

In Boston, the Right to Life group took a break from their Saturday-morning rosary recital in front of abortion clinics to send hundreds of telegrams to state senators admonishing them to vote no on legislation that would prohibit discrimination against gays in public employment. One state senator, who affirmed his membership in the John Birch Society, participated in a television debate and lauded Anita Bryant by parroting every argument she presented in Dade County.

In response to this new gathering of forces, the national leaders of the gay-civil-rights movement have arranged meetings with representatives of other civil-rights organizations in an attempt to build supporting coalitions.

Dade County has set the gay-civil-rights movement back. In addition to the escalation of violence, there is now an increased possibility of blackmail. How strange it is to remember the argument against having homosexuals in government employment. It was reasoned that closeted homosexuals were easy prey for blackmailers who might seek important information. The openly gay person, who has nothing to fear from blackmailers, is now told to go back to the closet.

In addition, if the public could be convinced that impressionable children can be converted, the next step will be screening literature and textbooks, and censorship of television programs that depict "happy, healthy homosexuals."

But what of other human-rights issues? If there is a new coalition among superreligious and superpatriot groups, opposition to gay civil rights is not their only common denominator. "Enough, enough, enough" by the "normal majority" means campaigns against sex education in schools, bussing, contraceptives for teen-agers, legalization of marijuana, the ERA, affirmative action for minorities, death with dignity, and abortion and campaigns for capital punishment, media censorship, and prayer in schools.

There was a time when civil libertarians could look to the Supreme Court for protection of constitutional rights. No longer, according to critics who suggest that the Nixon-packed court has abdicated its role to what appears to be majority rule as defined by Congress. The House and the Senate have rarely been known to tackle unpopular legislation. Even our "born-again" president has declined full affirmation of gay civil rights. While he has invited gay representatives into the White House and has said that laws should not punish homosexuals, he has refused to comment on whether or not homosexuals should be allowed to teach, indicating he "didn't want to get involved."

If the Gallup poll is correct, majority rule could be by Christian fundamentalists who, for the sake of our own good, will legislate life to comply with what they think is the essence of Scripture and Americana.

Observed C.S. Lewis: "Of all tyrannies, a tyranny exercised for the good of its victims may be the most oppressive. It may be better to live under robber barons than under omnipotent moral busybodies. The robber baron's cruelty may sometimes sleep, his cupidity may at some point be satiated; but those who torment us for our own good will torment us without end, for they do so with the approval of their own conscience."

His truth is marching on. . . .

If homosexuality were the normal way, God would have made Adam and Bruce.

ANITA BRYANT

A day without human rights is like a day without sunshine.

Gay bumpersticker

8.

MIDGE DECTER: Looting and Liberal Racism

On July 13, 1977, there occurred the second citywide blackout to afflict New York City in 12 years. But whereas the first—in 1965—had in a curious way become the occasion for a citywide party, this one soon became the occasion for widespread looting and arson. The blackout was followed by extensive soul-searching on the part of New Yorkers and others. Hearings were held to try to identify all those responsible for the electrical failure (most notably Consolidated Edison), and editorials were published placing the blame on attitudes of public and private citizens alike. In the opinion of some commentators, none of these investigations and allegations went to the heart of the matter. An interesting and eloquent account of and explanation for the 24 hours of civic rage and mayhem was offered by Midge Decter, a contributor to Commentary, *the well known conservative publication. Most of Decter's article is reprinted here.*

Source: *Commentary*, September 1977.

ON JULY 13, 1977, at 9:30 in the evening, New York City went suddenly and totally dark. The electric power had failed throughout the entire city. Within minutes several neighborhoods in the boroughs of Manhattan, the Bronx, and Brooklyn were aswarm with gangs of young men and little boys, lead pipes and gasoline in hand, on a rampage of looting and arson. Later, no doubt when the mayhem had become widespread and irresistible, a certain number of women and girls joined in. Small stores, restaurants, and supermarkets were broken into, their stocks cleaned out and fixtures smashed. In one neighborhood, the Bushwick section of Brooklyn, the fire department was literally unable to keep pace with the nightlong, and then daylong, setting of new fires.

It took twenty-four hours to achieve the full restoration of electricity. Meanwhile, havoc continued. In some areas the combination of daylight and continuous police surveillance brought a kind of spent, dazed quiet. In others—East Harlem, for instance, and the now infamous Bushwick—the pillage continued through much of the following day, interrupted only by the repeated appearance of the police, who arrived to carry off another and yet another wagonload of looters, and by occasional interviews granted to the press.

In any case, by the time the lights were all back on and the trains and elevators running, well over two thousand of New York's small businesses had been smashed, at a loss estimated at anywhere from $165 million to $1 billion, depending on how one did the computation. (Since most of the looted stores, because of their location, could not in the first place be adequately insured, the real figure will never be arrived at.) Nearly four thousand people

New York looters during the blackout of July 1977.

had been taken into custody for looting, thus swamping the city's jails and courts. Untold numbers of participants in the night's activities had been treated in hospital emergency rooms, some of these operating without power, for knife and glass wounds. More than four hundred policemen and firemen had been injured, several of them seriously.

So much is history. What cannot, of course, be captured in a telling of the facts and numbers, nor even in the more vivid newsphotos and TV news clips of the ongoing destruction, is the actual quality of the city's experience on that long, dark night. Much discussion has subsequently taken place, particularly on the editorial and Op-Ed pages of the New York *Times,* about whether or not their fellow citizens were justified in using the word "animals" to characterize the looters. But the term in any case seems inappropriate; for anyone watching them at work, surging out of the shadows in a horde and scurrying back

into the cover of darkness as the police cars came by, the imagery suggested is one taken from insect life—from urban insect life—rather than from the jungle or forest. Certainly the feeling left in the city by the night of July 14 was not so much of having been trampled as of having been given a sudden glimpse into the foundation of one's house and seen, with horror, that it was utterly infested and rotting away. No one will be at ease in the edifice again for a long time, if ever.

Now, people living in so famously troubled a city as New York are perhaps surprising candidates for a fresh experience of social trauma such as I have just described. After all, there have been arson and looting before, at least in some of the city's worst black ghettos. The South Bronx, for instance, having in the last few years become an arsonist's heaven, is by now a surrealist moonscape. And while during the riots that erupted in the aftermath of Martin

Luther King's assassination the city suppressed the truth of what was happening so that its then mayor, John Lindsay, might be congratulated for the success of his enlightened policy, anyone going through Harlem in the weeks after could clearly see all the detritus of a large-scale social explosion. Nor was the blackout itself a new experience. There had also been a total citywide (indeed region-wide) power failure once before, in 1965, during which New Yorkers had had ample opportunity to discover that the health and safety and general welfare of congested urban communities can nowadays hang by a single wire. And finally, as all the world knows, and some part of the world even views with a certain amount of malicious satisfaction, New York is currently engaged in a battle against fiscal, and with it possibly economic and social, ruin. It would seem that people might have expected nothing less of a power failure on a hot July night than what did in fact take place.

The problem was that after several years of being caught up in the fashion of pronouncing life in New York to be intolerable—a fashion made up in about equal parts of genuine weariness with street-corner violence, the chic gaspings and coughings of environmentalism, and a general political bad mood, faintly radical in origin—the city's inhabitants were beginning to feel a bit better, if not about their lot in life, then at least about themselves. This turn in mood, discernible in the language of the local press and the tone of public and private conversation more than in any measurable change in actual political and social conduct, was almost directly attributable to the fiscal crisis. If the prospect of being hanged concentrates the mind wonderfully, as Dr.

Johnson so usefully and quotably said, then the prospect of going bankrupt seemed to concentrate the affection of New Yorkers and help them to regain their sense of urban pride. Moreover, the discovery of how widespread was the hostility to New York, and with what equanimity other Americans were prepared to view its downfall, stirred a new spirit of loyalty: one of the most commonly enunciated sentiments about the crisis came to be that the city was in fiscal trouble because it was better than other places, more generous and compassionate with its citizenry, more alive to the beauties of racial, cultural, and class heterogeneity.

But there was another, more precise and particular, reason for the sense of trauma as well. The previous blackout, though more than a decade past, was still rather vivid in the memory of those old enough to have been around as a moment of neighborliness and civic cooperation and that special kind of gaiety that these produce in times of crisis. This time when the lights went out, people were able to recognize immediately the possible magnitude of the problem and at the same time to feel assured on the basis of experience that there was no cause for panic.

For a moment or two, that is. As things turned out, we know, civic cooperation was left largely to policemen and firemen who worked around the clock with little rest and to private citizens who stood with baseball bats and lead pipes of their own, prepared to fend off any advancing marauders and defend the ground for friends and neighbors. Thus, beyond the dangerous disruptions attendant on the withdrawal of electricity from a community of nearly eight million people living in fewer than three hundred square miles, beyond even the immeasurable, irrecoverable physical and economic damage done both to individuals and to New York as a whole, there was additional shock—perhaps the greatest shock of all—in the force with which the city had been caught spiritually off guard.

Whatever the outraged bewilderment of most ordinary New Yorkers in the face of twisted iron, broken glass, empty stores, and burnt-out buildings, however, it can at least be said that they were not left for very long with any unappeased hunger for an explanation. Even before the last fire engine had returned to its berth and the first looter taken from his temporary jail cell for arraignment, a group of important spokesmen for the conventional wisdom of what is nowadays called liberalism had reached a consensus on the meaning of the looting and were offering it confidently to the world.

The events of the night of July 13, according to this consensus, though deplorable, were a much-needed reminder of the way American society had failed. In the relative racial quiet of the past few years, many of us had been lulled into a false sense of security about the condition of the poor and black young, out of a wish to be shut of disquieting feelings of obligation to them and at the invitation of certain politicians to indulge that wish. But now we were being forced once more to confront our failure. . . .

Our callous indifference to ghetto conditions is both private—the luxury of those whom a benign fate had permitted to move to, or be born into, greener suburban pastures—and political: the urban riots in the late 60's should have given us ample warning that something must be done, and done

quickly, to overcome poverty, but we did not, said the *Times* in yet another editorial, "spend enough of our ingenuity and our affluence to solve the problems the riots of the 60's made evident. . . ."

Or, in the somewhat more sonorous recital of Clayton Riley: "We are building sports complexes and increasing our manufacture of luxury automobiles while failing to provide substance to the dreams of nothing more than shelter, clothes, food, and some occasional fun." Indeed, no less a spokesman for the enlightened consensus than the President of the United States himself saw the looting as a message that more programs were needed in the areas of housing, health, education, and jobs for urban areas that had, as he put it, been "neglected too long."

In other words, proclaimed the liberal consensus, the looting was an expression of the rage and desperation of minority youth at being the hopeless members of a hopeless community. Permit this rage and desperation to ferment unseen for long enough, as we have done, turn on the summer heat, turn off all the lights . . . and hark what bloody and sulphurous discord follows.

The first thing that strikes one about this explanation for what happened on the night of July 13—aside from the speed and the easy, one might almost say cheerful, assurance with which it was brought forth out of a moment of unforeseen chaos—is its complete familiarity. For well over a decade now there has been almost no form of urban unpleasantness, from purse-snatching to rioting, which has not instantly been imputed by those who have elected to speak in the name of liberalism to the inescapability of black poverty and the indifference of white society to it. . . .

But most familiar, and on the other hand most curious, of all is the general assertion—made in the teeth of how many hundreds upon hundreds of government programs and hundreds upon hundreds of millions (or is it billions?) of dollars of public expenditure—that the problems of the urban poor have been neglected. Many things have been, and no doubt will long continue to be, in dispute in the discussion of the relative success or failure of this or that aspect of that aggregate enterprise known as the poverty program. What we do know is that there has been a massive, whether or not adequate, effort to improve the social and economic condition of the poor—particularly and by all means the black poor. And what we do know further is that there has been, whether or not as a result of this effort and however inadequate we judge it to be, a substantial improvement in the social and economic condition of the black population. There are those who would say that government intervention in behalf of the racial minorities, by creating certain economic and social problems, actually impeded rather than aided their progress. Be that as it may, the terms "neglect" or "indifference" when applied in this case can have only, and perhaps are intended only to have, a liturgical effect. . . .

In New York City there has been a growing employment crisis in general, created not by the absence of good will but by the positive flight from the city of businesses unable to find a qualified and efficient labor force and yet constrained to pay high wages to an unreliable one. Labor-union opposition to the lifting of the minimum-wage requirements for adolescents would of course, and from labor's point of view justifiably, have been very strong. But so, one feels, would opposition from those very spokesmen for civic "compassion" who currently bid us to pay heed to the job needs of the enraged ghetto young, on the grounds that a malign and greedy business community was trying to exploit them. Just as it seems not to have occurred to Clayton Riley that the building of sports complexes and the manufacture of luxury automobiles are precisely the sorts of activity that create jobs and bring a bit of wealth to the working class, so many who are habitually quick and sure and virtuous in all their analyses of social problems often find it worthwhile to remain oblivious to any of the consequences of their views in the real world.

Many people have in the same way also found it worthwhile to remain unaware of just how knotty in the first place is the whole question of youth unemployment in the urban ghetto. To begin with, there is the problem of what actually constitutes unemployment and how percentages like 40 per cent and 50 per cent are arrived at. There is certainly no doubt—the simple evidence of one's senses in the course of a car ride through, say, Harlem or Bedford-Stuyvesant will suffice to confirm—that hordes of adolescent boys and post-adolescent young men hang out seemingly all day long on street corners, spending their time in a form of play which consists largely of offering menace to one another and to passers-by. That they are idle and as a consequence headed for trouble of one kind or another is obvious. That they mind being in this condition is less obvious. That they are all of them poor is less obvious still. And that they are unemployed, in the sense of having sought, and failed to find, a job, seems in many cases simply a laughable proposition. . . .

Naturally a major consideration in talking about jobs, not necessarily always included in the characterization "dead-end" but nonetheless surely important to it, is money. For large numbers of those young men on street corners it does not pay to take a job. Not only because there is nothing much they are qualified to do; and not only because welfare payments are at least adequate to keep them housed and fed; and not only because they have increasingly been brought up in, and seem content to perpetuate, a system of being kept by women; but because so many of them have access, or the occasional promise of access, to a different kind of money— money sometimes dangerously, but always easily, come by.

Another famous book of the 60's, much praised but obviously insufficiently attended to, is Claude Brown's *Manchild in the Promised Land,* which provides an illuminating account of the actual days and nights of many a Harlem youth. The book tells a terrible story; between drugs and jails, hardly any of Brown's old gang survived. Nevertheless, it is important to understand that Brown and his friends would not have been caught dead holding down a regular job. In their case, the income of preference happened to be that derived from the rolling of drunks. But the list of lucrative street occupations for the alert and hard-working is long and various: for the well-connected, there is running numbers or running errands for those who do; there are the many different levels of participation in the trafficking of drugs; there is stealing; there is mugging; there is (or used to be) contriving to get paid to go to school; and finally there is selling the services of one, or if you are very shrewd and talented, of a whole stable, of your girl

friends. This list of employments is not very pretty and has been intentionally somewhat narrowed for emphasis, but one pays those young men less than proper respect to imagine that President Carter can so easily afford the means to buy them away from their present life.

And if it is not true that they are to be seen day after day hanging about on stoops and parked cars because they are tired from having pounded the pavements in vain, it is even less true that the looting and arson were acts of desperation. Nothing at this moment seems more critical for the social and even political health of New York City than that we have done with at least some of the cant in which we have been threatening to drown ourselves.

It is cant to call the looters victims of racial oppression, and it is still worse cant to say that their condition is the result of our apathy. Immigrants from Cuba, the Dominican Republic, San Salvador, Haiti, and Puerto Rico— all of whom were prominently included among the looters—may have been the hapless victims of something, but not in the United States. They flock here and go to any lengths not to be sent home— hardly the behavior, no matter how hard a time they are going through, of victims. They are poor, to be sure, but like all immigrant groups they are *here* because they were even poorer before.

It is cant to say that the looting only took place in the city's worst slums. Manhattan's Upper West Side is hardly Eden, but no one lives there in unimaginable squalor, except perhaps for the community of the very old people and the insane—white more than black— who have been dumped in the neighborhood by children or welfare agencies or the enlightened new practice of shutting down the asylums and drugging their former inmates to the eyeballs so that they may wander up and down Broadway. And speaking from the point of view of social attitude, the Upper West Side may be the most naturally and unself-consciously integrated neighborhood in America.

It is cant to refer to the looters as animals, because on that fateful July night they were behaving in all-too-human a fashion. It is also cant to say, as the *New Yorker* did in a ludicrous "Talk of the Town" piece (August 8), that people's anger at the looting after it had occurred actually caused the looting (or in the *New Yorker's* own words, "the attitude toward the riots created the riots").

But it is cant above all to say of the looters' conduct—as Herbert Gutman did in a truly disgraceful piece (which also appeared on the *Times* Op-Ed page, July 21), in which he compared them with a group of Jewish housewives in 1902 who organized what turned into a rowdy protest against the high cost of kosher meat and threw meat into the street to rot—that they were giving us "a pained message." Anyone who actually watched the looters at work, as those of us who live in looted neighborhoods were privileged to do first-hand and as millions of Americans did briefly on television, knows that they were doing no such thing as expressing rage or even blindly giving vent to some pent-up experience of torment: they were having the time of their lives. To see them, or better yet to listen to them through the darkness, shouting instructions to one another and roaring with their exertions, was to understand that they were people getting intoxicated on their dumb luck. Possibly that is why so many got caught—for falling into a state

of drunken incaution and forgetting to take proper advantage of the dark. By the next day, of course, the looting was not so much drunken as obsessive, going on blindly in full daylight. Who among those listening to Group-W radio will ever forget, for the sake of any mere social theory, the voice of the young man in Bushwick being interviewed in front of a clothing store he had just ripped off saying distractedly and impatiently to the interviewer: "Hey, man, all right, I'll tell you. *It's the name of the game.* Aw Jesus, man, let me go now—I got to go!"

Nor will a month of Sundays' worth of sermons about poverty and alienation erase the image captured in the special report which appeared in the July 25 issue of *Newsweek:* a woman wandering through the second floor of a Brooklyn discount furniture store looking for end tables and complaining to the others who were busily carrying away furniture, "I just can't use a thing up here." . . .

To be sure, the combination of greed and the special opportunity afforded by the blackout, potent as such a combination might be, is not by itself enough to explain that uncontrollable bout of pillage. Greed, being one of the seven deadly sins, may be assumed to be in some degree present in all human affairs. As, surely, is some degree of opportunity. Even so God-given an opportunity as a citywide power failure had been presented once before without being acted upon. If the looting was not an explosion of despair and rage, a cumulative response to joblessness and hopelessness and the feeling of being abandoned, how are we to account for it?

The answer is that all those young

men went on their spree of looting because they had been given permission to do so. They had been given permission to do so by all the papers and magazines, movies and documentaries—all the outlets for the purveying of enlightened liberal attitude and progressive liberal policy—which had for years and years been proclaiming that race and poverty were sufficient excuses for lawlessness. They had been given permission to do so by all the politicians and government officials who had for years and years through their policies been expressing their belief that there was no other way to "tame" ghetto youth except through bribery and no other way to move them ahead in life except by special arrangement. And they had been given permission to do so by all the self-appointed foundation- or government-funded militant spokesmen for the interests of the black and Hispanic communities whose threats of "long hot summers" had been the key to their exercise of power with the political establishment. The previous blackout, it is important to remember, had taken place before all these various embodiments of liberal enlightenment on race had offered their blessings to the riots in Watts and Detroit or heaped encomiums on the likes of Huey Newton and H. Rap Brown.

"Pained messages" are being transmitted and received, all right, but in exactly the opposite direction from the one suggested by Herbert Gutman. Young blacks are getting the message from the liberal culture, more subtly but just as surely as from any old-time Southern sheriff, that they are, inherently and by virtue of their race, inferior. There are virtually no crimes they can commit that someone with great influence does not rush in to excuse on the grounds that we had no right to expect any-

thing else. Moreover, there is virtually no traditional form of manliness—fathering one's children, defending one's women—that is not considered a cruel and bigoted demand to make on them, given the difficulties it would bring them. They must not be judged by the standards that apply to everyone else in school or in applying for or performing jobs; because they cannot succeed, it is heartless to subject them to the possibility of failure. Sooner or later, if only for its own survival, society will simply have to become wise enough and kind enough, and spend enough money, to be able to maintain them, and their unfathered children and unhusbanded wives, in comfort and dignity. The message they are given, in short, is that they are not fully enough human to be held morally responsible for their own behavior. They are children, as the Southerners used to say, or ironically, they are, in the terminology the New York *Times* editorialist so much objected to but so inevitably himself implied, "animals."

This is the message that has for some time now, at least since the late 60's, been consistently transmitted by the "best" people, and certainly widely received by their intended interlocutors. It is, to be blunt about it, the message of liberal racism.

But the problem does not rest there. For no matter how passionately the liberals argue against it, everyone at bottom holds himself morally responsible for what he does. Being told over and over again in a hundred different ways, as these ghetto youths are, that they are blameless victims does not convince them but only saps their ever-dwindling store of self-respect. Anyone who knows them or who has ever truly looked at them at their sidewalk stations can see, year by year, from little-boyhood to young manhood, the dying away of self-esteem: the special swaggering walk so full of uncertainty, the nearly insane scrutiny of every word, gesture, look, tone of voice directed to them for evidence of insult. They are people who have come dangerously to share in their would-be sympathizers' contempt for them.

It is possible for some of these young men to resist the idea that they are entitled to the special status of irresponsibles. Though one would not necessarily know it from reading the liberal press, many, many have resisted it, are resisting it, and will do so in the future (the "invisible" blacks, of course, are the millions of blacks, particularly young men, who lead ordinary lives). But it is an unfair burden—here is where the true cruelty and injustice lies—for a boy to have to bring himself to moral maturity, as well as for the parents who are trying to help him do so, without any support or confirmation from the society around him for the moral weight of his actions. . . .

In the course of the radio coverage of July 14, two little black boys, sounding about twelve years old, were interviewed and announced that they had taken no part in the looting going on all around them. They seemed a bit sheepish. When asked by the interviewer, "Why not?" one of them said, "I was scared of the cops," and the other one said, "Because my mama would have killed me."

A brave and lucky woman, that mama—no thanks to the culture intent on whispering sweet *nada* into her little boy's ear.

9.

Jimmy Carter: Amnesty for Illegal Aliens

It had become apparent by the later 1970s that the problem of illegal aliens was one of the most pressing in the United States. Such persons, who numbered as many as ten million according to some estimates, mainly lived in the southwestern states (since most of them came from Mexico), but there were large numbers in the large northern cities as well. They were exploited and lived in constant fear of the authorities, but they also performed essential economic services. Many proposals had already been put forth when President Carter, on August 4, 1977, sent to the Congress a message concerned with illegal aliens. That portion dealing with "amnesty" for illegal residents in the country is reprinted here.

Source: *Congressional Digest*, October 1977.

The fact that there are millions of undocumented aliens already residing in this country presents one of the most difficult questions surrounding the aliens phenomenon. These aliens entered the U.S. illegally and have willfully remained here in violation of the immigration laws. On the other hand, many of them have been law-abiding residents who are looking for a new life and are productive members of their communities. I have concluded that an adjustment of status is necessary to avoid having a permanent 'under-class' of millions of persons who have not been and cannot practicably be deported, and who would continue living here in perpetual fear of immigration authorities, the local police, employers and neighbors. Their entire existence would continue to be predicated on staying outside the reach of government authorities and the law's protections.

First, I propose that permanent resident alien status be granted to all undocumented aliens who have resided continuously in the U.S. from before January 1, 1970, to the present. These aliens would have to apply for this status and provide normal documentary proof of continuous residency. If residency is maintained, U.S. citizenship could be sought five years after the granting of permanent status, as provided in existing immigration laws.

Second, all undocumented aliens, including those (other than exchange and student visitors) with expired visas, who were residing in the United States on or before January 1, 1977, will be eligible for a temporary resident alien status for five years.

Those eligible would be granted the temporary status only after registering with INS; registration would be permitted solely during a one-year period. Aliens granted temporary status would be entitled to reside legally in the United States for a five-year period.

The purpose of granting a temporary status is to preserve a decision on the final status of these undocumented aliens, until much more precise information about their number, location, family size and economic situation can be collected and reviewed. That information would be obtained through the registration process. A decision on their final status would be made sometime after the completion of the registration process and before the expiration of the five-year period.

Temporary resident aliens would not have the right to vote, to run for public office or to serve on juries; nor would they be entitled to bring members of their families into the U.S. But they could leave and re-enter this country, and they could seek employment, under the same rules as permanent resident aliens.

Unlike permanent resident aliens, temporary resident aliens would be ineligible to receive such Federal social services as Medicaid, Food Stamps, Aid to Families with Dependent Children, and Supplemental Security Income. However, the allocation formulas for Revenue Sharing, which are based on population, would be adjusted to reflect the presence of temporary resident aliens. The adjustment would compensate states and local communities for the fact that some of these residents—undocumented aliens—are currently not included in the Census Bureau's population counts. That undercount deprives certain states and communities of Revenue Sharing funds which, if Census figures were completely accurate, would be received and used to defray certain expenses caused by the presence of undocumented aliens. Those receiving adjustments of status through the actions I am proposing would be included in the 1980 Census, so that the allocation charges would have to be made only through 1980.

Third, for those undocumented aliens who entered the United States after Jan-

uary 1, 1977, there would be no adjustment of status. The immigration laws
would still be enforced against these undocumented aliens. Similarly, those undocumented aliens, who are eligible for
adjustment of status, but do not apply,
would continue to have the immigration
laws enforced against them.

In addition, the INS would expedite
its handling of the substantial backlog of
adjustment of status applications from
those aliens entitled to an adjustment
under existing law.

Finally, those persons who would be
eligible for an adjustment of status under these proposals must not be ineligible under other provisions of the
immigration laws.

10.

HERMAN BADILLO, HANS F. SENNHOLZ, RICHARD S. SCHWEIKER, and MORGAN F. MURPHY: Controversy About Illegal Aliens

*President Carter's proposal for "amnesty" for illegal aliens (see Selection 9)
provoked heated debate. Actually, the debate had been going on for months, if
not years. Reprinted here are several responses. The first item, from remarks
on the floor of the House of Representatives by Representative Badillo (D-N.Y.),
antedated the President's message by several months; Badillo to a large extent had
anticipated Carter's program. Dr. Sennholz was chairman of the Department of
Economics of Grove City (Penn.) College; his remarks are drawn from a position
paper he prepared in his capacity as Secretary of the Treasury in the Conservative
Caucus "shadow cabinet." The negative responses by Senator Schweiker (R-Penn.)
and Representative Murphy (R-Ill.) were issued shortly after the President's
proposal was received by Congress.*

Source: *Congressional Digest,* October 1977.

PRO
HERMAN BADILLO

LAST YEAR, I introduced a bill to grant
amnesty to illegal aliens living in this
country. I am reintroducing this legislation, with one major change—a change
I was moved to make by what I have
seen as a new spirit in our administration, a new and realistic awareness of
the need for "forgiveness," a need expressed by the President in his granting
of amnesty to draft evaders. Because my
bill is being introduced in the first year
of our Nation's third century, I have
decided to place the effective date on
the day of our Bicentennial: my bill will
grant amnesty to all those unregistered
aliens who have resided in this country
prior to July 4, 1976.

Since the new President's election,
perhaps sparked by the visit by the
President of Mexico, there has been an
increasing concern about our Nation's
immigration policies, and subsequently
a growing pressure on the Congress for

legislative action. This activity has been exacerbated by our economic problems, as the lack of available bluecollar jobs has been equated, wrongly, with the number of illegal aliens now in America.

As a member of the Spanish-speaking community, I am acutely aware of what the problems are—and I am equally aware as to what the problems are not. There are now between 8 and 10 million illegal residents in this country. Many of them have been in this country for several years, and have established productive lives and are making real contributions to our country. Many of them pay taxes, and share in the responsibilities of citizenship. The only thing that differentiates them from those of us in this room is that they do not have the proper papers. These are people who have committed themselves to the United States, and we can no longer treat them inhumanely.

It is time that Congress address the question of illegal aliens, and I concur with those of my colleagues who have called for immediate action. But we cannot let illegal aliens become the scapegoats for our country's economic ills, and we cannot threaten legitimate citizens with the loss of their livelihoods by imposing fines on employers or taking other sanctions against them. That approach would only lead to one thing: employers would cease hiring all those who even appear foreign to avoid the possibility of hiring an illegal worker. Another possibility that I oppose strenuously is that which would eventually mean a national identity card. I find this a gross abridgement of civil rights. We cannot, in 1977, tolerate the passage of legislation that would perpetuate the kind of discrimination we have spent so many years trying to overcome.

Many of us are aware of the raids that have taken place in large urban areas to round up large numbers of illegal residents at the same time. These raids have pointed up the preposterous notion that we can deport all 8 or 10 million people who have come here without papers. In order to deport that great number of people I believe we would need more troops than we sent to Indochina—a patently absurd concept.

The only viable solution is to grant an amnesty to those people who are now here—an amnesty that would give these people not, as is commonly suggested, citizenship, but only "green card"— resident alien—status, and permit these people to work toward becoming full citizens of the United States.

It is the beginning of a solution to an international problem, and once such legislation is passed, we must then move forward toward a permanent way in which we can deal with a problem that can only be exacerbated as time goes by. We must realize that illegal immigration is a diplomatic problem as well as an employment problem. We must develop approaches to our foreign aid programs that will enable developing countries in our hemisphere to provide enough jobs for their citizens to keep pace with their growing populations.

Immigration is a complex problem, and it will take many years of debate and hard work until we find a light at the end of this very long tunnel. But there is an increasing awareness that some kind of amnesty must be granted. And it is fitting that the date marking the anniversary of a country that has always welcomed refugees from economic, social, and religious repression should mark another great step forward in our history of freedom.

The bill's provisions provide:

That the Attorney General make a

record of lawful admission for permanent residence in the case of any alien, and that each alien will provide that he or she is not inadmissible;

He or she must establish that he or she entered the country prior to July 4, 1976;

Has been continuously in this country since entry;

Is the spouse, parent, son, or daughter of a U.S. citizen or a resident alien;

Is a person of good moral character;

Is not ineligible for citizenship;

Application for residence must be made one year from the date of enactment.

PRO
HANS F. SENNHOLZ

WITH UNEMPLOYMENT at chronically high rates in nearly all countries, it is not surprising that the number of explanations and interpretations is on the rise. In less developed countries, we are told, the high birth rates and population growth rates exceed the ability of agriculture and industry to absorb the new population, with the result of increasing unemployment. In the industrial countries, where the rates of growth of population are much lower, the explanations cover a wide spectrum from the Marxian exploitation doctrine to the Keynesian inadequate-spending theory. In the U.S., the oldest explanation of them all is coming to the fore. Rooted in the fear and resentment of foreigners, many of whom are illiterate and poor, more and more Americans are pointing at the newcomers as the cause of their difficulties. Labor leaders, especially, are quick to vilify "the illegal aliens" for the chronic unemployment that is plaguing organized labor.

Their explanation is almost 300 years old. The descendants of the original English settlers used it, viewing with alarm the influx of Germans and Scotch-Irish. They in turn later protested the arrival of southern and eastern Europeans.

Their intellectual descendants now are pointing at millions of "illegal aliens" from Latin America who are blamed for our high unemployment rates, for lowering our enviable wage rates, for corrupting our political and social institutions, and their reluctance to conform and "Americanize."

The estimate of some 8 million illegal aliens in the U.S. suggests a simple solution to our unemployment problem. Let us expel the 8 million aliens after we have inflicted appropriate punishment for illegal entry, and our chronic unemployment will cease to exist. Now every native American will cheerfully find his job.

In reality, unemployment is a cost phenomenon. There is always employment for anyone whose productivity exceeds his employment costs. And unemployment is awaiting anyone whose costs exceed his usefulness. This is true whether or not he is a citizen.

No one can possibly know how many illegal aliens actually have entered the U.S. But we do know that they are earning a living through rendering services in agriculture, commerce and industry. You may find them in the fruit orchards of California, Oregon and Washington, on the farms and ranches of Arizona, Texas, Louisiana, and Mississippi, in the hotels and motels in our cities, and in other service industries from coast to coast. They are working because their services are useful and economical. Eight million Americans are unemployed because their employment costs consisting of wages and social benefits exceed their usefulness. How would they become more productive and economical through expulsion of foreigners? How could a black teenager in New York City whose employment costs exceed $3 an hour (minimum wage $2.30 plus fringe benefits) and whose labor may be worth only 75¢ find employment after a Latin chambermaid at the Park Hotel was arrested and expelled? The expulsion of eight million foreigners would not vacate eight million jobs for deserving Americans. In fact, it is likely to create even more unemployment.

Productive alien employees cannot forcibly be replaced by native labor that inflicts losses on employers. They can be removed and deported, which would withdraw useful labor, restrict service and production, inflict losses on employers, and thus cause a contraction of economic activity. The hotel and motel industry, for instance, would be severely hampered in service and capacity. The fruit orchards would harvest less fruit, which would cause prices to rise and the industry to contract. And the American people would suffer a significant reduction of living standards through the loss of wholesome fruit in their diets.

Economists readily admit that in a stagnant economy the influx of new labor, native or foreign, tends to reduce wage rates. The given amount of capital is distributed over a greater number of workers, which reduces individual labor productivity and wage rates. But this admission does not apply to labor markets in which generous unemployment compensation, multiple benefits, and liberal foodstamps keep millions of workers from seeking employment. The institutional benefits that are creating the unemployment are not reduced when aliens illegally enter the U.S.

In constant fear of detection and deportation few illegal aliens, if any, are seeking the social benefits that induce so many natives to prefer unemployment. There are no jobless benefits, no foodstamps, not even public assistance for illegal aliens. They live, and in many respects are like those old-fashioned Americans before the dawn of the New Deal and its redistribution programs. And they probably feel like American colonists who were illegal aliens in the eyes of all Indians.

While the fear of detection may prevent illegal aliens from collecting transfer benefits, it is more difficult to escape the taxes that are levied on labor. Surely, there are many who by arrangement with their employers pay neither income nor social security taxes. But this makes employers accomplices to illegal employment and tax evasion, which is a risk no large employer can possibly take. Therefore, it is rather likely that most illegal aliens suffer tax withholdings like anyone else. They are probably paying "their share" in the expenses of our social institutions.

And yet, illegal aliens stand accused of corrupting our political and social institutions, favoring political and social radicalism, agitating for more transfer programs, etc., etc. All of this may be true. But we wonder about the political and ideological dangers of a California fruitpicker or an Atlanta chambermaid who, in constant fear of detection and deportation, timidly inquires about membership in a labor union. Surely, every native newspaper publisher, editor, commentator, writer, or professor can be, and probably is, immeasurably more effective in propagating radical ideas than an illiterate alien.

He stands accused of refusing to conform and "Americanize." But he may be at a loss about the standard to which he is to conform and about the mean-

ing of "Americanization." As there is
no standard, and cannot be one in this
nation of refugees from all corners of
the world, he, the illegal alien from
Latin America, must be acquitted of
this charge. It must suffice that he con-
forms to the only standard of a civilized
society, that he is a human being who
was born with inalienable human rights.

CON

RICHARD S. SCHWEIKER

I OPPOSE PRESIDENT CARTER'S PLAN to
grant amnesty to illegal aliens. I believe
this proposal is ill-conceived, based on
erroneous assumptions, and mischievous
in impact.

In his recent message to Congress,
the President accurately stated the problem: "In the last several years, millions
of undocumented aliens have illegally
immigrated to the United States. They
have breached our nation's immigration
laws, displaced many Americans from
jobs, and placed an increased financial
burden on many states and local governments." The Immigration and Naturalization Service estimates that one
million jobs are now held by illegal
aliens. And yet, the essence of the President's plan is to reward this illegal
conduct with special benefits for which
aliens who have obeyed the law will be
ineligible.

Although there are precedents in our
history for granting an amnesty or pardon to lawbreakers to remove the adverse consequences of law enforcement,
the illegal alien amnesty plan goes much
further. It puts the government squarely
behind the lawbreaker, and, in effect,
says, "Congratulations, you have successfully violated our laws and avoided
detection—here is your reward."

Millions of people throughout the

UPI/Bettmann

A way over the U.S.–Mexico border for
Mexicans trying to get past Border Patrol agents.

world, including legal aliens temporarily in the United States and relatives of
American citizens, have tried to work
patiently within the confines of the
immigration laws to obtain permanent
status and eventually American citizenship. If the Administration's proposal is
adopted, the government will be saying
to them, "Sorry, we have nothing for
those who obey the law." We are fond
of saying America is a nation of laws.
By accepting the President's plan, we
would be setting a nasty precedent of
putting the government on the side of
the lawbreaker by rewarding his illegal
conduct and undermining the efficacy
of our laws.

The amnesty proposal is not only
misguided in approach, but also based
on erroneous assumptions. Administration spokesmen have conjured up images of massive dragnets of federal
officials having to comb communities
throughout the nation for illegal aliens
unless amnesty is granted. Obviously,
this could not and would not happen.

Enforcement of the immigration laws against illegal aliens has been a very difficult task. But one of the primary reasons is that employers at present can lawfully hire illegal aliens. Easy employment in the United States is the primary attraction for illegal aliens. We need effectively to cut off this source of jobs which rightfully belong to Americans and legal immigrants. When this is accomplished, I suspect many illegals would return to their homes, and others who are deported would have no incentive to return to the United States. The assumption that the only alternative to a massive round-up and deportation of millions of illegal aliens is to grant a general amnesty is simply erroneous.

Although the Administration emphasizes difficulties in enforcing the immigration laws against illegal aliens, there appears to be no adequate appreciation of the problems involved in enforcing the proposed amnesty plan. Under the President's proposal, aliens without legal status who have been in the United States since before January 1, 1977, but not as early as January 1, 1970, will be placed in a new category called "temporary resident alien." Almost certainly, the Administration contemplates that these people will in several years be granted full amnesty and adjusted to permanent resident status, the last step before American citizenship. Apparently, all that will be necessary to establish residency since prior to January 1, 1970, is to show rent receipts, wage records, or the like. It is unclear how the Immigration and Naturalization Service will be expected to detect fraudulent records.

The possible ease with which even newly arriving illegal aliens will be able to take advantage of the amnesty compounds the mischief of the proposal.

Recent reports from Immigration officials at our southern border show a significant increase in illegal alien traffic since talk of amnesty began. Although the proposal on its face may appear not to benefit new arrivals, the lack of understanding of the limits of the plan and the difficulties in enforcing it actually aggravate this very burdensome problem.

For these reasons, I oppose the Administration's amnesty plan. But I support the President's recent call for sanctions against employers who knowingly hire illegal aliens. Some months ago I introduced legislation (S. 1601) to make it unlawful to knowingly employ an illegal alien and to provide stiff fines for those who choose to violate the law. Although my bill prescribes a stronger arsenal of penalties to deter violations than the Administration proposal, I welcome this part of the President's program. Drying up employment opportunities, not rewarding illegality, should be the cornerstone of our nation's policy toward illegal aliens. We should open up the jobs illegal aliens now hold to unemployed Americans and legal immigrants, not make permanent the unfair labor competition. I believe strong employer sanctions can go far toward accomplishing this goal. I feel employer sanctions are a workable program to deal with the problem of illegal aliens without rewarding illegality.

CON
MORGAN F. MURPHY

THE PRESIDENT HAS TAKEN some positive steps in dealing with a very complex issue. But the plan contains some serious pitfalls. On the positive side, Carter rightly intends to see that wage-and-hour laws are strictly enforced. This is necessary if the U.S. aims to stop aliens from working for subminimum wages. Illegals are now taking hundreds of thousands of jobs from teenagers, the unskilled, and poor blacks. They also depress wage scales and working conditions of other U.S. workers. The AFL-CIO has testified that American workers annually lose $10 billion in wages due to competition from illegal aliens.

The President's call for beefing up the border patrol is also commendable. However, the President should consider adding as many as twice the number of border patrol guards as he now proposes. While 4,000 new guards might seem to be a large number, the fact is our country has sorely neglected the illegal alien problem for the past ten years. Our preoccupation with Vietnam, the recession and Watergate have prevented us from focusing on the true dimensions of this problem. Therefore, we have a great deal of catching up to do to meet the budgetary and man-power needs of the Border Patrol and INS. While efforts to halt immigration will cost the U.S. money, America will pay a much higher price if it decides to let this problem go.

Fining employers who hire illegal aliens is imperative so the U.S. can turn off the "magnet" of jobs that attracts illegal aliens. Since currently there are no penalties for hiring illegal aliens, Carter's recommendation of civil fines is a needed improvement. Criminal sanctions would be more effective, as many employers—not having to risk prison— will simply consider fines part of the cost of doing business. Nevertheless, because the Senate has failed to act on bills requiring criminal penalties in the past, Carter's proposal appears to be the toughest sanction possible.

A sticky question related to penalizing empoyers is how to provide them with the means to identify illegal aliens. Since so many illegal immigrants have forged birth certificates and Social Security cards, how are employers supposed to determine whether a person is an illegal? Clearly, the effectiveness of Carter's plan is jeopardized if employers have no reliable way to check a person's citizenship.

To remedy this, some have suggested that a national identification card be issued to every American. This way, every person applying for a job could present proof of his citizenship or legal residence. To be sure, fears have been expressed that such a card could become a kind of "work permit" that the government could withdraw for political or simply arbitrary reasons. But such fears are exaggerated. After all, every American is now issued a social security card that is widely used for identification purposes. Yet no abuses have occurred along the lines that civil libertarians fear. And columnist Tom Braden recently pointed out: "European democracies have used national identity cards for years without turning them into instruments for the benefit of gestapos."

A national ID card may be the only effective way of prohibiting the hiring of illegal aliens. As former Undersecretary of Labor Richard Schubert testified in 1975: "I don't think there is anything repugnant in asking an employer to check a person's citizenship. The (illegal alien) problem is serious enough to warrant extraordinary measures."

11.

Paul Simon and Jesse Helms: The Panama Canal Treaties— Pro and Con

On September 7, 1977, President Carter and Panamanian dictator Brig. Gen. Omar Torrijos Herrera signed accords that, after ratification by both countries, would give Panama eventual control over the Panama Canal and the Panama Canal Zone. Representatives from 26 other Western Hemisphere countries supported the measure by attending the ceremony at the invitation of Carter, who, despite the fact that every President since Eisenhower had been in favor of renegotiating the relationship between the United States and Panama, was well aware that the majority of Americans were probably opposed—often for emotional reasons—to "giving up the Canal." The Senate would have to ratify the treaties, he also knew, and there it was a question, he felt, of their coming to know "the facts." Throughout 1977 and early 1978 the question of ratification became the leading political issue facing the Carter Administration. Liberals and centrists tended to support the treaties, partly because the Panama Canal was being less and less used by American commerce as time went on. Conservatives, including Ronald Reagan, Strom Thurmond, and Jesse Helms, vigorously opposed ratification. The President won this battle: the Senate ratified the treaties in March and April 1978, although by only a single vote over the two-thirds needed. Reprinted here is a pair of statements for and against the treaties by Paul Simon, then a congressman from Illinois, and Senator Helms of North Carolina.

Source: *The American Legion Magazine,* January 1978.

A: PAUL SIMON
FOR THE TREATIES

What does the United States have to gain from the Panama Canal treaties?

Plenty, and don't let anyone fool you with appeals to your emotions but not to your head. The treaties provide enough advantages to the United States that the Communists in Panama are fighting them.

Consider some of the advantages:

(1) It is the only practical way to keep the canal open. The chairman of the Joint Chiefs of Staff has described the canal as "defenseless as a baby." A properly placed hand grenade or small mortar shell would close it. The Monday morning quarterbacks here who view the canal as some easily defended fortress are not facing reality.

(2) The top military people who know the facts are for the treaties. Some will respond, "They're for it because they got orders." That happens sometimes. The proposal to pull troops out of Korea, for example, is a case where our military officials have been given or-

ders on how to respond. But when you talk to them privately, they are virtually unanimous that we should stay in Korea. Panama is different. Talk to the top military people privately and they are strongly for the treaties.

(3) The treaties keep open the possibility of a newer, larger canal. None of our large military, freight or oil ships can use the present canal. The treaties give the United States the exclusive right to work with Panama for construction of a new, larger canal. If the treaties are not approved, any possibility of a new canal is dead.

(4) The treaties are a good deal for the American taxpayer. The only payments to Panama come from canal tolls. A separate agreement (not part of the treaties) calls for some U.S. loans to Panama. The treaties give us the right to three large areas with 14 military installations—for nothing. Compare that with the millions we pay Spain and other countries for our bases abroad.

(5) The treaties permit the United States to stay on the offensive in international politics. Not a single other country supports our keeping the canal. If we stand for colonialism, for keeping a strip of land through the middle of another country on the basis of a treaty that no Panamanian citizen even signed, we will be hurting our leadership role immensely.

(6) The treaties protect U.S. business interests and jobs. Shippers, U.S. labor leaders and others with economic interests in Latin America generally favor the treaties. They know it is a practical way to protect our business interests abroad—and those business interests mean jobs for Americans at home.

One final point: I want my nation to stand for justice, not injustice. I want us to avoid senseless wars.

I've worn our uniform with pride and I want us to stand for what is good and right and noble.

B: JESSE HELMS
AGAINST THE TREATIES

EMPTY SLOGANS now proclaim that our true national interest in the Panama Canal lies in use, not sovereignty. But the real question is whether our present treaties or the proposed treaties give the better basis to keep the Canal open, safe and efficient.

The 1903 Treaty wisely made a bloc grant of full sovereign rights in the Canal Zone to the United States; Panama was excluded from exercising any sovereignty whatsoever. This means that the United States has the supreme dominion or power in the Zone.

We own it too. As early as 1907, the U.S. Supreme Court declared that our title to the Canal Zone is perfect under law. Indeed, the Court specifically said that our title to the Zone is every bit as good as our title to Alaska. That's why Congress has always treated it as U.S. territory under Article IV, Section 3, of the U.S. Constitution.

Moreover, over the past 74 years, American taxpayers have invested more than $7 billion in building and defending the Canal, and they deserve to see that investment protected. It is nonsense to claim that we don't exercise full sovereignty or that we don't own the Zone.

The proposed treaties would surrender our sovereign rights immediately, and establish a timetable for the complete nationalization of our properties by Panama. Within five years, 20 percent of the U.S. citizens now employed by the Canal would have to be gone, and the rest would be phased out on similar schedules. Without U.S. citizens in key executive and security positions, we would have no practical way to operate the Canal if there were a dispute with Panama. Moreover, as soon as the treaties go into effect, Panama's defense forces would be combined with ours in the daily defense operations, thereby becoming privy to our plans and preparations.

The fatal flaw of the treaties is that they assume the participation of a friendly Panama. But they provide no viable options if Panama were controlled by a Communist or hostile government. The treaties are premised on the scare theory that we cannot presently defend the Canal against sabotage by disgruntled Panamanians. But our present position of undisputed command and control is far better to defend against that threat than the confusing mixed administration and combined defense system proposed to operate under Panama's sovereignty.

Even the so-called "neutrality" treaty fails to spell out what rights we would have to maintain neutrality after the year 2000. In practice, any dispute would be governed by the United Nations Charter, not by the Panama treaties. The new treaties cannot reasonably guarantee uninterrupted use of the Canal.

The fatal flaw [in the treaties] is the risk they contain for our national security and for hemispheric defense. No one can guarantee that we can keep this waterway open without the right of sovereignty, which we are giving away.

RONALD REAGAN

We could defend the Panama Canal, and if it is attacked by any means, I will defend it.

JIMMY CARTER

12.

EDWARD M. KENNEDY: The Case for Airline Deregulation

Franklin D. Roosevelt's New Deal administrations of the 1930s were marked, among other things, by their enthusiasm for federal regulation of many activities, most notably finance, communication, and transportation. The Civil Aeronautics Authority was established in 1938, became the Civil Aeronautics Board (CAB) in 1940, and continued its career under the Department of Transportation when that was created in 1966. The CAB regulated fares, schedules, and services, and saw to it that there was at least some air service to and from most cities of the United States. It did so at a cost, however, for air fares tended to be higher on interstate flights, where the federal government had jurisdiction, than on intrastate flights, where it did not. By the 1970s there was a strong movement for deregulation of the commercial airline industry, which began to be freed from federal control in 1978. The results were generally good, it was agreed, although some cities lost air service once the CAB no longer could require it, and diversity of air fares continued, becoming in fact much greater than before. Senator Edward M. Kennedy (D-Mass.) was a leading proponent of deregulation, as this November 1977 article shows.

Source: *Enterprise*, November 1977.

IT COSTS $56 to fly a modern jet the 399 miles between Boston and Washington on the federally regulated airlines, but only $31 to fly the same type of airplane the 456 miles between San Diego and San Francisco on an intrastate airline over which the federal government has no jurisdiction.

States like California, Texas and more recently Florida have safe, efficient commercial airlines carrying millions of passengers every year at air fares ranging from 20 to 60 percent lower than those charged by federally regulated interstate airlines whose basic fares are fixed by the Civil Aeronautics Board. The CAB's rigid fare regulation makes it unlawful for airlines to cut their prices without first obtaining government permission.

Historically, the labyrinth of administrative roadblocks and the CAB's highly protected environment have combined to seriously discourage price competition. As a result, federal regulation is costing travelers and shippers about $1.5 billion a year, according to the more conservative estimates.

But wasted money is not the only price. Restrictive entry policies have frustrated and discouraged qualified firms which have tried to begin commercial air service. Since 1950, more than 80 applications for authority to provide trunk air service have been filed by new companies but not one has been granted. In the 1930s, a prophetic Amelia Earhart warned a Senate committee considering airline regulation proposals that such a regulatory scheme might serve to thwart the pioneer and little guy with a new idea in the emerging field of aviation. Today— 40 years of federal regulation later— more than 90 per cent of the commercial aviation business is controlled by those firms grandfathered by Congress in 1938. The "little guy" shares only 10 per cent.

Nor has regulation brought forth profits and sufficient capital for the airline industry itself. Age, energy-consciousness and environmental considerations mean that hundreds of commercial airliners must be replaced. The industry will have to spend an estimated $60 billion in the next 13 years for new equipment. Yet, under current regulation airlines have posted a mere 3.6 per cent rate of return over the last 5 years. If private capital is to continue to fuel this important industry, and if private management is to begin making the pricing and marketing decisions of the airlines, then government regulation must be substantially reduced.

The time for change has come. Sen. Howard Cannon (D-Nev.), chairman of the Senate aviation subcommittee, and I have developed over the last two years legislation to reduce CAB regulation over prices and routes, and gradually shift the management of the airline industry from government employees to company officers.

This effort is supported by President Jimmy Carter, former President Jerry Ford, Ralph Nader and the National Association of Manufacturers, Sears Roebuck and Common Cause, to name just a few. The chairman of the House aviation subcommittee, Glenn Ander-son (D-Cal.), recently introduced aviation regulatory reform legislation in the House of Representatives.

Most of the major CAB regulated airlines are opposing meaningful reform. They prefer the coziness and comfort of federal bureaucratic protection from the rigors of competition. But, there are exceptions. The largest domestic carrier, United Airlines, and two relatively small regional airlines, Frontier and Hughes AirWest, support reduced regulation. They are joined by Pan American, Federal Express, and the nation's commuter air carriers.

Reducing regulation is an important national issue that transcends the airline industry. For example, in the area of surface transportation—especially the trucking industry—government regulation by the Interstate Commerce Commission has inflated shipping costs and imposed artificial operating restrictions on all classes of carriers.

As chairman of the Senate subcommittee on antitrust and monopoly, I am especially concerned that the federal government is not allowing competition to operate in various sectors of our nation's economic and industrial system. Whether reducing federal interference in private economic activity remains in the realm of rhetoric or becomes a practical legislative reality partly depends on whether the Congress acts on airline reform proposals. But, it also depends on whether business and industry are willing to come forward on economic and regulatory issues of general financial interest.

To refuse to get involved or devote the resources to such important public issues, except those that mean hard dollars and cents, is a sure way to limit effectiveness and credibility. Commercial interests must and should be represented. But, to fight only the fights where there is a direct financial interest is to forfeit the opportunity to nurture credibility by participating in the policymaking processes on other issues.

Numerous business organizations have been active for several years in efforts to influence public policy, and lately have done so under the banner of reducing federal interference in the private sector. But, when consumer groups approached the business groups to form a coalition to support less airline regulation, the response they often heard was "what's in it for us?" and "how does it affect our profits?"

The National Association of Manufacturers has been a notable exception. It has taken a forthright and visible stand in favor of less federal regulation of the airline industry. The free enterprise system is praised and enshrined in hundreds of speeches before business organizations. It is expounded in business and trade journals, and practiced skillfully and successfully by the executives of thousands of companies. It generally deserves the good press it has gotten, but it also should have a more central place in the practical workings of important industries, and not be just exiled to the editorial page of company newspapers.

Of course, a number of businessmen and women who pay lip service to this important economic tradition balk when it is suggested that their regulated industry or business begin to operate under the same rules that guide most other industries of this nation. This is quite true of a number of airline executives. But, our important traditions must apply to industries even if the executives of those industries would prefer that they did not.

The NAM deserves recognition for its faithfulness to this principle.

The challenge of airline reform is the challenge of regulatory reform in general. We must rethink all regulation to update what is outmoded, improve what is inadequate, discard what is unnecessary and soften what is oppressive.

If the laws and regulations we in Washington toil over are to be responsive to the nation's economic and technological spirit, we must act with appropriate caution, but we must be bold as well, and be willing to choose different solutions and new approaches.

The basic distrust of a market economy by a depression-weary Congress in the 1930s and that era's technological infancy help explain the rigid regulatory choice for air transportation made 40 years ago.

But the 1970s are not the 1930s. We recognize today that healthy growth in the travel and the air transportation industries is more likely to be stunted by trifling regulation than competitive market forces. Reduced regulation is an achievable and worthwhile goal that offers a promising reprieve from the inertia of the status quo. The stifling regulatory mantle should be lifted from the air transportation system.

13.

Knut Hammarskjöld: What to Do About Hijacking

On November 18, 1977, a West German commando unit, flown to Somalia, attacked a hijacked Lufthansa 737 with explosives, "blinding" grenades, and automatic firearms early in the morning. Three of four hijackers were killed, but all 86 hostages were freed. Amid applause for "the German Entebbe," calls were made for some kind of international response to the threat of hijacking. On November 22 the United Nations agreed to debate airline security, but the initiative was not endorsed by Arab nations, the Soviet Union and its allies, and African nations. Reprinted below is a review by Knut Hammarskjöld, director general of the International Air Transport Association, of the legal problems facing efforts to control air piracy.

Source: *International Review of Criminal Policy*, No. 32, 1976.

IN RECENT YEARS a new pattern of transnational crime has emerged and has taken the form of what is now known in legal parlance as "unlawful acts against the safety of international civil aviation." However, these acts are more frequently referred to as acts of air piracy. They include hijacking, sabotage and threats against civil aviation, as well as interference with air navigation facilities. The motivation behind these acts is usually blackmail of some sort. However, whether they are committed for blackmail of a political or a purely mercenary nature or for some other reason, it is contended that such acts are crimes which must be punished and deterred in order to restore the safety of international civil aviation. At a period when the world has begun to reap the benefits of safe and rapid international communications, misguided individuals or groups of individuals must not be allowed to play havoc with this most useful gift of progress.

Crimes against international civil aviation, especially those committed in the air, are particularly difficult to prevent and punish because of the international nature of air transportation and also because of its speed and range. While the criminal who operates in other spheres can usually be followed and tracked down within the confines of a given geographical area, the air criminal is in a position to pick and choose to a certain extent the country in which he wishes to seek asylum after having committed his deed, irrespective of physical obstacles, such as road blocks or closed borders, which may be set up to capture him. When one adds to this the fact that the air pirate may enjoy, if he wishes, the shield of a large number of conveniently gathered and mobile hostages, one begins to appreciate the special position of vulnerability of civil aviation.

Furthermore, the air pirate unfortunately enjoys unwarranted advantages in the legal sphere. As the air pirate generally commits his deed on board an aircraft, he enjoys all the benefits of the uncertainty which often enshrouds delicate questions of jurisdiction and which makes it very difficult for the authorities of many countries to exercise their right to punish. In former years before the advent of air transportation, the problem of who had jurisdiction over a sea-craft presented no problem. International law considered vessels on the open sea to be part of the territory of the flag State and granted this State jurisdiction over them for most purposes. However, this principle was developed in customary international law over a long period of time to meet the needs of the law of the sea and cannot be said to apply to aircraft in international law as it stands at present. Furthermore, States frequently encounter many practical problems in asserting their jurisdiction over acts that occur on board aircraft overflying their own territory.

Another undesirable legal advantage of the hijacker stems from the traditional rules of extradition. Even when the authorities of a country can successfully try a suspected hijacker, they often cannot secure his presence before the courts because of inapt extradition laws.

There is a further series of problems affecting international air transportation. These problems relate to the matter of developing adequate security standards for world-wide application. Many States have not felt the necessity of adopting such rules for the protection of passengers and aircraft, while others are awaiting guidance from the international community. Furthermore, there is a need for standardizing certain security measures on a world-wide basis. It is for these reasons that the International Civil Aviation Organization (ICAO) is in the process of developing certain minimum standards and has adopted certain guidance material which it is hoped will alleviate the problem of unlawful interference with civil aviation.

In the following pages we shall attempt to examine the problems that we have just outlined, and we hope to make some useful suggestions for international action in combating crimes against the safety of civil aviation.

We shall examine the shortcomings of the legal framework, the remedial role played by certain international conventions and the efforts deployed by the International Civil Aviation Organization to develop practical measures by which the international community can prevent and minimize the effects of acts of unlawful interference.

It has long been said that the concept of "law" involves at least two facets: first, the law specifies a norm of conduct; and secondly, the law punishes deviations from this norm. Without these two facets there is no law. With regard to acts of unlawful interference with the safety of civil aviation, we shall see that for a long period of time there was no law, and therefore morally reprehensible acts of interference went unpunished because they were not characterized as crimes under the law. This situation remains unchanged today in certain countries and for certain acts.

Generally, the diverse forms of unlawful interference with the safety of international civil aviation are not considered as specific crimes in customary international law. It should be noted that although customary law has long looked upon piracy on the open sea as an international crime, the author of which could be brought to justice anywhere, it has never been seriously contended that this notion applied to what might be termed piracy in the air.

The matter was therefore left to the domestic law of each State, which was very often ill-equipped to deal with most crimes which occurred beyond the territorial limits of that State. . . .

There is a further procedural problem which one encounters in trying to punish acts of interference with the safety of civil aviation. . . . There is no universal rule of customary international law in existence which imposes the duty of extradition. No such rule obliges a State to deliver an accused or a convicted individual to another State whose penal laws he is alleged to have broken or has been convicted of breaking. Therefore it can be said that for most countries of the world, extradition is not a right that can be demanded, unless there is some international instrument granting it.

The right to request extradition is usually granted in bilateral treaties which have been negotiated over a long period of years. Because monarchs in the past have tended to cultivate excessively the old right of asylum and modern States continue to be jealous of their sovereignty, the forms and conditions of extradition are very restrictively regulated. Usually extradition is granted only for crimes specifically enumerated in the relevant treaty. Frequently this instrument will stipulate that these offences will be extraditable only when committed on the territory of the requesting State. This in itself gives some idea of the inadequacy of the present system, since the unlawful acts which are being committed against the safety of civil aviation are rarely included in the enumeration of extraditable crimes; furthermore, even when they are, they might not be actionable if they were committed on board an aircraft in flight outside of the requesting country.

Two other aspects of the law of extradition are worth mentioning. First, frequently treaties of extradition do not apply to crimes for which the suspect might suffer the death penalty in the country that is seeking to try him. Since hijackings and other acts of unlawful interference frequently involve the commission of acts for which capital punishment can be demanded in many countries, offended States are faced with a further obstacle to redress. Secondly, there is a long-standing tradition to the effect that extradition is not to be granted in cases involving crimes of a political nature. In view of the fact that the perpetrators of many of the recent hijackings claim to be politically motivated, it would appear that as far as hijacking is concerned, political motivation should not be a bar to extradition, or if it should remain a bar, it should be interpreted very restrictively. . . .

As was the case in 1958 when the Convention on the High Seas was signed, in 1963 when a diplomatic conference was convened in Tokyo by the International Civil Aviation Organization, hijacking was not the pressing problem that it was to become. The main task undertaken by the framers of the Convention signed in Tokyo was to solve some of the procedural difficulties encountered by States in trying to prosecute offences committed on board aircraft in flight. This Convention did not therefore create any new offences, as was to be the case in later conventions.

The prime merit of the Tokyo Convention is that it attempts to solve the general problem of who has jurisdiction over offences committed on board an aircraft in flight. This jurisdiction is granted primarily to the State of registration of the aircraft on board which the reprehensible act took place (article

3). Other States are also given concurrent jurisdiction over such acts. These are the State on whose territory the offence has effect; the State whose national or permanent resident has suffered from the offence; the State whose security has been prejudiced by the offence; the State whose rules or regulations relating to the flight and manoeuvre of aircraft have been breached; and the State for whom the exercise of jurisdiction is necessary to ensure the observance of its obligations under a multilateral international agreement (article 4).

A second procedural difficulty which the Tokyo Convention endeavours to solve concerns extradition. Although the Convention does not oblige States to extradite, it does tend to facilitate the process by deeming that an offence which has been committed on an aircraft is to be treated as if it had been committed in the territory of the State of registration of this aircraft (article 16). This provision attempts to get around some of the inconvenient wording to which we referred previously and which is used in a multitude of outdated bilateral extradition treaties and requires the offence for which extradition is sought to have been committed on the territory of the State requesting extradition. . . .

The inadequacy of the Tokyo Convention in dealing effectively with the problems of aerial hijacking was soon recognized by the international community. The number of hijackings increased drastically during the end of the 1960s, and by December 1970 there had been over 90 instances of hijacking involving more than 8,000 passengers in that year alone. The preceding year the United Nations General Assembly had adopted a resolution in which it had expressed its deep concern about the increase in unlawful acts of interference with international civil aviation and had urged that effective legal measures be taken against unlawful seizure of aircraft in flight.

In response to the United Nations call, the International Civil Aviation Organization convened an extraordinary session of its members to find a solution to the problem of air piracy. The ICAO Assembly, which was held at Montreal from 16 to 30 June 1970, accomplished a tremendous amount of work in developing measures for the protection of civil aviation. It urged a wider acceptance of the Tokyo Convention and called upon States to convene at a diplomatic conference in The Hague and to consent to be bound by a convention that would make hijacking an international offence.

The Hague Diplomatic Conference was held in December 1970 and did develop a convention which made hijacking such an offence. Article 1 of the Hague Convention defines the new offence in the following terms:

"Any person who on board an aircraft in flight:

"(a) unlawfully, by force or threat thereof, or by any other form of intimidation, seizes, or exercises control of, that aircraft, or attempts to perform any such act, or

"(b) is an accomplice of a person who performs or attempts to perform any such act,

"commits an offence (hereinafter referred to as 'the offence')."

The States who ratify this Convention undertake to make the offence punishable by severe penalties (article 2).

This Convention marks the first time that a useful international norm of conduct of this type has been enacted by a fair-sized segment of the international community. Although the norm does not extend as far as it would if it were part of the customary international law, it nevertheless constitutes a giant step forward; and it is hoped that a sufficient number of countries will ratify this Convention so as to make this norm universal. . . .

Finally, the Convention holds that if a State in the territory of which an alleged offender is found does not extradite him, it is obliged without exception whatsoever and whether or not the offence was committed in its territory to submit the case to its competent authorities for the purpose of prosecution (article 7). Therefore, if a State feels that it cannot extradite a hijacker because his crime was politically motivated, it is under the obligation to prosecute him itself as if the crime were any ordinary offence of a serious nature under the law of that State. The obligation either to prosecute or extradite, irrespective of the place of commission of the offence, therefore ensures that whenever and wherever the hijacker is found, so long as it is within the territory of a contracting State, he will be subject to due process of law. This is a substantial break-through in the battle against aerial piracy.

The signing of the Hague Convention was undoubtedly a great step forward, and the work done there was extended and completed in Montreal one year later.

It was quickly realized that the acts of violence being perpetrated against civil aviation went beyond the simple act of hijacking. Aircraft were being sabotaged while on the ground, bombs were being placed on board, air navigation facilities were in danger of being interfered with and bomb hoaxes were multiplying. A

new and broader international instrument was needed to extend the offences created at The Hague.

A diplomatic conference was therefore convened at Montreal in September 1971. Except for the new offences created, the Convention signed at Montreal is quite similar in tenor to the Hague Convention. . . .

The new definitions cover a multitude of acts which are prejudicial to civil aviation. Sabotage of ground installations and mid-air bombings and bomb threats are now international crimes, the authors of which must be either tried or extradited.

The Montreal Convention confers jurisdiction much in the same manner as the Hague Convention. One heading of jurisdiction was added, however, because of the nature of some of the new international crimes: as it is no longer required that the offence be committed on an aircraft in flight, jurisdiction now lies also with the State in whose territory the offence was committed (article 5).

It should be noted that the Montreal instrument facilitates extradition in much the same manner as the Hague Convention (article 8). One new feature of the later Convention is that it requires contracting States which have reason to believe that one of the offences defined by the Convention is about to be committed to furnish any relevant information to the States that would have jurisdiction in the case of the projected offence (article 12). This obligation to "tip off" is quite new in international law and will, it is hoped, be of great use in the fight against unlawful acts which are prejudicial to the safety of civil aviation.

The increasing number of unlawful acts against the safety of international civil aviation, better known as acts of air piracy, have posed a serious challenge to our traditional legal framework, both domestic and international. In the past customary international law had practically ignored this new problem, while domestic law had revealed itself to be clearly incapable of solving a problem of such far-reaching international dimensions. The international community lacked a standard definition of the crimes involved, reasonable and universally acceptable rules to assign jurisdiction over such crimes and a clear set of extradition rules tailored to ensure the punishment of the air criminals.

These deficiencies were painstakingly ironed out over a period of less than 10 years, a remarkable feat in international affairs. The Tokyo, Hague and Montreal Conventions have given us clearly defined and extraditable international crimes which contracting parties agree to make punishable by severe penalties, a set of jurisdictional rules which leave little to be desired, an obligation for parties who find an air pirate on their territory either to try him or extradite him, and measures to alleviate the suffering of the innocent victims of hijackings. Unfortunately the three Conventions have not yet been universally ratified. Havens for air pirates have thus been created. When one considers the degree of mobility afforded the air pirate by the very aircraft he hijacks, one realizes how easy it is to frustrate the efforts of the nations of the world to find a legal solution for the elimination of the crimes of violence which have been thrust upon civil aviation.

An attempt was made in August and September of 1973 in Rome to find some way of imposing sanctions on States that provide havens for hijackers. Diverse solutions to the problem were proposed, ranging from the compulsory extradition of offenders under the Montreal Convention to the State in which the stricken aircraft is registered, as suggested by the Soviet delegation, to the incorporation of the Hague Convention into the body of the Chicago Convention, as suggested by the French delegation. Regrettably none of the proposals had a sufficient number of adherents to survive. . . .

It is well recognized that the fundamental responsibility for the protection of citizens rests with Governments, both in their individual capacities and as members of the international community of States. Governments are particularly answerable to the community for safeguarding the security of vulnerable public services which contribute to the social and economic welfare of their citizens. The airlines have done much on their own already to ensure the maximum possible safety and reliability of civil air transportation. They have assumed a heavy financial and physical burden which must now be shared by Governments, which alone have the necessary executive and legal powers to effectively safeguard the security of their citizens. . . .

We should therefore urge all States which have not yet acceded to the above-mentioned conventions to reconsider with great care their position on aerial piracy. For the protection of the world's airways and their users, all States should ratify these conventions and apply the Security Standards and Recommended Practices which are presently being worked out by the International Civil Aviation Organization. States that cannot for some reason of policy enter into such multilateral agreements should undertake to negotiate bilateral or regional agreements for solving the problem.

14.

Marilyn French: The National Women's Conference

The first national meeting of women since the Seneca Falls Convention of 1848 occurred in Houston on November 19–21, 1977. Nearly 2,000 women, including 1,442 voting delegates, convened on the mandate of a 1975 federal law. Resolutions were approved urging equal opportunities for women in education, employment, and health care; special attention to the problems of older, disabled, rural, and minority women; the involvement of women in international affairs; and the encouragement of women to seek elective and appointive office. Controversial planks included those endorsing the adoption of the Equal Rights Amendment, civil rights and child custody for lesbians, abortion, and federally funded child care. Only one resolution was defeated: it called for a Cabinet-level Women's Department. The resolutions and a report on the conference were to be delivered to President Carter and Congress by March 1, 1978; first lady Rosalynn Carter addressed the opening session and told the delegates that the President's "concern about the outcome of your agenda is deep." She added: "Never before in our history has there been such a women's meeting—in numbers, in preparation, in diversity, in long-range effect." Many accounts of the conference were published in the next few months. The article reprinted here, by Marilyn French, author of The Women's Room, *captured the spirit of the meeting.*

Source: "The Fearful and the Innocent," *Horizon*, January 1978.

HOUSTON, LIKE MANY American cities, appears to have been constructed from a kit produced by the creators of the General Motors Futurama at the 1939 New York World's Fair. Concrete-and-glass towers and well-behaved clumps of trees dot the landscape, which is embraced by curving, sensuous sweeps of superhighway. It is an automobile manufacturer's dream (there is almost no public transportation) that takes for granted the continuing availability of a manmade environment, of control over nature.

There are no dwellings at all in the center of the city, no markets, and except for the women who came last November to attend the International Women's Year National Women's Conference, there were few people on the streets. The city was not built for walking. Its amenities—glass-walled elevators, sparkling lights, artificial plants, and restaurants that are supposed to imitate French cafés, British pubs, or Continental gourmet spots but that derive more from Hollywood than from Europe—are all indoors.

Houston is the home of the Astrodome and the Astroworld amusement park, of the Rothko Chapel and Barnett Newman's *Broken Obelisk,* which is dedicated to Martin Luther King, Jr. The last two comment on the prevailing ethos even as they participate in it. The Mark Rothko paintings are housed in a windowless brick interfaith chapel, cooled by a huge air conditioner set in the lawn, which fills the quiet neighborhood with a continual roar. They are dark, these paintings— huge, monotonous wine or brown-and-black panels offering the observer contemplation of oblivion, while the Newman sculpture, standing in a pool in the neat chapel garden, soars upward in assured technological thrust only to end in jagged failure long before it has reached its presumed goal.

Central Houston, glittering with newness, is also a clean city, and the few Houstonians one meets are open and friendly. Yet, despite its general friendliness, Houston was not entirely welcoming to the IWY conference. The day before it opened, Jerry Smith, a lawyer with the firm of Fulbright and Jaworski and the new Harris County Republican chairman, denounced the participants as "a gaggle of outcasts, misfits, and rejects" with "perverted views." On a back page of the Houston *Chronicle,* which reported his comments, was a story of the sentencing to 15 years in prison of George Daniels, who told his wife she should "have her brains blown out" for attending a union meeting instead of cooking his dinner, and then proceeded to do it.

Delegates to the IWY conference began arriving on Thursday, November 17, holding confirmed reservations either at the Hyatt Regency or the Sheraton-Houston, the two hotels in which most of the workshops of the conference were to take place. On the way to town, taxi drivers warned that there were no rooms, that the National Building Materials Association had extended their stay by an extra day and had left no accommodations at the Hyatt Regency for the women. And indeed whole delegations were turned away, among them those from Wisconsin, Pennsylvania, Ohio, Arizona, Virginia, California, Puerto Rico, and the District of Columbia. Hundreds of women who arrived on Thursday went without beds, or if they were lucky stood in line for hours waiting to be shipped to some motel across the sprawling city, where they ended up separated from their delegations.

The hotel managers, while admitting to some overbooking and a few lingering guests, blamed the women, who, they suggested carefully, had no experience in travel: they had held reservations for the 18th, the managers said, but had arrived on the 17th. (If this were so, all the women should easily have been handled next day, on the 18th, but they were not.) Lines of women, four deep, wound around the Hyatt Regency lobby from eight in the morning until midnight. Close to 1,000 stood in line for six to ten hours; many were forced to go through the line two or three times before they finally got a room. Some women had to pay for their rooms in advance. Richard Nelson, a manager of the Hyatt Regency, claimed the long lines were caused by the women's "hysteria." I had been in and out all day and had spent several hours talking with women in the lobby, and had seen no hysteria. Well, he said, there had been an incident of pushing and a nasty retort to a bellhop.

Rooms were one problem; services and elevators were another. People waited twenty to thirty minutes for a down elevator or climbed down twenty-odd flights of stairs. When a man wearing a badge that said "engineer" forced his way rudely into an overcrowded elevator, one of the women teased him. "What a mess!" she laughed. "You're an engineer. Why don't you do something about it?" "It's you people," he retorted angrily. "You stand talking, holding the elevator doors open."

This, then, was the environment in which the conference began: hostile, difficult, and wearying, with the blame being laid on the women in stereotypic terms—women are ignorant, hysterical, and stand around gabbing. But perhaps no city in the country would have been entirely welcoming to the roughly 20,000 women who finally arrived in Houston; no city could guarantee freedom from sexist comment and attitudes. In any case, the response of the women was remarkable.

Late Thursday night many good-humoredly made plans to bunk together; some slept six or eight to a room. Audrey Colom, a hardworking commissioner of the conference, slept on the floor. She was not the only one. Twenty-four hours later, as women still stood queuing in the Hyatt lobby, some spelled each other in line while a few went out, found a friendly cab driver, and came back loaded with bags of hamburgers and Cokes for the others. Those waiting for elevators chatted easily with strangers. One group discovered that among their number was the lieutenant governor of New York, Mary Anne Krupsak. They gave the fact an appreciative "Oh!" but then returned easily, unawed, to the discussion. Everywhere one went there was laughter at the absurdity, the predictability of the mess. Everywhere there was good-natured cooperation. And the conferees

did not allow the initial confusion and unpleasantness to deflect their energies: as soon as they had beds, showers, some food, and had found their delegations, they moved with dispatch to business.

Nevertheless, the situation at the hotels reflected the contradiction that lies at the heart of the women's movement, a paradox that cannot be dislodged and that pervaded the entire conference. This contradiction is the apparent irreconcilability of two modes of existence: that of virtue and that of power. In her keynote address to the conference, Representative Barbara Jordan asserted that women already possess virtue and must now move to acquire power. The intrinsic difficulty of doing this was not discussed by any of the speakers, but the problems of integrating power and virtue continually cropped up in concrete form. Some women suggested that if they had not been so accepting and agreeable, hotel officials would have been quicker to respond. Others thought they should have given the hotel clerks hell, or behaved pompously, or been unruly. "Yes," one woman sighed sadly. "But do we really want that? To behave like men?" The group around her pondered, silently.

The moral division of virtue and power and the assignment of the first quality to women, the second to men, is ancient and is connected with, among other things, women's bearing and nursing of children and men's training for hunting and war. The split in roles that has structured civilization for thousands of years has been perpetuated on the grounds of efficiency: men, through war and rulership, provide the means whereby a culture survives; women, through procreation and service, assure the ends of that culture—its continuation in children and in a safe, nurturing,

AP/Wide World

Receiving applause at the Houston ERA rally are, from left: Liz Carpenter, former press secretary to Lady Bird Johnson; first lady Rosalynn Carter; former first lady Betty Ford; and Elly Peterson, co-chairman of ERAmerica.

and pleasant living place, a home. But the moral schizophrenia implicit in this dichotomy has, as often as not, resulted in the obliteration or the forgetting of ends, in the transformation of means into their own ends, in power that is designed to extend and maintain only power.

This perception lies at the root of feminism. But so deeply is the moral split ingrained in our traditions, our artifacts, our thinking, and our language, that both personal and cultural upheaval are required to imagine the integration of the two qualities.

There were two conferences held in Houston on November 18–21, 1977. One opened with a moving ceremony— the delivery of a torch that had been carried to Houston from Seneca Falls, New York, by 2,000 different runners—and proceeded in parliamentary session at the Sam Houston Coliseum to consider resolutions on 26 issues of deep concern to women, such as child abuse, child care, battered wives, the Equal Rights Amendment, abortion, and mi-

nority rights. This conference, government-financed by $5 million (a fraction of what the Republicans and Democrats spend on their political conventions), was made up of delegates elected in 50 state and 6 territorial conventions. To this observer's eye, at least one-third of the women were from minorities, and there were also substantial groups of elderly women, disabled women, and supporters of gay rights. Some women came with their children, for whom free day care was provided. In some cases expenses were paid by IWY, allowing poor as well as middle-class women to attend. There were political, government, and business leaders from all over the country, but 50 per cent of the women had never before attended a convention, and many had never before participated in a political process other than voting. It was probably the most diverse group of women ever assembled.

Across the city, with headquarters at the Ramada Inn, another group gathered—not just women but whole families. Women, men, and children, they came by the thousands on chartered buses and jammed into the Astro Arena Saturday afternoon for speeches, gospel singing, country music, and sermons. Most were members of conservative groups and religious organizations. There were few blacks or members of other minorities. More than half the speakers were men, and the emphasis of the meeting was on the Bible. The people gathered around Phyllis Schlafly's anti-ERA banner and raised their own, declaring themselves profamily, prolife.

And indeed they are. They too believe in virtue and feel they possess it. They too want to assert the importance of a safe, nurturing living place, want to protect their children and the women who create and maintain the home. But their focus is such that they perceive the women of the IWY conference as inimical and threatening. They see feminists as concerned only with power— power in the world, power over their own bodies, power to live individualistic emotional and economic lives. They are frightened by what seems to them a massive defection by women from "women's" values and from the traditional nutritive, compassionate, dependent female role.

They listen to their speakers as if they were authorities, credulously and in fear. The master of ceremonies introduces each in similar fashion, as someone "who believes like we do." One speaker cries out, "Only the good Lord can deliver you from homosexuality," and the crowd roars. A Vietnam veteran, a Green Beret, equates the IWY women with communists and subversives, warns that another war is inevitable, and announces after a meaningful pause, in triumphant voice, that the volunteer army is a failure. The single congressman in attendance empha-

sizes his singularity and the presence on the stage of the IWY conference of Rosalynn Carter and two former first ladies, who support, as he describes it, sexual license. In fact, sex is the bugaboo, the pervasive underlying terror, the temptation that opens the gates of hell. Sex threatens both virtue and power and is, after all, what connects the genders that exemplify those qualities.

The literature of the prolifers contains titillating references to sexual devices supposedly sold, and outrageous sexual acts supposedly performed, by lesbians at the state meetings that preceded the national conference. The imaginations of the thousands of people packed into the hall are febrile with sex. Only traditional family structure and strong male control can protect the women and children from abandoning themselves to its overwhelming and sinful allure.

They uphold what they call Biblical/patriarchal values against what they call humanist/feminist values intended to "restructure society." It is impossible to stand among them without sympathy. Inadequate and unsatisfying as present roles may be, unsuccessful as present institutions may be at guarding the "feminine" values they cherish, these frightened people cling to whatever exists because something is better than nothing. Impersonal, intrusive categorization compresses and compiles their lives on computer tape. Human control over nature threatens to obliterate human ties to nature; it is extended even to that most recalcitrant area, fertility in women. Sex will soon be, indeed already is, something that can now be indulged in just for fun. The group in the Astro Arena are willing to submit to any kind of patriarchal demand to avoid such sexual freedom.

The antifeminists stand together, tightly bound to each other by the impotence they feel in the face of the world around them. They have no faith that "feminine" values can support themselves, and insufficient imagination to conceive of virtue and power integrated. They have an embattled air; they watch bitterly as other women, who are supposed to be their allies—who, indeed, claim some similar values—fire torpedoes directly at their already sinking ship.

It does not occur to them that feminists are firing not at them but at their enemies; that if feminists support abortion, it is because the alternative is not the end of abortion but *illegal* abortion; that if feminists exhort government to act on their proposals, it is as much as anything else an exhortation that institutions shift their focus to women and children as people rather than as property.

Meanwhile, the wicked women on the other side of town were cheering every proposal that showed concern for the disinherited. They cheered for the disabled, the elderly, the battered wives, the rights of minorities. Every spoken word was interpreted in sign language by two experts onstage. By the end of the conference the delegates had passed a plan that, if it could be put into action, would lay the foundation for heaven on earth. So much on the side of the angels, they did not as a group seem to have any sense that most of what they were doing was exercising virtue, not power (although no doubt some individuals were aware of this, as were newspaper editors who relegated reports of the Houston conference to the women's pages).

Sitting for hours through the tedious parliamentary business, the delegates felt they were doing something important, in which, moreover, they believed. They were, as a group, politically naive and argued over each plank, passed each plank but one, as if those planks were being nailed down firmly to a foundation. As a group they were innocent. It never seemed to occur to them that the proposals, argued over, carefully phrased, causes at times of tremendous division among the women, were just that—proposals. They were designing the new world, creating a blueprint for utopia, and their joy, their innocence, their enthusiasm waved over the hall like a strong sweet wind. They felt that the rightness of their values and the power of their combined voices would inevitably succeed.

When the proposal for "sexual preference," a euphemism for lesbian rights, was passed, hundreds of colored balloons reading "We Are Everywhere" were released to float above the huge auditorium. They were symbolic of the whole conference: beautiful but vulnerable ideas for human possibility.

But after all why should cynical, disappointed minds refuse to entertain a possibility? It is just possible that the conferees' delighted conviction in their own power and rightness, their joy in the communality of women with similar values, and their enthusiasm for humane proposals can indeed wash over more space than that of the Sam Houston Coliseum, can sweep across the country like a Nile flood, unabating, unopposable, and leaving in its wake acres of land richly fertile, waiting for the next planting. However skeptical of political process one may be, however much one doubts the possibility of the integration of virtue and power, how can one wish them anything but the warm bloom of a new crop, fat ears of corn?

Video games became enormously popular in 1979–81. Arcades like the one above were so jammed that customers could hardly get through the doors. Later home video drew much of the play, but in 1986 arcades started to come back.

FUN, FITNESS, & TECHNOLOGY

Improvements in electronic and digital technology made an enormous impact on life and work during the 1970s and 1980s. Personal computers and fax machines quickly became essential equipment in most business offices. Microwave ovens, video cassette recorders, and cable television entered many American homes during this time. Video games made their debut as well. Games such as Space Invaders, Asteroids, and Pac-Man attracted millions of children (and a large number of adults) to gaming arcades. The old electric pinball machine was also revolutionized by new changes in technology. The Atari company introduced the 2600 VCS video computer console in 1977. The device turned the household television into a private video arcade. Although work and play became more sedentary for many in this new era of technology, others sought out new ways of maintaining physical fitness.

Photos by John Bevans

The arrival of the video cassette recorder (VCR) in the 1970s allowed users to record television shows while they were elsewhere and to watch favorite films at their own convenience. Suddenly, video rental stores were springing up in every hamlet across the nation, providing comedy, drama, instruction, and pornography for anyone who owned a VCR and a television set. The introduction of small, hand-held videocassette cameras also made it possible for anyone to make his or her own films for home use. Cable and dish antennas made as many as 100 channels of television fare available. Musical compact discs (CD) and their players offered greater durability and cleaner sound reproduction than vinyl records.

(Top) People who own video cassette recorders (VCRs) have access to all forms of entertainment as well as instruction; (center) dish antennas that receive from satellites have sprouted all over the country, especially in areas where television reception is poor; (bottom) compact discs are almost indestructible and compact disc players reproduce music from them with great accuracy.

A fad of the 1980s, perhaps less transitory than others, was the quest for fitness. Exercise, along with concern for proper nutrition, became a national pastime for millions. The most visible form was jogging. Other people got their exercise at home using their own equipment. Sometimes they were assisted by television, using perhaps the best-selling workout cassettes by Jane Fonda. Others joined health clubs, which proliferated in every city and suburb. Still others went to aerobics classes or took part in other workouts at schools, YMCAs, and other institutions. For younger adults, health clubs became social centers, replacing the singles bars of the 1970s. All the concern for fitness did not mean, however, that the people of the United States were all that healthy. Obesity and other health problems—caused largely by poor eating habits—still plagued millions of Americans.

(Top) Muscle-building becomes a social event as friends gather in a home gym in Beltsville, Maryland; (bottom) the footfalls of millions of joggers of all ages were heard across the land in the 1980s.

IBM

IBM

In the four decades after World War II the workplace changed dramatically. The changes were due mostly to the same innovations that had made possible video games and other amusements. Computers made their appearance during the war, and over the years they were remarkably refined. The development of the personal computer made for quicker processing of vast amounts of information and data. Information became the key to success or failure in almost every endeavor. To that end, the technology of the future would depend more on photons, the basic elements of light transmission, than on electrons, the basic elements of electricity. Light passing untouched through dark caverns and bending around corners, as at left, was expected to vastly speed up the transmission of information. The first compact discs carried more than half a billion words on a single five-inch disc.

(Top) In the 1980s computers and word processors replaced typewriters in offices; (center) computer production of sophisticated three-dimensional graphics as well as words, numbers, and graphs changed design and planning in the workplace; (bottom) an optical glass cable that carries over 1,000 telephone transmissions; the standard copper cable beside it takes 256 pairs of wires to carry the same number. (Opposite top) This aluminum disc, when prepared, stored up to four billion characters of information on a single side; (bottom) the speech recognizer in a prototype computer that is operated by spoken instructions.

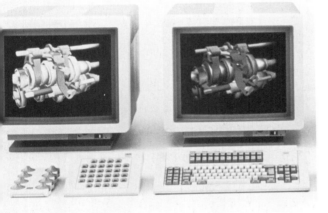

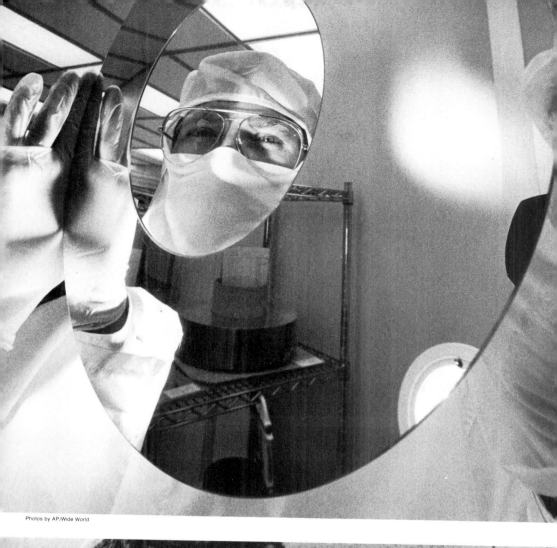

(Top) ENIAC, the first all-electronic digital computer, performed a mathematical calculation in 1946 that would have taken 40 hours to complete; (bottom) the Cray-2 supercomputer was, in 1985, able to process 400 million calculations per second over 60 miles of wiring.

Supercomputers, like the Cray-2 at left, stored amounts of information and processed data at speeds that were unimaginable a generation earlier. The variety of uses to which they were put ranged from military application in the nation's defense systems to operation of the largest corporations. With these machines it was possible to solve heretofore "unsolvable" mathematical puzzles and problems. These high-speed calculators, which processed as many as a billion operations per second, opened up whole new fields of mathematical investigation. The ENIAC was put into operation only some 40 years before the creation of the Cray-2.

1978

15.

A Declaration for Older Persons

In the first half of this century, progressive forces strove to reduce the hours per day, the weeks per year, and the total number of years that workers must labor. As a result, eight hours a day became first the norm and then a maximum, paid vacations became mandatory, and retirement at age 65 was required by law. But just as manadatory retirement became universal, voices began to be heard protesting against it, for reasons that are expressed in the Declaration reprinted here, signed by many well known persons, including four U.S. senators and nearly 100 members of the House of Representatives. On April 6, 1978, President Carter signed legislation raising the mandatory retirement age for most workers—police and firefighters, high-salaried executives, and a few other categories excepted—from 65 to 70.

Source: *The Humanist*, September/October, 1977.

VOLUNTARY RETIREMENT AND THE RIGHT TO EMPLOYMENT

WE, THE UNDERSIGNED, oppose mandatory retirement and are committed to work for its elimination in all areas of employment. We believe in making retirement a matter of voluntary choice, not a requirement.

Mandatory retirement is morally wrong. It is another name for dismissal from employment, a firing based not upon loss of skill, competence, or productivity, but upon attainment of an arbitrarily selected age. Mandatory retirement is a denial of a fundamental right—the right to earn a living, a right the United States Supreme Court once called "the very essence of personal freedom and opportunity."

Federal law, the Age Discrimination in Employment Act of 1967, states that no worker between the ages of forty and sixty-five can be denied employment, be refused a promotion, or have his employment terminated because of age. Not only can that worker be fired as soon as he or she is sixty-five, but that individual can be involuntarily retired before sixty-five if the provision for discharge is written into an employee benefit plan.

The law prohibits discrimination in employment based upon race, sex, religion, or national origin. Much more progress is needed to eliminate such discrimination, but the national commitment is clear.

Discrimination in employment based upon age is another matter. So long as mandatory retirement is sanctioned, our society places a stamp of approval on age discrimination.

Mandatory retirement may be a convenient tool for the employer but is often destructive of the health and well-being of the individual who is arbitrarily discharged when he or she is still able and willing to work.

The Committee on Aging of the American Medical Association found that mandatory retirement robs the individual of initiative and independence, "narrows physical and mental horizons," and impairs the health of those "whose jobs represent a major source of status, creative satisfaction, social relationships, or self-respect." It is hardly astonishing that a Louis Harris survey reports that half of all those mandatorily retired feel a loss of self-respect and a lack of usefulness.

Mandatory retirement does not make economic sense. Studies show that the belief that mandatory retirement creates new job opportunities for the young rests upon no factual foundation. For many employers, the loss of able, skilled, competent, reliable workers exacts an economic penalty. And mandatory retirement works a hardship on both the individual and the American economy. The median income for men forced to retire drops from $7,880 annually to $3,380. The impact upon individuals and families is devastating. The loss to the economy is immeasurable in terms of creativity; the reduction in purchasing power and the increased costs in welfare benefits and social-security payments is staggering.

Much needs to be done to eliminate all artificial barriers to employment— including removing the earnings-limitation test for social-security benefits, increased incentives to employ older workers, more and better flexible and gradual retirement programs. Arbitrary firing based on age needs to be replaced by fair and objective performance standards, applied systematically to workers of all ages.

Elimination of mandatory retirement is the necessary first step. So long as it remains, it stands as a symbol of what Dr. Alex Comfort calls "the ejection from a citizenship based on work." That citizenship must be restored.

16.

Cy Brickfield: Our Aging Workforce

The social and economic effects of the legislation raising the mandatory retirement age from 65 to 70 (see Selection 15) would be far-reaching, in the view of many commentators. Some feared that employers would extract more payments from workers during the extra years of labor in order to shore up their underfunded pension plans, while others pointed to the damaging effect on younger workers of a reduced number of job openings at the top of the age scale. Most believed, however, that the new freedom to work or not to work was a natural expansion of the century's push toward increased equality in the work place—after all, professionals, entrepreneurs, and other independents had always been able to work as long as they desired (and to quit when they wanted). At the same time, it was recognized that more general considerations lay behind the retirement age controversy. The U.S. workforce was changing in many ways, not just one. The economic and political consequences of the demographic shifts are discussed in this 1978 article. The author was executive director of the 12 million-member National Association of Retired Persons.

Source: *Enterprise*, June 1978.

IN RECENT YEARS, one of the biggest problems for a boss was figuring out how to entice "Old Joe" into retiring. Many employers were not able to come up with a solution and had to resort to making everyone retire at the same age, regardless of their ability and willingness or need to continue working. Thus did the practice of "mandatory retirement"—almost unheard of 30 years ago—become widespread.

But times are changing. Not only does "Old Joe" now refuse to accept the nickname and its accompanying negative stereotype, he is also fighting back against the practice of forced retirement at an arbitrary and irrelevant age. And, as was seen in the recent signing by President Carter of a new law pro-

hibiting mandatory retirement prior to age 70 for most American workers (and outlawing it altogether for 95 per cent of federal employees), he is winning that fight.

Age Potential

The business community should be encouraging him. For in the next three decades will come a dramatic change in our society from one that is oriented toward youth to one in which the old have far more influence.

In that period, older workers will become more important than ever before to business and industry; the strength and vitality of the workforce will depend on them. Mandatory retirement will become extinct, not just because it is discriminatory, but also because it will be an impediment to a full and productive labor force.

To understand these changes, one need only look at recent demographic history and population projections for the next 30 years.

Baby Boom a Bust

Several dramatic and unforeseen shifts in the birth rate have occurred, beginning with a sharply reduced birth rate caused by the Depression and World War II. This was followed by the "baby boom" which began at the end of the war and lasted into the early 1960s. The birth rate then began dropping again and continued to drop in the late 1960s and much of the 1970s.

Persons born during the "baby boom" period are already beginning to place tremendous stress on the labor force and the economy because of their numbers. They are now competing with each other for a limited number of jobs, resulting in chronically high unemployment rates. And as they seek promotions, they will be vying with each other for limited management slots.

But what will happen when they are ready to retire? Because of the low birth rate in the 1960s and the 1970s, there will be fewer workers around in the year 2000 and beyond to support the older population through payment of Social Security and income taxes. Social Security tax burdens may become intolerable 25 years from now unless we stop encouraging older workers to drop out of the labor force. And instead of the high rates of unemployment we are used to today, actual labor shortages may occur in certain sectors of the economy, demanding the continued employment— or reemployment—of older persons.

AP/Wide World

An 84-year-old Michigan tool worker.

Pressure to use older workers will build over the next 20 to 30 years not only because of a growing shortage of younger workers, but also because the older population will be living longer. By the turn of the century, the average life expectancy for men and women is predicted to jump from the present 73 years to 76. And this does not take into account the possible medical breakthroughs against "killer" diseases such as heart attack, cancer or stroke.

Methuselah in Our Time

This means that more people than ever before will live to be "old." Some of them will still have health problems and will need to be institutionalized or receive home care, thus requiring increased public tax support. But many more will live into their 70s and even 80s in generally good health, and will be both willing and able to continue making contributions to society—whether through paid employment or volunteer work.

To   illustrate   these   demographic

changes, the number of persons over 65 will have grown by 44 per cent between 1970 and 1990—twice as fast as the rest of the population. The present total of approximately 23 million Americans age 65 and older will rise to nearly 40 million by the turn of the century. Within the next 50 years, one in every five Americans will be over 65, compared with the present one in 10.

This dramatic increase in the number of older Americans—not to mention an equally important increase in their political and economic clout—will undoubtedly bring about significant changes in the nature of the workforce. While experts may disagree on specific changes, here are some of the areas in which industry and government will have to adjust their thinking:

Social Security at an Impasse

With all of the hue and cry that has surrounded congressional attempts to deal with the short-term financing problems of Social Security—problems caused by the recent high inflation and high unemployment creating a shortfall in revenues—our political leaders haven't even begun to come to grips with the effects on the system of a larger older population and smaller workforce in the years to come.

When Social Security was established in 1935, three Social Security recipients were being supported by 100 workers; the ratio in 1975 was 30 recipients per 100 workers. If present trends continue, 100 workers in the year 2020 will have to support at least 45 recipients.

One solution would be to encourage people to continue working so that they will be contributing to the system rather than drawing funds from it. Another would be the use—at least on a limited

basis—of general tax revenue to help support Social Security. Despite its controversial nature, this is not a new proposal; many of the people who founded Social Security envisioned someday a three-way sharing of the cost among employers and employees (through the payroll tax) and the federal government (through general tax revenue). This is clearly an idea whose time has come.

By the turn of the century, it is also quite possible that the goal of "universal" Social Security coverage will be achieved. This would not only bring into the system new revenues from millions of workers not now covered, it would also save the government millions of dollars yearly in administrative costs for the myriad of retirement plans (such as Civil Service, Military and Railroad Retirement) which it now oversees. If universal coverage extends to members of Congress—who now have their own very special retirement program—maybe the benefit program will also continue to be improved.

Private Pensions Also Under Pressure

The private pension system will be subject to the same pressures as Social Security over the next few decades. The continued solvency of the private pension system will be vital not only because it will affect the financial security of retirees, but also because it constitutes one of the nation's most important sources of investment capital.

One research organization, the Futures Group of Glastonbury, Conn., predicts that the federal government will continue to tighten its regulatory control of private pensions in the future to help insure their solvency.

Other experts foresee a greater trend toward pension portability because of the continued mobility of the workforce. Some even envision a sort of universal private pension plan in which any employee in any industry could participate.

Labor Market Changes

Where workers today have to compete for a limited number of jobs, employers in the year 2000 may have to compete with each other to attract qualified workers—and, in some extreme instances, any workers at all if the job is more arduous than rewarding. Some indications of this are already being seen at both ends of the employment spectrum: high technology employers fighting to outbid each other for workers with desirable, but not particularly prevalent, skills; and low-salaried drudgery jobs going unfilled because the pay offered is less attractive than unemployment compensation or welfare.

Doing What You Want to Do

The middle-class American worker 20 to 30 years from now will generally have a greater choice in the type of work he or she wants to do. This will lead to increased mobility (a tendency already apparent in a handful of fields) and to the development of serial (or multiple) careers. Where a worker may now hold seven or eight jobs during the course of an adult worklife (a figure that will probably not change in the future), there will be a higher incidence of people changing careers as well as jobs; thus, a person in the course of a worklife may have two, three or even more careers. In some cases, this will be a simple matter of survival as skills and/or entire professions become obsolete; in other instances, it will result from workers seeking new challenges and/or better remuneration.

Lower echelon workers and the structurally underemployed may be affected by this but to a considerably lesser degree. In other words, the further down the economic pole one is, the fewer the options available to him or her. But, then, that's nothing new.

Workforce Diversity

More women, especially those in their child-bearing years, are expected to join the labor force. Thus, there will be more female professionals and managers than ever before, achieving more balance between the sexes on the job.

If present inflationary trends continue, an increasingly large percentage of these working women will also be wives and mothers whose income is needed (more than just desired) to support the family lifestyle. As a result, the need for day care facilities may increase. Already we are seeing some companies allowing workers to bring infants or preschool children to work with them. Playgrounds on company grounds, lunchtime shared with children and other family-oriented worklife developments may become commonplace.

Education and Leisure

Paralleling these worklife changes will be an increased emphasis on education and leisure as integral components throughout the lives of workers.

There are, for instance, predictions that it will not be uncommon for workers to continue going to school after graduation—either on a part-time basis while working full-time, or on a part-time basis while working part-time, or on a full-time basis during a sabbatical leave from one's employment. Such continuing education can also be the basis for establishing new careers or obtaining better jobs.

An increasing emphasis on leisure is already beginning to be seen, and will undoubtedly continue into the future. Even as older workers fought to eliminate mandatory retirement, there was a growing tendency by many to take early retirement voluntarily. In some cases, this demonstrates a desire for a comfortably pensioned leisure, but it also indicates the beginning of second careers and personal entrepreneurship.

Happy Means Productive

If workers are happy in their free time, there is the assumption they will be more productive on the job. Working on this basis, the National Cash Register Company of Dayton, Ohio, has established a family camp for its employees, and the Upjohn Company of Kalamazoo, Mich., has hired a full-time recreation specialist to plan leisure activities for workers and their families.

Workers polled in several studies have indicated a preference for more free time (especially in large blocks such as long weekends or an additional week's vacation, etc.) rather than additional income, and are beginning to receive it through union contracts and employer agreements. However, once the expenses of a leisure lifestyle have to be met, there may be some changes in their preferences.

One area of concern that we have left untouched—as have many businesses— is the role of the future older person as a consumer. Their needs and desires are not necessarily going to be identical with today's older consumer, and, if they remain in the workforce longer, their buying power—while working, and when collecting greater Social Security and pension benefits after retiring—will be a factor with which future merchandisers will have to contend.

A small indication of this can be seen among menswear manufacturers, some of whom have begun adapting styles meant for a youthfully svelte physique to the more prevalent middle-aged bodies buying their wares. For instance, there is the item known as "gentlemen's jeans," which are a lot like the youth cult's jeans except they've been expanded in certain anatomical areas in deference to the demands of an expanding market.

We Should Have Foreseen

Back in the late 1940s we knew that the baby boom existed. All we had to do was look at the annual birth figures, and we could have foreseen the growth-related problems with which we would be plagued a decade or two hence. We didn't look, and were caught by surprise by the demands for schools and other facilities in the 1950s.

Today, we are faced with a similar situation. We know the birth rate has dropped (although no one can accurately predict how long it will stay down) and we know the workforce is aging. It would profit all of us not to make the same mistakes again.

17.

Proposition 13

On June 6, 1978, California voters overwhelmingly approved a state constitutional amendment to reduce property taxes more than fifty percent. The outcome, closely watched by voters and politicians everywhere, was viewed as the first salvo in what might be a national "tax revolt" by citizens who felt that recent tax increases were outrageous and that spending at all levels of government was out of control. The sponsor of the initiative, 74-year-old Howard A. Jarvis, argued that "the only way to cut the cost of government is not to give them money in the first place." Superficially, this idea was attractive to many persons, both in and outside of California, but whether in fact limiting one type of tax—on real property—would have the desired effect was questionable. This selection consists of two items. The first is an article by Jerry McCaffery and John H. Bowman of Indiana University on the effects, both financial and administrative, of the passage of Proposition 13. The second is a summary of comments by William A. Norris, a Los Angeles attorney, on the constitutionality of the popular initiative process itself.

Sources: *Public Administration Review,* November/December 1978.

The Center Magazine, November/December 1978.

A: JERRY McCAFFERY AND JOHN H. BOWMAN

PARTICIPATORY DEMOCRACY: THE EFFECTS OF PROPOSITION 13

PERHAPS THE MOST spectacular attempt at budget control through tax limitations is represented by the passage of Proposition 13, the Jarvis-Gann Initiative, in California on June 6, 1978. Limitations on taxes are not new. However, Proposition 13 has some unique features and special impacts which make it all the more interesting since it quickly became the prototype for limitation attempts in other states. This article explores the complexities of Proposition 13 in the context of fiscal policymak-ing. One of the major issues to be kept in mind in what follows is that the initiative as an electoral device is generally classified as one of the package of reforms growing out of the Progessive movement of the early 1900's; it permits direct democratic participation. Yet the study of Proposition 13 raises serious questions about the feasibility of participatory democracy in a policy area which commonly has been dominated by experts.

Even the smallest governmental unit exists in an intergovernmental context with diverse revenue structures at its own level and multiple sources of monies and controls stemming from other levels of government. Proposition 13's "meataxe" approach to taxing—and budget-ing—disrupted many of these relation-ships. What was headlined in petitions as a "property tax limitation" evolved into a complicated and extensive set of con-sequences. These include a property tax reduction of major proportions (spread unevenly over California's governmen-tal structure), and property tax relief captured only partially by Californians, serious problems of taxpayer equity, and a restructuring of intergovernmen-tal relationships in California. Further-more, the stringency of that "simple" property tax limit raises the prospect of defaults on certain non-voted debts and may greatly limit the use of general obligation debt instruments. Moreover, the stringency of the limit also will have a direct impact on many of California's cities which have traditionally under-funded pension plans, since these past obligations now must compete with cur-rent services for significantly reduced revenues. Ironically, this simple tax limit jeopardizes California's solution to the *Serrano vs. Priest* school finance case. Finally, given the initiative's two-thirds voting requirement for passage of new and/or increased taxes at both state and local levels, what has been done electorally will be even harder to undo. Each of these points will be discussed in more detail below.

INITIAL LOCAL RESPONSES AND STATE BAIL-OUT

In February, 1978, the staff of the California Assembly Revenue and Tax-ation Committee estimated that passage of Proposition 13 would cost local gov-ernments $7 billion out of an anticipated $33.9 billion in total local revenues—a drop of 20.8 per cent. The $33.9 bil-lion figure represented the controller's

estimate of a 17.7 per cent increase over the actual 1976–77 total of $28.8 billion for local revenues; the $7 bil-lion reduction threatened to cut local revenues almost $2 billion below the 1976–77 dollar base. Consequently, in the middle of the 1977–78 fiscal year, local government budgeters knew that passage of Proposition 13 would not only cut property taxes nearly 60 per cent and total revenues 20.8 per cent below the levels otherwise expected to be available for the *next* (1978–79) bud-get year, but that it would put them 6.6 per cent below the base of the *previous* (1976–77) year.

Thus, direct democratic participation limiting the property tax would impose a severe revenue cut on local govern-ments, and a 7 per cent inflation rate for government goods and services made the bite even deeper. Not only would there be 20.8 per cent fewer dollars than expected, but last year's dollars would buy only 93 per cent of what they purchased in 1977–78 and about 86 per cent of what they had purchased in 1976–77. For the 1978–79 budget year, therefore, the total decrease ap-proximated a cut of 26 per cent. On June 6, 1978, the handwriting on the wall was no longer something that could be wished away. Proposition 13 was passed by about as large a majority as those which had squelched two previous tax limitation attempts.

Andrew Glassberg argues that there is a difference between small or incre-mental declines in available resources and substantial or "quantum" decreases. If there is an expectation that the cut can be restored by resorting to proper strategies, then the cut may be treated as incremental. Quantum cuts are defined by size and a low leadership expectation of revenue restoration; consequently, says Glassberg, ". . . post-crisis managers are operating in a fundamentally different environment . . ." and their familiar strategies for dealing with incremental changes ". . . are unlikely to be applicable . . . ," although many of their initial reactions ". . . will be of the traditional sort developed to deal with incremental budget declines . . . ." Clearly, California local governments faced a quantum revenue decrease, although with a well-publicized state surplus of some $5-6 billion and a legislature in session, an obvious strategy was to replace local revenues with state revenues.

The size of the potential revenue reduction forced local governments to respond immediately. Changes were made to both sides of the revenue-expenditure equation. New budget estimates were called for; increased fees, lay-offs, and service cuts were threatened and often implemented. The largest immediate service reduction occurred in education; in 70 southern California school districts surveyed by the *Los Angeles Times,* about two-thirds eliminated or sharply curtailed summer school. Los Angeles, the biggest school district in the state, not only eliminated summer school, but also closed down its regional occupational training centers and slashed summer recreation by about 60 per cent. Additionally, 10,000 clerical employees, who normally worked on an annual basis, were laid-off for two months. Since schools were major users of the property tax, most had prepared a budget in anticipation of the passage of Proposition 13. In its "doomsday" budget, the Long Beach school board had slashed all interscholastic sports, eliminated adult education, drastically cut the length of the school day and sent lay-off notices to nearly half of its 2,916 teachers. Nor did schools eschew

raising or creating new fees and charges of various kinds aimed at community use of school facilities, including swimming pools, racquet ball courts, playing fields, and classrooms for night meetings, adult education, driver education, public lectures, and student health services. At El Camino College, the school catalog now costs $1.00. The San Diego school board decided to charge community groups $70 for use of the school auditorium and the Los Angeles Community College system set a fee of $1.00 an hour for the use of tennis courts and $2.00 if the lights were on.

Cities, counties, and special districts were not idle during this period. Proposition 13 would become law on July 1. After that date local governments would need a two-thirds popular vote to raise taxes, fees and charges. Consequently, for the remainder of June most local governments concentrated on raising various fees, charges, and other non-property taxes. Some also made cuts in services, but service reductions could always be made later in the summer. After July 1, the tax structure would be very difficult to change. The League of California Cities estimated that over a quarter of the state's 417 cities had raised or were considering raising fees and charges during June. The most popular increase seemed to be business licenses, followed by increases in various utilities, e.g., water, gas, electricity, telephone, cable television, but no source of income was too small to be overlooked.

Seal Beach, which has a long and pleasant beach front, increased beach parking fees from $2 to $3; it also increased business license taxes by 100 per cent. San Francisco raised its zoo admission from $1 to $2 for adults and from 50¢ to 75¢ for children and eliminated free days. Moreover, museum admissions also were increased. The large cities, although they talked about disastrous cuts, tended to wait for state action. Los Angeles froze salaries for 18 elected officials and 44,000 municipal employees. In June, Los Angeles County had laid off only 67 flood control workers. San Diego rescinded its four per cent pay raise and San Diego County established user fees for the flood control district, raised transit district fares by five cents, and eliminated night service. Some of the communities raised fees and charges dramatically. Beverly Hills' commercial rental tax jumped from $1.25 to $23.50 per $1,000 of gross receipts. Baldwin Park boosted license fees by 40 per cent and raised fees for issuing and processing various city permits by 50 per cent. Buena Park established a $40 paramedic fee for residents and $50 for out-of-towners. Inglewood enacted a fire service fee which included a levy against any structure requiring more fire protection capability than a home. Laguna Beach increased animal and business license fees by almost 100 per cent. Lynwood, in a series of moves that was not atypical, established a fee for almost everything: sewers, fire clearance, fire service, water turn-on and turn-off, the city dump, tree trimming, and sidewalks. Business license fees were increased, as were water rates. Recreation, park maintenance, tree trimming, and sidewalk repair services were reduced. Finally, twenty-six employees were laid off.

Rancho Palos Verdes took out an insurance policy by adding an inflation clause to the existing fee structure. Arcadia provided for street sweeping charges based on front footage of properties. Oakland adopted several new taxes, including a five per cent admission tax on entertainment events; it also increased the real estate transfer tax by 50 per cent and raised the annual business license tax from 90 cents to $14 per $1,000 of gross revenues. The business tax rate on auto dealers was increased from 30¢ to 60¢ per $1,000 of gross receipts. On the service side, the transit district reduced schedules and personnel by 40 per cent. Downey doubled its dog license charge from $5 to $10. Sacramento increased the 18 hole golf fee from $3.50 to $4.50 and raised parking meter fees from 10¢ to 25¢ an hour. Inglewood instituted a "tippler's tax," a 10 per cent surcharge on drinks served at bars. Localities with harbor or marina facilities either created or increased fees and charges. Orange County more than doubled charges for guest slips, moorings, and boat storage at Dana Point and Newport Beach, as well as for the county's 14 regional parks, beaches, and campgrounds. Newport Beach also froze salaries of all public employees and cut trash collections from twice to once a week.

Actions taken by communities during the month of June also included cuts in services. For example, Camarillo extinguished 1,000 street lights; Cerritos eliminated school crossing guards; Compton eliminated its public information and centralized purchasing offices, reduced its senior citizens' and recreation activities by 80 per cent, cut its public works crews by 30 per cent, and closed 25 per cent of its fire stations. Covina cut its library staff in half and reduced hours, eliminated crossing guards, and reduced street sweeping from a weekly to monthly basis. Monrovia eliminated most free recreation programs, cut library hours from 56 to 30 a week, and reduced counter time for the public at the planning, building, and safety counters from nine to six hours.

Needles closed its city park and recreation department, and transferred the workers to other jobs. Pasadena reduced library hours and maintenance of streets and recreation buildings. Petaluma cut its swimming pool season from eleven months to six. Piedmont eliminated its summer playground program. Riverside imposed fees on swimming pool use and reduced community center hours.

For special districts primarily financed through the property tax (non-enterprise), Proposition 13 was a disaster. About 80 per cent of the expenditures of California's 3,407 non-enterprise districts were made by fire (23.0 per cent), flood (17.7 per cent), planning (29.3 per cent), and parks (9.9 per cent) districts. The property tax accounted, on average, for funding of 89 per cent of the expenditures of fire protection districts, 77 per cent of flood control districts, and 71 per cent of the funding of recreation and parks districts, while planning districts relied on property taxes for less than 1 per cent of their revenues. With the passage of Proposition 13 the total revenues available to the fire, flood, and parks districts would be reduced 51 per cent, 44 per cent, and 41 per cent respectively. These districts now would either have to be supported by other units or get legislative authorization to use a new fee, charge, or tax to replace the property tax revenue loss. Those districts which were able to impose special charges for their services (enterprise districts) tended not to rely heavily on the property tax for revenue. Although the average reliance (14 per cent) for these districts was low, some used it as a major revenue source. Moreover, all would suffer some reduction. Consequently, while some waited to see if the state would make up for the property

tax loss, others began to shift more of the burden to their fee structure. For example, the Los Angeles Metropolitan Water District took steps, only a day or two after Proposition 13 passed, to shift its revenues to sales and away from the taxing power. This involved a hearing and rate setting procedure. It was estimated that the District's 12 per cent fee increase would represent a 75 per cent to 100 per cent increase by the time it reached consumers.

In sum, immediately after its passage Proposition 13 was producing visible fee increases and service cutbacks, many of which affected leisure time activities in the season when leisure is most valued, as local governments, large and small, attempted to cope with the prospect of drastically reduced revenues and uncertainty about what the state would do to help them. As Glassberg suggests, even in time of a perceived quantum decrease, they relied mainly on familiar mechanisms, which by and large have some theoretical underpinning, be it an ability-to-pay test (rate based on gross receipts) or economic efficiency (user charges). Meanwhile, threatened cuts in vital services and estimates of Proposition 13 lay-offs continued to appear. On July 1, the Employment Development Division estimated that as of June 28, 3,252 lay-offs had occurred as a result of Proposition 13, with 1,104 occurring in the week of June 21–28. Future lay-offs were estimated to be as high as 165,000.

The State's response came near the end of June. Senate Bill 154 drew upon the large state surplus to provide California local governments with about 90 per cent of what they had expected before the tax limitation. However, restrictions accompanied the money. Cities were required to use the state aid ". . . first to ensure continuation of the same level of police and fire protection as was provided in 1977–78." However, cities were authorized to effect cost savings so long as they did not impair the protection provided. The same stipulation was applied to counties. Additionally, counties which accepted any bailout money were barred from disproportionately reducing health services, and their budgets were to be reviewed by the state director of health services. The largest part of the county aid went for a variety of health and welfare related programs ($1 billion), not including a one-year waiver of the state's 10 per cent matching requirement for the mental health, alcohol, and drug abuse programs. Money for special districts was distributed to the county boards of supervisors for allocation to the special districts within each county. Most of the money went to fire protection districts, while those districts with authority to levy fees and charges were encouraged to do so. Again, fire and police protection levels were given the highest priority. A $2 billion block grant was extended to school districts to guarantee an average of 90 per cent of estimated 1978–79 budgets, but it incorporated a sliding scale so that high spending districts would be guaranteed 85 per cent of their 1978–79 budgets and low spending districts 91 per cent of theirs. The county office of education also was given a 90 per cent budget guarantee, primarily for special education and vocational education service provision, and community colleges were guaranteed 85 per cent of their 1978–79 budgets. A $900 million state emergency loan fund was created as a loan of last resort, and finally, a very strict local pay raise control was written in which allowed local discretion only in

merit increases and legitimate promotions, but lock-stepped state and local cost-of-living raises (if state employees received no cost-of-living raise, neither would anyone else.) Those who had voted for Proposition 13 in an effort to trade-off property tax increases for part of the state surplus had succeeded, but their victory set in motion a chain of events which would have serious repercussions among taxpayers and for the state and its subunits.

EFFECTS OF PROPOSITION 13

Property tax controls typically affect other aspects of government finance (e.g., grants, revenue diversification), and California's Proposition 13 is no exception. Indeed, a bewildering array of consequences is traceable to the deceptively simple 400-odd word initiative. The following discussion illustrates the pervasiveness of the effects in California.

Proposition 13 drops 1978–79 California property taxes some $7 billion (nearly 60 per cent) below what they otherwise would have been. This sharp reduction is perhaps the most unique—and newsworthy—feature of Proposition 13, although the feature may soon spread to other states. The severity of the property tax cut is quite uneven, both among counties and among types of governments. Intercounty variation occurs because pre-Proposition 13 county-average tax rates per $100 of assessed value ranged from $4.75 to $13.15 (average of $11.19) compared to the new limit of $4.00 (net of bond-service levies). Variation among types of governments occurs because local governments have relied on property taxes to differing degrees and because Proposition 13 stipulates that constituent units within a county share in the new, lower, county-collected property tax "according to law," a phrase defined by the legislature to mean previous years' (one year for schools, 3-year average for others) relative property tax shares. The first-year legislative response to Proposition 13 matches increased state assistance closely to lost property taxes, however, so that the overall loss of revenues averages about 10 per cent for each of the major types of local governments.

Because the increased state aid for 1978–79 comes from accumulated state surpluses, local governments' property tax losses should translate into tax savings (ignoring for now local revenue adjustments). Not all of the property tax cuts, however, will be captured by Californians. The portion of the $7 billion reduction most likely to remain largely within the state is that on owner-occupied residences, which accounts for about 35 per cent of the total (or roughly $2.5 billion). A significant part of this will redound to the federal government in the form of higher income taxes resulting from reduced property tax deductions. The remaining 65 per cent will go in the first instance to business, including owners of residential rental units, agriculture, and public utilities. How much of this will remain in California is difficult to estimate. Depending upon a variety of circumstances (e.g., extent of market competition, mobility of resources), the property tax—and property tax cuts—may rest with the owners of taxed property (shareholders, in the case of corporations), be passed forward to consumers through prices, and/or be passed backward to labor (and other resource suppliers) through wages. The combination of these three tax treatments practiced by California businesses

and the representation of Californians in the three groups which ultimately bear taxes jointly will determine the extent to which Californians will share in the business tax reduction, and solid data on these points do not exist. Additionally, the property tax cut will lower California's tax effort and, thereby, its share of federal revenue sharing (with a lag of a couple of years); matching monies for attracting other federal grants also will be harder to come by. In short, Californians may find that a major part of the property tax cut will leak out of the California economy.

Tax savings also will be less to the extent that replacement revenues are raised at either the local or the state levels. It will be difficult, however, to raise taxes for two reasons. One is that the post-Proposition 13 mood at the state level favors tax *cuts*—the legislature enacted a $1 billion state income tax cut in late August, featuring increased personal credits and inflation-index brackets. Indexing will slow the growth of the income tax (and the state surplus). Moreover, Proposition 13 imposes a two-thirds vote requirement for new and increased state and local taxes. For local units, however, it provides that "special taxes" may be imposed with the approval of two-thirds of a jurisdiction's "qualified electors." Neither of these terms is used in California law, so the meaning is not clear. With regard to "special taxes," possible interpretations range from opening to localities revenue sources not previously authorized by the state (e.g., income taxes) if the voters will approve them to removing from local officials the right to adopt or increase the rates of taxes previously authorized by the state. In either case, though, the two-thirds vote requirement may be insuperable. The hurdle would be most easily cleared if "qualified electors" is interpreted to mean those actually voting, but a case can be made for interpreting this to mean those registered to vote, or even those *eligible* to vote—whether registered or not. Interestingly enough, although Proposition 13 is generally said to have received "overwhelming" public support, it would not have passed under any of the above possibilities: those voting yes on Proposition 13 amounted to only 64.7 per cent of those voting (the yes vote exceeded 66 per cent in only 26 of the 58 counties), 42.3 per cent of the registered voters, and perhaps only one-fourth of all potentially eligible voters.

As noted above, many local governments already have turned to new and increased fees and charges to make up part of their revenue losses. It is both appropriate and possible to exact from users the revenues necessary to support some types of publicly provided services, and in these cases greater reliance on user charges should be considered a positive result of Proposition 13, producing improvements in both allocative efficiency (either under- or over-supply can result from divorcing payments from benefits) and equity (non-beneficiaries do not have to subsidize beneficiaries). For other types of services, however, it is either not technically feasible or not desirable (on distributional grounds) to link payments and benefits. These services must be funded from general tax revenues, such as the property tax. Unfortunately, Proposition 13 will present some serious equity problems. One of these results from the large cut in the level of property taxes: there is some evidence that higher levels of taxation are associated with greater assessment uniformity (equity). This source of diminished equity, however, is certain to

be dwarfed by inequities resulting from shifting of tax shares among classes of property owners. Proposition 13 requires that new or transferred properties be valued for tax purposes according to their market values at the time of construction or transfer (sale or otherwise), while properties not exchanged since 1975 are valued at 1975 prices, adjusted upward by the lesser of the rate of the state consumer price index increase or 2 per cent per year. (These values constitute "full cash value," on which the tax cannot exceed 1 per cent). This guarantees inequities—on the standard presumption that current market value is the best measure of value for tax purposes—because only recently-sold properties can be valued at market value. In some assessment systems, reassessments between mass reappraisals in fact are triggered by sales, but California has the dubious distinction of being first to require this method, while precluding ever putting all properties on the same footing through mass reappraisal—and by constitutional provision! The effect is to make the "property tax" more dependent upon mobility and property turnover than on property value, and to cause newcomers to a community to bear a disproportionate share of the cost of local services. Because business properties sell less frequently than residential properties, this same provision will cause residential properties to bear an increasing share of the property tax over time—probably not a result contemplated by the typical supporter of Proposition 13. Some offset to this business-to-residential tax share shift is provided by the fact that Proposition 13's valuation provisions (although not its rate limitations) apply only to real property, for in California the only tangible personal property that is taxable is that of business, and it is revalued annually. The offset is unlikely to be complete, however, since tangible personal property accounted for less than 15 per cent of taxable property values before Proposition 13.

Relationships among governmental units, as well as among taxpayers, are affected by Proposition 13 and the state legislation implementing it. In general, the changes are toward greater centralization and decreased local control. At the root of the changes, of course, is the nearly 60 per cent reduction of the property tax which dropped this tax's share of total 1978–79 revenues for California local governments from 40 per cent to 18 per cent. The argument has been made by some that, because of the historically high reliance of local governments on property taxation and the notion that this tax is better suited than other major taxes to local use, anything that weakens the property tax weakens local government (and conversely for strengthening the tax). In California, this tendency of the property tax reduction itself has been reinforced by several provisions of S.B. 154, the statute clarifying Proposition 13 and providing for state assistance to make up much of the revenue loss. State-local and inter-local relationships both are affected. Whereas nearly 6,300 units of local government had imposed property taxes, now only the 58 counties (including the independent city of San Francisco) can levy a property tax because Section 1 of Proposition 13 provides that the property tax is ". . . to be collected by the counties and apportioned according to law to the districts within the counties" and S.B. 154 gives meaning to this by stipulating that the counties also *levy* the tax and then divide the proceeds on the basis of historic shares of property tax collec-

tions. This greatly reduces the ability of local units to effect their own fiscal policies; the county and state roles have increased at the expense of all other units formerly having authority to levy property taxes. This is particularly true for special districts, whose tax-replacement aid goes first to county governments. Each county will receive an allocation of money for special districts (based on the counties' shares of special district property tax losses), but "the county will have complete discretion in allocating the assistance [within state-prescribed] guidelines." While many government "reformers" will applaud this apparent victory of the elected generalists over the special-purpose units, the change will not necessarily be for the better in all cases; special-purpose units with boundaries differing from those of the multi-purpose units often will permit clear equity and efficiency gains—e.g., better correspondence between actual and desired service levels and between benefit and financing areas. Moreover, if "fiscal pressures" are a poor basis for determining the assignment of functional responsibilities, it is not clear that the pressure produced by Proposition 13 will produce the optimal functional realignment.

The advent of uniform county-wide property taxes will have other effects, as well. For example, intra-county tax rate differentials which may distort locational decisions will be eliminated. Another *potentially* beneficial effect would be the reduction of fiscal capacity disparities and the consequent removal of one source of expenditure variation, but as long as the proceeds from these levies are distributed on the basis of prior years' property tax collections, this gain cannot occur (except to the extent that *future* decisions that would have worsened matters are averted). The current combination of uniform tax rates within a county and allocation among units based on historic tax patterns means that rural areas (where taxes generally have been relatively low) will tend to subsidize urban areas (where tax rates generally have been higher), a result that may be either desirable or undesirable depending upon the circumstances of a particular situation (and, of course, the criteria used to evaluate such a shift). Other results more obviously tend to be undesirable. For example, rapidly growing areas will have no control over their property tax revenues and may be unable to serve expanded populations and/or new properties (e.g., factories, shopping malls) without lowering the overall level of service; growth in a *single* small unit will translate into increased revenues for the entire county area and for *all* units within the county (other than special districts) in proportion to pre-FY 1979 tax shares. This is Twin Cities-style tax-base sharing carried to the extreme. This may affect special districts with no revenue source other than property taxes (and property tax replacement aid) the hardest— e.g., many fire protection districts—but cities and school corporations could fare worse, however, due to the inflexibility of current (S.B. 154) aid distribution provisions; special districts at least have the opportunity to press their cases for increased revenues with the county, which determines intra-county special district tax-replacement shares.

In addition to the largely inter-local effects discussed above, the post-Proposition 13 situation also changes previous state-local relationships. As already noted, the major property tax replacement funds to date have come from an accumulated state surplus, and in-

creased state funding has brought increased state control. Thus, for example, no local unit can receive state tax-replacement aid or loan funds under S.B. 154 if it grants cost-of-living pay increases for 1978–79 to its employees, welfare recipients, or others, in excess of those granted to state employees; the state's police powers are invoked to render "null and void" any contractual provisions to the contrary, and these provisions also ". . . supersede any inconsistent provisions in the charter of any county or city." Other "strings" attached to increased state aid, already noted, include the requirement that counties, cities, and appropriate special districts give first priority to police and fire service so that local units will not drop below 1977–78 levels of *service* in these functional areas; provisions concerning health service reductions; provisions which make special districts dependent upon overlying general-unit discretion for tax-replacement distributions (which could provide leverage for other county- or city-initiated controls); and various provisions pertaining to education finance.

Proposition 13, as noted, threatened to undo the legislature's response to the California Supreme Court's demands in *Serrano vs. Priest* for school finance restructuring, a further intergovernmental problem. The Assembly Education Committee argued that the tax limits would preclude high-wealth district tax increases which were to transfer money to the state starting in 1978–79 as part of the equalization provisions, make it impossible for districts to raise the local share of foundation-program funding, and render revenue limits meaningless. S.B. 154's education provisions, described earlier, represent the initial reworking of the *Serrano* solution, and it appears that the state's guarantee of a higher percentage of estimated 1978–79 budgets for low-spending districts than for high-spending districts (91 per cent vs. 85 per cent)—combined with the Proposition 13 tax limits—will cause per pupil expenditure disparities to be reduced more quickly than otherwise.

In short, Proposition 13 has served as the vehicle for some extensive changes in California intergovernmental relations, including structural and functional adjustments as well as increased centralization of both decision-making authority and financing.

Other effects of Proposition 13 are numerous (and some no doubt have not yet been identified), but only a few more can be noted here. The Assembly Revenue and Taxation Committee notes that, "Many cities have seriously underfunded employee pension and retirement systems. . . ." This situation may mean even deeper cuts in current services than otherwise would be necessary, for current services must compete for strictly limited (and reduced) revenues with unliquidated obligations from prior years. The competition between current services and debt service also is intensified. Outstanding debt issued without voter approval (unlike voted debt approved before July 1, 1978) does not entitle the issuing jurisdiction to property taxes in excess of those available under the new general limits. For units with such debt, an already tight fiscal situation is made even tighter. Possible outcomes include one or more of the following: further cuts in current services, default, and New York-style state and/or federal rescue. Future debt issues, whether voted or not, must be serviced within the Proposition 13 tax limitation. This means general obligation borrowing may be infeasible in

many—perhaps most—instances in the future, especially if tax-replacement aid is reduced and/or continues to be tied to historic property tax shares. In any event, the fact of property tax reduction and limitation is likely to result in higher bond interest rates.

CONCLUSION

The complexities associated with Proposition 13 provide a lesson in the hazards of fiscal policymaking through direct voter participation. While the full effects of Proposition 13 are not yet known, it is clear that it has reshaped California local government finance overnight. The financing role of property taxes has been cut from 40 per cent to 18 per cent for local governments on average. Furthermore, the tax now can be levied by only 58 counties at a county-wide uniform rate (excluding levies for old debt) rather than by some 6,300 local units, although these other units still share in property tax revenues on the basis of prior years' levies. Even if a community within a county were to agree unanimously to increase property taxes, it now has no authority to do so. Moreover, within any county this new system will fail to target increased revenue to units with rapidly increasing needs, and the tax-base incentive for cultivating new business development is diminished. Ironically, it appears that much of the property tax savings from this reduction will flow outside California. Homeowners clearly will enjoy some relief from recent high property taxes, but the extent of relief going to renters remains uncertain. In addition, mass reappraisals are now barred and all reassessments (other than an across-the-board increase of up to 2 per cent) are triggered by transfer of property or new construction. Over time, this will shift an increasing share of property taxes toward homeowners (and within this group, those who change residences) and guarantee inequities because only recently sold properties can be valued according to current market value; thus, the tax increasingly will become a tax on mobility.

The diminished role of this traditional local tax workhorse dramatically increases the importance of state aids. At least in the first year, increased state aids have meant increased state control over local government finances and structures—a development that is not likely to be reversed.

A huge state surplus played a role that cannot be overestimated. On the one hand, the surplus may have contributed strongly to the passage of Proposition 13. On the other hand, it was essential to an orderly transition. The essential question is whether a surplus of such magnitude will continue to be available for future rescue operations.

B: WILLIAM A. NORRIS
THE CONSTITUTIONAL ATTACK

IT IS ARGUABLE that the entire initiative process violates the guarantee clause of the United States Constitution, that clause which has been described as perhaps the sleeping giant of the Constitution, one which may be stirring again in our time. That really goes deep into political theory and into the question as to how we are going to govern ourselves, now and in the future.

The guarantee clause is Article IV, Section 4, and it says: "The United States shall guarantee to every state in this union a republican form of government, and shall protect each of them against invasion; and on application of the legislature, or of the Executive (when the legislature cannot be convened) against domestic violence."

The subsequent constitutional history of this clause goes back to 1849. In *Luther v. Borden*—a dispute between two rival factions in the State of Rhode Island as to whether or not Rhode Island's government was really republican in form—Chief Justice Roger Taney held that that was a political question, not a justiciable issue, and therefore it was not appropriate for the Court to decide it. That decision gave birth to the political question doctrine that stayed with us for more than a hundred years. Indeed, in 1912, the second of three important United States Supreme Court cases relating to the guarantee clause was decided. The State of Oregon had recently adopted the initiative process— as California had—and, through that process, had imposed a special tax on public utilities. The telephone company litigated the question as to whether the initiative process itself violated the guarantee clause of the U.S. Constitution. The question is whether we can govern by direct democracy without offending the guarantee clause. The Court disposed of that easily enough by citing *Luther v. Borden*. It said the Oregon case was a political question, therefore non-justiciable.

Then along came *Baker v. Carr,* a reapportionment case, in 1962. With Justice Felix Frankfurter dissenting vigorously, because he loved the political question doctrine, the United States Supreme Court scrapped the political question doctrine and decided this very important reapportionment case on the basis of the equal protection clause of the Fourteenth Amendment. Justice William O. Douglas, in his concurring opinion, wanted to talk about the guarantee clause. He thought that those malapportioned districts so diluted individual voting power that the principles underlying the guarantee clause were offended.

In any event, we no longer have the political question doctrine standing as a bar to a resolution of that issue by the State Supreme Court of California.

Arguably, the unrestrained use of the initiative process surely runs afoul of the constitutional principle that state governments must be republican in form. Whatever "republican" means, it certainly does not mean government by direct democracy. Two things were clear to me, as I reviewed all that history: the republican form of government is mutually exclusive with a monarchy, and it is mutually exclusive with direct democracy. James Madison and the other framers of the Constitution were as concerned about direct democracy as they were about a monarchy.

California has adopted the federal constitutional model in this sense: the framers of the California Constitution provided a system for establishing government and distributing the powers of government among its various institutions. The horizontal distribution is among the judicial, executive, and legislative branches. The obvious vertical distribution of power is between the state and local governments.

I do not claim that Californians were compelled by the U.S. Constitution to have this vertical distribution. What I do say is, that California started out with a state constitution vesting all power at the state level. That did not work. At the constitutional convention of 1878, the principal complaint seemed to be that local government should have some power, so that there would be limits, or checks, on the power of the state. Out of that constitutional convention, came certain constitutional changes, adopted in 1879, which provided for a vertical distribution of governmental power, including the taxing power.

My argument is that you just cannot now treat local governments in California as merely spending agents of the state. The California Constitution vests genuine governmental power in local governments, power that cannot be infringed by state action.

Chicken Little was wrong. Proposition 13 came and went and the sky over California has not fallen. The state did not drop off into the ocean after the quake of voters at the polls June 6.
CHARLES S. CRAWFORD, National Taxpayers Union

18.

Arthur F. Burns and Jimmy Carter: "Our Most Serious Domestic Problem"

The two most vexing problems of Jimmy Carter's administration were the Iran hostage crisis and inflation. Despite the greater emotional impact of the hostage situation, inflation was probably the more serious problem in the long run, in terms of its political as well as economic effects. The annual inflation rate rose into the high teens despite Carter's efforts to control it, and knowledgeable persons in the financial community began to express their fear that so-called hyperinflation — with annual rates in three digits, as in Argentina and Brazil — might take its terrible toll of the American economy. Hyperinflation did not happen, but Jimmy Carter never really controlled inflation, either; it was left to his successor to do so. Reprinted below are portions of a speech by Arthur F. Burns, retiring head of the Federal Reserve, and part of an address to the nation by President Carter on October 24.

Sources: *Across the Board*, May 1978.

Presidential Documents, October 1978.

A: ARTHUR F. BURNS

THE ECONOMIC EXPANSION that began almost three years ago still has vitality in my estimation and I see no serious risk that it will peter out soon. The upsurge in sales with which 1977 ended caused inventories to be drawn down in numerous businesses, thus creating a likelihood that overall economic activity will receive a special fillip for a while from businessmen's efforts to rebuild stocks. And with consumer activity, housing activity and governmental activity all still exhibiting expansionary tendencies, I believe that further gains in employment and income lie ahead.

Business investment activity, to be sure, is still not showing decisive robustness. This reflects the uncertainties and unease that continue to haunt our business and financial environment. I expect, nevertheless, that the tax relief that the President has proposed for business will lead to a strengthening of investment commitments as 1978 unfolds. In saying this, I do not mean to embrace each and every aspect of the Administration's tax and budgetary strategy. A tax program structured to my liking would be tilted more decisively toward the stimulation of savings and investment. I feel that tax reduction at this stage of economic expansion should be primarily accommodated by limiting expenditures, so that significant shrinkage in the Federal budget deficit might still be achieved. But on the specific issue of tax reduction for business, I do believe that what has been proposed will help to relieve the low level of corporate profitability that has prevailed in recent times and thus constitutes an important plus for the capital-goods outlook this year and next.

So much for the bright side of the coin. The generally good record of our economy in terms of recovery from recession stands in marked contrast to a virtual absence of progress in coping with the overlay of our longer-term economic problems. I am thinking particularly, of course, of the dispiriting failure we have experienced in making headway against inflation. I am thinking also of our inability to solve the structural unemployment that is causing so many young people and blacks to be left outside the mainstream of national progress. And while most people probably think of our well-publicized balance-of-payments difficulties as being of recent origin, they are also the product, to a considerable extent, of deep-rooted ailments that we have not dealt with effectively.

Last year witnessed no progress toward a less inflationary environment. Rather, the basic inflation rate settled in the 6 percent area, reflecting the difference between average annual pay increments of labor that are running about 8 percent and productivity gains that are averaging little more than 2 percent.

While the discrepancy between wage and productivity increases is tending at present to perpetuate inflation, it is important to recognize that the inflationary problem with which this nation is burdened did not originate with an irresponsible wage push on the part of American workers or their unions. Rather, the tragic skein of events in which we are caught is chiefly traceable to fundamental mistakes of governmental policy made in the mid-1960s. Those mistakes involved overstimulation of the economy at the very time our military involvement in Vietnam was escalating and when we were also embarking upon Great Society programs that were to become an increasingly heavy drain on the Federal budget. The pressures on available resources generated in the mid-1960s started us on a path of enormous budget deficits and rapid inflation from which we have not been able to disengage ourselves. Indeed, we have continued to compound our problem by seeking to fine-tune the economy by governmental fiscal actions that, in my judgment, have weakened the private sector's dynamism and efficiency.

Events of recent years, such as major crop failures and the sharp rise in oil prices, have merely aggravated the underlying inflationary bias that our government, under both Republican and Democratic Administrations, has imparted to the economy. Other developments—such as the escalator arrangements sought and achieved by various economic groups—have speeded the transmission of inflationary impulses across the economy. In sum, over an extended span of time, we as a nation first created enormous upward pressures on the price structure, and we then devised elaborate arrangements that tend to perpetuate those pressures even under conditions of economic slack.

The inflation plaguing our economy may not end quickly. Government has, however, a special leadership role in the pursuit of moderate fiscal and monetary policies, in encouraging wage restraint by way of example, and in many other particulars. But private actions are critical, too, ranging from more determined pursuit of productivity gains to the conduct of collective bargaining in ways

UPI/Bettmann

Arthur Burns, Chairman of the Federal Reserve System, with President Jimmy Carter.

that are more responsible in a broad social sense. We see nowadays too many excessive wage settlements entered into by managements and trade unions, who then band together in seeking governmental protection from the market consequences of their own actions.

The need to fight inflation is widely recognized in our country, but the will to do so is not yet strong enough. I have no doubt that the will to get on energetically with the job of unwinding the inflation will be forged someday. I only hope this will come through a growth of understanding, not from a demonstration that inflation is the mortal enemy of economic progress and our political freedom.

And just as we need a more determined approach to the challenge of inflation, so too do we need fresh initiatives for dealing with structural rigidities in the job market. The heavy incidence of unemployment among young people and blacks will not be remedied by general monetary and fiscal policies. We need, instead, specialized efforts; first, efforts to overcome serious educational deficiencies so that individual

job seekers will possess greater marketable skills; second, efforts to eradicate impediments that stand in the way of job opportunities for young people and minorities even when the potential for effective job performance is present. These impediments include Federal and state minimum-wage laws, restrictive practices of various craft unions in limiting membership, unnecessary licensing and certification requirements for many jobs and business undertakings, and— I must add to our shame—continuing racial discrimination. This nation can have no greater priority than to end the tragic human wastage that we have been allowing to occur.

B: JIMMY CARTER

I WANT TO HAVE a frank talk with you tonight about our most serious domestic problem. That problem is inflation. Inflation can threaten all the economic gains we've made, and it can stand in the way of what we want to achieve in the future.

This has been a long-time threat. For the last 10 years, the annual inflation

rate in the United States has averaged
6½ percent. And during the 3 years before my Inauguration, it had increased
to an average of 8 percent.

Inflation has, therefore, been a serious problem for me ever since I became
President. We've tried to control it, but
we have not been successful. It's time
for all of us to make a greater and a
more coordinated effort.

If inflation gets worse, several things
will happen. Your purchasing power will
continue to decline, and most of the
burden will fall on those who can least
afford it. Our national productivity will
suffer. The value of our dollar will continue to fall in world trade.

We've made good progress in putting
our people back to work over the past
21 months. We've created more than
6 million new jobs for American workers. We've reduced the unemployment
rate by about 25 percent, and we will
continue our efforts to reduce unemployment further, especially among our
young people and minorities.

But I must tell you tonight that inflation threatens this progress. If we do not
get inflation under control, we will not
be able to reduce unemployment further, and we may even slide backward.

Inflation is obviously a serious problem. What is the solution?

I do not have all the answers. Nobody does. Perhaps there is no complete
and adequate answer. But I want to let
you know that fighting inflation will be
a central preoccupation of mine during
the months ahead, and I want to arouse
our Nation to join me in this effort.

There are two simplistic and familiar answers which are sometimes proposed—simple, familiar, and too extreme. One of these answers is to impose
a complicated scheme of Federal Government wage and price controls on our

entire free economic system. The other
is a deliberate recession, which would
throw millions of people out of work.
Both of these extreme proposals would
not work, and they must be rejected.

I've spent many hours in the last few
months reviewing, with my own advisers
and with a number of outside experts,
every proposal, every suggestion, every
possibility for eliminating inflation. If
there's one thing I have learned beyond
any doubt, it is that there is no single
solution for inflation.

What we have, instead, is a number
of partial remedies. Some of them will
help; others may not. But we have no
choice but to use the best approaches
we have and to maintain a constant
search for additional steps which may
be effective.

I want to discuss with you tonight
some of the approaches we have been
able to develop. They involve action by
Government, business, labor, and every
other sector of our economy. Some of
these factors are under my control as
President—especially Government actions—and I will insist that the Government does its part of the job.

But whether our efforts are successful
will finally depend on you as much as on
me. Your decisions—made every day
at your service station or your grocery
store, in your business, in your union
meetings—will determine our Nation's
answer to inflation as much as decisions
made here in the White House or by
the Congress on Capitol Hill.

I cannot guarantee that our joint effort will succeed. In fact, it is almost
certain not to succeed if success means
quick or dramatic changes. Every free
government on Earth is wrestling with
this problem of inflation, and every one
of them knows that a long-term disease
requires long-term treatment. It's up to

us to make the improvements we can, even at the risk of partial failure, rather than to ensure failure by not trying at all.

I will concentrate my efforts within the Government. We know that Government is not the only cause of inflation. But it is one of the causes, and Government does set an example. Therefore, it must take the lead in fiscal restraint.

We are going to hold down Government spending, reduce the budget deficit, and eliminate Government waste.

We will slash Federal hiring and cut the Federal work force.

We will eliminate needless regulations.

We will bring more competition back to our economy.

And we will oppose any further reduction in Federal income taxes until we have convincing prospects that inflation will be controlled.

Let me explain what each one of these steps means.

The Federal deficit is too high. Our people are simply sick and tired of wasteful Federal spending and the inflation it brings with it.

We have already had some success. We've brought the deficit down by one third since I ran for President—from more than $66 billion in fiscal year 1976 to about $40 billion in fiscal year 1979—a reduction of more than $25 billion in the Federal deficit in just 3 years.

It will keep going down. Next year, with tough restraints on Federal spending and moderate economic growth in prospect, I plan to reduce the budget deficit to less than one-half what it was

when I ran for office—to $30 billion or less.

The Government has been spending too great a portion of what our Nation produces. During my campaign I promised to cut the Government's share of our total national spending from 23 percent, which it was then, to 21 percent in fiscal year 1981. We now plan to meet that goal 1 year earlier.

Reducing the deficit will require difficult and unpleasant decisions. We must face a time of national austerity. Hard choices are necessary if we want to avoid consequences that are even worse.

I intend to make those hard choices. I have already vetoed bills that would undermine our fight against inflation, and the Congress has sustained those vetoes. I know that the Congress will continue to cooperate in the effort to meet our needs in responsible, noninflationary ways.

I will use the administrative and the budgetary powers of my office, including the veto, if necessary, to keep our Nation firmly on the path of fiscal restraint.

Restraint involves tax policy as well as spending decisions. Tax reduction has never been more politically popular than it is today. But if future tax cuts are made rashly, with no eye on the budget deficits, they will hurt us all by causing more inflation.

There are tax cuts which could directly lower costs and prices and help in the fight against inflation. I may consider ways to reduce those particular taxes while still cutting the budget deficit, but until we have a convincing prospect of controlling inflation, I will oppose any further reductions.

19.

The Bakke Case

Allan Bakke, a 38-year-old white engineer, was twice in the early 1970s refused admission to the medical school of the University of California at Davis. To ensure minority representation in the student body, the university had set aside 16 out of the 100 places in each class for minority applicants. Bakke sued, contending that without this rigid preference system he would have been admitted because some minority students having inferior qualifications had been accepted. The California supreme court ruled in favor of Bakke, and the university appealed. After eight months of deliberation the U.S. Supreme Court handed down its decision on June 28, 1978. Universities may not, it said, set aside a quota of seats in each class for minority representatives, denying white applicants the right to compete for those places. At the same time, the court held that it was constitutionally permissible for admissions officers to consider race as one of the complex of factors that determine which applicants are refused and which accepted. The votes of the justices were divided. Four found the university's rigid preference system illegal; four others found it justifiable to compensate minority groups for decades of discrimination. Justice Lewis F. Powell, Jr., voted with the first group here, thus striking down the special admissions program and ordering Bakke admitted. But on another aspect of the case, Powell voted with the other group to hold, 5-4, that race-conscious programs intended to remedy the damage of past discrimination are not unconstitutional. Thus Bakke gained his place in medical school, but so-called affirmative action programs in education, industry, and elsewhere gained a new lease on life. Reprinted here are an article by Charles Lawrence III, associate professor of law at the University of San Francisco, reviewing in advance of the decision the complex issues in the case, and an eloquent editorial about the decision that appeared shortly after it was handed down.

Sources: *Saturday Review*, October 15, 1977.

The New York Times, July 2, 1978.

A: CHARLES LAWRENCE III
THE BAKKE CASE: A PREVIEW

THIS MONTH [October], the United States Supreme Court is hearing oral argument in what may be the single most important constitutional case since the 1954 *Brown* decision outlawed seg- regated schooling. In *Regents of the University of California v. Bakke,* the issue in question is narrow enough: the constitutionality of a special admissions program used by the medical school at the Davis campus of the University of California to ensure the enrollment of a representative number of minority students.

The verdict, however, will have implications that go so far beyond the parties involved that the case will become nothing less than a major historical event.

If the Court decides in Bakke's favor, it will be a serious setback for meaningful integration of America's middle class. The nation's leading educators have alerted the Court that the "for whites only" signs would be effectively restored in our professional schools and colleges. Thousands of private corporations and public agencies might follow suit by abandoning "affirmative action" programs designed to give minorities an equal chance in the job market. Moreover, if Bakke succeeds, his case may become the vehicle for legitimizing a massive public misunderstanding of the meaning of racial equality. Unless the Court is prepared to take the kind of morally courageous stand against public sentiment that it did in *Brown,* the prospects for a constructive outcome are dim.

Affirmative action has been a highly controversial issue since its inception in the late Sixties, but *Bakke* marks the first time the nation's most authoritative court will face the issue head on. It will be doing so not after months and months of arduous and exhaustive evidentiary hearings, but in the absence of real debate and adequate information on the trial record. Worse still, the Court, as it must know, will be handing down its decision to a public that unfortunately has been misled into believing that affirmative action means "reverse discrimination." The story of the *Bakke* case to date contains a string of intentional and accidental misunderstandings that may ambush all those who are struggling to achieve equality in these hard economic times.

In 1973 and again in 1974, Allan Bakke, a thirty-seven-year-old civil engineer, applied for admission to the medical school at the Davis campus of the University of California. He was rejected on both occasions. During those same years, the university initiated a special admissions procedure that enabled about 16 "disadvantaged" applicants to join its freshman class of 100 students. Admission to the medical school under the regular procedures depended heavily on the applicant's college grades and performance on the Medical College Admissions Test (MCAT), a standardized entrance examination. Because very few blacks, Mexican-Americans, native Americans, or Asian-Americans could compete with white applicants under these traditional measures, the medical school had remained lily-white. In an effort to correct the inequity, the school in 1970 adopted a procedure under which applicants were judged by criteria that placed less emphasis on college grades and entrance test scores and more emphasis on subjective evaluations.

Bakke went to court. He complained that the special procedure admitted students who were less qualified than he and that he had been denied admission solely because he was white. This, he argued, violated the equal protection clause of the Fourteenth Amendment. The trial court agreed with Bakke and held the special admissions procedure unconstitutional. The California supreme court, by a six-to-one majority, affirmed the judgment.

Ours is a nation of many minorities, and of course all these groups deserve as much protection from discrimination as blacks. But Bakke is not claiming that he was denied admission because of his religion or national origin. Bakke's claim is that he is being discriminated against because he is white. It is simply absurd to argue that the purpose of the university's admissions program is the subjugation or oppression of whites.

Perhaps the most frightening aspect of the case has been the eagerness with which some white Americans have bought Bakke's "reverse discrimination" argument. The university's initial mishandling of the case, the California supreme court's refusal to hear all of the evidence, the assumption by opponents and supporters alike that white applicants are automatically "better qualified" and that minorities must therefore be arbitrarily "preferred" to gain admission—all are symptomatic of a prevailing attitude that says, "Perhaps we have gone far enough with this equal opportunity nonsense"; an attitude that denies any responsibility for correcting the effects of this nation's past inhumanities and that refuses to acknowledge the existence of racial oppression today.

Part of the problem is that there has been very little informed and enlightened public discussion of the issues. But the opposition to affirmative action is rooted, I think, in the fear of many former allies in the civil rights struggle that they will be hurt by this version of equal opportunity for minorities. Access to the many benefits of professional status has always been hard to come by, but nowadays one feels lucky just to have a paying job. When it is your own job or promotion that may be at stake, or your own son's or daughter's chance to get into a good college or go to medical school, it's difficult to make dispassionate decisions in the best interests of society.

In the final analysis, the result of the *Bakke* case and the chances for American minorities to achieve true equality in the foreseeable future will turn on just how much privilege white America

is willing to relinquish in exchange for racial parity. Despite the grand strides we have made during the past two decades toward eradication of inequality, a disproportionate number of black, brown, yellow, and red people in this country continue to belong to an underclass. And there they will remain until people in higher classes are willing to give them room. When all is said and done, each of the nine Justices will be choosing not so much between Bakke and the university as between ensuring equality for minorities and protecting the privileges of the majority.

Though damaging, a decision for Bakke need not be totally disastrous; given that sorry eventuality, civil rights groups should by no means cease their efforts. Some of the amicus briefs already submitted—even some that side with Bakke—contend that only those admissions policies requiring outright quotas are unconstitutional; those that give preference to underprivileged races, they hold, are not only legal but desirable.

Nevertheless, the omens cannot be considered propitious. While it is probably true that a narrow decision would allow a technical distinction to be made between the admissions policy at Davis and more carefully worded affirmative action programs, it must be remembered that the Court cannot always control the manner in which its decisions are intepreted and implemented. Two decades of struggle to implement the "all deliberate speed" of the *Brown* decision starkly testify to the need for the Court to be definitive in the face of strong public opposition.

Public response to the California decision, some civil rights groups add, may also serve as a harbinger should the U.S. Supreme Court rule in Bakke's favor. Immediately following the state's decision, California's Fair Employment Practices Commission was deluged by calls from private business, all hoping that the Bakke verdict gave them license to kill their fledgling affirmative action programs. If Bakke wins on the federal level, even institutions genuinely committed to affirmative action may be hesitant to adopt programs that could subject them to legal liability. The University of California has flatly stated, for example, that it will not adopt an admissions program that is simply a subterfuge for considering race. Numerous professional schools and colleges have indicated in amicus briefs that an upholding of the California opinion will make the end of all but token integration of their campuses.

Now that the case is in the United States Supreme Court, the University of California has retained the most talented and experienced of outside counsel to defend its position. A prestigious San Francisco law firm and several Berkeley law professors have been involved in the preparation of the university's brief, and none other than Harvard law professor and former special prosecutor Archibald Cox has been retained to present oral argument before the Court. Why the university is retaining such well-known counsel only at this late stage is perhaps a classic example of "too little, too late."

The university's initial handling of the defense of the Davis admissions program left much to be desired. Many members of California's minority community believe that the university set the case up to rid itself of a program it never wanted. They point to the fact that special admissions programs were begun only after the substantial political pressure and urban unrest of the mid-Sixties. The charges of collusion are not

entirely unwarranted, and the best that can be said for the university's legal efforts in the trial court is that they were lackadaisical.

Bakke was encouraged to file the suit, it has been discovered, by an admissions official at Davis who provided names of attorneys who might be helpful, shared his own thoughts on the best strategy, and even leaked information concerning the academic performance of students admitted under the special program. That behavior set the mold for events to follow. University counsel approached the trial of the case in an almost perfunctory fashion. They agreed with Bakke's counsel to try the case without oral testimony—the direct result being that the all-important trial court record is completely lacking in the kind of evidence crucial to framing a proper appellate level argument. No expert testimony describes the purpose of the program or explains why traditional criteria are inadequate to judge the true potential of minority candidates. No statistics demonstrate the compelling need for doctors in California's minority communities or show that the number of minority doctors cannot be increased if traditional admissions standards continue to be applied to disadvantaged students.

Nor did the university question the very assertion that Bakke was indeed "better qualified" than the minority applicants who were accepted. Had the university not agreed to this unsupportable assumption, Bakke would never even have had a case. Worst of all, university lawyers made no mention of the dean's special admissions program, under which white children of politically well-connected university supporters or substantial financial contributors have been admitted in spite of being less qualified than other applicants, including Bakke.

Another glaring inadequacy in the record is that past discrimination against minorities by the university is wholly disregarded. This omission is particularly damaging because the Supreme Court has created a special exception to the rule that race may not be a consideration in any government policy. In school desegregation, employment, and housing cases, the Court has held that where past discrimination or purposeful segregation on the part of the defendant has been proven, race may be taken into account in order to remedy the situation.

Only a severe case of myopia could prevent one from seeing rampant racial discrimination in the University of California's history. Between 1866 and World War II, there was only one black graduate from the university's medical school in San Francisco. Blacks were once not even allowed to live on the Davis campus.

The California supreme court, in a brilliant display of judicial sleight of hand, was able to evade this issue because no evidence of past discrimination against minorities was cited in the trial record of the lower court. Nonetheless, it refused a subsequent request by the California branch of the National Association for the Advancement of Colored People to allow the case to be sent back to trial so that the evidence could be presented and put on record.

The California court even failed to note its own findings in other cases involving racial discrimination by the state's educational system. In numerous desegregation and bilingual education cases, the state supreme court has held that the state unconstitutionally deprived minorities of an equal education.

It is difficult to understand how the state, having handicapped minority students at an earlier point in their education, can legally disclaim responsibility for their difficulties at a later juncture in their schooling.

The university's brief for the U.S. Supreme Court makes this reasoning quite clear. It points out that most of the applicants to medical school in 1974 entered elementary school in 1954, when the Court held segregated schooling illegal. In the words of the brief, these students received "the promise and not the actuality of *Brown*." It remains to be seen whether the Supreme Court, like the California court, will use a poor trial record to defer the promise of *Brown*.

There is no doubt that Mr. Cox's legal skills, commitment to the case, and integrity are unimpeachable. The brief filed by the university in the U.S. Supreme Court is forcefully written, and it documents a great deal of the evidence not presented at trial. But the rules for cases on appeal allow the Court to ignore evidence that is not on the trial court record. Mr. Cox will be forced to argue from a record which gives him little to work with.

The issues that have been ignored by the California courts and the parties to the case are being further buried by an avalanche of erroneous assumptions reported by the media. The measure of the magnitude of this avalance is evident in a recent *New York Times* headline: "83 percent in Poll Oppose Reverse Bias Plans—Ability Rather than Preferential Treatment Favored on Hiring and Admission to College." It is worthwhile to consider the underlying misunderstandings that led to the results of the Gallup poll on which the *Times* article was based.

Opponents of affirmative action argue that special admissions programs constitute "reverse discrimination." They say that if the Constitution prohibits exclusion of blacks and other minorities on racial grounds, it cannot permit the exclusion of whites on racial grounds. Special admissions programs, they argue, destroy the right to be judged on individual merit and violate the constitutional guarantee of equal protection.

Supporters of these programs, on the other hand, contend that racial discrimination has deprived minorities of educational and employment opportunities for generations. The "reparations" or "preferential treatment" argument holds that minorities should be "preferred" because the only way to remedy inherited disadvantage is to transfer some opportunity from the advantaged majority to the injured minority.

Both of these positions—whatever their merit as abstract principles of justice—miss the point of the *Bakke* case entirely. Moreover, they have uncovered an inherent racism among opponents as well as among many supporters of affirmative action.

The opinion of the California supreme court begins by pondering "whether a special admissions program which benefits disadvantaged minority students who apply for admission . . . offends the constitutional rights of *better qualified* [emphasis added] applicants denied admission because they are not identified with a minorty."

The court's opinion, then, is based on the unfounded assumption that Bakke and many of the other white applicants who were rejected are "better qualified" than the minority students who were admitted. This assumption implies that the minority students accepted through these programs are less qualified and

are lowering the school's and the profession's standards.

What makes Bakke better qualified? The most simplistic answer to that question, the one that both the California court and the university find acceptable, is that his "bench mark score" (a number determined by combining scores on standardized tests, undergraduate grade point average, and an interview score) was higher than that of some of the minority students admitted. In fact, the answer is not nearly so simple.

Each year thousands of highly qualified students apply to the various University of California medical schools to fill a few hundred places. Obviously many of those turned away are capable of completing a medical degree and going on to practice medicine successfully. Medical students are among the most highly subsidized students in the nation, and the present economics of medical education make it impossible to provide an opportunity to everyone who is qualified. The real issue, then, is how this scarce resource should be allocated.

It was thought that "objective testing" would eliminate favoritism and ensure the highest level of technical competence. But there appears to be little correlation between applicants' test scores and their subsequent performance as medical students. A study of 1,088 students in 14 classes at the University of California School of Medicine in San Francisco concluded that there is virtually no relationship between those scores and medical school grades. Standardized tests have often eliminated those persons who are most humane and empathetic. Other studies, moreover, have determined that high MCAT scores do not always accurately indicate which students will be most effective in clinical situations. Comparisons between students' test scores and their subsequent performance as physicians have yielded similar findings.

If test scores mean relatively little among otherwise qualified applicants, then the determining factors of acceptance must be based on the applicant's potential for fulfilling the goals of the school and society at large. Logically, minority applicants are probably better qualified to fulfill one of the most important of those goals: providing medical services to minority communities.

If minority admissions programs are characterized as giving the advantage to underqualified minority applicants because of their skin color, the programs do indeed seem to reek of "reverse-discrimination." But try this description: "A certain number of capable minority students are admitted each year because their life experience as members of minorities in this country makes them better qualified than white applicants to meet the important university goal of training doctors to work in minority neighborhoods."

Bakke does not have an equal protection argument; he was excluded not because of the color of his skin, but because there were others who could do the job better. Just as the person who has a graduate degree in chemistry may be better qualified to fulfill the medical school's goal of producing a certain number of doctors to do medical research, just as a woman may be better qualified to become a sensitive and effective gynecologist, so is the person who has experienced a lifetime of racial discrimination better qualified to understand and solve the problems of people in similar circumstances. A black doctor in Oakland, for example, tells of making rounds with a white chief resident in an inner city hospital. The resident suggested that a black male patient showed signs of paranoia because he was wearing sunglasses in a dimly lighted room. The black doctor informed his senior colleague that the patient was not neurotic; he was simply hip.

In its most glaring failure to face reality, the California supreme court claimed that it is not necessary to produce minority doctors to serve minority communities. The court said, "The Purpose of the University . . . cannot be to produce Black (doctors) for Blacks, Polish (doctors) for Poles, Jewish (doctors) for Jews, Irish (doctors) for Irish. It would be to produce good (doctors) for Americans." A noble sentiment but an unrealistic one. For the most part white doctors will not work in minority communities, and many of those who do work there lack empathy with their patients or display paternalistic feelings that make it impossible for them to gain the trust necessary for a good doctor-patient relationship.

As the Supreme Court begins its deliberations on the *Bakke* case, it must make a choice. Will it confine itself to a wholly inadequate record and disregard the inadequacy of traditional standards, the past and present discrimination against minorities, and the need for more minority doctors? Will it be influenced by the public cries of "reverse discrimination," ignoring the fact that the vestiges of slavery cannot be eliminated unless the descendants of the slaves are protected from institutionalized and subconscious forms of racism? Or will it cut through the convenient slogans and declare that since society has adopted a rational policy for healing its wounds and providing important health and welfare needs, the highest court in the land will not stand in its way?

The United States Supreme Court

has always been a political institution. There is ample precedent and high-minded language to support both sides in this case. I am not overly sanguine about the outcome of the Bakke case. The public mood is against affirmative action, and the Burger Court has not always been sensitive to minority interests. Still, there is reason to hope that the Court will have the foresight to understand that no one's interest will be served if we continue to exist as two nations divided by color and opportunity.

B: EDITORIAL
THE BAKKE CASE IN A HIGHER COURT

When King Solomon ordered the baby cut in half, he could safely count on a natural law, rooted in a mother's love, to rescue the secular power from committing an outrage. Now that the Supreme Court has narrowly carved up the legal equities in the Bakke case, only a higher law can assure that Americans respond justly. If we seek it, we too shall find it rooted in love.

Americans love law because it is, in the end, a sport that confines our passions and channels our competitions in safe if not always satisfactory ways; law contains the chaos of living with ground rules that we can comprehend. A California medical school has been found breaking the rules by barring whites from some student places; Mr. Bakke will now be admitted. Yet the movement to expand opportunity for blacks and other minorities has been ruled legal; reparation for past injustice may continue if it avoids crude racial classification. Faced with competing claims of principle, wise law can try only to balance them.

So the heart of the matter transcends the capacity of a mere court. In the sporting image of Lester Thurow (here embellished), the questions of Bakke and affirmative action turn on the competition in which we all must run. Plainly, many of the runners are variously handicapped; they must carry heavy weights. Remove those handicaps — namely, create equal opportunity — and still the race remains unfair; everyone did not start from the same point at the same time. Even where equal opportunity prevails, those who start ahead usually finish ahead, even if they are less able. To have a truly fair race, those who once ran with weights must have them lightened and those who ran without must be to some degree handicapped. This is true even if those who lead the race did not themselves impose the handicaps; they have benefited even if they have in conscience opposed them.

How then do we serve the great goal of equal opportunity among runners of marked inequality? How, especially, when only some of their handicaps were forced upon them, by competing runners and by government disguised as referee, while other handicaps were endowed to them by the Creator? Neither religion nor science has been able to differentiate among the burdens that each of us carries; even the most cruel weights on the back of every American black do not — alone — explain every black's position in the contest. Are we helpless before this ultimate mystery of the handicaps? Should Government simply chalk the lines of the running track and enforce sportsmanlike conduct? Or is it obligated to promote a larger vision of fairness in which society strives to eliminate the handicaps that society has added to the unfathomable distinctions among us?

The love of fairness, which is the

ultimate American faith, insists on the uncomfortable answer—even when it challenges other faiths. Those who are running a good race tend to believe that they have earned their advantage and, for deeper reasons than selfishness, resist the idea of having it diminished by law. Even some who straggle far behind often prefer the illusion of a formally equal contest to a redistribution of handicaps by official judgment. Thus is stability served even while conscience cries for change.

To get beyond racism, wrote Justice Blackmun in the Bakke case, we must first take account of race; to treat some persons equally, we must treat them differently. To rid the race of handicaps, in other words, we must advance some, and restrain others. Whom? And how much? And for how long? The Court invites us to reveal our devotion to a higher law.

It has ordered unspecified reparation for the millions maimed by slavery and the legal horrors that followed. It tries imperfectly to measure assorted remedies against perceivable damage. And it keeps chalking the lines: No one, the Court said last week, may be disqualified in the contest solely on account of race; but handicaps distributed to favor previously injured races or ethnic groups are often permissible, even desirable. What no court can measure is the full weight of the burden over the generations. What no court can know is how much inequality Americans will tolerate in the pursuit of truly equal opportunity. There should be no doubt, however, that we shall be judged by our answer.

The experience of Negroes in America has been different in kind, not just in degree, from that of other ethnic groups. The dream of America as the great melting pot has not been realized for the Negro; because of his skin color he never even made it into the pot.
JUSTICE THURGOOD MARSHALL, opinion, Bakke case

20.

ANDREW YOUNG: U.S. Political Prisoners

Andrew Young, reared in a middle-class African American family, was graduated from a theological seminary with a divinity degree. A pastor of several churches in the South, he became active in the civil rights movement and joined with Dr. Martin Luther King, Jr., in leading the Southern Christian Leadership Conference (SCLC). Starting in 1970, Young turned to a political career and was elected to Congress two years later. An early supporter of Jimmy Carter, he was made UN ambassador after Carter's election. Young's sympathy with the aspirations of the Third World made him highly controversial, and he was finally forced to resign in 1979 after it became known that he had met with a representative of the Palestine Liberation Organization (PLO). In 1981 he was elected mayor of Atlanta. Among many controversial statements, perhaps the most inflammatory was Young's charge that the United States also—not just the Soviet Union—possessed political prisoners. His remarks were published in a French daily on July 12, and then translated in The New York Times *the next day. Below is an excerpt from the French interview, as well as the text of a statement made by Young in Geneva some hours later.*

Source: *The New York Times,* July 14, 1978.

EXCERPTS FROM INTERVIEW

Question: How do you explain the opening of the trials of Shcharansky and Ginzburg on the eve of a Vance-Gromyko meeting?

Answer: Oh, it's certainly a challenge, a gesture of independence on their part. But that will not prevent them from pursuing the SALT negotiations. And then, one doesn't know what can happen to the dissidents. After all, in our prisons, too, there are hundreds, perhaps even thousands of people whom I would call political prisoners. Ten years ago I myself was tried in Atlanta for having organized a protest movement. And, three years later, I was a Georgia Representative. It's true that things do not change that quickly in the Soviet Union, but they do change.

Q: But one cannot compare the two systems. . . .

A: I do not agree that these systems should be considered as opposing each other. Take the United States, for example. The society of today has nothing in common with the pre-Roosevelt one. In the years 1930-40 the trade union movement launched a radical revolution in American life, a revolution without which we certainly couldn't produce nine million automobiles a year today. In the 1950's there was a revolution in civil and racial rights. Today it is women who are participating more and more in our economy. And this constant evolution is the rule everywhere. I think the current Soviet dissidents could well be the salvation of the Soviet Union. They are a natural development of Soviet society, but the leadership has not yet realized it.

STATEMENT IN GENEVA

A lengthy interview has been excerpted to give an erroneous impression of my views on the trial of Mr. Anatoly Shcharansky.

Let me assure you that I am fully in accord with the strong statements condemning the persecution of Soviet dissidents issued by President Carter and Secretary Vance and have actively supported the movement for universal human rights and freedoms and especially the cause of Soviet Jewry from my earliest days in the U.S. Congress.

Nor have I ever equated the status of political freedom in the United States with that in the Soviet Union. I know of no instance in the United States where persons have received penalties for monitoring our Government's position on civil or human rights.

Last June in Atlanta at a service of worship memorializing the Holocaust, I met the younger brother of Mr. Shcharansky and I was greatly impressed by the courage and determination he expressed toward the pursuit of full cultural and religious freedom in his country. He said that Soviet citizens wanted and needed strong reactions from all freedom-loving people and praised the human rights concerns that we have expressed.

21.

Vine Deloria, Jr.: Civilization and Isolation—a Native American View

Interest in Native American history and culture has endured even in a technological era. It is especially interesting when an American Indian analyzes white American society and culture. Vine Deloria, Jr., the author of the following selection, is descended from members of the Sioux Nation.

Source: *The North American Review*, 1978.

"Men can be provincial in time, as well as in place," Alfred North Whitehead once remarked. When we apply this insight to the realm of human knowledge, quite frequently we refer to the nonwestern peoples and point out that they have failed to keep pace with the technical developments that other peoples, particularly western peoples, have made. Thus non-western societies are considered by many social scientists as remnants of stages of human evolutionary growth struggling to reach levels of sophistication that were achieved and surpassed by Europeans many centuries ago. Rarely is the question of provinciality applied directly to western European peoples, and on those occasions we find that provinciality is applied as a criterion to determine efficiency and sophistication within the world view of that tradition.

Provinciality, however, is a characteristic of societies and individuals who fail to conduct periodic critiques of their beliefs and who assume, with some degree of smugness, that the knowledge they possess, because it has been their possession for so long, provides the basis for intelligent existence in a world of sudden and unexpected change. Western Europeans have been so much dazzled by their own technology that they have fallen into a provinciality in regard to human knowledge so narrow as to exclude major portions of human experience. Whitehead called this attitude the "fallacy of misplaced concreteness," and he meant by this the exclusionary approach to the physical world coupled with the belief that whatever approach one did use properly excluded things that have no value.

When Native Americans have been forced to confront this attitude on the part of non-Indian neighbors we have generally come off second best. A good many factors must be included in any analysis of our failure to confront and overcome the attitude of superiority which non-Indians have thrust upon us. The most important factor would probably be the efficiency of technology which non-Indians brought with them. Marvelous instruments and tools of iron and other metals blinded us and produced an uncritical assumption that whatever the white man was doing must be based upon some superior insight into the world of nature. We forgot, to our detriment, that the first European we encountered thought they were going to sail over the edge of the world, that succeeding expeditions had fantasies about Fountains of Youth, Cities of Gold, and northwest passages to Cathay.

Native Americans did not realize that Europeans felt a dreadful necessity to classify us within a view of the world already made obsolete by discovery of our continent. While we could not participate in the heated theological discussions concerning our origins—whether we derived fron Noah's Ark or were survivors of the Ten Lost Tribes of Israel—we perhaps could have been more insistent on making the non-Indians provide more and better arguments for their version of world history and human knowledge. Any group that frantically dug gold in the west in order to transplant it to the east and bury it cannot be quite right and their insights cannot form the highest achievement of our species.

The world is much more sophisticated today, and groups of widely varying backgrounds can communicate with each other even though they form the minority of particular societies. Thus the modern emergence of Indian peoples and the concentration by them on revival and revitalization of culture should include a persistent emphasis on the validity of their own histories, technologies, and social and political institutions. In some measure Indian groups have already begun this process of defending and justifying cultural insights tribes have preserved over the centuries of contact with Europeans. Unfortunately, much of this activity has been phrased in an anti-white format which does not produce a justification of the Indian tradition but merely points out the inadequacies of the non-Indians. We do not take time to adapt this approach to the problem. One glance at the western democracies and we discover that the political leaders, when they are not lusting in their hearts after forbidden fruit, are demonstrating that intelligent life probably does not exist on the planet or, in the alternative, are planning ways to extinguish whatever intelligent life might accidentally arise here.

Transcending this childish tactic of accusatory relationship with non-Indians is not difficult but it involves creating or re-creating a confidence in the Indian traditions. Such a task initially involves a determination of the techniques which Indians used to accumulate, evaluate, and perpetuate their knowledge of the world and to translate this knowledge into western terms that can speak rationally and intelligently to those people within the western cultural milieu who are prepared to listen. That is a lot of "lates," but above all it is not *too* late. So I will attempt to outline the variances which I see between the western European traditions and the Indian traditions, primarily the North American peoples, with the hopes that the differences—and there are radical differences to be seen—will be illustrated so clearly as to enable us to embark on a new interpretation of human knowledge which is not provincial in either time or space.

If I were to choose the single attribute that characterizes the western approach to human knowledge, indeed to almost all human activities, I would unhesitantly choose "isolation." In scientific and philosophical terms we are perhaps speaking of William of Occam and his famous razor which has cut the throat of more than one effort to synthesize human knowledge. Briefly, we can rephrase this doctrine as the belief that by continual subdivision of any problem we can reach a certain and ultimate knowledge. For most of the

last couple centuries the scientific concern with finding the tiniest element of the atom demonstrated the potency of this belief. It also, incidentally, illustrated the basic western belief in the primacy of matter over spirit. But isolation remains the dominating attitude which western peoples have adopted toward the world. We see this approach eloquently in our political institutions and the assumption that one human being is interchangeable with another and that the conglomerate of human decisions, counted statistically, produces the proper course of action for a nation to adopt. This belief reduces wisdom to public opinion polls and produces those nasty and distasteful compromises which substitute for intelligent activities in most of the western democracies.

We find additional confirmation of this belief in isolation in the various religious traditions that are characteristic of western peoples. Almost always, in the last analysis, we find the solitary individual in the hands of an angry, or at least disgruntled, god. Even those western peoples who have rejected the traditional religious denominations of their culture have not found another approach to the religious question but have simply adopted the Oriental version of solitude, listening to one hand clapping, and other symbolic gestures, and are now contentedly recycling their own energies endlessly. Even the atheists and humanists ground their justifications in the primacy of the individual rather than the maturity of the species.

One reason for the scientific and philosophical isolation of the elements of experience is the belief, deeply held although rarely practiced, that one cannot trust sense perceptions, human emotions, or the intuitional abilities of the human personality. This article of faith must certainly go as far back as the Greek philosophers and the prophetic movement in Israel, but was not a dominating factor in western existence until the relatively late period when Descartes, Leibnitz, and Newton demonstrated the efficiency of the mathematical descriptions of the physical world. Since that time western peoples have increasingly depended upon mathematics for their analyses and insights of nature. The approach has proven spectacular in the physical sciences, particularly physics, and the technology that has been produced as a by-product of physical theory has only served to entrench in western minds the belief that mathematics is the proper description of reality. So influential is this attitude that in the last century we have seen the development of social sciences which seem to suggest that statistical truth is equivalent to ultimate reality. The social sciences now insist that all human activities can be described as functions of complicated formulas. I have seen this attitude applied to elections in the United States, but I have generally rejected that approach and bet on the people who counted the votes rather than on those statistics which projected who would vote. Mayor Richard Daley of Chicago, now deceased, never failed me in this respect.

As mathematics has been more influential in representing the scientific quest, and as the scope of human knowledge has expanded, the old tendency toward isolation has produced a strange phenomenon in which human knowledge is divided into separate categories variously called disciplines, fields of study, or what have you. As sciences have given rise to subgrouping of knowledge and specialties have been developed, knowledge itself has suffered a fragmentation and the sole guarantee of the validity of knowledge has been in the similarity of techniques employed to accumulate and interpret data. Briefly, even this field of methodology has degenerated as the various disciplines have moved away from each other, so that the sole criterion of truth today seems to lie in the sincerity of the researcher and his or her relative status within the specific field of endeavor. Sincerity is no guarantee of anything except an emotional state and quite often not much of a characterization even of that. . . .

Perhaps the final consequence of approaching the world with the intent to isolate and thereby achieve dominance over things is the belief that the way we see things is the proper manner of describing them. Thus we approach and reunite with the original contention that we are dealing with the fallacy of misplaced concreteness. But we have not engaged in a reasoning process as much as taken a tour around the intellectual and conceptual universe of the western European to illustrate the various modes that this basic error can take. A few illustrations may be in order, to demonstrate both the provinciality of the western attitude and the manner in which Indians and dissatisfied non-Indians can begin to move away from this mooring and expand the horizons of all concerned. The treatment of nonwestern peoples, particularly North American Indian peoples, provides a perfect setting in which we can examine the manner of escape.

The Europeans, arriving in North America, discovered a people that had no written language, laws, religions, or customs, yet governed themselves so well that the American constitutional fathers were encouraged by Benjamin Franklin to model themselves after the

Iroquois League when they came to devise a constitution. Europeans, looking at Indian societies, decided that these people lived in savagery because they had no written rules and regulations to govern them. Here we find the intense desire to objectify, to render human activities to mechanical form, and to accord respect by discovering similarity and homogeneity. Finding a qualitative difference between Indians and themselves, the Europeans promptly characterized the North American peoples as a lawless breed devoid of the attributes of civilized society. A great many wrongs were done to Indians because non-Indians believed them to be without laws and therefore unable to make intelligent or just decisions regarding their lives.

All of these beliefs about Indians changed as social science became more influential in western society and more sophisticated in its observations. In 1926, with the publication of Malinowski's famous book, *Crime and Custom in Savage Society,* which demonstrated that customs could be as restrictive and socially integrating as written codes and laws, the perception of people made a radical shift and Indians were considered savages because they were so tightly bound by custom and lacked the freedom of western democratic peoples. How a whole race could shift in one century from most lawless to most law-bound remained a mystery to the Indians who came into contact with western intellectual history, but it should have been an indication to non-Indians that all was not well with the western way of perceiving human activities.

This example illustrates that much of what western peoples have understood as knowledge is simply a reorientation, within their own framework, of the thesis used to interpret phenomena, and is

not a corresponding development in the phenomena itself. Even more, the example indicates that no final statement, and perhaps no reliable statement, can ever be made concerning knowledge of the world. There is always another viewpoint by which interpretations of data can be made and when this situation becomes entrenched in the academic worldview of a culture, inevitably the reality that it describes becomes a verbal or mental reality. When phenomena do not fulfill our expectations, they are disregarded, downgraded, or derided and the opportunity to come to grips with another facet of reality escapes us.

When we turn to the North American Indian worldview we discover an entirely different perspective on the world. Instead of isolating things, Indians encompassed them; togetherness, synthesis, and relatedness characterized their experiences of the universe. The ordinary distinctions between mind and matter, human and other life forms, nature and human beings, and even our species and the divinity were not considered valid ways of understanding experience. Life was a complex matrix of entities, emotions, revelations, and cooperative enterprises and any abstraction was considered stupid and dangerous, destructive of spirit and reductionist in the very aspects that made life important. A great many non-Indians have intuited this "togetherness" from observing Indians and reading of the "Indian way," but have failed to understand the remarkable system of relationships which undergirds a seemingly innocent and simple life.

Relatedness is a much better description of the Indian way of looking at the world. Here we are not describing a comparative knowledge in which no absolute value exists. Indeed, all values are absolute because they are experiences and because they deal with specific relationships between specific individuals. A good example of this specificity is the manner in which the Osage Indians fed themselves. In the early spring they would plant their corn along the bottomlands of the Missouri River about the place where St. Louis is today. After they had sown their crop they would depart for the far Rocky Mountains in Colorado and Wyoming to do their summer hunting. The Osage would spend most of the summer in the high mountains hunting deer, buffalo, antelope and other large game animals, and they would dry their meat in the sun, making it suitable for preservation.

In the middle of July they would begin to examine one of the mountain flowers and when this flower began to turn to seed they would know that it was time to begin their journey back to their winter homes. They would pack up their summer's hunting surplus and return to Missouri where their corn would now be ready for the harvest. Such behavior may seem the utmost of simplicity except that to accomplish such a task required that the Osage know the relationships of plants, animals, and lands over a distance of some 1,000 miles and know these complex relationships so well that they could transfer an abstract sense of time, time in the sense of organic growth, from plant to plant over that distance and use the growth of a mountain plant as a gauge or calendar for their corn.

Here we have no general knowledge, no principles valid in all cases, no knowledge that can be tested in the laboratory. We have a knowledge totally unlike western scientific knowledge and yet an understanding of great profundity. Within this scope of knowledge we have an intuitive understanding of the spiritual nature of life which enables people to act in a purposive and predictive sense. Classifications, in this system of thinking, defy western categorization; they are not deductive and cannot be reached through any complicated logical path. Yet they exist and serve amazingly well in determining how a specific people will relate to an environment. Thus if we can learn anything from this example the first lesson must be that classifications, as we have been used to them in the western schemata of knowledge, are useless when we approach a more intimate relationship with the universe.

The hallmark of relatedness or synthesis is experience rather than interpretation. In the synthetic process we first experience the unity of existence and then, upon reflection and further experience, we begin to separate elements of that experience into useful categories of knowledge in which similarities and intimacies are the most important criteria. For that reason most Indian classifications of birds, animals, reptiles, and other life forms begin with the activities of these creatures and seek to identify similar purposive behaviors. Simple morphologies, as western peoples have conceived the organic world, have little part in the Indian format; when they do, the morphological features that are chosen are understood as indicating similarity of temperament, not evolutionary origins. Thus our species, birds, and bears are considered to be the "two-leggeds," and we behave in many respects as if we were a single species. A good Indian medicine man can conduct a sophisticated tour of human and animal personality by describing the traits that convinced Indians long ago that the "two-leggeds" were a specific group.

The shift from isolating things to relating them involves the recognition of a different form of preserving knowledge. When we isolate and then interpret phenomena, our basic intent is to derive principles from which we can predict future behavior, illustrate mechanical operations, or analyze into further component parts. Our interpretation and rearrangement of data is most important. In the tradition which relates everything in specific terms the immediate experience is most critical and everything is oriented toward a preservation of the exact conditions under which something happened. Little effort is devoted to rearranging the elements of the incident or experience, for it was the uniqueness of that particular experience that first attracted us and made it seem important. Thus the tradition seeks to preserve as accurately as possible everything that took place.

When we look at the traditions of the North American peoples we discover that they have carried down over the generations many accounts of phenomena we would consider amazing today. The Ojibway of western Ontario, for example, relate stories of the water monster who lived in the lakes and rivers and tipped over the canoes of the unwary and unlucky. Pictures of this creature are liberally scattered over much of Ontario and eastern Canada. The Sioux also relate the story of water monsters and their description correlates to an astounding degree with the Ojibway tale. Further west the Indians of the Pacific Northwest have traditions that the lakes of the region were formerly much larger and contained monsters who stirred the waves unmercifully whenever humans ventured out on the water. A correlation of all accounts, of petroglyphs and pictographs of the various tribes, and an acknowledgment that this particular set of stories is always intimately tied to specific lakes should be sufficient to inform us that at one time within the memory of these tribes, a different and perhaps most spectacular form of life inhabited this continent. If we use our imaginations we can see in this tradition the presence of the group that we have always called "dinosaurs."

Now to suggest that human beings have been living in North America since the mesozoic is radical only when we restrict our interpretation of human knowledge to that already accumulated by western peoples through the process of isolating elements of experience. The suggestion seems less radical when we remember that the oral traditions do not seek to interpret as much as they attempt to recall and remember precisely the unusual events of the past. The possibility that these stories contain the elements of past experiences is heightened considerably when we view contemporary research on the dinosaurs and discover that the latest and most precise interpretation of this group conceives them as warmblooded, bearing their young live, and traveling in herds, all characteristics of mammals and not reptiles, and possessing behavior patterns not unlike those which the Indian water monster tales relate.

What are we to do when a tradition which has always been seen by western peoples as primitive and superstitious now threatens to become an important source in a new and important revolution in paleontology? Are there other important areas of experience that have been preserved by oral traditions that have been neglected or discarded by the scientific mind because of the all-consuming goal of achieving truth by the isolation of elements of experience?

Here we have a dilemma of major proportions which strikes the western mind at precisely the most vulnerable point. Isolation has not produced truth as much as it has produced specialists who studiously avoid synthesis in favor of a continuing subdivision of information into increasingly separated disciplines. We finally arrive at the fundamental question underlying the scope of human knowledge: is truth divisible into categories or is it synthetic, incorporating all aspects of experience and understanding?

The present situation calls for a sense of maturity between cultures that no other period of human history has required. We must now begin to transcend all other parochial considerations in our understanding and move forward into a new period of synthesis in which all information is brought into a coherent whole.

Alfred North Whitehead remarked rather casually in *Science and the Modern World* that "it takes a very unusual mind to undertake the analysis of the obvious." Now the obvious always refers to those things that are so commonly accepted as to be considered beyond serious consideration by scholars. So the task of moving human knowledge forward has generally fallen to the amateur, to those who simply wish to know, and to the humble souls who refuse to surrender an idea to the guardians of human knowledge, the academics; those souls who understand knowledge as the possession of the whole human species and not the plaything of the specialist.

North American peoples have an important role to play in the determination of knowledge in the future. They represent thousands of years of experience in living on this continent and their customs and traditions, the particular and sometimes peculiar ways they have of approaching problems, of living, and of protecting the lands, are not simply the clumsy adjustments of primitives but the seasoned responses of people who synthesized and summarized the best manner of adapting themselves to the world in which they lived. Insofar as their insights can be translated into principles which can reorient western thinking, scientific and social, and insofar as North American peoples can understand their own traditions and abide by them, to that degree we can produce a more sophisticated, humane, and sensible society on this continent.

So the provinciality of which Whitehead speaks is really the provincial manner in which we today look at the experiences and memories of our ancestors and define the history of our species and planet. World history, Arnold Toynbee once remarked, is a parochial affair comparable to a map of the Mediterranean area being considered a true and accurate map of the world. Human knowledge cannot be provincial, but must enclose the planet and render an accurate account of its nature and growth. We are today on the threshold of a new era in which this task will be accomplished—and it is perhaps the most exciting time of any that our species has experienced. Let us have the emotional and intellectual maturity to bring it to pass.

22.

The Camp David Accords

On November 15, 1977, President Anwar Sadat of Egypt received from Prime Minister Menahem Begin of Israel a most unusual communication, namely, a formal invitation to visit Jerusalem. Sadat's response was if possible more unusual, considering that his country had been at war with Israel four times in 30 years: he accepted. Sadat arrived in Jerusalem on November 19 and addressed the Knesset the next day. Begin returned the visit a month later, meeting Sadat at Ismailia on Christmas Day. The world, and especially the peoples of Egypt and Israel, welcomed the meetings as the first sign of peace in the war-torn Middle East, and both Sadat and Begin vowed to continue talking. But by the next spring negotiations had slowed, and visits to Washington by both men did not get things moving again. President Carter was not content with this state of affairs, and he invited Sadat and Begin to come to Camp David, the presidential retreat near Washington, to remain — in seclusion — until at least the basis of peace had been attained. The President's action was recognized as courageous. As the Wall Street Journal *said, "He took a tremendous personal risk inviting Mr. Begin and Mr. Sadat to a summit meeting when peace efforts were near collapse. Failure certainly would have been labeled the President's failure, another example of well-intentioned amateurism." The meeting, of course, was a brilliant success. The three men and their staffs met at Camp David for two weeks, working day and night to produce two crucial documents that Begin and Sadat signed for their respective countries, and that Carter witnessed. These laid the groundwork for peace between Israel and Egypt, and this indeed came about within the next few months. Hopes for a wider Middle East peace were high at the end of the meetings, but progress in that regard was much slower. Reprinted here is most of the text of the remarks by Carter, Sadat, and Begin at the conclusion of the meeting.*

Source: Presidential Documents, September 17-18, 1978.

PRESIDENT CARTER. When we first arrived at Camp David, the first thing upon which we agreed was to ask the people of the world to pray that our negotiations would be successful. Those prayers have been answered far beyond any expectations. We are privileged to witness tonight a significant achieve-ment in the cause of peace, an achieve-ment none thought possible a year ago, or even a month ago, an achievement that reflects the courage and wisdom of these two leaders.

Through 13 long days at Camp David, we have seen them display de-termination and vision and flexibility which was needed to make this agreement come to pass. All of us owe them our gratitude and respect. They know that they will always have my personal admiration.

There are still great difficulties that remain and many hard issues to be settled. The questions that have brought warfare and bitterness to the Middle East for the last 30 years will not be settled overnight. But we should all recognize the substantial achievements that have been made.

One of the agreements that President Sadat and Prime Minister Begin are signing tonight is entitled "A Framework For Peace in the Middle East."

This framework concerns the principles and some specifics, in the most substantive way, which will govern a comprehensive peace settlement. It deals specifically with the future of the West Bank and Gaza and the need to resolve the Palestinian problem in all its aspects. The framework document proposes a 5-year transitional period in the West Bank and Gaza during which the Israeli military government will be withdrawn and a self-governing authority will be elected with full autonomy. It also provides for Israeli forces to remain in specified locations during this period to protect Israel's security.

The Palestinians will have the right to participate in the determination of their own future, in negotiations which will resolve the final status of the West Bank and Gaza, and then to produce an Israeli-Jordanian peace treaty.

These negotiations will be based on all the provisions and all the principles of United Nations Security Council Resolution 242. And it provides that Israel may live in peace, within secure and recognized borders. And this great aspiration of Israel has been certified

without constraint, with the greatest degree of enthusiasm, by President Sadat, the leader of one of the greatest nations on Earth.

The other document is entitled, "Framework For the Conclusion of a Peace Treaty Between Egypt and Israel."

It provides for the full exercise of Egyptian sovereignty over the Sinai. It calls for the full withdrawal of Israeli forces from the Sinai and, after an interim withdrawal which will be accomplished very quickly, the establishment of normal, peaceful relations between the two countries, including diplomatic relations.

Together with accompanying letters, which we will make public tomorrow, these two Camp David agreements provide the basis for progress and peace throughout the Middle East.

There is one issue on which agreement has not been reached. Egypt states that the agreement to remove Israeli settlements from Egyptian territory is a prerequisite to a peace treaty. Israel states that the issue of the Israeli settlements should be resolved during the peace negotiations. That's a substantial difference. Within the next 2 weeks, the Knesset will decide on the issue of these settlements.

Tomorrow night, I will go before the Congress to explain the agreements more fully and to talk about their implications for the United States and for the world. For the moment, and in closing, I want to speak more personally about my admiration for all of those who have taken part in this process and my hope that the promise of this movement will be fulfilled.

During the last 2 weeks, the members of all three delegations have spent endless hours, day and night, talking, negotiating, grappling with problems that have divided their people for 30 years. Whenever there was a danger that human energy would fail, or patience would be exhausted or good will would run out—and there were many such moments—these two leaders and the able advisers in all delegations found the resources within them to keep the chances for peace alive.

Well, the long days at Camp David are over. But many months of difficult negotiations still lie ahead. I hope that the foresight and the wisdom that have made this session a success will guide these leaders and the leaders of all nations as they continue the progress toward peace.

Thank you very much.

PRESIDENT SADAT. Dear President Carter, in this historic moment, I would like to express to you my heartfelt congratulations and appreciation. For long days and nights, you devoted your time and energy to the pursuit of peace. You have been most courageous when you took the gigantic step of convening this meeting. The challenge was great and the risks were high, but so was your determination. You made a commitment to be a full partner in the peace process. I'm happy to say that you have honored your commitment.

The signing of the framework for the comprehensive peace settlement has a significance far beyond the event. It signals the emergence of a new peace initiative, with the American nation in the heart of the entire process.

In the weeks ahead, important decisions have to be made if we are to proceed on the road to peace. We have to reaffirm the faith of the Palestinian people in the ideal of peace.

The continuation of your active role is indispensable. We need your help and the support of the American people. Let me seize this opportunity to thank each and every American for his genuine interest in the cause of people in the Middle East.

Dear friend, we came to Camp David with all the good will and faith we possessed, and we left Camp David a few minutes ago with a renewed sense of hope and inspiration. We are looking forward to the days ahead with an added determination to pursue the noble goal of peace.

Your able assistants spared no effort to bring out this happy conclusion. We appreciate their spirit and dedication. Our hosts at Camp David and the State of Maryland were most generous and hospitable. To each one of them and to all those who are watching this great event, I say thank you.

Let us join in a prayer to God Almighty to guide our path. Let us pledge to make the spirit of Camp David a new chapter in the history of our nations.

Thank you, Mr. President.

PRIME MINISTER BEGIN. *Mr. President of the United States, Mr. President of the Arab Republic of Egypt, ladies and gentlemen:*

The Camp David conference should be renamed. It was the Jimmy Carter conference. [*Laughter*]

The President undertook an initiative most imaginative in our time and brought President Sadat and myself and our colleagues and friends and advisers together under one roof. In itself, it was a great achievement. But the President took a great risk for himself and did it with great civil courage. And it was a famous French field commander who said that it is much more difficult to show civil courage than military courage.

And the President worked. As far as

President Jimmy Carter applauds as Israeli Prime Minister Menahem Begin and Egyptian President Anwar Sadat embrace at the conclusion of the Camp David Summit.

my historic experience is concerned, I think that he worked harder than our forefathers did in Egypt building the pyramids. [*Laughter*]

Yes, indeed, he worked day and night, and so did we—[*Laughter*]—

PRESIDENT CARTER. Amen.

PRIME MINISTER BEGIN. Day and night. We used to go to bed at Camp David between 3 and 4 o'clock in the morning, arise, as we are used to since our boyhood, between 5 and 6, and continue working, working.

The President showed interest in every section, every paragraph, every sentence, every word, every letter—[*Laughter*]—of the framework agreements.

We had some difficult moments—as usually there are some crises in negotiations, as usually somebody gives a hint that perhaps he would like to pick up and go home. [*Laughter*] It's all usual. But ultimately, ladies and gentlemen,

the President of the United States won the day. And peace now celebrates a great victory for the nations of Egypt and Israel and for all mankind.

Mr. President, we, the Israelis, thank you from the bottom of our hearts for all you have done for the sake of peace, for which we prayed and yearned more than 30 years. The Jewish people suffered much, too much. And, therefore, peace to us is a striving, coming innermost from our heart and soul.

Now, when I came here to the Camp David conference, I said, perhaps as a result of our work one day people will, in every corner of the world, be able to say, *Habemus pacem,* in the spirit of these days. Can we say so tonight? Not yet. We still have to go a road until my friend President Sadat and I sign the peace treaties.

We promised each other that we shall do so within 3 months. Mr. President [*referring to President Sadat*], tonight, at this celebration of the great historic event, let us promise each other that we shall do it earlier than within 3 months.

Mr. President, you inscribed your name forever in the history of two ancient civilized peoples, the people of Egypt and the people of Israel. Thank you, Mr. President.

PRESIDENT CARTER. Thank you very much.

PRIME MINISTER BEGIN. Oh, no, no, no. I would like to say a few words about my friend, President Sadat. We met for the first time in our lives last November in Jerusalem. He came to us as a guest, a former enemy, and during our first meeting we became friends.

In the Jewish teachings, there is a tradition that the greatest achievement of a human being is to turn his enemy into a friend, and this we do in reciprocity. Since then, we had some difficult days. [*Laughter*] And he then came to visit me. We shook hands. And, thank God, we again could have said to each other, "You are my friend."

And, indeed, we shall go on working in understanding, and in friendship, and with good will. We will still have problems to solve. Camp David proved that any problem can be solved if there is good will and understanding and some, *some* wisdom. . . .

I looked for a precedent; I didn't find it. It was a unique conference, perhaps one of the most important since the Vienna Conference in the 19th century.

And now, ladies and gentlemen, allow me to turn to my own people from the White House in my own native tongue. [*At this point, the Prime Minister spoke briefly in Hebrew.*]

Thank you, ladies and gentlemen.

PRESIDENT CARTER. The first document that we will sign is entitled, "A Frame-work for Peace in the Middle East Agreed at Camp David," and the texts of these two documents will be released tomorrow. The documents will be signed by President Sadat and Prime Minister Begin, and it will be witnessed by me. We have to exchange three documents, so we'll all sign three times for this one.

[*At this point, President Sadat, Prime Minister Begin, and President Carter signed the first document.*]

I might say that the first document is quite comprehensive in nature, encompassing a framework by which Israel can later negotiate peace treaties between herself and Lebanon, Syria, Jordan, as well as the outline of this document that we will now sign.

And as you will later see, in studying the documents, it also provides for the realization of the hopes and dreams of the people who live in the West Bank and Gaza Strip and will assure Israel peace in the generations ahead.

This second document is the one relating to a framework for a peace treaty between Egypt and Israel. This is the document that calls for the completion of the peace treaty negotiations within 3 months. And I have noticed the challenge extended by these two gentlemen to each other. They will complete within 3 months—I might say that this document encompasses almost all of the issues between the two countries and resolves those issues. A few lines remain to be drawn on maps, and the question of the settlements is to be resolved. Other than that, most of the major issues are resolved already in this document.

We will now sign this document as well.

[*At this point, President Sadat, Prime Minister Begin, and President Carter signed the second document.*]

23.

David G. Winter, Abigail J. Stewart, and David C. McClelland: Advantages of a Liberal Arts Education

One of the oldest ideas in education — it goes back at least to the time of Plato — is that a liberal arts education makes us think more clearly and act more wisely. In recent years, however, many have questioned whether this is really so. The three psychologist-authors of this article were strongly of the opinion that the answer to the question is yes, and that they had a way to prove it.

Source: *Psychology Today*, September 1978.

For more than 2,000 years, a liberal education has been the ideal of the West—for the brightest, if not for all, students. The tradition goes back to Plato, who argued in *The Republic* that leadership should be entrusted to the philosopher—"a lover not of a part of wisdom only, but of the whole . . . able to distinguish the idea from the objects which participate in the idea." More recently, in a World War II-era treatise, a Harvard University committee concluded that a liberal education best prepared an individual to become "an expert in the general art of the free man and the citizen." The report, which led to the introduction of Harvard's general education curriculum, concluded, "The fruit of education is intelligence in action. The aim is mastery of life."

In recent years, the fruit has spoiled and such high-sounding rhetoric has been increasingly challenged. Critics have charged that liberal arts education is elitist education, based on undefined and empty shibboleths. Caroline Bird, social critic and author, argues in *The Case Against College* that the liberal arts are a religion, "the established religion of the ruling class." Bird writes, "The exalted language, the universalistic setting, the ultimate value, the inability to define, the appeal to personal witness . . . these are all the familiar modes of religious discourse."

Students in the 1960s charged that such traditional liberal arts courses as "Western Thought and Institutions" and "Contemporary Civilization" were ethnocentric and imperialistic. Other students found little stimulation in a curriculum that emphasized learning to both formulate ideas and engage in rational discourse. They preferred, instead, to express themselves in experience and action; they favoured feeling over thought, the nonverbal over the verbal, the concrete over the abstract. In the inflationary, job-scarce economy of the 1970s, many students argue that the liberal arts curriculum is "irrelevant" because it neither prepares them for careers nor teaches them marketable skills. In its present form, moreover, liberal arts education is expensive education.

Partly in response to these charges and, more immediately, to faculty discontent, Harvard recently approved a redesigning of the liberal arts program. Faculty had complained that the growing numbers and varieties of courses had "eroded the purpose of the existing general education program." Students, they felt, could use any number of courses to satisfy the university's minimal requirements, making those requirements meaningless. The new core curriculum will require students to take eight courses carefully distributed among five basic areas of knowledge.* The Harvard plan proposed to give students "a critical appreciation of the ways in which we gain knowledge and understanding of ourselves." Plausible as this credo may be, it rests on rhetoric and not solid research evidence—like curriculum innovations of the 1960s.

In an era of educational accounting and educational accountability, it would be helpful to have a way of determining what the essential and most valuable "core" of a university education is and what is peripheral and mere tradition. What are the actual effects of a liberal education, this most persistent of Western ideals? It is sobering to realize that we have little firm evidence.

Against this background, we recently designed and carried out a new study to get some of the evidence. Our findings suggest that liberal arts education does, in fact, change students more or less as Plato envisioned, so that the durability of this educational ideal in Western civilization may not be undeserved. In our research, liberal education appears to promote increases in conceptual and social-emotional sophistication. Thus, ac-

*These are (1) letters and arts; (2) history; (3) social and philosophical analysis; (4) science and mathematics; (5) foreign languages and cultures.

cording to a number of new tests we developed, students trained in the liberal arts are better able to formulate valid concepts, analyze arguments, define themselves, and orient themselves maturely to their world. The liberal arts education in at least one college also seems to increase the leadership motivation pattern—a desire for power, tempered by self-control.

The precise content of a liberal education remains unclear. Is it the study of certain "core" disciplines or bodies of knowledge—courses in Western civilization or modern literature, or a particular set of "Great Books"? Does it require a multidisciplinary approach, as, for example, in courses entitled "Science and Responsibility" or "Freedom and Authority in the Modern Novel"? Many professors argue that the essence is not *what* is learned, but *how* it is taught—with an emphasis on concepts rather than facts, on independent inquiry rather than learning by rote. Some educators, perhaps half-facetiously, contend that liberal arts include everything that is not of obvious practical or vocational use!

The Harvard committee during World War II theorized that general education fostered four traits of mind: thinking effectively, communicating thought, making relevant judgments, and discriminating among values. Some 33 years later, the committee headed by present dean Henry Rosovsky characterized the goals of the liberally educated person in similarly luxuriant language: to "think and write clearly and effectively"; to have "some understanding of, and experience in thinking about, moral and ethical problems"; and to use experiences in the context of "other cultures and other times."

Still, these traits and skills remain

largely unmeasured and ignored by psychologists who, even when they study "thinking," focus on much more elemental and simple processes. Most of the abundant research on the effects of higher education have focused on changes in personality, values, and beliefs. Even here, the conclusions are largely equivocal: many college "effects" are due to the process by which the students were chosen in the first place and not to the changes that occur during college. Studies have shown, for instance, that attitudes are stabilized as much as they are altered during college.

We started our study from two fundamental premises: first, that the evidence to date was probably more a reflection of the testing procedures used than of the efficacy of higher education; and, second, that new tests should be modeled on what university students actually do rather than on what researchers can easily score. If liberal education teaches articulate formation of complex concepts, then student research subjects should be asked to form concepts from complex material and then scored on how well they articulate them, rather than being asked to choose the "best" of five concepts by putting a check mark in one of the boxes. In more formal terms, tests of the effects of education should be *operant* tests that require operating on material and making up answers, rather than *respondent* tests that merely ask for choices from among precoded alternatives.

Any study of the effects of higher education has the difficult task of distinguishing educational effects from simple maturational effects. In order to have some control over the effects of maturation, therefore, we tested students who were receiving three different *kinds* of higher education:

1. A traditional four-year liberal arts education at a prestigious Eastern U.S. institution. By any definition, students attending this school enjoy a curriculum that is considered liberal arts. It is a well-endowed, private college with a tradition of scholarly excellence, an eminent faculty, and great prestige. Its students, drawn from this country and abroad, must satisfy very competitive admissions standards. The college accepts 20 percent of all applicants. Approximately two-thirds of its students are men and one-third women. The curriculum emphasizes broad, interdisciplinary survey courses in the sciences, humanities, and social sciences, and individualized scholarship at all stages of the college career.

2. A four-year undergraduate program for training teachers and other professionals. The offerings at this state-controlled institution have been expanded in recent years to include such general and career programs as law enforcement and health education. The college's students, drawn from a large metropolitan area, must pass moderately competitive admissions standards; about one-half of those who apply are accepted. The student body is about evenly divided between men and women.

3. A two-year community college that offers career programs in data processing, electronics, nursing, secretarial skills, and business administration. A publicly controlled institution, our community college is situated in a city and draws most of its students from nearby suburbs. It has a relatively nonselective admissions policy, accepting about 70 percent of those who apply. The student body is 60 percent male.

We administered three kinds of tests to a total of 414 students, half men and half women, drawn from the first-year and last-year classes of the three colleges. We controlled statistically for intelligence and social class, to eliminate differences in performance based on these two characteristics. By comparing the test scores of first- and last-year students at each school, we hoped to determine the degree and nature of any changes brought about by the educational programs. By evaluating all three schools together, we hoped to find out whether the liberal arts school has a unique impact on its students.

With our new Test of Thematic Analysis, we examined the students' abilities to create and express sophisticated concepts. We asked them to read two groups of brief, imaginative stories, and then to describe the differences between the two in any way they liked. We awarded positive values to their work when they perceived characteristics of both story groups that could sensibly be compared and contrasted, used examples and qualifications to strengthen their arguments, legitimately redefined aspects of stories to support their theses, and found general categories to group apparently unrelated elements. When they compared unlike things or used affective and subjective phrasing such as "It makes the reader nervous" or "It left me satisfied," we awarded negative values.

At all three institutions, last-year students scored higher than first-year students, but seniors at the liberal arts college far outdistanced their counterparts at the teachers' and community colleges.

Thus, a typical freshman at any of the schools might describe the differences between the two groups of stories in rather wandering terms: "Group B stories are more exciting than Group A

stories. They were about nasty leaders and I don't like that. Group B stories show people as not trusting each other." A typical final-year student at our liberal arts college might put what is essentially the same contrast in these terms: "Both groups of stories involve relations to authority. In Group A, authority is either accepted or actively rejected; while Group B stories involve moderate suspicion of authority. While story A-4, an animal fable, might seem an exception to the rule, it does, in fact, fit if one considers the phrase 'king of the beasts' as representing symbolic authority."

Liberal education, then, seems to affect the way in which people marshal, organize, and "operate" on facts. These processes are spontaneous, self-initiated, and active, and are the same ones called for by an essay assignment to "compare and contrast the Renaissance and the Reformation," or an examination question asking, "What are the essential differences between normal and malignant cells?" We believe these processes are more central to a liberal education than learning simple concepts and memorizing detailed facts. Indeed, we gave the students an adaptation of a standard reading-comprehension test and found that none of the three schools significantly affected the ability to learn and remember isolated facts.

As another means of probing the conceptual processes and reasoning abilities of the three groups of students, Abigail Stewart devised an Analysis of Argument test. The test first quotes an extreme, unpopular, and rather badly argued position on a controversial issue. Students must attack this position and support their own stance with reasoned argument. Again, the quality of the attack improved from first to final year at all three schools, but more so at our liberal arts institution. Thus, a typical first-year student would dispute a series of facts: "*X* is wrong when he says that . . ." A final-year attack focused on a more abstract, general principle, such as faulty logic: "*X*'s arguments all derive from a confusion of association with causation."

In the second step of Stewart's test, students switched sides and had to defend the position they had formerly attacked. Most floundered and simply substituted a blank endorsement for a blanket attack. Only our final-year liberal arts students were able to craft a limited, qualified endorsement of a position they had opposed. They could respond: "While there are flaws in *X*'s whole line of reasoning, it must be admitted that some of his particular claims and examples are true." In other words, the liberally educated students were better able to argue both sides of a question, but with integrity and intelligence rather than by simply espousing the other point of view uncritically.

The other changes in student ability unique to, or more pronounced at, the liberal arts college involved measures in the Thematic Apperception Test (TAT), a "projective" test that clinicians have used for over 40 years to assess personality. Subjects see a series of vague and ambiguous pictures—a man wearing the uniform of a ship's captain talking with a man in a business suit, for example, or two women in lab coats using equipment such as a test tube—and must tell or write stories about the pictures. Researchers may use any number of scoring systems to analyze the results, depending on the personality characteristics that interest them. We were looking for three elements in the responses: self-definition, maturity of adaptation to the environment, and the leadership motivation pattern.

A story that scores high in self-definition uses causal words such as "because" and "in order to," and portrays characters who take actions for reasons, for example: "After being miserable for a while, the woman in the picture will realize that her love affair won't work and will leave." Low-scoring stories portray ineffective actions, events with no apparent causes, and characters who experience intense feelings in response to others' actions, but who are unable to act themselves: "The man and woman pictured will try desperately to establish a love relationship, but will end up feeling only more alone." In a number of studies, people who score high in self-definition act instrumentally (that is, effectively and constructively), often in ways that go beyond ascribed roles. Self-defining women, for example, tend to seek careers as well as marriage, and in many different ways are not limited by traditional sex roles. Thus, self-definition is associated with an instrumental, effective style of translating thought into action. When compared with the teachers' and community colleges, the liberal arts college produced unique and significant gains in student self-definition.

Maturity of adaptation to the environment refers to success in developing characteristics that personality theorists have identified as representing the highest levels of personality growth of maturity. Drawing on the ideas of Freud and Erik Erikson, who described the "stages" of development, Stewart recently worked out a TAT measure of this adaptation. As we expected, students at all these institutions showed higher stages of adaptation over time, but those at the liberal arts college showed larger, more significant gains.

In terms of particular scoring categories from the Stewart measure, this means that students, our liberal arts students in particular: (1) see authority in complex, versus simplistic, pro and con terms; (2) view other people as differentiated beings in their own right, rather than as simple means of gratifying their (the students') desires; (3) integrate both joy and sorrow into their moods; (4) are able to work without falling victim to passivity, self-doubt, or anxiety about failure.

Seniors at the teachers' and community colleges scored higher than freshmen in both maturity of adaptation and self-definition, suggesting that almost any kind of higher education, or even just physical and social maturation, has some influence on these variables. But for all measures, the gains at the liberal arts college were significantly greater.

It appears that the liberal arts college also fosters a unique pattern of motivation in its students: strong concern for power and weak concern for affiliation, combined with high self-control or ability to inhibit activity. Thus, the final-year liberal arts students wrote more TAT stories with the following combination of characteristics: (1) one character has an impact (or tries to) on another; (2) activity is restrained or inhibited— as indicated by the use of such words as "not" or "cannot"; and (3) characters do not show concern with establishing and maintaining warm, friendly relations with others.

David McClelland, of Harvard, has called this set of characteristics the leadership or "imperial" motive pattern. In a series of experiments, McClelland has demonstrated that it is usually found in individuals who are considered effective leaders—managers who have a talent for creating in their subordinates such qualities as high morale, a sense of responsibility, organizational clarity, and "team spirit." For, while the qualities of an imperial motive suggest that a person is not compassionate, they generally dictate that he will be fair, treating others in an impartial manner that subordinates seem to appreciate.

The present study of only three colleges limits inference and further speculation. We must study other liberal arts schools to discover whether they have the same impact on the students as the liberal arts college discussed here. The issue will likely be complex. Indeed, data we recently collected from another college similar to the liberal arts school we examined suggest that liberal education there increases self-definition, but decreases maturity and has little or no effect on the imperial pattern.

When we know more about what causes the kinds of changes in students detailed here, then our research can contribute to shaping educational policy. But who can say, from the evidence now at hand, that the effects of liberal education at our liberal arts college, or anywhere else, are caused by course requirements at all? It may be that the worth of an education at any school is determined more by the self-fulfilling anticipations and beliefs of faculty and students. We are currently seeking answers to these questions, taking our new test procedures to students at more than 15 different post-secondary-school institutions. During the next year or two, we hope to point to specific qualities of liberal arts colleges that leave their particular imprints on the students.

Still, the changes unique to, or enhanced by, attendance at our liberal arts college do establish at least a prima-facie case for education in the liberal arts. The pious goals and extravagant language of liberal arts educators must yet be analyzed, broken down into specific skills. With tests to measure student abilities in these skills, we can determine whether liberal arts education is doing what its proponents claim and how its performance can be improved.

24.

FRED FRIENDLY: The Public's Right to Know

One of the most bitter and divisive newspaper strikes in New York City's history ended on November 6, 1978, after 88 days. Radio, TV, and weekly magazines had thrived during the deadlock, and some interim newspapers had tried to fill the gap. But the gap could not be filled by these means, and the public became increasingly irritated by the intransigent pose of both sides in the dispute. In this article Fred Friendly, a professor of journalism at Columbia University, raised questions about the obligation of newspapers to continue publication short of a debacle.

Source: *The Wall Street Journal,* October 5, 1978.

"EXPLAIN SOMETHING to me about you journalists. You proclaim that you have the right to print stolen government secrets. You claim your right to withhold evidence from judges and juries exceeds the Sixth Amendment rights of a man on trial for his life. You say you would go to jail to protect my right to know. What's happened to my right to know during the last eight weeks?"

That question, or one like it, is asked every day by judges, grocery clerks, university presidents, doctors and one very angry teacher. A lady who is tired of reading two-day-old Die Zeits and the Yonkers Herald Statesman recently barked: "You make speeches about the First Amendment—do something about it." She was only half-kidding.

The question is a serious one, posed by people who favor neither side in New York's current newspaper strike.

The facts seem to be on the publishers' side—everyone recognizes the existence of feather-bedding in the pressroom—but the emotional specter of pickets protesting lost jobs still has poignant appeal. But the merits of the issues have little to do with the rising tide of anger against everyone responsible for robbing the world's greatest city of the essential stimuli to its central nervous system—information and probing news analysis. New Yorkers, fighting for their city's fiscal survival, amidst gubernatorial and congressional elections, untangling the strands of the Camp David summit, befuddled by a constitutional maze called the Farber case and the intricacies of a natural gas row in Congress, have been short-changed by their newspapers. The New York Times and The Daily News seem more anxious to win than to publish.

AP/Wide World

Professor Fred W. Friendly of the Columbia School of Journalism.

The labor-management questions are not new—machines can replace people and save money. But ancient equipment gives way to modern technology only under the pressure of long term accommodation and programmed attrition.

The presses may be overmanned, but trade union leaders risk their positions when they yield too much too quickly. The rank and file do not reward statesmanship when it forfeits their jobs.

NO VICTORS OR VANQUISHED

In moving from conflict to resolution, face saving is a central ingredient— there can be no victors or vanquished. In this confrontation one has the impression that the New York publishers, aware of Katharine Graham's crushing victory in The Washington Post strike of 1975, thirsted for an early knock-out. So they unilaterally revised work rules enabling them to reduce press crews by 40%, thus precipitating the strike.

But New York is not Washington. It is a union town whose shrewd if sometimes impossible labor leaders will not permit their members to commit a fatal error such as smashing the presses. Without such an incident the nearly 4,000 reporters, editors and other white-collar workers who comprise the Times, News and Post units of the Newspaper Guild are not likely to allow their Washington Post counterparts across picket lines.

As the calculated stalemate grows more bitter and the summer weeks become autumn months, the cynical strategy begins to emerge: "If we can hold out long enough we can break the back of the other side. Whatever the price to the news-starved reader, the rout of the opposition will be worth it."

But will it really be worth it? In 1962, a tragedy of errors and mismanagement on all sides extended a newspaper strike for 114 days. When it was over, four newspapers lay dying and fewer people would read the ones that survived.

The survivors swore it would never happen again. A. H. Raskin, who for 40 years chronicled labor disputes for The New York Times, wrote a post-mortem on the '62 strike: "Both sides see hope for an unspectacular but useful growth in mutual understanding through the joint industry board initiated last month by Mayor Wagner. They are confident that the board will produce answers for the difficulties raised by automation and antiquated machinery."

Sixteen years and 190 missed publication dates later, we know it didn't happen that way. "The integrity of newspapers may be too important to be left to profit maximizing owners and trade union hacks," one honored editor said.

What emerges is that publishers act just like other businessmen as they mouth platitudes about the people's right to know and their solemn rights under the First Amendment. But it is the truth behind those platitudes that makes a newspaper shut-down different from a steel or auto strike or one involving baseball umpires or garbagemen.

The difference may be that for 190 years newspapermen from Ben Franklin to Ben Bradlee have been telling themselves and the court that they are special, that they perform a unique and indispensable function. They argue that the Constitution itself grants them unique rights—privileges indispensable to the Republic.

Our nation has decided that there can be no prior restraints against publication of classified information unless the government can prove that publication would cause irreparable damage to the nation. Our libel laws are the most liberal in the world. The press is now battling for an absolute privilege to protect its sources of information.

On the business side, the Newspaper Preservation Act of 1967 permits exceptions to the antitrust laws. Special mailing rates date back to 1792, when it cost six or eight times more to mail a letter than it cost to mail a newsapaper. There was a time when newspapers resisted child labor laws and provisions of the Wages and Hours Act as violations of their First Amendment rights. Other privileges, from parking permits to press cards to the use of parkways closed to all other commercial traffic, are recognition of a special status reserved for newspapers.

The justification for such exemptions is rooted in the belief that they serve the cause of public awareness, the lifeblood of democracy. "Our rights are the public's rights," goes the newspaperman's refrain. If that is so, as most publishers and members of the Newspaper Guild argue, then is there not a moral obligation to maintain the continuity of serious newspapers?

If governments cannot stop publication, can labor disputes be permitted to do so? Whatever the faults of the unions, the current strike was not triggered by a demand for more pay or better working conditions, but by three newspapers, two of them highly profitable, exerting their collective clout to eliminate superfluous jobs and increase their net revenues.

Does a news organ which rationalizes its privileges as "a fourth branch of government" have a right to shut down in order to gain a financial advantage? Legally the answer is yes—morally the answer may be no.

A television station that permitted itself to be blacked out by a long labor dispute might well lose its license. Is there a moral license that absolves newspaper owners of the responsibility to go that extra mile to avert a strike? And how can the Newspaper Guild, which so often files amicus briefs in Supreme Court litigation involving free press issues, remain silent on a stopped press issue?

Newspapers are properly zealous in protecting their independence, but every institution must be accountable to someone. Editors and publishers always insist their accountability is to their readers, who will go elsewhere if the product does not measure up. But in most cities, where corporate monopolies dominate the news business, accountability by free-market competition is a mirage.

The present botched negotiation, complete with an adventure in labor relations Murdoch-style, indicates anew that scant cooperative planning exists in the newspaper industry. Although the three newspapers had agreed to bargain together in order not to be "whipsawed" by the unions, the Post, hungering for Columbus Day advertising, broke ranks. Mr. Murdoch agreed to match the terms negotiated with the Daily News and the Times on the pivotal issue of manning the pressrooms. The resulting pressure on the other two newspapers could prompt a settlement that does nothing to settle the basic problems of the industry.

ECONOMIC STUDY NEEDED

There needs to be a long-range study of the economic future of the American newspaper, examining all its technological, distribution and manpower revolutions. A reliable profile of the industry's coming decade may make possible the kind of foresight that will save money, face and jobs. Trying to negotiate settlements in the acrimonious heat of strike deadlines will only invite permanent discord.

Here in New York, where few newspapermen and even fewer citizens understand the anatomy of the dispute, both sides owe the public they protect innovative solutions to labor management problems in the news business. Since the rest of the press—particularly the broadcasters who have been profiting from the strike—has been sluggish in digging out the facts of the dispute, reliable fact-finding is vital.

The Council of Accountability, which 15 years ago promised to end all newspaper strikes, should be reconstituted and strengthened. If compulsory government arbitration is dangerous, as I think it is, there must at least be fact-finding, if not fact-finding with recommendations, so that the community, including the frustrated workers, can be made aware of what independent mediators might recommend.

Perhaps such nonbinding fact-finding, even with recommendations, would have achieved nothing but a postponement of the bitter and politicized stalemate, but at least it would have lifted the shroud of darkness which has prevented enlightened public opinion from becoming a force.

To do nothing is to deny newspapers their principal reason for being. It also makes mockery out of our ringing proclamation that we would go to jail to bring the news to the people. The present cavalier assumption that some settlement will magically emerge from our mutual suffering is a self-inflicted wound to the First Amendment.

25.

The Jonestown Tragedy

In November 1978 Congressman Leo J. Ryan and four aides visited Jonestown, a quasi-religious community established in the jungle of Guyana by the Rev. Jim Jones, the charismatic but paranoid leader of the People's Temple, a San Francisco-based cult. Ryan was investigating rumors that some members of the cult were being held against their will and that some were being subjected to physical and psychological abuse. When Ryan left Jonestown and journeyed to the small airport at Georgetown, he was followed by members of the cult. As he was about to board his plane, he and his aides were attacked. Ryan and several others were killed. When Jones learned that not all of the Ryan party had been murdered, he informed his followers that a previously rehearsed suicide ritual would be carried out. Babies were first given a cyanide-poisoned drink, then the others either willingly drank the deadly potion or were murdered. Only a few members of the cult escaped by fleeing into the jungle. When Guyanese police arrived at Jonestown after the airport murders they found over 900 corpses in and around the buildings. Jones had died from a bullet fired into his brain. Officials later discovered a cache of firearms, hundreds of passports stacked together, and $500,000 in U.S. currency; millions more had reportedly been deposited in bank accounts overseas. Reprinted below are several views of the tragedy as collected in a report prepared for the House Committee on Foreign Affairs.

Source: U.S. Government Printing Office, 1979.

LOG NO. 126:
Text of June 6, 1978
Cable from U.S. Embassy in Guyana
to U.S. Department of State

SUBJECT: People's Temple and the Community at Jonestown.

1. *Discussion.*—As the Department is aware considerable public, press and Congressional interest has been focused, over the last year, on the People's Temple settlement at Jonestown. Located in a remote part of northwest Guyana, this agricultural community consists of a group of American citizens thought to number in excess of 1,000 who have immigrated to Guyana from various parts of the U.S. The preponderance of attention has turned around the question of the welfare and whereabouts of individual members of the community raised by their next of kin in the U.S., either directly or by using the intermediary of various senators and congressmen.

2. Responding to this interest, the Embassy has established a procedure whereby one of the consular officers visits Jonestown on a quarterly basis to

perform routine consular functions and to communicate with various individuals within the community who may have been the subject of specific inquiries. (It should be noted that because of its remote location, travel to Jonestown from Georgetown and back requires some three to four days using the uncertain commercial transport facilities available. Travel to and from the site can be accomplished in one day but this requires that an aircraft be chartered and that ground transport from the nearest airstrip be provided by the nearest government of Guyana administrative office.) So far there have been three such visits and the procedure seems to be functioning satisfactorily.

3. During the consular visits it has been observed that the local Guyanese administration exercises little or no control over the Jonestown community, and that the settlement's autonomy seems virtually total. This is due to a variety of reasons which include the fact that the area in question is remote and thus the government's rather primitive administrative machinery is already overstrained by its obligations to the Guyanese citizens living in the region, as well as an understandable disinterest on the part of the local officials to bother with an apparently self-sufficient community of non-Guyanese who obviously are not actively seeking any extensive contact with the Guyanese environment in which their settlement is located.

4. What we have, therefore, is a community of American citizens existing as a self-contained and self-governing unit in a foreign land and which, for all intents and purposes, is furnishing to the residents all of the community services such as civil administration, police and fire protection, education, health care, etc., normally provided by a central government within its territory.

5. Given the nature of many of the inquiries, both private and congressional, concerning the welfare/whereabouts of various members of the residents of Jonestown, as well as many of the articles appearing in the press which have alleged that individuals were being held in the community against their will, the lack of any objective elected or appointed political presence in Jonestown raises a legal question which this mission is not qualified to answer.

6. The Embassy is not, of course, in a position to exercise any control over private American citizens: however, private Americans traveling to or resident in a foreign country are expected to observe and conform to the laws of the host government. Conversely, can the host government be obliged to extend its governmental control and the protection of its legal system over an individual or group of aliens residing within its territory?

7. *Recommendations.*—It is requested that the Office of the Legal Adviser review the situation described above, as well as other pertinent data concerning the People's Temple and the Jonestown community which are available in CA/SCS in the Department. If, after such review, and assuming that the answer to the question posed in the preceding paragraph is affirmative, it is requested that we be instructed to approach the government of Guyana at an appropriate level to discuss the People's Temple community and request that the government exercise normal administrative jurisdiction over the community, particularly to insure that all of its residents are informed and understand that they are subject to the laws and authority of the GOG and that they enjoy the protection of the Guyanese legal system.

LOG NO. 130:
Text of June 26, 1978
Cable from U.S. Department of State
in Response to June 6, 1978 Cable
from U.S. Embassy in Guyana

SUBJECT: People's Temple and the community of Jonestown.
Ref. Georgetown 1915.

1. Department can appreciate the uniqueness of the situation described in ref tel and the problems post has encountered in attempting to deal with this situation.

2. We agree with post's position set forth in paragraph 6 of ref tel and concur that host government has governmental jurisdiction over U.S. citizens and other aliens residing within its boundaries. Department assumes that both the Guyanese Government and the leader of the People's Temple are aware that the community is under the jurisdiction of the GOG and that all members of the community are subject to the laws and authority of the GOG. Department at present of view that any action initiated by the Embassy to approach the GOG concerning matters raised in ref tel could be construed by some as U.S. Government interference, unless Amcit member or family requests assistance or there is evidence of lawlessness within the community of Jonestown.

"JONESTOWN," *Michael Novak,*
American Enterprise Institute,
Reprint No. 94, March 1979

JONESTOWN: SOCIALISM AT WORK

IF JONESTOWN was a religious colony, why did it have no church, no chapel, no place of prayer? It had a day-care center, a school, a clinic. The religion of Jonestown was explicitly and unequivocally socialism, not Christianity. The cult in Jonestown was socialism. Jim Jones proclaimed mass suicide under the concept of "revolutionary suicide" and "suicide for the glory of socialism." He chose Guyana, the only socialist nation in Latin America, for his protective cover.

At his death, he was negotiating with the Soviet Union for a new home for his "experiment in socialism."

The evidence is overwhelming. But "progressive" writers in the press and in the public at large have failed to identify it, preferring to shuck the blame upon "fundamentalist religion." They do not wish to face the real supply of "true believers" today. Jim Jones easily fooled left-wing, progressive politicians. By his own testimony, Jonestown even fooled eyewitness Charles A. Krause of the *Washington Post,* author of *Guyana Massacre.* Right up until the time a bullet hit his leg, Krause says, he intended to write a piece describing how much he admired the ideals of Jonestown. The religion of Jonestown—as he saw it during two days—was in all its essentials the religion of progressive politics. He was impressed.

Krause tried to win the confidence of radical lawyer Mark Lane, as Lane tried to win his, by saying that he was "open-minded." Lane tried to give him favored access. Krause was captivated by two top aides of Jones, Sarah and Richard Tropp, veteran socialists and participants in the antiwar and civil rights movement. They explained how they had always hated American society. They loved Jonestown, they told him, because there they could build the experimental socialist community they had always worked for. For the Tropps, who were Jews, and others, Jonestown demanded no Christian commitment; its doctrine was "social change."

Other liberal politicians were just as easily fooled. Governor Jerry Brown, Lieutenant Governor Dymally, Mayor Moscone, the social action director for the Council of Churches (until, finally, he awoke, on religious grounds), and many in the liberal establishment of California were deceived by the ideals and principles of Jim Jones. How could they not be? He repeated back to them the catechism of radical politics. He could fill halls with enthusiastic political supporters. He could place 2,000 campaign workers in the fields. He gave money to radical causes. He controlled several thousand bloc votes. Radical politics was his religion, and it was in the air.

Even the name he chose was instructive. His Temple was not God's Temple. It was the People's Temple. Marcelline Jones told the *New York Times* in September 1977 that her husband was a Marxist who held that religious trappings were only useful for social and economic uplift. "Jim has used religion to try to get some people out of the opiate of religion," she said. She told how he had once slammed a Bible on the floor while exclaiming, "Marcie, I've got to destroy this paper idol."

"Neither my colleagues nor I are any longer caught up in the opiate of religion," Jones wrote in his organization's magazine, *People's Forum* (January 1978). After the "socialist suicides," two of his most trusted aides were dispatched with $500,000 to take to the Soviet embassy in Guyana.

Given a rude shock by nine hundred deaths, Krause dimly saw that he had gone to Jonestown as to a "Potemkin village," as so many "progressive" persons have gone to China, the Soviet Union, Cuba, and other socialist experiments over the years. The capacity of socialists to stage illusions for the true believers of the free world is always underestimated.

The techniques of indoctrination used at Jonestown were not original, but borrowed from those of other socialist experiments, in China, in the Soviet Union, in eastern Europe, in North Vietnam, and elsewhere. People were not permitted to emigrate. Family members were kept hostage. Egalitarianism was effectuated by force. "Socialization" was accomplished by breaking down the individual (bourgeois) ego, by public humiliation, by restricting permissible emotions. Experiments in socialism have, by now, a familiar pattern. Rhetoric which destroys the individual and exalts social consciousness clears the way for the socialization of all emotions and the surrender of individuality. The family is the main institutional defender against the collective; it must be destroyed. From being a bastion of privacy and individuality, sex must become publicly and socially administered.

The logic of socialism is anti-individualistic and leads, unless interrupted, to the submersion of the individual self. Egalitarianism is so opposed to the unequal patterns of natural gifts, to the variety and diversity of consciences, that it can only be imposed by force. Those who are attracted to socialism by its moral ideals—by a kind of religious feeling for equality and justice—find it hard to face its actual practical results. Of Jonestown, Mort Sahl said, "Socialists don't do that." The awful truth is that they do. Millions have died in our century showing that they do. In more places than Jonestown, socialism begins in mysticism and ends in terror. It is the fundamentalism of our time.

December 17, 1978

". . . AND WHAT GOVERNMENT CAN'T DO,"
William Raspberry,
Washington Post, *December 21, 1978*

ONE OF THE PERSISTENT threads running through conversations about the mind-numbing tragedy at Jonestown, Guyana, is that the U.S. government was somehow at fault.

The FBI, the CIA, the State Department—*somebody*—should have done something to stop Jim Jones and his followers before they went off the deep end.

Perhaps the clearest statement of the theme came in a recent column by Carl T. Rowan:

"The gruesome tragedy in Guyana is an appalling example of governmental failure to act," he wrote, "primarily because government officials are timid about breaching sanctuaries of 'religion' . . . .

"It is easy enough for the State Department, the FBI, the army and a host of other agencies to spring to action *after* a congressman and a news team are murdered and more than 700 [now at least 912] members of the People's Temple are found dead."

No less than Rowan and others who are faulting the timidity of the government, I wish the stupefying tragedy in Guyana could have been averted. Perhaps it could have been, if there had been some solid evidence that Jones had threatened beforehand to do in 900—or nine or even one—of his followers.

We did know some things that were deeply disturbing to a lot of us. We knew that Jones's followers seemed to have an unhealthy commitment to him, that thousands and thousands of dollars in Social Security and welfare checks were being endorsed over to the Peo-

AP/Wide World

Bodies of members of the People's Temple who died after their leader Jim Jones ordered them to drink a cyanide-laced soft drink. The vat that contained the poison is in the foreground.

ple's Temple, that hundreds of his members were signing their property to the organization and that there existed the opportunity for someone to become awfully rich as a result.

But what action would we have wanted the government to take?

Before answering that question with regard to Jim Jones and his People's Temple, ask yourself what government action you would recommend in the following situation:

You learn that a group of women, all of them single, many of them smilingly naive and some of them, quite frankly, "different," has been taken to some remote place and hidden away from the public view.

You learn that they have been talked into giving up their personal property for the good of the organization and that they now live in unbelievably modest circumstances, working long arduous hours for little or no pay. Even on those rare occasions when they are permitted to leave the compound, they must be accompanied by at least one other member.

For all you know, many of them may wish to escape, but perhaps they fear for their lives if they try to get away. Maybe someone has convinced them that some unspeakable thing worse than physical death will be their lot if they turn on their overseers. You simply don't know.

Question: Would you urge a government investigation of the organization to see what was going on? Or would you scream bloody anti-Catholic murder if the FBI raided the convent?

The point is, some things that look terrible when they are done by members of "cults" seem perfectly all right when they are done by members of established religions.

At what point does it become the government's role to decide which religious group is legitimate and which is only a "cult"?

Should Abraham have been convicted of attempted murder when he tricked his son Isaac up the mountain to do him in?

Should Moses have been brought up on charges for taking the children of Israel off into the wilderness, away from the fleshpots of Egypt, risking mass starvation in the process?

Should Jesus of Nazareth have been treated as a public threat (He *was* so treated) for talking ordinary hardworking citizens into quitting their jobs and abandoning their families in pursuit of His farfetched promises?

The point is not that Jim Jones (or Elijah Muhammed or Brother Gene Ewing or Rev. Ike) can be compared with Abraham, Moses or Jesus. The point is that all of these leaders were seen by their contemporaries as smooth-talking slicksters, and their followers were seen as naive fools.

But it is not against the law to be either slick or naive. The government must tread with great care in protecting people who do not wish to be protected.

And it must be a thousand times more careful when the impulse is to protect people from what appear to be misguided religious beliefs.

A lot of things went wrong—inside Jim Jones's head, among his followers and in the American society at large— to produce the tragedy at Jonestown.

But I'm not sure it's fair to lay much of the blame at the feet of governmental "timidity."

There are some things the government can't do for us—and shouldn't even try.

In New York, Oric Bovar, a 59-year-old former opera coach who asserted that he was Christ, was found praying over the decomposing body of a follower [of Jones] who had died of cancer and was charged with failing to report a corpse. On April 14, 1977, the day he was to stand trial, he jumped from a 10th-floor window and killed himself. He had once said, according to some reports, that if he jumped out a window, God would bounce him back.

The New York Times, January 21, 1979

The seventh launch of the space shuttle and the second lift-off of the *Challenger*. The crew included a woman, Sally Ride, for the first time in space from the United States; the mission lasted six days.

WARFARE AND SPACE

The Apollo program put men on the Moon in July 1969. This, along with the other striking achievements of the American space program, accustomed the American public to success in whatever the National Aeronautics and Space Administration (NASA) attempted. Television first amazed the world with live pictures of men walking on the Moon's surface, and later it brought to a worldwide audience intriguing pictures of Mars, Jupiter, and Saturn, relayed by unmanned space probes. To be sure, there were some setbacks in the space program. The most serious was the fire in which three astronauts died in 1967. Generally, however, success became so routine that the public began to lose its fascination with the frequent launchings of new satellites and the space shuttles. It was taken for granted that the technological expertise of the United States had worked out all the bugs and removed as far as possible the element of danger from manned space flights. The shuttles, with such names as *Columbia*, *Discovery*, and *Challenger*, seemed to promise so much in the way of new scientific undertakings. In an era when so much seemed wrong with government, it was a comfort to have an agency like NASA where everything seemed to go right. Then, suddenly, these aspirations turned to dust on one January morning in 1986. The whole American space program was put in jeopardy, and the brilliance of NASA's technology was called into question.

Those who were present at Cape Canaveral on the morning of January 28, 1986, got the shock at first hand. The impact on television viewers was almost as immediate. The space shuttle *Challenger* lifted off at 11:38 AM. About 75 seconds later the space shuttle blew up, killing all seven crew members. The best known of the crew was a high-school teacher from New Hampshire, Christy McAuliffe. The *Challenger* explosion was the worst disaster in the American space program. It sent the nation into mourning and postponed indefinitely all other launchings. McAuliffe was supposed to teach a lesson from space; all her pupils, and thousands of other pupils from other schools, would be watching her on TV. Six weeks later, when the remains of the command module were found under 100 feet of clear Caribbean water, it was learned that the part of the vessel where Christy McAuliffe had sat had been obliterated in the first explosion. In a waterproof plastic case, in another part of the water, her notes were found.

(Top) A NASA ice inspection team took this photo on the launch pad of the ill-fated *Challenger* on the morning of the final launch; (bottom left) the space shuttle *Challenger* as it lifts off moments before the explosion; (bottom right) the two solid rocket boosters continue to thrust away from the fire as the vehicle breaks up; the orbiter itself, engine still firing, is at the bottom of the photo.

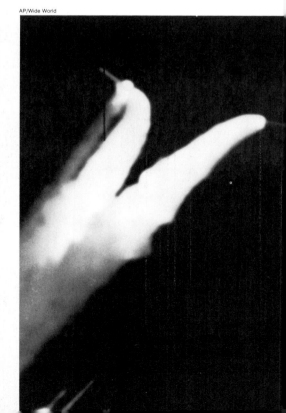

Crew members of the *Challenger* were, front row, left to right: Michael J. Smith, Francis R. (Dick) Scobee, and Ronald E. McNair; second row, Ellison S. Onizuka, Sharon Christa McAuliffe, Gregory Jarvis, and Judith A. Resnik. After the loss of *Challenger*, NASA suffered other setbacks as well, and by the summer of 1986 it was evident that the United States no longer had—for the moment at least—the capacity to launch anything, to say nothing of 2,200-ton space shuttles. There were military consequences of the disaster: the ability to spy on the Soviet Union and to deploy Star Wars satellites was at least temporarily impaired. There were commercial consequences as well. One of the main tasks of the shuttles had been to deploy new communications satellites and to reorient satellites that had drifted out of orbit. Without this capacity, it was possible that the quality of overseas telephone service would decline. It was possible, too, that television transmission would become too crowded on the remaining operational satellites.

(Top) Official portrait of the *Challenger* crew; (center) debris from the shuttle hauled up from waters 70 feet deep; (bottom) two mission specialists share a repair job on a satellite later lifted back into space from an earlier shuttle.

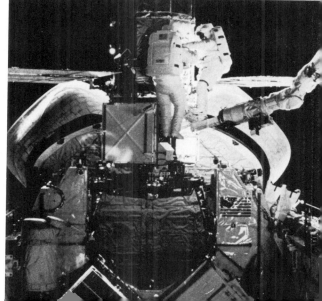

The Titan rocket has been a workhorse of the U.S. government space program. Though it saw use as space launch vehicles for research, its main use has been for military purposes, lifting spy satellites into space and being armed with warheads as intercontinental ballistic missiles (ICBMs). The Titan rocket has had at least one major failure. On September 19, 1980, at an underground missile silo in Arkansas, an accident occurred. A maintenance technician had dropped a three-pound socket wrench, which fell 71 feet and ruptured the missile's first-stage fuel tank. Toxic vapors began to fill the chamber, and despite valiant efforts to put out a fire in one of the engines, the missile exploded after six hours. The 10-megaton warhead was thrown 750 feet but did not detonate. Technicians denied that there had ever been any further danger because the warhead was equipped with a fail-safe device. Ten megatons means that the force of the warhead, if it had exploded, would have been equal to 10,000 tons of TNT. The Titan carried one warhead, while MX missiles, or Peacekeeper missiles, which came into use in 1986, carried several warheads, which could strike different targets. Multiple warheads have the appearance of several little black dunce caps, as evidenced by the photo of the nose cone of an MX Pathfinder, right. By the mid-1980s both the United States and the Soviet Union possessed many thousands of warheads. The British, French, and Communist Chinese governments also had nuclear warheads, as did a small number of other countries. In any case, there were enough such warheads in the world to create a real anxiety about the potential for nuclear war and to press the urgency for international agreements to stem the nuclear threat.

(Opposite top) Missile silo after the explosion of the Titan II rocket in 1980; (bottom) a Titan rocket explodes and sends flaming debris over Vandenberg Air Force Base seconds after launch. (Top) The successful first flight test of the Peacekeeper MX missile in 1983; (bottom) technicians place cones on the top of an MX Pathfinder missile's ring.

AP/Wide World

U.S. Air Force

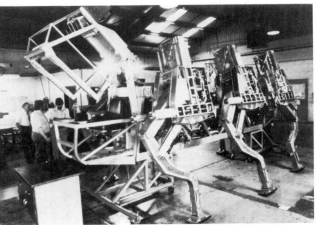

Missiles and rockets are not the only weapons that occasionally fail. There were numerous news stories in the 1980s about weapons that did not work and about the enormous cost run-ups of simple, hardware-store items. The Sergeant York tank (top left) is a case in point. With all of the brilliant technology that went into designing it, the tank was hard to drive, it overheated inside when the sun shone on it, and it broke down much too often. It was named, ironically, after a World War I infantryman, Alvin York, who captured 39 German soldiers single-handedly, with a single sub-machine gun cradled in his arms. When asked how he did it, he replied: "I surrounded 'em." Such a low-tech solution was a distant notion by the mid-1980s, when the armed forces sought out the most advanced new weapons systems. Some of them looked like they were derived from science fiction films, such as prototypes for mechanized transport (middle left) or highly complex ships that support guided missiles (bottom left). But the armed forces still must depend on personnel who are well-trained, well-armed, and experienced, such as the Special Forces ranger on the opposite page. In the long run wars are won or lost by human beings, who must be able to face death and still do their job.

(Top) The Sergeant York tank was declared a failure after seven years of development at a cost of $1.5 billion; (center) an experimental six-legged walking machine for rough terrain being developed at Ohio State University; (bottom) the guided missile frigate *Rentz*. (Opposite top) A Texas National Guard crew on maneuvers in Honduras is halted by a herd of cattle; (bottom) the army Special Forces are skilled rangers, paratroopers, demolitionists, and underwater men.

AP/Wide World

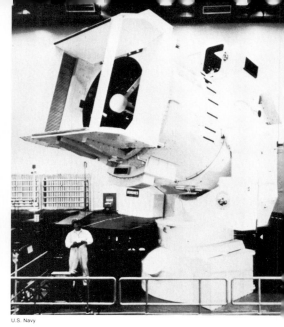
U.S. Navy

(Top left) U.S. Marines demonstrate a model of a new laser device that pinpoints targets for laser-guided weapons; (top right) a high-energy laser-beam director developed by Hughes Aircraft for the Navy; (bottom) an artist's conception of an Army Homing Overlay Experiment that tracks a target and destroys it.

Dept. of Defense

On March 23, 1983, President Reagan addressed the nation to announce what he called a strategic defense initiative (SDI), which would theoretically have the ability to destroy oncoming missiles from space. Because SDI was mainly a space-based system, it was quickly dubbed "Star Wars," after the movie of that name. Star Wars technology, the merits of which have been vigorously debated, are dependent on the use of lasers. Theoretically, laser beams could ward off, misguide, or pre-detonate any number of missiles heading toward the United States. Many scientists think the idea is no more than wishful thinking, but that does not mean that lasers are any the less useful. Some lasers are so incredibly powerful that they harness energies comparable to those of the Sun. Star Wars, if it is developed, might use less exotic means of intercepting enemy missiles. The artist's conception at right shows a device that could be shot into space and nip the warheads of any missiles that strayed into its path. The artist conceived this particular device some years ago.

1979

26.

The Reopened Door: Reestablishment of Relations with China

In a surprise announcement from Beijing and Washington on December 15, 1978, China and the United States declared that they would establish full diplomatic relations as of January 1, 1979. In a televised address in December, President Carter said the United States would recognize the government in Beijing "as the sole legal government of China." He added: "Within this context the people of the United States will maintain cultural, commercial and other unofficial relations with the people of Taiwan." At the end of January 1979, Vice Premier Deng Xiao-ping, the de facto leader of China, arrived in Washington at the start of a nine-day visit to the country. He met with President Carter for two days and on January 31 signed agreements for cultural and scientific exchanges; Deng noted that "there are many more areas of bilateral cooperation and more channels waiting for us to develop." Among the most important of these was trade. A nation of more than one billion persons constituted a potential new market for American exporters; at the same time, the Chinese could now look to the technological leader of the West for the solutions to some of their problems. Reprinted here are two discussions of the trade potential of the two countries, the first by George H. Dixon, a Minneapolis banker, the other by Sen. John Heinz, Republican of Pennsylvania.

Sources: *Vital Speeches of the Day*, November 15, 1979.

Senate Documents (Committee on Finance), November 15, 1979.

A: GEORGE H. DIXON:
SPEECH, DULUTH, MINNESOTA,
OCTOBER 29, 1979

IT IS THE CONSENSUS of most China watchers that the momentous event of the death of Chairman Mao has re- sulted in a fundamental change in the way that China views both itself and the rest of the world. But even before Mao died, there was as you know some tentative edging in the West's direction — sending Russian advisors home in the early 1960's, Kissinger's secret trip to visit Mao and Chou En-lai, then President Nixon's visit in 1972, the ping-pong days, and then rather cautiously yet quickly the opening of China's doors to a few, then more and more visitors from America. By a stroke of luck, I was one of those early and fortunate few who visited mainland China in 1975 in the company of then Minnesota Governor Wendell Anderson. Those of us on that trip who may have needed to do so learned very quickly what our young friend in the story discovered to his embarrassment; that the Chinese people are a warm, lively, energetic, alert and intelligent race and with a simply enormous economic potential, a potential which in the course of the next 25-50 years may come to full fruition now that this great country seemingly has begun to join the modern world.

No one, least of all the Chinese themselves, knows whether this pragmatization of the ancient nation of China will endure long enough to rival the dynasties, or even be a long-term trend. There is so much about China that remains unknown — some might even say unknowable. Virtually all of the hard data, the numbers we have on China, for example, are very uncertain. We must remember, too, when we study China that we are looking at an ancient eastern world through modern western eyes. The Chinese are, as a people, patient and poetic. We are impatient and pragmatic. We want hard facts and instant analysis and China defies both. The Chinese have a saying that aptly describes our desire to observe and deal with China. It is like, the saying goes, "trying to see wild flowers from a galloping horse." At the moment at least it seems a good bet that the turn to pragmatism and to the West will continue for a long time. That view rests more than anything else on two fundamental points.

One is the Chinese fear of Russia — a fear which is father to a perception by the Chinese rulers that rapid scientific and technical progress is the only way to meet the mounting challenge of the country which is regarded as China's ultimate enemy. The second fundamental is a sense of urgency born from within. It comes from the rising expectations of the Chinese people for a better life, sooner rather than later.

These two bedrock issues have fostered a commitment by China's leaders Deng Xiao-ping and Hua Kuo-feng to a program of modernization, one that's been labeled a "second revolution" or the "four modernizations"—of industry, agriculture, science and technology, and the military.

The change, coming as rapidly as it has, carries risks of course. There are bound to be tensions, from ideologists, the "believers" of the teachings of Chairman Mao; there must be dozens or hundreds of millions of them pulling and tugging at the country's social fabric. The Maoist Revolutionary Ideology over the last 30 years or so has developed a highly refined framework of thought and social order. In abandoning that framework for pragmatism, a new thought and social framework of substance and depth hasn't yet at least been put in its place.

China's leaders know that rapid strides toward their goals demand that they maintain social and political stability. For the immediate years ahead, to do so will at times be no easy task. There is an old Chinese saying which a recent story about that country in *The New Yorker* magazine reminds us. It is "when the snow thaws, the road is muddy."

Also part of this issue is that China's new leaders have encouraged the hope of rising expectations and as a consequence they are under great pressure to perform. But even if they are perceived to have failed and are replaced, or if their successors are simply appointed in the natural order of things it seems to me that those successors are likely to be equally pragmatic, with the same assignment; rapid and fairly dramatic efforts to bring China into the modern world, in a leading role.

China has many geopolitical parallels with the United States and the rest of the Western World.

For example, China needs food, and the West can provide it.

It needs huge amounts of capital to build virtually everything . . . its infrastructure first, then all the rest.

It needs personal productivity incentives which are truly effective.

It must modernize its defense capability.

Everywhere, from village to city, technology is desperately needed.

The entire system of higher education has lain dormant for decades, and must be reconstructed. This element of China's program is obviously essential if the managers and leaders of the rest of this second revolution are to be found.

During that lost decade before Mao's death, China's universities were decimated. Now the ruling regime is turning abroad to aid in its intellectual rebirth. Foreign scientists and other scholars are being welcomed to teach and lecture in Chinese universities. Foreign management consultants are being employed. And Peking is sending thousands of the nation's brightest students abroad to study in Japan, Western Europe and the U.S.

Energy and transport are also major bottlenecks in China today. Take rail transportation for example. If you superimpose a map of the U.S. rail system over that of China — incidentally the Chinese land mass is only about 4 percent larger than the continental 48 states — it is remarkable to see the tightly woven fabric of U.S. rail lines, most built in the early part of this century, and the thin, scattered lines across the Chinese landscape, many constructed since 1949 and serving 4 to 5 times our population.

Let's take a more specific look at the goals China is pursuing.

China says it means to join the front rank of industrialized nations by the year 2000 — about 20 years away.

Over the next six years, the PRC hopes to achieve 85 percent mechanization of agriculture, and to build or complete 120 large-scale industrial projects . . . including 10 iron and steel complexes, nine nonferrous metal complexes, eight coal mines, 10 oil and gas fields, 30 power stations, six new trunk railroads, and five key harbors. Moreover, light industry will be upgraded and export production expanded.

Large-scale imports of foreign industrial goods, technology and services must obviously play a key role in the pursuit of these goals . . . and, after years of stagnation, imports are projected to grow at an annual rate of 25 percent, to reach an estimated $50 billion by 1985.

You might have noticed I said "pursuit" of these goals rather than "attainment." That's because most western analysts believe, as do I, that the Chinese will have to scale down a great many of these targets in the coming years.

Nevertheless, the Chinese have begun their rapid march into the present and, for this journey, as I have suggested, the West is a far more logical travelling companion than is Russia and its satellites.

China's opening door to the West is a clear indication that its leaders agree that the West must be the source of knowledge and assistance in this modernization program. Already, fully 80 percent of all China's trade is with noncommunist nations.

So, given all that, what are the near-term prospects for trade with the PRC?

I say this is a coin with two sides, one dull and the other shiny.

First, the dull side.

The initial euphoria and excitement in the U.S. about the prospects for large volumes of trade with China is fading. Business people here are finding that the door to China is open only part way, that it's a narrow squeeze to get in and probably will remain so for some time to come. Accounts of the experiences of a delegation of business people from the twin cities, sponsored by the Minneapolis Chamber of Commerce, who have been visiting China this month seem to confirm this assessment.

This initial China trade fever happened just before and during Chairman Deng's recent visit to America, and it may well be that the Chinese themselves helped to create the overblown expectations in order to generate more competition for their favor, and thus more favorable terms for their nation.

A recent CIA study demonstrates convincingly that China's modernization goals are indeed overly ambitious, as I've mentioned.

The reality is that 70 percent of the labor force in China is still engaged in agriculture and that even the so-called modern industries there are decades out of date.

The rulers have said their modernization plan would cost $660 billion through 1985, and that's made much of the West skeptical that the Chinese can pay the bill.

From all I've seen, it is apparent that the Chinese are continuing to study and devise their analysis of where they are, where they want to be and how they are going to get there. Estimates of China's borrowing plans range from the U.S. Commerce Department's of $15-25 billion to a Japanese estimate of $200 billion. So as we scale down our total economic forecasts for China, we should scale down our trade expectations as well.

This year's estimated U.S.-China trade of $2 billion, a record high, will be largely food and grain shipments from America. Even if U.S. exports to China total $10 billion over the next five years, this is still well below our sales to Africa during the past five years.

Trade involves both import and export, and China's export potential is limited, too, by the same antiquated industrial technology it means to modernize.

In addition to the capital formation problem I've mentioned, the need to modernize military technology and capacity will drain many of the resources that might otherwise be turned toward more productive development.

China's opportunity to develop tourism will be restrained by a lack of transportation and accommodations that meet Western standards.

Oil export potential is limited because much of the PRC's current domestic production is needed for domestic use, and because Chinese crude has a heavy wax content. This makes it less desirable in nations whose refineries are equipped to handle lighter crudes, and which have heightened environmental concerns and restrictions.

There are other limitations to growth and, thus, to trade capacity.

Under Chairman Mao, China had a highly-centralized planning system, and it retains a large, entrenched bureaucracy. If progress is to occur, much decision-making must be decentralized, and priorities must be set . . . all of which will take a great deal of time, it would appear.

Scientific and managerial know-how are sorely wanting, as I've indicated, and the rebuilding of the managerial, scientific and technical skills will not occur overnight, even with western help.

Many of the present generation of Chinese have been raised under a system of communist ideology, and so do not now grasp the dynamics of capitalism, with its emphasis upon private initiative, competition, incentives and only partially-controlled markets. Moreover, millions of Chinese, particularly those who remember the "cultural revolution," must be bewildered, confused and cynical about the turn toward the West when so recently and for nearly 30 years it was we, the "imperialist, capitalist dogs" who were the barbarians, the ultimate enemy, the oppressors — when it was socialism that was superior, when it was part of one of the great social experiments in world history, where materialism was denounced. Small wonder if they proceed cautiously with the new themes, concerned about getting caught off base when and if the next turn of the political wheel comes.

The Chinese are by nature a conservative and frugal people who move carefully, especially in international affairs. So within the Chinese character there must be an internal contradiction in this desire to move ahead rapidly to modernization and to the knowledge and cultural barriers that must be dismantled and reassembled. Many people, Henry Kissinger among them, have noted that in its long, long history China has lived for centuries apart from much of the rest of the world, that many Chinese would still prefer it that way and that it is the fear of the Russian bear and only that that drives them toward us. Should that fear disappear, withdrawal within itself could occur again, though I must say that in a world which becomes daily more interdependent that seems more and more economically and politically difficult and therefore unlikely.

This cautiousness in foreign affairs, of course, stems from centuries of foreign exploitation of China. And it remains embodied in a clause in the modern Chinese constitution, which states that the nation's resources can't be appropriated to foreign powers.

Thus, embracing a capitalistic ideology and entering into joint ventures, for example, to achieve modernization goals cannot be automatic and easy for the Chinese mind.

So it seems clear that forecasts for dramatic increases in trade by 1985 are very likely to prove unrealistic. Knowledgeable China watchers believe that a 10 to 12 percent rate of real economic growth and trade per annum is closer to the mark.

I said this coin of China trade has two sides, and I think there is indeed a shiny side, too.

The Chinese are a lively, intelligent, energetic people. It is well-known that overseas Chinese are often the leaders of commerce and industry in the countries where they live.

A great many Chinese have been extremely successful in a capitalistic, free-market, profit-oriented culture.

The Chinese certainly have the ability to learn the Western system of business, trade and commerce very quickly. And they seem committed to do so. . . .

From the day Marco Polo arrived in China, the West has been fascinated with the Chinese people and the nation of China. Our fascination continues, but we are closer today than ever before to truly welcoming that magnificent, poor, backward, enormously interesting nation, whose human and natural resources have such unimaginable potential, into the ranks of the modern industralized world.

B: SEN. JOHN HEINZ:

STATEMENT CONCERNING RESOLUTION
TO APPROVE EXTENSION OF U.S.-CHINA
TRADE AGREEMENT, NOVEMBER 15, 1979

THIS AGREEMENT is important not just because it represents improved relations with the People's Republic of China, but because it also represents a major turning point in the development of economic relations with Communist nations.

I hope to be able to support this agreement, just as I have supported establishment of diplomatic relations with the PRC, although I have consistently disagreed with the way this Administration has handled that action. It is important, however, that such relations be established. As we have learned throughout the post-war period, progress and change come through contact, through discussion and exchange of ideas, through exchange of products as a result of trade. To open such doors to the PRC is not only to accept present reality, it is to influence the future by bringing the Chinese into the marketplace—of ideas as well as commodities.

At the same time, however, opportunities bring both promises and problems. We have the promise of better political relations expanding trade to the mutual benefit of both nations. We have the problem of potential trade disruption through import surges from this new market source, and through artificial pricing by an economy controlled by the government, where prices can be set to achieve political goals as well as economic ones, and where both lead far away from a free market climate.

It is this program I want to examine more closely in this hearing. We have sought to meet this challenge in one very important area—textiles and apparel—through the imposition of quotas when bilateral negotiations did not produce the desired result, and I am confident my colleagues at this hearing will be pursuing that issue in some detail. There are also other specific areas, such as ceramics and glassware, and mushrooms, that we should discuss.

Beyond particular commodities, there is also the conceptual problem of fitting various possible trade practices by a nonmarket economy such as the People's Republic into the legal framework we have established for dealing with unfair practices by our traditional, free market trading partners. Application of our dumping and countervailing duty laws is difficult when prices and costs are set by the government, and where the amount of a subsidy in an economy where everything is owned by the state is impossible to determine.

The Treasury Department has sought to cope with the problem through regulations, and the Congress has dealt with it though section 406 of the Trade Reform Act of 1974. Both approaches, in my view, are inadequate and in need of overhaul.

To stimulate public debate on such an overhaul, Senator Roth and I recently introduced S. 1966, which embodies new approaches to the problem of nonmarket economies and makes major changes in section 406 and the Antidumping Act of 1921. We introduced this bill to bring this issue to public attention. We are not irrevocably attached to every detail. We are, however, determined to see the issue debated and discussed, precisely because of the problems posed by this agreement and others which might be waiting in the wings. Today's hearing is an initial opportunity to raise some of these questions.

27.

Three Mile Island and the Future of Nuclear Energy

On March 28, 1979, a major nuclear accident occurred near Harrisburg, Pennsylvania, when the cooling system of the No. 2 reactor at the Three Mile Island nuclear power plant malfunctioned. On March 30 it was announced that a catastrophic meltdown of the core was possible. By April 2 the situation had stabilized and on April 9 Harold Denton, director of nuclear reactor regulation for the NRC, announced that the crisis was over. That may have been true at Three Mile Island, but it was not true for the nuclear power industry as a whole. For some time prior to the March 28 accident it had been fighting a rearguard action against antinuclear forces; after it, the industry's prospects were bleak indeed. Reprinted here are a strong statement in behalf of nuclear power by Sen. James A. McClure (R-Idaho) made a few weeks before the accident, and a "guest editorial" response to the accident by Ken Bossong summarizing the view of the Center for Science in the Public Interest.

Sources: *Vital Speeches of the Day,* March 1, 1979.

Chemical and Engineering News, May 1979.

A: SEN. JAMES A. McCLURE:
SPEECH, WASHINGTON, FEBRUARY 2, 1979

IN THE EARLY DAYS of nuclear power, the scare tactic was the threat of atomic power plants becoming atomic bombs. After that nonsense was discredited, the anti-nuclear types began the campaign about how deadly the radiation was that was emitted by these power plants. This, too, was thoroughly discredited, as was the subsequent scare campaign about how the cooling water discharges would boil our nation's rivers and lakes, destroying all fish and plant life. So, pre-1977, the nation was moving ahead with development of nuclear energy, despite the continuing propaganda efforts and guerilla attacks. But, then the anti-nuclear movement finally discovered a winning combination: (1) stop the breeder reactor program, using phony press releases concerning plutonium, (2) stop spent nuclear fuel reprocessing, while making vague threats about terrorists who somehow are immune to radiation, (3) create serious doubts as to the future availability of spent fuel storage facilities, and (4) cripple the opportunities for our domestic nuclear industry to survive through exports, using the reality that such prohibitions actually *increase* the threat of proliferation.

I believe that we are all aware of the success that each of these tactics has enjoyed. But, why, we should ask ourselves, do the opponents of nuclear energy continue to successfully advance, even though the facts, data, evidence, and realities concerning nuclear energy discredit their positions? The answer, I believe, lies in Congress.

The *proponents* of nuclear energy have surrendered the moral issues involved, the *opponents* have wrapped themselves in the invisible emperor's cloak of righteousness. They have assumed the role of good, while casting the proponents as evil. The validity of this proposition can be demonstrated by talking with some of the men and women who *support* nuclear energy.

Even while disagreeing with the anti-nuclear crowd, they still ascribe to them pure and sincere motives. They are just "misguided idealists," trying to save mankind, even though they do not have all their facts straight. The supporters, on the other hand, are imagined as being concerned with "only" such self-serving worries as jobs and profits. It is time that the record be set straight. This battle for the survival of nuclear energy cannot be won while conceding the moral position to the opposition.

It is indeed ironic that the moral defense offered for the American nuclear energy program comes from a Russian. Of course, he is no ordinary Russian. He is Andrei Sakharov, a Nobel Peace Prize winner in 1975 and prominent advocate of international disarmament, including the banning of nuclear weapons.

Doctor Sakharov has summarized the issue perfectly, regarding the development of nuclear energy. In his own words, "It is not just a question of comfort or maintaining what is called 'the quality of life.' It is a more important question—an issue of economic and political independence, of maintaining freedom for your children and your grandchildren."

And that is the decision before us today. Will the United States and its allies have the nuclear energy required during the decades ahead for national independence and military defense, or will we continue our disastrous increasing dependence on outside energy sources?

Continued American dependence on Middle East oil does not benefit us or the Arabs or our other allies. It serves the best interest of only one nation—the Soviet Union. Reducing this dependence is essential if we are to maintain our ability to discourage Soviet aggression, not to mention preventing further decay of our dollar and our national economy. . . .

When you debate the issue of nuclear energy, you are actually debating the issue of growth. Growth will be the key issue for the remainder of this century, and it is the resolution of that issue which will determine the lifestyles of most Americans for generations to come. To fully understand the implications of this debate, it is useful to take a look at who the opponents of growth are. Tom Wolfe has called them the "me generation," and Herman Kahn terms them "the new class." They often call themselves consumerists or environmentalists. Whatever label is used, however, what this group represents is an affluent, politically active, college-educated minority whose influence is far out of proportion to its numbers. This is partly because the members of this group often occupy key positions in the media and in federal agencies through which they can act on their beliefs and publicize them.

What then are they looking to do? First and foremost, the advocates of this "new class" philosophy want to limit economic growth. In a sense this is ironic, as they are the beneficiaries of the growth which has taken place to date. Having reaped the benefits of an expansionary economy, though, they are beginning to question the merit of further expansion. This is because they see such expansion as infringing on their ability to enjoy the material benefits they have been able to acquire. Perhaps I can draw an example which will make this more clear. If, for example, I, as a member of this group have been able to purchase a fast, sleek sports car in which I can experience the joys of motoring, I might not want to see too many more such automobiles on the road, because then there would be a traffic jam which would limit my capacity to enjoy the machine. If I have a cabin on a lake in the woods, I might not want to see others build in my area because they might infringe on my privacy. If I have a home in a comfortable neighborhood, with good schools, I might not want to see further development in my area so that the schools will remain uncrowded. The point is, of course, that one of the characteristics of this "new class" is to want to limit growth so that no one else's enjoyment of the goods of society will infringe on their own. . . .

On the surface, what this new class is advocating is a return to a simpler, less hectic existence. On the surface, at least, it is certainly attractive. It is a pastoral vision, out of late 19th century England, with every man a country squire. The only problem is that during this period every man was not a squire, and their vision bears no resemblance to what the society they advocate would really be like.

What their society, which they term a stable state economy, would resemble, would be more akin to the feudal era than to the last period of the industrial revolution. The reason is that an economy which does not grow makes no allowance for upward mobility. Of necessity, it would result in the creation of a permanent underclass. Were it imposed on our economy, those who were only just attaining the American dream would be the ones condemned to that fate.

How then, does the concept of a stagnant economic system relate to the question of energy advocacy? The answer simply is that economic growth has been inextricably linked to the growth of the supply of energy throughout history. The advocates of the stable state economy realize that if they can control the supply of energy, they can control the rate at which an economy is to grow. Energy is the one crucial variable in any economic system. You see, no matter what the cost of energy, a way can be found to pay for it. This lesson has been well learned in both Europe and Japan, both of which experience far higher energy costs than does the United States. In the case of these nations, adjustments have been made, and methods of conservation have been instituted.

On the other hand, if energy is not available, nothing can make up for its absence. For this reason, control of the supply of energy is tantamount to control of the economy. This, in turn, would give the Federal Government an unprecedented ability to control individual lifestyles. . . .

The most important thing to remem-

UPI/Bettmann

Three Mile Island nuclear power plant.

ber is to speak out. The only reason for the current advantage enjoyed by the advocates of the new class philosophy is that too many of us have been complacent. We have stood by and let the other fellow do it. For most of you in this room this is not the case, as you have already been involved in advocacy in some fashion, but that is not enough. Now is the time for you to go out and get your friends, neighbors, co-workers, and others who agree with you to add their voices to the debate.

Finally, don't let yourself be intimidated by the other side. They love to make statements they don't have to back up. Make them back them up. They love to use figures which have no basis. Challenge them. They love to talk about energy options which will be available in the middle of the next century. Make them talk about the middle of the next decade. If you do this they will quickly be shown up for the frauds that they are.

B: KEN BOSSONG:

EDITORIAL, MARCH 1979

THE VOCAL and increasingly active opponents of the nation's atomic energy programs invariably base their opposi-

tion on the potential dangers inherent in the generation of power from nuclear fuels. Are they hypothesizing problems that are of the one-in-a-million-chance variety? Are their concerns more fantasy than fact?

A review of the safety record of domestic nuclear facilities during the past three decades reveals a history of worker deaths, plant accidents, acts of terrorism, and other incredible mishaps. In fact almost every "one-in-a-million" occurrence has already occurred as well as a number of incidents whose probability was considered so statistically minute as to not be worth evaluating.

Whereas federal and industrial spokespersons have extolled the safety record of nuclear power, studies issued—but kept unpublicized—by the old Atomic Energy Commission, the Nuclear Regulatory Commission, and other agencies document a far different story. They report that in the previous 33 years, there have been over 10,000 disabling work injuries at domestic nuclear facilities including more than 300 fatalities. Hundreds of other workers are expected to die of radiation-induced cancers by 1990.

In the past seven years, there have

been 150 instances of threats against nuclear installations across the U.S. These have included three cases in which bombs were successfully planted on facility sites and several instances of arson in which major fire damage resulted. On the average, NRC loses (or has had stolen) as much as 100 lb of uranium and 60 lb of plutonium every year—enough to make more than 10 atomic bombs.

"Acts of God" also have taken their toll. Lightning and cold weather have disabled plant safety/security systems. Gale force winds damaged AEC's Amarillo, Tex., facility in 1967. A tornado passed through the site of a proposed plant in Dixon Springs, Tenn., and another came within 10 miles of an operating reactor in Athens, Ala. Several reactors are built near or astride geological faults either known to be or suspected of being still active, including several that have experienced quakes in this century. On at least two occasions, B-52 bombers have crashed within sight of nuclear facilities.

The power level of fissile systems has become uncontrollable on 26 occasions in the past three decades; that is, nuclear accidents either occurred or were just avoided. These include a core meltdown at the first experimental breeder reactor in 1955 as well as a partial fuel meltdown of the Fermi I breeder near Detroit in 1966. The well-publicized 1975 Brown's Ferry fire started with a worker carelessly using a candle to test for air leaks; it ended with most of the plant's safety systems rendered inoperable and more than $50 million in damages.

Thus, while nuclear supporters have glorified their industry in terms that have bordered on outright fabrication, serious mishaps have been occurring with frightening regularity.

There are alternatives, however, to continued exposure to such hazards. Nuclear power presently constitutes only 3% of total domestic energy consumption. That is a contribution to the nation's energy budget which could be easily eliminated through simple conservation strategies or through the implementation of presently available and cost-competitive solar technologies. Moreover, numerous studies issued by the Energy Research & Development Administration and the Federal Energy Administration confirm that future energy needs that would otherwise be met with nuclear power can also be satisfied with conservation, solar and wind technologies.

For these reasons, the U.S. should immediately declare a moratorium on new reactor construction and begin a phaseout of all existing nuclear programs other than perhaps some research efforts.

Our experience with nuclear facilities has already proven the truth of Murphy's Law: "If anything can possibly go wrong, it will"; further test data are not needed.

28.

John C. Sawhill: The Collapse of Public Schools

As the 1970s wound to an end, the furor about the public schools of America became ever more vocal. Speeches were made, programs were proposed, and studies were funded that would be highly publicized in the coming decade. Few statements were so pessimistic about the situation as this article by the president of New York University.

Source: *Saturday Review*, August 1979.

For more than two decades, America's public schools have been expected to cure society's discontents. In the mid-Fifties, we demanded that our schools create a harmony among races that existed nowhere else in American life. In the mid-Sixties, when our young were engaged in a rebellion that seemed to threaten virtually every ideal we embraced as a nation, we insisted that the schools restore social order and preserve the status quo. In the mid-Seventies, we instructed our schools to go one step farther—to look first to the wants of the individual, to nurture a child's discovery of self, while at the same time distracting him from his attempts to reduce his school to rubble.

Clearly, this prolonged and ill-advised effort to make the educational system the principal tool for social change has contributed to such problems as the sharply increased incidence of functional illiteracy.

To rehabilitate our schools, we must look to the hard realities of *why* our system of public education is not working and learn from them.

As we examine the performance of our schools, six basic truths—most of them a result of our mixing altruism and education—emerge time and again.

1. *Schools are asked to do too much.* Racial, economic, and sexual inequalities; poor parenting; malnutrition; crime; and a lengthy list of other social disorders unquestionably affect an individual's capacity to participate in society. But while education can enhance the student's ability to cope with, and to change, the conditions of life around him, it cannot, in and of itself, make them better. In thrusting the schools to the forefront of social change, we have diverted their energies from their basic purpose—education.

The issue of acculturation of ethnic minorities provides a case in point. Greater emphasis has been placed on bilingual education in the public schools as the number and variety of ethnic minorities have grown in the nation. We are insisting both that the schools improve the way they teach English, so that language is removed as a barrier to learning, and that they increase the number of courses taught in students' native tongues, so that the pace of learning begun in their homelands continues uninterrupted. The conflict that such demands create can be seen in Chicago, where, as a condition of $90 million in aid, the federal government exacted a pledge that the public schools offer bilingual courses in 20 languages, from Arabic to Vietnamese.

While we do not yet know what effect the study of major courses in a native tongue has on a child's ability to learn English, we may be allowed the suspicion that it will prove as counterproductive as it sounds. In addition, the burden these extra courses place on the schools is obvious. Once we stop asking the schools to do too much, they can get on with solving the more acute problem of performing their basic task—that of education—more effectively.

2. *Students cannot learn what they are not taught.* Current dismay over public education centers on the fact that substantial numbers of our children cannot perform even the most basic functions of reading, writing, and mathematics. Such poor performance is understandable, however, when we recognize that proficiency in basic skills no longer is required of public-school students.

"Minimum competency" is the result of the schools' misguided efforts to serve two masters at the same time. On one hand, they are trying to respond to the public demand for sound, basic education by requiring a specific level of achievement in certain subjects. On the other hand, in their attempt to correct social inequities, schools are often setting standards so low as to be meaningless and even detrimental.

Although the concept of minimum competency is not inherently bad, it does require careful implementation. The depth to which public education can sink under the weight of prob-

lematic minimum-competency levels was demonstrated in New York this past spring when educators and others engaged in a spirited debate over the question of whether freshman reading standards are too *high* for graduating seniors. What began as a tool for ensuring performance has become an excuse for failure. This situation must be corrected.

Electives are sometimes used by schools as another means of preventing students from failing when they cannot educate them. Nationally, we can see a trend that moves even farther away from requiring certain basics and toward instituting yet more electives— courses that range from studies amplifying basic skills to programs that can only be described as the marginalia of pop culture.

In Massachusetts, state educators compared a survey of elective courses developed between 1971 and 1976 with an analysis of Scholastic Achievement Test scores for students in 43 high schools. In this five-year period there was a 50 percent increase in English electives alone. The educators found that students with more electives showed greater than average declines in SAT scores.

Similarly, in New York, where the documented trend has been away from academic basics in recent years, two-thirds of the graduates of city high schools required additional pre-college study upon entering the City University.

In contrast, a survey of 34 high schools in which students have maintained or improved their SAT scores revealed that these schools encourage enrollment in advanced academic courses and allow electives to be taken only in addition to required classes rather than as a substitute for them.

Thus we must temper our dismay at our children's inability to read, write, and solve simple mathematical problems with the recognition that little goes on in the classroom to provide them with the skills to do better.

3. *We do not know what makes for an effective learning experience.* With the possible exception of one-to-one teaching, virtually all of our theories about factors that contribute to productive instruction have not held up. Even our most cherished socio-educational assumption—that racial and social integration contributes to learning (provided half of the class is white)—runs counter to the reality of public schools, where students are put in classes according to their abilities; ethnic minorities are thus effectively resegregated and educational inadequacies perpetuated.

As long as schools are diverted by social concerns from the experimentation essential to improving their performance, our students and teachers will continue to stumble through a succession of educational theories, reinventing the wheel daily out of necessity and, worse, becoming more entrenched in classroom practices that produce no positive results.

4. *What is good for the teacher is not always good for the pupil.* Increasingly in recent years, teachers have argued that higher salaries attract better teachers. Smaller classes, they have said, more time to prepare for class, and publicly financed teacher training—improve the performance of those already in the profession. The result, our teachers tell us, is better education for our children. None of these assertions is supported by fact. Teachers' salaries have risen steadily during the past 20 years. In the classroom, the ratio of one teacher for every 30 students in 1955 had dropped

to one for every 20 by 1976. There has also been a substantial increase in the amount of time teachers spend outside the classroom in course preparation and professional training. Yet students are performing dismally on almost every test we have thus far devised to measure their academic competence.

As is the case with the learning experience itself, we must recognize finally that we do not know what makes a teacher effective.

5. *The way we finance public education is discriminatory and contributes to chaos in the schools.* Getting and spending the money to finance our public schools are among the most serious problems we face as a nation today.

Taxation of private property in itself has become an explosive issue. Reliance on property taxes discriminates against our cities and poorer suburban and rural areas. Property-poor localities must tax themselves at a higher rate to generate the same amount of tax dollars as their property-rich neighbors. Those who can afford to, move to areas where taxes are lower, and the money available for public education is thus further eroded in those localities where it is most needed.

Efforts have been made in the state courts and legislatures to equalize funding. While these efforts generally have resulted in increased aid to poorer districts, they have not addressed the major issue of linking public education to property taxes.

Meanwhile, increases in property taxes meet with growing resistance. The "taxpayers' revolt" is surprising only in that it did not surface sooner. Neither the very poor nor the very rich pay as much of the cost of education as the middle-class property owner.

The inequities of the property tax

are also felt acutely by older property owners who enjoy only indirectly the benefits of public education. Many of those who must survive on fixed incomes have found that the value of their once-modest homes has tripled and even quadrupled in recent years. The result: steep increases in taxes that their incomes cannot grow to match.

While we have yet to see what longterm effects the taxpayers' revolt will have on public education, Cleveland provided us with a clue when voter rejection of a bond issue closed the schools twice in one year, left the city $130 million in debt, and pushed teachers' salaries months in arrears.

Getting the money to finance public education, however, is only half of the problem we face. Spending it wisely is equally important and sometimes even more perplexing.

Why is it, with increased teachers' salaries and per-pupil expenditures, that our students perform so poorly? Again, the answer can be found in our zeal to correct social disorders. Schools in localities with large low-income and minority populations must provide costly social services to their students, leaving even less money for actual education.

6. *Someone must be in charge.* Local, state, and federal government; community groups; unions; educational theorists; parents; and even students have all taken a crack at running our schools, and the results are about the same. None has run them well. Schools and their employees' unions have developed intricate bureaucracies of their own, which spend more time explaining their failures than seeking solutions to the problems they face.

The responsibility for making decisions, controlling resources, and planning and implementing programs has been taken away from principals and teachers and dispersed throughout the educational bureaucracy, from the local school system all the way to the federal government.

We cannot expect our schools to function well when those most directly involved lack the authority to manage them effectively.

Acceptance of these six realities will not provide all the answers to the problems our schools face today. But they do suggest directions we might pursue:

We must recognize that schools exist to educate, and that the task is monumental enough without the attempt to right the social wrongs that have originated elsewhere.

We must recognize that—if the function of education is to enable us to become the most that we can be—there is no such thing as a minimum acceptable standard.

We must insist that time and money be used to strengthen basic academic curricula.

We must scrutinize our beliefs about what makes for an effective learning experience and discard those that have proved ineffective and wasteful; further, we cannot rely on teachers and educational theorists alone in making such decisions.

We must revolutionize the way in which schools are financed and establish firm priorities for spending.

And finally, we must return the management of our schools to those most directly involved in the delivery of educational services to the public.

Our schools provide a key to the future of society. We must take control of them, watch over them, and nurture them if they are to be set right again. To do less is to invite disaster upon ourselves, our children, and our nation.

29.

Lee Iacocca: The Chrysler Bailout

By the summer of 1979 it was apparent to many analysts and to Lee Iacocca, head of the Chrysler Corporation, that the situation of America's third-largest automaker was desperate. Chrysler had done all it could do on its own, but the combination of poor management in the past, government demands for heavy spending to meet imposed regulations, and a sudden fuel shortage that made Chrysler's big fuel-hungry cars a drug on the market would bring the company crashing down if it did not receive help from outside. Iacocca turned to the White House, asking for loan guarantees that would allow the corporation to borrow enough money to carry it through until it could get its feet on the ground again. He was attacked from every side, but the Democratic administration and Congress, well aware of the vast number of jobs that would be lost if Chrysler failed, finally agreed to provide guarantees of up to $1.2 billion. Chrysler quickly borrowed the funds and, in one of the most dramatic turnarounds in American corporate history, was solvent again sooner than anyone—with the possible exception of Iacocca—had dreamed it could be. The splendid success story of the "Chrysler bailout" is told in detail in Iacocca's bestselling autobiography. A few passages from that book are reprinted here.

Source: *Iacocca: An Autobiography*, Ch.XVIII-XIX, 1984.

FROM THE VERY START, the prospect of government-backed loans for Chrysler was opposed by just about everybody. Predictably, the greatest outcry came from the business community. Most business leaders came out strongly against the plan, and many of them went public with their views, including Tom Murphy of General Motors and Walter Wriston of Citicorp.

For most of them, federal help for Chrysler constituted a sacrilege, a heresy, a repudiation of the religion of corporate America. The aphorisms started flowing like water as all the old clichés got dusted off. Ours is a profit-and-loss system. Liquidations and close-downs are the healthy catharsis of an efficient market. A loan guarantee violates the spirit of free enterprise. It rewards failure. It weakens the discipline of the marketplace. Water seeks its own level. Survival of the fittest. Don't change the rules in the middle of the game. . . . Failure is to capitalism what hell is to Christianity. Laissez-faire forever. And other assorted bullshit!

The National Association of Manufacturers came out strongly against federal loan guarantees. And at its meeting on November 13, 1979, the policy committee of the Business Roundtable approved the following statement on the Chrysler situation:

Lee A. Iacocca

A fundamental premise of the market system is that it allows for both failure and success, for loss as well as profit. Whatever the hardships of failure may be for particular companies and individuals, the broad social and economic interests of the nation are best served by allowing this system to operate as freely and fully as possible.

The consequences of failure and reorganization under the revised statutes [bankruptcy, in other words], while serious, are not unthinkable. The loss of jobs and production would be far from total. Under reorganization, the many viable components of the business could be expected to operate more effectively while other elements might be sold off to other producers. It is at this stage that a better case can be made for targeted federal assistance to deal with any resulting social problems.

At a time when government, business, and the public are becoming more and more aware of the costs and inefficiencies of government intervention in the economy, it would be highly inappropriate to recommend a course of even deeper involvement. Now is the time to reaffirm the principle of "no federal bailouts."

This statement made me furious. I tried to find out exactly who in the group had voted for it, but everybody I checked with seemed to have been out of town at the time. Nobody wanted to take responsibility for zapping us.

In reply, I sent the following letter:

Gentlemen:

I was deeply disturbed to learn that on the same day I testified in Washington on behalf of Chrysler Corporation's request for loan guarantees, the Business Roundtable, of which Chrysler is a member, issued a press release against "federal bailouts."

I have several observations to make.

First—the basic charter of the Roundtable is to contain inflation. Its goals have since been extended to a discussion of other economic issues of national importance. These discussions have traditionally taken place in an open and free atmosphere in which all points of view are considered. The fact that we did not have an opportunity to present the facts of the Chrysler case to the members of the Policy Committee runs directly counter to that tradition.

Second—it is ironic that the Roundtable took no similar position on federal loan guarantees to steel companies, to shipbuilders, to airlines, to farmers, and to the housing industry. Nor did it protest the establishment of "trigger prices" on foreign steel, or the provisions for federal assistance to American Motors.

Third—the Roundtable statement invokes the principles of the free market system which "allows for both failure and success." It totally ignores the fact that government regulatory intrusion into the system has contributed greatly to Chrysler's problem. It is in fact entirely consistent with the workings of a free market system for the government to offset some of the adverse effects of federal regulation. Federal loan guarantees to steel companies were made precisely for that reason.

Fourth—the Roundtable statement is wrong in its declaration that reorganization under the new bankruptcy statute is practical. Our need is not to scale down debt, but to raise huge amounts of new capital. It would be impossible for us to raise the necessary amounts of capital during a bankruptcy proceeding. We have consulted with one of the nation's leading experts on bankruptcy, Mr. J. Ronald Trost, of Shutan and Trost, whose analysis of the new law led him to testify that bankruptcy is not practical for Chrysler and would lead quickly to liquidation.

Your own Roundtable staff has indicated that no bankruptcy experts were consulted during the preparation of your statement. If they had been, I feel sure the statements would have been considerably less confident on the subject of the virtues of bankruptcy.

Fifth—it is most unfortunate that the Roundtable has chosen to engage in sloganeering in this campaign. To proclaim a policy of "no federal bailouts" in a press release is to reduce the discussion to its lowest level. The hundreds of thousands of workers across the country who depend on Chrysler for employment deserve far better in the debate over their future.

Finally, I believe my acceptance of your current invitation to become a member of the Roundtable would be a source of embarrassment to the other members. I had looked forward to joining a business forum that openly discusses vital economic and social issues in an atmosphere of mutual trust and respect. The Roundtable's press release indicates that such an opportunity does not exist in the Policy Committee. Therefore, please accept my sincere regrets and the resignation of Chrysler Corporation from Business Roundtable membership. . . .

During the debate, the bankruptcy "solution" for Chrysler was very popular. Under Chapter 11 of the Federal Bankruptcy Act, we'd be protected against our creditors until we got our house in order. A few years later, we would supposedly emerge as a smaller but healthier company.

But when we called in all kinds of experts, they told us, as we already knew, that in our case bankruptcy would be catastrophic. Our situation was unique. It wasn't like dealing with the government on defense contracts they've already given you. And it wasn't like the cereal business. If Kellogg's were known to be going out of business, nobody would say: "Well, I won't buy their corn flakes today. What if I get stuck with a box of cereal and there's nobody around to service it?"

But cars are different. Just the whisper of bankruptcy would shut off the cash flow to the company. We'd see a domino effect. Customers would cancel their orders. They'd worry about future warranty coverage and the availability of parts and service—not to mention the resale value of the car.

Here there was an instructive precedent. When the White Truck Company declared bankruptcy, they thought they could strong-arm their lenders by hiding under the rules of Chapter 11. Technically it might have worked. Except for one problem. Every one of their customers said: "Oh, no, they've gone bankrupt! I think I'll buy somebody else's truck."

Some of the banks wanted us to go that route. "What are you messing around with the government for? Go declare bankruptcy, and run your company out of bankruptcy." They'd give us examples of other companies that had done that. But we kept saying: "Look, we're a major consumer company in a consumer industry. We wouldn't survive for two weeks trying that."

In a bankruptcy, our dealers would lose their ability to finance purchases from the factory. Nearly all dealer vehicle financing would be shut off within a day or two by the banks and the finance companies. We estimated that about half our dealers would themselves be forced into bankruptcy. Many others would be recruited by GM and Ford, leaving us without outlets in major markets.

Suppliers would demand payment in advance—or on a COD basis. Most of our suppliers are small businesses with fewer than five hundred employees. The strain of a Chrysler bankruptcy would be impossible for thousands of small companies who depended on us for their very existence. Many of them, too, would have to declare bankruptcy, which in turn would deprive us of essential parts.

And forget about Chrysler. What would the largest bankruptcy in American history have done to the nation? A study by Data Resources estimated that the demise of Chrysler would ultimately cost the taxpayers $16 billion in unemployment, welfare, and other expenses.

So much for the bankruptcy option. . . .

As I write these words, it's been four years since the loan guarantees were passed. During that time, we've kept hundreds of thousands of people off the dole. We paid hundreds of millions of dollars in taxes. We preserved competition in the auto industry. We paid back the loans seven years early. We paid large fees to the Loan Guarantee Board. And the government enjoyed a windfall from selling our warrants.

In view of all this, you have to ask a philosophical question. By going to Congress, did we really violate the spirit of free enterprise? Or has our subsequent success actually helped free enterprise in this country? I don't think there's any doubt about the answer. Even some of our opponents from 1979 now concede that the Chrysler loan guarantees were a good idea.

Oh, there are still some diehards such as *The Wall Street Journal* and Gary Hart—but what the hell! You can't convert them all.

The problem is not that there aren't any alternatives but rather the man at the helm. The trouble with super leaders is their super egos. Lee [Iacocca]'s in a race to show Henry [Ford] what he can do. And in the process, he's likely to become a General Custer.

WILLIAM J. McGRATH, JR., auto industry expert

30.

Cyrus Vance, Paul H. Nitze, and Henry Kissinger: Views of SALT II

The first Strategic Arms Limitation Treaty (SALT I) was signed in 1972. Negotiations on a second treaty began almost immediately. At a meeting in Vladivostok in November 1974, President Ford and Secretary Brezhnev agreed on a basic framework for SALT II. In 1975 a joint draft text was prepared and numerous limitations were agreed on. Early in the Carter Administration, Secretary of State Vance proposed significant reductions and qualitative constraints on the ceilings that had been agreed on at Vladivostok. These "deep cuts" were rejected by the Soviet Union. The negotiations came to an end early in 1979 and the treaty, after being approved by America's NATO allies, was signed in Vienna by President Carter and President Brezhnev on June 18, whereupon it was presented to the U.S. Senate for review. It was never formally ratified, although both countries agreed to abide by its restrictions. Reprinted here are three statements made before the Senate Foreign Relations Committee in July 1979. Cyrus Vance was at the time still Secretary of State. Henry Kissinger had been Secretary of State at the time of the Vladivostok meeting. Paul H. Nitze, former Deputy Secretary of Defense, had been a leading U.S. arms negotiator during the 1970s.

Source: *Congressional Digest,* August-September 1979.

A: CYRUS VANCE

First and foremost, SALT II must be judged by its impact upon our national security. That is its transcendent purpose. We believe the treaty meets that test. It makes an important contribution to maintaining a stable strategic balance, now and in the future.

SALT II is not a substitute for a strong defense. It complements and reinforces our defense efforts. Together, SALT II and our defense modernization programs will give us the security we need as we meet other critical challenges to American's future.

Beyond its direct contribution to our security, the SALT II treaty must also be seen in the context of the larger fabric of international relations.

Approval of the treaty will help us meet several essential objectives of our foreign policy.

It will help us to defend our interests and promote our values in the world from a position of strength. For a strategic imbalance could lead some of our friends and allies to question our ability to protect our interests and theirs.

It will help us to fashion a balanced relationship with the Soviet Union in which we build on areas of mutual in-

Cyrus Vance

terest, but do not let the benefits of cooperative measures blind us to the reality of our continuing competition.

It will reinforce the confidence of our allies and help strengthen the alliances through which our own security is enhanced.

And it will enable us to broaden the work of arms control, so we can encourage the further transfer of attention and resources to steps which will lift the human condition.

We do not suggest that SALT II will by itself carry us to a new world of prosperity and peace. Even with this treaty there will be continued tests of our political will. Substantial new investments will be required to keep our defenses strong and ready. Nor do we suggest that if SALT is not approved, we could not survive. We could.

The issue is whether we would be in a better or worse position, whether our national security and foreign policy would be enhanced and strengthened or hurt and weakened, as some suggest, by the approval of this treaty.

The decision on SALT II will have a direct and important impact on our relationship with the Soviet Union.

The growth of nuclear arms has altered that relationship in fundamental ways. We continue to have sharply different values and different views on many issues. Yet, in a nuclear age, each nation understands the importance of seeking agreement where our interests coincide.

For the foreseeable future, our relationship with the Soviet Union will continue to have two strands. One is the steady pursuit of measures of cooperation and restraint. There is no reason why we cannot benefit from carefully negotiated arms control, economic or cultural agreements just because the Soviet Union also benefits.

At the same time, the process of seeking restraint and broadening areas of cooperation cannot be allowed for a moment to divert our attention and determination from the fact of continuing competition with the Soviet in many areas.

It is imperative, in an era of continuing competition, that we not allow a military imbalance which could offer the Soviets either political or military advantages.

Perceptions of our strength and resolve are crucial. If there were doubts about the credibility of our deterrent, third countries could feel more vulnerable to Soviet pressure. The result could be a lessening of American influence and a more dangerous world.

We have no way to measure precisely how large a military discrepancy would have to be to cause political harm. We also have no interest in experimentation. The surest way to prevent political harm is to preserve an essential equivalence between our forces and those of the Soviet Union. That is precisely what SALT II will help us to do. Indeed, equivalence is the premise of this treaty. With the future strategic balance more secure, we can most effectively compete wherever necessary.

What would happen to the U.S.-Soviet relationship if SALT II were rejected? We cannot know entirely. But it is clear that we would be entering a period of greater uncertainty.

I see no reasonable basis for believing that if SALT II is not ratified, the Soviet Union will be induced to moderate its defense spending or become more cooperative in the Third World. In the absence of SALT, however, we face unlimited nuclear competition and a serious increase in U.S.-Soviet tensions. In such an atmosphere, each crisis and each confrontation could become far more dangerous.

America's allies fully support the SALT II treaty. Just as our partners look to us for leadership in strengthening the military position of our alliances— which we are doing—they also expect and want us to lead in the quest for greater security and stability through arms control.

The NATO Allies have endorsed the SALT II treaty on two levels: they are convinced that it preserves all essential defense options, to sustain deterrence in Europe; and they believe the treaty serves a necessary role in the overall East-West political and strategic relationship.

Beyond Europe, this treaty is supported by our other friends and allies around the world.

Beyond its effects on East-West relations and the interests of our Allies, SALT II is important to all of our other efforts toward arms restraint.

In sum, the SALT II treaty and the commitments we have made to strengthen our strategic forces will have a profound influence on the character of American leadership in the world. Obviously, with or without this treaty, we will face an imposing array of challenges and problems. But if we are to meet them, SALT II is an important and necessary first step.

B: PAUL H. NITZE

THE ISSUE BEFORE the Senate is broader than merely whether or not to consent to the ratification of the SALT II agreements signed at Vienna on June 18th. The Constitution also places on the Senate the responsibility to advise with respect to treaties brought before it for consideration.

For some time the SALT II proponents have been explaining the agreements in a manner intended to praise them. In so doing, they have given what I believe to be a one-sided and misleading picture. The Senate is entitled to a more critical and balanced analysis.

Supporters of the agreements stress equality in the main provisions of the treaty. Despite the superficial appearance of equality, the agreements are unequal both in their legal and in their practical effects.

The supporters assert that the agreements put a cap on the so-called arms race and initiate a process of reductions in offensive strategic nuclear armaments. On the contrary, the limits in the agreements are so designed and are so high that they put no effective limit on Soviet offensive strategic nuclear capabilities. Rather than forcing a reduction, there will be a continuous and large increase in Soviet capabilities during the term of the treaty. There will be some increase in our capabilities as well; but in net terms, the strategic balance will move from a position not far from parity to one of Soviet strategic nuclear superiority.

The SALT II proponents assert that the agreements are adequately verifiable. Strict adherence to many of the provisions of the agreements cannot be confidently verified. But the agreements so one-sidedly favor the Soviet Union that verifiability is not the major issue. What could be gained by cheating would be less significant than the shift in strategic capabilities permitted without the necessity of cheating.

It is also asserted that, despite their shortcomings, the agreements are a good and necessary foundation for the negotiation of better future agreements—SALT III, SALT IV, etc. To the contrary, there is no evidence whatever that, as the strategic nuclear balance shifts further in favor of the Soviet side, they will become less resolute in pressing every possible advantage. It is almost certain that, if SALT II is ratified as signed at Vienna, SALT III will be less favorable to the U.S. and more favorable to the USSR than SALT II.

Further, there is the broader political question of how best to deal with the Soviet Union. Is unequal and one-sided accommodation by us the best way to assure the cooperation of the Soviet leadership toward world progress and toward peace? Again history gives no support to that hope. I believe we are headed for difficult times ahead in our relations with the world, and particularly with the Soviet Union, whether SALT II is ratified or not.

Finally, the Senate must resolve the question of whether, in times of increasing danger, including military danger, it is wise to let down our guard or whether it is time to pull the country together for the major effort that is required on many fronts. . . .

The Soviet leaders threaten us with dangers ahead if the Senate does not consent to the ratification of the SALT II terms as signed at Vienna. No one can guarantee that their threat is a mere bluff.

That there are dangers in failure to ratify might be the core of a valid issue if one could truly say that acceptance of the treaty as drafted would bring us safety. That is not the case. We are not at a crossroads between safety and perplexity. There is no formula for salvation in making these inequitable provisions into the supreme law of the land.

However the Senate may vote, there is trouble in prospect. Amendment of the treaty does not assure Soviet acceptance of the amended terms nor does failure of the treaty assure strategic balance. But neither will acceptance of the Vienna draft assure strategic balance; to the contrary, it will tend to nail down dangerous strategic imbalance.

That brings me to the heart of the problem posed by SALT II. To accept the case that is being made for the Vienna terms, with all its fallacies and implausibilities, can only incapacitate our minds and wills for doing the things necessary to redress the strategic imbalance.

The first step out of danger is to recognize danger. We have to come to terms with the plight we are in before we can correct it. In Lincoln's words, "First we must disenthrall ourselves, and then we shall save the country." . . .

Fundamental to the debate over SALT II and over our strategic nuclear program is the question of what strategy to follow, if deterrence were to fail, and the relationship of strategy to deterrence.

Some start from the assumption that a nuclear war is "unthinkable"; that deterrence has nothing to do with the military strategy either side intends to follow in the event deterrence were to fail; that, regardless of strategy and of the probable balance of the initially surviving and then enduring nuclear forces, there could be no meaningful winner or loser in a nuclear way.

Others believe that a nuclear war is thinkable, that the United States can best avoid a nuclear war, while preserving its independence and honor, by thinking seriously about nuclear war and taking prudent and timely actions to forestall it. They view the quality of deterrence to be importantly affected by the strategy we intend to follow and could effectively implement, if deterrence were to fail. They question the wisdom and credibility of a so-called minimum deterrence strategy. Under such a strategy, deterrence would depend on the United States' ability and will to launch, in response to a Soviet attack, a few hundred missiles, warheads or megatons (they are generally imprecise about which) against Soviet cities and industry protected by extensive active and passive defenses. The fact that the remaining U.S. military forces and U.S. population and industry would then be defenseless against ten thousand megatons or more of a Soviet third and fourth strike capability would be ignored.

Few now overtly support the minimum deterrence approach. They are more apt to describe their position with such phrases as "sufficiency" or "flexibility." This leads to the question of how much of what is enough? That judgment in turn must rest importantly upon the relative emphasis placed on the counterforce aspect of nuclear strategy and on the countervalue aspect. Neither aspect can be ignored. If our counterforce capabilities, survivable after an initial Soviet strike, were sufficient to out-fight Soviet residual forces, while our other forces were capable of holding Soviet population and industry in reciprocal danger to our own, the quality of deterrence would be high because the Soviets would know we were in a position to implement a credible military strategy in the event deterrence were to fail.

If our strategy were restricted to a revenge attack on, for instance, the 200 largest Soviet cities, the military forces required to support such a strategy would be relatively small. Such a strategy, however, would be suicidal if implemented, vastly more destructive to us than to the Soviet Union, and militarily hopeless. One could, therefore, have only limited confidence in deterrence based upon an implied determination to execute such a strategy to defend vital U.S. interests.

Those that claim that we are stronger than the Soviet Union now and will continue to be so during our lifetimes, more or less regardless of what we do, must equate forces designed to support such a minimum deterrence strategy with superiority. . . .

Some proponents argue a different series of points along the following lines:

a. The United States' March 1977 comprehensive proposal leaned over backward in attempting to be fair to the Soviet Union. It offered them complete assurance against any significant counterforce threat from the United States while not assuring comparable protection for the United States.

b. That proposal was wholly unacceptable to the USSR, and any proposal which would in fact assure stability and rough equivalence at lower levels of nuclear armaments would be even more unnegotiable.

c. To insist on such an equitable agreement would assure that there would be no success, at least in the next few years, in negotiating a SALT II set of agreements. Such a delay would risk a breakdown of detente.

d. Rather than risk such a breakdown, it is wiser to negotiate the best deal that is now reachable, preserve at least the outward forms of detente, and open the way to follow-on negotiations for a better deal in the future.

e. And in any case, a deterioration in the state of the strategic nuclear balance will have no adverse political or diplomatic consequences.

To some of us who lived through the Berlin crisis in 1961, the Cuban crisis in 1962, or the Middle East crisis in 1973, the last and key judgment in this chain of reasoning—that an adverse shift in the strategic nuclear balance will have no political or diplomatic consequences—comes as a shock. In the Berlin crisis of 1961 our theater position was clearly unfavorable; we relied entirely on our strategic nuclear superiority to face down Chairman Khrushchev's ultimatum. In Cuba, the Soviet Union faced a position of both theater inferiority and strategic inferiority; they withdrew the missiles they were deploying. In the 1973 Middle East crisis, the theater and the strategic nuclear balances were more balanced; both sides compromised.

It is hard to see what factors in the future are apt to disconnect international politics and diplomacy from the underlying real power balances. The nuclear balance is only one element in the overall power balance. But in the Soviet view, it is the fulcrum upon which all other levers of influence—military, economic, or political—rest.

In any international crisis seriously raising the prospect that the military arms of the United States and of the USSR might become engaged in active and direct confrontation, those directing U.S. and Soviet policy would have to give the most serious attention to the relative strategic nuclear capabilities of the two sides.

Unequal accommodation to the Soviet Union would then have resulted not in cooperation and peace but in forced withdrawal.

C: HENRY KISSINGER

I REGRET TO HAVE to say that the present treaty comes up for ratification at a time of grave danger to our national security and to the global equilibrium. The military balance is beginning to tilt ominously against the United States in too many significant categories of weaponry. The unprecedented Soviet use of proxy forces in Africa, the Middle East and Southeast Asia, and the turmoil caused by radical forces and terrorist organizations sponsored by Moscow's friends, mark ours as a time of profound upheaval. . . .

If present trends continue, we face the chilling prospect of a world sliding gradually out of control—with our relative military power declining, with our economic lifeline vulnerable to blackmail, with hostile forces growing more rapidly than our ability to deal with them, and with fewer and fewer nations friendly to us surviving. . . .

There is now general agreement that their improvements in missile accuracy and warhead technology will put the Soviets in a position to wipe out our land-based forces of Minuteman ICBM's by

1982. Whether this capability is ever exercised or not—and I consider it improbable—it reverses and hence revolutionizes the strategic equation on which our security and that of our friends have depended through most of the postwar period.

The revolution in the strategic balance is aggravated by a comparable buildup of Soviet aircraft and missiles that threatens to overturn the American advantage in theater-based nuclear forces. . . .

All this has been accomplished while the Soviet advantage in conventional forces has grown, and while the reach of Soviet power has been extended enormously. . . .

Rarely in history has a nation so passively accepted such a radical change in the military balance. If we are to remedy it, we must first recognize the fact that we have placed ourselves at a significant disadvantage voluntarily. This is *not* the result of SALT. It is the consequence of unilateral decisions extending over a decade and a half. By a strategic doctrine adopted in the '60s, by the bitter domestic divisions growing out of the war in Vietnam, and by choices by the present administration.

All these actions were unilateral—hence avoidable. They were not extracted from us by clever Soviet negotiators. We imposed them on ourselves by our choices, theories and domestic turmoil. It is therefore in our power to alter them. . . .

After the end of our involvement in Vietnam, new strategic programs could at last be funded: The B-1 manned strategic bomber, to become operational in 1979; the MX ICBM, to become operational in 1983; the Trident submarine and missile, expected to become operational in 1978; various kinds of cruise missiles for the 1980s—all of which would give the United States greater options, and some of which would bring about a new counterforce capability.

Every one of these programs has been canceled, delayed or stretched out by the current administration, so that we are at a point where only the Trident—with only the most limited counterforce capability—can be operational during the period of the projected SALT treaty. In addition, even the Minuteman production line was closed down, leaving us without an emergency hedge for rapid buildup in unexpected contingencies. We now face the challenge of the early '80s with forces designed in the '60s. . . .

As one of the architects of SALT, I am conscience-bound to point out that—against all previous hopes—the SALT process does not seem to have slowed down Soviet strategic competition, and in some sense may have accelerated it. . . .

Any fair-minded analysis must recognize the beneficial aspects of the SALT II agreements. The overall ceiling of 2,250 will force the Soviets to get rid of 250 strategic systems, including some modern ones, while giving us the right to equalize the numbers. The permitted number of land-based Soviet MIRV's—820—is some 100 below the maximum number that they probably intended to build in the absence of SALT. There are some restrictions on missile-testing procedures. There are limits on numbers of missile warheads on ICBM's and a prohibition on more than one "new" ICBM. There is for the first time an agreed base line of information on the Soviet forces. The counting rules are a useful way of dealing with the MIRV problem.

Regrettably, none of these very

real achievements affects the grave strategic situation which I have described and which must urgently be reversed. . . . And it does not enhance—indeed it may slightly inhibit—the possibility for the United States to catch up in the capacity of our strategic forces to attack military targets. . . .

The provisions of the protocol with respect to cruise missiles, especially, restrict exclusively American programs. They affect not a single Soviet program. They amount to a unilateral renunciation of an American capability. . . .

To sum up: I have serious reservations about the protocol. As for the treaty, I conclude that its terms do not improve our strategic situation, but neither do they prevent our remedying it during the remaining six years of its life. Undoubtedly, it imposes some inhibitions on us—the prohibition against "heavy" missiles for the United States, for example, as well as the protocol's ban on mobile missiles through 1981. But I believe that the Senate can deal with these during the ratification process. . . .

The crucial question is whether we can unite behind what is clearly necessary. Ratifying SALT—or rejecting SALT—makes sense *only* if it prompts a renewed dedication to our national defense and security. The Senate's judgment of the Vienna treaty should hinge, in my view, on what will be done to remedy existing trends and on the international impact of ratification or rejection. . . . Some argue that SALT is necessary lest we risk a return to the cold war. This is a curious argument. Whatever label we give to recent Soviet conduct—whether "cold war" or opportunism—it must be ended if there are to be any prospects for East-West coexistence or cooperation.

No leader serves his people by pretending that SALT is needed to perpetuate an acceptable state of affairs. It is *not* an acceptable state of affairs, and it cannot be continued. . . .

I am inclined to agree that the failure to ratify an agreement negotiated over seven years by three administrations would have a disruptive impact on East-West relationships, creating a crisis atmosphere for which we may have little public or allied support. This is undoubtedly one of the telling arguments in favor of ratification.

But the Senate will also wish to consider that to deal with SALT in isolation runs the risk of seriously misleading the Soviet Union. Moscow cannot have it both ways: The slogan of détente and the reality of the systematic undermining of the geopolitical equilibrium. We should use the SALT debate to force a decision.

The Senate will want to make clear that Soviet expansionism threatens the peace and that coexistence depends above all on restrained international conduct, for which the Senate should define some criteria. . . .

We thus return to our original problem. The Senate is in the anomalous position of being asked to ratify a treaty which is essentially peripheral to our basic security and geopolitical concerns but whose either simple ratification or simple rejection would have a profound and dangerous symbolic impact.

Failure to ratify an agreement negotiated over seven years would compromise international confidence in our ability to perceive our own interests or to harmonize the various branches of our government. But it is equally true that if the custodian of free-world security neglects its task, sooner or later panic will become inevitable. . . .

After much reflection, I have concluded that I can support ratification only with the following conditions:

First, if it is coupled with a defense program representing an obligatory understanding between the Congress and the President which overcomes on an urgent basis the grave peril posed by the current military balance.

Second, if it is accompanied by amendments—not requiring renegotiation—clearing up ambiguities in the treaty, defining the status of the protocol, the meaning of noncircumvention, and setting guidelines for follow-on negotiations.

And third, if it is accompanied by a vigorous expression of the Senate's view of the linkage between SALT and Soviet geopolitical conduct.

This approach would avoid the negative consequences of a collapse of SALT. But ratification must not become an end in itself.

In my view, it can only be justified if the administration is prepared to unite our country by demonstrating its determination to restore our military strength and the geopolitical equilibrium. This seems to me the sense of what Senator Nunn, among others, has proposed, and it points the way to a bipartisan resolution of the issue.

With respect to the military programs, I respectfully recommend that the Senate give its advice and consent to ratification of the Vienna treaty *only* after the administration has submitted, and the Congress has authorized and begun appropriating, a supplemental defense budget and a revised five-year defense program that will begin rectifying some of the shortcomings I have identified. The congressional recess provides an opportunity to prepare such a program, on which work should already be far advanced as part of the normal budgetary process.

If the administration is unable to put forward such a program to this session of Congress, I recommend that the Senate delay its advice and consent until a new military program has been submitted to and authorized by the next session of Congress.

I would be open-minded about other methods to achieve this end, provided they are unambiguous and represent an obligatory commitment by both branches of our government. . . .

The program must include accelerated development of a counterforce capability through the MX and Trident II, air defense against Backfire, immediate steps to restore the theater nuclear balance, and urgent measures to beef up our capacity for regional defense—including accelerated modernization and expansion of our Navy. Our current five-year program is deficient in all these categories. My support for ratification is *entirely conditional* on the development of a new program and doctrine given some binding form by the Congress.

The Joint Chiefs have testified that the rapid improvements required cannot be achieved at expenditures representing less than a 5 percent real increase over current programs, for at least the next five years. The burden of proof to the contrary should rest with the administration. . . .

The Senate should attach to its instrument of advice and consent an expression of the following principles:

That the absence of political restraint will seriously jeopardize continuation of the SALT process.

That the Senate understands this to include Soviet supply or encouragement of intervention by proxy military forces; the use of Soviet forces on the territory of its allies such as Cuba, to free Cuban forces to fight in Africa; the support, financing or encouragement by any member of the Warsaw Pact of groups and activities seeking to undermine governments friendly to the United States, or the exacerbation of regional conflicts.

That the administration be required to submit an annual report to the Senate on the degree to which the Soviet Union is living up to these criteria.

That the Senate vote every two years its judgment whether the Soviet Union has lived up to these criteria. If the judgment is negative, the Senate should then vote whether whatever SALT negotiations are taking place should be continued.

31.

Visit to the United States of John Paul II

From the very beginning of his papacy it was apparent that Karol Wojtyla would be one of the most peregrinatious of popes. Within a few years he was able to visit every continent and most of the major countries of the world outside of the Soviet sphere. His tour of the United States took him from Boston to New York to Philadelphia to Des Moines to Chicago and finally to Washington during the week of October 1-7, 1979. While in Washington the Pope met with President Carter, and the following statement was issued by the White House on October 6.

Source: Presidential Documents, October 6, 1979.

THE PRESIDENT. My friends, fellow Americans of every faith, I greet you here with a mixture of both pride and pleasure. We've been privileged to meet today at the White House with a truly extraordinary man—John Paul—one who will mean even more to us in the future as we in this world move in this century to meet the complex challenges which inevitably will confront us and all others who live on Earth.

Regardless of our faith, we look on him as a pastor, and he's come to know us and to talk to us about gentleness, about humility, about forgiveness, and about love. You've taught us, our beloved guest, that we in the United States are not perfect, that we in the United States are responsible for our own behavior. You show in your life and in your teachings a particular concern for human dignity. You know that many people are fearful, but that a person with faith need not be afraid. Our religious faith is, indeed, relevant to a modern world. . . .

This afternoon Pope John Paul and I met alone in the Oval Office and discussed . . . future prospects for peace. We share a belief that "the Church must in no way be confused with the political community, nor bound to any political system." But we also spoke of opportunities we might pursue together.

We will work to renew our spiritual strength that can bear us beyond the blind materialism which brings no joy and change that into true caring for one another—in our families, in our communities, in our nations, in our common world. We will pursue this goal through action, not just through words.

I join His Holiness in urging all individuals and nations of the world to alleviate the hunger of people and the homelessness of refugees—not as political acts, but as acts of humanitarian concern. We cannot profess to love humanity and watch hundreds of thousands of men, women, and children die in human tragedy, which we ourselves can help, as a nation and as people, to prevent. It's our responsibility to provide prompt and generous aid to them through action of our own.

In another area of opportunity—concern and action on behalf of human rights—we have long shared a common purpose. As His Holiness has written, "The essential sense of the State, as a political community, consists in that the society and the people composing it are master and sovereign of their own destiny."

We call on all people and all nations to look beyond ancient hatreds, beyond differences in race and customs, traditions and beliefs, to see the shared humanity of every other human life on Earth. Whenever state and religion can do that together, then violations of the human rights of any person anywhere in the world—whatever cause may be claimed in justification of those deprivations—will be seen to be, as Your Holiness has so accurately described them, "warfare on humanity" itself. . . .

All of us share full responsibility for seizing another opportunity: In a world filled with weapons there can be no more urgent human passion than to wage and to win the struggle for peace—for the

UPI/Bettmann

Pope John Paul II with President Carter at the White House during a reception for the pope.

sake of every living thing on Earth.

We must, above all, wrest the fateful lightning of nuclear destruction from the hands of man. We must successfully conclude our nuclear arms agreements, and in this continuing effort we must find a way to end the threat of nuclear annihilation in every nation on Earth. The age of nuclear weaponry can either be long or short, as we choose.

We must continue the common struggle—the church and governments—for peace. . . .

THE POPE. Mr. President, I am honored to have had, at your kind invitation, the opportunity for a meeting with you; for by your office as President of the United States of America, you represent before the world the whole American nation, and you hold the immense responsibility of leading this nation in the path of justice and peace. I thank you publicly for this meeting, and I thank all those who have contributed to its success. I wish also to reiterate here my deep gratitude for the warm welcome and the many kindnesses which I have received from the American people on my pastoral journey through your beautiful land. . . .

There is indeed no other way to put oneself at the service of the whole human person except by seeking the good of every man and woman in all their commitments and activities. Authority in the political community is based on the objective ethical principle that the basic duty of power is the solicitude of the common good of society and that it serves the inviolable rights of the human person. The individuals, families, and various groups which compose the civic community are aware that by themselves they are unable to realize their human potential to the full, and therefore they recognize in a wider community the necessary condition for the ever better attainment of the common good.

I wish to commend those in public authority and all the people of the United States for having given, from the very beginning of the existence of this Nation, a special place to some of the most important concerns of the common good. . . . It is superfluous to add that respect for the freedom and the dignity of every individual, whatever his origin, race, sex, or creed, has been a cherished tenet of the civil creed of America, and that it has been backed up by courageous decisions and actions.

Mr. President, ladies and gentlemen, I know and appreciate this country's efforts for arms limitation, especially of nuclear weapons. Everyone is aware of the terrible risk that the stockpiling of such weapons brings upon humanity. Since it is one of the greatest nations on Earth, the United States plays a particularly important part in the quest for greater security in the world and for closer international collaboration. With all my heart I hope that there will be no relaxing of its efforts, both to reduce the risk of a fatal and disastrous worldwide conflagration and to secure a prudent and progressive reduction of the destructive capacity of military arsenals.

The present-day relationships between peoples and between nations demand the establishment of greater international cooperation also in the economic field. The more powerful a nation is, the greater becomes its international responsibility; the greater also must be its commitment to the betterment of the lot of those whose very humanity is constantly being threatened by want and need. It is my fervent hope that all the powerful nations in the world will deepen their awareness of the principle of human solidarity within the one great human family.

America, which in the past decades has demonstrated goodness and generosity in providing food for the hungry of the world, will, I am sure, be able to match this generosity with an equally convincing contribution to the establishing of a world order that will create the necessary economic and trade conditions for a more just relationship between all the nations of the world, in respect for their dignity and their own personality. Since people are suffering under international inequality, there can be no question of giving up the pursuit of international solidarity, even if it involves a notable change in the attitudes and lifestyles of those blessed with a larger share of the world's goods.

32.

Orville Bach: The Little Fish and the Big Dam

The Endangered Species Act that took effect in December 1973 provided that all Federal agencies "insure that actions authorized, funded, or carried out by them do not jeopardize the continued existence" of an endangered species or "result in the destruction or modification of habitat of such species." The snail darter, a tiny fish that lived only in the Little Tennessee River, was an endangered species under the act, and as such it stood in the way of TVA's giant Tellico Dam. Conservationists, who had fought the Tellico Dam as an uneconomic boondoggle, finally were forced—or chose—to rely on the little snail darter as their champion. Their reliance was misguided. In a suit brought by TVA, the Supreme Court in 1978 ruled in favor of the fish—but Chief Justice Warren Burger's opinion was an open invitation to Congress to amend the Endangered Species Act. Congress soon did so, amid national hilarity about the inequality of the adversaries: little fish and big dam. On November 29, 1979, the story, which others saw as not at all funny, came to an end with the closing of the dam gates. One of those who deeply regretted the conservationist defeat and the loss forever of the Little Tennessee River was Orville Bach, who wrote this article early in 1980.

Source: "The Late Little T: A Lesson in Defeat," *Outdoor Life*, October 1980.

THIS MONTH MARKS a sad anniversary for sportsmen: Thursday, Nov. 29, 1979, the day one of the richest outdoor recreation resources in North America died. The last 33 miles of the Little Tennessee River, the "Little T," and 16,000 acres of its valley land, inundated forever by TVA's Tellico Dam. Sportsmen fought fiercely for the Little T and mourned its passing. Economics and nature were on the side of preserving the river, yet we lost. And in that there is a lesson.

It's too late for the Little T, but more rivers are endangered. If we are to stop environmentally devastating water projects, conservationists must understand what happened at Tellico. *Your* favorite stream could be next.

The Little Tennessee River was unique as far as Southeastern streams are concerned. Its cold, clear, trout-laden waters were reminiscent of famous Western trout streams. With the Great Smoky Mountains providing a spectacular backdrop, the Little T was like a little bit of the Rockies in east Tennessee. On a typical fall, summer or spring weekend, it attracted canoeists, trout anglers, float fishermen, picnickers, hikers and campers—rustic and RV.

The dam that put all this to an end was controversial from the very beginning. Tellico became the most litigated federal water project in history. Sportsmen, economists, biologists, historians, archeologists, religious groups,

the Cherokee Indian Nation, a Supreme
Court justice, a Tennessee governor,
the Tennessee Fish and Game Commission, Trout Unlimited and the Outdoor
Writers Association of America were
among those who expressed strenuous
opposition to the project.

The dam was designed to provide
recreation and industrial development.
Yet there were already 22 reservoirs
within a 50-mile radius of Tellico, and
TVA's impoundments had created 638,-
000 acres of water in lakes surrounded
by more shoreline than all the Great
Lakes. TVA's own studies showed that
more jobs could have been created by
leaving the valley for agriculture and
forestry than by flooding it.

Tellico Dam, which cost taxpayers
$138 million, was a fiscally irresponsi-
ble project. But it was the devastating
environmental costs that disheartened
recreationists.

The most productive trout fishery in
the eastern United States, the spiritual
homeland of the Cherokees, historic villages and archeological sites, prime farm
bottomland and some of the finest small
game habitat in the Southeast were sacrificed. How did it happen? Pork-barrel
politics at their worst, perhaps. And
then there was the snail darter. The
controversy over Tellico Dam became
so emotional, so feverish, so sensationalized that the basic economic issues were
obscured in the fray.

The dam was proposed in the mid-
60's. TVA officials promised the residents of the economically depressed
Tellico area that a model community
with high-paying industrial jobs would
be built on the shore of the new lake.
From the start, support of the project
was equated with progress. Opposition
came mostly from outside the immediate
area. At the height of the controversy,

AP/Wide World

Top, Tellico Dam across the Little Tennessee
River. Behind the dam is the area that will be
flooded when the project is completed. Below, a
preserved specimen of the tiny snail darter.

I pulled into a service station where the
attendant eyed the bright red canoe on
top of my car and asked, "You ain't one
of them anti-dam troublemakers, are
you?" And I don't even have a beard or
long hair!

Of course, this sequence of events is
not unique to TVA projects. When the
pork barrel starts to roll—when Congressmen begin promising to vote for
projects in each others' districts in return for votes for equally massive projects that will pump millions of federal
dollars into their own—it becomes next
to impossible to stop. Tennessee politicians don't want to be labeled anti-
growth or against federal expenditures
in the state. Sen. Howard Baker, who
should have been well aware of Tellico's
negative economics and environmental
costs, was one of its biggest backers.

Nearly three-quarters of all federal
water projects waste taxpayers' money.

When Jimmy Carter was elected President, he promised to stop the waste. Still, projects like the Tellico Dam proceed. With all the momentum on the side of the bulldozers, conservationists have to be especially careful because even a small mistake can tip the balance. In the case of the Little T, there were two very big mistakes.

The snail darter was one of the worst things that could have happened to the Tellico Dam controversy, at least from a conservationist's point of view.

No one had even heard of the snail darter when the dam was proposed. But this tiny fish existed naturally in the Little Tennessee River and nowhere else. When a scientist discovered the fish and announced that completion of the dam, already under construction by that time, would destroy its only known habitat, it seemed that the conservationists had an open and shut case. The Endangered Species Act would legally prevent any federal action that would wipe out the snail darter.

Looking back, it's easy to see why the conservationists chose the snail darter and the Endangered Species Act as the battlefield upon which to fight out the entire project. The economic boondoggle had been acknowledged from the start, yet that hadn't been enough to stop the project. Here was an issue that would *make it illegal* for TVA to proceed.

Some of the dam opponents saw the risk of backfire and elected to take it, having exhausted other routes. Others simply underestimated TVA's resourcefulness at exploiting the turn of events.

The energy crunch of the mid-70s gave the dam a boost. This was strange, because Tellico Dam contains no generators, and its total contribution to the TVA power system will be less than $\frac{1}{10}$ of 1 percent of 1985 capacity. Conservationists perhaps didn't see the threat when TVA began portraying the dam as a power project—in the first place because this was obviously false, and in the second place because the Endangered Species Act seemed likely to make this point moot.

It became something like one of those household arguments in which everybody gets so hot under the collar that it's hard to remember what started the whole thing and who was on which side at the beginning. The multimillion-dollar dam that couldn't stand on its own economic merit looked somehow better when its chief opponent was a miserable 3-inch fish that no one had known or cared about a few years earlier. People got used to hearing about hydroelectricity in connection with the dam (incredibly, 95 percent of the respondents in a 10-county survey said they thought that power production, not recreation, was the impoundment's primary purpose). News coverage was often sensational: "Some of those scaredy-cats are helping a 3-inch fish hold up a $100 million power project," said commentator Paul Harvey in a fairly typical column.

John Gibbons, director of the Congressional Office of Technology Assessment, sums it up this way:

"I think Tennessee's Congressional delegation misled people. The record is very clear that the amount of power produced by that dam will be negligible. We had a dam with a lot of money invested in it, and in order to keep the momentum going the delegation tried to focus on something else. And the something else in this case was the snail darter.

"The ground was carefully chosen to make it seem as if the issue were mankind versus a tiny minnow. That was false and misleading."

Maybe, as energy supplies got tighter, people really wanted to believe that the only thing standing between them and a return to past days of cheap electricity was an insignificant fish. Congress first created a special panel empowered to override the Endangered Species Act and authorize construction of projects that would threaten such species if completion, and extinction, were considered on balance to be in the public good. This applied to any project, not just Tellico, and seemed to indicate a severe weakening of the act. The commission, however, ruled against the completion of Tellico Dam. So the Tennessee delegation finally persuaded Congress to pass a bill exempting Tellico from the Endangered Species Act *and all other federal laws.* The battle was over; the conservationists had absolutely no grounds upon which to base further action.

Almost as unfortunate as the dam opponents' choice of issues was their timing. Although Cherokee Indians had voiced opposition to the dam for 15 years, they didn't file suit until Oct. 12, 1979, *after* President Carter had signed the bill exempting Tellico from federal laws. It was also after the bill was signed that Little T-area landowners, who had assumed the bill would be vetoed, staged a tractorcade to TVA headquarters in Knoxville and 2,000 dam opponents protested by camping out at Chota, ancient capital of the Cherokee Nation.

By then it was too late, and now the Little T is gone. How could it happen? And will it happen again? The answers are sobering.

The dam gates were finally closed because TVA is accountable to virtually no one. Critical reports by agencies in the executive branch of the federal government have had no effect, and Congress illustrated the strength of its muscle in the bill exempting Tellico from federal laws. As for judicial control, attorney Frank M. Fly of the Tennessee Scenic River Association has this to say:

"The courts can only require TVA to conduct certain studies, prepare an environmental impact statement and conduct a public hearing prior to initiating a project. Once these procedures are carried out, the courts are powerless to stop the project, regardless of the findings of the studies, and no matter how disastrous the consequences of the project may be."

Variations of the drama of the Little T continue even today, all over the United States. Early this year (1980) the House of Representatives passed a $4.2 billion public works authorizing money for more than 200 dams and various other projects. President Carter has argued that more than half those appropriations are wasteful and unnecessary, but the margin in the house was greater than 2-to-1. More than 50 of the projects authorized have not yet been studied for economic feasibility.

Back in Tennessee, another group of landowners and farmers has been organizing. The Duck River Farmers-Landowners Association vows that it will fight to keep TVA from completing the Columbia Dam, which would flood 12,600 acres, destroy 24,000 acres of wildlife habitat and cost an additional $125 million in taxpayer money ($44 million has already been spent) to provide flood control that could be equaled for $\frac{1}{20}$ of the cost by relocating 43 buildings. TVA documents show that all the benefits to be gained by building the Columbia Dam, two miles east of Columbia on the Duck River, could be obtained by controlling the releases from Normandy Dam, just a few miles upstream.

Will this group be successful where the Tellico Dam opponents failed? They can learn the lessons of the Tellico case and stick to their guns, fighting the dam on its economic merit. They can let their elected representatives know that the ballot box will be the place where those responsible for the death of the Little T will be held accountable. But the whole series of episodes dramatically illustrates the need for a rethinking of our federal water policy.

33.

JIMMY CARTER: A National Malaise

The second half of Jimmy Carter's presidency was a time of troubles, for him, for his administration, and for the nation. Inflation and the energy crisis persisted despite all efforts to deal with them, and the situation in Iran looked as if it would get worse and worse—which indeed it did. On July 15, 1979, Carter addressed the nation on the subject of energy for the fifth time. He spoke at length of his plans to solve the problem. But before discussing the energy problem he discoursed to the American people on another problem, a deeper one, he felt, and one that required a greater national effort to solve. He referred to a "crisis of confidence"; several days later he talked of "a national malaise." Reprinted here is a portion of the July 15th speech, in which he stated some ideas that will probably be remembered longer than most of his other presidential acts and words.

Source: Presidential Documents, week ending July 20, 1979.

I KNOW, OF COURSE, being President, that government actions and legislation can be very important. That's why I've worked hard to put my campaign promises into law—and I have to admit, with just mixed success. But after listening to the American people I have been reminded again that all the legislation in the world can't fix what's wrong with America. So, I want to speak to you first tonight about a subject even more serious than energy or inflation. I want to talk to you right now about a fundamental threat to American democracy.

I do not mean our political and civil liberties. They will endure. And I do not refer to the outward strength of America, a nation that is at peace tonight everywhere in the world, with unmatched economic power and military might.

The threat is nearly invisible in ordinary ways. It is *a crisis of confidence.* It is a crisis that strikes at the very heart and soul and spirit of our national will. We can see this crisis in the growing doubt about the meaning of our own lives and in the loss of a unity of purpose for our Nation.

The erosion of our confidence in the future is threatening to destroy the social and the political fabric of America.

The confidence that we have always had as a people is not simply some romantic dream or a proverb in a dusty book that we read just on the Fourth of July. It is the idea which founded our Nation and has guided our development as a people. Confidence in the future has supported everything else—public institutions and private enterprise, our own families, and the very Constitution of the United States. Confidence has defined our course and has served as a link between generations. We've always believed in something called progress. We've always had a faith that the days of our children would be better than our own.

Our people are losing that faith, not only in government itself but in the ability as citizens to serve as the ultimate rulers and shapers of our democracy. As a people we know our past and we are proud of it. Our progress has been part of the living history of America, even the world. We always believed that we were part of a great movement of humanity itself called democracy, involved in the search for freedom and that belief has always strengthened us in our purpose. But just as we are losing our confidence in the future, we are also beginning to close the door on our past.

In a nation that was proud of hard work, strong families, close-knit communities, and our faith in God, too many of us now tend to worship self-indulgence and consumption. Human identity is no longer defined by what one does, but by what one owns. But we've discovered that owning things and consuming things does not satisfy our longing for meaning. We've learned that piling up material goods cannot fill the emptiness of lives which have no confidence or purpose.

The symptoms of this crisis of the American spirit are all around us. For the first time in the history of our country a majority of our people believe that the next 5 years will be worse than the past 5 years. Two-thirds of our people do not even vote. The productivity of American workers is actually dropping, and the willingness of Americans to save for the future has fallen below that of all other people in the Western world.

As you know, there is a growing disrespect for government and for churches and for schools, the news media, and other institutions. This is not a message of happiness or reassurance, but it is the truth and it is a warning.

These changes did not happen overnight. They've come upon us gradually over the last generation, years that were filled with shocks and tragedy.

We were sure that ours was a nation of the ballot, not the bullet, until the murders of John Kennedy and Robert Kennedy and Martin Luther King, Jr. We were taught that our armies were always invincible and our causes were always just, only to suffer the agony of Vietnam. We respected the Presidency as a place of honor until the shock of Watergate.

We remember when the phrase "sound as a dollar" was an expression of absolute dependability, until 10 years of inflation began to shrink our dollar and our savings. We believed that our Nation's resources were limitless until 1973 when we had to face a growing dependence on foreign oil.

These wounds are still very deep. They have never been healed.

Looking for a way out of this crisis, our people have turned to the Federal Government and found it isolated from the mainstream of our Nation's life. Washington, D.C., has become an island. The gap between our citizens and our Government has never been so wide. The people are looking for honest answers, not easy answers; clear leadership, not false claims and evasiveness and politics as usual.

What you see often in Washington and elsewhere around the country is a system of government that seems incapable of action. You see a Congress twisted and pulled in every direction by hundreds of well-financed and powerful special interests.

You see every extreme position defended to the last vote, almost to the last breath by one unyielding group or another. You often see a balanced and a fair approach that demands sacrifice, a little sacrifice from everyone, abandoned like an orphan without support and without friends.

Often you see paralysis and stagnation and drift. You don't like it, and neither do I. What can we do?

First of all, we must face the truth, and then we can change our course. We simply must have faith in each other, faith in our ability to govern ourselves, and faith in the future of this Nation. Restoring that faith and that confidence to America is now the most important task we face. It is a true challenge of this generation of Americans.

On the old highway maps of America, the main routes were red and the back roads blue. Now even the colors are changing. But in those brevities just before dawn and a little after dusk—times neither day nor night— the old roads return to the sky some of its color. Then, in truth, they carry a mysterious cast of blue, and it's that time when the pull of the blue highway is strongest, when the open road is beckoning, a strangeness, a place where a man can lose himself.

WILLIAM LEAST HEAT MOON, *Blue Highways*, 1982

34.

The Iranian Hostage Crisis, 1979–1981

The Iranian revolution of February 1979 profoundly affected U.S. relations with Iran. The closeness of the U.S. to the Shah, in particular, produced deep suspicion and hostility among the revolutionary leadership. Since the fall of 1978 the U.S. Embassy in Tehran had been troubled by frequent demonstrations against the American presence in the city. On February 14, 1979, the embassy was attacked, and several embassy personnel were killed or wounded. The embassy survived this attack, but a new policy toward the new government was obviously called for. The staff was cut from over 1,400 civilian and military personnel before the revolution to about 70 men and women. In addition, attempts were made to arrive at a modus vivendi *with the Provisional Government. Things seemed to be looking up as spring turned into summer. But in October the State Department was informed that the deposed Shah of Iran was ailing and that he required medical treatment available only in the United States. The Shah arrived in New York on October 23. The initial public response in Iran was moderate. But on November 4, 1979, the U.S. Embassy in Tehran was attacked by some 3,000 armed men, who took 61 American men and women hostage, demanding that the Shah and all of his assets be returned to Iran in exchange for the hostages' freedom. Thus began the most memorable crisis of the Carter presidency — a crisis that endured until the very day on which his successor was sworn in as President. What happened during the 15 months from November 1979 to January 1981, together with why it happened, is told in detail in the document that is reprinted here. It was prepared by the U.S. State Department for a series of hearings conducted, at the behest of the new President, by the House Committee on Foreign Affairs.*

Source: House Documents, March 1981.

THE HOSTAGE CRISIS IN IRAN: 1979–81

I. *Summary*

Rarely in its history has the United States confronted a challenge as difficult, frustrating, and emotionally charged as that of freeing the hostages captured in Iran on November 4, 1979. During the long months of their captivity our extraordinary efforts to free them were joined by virtually all civilized nations and by hundreds of individuals who worked continuously, diligently, and courageously.

Throughout the ordeal that is described in this paper, certain themes are dominant:

—From the start the United States had two overriding objectives:

—protection of the honor and vital national interests of the United States; and,

—protection of the well-being of the hostages and their safe release at the earliest possible moment.

—The United States pursued these objectives starting from certain basic principles (*e.g.*, no trials, no apology) and through the exercise of flexible diplomacy against a background of steadily increasing international economic pressure on and political isolation of Iran. This approach involved:

—development of an international consensus and specific measures that would isolate Iran and bring home to the Iranian people and their leaders the high cost of holding our people hostage;

—identification of persons and groups who enjoyed influence with the Iranian leadership or could serve as a channel of communication to it in working out a peaceful solution; and

—pursuit of all possible humanitarian channels to establish contact with the hostages, to ease their conditions of confinement, and to enable them to communicate with their families.

—From the outset, we faced the internal power struggle in Tehran, which prevented the emergence of responsible leadership that could speak consistently and authoritatively for Iran and communicate effectively with us about how the crisis might be resolved. Changing demands and the prolonged detention of the hostages were determined mainly by the political balance in Tehran. Throughout the crisis, we were advised that progress must await specific stages in development of Iran's new political institutions, first the December constitution, then the election of a president in January, finally the election and organization of the Parliament.

—As the Iranian political process moved haltingly through its various stages of development, we shifted the emphasis of our approach between measures to increase Iran's isolation and steps to open the way to an agreed resolution. Only after almost a year, when a degree of political coherence had been achieved in Tehran, could there be useful discussions about a possible agreement. These discussions covered terms the United States had been willing to accept for the release of the hostages.

—For the most part, the terms were developed from positions established during the first three months of the crisis. Most of the terms that formed the basis of the final proposals we made in November 1980-January 1981 were essentially those set forth in November and December 1979 and elaborated in January 1980, when the first systematic effort to negotiate a scenario for release of the hostages began. Where the content of a possible agreement changed, it was to deal with changing circumstances in the volatile and complex revolutionary environment in Iran.

—The crisis in U.S. relations with Iran disrupted extensive and complex financial, business, and commercial relationships between U.S. firms and individuals and their Iranian counterparts. This has resulted in significant losses and sacrifice on both sides.

—The effort to free the hostages has involved hundreds of thousands of hours by officials in the U.S. Government, including the President and his most senior advisors. There has been an equally massive devotion of energy by the families of the hostages, pri-

AP/Wide World

President Jimmy Carter was the last of a long line of U.S. presidents who had tried since World War II to maintain good relations with Iran. Here, he welcomes the Shah in 1977.

vate American citizens, and dedicated officials and citizens of other nations.
—Rarely has an event so gripped the attention of the world in peacetime and rarely has the world been so united in its outrage at a violation of elementary principles of religion, international law, and common decency.

II. *Background*

American foreign policy since World War II has consistently recognized the strategic, political, and economic importance of Iran. Each American Administration has sought to develop close relations with the Iranian Government and the Iranian people to strengthen that country and to protect vital American interests in the Middle East. During the three decades after the war, the United States assisted materially in developing Iran's economic and military strength through aid programs and commercial ties. Great numbers of young Iranians were educated in the United States to

return home to participate in their nation's development.

The Iranian revolution of February 1979 profoundly affected U.S. relations with Iran. The closeness of our association with the government of the Shah produced deep suspicion and hostility among the revolutionary leadership. Iran's new leaders tended to attack all past U.S. actions, disregarding the positive contributions we had made to Iranian development. They charged that the United States had imposed on Iran since 1953 a government that was oppressive and corrupt, that consistently violated human rights, and that was insensitive to the traditional values of Iran's Islamic society.

The United States determined shortly after the success of the revolution to attempt to establish a new relationship based on the changing realities in Iran. We recognized that the unstable political and economic conditions in Iran would make it difficult for the Provisional Government of Prime Minister Barzagan to deal effectively with the United States. But the judgment was made that our substantial interests in Iran warranted maintaining a presence and attempting to build a new relationship.

Our Embassy staff in Tehran was instructed to proceed cautiously in seeking opportunities for a better relationship. The official staff was small—cut from over 1400 civilian and military personnel before the revolution to about 70 men and women in November 1979. Thirteen of the staff were Marine Guards, and many of the remainder were occupied primarily in cleaning up the residue from our relationship with the previous regime, straightening out hundreds of disrupted contracts, seeking access to U.S. facilities occupied by revolutionary groups, disposing of property, and packing and shipping household goods.

Dealing with the complex military program, which had fallen from an annual level of payments of about $3 billion to zero, was a major issue on our agenda with the new leadership. Iranian orders for two Spruance ships, 160 F-16 and seven AWACs aircraft and other major equipment had been cancelled.

We were aware that it would not be productive to attempt to move faster in our overall relationship than the Iranians wished to move with us. In the complex and fluid revolutionary environment, we sought to be open to contacts with all Iranians. Our posture was one of readiness to respond to Iranian initiatives and openness to any signs of Iranian desire to resolve the many commercial, military, and political problems that complicated our relationship. As the Secretary of State told the Iranian Foreign Minister in New York in October 1979, the United States wanted a relationship with Iran based on "mutual respect, equality and friendship."

Security at the American Embassy was a problem throughout this period. The Embassy was attacked on February 14, 1979, after which the Iranian Deputy Prime Minister personally led a group of revolutionary guards to obtain the release of the captured Embassy personnel. Those informal guards remained as the "protection" for the Embassy premises. Our Charge d'Affaires pressed to have the informal force replaced by uniformed Iranian police more directly responsive to the central government, and this transfer was achieved in late August. Subsequently the Embassy premises were patrolled by an external force of about 15 uniformed policemen. Effective working-level contacts were established with the area police office and the area's contingent of revolutionary guards. During the spring and summer extensive physical improvements were completed in the Embassy buildings to enhance protection for our staff. Security conditions were not ideal, but were sufficiently improved by early September to permit the Embassy to resume near normal consular operations. Many Iranians, including leaders of the government and of minority groups, had been urging us to reopen our visa office on a more normal basis.

Throughout the eight months of the Provisional Government, our relations with Iranian authorities were generally characterized by tension and their great sensitivity to criticism. Some Iranian leaders asserted that criticism of them in the U.S. press was directed by the U.S. Government, and many of them appeared to believe that the United States was determined to bring down the new revolutionary government. In fact our policy was to seek where possible to strengthen the institutional structure in Iran. Thus in August, when the solvency of the Iranian Trust Fund maintained by the Department of Defense had been assured, we agreed to a limited resumption in the supply of spare parts for U.S.-origin military equipment. The spare parts, valued at $3.2 million, that were shipped in September and October were those which had already been paid for by Iran but which had been blocked in the pipeline during the revolution. For new spare parts not previously ordered by the Iranian forces, we agreed to the establishment of small trust funds for the Air Force and the Army. These arrangements for the purchase of additional spares were never implemented. Hundreds of military contracts were in suspense as the new Iranian leadership struggled with the complexities of the Shah's ambitious defense programs. Our Embassy faced a major task in explaining and getting Iranian decisions on dismantling these contracts.

In an effort to cooperate in restoring Iran's economic health, in the spring of 1979 we cautiously began to advise American businessmen to resume contacts with their Iranian partners in order to resolve the many complex commercial disputes. We wanted to see a resumption in the flow of spare parts and components for Iran's industrial establishment as a means of helping the Iranian labor force return to work. A restored economy could support increased political stability. From March to November 1979 Iran's oil sales to the U.S. were maintained at about pre-revolution levels.

Some limited success was achieved in the search for solutions to bilateral problems during this period, but strong suspicions and hostility persisted on the Iranian side.

III. *Admission of the Shah to the United States and Seizure of the Embassy.*

The Shah left Iran on January 16. Before he left, we told him that he would be welcome if he chose to come to the United States. Instead, he decided to remain first in Egypt and then in Morocco. After the revolution had succeeded, there were approaches on behalf of the Shah regarding his possible residence in the United States. At that time, against the background of the February 14 attack on the Embassy, we were concerned about the effect of his arrival in the United States on American personnel in Iran. Word was passed to the Shah that there would be risks for our Embassy staff if he came to the

United States at that time. The Shah left Morocco in March, and after a brief sojourn in the Bahamas, settled in Mexico. During the summer, there was contingency consideration of a possible later move to the United States, but the subject was set aside.

In late September and October, the Department of State was advised that the former Shah's health was deteriorating and that he would require diagnosis and treatment of a kind available only in the United States and in a few other countries that were not willing to admit him. After tentatively concluding that humanitarian considerations strongly supported admitting the Shah for this purpose, the United States instructed its Charge in Tehran to inform the Iranian Prime Minister and Foreign Minister before a final decision was made. He did so on October 21, presenting a detailed description of the Shah's medical condition and requesting adequate security protection for the Embassy. The Iranian leadership indicated that the Shah's travel to the United States would produce a sharp reaction in Iran, but they assured the Charge that protection for the Embassy would be provided. Based on that assurance, the improved physical security of the Embassy, and the increased security precautions taken by the Embassy staff, the United States decided to admit the Shah for medical treatment. As the President said later, it would have been inconsistent with the humane tradition of the United States to deny a sick man access to vitally needed American medical treatment. The Shah arrived in New York on October 23. Iran's assurances of protection were twice reaffirmed by the Iranian leadership after our first approach. The Iranians had, during earlier attacks or threatening demonstrations, showed themselves willing and able to defend our Embassy staff and premises.

The initial public reaction in Iran to the Shah's arrival in the United States seemed controlled and moderate. Gradually, however, Iranian leaders, including the Ayatollah Khomeini, sharpened their criticism of the United States for having admitted the Shah. This criticism coincided with attacks on the Provisional Government by its internal opponents of the extreme left and right. Nevertheless, during a large demonstration against the United States in Tehran on November 1, the Embassy was adequately protected.

On November 4, at about noon, possibly 3,000 young Iranians swarmed over the Embassy walls and threatened to burn the Embassy Chancery where most of the employees had taken refuge. The Embassy staff was able to hold out against the assault for over $3\frac{1}{2}$ hours, while making repeated calls for assistance to the Iranian police and political leadership. Our charge, L. Bruce Laingen, Political Counselor Victor Tomseth, and Security Officer Michael Howland were at the moment of the attack driving from the Foreign Ministry to the Embassy. They returned to the Ministry where they sought to obtain assistance for the beseiged Embassy staff. The Provisional Government was unwilling or unable to fulfill the assurances of protection it had given and had fulfilled for almost two weeks.

In Washington, Department of State officers kept open telephone lines with the Embassy staff and other Americans in Tehran during the attack. The Department was also in continuous contact with the Iranian Embassy in Washington and our embassies in third countries in efforts to lift the Embassy siege and to free our diplomats.

From the first word of the attack, the Department has maintained a Working Group on 24-hour duty monitoring all aspects of the crisis. The President, key Cabinet members, senior officials, staff and hostage families have since spent hundred of thousands of hours in a continuous effort to free the hostages. The breadth and persistence of this effort may be unprecedented in peacetime diplomacy.

Taken hostage with 61 Embassy staff were two Americans who happened to be visitors at the time of the attack. Some of these Embassy personnel were trapped during the assult in the separate consular building or in other offices in the city. All of these men and women, with the exception of six persons, were captured within a few days by the militants and confined in the Embassy compound with the other hostages. The six others remained free in Tehran, moving between various locations, until they were given protection by the Ambassador and Embassy staff of Canada.

During the first 48 hours, there appeared to be a possibility that the Iranian leadership would assert its authority and free the hostages from the control of the militants. The Foreign Minister indicated that such a move was underway in a conversation with Charge Laingen on the first day of the attack. During this period, several Ambassadors in Tehran attempted to use their personal influence to obtain the release of the hostages. State Department officers made direct telephone contacts with Iranian leaders to urge release.

By November 6, it became apparent that the Iranian authorities were unwilling to free the hostages, especially after Ayatollah Khomeini had endorsed the taking of the Embassy by the militants. Faced with Iran's refusal to meet its responsibilities, the President decided to send two special envoys to Iran to meet with Ayatollah Khomeini in order to seek release of the hostages and to work toward solutions to serious U.S.-Iranian problems. The President selected former Attorney General Ramsey Clark, who had a long and close association with many of the new Iranian leaders and who had met with Khomeini in Paris early in 1979. Mr. Clark was accompanied by William Miller, Staff Director of the Senate Commitee on Intelligence, who had served in Iran as a Foreign Service Officer in the 1950's and 1960's and who also knew the Iranian revolutionary leaders. The Iranian Government initially indicated that it would receive the Clark-Miller mission. However, as Mr. Clark was about to board a commercial flight from Istanbul to Tehran on November 7, he was informed that the Iranian Government had decided, on instruction from Ayatollah Khomeini, that he should not come to Iran and that no officials in Tehran should have discussions with American representatives. This barrier to direct communications was only rarely breached and was a serious obstacle to our diplomacy throughout the crisis.

In all of our dealings with Iran after the revolution we faced a political situation marked by sharp divisions and contests for power. The Ayatollah Khomeini was clearly the dominant figure. It was also clear that he did not wish to impose his will on the various factions until they could be brought together into a broad consensus. He saw in the establishment of the constitution and of the institutions under that constitution a framework within which decisions could be made and responsibilities shared.

Because of the internal political struggle, Iranians were terribly fearful of any direct contact with the United States. Those who had contact or received messages from the United States were often quick to announce the fact publicly and to distance themselves from the U.S. position. There were some who saw very early the desirability of resolving the hostage question, but who had only limited influence on the leadership. The United States faced a situation in which, for many months, those with whom we dealt were themselves seeking to penetrate the political framework and convince the leadership.

The political struggle was basically, but not exclusively, between those who saw Iran's revolution in modern terms and those who saw it in more conservative Islamic terms. There were groups representing a spectrum from left to right. Within the Islamic group there were contests for power between individuals. The only element on which all agreed—or professed to agree—was a strong antipathy toward the United States because of its past association with the Shah. It was in that atmosphere that the United States was required to resolve the hostage crisis.

IV. *The First Stage of Diplomatic Efforts: Setting Basic Principles (November—mid-December).*

On November 6, the Bazargan Government resigned and power was assumed by the Revolutionary Council. It became evident that no political group in Iran was prepared to challenge the insistence by the militants that the Shah and his assets be returned in exchange for the hostages. The United States had explained to the Iranian authorities that, in the absence of an extradition treaty, it was impossible for the United

States to consider legal proceedings to extradite the former Shah. Despite this fact, each of the contending political factions in Iran was unable or unwilling to oppose the demands of the militants. The militants consistently affirmed that they would take instructions only from the Ayatollah Khomeini directly, and he refused to issue orders to free the hostages. Since we had no means of directly influencing either the Ayatollah or the militants, we had to concentrate on reaching persons who could influence them indirectly.

Anti-American feelings whipped up by the official media were extremely strong in Tehran in the first weeks of the crisis. Emotional rallies and demonstrations around the Embassy appeared to pose a serious risk to the safety of the hostages, and the hostile attitudes of Iranian leaders made rational consideration of U.S. overtures virtually impossible.

From the outset of the crisis, the President established two equal and overriding goals for American policy:

—protection of the honor and vital interests of the United States; and

—protection of the well-being of the hostages and their safe release at the earliest possible moment.

These objectives remained constant throughout the crisis.

In implementing them, we sought to develop three basic approaches:

—the development of an international consensus and specific measures that would isolate Iran and bring home to the Iranian people and their leaders the high cost of holding our diplomats;

—the identification of persons and groups who enjoyed special influence with the Iranian leadership; and

—the pursuit of all possible humanitarian channels to establish contact with the hostages and to ease their conditions of confinement.

In our multilateral efforts, the United States was very early in touch with the highest levels of all governments with which we have diplomatic relations. Throughout the crisis these contacts were repeated when special requirements arose. Support for our position was quick, strong, and virtually unanimous. At that stage, only the Governments of North Korea, Vietnam, and Albania supported the Iranian position. Virtually all other governments, either publicly or privately, made known their firm opposition to the Iranian violation of international law and religious norms of conduct. Some governments sent private messages to the Iranian leadership. Some instructed their Ambassadors in Tehran to work for the hostages' release. Others who were not represented in Tehran instructed their UN Ambassadors to contact the Iranian representatives. Iran's isolation on the hostage issue was tangible evidence of the damage being done to Iran and its revolution.

These approaches were of special value to the United States when it was unable to have effective exchanges itself with Iran's leaders. During those early days, although Department of State officers spoke daily with members of the Revolutionary Council and the militants, there were no productive conversations.

We were also in close touch immediately after the Embassy seizure with Secretary General Waldheim to explore through his offices possible means of ending the crisis. The President of the Security Council, after consultations with the Council membership, issued on November 9 a statement expressing the Council's profound concern over the detention of American diplomats and urging that they be released without delay and given protection.

The President met with members of hostage families on November 9 and later they joined him in issuing an appeal to all Americans to exercise restraint toward Iran and Iranians and to do nothing that would endanger the hostages. The judgment was made that every effort would be made to free the hostages through diplomatic means to avoid endangering their lives.

On November 12, then Acting Foreign Minister Bani-Sadr stipulated three Iranian demands for release of the hostages:

—admit that the property of the Shah was stolen;
—cease interference in Iranian affairs; and
—extradite the Shah to Iran for a "fair trial."

Subsequently, Bani-Sadr was to modify these demands to:

—return of the Shah's assets;
—an end to interference in Iran's affairs; and
—an apology for past U.S. "crimes" against Iran.

The United States responded by making clear on repeated occasions that its courts were open to Iran to pursue the Shah's wealth; that we would not intervene internally in Iran; but that we would not make an apology for so-called "crimes." There was, of course, no assurance that meeting the Iranian demands would result in release of the hostages.

By November 17, the United States worked out with Secretary General Waldheim four points that he conveyed to the Iranian authorities that day. These points made clear our desire to end the crisis on a fair basis:

1. We required release of all personnel held in Tehran.
2. We suggested the establishment of an international commission to inquire into allegations of violations of human rights in Iran under the previous regime.
3. We indicated that the courts of the United States would be available to the Government of Iran to hear its claims for return of the assets it believed had been illegally taken out of Iran.
4. We proposed an affirmation by the Government of Iran and the United States of their intention to abide strictly by the Declaration on Principles of International Law Concerning Friendly Relations and Cooperation Among States in Accordance with the Charter of the United Nations, and by the provisions of the Vienna Convention on Diplomatic Relations.

During this early period and later, the United States was in touch with a wide range of individuals, both American and foreign, believed to have useful connections in Tehran. These included Islamic religious leaders, American and foreign clerics, journalists, international human rights advocates, businessmen, academic leaders, and jurists. Throughout the crisis, many people volunteered their services as intermediaries, but only some had useful ties with key Iranians. At any particular moment after the first weeks of the crisis we were normally in touch with at least 15 channels to the Iranian leadership. The reports and views of these contacts were regularly considered in reaching our own decisions.

On November 17, Ayatollah Khomeini directed the militants to release the women and black hostages who were not considered "spies." Thirteen hostages were released and flown to Germany for medical examination prior to their return home. Unfortunately, this potentially positive development was counterbalanced by statements by Iranian officials threatening that the remaining hostages would be placed on trial for espionage and subversion. The United States made clear in public and private communications with the Iranian authorities that a trial or any other steps that could endanger the well-being of the hostages would be viewed by the United States with utmost gravity and could cause severe consequences for Iran. In late November, the President met with his advisors at Camp David to consider the threat of a hostage trial. He authorized a very blunt, private warning to the Iranians against pursuing that course. Subsequently, the President told the first meeting of hostage families on December 7 that Iran had been warned that the United States would interrupt its commerce if Iran took steps to try any of the hostages. In the weeks that followed, talk of a trial began to subside in Iran.

For several weeks after the hostages were taken, the United States had only a very limited idea of their conditions of confinement and the character of their captors. We knew from a visit to the hostages on November 10 by the Papal Nuncio, the Ambassadors of Sweden, Algeria, and Syria, and the Charge of France that the hostages were bound and not allowed to speak. Even more graphic descriptions of harsh confinement were given by the released 13 hostages. The captors had made threats to kill the hostages and we did not know whether those threats would be carried out. We did not know, in fact, whether all the hostages were alive. In an effort to pressure the Iranians to improve the conditions of the hostages, we informed all governments of the cruel conditions of detention. The international criticism that followed led, we believe, to improved conditions starting in December.

After the Embassy seizure, several international agencies with which we were in touch immediately attempted to provide humanitarian assistance. On November 11, the Pope made a personal appeal to Ayatollah Khomeini, and was rebuffed. The International Red Cross sought but was denied its usual role of providing humanitarian services to prisoners. During this period we had daily telephone contact with the captors in the compound, in which they agreed to take down short messages from the hostage families and to relay them to the individual hostages. We learned from the 13 who were released that none of these messages was delivered. The Iranians never gave a complete and accurate accounting for the hostages, and throughout the crisis mail delivery to and from the hostages was irregular and severely restricted. When clergymen were allowed to conduct services for the hostages at Christmas, there were seven hostages whom they did not see.

As the international consensus against Iran grew stronger and the level of frustration in this country and abroad increased, it became important to convey tangible signals of the seriousness of the crisis to Iran. To assure that Iran could not use the "oil weapon" against us, on November 12 the President ordered the cessation of all U.S. oil purchases from Iran. The Iranian Government then stated that Iranian deposits would be immediately withdrawn from U.S. financial institutions. In order to prevent economic disruption and to protect legitimate claimants, the President directed on November 14 that all Iranian assets, including deposits in U.S. banks and their foreign branches and subsidiaries, be frozen. The President's order was based on his finding that the "situation in Iran" was a threat to the United States. It was clear that the freeze could be lifted once the hostages were released in the context of arrangements that would prevent economic disruption and protect American interests.

Iran, also on November 14, closed its airspace to U.S. aircraft. (Pan American, the only U.S. line serving Iran, had suspended flights at the outset of the crisis.) During this initial period also, the shipment of all military equipment to Iran was halted and virtually all U.S. trade with Iran ceased. Other nations were not prepared at that time to take the significant step of invoking economic sanctions against Iran.

By mid-November basic U.S. principles for ending the crisis had been established and the Iranians were aware of them. However, the absence of any centralized authority in Tehran apparently made the Iranians incapable of considering and acting on those principles.

As the crisis continued into late November, the United States recognized that no decisive Iranian action was likely until after the completion of the principal religious ceremonies of Moharram on November 29 and 30, and the national referendum for a new constitution on December 2. It appeared possible that an opportunity for obtaining release of the hostages might open just after those events. When there was no indication in early December of Iranian movement toward a settlement, the UN Security Council on December 4 unanimously adopted Resolution 457, calling on Iran to release the hostages immediately, to provide them protection, and to allow them to leave the country, and

further calling on Iran and the United States to resolve peacefully the remaining issues between them and requesting the Secretary General to lend his good offices. The United States accepted the resolution, but Iran flatly rejected it.

On November 29, the United States applied to the International Court of Justice for a ruling that Iran's seizure and holding of the hostages violated international law and that they should be immediately released. The Court heard the case on December 10 and issued an interim order on December 15 that Iran should immediately release all the hostages, afford them full protection, and restore to the United States its diplomatic premises in Iran. The order was issued unanimously by the Court's 15 judges, whose nationalities include all of the major regions of the world. Iran rejected the order and refused to comply with its terms.

The situation around the Embassy in Iran remained volatile and dangerous, with frequent anti-American demonstrations. Other Embassies considered themselves threatened, and the British Embassy was briefly occupied in early November. Similar anti-American outbursts occurred that month in Pakistan and Libya, where mobs attacked American Embassies. During the attack in Pakistan four U.S. Government employees were killed.

On December 15, the Shah left the United States for Panama, thus removing the ostensible cause for the occupation of the Embassy. However, there was no change in the Iranian refusal to release the hostages. Thus, at mid-December the United States had enunciated basic principles for a settlement, but there was no movement by Iran to resolve the crisis, and there appeared to be little prospect for an early solution.

V. *The Second Stage: Moving Toward Sanctions (Mid-December–mid-January).*

The United States sought to apply additional pressure in order to persuade the Iranians that it did not serve their interests to continue to hold the hostages. The President directed on December 12 that the Iranian diplomatic and consular staffs in the United States be cut to a total of 35 persons. Iran was not directed to close its Embassy and consulates entirely because the United States wished to keep open a possible channel to Tehran and also to allow necessary consular services to be performed for the thousands of Iranians living in this country.

On December 24, our Ambassador to the UN wrote to the President of the UN Security Council, noting the earlier actions of the Council and the World Court and asking the Council to meet at an early date to consider measures designed to induce Iran to comply with its international obligations. The Secretary of State had visited European capitals earlier in December to underline for our allies the gravity of the situation and to build support for the U.S. position.

On December 31, the Security Council adopted a second Resolution, number 461. Adopted by a vote of 11-0 with four abstentions, that Resolution reaffirmed Resolution 457 and decided that the Council would meet on January 7, 1980, to review the situation and to adopt effective measures under Articles 39 and 41 (sanctions) of the Charter in the event of continued Iranian noncompliance with the earlier resolution. The Soviet Union abstained on Resolution 461, moving away from its prior support of the U.S. position as a result of new tensions between it and the United States arising out of the Soviet invasion of Afghanistan on December 27. The Soviets continued on rare occasions to state their formal opposition to the holding of hostages, but Soviet propaganda shifted to attempts to exacerbate tensions between the United States and Iran and to portray the United States as the offending party in the crisis. Even before the invasion of Afghanistan, the Soviet desire to maintain a good relationship with Iran had caused the Eastern Bloc countries to refuse to participate in any combined initiatives of the diplomatic corps in Tehran.

Following the second UN resolution, Secretary General Waldheim visited Tehran in an effort to persuade the Iranian authorities to move toward a settlement. Prior to his departure, the United States gave him on December 31 a five-point statement of the U.S. position—again emphasizing our readiness to reach a reasonable and peaceful solution to the issue. The five points were:

1. That all U.S. personnel must be released from Iran prior to the institution of any international tribunal.

2. That the United States was prepared to work out in advance a firm understanding on arrangements for the airing of Iranian grievances before an appropriate forum after the hostages had been released.

3. That the United States would not object to any Iranian suits in U.S. courts to recover assets allegedly taken illegally from Iran by the former Shah.

4. That the United States would affirm jointly with Iran its intention to abide by the Declaration of Principles of International Law Concerning Friendly Relations and Cooperation Among States in Accordance with the Charter of the United Nations, and by the provisions of the Vienna Con-

vention on Diplomatic Relations. The United States stated that it accepted the present government of Iran as the legitimate authority in Iran and reaffirmed the view that the people of Iran had the right to determine their own form of government.

5. That the United States was willing, once the hostages were safely released, to seek in accordance with the UN Charter a resolution of all issues between the United States and Iran.

When he arrived in Tehran, the Secretary General encountered large and hostile demonstrations against the UN and the United States. Although he met with Iranian leaders on several occasions, he was not able to persuade them to change their positions. On January 7, the Secretary General reported to the Security Council that the Iranians were not yet ready to release the hostages but that a commission on international inquiry to hear Iran's grievances might help to defuse the situation. On January 11, as the Security Council was preparing to vote on a resolution on economic sanctions, Iran asked that consideration be given to the establishment of a commission of inquiry that could help improve the atmosphere for resolution of the crisis. The United States agreed to defer the Security Council vote until January 13 to give the Secretary General time to explore the Iranian position. When it became clear that the Iranian proposal was not directly linked to release of the hostages, the Security Council moved to consider a sanctions resolution. The resolution imposing sanctions on Iran gained 10 votes but was vetoed by the USSR.

The United States indicated that it wished nonetheless to proceed with sanctions and urged its allies to do the same. Members of the European Community and Japan responded that the imposition of sanctions without a UN resolution would be legally difficult for them. Our allies asked the United States to delay imposition of sanctions until after the election of an Iranian President on January 29 and possible consideration of the hostage crisis by the Islamic Conference at the end of the month. As these developments seemed to hold some hope for movement on the crisis, the United States agreed to defer action on sanctions.

After Secretary General Waldheim had returned from Tehran and met with the President, it seemed that a more complete statement of the U.S. position might help to convince the Iranians that we were willing to agree to a mutually honorable end to the crisis. The pressures applied to Iran and the indications of probable further measures appeared to be having some effect. The Soviet invasion of Afghanistan and the resulting threat to Iran gave the Iranians an additional reason to seek a way out of the crisis. Several intermediaries suggested U.S. positions that might create greater flexibility in Tehran. The President reviewed the existing situation and these proposals with his advisors and decided to refine the earlier U.S. position. The President approved the following six-point statement:

1. The safe and immediate departure from Iran of all U.S. employees of the Embassy in Tehran and other Americans held hostage is essential to a resolution of other issues.

2. The United States understands and sympathizes with the grievances felt by many Iranian citizens concerning the practices of the former regime. The United States is prepared to work out in advance firm understandings on a forum in which those grievances may sub-

sequently be aired, so that the hostages could be released with confidence that those grievances will be heard in an appropriate forum after the release has taken place. The United States will not concur in any hearing that involves the hostages. The United States is prepared to cooperate in seeking through the auspices of the UN to establish such a forum or commission to hear Iran's grievances and to produce a report on them. The U.S. Government will cooperate with such a group in accordance with its laws, international law, and the Charter of the UN.

3. The U.S. Government will facilitate any legal action brought by the Government of Iran in courts of the United States to account for assets within the custody or control of the former Shah that may be judged to belong to the national treasury of Iran by advising the courts, and other interested parties, that the U.S. Government recognizes the right of the Government of Iran to bring such claims before the courts and to request the courts' assistance in obtaining information about such assets from financial institutions and other parties.

4. Once the hostages are safely released, the United States is prepared to lift the freeze of Iranian assets and to facilitate normal commercial relations between the two countries, on the understanding that Iran will meet its financial obligations to U.S. nationals and that the arrangements to be worked out will protect the legitimate interests of U.S. banks and other claimants. The United States is prepared to appoint members of a working group to reach agreement on those arrangements.

5. The United States is prepared to appoint a representative to discuss with Iranian representatives the cur-

rent threat posed by the Soviet invasion of Afghanistan and to recommend to their governments steps that the United States and Iran might take in order to enhance the security of Iran, including the resumption of the supply of military spare parts by the United States to Iran.

6. The U.S. Administration is prepared to make a statement at an appropriate moment that it understands the grievances felt by the people of Iran, and that it respects the integrity of Iran, and the right of the people of Iran to choose their own form of government. The U.S. Government recognizes the Government of the Islamic Republic of Iran as the legal government of Iran. The United States reaffirms that the people of Iran have the right to determine their own form of government.

The text of these points was given to the Secretary General and to other intermediaries, who transmitted them to Iranian leaders. The proposals made in November and December 1980 and January 1981 did not deviate substantially from these positions. But in January 1980 they drew no response from Tehran. There appeared to be no one in Iran at that time capable of responding meaningfully to the U.S. position.

On January 29, the six Americans who had been hiding with the Canadians departed Iran through the Tehran airport using assumed identities. Canada then closed its Embassy and withdrew all personnel. The presence of "the six" in Iran had been known to several journalists for some weeks, but fortunately they accepted the importance of keeping the information confidential. The return home of the six Americans on January 31 was greeted with an outpouring of American joy and gratitude for the courageous assistance of the Canadian Ambassador and his staff. Iranians reacted sharply, compaining of a "violation of international law"; in retaliation the Foreign Ministry severely limited our contacts with Bruce Laingen and his colleagues held in the Foreign Ministry.

VI. *The Third Stage: Development of a Written Scenario for Release (January-April).*

About one week after the Soviet veto of the sanctions resolution, the United States finally was contacted by two intermediaries who enjoyed special ties of confidence with persons in the Iranian leadership. A series of meetings, some 100 hours of discussion in all, were held in London, Washington, Paris, and Switzerland to design a written scenario that would secure the safe release of the hostages and at the same time assure that Iran received an appropriate international hearing for its asserted grievances. The President closely monitored and approved each of the steps taken in formulating and implementing the scenario.

The scenario was developed over several weeks in January and February, and we were assured that it had been fully discussed in the Revolutionary Council and accepted by all significant elements of the Iranian leadership. It involved the UN's dispatch of a five-man fact-finding commission to Iran to hear Iran's grievances and allow an early solution to the crisis. The scenario was laid out in a series of steps—each agreed to by the United States and Iran—that would permit each side to assure itself of the performance of the other as the scenario moved toward its final steps. The United States briefed UN authorities on the scenario, and they agreed to join in its implementation.

A five-man UN Commission was selected under the co-chairmanship of Andres Aguilar of Venezuela and Mohammed Bedjaoui of Algeria, and including Adib Daoudi of Syria, Harry W. Jayewardene of Sri Lanka, and Louis Edmond Petitti of France. They arrived in Tehran on February 23. On the same day, Ayatollah Khomeini announced that the fate of the hostages should be decided by the Iranian Parliament, which was to be elected in March. His announcement, which was not part of the agreed scenario, was the first indication that he had not fully approved the plan. Nevertheless, the Commission members began their work on the review of Iran's grievances, receiving documents and hearing testimony assembled by the Iranian authorities. The scenario called for the Commission to visit each of the hostages and for the hostages subsequently to be transferred to the authority of the Iranian Government. Again, the Ayatollah departed from the agreed scenario. Even after the militants had grudgingly announced their willingness to yield control of the hostages to the Revolutionary Council and the Council had issued a statement accepting the offer, the Ayatollah on March 10 called on the militants to prevent the Commission from seeing the hostages until after it had completed its report and made it public, and after the Iranian people had approved the Commission's findings. These were, of course, impossible conditions for the Commission.

As the Commission was unable to complete its agreed mandate by seeing the hostages and obtaining their transfer, it departed from Tehran on March 11, promising to return and to finish its report when conditions were more appropriate for it to perform its full mandate. During the weeks that followed, it was unclear whether or how the Commission might resume its work and reactivate the scenario.

Meanwhile, in Panama, the Shah, who was scheduled for surgery for the removal of his spleen, was becoming increasingly uneasy. Panama had given Iran's lawyers until late March to make the case for extradition of the Shah to Iran. The Shah, advised by his doctors that he needed urgent medical treatment, and displeased with a dispute between doctors in Panama, decided to reject the urging of the United States that he remain in Panama and instead accepted the longstanding offer of President Sadat to settle in Egypt. He departed for Egypt on March 23, where a few days later he underwent surgery. The decision to go to Egypt was the Shah's own choice in consulation with his physicians.

The atmosphere in Tehran was further confused at this time by the publication in the Iranian press of a false letter allegedly from President Carter to Ayatollah Khomeini. President Bani-Sadr revealed to the Iranian public the content of two authentic letters delivered by the Swiss from the United States, urging that the Iranian Government take custody of the hostages from the militants as a step toward their final release. On March 31, we received word that the Revolutionary Council was again attempting to deal with the hostage question.

On April 1, we learned that President Bani-Sadr had announced that the hostages would be transferred to government control if the United States would recognize the role of the Iranian Parliament in the hostage crisis and refrain from propaganda, provocation, or claims against Iran. Swiss Ambassador

Probst telephoned the White House to deliver the news early in the morning of April 1. President Carter went on television a short time later to welcome the announcement and to say that we would again delay the imposition of sanctions in light of this possibly positive development. Assurances along the lines of those sought by Bani-Sadr were passed to him and accepted as satisfactory. President Carter knew that there were no binding guarantees, but he sought to make sure that the Iranians understood that we wanted our people protected and released under peaceful and honorable conditions. Once the hostages were transferred to Iranian Government control, we believed, a new dynamic would be introduced which could expedite their release. A few days later, however, a minority of the faction-ridden Revolutionary Council undercut Bani-Sadr and prevented the transfer of the hostages.

During this period, the United States had established constant and effective communications through intermediaries with responsible Iranian officials and reached agreement with them on a basis for ending the crisis. But it had been unable to reach the other, more powerful political group, the religious leadership, which had blocked the agreed solution. The divisions within Iran continued to frustrate a resolution of the problem.

VII. *The Fourth Stage: Maximum Pressure and the Rescue Mission (April—May).*

It became plain in early April that the internal power struggle in Iran was preventing an early end to the crisis. The United States had made concerted efforts to resolve the matter through negotiation, which had failed because of the absence of centralized authority within Iran. A contest for control of the new Parliament stalled any constructive steps by the Iranian leadership to resolve the problem. With political divisiveness growing within Iran, it was the judgment of the Administration that precise and very firm action had to be taken to end the crisis before the hostages were further endangered.

Accordingly, on April 7 the President announced a series of actions against Iran which the United States had considered in the past but withheld in the interest of obtaining a negotiated release of the hostages. First, the United States broke diplomatic relations with Iran and declared all Iranian diplomatic and consular personnel and military trainees *persona non grata,* obliging them to leave the United States.

Second, the United States put into effect official economic sanctions in accordance with the provisions of the resolution vetoed in the UN Security Council on January 13. This provided a legal barrier to the shipment of U.S. goods—with the exception of food and medicine—to Iran. Trade between the United States and Iran had already come to a virtual halt because of political uncertainties, the pressure of public opinion, and the freezing of Iran's assets.

Third, the United States ordered a formal inventory of the assets of the Iranian Government frozen by the November order and of all claims against Iran, with the purpose of designing a possible program for handling the claims.

Fourth, all visas held by Iranian citizens were invalidated. The President directed that no new visas would be issued except for compelling and proven humanitarian reasons or where the U.S. national interest required. The United States earlier had directed that all Iranian applications for new visas be sub-

jected to a special security check to prevent potential terrorists from reaching the United States.

On April 17, as a further indication of U.S. determination to demonstrate to Iran the cost of holding hostages, the President announced additional measures against Iran:

—All financial transfers to Iran were prohibited, with the exception of those licensed by Treasury or those related to gathering news.

—All imports from Iran to the United States were banned.

—American citizens were prohibited from traveling to Iran, with the exception of journalists and persons expressly authorized by the Secretaries of State and Treasury.

—All military equipment previously purchased by Iran and impounded in the United States was to be made available for purchase by U.S. military forces or sale to other countries. Phoenix missiles and other items were purchased by the U.S. services with payment made to the Iran Trust Fund held by the Department of Defense.

In addition, the President mentioned other steps that might be taken—including legislation for processing of claims against Iran, prohibition of shipments of food and medicine, and interruption of Iran's access to international communications—if progress were not made toward release of the hostages.

During these weeks, the President and his advisors were also considering the feasibility of a rescue mission. The possibility of mounting a rescue mission had been explored from the outset of the crisis, and planning and practice for a rescue attempt were placed in motion early in November 1979. The planners faced a difficult set of circumstances, including the rapidly changing Iranian political scene, uncertainty about the captors' intentions and their capabilities, the hostility of Iranians toward the United States, and the harsh environment and distances to be covered.

By the end of November, planning and operations had progressed to the point that mission commanders had developed confidence in their ability to proceed with the rescue. The commanders recognized that substantial additional practice was needed, and they conducted training missions in the western United States throughout December. By January, helicopters and other equipment had been transferred to ships in the area and final landing sites selected. In early February the mission commanders concluded they had the capability to mount a successful rescue. There was a delay of several weeks, however, because diplomatic activity still held a serious prospect for obtaining the release of the hostages.

By April, when that diplomatic activity seemd blocked, the commanders of the joint task force recommended April 24 as the day for the rescue. The President personally approved the plan on April 11.

The mission began with 8 helicopters flying toward the staging point in the eastern desert. Two helicopters were lost en route. The failure of the third helicopter at the staging point necessitated a decision to terminate the mission. In the attempt eight airmen lost their lives and five others were seriously injured.

The rescue mission was planned as a precise action in Tehran to pick up the hostages, both in the Embassy compound and in the Foreign Ministry, and to remove them safely from Iran. No attack on the Iranian Government or on units not involved in holding the hostages was planned. However, the Iranian Government reaction to the mission was to describe it as an effort to overthrow the revolutionary regime.

Diplomatic discussions concerning the release of the hostages were naturally stalled in the immediate aftermath of the abortive rescue mission. Tehran was again agitated by anti-U.S. demonstrations. Considerable effort was required to secure the return of the bodies of the eight deceased servicemen to their families in the United States. Archbishop Hillarion Capucci, who had travelled to Iran in February to visit some of the hostages in the compound and again at Easter with American clergy, was helpful in arranging for the release of the bodies.

The reaction of the militants to the rescue mission was to threaten the lives of all hostages, to transfer them to separate locations in Iran, and to interrupt the very limited movement of mail to the families. Previously, there had been some slight improvement in contacts with the hostages. There were TV films of the religious services at Easter, and on April 14, for the first time, all of the hostages were visited by the Red Cross and allowed to send brief messages to their families. After April, no outsiders were permitted to visit the hostages until Christmas.

From the beginning of the crisis, volunteers, including hostage family members, worked with the Iran Working Group to maintain contacts with the widely scattered families of the hostages and to keep them informed of developments to the maximum extent possible. In April, the family members formed the Family Liaison Action Group (FLAG), which as its first act sent a delegation on April 22 to Europe to seek the support of European leaders for freeing the hostages. Later, FLAG sent appeals to the Islamic Conference. FLAG met regularly with the President and the Secretary of State and helped to organize meetings of hostage families throughout the United States. These efforts successfully emphasized the humanitarian interest in release of the hostages and provided important moral support to the deeply concerned families around the country. Without question, the steadfast performance of these troubled families during months of intense emotional strain was magnificent. These families were true heroes of the efforts to free the hostages.

On May 24, 1980, the International Court of Justice ruled conclusively in the United States' favor in its case against Iran, The Court issued a final judgment unanimously confirming that Iran's takeover of the Embassy and continued holding of hostages were inadmissible in a civilized international order and could not be justified by past or current grievances, real or imagined. The Court noted that the holding of the hostages "is unique and of particular gravity." It also unanimously decided that no hostage could be placed on trial or required to be a witness.

By a majority of 12-3, the Court decided that Iran had an obligation to make reparation to the United States for the injuries suffered as a result of the hostage seizure. The United States immediately called on the Iranians to comply with the Court's judgment and redoubled its efforts in the UN to ensure that all nations recognized the justice of its efforts to free the hostages.

Meanwhile, during April the United States had been in touch with the countries of the European Community and Japan about their imposition of sanctions on Iran. Their sanctions were agreed to on May 17, and went into effect shortly thereafter. The measures varied in details between countries, but their general effect was to make it increasingly difficult for Iran to purchase needed supplies from abroad. In addition, Iran's demand for higher oil prices led its Japanese and Western European customers to cease purchases of Iranian oil. This reduction in oil sales and available income dealt a significant blow to the Iranian economy.

The freeze of Iranian assets continued during this period, as it did throughout the crisis. In implementing the freeze, Treasury sought to maximize its impact on Iran by limiting exceptions to hardship, health, and hunger situations. At the same time, attempts were made to minimize harm to U.S. commercial interests. Thus, for example, licenses were issued allowing payments of up to $500,000 out of blocked funds to small U.S. entities whose existence might otherwise have been threatened and to authorize Iran to bring previously unblocked money into the United States to pay obligations to United States persons and entities. In order to avoid hardships and the development of new irritants that could adversely affect the hostage issue, Treasury also allowed Iran to bring in new money to provide for the support of Iranian students here. The overall impact of the freeze, however, was severely to curtail economic contact between Iran and the United States. This caused significant problems for banks and businesses that had previously been active in Iran.

In the first month of the freeze, regulations were adopted permitting the filing of litigation against Iran; and over 200 lawsuits were filed here and abroad. These suits generally asserted monetary claims against Iran or its entities and sought to attach various assets. The regulations allowed the lawsuits, but prohibited the entry of judgments affecting the frozen assets; and we urged judges to defer action on these lawsuits pending resolution of the hostage crisis. This position was not accepted by all judges, and rulings have been made by lower courts on issues in some of the lawsuits.

VIII. *The Fifth Stage: The Buildup of Pressure and Diplomatic Activity (May—August).*

At the end of May the Administration conducted a comprehensive review of past and possible new efforts to free the hostages. The Iranians steadfastly maintained that the new Parliament would determine Iran's position on the hostage question. The new Parliament had not yet been organized, nor had a Prime Minister and Cabinet been appointed to lead a new government. The political infighting in Iran foretold that such fundamental political decisions would be reached only with great difficulty.

In these circumstances the President decided that U.S. measures in the succeeding weeks should emphasize:

—Assuring that the sanctions were strictly applied and allowing time for their effect to sink in and for the Iranians to perceive that it was increasingly in their interest to end the crisis.

—Intensifying diplomatic activity and contacts by other parties to explain to the Iranians the harsh consequences for Iran and its revolution of allowing the hostage crisis to continue.

—Playing down the public diplomacy aspect of our crisis management in order to give the Iranians time and a certain degree of calm to work out a reasonable way out of the crisis.

This approach was pursued through-

out the summer, but especially in June, when there was a marked increase in the number of contacts with Iranian leaders and foreign diplomatic sources in Tehran. After the rescue mission Iranian spokesmen began again to demand that some or all of the hostages be placed on trial. We emphasized in our diplomatic contacts and those of our intermediaries our total opposition to any procedure that would endanger or humiliate the hostages in violation of international law. Apparently in response to this message, the threats of trial subsided.

In early June the Iranians convened an international conference to air evidence of "U.S. complicity" with the Shah's regime and alleged efforts to bring down the revolutionary government. We refused to validate passports for a group of Americans who wished to travel to the conference on the ground that it was strictly a propaganda device, unlikely to make any progress toward a fair resolution of the crisis. That judgment proved to be correct.

In June, European Socialist leaders in touch with the United States sought to persuade the Iranian authorities to release the hostages. Messrs. Kreisky of Austria, Palme of Sweden, and Gonzales of Spain traveled to Iran to attempt to convince the Iranians of the harm being done to their country by the continuing crisis. Similar arguments were put to the Iranian Foreign Minister when he met with the Socialist International in Oslo.

Throughout the summer, the atmosphere did slowly and haltingly improve, despite Iranian accusations in July of American backing for a military coup. There were fewer and smaller mobs in front of the Embassy, and Iranian rhetoric generally subsided. On July 11, hostage Richard Queen was suddenly released by the Iranian authorities for humanitarian reasons. Queen had been stricken by multiple sclerosis during his captivity and was returned home to a heartfelt national welcome.

On July 23, an Iranian who opposed the Khomeini regime was assassinated in Bethesda, and several Americans associated with Iranian revolutionaries in this country were linked to the attack. A few days later, at the end of clashing pro- and anti-Khomeini demonstrations in Washington, about 200 Iranian students were arrested. Their refusal to cooperate with the police and immigration authorities led to scuffles as they were arrested and to their detention for about 10 days. Television and news reports of the students' arrests again fanned anti-American feelings in Iran and led to large demonstrations against the United States. That response quickly subsided, however, when the students finally decided to cooperate with the authorities and were released.

On July 27, the Shah died in Cairo—thus removing entirely the original stimulus that triggered the seizure of the Embassy. However, there was no change in the Iranian position, which had shifted from demands for the return of the Shah to a generalized "attack on imperialism."

At the end of this stage, sanctions were clearly hurting the Iranian economy, which was already weakened by the revolutionary turmoil. President Bani-Sadr, an economist, acknowledged that the sanctions had added 25 percent or more to the high rate of inflation. Iran's industrial establishment was operating at less than 30 percent of normal. The continued freeze of Iranian assets (in excess of $8 billion) and the virtual cutoff in Iran's oil income were creating serious problems for Iran's banking and fiscal systems. Plainly, even to many hardline revolutionaries, the disadvantages to Iran of continuing to hold the hostages were beginning to be apparent.

IX. *The Sixth Stage; Intensified Diplomatic Exchanges (Mid-August—January).*

By mid-August, after months of bitter political struggle, the necessary Iranian political structure for dealing with the hostage crisis seemed to be in place. The Parliament had been organized and Ali Akbar Hashemi Rafsanjani was named President or Speaker. Mohammed Ali Rajai was approved as Prime Minister, along with a majority of his Cabinet. There were expectations that the Parliament would soon turn its attention to the hostages. The United States decided that the moment was ripe for more direct and intensive diplomacy.

The first of a series of personal letters from U.S. officials to the new Iranian leaders was sent in August. In an initiative that originated in the House of Representatives, 187 Members signed a letter to Rafsanjani urging that the new Parliament give priority attention to the hostages. Speaker Rafsanjani's oral reply, while critical of the Congressional approach, held out some prospect for further exchanges. Accordingly, a second Congressional letter signed by Congressmen Gilman and Hamilton was sent on September 15.

Throughout the crisis, the Administration had kept the Congress fully informed of developments. The President, Secretary, Deputy Secretary, and other officers met regularly with Senators and Congressmen to share assessments of events. The Congress clearly understood the difficulty and delicacy of the complex situation and was helpful and fully supportive of the efforts pursued by the Executive Branch to gain freedom for the hostages. The long months of the hostage crisis showed how effectively Congress and the Executive Branch can cooperate to protect the national interest.

On their own initiative, the families of the hostages wrote to Speaker Rafsanjani on September 13, urging that the Parliament consider release of the hostages on humanitarian grounds and offering to meet with him for discussions. Like the Congressional letters, this one was read to the Parliament, but there was no response.

The Secretary of State wrote to Prime Minister Rajai on August 31 and again on September 30. In addition, papers spelling out the U.S. general position on the basic elements of a settlement along the lines of the January six-point paper were conveyed to key Iranian leaders during September.

In August and early September, it became evident that the political situation in Tehran was beginning to coalesce and lines of authority were becoming clearer. Concurrently, the view that holding the hostages was more of a liability than a benefit appeared to gain strength among the Iranian leadership. The early widespread support for holding the hostages was outweighed by the very heavy price Iran was paying economically and in terms of international isolation. The judgment that the revolution was more endangered than helped by the hostage situation seemed increasingly to be accepted.

On September 12 Khomeini stated briefly in a speech on a larger subject the conditions that the Parliament should set for the release of the hostages. These were:
—return of frozen assets:
—return of property taken illegally by the Shah;
—cancellation of financial claims against Iran: and
—a pledge not to interfere in Iran's internal affairs.

Although broadly stated and not precisely defined, these conditions provided the structure for an agreement. An additional step was the establishment of a Commission in the Parliament to recommend to the Parliament the conditions for the hostages' release.

In private contacts in mid-September, arranged by the Government of the Federal Republic of Germany, we were able to clarify and explain in greater detail our position on the various conditions outlined by Khomeini. Further exchanges were envisioned to try to expedite the process in Tehran to permit the hostages to be returned as promptly as possible. However, before further exchanges could be arranged, positive movement on the hostage issue was sharply interrupted in late September by the Iraqi military strike against Iran and the outbreak of hostilities between the two countries.

The Iraq-Iran conflict had two effects on the hostage situation, one immediate and one more delayed. In the short term, the Iranian leadership shifted its attention almost exclusively to the war, and its interest in a resolution of the hostage situation was concomitantly reduced. However, as the war continued, the costs of holding the hostages were starkly felt by Iran. The combination of diplomatic isolation, an economy severely strained by sanctions, the draw-down of financial reserves which were not replenished by much-reduced oil sales, and the general unavailability of military resupply, all dramatized for Iran the high price it was paying for holding the hostages.

Although the hostilities had interrupted the momentum that was building on the hostage issue, we continued to press for release. We attempted to reinforce those in Tehran who were arguing that the war demonstrated Iran's need to resolve the hostage crisis and end its international isolation. During October we sent a number of indirect messages to the Iranian leadership, which stressed that a resolution of the issue was to our mutual benefit and refined further the actions we would be willing to take in the context of a general settlement of the hostage issue. With increasing frequency as the U.S. elections drew closer, Iranian leaders spoke in more positive terms of release.

Prime Minister Rajai visited New York on October 16-19. During the Prime Minister's effort to focus world attention on Iran's grievances in its conflict with Iraq, numerous interlocutors told him that Iran could not expect support from the world community as long as it continued to hold the hostages.

Illustrating the importance to Iran of a prompt resolution of the hostage crisis, the Parliament's Commission completed its work despite the war with Iraq and reported to the full Parliament during the last week of October. The Majlis (Parliament) held several closed sessions without reaching a decision. When a vote was scheduled for October 30, hard-line members blocked the session by preventing a quorum. Finally, on November 2 the Majlis adopted the Commission's recommendations elaborating Khomeini's conditions for releasing the hostages.

The Majlis Resolution demanded that the U.S.:
—pledge not to interfere in the affairs of Iran;
—lift the freeze on Iranian assets and put [them] at the disposal of Iran;

—cancel all economic and financial sanctions against Iran, cancel all U.S. claims against Iran, and assume financial responsibility for any claims made against Iran:
—return to Iran the assets of the Shah and his close relatives.

In return, Iran would release the hostages gradually as the U.S. implemented the stipulated conditions. If the U.S. did not meet Iranian demands, the hostages would be tried.

In a public statement that was conveyed to Iranian officials by the Swiss, the President termed the Majlis action of taking a position "a significant development" and a positive basis for moving toward an honorable and peaceful solution to the crisis. He said we would not be influenced by the impending U.S. elections in dealing with the issue and any action we took would be consistent with our vital national interests and national honor and in full accordance with our laws and Constitution. Deputy Secretary of State Christopher and a small team of advisors began at once to formulate a U.S. response to the Majlis Resolution.

A Committee headed by Minister of State for Executive Affairs Nabavi was also established in the office of Prime Minister Rajai to deal with all aspects of the hostage crisis. In the initial stages, this group had little flexibility and saw its role as the strict implementation of the Majlis Resolution as if it were a binding law. Rajai designated Algeria as the sole contact for communications between Iran and the U.S. on the hostage issue. On November 3, Algerian Ambassador Malek delivered the official text of the Majlis Resolution to the State Department.

Following the passage of the Majlis Resolution, the militant captors met with Khomeini and told him they wished to turn over custody of the hostages to the Government. Khomeini praised their revolutionary act and agreed to the transfer. Despite conflicting reports in the weeks that followed, the Government did not publicly acknowledge that it had definitely assumed custody of all of the hostages until early January.

On November 10 Mr. Christopher and his team flew to Algiers to deliver the U.S. response and to explain it in detail so that the Algerian representatives would be prepared to answer the questions of the authorities in Tehran. Prefacing his description of our response, Mr. Christopher told the Algerians that we accepted in principle the Majlis Resolution as a basis for ending the crisis and had sought to be as forthcoming as possible under our Constitution and legal system. At the same time, any solution of the issue must reflect American national interests and honor, and be perceived as equitable by both countries. This position was later stated publicly by Secretary Muskie.

The core of our response was a general statement of the U.S. position on each of the points in the Majlis resolution. We also shared with the Algerians examples of U.S. Government declarations which could be made effective with the safe release of all of the hostages.

A high level Algerian team left immediately after the Algiers meeting, taking the U.S. response and detailed U.S. position papers to Tehran. The Algerians stayed in Tehran ten days as the Nabavi Committee studied the U.S. response. The Iranian comments came in two separate submissions. First, there was a request cabled to Washington for five lists of data from us:

—a listing of all legal suits pending against Iran in U.S. courts;

—an inventory of Iranian assets held in U.S. banks here and abroad;

—a list of all loan offset measures taken by U.S. banks;

—an accounting of all Iranian Government assets and real estate property held by U.S. companies or private citizens here and abroad;

—a compilation of judgments rendered by U.S. courts.

We pointed out that some of the financial information had already been provided to the Algerians and all of the data should have been in the possession of the Iranian authorities or their lawyers in the U.S. After agreement had been reached on the principles for a settlement, we would be prepared to cooperate to the extent of our information.

The second Iranian statement, delivered by the Algerians to the Department of State on November 26, commented on the U.S. response. The U.S. response was termed by the Iranians to be "new proposals" or "obscure." The Nabavi Committee asked for explicit statements whether or not the U.S. would agree to nine specific elements in the Majlis Resolution.

Working over the Thanksgiving holidays and obtaining the President's final guidance that weekend, Mr. Christopher and his team were able to return to Algiers on December 2 to present the second U.S. response. Our response, in effect a statement of the previous U.S. position in a different form, was designed to meet the Iranian need for explicit answers to their nine questions related to the elements of the Majlis Resolution. In addition, the U.S. again described in a separate paper how each of the nine undertakings was to be accomplished. Affirming that the U.S. would restore the financial position of Iran insofar as possible to that which existed prior to November 1979, the U.S. explained the elements of our position and the constraints affecting it.

As they had on the previous occasion, the Algerian delegation left at once for Tehran following the conclusion of the meetings with the U.S. team and delivered our response on December 4. The comments of Rafsanjani and other Iranians who were briefed on the second U.S. response were less negative than they had been on earlier occasions about prospects for a settlement. Mail to the families from the hostages—blocked since the outbreak of war with Iraq—suddenly began to arrive again in the U.S. Presumably, humanitarian arguments by the Algerians in their meetings in Tehran had been persuasive.

The hope for release by Christmas that these developments produced was dashed, however, on December 19, when the Iranians presented their response to our paper of December 4, The Iranians stipulated that the U.S. should deposit with Algeria a total of almost $24 billion prior to the release of the hostages. These funds, described as financial guarantees, included not only all known Iranian assets (over $9 billion) frozen in U.S. institutions, but also $10 billion against the later return to Iran of assets of the late Shah and his family allegedly held in the U.S. and $4 billion in U.S. Government funds to cover other unidentified Iranian assets that might be located later. The total funds covering Iran's assets (over $13 billion), but not the Shah's wealth, were to be handed over to Iran with the release of the 52 hostages.

Although some of the demands contained in the Iranian response clearly exceeded the Constitutional and political authorities of the President, there were also certain positive elements. The

Iranians agreed to make good on outstanding loans and to settle bona fide debts through acceptable arbitration. Thus, we decided to make one further attempt to build on those elements and to reformulate our position.

During this period we sought through the Swiss and Algerians to arrange for pastoral visits at Christmas to the hostages. Although at first our requests were turned aside, on Christmas Eve the Papal Nuncio and three Iranian clergymen were allowed to visit the hostages and TV films were made. On Christmas day the Algerian Ambassador in Tehran was allowed to see each of the 52 hostages and to collect TV tapes, photographs and messages for the families. These were the first contacts the hostages had had with an outsider since April.

On December 28 Rajai made public the Iranian response and, in part, the U.S. position of December 4, adding his own comments. To remove any confusion we released to the press on December 29 the text of our position.

The revised U.S. response was given to the Algerians on December 30. In this formulation we offered a detailed proposal for settling claims through arbitration and the establishment of an escrow account in an agreed central bank for the deposit of presently frozen Iranian assets. Part of the proposal called for establishment by Iran of a Security Account with the same central bank to provide a means of making payment of claims under the proposed Claims Settlement Agreement. These proposals were worked out as a Declaration of the Government of Algeria which both sides would accept. When these arrangements were all in place and when Algeria certified that the 52 hostages had been safely released, the monies in the escrow account could be released to Iran but the Security Account would be maintained by Iran with a large balance during the settlement of claims. With the assurance of an acceptable agreement on arbitration of claims, the U.S. would seek to have the courts lift attachment orders affecting frozen assets so that those funds could also be placed in the escrow account. We explained that it would take time beyond the release of the hostages for these legal actions to be accomplished.

We made clear that in order for the complicated transactions in the U.S. proposal to be initiated during the time remaining to the Administration of President Carter, the Iranians would have to indicate their agreement by January 16. (At Iran's request and when prospects for an agreement improved, we dropped the stipulated date.) Minor changes in language were made in our formulation of the points on non-intervention in Iranian affairs and the Shah's assets, and these two points appeared no longer to be issues of contention.

On January 4, the Iranians announced that the three hostages held in the Foreign Ministry had been transferred to a more "appropriate location" with the other hostages. On December 23, revolutionary guards had attempted to transfer the three, but they had resisted and the attempt had been abandoned. On January 4, the Government clearly sanctioned the move. About a week later the Swiss Ambassador was told that the three had been taken to join the other 49 hostages and henceforth would not enjoy special access or privileges.

The Iranians reacted positively to the revised U.S. position, and on January 7 Mr. Christopher and his team flew to Algiers to facilitate further exchanges.

There the Algerians assisted in working out the final details and in developing a process for implementing the arrangements proposed by the U.S. The Bank of England was selected as the central bank to hold the escrow account in the name of the Algerian Central Bank.

The Iranians made very plain their desire to end the crisis before the expiration of President Carter's term of office by proposing on January 12 to the Parliament on an urgent basis a bill to authorize the Government to arbitrate disputed claims with the U.S. The bill passed after a day's delay, but a second proposed bill to nationalize the Shah's assets was deemed not urgent as it was not essential for the conclusion of an agreement with the U.S. It was deferred for later consideration.

Three categories of Iranian assets were covered by the agreement. In the first category were Iranian securities and gold in the custody of the Federal Reserve Bank in New York. Arrangements were initiated on January 16 to facilitate the subsequent transfer of these assets to the escrow account of the Bank of England on January 16 as a mark of U.S. good faith in seeking an agreement.

The second category of Iranian assets was funds held in foreign branches of U.S. banks. A portion of funds would be used to prepay bank loans while another part would remain in the escrow account until disputed bank loans were resolved by the arbitration commission. A third, smaller portion would also remain in escrow until all disputes were settled over interest rates allegedly owed by the banks. The undisputed balance would immediately go to Iran with the release of the hostages. Thus, the claims of the American banks would be either fully settled with the release of the hostages or protected in the escrow account until disputes were resolved.

The third category of funds to be deposited in the escrow account would be comprised of Iranian assets in domestic branches of U.S. banks and all other Iranian assets located in the U.S. or abroad in the custody of persons subject to U.S. jurisdiction. In the context of the transfer of these assets to the escrow account, Iran was committed to resolve claims by U.S. nationals under the agreed claims settlement procedure.

The U.S. also agreed to lift import and export sanctions under the agreement when the hostages were released. Our allies stated they would take parallel steps to remove their sanctions. These sanctions imposed increasingly heavy costs on Iran in terms of greatly curtailed economic activity and substantial diplomatic isolation. During our exchanges with the Iranians through the Algerians, they never raised the subject of Iranian-owned military equipment held here. The U.S. will decide at a later date whether any or all of this equipment should be released to Iran. In any event, under the agreements, the U.S. has no obligation to release any exports to Iran which were prohibited by law or regulation prior to the seizure of the hostages. Funds that Iran has deposited with the Department of Defense for the purchase of equipment will be returned in full when all Iranian obligations have been settled.

Throughout this crisis the U.S. has remained faithful to fundamental principles. We have obtained the safe release of the hostages and we have preserved national honor and national interests. We have not paid ransom; the money consigned to Iran is its own property. We did not agree to the return of the Shah's wealth, except insofar as U.S. courts upheld Iranian claims to the property. We have agreed to block the transfer of any properties belonging to the Shah's estate that may be located here while U.S. courts determine legal ownership. We told Iran, as we would any other country, that we would inform the U.S. courts of our position that claims by Iran seeking recovery of the Shah's assets were not legally barred here by sovereign immunity or by the act of state doctrine.

The good offices of Algeria during the final state of discussions were of crucial importance. The Algerian intermediaries carried out their responsibilities in a thoroughly professional and fair manner. The Governments of Algeria and of our protecting power, Switzerland, whose diplomats worked tirelessly throughout the crisis, have made a major and vital contribution to the settlement of this crisis. Other Governments were also extraordinarily helpful. The Soviet Union in contrast on January 17 issued a press statement that the U.S. was preparing to intervene militarily in Iran. The Secretary called in the Soviet Ambassador and demanded an immediate end to this scurrilous propaganda and warned him of serious and lasting effects on U.S.-Soviet relations and U.S. public opinion.

On January 19 agreement between the parties was reached and Mr. Christopher initialled the two Algerian Declarations after Behzad Nebavi had initialled for Iran in Tehran. It appeared that the hostages might be able to leave Tehran the following day. Once again, however, hopes were disappointed. The Iranian Central Bank objected to certain details of the financial arrangement and the negotiators were forced to return to their task.

Finally in the early morning on January 20 the White House was able to announce all of the necessary documents had been approved by the parties and funds from U.S. banks had been deposited in the Bank of England escrow account. Iran was informed. The hostages boarded the Algerian aircraft in Tehran and at about 12:30 p.m. EST left en route to Algeria where they were to rendezvous with USAF aircraft which would take them to Wiesbaden, Germany. After 444 days the good news was flashed to the families of the hostages and to the entire world.

X. *The Future*

The United States retains an interest in the preservation of Iran's territorial integrity and in the development of institutions in Iran that will permit stable government by leaders chosen by the Iranian people. There is no other route to political stability in post-revolution Iran. We want to see an Iran that is independent and strong and able to enjoy respect among the nations of the world through adherence to standards of international law and accepted conduct between nations.

At the same time, we realize that many Iranians believe they have serious grievances against the United States, just as many Americans believe they have been seriously wronged by Iran. The bitterness that exists on both sides will require much time to heal. But both countries share important mutual interests. Both want to see Iran preserve its integrity and avoid the fate of Afghanistan. The people of both Iran and the United States want to see Iran develop the free and effective political and economic institutions that will enable the country to realize its vast potential.

Seizing and holding the hostages was the greatest political gain in the social history of the world. Iran has forced the greatest satanical power to its knees.

PRIME MINISTER RAJAI of Iran, January 21, 1981

Q. What is your opinion of American companies that now want to resume business with Iran?

A. I hope they're going to do it by long distance. [Laughter.]

Excerpt from news conference with President Reagan,
January 29, 1981

1980

35.

George McGovern: The Soviet Grain Embargo of 1980

Following the Soviet invasion of Afghanistan in the fall of 1979, the Carter administration sought ways in which to punish the Soviets for their audacity. The embargo on grain sales to the Soviet Union, announced on January 4, 1980, was an attempt to hit the Soviets both in the pocketbook and in the stomach. The new policy was immediately attacked by many farmers and legislators from the Farm Belt, although some farm organizations supported it. Sen. McGovern, D-South Dakota, appeared before a Senate hearing on January 22 that was considering the matter. McGovern was an acknowledged expert on agricultural matters and was ranking majority member of the Senate Agricultural Committee. Portions of his testimony are reprinted here.

Source: Hearings before the Subcommittee on International Finance, U.S. Senate, January 22, 1980.

Mr. chairman, we are all familiar with the wisdom of George Santayana's thought that those who ignore the lessons of history are bound to repeat them. January 4th marked the fourth time in less than a decade that U.S. officials have embargoed or suspended sales of agricultural products.

In 1973, President Nixon suspended soybean export sales because of short domestic supply. Prices fell from $12 a bushel to $7 a bushel in a matter of weeks. More seriously, we so drastically disrupted the Japanese economy that they turned to Brazil for new soybean production that has permanently damaged American export sales.

In October of 1974, President Ford requested the voluntary withdrawal of 125 million bushels of wheat and corn to Russia and the United States Department of Agriculture adopted a "prior approval requirement." Markets dropped sharply and wheat went off 80¢ a bushel and corn about 60¢ in a six-week period.

In the summer of 1975 in the middle of the growing season, President Ford again ordered a slowdown of sales to the USSR. It amounted to an embargo of new sales of wheat, corn and soybeans. Involved also was a loading boycott by the longshoremen. Soybeans were down $1 by October first, wheat about 50¢ and corn 30¢ a bushel.

Later that year, on October 20, 1975, the U.S. and the USSR signed the five-year grain sales agreement.

On January 4, 1980, President Carter announced suspension of sales of 17 million metric tons of wheat and corn, but allowed the 8 million metric ton commitment under the 1975 agreement to go forward.

After a suspension of trading on the major exchanges for two days, commodities went down the limit.

Mr. Chairman, the obvious failure of past embargoes, at least in terms of the devastating effect they have on farmers and farm prices, lead all aspirants to high office to deplore them and promise not to make them a part of public policy. This includes the present occupant of the Oval Office. Food and food products have always been suspect as a tool of foreign policy on both humanitarian and economic grounds. Though I deplore the Russian presence in Afghanistan as an act of aggression, I think that the question of whether the blow we are delivering is equal to or greater than the blow we are called upon to absorb is open to debate. I will go into this later in my testimony. For the moment I want to make it clear that history is not on our side in view of past events and past embargoes.

WHO DOES THE EMBARGO HURT?

Mr. Chairman, let me be quick to point out that I do not in any way question the President's motives in announcing the embargo. He is an honest and compassionate President and I am

Senator George McGovern

confident that he feels that he has done the right thing. I do feel that the political process is such that every important announcement from the White House should be subject to the closest of public scrutiny. That is why we are here today.

The January 12th issue of *Congressional Quarterly* points out that total U.S.-Soviet trade in 1979 was valued at 3.4 billion dollars of export value to the U.S. Grains accounted for 2.6 billion dollars, manufactured-goods amounted to $600 million and high technology around $200 million. Agricultural products amounted to nearly 75% of all our business with the Soviets. Consequently, if we did anything at all, the farm community, amounting to only 3% of the population, would be called upon to bear 75% of the response.

1978 was a record year for Russian crop production and amounted to 237 million metric tons. 1979 was a disaster for the Soviets and domestic production fell to 180 million metric tons.

As a consequence, the Soviets had

planned to purchase 37 million metric tons of grain abroad—25 million from the U.S. and 12 million elsewhere in the world. Domestic needs were calculated at 217 million metric tons.

By denying the Soviets 17 million metric tons we are denying them only about 8% of their projected domestic needs.

Since the embargoed grain represents about 13 million tons of corn and 4 million tons of wheat all earmarked for animal feed, we are denying some Russians, at least at first blush, a slightly better meat and poultry diet for the present and the future.

Americans consume an average of slightly over 200 pounds per year retail weight of red meat and poultry. The Congressional Research Service of the Library of Congress estimates Russian red meat and poultry consumption at something like 120 pounds per year, retail weight. How much red meat and poultry are we denying the Soviets by cutting their feed allocations by 8%? Hardly enough for any real application of the term "belt tightening." Even Secretary Bergland estimates decreased Soviet meat production in the 5 to 8% range.

In the near term, all economists agree that any feed shortfall will result in expanded herd slaughter and deep herd culling. This means that at least for 1980, Russians will eat more meat and poultry. The long range effect is for years to come and is incalculable.

With possible expanded purchases elsewhere in the world and the possible transshipments of U.S. grain, I question that either the short term or the long term effects will devastate the Soviet Union, especially if the 1980 domestic crop returns to record levels.

On the U.S. side of the equation, experts predict that U.S. farmers will suffer a decline in prices estimated at 50¢ a bushel on wheat and 35¢ a bushel on corn. Additionally, American taxpayers will foot the bill for possibly 2.5 to 3 billion dollars in the purchases of 14 million metric tons from grain traders to isolate the embargoed grain from the market, over a half a billion dollars for a paid diversion program, 200 million dollars for an expanded P.L. 480 program, and other costs that make a grand total of 3.8 billion dollars as estimated by the Congressional Budget Office, with other estimates ranging to 5 billion dollars.

And these equations do not take into consideration the tremendous increase in cost of production for crop year 1980 for farmers, coupled by depressed markets, and a tremendous psychological overhang of the markets caused by C.C.C. ownership of 14 million metric tons of grain purchased from the traders. Even the dramatic upturn of the futures market on Thursday and Friday of last week can be traced to the artificial spurt in the price of gold rather than any intrinsic strength in the grain market itself.

I think the conclusion is clear. The U.S. domestic blow to the agricultural community can reasonably be concluded to be greater than the one we are delivering, at least in the long run and at least in economic terms. History again prevails.

As the world's largest exporter of agricultural commodities—one planted acre in three ends up in export status—the U.S. has a monumental stake in its credibility as a dependable supplier of agricultural commodities. We have carefully cultivated and expanded our export markets to the point where we sell well over 30 billion dollars of commodities each year. Agricultural exports amount to the largest single cushion in our balance of payments position and offset the high cost of energy imports to a greater degree than any other single segment of the domestic economy. This move must be viewed in the community of nations as making us at least suspect as a steady supplier to such important markets as Japan and the Economic Community. At the very least, it amounts to tampering with a finely tuned and carefully developed world trade market. If we want to keep the image of the American farmer as the world's model, as the modern day miracle of food production, we had better think twice or even more than twice before we tarnish that image through public policy decisions that make delivery of expanded production unavailable to the world's buyers. If we wish to continue as the most important supplier of food to the world, we must have the reputation of a dependable supplier.

Immediately after the announcement of the embargo the Department of Agriculture took immediate steps to bail out grain traders who had signed commitments to the USSR. This amounted to about 22 firms and 14 million metric tons of the 17 million that were embargoed. Trading on the major exchanges was suspended for two days. Pre-embargo prices received by farmers on a national average were about $3.85 for wheat and $2.40 for corn. Upon resumption of trading on January 9th, both commodities went down the limit and trading stopped. I am advised by my South Dakota grain elevators that wheat is still off between 40¢ and 50¢ a bushel and corn off about 30¢.

Though the Secretary has announced modest increases in loan rates, together with an expanded P.L. 480 program, waiver of first year interest rates for grain moving into the farmer-owned reserve, and the promise of a paid diversion program, these remedies are generally viewed as inadequate by producers. Uncertainty exists as to the status of farmers who participated in the program and those who did not. This is significant because only 20% of the 1979 corn acres and 55% of the wheat acres were program acres.

Mr. Chairman, the embargo is a reality and it is now national policy. Though its effects are open to question, let us move forward to protect our domestic producers with as much vigor as we seek to punish the enemy.

In this connection, let me advance a position taken only recently by the National Farmers Union. It is in N.F.U. terms a conservative position, at least in light of the past goals of that organization. The Farmers Union has expressed support for the action of the President, given the following safeguards for domestic producers:

1. Increase 1979–80 loan levels to $3.90 on wheat, $2.50 on corn and $6.25 on soybeans, with semi-annual adjustments.

2. Prohibit C.C.C. releases at less than 10% above the call levels or 20% above the loan.

3. Announce a paid diversion for 1980.

4. Provide effective safeguards to prevent transshipments through third world countries or trading firms.

5. Immediately initiate a strong and effective gasohol program to spur alcohol fuel production from feed grains diverted from export shipment, and a major expansion of the Food for Peace program with particular emphasis on market development activities.

Hopefully, such a program would stem the tide and prevent economic dislocation for domestic producers. It is a program that the Department could live with on an emergency basis if it in fact is fully committed to its announced position of making domestic farmers whole from the numerous financial consequences brought on by the embargo announcement.

36.

The Humanities in American Life

In April 1978 the Rockefeller Foundation decided to sponsor a Commission on the Humanities to assess the humanities' place and prospects in American life. Richard W. Lyman, then president of Stanford University, was appointed chairman. The members of the Commission met a number of times from September 1978 to January 1980 and produced a Report that was published later in 1980. Their views of the humanities were traditional ones, but no less important for that. Some educators attacked the report for being unoriginal and also for its failure to show how an expansive concept of the humanities could begin to influence American education. A portion of the Report is reprinted here.

Source: *Report of the Commission on the Humanities*, 1980.

DOMAINS OF THE HUMANITIES

The importance of the humanities cannot be quantified nor their needs reduced to enrollments and budgets. The humanities have no rigid institutional or intellectual boundaries. They occupy a central place in our national culture, they help shape the meaning of individuality and citizenship, and they pose fundamental questions about the human purposes of science and technology.

Culture and Citizenship

The humanities are often placed in the middle of a cultural debate that carries the shorthand description "elitism versus populism." Indeed, readers might view some arguments in this report as elitist or populist. We have not let these terms control our debate, however. We reject the elitist-populist formula as a misleading label for some real, diverse, and often confused issues in our culture.

Some people think it elitist to point out that our culture arose in what is generally described as the Western tradition; populist to affirm that Native and Latin American, African, and Asian cultures also form our heritage. Elitism is associated with high culture, which often refers to a finite list of works, authors, and standards; populism with popular culture, which has an inexhaustible list. The rich are thought elitist because they can afford educational and cultural activities the poor cannot. Those who emphasize our common culture are sometimes called elitist, whereas those who accentuate cultural pluralism are called populist. Maintaining traditional forms of cultural expression is often viewed as elitist, whereas admiring novelty and spontaneity is apparently a populist trait. It is allegedly elitist to advocate the preservation of cultural resources, populist to urge broad public access to them.

"Elitism versus populism" distorts these issues. The Western tradition includes popular culture and non-Western elements. Our common culture is not limited to the Western tradition nor restricted to the wealthy. An interpretive exhibit of Cézanne's paintings accessible to people across the country is neither elitist nor populist.

"Elitism versus populism" reduces debate to ideological categories and polarizes opinions. To be sure, the issues above express tension between cultural views that are sometimes irreconcilable and often must compete for limited resources, as we discovered in our deliberations as a Commission. Nevertheless, our discussions convinced us that we are not dealing with mutually exclusive cultural realms. Frequently the tensions can, at least in principle, be resolved. More often than not, they can generate creative energy if they are understood clearly and approached constructively.

The controversy over bilingualism exemplifies such tension. Proponents support bilingual education as the right road to full citizenship, with competence in both English and the language of origin. The President's Commission on Foreign Language and International Studies claims that denigrating the languages of immigrants and linguistic minorities has partly caused the present ignorance of foreign languages (*Strength Through Wisdom,* Washington, D.C., 1979). Critics of bilingual educa-

tion, on the other hand, fear that it may create permanent foreign language enclaves in the United States, or that some children, caught halfway between two cultures, may miss opportunities or become "alingual"—not competent in any language. Congress has recently authorized the Office of Bilingual Education (Department of Education) to conduct a national evaluation of bilingual education. This study must help end the needless politicization of the issue, which prevents an acceptable resolution of the two points of view. Just last year, such politicization produced a noisy and rancorous struggle in the California State Legislature that did nothing to shed light on the genuine problems of bilingual education, still less to contribute to their solution.

American society, among the world's most diverse in its cultural origins, should cherish that diversity as a source of constantly renewed strength. But there is danger in diversity when it is carried to extremes. No society can flourish if its citizens deny the possibility of a common culture that unites all despite differences in origin, education, and outlook. This Commission does not seek to preserve a narrow set of moral, social, and aesthetic values; nor do we believe that pluralism should lead to excessive cultural particularism, crude moral relativism, or the suspension of critical judgment. We propose three principles by which the humanities can help us all find common ground amid the competing interests and values in our national life.

First, our cultural tradition contains works generally regarded as classics. This tradition holds a special regard for the past, yet is flexible and alive. Western culture has always been enlarged and enriched by non-western cultures, by new works of art and scholarship, by the contributions of people never before given their due, and by concerns arising from our historical situation. These help define and redefine the canon of classics by forcing us to look at tradition in fresh ways.

Second, there are standards within standards. Some popular novels are more subtle than others, some Greek or Navajo myths more profound than others, some Black autobiographies more enlightening than others, some of Shakespeare's plays more effective dramatically than others. It is in no way undemocratic to recognize these distinctions, and only confusion and bigotry gain by denying them. All people have the capacity to reach for high standards of expression, interpretation, and discrimination; these are not exclusive privileges of one class or culture.

Third, education has a socializing dimension, as individuals share ideas, relate particular experiences to universal concerns, sharpen their moral faculties, and serve the community. The humanities, by emphasizing our common humanity, contribute especially to the social purpose of learning—to education for civic participation, which has been a strong theme in American society since the days of Thomas Jefferson.

No conception of the humanities is complete if it omits humanism as a civic ideal. In the European Renaissance many humanists connected learning with civic duty and decried what they took to be the pedantic, unworldly attitudes of medieval scholasticism. Since the Renaissance the connections between education and public life have multiplied. Democracy rests on the principle of enlightened self-rule by the entire citizenry. So, in a sense, does our modern system of cultural patronage.

In the Renaissance the humanities depended on a few patrons; today support for and participation in the humanities are public forces and public responsibilities on a large scale. Finally, though slowly, the meaning of cosmopolitanism has broadened, and with it the idea of citizenship. We cannot afford to look parochially at other cultures as curiosities, "like us" only insofar as their members have converted to Christianity or studied at Oxford or Yale.

These important social changes do not point to a simple or single ideal of civic virtue. Our republic stands on a belief that educated citizens will participate effectively in decisions concerning the whole community. Humanistic education helps prepare individuals for this civic activity. The humanities lead beyond "functional" literacy and basic skills to critical judgment and discrimination, enabling citizens to view political issues from an informed perspective. Through familiarity with foreign cultures—as well as with our own subcultures—the humanities show that citizenship means belonging to something larger than neighborhood or nation. Complementing the political side of citizenship is the cultural. A literate public does not passively receive cultural works from academic guardians, but actively engages in the interpretation, creation, and re-creation of those works. Participation in the republic of letters is participation in community life as well.

Although the humanities pertain to citizenship, they also have an integrity of their own. They are not always relevant to urgent social or political issues. They are not simply a means to advanced literacy or cultivation. Nor are they a duty, a requirement, or a kind of finishing-school concern—froth on the brew, embroidery on the blanket.

If to grow in wisdom—not simply in cleverness, or dexterity, or learning—is practical, then the humanities, properly conceived and conveyed, are decidedly practical. They help develop capacities hard to define clearly and without cliché: a sharpened critical judgment, a keener appreciation of experience. Study of the humanities makes distinctive marks on the mind: through history, the ability to disentangle and interpret complex human events; through literature and the arts, the ability to distinguish the deeply felt, the well wrought, and the continually engrossing from the shallow, the imitative, and the monotonous; through philosophy, the sharpening of criteria for moral decision and warrantable belief. These capacities serve much more than the notion that, as a member of a community or state, the individual has civic duties and virtues. There are other values besides civic ones, and they are often found in privacy, intimacy, and distance from civic life. The humanities sustain this second conception of individuality, as deeply rooted as the other in our cultural inheritance, in three important ways. First, they emphasize the individual's critical vigilance over political activity. This is a form of civic participation, but it demands judgment acquired through detachment and circumspection. Second, teaching and scholarship in the humanities frequently consider subjects beyond those of immediate public concern; the humanities pursue matters of value without defining value as social utility. Finally, the humanities offer intensely personal insights into the recesses of experience. Ultimately, the individual interprets what appears in the gold doubloon.

The humanities illuminate relationships between the public and private notions of individuality. The two sometimes reinforce each other, sometimes remain indifferent to each other. They often pull away from each other, and are at times irreparably divided.

Scientific research is sustained by the commonly accepted belief, or myth, that scientists are constructing an edifice of objective reality and that every bit of research, however small or insignificant it may appear to the outside, is a building block of that structure. This myth has served scientists well and there is a great deal of truth in it; science is cumulative. . . . Humanists have often tried to justify trivial research in much the same way, but unfortunately the same myth does not operate for them. What seems trivial or insignificant in the humanities probably is and is likely to remain so.
                    ROBERT M. BERDAHL, University of Oregon

Women scuffled with men carrying white supremacy signs outside the convention center in Houston, Texas, where the National Women's Conference took place in 1977.

THE NEW WOMEN

The movement for women's rights emerged in the late 1960s, subsequent to the civil rights movement of the blacks. Amid protest and counterprotest, it was sometimes difficult to discern the aims of the women's movement. One goal, of course, was an Equal Rights Amendment to the Constitution. This, after years of campaigning, failed—at least partly because of the furious opposition of some of the women themselves. Phyllis Schlafly, for one, spoke out against the amendment at many public forums. In the course of time, much of the harsh rhetoric that had characterized the movement's earlier years faded, and more definite goals were outlined—goals that often had as much to do with the broader issues of human rights as they did with women alone. The 1980s was declared by the United Nations to be the Decade of Women. In Nairobi, Kenya, an international gathering of more than 15,000 women from 130 nations met in the summer of 1985. There were challenges, disagreements, and demands. But the significant fact was that they were all together, sensing their power and demanding changes that would ultimately lead to the ancient dream of equality among women and men—or, to put it even more succinctly, the equality of the human race.

The ten years from 1977 to 1986 proved to be a time of gains as well as losses for women. Millions left off, at least in part, the task of housewife and went into the workplace. For many, work represented the possibility of achievement in a career. For others, with economic conditions deteriorating, it was a matter of sheer necessity. Many households came to depend on two paychecks to survive. In addition, analysts figured that the value of women's unpaid domestic labor, worldwide, exceeded $4 trillion—one-third of the gross world product. More women than ever went to college and to law and medical school, but there were not always jobs available for them commensurate with their experience and skills. Even when they held jobs, women's salaries or wages continued to be lower than those paid to men, often for the same work. Attempts to establish the principle of "comparable worth" in the workplace did not generally succeed.

(Top) When the National Women's Conference opened in Houston, delegates and observers filled every seat in the building; (bottom) an ERA rally in New York, where participants were celebrating the sixtieth anniversary of women's suffrage.

(Top left) Rosalynn Carter talks with children during a three-day trip to Brazil; (top right) Nancy Reagan watches students working with computers at a drug rehabilitation school in New York; (bottom) not all women are in favor of the Equal Rights Amendment.

Women in the 1980s discovered new opportunities and filled new economic niches. By 1985 nearly 40 percent of U.S. women had entered the work force, and, if too many women still held menial jobs, there were plenty of executives, too, and more than a handful of CEOs (chief executive officers) as well. Women had always distinguished themselves in the arts and entertainment, but now there were thousands of successful women in other fields, working as firefighters and astronauts, and much else. Many so-called "mainline" Protestant denominations found little difficulty with accepting female ministers, and even a few women became rabbis. More conservative Protestants held out against women in the ranks of the clergy. Most notably, the Roman Catholic Church, largest of the Christian denominations, held out. But even there the force for change was emerging, especially among the vanguard of American Catholics.

(Top left) Cheryl Crawford, at 83, is still producing Broadway plays; (bottom) Barbara McClintock received the 1983 Nobel Prize in medicine for her genetic work on corn; (top right) this former beauty shop owner has become an ironworker.

(Top left) Sally K. Ride was the first woman astronaut; (top right) Lynette Woodard was the first woman member of the Harlem Globetrotters; (bottom left) Patricia Kenneally, when she became a fire fighter, was the first woman to hold that job in Boston; (bottom right) Sally Priesand was the first woman rabbi in the U.S.

When a woman was chosen to fill a public post in the 1980s, it was first noted that a woman was chosen; only then was she specifically identified. So common was this practice that it became impossible to escape the notion that tokenism still prevailed when it came to promoting women to positions of authority. Barbara Mikulski of Maryland was the first woman Democrat to be elected to the Senate in her own right. Sandra Day O'Connor was named an associate justice of the Supreme Court. The two candidates for governor of Nebraska in 1986 were women. All of these women made headlines first because they were women and second because they were highly qualified. So too, when Geraldine Ferraro was nominated for the vice-presidency at the Democratic convention in San Francisco, there was a new kind of electricity in the air. She didn't win, perhaps partly because she was a woman and because the head of the ticket, Walter Mondale, was running against a landslide. But the fact that she was chosen as a presidential running-mate was seen as a landmark achievement.

(Top) Sandra Day O'Connor is shown as she was sworn in at her confirmation hearing before she became the first woman Supreme Court justice; (center) Geraldine Ferraro was the first woman vice-presidential candidate when she ran with Walter Mondale; (bottom) Rep. Barbara Mikulski and Linda Chavez of Maryland are the first two women to run against each other for the U.S. Senate; the winner, Rep. Mikulski, is at left.

37.

The Gold Boom

On January 18, 1980, the price of a troy ounce of gold on the London market reached $835. The price had been rapidly escalating since the beginning of the year; on January 2 the price had been $563. This was the most rapid runup in history, and the January 18 price was an all-time high. Fears were expressed in many quarters that the increased price of gold would have a destructive effect on the world's economy. But in fact after January 1980 the price began to fall, and it was soon back to its "norm" of about $350 an ounce. Silver followed much the same pattern. Some of the effects of the gold boom are discussed in this February 1980 article in BusinessWeek.

Source: *BusinessWeek*, February 11, 1980.

HAVING CUT THEIR TEETH at a time when gold was worth only $35 per oz., most U.S. economists are inclined to write off the current rise in its price as a sideshow. But, in truth, it appears to be the big tent event. Even if the gold price averages "only" $650 per oz. this year—a conservative figure—it will have major effects on interest rates, exchange rates, and inflation rates around the industrial world, as well as on the geopolitical balance between the West and the Soviets. And there is no way that these effects are going to make life easier for the industrial world's policy-makers or for U.S. strategic planners.

Even though the sharp runup in the price of gold is only three months old—its price was only $382 per oz. at the end of October—it is already having disruptive effects:

—The higher price of gold may be driving up the price of oil. Analysts have been inclined to view the gold boom as an effect on the surge in oil prices. This was probably initially true. But there are now also signs that the gold-oil price relationship has become a game of leapfrog. One of the potentially most explosive results of the gold surge is the unleashing of a wave of paranoia throughout the Middle East, where the money-men of the Organization of Petroleum Exporting Countries now believe that they are the victims of a massive plot to rig the gold market in a way that diminishes the "purchasing power" of their oil. If this belief grows, the world could be faced with still another round of major oil price rises. And while the recent Saudi Arabian $2-a-bbl. increase was designed mainly to get political unity among the Arabs prior to the Islamabad conference in Pakistan, future oil price rises may be linked to gold.

—Gold profits are feeding inflation. The direct effect of the higher gold price has been to make the holders of the world's 2 billion oz. of gold richer by nearly $1 trillion over the past year. The upshot is a massive "wealth effect." The combined gold reserves of Western governments have increased by $230 billion in the past three months, and there are temptations to trade on the increased wealth to finance deficits in domestic budgets and in the balance of payments. And if governments yield to these temptations (there are, for example, proposals for the U.S. to mint gold coins), the impact will be inflationary. Insofar as individuals own the gold (and Merrill Lynch International estimates that U.S. citizens hold 3,000 tons of it—more than even the Swiss government), the wealth effects are even more drastic. The richer people feel, the more they spend.

—Gold fever is spreading to other speculative markets. The higher price for gold is feeding commodity speculation, adding to price rises for other precious metals and for more prosaic items, such as copper. This probably helps explain why commodity price indexes continue to soar, even though world industrial growth stays sluggish.

—More expensive gold lessens the impact of the grain embargo on the Soviet Union. If the Soviets go back to their 1978 volume of gold sales, the new higher gold price will bring in some $6.3 billion in hard currency—enough to be able to pay for grain and technology at rates potential embargo-busters will find hard to refuse.

European bankers just back from the Persian Gulf say that OPEC financial officials are convinced that the rich industrialized nations holding most of the world's gold in their reserves have deliberately manipulated the market to reverse terms of trade with the Middle East that currently favor oil. The Arabs feel that by pushing up gold prices, the West can indirectly cheapen the value of oil. While this might be dismissed as the financial fantasies of an increasingly xenophobic group, the real economic consequences could prove dramatic. If OPEC thinks the true value of its oil is being whittled away by the West through the rise in gold prices, it can react, either by again raising the price of oil or by keeping a greater amount of its limited natural resource in the ground, which does the same thing. Already, Saudi Arabia, Kuwait, and the United Emirates have announced a $2-per-bbl. price increase, despite talk of a glut— and more increases may be in store.

In New York and London gold markets, there is universal agreement that Washington's freezing of Iranian assets held in U.S. banks triggered the current flight out of paper currency into gold. That movement has recently been reinforced by the buying of gold by thousands of rich Arab merchants, afraid for their lives in the wake of the Russian invasion of Afghanistan and the recent uprising in Saudi Arabia. Arab purchases have continued unabated through gold's sharp rise to $875 per oz., its low of $585, and its climb back to more than $700 because the metal is being bought out of fear—as a mechanism of escape. But OPEC money-men insist they are suffering the same "organized" terms of trade loss imposed on them from 1974 to 1978, when the prices of goods and food imported from the West outpaced the oil price increases and diminished the value of their oil. "I have just come back from a long trip in the Mideast, and I can tell you there is a general conviction that the U.S. and other countries are manipulating gold so that the terms of trade for industrialized countries in terms of reserves improve," says one Swiss banker, just back from the Gulf.

GOVERNMENT GOLD RESERVES

The key word is "reserves," and here the Arabs may have stumbled onto a major change in the Western global monetary system—one that is a direct result of the surge in gold prices. Gold has now become a major part of the petrodollar recycling process, and its rise has the potential for sharply influencing economic and financial policies in Europe and the U.S. for years to come.

The $400 to $500 jump in gold prices has raised the value of government reserves dramatically in the past 12 months. The value of gold held in reserve by industrial nations far exceeds any paper currency assets. More important, industrial countries, led by the U.S., Germany, and France, have seen the value of their reserves triple in a single year, far outpacing their oil import bills. This means industrialized countries that have large gold holdings—which include almost all except Japan and Britain—may be able to finance growing balance-of-payments deficits that have been generated by higher oil prices.

The higher value of gold reserves provides a great temptation for governments to translate this new wealth into some painless way of solving urgent economic problems. Last year the U.S. sold $3 billion worth of gold to help cover a $24.7 billion trade deficit. And there is growing pressure in Washington to sell gold to pay off the national debt, balance the government deficit, help exports, and sop up some of the $800 billion offshore in the Eurodollar markets.

Yet the most likely move by governments in the months ahead will be to use gold as collateral to borrow dollars floating around the global money markets to pay for higher oil import bills.

This prospect may intensify inflation and raise interest rates around the world. There is a growing fear that the prospective use of gold in the petrodollar recycling process may permit countries to delay the crucial adjustment process needed to accommodate economies to higher oil prices. The higher value of government gold reserves may also tempt nations to borrow their way out of oil-induced payments deficits and forgo domestic tightening of monetary and fiscal policies. "The increased value of reserves for those countries with a lot of gold has eased the balance-of-payments constraint," says Nicholas Krul, managing director of Gulf & Occidental, an investment managing company in Geneva. "That may give more leeway in handling payments deficits and allow less restrictive policies than otherwise." Krul points to such countries as Portugal, France, and Italy as the likely candidates to use gold as a means of borrowing to pay for oil imports, "and of course, the U.S.," he adds. During the last round of oil price increases and payments deficits Portugal and Italy did use their gold to collateralize borrowing from Germany. Had it not been for their gold, Germany probably would not have lent them the money, certainly not at the rates it charged. This time, the government gold hoard could be valued at nearly four times the price of gold in 1974–75 and much more can be borrowed, perhaps with better terms. "The key point is that higher gold prices will increase the credit ratings of several countries, enhancing their ability to borrow on international markets," says J. Paul Horne, vice-president at Smith Barney in Paris.

It is, of course, the rich countries that will get most of the gravy in the petrodollar recycling process. The surge in gold prices benefits the industrial countries far more than it does the less developed countries (LDCs). For the most part, LDCs do not have much gold in their official reserves, and the gap between the creditworthiness of European nations and those in Asia, Latin America, and Africa will increase in the months ahead. LDCs will have to pay even more for loans to pay for oil because they do not hold gold. "Gold will affect differentials in interest rates," says Brendan Brown, an economist at American Express International in London. "Italy has gold and will get lower rates. Most lesser developed countries are without gold and will get higher rates."

This lesson may not be lost on LDCs because persistent reports of central banks buying gold over the last six months probably originated from gold buys by Taiwanese, South Korean, and other Asian governments. Eastern European central banks have been buying gold as well. The International Monetary Fund statistics show that Korea has only 280,-000 oz. in its reserves and Brazil 1.61 million oz. Mexico, on the other hand, may have hit a bonanza on top of its oil reserves: It is one of the world's largest producers of silver and ranks No. 9 in gold. Taiwan is sitting on a 2.2 million-oz. gold hoard. The Philippines also has old gold mines, and one of the hottest stocks on the New York Stock Exchange in recent weeks has been Benguet Consolidated Inc., which owns gold mines around Manila. By comparison, the industrialized countries have gold holdings of at least 764 million oz., or 83% of all government-owned gold in the world.

Gold's potentially inflationary impact for government may be matched by an equivalent effect on business and investment. Says Lawrence R. Klein of the University of Pennsylvania: "Gold is not a sideshow. It introduces dynamics into the whole economic system that we simply do not understand. Nor can we model it into our forecasting equations." One thing that economists have difficulty in understanding is the psychological effect that the head-line-grabbing news about soaring gold prices exerts on consumer psychology. "Anytime an important commodity skyrockets in price," explains Leonard Rapping of the University of Massachusetts, people start to worry about all their assets, and "they do not want to get caught on the short end of the stick." For an economy to grow, the public must be fairly certain about its wealth position, he says. The market prices of those assets should be rooted in technology and the costs of production. But when gold prices soar, in effect they are wiping out the value of other assets relative to gold.

"This raises real questions about where wealth holders will put their assets," says Rapping. Franco Modigliani, of the Massachusetts Institute of Technology, puts it this way: "It creates the climate of escaping from normal types of investments like stocks and bonds into gold." And that produces more inflation because investing in gold, or for that matter in works of art, does not add to the stock of productive capital.

"The economy is sitting on a powder keg," says R. Keith Aufhauser of the City University of New York. The danger, he explains, is that there could be a general flight from paper money to commodities, which could send the 13% U.S. inflation rate even higher. And, he adds, when individuals begin to look for commodities in which to store their wealth, they bid up commodity prices, making the job of monetary authorities to control inflation that much harder. "It sets the psychological basis for hyper-inflation," he says. Rutgers University's Paul Davidson adds that it is difficult for workers to accept wage settlements within the Administration's guidelines of 7.5% to 9.5% annual increases when they see gold prices shooting up by 10% in one day.

The upsurge in gold is also affecting the price of silver, which is used in the photographic, electronic, and health-care industries. And the rise in precious metals prices has direct impact on the consumer price index: The 1.5% jump in the December wholesale prices of durable consumer goods was concentrated in jewelry prices, reflecting higher prices of precious metals.

Alan Greenspan, president of Townsend-Greenspan & Co., estimates that the recent gold price increases will add about 0.4% to the consumer price index. Far more troublesome is the spillover into the copper market. Copper prices are near their all-time peaks, despite the fact that the world economy is growing slowly and industrial demand for copper should be weak. Moreover, the search for gold and silver actually leads to the production of more copper, a byproduct, so the increased supply should actually be reducing copper prices.

If surging gold prices have made gold owners better off, they have tremendously improved the fortunes of the two largest gold producers—South Africa and the Soviet Union. Increasing gold prices are transforming South Africa's economy. For the Soviet Union, the impact is profound and will have geopolitical consequences. The Soviets have

been exporting oil to earn desperately needed foreign exchange. But with their oil fast running dry, according to most experts (including the Central Intelligence Agency), they will be relying more on gold sales. In 1978 the Russians exported 401 metric tons of gold; last year they sold 225 tons, which earned them about $2.5 billion.

If the Soviets go back to the 1978 level of volume sales, then the new, higher gold prices will bring some $6.3 billion in hard currency needed to import grain and Western technology for their sagging economy. "How can the U.S. embargo grain when the Russians go around and get it by bidding up prices?" asks Pennsylvania's Klein. "It gives the Soviet Union hard currency just when they were getting squeezed."

Ironically, so far, the gold runup has had a stabilizing effect on the foreign exchange markets. Far from hurting the dollar, the surging gold price has kept it steady. In fact, the price of gold has been increasing in terms of Swiss francs, German marks, and other hard currencies. Investors, in fact, have been shifting out of all paper money, not just the dollar.

How long the shifting will continue remains a question, and the dollar will be vulnerable as long as inflation remains in the double-digit range, the economy keeps out of recession, and the payments deficit runs at December's $3 billion rate. Moreover, although Germany, Japan, and Switzerland are also having inflation problems because of oil's high price, foreign exchange markets believe that monetary discipline will be stronger outside the U.S. in this Presidential election year.

For that reason, there is a strong movement to use the strength of gold to back a new IMF substitution account that would absorb billions of surplus dollars now washing around the world. The aim would be to give some gold backing to the accounting device—in much the way that the European Currency Unit, the ECU, is 20%-backed by official gold reserves. The goal of the IMF is to absorb much of the petrodollar surplus, which will grow even larger in the future—and the glitter of gold may be just the thing to give life to the now-moribund substitution account idea.

But even though the IMF has proved effective in forcing discipline on countries in balance-of-payments trouble in recent years, it has failed to impose a new grand design on the world's international money system. For this reason, the idea that higher gold reserves will act to restructure and stabilize the world's money system must still be viewed as a central banker's dream.

38.

JAMES R. ARNOLD: The Frontier in Space

During the morning hours of March 5, 1980, there occurred the long-awaited flyby of Jupiter by the Voyager I spacecraft. The event was highly dramatic, as incredible views of alien worlds—Jupiter and its satellites—began appearing on TV monitors at the Jet Propulsion Laboratory in California. There were many surprises—for example, at least six active volcanoes on Io, one of the largest of Jupiter's moons—and much valuable new information that was not immediately understood. But these notable results masked a sombre note in America's space program. Little, in fact, was being planned for the future; Voyager I and the other space probes currently in space had been launched years before. In fact, the Comptroller General of the United States had warned in a January 31 letter to Sen. Adlai Stevenson, D-Illinois, that "despite high expectations among U.S. scientists, only limited success can be expected in the next 20 years due to low funding and limited backing by the Administration and the Congress. This could let foreign competition rapidly overcome any technological lead . . . now enjoyed by the United States." James R. Arnold, a professor at the University of California and an old hand in the Manhattan Project, offered his vision of what might be in space if the country had the imagination to create it.

Source: *American Scientist*, May-June 1980.

THE HUMAN SPECIES distinguishes itself from its relatives by a number of attributes. One is range. Starting, as is now believed, from a center in Africa, human beings had already spread ten thousand years ago into every continent (except Antarctica) and every climatic zone on the planet. Long before the invention of writing and the appearance of cities, our ancestors had adapted not only to all habitable climates but to a wide variety of plant and animal food and to a range of technologies for providing basic human needs. This trait in humans is undoubtedly "culture-bound"—there are very rigid societies—but generally speaking we seem to be descended from the migrants and innovators. So far as we know, the chimpanzees and gorillas have not left home.

Twenty years ago it would have been unnecessary to remind people of this. "Progress" was taken for granted, especially in the United States, a country inhabited almost exclusively by immigrants and their more or less immediate descendants. The western frontier was an essential element of our historical vision of ourselves. Today our mood is more critical of technical adventure and exploration. On a finite earth this is reasonable, and indeed long overdue. However, it also tends to stifle the creative impulse. Where we formerly embraced novelties both good and bad, we may now be resisting them equally.

The purpose of this article is to explore one new idea: the possibility of people living and working away from the planet Earth. There may now be outlets for the deep human urge to move onward that were imagined only by a few dreamers even in the more expansive era of the fifties. The ideas set forth here owe very much to the leading exponent of space settlements, G. K. O'Neill (1978). The subject is illuminated beautifully from a different angle by Freeman Dyson (1979).

Of course, we have already been exploring space. So far, however, the tie between astronauts or cosmonauts and the ground has been close. The phrase "Mission Control" says it all. If a true frontier in space is to be created, we must move toward a far greater degree of autonomy for those who would live there. There seems little likelihood at present that the spirit of adventure or national pride alone can nourish such a frontier community. There must be some tangible value: the resources of space must be put to use.

What do we mean by use? Civilizations have always rested on supplies of four essentials: labor, materials, energy, information. The labor used until recently was that of masses of slaves, in name or in fact. It is the special character of a technical society that the conditions of labor are more and more transformed by increasing supplies of the other three components. It is the dramatic development of materials, energy, and information that has eased and equalized the burden of labor. Whatever basic decency our particular culture can lay claim to is made possible by this transformation.

Space provides a wide range of opportunities to continue this process. So far, all the major effects have been in the information segment. Telecommunication and weather forecasting use satellites on a large scale ever more effectively. Less measurable, but perhaps more significant, are our learned ability to succeed in complex and dangerous enterprises ("If they can go to the moon, why can't they . . . ?") and our slowly increasing grasp of the unity and fragility of the planet Earth.

To make use of the energy and material resources of space, we require at a minimum the improved transport capability to be provided by the Space Transportation System (Space Shuttle). The first flights of this system are expected soon. Each flight will be able to carry into near-Earth orbit something like the contents of a railroad box car—a few tens of tons—at a cost in round figures of some hundreds of dollars per kilogram. This is a marked reduction from earlier costs, but it is still not cheap.

A later generation of transport systems, such as those that might be available in the 1990s, can be expected to reduce this cost further, perhaps by ten times or even more (Bekey and Mayer 1976). It is not easy to do this, however, because the escape velocity from the Earth, 11.3 km/sec, is large. The minimum energy imparted to the payload must be 6.4×10^{11} ergs/g, to escape the Earth's gravitational field entirely.

This is larger than the energy content per gram of chemical fuels and imposes a requirement for large, complex, and precise launching systems such as the STS. The atmosphere of the Earth is a further hindrance to going out, though it can be very helpful (as a brake) in coming back in. If useful materials in space were available without going through this difficult lifting process, there would be marked advantages.

WHAT'S IN SPACE?

Advantages for what? Is there anything we think we can do uniquely, or better, or cheaper, or with less pollution in space than we can on Earth? There is reason to think so.

A useful way to view the possibilities is to look at three essential differences between the space environment and our own. The first is "weightlessness." The effective force on an object in a spacecraft is very small—typically on the order of 10^{-5} times Earth gravity or less. An object at rest in the local coordinate frame tends to remain so. This changes, for example, the meaning of the word "container."

A second difference is in the availability of solar heat. At a relatively short distance from the Earth there is no weather and no night, and thus solar energy becomes steady and virtually uninterrupted. Because of the day-night cycle, and the absorption and scattering of the Earth's atmosphere, the effective intensity of sunlight at the Earth's surface is only a small fraction of the 1.5 kW that fall on 1 m^2 at right angles to the solar beam. In space we get it all. Collectors for solar heat can be light and simple. Thus heat is available, at very low cost, at any reasonable scale required, in almost any desired place far enough outside the Earth's atmosphere. To convert this heat to electricity, at an efficiency on the order of 10%, is a known though still fairly expensive art.

The third major difference is the absence of an atmosphere. Far from human activity, the vacuum of interplanetary space is at a level ≤ 10 molecules/cm^3, or 10^{-15} torr—better than any attainable laboratory vacuum. Around a space habitat or space factory the vacuum would be much poorer, because of inevitable leakage of gases. However, even such a relatively poor vacuum is potentially useful—for example, as an environment for fabrication of reactive metals. Even a very high vacuum could be maintained with careful factory design. Because the vacuum is always present, the "pumping speed" would be very high, thus speeding up high-vacuum operations over the time for equivalent operations on Earth.

We can already give some simple examples of the usefulness of these properties. We cannot yet perceive the possibilities of combining them in new patterns, of mastering the art of working in space. The first automobiles and airplanes, and computers even up to the present, remind us that our mental blinders can delay for decades the realization of the best design and use of something really new. In space all this is still before us.

A clearly identified barrier to activities in space is the cost and difficulty of bringing material there from the deep gravitational well of Earth. Fortunately there are two alternative sources of useful materials—the moon and near-Earth asteroids.

Given the escape velocity, 2.3 km/sec, we can easily calculate the energy requirement for bringing material from the moon. It is 2.6×10^{10} ergs/g—less than 4% of the figure for the Earth. In one way this understates the relative cost, since we must put the mining and launching systems on the moon first, using terrestrial materials. How to do this most economically is at present a subject of active study. In another way, it overestimates the cost. The fact that 2.6×10^{10} ergs/g is small compared to the energies from typical chemical fuels means that simple, light propulsive systems will serve. O'Neill and his colleagues are developing a device called a "mass driver," which has the capacity to eject matter from the moon using modest amounts of electrical energy, without fuels or rockets (Chilton et al. 1976). This device has very attractive possibilities.

We have done a little prospecting on the moon. Twelve men have spent hours or days on its surface, collecting a few hundred kilograms of samples from six places, all at low latitudes on the front side. Soviet unmanned spacecraft have returned samples from three other sites in the same zone. Other American and Soviet spacecraft have provided data from the surface or from orbit. The Apollo 15 and 16 missions carried into orbit geochemical instruments that made remote analyses of about 20% of the lunar surface for several major elements and for the radioactive elements.

As a result we have a pretty good

AP/NASA

A geologist astronaut probes for samples among moon rocks and soil.

knowledge of the common materials on the lunar surface (Taylor 1975; Bielefeld at al. 1976). The soil and rocks we have surveyed fall mainly into three broad compositional classes. Like the major rocks of the Earth, all are silicates. Most of the moon's surface (but not most of the front-side equatorial zone) is "highland" material, comparatively light in color and low in density. The lightest materials there (in both senses) are anorthosites, rocks that are high in aluminum and calcium (Table 1).

In the dark lunar maria that are widespread on the front face of the moon, we find basaltic lavas from the lunar interior, which are rich in iron. They contain variable, sometimes strikingly high, concentrations of titanium. A more localized, but still abundant, material on the lunar surface was given the acronymic name KREEP—from K (potassium), Rare Earth Elements, and P (phosphorus)—by the late Paul Gast. KREEP contains high concentrations of a large number of minor and trace elements, including the radioactive elements potassium, thorium, and uranium.

Everywhere the soil (but not the rocks) contains a fraction of a percent of metallic iron and interesting quantities of several light elements, the result of billions of years of bombardment by the solar wind. These solar-wind components include hydrogen, carbon, nitrogen, and noble gases in the general range of 0.01% by weight. Sulfur is also widespread, at a level about 0.15%. These important materials appear to be more concentrated in finer soil fractions, but data are still incomplete.

We do not know if there are rich mineral deposits on the moon. Conventional wisdom does not encourage us to seek them, because most (but not all) valuable deposits on Earth were formed by processes involving abundant water. But conventional wisdom did not predict the presence of the remarkable "orange glass" deposits found by the Apollo 17 astronauts. We must conservatively assume that rich mineral concentrations are absent, but we may be wrong.

One commodity clearly absent on the areas of the moon we have explored is water. The rocks are all dryer than any known on Earth. The only local source of water would be through a chemical combination of the solarwind hydrogen embedded in the soil with the oxygen of the rocks, which might yield about 0.1% water by weight (one liter per ton of soil). Recovering such a tiny amount of water does not appear to be attractive economically, though as always there is room for ingenuity. But there is one other possibility.

Some time ago Watson and co-workers (1961) pointed out that craters near the lunar poles, into which sunlight never falls, make up about 0.5% of the lunar surface. With no atmosphere to

carry heat to the dark areas, they must be very cold—in the range of $-170°$ to $-250°$ C. In such places, ice has effectively a zero vapor pressure; put there it will presumably remain forever. These authors suggest that any water vapor liberated over the entire surface of the moon would be transported and stored as ice in these craters.

Today we know far more about the moon that we did in 1961. Many details of the discussion by Watson and co-workers are obsolete. In a reanalysis of the problem (Arnold 1979), I have estimated that 10^{16}-10^{17} g of ice may be found in the polar cold traps. But this is a paper study, not an observation, and we can settle the question only by an appropriate experiment, such as gamma-ray mapping from a polar-orbiting spacecraft. A spacecraft with present-day instrumentation could also give us far better information on the composition of the whole lunar surface than the Apollo missions provided for 20% of the surface.

Because we cannot count on finding rich deposits of minerals or water on the moon, we should plan to make use of ordinary lunar soil and rocks.

The elementary abundances shown in Table 1 must be compared to the needs for industrial production and for human comfort. On Earth, two hundred years after the start of the industrial revolution, we have become accustomed to using essentially all the elements of the periodic table for one purpose or another. During the early stages of space manufacturing, we will have to get along with only a fraction by mass (much less than unity) of lunar material in our products. The components to strive for are the materials needed in the largest quantities. These are few and predictable (Criswell and Waldron 1978): oxygen, water, construction materials (concrete and steel or their equivalents and perhaps glass), and electrical conductors.

Table 1. Compositions of lunar soils collected during three Apollo missions (percentages by weight). Apollo 11 soil is a titanium-rich material from a mare; Apollo 14 soil is the unusual pottassium-rich material called KREEP: Apollo 16 soil came from the highlands.

	Apollo 11	Apollo 14	Apollo 16
O	42.06%	44.16%	44.88%
Si	19.64	22.39	21.00
Al	7.37	9.31	14.13
Ca	8.58	8.00	11.13
Fe	12.23	8.06	4.27
Mg	4.77	5.57	3.59
Ti	4.48	1.04	0.35
Na	0.33	0.50	0.36
K	0.12	0.46	0.11
Cr	0.21	0.17	0.08
Mn	0.16	0.11	0.05
P	0.05	0.23	0.05

SOURCE: Taylor 1975

The elements that we are sure to need are oxygen, silicon, iron, aluminum and hydrogen. These are abundant in normal lunar materials, along with titanium (in some mare basalts)—also a very useful structural metal. Only the amount of hydrogen is doubtful. The next largest requirements are carbon, nitrogen, and sulfur (for food sources and organic synthesis) and alloying elements like manganese. These elements seem to be present in lunar soil in adequate amounts, though more concentrated sources would be welcome.

Now let us turn to the other potential source of materials, the near-Earth asteroids. In a short article I can give only a brief account of their supplementary role (see O'Leary 1977; Helin and Shoemaker 1977; Shoemaker et al., in press). We have only general indications

of their composition from direct observation, but we can infer that at least some of the meteorites in our museums are probably fragments of the same materials. Of special interest among them are the meteorites called carbonaceous chondrites, which contain bound water, and the so-called iron meteorites, which are composed of an alloy of iron, nickel, and cobalt. It has even been suggested that iron asteroids might someday prove to be a potential resource for use on Earth (Gaffey and McCord 1977).

The Earth-approaching asteroids are as yet little studied. The list of objects is now about fifty and growing fairly rapidly: there may be as many as a thousand large ones, on the order of 1 km or more in the longest dimension, and greater numbers in smaller size ranges. The escape velocities from asteroids are very small, but a lot of energy would be required to bring them (or fragments of them) close enough to the Earth to be used. There is as yet no known asteroid for which the energy needed is lower than it is for lunar materials to be brought near the Earth. Very likely some will be found in the future.

A way around this problem has been suggested by Bender and co-workers (1979). It has been known for a long time that asteroids or comets passing near a planet are subject to gravitational perturbations capable of causing major changes in shape, size, and period of orbit. This effect has been used deliberately to modify the orbits of exploring spacecraft, for example in the Mariner 10 mission to Venus and Mercury. According to Bender and co-workers, it is possible in the case of some known Earth-approaching asteroids to find schedules of propulsion which would cause the asteroid (or some portion of it) to make a series of close approaches to the moon, Venus, and perhaps the Earth (though safety questions arise here). If this could be done the requirement for propulsive energy to move an asteroid would be drastically lowered. In effect, the orbital energy of the planet approached would supply the difference. The disadvantages of this technique are that diversion is possible only at certain special times for a given asteroid and that the required transport times become much longer. Still, extending greatly the list of available asteroids improves the prospects of using asteroidal materials.

Thus we know that nearly all the materials most necessary for living, working and building in space are available on the moon. Unexplored lunar regions may contain others, as well as more convenient forms of the elements already known to be there. Water is the most serious potential gap. But it is almost surely available from some Earth-approaching asteroids, which may be very attractive in the long run as sources for other materials as well.

MEANS OF RECOVERY

The transformation of excavated ores into manufactured articles requires a long succession of operations which on Earth are carried out by separate industries. In a frontier environment, the processes must be simplified. The need for simplification and the extremely different conditions in the space environment force us to rethink everything. A few people have already devoted some thought to the problems and possibilities involved (see, for example, Arnold and Duke 1977; Rao et al. 1979; Bock 1979) and have formulated some guidelines.

The first step illustrates the contrast.

On Earth, with a well-explored planet at our disposal, the miners' rule is that "grade wins." That is, a small increase in content of the desired element in an ore pays for a large additional investment in equipment, labor, transportation cost, and so on. On the moon, with limited knowledge and high investment costs, there is every reason for ease and convenience to win. The top few meters, at least, of the lunar surface are already converted to fine particles by micrometeorite impact. The location of a mining site at a point where two or even three major surface materials are available nearby would permit a wider choice of materials. The "mining" could be done with simple soilmoving equipment. Of course, if we find rich deposits on the moon, we could revert to a more Earthlike pattern.

For the next step, the isolation of each desired element (at least in crude form), there is a wide assortment of possibilities. Four analyses of the problem to date have yielded four entirely different schemes (the most recent study, Bock 1979, summarizes earlier ones). My own choices are intuitive and arbitrary; more work is needed, especially in the laboratory.

It must be emphasized that the energy requirements to produce useful materials from lunar soil will be much greater than those needed to produce the same materials from ores on Earth. Not only are the concentrations lower but most chemical forms are more difficult to use (silicates rather than oxides or sulfides). The typical energy penalty may be as much as a factor of ten. However, as we have seen, solar heat energy is abundant in space, and thus heat requirements for processing are probably not an important constraint. Because electrical energy in large quantities will require a larger investment in solar cells or a competitive technology, most of the processes under consideration use heat energy, primarily or entirely.

For iron we can go either of two ways. A simple method is to make a magnetic concentrate of the raw lunar soil. The natural soil content of metallic iron, about 0.5%, can probably be increased to more than 10% by magnetic separation. Then melting, using concentrated solar heat, would yield a crude iron separate. This method is straightforward, but it does not recover the much larger iron content of the silicate minerals.

The simplest imaginable process by which to recover iron from silicate materials, without using reagents, is direct electrolysis of molten lunar soil or rock. The lunar soil could first be melted in place, with a minimum of processing, using solar heat. A shell of solidified material would hold the molten material, and electrodes could be inserted into it to produce the desired metallic products. Haskin and Lindstrom (1979) have recently shown (on a small laboratory scale) that iron and titanium can be recovered at the cathode, and oxygen under some conditions at the anode. It may be very difficult to produce aluminum by such a process.

The simultaneous production of oxygen is a major advantage of electrolysis. The uses of oxygen in a space economy are many. We will probably need more of it than any other purified substance.

HOW TO BEGIN

The old frontier was developed in different ways. The government supported discovery and exploration of new lands. Land companies, fur companies, and, later, railroads provided capital. With few exceptions, individuals were able to move out on their own only after the first stage had passed. Space exploration up to now has been supported by governments. To justify the next stage—assuming it to be investment based on hope of economic return—the economic expectations must be commensurate with the necessary investment. If a very large initial investment is required, a very large industry must be created to produce the cash. Only very rich players can join the game.

Until recently there has been a general perception that the entry stake must be very large indeed. Studies sponsored by NASA have yielded estimates of start-up costs in the range of $50-100 billion. This amount would allow the transport of lunar material, on the order of 10^5 tons/year—enough for quite a large industrial enterprise—to some assembly point in space. But the size of the "front end" investment has narrowed down the possible industries, in effect, to one: production of electrical energy for terrestrial use. The United States today buys $50-100 billion worth of oil from OPEC countries each year. Thus logically we should be prepared to consider an investment of this size for a program that could make a major reduction in our energy dependence.

The idea would be to manufacture and assemble in space very large arrays of solar cells. An array with an electrical output of 1000 MW (the size of a typical nulcear station) would have an area of 5 km² or more, depending on cell efficiency. Placed in a 24-hour (geosynchronous) orbit at any desired longitude, it would radiate its power at microwave frequencies to a fixed open-structured receiving antenna on the Earth's surface, which would then relay the energy to power transmission grids and eventually to the consumer.

The economically optimum size of such a power plant, it is asserted, is in the range of 5-10,000 MW (Glaser 1977; O'Neill 1975). This would require a solar-collecting area of tens of square kilometers, with a radiating antenna not much less than one kilometer across. An array of this size would dwarf man-made structures on Earth; the nearly force-free environment of space makes it possible.

These power stations, according to the calculations, could produce both energy and profits, based on projected costs of alternate sources (chiefly coal and nuclear). Such estimates at an early technical stage are, of course, vulnerable. However, as recent history suggests, nasty surprises can also crop up in other energy technologies. I believe the argument for pursuing satellite solar power as one of our energy options is very strong. It is to be hoped that the next step, a 25-kW prototype in space, will be authorized soon.

No new energy source can yet be accepted or rejected on economic grounds alone. Solar power has one obvious advantage not yet mentioned—it can be monopolized by no one country or small group of countries. On the other hand, the use of microwaves to radiate large amounts of power through the atmosphere has been questioned on environmental grounds. In my view, the health hazards of low-level microwave radiation have been greatly exaggerated. However, we must be sure. There may be other undesirable effects, for example on the ionosphere.

Whatever the assesment of the desirability of satellite solar power stations made from lunar materials over the next few decades, it is clear that the large entry cost is a serious deterrent, even though the Apollo project reminds us that huge enterprises in space can be managed and can achieve their goals within the original budget. Those of us who want to see the space frontier opened are currently rethinking the problem, in an effort to find paths that begin in a more natural way, with small-scale projects of use and profit, which can lead on as our experience grows to activities of increasing scale. Dyson (1979) has given persuasive arguments that this can be done. As one physical scientist to another, I cannot quite accept his economic arguments. We may have to work on an intermediate scale: the level of one to a few billion dollars, which is now actually available to very rich individuals, companies, and small countries.

We do not know yet what the first small steps will be. Very likely crystals of unusual size, perfection, and composition can be made in space and used in new ways. Composites of new kinds, including foams and fiber-reinforced metals, are another promising class of materials for manufacture in the space environment. The long-standing synergism between space technology and computer science can be expected to continue. Some remarkable consumer products (silent alarms? wrist telephones?) may use satellite links. Industrial robots in space may be one element in reducing manufacturing costs.

When can we expect to be well started on this process? Opinions will differ widely, but an experience of my own may be some guide. In 1950 I was on a panel of scientists asked to discuss before television cameras the expected scientific and technical advances of the next 50 years. When I suggested that we would have manned space satellites, and even trips to the moon, before the year 2000, the distance between me and my four fellow panelists grew dramatically. They did not simply disagree with this particular prediction, which might have turned out wrong: they refused to participate in predicting that any such revolutionary achievements were possible in the next fifty years. I asked them whether in 1900 they would have predicted heavier-than-air flight, or radio, or the dominance of the automobile. No one mentioned potential advances in genetics or integrated circuits—in these areas I saw no further than my colleagues.

In looking forward, our time estimates, it seems, are often too short on a time scale of years and too long on a scale of decades or centuries. I myself would never have imagined in 1974 that in 1980 there would still be so little public acceptance of the reality of the energy crisis and of the need for energy conservation as well as an active, constructive program. Many of us have been foolishly optimistic about the rate of progress toward some solution of this crucial problem. Still, technical and social revolutions of enormous magnitude, as the human habitation of space would be, have taken place within our lifetime. Some are unexpected; this one seems to me inevitable.

When people are moving in and out of space on the Shuttle, and when other people are permanently occupying the Soviet Salyut and its descendants, the change will begin. So long as these capabilities continue and grow, space will be the frontier in the literal sense of the word.

Space is the empty place next to the full place where we live. I believe we will be true to our nature and go there.

References

Arnold J. R. 1979. Ice in the lunar polar regions. *J. Geophys. Res.* 84:5659-67.

Arnold J. R., and M. B. Duke, eds. 1977. Summer workshop on near-Earth resources. *NASA Conference Publication 2031.* Houston: Johnson Space Center.

Bender, D. F., R. S. Dunbar, and D. J. Ross. 1979. Round-trip missions to low delta-V Asteroids and implications for material retrieval. In *NASA Report SP-428, Space Resources and Space Settlements,* ed. J. Billingham.

Bekey, I., and H. Mayer. 1976. 1980-2000: Raising our sights for advanced space systems. *Aeronautics and Astronautics* July, 34–63.

Bielefeld, M. J., R. C. Reedy, A. E. Metzger, J. I. Trombka, and J. R. Arnold. 1976. Surface chemistry of selected lunar regions. *Proc. Lunar Sci. Conf. 7th,* 2661-76.

Bock E. H., ed. 1979. Lunar resources utilization for space construction. *Final Report, NASA Contract NAS 9-15560.* San Diego: General Dynamics, Convair Division.

Chilton, F., B. Hibbs, H. Kohn, G. K. O'Neill, and J. Phillips. 1976. Electromagnetic mass drivers and mass driver applications. *Prog. in Astronautics and Aeronautics* 57:37-94.

Criswell, D. R., and R. D. Waldron. 1978. Commercial prospects for extraterrestrial materials. *J. Contemporary Business* 7: 153-69.

Dyson, F. 1979. *Disturbing the Universe.* Harper and Row.

Gaffey, M., and T. B. McCord. 1977. Mining outer space. *Technol. Rev.* June, 50-59.

Glaser, P. E. 1977. Solar power from satellites. *Physics Today* Feb., 30-38.

Haskin, L. A., and D. J. Lindstrom. 1979. Electrochemistry of lunar rocks. Paper 79-1380, 4th Princeton/AIAA Conference on Space Manufacturing Facilities, Princeton. (Summer Study 1978).

Helin, E. F., and E. M. Shoemaker, 1977. Discovery of Asteroid 1976AA. *Icarus* 31:415-19.

O'Leary, B. M. 1977. Mining the Apollo and Amor asteroids. *Science* 197:363-66.

O'Neill, G. K. 1975. Space colonies and energy supply to the earth. *Science* 190:943-47.

———. 1978. *The High Frontier. Human Colonies in Space,* 2nd ed. Bantam Books.

Rao, D. B., U. V. Choudary, T. E. Erstfeld, R. J. Williams, and Y. A. Chang. 1979. Extraction processes for the production of Al, Ti, Fe, Mg and O from nonterrestrial sources. In *NASA Report SP-428, Space Resources and Space Settlements*, ed. J. Billingham.

Shoemaker, E., J. G. Williams, E. F. Helin, and R. F. Wolfe. In press. Earth-crossing asteroids: Orbital classes, collision rates with earth, ori-

gin. In *Asteroids*, ed. T. Gehrels.

Taylor, S. R. 1975. *Lunar Science: A Post-Apollo View*. Pergamon.

Watson, K., B. C. Murray, and H. Brown. 1961. The behavior of volatiles on the lunar surface. *J. Geophys. Res.* 66:3033-46.

39.

Irvin B. Nathan: ABSCAM Ethics

On February 2, 1980, viewers of NBC's evening newcast learned of the existence of a two-year-old FBI undercover investigation with the code name ABSCAM that had turned up almost irrefutable evidence that a number of high U.S. government officials were willing to sell their influence for cash. The officials included a U.S. senator, several congressmen, and assorted state officials who had offered to act as intermediaries. On August 31, Representative Michael O. Myers of Pennsylvania and three co-defendants became the first persons convicted of bribery and conspiracy in a case arising from the ABSCAM investigation. Videotapes showed Myers accepting $50,000 in cash in return for a promise to introduce special immigration legislation that would allow certain Arab sheikhs (actually undercover FBI agents) to reside in the United States. Myers and certain other defendants, as well as many newspaper editors, raised issues about the fairness of the operation. Were the victims entrapped? Had the FBI embarked on a "fishing expedition"? Had there been a "hit list" of suspected corrupt officials? All of these questions and others were answered in a careful review of the operation by the deputy assistant attorney general in the Department of Justice who coordinated the ABSCAM prosecutions. Mr. Nathan's article was published in 1983, after all of the trials had been concluded.

Source: *ABSCAM ETHICS: Moral Issues and Deception in Law Enforcement*, ed. G.M. Caplan, The Police Foundation, 1983.

ALL OF THE MAJOR ABSCAM trials having been completed, the time has arrived for an assessment of the operation and an evaluation of the public policy questions of using undercover operations to detect political corruption.

In the series of ABSCAM prosecutions, eight juries in three cities unanimously found guilty of official corruption a senior United States senator; six members of Congress, including the chairmen of two powerful committees in the House; the mayor of Camden, who is also a state senator in New Jersey; the president of the Philadelphia City Council, along with its majority leader and a third member; an inspector for the United States Immigration and Naturalization Service; a Philadelphia lawyer; a New York accountant; and other assorted "business associates" of the public officials. Not one defendant who stood trial was acquitted, although two juries returned verdicts of not guilty on one or two counts.

For the first time in history, a sitting member of Congress, Michael O. Myers of Philadelphia, was expelled from the House of Representatives on the ground of official corruption. Two others, John Jenrette and Raymond Lederer, resigned on the eve of their anticipated expulsion. Five of the six indicted representatives were turned out of office by their constituents when they stood for reelection; only Representative Lederer, whose trial began after the elections, was reelected to his seat, which he vacated after conviction.

Of the 96 jurors, men and women drawn from broad cross-sections of society in Brooklyn, Long Island, Philadelphia, and Washington, D.C., there was not a single holdout. Few of the eight juries required more than a day's deliberation to reach the conclusion that the defendants were guilty beyond a reasonable doubt; most completed their deliberations in a matter of a few hours. In most of the trials, the videotapes were released to the media at the same time they were presented to the juries so that the public could assess the fairness of the juries' verdicts. The unanimity and swiftness of the verdicts reflect the fact-gathering techniques employed by the FBI, the skilled presentation of the evidence by career prosecutors, and the precision with which the charges in the indictments were drafted. They also, of course, reflect the potency of the videotaped capture of a crime in progress.

To date, the appellate courts have been equally unanimous in affirming the ABSCAM jury verdicts. Of four separate panels of appellate courts that have reviewed ABSCAM convictions, three of them have affirmed the convictions unanimously and the U.S. Court of Appeals for the Third Circuit, sitting *en banc,* affirmed the convictions by a 7-2 vote. Each of these courts expressly found that there had been no violation of any defendant's rights under the Constitution and rejected contentions that the government entrapped or otherwise treated the defendants unfairly. As of this writing, the Supreme Court has declined to review the only ABSCAM case to come before it, appeals to intermediate federal appellate courts are pending in two cases and a motion for a new trial is under consideration by a district court in a third case.

By any reckoning, ABSCAM must be considered the most extensive investigation and prosecution of legislative corruption in the nation's history. In no previous federal investigation—not in Watergate, not in Teapot Dome—have so many elected officials at the federal, state and local levels been found guilty and repudiated by their constituents.

The deterrent effect of the operation is not so easily measured, but the evidence of substantial deterrence is clear. In Philadelphia, after the jury verdicts were rendered, the council president pro tem said, "It means that the old politics, backroom politics, darkroom politics, has come to an end. You're going to see the leadership of leaders who are open, more responsive to the people." One need not accept that statement at full value, in Philadelphia or elsewhere, to realize that public officials, aware of such undercover operations, are either going to refrain entirely from such transactions or, at the very least, to be more circumspect in choosing their associates, transactions, and words.

Shortly after the disclosure of ABSCAM, FBI Director William Webster reported that there were more than 50 sophisticated undercover operations underway across the country, involving examinations into various crimes, including public corruption. According to recent testimony by FBI officials, undercover agents in some of these continuing investigations have reported conversations in which suspects attributed their caution to concerns about the possibility of ABSCAM-type probes. This and other evidence suggests that the verdicts of the juries and electorate have been heard and heeded.

Yet the results of the trials and appeals have not stilled the controversy surrounding the techniques employed in the investigation. While jurors and voters have spoken uniformly and unequivocally, questions continue to be raised by defense counsel, commentators, and at least two district court judges about the fairness and propriety of this operation and, more generally, about the future use of undercover operations to ferret out public corruption and white collar crime. Indeed, decisions in each of the cases await judicial review of defendants' post-trial motions, some of which challenge the basic fairness of the ABSCAM operation.

At the heart of the controversy are two questions: How were these public officials selected and what in the future will prevent unscrupulous prosecutors and investigators from employing these techniques to ensnare innocent political enemies? Both questions deserve serious responses.

One indisputable fact must constantly be borne in mind in assessing the fairness of ABSCAM: There was no targeting. There was no hit list. No one in the executive branch, in Washington or elsewhere, ever sat down and selected public officials at whom the ABSCAM operation was to be aimed. All of the

public officials who became involved in ABSCAM came into the operation as a result of the representations and actions of corrupt intermediaries. These "bagmen" boasted to people they believed were fellow criminals (but who actually were government agents) about their ability to produce these public officials for illegal actions, sometimes supporting their claims by citing past illegal ventures. The absence of any common thread linking the seven members of Congress found guilty underscores the lack of any governmental selection process. They came from five different states in the East and had widely differing politics, ranging from extreme conservatism to extreme liberalism.

No political official was put off limits; no allegation, regardless of the party, power, or position of the official involved was disregarded as too hot to pursue. When corrupt intermediaries, who had participated in criminal ventures with the undercover operatives, claimed that they could produce a public official to take a bribe, they were invariably invited to live up to their claims. They were told that they would have to produce the allegedly corrupt politician in the flesh and that the politician would have to acknowledge both the bribe and the services to be personally performed for it.

They did fail to produce on a number of occasions, for reasons ranging from outright lies about politicians whom the go-between had never even contacted to a prudent abundance of caution by seemingly predisposed officeholders and their close associates. But the failures were never the result of a veto from a Justice Department representative. As Philip B. Heymann, the head of the Justice Department's Criminal Division, who monitored the investigation and made final prosecutive decisions, testified before a congressional committee, "If a middleman had claimed that he could produce President Carter to take a bribe, we would have swallowed hard but we would not have backed off."

Detractors of ABSCAM attempt to portray an image of high-level Justice Department officials engaged in a crusade against selected public officials or seeking to test the honesty or morality of randomly chosen politicians. The truth of the matter, as shown by the evidence developed in eight public trials, is far different. At critical junctures in the investigation, high-level officials in the Criminal Division and the FBI were faced with essentially only one simple choice: either ignore serious allegations of corruption by refusing to allow contacts with those represented to be ready and willing to engage in criminal conduct, or authorize FBI operatives to pursue the leads they had developed during their investigation, up to and including meeting and offering bribes to public officials identified by proven criminals. It would have been scandalous to have refused to explore fully these serious allegations.

The origins and natural progressions in the ABSCAM investigation have been presented repeatedly in the trials and in congressional hearings. Unfortunately, they apparently have been obscured by the high drama in each case, the videotaped receipt of large amounts of cash by elected officials, often accompanied by such vivid statements as "Money talks, bull shit walks" or "I've got larceny in my blood." Thus, it may be useful to retrace briefly the beginnings and early developments of the operations.

ABSCAM began in the Hauppauge office of the FBI in Long Island in early 1978. Imaginative agents there, headed by group supervisor John Good, began working with a convicted swindler, Melvin Weinberg, who had agreed to cooperate with the government. The scope of the operation was limited at the outset to solving property crimes and recovering stolen or forged securities or art work. The basic setup was simple, and similar to one which Weinberg had run illegally before he had been caught and convicted. Weinberg and agents of the FBI posed as American representatives of fabulously wealthy Arab businessmen interested in shrewd investments in this country, the legality of which did not concern them at all. They created "Abdul Enterprises Limited" (from which the name ABSCAM derived), established an office in Long Island, and spread the word in the netherworld that easy money was available for shady transactions.

As a result of the efforts of Abdul Enterprises, the government was able to recover millions of dollars worth of stolen art and forged stocks, bonds, and certificates of deposit. Private insurance companies paid substantial rewards to Weinberg for his extraordinary efforts in securing return of the stolen works. To this point, there was nothing particularly unusual about the undercover operations, except perhaps the somewhat elaborate cover story. Through the summer of 1978, there was no political orientation to the relatively routine undercover operation.

Things began to change slowly in the fall of 1978, when one of the groups which had previously sold Abdul Enterprises phony certificates of deposit raised a new prospect. They offered to serve as a broker between a New Jersey politician and the fictional Arabs, who had indicated some interest in investing in the newly legalized gambling casinos in Atlantic City. These people described in detail the corrupt relationship they had had with this politician and the influence he claimed he could sell in the state. As a result, the Arab's representatives met with Angelo Errichetti, the mayor of Camden, New Jersey, who also served as a state senator from New Jersey. In short order, Errichetti and the undercover operatives developed a profoundly corrupt relationship.

In the spring of 1979, Errichetti furnished the FBI operatives, still believing them to be agents of the wealthy and unscrupulous Arab sheiks, with a written list of names of those who he claimed were corrupt federal and state politicians in and around New Jersey. He claimed he could put the operatives in touch with these allegedly corrupt politicians should the need arise. In the course of his continuing dealings with the operatives, Errichetti soon had an opportunity to fulfill his boast.

In late July 1979, aboard a yacht in Florida, a meeting was held with Errichetti and others to discuss a proposed casino transaction. Also present at the meeting were people whom Errichetti had introduced to the FBI operatives as instrumental in the casino deal, including Louis Johanson, a Philadelphia city council member, and his law partner Howard Criden. During the cruise, the glib and extremely effective undercover FBI agent Anthony Amoroso, posing as Tony DeVito, the Arabs' righthand man, remarked that the sheiks might have to flee their country and seek asylum in the United States. He said that the sheiks did not want to face a situation like the one that had confronted Anastasio Somoza, the deposed Nicaraguan leader, who had been expelled from this country shortly after his arrival. Amoroso did not suggest how this problem might be avoided. Errichetti and Criden took the initiative and embarked on a campaign of lining up members of Congress who, in return for cash, would take actions to guarantee asylum for the fictional sheiks. This was, in essence, the beginning of the congressional phase of ABSCAM.

To this point the Department of Justice in Washington had very limited involvement in the development of ABSCAM. Even more important, at this time, in late July 1979, the FBI and Justice personnel had no designs on any officials and had probably not even heard of Ozzie Myers, Raymond Lederer, or Richard Kelly.

The first mention of the names of Representatives Myers and Lederer was made by Errichetti on July 29, 1979, when he claimed that he had lined them up to meet with the sheiks' representatives in order to provide immigration assistance. In subsequent conversations, Errichetti said that the price for each would be $100,000. Weinberg later got the price reduced to $50,000.

Thus, when this phase of the ABSCAM-case came to Washington, the question was whether the agents would be authorized to offer and pay $50,000 bribes to Representatives Myers and Lederer, two public officials whom Mayor Errichetti represented as ready and willing to sell their offices for that amount. The decision Director Webster faced, in consultation with the head of the Criminal Division, was whether to authorize the agents to proceed or whether to call them off. If the director had disapproved the request, the serious allegations raised against two sitting congressmen would never have been proven or refuted. In effect, the allegations would have been covered up. By authorizing the approach, the director gave the

AP/Wide World

`08-22-79    12:43:25`

In this videotape played at the first ABSCAM trial, Representative Michael Myers, second from left, receives an envelope containing $50,000 from an undercover FBI agent.

named representatives an opportunity to clear themselves or to incriminate themselves. No conscientious law enforcement official could have made any other decision.

The ground rules communicated to all the FBI operatives were designed to thwart unscrupulous middlemen and eliminate any ambiguity. The operatives were directed to make it clear that the representatives themselves would be required to appear, would be told unequivocally what was expected of them and would have to accept or acknowledge receipt of the bribe. Every meeting between the operatives and a member of Congress at which a bribe was offered or passed was videotaped. These videotapes are there for all to see and to determine whether these conditions were met, whether the mutual exchanges of promises were unambiguous and whether the public officials were pressured or fooled in any way. The juries had no trouble with these questions.

Either Errichetti or Criden or both were involved in the introductions

to Representatives Myers, Lederer, Thompson, and Murphy. Indeed, it was Thompson who first raised Murphy's name and then introduced the operatives to him for a corrupt transaction. The same pattern held in the cases of Representatives Jenrette and Kelly. In each case, an intermediary claimed to be able to produce a legislator who, in return for cash, would be willing to assist in the immigration problems. In all cases, the names and predisposition were first raised by the intermediaries who had no reason to believe that they were dealing with the government and who had little incentive to lie.

In all of the cases, except that involving Jenrette, the intermediaries were told of the supposed immigration problems *before* they disclosed which members of Congress they could produce to lend assistance in return for a bribe. In the Jenrette case, the FBI operatives had been dealing with a South Carolina businessman, John Stowe, on a deal involving forged certificates of deposit. In the course of those discussions, Stowe said that he knew a representative who was "as big a crook as I am" and would assist in the certificates of deposit transaction. Stowe identified the legislator as John Jenrette. After the securities deal fell through, the operatives asked Stowe whether he thought Jenrette would be willing to assist in the immigration problem in return for cash. Stowe reported that Jenrette was interested and the meetings and the payoff to Jenrette ensued.

The case involving Senator Williams proceeded along a slightly different track, but the pattern was essentially the same. The testimony in the Williams trial showed that after Mayor Errichetti learned of the enormous wealth of the Arabs and their eagerness to seek political influence in this country, Errichetti communicated his find to Senator Williams. The senior senator from New Jersey then immediately directed his long-time associate, Alex Feinberg, to have Errichetti put Feinberg in touch with the Arab representatives. Feinberg advised the sheiks' agents of Senator Williams's interest in a titanium mine and of the urgent need for substantial financing. As a result, Senator Williams met repeatedly, face-to-face, with the undercover agents, promising to use his influence with the president of the United States, the vice president, the secretaries of defense and state, and others to secure government purchases of titanium from the mine in return for a $100-million loan.

Of course, the government had set the bait by having its undercover agents tell the corrupt intermediaries they were willing to pay for political influence. But the government had no idea which politicians would rise to the bait and made no effort to push the bait toward any particular public officials. Neither had the government any idea which of the politicians was in fact corrupt and which was not. The process was very similar to the ordinary undercover fencing operations, in which government agents spread the word that they are willing to purchase stolen property at a discount for ready cash. At the time the operation is set up and the word goes out, the agents have no idea which people are going to come in with stolen goods. The agents take all comers, whether it be the town's most notorious thief or its minister. Similarly, in ABSCAM, it would have been improper for the government to close up shop when, instead of two-bit con men, the names of powerful public officials were raised as ready and willing to deal.

It is also untrue that law enforcement officials were running around Washington "offering bribes, willy-nilly, in hopes someone" would accept something, as at least one newspaper editorial charged. Whether or not it would be unfair or improper to offer a bribe to randomly selected public officials, who like many others must face similar temptations every day, it would be an extremely imprudent and wasteful expenditure of scarce law enforcement resources. How could one justify the time and effort to go on a wild goose chase with no prospects of success? This was not done in ABSCAM, and it is unlikely that any law enforcement administrator, in the face of rising crime rates and reduced budgets and staff, would do so. As in ABSCAM, law enforcement officials will not devote resources unless they have been alerted to the dangers of a serious crime problem in the area, even if they do not know the particular culprits involved.

Some critics argue that the government should have solid evidence, something approaching probable cause, to believe a particular public official has engaged in similar illegal conduct in the past before a bribe can be offered. Such a requirement would be unreasonable, unnecessary, and unworkable.

Consider the analogy of the "granny squads" which are common in urban police forces. When a particular park or downtown street is plagued with muggings and other violent crime, police may disguise themselves as vulnerable, elderly women with handbags ready to be snatched. When the disguised police officers enter the crime area, neither they nor their colleagues in waiting have any idea who is going to try to rip them off. Thereafter, if the scenario goes as planned, a thug appears, grabs the purse, attempts to run off, and is captured. Only later do the police learn whether this thief has a record. While the existence of a record may make some difference with respect to ultimate punishment, it should make no difference with respect to whether or not the thief should be prosecuted.

Substitute a member of Congress taking a bribe and ask what difference should it make at the investigative stage whether the government can prove that this politician had ever before taken a bribe. The question is will he or she, as represented, engage in illegality on this occasion under circumstances that closely approximate the real world. For the government to undertake a full-scale investigation into the alleged previous incidents before a fast-breaking transaction is consummated would be time-consuming and not particularly worthwhile. In responding to the proffered bribe, the public official can either prove or disprove the outstanding allegation without any reference to previous behavior. Even first offenders should be prosecuted. It seems likely that those who would be caught in decoy transactions—whether it is ripping off "grannies" or taking bribes—are those who are likely to have engaged in such conduct in the past.

Further, in considering whether to pursue the allegations raised by corrupt intermediaries, the government had to consider the source of the allegations and the likelihood that they were telling the truth. If a total stranger were to come into the police station and make an allegation of corruption against a public official, the allegation should, of course, be fully explored, even if there is a substantial chance that the allegation is a fabrication. There could be many reasons why this person may be fabricating the story, but no self-respecting

investigator or prosecutor would ignore the allegation. How then could the investigators in ABSCAM have failed to pursue allegations coming from people with whom they had dealt reliably in the past?

The intermediaries had every reason to tell the truth to the Arabs' representatives. First, they had established continuing corrupt relationships with them and presumably desired to continue the relationships so long as they proved profitable. If their information proved unreliable, the relationship, along with the anticipated reward, would be damaged or destroyed. Second, they were advised that they would have to produce the public officials for blatant offers of bribes. There would, of course, be considerable embarrassment if, at the meeting, the public official were to protest complete ignorance about the transaction and storm out. This would jeopardize the intermediary's status with both the public official and with the Arabs' representatives. Bringing an innocent public official to such a meeting would involve the risk that the official would inform the authorities, leading to the possibility of prosecution and to retribution from the Arabs' representatives— a risk not lightly run. Indeed, no public official brought to a meeting in ABSCAM ever reported a bribe offer to any law enforcement agency.

Another source of concern for some of ABSCAM's critics is the question of entrapment. This concern is based on the clearly correct notion that it is unfair to trap or trick innocent persons into taking illegal action they had no previous inclination to pursue. The law of entrapment is well settled. When this defense is raised by a defendant who essentially admits engaging in the illegal transaction, the jury must decide whether the accused was ready and willing to commit the crime if an opportunity should be presented or whether a person not otherwise predisposed to wrongdoing was corrupted by some overreaching or special inducement. The focus in this defense is properly on the mental state of the defendant, and it is provable or rebuttable by many different factors, including the prior conduct and words of the defendant, his or her knowledge before engaging in the criminal act, the alacrity with which he or she enters into the criminal act, the language and body movements accompanying the commission of the criminal act, and actions and relationships to the others involved after the commission of the criminal act. It is an individual defense and one which must be passed upon by the jury based on particular facts presented to it.

Curiously, although entrapment is often mentioned in the press, and even though words like "traps" and "snares" were thrown about in court by defense counsel, very few of the defendants actually raised the formal defense of entrapment. In each case where it was raised, the jury rejected the defense. In only one case did a judge disturb the jury's verdict. In a Philadelphia case involving two city council members, the court was not satisfied with the evidence of predisposition and set aside the guilty verdicts. That decision was reversed by the U.S. Court of Appeals for the Third Circuit sitting *en banc.*

Eschewing the entrapment defense, many of those prosecuted raised novel and bizarre defenses. For example, Representative Myers did not claim that he was pressured or coerced into taking $50,000 in $100 bills or into demanding an additional $85,000. Instead, his defense was that he was "play acting," only pretending that he would introduce legislation or take other acts to guarantee asylum while ripping off "fat-cat" Arabs. Representative Kelly, a former state judge from Florida, contended that when he took the $25,000 and stuffed it in his pockets, it was only part of his own investigation, an investigation which he never bothered to document or report to anyone else. The principal defense raised by Representative Jenrette, who also claimed entrapment, was that he was in a state of incapacitating inebriation for several months before and after his demand for and receipt of $50,000 and therefore should not be held accountable for his actions. It is striking to contrast these defenses with the simultaneous requests by these men to their constituents that they be returned to positions of high trust.

Entrapment was rarely raised, and was never accepted by a jury, for a very simple reason: there was none. No pressure was brought to bear on any public official; there was no badgering, no intimidation, no coercion, no imploring, no pandering. Judge Jon Newman, who previously served as a top aide to a senior United States senator, spoke for a unanimous panel of the Second Circuit Court of Appeals when, in rejecting an argument that ABSCAM represented an unconstitutional abuse, he made the unanswerable observation: "Any member of Congress approached by agents conducting a bribery sting operation can simply say 'No'." Any of the seven members of Congress was free to turn down the proposition, leave the room, and report the matter to the FBI. None of them did so.

Courts have developed the entrapment defense to protect unsophisticated people who could be lured or pressured into criminality without a clear appreciation of the consequences of their actions. It is farfetched to suggest that members of Congress—some of whom had held their seats for more than 20 years—were so naive or impressionable that they could be tricked or trapped into doing something that they were not predisposed to do. It was the Congress which had determined that this conduct should be deemed criminal in the first place.

During the eight trials, all of the interaction between the government operatives and the public officials was presented to the juries on videotapes without any editing. Every statement, every blandishment, every facial expression, every body movement by all of the participants was there in plain sight for the juries to consider. If a single one of the 96 jurors had thought that the government's conduct was high-handed, overreaching, or otherwise unfair to the public officials, he or she could have voted to acquit. Yet not a single one indicated by his or her vote a belief that there was any unfairness in the ABSCAM operation.

For the future, the tougher question is whether the public can be assured that these techniques will not be abused by unscrupulous and unethical executive branch officials against their political enemies in the legislative branch. The short answer is that any effective law enforcement tool can, in the wrong hands, be abused, but that is no reason to eliminate or outlaw the technique. Further, the dangers of abuse can be reduced by establishing and adhering to certain guiding principles and continuing to have close judicial scrutiny, aided by vigilant defense counsel, after an operation is completed.

In the future, any sophisticated federal undercover operation will be conducted under a detailed set of guidelines, promulgated in January 1981 by outgoing Attorney General Civiletti. The guidelines, which for the most part set forth the principles followed in ABSCAM, establish elaborate review procedures within the Department of Justice and mandate certain criteria designed to minimize any possibility of entrapment or other unfairness to potential defendants. The guidelines require that no such operation can be approved unless there is a reasonable indication that the individual has engaged or is engaging in the contemplated illegal activity or that only those predisposed would be expected to enter the operation. Further, the guidelines require that the proposed operation be "based solely on the law enforcement considerations." In addition, the details of the operation must satisfy the reviewing board that:

(A) the corrupt nature of the activity is reasonably clear to potential subjects;
(B) there is reasonable indication that the undercover operation will reveal illegal activities; and
(C) the nature of any inducement is not unjustifiable in view of the character of the illegal transaction in which the individual is invited to engage.

The essence of the guidelines is to make sure that the opportunities for crime resemble those in the real world as closely as possible and to make sure that the illegal nature of the opportunity is unambiguous. In the real world, most people—whether they be bank tellers, lawyers, domestics, bookkeepers or legislators—are faced with temptations and opportunities almost daily. If the opportunities presented by a sting operation are commensurate with those faced regularly by a public official, there is no element of unfairness in prosecuting him or her for having willfully seized it. Actually, this is an area in which fairness and practicality coalesce. If the circumstances are not similar to those found in the real world—for example, if the proffered rewards are too large or the pressures too overbearing, juries will not convict and judges will not sustain convictions.

Finally, the most basic safeguards are trial and appellate courts. In the end, the courts must scrutinize the evidence to determine whether there is any credible proof that an operation was directed at political opponents or whether it was in any other way fundamentally unfair to the defendants. Fortunately, in this electronic era, courts will be able to rely, in large measure, on audio and videotaped reproductions of the pivotal events to rule on any allegations of government overreaching or other misconduct.

When courts determine the fundamental fairness of these operations, they should compare, among other things, the quality of evidence in such videotaped operations with, for example, the testimony of a disaffected participant in an alleged bribe transaction committed years earlier by a prominent public official of theretofore unblemished reputation. They should also consider the likelihood that there will ever be a report of a bribe between two consenting individuals, each of whom has profited from the transaction. The court should also consider whether an operation such as ABSCAM is not less intrusive and less coercive than other judicially sanctioned techniques. They should compare the consensually recorded conversations between public officials and strangers to court-ordered wiretaps and bugs, where no party to the conversation knows that it is being overheard or recorded; judicially issued search warrants executed in private homes and offices against the wills of the owners; and grand jury or trial testimony compelled against friends or even relatives. All that the undercover technique relies upon is the willingness of public officials to engage in criminal conduct and make damaging admissions voluntarily and intentionally to those they believe are colleagues in crime. They recognize, of course, the risk that at some later date these people could reveal damaging information to the authorities, but they believe either that this is a remote possibility or that if a case is brought they will be able to put their credibility on the line against these criminal actors. What they do not know is that their voluntary words or actions are being recorded and are available for future use against them.

When all of these factors are considered, it becomes apparent that sophisticated undercover operations are fair and effective and represent the wave of the future in combatting public corruption as well as a variety of other consensual crimes. I suggest that this is good news, at least for law-abiding citizens.

40.

MALCOLM E. WHEELER: The Pinto Case

On March 13, 1980, a jury in Winamac, Indiana, found the Ford Motor Company not guilty of reckless homicide in a case involving the death of three teenage girls who had been killed in August 1978 when the 1973 Pinto subcompact in which they were riding burst into flames after it was struck from behind by a van. The prosecution, headed by Michael A. Cosentino, state's attorney of Elkhart County, claimed that Ford knew of a design defect in the Pinto but had failed to correct it. Ford contended that other small cars, but also larger ones, could not have withstood the impact of such a crash without spilling a large amount of fuel, which in this case ignited and burned the three girls to death. Questions about the appropriateness of using the criminal law to deal with product liability matters are raised by Malcolm E. Wheeler in the selection reprinted here. It should be noted that Mr. Wheeler was one of the attorneys who participated in Ford's defense.

Source: *The Forum,* Fall 1981.

On September 13, 1978, the grand jury for Elkhart County, Indiana, returned an indictment that commenced the first criminal prosecution of a product manufacturer for allegedly having made and sold a defective product that caused the product user's death. The defendant was Ford Motor Company, the product a Pinto sedan. The indictment contained four counts: three for reckless homicide and one for criminal recklessness.

Newspapers called it the most important economic case of the century, and it may well have been. The case was rife with substantive criminal-law questions of first impression and criminal procedural questions, constitutional issues, ethical issues, factual issues, and tactical issues of the first order. This article provides a brief overview of the facts of the case, describes the basic manner in which counsel constructed its defense, and uses the case to explain some of the reasons why the use of general criminal laws, such as homicide statutes, to regulate the design of products disserves the public's interests.

1. THE FACTS OF THE PINTO CASE

On August 10, 1978, at about six o'clock in the evening, three teenaged girls were driving a 1973 Pinto sedan south on U.S. Highway 33 toward Goshen, Indiana. They stopped for gas at a self-service station, filled up, and drove back onto the highway. The driver, however, had neglected to put the filler cap on tightly. It fell off and rolled across the highway, coming to rest near the curb in the northbound lane.

The girls did a U-turn to retrieve the filler cap, pulled up where it lay, and drew to a stop in the right lane. They could not pull off the road, because it was designed with an eight-inch-high curb running its entire length, only inches from the traffic lane. Neither a shoulder nor periodically spaced turnouts existed to enable a vehicle in trouble to pull off for repairs. The curbed, shoulderless road was so dangerous that Elkhart County's Citizens' Safety Committee had written a letter to the Indiana State Highway Department asking that the road be modified to provide safe stopping spaces for emergencies.

AP/Wide World

Elkhart County officials and Ford representatives examine the Pinto in which three girls died.

The weather was clear; the road was dry; and visibility was unobstructed for more than a mile in both directions. But, as the girls drew to a stop alongside the filler cap, a Chevrolet van weighing more than 4,000 pounds, modified with a rigid plank in place of the original front bumper, driven by a man carrying open beer bottles, marijuana, and caffeine pills, and travelling at some fifty-five miles per hour, bore down on them. Without touching his brakes, the van driver plowed squarely into the back of the Pinto, knocking it some 170 feet down the road, spinning it around, and causing it to jump the eight-inch curb with its left side wheels.

The Pinto burst into flame. The two passengers died in the car, but the driver was partially ejected. She was rushed to the hospital and died several hours later. Before dying, however, she told two of the hospital employees, an orderly and a nurse, exactly what had happened.

The police inspected the van immediately after the accident. They found the open beer bottles, the marijuana, and what they reported as capsules of speed.

Based on those facts, one might have expected any of several occurrences. A civil action might have been filed against the Indiana Highway Department and the engineers who designed and approved Highway 33 and who failed to heed the request that it be modified for safety. A civil action might have been filed against the van driver. The van driver might have been criminally prosecuted for reckless homicide, speeding, reckless driving, possession of controlled substances, and driving with open liquor bottles in his possession. Or, because the Pinto driver had neglected to replace the cap and then had stopped her car on a highspeed highway, one might have concluded that, unless comparative negligence applied, no legal action would be brought based on the girls' deaths.

But the prosecutor of Elkhart County, Indiana, chose to seek an indictment against Ford Motor Company for reckless homicide and criminal recklessness, claiming that the cause of the deaths was the design of the Pinto and Ford's failure to "remove [the Pinto] from the highways" before August 10, 1978. He also obtained an information against the van driver for possession of amphetamines. (Rather than promptly proceeding to judgment and sentencing on that charge, he kept those charges hanging over the van driver's head until after March 1980, when the driver had testified against Ford and the trial of Ford had ended. Moreover, the pills reported as amphetamines in the official police report were later analyzed and determined to be caffeine pills; but that information was concealed from Ford's lawyers until after the driver took the stand at trial, and the charge of possessing amphetamines was kept pending throughout the trial.)

There the legal saga began. By the time we were asked to defend Ford, the prosecutor had already impounded the vehicles, arranged for three well-known plaintiffs' experts from California and Arizona to examine them, allowed one of those experts to remove the Pinto's carburetor, obtained full reports from the officers who had first been called to the accident scene, interviewed witnesses, and commenced a whirlwind grand jury proceeding that had resulted in an indictment only thirty-four days after the accident. In the ensuing months we would find that various state and local government employees would not talk to us, that the prosecutor was receiving documents and other help from plaintiffs' lawyers throughout the country, that federal agencies were assisting the prosecutor, that the coroner's office, the fire department, the highway patrol, and the sheriff's office, to name but a few, were providing personnel and facilities, and that the prosecutorial legal team included the prosecutor and deputy prosecutor; a private plaintiff's attorney from Goshen, Indiana; another attorney, the president of Indiana's prosecutors' association; two law professors; and numerous law students. When the case was moved to nearby Winamac, Indiana, the additional resources of the Pulaski County Prosecutor's office were added to that army. In addition, several nationally known plaintiffs' experts, including an out-of-state pathologist, several automotive experts, and a statistician from Washington, D.C., were providing advice or testimony either for free or at nominal cost. Finally, in addition to all of those resources, Elkhart County appropriated extra funds for the prosecutor to use for expenses incurred in the prosecution.

These facts demonstrate three important characteristics of a criminal prosecution of a manufacturer for an alleged product defect. First, even a well funded corporate defendant begins at a severe disadvantage. The prosecutor can make his case before the indictment issues. The prosecutor has control of much, if not most, of the key tangible evidence and most of the witnesses. He can impound evidence, instruct government employees not to talk, and, whether intentionally or not, induce private witnesses to be reluctant to talk. Because he is on the attack, the prosecutor can call news conferences, issue press statements, and otherwise use the media to create an overall atmosphere hostile to the defendant. By carefully timing his news releases of noteworthy information or contentions, he can prolong or intensify the adverse publicity almost at will. The prosecutor can use the state's employees, laboratories, vehicles, aircraft, and other resources to perform numerous tasks. The prosecutor can obtain substantial assistance from plaintiffs' lawyers and experts, because they can indirectly benefit from a conviction.

Second, the societal cost of such a prosecution is immense. The value of the services provided in the Pinto case by firemen, highway patrol officers, coroners, pathologists, laboratory personnel, film technicians, lawyers, and numerous other government employees must have exceeded a half-million dollars.

Third, the very commencement of such a prosecution has a devastating effect on a manufacturer-defendant, even if the manufacturer is innocent and is ultimately acquitted of the charges on the merits. A product manufacturer survives by the reputation of its product. If a manufacturer is prosecuted for manufacturing a criminally defective product, even a jury's pronouncement of innocence cannot unring the bell loudly sounded for months by the prosecutor and press. Unfortunately, but understandably, the media report the sensational news, and there is nothing sensational in a headline that says, "Manufacturer makes good product serving public's needs." Sensational is a picture of dead girls; sensational is a simplistic description of complicated documents; sensational is a charge of homicide; sensational is a one-liner like "sacrifices safety for profit," as opposed to a careful and thoughtful description of the difficulty of satisfying a massive public with widely varying conceptions of the proper balance to be struck among price, reliability, durability, safety, maintenance costs, appearance, comfort, convenience, performance, and all of the other factors that go into every consumer product.

Sensationalistic reporting not only seriously lessens the likelihood that the defendant can obtain a fair trial, but, to the extent that it damages an innocent company's reputation, it harms consumers by misleading them and by reducing their market choices because of the productivity retrenchment that lower sales will dictate. Thus, whereas the danger of criminally prosecuting an innocent individual seriously affects only that individual and his family and friends, the prosecution of an innocent corporation for manufacturing an allegedly defective product adversely affects the defendant's thousands of employees and their families, the company's suppliers and shareholders, and the consuming public. It is one thing to prosecute an antitrust or securities law violation, about which the general public knows little and cares less; it is an entirely different matter to charge a company with homicide.

II. THE DEFENSE OF THE PINTO PROSECUTION

The defense of Ford in the Pinto prosecution consisted of three principal efforts: (1) Moving to dismiss the indictment on statutory and constitutional grounds; (2) seeking to put the case in the best procedural posture for trial; and (3) developing substantive trial defenses and supporting evidence. . . .

Our defense at trial consisted of proving nine principal points:

1. In the 1973 model year, Ford was the only automobile manufacturer in the world that had voluntarily adopted a mandatory internal rear-impact fuel-system-integrity crash-test requirement.

2. The internal standard that had been adopted by Ford and met by the 1973 Pinto was a reasonable standard, the very one that had been proposed by the General Services Administration in 1966, by the Canadian Government, by the National

Highway Traffic Safety Administration in 1969, and by various private, non-manufacturer entities and researchers.

3. Any car manufactured in 1973, of any size and design, would have suffered a ruptured fuel system if hit by that van at that speed.

4. The 1973 Pinto was comparable in design, and the federal government's own statistics showed that it was comparable in safety performance, to other 1973 subcompact cars.

5. The 1973 Pinto had met all applicable governmental safety standards.

6. All of the key Ford engineering executives involved in the development of the Pinto had provided Pintos to their wives and children to drive, thereby demonstrating those executives' belief in the car's safety.

7. Even though Ford had believed the Pinto to have been reasonably designed, it had recalled the car in a manner that, during the relevant period, was accomplished as quickly as possible and under the guidance of the federal government.

8. The driver of the van had been the primary cause of the tragedy, but he was not even on trial.

9. The badly designed road had been the other cause of the tragedy, but its designers and the persons who approved it were not on trial.

There is, of course, a story behind each of those defenses, the accumulation of the evidence to prove them, the choice of how to present them, and the way the evidence went in at the trial. But time does not permit the telling. It must suffice to say that some combination of the factors succeeded, because the jury returned with an acquittal on all counts.

III. THE PINTO PROSECUTION: AN EXAMPLE OF WHY USE OF GENERAL CRIMINAL LAWS TO REGULATE PRODUCT DESIGN DESERVES THE PUBLIC'S INTEREST

At last year's annual meeting, the prosecutor in the Pinto case gave a presentation in which he attempted to justify the use of general criminal statutes, as opposed to the use of criminal sanctions for violations of governmental regulations governing the specific product in issue, on two grounds: to deter undesirable conduct and "to reinforce the norm against killing and the sanctity of life." One cannot, of course, question the general goal of deterring "undesirable conduct," because conduct that is undesirable is by definition something that, *ceteris paribus,* one wants to prevent. Similarly, one cannot question "the sanctity of life" as such, because that phrase lacks specific meaning and simply provides a sententious starting point, a fact amply demonstrated by the abortion controversy.

One can, however, question whether the type or amount of deterrence achieved by using general criminal statutes to regulate product design is in the public's interest; whether the monetary and nonmonetary costs to society of that method of deterrence outweigh the benefits; whether the same level of deterrence that would be achieved in that manner could, if desirable at all, be achieved in another manner that would better serve the public's interest; whether it is wise or just to single out a particular group—product manufacturers—by which to "sanctify life" through prosecutions for balancing safety needs against other needs of society; and whether one reinforces the "sanctity of life" or evokes disrespect for the fairness and logic of the law by pretending that there is something immoral about using cost-benefit analysis or risk analysis where safety is one of the variables. It seems fair to say that the person who advocates a dramatic change in the law that has existed for centuries, the criminal law that before the Pinto prosecution had never been used to regulate product design, bears the burden of showing that the change is necessary and desirable and will not entail other changes that, when all are considered together, will disserve the public's interests.

Consider, for example, whether more deterrence in product manufacturing is desirable and, if so, whether general criminal statues are a desirable means to achieve the desired additional amount. The theory of deterrence assumes that a person contemplating the commission of a particular act will commit that act only if the benefits he expects to reap outweigh the anticipated costs he expects to incur, where the anticipated costs are a function of the possible costs and the probability that those possible costs will be incurred. Thus, to increase deterrence, one can increase either the cost the actor might incur by engaging in the conduct or the probability that the actor will in fact incur those costs.

Even absent that threat of criminal sanctions, manufacturers, in deciding whether to implement any modification affecting product safety, must consider several costs they might incur by producing and selling products that could be made safer. These potential costs include civil lawsuits for compensatory damages, including lost income, medical expenses, property damage, and intangibles such as pain and suffering, loss of consortium, the mental distress

to family members, all of which can total several million dollars in a single lawsuit; civil lawsuits for punitive damages that can be several million dollars in a single lawsuit; civil lawsuits for fraud, breach of contract, or breach of warranty, including class actions in which purchasers who have not suffered physical injury seek equitable relief or damages; administrative or judicial proceedings by regulatory agencies to require recalls, warnings, or other actions that can cost the manufacturer several million dollars; critical publicized evaluations of the product, by government agencies or by private testing entities such as Consumers' Union, which may cause consumers to stop buying the particular product and, perhaps, other products made by the manufacturer; adverse publicity about injuries suffered by the product's users, about lawsuits brought against the manufacturer, or about proceedings instituted by regulatory agencies, all of which may cause additional consumers to stop buying the particular product and, perhaps, other products made by the manufacturer; and the costs of defending lawsuits and other proceedings, even where no adverse judgment or settlement ever occurs. Such a broad array of noncriminal deterrent forces attends few other activities engaged in by members of our society.

Further, the probability appears to be substantial and growing that at least some of these costs will be incurred by a manufacturer that makes and sells a product that could have been made safer and injures someone. In 1974, only 1,579 product liability cases were filed in federal courts; but 7,775 such cases were filed in federal courts in the year ending June 30, 1980. The magnitude of jury awards has risen so substantially that million-dollar verdicts are now common. Tort law has continually developed in a fashion that favors plaintiffs, both in liability and in damages issues. . . . And these are only highlights of the array of judicial and legislative actions taken in recent years to increase the probability that injured persons will sue and recover large sums from product manufacturers.

Despite the impressive array of potential costs that tend to deter manufacturers from producing and selling products that they think the courts, the regulators, the testing entities or the public are likely to consider defective, and despite the apparent magnitude of the probability that some of those costs will be incurred by manufacturers who market such products, one might contend that even more deterrence is socially desirable and can be efficiently achieved by the use of criminal sanctions. . . .

Before deciding whether more deterrence is needed or can efficiently be obtained through criminal sanctions, however, one must identify what one wishes to deter. Since the prosecutor's principal criticism of Ford was its use of a cost-benefit safety analysis, one might contend that criminal sanctions are needed to deter the use of any such analysis. That contention would be self-contradictory and unrealistic. The very essence of deterrence theory *requires* that an actor weigh the costs and benefits of contemplated conduct in deciding whether to engage in that conduct; it would be self-contradictory, therefore, to assert that society should deter the use of cost-benefit analysis by relying upon a theory that necessarily recognizes and encourages cost-benefit analysis. . . .

IV. CONCLUSION

From the point of view of an economist, a political scientist, or any other person concerned with maximizing the general public welfare and quality of life, one of the problems in human affairs is that the simplistic, emotional argument so often carries the day, even when the result will be quite the opposite of what the public really wants to achieve. This is especially true in the products liability area, where post-accident pictures or appearances of badly injured accident victims and sorrowful tales by friends and relatives so readily generate sympathy and horror that close the viewers' and listeners' ears to the necessarily complex, big-picture analysis by which major policy decisions should be governed.

It should be incumbent upon public representatives, such as legislators and prosecutors, not to exacerbate that problem by painting with broad, moralizing brush strokes where detail and clear definition are absolutely necessary. The decision whether to use general criminal laws to regulate product design, therefore, should not be made by casual references to the sanctity of human life, to the alleged overarching importance of absolute safety (which does not exist even in theory), or to the alleged immorality of the profit motive. The decision should, instead, be made only after a careful consideration of all of the effects that such a use is likely to entail and of the desirability of those effects. The Pinto prosecution strongly suggests that such a careful consideration will readily demonstrate that the use of general criminal laws to regulate product design will ill serve the public's interests.

41.

Walter Jacob: Refugees and Their Problems

Men and women and children, fleeing political repression, war's desolation, and economic miseries in their own countries, often have sought asylum in the United States because of its promise of peace, freedom, and opportunity. In every year the refugees have flooded America's shores, but especially during 1980, when tens of thousands of Cubans and Haitians arrived in small boats off the coasts of Florida and entered the country both legally and illegally, to create enormous problems in Miami. On March 17, President Carter signed the 1980 Refugee Act, which extended the definition of refugees to include persons from every part of the world and increased the number of refugees and immigrants allowed to enter the country each year from 290,000 to 320,000. But this number did not include notable exceptions, like many Cubans and most of the Haitians, to say nothing of the illegal entrants from Mexico. The article reprinted here (in part), by a knowledgeable journalist, details many of the problems and difficulties in resettling hundreds of thousands of refugees every year.

Source: *National Journal,* July 26, 1980.

In 1975, something new turned up on the television screens of Orange County, Calif.: advertisements publicizing the plight of thousands of Indochinese refugees and seeking help from the affluent community.

Many volunteered, and today an estimated 38,000 residents—1 of every 50 people in the county—are refugees from Vietnam, Cambodia and Laos. But in a period of recession, the 700 to 1,000 Indochinese who continue to arrive each month are receiving an increasingly hostile welcome.

"It's like a powder keg," said Gail McGee, Orange County's coordinator for refugee resettlement. And the national resettlement system, she said, has not made her life any easier. "This whole program," she said, "has been managed on a cut-and-paste theory. Everything is ad hoc."

Refugee coordinators in other states with heavy influxes of refugees—Florida, Texas and Illinois—echo her complaints about disorganization in the refugee resettlement system. So do federal officials and representatives of private resettlement organizations who also contribute to the confusing patchwork of responsibility for the approximately 231,700 refugees whom the government plans to let enter the United States this year—not counting the 116,000 Cubans and Haitians who have entered with less than full refugee status.

At the federal level, the State, Justice and Health and Human Services

(HHS) Departments share jurisdiction over refugees. In the private sector, 10 major voluntary agencies, each with its own philosophy and operating procedures, make first contact with refugees seeking to enter the United States and try to help provide for them when they arrive.

In the 1980 Refugee Act, which President Carter signed on March 17, Congress tried to impose some coherence on the resettlement system by assigning roles to the various agencies involved in it and assuring that all refugees will be entitled to the same federal benefits. But the act has many detractors, and by all accounts, it has left many organizational problems unsolved. It also proved not to be the last word on the federal government's financial obligation to refugees. Although the act says Washington will reimburse the states for their costs of providing for refugees during their first three years in this country, the Carter Administration announced last month that it would pay for only a portion of the resettlement costs of the Cubans and Haitians who have flooded southern Florida since April.

Even if the federal government pays for only a part of these costs, it will spend a total of $1.4 billion this year to resettle refugees in this country and provide for them, the State Department estimates. But to McGee, cold cash is no more important than the need for a coherent, smoothly functioning resettlement system that responds to the pressures that refugees exert on both governmental and private agencies.

"We are taking agencies that were set up to handle trickles of refugees and simply overwhelming them," she said. "National refugee resettlement has not yet been set up so that it can handle refugees responsibly."

HOW THE SYSTEM WORKS

While the waves of Cubans and Haitians are more recent, the Indochinese refugees, who have arrived in great numbers ever since the United States evacuated Vietnam in 1975, provide a more complete lesson in the fragmentation of refugee assistance. Of the 231,-700 refugees expected this year, 168,-000 are Indochinese and most of the rest are Soviet and Eastern European.

Vietnamese, Cambodians and Laotians who make their way to the refugee camps in Thailand and Malaysia are met by representatives of the voluntary U.S. resettlement agencies. Some, such as men with more than one wife, are rejected automatically for entry to the United States, and persons with communicable diseases must first recover.

For others, the voluntary agencies exercise discretion, and currently, under terms of the Refugee Act, they are giving priority to refugees who have relatives already settled in the United States. Bob White, associate director of refugee resettlement for Church World Service, a major voluntary agency, said 70 percent of the Indochinese entering the United States already have family members here.

The voluntary agencies help officers of the Justice Department's Immigration and Naturalization Service examine the applicants' claims to refugee status. To qualify, according to the Refugee Act, persons must normally be outside their home country and unable to return to it for fear of "persecution on account of race, religion, nationality, membership in a particular social group or political opinion."

The recently arrived Cubans and Haitians did not qualify for full refugee status in part because they arrived on

AP/Bettmann

Cambodian refugees who have fled to Thailand await help in a refugee camp.

U.S. shores in uncontrollable thousands without being processed abroad. Many Haitians remain in hiding in southern Florida, afraid that they will be shipped back, although the Carter Administration has said it will grant them provisional status if they were in Immigration and Naturalization Service proceedings as of June 19.

For Indochinese who are certified in Thailand or Malaysia as refugees, the American Council on Voluntary Agencies assigns each to one of its 12 member agencies. For each refugee, the voluntary agency finds a sponsor in the United States: a single family, a congregation or an entire resettlement service.

After the refugees are flown to the United States at State Department expense, the department provides the voluntary agencies with $500 per refugee to cover initial resettlement expenses, although many of the agencies estimate that their actual costs are more like $1,200. The agencies also qualify for grants from HHS if they provide social services.

Refugees who need them qualify for the full range of federal relief programs under relaxed standards. The Refugee Act provides that during refugees' first three years in the United States, the federal government reimburses the states for their share of the costs of such programs as medicaid and aid to families with dependent children (AFDC).

Sometimes the American system of refugee resettlement can function relatively smoothly, as it has with Soviet Jewish refugees. The Soviet Jews, who receive strong support from the private sector and who came to the United States in comparatively small though gradually increasing numbers each year up to 1979, are deemed so likely to find employment that their sponsoring agencies have accepted a fixed sum from HHS as reimbursement for their services for each refugee.

HHS provides $1,000 per Soviet Jew to such groups as the Hebrew Immigrants Aid Society, a worldwide Jewish migration agency, and in return receives an unwritten assurance that the refugees will find employment and will not become a burden to state and federal welfare systems.

Unfortunately, the resettlement system's record is not so good with larger waves of immigrants—particularly those that have appeared without much warning. While critics charge that the State Department could have anticipated the recent Cuban crisis on the basis of Central Intelligence Agency reports, the regular resettlement system probably could not have been expanded quickly enough to accommodate all the Cubans.

FEDERAL CONTRIBUTION

If the voluntary agencies and state and local governments are arguing among themselves, there is one point on which they all agree: that disorganization at the federal level has aggravated the situation. Until Feb. 28, 1979, when Carter established the office of U.S. coordinator for refugee affairs in the State Department and named former Sen. Dick Clark, D-Iowa, to head it, no office in the federal government was keeping tabs on the activities of all the component parts of the resettlement system.

Victor Palmieri, Clark's successor, has a staff of 15, including secretaries, to coordinate some $2.1 billion in federal, state and local expenditures that are going into the resettlement system each year. He said he needs over twice that staff to provide effective coordination. "I don't consider that a big bureaucracy by Washington standards," he said.

Fortunately for the states and localities, HHS has found that the need for cash assistance tends to diminish among Indochinese refugees as the resettlement process continues. While 43.9 per cent of refugee households that arrived in 1977 were on some kind of cash assistance in 1979, according to HHS, only 38 per cent of those that arrived in 1976 and 18.8 per cent of those that arrived in 1975 received such aid. It is also true, however, that the earliest refugees were also the most proficient in English, the most highly skilled and the most accustomed to Western culture.

Among the Vietnamese, who made up 85 per cent of all Indochinese refugees through early 1979, unemployment actually seems to be less than the national average. In the spring of 1979, according to a survey by Opportunity Systems Inc., the unemployment rate for Vietnamese men who had arrived between 1975 and 1977 was only 4.5 per cent, compared with a 4.9 per cent rate nationally for men. For Vietnamese women, the unemployment rate was just 1 per cent, against a national rate of 7 per cent.

Roger Conner, director of the Federation for American Immigration Reform (FAIR), argues that refugees are taking jobs at a time when many native-born Americans can't find work. "If they get jobs," he said, "it's clear in the short run that they will be in competition with the American people."

But Barry Chiswick, an economist at the University of Illinois, said the refugees' demands for goods and services create as many jobs as the refugees fill. "The notion that immigrants take jobs away from domestic workers is only true in a very narrow sense," he said.

Federal management of the resettlement of Cubans and Haitians has presented states and voluntary agencies with many of the problems that have arisen with the Indochinese—and then some. Instead of granting the new arrivals full refugee status, which would have entitled them to the benefits Indochinese currently receive under the Refugee Act, Carter dubbed them "Cuban/Haitian entrants (status pending)."

By the President's determination, the voluntary agencies receive only $300, not the full $500, for refugees still in camps such as Fort Chaffee, Ark., and Eglin Air Force Base, Fla. They get only $100 for those who have already been settled with families.

The federal government would not reimburse the states for their share of the costs of such joint federal-state programs as AFDC and medicaid. For special state educational and social services programs, Washington would provide 75 per cent reimbursement for one year.

Palmieri explained that the Administration does not have to provide the full benefits allowed under the Refugee Act because the Cubans and Haitians, who entered this country without first being processed elsewhere, are not regular refugees. "We are not going to use the Refugee Act," he said, "and thereby give people in the Caribbean and people abroad the impression that all they have to do is arrive here to get refugee status."

But in a 1980 supplemental appropriation, Congress made available $346 million to process and temporarily house the Cubans and Haitians and another $50 million to reimburse state and local governments—but not voluntary agencies—for their share of the costs of welfare, education and social services.

WHAT'S AHEAD

For all the complaints, a more stable period of refugee admissions may be on the way. The State Department is predicting a total influx of only 210,-000 refugees in 1981—21,700 fewer than this year—a figure that at least in part reflects the department's growing awareness of Congress's impatience with the refugee issue. . . .

Congressional action is only one way to limit refugees. Present acceptance of African and South American refugees may be low simply because the Immigration and Naturalization Service operates only one refugee processing center in all of Latin America and none in Africa. To gain refugee status, Africans must make their way to Rome, Athens or Frankfurt, the three nearest centers. While State Department officials maintain that Africans have no real desire to come to the United States, representatives from numerous human rights organizations and from the United Nations high commissioner for refugees disagree.

Palmieri said current restrictive U.S. policies reflect the economic condition of the country. "I think we will get over this reactionary period, especially as soon as we get out of this recession," he says. "I think people feel threatened now."

But before the country will be willing to accept increased numbers of refugees, the refugee resettlement system may have to prove itself capable of handling the task—and that means better organization. According to federal officials, however, the prospects for quick unification of the resettlement system are slim. . . .

Palmieri himself holds out hope. "What we're seeing now is a convergence of refugee and immigration issues," he said, "and there's no place to go but the coordinator's office." But the tough questions—whether Palmieri's office is the proper one to handle coordination and whether any agency, no matter how large, can oversee anything as complicated as the U.S. refugee resettlement system—have barely been asked.

42.

Lisa Birnbach: The Preppy Handbook

One of the surprise bestsellers of 1980 was The Preppy Handbook, *the first "official" guide to "The Tradition, Mannerisms, Etiquette, Dress Codes, The Family," and "How to Be Really Top Drawer." The project was very much tongue-in-cheek, but the book would not have been a success if it had not contained more than a grain of truth. A chapter of the book dealing with The Family is reprinted here.*

Source: *The Official Preppy Handbook*, 1980.

A Preppy begins grooming for Prep school at the moment of birth. Mummy and Daddy have carefully selected first and middle names (at least one of each) for the newborn that correspond to the names of dormitories at their Prep alma maters. An announcement of birth is sent by messenger to the alumni newsletter to alert the school's admission office of a future applicant. And Prep tots are carted along on Homecoming weekends so that the campus will seem like a second home by the time they are fifteen.

But just as important as guaranteeing their offsprings' entrée into the Right School is the Prep parents' need to impress their children with the desirability—nay, inevitability—of their going Prep. No use sacrificing Bermuda vacation money for tuition for a kid who's going to run off and join a modern dance troupe. Nor does the Prep parents' responsibility stop with simply ensuring their children's acceptance at a school: they've got to make certain that once the progeny are enrolled, they're not going to lock themselves in the computer lab for the whole four years and miss out on house party invitations, "after-hours alcoholic sprees," and the joy of shopping for madras.

Thus, the Prep child's indoctrination to the preferred way of life begins immediately. Mummy and Daddy make certain that he or she will not stray from the family fold because he or she won't know that other folds exist. The Prep child grows up surrounded by relatives who are all going, have gone, or, like him or her, will go to the same schools. Both sets of grandparents, Brother Bobo, Sister Biffy, Uncle Icky, Aunt Teeny, Cousin Amanda and Cousin Bob all rhapsodize about the fun they've always had with fellow Preppies, and what upstart is about to think otherwise? When you spend all your time with your family and other Prep families at the beach, on the slopes, at the country club, and at innumerable family reunions; when all your birthday and Christmas presents are either monogrammed or have Izod labels, it's unlikely that you will have the normal childhood aspirations of becoming a fireman or a nurse.

Preppies inherit from Mummy and Daddy, in addition to loopy handwriting and old furniture, the legacy of Proper Breeding. Preppies soon learn that any deviation from the prescribed style of life is bound to bring disaster. Attending a déclassé school, marrying wrong, selecting uncharted neighborhoods, choosing demanding vocations, or simply taking up bowling can unravel the tightly woven social fabric that binds the comfortable Preppy community.

Because Mummy and Daddy instruct their children in all matters of Taste and Tact, Preppies don't really have to worry about going astray. When the time comes, the children will know what to write on a Prep school application essay, who to marry, and how to ensure serenity and security for *their* children by putting their tooth-fairy dollars in a money market fund.

Like everything else, Preppiness begins in the home.

43.

JESSE HELMS, EDWARD M. KENNEDY, and THOMAS EMERSON:
School Prayer

In the spring of 1979 amendments attached by Senator Jesse Helms, R-North Carolina, to several Senate bills effectively added an amendment to the Constitution allowing voluntary prayer activities in the nation's public schools. The controversy about his proposal, which had been of long standing, grew more heated throughout the remainder of 1979 and throughout all of 1980, especially when the Republican presidential candidate supported the idea. Reprinted here are three comments on the proposal. The first is a statement by Senator Helms in the debate in the Senate on April 5, 1979. The second is drawn from a statement by Senator Kennedy, D-Massachusetts, in the course of Senate debate on a similar measure on April 9, 1979. The third is excerpted from testimony by a representative of the American Civil Liberties Union before a subcommittee of the House Judiciary Committee conducting hearings on the school prayer bill in August 1980.

Source: *Congressional Digest*, December 1980.

A: SENATOR HELMS

THIS MORNING as we joined with the Chaplain of the Senate in prayer, as we do each day the Senate is in session, I could not avoid the irony that while we in the Senate begin our day's activities by asking God's blessing on our efforts, the Supreme Court has effectively denied this same right and privilege to millions of schoolchildren across this Nation.

One would think that if the legislators of this country are entitled to ask for divine blessing upon their work, then so are schoolchildren. However, the Court has ruled to the contrary and in so doing has overturned more than 200 years of American custom. . . .

The interpretation of the first amendment used by the Supreme Court to strike down this practice of the American people has distorted the intent and language of the first amendment. The Justices of the Court held that a voluntary, nondenominational prayer constituted a violation of the "establishment of religion" clause of the first amendment. The Court's interpretation of the first amendment indicated not only what must be interpreted as an animosity toward the effect of religion in the public life of our Nation, but also a misunderstanding of its historic role.

Nearly 200 years after the drafting of the Constitution, the Supreme Court for the first time ruled that prayer and Bible-reading in public schools encouraged by the State constitutes an establishment of religion in violation of the first amendment. At the time of these decisions, 26 States permitted Bible reading in the public schools and 13 authorized the saying of the Lord's Prayer.

In each case, the Court ruled that voluntary school programs including Bible-reading or prayer violate the establishment clause of the first amendment.

In both rulings, the Court went beyond the language of the establishment clause to construct an interpretation of it which would overturn the long-standing State practices.

In Engel, Justice Black asserted: "Its first and most immediate purpose rested on the belief that a union of government and religion tends to destroy government and to degrade religion . . . . The Establishment Clause thus stands as an expression of principle on the part of the Founders of our Constitution that religion is too personal, too sacred, too holy, to permit its 'unhallowed perversion' by a civil magistrate."

Mr. Justice Clark argued in Schempp that the Court had previously "rejected unequivocally the contention that the Establishment Clause forbids only governmental preference of one religion over another." He maintained that the establishment clause must be considered together with the free exercise clause, and that they impose on government a "wholesome neutrality" toward religion—whatever that is. In Justice Clark's view, the first amendment prohibits Government from any action favoring one religious sect over all others, or religion in general over nonreligion.

Mr. Justice Clark, meanwhile, formulated a new standard by which to measure legislative action regarding the first amendment. "The test may be stated as follows: what are the purpose and the primary effect of the enactment? If either is the advancement or inhibition of religion the enactment exceeds the scope of legislative power as circumscribed by the Constitution. That is to say that to withstand the strictures of the Establishment Clause there must be a secular legislative purpose and a primary effect that neither advances nor inhibits religion."

The Court maintained that even though the prayer and Bible-reading activities were voluntary, this did not prevent them from violating the establishment clause. In Engel, the Court held that: "The Establishment Clause, unlike the Free Exercise Clause, does not depend upon any showing of direct governmental compulsion and is violated by the enactment of laws which establish an official religion whether those laws operate directly to coerce non-observing individuals or not."

AP/Wide World

In accordance with Massachusetts law, a fourth grader offers a prayer in a Boston school.

Thus, the Supreme Court reached a position which earlier the highest court of New York State had concluded "is so contrary to history as to be impossible of acceptance." Constitutional scholars also took issue with the Court's new interpretation. . . .

The Court reached its holdings in Engel and Schempp by way of a myopic and narrow view of the history of the Constitution. Only by a thorough distortion of the work of the authors of the Constitution is it even remotely possible to arrive at the sweeping condemnation of America's spiritual heritage presented in the Court's opinions.

The first amendment provides that Congress shall make no law respecting an establishment, let me emphasize that word—an establishment of religion. Those assembled at the Constitutional Convention did not arbitrarily choose the phrase "an establishment of religion." There was much history behind the term. Not only did England and Scotland have an established church, but

five of the States which later adopted the first amendment had establishment churches as well.

In the Engel and Schempp opinions, the Court ruled that the phrase "establishment of religion" really meant not just the creation of a national church, but any government action dealing with or touching religion. To cite Mr. Justice Clark's new test outlined in Schempp, the "primary effect" of any governmental act must not "advance religion."

Yet, it is just this view of what the first amendment should provide that the authors of the amendment specifically rejected. During the Constitutional Convention, the delegation from New Hampshire proposed that the first amendment should read: "Congress shall make no laws touching religion . . . ." Needless to say, that language was rejected.

An elementary rule of statutory construction provides that when a legislative assembly rejects language which has a broad application and substitutes in lieu of it language with a specific, narrow application, that the legislative intent is to exclude the broad application. Had the proposal that Congress make no law "touching religion" been accepted, it would undoubtedly have prevented Congress from doing much more than establishing a national religion. If applied to the States, it undoubtedly would have prohibited the type of prayer at issue in the Engel and Schempp cases. However, it is equally clear that this broad language was rejected and that Congress viewed the official encouragement of voluntary prayer, even on the national level, as not to be contrary to the first amendment's establishment provision. . . .

The Congress need not yield to any Justice of the Supreme Court in its respect for the words of the first amendment or for the principles or history behind them. Neither must Congress yield its responsibility under the Constitution to insure that the freedoms protected by the first amendment are not undermined by actions of other institutions. There is no more pressing duty facing the Congress than to restore the true spirit of the first amendment.

In anticipation of judicial usurpations of power, the framers of our Constitution wisely gave the Congress the authority, by a simple majority of both Houses, to check the Supreme Court by means of regulation of its appellate jurisdiction. Section 2 of article III states in clear and unequivocal language that the appellate jurisdiction of the Court is subject to "such exceptions, and under such regulations as the Congress shall make."

The limited and specific objective of my amendment is to restore to the American people the fundamental right of voluntary prayer in the public shools. I stress the word "voluntary." No individual should be forced to participate in a religious exercise that is contrary to his religious convictions, and the bill recognizes this important freedom.

At the same time, the bill seeks to promote the free exercise by allowing those who wish to recite prayers—and they are, I believe, the vast majority of our citizens—to do so, with or without the blessings of the Federal Government. . . .

Public schoolchildren are a captive audience. They are compelled to attend school. Their right to the free exercise of religion should not be suspended while they are in attendance. The language of the first amendment assumes that this basic freedom should be in force at all times and in all places.

B: SENATOR KENNEDY

THE AMENDMENT of the Senator from North Carolina would have a greater impact and assault on the Supreme Court of the United States and its jurisdiction than has taken place in this country over the 200 years of its history.

It is important that the membership of the Senate have some awareness and understanding of the extraordinary significance of this measure. Some of the most important decisions, perhaps the two most important decisions that have been made by the Supreme Court, were those that were understood by every student in law school—they learn it early—and by most college students: the Marbury against Madison decision, which permitted the Supreme Court's judicial review of acts of Congress; and the Martin against Hunter's Lessee decision, which recognized the Supreme Court's jurisdiction to rule on State laws. Those are, really, the two bedrock decisions which have established the importance of Supreme Court judicial decisionmaking.

We are asked to impede the second of those decisions by eliminating or restricting the judicial authority and power of the Supreme Court on one particular issue—school prayer decisions. At some time in the future, I—and I am sure my colleagues—would be willing to debate the appropriateness of the previous Supreme Court decisions, or the state of the law, or what this body ought to be doing on that issue. However, the Helms amendment reaches a significance far beyond this issue of prayer. Some can make the declaration or the statement that, on its face, it is unconstitutional. I believe that to be so, but I do not think that we really have to debate this issue. It is basically, I believe, extremely bad, and poor policy. I do think the Helms amendment reaches the foundation of this Nation in one of the most important decisions that our Founding Fathers made. That is on the separation of powers.

No one really questions that we in this body have the power effectively to destroy the judiciary. We could do that by curtailing or eliminating the authorizations and appropriations for U.S. attorneys, for the Federal judges, for magistrates, for the court buildings, for all the mechanisms which permit our Federal system to function. No one denies that we have at least that power.

The question is whether, by the exercise of that power, we should reduce and impact the jurisdiction of the judiciary. We understand that, under the Constitution, there are clearly housekeeping issues which affect the merits of decisions, which permit Congress to establish appropriate jurisdictional definitions—whether certain courts are going to be able to consider antitrust matters or not—and other similar items. But this is virtually the first assault on the Supreme Court of the United States in over 100 years, trying to define its jurisdiction in such a way as to affect the merits or the outcome of a particular Supreme Court decision.

It is for that reason and because this particular amendment affects the issues of the establishment clause and the free exercise clause of the Constitution of the United States that virtually every major religious group in this country is strongly opposed to the Helms amendment. We can ask ourselves, why are they opposed to this amendment?

It is because they see that if the Congress of the United States is prepared to exclude jurisdiction of the Supreme Court in one particular area,

in the area of voluntary prayer, why cannot the Congress of the United States—maybe not this year, maybe not next year, maybe not in 20 years, but, say, in 30 years or 50 years—virtually establish a religion in the United States of America and provide for the Supreme Court exclusion from ruling on the appropriateness of that enactment.

Or, on the other hand, with acceptance of the Helms amendment, what is going to prevent the Congress in some future years from violating the free exercise clause of the Constitution by tagging on a little line, and effectively saying that the Supreme Court of the United States will be prohibited from making any jurisdictional finding on the issue?

It is a fact of history, not only of this country but of democracies throughout the history of mankind, that religions have been more persecuted than protected under democracies, and the great religions have expressed strong reservations about tampering with the Constitutional provisions that deal either with the establishment clause or the free exercise clause.

I would think that others in this body would be somewhat leery of this particular procedure. It might not be long before Members of this body, at some future time, might say, "We are going to confiscate certain business properties in this country," and then, after the confiscation process add one little, final clause, and say that no Federal Court or Supreme Court will have jurisdiction over this matter, or over compensation, or due process for businesses.

I can see that, sometime in the future, the free press might be under assault or attack. Maybe we are just going to take this one, small action dealing with the free press, and then we are going to take the old Helms language and exclude the press from the jurisdiction of the Supreme Court of the United States. The Helms amendment establishes a precedent for all types of mischief.

C: PROFESSOR EMERSON

I WANT TO MAKE three basic points. The first is that the religious clauses of the First Amendment embody a principle that is rather unique in our system of individual rights because it provides not only that the government may not interfere or repress religious freedom but that it may not also support even benevolently religious freedom.

In other words, the concept of freedom of religion, the right to worship whatever God one pleases, is so sensitive and so delicate that the very presence of the government in the picture acts in a repressive way and, consequently, any adequate protection of the right to religious freedom must eliminate the government from the picture entirely.

Secondly, I want to point out that the provisions in the resolutions allowing prayers in the schools and other public buildings are clearly a violation of the principles of religious freedom as we have known them. The reason primarily is that the religious exercises in the schools take place under a blanket of government compulsion. The principals, the teachers and administrators of the school systems are public officials; they control the operation of the school lock, stock, and barrel.

The children are compelled to attend, thereby becoming a captive audience, and they are required to comply with the rules of the institution. If they were not, they do not have the maturity, the capacity, or the experience to act independently of the school authorities. . . .

Nor is it realistic to think that the opportunity for voluntary execution eliminates the element of coercion. School children tend to be conformists and vulnerable to both official and peer pressure. The very process of obtaining an exemption operates as a detriment to them. Withdrawal from group activities makes them feel odd or out of place and hence they have no real choice.

There is unfortunately no way to introduce freedom of religion into a compulsory authoritarian, government-dominated institution for minors, such as the public school system is. . . .

The third point I would want to make concerns the resolutions specifically before this committee. The resolutions purport to convey upon individuals, but in actuality, and in their operation, what they do is confer power upon the government to interfere with the religious freedom of individuals.

The reason for this is that the religious exercises which the resolutions purport to protect are religious exercises conducted in public buildings, and school buildings, and so forth. That in itself renders the amendments objectionable and they are not saved by the provision that the right is to engage in "voluntary prayer" or religious observance. . . .

In conclusion, let me just say the proposed amendments are intended to improve the understanding and encourage the practices of religion. The objective may be a laudable one but the means chosen are ill-conceived and dangerous to our system of individual rights.

44.

Red Smith: On Playing in Ivan's Yard

On January 20, 1980, President Carter wrote to the president of the U.S. Olympic Committee to inform him that, in the opinion of the President, it would not be permissible for the United States to compete in the 1980 Olympic Games, which would be held in Moscow. The reason was the Soviet invasion of Afghanistan the previous fall, when Russian troops had rolled into Kabul, overwhelmed the city, captured the president, shot him, and then announced that they had been invited. "We must make clear," said Carter, that the Soviet Union "cannot trample upon an independent nation and at the same time do business as usual with the rest of the world." The U.S. Olympic Committee, after much soul-searching, decided to obey the President of the United States and not send a team to Moscow, but the International Olympic Committee, citing its old contention that the "games are not political," allowed them to proceed, and some of America's allies sent teams. Red Smith, the dean of American sports columnists, was one of those who enthusiastically supported the President's position, as this February column shows.

Source: *The Red Smith Reader*, 1982.

PRESIDENT CARTER has warned that the United States might withdraw from the Moscow Olympics if the Soviet Union's aggression in Afghanistan continues. Some voices have seconded the motion, Saudi Arabia has already pulled out, and sentiment in favor of a boycott will spread as Soviet tanks and troops press on with their bloody work.

It is unthinkable that in the present circumstances we could go play games with Ivan in Ivan's yard. The United States should lead a walkout now, making it clear to the Russians that even if the shooting ends and the invading forces go home, the rape of a neighbor will not be quickly forgotten. With their parades and flags and anthems and the daily count of medals won, the Olympic Games are a carnival of nationalism.

The festival is a showcase for the host nation to display its brightest face to the world. It is inconceivable that we should lend our presence to a pageant of Soviet might.

Dispatches from Moscow tell of an "Olympic purge" already under way to present the Communist society as an ideal surpassing even the dazzled view that Lincoln Steffens got. ("I have been over into the future, and it works.") To scrub up the capital for an anticipated 300,000 visitors, "undesirables" will be sent out of the city and contact with foreigners will be discouraged. Dissidents, drunkards, psychotics and Jews who have applied for emigration are undesirable. School children will be sent to summer camps. Kevin Klose, the *Washington Post* correspondent, reports that

AP/Wide World

Viktor Saneev, Soviet triple jump star, carries the Olympic torch past Afghanistan's athletes at the opening of the Moscow Olympics.

some teachers are telling their pupils that American tourists will offer them poisoned chewing gum.

Unofficial sources, Klose writes, "sardonically use the Russian word *chistka* or 'cleaning' to describe what is going on. It is a word with dread connotations for Soviets because it is the term used in designating the Stalinist purges that swept millions to their death in slave labor camps beginning in the late 1930s."

All of this hints at how important the Olympics are to the government. Diminishing their vast propaganda show or possibly causing its cancelation would be a sterner measure than many might think. And the millions of tourist rubles involved are no small matter.

It was inevitable that as soon as the President mentioned the possibility of a boycott, the stuffed shirts in the Olympic movement would revive the threadbare argument that politics should not be injected into the Olympics—as if the games ever had been free of politics, as if the Olympic movement itself weren't

shot with politics. Not that the playground directors have a monopoly on unrealistic thinking or fatuous speech. Consider the statement of Gerhart Baum, West Germany's Interior Minister:

"In the opinion of the government, sports cannot be used as a means for political ends. Sports cannot solve problems whose solution can only be achieved politically."

In 1956, Egypt, Lebanon, and Iraq withdrew from the Melbourne Olympics to protest an Israeli invasion of the Sinai and the Gaza strip. Spain, Switzerland and the Netherlands walked out to protest the Soviet march into Hungary. In 1976 the entire African continent boycotted the Montreal games because of the presence of New Zealand, which countenanced athletic relations with South Africa. The quadrennial quarrel over the two Chinas remains unresolved.

And still the Olympic brass clings to the fantasy that these are contests for individuals, not nations. Then after each contest they raise the winner's national flag and play his national anthem. Between games, Olympic fund raisers beg for contributions to help beat the Russians.

Aside from the garbage about politics, the only argument against withdrawal is that it would penalize American kids who have endured the drudgery of training for four years or more with their dreams fixed on this one opportunity for international competition.

It would, indeed, be a disappointment, perhaps not their first and surely not the last they will ever experience. But any measures taken against Soviet aggression will demand sacrifices from someone. As Mary McGrory observed in her *Washington Post* column, if we got into war, those kids are the ones who would do the fighting.

Chances are the savants who write editorials in *The New York Times* today weren't even reading that page in 1936, but the paper opposed American participation in the Nazi Olympics of that year.

When the Nazis "deliberately and arrogantly offend against our common humanity," the *Times* said, "sport does not 'transcend all political and racial considerations.' "

"Deliberately and arrogantly" sound like the words Jimmy Carter used last week. Considering the provocation, they are mild. The Soviets invaded an independent nation—which happens, incidentally, to be a member of the Olympic family—executed the leader of that nation's government and then said the government had invited them in.

In ancient Greece, wars were suspended when the Olympics rolled around. It says here the Olympics should be suspended when the caissons roll.

45.

Ronald Reagan: Acceptance Speech

Republicans meeting in Detroit in July 1980 chose Ronald Reagan, ex-movie actor and ex-governor of California, as their candidate for President in the upcoming election. Reagan was nominated by a landslide; the most dramatic event of the convention involved the choice of a running mate. Many wondered whether Reagan was sufficiently experienced, and they welcomed rumors that former President Ford had been offered extraordinary powers as Vice President if he would agree to run—in effect, Reagan would be the Chief Executive Officer of the nation, with Ford the Chief Operating Officer. In the end Ford turned down the offer, and George Bush became the Republican candidate. The GOP platform withdrew support for the Equal Rights Amendment, called for a constitutional ban on abortion, and proposed across-the-board tax cuts of ten percent for three years. It also strongly advocated a large increase in America's defense capability. Reagan's acceptance speech, delivered on July 17th, touched on all these matters and emphasized a new kind of federalism, in which the half-century increase in Washington's power would be reversed. Excerpts from the speech are reprinted here.

Source: *Vital Speeches of the Day,* August 15, 1980.

THE MAJOR ISSUE of this campaign is the direct political, personal, and moral responsibility of Democratic Party leadership—in the White House and in the Congress—for this unprecedented calamity which has befallen us. They tell us they've done the most that humanly could be done. They say that the United States has had its day in the sun, that our nation has passed its zenith. They

Ronald Reagan delivers his acceptance speech at the 1980 Republican Convention.

expect you to tell your children that the American people no longer have the will to cope with their problems; that the future will be one of sacrifice and few opportunities.

My fellow citizens, I utterly reject that view. The American people, the most generous on earth, who created the highest standard of living, are not going to accept the notion that we can only make a better world for others by moving backward ourselves. And those who believe we can have no business leading this nation.

I will not stand by and watch this great country destroy itself under mediocre leadership that drifts from one crisis to the next, eroding our national will and purpose. We have come together here because the American people deserve better from those to whom they entrust our nation's highest offices, and we stand united in our resolve to do something about it. . . .

Together, let us make this a new beginning. Let us make a commitment to care for the needy; to teach our children the virtues handed down to us by our families; to have the courage to defend those values and virtues and the willingness to sacrifice for them.

Let us pledge to restore, in our time, the American spirit of voluntary service, of cooperation, of private and community initiative; a spirit that flows like a deep and mighty river through the history of our nation.

As your nominee, I pledge to you to restore to the Federal Government the capacity to do the people's work without dominating their lives. I pledge to you a Government that will not only work well but wisely, its ability to act tempered by prudence, and its willingness to do good balanced by the knowledge that government is never more dangerous than when our desire to have it help us blinds us to its great power to harm us. . . .

Ours are not problems of abstract economic theory. These are problems of flesh and blood; problems that cause pain and destroy the moral fiber of real people who should not suffer the further indignity of being told by the Government that it is all somehow their fault. We do not have inflation because—as Mr. Carter says—we've lived too well.

The head of a Government which has utterly refused to live within its means and which has, in the last few days, told us that this coming year's deficit will be $60 billion, dares to point the finger of blame at business and labor, both of which have been engaged in a losing struggle just trying to stay even.

High taxes, we are told, are somehow good for us, as if, when government spends our money it isn't inflationary, but when we spend it, it is. . . .

I believe it is clear our Federal Government is overgrown and overweight. Indeed, it is time our Government should go on a diet. Therefore, my first act as chief executive will be to impose an immediate and thorough freeze on Federal hiring. Then, we are going to enlist the very best minds from business, labor and whatever quarter to conduct a detailed review of every department, bureau and agency that lives by Federal appropriation.

And we are also going to enlist the help and ideas of many dedicated and hard-working Government employees at all levels who want a more efficient Government just as much as the rest of us do. I know that many of them are demoralized by the confusion and waste they confront in their work as a result of failed and failing policies.

Our instructions to the groups we enlist will be simple and direct. We will remind them that Government programs exist at the sufferance of the American taxpayer and are paid for with money earned by working men and women, and programs that represent a waste of their money—a theft from their pocketbooks—must have that waste eliminated or that program must go. It must go by Executive Order where possible, by Congressional action where necessary.

Everything that can be run more effectively by state and local government we shall turn over to state and local government, along with the funding sources to pay for it. We are going to put an end to the money merry-go-round where our money becomes Washington's money, to be spent by states and cities exactly the way the Federal bureaucrats tell us it has to be spent.

I will not accept the excuse that the Federal Government has grown so big and powerful that it is beyond the control of any President, any administration or Congress. We are going to put an end to the notion that the American taxpayer exists to fund the Federal Government. The Federal Government exists to serve the American people and to be accountable to the American peo-

ple. On January 20, we are going to reestablish that truth. . . .

The American people are carrying the heaviest peacetime tax burden in our nation's history—and it will grow even heavier, under present law, next January. We are taxing ourselves into economic exhaustion and stagnation, crushing our ability and incentive to save, invest and produce.

This must stop. We must halt this fiscal self-destruction and restore sanity to our economic system.

I've long advocated a 30 percent reduction in income tax rates over a period of three years. This phased tax reduction would begin with a 10 percent "down payment" tax cut in 1981, which the Republicans in Congress and I have already proposed.

A phased reduction of tax rates would go a long way toward easing the heavy burden on the American people. But we shouldn't stop there.

Within the context of economic conditions and appropriate budget priorities during each fiscal year of my Presidency, I would strive to go further. This would include improvement in business depreciation taxes so we can stimulate investment in order to get plants and equipment replaced, put more Americans back to work and put our nation back on the road to being competitive in world commerce. We will also work to reduce the cost of government as a percentage of our gross national product.

The first task of national leadership is to set realistic and honest priorities in our policies and our budget, and I pledge that my Administration will do that.

When I talk of tax cuts, I am reminded that every major tax cut in this century has strengthened the economy, generated renewed productivity and ended up yielding new revenues for the Government by creating new investment, new jobs and more commerce among our people. . . .

I have thought of something that's not a part of my speech and worried over whether I should do it. Can we doubt that only a Divine Providence placed this land, this island of freedom, here as a refuge for all those people in the world who yearn to breathe free? Jews and Christians enduring persecu-

tion behind the Iron Curtain; the boat people of Southeast Asia, Cuba and of Haiti; the victims of drought and famine in Africa; the freedom fighters in Afghanistan; and our own countrymen held in savage captivity.

I'll confess that I've been a little afraid to suggest what I'm going to suggest. I'm more afraid not to. Can we begin our crusade joined together in a moment of silent prayer?

God bless America.

46.

RICHARD M. SCAMMON and BEN J. WATTENBERG: Is It the End of an Era?

Both Ronald Reagan and Jimmy Carter were nominated by their respective conventions on the first ballot, and although Reagan was perceived to have a strong lead in early polls, by mid-September the upcoming election was being termed "too close to call." Some pundits, however, were certain that, whoever won the presidency, a deep and probably enduring change had occurred in American political life. This view was not unanimous; even some of Scammon and Wattenberg's colleagues on Public Opinion *disagreed with their belief that a major realignment was imminent. (It was a widely held opinion among Democrats, for example, that the problem was not so much a shift in public attitudes as a failure of liberals to make their positions clear.) In the end, of course, Scammon and Wattenberg turned out to be correct. Reagan, although his lead had been said to be "paper-thin" as late as October 15th, won in November by a landslide, taking an absolute majority of votes cast. Furthermore, the Republicans did not have to wait until 1982 to win the Senate, which shifted to their party in the 1980 election; they also decreased the Democratic majority in the House substantially and won a number of key governorships.*

Source: *Public Opinion*, October-November 1980.

SOMETHING VERY IMPORTANT has happened in America in recent years: people have changed their minds. Something else may happen in the course of the next few years: people will change

their politics. And so, we hear talk (once again) of the much-storied, much-fabled, powerful virus that periodically infects the political community: "realignment." But what political scientists think of as a realignment travels under a simpler flag to more common folk who simply say, "it's the end of an era."

It is our view that because people have changed their minds, a political era characterized by a distinct political philosophy has indeed come to an end. We further believe that the philosophy in question—American liberalism—has rendered healthy, vigorous and constructive service to the republic: that its impact will continue to be felt, and that there will be no going back to yesteryear—but, still, *it is over.* The center of the political spectrum is moving; politicans will gain or keep power only insofar as they can appeal to that moving center.

Moreover, this case holds almost regardless of who wins what in the next few years; whether or not the Republicans this fall capture the presidency, whether or not they capture the Senate in 1982, whether or not they (someday) carry the House or the governorships or the state legislatures.

The changed political climate, mind you, gives Republicans a chance for all these things; but what is most important for the nation, if not for politicians, is the change in direction, not the change in party. Thus, the Democratic party can change its direction and scrub its image clean in conformity with its voters' current views and plausibly remain the dominant party; or it can *not* scrub and become the minority view in America; but it can't do both. For new conditions seek new solutions and new images. And politics in a democracy is the ultimate Darwinian activity: adapt or die.

In this article we propose to deal with both *actual* change in the climate of opinion and the *potential* for change, from Democratic to Republican.

REALIGNMENTS

Wood rots. Iron rusts. Those are sometimes the wrong metaphors for political realignments. Plastic may be better. For, under stress, plastic breaks suddenly, swiftly and cleanly.

In earlier times in America, major realigning elections often sounded like the quick snap of plastic—at least in retrospect.

William Jennings Bryan's Cross of Gold speech electrified the Democratic Convention in 1896, but the issue of Free Silver was a loser on the national scene. It was not Bryan, but the Republican nominee, William McKinley, who went to the White House. That election firmly established in the public mind that the Democrats were a somewhat radical party and that the Republicans were the party of stability and "the full dinner pail." Thus, an *idea* was implanted in the American psyche— a partisan idea—with massive political repercussions. For the next third of a century that partisan idea—Republican stability versus Democratic radicalism— hung on. Republicans dominated the Congress, the presidency and the State houses. When the dust settled, it was clear that the plastic had snapped during the 1896 election. And it was called, in the political science trade, a realigning election. That realigning election had two noticeable criteria: a change in partisan perception and a subsequent change in voting patterns.

In 1932, a new partisan perception began to take shape. Under the lash of the Depression, Democrats took power under the leadership of Franklin Delano Roosevelt. In a dozen years as President, FDR worked one rich political vein. The Democratic party, he intimated, was the party of "the people," "the forgotten man," "the little guy" and "the common man." By contrast, the Republicans were the party of "economic royalists"—or in later parlance, "fat cats" who felt at home in "corporate board rooms" and "country clubs."

Under the rubric of such (sometimes valid) imagery, Democrats have become powerful, wealthy and prominent for almost half a century. They captured the presidency five times in a row; they have had majorities in the Congress almost constantly, and won a majority of the governorships much of the time.

More important, their ideology—liberalism—became the regnant received wisdom of the time. Liberalism both reflected changed opinions in America and helped to change opinions in America. So, a third criterion for realignment became apparent. *Partisan perceptions* had changed as in the earlier realignment; *politics* had changed as in the earlier realignment; and in *this* one *opinions* changed.

Looking now toward the possibility of a new realignment, it is useful to explore whether these three criteria are satisfied in the present instance.

CRITERION NUMBER ONE: OPINIONS

So we come to 1980. As this is written in the early fall of that year, what is important about the notion of political realignment is not that anyone can say "It is here." After all, other realignments were confirmable and noticeable only long after they occurred and were in some measure dependent on both subsequent unforeseen events and remarkable political personalities (like FDR and World War II). No, what is important this year is that for the first time one can look at substantial evidence and say

"this has all the earmarks; it may turn out to be an ear."

Consider first the evidence of *changing opinions.* In the field of survey research there is almost always some countervailing evidence available, but in scanning the decade of the 1970s, one is struck by the powerful themes of change that emerge. Like it or not, almost all of these changes are in general concert with recent perceived Republican doctrine—not perceived Democratic doctrine.

What is the current Republican doctrine?

In shorthand, try this: *economic stagnation and inflation are the real problems. Their major cause is big taxation which feeds big government which, in any event, is not doing well what it is supposed to do and is, moreover, making it difficult for private enterprise to do well what it is supposed to do. Furthermore, the government has been taken over by high-minded elitists who have lost touch with everyday concerns of everyday citizens. Meanwhile, America has grown militarily weak and is being pushed around all over the world.*

Those are important political thoughts and, to be fair, have not been mainstream liberal Democratic views (at least until very recently). Liberal ideology, after all, was predicated on the idea that a bigger, centralized government would help less fortunate people become more fortunate people. And if more government spending led to a little deficit spending which led to a little inflation, why a little inflation was not such a bad thing. After all, it let poor people pay off their debts more cheaply. In recent years—at least since Vietnam—the most vocal wing of the Democratic party has also said we're spending too much, not too little on national defense (the "bloated military-industrial complex") and that America is suffering from an "arrogance of power." Finally, it has been liberal Democratic credo that "social engineering" was a discipline whose time had come. Busing, quotas, environmentalism-impinging-on-life-style, were all part of the agenda.

Against that backdrop, consider a few selected poll results:

—Between 1959 and 1978 the percentage of Americans who thought that "big government" was the major cause of inflation went from 14% to 51% (!)

That's the Republicans' issue, and if reinforcement of that idea is needed let it be noted that by 1978 fully 76% of Americans thought that "Washington had become too powerful" and 84% believed that "Washington was spending too much."

A similar pro-Republican point of view has emerged on the issue of national defense. Consider what has happened as Vietnam has receded from the public consciousness:

	Increase defense spending	
	Favorable	Unfavorable
1971	11%	49%
1979 (pre-Iran)	60	9

Furthermore, the spirit of what was called "neoisolationism" has receded in the land. Democrats of the "New Politics" persuasion who made political hay on the idea that America was "overextended" and shouldn't be "the world's policeman" should consider data generated recently by Lloyd Free and William Watts. Under the Free-Watts scheme, a wide-ranging series of questions about foreign policy yields an index to measure the percentage of "total internationalists" in the American population.

—In 1964 (pre-Vietnam when *Pax*

Americana was still thought of as a good idea), 65% of the American public were "total internationalists."

—In 1974, just before the final death throes in Vietnam the percentage of "total internationalists" had plummeted to 41%.

—In 1980 the percentage of "total internationalists" was back to 61%.

These are, as noted, selected data. To be sure there are other data that show that people don't want cutbacks on services, and inflation induced data that yield positive responses to the idea of wage and price controls. The idea of national health insurance is still popular. But, notwithstanding these counterbalances, there are few analysts these days who would deny what the general run of numbers tends to point up: inflation has become the nation's number one concern, the bloom is off the rose for the idea of further governmental activism, the public is substantially more hawkish than it was a few years ago. (Proposition Thirteen and the hostage issue seem to be the best attitudinal pointers in recent years.)

Agree or disagree on substance, these have been Republican themes. In a just world (which, in fairness, is not always the best way to describe the political arena) these are themes that should help Republicans—perhaps enough to kick off a new political era.

The change of attitudes has not only proceeded among the public. Consider the Congress. Ideas that were unpopular five years ago are seen now as the wave of the future. The capital gains tax has been lowered. The defense budget has been raised. Oil prices have been deregulated. Airlines and trucking are deregulated. Democrats and Republicans issue *joint* reports praising "supply side" economics. And for a brief, shining moment, the budget was balanced, at least in committee. And members of both parties compete with one another to make a point of how much they want to cut domestic spending.

It's happening in expert-land, too. Economists of almost every persuasion beam proudly upon the idea of letting the market work its will and encouraging business investment. President Carter's new "revitalization" plan features business incentive tax cuts unheard of in previous Democratic programs. And when the chairman of the Council of Economic Advisers Charles Schultze is asked on television to explain why the proposed personal tax cuts only offset the social security tax increases, he reaches back to the Country of Friedman and says, "Well, you know, in economics there's no free lunch."

In short: opinions have changed among the public, the Congress, and the experts. We've changed our minds.

A SECOND CRITERION: ELECTIONS

Election Results: Beyond attitude, opinion and ideology, there is at least some evidence to suggest that attitudinal changes have already begun to yield election results.

Consider the senatorial races of 1978. Five Democratic incumbent senators lost their seats. All were perceived to be liberal. Their liberalism was an issue in their campaigns. The only Democratic senators who lost were liberals. All of the liberals running but one (Pell) lost.

Of course, one set of elections in one year doesn't necessarily make a rigid pattern. Even in geometry, two points are needed to define a straight line. Each of the defeated liberal senators

surely faced unique local situations that could have accounted for his defeat.

On the other hand, if "politics ain't beanbag" as Mr. Dooley said, it ain't geometry either. *Fear* operates in politics if not geometry. If five of six liberal senators get voted out of office—their remaining colleagues get nervous indeed. Those who seek political survival begin to wonder about trimming their political philosophy here, there and everywhere. This has already happened in Congress, as has been noted.

Moreover, something else quite potent is at work. A second point on the graph seems to be emerging. Of course, the 1980 election hasn't been held yet, and to coin a rich phrase, anything can happen. Still, it is instructive to ask the perennial political question: "Who's in trouble?"

For the second straight election, it is mostly *liberals* who are said to be "in trouble." . . .

And who isn't in trouble in the Democratic Party? The not-so-liberals are not-so-in-trouble. . . .Most of the non-liberals are not in much trouble.

Now, the Democrats control the Senate rather substantially: 58–41 (with one Independent). It will take a *shift* of *nine* seats to break Democratic control of the Senate. Even with a big Reagan win, such a swing is quite unlikely—even though, as the luck of the draw would have it, far more Democrats than Republicans must face the voters this year (24–10).

But suppose the Republicans have a net gain of, say, four or five seats—which is not unlikely. After all, that still means winning less than half the contested seats. Then, in 1982, with the Republicans only needing four or five seats for control, the luck of the draw again becomes important. For then, as now, more Democratic seats are up than Republican—19 to 14. The Republicans would have to do only slightly better than an even split among the contested seats to control the Senate—for the first time in 52 years. . . .

THE THIRD CRITERION: PARTISAN PERCEPTION

A political realignment, should it come, and should it be a big, bouncing, healthy realignment, needs more than the "evidence" of opinion and of politics that it *may* happen, as laid out above. A political realignment of Rooseveltian magnitude also seems to need a big, bouncing change in partisan perception, a change rich enough so that 30 years from now pundits might write about the "genius" behind this realignment as they now write of the "genius" of the "FDR coalition."

Politics ain't beanbag or geometry— or philosophy or plasma physics for that matter. Big motive partisan ideas in politics are straightforward ones, simply stated. The big idea of FDR's New Deal was clear enough: "We are the party of the people," said Roosevelt. Simple idea, not entirely accurate but fecund with political potential. Fecund enough, at least, to transform a nation (for the better, we think) and, by the way, make three generations of politicians fat and powerful.

Is there such a new, big idea on the Republican side this time around?

There is indeed. It is this: "We are the party of the people"(!).

Not exactly $E=MC^2$, but no matter; it is, like its predecessor, a big, bouncing, rich idea fecund with potential— and not entirely accurate.

Of course, Republicans have been trying the party-of-the-people number

for many years. The last fellow to give it a serious whirl was a dapper man-about-Washington named Spiro Agnew. It didn't quite work. Aside from his other well-publicized problems, Vice President Agnew had a tendency to snarl in making his pitch.

But Ronald Reagan doesn't snarl. He has been called an "affable ideologue." And he says he represents the "party of the people" with some credibility. He was, after all, a union president. Remember, it was not Reagan, but John Connally, who was called the candidate of "the corporate board room."

Or consider Congressman Jack Kemp, one of the most interesting and able politicians on the national scene. His congressional district includes Buffalo, a large, dreary, industrial city once called "the armpit of America." It is surely not a place from whence Republicans, ostensible party of the country-club set, are supposed to hail. And Kemp is a former football player. But Republicans are supposed to own football teams, not play for them.

Now, Kemp's economics—economics which have been smiled upon by Reagan and the Republican platform—may leave much to be desired. Many astute economists, Democratic and Republican, believe the Kemp-Roth tax reduction plan as originally written is a funny-money scheme. Perhaps it is.

But that is not the point. Economics, like politics, is at least partly symbolic. As a political metaphor Kemp-Roth plus the other aspects of "supply side economics" are not only right on target but more than vaguely reminiscent of certain earlier Democratic party rhetoric: Get America moving again (but don't mindlessly slash government expenditures). Tax cuts are offered, say Kemp-Rothniks, not to help fat-cats but because high taxes are strangling middle class people and because America needs to provide incentives to make capital work again so that all those blue-collar workers can get jobs. Hyper-regulation, too, strangles productivity say the supply siders. To square the circle, supply siders say that only if we get America moving again can the welfare state be funded without continuing inflation.

These supply side economics are, if you will, *growth economics*. As such they are far removed from one strand of Wing A Democratic economics that at times seemed to influence at least some aspects of the early Carter presidency: conservation without production incentives in the energy field, a smattering of ideological no-growth, slow-growth, and era-of-limits, a dose of anti-nuclear environmental purity and an early shot of hyper-regulation.

Indeed it was *growth economics* (along with a strong defense) that was the key theme of the Detroit Republican convention. The GOP said that the Wing A era-of-limits ideology was a betrayal of the American dream—and that is a potent theme.

Having allowed growth economics to be stolen by the Republicans (while they were perceived to be diddling with solar power), in this election year the Democrats are now in the ironic position of saying "me too" to an economic philosophy (growth) that was once their own meal ticket. The Carter plan for "reindustrialization" represents supply side catchup ball. Democrats hope that it will not be seen as too little and too late.

A fascinating process is apparent in the current economic jousting. The *Democratic* plan has greater incentives for *business* (!); the Republican plan has more for *consumers* (!!). This role rever-

sal is either (A) crazy or (B) a classic example of the critical electoral game called Capture the Center, with each side attempting to raid the other's constituency. We lean toward explanation (B).

And in the meanwhile Mr. Reagan will keep on making those pernicious and malign noises that say, "*We* are the party of the people, *they* are the elite royalists."

If the Republicans can make that partisan perception stick, they can remind voters of that wonderful dictum of the football fan: "fire the coach." If that happens, in that way, which is possible, realignment will be on its way.

DOES IT MATTER?

Possible realignment.

So what? Does it matter much if it happens?

Let us consider two alternate scenarios: with realignment, and without.

We have been in a political netherworld for a generation: the presidency rotates, the Congress is Democratic only because of an anomaly that has the most conservative part of the country (the South) helping the more liberal party. But suppose Reagan wins in 1980. And Democratic liberals lose further seats in 1980 and even lose the Senate in 1982. Suppose the governorships and the legislatures start moving toward the Republican column. Suppose the Republicans indeed become known as the party of the people; suppose the polls begin to show ever greater numbers of voters self-identifying as Republicans.

This will, to be sure, change American politics. But will it change America?

Yes, but probably not as much as one might think.

Such a Republican era would likely

be characterized by increased military spending and an attempt at a reassertion of American power in some parts of the world. (There will be no big war; hawks know how to count—and we are out-gunned now.)

Such a Republican era would be pro-growth in a private-sector-incentive manner.

But here we run into the Grand Conundrum of the Center.

Will such a Republican era be anti-civil liberties? If that attempt is made—it won't be a Republican era for long. Will such a Republican era cut through the entitlements programs like a hot scythe through a vat of axle grease? If that happens, if the Republicans try to repeal rather than contain the welfare state, it won't be a Republican era for long. Will such a Republican era try to savage unions in America? Only if it wants to risk slipping back into minoritarian status. Will such a Republican era turn power back to the states? If you believe that government officials *give back* power—to anyone—go back three spaces and re-enroll in Politics 101.

So, the realignment we speak of—if it occurs—is a realignment within the moderate center of the political spectrum, between the forty-yard lines. The "center" we spoke of ten years ago in *The Real Majority* still lives; an extreme party of left or right will not become dominant in America; the only thing extremism in either party can do is guarantee victory for the other party.

The Grand Conundrum of the Center is simple enough as politics goes: You can capture the center if you are a centrist; if you are not a centrist you won't capture or keep the center.

In short: a Republican realignment would do those things Americans have already decided they want done. That is reinforced by the likelihood that any realignment, although viewed historically as a sudden break at a particular election, is more likely to be a process rather than an event. Reagan, for example, may well be elected by less than a majority of voters. That could be a first step, but sustainable only if Republican policies were deemed worthy by specific groups. Remember, blacks voted for Hoover in 1932—not for FDR until 1936.

Republican prime targets in the eighties would be Southerners, union members, ethnics, Jews—yet they can add numbers if and only if they stay near the potent center.

But suppose there is no political realignment. Suppose the Democrats stay in the saddle. Our formal politics might not change, but would America change?

Yes.

Again, because of the Grand Conundrum of the Center.

Entering the 1980s, it is clear that Democrats will not retain hegemony unless they move to a guns-and-margarine position on defense—until we can afford butter again. They will not retain hegemony unless they reinvigorate the private sector economy.

In short, the people have spoken. A new consensus is forming. The center has moved. Both parties will respond. Change is in the air. It is a new moment. The party that listens best to the people will be known as "winners." The differences will be fewer than the similarities.

1981

47.

Clifford M. Hardin: Can a President Control His Own White House?

Between Ronald Reagan's election to the presidency, at the beginning of November 1980, and his inauguration late in January 1981, there was the usual scramble to set up and organize a new administrative apparatus in the White House. For many years it had seemed to some observers that presidents were tending more and more to become the creatures of their own organizations, rather than vice versa. With a government grown vastly larger and more complex, was there any way that a single individual could retain a measure of control over his administration's policies, and the execution thereof? The speech reprinted here, which was delivered in November 1980 but not published until January 1981, was by a scholar-in-residence at the Center for the Study of American Business. It addresses a number of important issues that any president must consider upon taking office.

Source: *Vital Speeches of the Day,* January 1, 1981.

CAN A PRESIDENT really control his own White House? Yes, he can—if, before he takes office, he insists on a basic restructuring which is put in place immediately. But if President-elect Reagan accepts the traditional pattern and fills all the job slots that will be available, he will be frustrated eventually, just as his predecessors have been.

My remarks this evening will focus, therefore, on the structure of that institution known as the Executive Office of the President, and on how the very organization and size of that establishment often hinders the President in achieving what he believes is best for the country.

I believe that the White House staff group has become much too large. I further believe that the excess staffing contributes to loading the President's "in basket" with many items that might better be handled elsewhere, that too many people invite intrigue, and that they tend to add to confusion throughout government.

The "bottom-line" issue involves preserving the President's time for those items that must have his personal attention, gaining the time he needs for study and reflection—which he must have if he is to lead and not merely react—and providing him with ready access to the thinking of the best brains in government.

Dr. James S. Young, of the White Burkett Miller Center for the Study of the Presidency at the University of Virginia, writing in the New York *Times* on December 7, 1978, stated the issue quite effectively. After discussing the need for redefining the presidency, he stated:

> It means disengaging the Presidency from many of the problems that public expectations, campaign exigencies, news-media pressures and the Washington Establishment will demand that the President do something about. It means substantially abandoning White House efforts to presidentialize the bureaucracy that only ends up bureaucratizing the Presidency. It means getting the Presidency substantially out of the business of managing the executive branch: ceding large parts of that domain to Congress, courts and Cabinet, but not ceding the President's power to pre-empt or intervene when reasons of state require. It means putting distance between the Presidency and the permanent government in Washington—distance enough to enable a president to watch the Government as the outsider he really is, to know when it is getting the country into serious trouble and when it isn't, to know when to step in and when to stay out.

I believe firmly that a president, once elected, should be free to determine and exercise his own style of leadership—how he communicates with the Congress, how he works with his close associates whom he himself has selected, how he relates to the American people, and how he administers foreign policy. What's new about that? Don't all presidents do just that? Yes and no. Yes, they do announce how they intend to handle all of those functions, but sometimes those goals and desires are not realized. Why?

LESSONS FROM THE RECENT PAST

Nearly all, if not all, recent presidents have announced that they will make broad delegations for decision making to the members of the Cabinet and to the Vice President, and that they will become involved in the affairs of departments only in exceptional instances where concerns extend far beyond normal operation. Recent administrations, both Republican and Democratic, have begun that way, but invariably, decision making has begun to flow back to the White House—not necessarily because of any overt action or policy expressed by the President, but because the nature of the structure surrounding the White House encourages it.

Paul Nitze, in the context of foreign policy and national defense, has spoken to this point in a paper published in the Miller Center Forum. He favors, as I do, transferring back some or all of the staff functions that have been going to the White House to the operating departments, and he states, "Frankly, I think the White House staff is too big, deals with too many diverse questions and isn't focused on the control issues. . . ." He concludes, "The main problem with the presidency is the economy of time. What we have is one man with a twelve-hour day. . . . How do you prevent everything going to the President? I think you prevent it mainly through decentralization of authority. In the Truman years . . . the great factor was Mr. Truman's confidence in General Marshall, Dean Acheson, Robert Lovett and a few others, confidence that gave them credibility in speaking and acting for him." While Mr. Nitze was discussing foreign policy, I feel that his summary could and should apply to domestic matters as well.

Although I wasn't there, I have a feeling that the Truman pattern of utilizing Cabinet officers and their staffs continued with President Eisenhower, and that he also succeeded in delegating to other officials many items that in recent administrations have moved to the White House. But the White House staff wasn't as large in the 1950s as it has become in the 1960s and 1970s.

GROWTH OF THE WHITE HOUSE STAFF

Meaningful numbers showing the size of the White House staff are hard to find. The published number for 1979 is 315, but that is only the designated personal staff, and it does not include huge numbers of people who appear in other government budgets, but who are loaned on a more or less permanent basis to the White House. The number of 315 does not include the people in a long list of other offices which are active parts of the White House establishment. These include the Office of Management and Budget, the Council of Economic Advisers, the National Security Council, the Office of Science and Technology Policy, the Office of the Special Representative for Trade Negotiations, the Council on Environmental Quality and the Office of Environmental Quality, the Domestic Policy Council staff, the Office of Administra-

tion, the Office for Special Assistance to the President, the Special Action Office for Drug Abuse Prevention, the Council on Wage and Price Stability, the Intelligence Oversight Board, and several others. Perhaps the number of people may be as many as 2,000.

Additionally, there are some 60 to 70 independent agencies that are part of the Executive Branch and also report directly to the President—if indeed they report anywhere. Finally, there are 13 Cabinet departments. In industry by contrast, the span of control that is generally considered maximum for efficient operation, in a direct reporting relationship, is six to eight people.

Even if the President is an experienced executive, skilled in the art of delegation and coordination, the management task itself is formidable. Add to it all the other roles the modern president is expected to play, all the issues and circumstances he is expected to react to on an almost daily basis, and you can wonder how anyone who occupies the office can find the time for study and reflection that are so necessary.

Staff numbers grow for a variety of reasons. First, presidents sometimes desire to elevate an issue to White House status and appropriately create a small, ad hoc group to help with it. Even though initially regarded as temporary, such groups often continue in place after the emergency has passed, continue to find things to do and to grow. Numbers increase also because of the age-old tendency for everyone to want an assistant.

Then why doesn't the President trim the size of the staff? President Carter announced that he intended to do just that, and a few more moves were made in this direction in the early days of his administration. It is risky to ascribe motives when you were not present and part of the action. But we do know that in several administrations, many of the positions on the White House staff have gone to people who were active in the campaign—perhaps as a reward for their help and perhaps also because there will soon be another election to plan for. Furthermore, these people are known to the new President and he is comfortable with them. Once in place, they are difficult to remove, especially the former campaign workers.

COMPETITION AND IN-FIGHTING

Many White House staffers are inexperienced in government, but they tend to be both bright and ambitious. There is great competition among them to get close to the Oval Office. One way to get the President's attention is to surface an issue that may spark his interest. Once an issue has been staffed-out and an "option paper" prepared, it nearly always reaches the President's desk.

In addition, there is a strong tendency for the staffers to consider themselves the "insiders," and, in their view, for Cabinet officers and agency heads to be "outsiders" whose loyalties to the President are not as intense or pure as their own—and who, therefore, must be constantly watched. Add to this the fact that the President normally spends many more hours with staffers than with his Cabinet officers, and a climate has been created which can lead to "second guessing" and perhaps distrust.

It doesn't stop at that point. The White House staff quickly becomes an institutional entity in its own right, with considerable power over what the President sees and finally over what he decides. In a new book entitled *Palace Politics, An Inside Account of The Ford Years,*

Robert T. Hartmann, who was President Ford's closest personal aide for more than a decade—from Congress to the White House—describes, in great detail, the inner struggles and clashing ambitions that infected at least one White House staff. At one point, he states, "The Praetorian pattern was a thing of beauty. What they could not prevent they could delay. What they could no longer delay they could cause to fail. What they could not make fail they could alter. What they had altered was no longer the President's idea and should be discarded. After a while, initiators of new ideas simply gave up."

As an example, Hartmann describes President Ford's announcement in New York that Vice President Rockefeller would head the Domestic Council for him. He quotes President Ford as follows:

I want the Domestic Council to undertake the following responsibilities: First, assessing national needs and identifying alternative ways of meeting them; second, providing rapid response to Presidential needs for policy advice; third, coordinating the establishment of the allocation of available resources; fourth, maintaining a continuous policy of review of our ongoing programs and, as we look down the road, proposing reforms as we need them.

That is why I personally, with the deepest conviction and support have asked the Vice President to serve as Vice Chairman of the Council and to personally and vigorously oversee its work.

This announcement by the President was widely acclaimed. For once a Vice President was being used. But it never happened, and Hartmann describes in his book how it was accepted by the staff and then completely frustrated by the same group. Vice President Mondale has stated that he was used more than any other Vice President, and while this may be true, he did not appear to be a regular part of the decision making process.

Hartmann then quotes from George Reedy's book on the Johnson Presidency in these terms:

> The White House does not provide an atmosphere in which idealism and devotion can flourish. Below the President is a mass of intrigue, posturing, strutting, cringing and pious windbaggery. For the young, the process is demoralizing.
>
> It is possible for a president to assemble a staff of mature men who are past the period of inordinate ambition that characterizes the courtier. But this rarely, if ever, happens. The White House is a court. Inevitably, in a battle between courtiers and advisers, the courtiers will win out.

These examples are given, not to highlight any one administration, but because they are characteristic of the struggle for power and position that has become typical of all recent administrations.

THE VICE PRESIDENT AS CHIEF OF STAFF

Let us return once again to the Vice President. Invariably, his staff is resented by the President's staff. The Vice President usually sits with the Cabinet; he attends other meetings on occasion, but quite soon he becomes an outsider. For several years, I have felt that a President, when selecting a running mate, should do so with the objective of making him his "chief of staff." What better training could there be for the person

who might become President without notice? Furthermore, the Vice President is typically one of two people in the entire executive branch of government who is there by election of the American people.

Interestingly, former President Ford, writing in the November 10, 1980, issue of *Time,* makes the same point. He recommends using "the Vice President as a real Chief of Staff, both to control the administrative bureaucracy and to see that Administration relations with the Congress really mesh." He continues, "Having been the Vice President and having been the President, I know that there has to be a better delegation of responsibility between the two officers. I don't care how well intentioned a President or a Vice President is—and I have seen both Democrats and Republicans try to work it out—no Vice President that I have known has been a full partner."

Using the Vice President as Chief of Staff puts him in the position of helping to make government work and it leaves the decision-making with the Oval Office.

DELEGATION

If delegation and decentralization are to be effective, Cabinet officers must be people in whom the President has great confidence and who merit such confidence. They must be people who are sympathetic with the President's philosophy and goals, and who are knowledgeable in the areas they will manage; they must be people who will always be open and candid with the President. Once these conditions have been met, they can be as effective as the President's public expressions of confidence in them will permit.

Something needs to be done also with the 60 to 70 independent federal agencies. I don't think the answer lies in grouping them all into a new Department of Potpourri, but perhaps they could, on a selective basis, be made part of appropriate existing departments.

But span of control is only part of the problem. Associated with it is the quality of staff work and background papers. Increasingly, the background material and the option papers are originating within the White House staff. The system is not only funneling more decisions into the White House, but more and more of the "staffing out" is being done there also.

Yet, the experience, expertise, and general capability for developing position papers in both foreign policy and domestic areas exist, to a much greater degree, in the departments than they do in the White House staff. As a matter of fact, it has been my observation that in every Cabinet department there are a few top career people who can only be described as superb people—among the very best in the country in their fields of specialization. They are mature and "game wise" and they have long memories. Typically, they are nonpolitical and are the kind of people who are able to be helpful on a professional basis, and who are able to transfer their loyalties to succeeding administrations.

The President needs the input of these unusual professionals. They are part of the glue that holds government together; they provide for continuity when there is a change of administration.

SOME POSITIVE APPROACHES

As with so many things that happen, it is relatively easy to be critical or to analyze with the benefit of hindsight. It is difficult to recommend positive, workable and effective solutions. In this kind of forum, however, I feel an obligation to try.

First, I repeat, I believe that each President should and must have the freedom to organize his own White House. It would be wrong for the Congress to impose a structure on a President.

Second. If meaningful reorganization is to occur, it must begin to take form during the transition period between election and "swearing in." The successful candidate simply must have a clear picture in mind, and this must influence his choice of people. If he waits until he is the President, he will have neither the time nor the flexibility.

Third. I would recommend to a successful candidate that he refrain from filling at least half the slots that will be provided on the transition budget sheets. If he feels compelled to reward some of his key campaign workers, that can be done by placing them elsewhere in government.

Fourth. It is paramount that organization and reporting patterns be clearly established. The Chief of Staff—and I think there must be one, whether he is the Vice President or not—must be a person who clearly understands the President's desires and in whom the President has complete confidence. That person must also be a skilled manager.

Fifth. The President must begin immediately to express confidence in his Cabinet officers. This must be done with actions as well as words. It must be clear that they individually speak for the President in their fields of responsibility. As a matter of good management, utilization of Cabinet Secretaries to make decisions and announcements that may become controversial is an excellent technique. It buys time for the President. The President can observe reactions and is still available to apply a patch if that should prove necessary. If the President makes the announcement himself, there is no room left for maneuvering. Above all else, the President must make it clear at all times to his staff that the Cabinet officers are decision makers who are authorized and commissioned to speak for the President.

Sixth. The President should solicit background materials from appropriate departments and agencies, utilizing the wisdom and memories of some of the experienced and able civil servants. The President does not have to follow their advice, but he definitely should know their views, especially on sensitive issues.

Seventh. I believe every President needs one individual who is wise and experienced in Washington to be a personal advisor and counselor. This person should have Cabinet rank, be "without portfolio," and have full access to all parts of the White House organization. Arthur Burns performed this function early in the Nixon administration.

Eighth. The President should decree, and enforce such decree, that no one on his staff is authorized to call anyone in or outside of government and say "The President wants . . ." unless that person has been specifically authorized to do so. Normally, only three or four people shall be calling at the direct request of the President.

Ninth. The President must be alert at all times to actions by his staff that will undermine the effectiveness and authority of his Cabinet officers. There is something about the White House atmosphere that sooner or later infects even nice people with an inner feeling of superior knowledge and judgment.

Tenth. Consideration should be given to removing certain entities from the White House complex. The National Security Council is a case in point. If it cannot be removed from the White House, then perhaps it should be headed by the Secretary of State. Does the Council on Environmental Quality need to be in the White House, or the Special Action Office for Drug Abuse Prevention?

Reform will not come easily, but the stakes are high. As we begin the decade of the 80's, the leadership of the United States is being challenged. The need for a strong and clear voice from the White House is paramount. A well-disciplined staff that focuses on the control issues may not guarantee an effective presidency, but it will greatly increase the likelihood of success.

48.

Ronald Reagan: First Inaugural Address

Ronald Reagan was sworn in as the 40th President of the United States on January 20, 1981. At 69, he became the oldest person ever to assume the presidency. His predecessor, Jimmy Carter, was twice during the ceremony told that the U.S. hostages had not left Iran—once during the motorcade and again during Reagan's inaugural address. But Reagan was able to announce shortly after he became President that the hostages had cleared Iranian air space. They arrived in Wiesbaden, West Germany, later in the day. In his speech, reprinted below, Reagan emphasized certain points that he had reiterated throughout his campaign: the perilous economic condition of the country, the need to reduce the size of government, and the opportunities that still existed in America for heroic deeds.

Source: Public Papers of the Presidents of the United States.

Senator Hatfield, Mr. Chief Justice, Mr. President, Vice President Bush, Vice President Mondale, Senator Baker, Speaker O'Neill, Reverend Moomaw, and my fellow citizens:

To a few of us here today this is a solemn and most momentous occasion, and yet in the history of our nation it is a commonplace occurrence. The orderly transfer of authority as called for in the Constitution routinely takes place, as it has for almost two centuries, and few of us stop to think how unique we really are. In the eyes of many in the world, this every-4-year ceremony we accept as normal is nothing less than a miracle.

Mr. President, I want our fellow citizens to know how much you did to carry on this tradition. By your gracious cooperation in the transition process, you have shown a watching world that we are a united people pledged to maintaining a political system which guarantees individual liberty to a greater degree than any other, and I thank you and your people for all your help in maintaining the continuity which is the bulwark of our Republic.

The business of our nation goes forward. These United States are confronted with an economic affliction of great proportions. We suffer from the longest and one of the worst sustained inflations in our national history. It distorts our economic decisions, penalizes thrift, and crushes the struggling young and the fixed-income elderly alike. It threatens to shatter the lives of millions of our people.

Idle industries have cast workers into unemployment, human misery, and personal indignity. Those who do work are denied a fair return for their labor by a tax system which penalizes successful achievement and keeps us from maintaining full productivity.

But great as our tax burden is, it has not kept pace with public spending.

For decades we have piled deficit upon deficit, mortgaging our future and our children's future for the temporary convenience of the present. To continue this long trend is to guarantee tremendous social, cultural, political, and economic upheavals.

You and I, as individuals, can, by borrowing, live beyond our means, but for only a limited period of time. Why, then, should we think that collectively, as a nation, we're not bound by that same limitation? We must act today in order to preserve tomorrow. And let there be no misunderstanding: We are going to begin to act, beginning today.

The economic ills we suffer have come upon us over several decades. They will not go away in days, weeks, or months, but they will go away. They will go away because we as Americans have the capacity now, as we've had in the past, to do whatever needs to be done to preserve this last and greatest bastion of freedom.

In this present crisis, government is not the solution to our problem; government is the problem. From time to time we've been tempted to believe that society has become too complex to be managed by self-rule, that government by an elite group is superior to government for, by, and of the people. Well, if no one among us is capable of governing himself, then who among us has the capacity to govern someone else? All of us together, in and out of government, must bear the burden. The solutions we seek must be equitable, with no one group singled out to pay a higher price.

We hear much of special interest groups. Well, our concern must be for a special interest group that has been too long neglected. It knows no sectional boundaries or ethnic and racial divisions, and it crosses political party lines.

It is made up of men and women who raise our food, patrol our streets, man our mines and factories, teach our children, keep our homes, and heal us when we're sick—professionals, industrialists, shopkeepers, clerks, cabbies, and truck-drivers. They are, in short, "We the people," this breed called Americans.

Well, this administration's objective will be a healthy, vigorous, growing economy that provides equal opportunities for all Americans, with no barriers born of bigotry or discrimination. Putting America back to work means putting all Americans back to work. Ending inflation means freeing all Americans from the terror of runaway living costs. All must share in the productive work of this "new beginning," and all must share in the bounty of a revived economy. With the idealism and fair play which are the core of our system and our strength, we can have a strong and prosperous America, at peace with itself and the world.

So, as we begin, let us take inventory. We are a nation that has a government—not the other way around. And this makes us special among the nations of the Earth. Our government has no power except that granted it by the people. It is time to check and reverse the growth of government, which shows signs of having grown beyond the consent of the governed.

It is my intention to curb the size and influence of the Federal establishment and to demand recognition of the distinction between the powers granted to the Federal Government and those reserved to the States or to the people. All of us need to be reminded that the Federal Government did not create the States; the States created the Federal Government.

Now, so there will be no misunderstanding, it's not my intention to do away with government. It is rather to make it work—work with us, not over us; to stand by our side, not ride on our back. Government can and must provide opportunity, not smother it; foster productivity, not stifle it.

If we look to the answer as to why for so many years we achieved so much, prospered as no other people on Earth, it was because here in this land we unleashed the energy and individual genius of man to a greater extent than has ever been done before. Freedom and the dignity of the individual have been more available and assured here than in any other place on Earth. The price for this freedom at times has been high, but we have never been unwilling to pay that price.

It is no coincidence that our present troubles parallel and are proportionate to the intervention and intrusion in our lives that result from unnecessary and excessive growth of government. It is time for us to realize that we're too great a nation to limit ourselves to small dreams. We're not, as some would have us believe, doomed to an inevitable decline. I do not believe in a fate that will fall on us no matter what we do. I do believe in a fate that will fall on us if we do nothing. So, with all the creative energy at our command, let us begin an era of national renewal. Let us renew our determination, our courage, and our strength. And let us renew our faith and our hope.

We have every right to dream heroic dreams. Those who say that we're in a time when there are no heroes, they just don't know where to look. You can see heroes every day going in and out of factory gates. Others, a handful in number, produce enough food to feed all of us and then the world beyond.

You meet heroes across a counter, and they're on both sides of that counter. There are entrepreneurs with faith in themselves and faith in an idea who create new jobs, new wealth and opportunity. They're individuals, and families whose taxes support the government and whose voluntary gifts support church, charity, culture, art, and education. Their patriotism is quiet, but deep. Their values sustain our national life.

Now, I have used the words "they" and "their" in speaking of these heroes. I could say "you" and "your," because I'm addressing the heroes of whom I speak—you, the citizens of this blessed land. Your dreams, your hopes, your goals are going to be the dreams, the hopes, and the goals of this administration, so help me God.

We shall reflect the compassion that is so much a part of your makeup. How can we love our country and not love our countrymen; and loving them, reach out a hand when they fall, heal them when they're sick, and provide opportunity to make them self-sufficient so they will be equal in fact and not just in theory?

Can we solve the problems confronting us? Well, the answer is an unequivocal and emphatic "yes." To paraphrase Winston Churchill, I did not take the oath I've just taken with the intention of presiding over the dissolution of the world's strongest economy.

In the days ahead I will propose removing the roadblocks that have slowed our economy and reduced productivity. Steps will be taken aimed at restoring the balance between the various levels of government. Progress may be slow, measured in inches and feet, not miles, but we will progress. It is time to reawaken this industrial giant, to get government back within its means, and to lighten our punitive tax burden. And these will be our first priorities, and on these principles there will be no compromise.

On the eve of our struggle for independence a man who might have been one of the greatest among the Founding Fathers, Dr. Joseph Warren, president of the Massachusetts Congress, said to his fellow Americans, "Our country is in danger, but not to be despaired of. . . . On you depend the fortunes of America. You are to decide the important questions upon which rests the happiness and the liberty of millions yet unborn. Act worthy of yourselves."

Well, I believe we, the Americans of today, are ready to act worthy of ourselves, ready to do what must be done to ensure happiness and liberty for ourselves, our children, and our children's children. And as we renew ourselves here in our own land, we will be seen as having greater strength throughout the world. We will again be the exemplar of freedom and a beacon of hope for those who do not now have freedom.

To those neighbors and allies who share our freedom, we will strengthen our historic ties and assure them of our support and firm commitment. We will match loyalty with loyalty. We will strive for mutually beneficial relations. We will not use our friendship to impose on their sovereignty, for our own sovereignty is not for sale.

As for the enemies of freedom, those who are potential adversaries, they will be reminded that peace is the highest aspiration of the American people. We will negotiate for it, sacrifice for it; we will not surrender for it, now or ever.

Our forbearance should never be misunderstood. Our reluctance for conflict should not be misjudged as a failure of will. When action is required to preserve our national security, we will act.

We will maintain sufficient strength to prevail if need be, knowing that if we do so we have the best chance of never having to use that strength.

Above all, we must realize that no arsenal or no weapon in the arsenals of the world is so formidable as the will and moral courage of free men and women. It is a weapon our adversaries in today's world do not have. It is a weapon that we as Americans do have. Let that be understood by those who practice terrorism and prey upon their neighbors.

I'm told that tens of thousands of prayer meetings are being held on this day, and for that I'm deeply grateful. We are a nation under God, and I believe God intended for us to be free. It would be fitting and good, I think, if on each Inaugural Day in future years it should be declared a day of prayer.

This is the first time in our history that this ceremony has been held, as you've been told, on this West Front of the Capitol. Standing here, one faces a magnificent vista, opening up on this city's special beauty and history. At the end of this open mall are those shrines to the giants on whose shoulders we stand.

Directly in front of me, the monument to a monumental man, George Washington, father of our country. A man of humility who came to greatness reluctantly. He led America out of revolutionary victory into infant nationhood. Off to one side, the stately memorial to Thomas Jefferson. The Declaration of Independence flames with his eloquence. And then, beyond the Reflecting Pool, the dignified columns of the Lincoln Memorial. Whoever would understand in his heart the meaning of America will find it in the life of Abraham Lincoln.

Beyond those monuments to heroism is the Potomac River, and on the far shore the sloping hills of Arlington National Cemetery, with its row upon row of simple white markers. . . . They add up to only a tiny fraction of the price that has been paid for our freedom.

Each one of those markers is a monument to the kind of hero I spoke of earlier. Their lives ended in places called Belleau Wood, The Argonne, Omaha Beach, Salerno, and halfway around the world on Guadalcanal, Tarawa, Pork Chop Hill, the Chosin Reservoir, and in a hundred rice paddies and jungles of a place called Vietnam.

Under one such marker lies a young man, Martin Treptow, who left his job in a small town barbershop in 1917 to go to France with the famed Rainbow Division. There, on the western front, he was killed trying to carry a message between battalions under heavy artillery fire.

We're told that on his body was found a diary. On the flyleaf under the heading, "My Pledge," he had written these words: "America must win this war. Therefore I will work, I will save, I will sacrifice, I will endure, I will fight cheerfully and do my utmost, as if the issue of the whole struggle depended on me alone."

The crisis we are facing today does not require of us the kind of sacrifice that Martin Treptow and so many thousands of others were called upon to make. It does require, however, our best effort and our willingness to believe in ourselves and to believe in our capacity to perform great deeds, to believe that together with God's help we can and will resolve the problems which now confront us.

And after all, why shouldn't we believe that? We are Americans.

God bless you, and thank you.

This—for the benefit of the oral press—this is an order that I am signing, an immediate freeze on the hiring of civilian employees in the executive branch. I pledged last July that this would be a first step toward controlling the growth and the size of Government and reducing the drain on the economy for the public sector. And beyond the symbolic value of this, which is my first official act, the freeze will eventually lead to a significant reduction in the size of the Federal work force.

RONALD REAGAN, remarks on signing Hiring Freeze
Memorandum, January 20, 1981

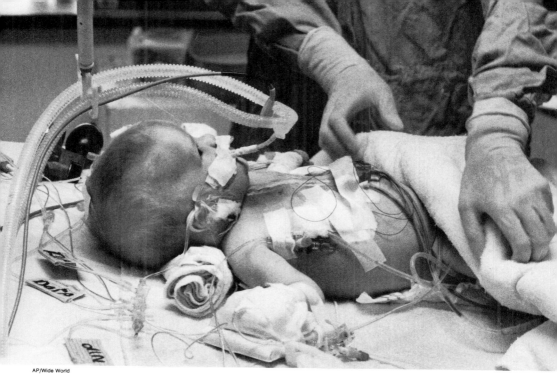

This elaborate apparatus is the support system for a five-and-a-half month old baby who is recovering from a heart transplant operation in the intensive care unit of a Philadelphia hospital.

SCIENCE AND MEDICINE

In the 1970s there was a growing awareness that despite the fact that the United States had some of the best health care facilities in the world, most Americans were not well served by them. At the heart of the matter were the problems of cost and availability. Medical science in the period made remarkable progress, and advances in technology had greatly facilitated the diagnosis and treatment of sickness and disease; however, in the process the costs of health care delivery increased dramatically. For diseases that were well understood and preventable (or readily curable), the costs may have been relatively low. It was, for instance, far cheaper to get a vaccine for polio than to treat the condition once it had arisen. But for other conditions that could not be treated so simply the costs could be enormous. Some contended that only the very rich and the very poor were able to receive adequate health care and that those in the middle,

if left to depend on their own resources, hardly dared to become ill. Continuing with increasing fervor, this debate would remain one of the most prominent and contentious features of the American social and political landscape. As remarkable medical discoveries were made and tested—devices such as the Jarvik artificial heart, for example—the high cost of funding such research and development also became an important issue, as it did in other areas of science and technology. The United States was more fortunate in this regard, in that its many institutions for advanced research were often funded by the federal government, allowing scientists to work for years in fields of their own choosing before ever having to produce results. This freedom was envied by scientists in countries such as the Soviet Union, Japan, or West Germany, where such research could be viewed as a waste of time and resources.

Photos by AP/Wide World

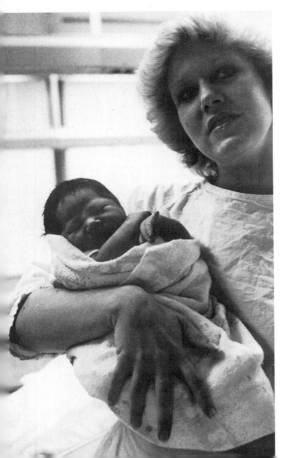

Some of the paradoxes of American medical science in the 1970s and 1980s are displayed on these two pages. The high standard of living generally enjoyed by Americans meant that many more people lived to an old age than had before been the case, but living longer also meant that these senior citizens were more likely to encounter diseases of senescence. The dangers of heart disease and cancer had been known to afflict the elderly for a long time, but in this period new diseases were discovered, including Alzheimer's disease, a progressive deterioration of the brain that brings about loss of memory, confusion, erratic behavior, and finally death. Alzheimer's is a chronic, not an acute, affliction, and as such its treatment was complicated by a family's ability to pay for long-term care. Some Americans were also troubled by the era's proliferation of medical malpractice litigation. The necessity of malpractice suits in general was not questioned, but many believed that juries were tending to award unnecessarily high monetary compensation to the plaintiffs. Critics argued that high legal settlements and the resulting increases in premiums for malpractice insurance were reaching such levels that many good doctors were choosing to leave the practice of medicine.

(Top) A social worker reassures a woman who has Alzheimer's disease; (bottom) this baby was the third "test-tube baby" born in the U.S.

The advances in medical procedures during this period were offset by the ill effects of newly discovered diseases. Pictured on the previous page is a "test-tube baby," a result of in vitro fertilization of the mother's egg. The first such birth occurred on July 25, 1978, to Louise Brown, through the efforts of doctors Patrick Steptoe and Robert Edwards of Britain. In the years following, thousands of babies were born as a result of assisted reproductive technology, often to infertile parents. Pictured below is a less fortunate baby, one afflicted by acquired immunodeficiency syndrome (AIDS). The infant is unprotected from infections as a result of the human immunodeficiency virus that has weakened its immune system. By the mid-1980s, AIDS was one of the most feared diseases in the world—the modern equivalent of the plagues that decimated entire populations in medieval Europe. Nearly half a million Americans would die from the virus that causes AIDS by the end of the century.

(Top) A malpractice attorney shows some of the anatomy models he uses in the courtroom; (bottom left) all but the daughter in this family have been infected with AIDS, contracted from the father, a hemophiliac, passed to the mother, and thus to the baby; (bottom right) digital subtraction angiography is demonstrated in 1981; the method can be used to study heart disease without use of X rays.

Photos by AP/Wide World

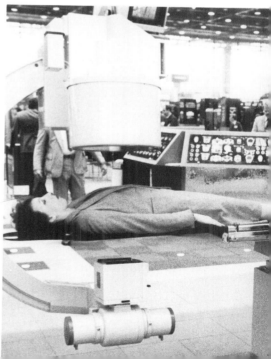

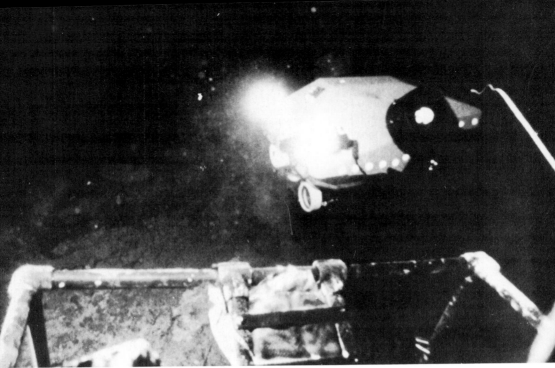

Photos by AP/Wide World

(Top) The robot "Jason, Jr.," leaves the manned submersible _Alvin_ to photograph the sunken liner _Titanic_; its movements are controlled by a pilot in the submersible; (bottom) the _Gossamer Albatross_ reaches the end of its man-powered English Channel crossing; the trip took 2 hours and 50 minutes.

Photos by NASA

Modern technology has provided invaluable aids in the exploration of what may well be humanity's last frontiers: the oceans and outer space. In April 1912 the unsinkable ocean liner *Titanic* struck an iceberg during its first voyage across the Atlantic. Although there were many survivors who escaped in lifeboats, hundreds went down with the ship. For 74 years the wreck's whereabouts were a mystery, and then, in the summer of 1986, it was found, and "J.J.," the versatile robot, explored its interior. To the right are pictures sent by equally versatile discoverers, Voyager 1 and 2, and Pioneer 10. Voyager 2 photographed the Great Red Spot of Jupiter on June 6, 1979. Even this small black and white reproduction suggests the enormous energies on the swirling surface. Voyager flew by Saturn in July and August of 1981. Dramatic pictures radioed back to Earth showed aspects of Saturn's famous rings never before seen or understood. Little Pioneer, the first manmade object ever to escape from the Solar System and journey into interstellar space, carried with it—and presumably still does—a cosmic message for someone in a far-off system revolving around another star. The symbolism of this message etched into a gold-anodized aluminum plate is complex and requires an enormous amount of scientific knowledge to interpret it. But anyone capable of intercepting Pioneer, perhaps a billion or more years from now, will probably be able to understand what it is trying to convey. (For another picture of Pioneer's famous plaque, see page 428.)

(From top) Jupiter's Great Red Spot in a photo sent back by Voyager 1 in 1979; Voyager 2 took this photo of Saturn in 1981; the Uranian satellite Miranda, photographed in 1986 by Voyager 2, has many fault valleys and ridges; Pioneer 10, which may find inhabitants of some other star system, carries this plaque to explain its origin to scientists there.

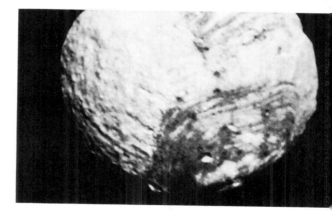

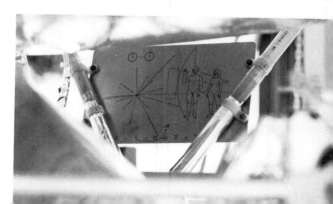

Photos by AP/Wide World

Pictured on the previous page, Voyager 2, an unmanned U.S. interplanetary probe launched in 1977, was seen as a triumph of American science. Originally designed to last for only five years or so, it reconnoitered Jupiter (1979), Saturn (1981), and Uranus (1986) and continued to report data long afterward. It was a bright spot for NASA, which was beset with the failure of the space shuttle *Challenger,* which had exploded moments after its launch in January 1986, killing all seven astronauts aboard. Some of the heroes of American science are pictured on this page, all of whom were recipients of the Nobel Prize. In fact, in the century since the Nobel Prizes were established, more awards have been won by Americans than by any other nationality.

(Left top) Rosalyn Yalow of New York bows to the audience after receiving the 1977 Nobel Prize in medicine; (left center) Walter Gilbert, winner of the 1980 Nobel Prize in chemistry, stands next to a model of DNA at Harvard University; (left bottom) Stanley Cohen of Vanderbilt University in Nashville, Tennessee, won the 1986 Nobel Prize in medicine; (below) William Fowler receives the Nobel Prize in physics from King Carl Gustav of Sweden in 1983. All winners shared their prizes with other scientists.

49.

Ronald Reagan: Address to the Nation on the Economy

Throughout his campaign and in the months between his election and his inauguration President Reagan had never ceased to reiterate his belief that the state of the nation's economy was both perilous and frightening. He had emphasized this point in his Inaugural Address, and he had promised that he would not delay in proposing measures to deal with what he called, in the address reprinted here — his first televised speech from the White House — "the worst economic mess since the Great Depression." He called upon all Americans — lawmakers and ordinary citizens alike — to support his dramatically new economic program so as to prevent "an economic calamity of tremendous proportions." He asked for three successive 10 percent reductions in income tax rates for individuals, accelerated depreciation allowances for businesses, and a drastic reduction in the growth of government spending. The plan, he said, was designed to slow the rate of inflation, increase productivity, and decrease unemployment. Although the President warned that his proposed budget cuts would affect practically every department of government (except the military, which would increase), he gave assurances that "the truly needy" would be cared for. The speech was broadcast on February 5, 1981.

Source: Public Papers of the Presidents of the United States.

Good evening.

I'm speaking to you tonight to give you a report on the state of our Nation's economy. I regret to say that we're in the worst economic mess since the Great Depression.

A few days ago I was presented with a report I'd asked for, a comprehensive audit, if you will, of our economic condition. You won't like it. I didn't like it. But we have to face the truth and then go to work to turn things around. And make no mistake about it, we can turn them around.

I'm not going to subject you to the jumble of charts, figures, and economic jargon of that audit, but rather will try to explain where we are, how we got there, and how we can get back. First, however, let me just give a few "attention getters" from the audit.

The Federal budget is out of control, and we face runaway deficits of almost $80 billion for this budget year that ends September 30th. That deficit is larger than the entire Federal budget in 1957, and so is the almost $80 billion we will pay in interest this year on the national debt.

Twenty years ago, in 1960, our Federal Government payroll was less than $13 billion. Today it is $75 billion. During these 20 years our population has only increased by 23.3 percent. The Federal budget has gone up 528 percent.

Now, we've just had 2 years of back-to-back double-digit inflation—13.3 percent in 1979, 12.4 percent last year. The last time this happened was in World War I.

In 1960 mortgage interest rates averaged about 6 percent. They're $2\frac{1}{2}$ times as high now, 15.4 percent.

The percentage of your earnings the Federal Government took in taxes in 1960 has almost doubled.

And finally there are 7 million Americans caught up in the personal indignity and human tragedy of unemployment. If they stood in a line, allowing 3 feet for each person, the line would reach from the coast of Maine to California.

Well, so much for the audit itself. Let me try to put this in personal terms. Here is a dollar such as you earned, spent, or saved in 1960. And here is a quarter, a dime, and a penny—36 cents. That's what this 1960 dollar is worth today. And if the present world inflation rate should continue 3 more years, the dollar of 1960 will be worth a quarter. What initiative is there to save? And if we don't save we're short of the investment capital needed for business and industry expansion. Workers in Japan and West Germany save several times the percentage of their income that Americans do.

What's happened to that American dream of owning a home? Only 10 years ago a family could buy a home, and the monthly payment averaged little more than a quarter—27 cents out of each dollar earned. Today, it takes 42 cents out of every dollar of income. So, fewer than 1 out of 11 families can afford to buy their first new home.

Regulations adopted by government with the best of intentions have added $666 to the cost of an automobile. It is estimated that altogether regulations

of every kind, on shopkeepers, farmers, and major industries, add $100 billion or more to the cost of the goods and services we buy. And then another $20 billion is spent by government handling the paperwork created by those regulations.

I'm sure you're getting the idea that the audit presented to me found government policies of the last few decades responsible for our economic troubles. We forgot or just overlooked the fact that government—any government—has a built-in tendency to grow. Now, we all had a hand in looking to government for benefits as if government had some source of revenue other than our earnings. Many if not most of the things we thought of or that government offered to us seemed attractive.

In the years following the Second World War it was easy, for a while at least, to overlook the price tag. Our income more than doubled in the 25 years after the war. We increased our take-home pay in those 25 years by more than we had amassed in all the preceding 150 years put together. Yes, there was some inflation, 1 or $1\frac{1}{2}$ percent a year. That didn't bother us. But if we look back at those golden years, we recall that even then voices had been raised, warning that inflation, like radioactivity, was cumulative and that once started it could get out of control.

Some government programs seemed so worthwhile that borrowing to fund them didn't bother us. By 1960 our national debt stood at $284 billion. Congress in 1971 decided to put a ceiling of $400 billion on our ability to borrow. Today the debt is $934 billion. So-called temporary increases or extensions in the debt ceiling have been allowed 21 times in these 10 years, and now I've been forced to ask for another increase in the debt ceiling or the government will be unable to function past the middle of February—and I've only been here 16 days. Before we reach the day when we can reduce the debt ceiling, we may in spite of our best efforts see a national debt in excess of a trillion dollars. Now, this is a figure that's literally beyond our comprehension.

We know now that inflation results from all that deficit spending. Government has only two ways of getting money other than raising taxes. It can go into the money market and borrow, competing with its own citizens and driving up interest rates, which it has done, or it can print money, and it's done that. Both methods are inflationary.

We're victims of language. The very world "inflation" leads us to think of it as just high prices. Then, of course, we resent the person who puts on the price tags, forgetting that he or she is also a victim of inflation. Inflation is not just high prices; it's a reduction in the value of our money. When the money supply is increased but the goods and services available for buying are not, we have too much money chasing too few goods. Wars are usually accompanied by inflation. Everyone is working or fighting, but production is of weapons and munitions, not things we can buy and use.

Now, one way out would be to raise taxes so that government need not borrow or print money. But in all these years of government growth, we've reached, indeed surpassed, the limit of our people's tolerance or ability to bear an increase in the tax burden. Prior to World War II, taxes were such that on the average we only had to work just a little over 1 month each year to pay our total Federal, State, and local tax bill. Today we have to work 4 months to pay that bill.

Some say shift the tax burden to business and industry, but business doesn't pay taxes. Oh, don't get the wrong idea. Business is being taxed, so much so that we're being priced out of the world market. But business must pass its costs of operations—and that includes taxes—on to the customer in the price of the product. Only people pay taxes, all the taxes. Government just uses business in a kind of sneaky way to help collect the taxes. They're hidden in the price; we aren't aware of how much tax we actually pay.

Today this once great industrial giant of ours has the lowest rate of gain in productivity of virtually all the industrial nations with whom we must compete in the world market. We can't even hold our own market here in America against foreign automobiles, steel, and a number of other products. Japanese production of automobiles is almost twice as great per worker as it is in America. Japanese steelworkers outproduce their American counterparts by about 25 percent.

Now, this isn't because they're better workers. I'll match the American working man or woman against anyone in the world. But we have to give them the tools and equipment that workers in the other industrial nations have.

We invented the assembly line and mass production, but punitive tax policies and excessive and unnecessary regulations plus government borrowing have stifled our ability to update plant and equipment. When capital investment is made, it's too often for some unproductive alterations demanded by government to meet various of its regulations. Excessive taxation of individuals has robbed us of incentive and made overtime unprofitable.

We once produced about 40 percent

AP/Wide World

A worker finishes the last Corvette to be made at General Motors' St. Louis plant. Production was shifted to a factory in Kentucky because the manufacturer could not afford to make the changes at the St. Louis assembly plant required by the Federal Clean Air Act.

of the world's steel. We now produce 19 percent. We were once the greatest producer of automobiles, producing more than all the rest of the world combined. That is no longer true, and in addition, the "Big Three," the major auto companies in our land, have sustained tremendous losses in the past year and have been forced to lay off thousands of workers.

All of you who are working know that even with cost-of-living pay raises, you can't keep up with inflation. In our progressive tax system, as you increase the number of dollars you earn, you find yourself moved up into higher tax brackets, paying a higher tax rate just for trying to hold your own. The result? Your standard of living is going down.

Over the past decades we've talked of curtailing government spending so that we can then lower the tax burden. Sometimes we've even taken a run at doing that. But there were always

those who told us that taxes couldn't be cut until spending was reduced. Well, you know, we can lecture our children about extravagance until we run out of voice and breath. Or we can cure their extravagance by simply reducing their allowance.

It's time to recognize that we've come to a turning point. We're threatened with an economic calamity of tremendous proportions, and the old business-as-usual treatment can't save us. Together, we must chart a different course.

We must increase productivity. That means making it possible for industry to modernize and make use of the technology which we ourselves invented. That means putting Americans back to work. And that means above all bringing government spending back within government revenues, which is the only way, together with increased productivity, that we can reduce and, yes, eliminate inflation.

In the past we've tried to fight inflation one year and then, with unemployment increased, turned the next year to fighting unemployment with more deficit spending as a pump primer. So, again, up goes inflation. It hasn't worked. We don't have to choose between inflation and unemployment—they go hand in hand. It's time to try something different, and that's what we're going to do.

I've already placed a freeze on hiring replacements for those who retire or leave government service. I've ordered a cut in government travel, the number of consultants to the government, and the buying of office equipment and other items. I've put a freeze on pending regulations and set up a task force under Vice President Bush to review regulations with an eye toward getting rid of as many as possible. I have decontrolled oil, which should result in more domestic production and less dependence on foreign oil. And I'm eliminating that ineffective Council on Wage and Price Stability.

But it will take more, much more. And we must realize there is no quick fix. At the same time, however, we cannot delay in implementing an economic program aimed at both reducing tax rates to stimulate productivity and reducing the growth in government spending to reduce unemployment and inflation.

On February 18th, I will present in detail an economic program to Congress embodying the features I've just stated. It will propose budget cuts in virtually every department of government. It is my belief that these actual budget cuts will only be part of the savings. As our Cabinet Secretaries take charge of their departments, they will search out areas of waste, extravagance, and costly overhead which could yield additional and substantial reductions.

Now, at the same time we're doing this, we must go forward with a tax relief package. I shall ask for a 10-percent reduction across the board in personal income tax rates for each of the next 3 years. Proposals will also be submitted for accelerated depreciation allowances for business to provide necessary capital so as to create jobs.

Now, here again, in saying this, I know that language, as I said earlier, can get in the way of a clear understanding of what our program is intended to do. Budget cuts can sound as if we're going to reduce total government spending to a lower level than was spent the year before. Well, this is not the case. The budgets will increase as our population increases, and each year we'll see spending increases to match that growth. Government revenues will increase as the economy grows, but the burden will be lighter for each individual, because the economic base will have been expanded by reason of the reduced rates.

Now, let me show you a chart that I've had drawn to illustrate how this can be.

Here you see two trend lines. The bottom line shows the increase in tax revenues. The red line on top is the increase in government spending. Both lines turn upward, reflecting the giant tax increase already built into the system for this year 1981, and the increases in spending built into the '81 and '82 budgets and on into the future. As you can see, the spending line rises at a steeper slant than the revenue line. And that gap between those lines illustrates the increasing deficits we've been running, including this year's $80 billion deficit.

Now, in the second chart, the lines represent the positive effects when

Congress accepts our economic program. Both lines continue to rise, allowing for necessary growth, but the gap narrows as spending cuts continue over the next few years until finally the two lines come together, meaning a balanced budget.

I am confident that my administration can achieve that. At that point tax revenues, in spite of rate reductions, will be increasing faster than spending, which means we can look forward to further reductions in the tax rates.

Now, in all of this we will, of course, work closely with the Federal Reserve System toward the objective of a stable monetary policy.

Our spending cuts will not be at the expense of the truly needy. We will, however, seek to eliminate benefits to those who are not really qualified by reason of need.

As I've said before, on February 18 I will present this economic package of budget reductions and tax reform to a joint session of Congress and to you in full detail.

Our basic system is sound. We can, with compassion, continue to meet our responsibility to those who, through no fault of their own, need our help. We can meet fully the other legitimate responsibilities of government. We cannot continue any longer our wasteful ways at the expense of the workers of this land or of our children.

Since 1960 our government has spent $5.1 trillion. Our debt has grown by $648 billion. Prices have exploded by 178 percent. How much better off are we for all that?

Well, we all know we're very much worse off. When we measure how harshly these years of inflation, lower productivity, and uncontrolled government growth have affected our lives,
we know we must act and act now. We must not be timid. We will restore the freedom of all men and women to excel and to create. We will unleash the energy and genius of the American people, traits which have never failed us.

To the Congress of the United States, I extend my hand in cooperation, and I believe we can go forward in a bipartisan manner. I've found a real willingness to cooperate on the part of Democrats and members of my own party.

To my colleagues in the executive branch of government and to all Federal employees, I ask that we work in the spirit of service.

I urge those great institutions in America, business and labor, to be guided by the national interest, and I'm confident they will. The only special interest that we will serve is the interest of all the people.

We can create the incentives which take advantage of the genius of our economic system—a system, as Walter Lippmann observed more than 40 years ago, which for the first time in history gave men "a way of producing wealth in which the good fortune of others multiplied their own."

Our aim is to increase our national wealth so all will have more, not just redistribute what we already have which is just a sharing of scarcity. We can begin to reward hard work and risk-taking, by forcing this Government to live within its means.

Over the years we've let negative economic forces run out of control. We stalled the judgment day, but we no longer have that luxury. We're out of time.

And to you, my fellow citizens, let us join in a new determination to rebuild the foundation of our society, to work together, to act responsibly. Let us do so with the most profound respect for that which must be preserved as well as with sensitive understanding and compassion for those who must be protected.

We can leave our children with an unrepayable massive debt and a shattered economy, or we can leave them liberty in a land where every individual has the opportunity to be whatever God intended us to be. All it takes is a little common sense and recognition of our own ability. Together we can forge a new beginning for America.

Thank you, and good night.

50.

George Gilder: Supply-Side Economics

The greatest of economic laws is the law of supply and demand, which are said inevitably to balance in a free economy. According to a school of economists who had been dominant in Washington for a generation, the way to control the economy was to manipulate the demand side by influencing consumer choices and dictating prices. Now a new school was coming to the fore, which emphasized the supply side, and claimed that if production was encouraged, demand would follow suit. In his book, Wealth and Poverty, *economics writer George Gilder argued that America had been following paths toward poverty rather than plenty. In the excerpts from the book reprinted here, he discusses the theory of supply-side economics in a particularly lucid manner. The book was a best-seller in the spring of 1981, when many persons, both in and outside of Washington, were trying to understand the new ideas —"Reaganomics"—that were inspiring the Reagan administration.*

Source: *Wealth and Poverty.*

As Thomas Sowell has explained in two books (*Say's Law: An Historical Analysis* and *Classical Economics Reconsidered*), the theorem associated with the name of the French economist Jean-Baptiste Say essentially maintains that the sum of the wages, profits and rents paid in manufacturing a good is sufficient to buy it. This does not mean that the same people who make a thing will necessarily buy it, but that they could. The sum of money paid to the factors of production, chiefly in rents, wages, salaries and profits, for the making and marketing of an automobile, for example, is precisely enough to purchase it. Therefore, across an entire system, purchasing power and producing power can always balance: There will always be enough wealth in an economy to buy its products. There cannot be a glut of goods caused by inadequate total demand. Producers, collectively, in the course of production, create demand for their goods. This idea is obviously simplistic in many ways, but it bears a number of key economic truths and implications never refuted by John

Maynard Keynes or anyone else. These truths are the foundation of contemporary supply-side theory. . . .

Capitalist creativity is guided not by any invisible hand, but by the quite visible and aggressive hand of management and entrepreneurship. Businesses continually differentiate their products, their marketing techniques, their advertising and their retailing strategies in order to find some unique niche in the system from which they can reap, as long as possible, monopoly profits. Without the aid of government, protecting patents or otherwise excluding competitors, these monopoly positions tend to be shortlived. But they are the goal of business strategy, the focus of creative entrepreneurship, the motivation of original research and development.

The monopoly positions, moreover, are not at all unlimited, because they are always held—unless government intercedes to enforce them—under the threat of potential competitors and substitutes at home or abroad. To the question of how many companies an industry needs in order to be competitive, economist Arthur Laffer answers: one. It will compete against the threat of future rivals. Its monopoly can be maintained only as long as the price is kept low enough to exclude others. In this sense, monopolies are good. The more dynamic and inventive an economy, the more monopolies it will engender. The ideal of perfect competition, like the ideal of an economy without business power, translates into an economy without innovations. A rapidly developing system will be full of monopolies as new industries repeatedly crop up and have a lucrative run before the competition can emerge and catch up, benefiting from the advantages of imitation. Every now and then, a company like IBM or Polaroid will get such a lead and exploit it so efficiently that it retains dominance for decades, to the great benefit of the country.

This form of "monopoly capitalism" does not readily or automatically result in the fulfillment of the preexisting desires of consumers, for consumers do not know what they desire until they have tried a sample at a specified price. Consumers respond to the creative experiments of business. Demand, as John Kenneth Galbraith points out, "does not arise in spontaneous consumer need. Rather the dependence effect means that it grows out of [depends on] the process of production itself. If production is to increase, the wants must be effectively contrived." Exactly. The quality of capitalist society depends not on automatic mechanisms, but on the quality, the creativity and leadership of the capitalists.

The contemporary Left prefers economic leadership from government. But Say's Law, in general terms, is a rule of all organized human behavior. The will of the people is often no more "spontaneous" or free of elite initiative and manipulation in politics than in economics. Democratic masses cannot be generative or creative; they can merely react and ratify. They affirm or reject the creative offerings of entrepreneurs in both business and politics. Howard Jarvis was no less an enterpriser in launching the Proposition 13 tax cut movement in California than was Ray Kroc in launching McDonald's. Both gave specific form to the previously amorphous though finally sovereign wishes of the public.

An economy can be democratic chiefly in proportion to its diversity of choices—the proliferation of monopoly experiments—corresponding to the huge multiplicity of individual tastes and desires. In its cornucopia of choice the capitalist marketplace contrasts vividly with even the most democratic political marketplace with its near monopoly of power vested at every election and with the requirement that voters select a whole cluster of policies in order to get the one desired. Representative democracy is a better system than any other, chiefly because it evokes the experimental competition of elites. There is little evidence, moreover, that capitalism corrupts democracy and much evidence that capitalism is essential to it. The widespread belief that capitalist societies, perverted by corporate power, show a persistent bias in favor of business goods and against public services has not stood up well under recent experience. Government has been growing faster than business in most democratic countries.

Nonetheless, the crucial source of creativity and initiative in any economic system is the individual investor. Economies do not grow of their own accord or by dint of government influence. They grow in response to the enterprise of men willing to take risks, to transform ideas into monopolies, and monopolies into industries, and to give before they know what they will get in return.

The essential thesis of Say's Law remains true: Supply creates demand. There can be no such thing as a general glut of goods. There can be a glut of "bads," but in the world of necessary scarcity in which the very science of economics finds its meaning, an apparent glut of all goods merely signifies a dearth of creative production, a lack of new supplies and fresh demands. Private savings, moreover, in the current inflationary period, are invested. Saving, in fact, signifies a commitment to

the future, a psychology of production and growth. Since World War II, the countries that have saved most, preeminently Japan and other Asian capitalist lands, have grown fastest. The apparent gluts of goods have emerged chiefly in countries that fail to save.

This situation illuminates a central fallacy of demand-oriented economics. Like the politician in the thrall of "public opinion," who lives always in the past, demand-oriented businesses rarely create new goods, for there is no measurable demand for what is not already familiar. The market surveys are mute on most innovations. Without a flow of new products, the marketplace can be filled with stale items, produced with ever greater efficiency, continually redesigned in trivial ways, repackaged in brighter colors, and marketed with a more expensive and harder sell. "Jaws III" will be followed by "IV" and "V"; Cheerios become Sugar Cheerios; and corporations grow chiefly by purchasing proven firms. New businesses that provide new products, new hierarchies, new opportunities, new patterns of jobs and skills, more rarely emerge and acquire the resources for rapid growth. The employment market becomes more stratified, bureaucratized and alienating; the consumer market seems less diverse and savory; advertising appeals grow more strident and clamorous. The public becomes jaded, and pressures mount on government for further expansion of demand. It is a vicious circle that steadily erodes the creative forces of capitalism.

Originating in a liberal effort to respond to the popular will and relieve the pressures of poverty, demand-oriented politics ends in promoting unemployment and dependency and creating a less open and accessible economy and a more stratified and hierarchical political order. Government bureaucracies proliferate to furnish the services that overtaxed businesses no longer can provide and to subsidize the favored private interests of a depleted capitalism. As bureaucracy grows, moreoever, industrial progress declines. For progress is always dependent on the creativity of suppliers.

Say's Law in all its variations is the essential enactment of supply-side theory. But its value does not reside in its mathematical workings. In economics, mathematical models, however elegant, must always defer to the behavior and psychology of persons with free will, who often act, and interact, in unexpected ways. The importance of Say's Law is its focus on supply, on the catalytic gifts or investments of capital. It leads economists to concern themselves first with the motives and incentives of individual producers, to return from a preoccupation with distribution and demand and concentrate again on the means of production.

This return is crucial to understanding the current predicament of capitalism. But it will be difficult for economists. Reversion to the supply side means leaving the comfort of rigorous models and computations and again entering the fray of history and psychology, business and technology. Economists should again focus on the multifarious mysteries of human social behavior and creativity which Adam Smith luminously addressed in *The Wealth of Nations,* which Marx stuffed into the maw of his theory, which Keynes treated in most of his writings and which even Galbraith, in his often perverse way, delights in describing. . . .

Living at a time when government and taxes were seen as a relatively minor force in capitalist economies, Keynes did not apply his mode of thinking to governmental activity. But Keynes' paradox of savings applies just as much to forced savings by taxation as to consumption voluntarily forgone by private citizens. Like any group of individuals, the government may intend to save, but if it cannot generate real investments, the result will be merely a decline in total incomes and a tendency toward stagnation.

Through the progressive tax structure, government revenue tends to come from funds that might otherwise have been invested. But Washington itself does relatively little productive investment. As the federal budget grows, much of it goes to transfer payments that are spent heavily on the bundle of goods in the rapidly rising consumer price index, from gasoline to hamburgers, and to federal pay and contracts that go to bid up the price of real estate in the District of Columbia. Some money does go to "investments" in public works of various kinds and in education, but many appropriations are motivated less by their economic and social benefits than by political pressures.

Furthermore, from Keynes' theory of the sources of poverty arise vital new reasons for concern about the nature of government growth. Throughout human history, he wrote, "The weakness of the inducement to invest has been at all times the key to the economic problem. . . . The desire of the individual to augment his personal wealth by abstaining from consumption has usually been stronger than the inducement to the entrepreneur to augment the national wealth by employing labor on the construction of durable assets."

One reason for this gap, according to Keynes, has been the continual existence of sumps of wealth, sinks of purchasing powers, which divert money from productive use.

Like Henry George, the eloquent author of economics' leading best-seller, *Progress and Poverty,* Keynes believed that during many historic periods land played this role. Since mortgage rates were often higher than the yield of the land in farming, it often could be purchased only by people inexpert in using it, chiefly urban speculators. Other important sinks of purchasing power have been gold, jewelry, art and collectibles, such as stamps and coins.

The purchase of such goods—the sinking of money into these sumps of wealth—does not itself directly reduce investment, production or purchasing power. If I have an ounce of gold and you give me $600 for it, you have simply transferred your investing or buying power to me; no wealth is lost. The problem arises when throughout an entire economy an ever-increasing number of people choose to spend their money on gold or other sumps of wealth. Then the price of gold will continually rise, absorbing more and more purchasing power. A rising price means that there is a steady increase of buyers or demand over sellers or supply. The problem becomes worse when the sellers (in this instance me with my $600) spend it on other relatively nonreproducible objects—land, works of art, historic buildings or durable consumer luxuries—and then the men who profit from these transactions also tend to refrain from creative investment and instead themselves bid up the price of gold and Van Goghs, antiques and old autos, Rembrandts and real estate. . . .

Over the decades, government steadily acquired most of the character-istics that Keynes listed as signs of a "limitless sink" of wealth. There is no obvious limit on governmental expansion or forced profitability through taxes, few supply-side constraints on its size, no tendency for demand for government to slop over onto other products and little short-run tendency for government to decline when the economy fails. When people want the Keynesian "moon," which he described as liquidity but which is now better seen as security, they turn to Washington and its outland satellites.

During the 1970s, these enterprising bureaucrats gathered, bringing all their human capital and entrepreneurial aggressiveness to the ventures of the state. Many of them were lawyers, because governmental expansion is best achieved through exploiting the fertile chinks and fissures in the tomes of federal regulation. They joined with congressmen in mobilizing constituencies of private interests that could be profitably served. The programs multiplied, the money supply grew, inflation raised taxes, and the spurious yield of federal programs—which often gave no valuable service—and of government bonds—which often financed waste—remained as high or higher than the real profits of private capital. In fact, one could say that the yield of government from inflation has risen to 60 percent, since each percent of increase in the price level results in a 1.6 percent jump in federal revenues. As government expanded, in a vicious circle it also enlarged its tax receipts.

This is the new Keynesian source of stagnation and poverty in the nations of the West. What politicians are essentially selling—the new liquidity—is tenure and security, and there seems to be no end to the demand for these services. Yet security, too, like thrift, liquidity and leisure, has its own paradox of aggregation. Some people can gain exemption from risk, and safety from inflation, by turning to the state. But when a majority does, the security and stability of the nation declines.

As the enterprising spirit is channeled increasingly into law and other professional schools, and thence into government, its lobbies, consultant groups and organized clientele—as great tycoons arise more readily selling "security" in HEW than in selling securities in private firms, or selling real products to the public—the crucial inducement to invest once again sinks below the attractions of other wealth. People without access to the state buy gold and yachts, government bonds and foreign money, or parlay private housing—with its special government protections—into a trillion-dollar sum exceeding in nominal value all the assets of American corporations. . . .

What has happened is emergence of a final corollary of Say's Law: Subsidized supply destroys demand. Production without a willing market is a form of disguised consumption, and despite first appearances it does not stimulate an economy. Nonproductive government spending, even when designed to spur demand, actually soon reduces it, regardless of any statistical increase in "purchasing power." The artificial stimulus, like an addiction, requires ever greater injections to sustain the initial effect.

When government gives welfare, unemployment payments and public-service jobs in quantities that deter productive work, and when it raises taxes on profitable enterprise to pay for them, demand declines. In fact,

nearly all the programs that are advocated by economists to promote equality and combat poverty—and are often rationalized in terms of stimulating consumption—in actuality reduce demand by undermining the production from which all real demand derives. Buying power does not essentially "trickle down" as wages or "flow up" and away as profits and savings. It originates with productive work at any level. This is the simple and homely first truth about wealth and poverty. "Give and you will be given unto." This is the secret not only of riches, but also of growth.

This is also the essential insight of supply-side economics. Government cannot significantly affect real aggregate demand through policies of taxing and spending—taking money from one man and giving it to another, whether in government or out. All this shifting of wealth is a zero sum game, and the net effect on incomes is usually zero, or even negative.

Even a tax cut does not work by a direct impact on total disposable incomes, since every dollar of resulting deficit must be financed by a dollar of government debt, paid by the purchaser of federal securities out of his own disposable income. Even in the short run, real aggregate demand is an effect of production, not of government policy. The only way tax policy can reliably influence real incomes is by changing the incentives of suppliers. By altering the patterns of rewards to favor work over leisure, investment over consumption, the sources of production over the sumps of wealth, taxable over untaxable activity, government can directly and powerfully foster the expansion of real demand and income. This is the supply-side mandate.

51.

Reagan Administration Review of the Iran Hostage Agreements

During the last months, and especially the last weeks and days of his administration, Jimmy Carter had struggled frantically to resolve the hostage crisis and free the American men and women who had been held captive in Teheran since November 1979. Negotiations continued nonstop throughout the first three weeks of January 1981, and success was finally obtained — with the help of Algerian intermediaries — on January 20 (President Reagan's Inauguration Day). The hostages were freed, but there was some doubt whether the Reagan administration would honor the agreements that had been arrived at by Carter and his people. On February 18, 1981, the U.S. State Department issued the following statement, declaring that although not all aspects of the agreements could be approved, all would be honored.

Source: State Department Bulletin, February 18, 1981.

OUR POSITION up until now has been that the U.S. will, of course, honor its obligations under international law. Because of the complexity of the agreements and the extraordinary conditions under which they were negotiated, we have undertaken a review to determine precisely what our obligations are under them.

That review has been completed. Having considered all the circumstances carefully, we have decided to approve implementation of the agreements in strict accordance with the terms of the agreements.

The review considered the impact of implementing or not on: the rights of U.S. claimants; U.S. terrorist policy; U.S. international interests, including U.S. obligations to third parties, particularly Algeria, who had themselves made commitments during the course of these negotiations; long-term U.S. interests in the Persian Gulf, including Iran.

It did not consider several questions, of great potential interest to historians and of possible value for drawing lessons with respect to future policy but of no practical bearing on the immediate question of whether or not to implement the agreements.

THE ISSUES NOT CONSIDERED

The review just completed did not consider: how could the whole crisis have been handled better; could a better set of agreements have been negotiated; we did not consider whether these agreements should have been signed.

We are confronted with an accomplished fact. We have an agreement signed by a President of the U.S. and the question is whether— given the existence of the agreement and the consequences (legal, financial and political)

UPI/Bettmann

After a ticker tape parade up Broadway in New York City on January 30, the hostages are honored at City Hall.

of implementing it or not, what should this country do.

The conclusion of the agreements was a legal exercise of Presidential authority. This authority will be subject to challenge in our courts, and the executive branch will, of course, abide by the determination of our judicial system. We did not find it necessary to reach a conclusion as to the legally binding character of these agreements under international law. We are proceeding because we believe it is in the overall interests of the United States to carry out the agreement.

THE STATUS QUO ANTE

The decision represents a practical judgment that implementation provides the surest resolution of the issue consistent with the best interests of the United States in the Gulf region and throughout the world. Iran has not profited from these agreements. It was ultimately forced to settle on terms that simply restored the status quo ante because the advent of the new Administration finally confronted it with a serious deadline. The funds already returned to Iran and those which may be returned following the implementation of these agreements and the settlement of commercial and financial claims are funds which belonged to Iran before the seizure of the American hostages.

It should be well understood that the decision to faithfully implement the agreements does not represent a precedent for future actions by the United States Government in similar situations. The present Administration would not have negotiated with Iran for the release of the hostages. Future acts of state-sponsored terrorism against the U.S. will meet swift and sure punishment.

52.

Russell Baker: Indians Did It in Smoke

The situation in Central America seemed especially troublesome to the Reagan administration when it took over the government in January 1981. El Salvador, in particular, was the site of continuing, and highly disturbing, agitation by leftist guerrillas who, according to Secretary of State Alexander Haig, were receiving military supplies from outside the country. The Soviets were suspected, although a senior Soviet diplomat declared in Washington on February 14 that his government was not supplying arms to the Salvadoran rebels. Not directly, perhaps, replied the State Department, but indirectly—via Cuba and Ethiopia. Secretary Haig's pleas were heeded by the Congress, which sent aid later in February to the strife-torn government of El Salvador. The situation was not yet as serious as it would later become, and columnist Russell Baker, in The New York Times, *could pen the following sardonically humorous account of the administration's action.*

Source: *The New York Times,* March 4, 1981.

DIPLOMACY NOWADAYS is mostly a matter of sending signals. Suppose you want to let country X know you are sick and tired of its insolence and likely to give it a rap on the snout unless you start getting a little respect. How do you send the message?

In the old days you wrote a letter—"I am fed up with your high-handed attitude" and so on—and gave it to an ambassador to deliver. This no longer works. Thanks to the telephone, nobody remembers how to write a letter. And of course telephoning the message we have in mind is out of the question.

Suppose you dial country X, of whose insolence you are sick and tired. What happens? A telephone-answering machine says, "I am not here at the moment, but if you leave your name after the sound of the beep. . . ."

You are certainly not going to leave your name, not for insolent country X. It would be an invitation for country X to heap on fresh humiliation by refusing to return your call.

Once the telephone destroyed letter writing, new ways of getting through had to be contrived. For a while spies were the answer. You encouraged country X to keep a large supply of spies around your premises. When you wanted something sent to their masters you stamped it "Absolutely Top Secret" and left it lying around so they could easily filch it.

Since all countries love other countries' secrets, especially secrets of the absolutely top variety, it was a sure bet that country X would drop everything for a few minutes and give full attention to your message.

Transmission via spy worked very well, but only for a short time. Country

X, being nobody's dummy, soon figured out what was going on and began examining its spygrams with the same cunning that you employ in riffling through the daily mail.

Most of that mail, you know from bitter experience, is cleverly packaged to present you with messages you don't want to receive. Announcements of miraculous new bargains in phonograph records, fantastically low magazine subscription rates, stupendously needy alumni funds. Into the trash it goes unopened.

When country X realized its spies were being used to deliver messages it did not want to receive, a new transmission system had to be developed. Thus, today we have signals. All over the world foreign ministries have been converted into signal corps busily sending, receiving and interpreting signals.

This explains the Reagan Administration's bellicose absorption in El Salvador. "Why all this fuss," you must have asked yourself, "about a country no bigger than a coffee bean?"

Well, this fuss, as you so quaintly put it, may look like a fuss to you, but what it actually is, you see, is a signal.

After the Reagan people took power, they wanted to notify Moscow that they were tougher and meaner than the Carter Administration.

"We have to let them know," said President Reagan, "that we are sick and tired of their insolence and will give them a rap on the snout unless we start getting a little respect. Compose a signal to that effect and send it right away."

After studying the semaphore supplies, Secretary of State Haig came back with a proposal. "Have you ever heard of El Salvador?" he asked.

"Sure," said the President. "That Mexican nightclub way out on Wilshire Boulevard. Didn't it burn down in 1937 because of a frijole fire in the kitchen?"

"No, sir," said Mr. Haig. "You're thinking of Al Salvatore's, which was an Italian restaurant on La Cienega and went bankrupt in 1940 after rumors spread that somebody had been served a cockroach in the antipasto. El Salvador is a country in Central America. A very, very small country."

"Al," said the President, "if you're proposing we send it to the Russians as a signal, I have to say no. Start by sending them a little country and it will whet their appetite for bigger and bigger signals. We'd end up having to send them Brazil."

Haig explained that El Salvador would not be sent; it would be saved. Saved from Castro, saved from Moscow, saved from aggressive international Communism, all of which were threatening it. "When the Russians see us moving into El Salvador with guns and soldiers if necessary, they will read our signal," he said.

"Which will say what?" asked the President.

"That we are tougher and meaner than the Carter crowd and they had better start giving us a little respect."

"There's no chance we could get our nose bloodied, is there, Al?"

"Not a chance. El Salvador is not much bigger than a baseball park and it's right in our own backyard. If we can't whomp the bejeebers out of Communism there we might as well hang up our ghost writers and go home."

So it was decided, and we are signaling Moscow that we are tougher and meaner than we were last year by showing we can manhandle the smallest kid on the block. This is the kind of logic you fall into when you lose the habit of mental discipline imposed by letter writing.

53.

IRA BERKOW: The Baseball Effect on America

A dispute between the Major League Baseball Players Association and the owners of major league teams had been simmering for over a year before it broke out into open flame in the spring of 1981. Up until the mid-1970s, a baseball player had been tied by his basic contract to a particular team until he retired, was traded, or was dropped outright. A series of court decisions created a new entity, the free agent, who could "play out his contract" and, after six years with a club, become free to sign with another. The dispute in 1981 involved the question of compensation for the club that would lose the player, often a valuable one, to another club that was willing to pay him more. The players threatened to strike, but negotiations continued at a surprisingly unhurried pace. The strike began on June 12, 1981, and continued for weeks; when the players returned after an agreement unsatisfactory to both sides had been concluded, the season was more or less in ruins. The following article by sports writer Ira Berkow appeared on May 31, when there was still hope that a strike against "America's pastime" could be avoided.

Source: *The New York Times,* May 31, 1981.

WARS COULDN'T stop major league baseball, the Depression couldn't stop major league baseball; it seems the only thing that could is major league baseball itself. By the very threat of the players' strike, the idea that the great stadia would be empty this summer—and the crack of bat against ball merely an echo in the mind—gives pause to reflect on baseball and its meaning in the warp and woof of life.

"Whoever wants to know the heart and mind of America had better learn baseball," Jacques Barzun, the social commentator, wrote more than a quarter of a century ago.

"Fundamentally," Barzun said in an interview last week, "things haven't changed. Baseball still reflects our so-ciety, it's just that our society has changed."

Baseball, Barzun says, once expressed the unification of America, the teamwork involved. "When we look at the triumphs of American technology on a large scale," he says, "we see the fine workings of a national machinery—everybody in every department cooperating effectively with no gaps in time.

"It was like the making of a double play perhaps. Or a relay in which nine men speedily clicked together to achieve a desired result. It's a beautiful thing to observe.

"But now, the contentions in baseball parallel the enormous unrest in our society—there's more litigation, for example, than ever before. And the star system has gotten out of hand. The teamwork that once marked the beauty of baseball is now scorned, and along with the diminishing appreciation for the rich qualities of baseball, there has developed diminished appreciation for the rich qualities of American life."

A DIMENSION OF SUMMER

But a summer without baseball would not be quite the same for Barzun—who is still a casual fan—or for Jake Rabinowitz, proprietor of A & J Grocery on Second Avenue, who said, "I wouldn't have all the aggravation watching the Mets and Yankees, especially this season, but sometimes they give me pleasure— once in a while they win."

For Roger Angell, a writer for The New Yorker magazine, baseball would be missed. "It's part of my summer habits—and maybe my winter habits, too," he said. "I suppose I'd get along all right without it, but I'd rather not. There is a continuity with baseball— and there'd be a feeling of loss without it, like, there goes something else in our lives."

One of the qualities that Angell likes best about baseball has been its relative stability. He wrote: "Within the ball park, time moves differently, marked by no clock except the events of the game. This is the unique, unchangeable feature of baseball and perhaps explains why this sport, for all the enormous changes it has undergone in the past decade or two, remains somehow rustic, unviolent and introspective. Baseball's time is seamless and invisible, a bubble within which players move at exactly the same pace and rhythms as all their predecessors."

The late Bruce Catton, the historian, said that "baseball is a . . . pageant and a

AP/Wide World

A double play in the 1981 World Series.

ritualized drama, as completely formalized as a Spanish bullfight, and although it is wholly urbanized it still speaks of the small town in the simple rural era that lived before the automobile came in to blight the landscape. One reason for this is that in a land of unending change, baseball changes very little."

But it seems to have often reflected the mood of the nation, and its ambitions.

Mark Twain wrote at the turn of the century that baseball was "the very symbol of the outward and visible expression of the drive and push and rush and struggle of the raging, tearing, booming 19th century."

For many it remained that way into the 20th century. "America was the land of opportunity where even a poor boy could grow up to be Babe Ruth," wrote Douglass Wallop, in "Baseball: An Informal History."

Once those sentiments were expressed about the Presidency. But, Wallop went on, "Cal Coolidge moved through life with careful sidesteps, smiling sour smiles. Babe Ruth laughed a mighty laugh, strode with the stride of a giant, slamming the door of his Stutz Bearcat and wading through the crowds, long camel hair coat flapping near his ankles, big brown eyes shining, a long cigar stuck between the fat lips, and grinning as they all say, 'Hiya, Babe,' and yelling back, 'Hiya, Kid . . . Sure, Kid . . . Atta boy, Kid, keep swinging from the heels.' "

Surely there were those who resented Ruth making more than the President of the United States, but his larger-than-life qualities overshadowed the money aspect. Today, though, the big bucks intrude on our summer devotions, says Angell. "A lot of people find it insupportable, and against the work ethic, that young men can make so much money. You're supposed to work hard for not much money at something you don't like when you're young, and improve on that as you get older.

"And this idea of players making large amounts of money also says something uncomfortable about our society, where a ballplayer can make so much more than, say, a teacher. But it's not the fault of the players. The money is obviously there. It seems like the owners have a death wish about the game."

Above the noise of the machines in the United Features Syndicate pressroom Raymond Ruiz, in a blue smock, says he has sometimes resented the big money the players are making. "But if I was a player," he said, "and the owners were giving it to me, I'd take it, too. I sure would."

IN THE MINDS OF A NATION

Baseball is part of the tradition of many American families. "It may be on the periphery of our lives, but it is ingrained in our psyches," said Dr. Peter Berczeller, a Manhattan physician. "We grow up with it being an integral part of our childhood, and we never really divest ourselves of it. I still root for the Giants—even though they've moved from New York to San Francisco. And now I see my son following the teams and players, as I did."

At least twice a year, Paul Weiss, professor of philosophy at Catholic University in Washington, and author of "Sport: A Philosophic Inquiry," says he meets his son, Jonathan, a New York attorney, in Baltimore to take in an Orioles game. "Baseball is something we've shared for a long time," said Dr. Weiss. "It is a beautiful, graceful game and it is social in a way that football and hockey aren't. Those two sports are adventitious. It seems that beating up opponents is of as much interest to fans in those sports as the game itself; and basketball is a sport limited to the technically knowledgeable."

If there is a baseball strike, Dr. Albert Ellis says he is sure to hear about it from some of his clients. "It will disturb a few of them greatly," says Dr. Ellis, a psychologist and executive director of the Institute for Rational-Emotive Therapy. "They're devoted to it, and some of these people have a very low frustration tolerance. They'll whine and scream that there's no baseball."

There are other citizens who have a different view of baseball. "I don't have the slightest interest in the thing," says Lillian Hellman, the playwright. "Mr. Dashiell Hammett spoiled me of all sports. He was such a sports fan— a sports *fiend*, I should say—that he drove me crazy. He'd be listening to a baseball game and shouting about this player and that, and I'd have to leave the room. He'd holler, 'You're the only person in America who doesn't give a damn about baseball.'"

Not so. "I went to my last baseball game in 1934 in Washington," said John Kenneth Galbraith, the economist, with a chuckle. "It was between the Senators and an otherwise unspecified team. Unless I'm in Washington and unless the Senators come back to town, I don't plan on seeing another." About the possible baseball strike? "I am totally unaffected by these grievous undevelopments," he added.

Baseball doesn't always travel well and it has had its detractors overseas. In the fall of 1924 George Bernard Shaw wrote about an exhibition game in London between the Chicago White Sox and the New York Giants.

"It was as a sociologist, not as a sportsman—I cannot endure the boredom of sport—that I seized the opportunity of the London visit of the famous Chicago Sioux and the New York Apaches (I am not quite sure of the names) to witness for the first time a game of baseball," wrote Shaw.

"I found that it has the greater advantage over cricket of being sooner ended."

Perhaps baseball held the kind of impenetrable mysteries for Shaw that it did for Albert Einstein. When Professor Einstein met Moe Berg, the esteemed linguist and major league catcher, he suggested, "Mr. Berg, you teach me baseball, and I'll teach you mathematics." He paused, and added, "But I'm sure you'd learn mathematics faster than I'd learn baseball."

Such is not the case for Seymour Siwoff, president of Elias Sports Bureau, the sports statistics company. "I'd miss everything about baseball that we grew up with—from the pennant races to the batting averages," said Siwoff. "A real part of our history would be lost. Take for example the box score, it is a treasure.

"Baseball in the summer is like a journey, it's played every day," continued Siwoff. "We follow it. There'd be a great void without it. I'm sure we'd find something to take its place. The question is, what?"

It's a little bit of history, don't you think? The players have never gone out during a season before. I got here around 10 o'clock, and the flags were flying from the scoreboard, the way they do when there's a game. The sun was out, it was the best weather we've had in a long time, and the Cubs have won five out of six. What a time for a strike!

MARK DITLER, Chicago Cubs fan, at Wrigley Field on June 12, 1981 (the first day of the strike)

54.

RONALD REAGAN: Responses to an Assassination Attempt

On March 30, 1981, President Reagan was shot in the chest from close range by a lone gunman who was lying in wait outside a Washington hotel. The President's press secretary, James Brady, was severely wounded by a bullet that pierced his brain. A secret service agent and a local police officer were also wounded. All four victims were rushed to hospitals, where they underwent emergency surgery. Doctors were optimistic about the President after removing a bullet from his left lung, and the two officers were considered likely to recover, and though Brady's chances were considered slight, he did recover almost completely after many months. The assailant, who was apprehended at the scene, was identified as John W. Hinckley, Jr., of Evergreen, Colorado. He had used a .22-calibre pistol loaded with devastator bullets that fragment on impact. On June 16, 1981, President Reagan held his first press conference following the assassination attempt . He was asked whether he intended to change his habits as far as meeting people were concerned, and whether his views had changed about gun control. Excerpts from the press conference are reprinted here.

Source: Weekly Compilation of Presidential Documents, June 22, 1981.

Q. Thank you, Mr. President. As everyone knows, this is your first news conference since you were shot, and I think everybody has the impression that you have fully recovered. My first question is, have you fully recovered? And secondly, can you tell us how having been shot has changed you? Have you become more cautious, or are there any differences?

THE PRESIDENT. I have recovered. I feel fine. And the doctors say I've recovered. So, if I'm a medical miracle, I'm a happy one.

No, you can't spend your life worrying about that. I'm quite sure that there will be and have been changes in—I look back now and wonder why it didn't happen 30 times before—changes in alertness on the part of security and so forth. But it hasn't made too much of a change in how we do, and I still want to be able to see the people and meet them . . . .

Q. Mr. President, at a recent White House meeting Senator Edward Kennedy asked if you'd refuse to lead the fight against his legislation on handgun control, or Saturday night specials, sales of Saturday night specials. What was your answer?

THE PRESIDENT. Would I lead the fight against his—

Q. No, he asked that you not lead the fight against his legislation.

THE PRESIDENT. Oh.

Q. What was your answer?

THE PRESIDENT. Well, we had a very

nice talk. And I told him that I believe that some of the things that we had tried in California served better, and that is to make the penalties for the carrying of a weapon, particularly in the commission of a crime, much stiffer than they are. California—we added 5 to 15 years to the prison sentence for anyone carrying a gun in the commission of a crime—convicted of that crime, whether they used the gun or not. And since, that's been augmented to include no probation—mandatory prison sentence.

I believe in that, because my concern about gun control is that it's taking our eyes off what might be the real answers to crime. It's diverting our attention.

There are today more than 20,000 gun control laws in effect—Federal, State, and local—in the United States. Indeed, some of the stiffest gun control laws in the Nation are right here in the District, and they didn't seem to prevent a fellow a few weeks ago from carrying one down by the Hilton Hotel. In other words, they are virtually unenforceable.

So, I would like to see us directing our attention to what has caused us to have the crime that continues to increase as it has and is one of our major problems in the country today.

55.

Overselective Service

On June 25, 1981, the U.S. Supreme Court announced its ruling on the constitutionality of having only males register for a potential military draft. The Court did not consider directly the advisability of having women drafted into military service; instead, it emphasized the constitutional right of Congress "to make rules for the government of the land and naval forces." That authority, the Court declared, includes the right to decide who should be required to register for the draft. Justice William Rehnquist, writing for the 6-3 majority, also commented that it was not the Court's affair to agree or disagree with any such judgment because Congress is a separate branch of government. The decision was met by protests from many quarters, particularly women's groups, who felt that the Court was showing signs of backing away from its earlier stance against sex discrimination. A negative editorial response to the decision is reprinted here.

Source: *The New Republic*, July18, 1981.

IT'S PERFECTLY constitutional for Congress to register men and not women for the draft. So says the Supreme Court in *Rostker v. Goldberg*, one of those blockbuster social cases reserved—for some reason—for the end of the Court's October to July term. Six of the nine justices say legislators have every right to decide that soldiering is not women's work. This is bad policy and bad constitutional law.

It is bad constitutional law because the high court, disliking the implications of its own equal protection precedents, has made a sham of adhering to the "well-settled" (as lawyers say) sex discrimination test. That test says that if Congress wants to discriminate on the basis of sex, it must do two things. First it must point to a goal (in this case raising an army) and convince the Court that goal is important. Then it must show that the sex discrimination is "substantially" related to achieving the goal—in other words, that discriminating achieves the goal better than a sex-neutral plan would.

This two-part sex discrimination standard is known as the *Craig* test, after the pathbreaking case *Craig v. Boren,* which struck down a state law setting a higher drinking age for boys than for girls. The *Craig* test was supposed to be a compromise between the traditional poles of equal protection law. Most "discrimination" by Congress is presumed to be constitutional, since Congress can't help using categories (income levels, say, or age group or geographical location) to distribute costs and benefits. But some classifications, notably those based on race, have been considered "invidious" and presumed unconstitutional. The Supreme Court never could decide which category to put sex discrimination into since some sex classifications are hard to argue with (maternity benefits for women but not men, for example) while others are plainly indefensible (requiring all nurses to be female, for example)—so it split the difference.

But in *Rostker* the Court makes only a sophisticated pretense of applying the *Craig* test to the all-male draft. Justice William H. Rehnquist, writing for the majority, rounds up the usual precedents. Then he more or less ignores them. He reasons as follows. Women are precluded by statute from combat duties. Yet combat troops are precisely what Congress says the military will need in any future draft. Thus there is no military need to register women, and any argument for including them must be based instead on equity. And, Rehnquist says, "Congress was certainly entitled . . . to focus on the question of military need rather than 'equity.' "

All of which leaves some questions unanswered. Why, for example, is the concept of equity so alien or distasteful to a majority of the high court that Rehnquist feels the need to place the word in quotation marks? Why must equity and military need be portrayed, without explanation, as somehow mutually exclusive? And above all, why, as Thurgood Marshall's dissent asks, can't Congress be required to find a way to meet the country's legitimate military needs in a fashion that *is* equitable?

Had the Supreme Court applied *Craig* in good faith, it would have left to Congress the burden of proving that the *exclusion* of women from draft registration relates closely to the goal of raising an army. Rehnquist's majority opinion argues instead that the *inclusion* of women is pointless, since, the Court claims, a draft is for combat troops and women are banned from combat. This not only turns the proper question on its head, it is not even true. Congress, in attempting to justify all-male draft registration, does not pretend that every person inducted will have to be eligible for combat. (If Congress did make that claim, it might also wish to explain why its registration scheme includes large numbers of men who are ineligible for combat because of physical handicap or conscientious objector status.) Testimony in the Senate, in fact, established that women could fill at least 80,000 positions in any likely draft—even under the present combat ban.

AP/Wide World

A woman soldier negotiates a demanding obstacle course as part of her training.

Why, then, is the Court so eager to "defer" to Congress's sexually discriminatory decision? It is true, as Rehnquist points out, that Congress has more constitutional latitude on military matters than perhaps in any other area. It also is true that the Republic will not crumble if men, rather than men and women, fill those 80,000 non-combat posts. But the Court would not stand by while Congress registered blacks and not whites (or vice versa) or Protestants and not Catholics. The burden is on Congress to explain what important interest is served by drawing a sexual distinction where none appears relevant. Congress did not meet that burden.

What may be lost in this legal thicket is why the rest of us should care about the Court's constitutional mugwumpery. There are two good reasons. First, the high court appears to be backing away fast from the *Craig v. Boren* line of cases, which is to say backing away from constitutional protections against sex discrimination. By just barely blundering through the motions of the *Craig* test, Rehnquist has sabotaged the precedent and made mush of the commonsensical notion that high-sounding motives ("national defense") are no excuse for discriminatory behavior unless somebody can suggest a clear relationship between them. If the Court is going to fudge the standard when the stakes are this high— life and death, perhaps, or at least many months of conscripted labor—it may well feel free to fudge the standard elsewhere. What about sex discrimination, say, in pension funds, or in child custody laws—both of which have been litigated extensively under the *Craig* test? And there is no doubt that Rehnquist, touted so often as one of the best legal minds on the Court, knows this. In fact, he has never subscribed to the Court's treatment of sex discrimination, having dissented not only in *Craig* but in virtually every sex bias case since. That five justices should choose to go along with him now is disturbing.

But if *Rostker v. Goldberg* is bad constitutional law, it is worse policy. Even conceding combat restrictions, there is no acceptable reason to exclude women. . . . To do so is to discriminate against both men and women. A male-only draft disfavors men, obviously, because they must bear the entire burden of staffing the armed forces—and the cost in time, to say nothing of the risk to life and limb, is unparalleled by any other obligation of the citizen. It disfavors women, perhaps, even more—for the cost is the continued social imprimatur on a set of values that say women are too frail and too emotional to be entrusted with any direct role in the serious business of protecting national security.

Still, we don't have to talk about equity (or even "equity") to make the case for unisex draft registration. The plain fact is that women have made and continue to make a much greater contribution to the armed services than most chest-thumpers imagine. Military statistics show that female volunteers—who now number some 150,000—are easier to recruit, more mature, better educated, more quickly promoted, more inclined to re-enlist, and less inclined to have drug or disciplinary problems than their male counterparts. Even the Senate Armed Services Committee, no great fan of female draft registration, concedes that women have made an "important contribution" to the armed forces. Education and ability to learn sophisticated skills have come close to replacing simple physical prowess as the prime attribute of the soldier in many parts of the modern military, and women are demonstrably as good as or better than men by this standard.

Of course, it was politics, not policy, that doomed female draft registration in Congress. (All four military service chiefs, after all, recommended register-

ing women.) And another sort of politics probably helped doom it before the Supreme Court. There is little doubt that the Court would have ruled differently had the Constitution included the Equal Rights Amendment, which is yet another reason why we're sorry to acknowledge to all the Phyllis Schlaflys that there will be no ERA this time around. This is not destined to be the time for new social initiatives—either in Congress or in the state legislatures— and, with the high court "deferring" left and right to the other branches of government, the nation will get what it voted for.

To a certain point, we agree with the court's inclination to deference. We too would rather see 535 representatives than nine appointed jurists make a historic change in the way the country raises its armies. In many cases the Court would be overstepping its mandate to strike down misguided legislation. But a male-only registration scheme is not simply misguided. It flouts established and persuasive constitutional doctrine. The constitutional question was for the Court to decide, and it decided wrong.

56.

The Strike of the Air Traffic Controllers

On August 3, 1981, more than 85 percent of the members of the Professional Air Traffic Controllers Organization (PATCO) went on strike across the United States despite repeated government warnings that any controller who refused to work would be fired. Government negotiators had offered a compromise settlement, but it was judged unacceptable by the union. PATCO's demands included a four-day, 32-hour workweek, a $10,000 across-the-board raise, and additional retirement benefits. The union was found in contempt of court and fined $250,000 for the first three days and $1 million a day thereafter. On August 5 five union officials were jailed and 55 controllers were fired. Meanwhile, some 2,000 nonstriking PATCO members and an equal number of nonunion controllers manned the towers with the help of supervisory personnel. The botched strike showed that the PATCO leadership had badly overrated the effect of their endorsement of Ronald Reagan in the 1980 campaign, ignored his often stated revulsion against strikes by federal employees, erroneously expected the strike to create chaos in the skies, and failed to muster support from other unions prior to walking off the job. As a result 12,000 men and women lost their jobs, and undeniable proof was provided of the featherbedding that had existed in the union. The government's firm action, however, sent shock waves through the ranks of organized labor in many other industries. Reprinted here is the text of a statement read to reporters in the Rose Garden at the White House on the morning of August 3, together with questions by reporters and responses by President Reagan and other government officials.

Source: Weekly Compilation of Presidential Documents, August 10, 1981.

THE PRESIDENT. This morning at 7 a.m. the union representing those who man America's air traffic control facilities called a strike. This was the culmination of 7 months of negotiations between the Federal Aviation Administration and the union. At one point in these negotiations agreement was reached and signed by both sides, granting a $40 million increase in salaries and benefits. This is twice what other Government employees can expect. It was granted in recognition of the difficulties inherent in the work these people perform.

Now, however, the union demands are 17 times what had been agreed to— $681 million. This would impose a tax burden on their fellow citizens which is unacceptable.

I would like to thank the supervisors and controllers who are on the job today, helping to get the Nation's air system operating safely. In the New York area, for example, four supervisors were scheduled to report for work, and 17 additionally volunteered. At National Airport a traffic controller told a newsperson he had resigned from the

UPI/Bettmann

Supervisors work in the control tower at O'Hare International Airport in Chicago during the air traffic controllers' strike.

union, and reported to work because, "How can I ask my kids to obey the law if I don't?" This is a great tribute to America.

Let me make one thing plain. I respect the right of workers in the private sector to strike. Indeed, as president of my own union, I led the first strike ever called by that union. I guess I'm maybe the first one to ever hold this office who is a lifetime member of an AFL-CIO union. But we cannot compare labor-management relations in the private sector with government. Government cannot close down the assembly line. It has to provide without interruption the protective services which are government's reason for being.

It was in recognition of this that the Congress passed a law forbidding strikes by Government employees against the public safety. Let me read the solemn oath taken by each of these employees, a sworn affidavit when they accepted their jobs: "I am not participating in any strike against the Government of the United States or any agency thereof,

and I will not so participate while an employee of the Government of the United States or any agency thereof."

It is for this reason that I must tell those who fail to report for duty this morning they are in violation of the law, and if they do not report for work within 48 hours, they have forfeited their jobs and will be terminated.

Q. Mr. President, are you going to order any union members who violate the law to go to jail?

THE PRESIDENT. Well, I have some people around here, and maybe I should refer that to the Attorney General.

Q. Do you think that they should go to jail, Mr. President, anybody who violates this law?

THE PRESIDENT. I told you what I think should be done. They're terminated.

THE ATTORNEY GENERAL. Well, as the President has said, striking under these circumstances constitutes a violation of the law, and we intend to initiate in appropriate cases criminal proceedings against those who have violated the law.

Q. How quickly will you initiate criminal proceedings, Mr. Attorney General?

THE ATTORNEY GENERAL. The process will be underway probably by noon today.

Q. Are you going to try and fine the union $1 million per day?

THE ATTORNEY GENERAL. Well, that's the prerogative of the court. In the event that any individuals are found guilty of contempt of a court order, the penalty for that, of course, is imposed by the court.

Q. How much more is the Government prepared to offer the union?

THE SECRETARY OF TRANSPORTATION. We think we had a very satisfactory offer on the table. It's twice what other Government employees are going to get—11.4 percent. Their demands were so unreasonable there was no spot to negotiate, when you're talking to somebody 17 times away from where you presently are. We do not plan to increase our offer to the union.

Q. Under no circumstances?

THE SECRETARY OF TRANSPORTATION. As far as I'm concerned, under no circumstance.

Q. Will you continue to meet with them?

THE SECRETARY OF TRANSPORTATION. We will not meet with the union as long as they're on strike. When they're off of strike, and assuming that they are not decertified, we will meet with the union and try to negotiate a satisfactory contract.

Q. Do you have any idea how it's going at the airports around the country?

THE SECRETARY OF TRANSPORTATION. Relatively, it's going quite well. We're operating somewhat in excess of 50-percent capacity. We could increase that. We have determined, until we feel we're in total control of the system, that we will not increase that. Also, as you probably know, we have some rather severe weather in the Midwest, and our first priority is safety.

Q. What can you tell us about possible decertification of the union and impoundment of its strike funds?

THE SECRETARY OF TRANSPORTATION. There has been a court action to impound the strike fund of $3.5 million. We are going before the National Labor Relations Authority this morning to ask for decertification of the union.

Q. When you say that you're not going to increase your offer, are you referring to the original offer or the last offer which you've made? Is that still valid?

THE SECRETARY OF TRANSPORTATION. The last offer we made in present value was exactly the same as the first offer. Mr. Poli asked me about 11 o'clock last evening if he could phase the increase in over a period of time. For that reason, we phased it in over a longer period of time. It would have given him a larger increase in terms of where he would be when the next negotiations started, but in present value it was the $40 million originally on the table.

Q. Mr. Attorney General, in seeking criminal action against the union leaders, will you seek to put them in jail if they do not order these people back to work?

THE ATTORNEY GENERAL. Well, we will seek whatever penalty is appropriate under the circumstances in each individual case.

Q. Do you think that is an appropriate circumstance?

THE ATTORNEY GENERAL. It is certainly one of the penalties that is provided for in the law, and in appropriate cases, we could very well seek that penalty.

Q. What's appropriate?

THE ATTORNEY GENERAL. Well, that depends upon the facts of each case.

Q. Can I go back to my "fine" question? How much would you like to see the union fined every day?

THE ATTORNEY GENERAL. Well, there's no way to answer that question. We could just have to wait until we get into court, see what the circumstances are, and determine what position we would take in the various cases under the facts as they develop.

Q. But you won't go to court and ask the court for a specific amount?

THE ATTORNEY GENERAL. Well, I'm sure we will when we reach that point, but there's no way to pick a figure now.

Q. Mr. President, will you delay your trip to California or cancel it if the strike is still on later this week?

THE PRESIDENT. If any situation should arise that would require my presence here, naturally I will do that. So that will be a decision that awaits what's going to happen. May I just—because I have to be back in there for another appointment—may I just say one thing on top of this? With all this talk of penalties and everything else, I hope that you'll emphasize, again, the possibility of termination, because I believe that there are a great many of those people, and they're fine people, who have been swept up in this and probably have not really considered the result—the fact that they had taken an oath, the fact that this is now in violation of the law as that one supervisor referred to with regard to his children. And I am hoping that they will in a sense remove themselves from the lawbreaker situation by returning to their posts.

I have no way to know whether this had been conveyed to them by their union leaders who had been informed that this would be the result of a strike.

Q. Your deadline is 7 o'clock Wednesday morning for them to return to work?

THE PRESIDENT. 48 hours.

THE SECRETARY OF TRANSPORTATION. It's 11 o'clock Wednesday morning.

Q. Mr. President, why have you taken such strong action as your first action? Why not some lesser action at this point?

THE PRESIDENT. What lesser action can there be? The law is very explicit. They are violating the law. And as I say, we called this to the attention of their leadership. Whether this was conveyed to the membership before they voted to strike, I don't know. But this is one of the reasons why there can be no further negotiation while this situation continues. You can't sit and negotiate with a union that's in violation of the law.

THE SECRETARY OF TRANSPORTATION. And their oath.

THE PRESIDENT. And their oath.

Q. Are you more likely to proceed in the criminal direction toward the leadership than the rank-and-file, Mr. President?

THE PRESIDENT. Well, that again is not for me to answer.

Q. Mr. Secretary, what can you tell us about the possible use of military air controllers—how many, how quickly can they get on the job?

THE SECRETARY OF TRANSPORTATION. In answer to the previous question, both civil and criminal, probably more civil than criminal, and we now have papers in the U.S. Attorney's offices, under the Attorney General, in about 20 locations around the country where two or three principal people would be involved.

As far as the military personnel are concerned, they are going to fundamentally be backup to the supervisory personnel. We had 150 on the job, supposedly, about a half-hour ago. We're going to increase that to somewhere between 700 and 850.

Q. Mr. Secretary, are you ready to hire other people should these other people not return?

THE SECRETARY OF TRANSPORTATION. Yes, we will, and we hope we do not reach that point. Again, as the President said, we're hoping these people come back to work. They do a fine job. If that does not take place, we have a training school, as you know. We will be advertising. We have a number of applicants right now. There's a waiting list in terms of people that want to be controllers, and we'll start retraining and reorganize the entire FAA traffic controller group.

Q. Just to clarify, is your deadline 7 a.m. Wednesday or 11 o'clock?

THE SECRETARY OF TRANSPORTATION. It's 11 a.m. Wednesday. The President said 48 hours, and that would be 48 hours.

Q. If you actually fire these people, won't it put your air traffic control system in a hole for years to come, since you can't just cook up a controller in— [inaudible].

THE SECRETARY OF TRANSPORTATION. That obviously depends on how many return to work. Right now we're able to operate the system. In some areas, we've been very gratified by the support we've received. In other areas, we've been disappointed. And until I see the numbers, there's no way I can answer that question.

Q. Mr. Lewis, did you tell the union leadership when you were talking to them that their members would be fired if they went out on strike?

THE SECRETARY OF TRANSPORTATION. I told Mr. Poli yesterday that the President gave me three instructions in terms of the firmness of the negotiations: One is there would be no amnesty, the second, there would be no negotiations during the strike, and third is that if they went on strike, these people would no longer be Government employees.

Q. Mr. Secretary, you said no negotiations. What about informal meetings of any kind with Mr. Poli?

THE SECRETARY OF TRANSPORTATION. We will have no meetings until the strike is terminated with the union.

Q. Have you served Poli at this point? Has he been served by the Attorney General?

THE ATTORNEY GENERAL. In the civil action that was filed this morning, the service was made on the attorney for the union, and the court has determined that that was appropriate service on all of the officers of the union.

Q. My previous question about whether you're going to take a harder line on the leadership than rank-and-file in terms of any criminal prosecution, can you give us an answer on that?

THE ATTORNEY GENERAL. No, I can't answer that except to say that each case will be investigated on its own merits, and action will be taken as appropriate in each of those cases.

Q. Mr. Lewis, do you know how many applications for controller jobs you have on file now?

THE SECRETARY OF TRANSPORTATION. I do not know. I'm going to check when I get back. I am aware there's a waiting list, and I do not have the figure. If you care to have that, you can call our office and we'll tell you. Also, we'll be advertising and recruiting people for this job if necessary.

Q. Mr. Secretary, how long are you prepared to hold out if there's a partial but not complete strike?

THE SECRETARY OF TRANSPORTATION. I think the President made it very clear that as of 48 hours from now, if the people are not back on the job, they will not be Government employees at any time in the future.

Q. How long are you prepared to run the air controller system—[*inaudible*].

THE SECRETARY OF TRANSPORTATION. Four years, if we have to.

Q. How long does it take to train a new controller, from the waiting list?

THE SECRETARY OF TRANSPORTATION. It varies; it depends on the type of center they're going to be in. For someone to start in the system and work through the more minor office types of control situations till they get to, let's say a Chicago, or a Washington National, it takes about 3 years. So in this case, what we'll have to do if some of the major metropolitan areas are shut down or a considerable portion is shut down, we'll be bringing people in from other areas that are qualified and then start bringing people through the training schools in the smaller cities and smaller airports.

Q. Mr. Secretary, have you definitely made your final offer to the union?

THE SECRETARY OF TRANSPORTATION. Yes we have.

THE PRESS. Thank you.

You can rest assured that if I am elected President, I will take whatever steps are necessary to provide our air traffic controllers with the most modern equipment available and to adjust staff levels and work days so that they are commensurate with achieving a maximum degree of public safety. . . . I pledge to you that my administration will work very closely with you to bring about a spirit of cooperation between the President and the air traffic controllers.

RONALD REAGAN, in letter to PATCO president Robert Poli, October 20, 1980

It's possible to bargain [without a right to strike]. But it is not real bargaining unless the individual or the group can withhold their labor. And it is not true bargaining when the price for withholding their labor is instant dismissal. That is "economic capital punishment."

MOE BILLER, president, American Postal Workers Union

57.

JAMES G. WATT: Interview

James G. Watt was named a deputy assistant Secretary of the Interior in 1969, director of the Bureau of Outdoor Recreation in 1972, commissioner of the Federal Power Commission in 1974, and vice chairman of the commission in 1977. He met Ronald Reagan in December 1980 after having been proposed as the new Secretary of the Interior. "I outlined what I thought his administration should do." says Watt in the interview reprinted here. "He added to my proposals. So I know what he wants done, and I know how he wants it done." If the incoming President was satisfied with his new Interior boss, the confraternity of American environmentalists and conservationists was highly dissatisfied. They were almost unanimous in protesting the new policies put into effect by Watt, and heavy mail campaigns by various environmentalist organizations resulted in widespread disapproval of the situation at Interior. The energy, mining, and timber industries were, however, enthusiastic about what he was doing. Watt managed to hang on as Secretary of the Interior for three years. He accomplished some important things and ended up doing less harm than his critics had feared. He was certainly the most controversial member of the Reagan administration. His views of his mandate are expressed in the following August 1981 interview.

Source: *Nation's Business*, September 1981.

Sen. Malcolm Wallop of Wyoming says you are "the first real Secretary of the Interior that the country has had in a couple of decades."

He's probably the wisest man on the Hill.

What are you doing differently that would prompt such a remark?

I have approached the management of our national resources with the realization that they are there to benefit Americans in all walks of life, and so I have implemented some policies that allow energy development, mineral extraction, grazing and timber cutting as well as preservation and recreation.

In the past, the state of Wyoming, as well as the other states, had just been locked up to economic development and set aside for a few backpackers rather than the rest of us who might want to use a four-wheeler or go horseback riding or develop some energy.

We intend to see that these public lands, which amount to one third of the nation—768 million acres, are used for all Americans. Everybody has a right to benefit from these lands.

You have mentioned four corner-stones for Reagan administration conservation policy. What are they?

In addressing the North American Wildlife and Natural Resources Conference, I listed these points.

First, America must have a sound economy if it is to be a good steward of its fish and wildlife, its parks and all its natural resources.

Second, America must have orderly development of its vast energy resources to avert a crisis development, which could be catastrophic to the environment.

Third, America's resources were put here for the enjoyment and use of people, now and in the future, and should not be denied to the people by elitist groups.

Fourth, America has the expertise to manage and use resources wisely, and much of that expertise is in state government and in the private sector.

All actions President Reagan or I have taken that affect conservation grow out of those principles.

Critics, such as California Sen. Alan Cranston, say you have gone beyond the administration's position on the environment.

I'm fortunate in that I am probably the first Secretary of the Interior to work for a President who understands the Department of the Interior.

President Reagan, while serving as governor of California for eight years, had to deal with the department on a daily basis. More than 40 percent of California is owned by the federal government and subject to the dictates and the reactions of the Secretary of the Interior.

So when we're dealing with environmental issues, he has a keen awareness. He understands the mission of the department. In December I outlined what I thought his administration should do. He added to my proposals. So I know what he wants done, and I know how he wants it done. We are doing it, and our department has had full support.

How have the career employes reacted?

In many instances, I had to turn the bureaucracy 180 degrees to make major changes in the direction they were marching. I yelled out some orders. I was harsh in some instances, but I got their attention.

What surprised all of us was how quickly they came around. We've made great strides. We're 8 to 10 months ahead of our own schedule. The career government employees have been just phenomenal.

What do you consider your major accomplishments in your seven months in office?

I have focused Congress' attention on the need to restore the National Park System to its proper shape; we have committed ourselves to a billion-dollar program on that, and Congress is supporting us enthusiastically.

I have opened for energy exploration and development lands that had been locked up for 10 to 15 years in an unreasonable manner.

We have stimulated the hard-rock mining industry and given it hope that there is a future for domestic mining in America.

We have focused attention on the states' role in land-use planning, in providing recreational opportunities for their citizens, and we have helped them realize that they must expand the opportunities for such recreation, that it is not the role of the federal government.

Is it true that, in comparison with Congress, you really have little authority to make drastic changes in managing public lands?

When [former Secretary of the Interior Cecil D.] Andrus left, he told *The New York Times* it didn't make any difference who was going to be named

AP/Wide World

James G. Watt

Secretary of the Interior because there wasn't anything that a Secretary could really change. Andrus said that was because of the cumbersome bureaucracy and the special-interest groups.

Now I have come in, and within 30 days the Sierra Club started its drive to run me out of here because I'd made too many changes. And the National Wildlife Federation is concerned that I'm bringing about too much change.

I am trying to bring about change and I'm trying to do it in an aggressive way that will be filled with common sense and a balanced perspective.

So how much discretion is there? In some people's minds, not very much; in others', way too much.

The responsibilities of the Secretary of the Interior seem to be in conflict. On the one hand, the Secretary is charged with preserving the land, and on the other he is responsible for making these lands productive.

True, there is an absolute conflict built into the Department of the Interior. I am called, on one hand, the chief environmental officer for the nation, and the special-interest groups refuse to look at anything else.

I suppose I might also be called the chief miner on Department of the Interior lands, the chief harvester of timber, the chief Indian. And these missions, outlined by statute, are contradictory in many instances.

To the various special-interest groups, the Secretary has a statutory duty to do A, B and C, but they refuse to look at any of the other responsibilities of the office.

That's why I'm so critical of the narrow special-interest groups on both the development and the preservation sides. I must search for balance. Yet, if I do an effective job, I will receive criticism at different times from the different groups.

How do your definitions of "national need" and "national interests," when applied to the parks and wilderness areas, differ from environmentalists' definitions?

I believe that these lands need to be primarily preserved in their natural state so they can be used by us and by many generations yet to come, but I believe—and here's where the difference comes—that they must be made available in that natural state to the handicapped, to the family, to the camper, to the older couple, to the young couple with not so much money and to the children.

I do not think they ought to be set aside for just the few backpackers who are rugged enough and affluent enough and have enough time.

You have asked that instead of buying more parkland, money from the Land and Water Conservation Fund be spent on fixing up present parks. Critics say that because the parks are deteriorating from overuse, more parkland should be purchased. How do you respond?

Right now, the system is skewed to acquiring more and not taking care of what we have. We're changing that. We have increased by 225 percent the money to be used for restoration.

I am critical of the special-interest groups for encouraging department policies that permit deterioration of our park system. I don't think we can afford to lose what we have.

What is needed most is to build proper sewage treatment facilities. That means increasing drinking water supplies, building proper roads, restoring buildings that are deteriorating just through age, replacing tunnels, repairing what needs repairing.

Most of that has nothing to do with use, it has to do with neglect. The greed of those who want to expand the federal estate and take private property off the tax rolls was such that money had been flowing to further acquisition rather than restoration.

So you want a change in the law?

We think good stewardship is taking care of what we have, and so I asked for a change in the law regarding the use of the fund's money. Government officials ought to be held accountable for their actions. You take a government employee and give him hundreds of millions of dollars to acquire land, but then you do not expect him to exercise any judgment on acquisition and development.

What does he do? He just does what he is told—acquire, acquire, acquire. Then he doesn't have to take care of it because he doesn't have any money left to do so. The entire procedure requires no value judgments.

That's not good stewardship. A responsible government decision maker should determine whether he needs to

maintain what he has or can afford to take more.

Your critics also say you intend to open up wilderness areas and national parks to timber and mining companies, to oil and gas exploration. Aren't some of these wilderness areas, parks and wildlife refuges exempt from such multiple use?

Yes they are. And the critics have fabricated the story in an effort to raise dollars. We have never suggested, nor would we, that there would be mining or timbering or drilling in parks unless Congress has dictated it. For those people to try to confuse the public is unfair. I have never suggested those things, never will—and it will never happen. The law protects the parks, as it should, and we're not asking that the law be changed.

You speak of inventorying all public lands to determine the best uses for them. Is this a policy you initiated?

Congress has repeatedly asked for an inventory, and it just has not been effectively done. Congress has done some of the inventorying itself by setting aside a national park and saying that is its highest use; there is no going back to see what other values are there, since Congress has already determined that.

But we ought to look at the millions and millions of acres that we do need to know the values of. For example, BLM—the Bureau of Land Management—has 341 million acres to manage. That's in addition to the more than 190 million National Forest Service acres and the 156 million acres set aside for parks and wildlife refuges.

Now the 341 million acres managed by BLM—an area twice the size of Texas—is land that has a variety of values. We really have not ever inventoried those lands. We should know what strategic minerals they hold.

For example, the United States is critically dependent on foreign sources for 22 of the 36 most needed strategic minerals. At the moment, less than one half of 1 percent of our lands is subject to mining. I don't think that is an excessive amount, but I do think we'd better determine what minerals we have in this country.

Do we have the capability to be independent, or are we vulnerable to a natural resource war? I think we're vulnerable today. We'd better correct that.

You've proposed bringing the private sector more into the operation of the parks— concessionaires, for example. Some say that plan will commercialize and ruin the parks.

The critics continue, by design, to ignore facts. The private enterpreneur had been invited into the national parks long before there was a National Park Service. At our major parks, visitors' services, for the most part, have always been provided by concessionaires. And they should be.

The question is: Can government or the private sector provide better eating facilities, sleeping accommodations and campground facilities? I have faith that the private sector can. There are not sufficient taxpayer dollars to meet the growing needs of the parks, and I think we ought to invite the private sector in and let it do the job and do it properly.

The National Park Service, you have said, should get out of the business of managing urban parks. Will local communities be able to finance and manage these parks if the Park Service withdraws?

First, I have not proposed turning any national parks over to city or local government. There is no park "hit list."

I have raised the question, however, of just how far the federal government should go in purchasing and managing parks or playgrounds.

Until relatively recently, local parks and playgrounds were the province of municipal and county governments. Tradition and law required that national parks be areas of significant national interest—places you or I might drive a couple hundred miles to visit.

Now, some mayors, some congressmen think the federal government should also pick up the tab for parks that have, at best, questionable national significance. If the people in New York City don't want to pay for their local parks, why should the people of Denver have to foot the bill—or vice versa? This debate has been going on for decades in the National Park Service. I just laid the issue on the table so there could be some frank discussion. I have not set any time frame.

Getting back to the land's resources, it has been charged that you are being shortsighted, that your policies risk spoiling our environment.

Every decision I have made has been, I feel, for the long-term benefit of the environment. I've been concerned for a long time that we do not properly manage our public lands, and that includes our energy resources—in the West, particularly. The West has 90 percent of the nation's uranium, 80 percent of its coal and so on. It can become the most energy-productive area of the world, bar none; oil shale, coal, uranium, oil and gas. There's enough energy there to meet America's needs for thousands of years.

Enough to solve the energy crisis?

We do not have an energy crisis; we

have a crisis in government management. If we do not allow the private marketplace to go in and develop those energy sources in a systematic, methodical and environmentally sensitive way, we will create such a political and economic crisis in America that Washington will nationalize the industries and attack our energy-rich West in such a manner as to destroy the ecology, primarily because it will decide it must get to that energy to heat the homes of the Northeast and keep the wheels of industry going in the Midwest.

And that we cannot afford.

So to protect the environment, we must develop our energy in an orderly and environmentally sensitive way. We have not done that in recent years. In fact, to the contrary, we have prohibited it. That's one of the things I have changed.

For a nation to be great, it must manage properly both its human resources and its natural resources. America is blessed with both—an abundance of talented human resources and an abundance of natural resources.

If we will manage these resources for the benefit of America, we can be a great, great nation.

Would you spell out your views on offshore oil drilling in general and the controversial leasing of drilling sites off Northern California in particular?

One of our important and thus far underdeveloped energy resources lies under our territorial waters. We have explored only a small percentage of the outer continental shelf under federal jurisdiction. The OCS is not the only solution to our energy crisis, but it is an extremely important element.

The state of California has allowed the drilling of 3,000 wells in state wa-

ters, and the federal government has already permitted the drilling of more than 500 wells on the OCS off California. So what we are talking about is simply extending a program already in operation. However, we have decided to defer possible offshore Northern California leasing pending the outcome of our appeal of a recent federal court decision.

U.S. offshore drilling has an outstanding environmental record. We are convinced that OCS development, on balance, is far less risky for the environment than the alternatives. A great deal of study, thought and care has gone into the decison-making process for all OCS decisions.

You have announced that the department intends to lease 1 billion acres over the next five years. How can the oil and gas companies, which are already drilling at a high rate, explore that many acres?

Industry isn't going to rush out and explore a billion acres in the next five years—they know that and I know that. What we are offering is a chance for industry to go after gas and oil in areas where industry believes gas and oil to be. Some companies have quibbled with my proposal, but the industry as a whole supports it. I think the oil industry will meet this challenge. The only way we as a nation can lose is by offering too little, not too much.

Many statements that have raised the hackles of environmentalists have been attributed to James Watt. Are the media reporting accurately?

I am surprised that the media can be manipulated repeatedly by narrow special-interest groups. Most of what has been attributed to me was made up by a critic and then repeated by the press.

Now, I have found a great dichotomy between the reporters and the editorial writers. The reporters frequently call to check out something to see whether there is some truth to it. But it seems that a search for truth doesn't slow up editorial writers much.

A recent National Wildlife Federation survey measured members' opinions of your environmental priorities. The results were used to support calls for your resignation. Yet to one question, 44 percent of the respondents answered that they didn't know enough about your policies to make a judgment. What did you think of the survey?

I looked at one of the questions, and it gave me four alternative answers. Answer A was so reasonable and well written and understandable that, of course, I selected it. The other three answers were really off the wall. It turned out 95 percent of the respondents also picked choice A.

Choice B was the answer they had attributed to me, which was ridiculous and totally unfair. By voting the way I did on that one question, I was voting, I learned, to force the resignation of Jim Watt as Secretary of the Interior.

If the rest of the poll was similar to what I saw in that one question I answered, it was so rigged and unfair that it wasn't worth studying. I dismissed it entirely.

Have you solicited views from the environmentalists' side? Do you ever invite them to your regular breakfast sessions?

Yes, they've all been in—and as they left, they called news conferences to denounce us.

Politics is often called a game of compromise. You've been accused of not compromising on issues, of following the letter of the law. Are you inflexible?

We've seen parks deteriorating, we've seen the grazing lands threatened, we've seen our economy suffer double-digit inflation, we've seen economic development brought to a halt by poor decisions coming out of the Department of the Interior.

When I came here, the pendulum was swinging way out in left field. I've got to bring it into the middle, into mainline America.

And so I am being tough—and I am not compromising with those who seek to block economic activity. I am going to bring about a commonsense approach, which is incorporated into the law, to see that these resources are managed for the benefit of all Americans, not just for the select few.

A black, a woman, two Jews and a cripple.
> JAMES WATT, flippant description of the balance
> reflected in a coal-leasing advisory panel he
> had appointed; the remark, widely reported, led
> to his resignation on October 9, 1983

58.

The Environmental Super-Fund: Moynihan vs. Gorsuch

Anne M. Gorsuch (later Anne Burford) was named by President Reagan the new head of the Environmental Protection Agency (EPA) in early 1981. Mrs. Gorsuch tangled with liberal members of Congress during her confirmation hearings and frequently thereafter, owing to her obvious reluctance to spend moneys provided by Congress for the protection of the environment, and particularly for cleaning up toxic wastes. Mrs. Gorsuch claimed that she was under severe pressure from the President to save funds even if they had been appropriated. The dispute came to a head in a hearing before the Committee on Environment and Public Works of the Senate on October 15, 1981. The text of an extremely spirited interchange between Sen. Daniel Patrick Moynihan, D-New York, and Mrs. Gorsuch is reprinted here. The other speakers are Sen. Robert T. Stafford, R-Vermont, chairman, and Sen. Alan K. Simpson, R-Wyoming.

Source: U.S. Government Printing Office, 1982.

SENATOR STAFFORD. Thank you very much, Senator Hart.

The Chair would like to go ahead and finish the hearings this morning for everybody's sake. Senator Moynihan has had no time yet and would be recognized next. The Chair has already reserved the right to members to submit questions in writing. The Chair has a few more questions to ask on a second round.

Senator Mitchell, do you have further questions?

SENATOR MITCHELL. Well, I did, but I don't want to prolong this.

SENATOR STAFFORD. We will keep it going.

SENATOR MITCHELL. I could submit them in writing.

SENATOR STAFFORD. In that event, Senator Moynihan, the floor is yours.

SENATOR MOYNIHAN. Thank you, Mr. Chairman.

I will confine myself to one topic in order to move along, and we can submit some other questions in writing.

I would like to raise the question of the superfund, which this committee was responsible for creating a year ago, for the elimination of toxic wastes. It is a fund that is provided by a tax on chemicals, a certain list of chemicals. As they are produced, producers pay a tax into this fund. And it was the chairman of our committee who most particularly took the initative and made possible this legislation during the postelection session last year.

And we regard, I think this committee would regard, these as dedicated moneys. There is a special tax for the purpose of cleaning up toxic wastes. And the initiative is especially important to me because the event that led to this fund was the Love Canal discovery in Niagara County. That was sort of the catalyzing event that made us realize we have toxic waste dumps all over the country. We find them and find out who is responsible and go through 5 years of lawsuits. Our proposition is clean them up first and have the lawsuits later.

We think of these as dedicated moneys just as we do the highway trust fund. Yet, we find the administration not evidently intending to spend these moneys at all. President Carter proposed a $250 million budget. Reagan then came in with a $200 million budget and now a $176 million budget. What we see is 140-percent reduction from President Carter's proposals, and in point of fact a proposal to spend in fiscal 1982, $176 million, when the revenues will be $397 million. What some of us feel is what we are seeing here is what was attempted unsuccessfully in social security, which is steal the money from funds dedicated to one purpose for the simple purpose of offsetting a budget deficit elsewhere.

I would like to ask you do you think it is right, when the superfund which will produce almost $400 million this year for cleaning up toxic wastes, that you propose to spend less than half that, or have you a different view?

MRS. GORSUCH. Well, Senator, let me share with you my understanding of the superfund. It is indeed dedicated money raised from a special tax for a specific purpose. We clearly understand that. Our administration considers the implementation of superfund certainly among its most significant priorities. We are fully aware also that the moneys appropriated by Congress for this purpose will not remediate every hazardous waste site throughout the country. It was never the congressional intent. It was to address those priority sites that

posed the greatest hazard to the health and welfare of the people of this country. We have a strong commitment to fulfilling that congressional intent and feel there is a proper purpose of the Federal Government interfering in this time and using the funds that have been earmarked for this purpose.

As you probably are aware, in addressing the cleanup of any hazardous waste site, and they do differ in characteristics one from another, the first step will be in terms of planning, second in terms of design, and third in terms of real construction or cleanup work. And I think it makes sense we will see in the initial years, the lesser flow of actual moneys which are in the planning and design functions, and in later years the larger flow of money where actual construction costs begin to be part of the overall program. That is just an overview.

SENATOR MOYNIHAN. Has the Office of Management and Budget told you how much money you can spend from the supurfund this year?

MRS. GORSUCH. This year, no.

SENATOR MOYNIHAN. Are you free to spend as much as you like?

MRS. GORSUCH. I am certainly free to spend as much as I like.

SENATOR MOYNIHAN. How much do you intend to spend?

MRS. GORSUCH. That, Senator, I would have to refer to the people who advise me in terms of specific dollars.

SENATOR MOYNIHAN. You mean somebody else decides?

MRS. GORSUCH. No, Senator. I would hope you respect I don't carry these figures in detail in my mind.

Sen. Daniel Patrick Moynihan

Anne M. Gorsuch

SENATOR MOYNIHAN. Let me say the fund is limited to revenues of roughly $397 million. Do you expect to spend $397 million?

MRS. GORSUCH. No, we don't.

SENATOR MOYNIHAN. Do you expect to spend $396 million, $395, $394? I mean do you know what you are talking about?

MRS. GORSUCH. $200 million has been appropriated by Congress.

SENATOR MOYNIHAN. It is proposed this be reduced further. Do you mean to go along with that proposal? I told you the first budget request of the President was $200 million. It is now $176 million. Is that your idea of what should be spent?

[No response.]

SENATOR MOYNIHAN. Has this subject come to your attention, that there is a superfund?

MRS. GORSUCH. Senator, I appreciate your good wit.

$200 million was appropriated by Congress. If the President's proposals are enacted by Congress, it would be affected.

SENATOR MOYNIHAN. And that is satisfactory to you?

MRS. GORSUCH. In terms of our proper implementation of that law, yes, I think we can conform with the desires of Congress to meet the planning, design.

SENATOR MOYNIHAN. You find this new proposal of a reduction satisfactory, and do you support it?

MRS. GORSUCH. Yes I do.

SENATOR MOYNIHAN. Let me say I have been in the subcabinet of four previous Presidents, and one of the things you learn is there comes a time when things are being done to your program which require you to resign. Is there any point at which the toxic waste program would be so reduced as a budgetary matter that you would, in fact, resign?

MRS. GORSUCH. Senator, I think it is highly unprofitable to engage in that kind of speculation.

SENATOR MOYNIHAN. You mean nothing would make you resign?

MRS. GORSUCH. I think the President's proposal is to make a reduction in the budget of 12 percent. I think although the proposal is to do that account by account, there are ways we will be discussing with the Appropriations Committee which can tailor the reductions more adequately to our needs.

SENATOR MOYNIHAN. Will you have the kindness to understand that it is this committee that passed that legislation and dedicated those revenues, and we expect you to speak to the matter with us. Now we are serious. We are not going to let money be stolen from this to offset something the President's people have created all on their own, and we do not expect the Administrator will allow this to happen. There are more important things than getting through the next 12 months or so. You will have to live with the reputation you leave behind. And there are things on which it is not worth staying. And I have to tell you it is the impression of many members of this committee that you are getting close to the point where other persons who have preceded you would have resigned. I am not asking you to do so, but I am asking you to know in the life of an honorable public servant there comes that time, and I haven't the doubt in my mind, and when it comes

you will recognize and you will give it thought.

MRS. GORSUCH. Senator, I appreciate your confidence in my honor and integrity.

Getting back to the substance of your question of implementing superfund, we have every intention of using those moneys that are appropriated by this Congress for that purpose in addressing the most hazardous waste sites that we can identify on a national basis.

SENATOR MOYNIHAN. I would like to remind you that those amounts are continually being reduced at the behest of the administration, and when they do so it is assumed they do it with your approval. And if you do approve, it seems to me you have more to explain to this committee than you have done. And if you don't approve, I think you ought to consider resigning.

MRS. GORSUCH. I appreciate your advice.

SENATOR MOYNIHAN. Thank you, Mr. Chairman.

SENATOR STAFFORD. Thank you, Senator Moynihan.
Senator Simpson.

SENATOR SIMPSON. Welcome to the pit. It is a spirited group.

MRS. GORSUCH. Yes, sir, it is indeed.

SENATOR SIMPSON. When I was a member of the minority, I was always asking people to resign. And when the time comes, as my good colleague from New York says, the time to resign, I hope you will not recognize it.

So, enough of that. Pat will catch me later and discuss this with me.

59.

WILLIAM GREIDER: The Education of David Stockman

A story in The New York Times *for November 11, 1981, discussed what the "Reagan people" were said to feel was a need for "a show of confidence and unity" in order to maintain the administration's political momentum. On the same day copies of the December issue of* The Atlantic *hit the newsstands. The issue contained the famous article, "The Education of David Stockman," by William Greider, that is reprinted in part below. Stockman, a young, brilliant, and ambitious Congressman from Michigan, had been named director of the Office of Management and Budget (OMB) by Reagan in December 1980. Stockman's success in manipulating the President's Cabinet and the heads of important Senate and House committees to carry through Congress the administration's budget-cutting bills was considered by veteran Washington hands as almost miraculous. But Greider's revealing article showed that Stockman, in the course of a year in power, had come to have serious doubts about the validity of Reaganomics. He was particularly concerned whether it was really possible, as the President had claimed, to accomplish the task that John Anderson had said could not be accomplished: namely, to raise defense spending, lower taxes, and balance the budget all at the same time. By the end of the year Stockman was aware that America faced massive increases in the federal deficit rather than a balanced budget, and he said so to Greider. After the article appeared Stockman was severely reprimanded by the President but retained as head of the OMB, a position he held until 1985. He was right about the deficits, of course; they grew even larger in the ensuing years than anyone in the administration could foresee in 1981.*

Source: *The Atlantic,* December 1981.

THREE WEEKS before the inauguration, Stockman and his transition team of a dozen or so people were already established at the OMB office in the Old Executive Office Building. When his appointment as budget director first seemed likely, he had agreed to meet with me from time to time and relate, off the record, his private account of the great political struggle ahead. The particulars of these conversations were not to be reported until later, after the season's battles were over, but a cynic familiar with how Washington works would understand that the arrangement had obvious symbiotic value. As an assistant managing editor at *The Washington Post,* I benefited from an informed view of policy discussions of the new administration; Stockman, a student of history, was contributing to history's record and perhaps influencing its conclusions. For him, our meetings were another channel—among many he used—to the press. The older generation of orthodox Republicans distrusted the press; Stockman was one of the younger "new" conservatives who cultivated contacts with columnists and reporters, who saw the news media as another useful tool in political combat. "We believe our ideas have intellectual respectability, and we think the press will recognize that," he said. "The traditional Republicans probably sensed, even if they didn't know it, that their ideas lacked intellectual respectability."

In any case, for the eight months that followed, Stockman kept the agreement, and our regular conversations, over breakfast at the Hay-Adams, provided the basis of the account that follows.

In early January, Stockman and his staff were assembling dozens of position papers on program reductions and studying the internal forecasts for the federal budget and the national economy. The initial figures were frightening—"absolutely shocking," he confided—yet he seemed oddly exhilarated by the bad news, and was bubbling with new plans for coping with these horrendous numbers. An OMB computer, programmed as a model of the nation's economic behavior, was instructed to estimate the impact of Reagan's program on the federal budget. It predicted that if the new President went ahead with his promised three-year tax reduction and his increase in defense spending, the Reagan Administration would be faced with a series of federal deficits without precedent in peacetime—ranging from $82 billion in 1982 to $116 billion in 1984. Even Stockman blinked. If those were the numbers included in President Reagan's first budget message, the following month, the financial markets that Stockman sought to reassure would

instead be panicked. Interest rates, already high, would go higher; the expectation of long-term inflation would be confirmed.

Stockman saw opportunity in these shocking projections. "All the conventional estimates just wind up as mud," he said. "As absurdities. What they basically say, to boil it down, is that the world doesn't work."

Stockman set about doing two things. First, he changed the OMB computer. Assisted by like-minded supply-side economists, the new team discarded orthodox premises of how the economy would behave. Instead of a continuing double-digit inflation, the new computer model assumed a swift decline in prices and interest rates. Instead of the continuing pattern of slow economic growth, the new model was based on a dramatic surge in the nation's productivity. New investment, new jobs, and growing profits—and Stockman's historic bull market. "It's based on valid economic analysis," he said, "but it's the inverse of the last four years. When we go public, this is going to set off a wide-open debate on how the economy works, a great battle over the conventional theories of economic performance."

The original apostles of supply-side, particularly Representative Jack Kemp, of New York, and the economist Arthur B. Laffer, dismissed budget-cutting as inconsequential to the economic problems, but Stockman was trying to fuse new theory and old. "Laffer sold us a bill of goods," he said, then corrected his words: "Laffer wasn't wrong—he didn't go far enough."

The great debate never quite took hold in the dimensions that Stockman had anticipated, but the Reagan Administration's economic projections did become the source of continuing controversy. In defense of their counter-theories, Stockman and his associates would argue, correctly, that conventional forecasts, particularly by the Council of Economic Advisers in the preceding administration, had been consistently wrong in the past. His critics would contend that the supply-side premises were based upon wishful thinking, not sound economic analysis.

But, second, Stockman used the appalling deficit projections as a valuable talking point in the policy discussions that were under way with the President and his principal advisers. Nobody in that group was the least bit hesitant about cutting federal programs, but Reagan had campaigned on the vague and painless theme that eliminating "waste, fraud, and mismanagement" would be sufficient to balance the accounts. Now, as Stockman put it, "the idea is to try to get beyond the waste, fraud, and mismanagement modality and begin to confront the real dimensions of budget reduction." On the first Wednesday in January, Stockman had two hours on the President-elect's schedule to describe the "dire shape" of the federal budget; for starters, the new administration would have to go for a budget reduction in the neighborhood of $40 billion. "Do you have any idea what $40 billion means?" he said. "It means I've got to cut the highway program. It means I've got to cut milk-price supports. And Social Security student benefits. And education and student loans. And manpower training and housing. It means I've got to shut down the synfuels program and a lot of other programs. The idea is to show the magnitude of the budget deficit and some suggestion of the political problems."

How much pain was the new President willing to impose? How many sa-

cred cows would he challenge at once? Stockman was still feeling out the commitment at the White House, aware that Reagan's philosophical commitment to shrinking the federal government would be weighed against political risks.

Stockman was impressed by the ease with which the President-elect accepted the broad objective: find $40 billion in cuts in a federal budget running well beyond $700 billion. But, despite the multitude of expenditures, the proliferation of programs and grants, Stockman knew the exercise was not as easy as it might sound.

Consider the budget in simple terms, as a federal dollar representing the entire $700 billion. The most important function of the federal government is mailing checks to citizens—Social Security checks to the elderly, pension checks to retired soldiers and civil servants, reimbursement checks for hospitals and doctors who provide medical care for the aged and the poor, welfare checks for the dependent, veterans' checks to pensioners. Such disbursements consume forty-eight cents of the dollar.

Another twenty-five cents goes to the Pentagon, for national defense. Stockman knew that this share would be rising in the next four years, not shrinking, perhaps becoming as high as thirty cents. Another ten cents was consumed by interest payments on the national debt, which was fast approaching a trillion dollars.

That left seventeen cents for everything else that Washington does. The FBI and the national parks, the county agents and the Foreign Service and the Weather Bureau—all the traditional operations of government—consumed only nine cents of the dollar. The remaining eight cents provided all of the grants to state and local governments, for aiding handicapped children or building highways or installing tennis courts next to Al Stockman's farm. One might denounce particular programs as wasteful, as unnecessary and ineffective, even crazy, but David Stockman knew that he could not escape these basic dimensions of federal spending.

As he and his staff went looking for the $40 billion, they found that most of it would have to be taken from the seventeen cents that covered government operations and grants-in-aid. Defense was already off-limits. Next Ronald Reagan laid down another condition for the budget-cutting: the main benefit programs of Social Security, Medicare, veterans' checks, railroad retirement pensions, welfare for the disabled—the so-called "social safety net" that Reagan had promised not to touch—were to be exempt from the budget cuts. In effect, he was declaring that Stockman could not tamper with three fourths of the forty-eight cents devoted to transfer payments.

No President had balanced the budget in the past twelve years. Still, Stockman thought it could be done, by 1984, if the Reagan Administration adhered to the principle of equity, cutting weak claims, not merely weak clients, and if it shocked the system sufficiently to create a new political climate. He still believed that it was not a question of numbers. "It boils down to a political question, not of budget policy or economic policy, but whether we can change the habits of the political system."

The struggle began in private with Ronald Reagan's Cabinet. By inaugural week, Stockman's staff had assembled fifty or sixty policy papers outlining major cuts and alterations, and, aiming at the target of $40 billion, Stockman was anxious to win fast approval for them, before the new Cabinet officers were fully familiar with their departments and prepared to defend their bureaucracies. During that first week, the new Cabinet members had to sit through David Stockman's recital—one proposal after another outlining drastic reductions in their programs. Brief discussion was followed by presidential approval. "I have a little nervousness about the heavy-handedness with which I am being forced to act," Stockman conceded. "It's not that I wouldn't want to give the decision papers to the Cabinet members ahead of time so they could look at them, it's just that we're getting them done at eight o'clock in the morning and rushing them to the Cabinet room. . . . It doesn't work when you have to brace these Cabinet officers in front of the President with severe reductions in their agencies, because then they're in the position of having to argue against the group line. And the group line is cut, cut, cut. So that's a very awkward position for them, and you make them resentful very fast."

Stockman proposed to White House counselor Edwin Meese an alternative approach—a budget working group, in which each Cabinet secretary could review the proposed cuts and argue against them. As the group evolved, however, with Meese, chief of staff James Baker, Treasury Secretary Donald Regan, and policy director Martin Anderson, among others, it was stacked in Stockman's favor. "Each meeting will involve only the relevant Cabinet member and his aides with four or five strong keepers of the central agenda," Stockman explained at one point. "So on Monday, when we go into the decision on synfuels programs, it will be [Energy Secretary James B.] Edwards defending them against six guys saying that, by God, we've got to cut these back or we're not going to have a savings program that will add up.''

In general, the system worked. Stockman's agency did in a few weeks what normally consumes months; the process was made easier because the normal opposition forces had no time to marshal either their arguments or their constituents and because the President was fully in tune with Stockman. After the budget working group reached a decision, it would be taken to Reagan in the form of a memorandum, on which he could register his approval by checking a little box. "Once he checks it," Stockman said, "I put that in my safe and I go ahead and I don't let it come back up again."

The check marks were given to changes in twelve major budget entitlements and scores of smaller ones. Eliminate Social Security minimum benefits. Cap the runaway costs of Medicaid. Tighten eligibility for food stamps. Merge the trade adjustment assistance for unemployed industrial workers with standard unemployment compensation and shrink it. Cut education aid by a quarter. Cut grants for the arts and humanities in half. "Zero out" CETA and the Community Services Administration and National Consumer Cooperative Bank. And so forth. "Zero out" became a favorite phrase of Stockman's; it meant closing down a program "cold turkey," in one budget year. Stockman believed that any compromise on a program that ought to be eliminated—funding that would phase it out over several years—was merely a political ruse to keep it alive, so it might still be in existence a few years hence, when a new political climate could allow its restoration to full funding.

"I just wish that there were more hours in the day or that we didn't have to do this so fast. I have these stacks of briefing books and I've got to make decisions about specific options. . . . I don't have time, trying to put this whole package together in three weeks, so you just start making snap judgments." . . .

The only Cabinet officer Stockman did not challenge was, of course, the Secretary of Defense. In the frantic preparation of the Reagan budget message, delivered in broad outline to Congress on February 18, the OMB review officers did not give even their usual scrutiny to the new budget projections from Defense. Reagan had promised to increase military spending by 7 percent a year, adjusted for inflation, and this pledge translated into the biggest peacetime arms build-up in the history of the republic—$1.6 trillion over the next five years, which would more than double the Pentagon's annual budget while domestic spending was shrinking. Stockman acknowledged that OMB had taken only a cursory glance at the new defense budget, but he was confident that later on, when things settled down a bit, he could go back and analyze it more carefully.

In late February, months before the defense budget became a subject of Cabinet debate, Stockman privately predicted that Defense Secretary Caspar Weinberger, himself a budget director during the Nixon years, would be an ally when he got around to cutting back military spending. "As soon as we get past this first phase in the process, I'm really going to go after the Pentagon. The whole question is blatant inefficiency, poor deployment of manpower, contracting idiocy, and, hell, I think that Cap's going to be a pretty good mark over there. He's not a tool of the military-industrial complex. I mean, he hasn't been steeped in its excuses and rationalizations and ideology for twenty years, and I think that he'll back off on a lot of this stuff, but you just can't challenge him head-on without your facts in line. And we're going to get our case in line and just force it through the presses."

Stockman shared the general view of the Reagan Administration that the United States needed a major build-up of its armed forces. But he also recognized that the Pentagon, as sole customer for weapons systems, subsidized the arms manufacturers in many direct ways and violated many free-market principles. "The defense budgets in the out-years won't be nearly as high as we are showing now, in my judgment. Hell, I think there's a kind of swamp of $10 to $20 to $30 billion worth of waste that can be ferreted out if you really push hard."

Long before President Reagan's speech to Congress, most of the painful details of the $41.4 billion in proposed reductions were already known to Capitol Hill and the public. In early February, preparing the political ground, Stockman started delivering his "black book" to Republican leaders and committee chairmen. He knew that once the information was circulating on the Hill, it would soon be available to the news media, and he was not at all upset by the daily storm of headlines revealing the dimensions of what lay ahead. The news conveyed, in its drama and quantity of detail, the appropriate political message: President Reagan would not be proposing business as usual. The President had in mind what Stockman saw as "fiscal revolution."

But it was not generally understood that the new budget director had already lost a major component of his revolution—another set of proposals, which he called "Chapter II," that was not sent to Capitol Hill because the President had vetoed its most controversial elements.

Stockman had thought "Chapter II" would help him on two fronts: it would provide substantially increased revenues and thus help reduce the huge deficits of the next three years; but it would also mollify liberal critics complaining about the cuts in social welfare, because it was aimed primarily at tax expenditures (popularly known as "loopholes") benefiting oil and other business interests. "We have a gap which we couldn't fill even with all these budget cuts, too big a deficit," Stockman explained. "Chapter II comes out totally on the opposite of the equity question. That was part of my strategy to force acquiescence at the last minute into a lot of things you'd never see a Republican administration propose. I had a meeting this morning at the White House. The President wasn't involved, but all the other key senior people were. We brought a program of additional tax savings that don't touch any social progams. But they touch tax expenditures." Stockman hesitated to discuss details, for the package was politically sensitive, but it included elimination of the oil-depletion allowance; an attack on tax-exempt industrial-development bonds; user fees for owners of private airplanes and barges; a potential ceiling on home-mortgage deductions; and other items, ten in all. Total additional savings; somewhere in the neighborhood of $20 billion. Stockman was proud of "Chapter II" and also very nervous about it, because, while liberal Democrats might applaud the closing of "loopholes" that they had attacked for years, powerful lobbies—in Congress and business—would mobilize against it.

Did President Reagan approve? "If there's consensus on it, he's not going to buck it, probably."

Two weeks later, Stockman cheerfully explained that the President had rejected his "tax-expenditures" savings. The "Chapter II" issues had seemed crucial to Stockman when he was preparing them, but he dismissed them as inconsequential now that he had lost. "Those were more like ornaments I was thinking of on the tax side," he insisted. "I call them equity ornaments. They're not really too good. They're not essential to the economics of the thing."

The President was willing to propose user fees for aircraft, private boats, and barges, but turned down the proposal to eliminate the oil-depletion allowance. "The President has a very clear philosophy," Stockman explained. "A lot of people criticize him for being short on the details, but he knows when something's wrong. He just jumped all over my tax proposals."

Stockman dropped other proposals. Nevertheless, he was buoyant. The reactions from Capitol Hill were clamorous, as expected, but the budget director was more impressed by the silences, the stutter and hesitation of the myriad interest groups. Stockman was becoming a favorite caricature for newspaper cartoonists—the grim reaper of the Reagan Administration, the Republican Robespierre—but in his many sessions on the Hill he sensed confusion and caution on the other side.

"There are more and more guys coming around to our side," he reported. "What's happening is that the plan is so sweeping and it covers all the bases sufficiently, so that it's like a magnifying glass that reveals everybody's pores. . . . In the past, people could easily get votes for their projects or their interests by saying, well, if they would cut food stamps and CETA jobs and two or three other things, then maybe we would go along with it, but they are just picking on my program. But, now, everybody perceives that everybody's sacred cows are being cut. If that's what it takes, so be it. The parochial player will not be the norm, I think. For a while." . . .

In political terms, Stockman's analysis was sound. The Reagan program was moving toward a series of dramatic victories in Congress. Beyond the brilliant tactical maneuvering, however, and concealed by the public victories, Stockman was privately staring at another reality—a gloomy portent that the economic theory behind the President's program wasn't working. While it was winning in the political arena, the plan was losing on Wall Street. The financial markets, which Stockman had thought would be reassured by the new President's bold actions, and which were supposed to launch a historic "bull market" in April, failed to respond in accordance with Stockman's script. The markets not only failed to rally, they went into a new decline. Interest rates started up again; the bond market slumped. The annual inflation rate, it was true, was declining, dropping below double digits, but even Stockman acknowledged that this was owing to "good luck" with grain harvests and world oil supplies, not to Reaganomics. Investment analysts, however, were looking closely at the Stockman budget figures, looking beyond the storm of political debate and the President's winning style, and what they saw were enormous deficits ahead—the same numbers that had

AP/Wide World

David Stockman

shocked David Stockman when he came into office in January. Henry Kaufman, of Salomon Brothers, one of the preeminent prophets of Wall Street, delivered a sobering speech that, in the cautious language of financiers, said the same thing that John Anderson had said in 1980: cutting taxes and pumping up the defense budget would produce not balanced budgets but inflationary deficits.

Was Kaufman right? Stockman agreed that he was, and conceded that his own original conception—that dramatic political action would somehow alter the marketplace expectations of continuing inflation—had been wrong. "They're concerned about the out-year budget posture, not about the near-term economic situation. The Kaufmans don't dispute our diagnosis at all. They dispute our remedy. They don't think it adds up . . . . I take the performance of the bond market deadly seriously. I think it's the best measure there is. The bond markets represent worldwide psychology, worldwide perception and

evaluation of what, on balance, relevant people think about what we're doing . . . It means we're going to have to make changes . . . I wouldn't say we are losing. We're still not winning. We're not winning."

The underlying problem of the deficits first surfaced, to Stockman's embarrassment, in the Senate Budget Committee in mid-April, when committee Republicans choked on the three-year projections supplied by the nonpartisan Congressional Budget Office. Three Republican senators refused to vote for a long-term budget measure that predicted continuing deficits of $60 billion, instead of a balanced budget by 1984.

Stockman thought he had taken care of embarrassing questions about future deficits with a device he referred to as the "magic asterisk." (Senator Howard Baker had dubbed it that in strategy sessions, Stockman said.) The "magic asterisk" would blithely denote all of the future deficit problems that were to be taken care of with additional budget reductions, to be announced by the President at a later date. Thus, everyone could finesse the hard questions, for now.

But, somehow or other, the Senate Budget Committee staff insisted upon putting the honest numbers in its resolution—the projected deficits of $60 billion-plus running through 1984. That left the Republican senators staring directly at the same scary numbers that Stockman and the Wall Street analysts had already seen. The budget director blamed this brief flare-up on the frantic nature of his schedule. When he should have been holding hands with the Senate Budget Committee, he was at the other end of the Capitol, soothing Representative Delbert Latta, of Ohio, the ranking Republican in budget matters, who was pouting. Latta thought that since he was a Republican, his name should go ahead of that of Phil Gramm, a Democrat, on the budget resolution: that it should be Latta-Gramm instead of Gramm-Latta.

After a few days of reassurances, Stockman persuaded the Republican senators to relax about the future and two weeks later they passed the resolution—without being given any concrete answers as to where he would find future cuts of such magnitude. In effect, the "magic asterisk" sufficed.

But the real problem, as Stockman conceded, was still unsolved. Indeed, pondering the reactions of financial markets, the budget director made an extraordinary confession in private: the original agenda of budget reductions, which had seemed so radical in February, was exposed by May as inadequate. The "magic asterisk" might suffice for the political debate in Congress, but it would not answer the fundamental question asked by Wall Street: How, in fact, did Ronald Reagan expect to balance the federal budget? "It's a tentative judgment on the part of the markets and of spokesmen like Kaufman that is reversible because they haven't seen all our cards. From the cards they've seen, I suppose that you can see how they draw that conclusion."

"It means," Stockman said, "that you have to have some recalibration in the policy. The thing was put together so fast that it probably should have been put together differently." With mild regret, Stockman looked back at what had gone wrong:

"The defense numbers got out of control and we were doing that whole budget-cutting exercise so frenetically.

In other words, you were juggling details, pushing people, and going from one session to another, trying to cut housing programs here and rural electric there, and we were doing it so fast, we didn't know where we were ending up for sure. . . . In other words, we should have designed those pieces to be more compatible. But the pieces were moving on independent tracks—the tax program, where we were going on spending, and the defense program, which was just a bunch of numbers written on a piece of paper. And it didn't quite mesh. That's what happened. But, you see, for about a month and a half we got away with that because of the novelty of all these budget reductions."

Reagan's policy-makers knew that their plan was wrong, or at least inadequate to its promised effects, but the President went ahead and conveyed the opposite impression to the American public. With the cool sincerity of an experienced television actor, Reagan appeared on network TV to rally the nation in support of the Gramm-Latta resolution, promising a new era of fiscal control and balanced budgets, when Stockman knew they still had not found the solution. This practice of offering the public eloquent reassurances despite privately held doubts was not new, of course. Every contemporary President—starting with Lyndon Johnson, in his attempt to cover up the true cost of the war in Vietnam—had been caught, sooner or later, in contradictions between promises and economic realities. The legacy was a deep popular skepticism about anything a President promised about the economy. Barely four months in office, Ronald Reagan was already adding to the legacy.

Indeed, Stockman began in May to plot what he called the "recalibration" of Reagan policy, which he hoped could be executed discreetly over the coming months to eliminate the out-year deficits for 1983 and 1984 that alarmed Wall Street—without alarming political Washington and losing control in the congressional arena. "It's very tough, because you don't want to end up like Carter, where you put a plan out there and then, a month into it, you visibly and unmistakably change postures. So what you have to do is solve this problem incrementally, without the appearance of reversal, and there are some ways to do that."

Stockman saw three main areas of opportunity for closing the gap: defense, Social Security, and health costs, meaning Medicare and Medicaid. And there was a fourth: the Reagan tax cut; if it could be modified in the course of the congressional negotiations already under way, this would make for additional savings on the revenue side. The public alarm over the deficits was, to some extent, "fortuitous," from Stockman's viewpoint, because the Wall Street message supported the sermon that he was delivering to his fellow policy-makers at the White House: the agonies of budget reduction were only beginning, and, more to the point, the Reagan Administration could not keep its promise of balanced budgets unless it was willing to back away from its promised defense spending, its 10-10-10 tax-cut plan, and the President's pledge to exempt from cutbacks the so-called "safety-net" programs. Stockman would deliver this speech, in different forms, all through the summer ahead, trying to create the leverage for action on those fronts, particularly on defense. He later explained his strategy:

"I put together a list of twenty social programs that have to be zeroed out completely, like Job Corps, Head Start, women and children's feeding programs, on and on. And another twenty-five that have to be cut by 50 percent: general revenue sharing, CETA manpower training, etc. And then huge bites that would have to be taken out of Social Security. I mean really fierce blood-and-guts stuff—widows' benefits and orphans' benefits, things like that. And still it didn't add up to $40 billion. So that sort of created a new awareness of the defense budget. . . .

"Once you set aside defense and Social Security, the Medicare complex, and a few other sacred cows of minor dimensions, like the VA and the FBI, you have less than $200 billion worth of discretionary room—only $144 billion after you cut all the easy discretionary programs this year."

In short, the fundamental arithmetic of the federal budget, which Stockman and others had brushed aside in the heady days of January, was now back to haunt them. If the new administration would not cut defense or Social Security or major "safety-net" programs that Reagan had put off limits, then it must savage the smaller slice remaining. Otherwise, balancing the budget in 1984 became an empty promise. The political pain of taking virtually all of the budget savings from government grants and operations would be too great, Stockman believed; Congress would never stand for it. Therefore, he had to begin educating "the West Wing guys" on the necessity for major revisions in their basic plan. He was surprisingly optimistic. "They are now understanding all those things," Stockman said. "A month ago, they didn't. They really thought you could find $144 billion worth of waste, fraud, and abuse. So at least I've made a lot of headway internally."

Revisions of the original tax-cut plan would probably be the easiest compromise. A modest delay in the effective date would save billions and, besides, many conservatives in Congress were never enthusiastic about the supply-side tax-cutting formula. In order to win its passage, the administration was "prepared to give a little bit on the tax bill," Stockman said, which would help cure his problem of deficits.

Social Security was much more volatile, but Stockman noted that the Senate had already expressed a willingness in test votes to reconsider such basic components as annual cost-of-living increases for retirees. In the House, the Democrats, led by J.J. Pickle, of Texas, were preparing their own set of reforms to keep the system from bankruptcy, so Stockman thought it would be possible to develop a consensus for real changes. He didn't much care for Pickle's proposals, because the impact of the reforms stretched out over some years, whereas Stockman was looking for immediate relief. "I'm just not going to spend a lot of political capital solving some other guy's problem in 2010." But he felt sure a compromise could be worked out. "If you don't do this in 1981, this system is going to land on the rocks," he predicted, "Because you won't do it in '82 [a congressional election year] and by '83, you will have solvency problems coming out of your ears. You know, sometimes sheer reality has a sobering effect."

Finally, there was defense. Stockman thought the sobering effects of reality were working in his favor there, too, but he recognized that the political tactics were much trickier. In order to get the first round of budget cuts through Congress, particularly in order to lure the southern Democrats to the President's side, there must be no hint of retreat from Reagan's promises for the Pentagon. That would mobilize the defense lobby against him and help the Democrats hold control of the House. Still, when the timing was right, Stockman thought he would prevail.

"They got a blank check," Stockman admitted. "We didn't have time during that February-March period to do anything with defense. Where are we going to cut? Domestic? Or struggle all day and night with defense? So I let it go. But it worked perfectly, because they got so goddamned greedy that they got themselves strung out on a limb."

As policy-makers and politicians faced up to the additional cuts required in programs, the pressure would lead them back, inevitably, to a tough-minded re-examination of the defense side. Or so Stockman believed. That combination of events, he suggested, would complete the circle for Wall Street.

"The markets will respond to that. Unless they are absolutely perverse." . . .

Stockman was wrong, of course, about the bull market. But his misinterpretation of events was more profound than that. Without recognizing it at the time, the budget director was headed into a summer in which not only financial markets but life itself seemed to be absolutely perverse. The Reagan program kept winning in public, a series of well-celebrated political victories in Congress—yet privately Stockman was losing his struggle.

Stockman was changing, in a manner that perhaps he himself did not recognize. His conversations began to reflect a new sense of fatalism, a brittle edge of uncertainty.

"There was a certain dimension of our theory that was unrealistic. . ."

"The system had an enormous amount of inertia. . ."

"I don't believe too much in the momentum theory any more. . ."

"I have a new theory—there are no *real* conservatives in Congress. . ."

The turning point, which Stockman did not grasp at the time, came in May, shortly after the first House victory. Buoyed by the momentum, the White House put forward, with inadequate political soundings, the Stockman plan for Social Security reform. Among other things, it proposed a drastic reduction in the benefits for early retirement at age sixty-two. Stockman thought this was a privilege that older citizens could comfortably yield, but 64 percent of those eligible for Social Security were not taking early retirement, and the "reform" plan set off a sudden tempest on Capitol Hill. Democrats accused Reagan of reneging on his promise to exempt Social Security from the budget cuts and accused Stockman of trying to balance his budget at the expense of Social Security recipients, which, of course, he was. "The Social Security problem is not simply one of satisfying actuaries," Stockman conceded. "It's one of satisfying the here-and-now of budget requirements." In the initial flurry of reaction, the Senate passed a unanimous resolution opposing the OMB version of how to reform Social Security, and across the nation, the elderly were alarmed enough to begin writing and calling their representatives in Congress. But Stockman seemed not to grasp the depth of his political problem; he still believed that congressional reaction would quiet down eventually and Democrats would cooperate with him.

"Three things," he explained. "First, the politicians in the White House are over-reacting. They're overly alarmed. Second, there is a serious political problem with it, but not of insurmountable dimensions. And third, basically I screwed up quite a bit on the way the damn thing was handled."

Stockman said that Republicans on Ways and Means were urging him to propose an administration reform plan as an alternative to the Democrats'; Stockman misjudged the political climate. The White House plan, put together in haste, had "a lot of technical bloopers," which made it even more vulnerable to attack, Stockman said. "I was just racing against the clock. All the office things I knew ought to be done by way of groundwork, advance preparation, and so forth just fell by the wayside. . . . Now we're taking the flak from all the rest of the Republicans because we didn't inform them."

Despite the political uproar, Stockman thought a compromise would eventually emerge, because of the pressure to "save" Social Security. This would give him at least a portion of the budget savings he needed. "I still think we'll recover a good deal of ground from this. It will permit the politicians to make it look like they're doing something *for* the beneficiary population when they are doing something *to* it which they normally wouldn't have the courage to undertake."

But there was less "courage" among politicians than Stockman assumed. Indeed, one politician who scurried away from the President's proposed cuts in Social Security was the President. Stockman wanted him to go on television again, address the nation on Social Security's impending bankruptcy, and build a popular constituency for the changes. But White House advisers did not.

"The President was very interested

[in the reform package] and he believed it was the right thing to do. The problem is that the politicians are so wary of the Social Security issue per se that they want to keep him away from it, thinking they could somehow have an administration initiative that came out of the boondocks somewhere and the President wouldn't be tagged with it. Well, that was just pure naive nonsense. . . . My view was, if you had to play this thing over, you should have the President go on TV and give a twenty-minute Fireside Chat, with some nice charts. . . . You could have created a climate in which major things could be changed."

The White House rejected that idea. Ronald Reagan kept his distance from the controversy, but it would not go away. In September, Reagan did finally address the issue in a televised chat with the nation: he disowned Stockman's reform plan. Reagan said that there was a lot of "misinformation" about in the land, to the effect that the President wanted to cut Social Security. Not true, he declared, though Reagan had proposed such a cut in May. Indeed, the President not only buried the Social Security cuts he had proposed earlier but retreated on one reform measure—elimination of the minimum benefits—that Congress had already, reluctantly, approved. As though he had missed the long debate on that issue, Reagan announced that it was never his intention to deprive anyone who was in genuine need. Any legislative action toward altering Social Security would be postponed until 1983, after the 1982 congressional elections, and too late to help Stockman with his stubborn deficits. In the meantime, Reagan accepted a temporary solution advocated by the Democrats and denounced by Stockman as "irrespon-

sible"—borrowing from another federal trust fund that was in surplus, the health-care fund, to cover Social Security's problems. Everyone put the best face on it, including Stockman. The tactical retreat, they explained, was the only thing Reagan could do under the circumstances—a smart move, given the explosive nature of the Social Security protest. Still, it was a retreat, and, for David Stockman, a fundamental defeat. He lost one major source of potential budget savings. The political outcome did not suggest that he would do much better when he proposed reforms for Medicare, Social Security's twin.

Where would Stockman find the money to cover those deficits, variously estimated at $44 to $65 billion? The tax-cut legislation itself became one of Stockman's best hopes. The tax bargaining had begun in the spring as a delicate process of private negotiations and reassurances with different groups—with Democrats needed for a House majority, with nervous Republicans still leery of the supply-side theology, and with the supply-side apostles zealously defending their creed. Stockman was a participant, though not the lead player, in this process; he met almost daily with the legislative tactical group at the White House—Edwin Meese, Jim Baker, Donald Regan, presidential assistant Richard Darman, and others—that called signals on both the tax legislation and budget reconciliation.

Stockman's interest was made clear to the others: he wanted a compromise on the tax bill which would substantially reduce its drain on the federal treasury and thus moderate the fiscal damage of Reaganomics. Stockman thought that if the Republicans could compromise with the Ways and Means chairman, Representative Dan Rostenkowski, the tax legislation would still be a supply-side tax cut in its approach but considerably smaller in size. More important, they would avoid a bidding war for votes. "We're kind of divided, not in an antagonistic sense, just sort of a judgment sense, between those who want to call off the game . . . and those of us who want to give Rostenkowski a few more days to see what he can achieve."

The negotiations with Rostenkowski ended in failure, and the Reagan team agreed that it would have to modify its own tax-cut plan in order to lure fiscal conservatives. Under the revised plan, the first-year reduction was only 5 percent and, more important, the impact was delayed until late in the year, substantially reducing the revenue loss. The White House also made substantial changes in the business-depreciation and tax-credit rules, which were intended to stimulate new industrial investments, reducing the overly generous provisions for business tax write-offs on new equipment and buildings.

Stockman was privately delighted: he saw a three-year revenue savings of $70 billion in the compromise. The depreciation rules that big business wanted were "way out of joint," Stockman insisted. But he was nervous about the $70 billion figure, because he feared that when Representative Jack Kemp (co-sponsor of the original supply-side tax proposal, the Kemp-Roth bill) and other supply-side advocates heard it, they might regard the savings as so large that it would undermine the stimulative effects of the major tax reduction. "As long as Jack is happy with what's happening," Stockman said, "it's hard for the [supply-side] network to mobilize itself with a shrill voice. Jack's satisfied, although we're sort of on the edge of thin ice with him."

The supply-side effects would still be strong, Stockman said, but he added a significant disclaimer that would have offended true believers, for it sounded like old orthodoxy: "I've never believed that just cutting taxes alone will cause output and employment to expand."

Stockman himself had been a late convert to supply-side theology, and now he was beginning to leave the church. The theory of "expectations" wasn't working. He could see that. And Stockman's institutional role as budget director forced him to look constantly at aspects of the political economy that the other supply-siders tended to dismiss. Whatever the reason, Stockman was creating some distance between himself and the supply-side purists; eventually, he would become the target of their nasty barbs. For his part, Stockman began to disparage the grand theory as a kind of convenient illusion—new rhetoric to cover old Republican doctrine.

"The hard part of the supply-side tax cut is dropping the top rate from 70 to 50 percent—the rest of it is a secondary matter," Stockman explained. "The original argument was that the top bracket was too high, and that's having the most devastating effect on the economy. Then, the general argument was that, in order to make this palatable as a political matter, you had to bring down all the brackets. But, I mean, Kemp-Roth was always a Trojan horse to bring down the top rate."

A Trojan horse? This seemed a cynical concession for Stockman to make in private conversation while the Reagan Administration was still selling the supply-side doctrine to Congress. Yet he was conceding what the liberal Keynesian critics had argued from the outset—the supply side theory was not a new economic theory at all but only new language and argument to conceal a hoary old Republican doctrine: give the tax cuts to the top brackets, the wealthiest individuals and largest enterprises, and let the good effects "trickle down" through the economy to reach everyone else. Yes, Stockman conceded, when one stripped away the new rhetoric emphasizing across-the-board cuts, the supply-side theory was really new clothes for the unpopular doctrine of the old Republican orthodoxy. "It's kind of hard to sell 'trickle down,' " he explained, "so the supply-side formula was the only way to get a tax policy that was really 'trickle down.' Supply-side is 'trickle-down' theory."

But the young budget director once again misjudged the political context. The scaled-down version of the administration's tax bill would need to carry a few "ornaments" in order to win—a special bail-out to help the troubled savings-and-loan industry, elimination of the so-called marriage penalty—but he was confident that the Reagan majority would hold and he could save $70 billion against those out-year deficits. The business lobbyists would object, he conceded, when they saw the new Republican version of depreciation allowances, but the key congressmen were "on board," and the package would hold.

In early June, it fell apart. The tax lobbyists of Washington, when they saw the outlines of the Reagan tax bill, mobilized the business community, the influential economic sectors from oil to real estate. In a matter of days, they created the political environment in which they flourish best—a bidding war between the two parties. First the Democrats revealed that their tax bill would be more generous than Reagan's in its depreciation rules. Despite Stockman's self-confidence, the White House

quickly retreated—scrapped its revised and leaner proposal, and began matching the Democrats, billion for billion, in tax concessions. The final tax legislation would yield, in total, an astounding revenue loss for the federal government of $750 billion over the next five years. . . .

The final reconciliation measure authorized budget reduction of $35.1 billion, about $6 billion less than the President's original proposal, though Stockman and others said the difference would be made up through shrinking "off-budget" programs, which are not included in the appropriations process. The block grants and reductions and caps that Reagan proposed were partially successful—some sixty major programs were consolidated in different block-grant categories—though Stockman lost several important reforms in the final scrambling, among them the cap on the runaway costs of Medicaid, and user fees for federal waterways. The Reagan Administration eliminated dozens of smaller activities and drastically scaled down dozens of others.

In political terms, it was a great victory. Ronald Reagan became the first President since Lyndon Johnson to demonstrate both the tactical skill and the popular strength to stare down the natural institutional opposition of Congress. Moreover, he forced Congress to slog through a series of unique and painful legislative steps— a genuine reconciliation measure—that undermined the parochial baronies of the committee chairmen. Around Washington, even among the critics who despised what he was attempting, there was general agreement that the Reagan Administration would not have succeeded, perhaps would not even have gotten started, without the extraordinary young man who had a plan. He knew what he wanted to attack and he knew Congress well enough to know how to attack.

Yet, in the glow of victory, why was David Stockman so downcast? Another young man, ambitious for his future, might have seized the moment to claim his full share of praise. Stockman did appear on the Sunday talk shows, and was interviewed by the usual columnists. But in private, he was surprisingly modest about his achievement. Two weeks after selling Congress on the biggest package of budget reductions in the history of the republic, Stockman was willing to dismiss the accomplishment as less significant than the participants realized. Why? Because he knew that much more traumatic budget decisions still confronted them. Because he knew that the budget-resolution numbers were an exaggeration. The total of $35 billion was less than it seemed, because the "cuts" were from an imaginary number—hypothetical projections from the Congressional Budget Office on where spending would go if nothing changed in policy or economic activity. Stockman knew that the CBO base was a bit unreal. Therefore, the total of "cuts" was, too. . . .

All in all, Stockman gave a modest summary of what had been wrought by the budget victory: "It has really slowed down the momentum, but it hasn't stopped what you would call the excessive growth of the budget. Because the budget isn't something you reconstruct each year. The budget is a sort of rolling history of decisions. All kinds of decisions, made five, ten, fifteen years ago, are coming back to bite us unexpectedly. Therefore, in my judgment, it will take three or four or five years to

subdue it. Whether anyone can maintain the political momentum to fight the beast for that long, I don't know."

Stockman, the natural optimist, was not especially optimistic. The future of fiscal conservatism, in a political community where there are "no real conservatives," no longer seemed so promising to him. He spoke in an analytical tone, a sober intellect trying to figure things out, and only marginally bitter, as he assessed what had happened to his hopes since January. In July, he was forced to conclude that, despite the appearance of a great triumph, his original agenda was fading, not flourishing.

"I don't believe too much in the momentum theory any more," he said. "I believe in institutional inertia. Two months of response can't beat fifteen years of political infrastructure. I'm talking about K Street and all of the interest groups in this town, the community of interest groups. We sort of stunned it, but it just went underground for the winter. It will be back . . . Can we win? A lot of it depends on events and luck. If we got some bad luck, a flareup in the Middle East, a scandal, it could all fall apart."

Stockman's dour outlook was reinforced two weeks later, when the Reagan coalition prevailed again in the House and Congress passed the tax-cut legislation with a final frenzy of trading and bargaining. Again, Stockman was not exhilarated by the victory. On the contrary, it seemed to leave a bad taste in his mouth, as though the democratic process had finally succeeded in shocking him by its intensity and its greed. Once again, Stockman participated in the trading—special tax concessions for oil-lease holders and real-estate tax shelters, and generous loopholes that virtually eliminated the corporate income tax. Stockman sat in the room and saw it happen.

"Do you realize the greed that came to the forefront?" Stockman asked with wonder. "The hogs were really feeding. The greed level, the level of opportunism, just got out of control." Indeed, when the Republicans and Democrats began their competition for authorship of tax concessions, Stockman saw the "new political climate" dissolve rather rapidly and be replaced by the reflexes of old politics. Every tax lobby in town, from tax credits for wood-burning stoves to new accounting concessions for small business, moved in on the legislation, and pet amendments for obscure tax advantage and profit became the pivotal issues of legislative action, not the grand theories of supply-side tax reduction. "The politics of the bill turned out to be very traditional. The politics put us back in the game, after we started making concessions. The basic strategy was to match or exceed the Democrats, and we did."

But Stockman was buoyant about the political implications of the tax legislation: first, because it put a tightening noose around the size of the government; second, because it gave millions of middle-class voters tangible relief from inflation, even if the stimulative effects on the economy were mild or delayed. Stockman imagined the tax cutting as perhaps the beginning of a large-scale realignment of political loyalties, away from old-line liberalism and toward Reaganism. . . .

When Congress recessed for its August vacation and President Reagan took off for his ranch in the West, David Stockman had a surprising answer to one of his original questions: could he prevail in the political arena, against

the status quo? His original skepticism about Congress was mistaken; the administration had prevailed brilliantly as politicians. And yet, it also seemed that the status quo, in an intangible sense that most politicians would not even recognize, much less worry over, had prevailed over David Stockman.

Generally, he did not lose his temper, but on a pleasant afternoon in early September, Stockman returned from a meeting at the White House in a terrible black mood. In his ornately appointed office at OMB, he slammed his papers down on the desk and waved away associates. At the Oval Office that afternoon, Stockman had lost the great argument he had been carefully preparing since February: there would be no major retrenchment in the defense budget. Over the summer, Stockman had made converts, one by one, in the Cabinet and among the President's senior advisers. But he would not convince the only hawk who mattered—Ronald Reagan. When the President announced that he would reduce the Pentagon budget by only $13 billion over the next three years, it seemed a pitiful sum compared with what he proposed for domestic programs, hardly a scratch on the military complex, which was growing toward $350 billion a year.

"Defense is setting itself up for a big fall," Stockman had predicted. "If they try to roll me and win, they're going to have a huge problem in Congress. The pain level is going to be too high. If the Pentagon isn't careful, they are going to turn it into a priorities debate in an election year."

Two days later, when we met for another breakfast conversation, Stockman had recovered from his anger. The argument over the defense budget, he insisted crankily, was a tempest stirred up by the press. The defense budget was never contemplated as a major target for savings. When Stockman was reminded of his earlier claims and predictions—how he would attack the Pentagon's bloated inefficiencies, assisted by a clear-eyed secretary of defense—he shrugged and smiled thinly. . . .

Stockman was boxed in, and he knew it. Unable to cut defense or Social Security or to modify the overly generous tax legislation, he was forced to turn back to the simple arithmetic of the federal budget—and cut even more from that smaller slice of the federal dollar that pays for government operations and grants and other entitlements. For six months, Stockman had been explaining to "the West Wing guys" that this math wouldn't add. When Reagan proposed his new round of $16 billion in savings, the political outrage confirmed the diagnosis. Stockman was accused of breaking the agreements he had made in June: Senate Republicans who had accepted the "magic asterisk" so docilely were now talking of rebellion—postponing the enormous tax reductions they had just enacted. While the White House promised a war of vetoes ahead, intended to demonstrate "fiscal control," Stockman knew that even if those short-range battles were won, the budget would not be balanced.

Disappointed by events and confronted with potential failure, the Reagan White House was developing a new political strategy: wage war with Congress over the budget issues and, in 1982, blame the Democrats for whatever goes wrong.

The budget director developed a new wryness as he plunged gamely on with these congressional struggles; it was a quality more appealing than certitude. Appearing before the House Budget Committee, Stockman listed a new budget item on his deficit sheet, drolly labeled "Inaction on Social Security." With remarkable directness and no "magic asterisks," he described the outlook: federal deficits of $60 billion in each of the next three years. Some analysts thought his predictions were modest. In the autumn of 1981, despite his great victories in Congress, Ronald Reagan had not as yet produced a plausible answer to John Anderson's question.

Still, things might work out, Stockman said. They might find an answer. The President's popularity might carry them through. The tax cuts would make people happy. The economy might start to respond, eventually, to the stimulation of the tax cuts. "Who knows?" Stockman said. From David Stockman, it was a startling remark. He would continue to invent new scenarios for success, but they would be more complicated and cloudy than his original optimism. "Who knows?" The world was less manageable than he had imagined: this machine had too many crazy moving parts to incorporate in a single lucid theory. The "random elements" of history—politics, the economy, the anarchical budget numbers—were out of control.

Where did things go wrong? Stockman kept asking and answering the right questions. The more he considered it, the more he moved away from the radical vision of reformer, away from the wishful thinking of supply-side economics, and toward the "old-time religion" of conservative economic thinking. Orthodoxy seemed less exciting than radicalism, but perhaps Stockman was only starting into another intellectual transition. He had changed from farm boy to campus activist at Michigan State, from Christian moralist to neo-conservative at Harvard; once again, Stockman was reformulating his ideas on how the world worked. What had he learned?

"The reason we did it wrong—not wrong, but less than the optimum—was that we said, Hey, we have to get a program out fast. And when you decide to put a program of this breadth and depth out fast, you can only do so much. We were working in a twenty or twenty-five-day time frame, and we didn't think it all the way through. We didn't add up all the numbers. We didn't make all the thorough, comprehensive calculations about where we really needed to come out and how much to put on the plate the first time, and so forth. In other words, we ended up with a list that I'd always been carrying of things to be done, rather than starting the other way and asking, What is the overall fiscal policy required to reach the target?"

That regret was beyond remedy now; all Stockman could do was keep trying on different fronts, trying to catch up with the shortcomings of the original Reagan prospectus. But Stockman's new budget-cutting tactics were denounced as panic by his former allies in the supply-side camp. They now realized that Stockman regarded them as "overly optimistic" in predicting a painless boom through across-the-board tax reduction. "Some of the naive supply-siders just missed this whole dimension," he said. "You don't stop inflation without some kind of dislocation. You don't stop the growth of money supply in a three-trillion-dollar economy without some kind of dislocation. . . . Supply-side was the wrong atmospherics—not wrong theory or wrong economics, but wrong at-

mospherics. . . . The supply-siders have gone too far. They created this non-political view of the economy, where you are going to have big changes and abrupt turns, and their happy vision of this world of growth and no inflation with no pain."

The "dislocations" were multiplying across the nation, creating panic among the congressmen and senators who had just enacted this "fiscal revolution." But Stockman now understood that no amount of rhetoric from Washington, not the President's warmth on television nor his own nimble testimony before congressional hearings, would alter the economic forces at work. Tight monetary control should continue, he believed, until the inflationary fevers were sweated out of the economy. People would be hurt. Afterward, after the recession, perhaps the supply-side effects could begin—robust expansion, new investment, new jobs. The question was whether the country or its elected representatives would wait long enough.

His exasperation was evident: "I can't move the system any faster. I can't have an emergency session of Congress to say, Here's a resolution to cut the permanent size of government by 18 percent, vote it up or down. If we did that, it would be all over. But the system works much more slowly. But what can I do about it? Okay? Nothing. So I'm not going to navel-gaze about it too long."

Still trying, still energetic, but no longer abundantly optimistic, Stockman knew that congressional anxieties over the next election were already stronger, making each new proposal more difficult. "The 1982 election cycle will tell us all we need to knew about whether the democratic society wants fiscal control in the federal government," Stockman said grimly.

The alternative still energized him. If they failed, if inflation and economic disorder continued, the conservative reformers would be swept aside by popular unrest. The nation would turn back toward "statist" solutions, controls devised and administered from Washington. Stockman shrugged at that possibility.

"Whenever there are great strains or changes in the economic system," he explained, "it tends to generate crackpot theories, which then find their way into the legislative channels."

The whole episode of Dave Stockman's humiliation speaks to the fairyland mentality and rhetoric that surround serious political discussion of the economy. Stockman's sin was to admit that he no longer believes in fairy tales. It would not have been a sin if the nation's major political leaders— including the President and the most prominent Members of Congress— were not themselves such peddlers of economic fantasies.
    ROBERT J. SAMUELSON, *National Journal,* November 21, 1981

David Stockman has faded from the headlines, but what remains is that he has given the coup de grace to the politics of instant economic gratification.
    ASHBY BLADEN, *Forbes,* December 21, 1981

The "Education of David Stockman" is not just the story of an ambitious and complicated young man learning more about himself and politics, but an education for us all.
    BRUCE MAZLISH, *The New Republic,* December 23, 1981

VIOLENCE, DRUGS, AND CRIME

Youth gangs have been a regrettable feature of American cities since at least the early 19th century. It was perhaps natural that gangs would develop among enclaves of urban immigrant populations. America was conceived of as the land of opportunity, and many uneducated youths took their opportunities where they found them. Gangs also gave security in numbers, as neighborhood thugs marked off their turf. From the early 1800s until well into the 20th century New York City had its Irish, Jewish, and Italian gangs—all members of ethnic groups that were beginning their climb toward acceptance and prosperity. These facts held true for the late 20th century as well, and for the same reasons. New waves of immigrants—many of them illegal aliens—found their way into American cities from Mexico and Central America, the Caribbean islands, and Asia. Among them were young people with few skills and seemingly little interest in schooling. In addition to these were millions of young black people for whom the promise of America had not meant much. Faced with high unemployment, a poor education, and few personal prospects, they turned to violence and crime. They were tempted to attain the same affluence they saw all around them and on television. The newer gangs of black, Hispanic, and Asian youths may well have been far more violent than previous ones. And many of them, in addition to more traditional forms of criminal endeavor, found drug dealing to be a major source of income. Drug dealing meant, for many gangs, organizing themselves as businesses. They often had intercity, and even international, connections. Most of the drugs were brought into the United States from elsewhere—mainly Latin America—and the chief port of entry was southern Florida.

Photos by AP/Wide World

In the 1980s there was heightened awareness of the dangers of drug and alcohol abuse. Concerns over the growing use of illegal "recreational" drugs and the high number of crimes that involved drugs led the federal government to declare a "war on drugs." One of the most popular and troubling drugs of the period was cocaine, which is known to be highly addictive. A smokable version of cocaine known as "crack" was cheap, easy to take, and soon creating addicts across the nation. The profitability of selling crack also led to increased street violence as rival gangs sought to control local markets for the drug. Alcohol abuse was also put under greater scrutiny as groups such as Mothers Against Drunk Driving (MADD) pushed for stiffer punishments of those who drove while intoxicated as well as those who served alcohol to minors. In 1984 a new federal minimum drinking age (21) was established.

(Top) Vials of "crack," a refined form of cocaine; (center) buyers are making drug deals on a Lower East Side street in Manhattan; (bottom) four members of a family were killed in this car, driven by a drunken driver. (Opposite top) A county sheriff takes four men to jail after they have been charged with possessing 673 pounds of cocaine; (bottom) U.S. troops stand waiting to raid jungle cocaine factories in Bolivia.

Photos, AP/Wide World

Violence seemed to be everywhere in the America of the 1980s, and not just in the cities. But it was more evident in cities than elsewhere, and reactions to it were beginning to be seen in cities as well. On a subway train in New York City on the afternoon of December 22, 1984, four black teenagers surrounded Bernhard Goetz and asked him to "lend" them $5.00. Instead he pulled a gun from his pocket and shot them all. His action aroused an immediate and furious controversy. Thousands of Americans all around the country applauded his act. At last, they said, somebody fought back against the punks, the muggers, the bums who want to rob and maim. Public officials, on the other hand, denounced Goetz as a reckless vigilante. Amidst the violence of society there were many individuals seeking to curtail it, like the neighborhood patroller in the bottom photo. Sometimes the neighborhood patrollers turned into vigilantes, too, or at least they were so accused by law enforcement officials. A doctor in Michigan was shot and badly wounded by a booby-trap of his own making; police went to his house and disarmed 17 other such crude weapons. Such was the public frustration with crime in the 1980s that individuals were driven to take the law into their own hands.

(Top) Heroin addicts discuss their treatment; (center) Bernhard Goetz arrives at court after shooting four youths he accused of trying to rob him in the New York subway; (bottom) a member of a neighborhood patrol in Cleveland, Ohio.

So pervasive did violence and random acts of terrorism become that even ordinary, law-abiding citizens began to see irrational solutions to problems. Those who espoused goals that many deemed noble often justified violent deeds by the merits of their cause. Anti-abortion groups were an example. The "pro-lifers" in many American communities bombed abortion clinics, harassed physicians who performed abortions, and tried to humiliate women on the way to or from a clinic. Even law enforcement officials seemed to overreact when faced with groups that flaunted society's values. The Philadelphia police, in May 1985, bombed the headquarters of a radical cult called Move; and in the process 11 people were killed, 61 houses were burned down, and about 250 people were left homeless. Mayor Wilson Goode said he had been wrong to order the attack, considering the devastating results.

(Top) A pro-life group planted a bomb that ripped through this abortion clinic in Maryland; (bottom) the rubble of 61 buildings set afire when the police bombed one occupied by the cult group Move in Philadelphia.

AP/Wide World

UPI/Bettmann

(Top) Agents tend to the wounded, and police and agents surround John W. Hinckley, Jr., who has just attempted to kill President Reagan; **(bottom left)** America's pop hero, Rambo, called a "pure fighting machine" and, inset, the Rambo doll; **(bottom right)** Gary Lee Yarbrough, member of a neo-Nazi group, The Order, and KKK member David Lane, both wanted for questioning in a murder.

No one in the world of the 1980s was safe from the violent tenor of the times. On March 30, 1981, President Reagan and three others were gunned down by John W. Hinckley, Jr., outside a Washington, D.C., hotel. A bullet was removed from Reagan's left lung, and a few weeks later he seemed little the worse for the ordeal. Six weeks later Pope John Paul II was shot in Rome. Violence was contagious, and groups like the KKK, The Order, and Christian Identity began arming to make war on the government. Sylvester Stallone's enormously successful movie *Rambo* typified the morbid fascination with violence, and before long Rambo dolls appeared in toy stores.

1982

60.

RONALD REAGAN: The State of the Union

In his first State of the Union address, delivered to a joint session of Congress on January 26, 1982, President Reagan reviewed the events and achievements of his first year in office and outlined his plans for the coming year. He dealt mainly with three subjects: foreign policy, his controversial economic program, and a new initiative that he called "the new federalism." Included here are those parts of the speech that dealt with the latter two subjects. The plan for a "new federalism" envisioned a changed relation between the federal government and the governments of the states and municipalities, whereby the latter would take over both financial and administrative responsibility for many programs hitherto funded, and administered, by Washington.

Source: Presidential Documents, week ending January 29, 1982.

Mr. Speaker, Mr. President, distinguished Members of the Congress, honored guests, and fellow citizens:

Today marks my first State of the Union address to you, a constitutional duty as old as our Republic itself.

President Washington began this tradition in 1790 after reminding the Nation that the destiny of self-government and the "preservation of the sacred fire of liberty" is "finally staked on the experiment entrusted to the hands of the American people." For our friends in the press, who place a high premium on accuracy, let me say: I did not actually hear George Washington say that.

[*Laughter*] But it is a matter of historic record. [*Laughter*]

But from this podium, Winston Churchill asked the free world to stand together against the onslaught of aggression. Franklin Delano Roosevelt spoke of the day of infamy and summoned a nation to arms. Douglas MacArthur made an unforgettable farewell to a country he loved and served so well. Dwight Eisenhower reminded us that peace was purchased only at the price of strength. And John F. Kennedy spoke of the burden and glory that is freedom.

When I visited this chamber last year as a newcomer to Washington, critical of past policies which I believed had failed, I proposed a new spirit of partnership between this Congress and this administration and between Washington and our State and local governments. In forging this new partnership for America, we could achieve the oldest hopes of our Republic—prosperity for our nation, peace for the world, and the blessings of individual liberty for our children and, someday, for all of humanity.

It's my duty to report to you tonight on the progress that we have made in our relations with other nations, on the foundation we've carefully laid for our economic recovery, and finally, on a bold and spirited initiative that I believe can change the face of American government and make it again the servant of the people . . . .

And so, the question: If the fundamentals are in place, what now? Well, two things. First, we must understand what's happening at the moment to the economy. Our current problems are not the product of the recovery program that's only just now getting underway, as some would have you believe; they are the inheritance of decades of tax and tax and spend and spend.

Second, because our economic problems are deeply rooted and will not respond to quick political fixes, we must stick to our carefully integrated plan for recovery. That plan is based on four commonsense fundamentals: continued reduction of the growth in Federal spending; preserving the individual and business tax reductions that will stimulate saving and investment; removing unnecessary Federal regulations to spark productivity; and maintaining a healthy dollar and a stable monetary policy, the latter a responsibility of the Federal Reserve System.

The only alternative being offered to this economic program is a return to the policies that gave us a trillion-dollar debt, runaway inflation, runaway interest rates and unemployment. The doubters would have us turn back the clock with tax increases that would offset the personal tax rate reductions already passed by this Congress. Raise present taxes to cut future deficits, they tell us. Well, I don't believe we should buy that argument.

There are too many imponderables for anyone to predict deficits or surpluses several years ahead with any degree of accuracy. The budget in place, when I took office, had been projected as balanced. It turned out to have one of the biggest deficits in history. Another example of the imponderables that can make deficit projections highly questionable—a change of only one percentage point in unemployment can alter a deficit up or down by some $25 billion.

As it now stands, our forecast, which we're required by law to make, will show major deficits starting at less than a hundred billion dollars and declining, but still too high. More important, we're making progress with the three keys to reducing deficits: economic growth, lower interest rates, and spending control. The policies we have in place will reduce the deficit steadily, surely, and in time, completely.

Higher taxes would not mean lower deficits. If they did, how would we explain that tax revenues more than doubled just since 1976; yet in that same 6-year period we ran the largest series of deficits in our history. In 1980 tax revenues increased by $54 billion and in 1980 we had one of our alltime biggest deficits. Raising taxes won't balance the budget; it will encourage more government spending and less private investment. Raising taxes will slow economic growth, reduce production, and destroy future jobs, making it more difficult for those without jobs to find them and more likely that those who now have jobs could lose them. So, I will not ask you to try to balance the budget on the backs of the American taxpayers.

I will seek no tax increases this year, and I have no intention of retreating from our basic program of tax relief. I promise to bring the American people—to bring their tax rates down and to keep them down, to provide them incentives to rebuild our economy, to save, to invest in America's future. I will stand by my word. Tonight I'm urging the American people: Seize these new opportunities to produce, to save, to invest, and together we'll make this economy a mighty engine of freedom, hope, and prosperity again . . . .

I am confident the economic program we've put into operation will protect the needy while it triggers a recovery that will benefit all Americans. It will stimulate the economy, result in increased savings and provide capital for expansion, mortgages for homebuilding, and jobs for the unemployed.

Now that the essentials of that program are in place, our next major undertaking must be a program—just as bold, just as innovative—to make government again accountable to the people, to make our system of federalism work again.

Our citizens feel they've lost control of even the most basic decisions made about the essential services of government, such as schools, welfare, roads, and even garbage collection. And they're right. A maze of interlocking jurisdictions and levels of government confronts average citizens in trying to solve even the simplest of problems.

They don't know where to turn for answers, who to hold accountable, who to praise, who to blame, who to vote for or against. The main reason for this is the overpowering growth of Federal grants-in-aid programs during the past few decades.

In 1960 the Federal Government had 132 categorical grant programs, costing $7 billion. When I took office, there were approximately 500, costing nearly a hundred billion dollars—13 programs for energy, 36 for pollution control, 66 for social services, 90 for education. And here in the Congress, it takes at least 166 committees just to try to keep track of them.

You know and I know that neither the President nor the Congress can properly oversee this jungle of grants-in-aid; indeed, the growth of these grants has led to the distortion in the vital functions of government. As one Democratic Governor put it recently: The National Government should be worrying about "arms control, not potholes."

The growth in these Federal programs has—in the words of one intergovernmental commission—made the Federal Government "more pervasive, more intrusive, more unmanageable, more ineffective and costly, and above all, more [un]accountable." Let's solve this problem with a single, bold stroke: the return of some $47 billion in Federal programs to State and local government, together with the means to finance them and a transition period of nearly 10 years to avoid unnecessary disruption.

I will shortly send this Congress a message describing this program. I want to emphasize, however, that its full details will have been worked out only after close consultation with congressional, State, and local officials.

Starting in fiscal 1984, the Federal

Government will assume full responsibility for the cost of the rapidly growing Medicaid program to go along with its existing responsibility for Medicare. As part of a financially equal swap, the States will simultaneously take full responsibility for Aid to Families with Dependent Children and food stamps. This will make welfare less costly and more responsive to genuine need, because it'll be designed and administered closer to the grassroots and the people it serves.

In 1984 the Federal Government will apply the full proceeds from certain excise taxes to a grassroots trust fund that will belong in fair shares to the 50 States. The total amount flowing into this fund will be $28 billion a year. Over the next 4 years the States can use this money in either of two ways. If they want to continue receiving Federal grants in such areas as transportation, education, and social services, they can use their trust fund money to pay for the grants. Or to the extent they choose to forgo the Federal grant programs, they can use their trust fund money on their own for those or other purposes. There will be a mandatory pass-through of part of these funds to local governments.

By 1988 the States will be in complete control of over 40 Federal grant programs. The trust fund will start to phase out, eventually to disappear, and the excise taxes will be turned over to the States. They can then preserve, lower, or raise taxes on their own and fund and manage these programs as they see fit.

In a single stroke we will be accomplishing a realignment that will end cumbersome administration and spiraling costs at the Federal level while we ensure these programs will be more responsive to both the people they're meant to help and the people who pay for them.

Hand in hand with this program to strengthen the discretion and flexibility of State and local governments, we're proposing legislation for an experimental effort to improve and develop our depressed urban areas in the 1980's and '90's. This legislation will permit States and localities to apply to the Federal Government for designation as urban enterprise zones. A broad range of special economic incentives in the zones will help attract new business, new jobs, new opportunity to America's inner cities and rural towns. Some will say our mission is to save free enterprise. Well, I say we must free enterprise so that together we can save America.

Some will also say our States and local communities are not up to the challenge of a new and creative partnership. Well, that might have been true 20 years ago before reforms like reapportionment and the Voting Rights Act, the 10-year extension of which I strongly support. It's no longer true today. This administration has faith in State and local governments and the constitutional balance envisioned by the Founding Fathers. We also believe in the integrity, decency, and sound, good sense of grassroots Americans.

Our faith in the American people is reflected in another major endeavor. Our Private Sector Initiatives Task Force is seeking out successful community models of school, church, business, union, foundation, and civic programs that help community needs. Such groups are almost invariably far more efficient than government in running social programs.

We're not asking them to replace discarded and often discredited government programs dollar for dollar, service for service. We just want to help them perform the good works they choose and help others to profit by their example. Three hundred and eighty-five thousand corporations and private organizations are already working on social programs ranging from drug rehabilitation to job training, and thousands more Americans have written us asking how they can help. The volunteer spirit is still alive and well in America.

61.

David Durenberger: The New Federalism

President Reagan's plans for a new relationship between Washington and the states had been widely discussed even before his State of the Union address in January 1982. The main lines of the program had become clear, especially to those in the Congress and in the state governments who would be most affected by it. Senator Durenberger, R-Minn., although in general a supporter of the President, had not been overly impressed by the plan to transfer certain government functions from the federal government to the states. In the following speech, delivered on November 18, 1981, to the Public Affairs Council in Washington, D.C., Senator Durenberger covered most of the actions of the new administration during its first year in the office. That part of the speech dealing with the "new federalism" is reprinted here.

Source: *Vital Speeches of the Day,* January 1, 1982.

Federalism. In its first months every new administration invents a theory of federalism to reflect its philosophy in domestic policy. We've had dual federalism, cooperative federalism, creative federalism, new federalism, layer-cake federalism, marble-cake federalism, fruit cake federalism. Today, we have the *worst* of all federalisms—budget federalism. The intergovernmental partnership is seeing its baddest days since Reconstruction.

This federalism combines the worst principles from three federalisms of different periods. The "Big Daddy" federalism of the Great Society. The "Dump and Run" federalism invented in our year of cut, cap and block. And a "Beggar Thy Neighbor" federalism based on principles of states' rights not credible since the Articles of Confederation.

The intergovernmental partnership built in the Great Society is primarily an $85 billion pipeline of federal grants-in-aid to state and local governments. That $85 billion accounts for *one-third* of the resources spent by governors and mayors and county commissioners to deliver services at the state and local level. As you will recall, it is one-half of the 15 percent of the federal budget labeled discretionary social programs.

Discretion in this context has a hollow ring to a governor or a mayor. The $85 billion is delivered through 500 separate grant programs the vast majority of which are narrow purpose categorical instruments awarded at the discretion of federal bureaucrats—with no discretion for the *elected* official in the statehouse or the courthouse.

Just finding out what's available and who is eligible is beyond the capacity of many local officials. In addition to the fragmentation, state and local governments find thousands of mandates—regulatory requirements attached to specific grants—and three score general requirements that apply to all recipients of federal aid. These general requirements include handicap access, equal employment opportunity, Davis-Bacon, the National Environmental Policy Act, and the many circulars of OMB.

Great Society federalism wastes national resources, distorts local priorities, and betrays the principle of accountability at every level in our political system. It has for a decade prompted the complaint that state or local governments are no more than administrative provinces directed by the agencies in Washington.

The newest federalism is a promise by the President that says, "We will return significant responsibilities to state and local government and the resources to pay for them." The instrument of this federalism is the block grant.

We authorized nine block grants to consolidate 57 specific categoricals in the Reconciliation Act this July. They were proposed on the theory that we could cut back funding by 25 percent, if we cut back the mandates by 100 percent. But Congress left the regulations intact and ear-marked funds within many of the blocks for specific categorical purposes.

And even though we authorized these new blocks in the reconciliation process, we have not appropriated the money, as yet. The President has proposed a further 12 percent across-the-board reduction in funding. The governors and mayors are five months into their fiscal year and they don't even know how much money they will have to spend, as yet. Remember that intergovernmental grants are one-third of their financial resources. And we tell them in a thousand ways how they must spend the money.

The promise of a new federalism is quickly becoming no more than a constant hammering on the $85 billion pipeline of intergovernmental grants to sweat out a much larger deficit in the federal budget. We are on the brink of discrediting the President's promise, by making life unbearable for state and local officials.

Some states would do very well under the "Dump and Run" theory of federalism. They are largely exporting the costs of general government to citizens in other states through taxes on energy resources. Large cuts in federal grants are easy for North Dakota to absorb, they simply increase their tax on Minnesotans by boosting the severance tax on oil and gas. Seven states now export more than 20 percent of their state budgets through energy taxes.

The senior policy advisor at the White House told me this was primarily an issue of states' rights. Baloney. What rights do you have when the legislator proposing an increase in your taxes is running for office in another state. Taxation without representation is intolerable. Shall the newest federalism be a throwback to the Articles of Confederation where beggar thy neighbor taxes and tariffs threatened the very existence of the new nation?

If we can quit being "Big Daddy" to the governors and the mayors and treat them as equal partners in the federal system . . . If we can get out of the

"Dump and Run" psychology of the budget process . . . If we can once again repudiate the "Beggar Thy Neighbor" theory of states' rights . . . maybe we can find time to concentrate on some more serious problems in the federal structure of our government. There is one that deserves the President's immediate attention. You may hear it called the infrastructure problem.

Business Week recently described it as a significant threat to the hoped-for economic recovery of the 1980s. I have been describing it as a problem of fiscal disparities in the hearings of my Subcommittee on Intergovernmental Relations. Let me start from the fiscal disparities side of the issue. In large part Great Society federalism—the pipeline of intergovernmental grants—has been used to fill a gap between the political and fiscal structure of state and local government and the economic structure of our society.

When the explosion in grant programs began, states and cities and counties simply did not have the capacity to respond to the challenge presented by the boom of post war growth. By capacity, I do not mean, as the special interests sometimes imply, that state and local government was dominated by mean spirited, country bumpkins who couldn't recognize the call of a new age. I mean that their fiscal instruments, primarily property and excise taxes, couldn't tap the new wealth reflected in rapidly rising incomes and that the political structure of local government did not allow for rational growth in most metropolitan communities.

There have been many changes over the past 20 years, particularly at the state level, and in part because of the grant programs offered by the federal government. But there is one aspect of the capacity problem that we have not solved and we continue to pay for the failure every day. We have not matched the boundaries of local government with the boundaries of local economic systems. States, especially in the Northeast and Midwest, have refused to let central cities grow to their economic horizons or to use fiscal instruments that can capture the wealth created by the services they provide.

A large part of the infrastructure problem that you will hear described is created by wealth chasing lower tax rates to the periphery of our metropolitan economic systems. Your companies do it all the time. It's a continuing transformation of the economic landscape. It causes disinvestment in the built-up infrastructure of the central city and at the same time creates demand for new infrastructure investments in the outlying suburbs.

There are many political and fiscal mechanisms that could be used to attack this problem. All of them are in the hands of state legislators. So why do I recommend the issue to the President's attention? Because, with him, I dream of a government that accomplishes more of its purposes closer to the people. With his leadership we might make a new beginning on that dream by telling the states that it is time to cut the cities free and let them be integrated units of economic and political life.

62.

John Kenneth Galbraith: Mr. Reagan's Deficit

John Kenneth Galbraith, Harvard economics professor and sometime ambassador to India, was a liberal Democrat and therefore not likely to approve of Reaganomics. His disagreement with the Reagan economic policy is expressed with his customary clarity and wit in this article, which was originally published in the New Republic *in March 1982. Professor Galbraith did not only disagree; he also proposed some alternate strategies, which, perhaps not surprisingly, were not adopted by the Reagan team, if they were ever even considered by them.*

Source: *Current,* May 1982.

ON THE CONSEQUENCES of President Reagan's budget I find myself in harmony with the great majority of other economists and the instincts of the American people at large. Indeed, for the first time in my professional life, stretching now over half a century, there is a broad unity of view extending from Wall Street and the conservative economists of the American Enterprise Institute to my liberal co-religionists. All manifest a concerned opposition to the economic design being offered for the years 1983 and thereafter.

The surface concern is with the deficits that are being projected: $91.5 billion in 1983, similarly massive figures for the years following. This concern has been deepened by the imaginative fudging of the figures to get the deficit down to the stated levels. It is likely that the gap between revenues and real expenditures will be much greater; indeed, the reliance on monetary policy to curb inflation ensures it. The sound instinct of the American people is that deficits of this magnitude are unwise and dangerous. Nor do I believe that people accept as a defense that all budget problems—indeed, all economic problems—are the inheritance of previous Administrations. This, the archaeological alibi, must never be taken seriously. All Administrations, of whatever political color, must be held firmly responsible for what happens in their own time. Otherwise, one day, some imaginative economist will attribute his failures to the erroneous economic framework established by Alexander Hamilton.

The problem of the deficit lies deeper than in the fact that more money is spent than received. It lies in the constraints and contradictions that this imposes on other economic policy.

Specifically, in an economy with a strong tendency to inflation, there are only three countering lines of policy. One is direct restraint on wages and prices in the highly organized sector of the economy. This the Administration eschews. The second is restraint on inflation through the budget. This the prospective deficit denies; as one cannot

UPI/Bettmann

John Kenneth Galbraith

working now. The question is the cost. There is no mystery in how monetary policy works against inflation. It works by restraining bank lending and the subsequent bank deposit and other money creation, and the spending therefrom. It does this primarily through high interest rates; these put the price of credit beyond the reach of would-be borrowers. From the constraint imposed on lending comes reduced spending for capital and consumer goods, a recession in economic activity, and, if not lower prices, at least a lessened rate of inflation. That has been the effect of the policy in these last months. The recession we now experience was not an adventitious or accidental thing. It was the scheduled result of the policy we are now using against inflation, for it is through a recession such as we are now experiencing that monetary policy works.

A further contradiction in the budget prospect will now be obvious. The budget deficit, as currently projected, assumes an expansion in real output in calendar year 1983 of 5.8 percent. But if inflation is to be controlled, the monetary policy will have to be sufficiently restrictive so as to deny any considerable expansion in output. Perhaps, as in these last months, it will require a contraction in output. (Inflation is not a one-time thing that, once extruded from the system, is like some poison gone for good.) The effect of the restrictive money policy that the deficit requires will, in turn, cut down on tax revenues and increase payments under the various entitlement programs—and thus increase the deficit. There is nothing hypothetical about this prospect. It is precisely what has happened in Britain as the British government has followed similar budget policies with a similar reliance on monetary policy. Economics is

sink and swim at the same time, so one cannot have a large budget deficit and fiscal restraint at the same time.

There remains only monetary policy as an agent against inflation. Prayer aside, it is the only recourse. That a flaccid fiscal policy places the burden on monetary policy the Administration does not deny. It so affirms. This year's *Economic Report of the President* says flatly that a "deficit financed by money creation will have persistent inflationary consequences." These inflationary consequences, it follows, can only be avoided by a firm refusal of the Federal Reserve to allow such money creation: in short, by rigorously stern monetary policy.

Here we encounter the first of the contradictions. Control of the money supply, the essence of monetary policy, is far more difficult than once imagined by its advocates. But if the effort is sufficiently pressed, it will work. It is not a compassionate thing. It does not deal gently with those who pursue such basically contradictory policies.

A recession has a restraining effect on spending in general and thus on prices. But monetary policy also has a more specific effect on those industries that are particularly dependent on borrowed money—what are coming to be called the credit-sensitive industries. Thus it works generally on the auto industry by causing fewer people to buy cars. But it has a more specific effect by cutting back, through high interest rates, on lending for the purchase of cars. It also raises the cost of credit to dealers and thus the cost of carrying inventory, with the further effect of putting some out of business. These effects we shall continue to have so long as we are forced by deficit financing to rely on monetary policy to dampen inflation—for that, to repeat, is the way it works.

There is a similar selective effect on the other credit-sensitive industries. Reduced demand from the recession acts against farm prices in general, with ancillary and highly visible effects on the farm equipment industry. The policy similarly singles out the housing, construction, and real estate industries, and small business in general, where the failure rate last year reached the highest level, one year excepted, since the Great Depression. This is the way monetary policy is working and is meant to work. These are the consequences we must expect if budget deficits require a continued reliance on monetary policy as the alternative to severe inflation.

MONETARY POLICY AND EMPLOYMENT

We have heard much from liberals and the trade unions of the effect of monetary policy on employment— of the social cruelty of a policy that works by making unemployment the restraining influence on wages, and that, at the most optimistic, promises unemployment in the range of eight percent of the labor force. (It would be much less painful to have a direct restraint on wages rather than the sanguinary, indirect restraint of the present monetary policy.) But the cruelty of the policy extends also to car dealers, home builders, construction firms, merchants, and farmers. This is small business; most small-business people are Republicans; they have often been called the backbone of the party. No one can accuse this Administration of sparing its own.

This is the policy and punishment that, in the absence of any fiscal restraint, will have to be continued and intensified in the months ahead—the policy that is made necessary, always assuming that inflation is to be contained, by the deficits.

There are three further consequences of the present policy. First, it is from borrowing for investment that we get improvement in productivity. High interest rates squelch such investment, especially by smaller enterprises. The recession by which monetary policy suppresses inflation also has an adverse effect on productivity. There is no mystery as to why this should be so. It is when business is expanding and firms are operating at or near capacity that new plant is wanted and new investment made. New plant is almost always more efficient than old. The years of high interest rates have, in virtually all countries, been years of low productivity gains.

A continuation of the monetary policy that the prospective large deficits will require will also have a deeply damaging effect on the international financial system. The high interest rates here draw funds from the other industrial countries. In defense, they are forced to raise *their* interest rates. In such fashion we export our economic policy—including the associated unemployment and recession—to our friends abroad. This is no hypothetical prospect: in recent weeks, the British Chancellor of the Exchequer, the German Chancellor, the head of the Bundesbank in Germany, the President of France, the Belgian Prime Minister, and the Prime Minister of Canada have all expressed deep concern, verging on anguish, over our policy. Rarely have we promoted such unity. If our policy continues, the European countries, acting through European monetary arrangements now in place, will be strongly tempted to control capital outflows, therewith to lower their interest rates and thus get control over their own policy. Few European leaders wish to see the world economic system broken in two; but many would accept it as an alternative to the disastrous policies that Washington's fiscal policy is otherwise forcing upon them.

Finally, the deficits now in prospect and the countering monetary action make nonsense of the talk of a supply-side economics—of a vigorous expansion in the economy unleashed by the tax cuts. This was always an exceptionally dubious design. But not even the most ardent advocates, men who have shown that they will believe anything, can suppose that there can be a vigorous supply-side expansion in combination with tight monetary restraint to control inflation. Those who so suggest, were they doctors, would tell an obese patient with a large appetite that he had only to eat a great deal more in order to grow thin. This is an economics guided

not by what is right, but by what people looking for a painless life prefer to hear.

Let it be noted that it is no case for the present budget that governments in the past deliberately resorted to deficit-financing. The deficit-financing of the Depression era was undertaken when prices were falling and interest rates at all-but-nominal levels. The massive deflationary tendencies of the time allowed, indeed required, *both* an easier monetary policy and an expansive fiscal policy. The case of the Kennedy-Johnson tax reductions is also cited. That too was a time of nearly stable prices and of low interest rates; and with the tax reduction of that time also went pressure on the Federal Reserve to lower interest rates. No lessons from these periods are applicable to a time when inflation is a central concern and when fiscal irresponsibility enhances the emphasis on monetary policy.

Let me now turn to remedies—to what needs to be done. I shall pass over the proposed cuts in social and other civilian expenditures. Much has been said about this and about the consequences. This expenditure, much of it on behalf of the poorest of our people, is not wasteful, dishonest, or out of control. Rather, it is the expression of compassion and concern that all modern industrial states have manifested for the least protected of their citizens. Our expenditures for this purpose have not, in relative terms, been high; in relation to gross national product they have been lower than those of the other major industrial countries with the exception of Japan. It is such expenditure that has tempered the rough edges of the economic system and helped ensure its survival. Social tranquility is not less important for conservatives than for liberals. It serves all.

The military budget does call for comment and action. All know of the factors that determine its scale; some of them have nothing to do with defense. To the calculation of military need is added what serves bureaucratic interest, what serves the competition between the services, and what serves, often at military cost, the technical dynamic of gadgetry—the belief that whatever is technically more arcane is always better. To this is added the large influence, which no one denies, of the weapons firms. Finally there is the protection that comes from political fear. In this day and age motherhood can be criticized; but mention Russia and the bravest men, politically speaking, take to the hills.

There is a question as to whether military expenditures at their present and projected levels add to our national strength. The history on this mattter is persuasive. During the 1970s we spent, in round figures, a hundred billion dollars annually on the defense establishment, for a total for the decade of roughly a thousand billion (in constant 1976 dollars). Capital in this magnitude could be used for arms; it could be used for private capital investment; it could not be used for both. If an appreciable part of this outlay had gone into the improvement of our industrial plant— as it would have, had it not been requisitioned by the government—no one can doubt that the American economy would be stronger today. And from this stronger economic position would have come, in turn, the economic primacy and political prestige that were enjoyed in the early years following World War II. It was economic, not military, strength on which the American world position then depended.

There is striking empirical evidence of the industrial effect of the arms race, as I have argued recently in the *Bulletin of Atomic Scientists*. In modern times the American competitive position has declined, specifically in relation to that of Germany and Japan. We are not, it is generally believed, less intelligent than the Germans or Japanese. The American raw material and energy base is not less good—indeed, it is far better. Germany spends more per capita on social services than does the United States; Japan does not spend greatly less. The difference is that the Germans and Japanese have been using their capital to replace old civilian plant and build new and better plant. The United States has been using much more of its capital for industrially limited or sterile military purposes.

Through the 1970s the United States used from 5 to 8 percent of its gross national product for military purposes. The Germans during this decade used between 3 and 4 percent—in most years relatively about half as much. The Japanese in these ten years devoted less than 1 percent of their gross national product annually to military use. In 1977, a fairly typical year, American military spending was $441 per capita; that of Germany was $252 per capita; that of Japan a mere $47 per capita.

TO FREEZE THE MILITARY BUDGET

It was from the capital so saved and invested that a substantial share of the civilian investment came which brought these countries to the industrial eminence that now so successfully challenges our own. Again the figures are striking. Through the 1970s our investment in fixed nonmilitary and nonresidential investment ranged from 16.9

percent of gross national product to 19 percent. That of Germany began where ours reached its peak; it ranged upward from 20.6 to 26.7 percent of gross national product. The Japanese range in these years was even greater—from 31 percent to a towering 36.6 percent. The investment in improvement of civilian plant was broadly the reciprocal of what went for weapons. No one looking at these figures can doubt that our military spending has been at cost to our industrial eminence and to the prestige and influence that go therewith. Certainly no one looking at these figures from the past can view the projected increases in the military budget with equanimity. The Administration itself affirms in the *Economic Report of the President* that these increases will be at cost to private capital formation. Is it really sensible to sacrifice our industrial eminence to a military budget that comprises so many elements so slightly related to any valid national concept of security? Lurking at the back of much past defense calculation has been the notion that we could somehow spend the Soviet Union into submission. It is a thought we can no longer tolerate, if, indeed, we ever could.

So, by all means, let us freeze the military budget along the lines proposed by Senator Ernest Hollings. Let us then have a serious look for savings—a look at the rehabilitation of those two old battleships, museum pieces both; at the B-1 bomber with its four or five years of useful survival; at aircraft carriers that in modern conflict would have to be rushed to the nearest harbor and might not make it; at the massive overkill in the strategic forces. And let there be serious pressure for an arms control agreement. (The issues here, needless to say, go beyond economics to survival.)

The military budget has a highly leveraged relationship to the civilian budget. A modest reduction in marginal military gadgetry frees a large number of dollars for civilian need or for covering the deficit. We would be wise to use this leverage to the full.

However vigorous and sustained the movement on the military budget, the deficit, or some of it, will remain. That means taxes must be raised. Let there be no flinching at this prospect; and let there be no doubt on one basic and indispensable point. Higher taxes are far better for the economy than higher interest rates. Investment, productivity, and economic growth are consistent, or can be made consistent, with higher taxes. They cannot be reconciled with the high interest rates which are the alternative.

There should be prompt repeal of the corporate tax concessions, including the transfer of tax credits. I would also make a strong case for the windfall tax on gains from oil and gas deregulation. But the obvious and practical action is to defer the tax reductions scheduled for this coming summer and for a year hence. Nothing would have a more immediate and positive effect. There would be a prompt rally in the stock market; interest rates would fall and bond prices would rise; economic activity in the credit-sensitive industries would respond. I am never sanguine about economic predictions, including, and perhaps especially, my own. This one I make with a confidence that would be widely shared.

I urge two final points. Let us be very careful about any action, however disguised by rhetoric, which praises local responsibility or a new federalism and which transfers costs to state and especially to local governments. All public action must take account of one of the major features, one can say flaws, of the American fiscal system. The government of the United States, with its access to diverse tax sources and the tendency of its revenue sources to keep abreast of inflation, is by nature one of the best-financed units of government anywhere in the world. And, over the last half-century, nothing has been so persistently evident and so grievously underestimated as the costs of operating the modern large city at any tolerable level of safety, decency, and compassion. When people live in close juxtaposition, the costs of government go up exponentially. And they go up on a tax base that, unlike the taxable resources of the federal government, is circumscribed. We have already had, in the last budget, a major shift in fiscal responsibility from the best-financed unit of our system of government to the ones in the greatest inherent difficulty. It is a path on which we should proceed no farther. So to proceed will not strengthen local governments; it will weaken them. The new federalism, there is little doubt, is a singularly transparent device for shifting public costs away from the personal and corporate income tax bases of the federal government, with the particular incidence on the affluent, to the more regressive sales and property tax bases of states and localities.

Mr. David Stockman, with admirable candor, said last year that the concept of supply-side economics and its associated rhetoric were a cover for the reduction of income taxes in the upper brackets. That conservatives should seek a reduction in the upper-income tax brackets is not remarkable; no less than liberals, conservatives have their constituency. What is not forgivable is that conservatives should disguise their purposes behind supply-side or new federalist rhetoric. Plain speech is proper to people of all political faiths.

Conservatives especially should not accept the deficit in its prospective magnitude. There is room for ideological difference on how public services should be financed. There is no room for difference on the question of whether or not it should be financed. Deficits on the scale now projected effectively remove all freedom of economic action and commit the government to a monetary policy that we are learning—as the British have learned—is painfully repressive and potentially disastrous.

I've never believed that just cutting taxes alone would cause output and employment to expand.

DAVID STOCKMAN, 1981

63.

RONALD REAGAN: Address on Tax and Budget Reconciliation

The Reagan administration, sensitive to criticism of the large deficit forecast in its budget for the 1983 fiscal year (and no doubt deeply concerned as well), allowed a bipartisan bill increasing taxes to come before the Congress in August 1982. The President himself was apparently even more concerned lest people believe that he had been a willing party to the promulgation of "the largest tax increase in history," when throughout his campaign and since his election he had never ceased to oppose strongly any general increase in personal taxes; and in this address to the nation, delivered on August 16, he attempted to reconcile what some saw as contradictions in his economic policy. The actual deficit for 1983 turned out to be vastly greater than had been forecast, and budgets in subsequent years were also huge, making Reagan, despite his protests, the greatest "deficit spender" in the history of the Presidency.

Source: Presidential Documents, week ending August 20, 1982.

My fellow Americans:

There's an old saying we've all heard a thousand times about the weather and how everyone talks about it but no one does anything about it. Well, many of you must be feeling that way about the present state of our economy. Certainly there's a lot of talk about it, but I want you to know we're doing something about it. And the reason I wanted to talk to you is because you can help us do something about it.

Believe me, if some of you are confused, I can understand why. For some time, ever since we started planning the 1983 budget for the fiscal year beginning this coming October 1st, there's been a steady drumbeat of "reports" on what we're supposed to be doing.

I know you've read and heard on the news a variety of statements attributed to various "authoritative government sources who prefer not to have their names used." Well, you know my name, and I think I'm an authoritative source on this since I'm right in the middle of what's going on here. So, I'd like to set the record straight on a few of the things that you might have heard lately.

I'm sure you've heard that "we're proposing the largest single tax increase in history." The truth is, we're proposing nothing of the kind. And then there's the one that "our economic recovery program has failed, so I've abandoned it and turned to increasing taxes instead of trying to reduce Federal spending." Well, don't you believe that one either.

Yes, there is a tax bill before the Congress tied to a program of further cuts in spending. It is not, however, the "greatest single tax increase in history." Possibly it could be called the greatest tax reform in history, but it absolutely does not represent any reversal of policy or philosophy on the part of this administration or this President.

Now, you may have heard that some special interests oppose this bill. And that's right; some do. As a matter of fact, some in the Congress of my own party object to this bill—and strongly. I'm told by many that this bill is not politically popular, and it may not be. Why then do I support it? I support it because it's right for America. I support it because it's fair. I support it because it will, when combined with our cuts in government spending, reduce interest rates and put more Americans back to work again.

Now, you'll recall that when our administration came into office a year ago last January, we announced a plan for economic recovery. Recovery from what? From a 1980 recession that saw inflation in double-digit figures for the second year in a row. It was 12.4 percent when we arrived. Interest rates had gone into outer space. They were at the highest they'd been in a hundred years with a prime rate that hit 21 1/2 percent. There were almost 8 million Americans out of work. And in several hard-hit industrial States, there already were pockets of unemployment reaching figures of 15, 18, and even 20 percent. I went to those areas; I know.

The cost of government was increasing at a rate of 17 percent a year. There was little we could do about the budget already in place. But we could do something about the one that had been proposed for the fiscal year beginning in October of our first year.

I'd campaigned on the belief that government costs should be reduced and that the percentage of the people's earnings taken by government in taxes should also be reduced. I also said that

one area of government spending could not be reduced, but must instead be increased. That was the spending necessary to restore our nation's defenses, which had been allowed to deteriorate to a dangerous degree in the preceding 4 years.

Interest rates continued high as the months went by, and unemployment increased, particularly in the automobile industry and housing contstruction. Few could or would afford the high interest rates for home mortgages or installment buying of an automobile.

Meantime, we were putting our economic recovery program in place. It wasn't easy. We didn't get all the cuts we wanted. And we got some tax measures we didn't want. But we were charting a complete turnaround in government policy, and we did get the major part of what we proposed. The Congress mandated spending cuts of $130 billion over 3 years and adopted the biggest tax cut in history.

Now, this, too, was to be implemented over a 3-year period. It began with a 5-percent cut in the personal income tax beginning October 1st, 1981, then a 10-percent cut this last July, and another scheduled for July 1st, 1983. These will be followed by indexing of the tax brackets so workers getting cost-of-living pay raises won't be moved up into higher brackets. We have to realize inflation itself is a tax. Government profits by inflation, but indexing will put a stop to that.

There were tax cuts for business and industry to help provide capital for modernization of plant and equipment, changes in the estate tax, capital gains tax, and the marriage-penalty tax. Some who supported us on the spending cuts were fearful about cutting taxes in view of the continuing budget deficits. We felt that tax cuts had to be a part of our plan in order to provide incentive for individuals and for business to increase productivity and thus create jobs for the unemployed.

Now, it's only been 10 months since the first phase of our program went into effect. As I said earlier, there are those who say it's been tried and it failed. Well, as Al Smith used to say, "Let's look at the record."

Start with interest rates, the basic cause of the present recession: The prime rate was, as I said, 21½ percent. Well, last week it was 14½ percent. And as of today, three major banks have lowered it to 14 percent. Last week 90-day Treasury bills were paying less than 9 percent interest. One year ago they were paying 15½. That double-digit inflation, 12.4 percent, has been cut in half for the last 6 months. Real earnings are at last increasing for the first time in quite a long time. Personal savings, which trended downward throughout the last decade, are increasing. This means more money in the pool of investment capital. This will help further reduce interest rates.

All of this in only 10 months hardly looks like a program that failed to me. Oh, yes, I failed to mention that in the quarter just ended there was an increase in economic growth—the first such increase in a long time.

Our biggest problem—the last one to be solved in every recession—is unemployment. I understand how tough it is for those who are waiting for the jobs that come with recovery. We can have no rest until our neighbors, our fellow citizens who want to work, are able once again to find jobs. Again, let me say, the main obstacle to their doing so is continued high interest rates.

Those rates should be lower now than they are, with the success we've had in reducing inflation. But part of the problem is psychological—a pessimism in the money markets that we won't stay the course and continue lowering the cost of government. The projected increase in budget deficits has added to that pessimism and fear. And this brings us back to that so-called greatest tax increase in history and the budget proposals now before the Congress.

When I submitted the 1983 budget to the Congress in February, it contained very significant spending cuts on top of those we obtained last year. This time, however, we couldn't get the support we had last year. Some who had not been happy about the tax cuts then were now insisting we must have additional tax revenues. In fact, they wanted to cancel the reduction scheduled for next July and cancel the indexing of tax brackets. Others proposed tax increases mounting to about $150 billion over a 3-year period. On top of this, there was resistance to the spending reductions we asked for, and even attempts to eliminate some of last year's cuts so as to actually increase spending.

For many months now we've been working to get a compromise budget that would further reduce spending and thus reduce the deficits. We also have stood firm on retaining the tax cuts already in place, because, as I said, they're essential to restoring the economy.

We did, however, agree to limited revenue increases so long as they didn't harm the incentive features of our economic recovery program. We ourselves, last year, had called attention to the possibility of better compliance with the tax laws—collecting taxes legitimately owed but which were not being paid.

Well, weeks and weeks of negotiations resulted in a congressional budget resolution combining revenue increases and further spending reductions. Revenues would increase over a 3-year period by about $99 billion, and outlays in that same period would be reduced by 280 billion. Now, as you can see, that figures out to about a 3-to-1 ratio—$3 less in spending outlays for each $1 of increased revenue.

This compromise adds up to a total over 3 years of a $380 billion reduction in the budget deficits. And remember, our original tax reduction remains in place, which means your taxes will still be cut $335 billion in these next 3 years, even with the passage of this present tax bill.

Now, let me take that $99 billion tax program apart, and you decide whether it's the biggest tax increase in history. Of the entire $99 billion, 32 billion is collection of tax presently owed under the present laws and which is not being paid. Now, to all of you who are paying your tax, simple fairness says we should collect from those who are freeloading. Roughly 48 billion of the 99 billion represents closing off special-interest loopholes which have resulted in unintended tax advantages for some—not all—taxpayers, some who are financially well able to pay their share. Now, this is also a matter of simple fairness. So, more than 80 percent of the tax bill is not new tax at all, but is better collecting and correcting of flaws in the system.

Now, this leaves $19 billion over 3 years of actual new taxes, which is far outweighed by the tax cuts which will benefit individuals. There is an excise tax on cigarettes, another on telephones. Well, for people who smoke a pack a day, that tax will mean an increase of only $2.40 a month. The telephone tax increase is only about 54 cents a month for the average household. Right now

the tax reduction that we passed last year is saving the average family about $400 per year. Next year, even after this new tax bill is passed, the savings will almost double; they'll go to $788.

And here's what the totals look like. The new tax reform will raise in 3 years about, as I say, 99 billion. In the same 3 years, as I said a moment ago, our tax-cut program even after this increase will save you 335 billlion.

Within the new bill there has, of course, been disagreement over some of the specific provisions. For example, there's considerable confusion over the proposal to have withholding of tax due on interest and dividends, just as it's withheld now on your wages and salaries. Many senior citizens have been led to believe this is a new tax added on top of the present income tax. Well, there is no truth whatsoever to that. We found that while the overwhelming majority of Americans faithfully report income from interest and dividends and pay taxes on it, some do not. It's one of the significant areas of noncompliance and is costing the government about $9 billion a year.

In the case of those over age 65, withholding will only apply to those with incomes of $14,450 and up per individual and $24,214 for couples filing a joint return. Low-income citizens below 65 will be exempt if their income is less than about $8,000 for an individual or $15,300 for those filing joint returns. And there will be an exemption for all interest payments of $150 or less. The only people whose taxes will be increased by this withholding are those who presently are evading their fair share of the tax burden. Once again, we're striving to see that all taxpayers are treated fairly.

Now, this withholding will go into effect next July, not this January 1st, as was earlier reported. Back during the campaign—on September 9th, 1980, to be exact—I said my goal was to reduce by 1985 the share of the gross national product taken by the government in taxes, reduce it to 20.5 percent. If we had done nothing, it would have risen to almost 25 percent. But even after passage of this bill, the Federal Government in 1985 will only be taking 19.6 percent of the gross national product.

Make no mistake about it, this whole package is a compromise. I had to swallow hard to agree to any revenue increase. But there are two sides to a compromise. Those who supported the increased revenues swallowed hard to accept $280 billion in outlay cuts. Others have accepted specific provisions with regard to taxes or spending cuts which they opposed. There's a provision in the bill for extended unemployment payments in States particularly hard hit by unemployment. If this provision is not enacted, 2 million people will use up their benefits by the end of March.

I repeat: Much of this bill will make our tax system more fair for every American, especially those in lower income brackets. I'm still dedicated to reducing the level of spending until it's within our income, and I still want to see the base of the economy broadened so that the individual's tax burden can be further reduced.

Over the years, growth in government and deficit spending have been built into our system. Now, it'd be nice if we could just cut that out of our system with a single, sharp slice. That, however, can't be done without bringing great hardship down on many of our less fortunate neighbors who are not in a position to provide for themselves. And none of us wants that.

Our effort to restore fiscal integrity and common sense to the Federal establishment isn't limited to the budget cuts and tax policy. Vice President Bush heads up a task force that's been reviewing excessive regulations. Already enough unnecessary and duplicative regulations have been eliminated or revised to save an estimated $6 billion every year.

Our Inspectors General have been mobilized into a task force aimed at ferreting out waste and fraud. They've conducted tens of thousands of audits, secured thousands of indictments resulting in many convictions. In the first 6 months of fiscal 1982 alone, they found $5.8 billion of savings and improved use of funds. Computer cross-checking has uncovered thousands of government checks still going to people who've been dead for several years.

Task forces from the private sector are engaged in a study of the management structure of government. What they've learned already indicates a great potential for savings by simply bringing government procedures up to ordinary modern business standards. Our private sector initiatives force, under William Verity, has uncovered hundreds of community and statewide projects performing services voluntarily that once were thought to be the province of government. Some of the most innovative have to do with job training and placement, particularly for young people.

What we need now is an end to the bickering here in the Capital. We need the bipartisan, comprehensive package of revenue increase and spending cuts now before the Congress. We need it to be passed.

We're not proposing a quick fix, an artifical stimulant to the economy, such as we've seen in the several recessions in recent years. The present recession is bottoming out without resorting to quick fixes.

Now, there won't be a sudden boom or upsurge. But slowly and surely, we'll have a sound and lasting recovery based on solid values and increased productivity and an end to deficit spending. It may not be easy, but it's the best way, the only way to real and lasting prosperity for all our people.

Think of it, we've only had one balanced budget in the last 20 years. Let's look forward to the day when we begin making payments to reduce the national debt, instead of turning it all over to our children . . . .

The measure the Congress is about to vote on, while not perfect in the eyes of any one of us, will bring us closer to the goal of a balanced budget, restored industrial power, and employment for all who want to work. Together we can reach that goal.

64.

BRUCE J. ENNIS: The Insanity Defense

On May 4, 1982, the federal trial of 26-year-old John Hinckley, Jr., for shooting President Reagan and three others in 1981 got under way in Washington, D.C. Hinckley had pleaded not guilty by reason of insanity; the prosecution tried to persuade the jury of Hinckley's guilt by arguing that the assassination attempt had been carefully planned and executed. On June 21 the jury, after four days of deliberation, found Hinckley not guilty by reason of insanity. The verdict shocked many and brought forth demands for a change in the law that permitted such an acquittal. After the verdict, Hinckley was committed to a Washington, D.C., hospital for an indefinite period. The author of the following measured examination of the insanity defense was a partner in the Washington, D.C., firm of Ennis, Friedman, Bersoff & Ewing, and was a member of the American Bar Association task force studying the laws governing mentally disabled defendants.

Source: *The Nation*, July 24–31, 1982.

A WASHINGTON, D.C., jury's finding that John Hinckley was not guilty by reason of insanity of the attempted assassination of President Reagan triggered widespread outrage among Americans. Pundits rushed to their typewriters to denounce the verdict and call for changes in the insanity defense. Columnist George F. Will understandably criticized the "incompatible marriage of psychiatry and law," which allows culprits like Hinckley to escape responsibility for their actions. In *The New Republic*, law professor Stephen Cohen reviewed the arguments for the insanity defense and concluded that "as it now exists it should be abolished." A *New York Times* editorial rejected abolishment but discussed some "changes worth considering." *The Washington Post* agreed:

"Something new has to be considered."

In Congress, which must do the considering, there are a raft of proposals, some old, some new, in the legislative hopper. They range from abolishment of the defense to creation of a "guilty but insane" verdict. While I agree that reforms are in order, the remedies now before Congress reflect confusion about the insanity plea and would radically revise not only the definition of what constitutes a *defense* to a crime but also the definition of crime itself.

In order to grasp why that is so it is necessary to understand the concepts underlying the insanity defense. Unfortunately, there is no agreement on the definition of those concepts. In fact, one of the reasons it is so difficult to make sense of the insanity defense is that people are not talking the same language.

The first concept involved is *mens rea* ("culpable mind"). With most crimes, conviction requires proof not only of a particular act (*actus reas*) but also of a particular mental state accompanying the act (*mens rea*). These are the necessary "elements" of the crime. Each element must be proved in order to establish a prima facie case—that is, a case in which the evidence will be sufficient to justify conviction unless the defendant rebuts it. The prosecution has the burden of proving these elements, including *mens rea,* and it must prove each of them "beyond a reasonable doubt."

The *mens rea* element is not the same for all crimes. Some crimes require only proof of a negligent state of mind; others require proof of a reckless state of mind. But for most serious crimes, the prosecution must prove that the defendant intended to commit the proscribed act, whatever his state of mind. However, there is no consensus on what is meant by intent. In jurisdictions adopt-

UPI/Bettmann

John W. Hinkley, Jr. in custody after his attempted assassination of President Reagan.

ing a narrow interpretation of the intent requirement, intent means only that the defendant had a conscious objective to commit the proscribed act. Whether he could appreciate the wrongfulness of his conduct or could conform his conduct to the law would be irrelevant to that narrow *mens rea* requirement (although it might be relevant to an "affirmative defense" of insanity, as I will explain later). In jurisdictions adopting a broad interpretation, intent means *sane* intent—that is, the defendant not only consciously knew what he was doing but also could appreciate the wrongfulness of his act and could control his behavior.

Obviously, in a jurisdiction where intent is broadly defined, the prosecution has to prove much more about the defendant's mental state in order to make out a prima facie case than in a jurisdiction where intent is narrowly defined. It is difficult to say whether the intent requirement is constitutionally required. But most courts and scholars agree that the Constitution requires at least proof of a narrow intent, in the sense of conscious objective, as an element of all serious crimes. Accordingly, I shall assume that the prosecution has to prove intent, but only in the narrow sense of conscious objective, in order to establish a prima facie case. Once the prosecution has introduced sufficient evidence to establish such a case, the defendant has to either rebut that case by introducing contrary evidence or overcome it by establishing what the law calls an affirmative defense.

An affirmative defense is a legally sufficient justification for a defendant's behavior, even if that behavior would otherwise warrant conviction. In effect, an affirmative defense overcomes an unrebutted prima facie case. For example, even after the prosecution establishes a prima facie case of murder by proving that the defendant consciously caused the death of a human being, the defendant could escape responsibility by establishing that he acted in self-defense. Similarly, the defendant could overcome a prima facie case by convincing the judge or the jury that although he consciously intended to take a human life, he did not know his conduct was wrongful or he could not control his behavior because he was insane.

Three examples will illustrate the difference between the mental state the prosecution would have to prove to establish a narrow, prima facie case of conscious intent and the mental state the defendant would have to prove to establish an affirmative defense of insanity.

(1) A blatantly psychotic person opens his car door without looking. A passing bicyclist hits the door and dies. The defendant caused the death, but he did not consciously intend to do so. In those circumstances, the defendant would not be guilty of murder because one of the elements of that crime—conscious intent—would be missing. The defendant would not have to rely on an affirmative defense of insanity, or on any other affirmative defense, because the prosecution did not make out a prima facie case of murder.

(2) A blatantly psychotic person suffocates a baby. Evidence introduced by the prosecution shows that the defendant, though psychotic, consciously intended to kill something but thought he was suffocating a kitten, not a baby. Would the defendant need to rely on an affirmative defense of insanity? No, because the prosecution would not have proved one of the elements of murder, the conscious intent to take a *human* life.

(3) A blatantly psychotic person kills a Presidential candidate. The prosecution shows that the defendant, though psychotic, knew he was taking a human life and consciously intended to do so. Would the defendant need to rely on an affirmative defense of insanity? Yes, because even though he was blatantly psychotic, he consciously intended to take a human life. The defense might be able to overcome the prosecution's case by showing that although the defendant consciously intended to take a human life, he did not appreciate the wrongfulness of his act—for example, he believed creatures from another world had instructed him to kill the candidate before he gained power and launched a nuclear war.

Another conceptual confusion is the important but usually ignored difference between an ordinary defense and an affirmative defense. The prosecution must prove that all the necessary elements of a crime were present. In a prosecution for murder, the defense might contend, for example, that there was no proof that the defendant caused the death of a human being. Even though this is called a defense, the defendant is not compelled to establish that he did not cause the death. Rather, the prosecution must prove that he did. Similarly, the defendant could escape conviction for murder if the prosecution failed to prove that he consciously intended to cause the death of a human being, and the defendant would be acquitted without having to raise an affirmative defense.

In an ordinary defense, the burden of proof is always on the prosecution, and properly so. But in a true affirmative defense, the burden shifts to the defendant. If the insanity defense were treated like any other affirmative defense, the defendant should bear the burden of proving it, and that is indeed the rule in several states. But in most states, once a defendant introduces evidence that he was legally insane at the time the proscribed act was committed, the prosecution is required to prove he was not. That is sometimes difficult to do, as the Hinckley verdict shows.

Although the point is certainly debatable, I believe legislatures could not constitutionally eliminate mental state, or *mens rea,* requirements as elements of certain serious crimes, but they could constitutionally eliminate the affirmative defense of insanity. That would be a harsh measure, and without major changes in the *mens rea* requirement, sentencing procedures and options, and the civil commitment process, it would be an unwise one. But once a legislature has provided that the prosecution must prove whatever mental-state element the Constitution would require for a particular crime, there would be no Constitutional obligation to provide for an affirmative defense of insanity.

Many of the bills now pending in Congress ignore *mens rea* and the important distinctions between an ordinary defense and an affirmative defense. For example, H.R. 6653 (introduced by Representative John Myers on June 22, 1982) provides that "mental condition shall not be a defense to any charge of criminal conduct." If "defense" means affirmative defense, the bill is probably constitutional (although it may not be wise). But if by "defense" the bill means that a defendant can be convicted of murder when the prosecution has failed to show even conscious intent, it is, in my view, unconstitutional.

Several bills provide that "a defendant is guilty but insane if his actions constitute all necessary elements of the offense charged other than the requisite state of mind, and he lacked the requisite state of mind as a result of mental disease or defect." These bills effectively eliminate the *mens rea* element from the definition of the crime, at least when that element is missing because of a mental disease or defect.

The elements required to establish guilt of a particular crime reflect a consensus, developed over hundreds of years, of the circumstances in which society believes criminal conviction and punishment is appropriate. That consensus is based on complex value judgments on such questions as how much individual freedom society can tolerate; how much security and public order society needs; how important it is to punish or deter the conduct in question; whether the punishment prescribed for the crime is disproportionate to its impact on the victim or on society; and whether others whose mental state is similar to the defendant's could or would be deterred by the prospect of conviction.

Strong arguments can be made for abolishing or substantially revising the affirmative defense of insanity. As I have indicated, I would favor placing the burden of proof on the defendant. Such a rule would be easier for juries to understand. It seems fair to place on the defendant the burden of justifying conscious and intentional conduct which, if not justified, would violate criminal law. And I believe expert witnesses should not be permitted to offer opinions on questions that are ultimately for the jury to decide, such as whether a defendant pleading insanity knew right from wrong. Such a reform would help juries understand that the final decision is up to them rather than to the experts.

Some of the bills now pending in Congress and state legislatures that would effectively eliminate any mental-state requirement in prosecutions for crime are a drastic revision of an ancient consensus that *some* level of mental culpability should be proved by the prosecution before an individual can be subjected to criminal punishment. Such a revision should not be achieved indirectly under the guise of revising the insanity "defense."

65.

David C. Anderson: 30 Million Handguns

Whether he was legally insane or not, John Hinckley, Jr., the would-be assassin of President Reagan, had had little difficulty obtaining the .22 caliber Roehm RG 14 pistol with which he had shot the President and three other persons on March 30, 1981. The assassination attempt, and the subsequent trial of Hinckley, heated up once again the always simmering American controversy about handguns, and about whether there was some way to control their ever wider distribution among the population. Across the Board, the magazine of the Conference Board, gathered together a series of articles on the subject in its February 1982 issue. Reprinted here is an article by David C. Anderson, who until shortly before publishing it had been editor of Criminal Justice Publications. Mr. Anderson's article seems to draw a fine, careful line between the views of more extreme apologists on either side of the controversy.

Source: *Across the Board*, February 1982.

JEAN HARRIS, Mark David Chapman and John Hinckley generated a new national debate over gun control, and for a reason that is less than obvious. Harris, convicted of murdering Dr. Herman Tarnower with a .32 caliber Harrington & Richardson revolver, Chapman, who pleaded guilty to killing John Lennon with a .38 caliber Charter Arms revolver, and Hinckley, accused of wounding President Reagan and his aides with a .22 caliber Roehm RG 14 pistol, did not emerge from some criminal netherworld; instead all are familiar-seeming, middle-class folks.

In addition to reflecting the potential

for violence in all of us, their proven or alleged crimes are disturbing reminders that the handgun is a pervasive element of American life. It makes that violent potential deadlier than ever.

Guns are intimately bound up with American history: Unlike Europe, America was settled after the invention of the gun; early settlers of the Eastern Seaboard and then the West used guns to hunt food, fight Indians and keep the peace. But for decades guns remained a part of rural life; the law-abiding city dweller had little use for them.

In the 1960s, however, in the wake of urban riots and perceived increases in urban crime, handgun sales increased dramatically from fewer than 750,000 in 1964 to more than 2 million in 1968, where they remain today. Most of the new sales, experts believe, were to fearful homeowners. Today about half of all American households contain some kind of firearm, and half of them are handguns.

This increase of the handgun supply in crowded urban areas is an unprecedented national phenomenon that poses questions of policy far more subtle and complex than those suggested by the cases of Harris, Chapman and Hinckley—or, for that matter, the latest liquor-store stickup in your own neighborhood.

A recent issue of the *Annals of the American Academy of Political and Social Science,* a scholarly journal, collects a number of articles . . . that summarize recent thinking of criminal justice experts about gun control. The points they make permit a fresh look at a debate that often deadlocks between gun foes who equate an interest in firearms with sexual hang-ups and National Rifle Association devotees who believe gun control is an effort to soften up America for Communist takeover.

In the first place, articles in the special issue, titled "Gun Control," suggest that the proliferation of urban household handguns clearly increases the dangerousness of life rather than making it any safer, and not just by creating the potential for more accidents. "If current rates of handgun violence persist, the approximately 2 million new handguns sold this year will eventually be involved in almost 600 thousand acts of violent crime—a rate of involvement that vastly exceeds the corresponding rate for rifles and shotguns," write Philip J. Cook and James Blose.

Harvard professor Mark H. Moore, in a fascinating study, traces the ways a vast arsenal of guns falls into the hands of "proscribed persons" each year. Between 300,000 and 700,000 change hands in private transactions, with an unknown number winding up in the clutches of criminals. And a huge number—between 60,000 and 200,000—are stolen. By definition, they wind up in criminal possession, and almost certainly are bound for criminal use.

But if all those criminals were denied guns, wouldn't they just use other weapons to commit crimes? Perhaps, says Cook in another study, but the results wouldn't be so deadly. "The type of weapon matters in violent crime, both in terms of its seriousness and its distribution." The number of deaths resulting from robberies and assaults would decline, he concludes, though that benefit would have its price: nondeadly robberies and assaults might increase, and predatory criminals would shift their sights from the young and strong to the old and weak.

Such a conclusion about reducing the deadliness of crime is reinforced by a study of the Bartley-Fox gun law in Massachusetts, which permits ownership of handguns but bans carrying them out of the house. After the law was introduced with a big publicity campaign, report Glenn Pierce and William Bowers, gun robberies and gun assaults declined, though nongun crimes of the same type increased throughout the state. And in Boston, the law appears to have prevented some gun-related homicides, without any accompanying increase in nongun homicides. "A gun control measure that increases the average cost and hassle of a youthful urban male acquiring his first handgun may at least delay acquisition for a year of two—with noticeable effect on the gun crime rate," concludes Mr. Cook.

While wrangling between politicians and lobbyists frustrates efforts to enact serious gun control laws, public opinion remains fairly unified on the issue. Sociologist James Wright points out that, although most Americans believe they have a right to possess guns, they also realize that guns are dangerous and ought to be regulated by the government. Wright compares two opinion surveys, one sponsored by the National Rifle Association and the other by the Center for the Study and Prevention of Handgun Violence. Naturally, the organizations used the results to promote opposing views, but Wright found many similarities in the responses, which provide interesting insights into gun-toting America and confirm a remarkable popular consensus. The surveys agreed that between 20 and 25 percent of Americans have handguns in their homes (about 30.85 million guns), with 40 percent of those citing protection or self-defense as the reason. Analysis of the surveys also showed widespread belief

that private citizens have a right to own guns, and that criminals will find ways to obtain guns no matter what. But they also indicated wide support for registration and licensing of all privately owned handguns, and a belief that such registration would not violate the individual's right to own a gun.

"The thrust of majority thinking on gun control," Wright concludes, "seems to be that the government should be just as careful about who is allowed to own and use a firearm as it is about who is allowed to own and use automobiles or other potentially hazardous commodities." That notion, too restrictive for the NRA, yet too permissive for serious handgun foes, may still offer a basis for national policy. The various authors of "Gun Control" don't attempt to propose one, but they offer plenty to a reader inclined to speculate.

A nationally coordinated registration program could create an important tool for law enforcement. Criminal suspects caught with unregistered guns could be detained for that reason in the absence of other evidence; computer gun-registration checks, similar to the auto-registration check a highway patrolman runs on you when he pulls you over for a moving violation, would become useful investigative procedures. Universal registration, especially if accompanied by a law requiring owners to report lost or stolen guns, would permit police to trace the ways guns move into the illicit market.

The public support for government regulation of the gun trade might also indicate support for other sensible measures. Cook and Blose, in their article, point out, for example, that 23 states, including 64 percent of the population, now already require that police be notified and permitted to check into the

UPI/Bettmann

Rows of confiscated handguns shown at police headquarters in Chicago.

background of a customer before he may purchase a handgun. Writing such a requirement into Federal law would strengthen existing legislation that prohibits sales of guns to categories of people considered dangerous.

A national gun-registration policy might also crack down on gun dealers. One proposal currently before Congress would raise the Federal dealer's license fee from $10 to $500, thereby reducing their number and making it easier to keep them under government supervision. The law would even make dealers liable for civil damages should they knowingly sell a handgun to an ineligible person who uses it to hurt somebody. (Their responsibility may be compared to that of the bartender who sells liquor to a drunk.)

A public that favors regulating guns

the way we regulate automobiles would not be likely to oppose such measures. They would constitute the politically feasible first step that, in the opinion of Cook and Blose, would cause "modest reduction in firearms violence rates." They would also give the government a handle on the problem, with the potential for more than modest reduction as time goes on.

In light of these speculations, two further points contained in this substantive volume are worth noting. The first is Moore's conclusion that since stolen handguns are such an important part of the illicit traffic, local police departments, rather than Federal agencies, are the best places to mount major efforts to control the criminal gun trade. "The best approach is likely to be high volume, relatively unsophisticated undercover investigations aided by patrol efforts and a few informants." In other words, he suggests, local cops should treat illegal guns like illegal drugs, and go after their users in the same ways. The possibilities of handgun squads— already being tried in some police departments—beefed up with Federal funding and tough universal gun-registration laws are more than interesting to contemplate.

The second point is contained in an article by Franklin Zimring, perhaps the nation's most respected authority on handguns and crime, who contemplates the future of handgun use and policy for the rest of the century. A basic problem, Zimring says, is that existing inventory of some 30 million handguns, to which another 2 million are added each year. The prospect that police will show up one day to search your home and confiscate your handguns is remote; but short of that, it's hard to see how any Federal policy can reduce the number of handguns in circulation. In fact, a Federal registration program would legitimize ownership as much as limit it.

A far more powerful factor, he suggests, is public opinion. "An increase in the social stigma associated with household defense guns will influence the demand for handguns long before it affects national policy toward handgun supply," Zimring writes. Once it becomes fashionable to talk about your guns at middle-class dinner parties, he suggests, no effective limits on the supply would be possible. But should gun ownership remain a little embarrassing, a sign of an extreme personality, then some hope remains for an eventual decline.

Which prompts a final suggestion: Perhaps the people who oppose the spread of handguns should take their money out of Washington lobbying efforts and put it into television commercials. They worked quite well, after all, for antismoking groups who wanted to counter the fashionable image of cigarettes.

And the dramatic possibilities are clear: In Mount Airy, Maryland, recently, a three-year-old boy picked up the family handgun, pointed it at his mother, pulled the trigger and shot her through the chest. What might a creative ad agency do with that?

66.

The "Law of the Sea" Treaty

On April 30, 1982, after eight years of complicated negotiations, delegates to the United Nations Law of the Sea Conference overwhelmingly adopted a final version of a comprehensive treaty governing the use of the seas and their natural resources. There were 130 affirmative votes, 4 negative, and 17 abstentions. Among its many provisions the treaty was to impose international controls on seabed mining and require mining companies to sell their technical expertise to an international group operating for the benefit of third world countries. The United States was one of the four nations voting against the treaty. The reasons for this negative vote are stated below by President Reagan. A dissenting view of the U.S. action is expressed by Rep. Lee H. Hamilton, D.-Ind., chairman of the House Subcommittee on Europe and the Middle East.

Source: Presidential Documents, week ending July 9, 1982.

Congressional Digest, January 1983.

STATEMENT BY THE PRESIDENT
JULY 9, 1982

THE UNITED STATES has long recognized how critical the world's oceans are to mankind and how important international agreements are to the use of those oceans. For over a decade, the United States has been working with more than 150 countries at the Third United Nations Conference on Law of the Sea to develop a comprehensive treaty.

On January 29 of this year, I reaffirmed the United States commitment to the multilateral process for reaching such a treaty and announced that we would return to the negotiations to seek to correct unacceptable elements in the deep seabed mining part of the draft convention. I also announced that my administration would support ratification of a convention meeting six basic objectives.

On April 30 the conference adopted a convention that does not satisfy the objectives sought by the United States. It was adopted by a vote of 130 in favor, with 4 against (including the United States) and 17 abstentions. Those voting "no" or abstaining appear small in number but represent countries which produce more than 60 percent of the world's gross national product and provide more than 60 percent of the contributions to the United Nations.

We have now completed a review of that convention and recognize that it contains many positive and very significant accomplishments. Those extensive parts dealing with navigation and overflight and most other provisions of the convention are consistent with United States interests and, in our view, serve well the interests of all nations. That is an important achievement and signifies the benefits of working together and effectively balancing numerous interests. The United States also appreciates the efforts of the many countries that have worked toward an acceptable agreement, including efforts by friends and allies at the session that concluded on April 30.

Our review recognizes, however, that the deep seabed mining part of the convention does not meet United States

objectives. For this reason, I am announcing today that the United States will not sign the convention as adopted by the conference, and our participation in the remaining conference process will be at the technical level and will involve only those provisions that serve United States interests.

These decisions reflect the deep conviction that the United States cannot support a deep seabed mining regime with such major problems. In our view, those problems include:

—Provisions that would actually deter future development of deep seabed mineral resources, when such development should serve the interest of all countries.

—A decision making process that would not give the United States or others a role that fairly reflects and protects their interests.

—Provisions that would allow amendments to enter into force for the United States without its approval. This is clearly incompatible with the United States approach to such treaties.

—Stipulations relating to mandatory transfer of private technology and the possibility of national liberation movements sharing in benefits.

—The absence of assured access for future qualified deep seabed miners to promote the development of these resources.

We recognize that world demand and markets currently do not justify commercial development of deep seabed mineral resources, and it is not clear when such development will be justified. When such factors become favorable, however, the deep seabed represents a potentially important source of strategic and other minerals. The aim of the United States in this regard has been to establish with other nations an order that would allow exploration and development under reasonable terms and conditions.

B: LEE H. HAMILTON
SPEECH TO THE HOUSE,
SEPTEMBER 8, 1982

WHEN THE UNITED STATES voted against the Law of the Sea Treaty, the action hardly made a headline. Even though the treaty took more than a decade to complete and contained several important rules governing the uses of the seas, few Americans seemed worried about its rejection. Yet, the decision is a significant one for Amercian foreign policy.

The seas have always been important in the scheme of things, and the ability of vessels to travel the seas freely has been of interest for hundreds of years. For the United States, one of the world's leading maritime powers, freedom of the seas is so vital that we fought wars to preserve it before our nation was a century old. Our trade depends heavily on the unimpeded movement of the merchant fleet. The value of our Navy would diminish if the seas were not open to our warships. History shows our strong commitment to the freedom of the seas—a commitment which we have honored in war and peace.

Since the 1700's, the only thing protecting the freedom of the seas has been its acceptance among nations. In this century that acceptance has been eroding. Many nations have different views of the seas and their uses. Oil and gas on the continental shelf and mineral-laden nodules on the seabed have caused conflict and may result in a division of the seas among the powerful nations.

In 1958 and 1960, the United Nations convened conferences to codify rules on the uses of the seas. The first conference produced agreements on the continental shelf, the high seas, and the conservation of marine wildlife. The second conference considered the width of territorial waters, but reached no agreement. The expansion of territorial waters (in some cases, up to 200 miles) and technological advances not anticipated by the 1958 agreement made further negotiations necessary, so the United Nations, with American support, again took up the question of the uses of the seas and called for a third conference. The conference convened in 1973 amid speculation that a consensus among nations could produce a treaty to cover all maritime activities. Presidents Nixon, Ford, and Carter pursued the negotiations with vigor. By the summer of 1980, all but three issues were decided. Tentative accords were reached on the width of territorial waters, passage through straits, responsibilities and rights of states in territorial waters, in economic resource zones, on the continental shelf, and on the high seas, conservation of fisheries, protection of the marine environment, marine research, and mining of minerals on the seabed. With regard to the last point, the treaty set up a body to regulate seabed mining so that the poor nations would have a role. The body would get its technology from the rich nations.

Critics of the treaty were found mainly among isolationists and among certain parts of the seabed mining industry. When President Reagan took office, however, these critics gained an influential ally. One of the President's first acts was to withdraw from the conference pending a full review of the American position. During the review, there was an intense battle within the bureaucracy between those who opposed the treaty outright and those who wanted certain changes, mainly in the provisions on seabed mining. In January of 1982, the President decided to return to the conference to pursue such changes.

The United States was unable to get all its changes at the 1982 session. Many delegates thought that the United States was inflexible in its view, pushing for changes but refusing to negotiate. Members of the American delegation said that their instructions, drafted largely by opponents of the treaty, were designed to prevent agreement. When a compromise was offered by some of our allies, we turned it down. The final session ended with the adoption of the treaty by 130 nations, but the United States, along with Israel, Venezuela, and Greece, cast negative votes. We said "no" despite some gains at the bargaining table, including the power to veto funding for national liberation movements and a guaranteed seat on the seabed mining authority.

The President argued that the seabed mining provisions would not encourage investment and would not guarantee our access to minerals on the seabed. He hoped that other nations would recognize certain provisions as international law, not denying their benefits to the United States, but that the seabed mining provision would not be accepted as international law because the United States, the major mining nation, would not follow them. He is now trying to get our friends to sign a separate "mini-treaty" on seabed mining.

Treaty supporters disagree. They think that the treaty protects our interests, and that we should try to change the provisions on seabed mining. They say that we will be unable to select the provisions of the treaty we like, and that we could lose our navigation rights. Since many of our friends appear unwilling to sign any mini-treaty, treaty supporters assert that we could jeopardize our own seabed mining industry and lose our assured access to minerals on the seabed.

I doubt that the Reagan Administration gave enough consideration to the implications of rejecting the treaty. Because the treaty also regulates territorial waters and navigation rights, treaty supporters are correct when they contend that any straits in the world could be closed to us in times of crisis. Also, any attempts by American companies to mine the seabed could be attacked by nations which have signed the treaty. These companies could then be forced to relocate abroad, and America could find itself with no means to reach minerals on the seabed. The President hopes to negotiate individual agreements if our interests are not adequately protected. The costs of such an approach could be high since we would be forced to make concessions to gain rights now protected under the treaty. Just as important, by rejecting the treaty we relinquish our leadership in the struggle to establish norms of behavior to guide nations.

The United States should not have given up on negotiations to change the treaty. I hope that we will reconsider sooner rather than later.

67.

Louis Harris: Public Attitudes Toward the Threat of Nuclear War

On June 12, 1982, a massive parade and peace rally, organized by religious and secular groups, was held in New York City to coincide with the second United Nations special session on disarmament. The crowd, including those who lined the sidewalks, was estimated to be more than 600,000; some estimates went as high as one million persons, making it one of the largest peace rallies in history. It was also colorful, with placards, effigies, masks, floats, balloons, banners, costumes, huge puppets, people dancing on stilts, and an enormous inflatable rubber whale labeled "Save the Humans." The New York Times *called it a "rainbow spectrum of religions, ethnic groups, trades, professions, unions, cultural and educational institutions, and political organizations." And its lead editorial proclaimed that "Hundreds of thousands of demonstrators in. . .Central Park can't be wrong." A few weeks later the* Bulletin of the Atomic Scientists *published an interview (conducted by Jamie Kalven) with Louis Harris, the public opinion analyst, dealing with the results of a recent poll of public attitudes toward the threat of nuclear war. The interview is reprinted here.*

Source: *Bulletin of the Atomic Scientists,* "A Talk with Louis Harris," August-September 1982.

"An incredible phenomenon"—these are the words public opinion analyst Louis Harris used in a recent interview with the *Bulletin* to describe his latest findings on public attitudes toward the threat of nuclear war.

Few people bring a more seasoned perspective to bear on questions of public opinion than Harris. Director of one of the most respected polling organizations in the country, he has been taking soundings on the attitudes of the American people for more than 30 years. And he says he can recall nothing quite like the "urgent hunger for peace" disclosed by his recent polls.

Consider the following findings on attitudes toward a nuclear arms freeze and toward a nuclear arms reduction agreement with the Soviet Union:

• A large majority (73 to 23 percent) favors every country that has nuclear weapons banning the production, storage, and use of those weapons.

• An even larger majority (86 to 11 percent) wants the United States and the Soviet Union to negotiate a nuclear arms reduction agreement.

• Another large majority (81 to 16 percent) wants the United States and the Soviet Union to agree not to produce any new nuclear weapons, provided both have a rough equivalence of such weapons today.

"These results are startling and simply cannot be ignored," says Harris. And

AP/Wide World

Louis Harris

it is unlikely that they will be ignored by elected officials, in view of figures like this: 56 percent of the voters say that they would vote *against* a candidate for Congress who favored escalation of the nuclear arms race, even if they agreed with him on almost every other issue; while only 14 percent say they would vote *for* him under such circumstances.

One of the most remarkable characteristics of the public's thinking, in Harris's view, is that it goes beyond the proposals that are presently under consideration. "Perhaps the most striking number in all the research we've done on the subject," he reports, "is that by 74 to 22 percent, a big majority of the American people, say that they want all countries that have nuclear weapons to destroy them." Another large majority (66 to 31 percent) think it is immoral for any country to produce more nuclear weapons.

Harris interprets these findings to mean that if an agreement were reached between the two superpowers to freeze or reduce nuclear weapons, the public would demand further reductions, and then further reductions beyond that, until the last nuclear weapons were eliminated.

How does he account for this phenomenon? The single most important factor, he says, is probably "a growing distrust of the rulers of the two superpowers." People have long been aware "in a passive kind of way" of the threat of nuclear destruction. But now they are "genuinely frightened"— "frightened in an activated as opposed to a passive way"—by the perception that "the leaders of the Soviet Union and the leaders of the United States are heading toward a nuclear confrontation." This fear is reflected in the 52 to 45 percent majority of the American people who are worried that President Reagan will get us into another war. And it is reflected in the portrait of the Soviet leaders that emerges from the following figures:

• A large majority of the American people (84 percent) see the Soviet Union as a threat to the security of the United States.

• A 2-to-1 majority (63 to 23 percent) think that there is a likelihood over the next 40 years that the Soviet Union will attack the United States.

• A substantial majority (69 to 24 percent) think the Soviet leaders would not hesitate to use nuclear arms, if they were desperate enough.

• Fully 49 percent of the American people view the Soviet Union as an outright "enemy," while another 31 percent think the Soviet Union is unfriendly toward the United States even if not our enemy. Thus, an 80 to 10 percent majority see the Soviet Union as a power hostile to the United States. These figures reflect a marked deterioration since 1976 when a 69 to 21 percent majority saw the Soviet Union as hostile—a deterioration Harris attributes to the impact of Afghanistan and Poland. (According to Harris, only three other powers in the world are viewed with a comparable degree of suspicion: Iran is viewed as hostile by 80 to 16 percent; Libya by 66 to 22 percent; and the Palestine Liberation Organization by 73 to 15 percent.)

In sharp contrast to their feelings about the Soviet state, Harris notes, the American people "feel remarkably little hostility toward the Russian people on a people-to-people basis." Thus, while 80 percent regard the Soviet Union as a power hostile to the United States, no more than 19 percent think the Russian people are unfriendly toward the American people; and only 9 percent feel unfriendly toward the Russian people.

Harris also points out that American distrust of the Soviet Union cannot be attributed entirely to the fact that it is a communist country, for there is a major communist country which is now seen as a close ally by 15 percent of Americans and as a friendly power, if not a close ally, by another 55 percent: the People's Republic of China. Viewed in light of the fact that in 1976 a 74 to 17 percent majority saw China as a hostile power, the finding that 70 percent of the American people now regard China as a friend should serve as a reminder that the enmities that fuel the nuclear arms race may prove more temporary, more ephemeral, than they seem at the moment.

One of the central themes that emerges from Harris's findings is the strength of the American people's desire to seek areas of agreement with the Soviets. This desire is all the more striking, Harris notes, because it moves against the undertow of such deep distrust. By a "huge margin" of 78 to 7

percent, the American people believe that the Soviets only want agreements when they can gain an advantage; and by another large margin of 75 to 21 percent, they are skeptical that the Soviets will keep their end of agreements. Yet despite this, 8 out of 10 Americans (83 to 15 percent) think it is important for the United States to try to establish better relations with the Soviet Union.

This general attitude is reflected in strong support for a wide range of potential agreements between the two countries:

• A large majority (82 to 16 percent) would like to see the START talks end in agreement.

• An almost identical majority (83 to 14 percent) think it is urgent for the two countries to reach agreement on capping, limiting, or reducing nuclear arms in each country.

The desire for agreement also reaches into a number of other areas:

• Nearly all Americans (90 to 5 percent) would like an agreement to help end the world's energy problems.

• Another big majority (88 to 6 percent) would favor agreement on a joint undertaking to curb air and water pollution.

There is a desire for agreements on matters the Soviets are not particularly eager to negotiate:

• A big majority (85 to 3 percent) would like a U.S.-Soviet agreement that would enable Jews to leave the Soviet Union more easily.

• Another large majority (85 to 5 percent) would like an agreement that would give more freedom to writers and scientists within the Soviet Union.

And there is as well a desire for agreements in areas where the United States has shown a reluctance to negotiate:

• A large majority (72 to 16 per-

Erv Kaczmarek

"I HAVE NONE. I MOVE AROUND
A LOT."

cent) would favor an expansion of U.S.-Soviet trade.

• A plurality (49 to 32 percent) would support giving the Soviet Union a "most favored nation" status in trade.

Thus, despite their skepticism about the good faith of the Soviet government, the American people want their government to seek out as many areas of agreement with the Soviet Union as possible. Harris characterizes their attitude this way: "They're saying we've got to try it, because the alternative to having agreements is building tensions which could lead to war—and to oblivion. The alternative has become unacceptable."

Harris cautions that this does not mean "that America has lost the will to defend itself" or that the public is moved to negotiate out of a sense of weakness. "The only kind of agreements people here want," he emphasizes, "are those which are to the mutual advantage of both parties."

It is precisely this concern with mutuality, he reports, that makes the present moment "seem particularly ripe to the American people" as a time to negoti-

ate nuclear arms agreements with the Soviet Union. For a majority of Americans now feel that there is rough equivalence in nuclear strength between the two countries and hence that "this is the right time to do something." The shift in public opinion on this point over the last two years has been dramatic: In 1980 a 57 to 37 percent majority felt the United States was weaker than the Soviet Union. Today, by contrast, a 59 to 38 percent majority feel the United States and the Soviet Union are roughly in parity.

The public's insistence on mutuality is also apparent in the response Harris and his colleagues received when they recently asked the following question: "Would you favor or oppose the U.S. deciding to gradually dismantle our nuclear weapons before getting an agreement from other countries to do the same?" By 82 to 15 percent, people who had favored a nuclear freeze by 6 to 1 declared that they would oppose any such move. The moral, as Harris sees it, is that "the American people want to negotiate from a position of rough parity and want a freeze or reduction of nuclear weapons to leave each country in a state of rough parity." Any suggestion that the United States disarm unilaterally, he warns, will "blight" the emerging public constituency for nuclear arms control.

What other dangers does he foresee? There is, he says, one other "very important" danger: It would, in his view, be "a mistake" to couple the nuclear war issue with other issues—for example, to argue that money being spent on the nuclear arms race should be spent on various social programs. Such a strategy would, he argues, "weaken rather than strengthen the movement, because what you're doing then is saying to people: 'Look, in order for you to join my anti-nuclear movement, you have to agree to call for a restoration of food stamps or something.' "

He advises: "If you want to be *effective* on this issue, you must zero in on it. The movement is much stronger on a straight-forward, simple basis. I don't think it's an oversimplification simply to say: 'We demand that this potential scourge of humanity be halted and finally ended.' The more you diffuse the issue with a whole series of other issues, the more you weaken the movement."

In Harris's view, any such effort to integrate the nuclear war issue with other issues misconceives—and undermines—the unique strength of the movement. That strength resides in the fact that this is an issue that affects everyone equally, an issue that has aroused the common concern of people who may agree about little else.

"There is no way," says Harris, "to paint the people who are affected by this issue into a simple mold and say they check out on this or that stereotype. They don't. This cuts right across the spectrum of social and political divisions in this country. It's an idea that will not go away. It's going to be with us until the final weapons are obliterated."

68.

William J. Brennan, Jr., and Warren E. Burger: Educational Rights of Illegal Aliens

On June 15, 1982, the Supreme Court, in a decision in Plyler v. Doe, overturned a Texas law that permitted local school districts to either bar children of illegal aliens from public schools or charge them tuition. The ruling meant that children of undocumented aliens had to be granted access to free public education. Secretary of Education T.H. Bell complained that the ruling was a federal intrusion into state affairs, but he agreed that the decision was, in principle, a just one. Texas Governor Bill Clements noted that he thought the problem "has been vastly overblown in the press" and added: "I'm sure we'll handle it in Texas in good form." The state's education commissioner reported that the number of illegal aliens in Texas public schools would reach 30,000 by the end of 1982 and that it would cost the state $100 million to educate them. Reprinted below are excerpts from the court's majority opinion, by William J. Brennan, Jr., and from its minority opinion, written by Chief Justice Burger.

Source: *The New York Times*, June 16, 1982.

A: JUSTICE BRENNAN

The question presented by these cases is whether, consistent with the equal protection clause of the 14th Amendment, Texas may deny to undocumented school-age children the free public education that it provides to children who are citizens of the United States or legally admitted aliens.

Unsanctioned entry into the United States is a crime. But despite the existence of these legal restrictions, a substantial number of persons have succeeded in unlawfully entering the United States, and now live within various states, including the State of Texas.

VIOLATION OF EQUAL PROTECTION

The 14th Amendment provides that "No state shall . . . deprive any person of life, liberty, or property, without due process of law; nor deny to *any person within its jurisdiction* the equal protection of the laws." Appellants argue at the outset that undocumented aliens, because of their immigration status, are not "persons within the jurisdiction" of the state of Texas, and that they therefore have no right to the equal protection of Texas law. We reject this argument. Whatever his status under the immigration laws, an alien is surely a "person" in any ordinary sense of that term.

Use of the phrase "within its jurisdiction" thus does not detract from, but rather confirms, the understanding that the protection of the 14th Amdendment extends to anyone, citizen or stranger, who *is* subject to the laws of a state, and reaches into every corner of a state's territory.

Our conclusion that the illegal aliens who are plaintiffs in these cases may claim the benefit of the 14th Amendment's guarantee of equal protection only begins the inquiry. The more difficult question is whether the equal protection clause has been violated by the refusal of the State of Texas to reimburse local school boards for the education of children who cannot demonstrate that their presence within the United States is lawful, or by the imposition by those school boards of the burden of tuition on those children.

Sheer incapability or lax enforcement of the laws barring entry into this country, coupled with the failure to establish an effective bar to the employment of undocumented aliens, has resulted in the creation of a substantial "shadow population" of illegal migrants—numbering in the millions—within our borders. This situation raises the specter of a permanent caste of undocumented resident aliens, encouraged by some to remain here as a source of cheap labor, but nevertheless denied the benefits that our society makes available to citizens and lawful residents. The existence of such an underclass presents most difficult problems for a nation that prides itself on adherence to principles of equality under law.

The children who are plaintiffs in these cases are special members of this underclass. Persuasive arguments support the view that a state may withhold its beneficence from those whose very presence within the United States is the product of their own unlawful conduct. These arguments do not apply with the same force to classifications imposing disabilities on the minor *children* of such illegal entrants. At the least, those who elect to enter our territory by stealth and in violation of our law should be prepared to bear the consequences, including, but not limited to, deportation. But the children of those illegal entrants are not comparably situated. Even if the state found it expedient to control the conduct of adults by acting against their children, legislation directing the onus of a parent's misconduct against his children does not comport with fundamental conceptions of justice.

THE PROBLEM OF ILLITERACY

Public education is not a "right" granted to individuals by the Constitution. But neither is it merely some governmental "benefit" indistinguishable from other forms of social welfare legislation. Both the importance of education in maintaining our basic institutions, and the lasting impact of its deprivation on the life of the child, mark the distinction. We have recognized the public school as a most vital civic institution for the preservation of a democratic system of government, and as the primary vehicle for transmitting the values on which our society rests.

Paradoxically, by depriving the children of any disfavored group of an education, we foreclose the means by which that group might raise the level of esteem in which it is held by the majority. Illiteracy is an enduring disability. The inability to read and write will handicap the individual deprived of a basic education each and every day of his life. The inestimable toll of that deprivation on the social, economic, intellectual and psychological well-being of the individual, and the obstacle it poses to individual achievement, makes it most difficult to reconcile the cost or the principle of a status-based denial of basic education with the framework of equality embodied in the equal protection clause.

These well-settled principles allow us to determine the proper level of deference to be afforded Section 21.031. Section 21.031 imposes a lifetime hardship on a discrete class of children not accountable for their disabling status.

The stigma of illiteracy will mark them for the rest of their lives. By denying these children a basic education, we deny them the ability to live within the structure of our civil institutions, and foreclose any realistic possibility that they will contribute in even the smallest way to the progress of our nation. In determining the rationality of Section 21.031, we may appropriately take into account its costs to the nation and to the innocent children who are its victims. In light of these countervailing costs, the discrimination contained in Section 21.031 can hardly be considered rational unless it furthers some substantial goal of the state.

Appellants argue that the classification at issue furthers an interest in the "preservation of the state's limited resources for the education of its lawful residents." Of course, a concern for the preservation of resources standing alone can hardly justify the classification used in allocating those resources. The state must do more than justify its classification with a concise expression of an intention to discriminate.

It is difficult to understand precisely what the state hopes to achieve by promoting the creation and perpetuation of a subclass of illiterates within our boundaries, surely adding to the problems and costs of unemployment, welfare, and crime. It is thus clear that whatever savings might be achieved by denying these children an education, they are wholly insubstantial in light of the costs involved to these children, the state and the nation.

B: CHIEF JUSTICE BURGER

Were it our business to set the nation's social policy, I would agree without hesitation that it is senseless for an enlightened society to deprive any children—including illegal aliens—of an elementary education. However, the Constitution does not constitute us as "Platonic Guardians" nor does it vest in this Court the authority to strike down laws because they do not meet our standards of desirable social policy, "wisdom" or "common sense." We trespass on the assigned function of the political branches under our structure of limited and separated powers when we assume a policymaking role as the Court does today.

The Court's holding today manifests the justly criticized judicial tendency to attempt speedy and wholesale formulation of "remedies" for the failures—or simply the laggard pace—of the political processes of our system of government. The Court employs, and in my view abuses, the 14th Amendment in an effort to become an omnipotent and omniscient problem solver. That the motives for doing so are noble and compassionate does not alter the fact that the Court distorts our constitutional function to make amends for the defaults of others.

In a sense, the Court's opinion rests on such a unique confluence of theories and rationales that it will likely stand for little beyond the results in these particular cases. Yet the extent to which the Court departs from principled constitutional adjudication is nonetheless disturbing.

The dispositive issue in these cases, simply put, is whether, for purposes of allocating its finite resources, a state has a legitimate reason to differentiate between persons who are lawfully within the state and those who are unlawfully there. The distinction the State of Texas has drawn—based not only upon its own legitimate interests but on classifications established by the Federal Government in its immigration laws and policies—is not unconstitutional.

The equal protection clause protects against arbitrary and irrational classifications, and against invidious discrimination stemming from prejudice and hostility; it is not an all-encompassing "equalizer" designed to eradicate every distinction for which persons are not "responsible."

"FUNDAMENTAL RIGHTS"

The importance of education is beyond dispute. Yet we have held repeatedly that the importance of a governmental service does not elevate it to the status of a "fundamental right" for purposes of equal protection analysis. The Court points to no meaningful way to distinguish between education and other governmental benefits in this context. Is the Court suggesting that education is more "fundamental" than food, shelter or medical care?

Without laboring what will undoubtedly seem obvious to many, it simply is not "irrational" for a state to conclude that it does not have the same responsibility to provide benefits for persons whose very presence in the state and this country is illegal as it does to provide for persons lawfully present. By definition, illegal aliens have no right whatever to be here, and the state may reasonably, and constitutionally, elect not to provide them with governmental services at the expense of those who are lawfully in the state.

Today's cases, I regret to say, present yet another example of unwarranted judicial action which in the long run tends to contribute to the weakening of our political processes.

69.

William Safire: The Computer Tattoo

On August 12, 1982, the U.S. Senate approved a new immigration bill that, while granting resident status to illegal aliens who had arrived in the United States before 1980, would make all those arriving after December 31, 1979, subject to deportation. For the first time, employers who knowingly hired illegal aliens would be fined; and repeated convictions could lead to imprisonment. The question, of course, was how employers were supposed to know that job applicants were undocumented; the bill envisioned a national identification system, so employers could tell who was legal. The result: an identity card that every citizen would have to carry. Many were the objections of libertarians to this intrusion on the freedom of Americans, objections that were summed up in this blazing comment by New York Times *columnist William Safire.*

Source: *The New York Times,* September 9, 1982.

In a well-meaning effort to curb the employment of illegal aliens, and with the hearty good wishes of editorialists who ordinarily pride themselves on guarding against the intrusion of government into the private lives of individual Americans, Congress is about to take this generation's longest step toward totalitarianism.

"There is no 'slippery slope' toward loss of liberties," insists Senator Alan Simpson of Wyoming, author of the latest immigration bill, "only a long staircase where each step downward must be first tolerated by the American people and their leaders."

The first step downward on the Simpson staircase to Big-Brotherdom is the requirement that within three years the Federal Government come up with a "secure system to determine employment eligibility in the United States."

Despite denials, that means a national identity card. Nobody who is pushing this bill admits that—on the contrary, all sorts of "safeguards" and rhetorical warnings about not having to carry an identity card on one's person at all times are festooned on the bill. Much is made of the use of passports, Social Security cards and driver's licenses as "preferred" forms of identification, but anyone who takes the trouble to read this legislation can see that the disclaimers are intended to help the medicine go down.

Most Americans see no danger at all in a national identity card. Most people even like the idea of a piece of plastic that tells the world, and themselves, who they are. "I'm *me*," says the little card. "I'm entitled to all the benefits that go with being provably and demonstrably *me*." Good citizens—the ones who vote regularly, and who don't get into auto accidents—might get a gold card.

Once the down staircase is set in place, the temptation to take each next step will be irresistible. Certainly every business would want to ask customers to insert their identity cards into the whizbang credit checker. Banks, phone companies, schools, hotels would all take advantage of the obvious utility of the document that could not be counterfeited. Law enforcement and tax collection would surely be easier, because the Federal Government would know at all times exactly where everybody was and what they were spending.

And then you might as well live in the Soviet Union. One of the great differences between free and enslaved societies is the right of the individual to live and work without the government knowing his every move. There can sometimes be privacy without freedom, as those in solitary confinement know, but there can be no freedom without privacy.

When Patty Hearst managed to remain a fugitive for 591 days, that did not mean the F.B.I. was bad at catching fugitives; it meant that America was a free society. In China or the Soviet Union she would have been captured in days, because it is impossible for ordinary citizens to move about without

permission. If our values mean anything at all, they mean that it is better to tolerate the illegal movement of aliens and even criminals than to tolerate the constant surveillance of the free.

The Attorney General, who evidently has no grasp of libertarian conservative principles, will not fight this legislation. When an outside adviser, Martin Anderson—who with his wife, Annelise, at O.M.B. represent what is left of the conservative conscience of the Reagan Administration—objected in a Cabinet meeting to this danger of Federal intrusion, William French Smith was forced to tell Congress of "a small but serious objection" to the identity card clause. He later made his objection meaningless by pretending it was "inappropriate to presume" he would have to do what the bill mandates him to do—come up with a foolproof identity system.

We are entering the computer age. Combined with a national identity card—an abuse of power that Peter Rodino professes to oppose in the House, as he makes it inevitable—government computers and data banks pose a threat to personal liberty. Though aimed against "undocumented workers," the computer tattoo will be pressed on you and me.

The bureaucratic apparatus needed to assign and administer a standard universal identifier (SUI) would represent another imposition of government control on an already heavily burdened citizenry.
DEPARTMENT OF HEALTH, EDUCATION, AND WELFARE, 1973

70.

JOHN EGERTON and JOHN HOLT: Can We Save the Schools?

Early in 1982 the editors of The Progressive *asked two noted writers on education to respond to the question, Can we save the schools? It was a question that was being asked by many persons, educators and nonprofessionals alike. The answers given by Egerton and Holt neatly spanned the controversy as it was then developing. It should be noted that while Egerton responds to the question in the affirmative, he too is extremely pessimistic about the chances of anything being done.*

Source: *The Progressive,* March 1982.

A: JOHN EGERTON
CAN WE SAVE THE SCHOOLS?
YES, BUT THERE ISN'T MUCH TIME.

ANYONE WHO DOUBTS that public education in the United States is in deep trouble has not been paying attention. Beyond the grim prospects of Reaganomics, beyond all the thorny problems of school finance, an imposing mountain of difficulties has been rising year by year. The woes of the schools have to do with quality and effectiveness, with student achievement and teacher competence, with administrative and governing-board leadership, with basic skills and comprehensive curricula, with standards and values, with the increase in private and parochial school enrollments and the decline in the birth rate, with the weakening of authority and the worsening of violence and disorder, with the pervasive strains of race and class and sex bias, with the acute needs of the poor, the handicapped, the non-English-speaking. More money might shrink problems, but it cannot completely solve them, or restore public confidence in the schools, or develop a national consensus on the means and ends of education.

No such consensus exists now. The rising chorus against Federal aid to education is being joined by voices opposing state aid or even local aid—and the proponents of more money for schools from any level of government are losing on every front. Pressure groups demanding specific moral or religious or patriotic content in curricula are countered by opponents who have their own notions of what consitutes "value-free" or "value-fair" material. Sociologist James Coleman's latest education study—a report which holds that private schools are superior to public schools—sets off a furious argument among "experts" over the relative quality of schools (and the validity of Coleman's data).

Anti-busing advocates want neighborhood schools. Textbook crusaders want the power to dictate content. Opponents of standardized testing want abolition of all such tests. New schemes to organize, conduct, and finance education are regularly advanced by all manner of critics and strategists arrayed across the ideological spectrum. Their proposals range from blatantly self-serving to blindly simplistic: tuition tax credits for private school patrons; government vouchers to finance "free-market" schools; segregation by subject matter or test scores or sex or race or socio-economic class; home teaching; instruction through computer terminals and television; the abolition of compulsory education; the "de-schooling" of society.

With so much turmoil and frustration abroad in and around the schools, the temptation is almost overpowering to long for bygone times when things supposedly were better. But were they? Those who think so argue that schools are now seized with violence and fear, immobilized by bureaucracy, fragmented by special interests, bankrupted by waste and inefficiency, split by philosophical and ideological differences, preoccupied with race and class divisions, filled with incompetence. And yet a persuasive counterargument exists: *There has never been a time when a larger number or percentage of American young people completed the requirements of schooling, left with a greater and more diverse store of knowledge, and went on to advanced training in such a multitude of endeavors.*

Whether for better or worse, the nation's schools have always been more nearly a reflection of the larger society than an expression of its ideals—and now they reflect the soul and substance of a nation gagging on its own divisive juices. Schools are essentially political institutions—they are, after all, the chief instrument for reproducing society—and it is unrealistic to expect them to be otherwise. They will not be agents for social change unless the larger society, through its political forces, is committed

to social change. But they will be battlegrounds for competing factions whose interests range from a particular vision of the society of the future to a general determination to preserve and perpetuate educational institutions as they are.

Regardless of our greatly differentiated perceptions and expectations of schools, we are faced with questions we cannot easily answer: How will we pay for education's mission of reproducing society? Can a distinction be maintained between public and private schools? Is such a distinction vital to our democracy or merely an exercise in semantics? Do schools transmit values and indoctrinate the young? Should they? How? Whose values and what doctrines should they impart? Can schools become guarantors of equal opportunity? Can they nourish pluralism and diversity as well as equality? Should formal schooling for the young be focused only on the basic skills? Could other functions of schools, from the arts and sciences to sports, be better provided by other institutions? Is the advance of technology in schools a promise or a threat to the education of the nation's children?

There is not much evidence that we fully understand the questions, let alone the answers. As taxpayers and parents, we seem instead to be endlessly preoccupied with arguments over taxes and appropriations and budgets, over pupil-teacher ratios and racial percentages and test scores, over credit hours and credentials, over a maze of abstract numbers that obscures our vision and our purpose. Schools have always been a focus of debate and controversy in this country; what is unclear just now is whether the present crisis in education is simply a replay from the past or a new warning sign of impending collapse.

I have always assumed, without really knowing, that faith in public education was rooted in our history; that the rise of schools for "the masses" in the Nineteenth Century was a belated but genuine attempt to fulfill the egalitarian ideal of the Declaration of Independence.

But in recent years a number of revisionist historians and educational critics have gone beyond the missionary zeal from which so much educational history has sprung, and in the works of this new wave of writers can be found some starkly different perspectives.

It is perhaps oversimplifying, and misleading as well, to paint in one brush-stroke the broad surface of views held by such writers as Bernard Bailyn, Lawrence Cremin, Paul Goodman, Charles Silberman, John Holt, Jonathan Kozol, Michael Katz, Herbert Kohl, Ivan Illich, Peter Schrag, Colin Greer, Joel Spring, Samuel Bowles, and Herbert Gintis. Certainly they are not of one mind about how we got into the mess we're in or how we might best get out of it. But there is in their investigations and insights a wealth of informed opinion that sheds light on both the past and the present. For example:

¶ The start of public education in this country was not a self-conscious attempt by the State to guarantee equality in the larger society; it was rather an attempt to reinforce tradition and authority and to keep control of a rapidly growing and diversifying population.

¶ The English principle of politics— that power (and thus education) should be preserved as an exclusive privilege of the rich and well-born—dominated the first 200 years of white settlement in this country and not even the Revolution altered that fact. It was not until democracy was born on the frontier and swept back East that education, like the

franchise, came to be considered a right of the many rather than a privilege of the few—and even so, "the many" were understood to include only white males.

¶ Waves of immigrants from Europe in the decades preceding the Civil War led liberals and conservatives alike to see schools as a device to encourage assimilation and perpetuate control. Far from giving the native and immigrant masses equal educational opportunity with the upper classes, public schools gave them a general indoctrination in the political, religious, and economic rules of the game—and a little taste of the three Rs for good measure.

¶ The educational reform movements generally associated with Horace Mann in the antebellum decades and John Dewey in the early part of this century were not intended to raise the opportunities and the status of the poor, or even to broaden the middle class. Their more fundamental objectives were to Americanize foreigners, to train workers for an urban/industrial society, to develop cooperative and compliant attitudes as a means of maintaining social order, and to legitimate inequality by excluding or segregating blacks and others deemed inferior.

I find these views compelling, if not totally convincing. All of us who are old enough to remember the shameful years of legalized segregation must know that however much the public schools promised full freedom and equality for whites, they held no such realistic promise for blacks. We should have known, if we did not, that the economic and social divisions among whites were hardly lessened by the schools; they were, in fact, reinforced.

But even when I suspend belief in the questionable claims of the old missionary historians of education, I am still left with concerns that neither the revisionists nor the contemporary critics of schools have addressed. Two things in particular disturb me.

The first is this: *Public education, for all its flaws and shortcomings, is the nearest thing we have to a publicly owned and operated institution devoted to the general welfare.* (If our mines or our manufacturing plants were so owned and operated, we would properly call them socialist.) From Mann to Dewey to school officials of the present day, there has been and is at least the *rhetoric* of equal opportunity; surely the *reality* of it is closer to our grasp there than in alternative institutions yet to be formed—not to mention private alternatives that already exist.

Until recent years, the strongest attacks on public education came from authoritarian and undemocratic forces opposed to schooling for all at the expense of the state. It would be tragically ironic if the new critics and reformers of the Left gave reactionary opponents on the Right the ammunition that they need to blow public education away once and for all.

Yet opportunities for such destructive mischief already exist. A prime example can be found in current pursuit of tuition tax credits and educational vouchers. Tax credits would bolster private and parochial schools at the expense of the public systems—and that would include the alternative schools of many middle-class liberals as well as those of churches and segregationist groups. Vouchers, or government-issued checks to parents for free-market purchase of educational services for their children, would have essentially the same effect.

In compelling children to attend school, and in compelling the public schools to welcome and teach all who come to them, the State has assured universal exposure to education. The supply-and-demand forces of a so-called free economy do not apply to that process. But with vouchers or tax credits, there could be no more required attendance or required admission. The only compulsion affecting students, parents, and schools would be governed essentially by money—the need for it and the lack of it. Vouchers would create a seller's market, with school administrator-entrepreneurs taking only those students who bring the most money and the least needs and problems with them. Parents, on the other hand, would be limited to what they and their children could "qualify" for—financially, academically, socially. The voucher money from the government would never be enough to buy an equitable and effective school experience for the poor, the handicapped, the underprepared, the unmotivated, the "problem kids"; they would end up in the most marginal schools, while the affluent supplemented their dole from the public treasury with private funds to widen the gap.

The second thing that bothers me about attacks on public education from the Left is that the alternatives advocated by the critics are, to put it mildly, disappointing. Some of them are simply poor imitations of conventional schools; others have attractive features that offer no realistic promise of broad application; still others are riddled with ideological contradictions or based upon pure fantasy.

Ivan Illich led off the contemporary search for alternatives with his proposal in 1970 for deschooling of society by which he meant that "the State shall make no law with respect to the establishment of education." School, he said, "is the advertising agency which makes you believe that you need the society as it is." Others have followed with all sorts of alternative proposals to the present structure. The latest comes from John Holt, whose new book, *Teach Your Own,* advocates abandoning schools which he calls "babysitting services" and teachers whom he describes as "no more professional than bus drivers" and leaving your kids at home alone with their books.

Such anarchism flavored the proposals of frustrated critics of education in the past, long before Illich and Holt. There was, for example, the Modern School in Shelton, New Jersey more than a half-century ago, and there have been others similarly devoted to radical re-creation of educational institutions. But now as then, while the alternatives may be interesting or even valuable, they cannot begin to meet the needs of millions of children. It is only the middle and upper classes who can afford to experiment with exotic new forms of schooling, whether their goal is the realization of equality or the enhancement of economic and social advantage.

The poor have less money, more needs and—most important—more children. As the costs of education rise, as the effectiveness of schools diminishes, as more and more unskilled jobs disappear from the nation's economy, and as the affluent, whatever their ideological bent, wander farther in search of educational alternatives for their children, the middle and upper classes are becoming as unmotivated to pay for public schools they'll never use as many of the wealthy are to pay for legal services for the indigent or public transportation or national health insurance or even Social Security.

We are dangerously near a time when public schools could become, like pub-lic housing or public jails, places where the poor are confined against their will. If we allow that to happen, it will not be the poor alone who lose; it will be all of us.

Saying the schools have failed and are hopeless is like saying racial integration has failed and can never be achieved. We have, in fact, never agreed upon the goals of education (or integration) or given them a fair trial. It is the society, the system, that has failed, not its ideals—and to give up now is to strengthen the hands of those who want the ideals to succumb.

To the extent that fighting for reform in public education requires or implies defense of it in its present condition, such a posture is at best uncomfortable and at worst indefensible. There is so much wrong with schools as they are, so much to be critical of, and not enough to inspire spirited defense. Schools that leave thousands of young people illiterate deserve condemnation; so do schools and teachers and administrators and boards of education that value order above freedom, control above creativity, and self-preservation above all.

But realism draws me back to the central question: Where is there an alternative to the present structure of public education that offers any promise at all of genuine equality and opportunity for almost fifty million school-age children in the United States? I can see none. We will realize a society equal to its ideals—and a school system worthy of it—or we will, literally, die trying.

B: JOHN HOLT
CAN WE SAVE THE SCHOOLS?
NO, AND THEY'RE NOT WORTH SAVING.

I HAVE TO DECLINE your kind invitation to submit a companion article to John

Egerton's. I am finishing a book against a tight deadline. With the other work I have to do here, that keeps me busy seven days a week. Sometime in the near future, I expect to begin a book about what kinds of changes in structure, function, philosophy, and methods might lift the "public" schools out of their downward spiral and into the beginnings of an upward one. But I can't get into that now.

Nonetheless, I want to respond briefly in letter form to some of the points Egerton raises. In the first place, I can think of no meaningful sense in which the "public" schools are public. They are about as public as the Pentagon. In Chicago, the schools are controlled by a small board of businessmen. In many cities, including my own, the day-to-day operations of the schools are controlled by judges who are completely outside the political process. In no communities do the citizens and voters exercise any effective control over choice of teachers, curricula (which are more and more determined at the state level), methods, or materials. Indeed, in thousands of communities effective local schools have been closed over the furious protests of the citizens.

The "public" schools are, in fact, a government monopoly, rather like our nuclear monopolies, and about equally sensitive and responsive to public input.

The public schools were never formed for a "public" purpose, and John Egerton half admits that. They were formed primarily to serve the interests of the rich and powerful—specifically, to make sure that the children of the great mass of Americans would turn into obedient and politically passive workers.

The "public" schools—which I call government schools—never did help

the poor. My authority for this is Fred Hechinger of *The New York Times,* who wrote in one of his columns that for seventy years and more it has been primarily the children of the poor whom the schools have failed, dropped out, pushed out. No one can dispute this; the record is plain. The government schools have long been bad for most children, but they have always been worst for poor children. They have not increased but decreased the chances of upward mobility in this country. All large schools track or ability-group their students, and every study of these groups has shown that they correlate almost perfectly with social class—the poorer the kids, the lower the group.

In my new book, *Teach Your Own,* I assert that with very few exceptions, the social life of schools and classrooms is mean-spirited, cruel, and violent. I have said exactly the same thing face-to-face to more than 5,000 educators. Not one has ever contradicted me, even after I point out that no one has ever contradicted me. What they say, without exception, is, "That's what the real world is like." I have been told over the years more times than I could count that the schools had to do this or that to get the children ready for "reality." Not one person who has ever said that to me has spoken of this reality, this "real world," as if it were a good place or could be made good, or even better. (I suspect this was not true fifty years ago, when many teachers thought part of their mission was to prepare children to make a better world.)

Indeed, this loss of any sense of humane or noble mission is one of the chief reasons why the schools are worse than they used to be and why their authority and discipline are breaking down so badly. They think, naively and wrongly, that authority and discipline can be made to rest entirely on force, fear, punishment, and the threat of punishment. Any half-smart Army sergeant knows better—and we learned in Vietnam that even an Army cannot maintain its discipline when it loses its sense of mission.

In the late 1960s Charles Silberman and a large team of researchers spent four years examining the government schools all over the United States. It was almost certainly the broadest and most intensive survey of our schools ever made. In his book, *Crisis in the Classroom,* Silberman had this to say about the schools—and please note that this was at the height of the supposed "permissive" revolution.

"Adults . . . fail to appreciate what grim, joyless places most American schools are, how oppressive and petty are the rules by which they are governed, how intellectually sterile and barren the atmosphere, what an appalling lack of civility obtains on the part of teachers and principals, what contempt they unconsciously display for children as children."

I don't know why he says "unconsciously"; many of them do it explicitly and repeatedly. Beyond that, Silberman says nothing at all about the extraordinary amount of physical violence to which children, above all poor children, are subjected in schools.

What we have in these government schools—and many of the private schools are just as bad—is not a preparation for freedom and democracy but a preparation for slavery and fascism. I can understand why the political Right should approve of this, but that the political Left, the "liberals" and "radicals," should do so surpasses belief. If you had talked as much as I have to Middle American audiences, you would know that there is nothing in the world they distrust, fear, and even hate as much as the idea of freedom, the idea that people—above all children— should have some real choices in their lives, should have the right to say No to Authority. In fact, I suspect that the only thing many Americans hate more than freedom is children themselves, perhaps because they are such a living embodiment of it.

Samuel Johnson said, "Patriotism is the last refuge of a scoundrel." We could equally say that it is the last refuge of the incompetent. Having failed dismally to do what they are supposed to do, the schools respond by wrapping themselves in the flag. What astonishes me is that people of the Left let them get away with this. When Charlie Wilson said, "What's good for General Motors is good for the country," liberals were smart enough to give him the horselaugh. But when the $100 billion per year government school monopoly, crammed to bursting with featherbedding administrators, says the same thing, liberals nod in agreement.

Amazing! And frightening!

George Dennison wrote in his wonderful book, *The Lives of Children,* still must reading for anyone concerned about education and especially about the education of poor kids, that even if we had an ideal democracy (which we are far from having) it would not take much more than a generation of government schooling to destroy it. I believe it is fair to say this has already happened. Only a tiny minority of Americans really understand what political and constitutional liberties mean and why they are worth defending. Should we expect otherwise? If we put children, for a large part of their waking lives, into miniature fascist states, why should we expect that at the end of twelve years they will come out understanding or believing in human liberty?

I cannot understand why liberals should object to the idea that poor people, or people of moderate income, should have some of the kinds of choices in education that rich people have always had. The logic is astonishing. Rich people should be able, as they are, to send their children to school wherever they want, but poor people should not have that right, *because it might hurt the government schools.*

Well, enough. I doubt that any of this will seem very convincing to you. But Egerton's piece thrust these thoughts into my mind, and I had to get them down before I could go on to something else.

C: JOHN EGERTON
A REJOINDER: BUT WHAT ARE THE ALTERNATIVES?

I ADMIRE THE CLARITY and quality of John Holt's criticism, and agree completely with most of it. But I am disappointed that my piece only provoked him to repeat the criticisms he has been offering now for a number of years, rather than to address the hard questions I have tried to raise. He says that "sometime in the near future" he intends to "begin a book about what kinds of changes in structure, function, philosophy, and methods might lift the 'public' schools out of their downward spiral and into the beginnings of an upward one." I only wish he would turn his mind to those crucial issues now, instead of giving us yet another analysis of what is wrong.

I can only assume from Holt's comments that he considers public schools and the people who run them beyond redemption since there is no hint in his letter of anything at all that might be tried to make them more effective or more equitable or more productive. So what do we do next? That is the fundamental issue, as far as I am concerned.

Holt seems to suggest that some sort of tuition tax credit or voucher system would serve us well. "I cannot understand," he writes, "why liberals should object to the idea that poor people, or people of moderate income, should have some of the kinds of choices in education that rich people have always had." I have stated my objections to such schemes; I won't go further here, except to note what an irony is embedded in the notion that so-called free and competitive private enterprise— the folks who brought us Exxon, Ma Bell, Texaco—might bring salvation to a publicly owned and operated school system that has failed us.

The shortcomings of this people's school system must surely be familiar to all of us by now, thanks to the well-aimed critical lights of Holt and others. But the solutions will not be found in transferring the system from the reach of the people to the grasp of the capitalist moneychangers. It is past time for John Holt and all the rest of us to figure out what we're going to do when the school bell rings Monday morning. It would be wonderful to invent a new and better approach to education, if only we had the time.

71.

MORTIMER J. ADLER: The Paideia Proposal

The question to which the previous Selection gives two pessimistic responses was also in the mind of Mortimer Adler when he published The Paideia Proposal *late in 1982. But where most other writings on education at the beginning of the 1980s were long on criticism and short on concrete proposals,* The Paideia Proposal *was a blueprint for the salvation of the American public schools. It urged that a single, uncomplicated course of study be adopted in all schools for all children, and it insisted that no less revolutionary a change was required of a nation that claimed to be a democracy. The Paideia program emphasized the basic skills of learning—reading, writing, speaking, listening, figuring, judging—but it also laid great stress on seminars: discussions in which the teacher descended from his or her symbolic podium, sat down with the children, and talked about ideas. These ideas could be great or little; it did not matter much as long as they talked together and sought some further understanding in each others' company. The* Paideia Proposal *was attacked by many educators, but it was also adopted in many schools by many teachers who saw it as the breath of fresh air they had been seeking for so long.*

Source: *The Paideia Proposal*, chs. 1, 11.

WE ARE on the verge of a new era in our national life. The long-needed educational reform for which this country is at last ready will be a turning point toward that new era.

Democracy has come into its own for the first time in this century. Not until this century have we undertaken to give twelve years of schooling to all our children. Not until this century have we conferred the high office of enfranchised citizenship on all our people, regardless of sex, race, or ethnic origin.

The two—universal suffrage and universal schooling—are inextricably bound together. The one without the other is a perilous delusion. Suffrage without schooling produces mobocracy, not democracy—not rule of law, not constitutional government by the people as well as for them.

The great American educator, John Dewey, recognized this early in this century. In *Democracy and Education*, written in 1916, he first tied these two words together and let each shine light upon the other.

A revolutionary message of that book was that a democratic society must provide equal educational opportunity not only by giving to all its children the same quantity of public education—the same number of years in school—but also by making sure to give to all of them, all with no exceptions, the same quality of education.

The ideal Dewey set before us is a challenge we have failed to meet. It is a challenge so difficult that it is understandable, perhaps excusable, that we have so far failed. But we cannot continue to fail without disastrous consequences for all of us. For the proper working of our political institutions, for the efficiency of our industries and businesses, for the salvation of our economy, for the vitality of our culture, and for the ultimate good of our citizens as individuals, and especially our future citizens—our children—we must succeed.

We are all sufferers from our continued failure to fulfill the educational obligations of a democracy. We are all the victims of a school system that has only gone halfway along the road to realize the promise of democracy.

At the beginning of this century, fewer than 10 percent of those of an age eligible for high school entered such schools. Today, almost 100 percent of our children enter, but not all complete such secondary schooling; many drop out for many reasons, some of them understandable.

It has taken us the better part of eighty years to go halfway toward the goal our society must achieve if it is to be a true democracy. The halfway mark was reached when we finally managed to provide twelve years of basic public schooling for all our children. At that point, we were closer to the goal that Horace Mann set for us more than a century ago when he said: "Education is the gateway to equality."

But the democratic promise of equal educational opportunity, half fulfilled, is worse than a promise broken. It is an ideal betrayed. Equality of educational opportunity is not, in fact, provided if it means no more than taking all the children into the public schools for the same number of hours, days, and years. If once there they are divided into the sheep and the goats, into those destined solely for toil and those destined for economic and political leadership and for a quality of life to which all should have access, then the democratic purpose has been undermined by an inadequate system of public schooling.

It fails because it has achieved only the same quantity of public schooling, not the same quality. This failure is a downright violation of our democratic principles.

We are politically a classless society. Our citizenry as a whole is our ruling class. We should, therefore, be an educationally classless society.

We should have a one-track system of schooling, not a system with two or more tracks, only one of which goes straight ahead while the others shunt the young off onto sidetracks not headed toward the goals our society opens to all. The innermost meaning of social equality is: *substantially the same quality of life for all.* That calls for: *the same quality of schooling for all.*

We may take some satisfaction, perhaps, in the fact that we have won half the battle—the quantitative half. But we deserve the full development of the country's human potential. We should, therefore, be vexed that we have not yet gone further. We should be impatient to get on with it, in and through the schools . . . .

When we hold before us the equally important results that our proposed reform of basic schooling aims at—earning a better living and enjoying a better quality of life—we are brought face to face with two obstacles that must be overcome. Even if all the others were surmounted, two things would still stand in the way of achieving the needed reform.

One is the uncertain economic status of a substantial part of the school population. The other is the understandable but nevertheless one-sided emphasis that too many parents place on economic and material advantages in thinking of their children's futures.

A basic human right is the right to obtain a decent livelihood by working for it under decent conditions. Those whom the economy leaves unemployed through no fault of their own are unjustly deprived of an essential human right which is indispensable to their pursuit of happiness.

As things stand now, that part of the school population which comes from severely disadvantaged minorities can look forward to unemployment after leaving school—thrown on the waste heap of a society that is squandering its human resources. Hopelessness about the future is bound to affect motivation in school. Why do the hard work that good basic schooling would demand if, after doing it, no opportunity exists to work for a decent living? This bleak prospect makes for the dropout, or, what is just as bad, turns the energetic into the delinquent. While still in school, they regard themselves as prisoners serving time.

The other face of the picture is the attitude of parents who regard all schooling as having no purpose beyond helping graduates to earn a living and get ahead materially.

The truth, hidden from too many, is that more than money and material advantages are necessary for the good life. Children should be prepared and motivated to make themselves the best human beings they are capable of becoming. If a better quality of schooling for all enables them to make a better use of their talents, their energies, their free time, it will also help to improve the quality of life for all.

Two things, then, must go hand in hand with the recommended reform of basic schooling. One is the commitment of our society to a policy of full employment, securing for everyone his or her right to earn a living. The other is the enlightenment of parents with regard to the goals of basic schooling—not just earning a living, but living well.

To put it another way, the monumental effort it will take to improve the quality of basic schooling cannot be justified solely by reference to economic and material advantages. It needs to be undertaken to improve the quality of human life for all.

An unidentified young man, concealed behind a curtain, tells of his experiences as a child prostitute during a meeting of a commission on pornography in 1985.

THE YOUNG AND THE OLD

In the late twentieth century the problems facing young people in America became more evident and more complex. Young people were frequently confronted with opportunities to use drugs and alcohol. The physical and emotional abuse of children by adults was more widely reported, and suicide rates among the young increased dramatically. Sexual activity among teenagers proliferated, as did the numbers of sexual abuse cases and unwanted pregnancies. At the other end of the life cycle were the elderly. In the 1980s there were more senior citizens than ever before, and they were more affluent than ever, thanks to pension plans, social security, and health insurance. While they had greater mobility and independence than ever, many elderly still suffered. Organizations such as the Gray Panthers and the American Association of Retired Persons (AARP) worked to protect the rights and interests of senior citizens.

Photos by AP/Wide World

(Top) A teacher in an elementary school in Harrisburg, Pennsylvania, helps her students learn to use computers; (bottom) four boys of the South Bronx in New York manage to enjoy playing ball among the ruins of houses in a wasteland of lots empty of everything except rubble and garbage.

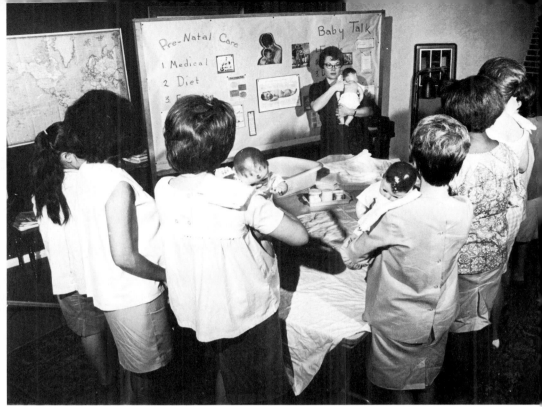

Photos by AP/Wide World

(Top) Pregnant teenagers are given instruction in baby care by a nurse in a Sacramento, California, school that gives them a chance to continue their studies instead of dropping out; (bottom) an eight-day-old baby is held by her mother after having been kidnapped from a hospital by a woman dressed as a nurse.

The welfare of America's youth was a growing concern in the 1970s and 1980s. First Lady Nancy Reagan launched a "Just Say No" anti-drug campaign that was targeted at young people. It was also important that the educational system respond to the perceived crisis facing American children. Introduction of computers into schools was essential to preparing youths for the modern workplace. The conditions facing infants were also a cause for concern. Nearly one-third of the babies born in 1986 were born out of wedlock, and a high proportion of them were born to teenage mothers, who often dropped out of school after giving birth.

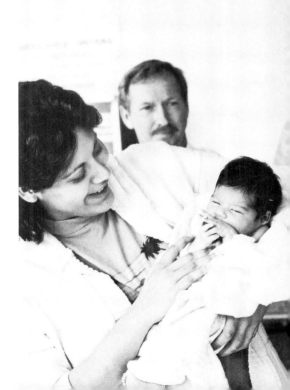

(Top) A young boy shows a photograph he has taken to a resident of a home for the aged during a program to promote communication between children and the elderly; (bottom) a nursing home can be an empty and lonely place for those who have no family to live with. (Opposite top) A homeless man huddles near the boxes he uses for shelter; (center) Maggie Kuhn, founder and leader of an activist group called the Gray Panthers, practices her panther snarl; (bottom) U.S. Rep. Claude Pepper of Florida was a leading advocate for the rights of the elderly in the 1980s.

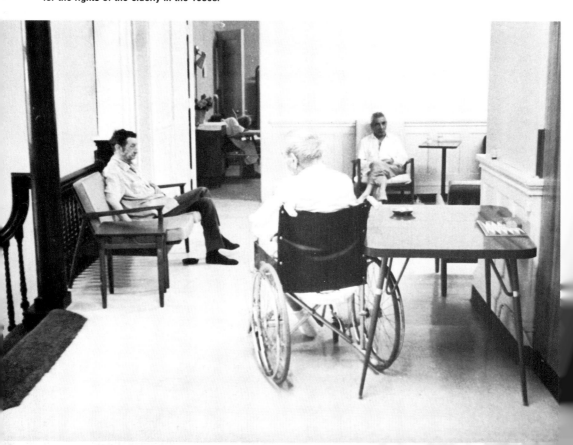

Not all of the older generation were healthy and affluent in the 1980s. Many were trying to live on fixed incomes and, without the benefit of relatives or friends, received little help. For many, additional years brought physical disabilities and mental deterioration, as well as deep pain and sadness. Maggie Kuhn's Gray Panthers were unwilling to accept the second-class status that older people often had to endure. Claude Pepper was equally tireless in fighting for the rights of the elderly, whose concerns he gave voice to as a representative in Congress. The efforts of Pepper and the Gray Panthers were highly effective, partly because a higher proportion of older people vote than of any other age group; they have become a potent special interest group. In 1978 the mandatory retirement age was raised to 70.

Older Americans who made vital contributions in the 1980s included Rear Admiral Grace Hopper, a pioneer in computer technology, and Armand Hammer, who long sought to establish better relations with the Soviet Union. Some young people also made important contributions. Samantha Smith was such a young person. She visited the Soviet Union on a quest for world peace in 1983, when she was 11. After her death in a plane crash in 1985, the Russians attached her name to an enormous Siberian diamond, a hybrid violet, a street in Yalta, and a postage stamp. They have also named a mountain after her, a 13,000-foot peak in the Caucasus.

(Top left) Rear Admiral Grace M. Hopper, at 79 the oldest active duty military officer, announced her coming retirement in 1985; Congress had approved her continued service after age 62; (top right) Armand Hammer, 87-year-old industrialist, has good relations with the Soviet Union and has acted frequently as a go-between for the U.S. and the U.S.S.R.; (bottom) Maine schoolgirl Samantha Smith, who visited the Soviet Union in 1983 at the invitation of Yuri Andropov, wears a folk costume given her by Russian schoolchildren; she died tragically in a plane crash after her return home.

72.

Geraldine A. Ferraro: Who Will Fight for the Worth of Women's Work?

Efforts to pass the Equal Rights Amendment (ERA) to the U.S. Constitution ended in failure when legislators in three additional states could not be persuaded to vote approval before the June 30, 1982, deadline. The National Organization for Women (NOW) stated that it would concentrate on electing women to state and federal legislatures before reviving the ERA issue. The amendment, however, was reintroduced in Congress on July 14; but again it failed to pass. One of the basic reasons for the failure, in the view of columnist Caryl Rivers, was the widespread fear that the world would change in a profound way if women changed and that the kind of caring that women do and men do not do would vanish if women obtained the equality represented by ERA. Whatever the merits of this argument, it or something very like it seems to be at the heart of this impassioned speech by a congresswoman who a mere two years later would become one of the most famous women in the United States.

Source: *Vital Speeches of the Day,* November 15, 1982.

When I was an assistant district attorney in Queens it used to make me terribly nervous to get up and argue a motion in front of one judge. So you can imagine how I feel standing up here in front of hundreds of judges. Of course, I am not here today to argue. But I am here to plead a case. My case is that women in leadership positions make a real difference in the way our society works. And I believe that women like us must continue to make that difference.

All of our futures, and our daughters' futures, are at stake. I am talking about the future of every woman, from the migrant farm worker or ghetto mother to United States Supreme Court Justice Sandra Day O'Connor, a founder of this organization and your honoree earlier today.

I speak to you as a member of Congress who has not forgotten that she is a lawyer who never forgets she is a woman. How could I?

I was one of just two women in my law class at Fordham in the late 50's. In 1960, five job interviews at one of our prestigious New York law firms culminated with a "you're terrific . . . but we're not hiring any women this year." As a bureau chief in the DA's office many years later, I learned that I was being paid less than men with similar responsibilities. When I asked why, I was told "you don't really need the money, Gerry, you've got a husband."

Getting to Congress wasn't easy either. The biggest problem in running as a woman, if by some quirk you get the organization endorsement, is raising money. I remember going from bank to bank in 1978 for a campaign loan and being told that my husband had to cosign. Forget that I was a lawyer with a good deal of trial experience. Just remember that even if I wanted my husband to sign, I couldn't because I would be in violation of the FEC laws. Once elected, I applied to Eastern Airlines for a Wings card to make billing for the shuttle flights to Washington a bit easier. Despite the fact I was a member of the Aviation Subcommittee of the House Public Works and Transportation Committee, I was turned down. It was only after I mentioned it, to everyone's embarrassment, at an ERA luncheon with an Eastern Airlines lobbyist present, that I received my card. I know what the law is, and so do you. But that doesn't mean it is observed.

Four months ago, I applied to Citibank for a VISA card, listing my salary, American Express, and Eastern Airlines as credit references, my savings banks, and my employer. Again, I was turned down. It was only after I commented to a friend of mine who is a Vice President of Citibank that I was going to write to inquire the basis on which my credit had been disapproved, that I received a note from the Credit Department, along with my card, welcoming me to the fold. There was no reason to turn me down other than I am a woman. Fortunately for me, I am a woman with clout. But what about the woman who is not a member of Congress?

As recently as two weeks ago, Capitol Hill police stopped me at four different locations, the last when I entered the House for a roll call vote, and demanded identification. Four years I've been working in and out of those hallowed halls. Clearly, they found it more difficult to recognize me—one of just 20 women in the House—than any of the 415 men.

Yes, the Old Boy Network is alive and well and living in our courthouses and our legislatures and our boardrooms. As women, we still have to be better than men at most of the things we do, we have to work harder and we have to prove our worth over and over and over again.

It is not just those of us who have reached the top who are fighting this daily battle. It is a fight in which all of us—rich and poor, career and home-oriented, young and old—participate, simply because we are women.

Look at the facts. More women than men are poor and it is harder for them to escape poverty. Indeed, more and more women are struggling to support children alone, earning 59 cents for each dollar a man earns and lower pay translates into smaller pensions or checks from Social Security in old age. As a result, more and more women are sinking deeper and deeper into poverty. In our wealthy society, poverty is becoming a women's issue. Cuts in domestic programs, seemingly gender-neutral, actually hit women and children twice as hard as they do men because women are the greater number of recipients. Ninety-two percent of the participants in Aid for Dependent Children are women and children. Sixty-six percent of the recipients of subsidized housing are women. Sixty-nine percent of Food Stamp recipients are women. Sixty-one percent of Medicaid recipients are women. And why are women dependent on federal help? It is not because they are lazier than men or less moral than men. Or less intelligent.

Women are in greater need because they often have less education. They are the ones who must care for the chil-

Geraldine A. Ferraro

cial Security Administration cuts their benefits. Yet—this Administration has persistently tried to abolish this source of legal hope and help by eliminating funding. So far Congress has refused to go along.

Cuts to Legal Services becomes a double-edged sword for women. Not only are women 67 percent of the Legal Services clients, but this public benefit agency has served as an important training ground for women attorneys. It has provided jobs for well-qualified lawyers who still find the doors of many rich corporate law firms open to "old boys" but closed to young women.

At a time when 29 percent of law school graduates are women—an amazing development in itself—almost 36 percent of Legal Services 5,678 lawyers are women.

And what about the working women? Is it any better for them? Our society has changed over the past thirty-five years—but our attitudes have not.

More and more women are working outside the home. Many work for personal satisfaction and achievement like many of us here. But most—two-thirds—work to support themselves and their children and husbands who cannot earn enough alone to keep the family above the poverty line. There are now 43 million women in the workforce, triple the number just prior to World War II. Sixty percent of all women between the ages of eighteen and sixty-four are workers, with eighty percent of all women who work concentrated in so-called "pink collar" jobs—jobs dominated by females and dominated by low salaries.

A woman with a college education can expect lifetime earnings equal to those paid to a man who never finished eighth grade. Groundskeepers are paid

dren. They must work part-time or in menial jobs and they get paid less for the work that they do. After a lifetime of work, in or outside their homes, they often enter old age dependent solely on Social Security benefits.

There are nine million families in the United States where a woman, not a man, is the breadwinner. Fully a third of these families are welfare cases. Still more of them require other federal aid—food stamps, Medicaid, public housing. Women and children are 75 percent of all Americans living in poverty.

What can women do when their government and, I admit, that includes Congress, takes a meat ax to the programs they depend on so heavily? They can, and do, turn to the Legal Services Corporation when the welfare office stops the food stamps, the landlord shuts off the water, the ex-husband forgets the child support check, or the So-more than nurses. Parking lot attendants are often paid more than experienced secretaries. We entrust our children—our most precious resource—to teachers who frequently earn less than truck drivers.

Who will fight for the worth of women's work? A series of hearings I conducted recently in Washington with two other Congresswomen provided some interesting answers.

We found that the fight for equity in the workforce is in full swing. But it is not happening in the marble halls of Washington. It is happening in the statehouses, the union offices, and the courts.

More than twenty-five states and local governments have launched studies of the comparative value of the work their male and female employees do. Spurred on by public employee unions, they are beginning to question the assumption that a tree trimmer should be paid more than an intensive care nurse.

In 1981, Minnesota became the first state to pass a law establishing a state commitment to comparable worth and earmarked budget funds for pay adjustments that might result.

Unions in the private sector have also brought successful pressure to bear on companies like AT&T. Non-union groups like 9 to 5—The National Association of Working Women—have embarrassed companies like John Hancock Insurance into granting raises for clerical workers.

In the courts, 1981 saw the crucial decision of Gunther *vs.* Washington which explicitly links the Civil Rights Act to the issue of wage discrimination against women whose jobs are similar, but not identical, to those performed by men.

At a time when the federal government seems to lack the funds, or the staff, or the will to vigorously enforce laws which promote fairness in the workplace, it is only before judges such as yourselves that these vital issues can, literally, have their day in court.

So what does this all mean to us? I did a little research the other day. I wanted to find out how many women in America earn more than $60,000 a year. I picked that number, frankly, because that is what I, as a member of Congress, earn. I learned that there are only 18,000 women in the entire United States, working full-time who earn more than $60,000. We represent just one-tenth of one percent of all the women who work full-time in America. By contrast, 885,000 men, 2.1 percent of full-time male workers, are in the $60,000-plus bracket.

It would be easy to say "gee, it's great to be part of such a tiny minority." It would be easy to say, "I'm all right, Jack—or Jill" and leave it at that. But that would be denying the real role we can—and must—play as female legislators and judges.

I said earlier that I believe women in leadership make a real difference in our society.

Now, there are really two reasons why there need to be more women in leadership—more than the bare five percent of Congress, more than the eight percent of the federal judiciary. More than the six hundred women in state court systems.

The first reason could be called the "Me-First" reason. We are smart, we worked hard, we deserve this job, we are entitled to it and we will do anything necessary to get and keep it. Women of merit do indeed deserve their fair share of society's reward—a share previously denied to us only because we were women.

The second reason, though, is more important. Women leaders are different. Despite our frequent political and philosophical differences, there are certain generalizations that can be made about women judges and women legislators. We care more about other women. We show more concern for children. We try to resolve controversies by co-operation, rather than conflict.

Harvard University Professor Carol Gilligan has written a book entitled *In a Different Voice* in which she discusses how men and women make decisions. Women, she suggests, are more likely to think about human relationships when they make decisions. They think about what the impact of their decision will be on the people it will affect. Men, on the other hand, are more likely to follow a set of rules and procedures to a conclusion. Women worry more about the effect of their decisions. Men worry more about making the decisions the right way. In short, men often worry more about rules and processes. Women often worry more about outcomes.

We have an obligation to use our unique perspective when we make the laws, as I do, and interpret the laws, as you do.

Your distinguished honoree, Justice O'Connor, has made this kind of difference on the Supreme Court even though I am sure we would all agree that she is neither a professional feminist nor, certainly, a liberal Democrat.

In fact, if I may be so bold as to characterize Justice O'Connor's first year, she has shown herself a staunch supporter of states' rights and a reduced court presence in legislative affairs.

Yet, in at least one opinion, pitting a male nurse against a Mississippi nursing college for women only, Justice O'Connor focused the arguments against sex discrimination in a way which may not have occurred, had our highest court still been an all-male enclave.

Let me quote her opinion: "Rather than compensate for discriminatory barriers faced by women, Mississippi University for Women's policy of excluding males tends to perpetuate the stereotyped view of nursing as an exclusively women's job."

Justice O'Connor went further. She added a footnote citing evidence that the small number of men in nursing keeps nursing wages down. So, the Justice argued, keeping men out of an all-women's nursing school actually punishes women, rather than helps them.

I am not here to give you a campaign speech. You know that I am a Democrat and you know that, with the exception of the appointment of Sandra Day O'Connor, I have not had very many good things to say about President Reagan.

But I do not think that you have to look at the world through Democratic spectacles to see that women judges made greater strides under President Carter than in any other period of our history.

Sixteen percent of Carter's appointments to the federal bench were women. Forty-one women out of 260. More than all of his predecessors combined. Not enough, after years of exclusion, but a good start compared to Reagan's percentage of four percent.

Four percent. At a time when our federal judiciary is eight percent female, the Reagan Administration is not even keeping up.

The President's record of female appointment to other top jobs is also poor. U.N. Ambassador Jeane Kirkpatrick is the only woman of Cabinet rank—but she is not a member of the Cabinet. Given a chance to name the highly qualified Republican Betty Southard Murphy as Secretary of Labor, Reagan instead chose Raymond Donovan. Need I say more?

What the President does—especially in the area of minority and women's rights—creates a national climate. That climate can be a climate of fairness for women in our society. Or it can be a climate of regression. It can be a return to an era when women were not vital participants in public policy-making.

I have long supported the Equal Rights Amendment—and have sponsored its reintroduction—because I see how government can lose the will to protect the rights of all citizens without the Constitutional imperative.

When women are named to federal courts, there is pressure to name them to state and municipal benches as well. Significantly, it was not until 1979, during the Carter Administration, that every one of our states could finally say it had a woman in its judiciary system.

When women become judges, when more and more women graduate from law school, not only government, but private enterprise, has to realize that women are a force to be dealt with and treated with respect.

On the other hand, the sight of top Administration officials capering at Bohemian Grove, that sexist California summer camp for overgrown boys, probably made it easier this past summer for the American Bar Association to undo a progressive new policy. That policy would have put the ABA on record against private clubs which refuse to admit women.

It is not my place, as a maker of laws, to tell you how to do your job of interpreting that law. I am a firm believer in the system of checks and balances established by our Constitution. I am strongly opposed to the efforts that are being made by some members of Congress to strip our courts of their proper jurisdiction.

Yet I do not think it is presumptuous of me to remind you that the courts in this country are in every sense courts of last resort for the poor and the powerless. Increasingly, those poor and powerless are women and children. If we, as women, don't look out for other women, who will? If we as women don't care what happens to women it will not just be the waitress or the welfare mother who loses. It will be every one of us. Every one of us who thought when we made it, all women had it made. Or who thought "if I make it, it doesn't matter who else makes it."

It is too easy to divide the world into "us" and "them." And it is far too easy for us—secure, successful, well-off—to become them. A simple thing—an illness, a divorce, widowhood, alcoholism, economic depression—could turn any of our hard-won gains into a struggle for mere existence.

I didn't go to Washington to represent the women of this nation. But if I don't, who will? I ran, and was elected, not as a feminist, but as a lawyer. And as a lawyer I can argue more effectively for equity and fairness of all Americans.

As I was preparing for this speech tonight I was reminded by one of your publicity aides that "judges are people too."

Women judges are women, too. Congresswomen are women in Congress. As each of us devotes energy, talent, and time to the "man's" work we are doing, we owe it to our nation to remember that we are in the same boat with more than half of all Americans. As women, as judges, as lawyers—we must make a difference.

As women we are a majority but as judges and legislators we are still an all-too-small minority in America. As a minority, our responsibilities—to our sex, our professions, and our nation—are heavy ones.

A majority may have the luxury of being a "silent majority." A minority in defense of its rights must speak up.

As members of a minority we have a responsibility to be role-models for all women. As a minority, we bear the burden of expressing the minority viewpoint and keeping it ever before the American public.

Our responsibilities are heavy but they are not oppressive. We have an opportunity as well as an obligation—an opportunity to help create a better society for all Americans, men and women.

Madam Justices, I rest my case. The verdict is yours.

73.

LUDMILLA THORNE: The Littlest Defector

Walter Polovchak arrived in the United States with his sister Natalie, his younger brother, and his parents in January 1980. They were Christians from the Ukraine, in the Soviet Union, and like millions of immigrants before them they hoped to find a better life for themselves. But things did not go well for Mr. Polovchak, and he soon announced to the family that they were going back home. Natalie, who was almost 18, refused to go; and her younger brother Walter said he wanted to stay in America, too, and not return to the USSR. The parents insisted, but Natalie and Walter asked for asylum in the United States. Natalie was granted it immediately; she was nearly old enough to be treated as an adult. Walter was 12. Was he too young to know his own mind? Should the wishes of his parents be given primary consideration, or the wishes of a youngster who had strong feelings about where and how he wanted to live? The story of what happened after Walter Polovchak asked for political asylum, and finally won it, is told in this article by Ludmilla Thorne, a specialist in the affairs of recent Russian immigrants to America.

Source: *National Review*, March 1983.

MICHAEL AND Anna Polovchak, aged 41 and 39, arrived in Chicago in January 1980 from Sambir, a small town in the western Ukraine, with their three children, Natalie, 17, Walter, 12, and Michael, five. They were not among the largest category of recent émigrés— Jewish refugees—but rather Christian believers who were to be reunited with the father's two older sisters. In the Soviet Union Michael was a cross-country bus driver and Anna worked in a candy factory.

Within three months of their arrival, Michael Polovchak was talking about returning to the Soviet Union and had begun calling the Soviet Embassy in Washington. He said that his expectations of life in America hadn't been fulfilled. Anna, a docile woman with a seventh-grade education, went along with her husband's decision, but when he told their two older children they were going back, all hell broke loose. "No way," was Natalie's response. The children were going to school, they were learning English and adjusting well to their new lives.

At this point Michael Polovchak was employed at the same valve company as his sister's husband, Dmitri Gusiev, who got him the job. Then, according to Gusiev, Polovchak developed a headache and, soon afterward, a pain in his leg; he left the factory after seven and a half months and didn't work again during the remainder of his time in the United States. By the time he left, he had been out of work for a year, and he was receiving $120 per week in welfare.

"My father thought that in the United States dollars would be falling off trees," Natalie told me. "As for me, from the first day here, I made up my mind that I would never go back to the Soviet Union. Over there, we were told that America is a slave country, and that people are starving in the streets, but when you come here and see everything for yourself, you think—where is all this misery? They lied to me."

In July of 1980 Natalie moved into the apartment of her cousin, Walter Polowczak, and little Walter insisted on going along. Natalie told him that he couldn't, that he had to remain with his parents. Nonetheless, the next day Walter also left, and joined his sister and cousin. Within a week, on July 21, the Immigration and Naturalization Service (INS) granted Walter Polovchak federal asylum. Because Natalie was almost

18 years old and had her own Soviet passport, her decision to remain in the United States was not challenged.

Why did you decide not to return to the Soviet Union? I asked Walter, a pensive boy with a sturdy Slavic frame, who looked thoroughly American in faded blue jeans and a T-shirt. He answered in fluent English, amply sprinkled with teenage slang.

"Well, I have more freedom here," he said. "I can believe in God, go to church, and all that. In the Soviet Union, when you go to church, the teacher or someone watches you by the church and next day, when you come to school, you're gonna get in trouble."

"On Christmas Eve the kids were told to come to school at six o'clock in the evening and clean our desks, wash the walls and the floors. They did that on purpose, so we couldn't be with our families on Christmas."

Are there other reasons why you didn't want to go back? I asked. "Over there, when you go to a store to buy something," he explained, "you can't get the stuff you want unless you have some friends working behind the counter. You also have to give them extra money, so they'll give you what you want. Over here it isn't like that."

Anything else? I asked. He paused for a moment and then replied: "I can go anywhere I want here, and I don't have to sign any papers. In the Soviet Union you have to get permission if you want to move."

Walter was quick to add that he made the decision not to return to the USSR by himself. "I told my dad I wasn't going," he told me. After the parents arrived in Moscow the government press agency, TASS, repeated the accusation that Walter had been "kidnapped," and Mrs. Polovchak was quoted as saying: "I know that Walter wants to come back home, but he is prevented from doing so . . . they surely poison him with narcotics."

In the United States the boy was processed as a "minor in need of supervision," a term that is usually applied to runaways, and the Juvenile Division of the Cook County Circuit Court declared him a ward of the state. The Illinois Division of the American Civil Liberties Union, which chose to represent the parents, contended that the only reason Walter was not returned to his parents was that they were Soviet citizens. "Runaways are practically always returned to their parents," says Harvey Grossman, the leading spokesman for the Illinois ACLU.

Judge Joseph C. Mooney explained his decision by saying, "The next time, if Walter runs, he may not run to cousin Walter. He may run some place where he will be harmed." At the adjudicatory hearings held July 30 and August 4, 1980, Walter did testify that if he couldn't have gone to his cousin's house, "I would have gone anywhere . . . I would have gone somewhere." . . .

The issue of state interference in family life is perhaps the most debated and the most emotional aspect of the Polovchak case. The ACLU's Harvey Grossman sees the granting of asylum to a 12-year-old boy as "classical abuse of the Federal Government's intervention." He also believes that the fact that Walter was from the Soviet Union played a major role in the decision. "It seems that it all depends on the United States' political stance toward the other country," he says. "Why aren't Haitian or Nicaraguan refugees given speedy asylum by the Federal Government?" Grossman's interpretation of the government's role in Walter's case is not shared by all ACLU representatives. In response to a *New York Times* editorial which asserted that "government officials have no business intervening in family life," Harriet F. Pilpel, a general counsel of the ACLU and vice-chairman of its National Advisory Council, pointed out in a letter published in the *Times* on January 20, 1982, that during the past 15 years various courts and legislatures, and the Supreme Court, have clearly established the concept that children do have rights of their own. "The Polovchak case must be viewed against the wishful thinking on the part of the *Times* . . . .Where the parents act in a manner detrimental to the best interests of the child," she continued, ". . . the government will step in to protect the child. That's neither new nor political posturing—it's the only rule that a nation committed to the promotion of basic human rights even for children can follow."

But did Walter Polovchak, at age 12, really understand the meaning of asylum? Should asylum indeed have been granted? Holzer's [Henry Mark Holzer, a professor of law at Brooklyn Law School] response is short and to the point: "Anyone who is old enough to ask for asylum is old enough to get it." In Harvey Grossman's contrary opinion, "Walter could never articulate political distinctions." A federal court will have to decide. Perhaps that's the bottom line of this unique case, which will undoubtedly set a precedent for other minors seeking haven in the United States.

There is another precedent-setting aspect to the Polovchak affair. Whereas the courts have ruled that people have a right to asylum—as dramatized by the granting of this privilege to Russian ballet dancers and other luminaries—the narrow question here is, What are a mi-

AP/Wide World

Walter Polovchak at age 14, two years after he began his effort to stay in the United States. In 1985 his request was finally granted.

nor's rights in applying for asylum when he has living parents? "And the answer is," says Holzer, "that nobody knows, because the court has never said."

Harvey Grossman holds that the initial asylum proceedings, having been conducted without consulting Walter's parents, had no right to be heard or to seek judicial review. In Holzer's opinion, an overwhelming argument can be made that nobody's consent is required, except the person who is applying for asylum, "given the very nature of asylum, the exigency, the urgency. It's not the kind of decision you could put in somebody else's hands," he says, "even under the circumstances of a minor."

A lurking issue in the Polovchak case is the question of parental abuse, although this case has not been formally treated as a case of child neglect. But it does relate to the pivotal concept of "what is in the best interests of the child"—to remain with the parents or not.

"We observed the Polovchaks with their younger son, Michael," says Grossman. "They were not abusive parents." Julian Kulas [a prominent attorney in the Chicago Ukrainian Community] asserts that the parents were abusive toward Walter and Natalie both in the Ukraine and in Chicago. "We found that Walter needed glasses very badly, he could barely read, and it wasn't until after he left his home that the state of Illinois provided glasses for him. We also noticed that both Walter and Natalie needed extensive dental care. And as you know, in the Soviet Union, dental care is free. All the father had to do was to take his children by the hand and bring them to the dental office." During court proceedings Kulas asked Mr. Polovchak whether he had ever taken Walter to a movie, and the father said, "Oh no, movies are provided by the state." When he was asked whether he had ever seen his son play soccer, for Walter is a good soccer player and was on a local team, Michael Polovchak replied that he was too busy. "It's true that Michael is Walter's biological father," says Kulas, "but I don't believe that there was really a father-son relationship." "I was never close to my father," Walter told me. "In the Ukraine I saw him only once or twice a week, and here it wasn't too different."

There are numerous other indications that the parents' attitude toward the two older children was less than caring. Natalie told me, for instance, that even though both parents were working soon after they arrived, they didn't give her or Walter any lunch money or carfare. "Our aunt in California sent us each $25 every month," she said, "but often this wasn't enough." Both parents used to ask her: "Why are you going to school instead of earning your own money?"

Professor Holzer insists that the very fact that the parents wanted to take their child back to the Soviet Union against his will is *per se* abusive, "given the country's track record, in terms of the rights that don't exist, the Gulag, the repressions, and the lack of free speech and all the other things which the ACLU purportedly values so highly."

"We recognize that this is the free world," says Harvey Grossman. "But we also believe that there are some interests that are paramount to political or economic considerations in the child-rearing process. There is a parenting function. The total needs of a child must be considered, and age is a critical question."

"He's saying that people who are older have a greater right to be free than children, who are younger," Holzer replies. "All he's saying is that the right of a child to be free can be made subject to his parents' desire to return him to a dictatorship. Would the ACLU defend the rights of parents who wanted to take their child back to South Africa, Cambodia, or Jonestown?"

"Obviously, people who may return to totalitarian or authoritarian regimes will live with less freedom," says Grossman, "but I don't think that we as a country can follow a policy that says that whenever we want to, we can take your kid."

"The United States or the state of Illinois did not take Walter," says Holzer. "Walter left. Walter defected. He wanted to be free, and he enlisted the United States Government's help to be a free boy and, eventually, a free man. So nobody took him. And I'm proud that our government, unlike its action with Simas Kudirka, the Lithuanian seaman who tried to defect, didn't throw this little boy back into the water and condemn him to a life of slavery."

Julian Kulas recently added a new twist to the Polovchak story by revealing that at the very beginning, the father wanted to leave the family in the United States and return to the USSR alone. He asked Kulas to give him a document showing that the children were being taken from him, which he could present to the Soviet Embassy and then get a Soviet visa. Polovchak also told his daughter that he wanted to go back by himself.

Julian Kulas's hypthosis is that when Polovchak applied at the Soviet Embassy for a visa, Soviet officials felt it would look very bad if he were to go back by himself. "After all, what would people say over there, if the United States was such a bad place to live, and the family didn't return? There are many indications that, after that, Soviet authorities put tremendous pressure on Polovchak to take the entire family back to the USSR, and that is why he went to the Chicago police and asked that his son be forced to come home. He told Natalie that the Soviet Embassy was paying for the family's telephone, presumably to keep in closer contact. "Let them pay for it," he said. "I'm not working, I can't pay." . . .

The image of the Polovchaks' life in Chicago which emerges from Harvey Grossman's description and from Michael Polovchak's statement is that from the very beginning, the Polovchaks were ostracized by the Ukrainian community, in part because they were Eastern Rite Catholics and most of their relatives were Baptists, in part because, in Grossman's words, "they had bad adaptive skills," and in part because they were living in a Polish and Latino neighborhood, instead of in the Ukrainian section.

However, a vastly different picture emerges from lengthy conversations with the Polovchak children, their relatives, and Ukrainian community leaders. Dr. Pawlo Turula, secretary of the Ukrainian Social Services Bureau, told me that friends had brought the family clothes, food, and presents. And when Mr. Polovchak reported to Turula that his younger son, Michael, was treated badly at school, Turula made arrangements for the boy to attend a private Ukrainian school for free. He also offered Polovchak his choice of two apartments in the northwestern part of town, the heart of the Ukrainian section. "However, he didn't even want to look at the apartment," says Turula, "but simply kept repeating 'I cannot move here,' as if he were under someone else's instruction."

Turula described Polovchak as an "explosive" person, somewhat unbalanced. "One time, he physically attacked me, screaming that I was helping Kulas deprive him of his son. Anna had to pull him away. And when he saw journalists waiting for him he burst into tears."

When the Polovchaks finally left the United States, a year after Natalie and Walter had moved out, they didn't inform the two children of their departure, and they didn't say good-bye. Natalie found out about it by watching the news. "I turned on the television, and saw my parents in the Soviet Union, holding a flower. I couldn't believe it! I turned to another channel and saw the same thing. It really upset me. They left without even saying *good-bye?*"

Walter was in summer camp in Wisconsin when he was informed that his parents had left. "I was shocked, because they were lying to me," he told me. "They said they were moving to another apartment, but they moved back to the USSR. My parents didn't really care about me. First they wanted to take me back, and then they didn't even want to say good-bye."

I've lived in both countries. You don't have to be smart, you don't have to be a certain age to tell the difference.
WALTER POLOVCHAK, October 2, 1985—his 18th birthday, on which day he became free to ask for legal asylum in the United States.

74.

Prolonging Death Is No Triumph

On December 2, 1982, Barney B. Clark, a 61-year-old retired dentist, received the world's first permanent artificial heart during surgery at the University of Utah Medical Center in Salt Lake City. Clark was chosen because his own heart had failed and he was fast approaching death, and because in the opinion of the doctors at the medical center he had all the psychological attributes desired in a patient undergoing such a critical operation. Barney Clark was tough, and he wanted very much to live. Soon after the plastic heart began beating his vital organs showed remarkable improvement, and doctors at the center were cautiously optimistic that he could survive for a considerable period. Unfortunately, this did not turn out to be true, and Clark died 112 days after the operation. In the interim many editorials appeared in U.S. newspapers criticizing the procedure. The editorial reprinted here appeared in The New York Times *twelve days after the operation.*

Source: *The New York Times,* December 14, 1982.

WHEN BARNEY CLARK consented to receive a mechanical heart at the Universty of Utah Medical Center, he was told what might go wrong, and a lot has. For two weeks the public has shared his sufferings as the initial operation was followed by one to mend his damaged lungs, by a prolonged seizure and now by a third operation, to repair a broken valve. Dr. Clark's courage is admirable and we truly wish him well.

But can all that pain and exertion be worthwhile? The purpose of medicine is to improve life's quality, not to make Methuselahs of us all. To prolong life beyond its natural span is no favor unless reasonable quality is also provided. Without it, the physician has succeeded only in prolonging death. Dr. Clark made his own choice, but many would decide death is preferable to being per-

manently tethered to a bulky machine, without hope of release.

Doctors who pioneer new operations may be led by natural enthusiasm, or a passion for the spotlight, to test them prematurely. To protect patients from such zeal, permission for experimental procedures must first be sought from institutional review boards, as was done by the developers of the mechanical heart. Although the device has been extensively tested in animals, in Dr. Clark's case half of the initial artificial heart had to be replaced at the time of operation, and now its mitral valve has failed from mechanical stress. Don't these failures suggest that the review board should have required even more testing in animals before using a patient as a guinea pig?

Should this type of device be used in

humans at all? The National Institutes of Health and the Utah team are working toward heart devices that will be portable and almost totally implantable. Why not wait for them? The N.I.H. has invested $8.4 million in the Utah project and $161 million in artificial hearts since 1964, yet it has failed to draw up criteria for what kind of device is acceptable therapy.

In the absence of thought, the technological bent of modern medical training seems to be taking over. The primitive belief that the heart is the seat of life endows heart surgery with a mystical glamor; the artificial heart is seen as a defiance of death. But medicine's real triumphs lie in improving the quality of life for everyone, not in death-defying heroics that benefit, or torment, a few.

75.

ANNIE DILLARD: Living Like Weasels

Annie Dillard's book of nature essays, Tinker at Pilgrim Creek, *won the Pulitzer Prize in 1975, but this did not surprise those who knew what a good writer she was, and how passionately she cared about all the living things in the world, and especially about the things that lived near her, in Tinker Creek and in Hollins Pond and in the fields and woods close by. "Living Like Weasels," which appeared in her book* Teaching a Stone to Talk, *is typical of the profound simplicity of her writings. But is this essay so very simple after all? Many readers have applied it to their own lives—and come to apparently different conclusions from Annie Dillard's. Thus you should read it for yourself, and decide for yourself.*

Source: *Teaching a Stone to Talk*, 1982.

A WEASEL IS WILD. Who knows what he thinks? He sleeps in his underground den, his tail draped over his nose. Sometimes he lives in his den for two days without leaving. Outside, he stalks rabbits, mice, muskrats, and birds, killing more bodies than he can eat warm, and often dragging the carcasses home. Obedient to instinct, he bites his prey at the neck, either splitting the jugular vein at the throat or crunching the brain at the base of the skull, and he does not let go. One naturalist refused to kill a weasel who was socketed into his hand deeply as a rattlesnake. The man could in no way pry the tiny weasel off, and he had to walk half a mile to water, the weasel dangling from his palm, and soak him off like a stubborn label.

And once, says Ernest Thompson Seton—once, a man shot an eagle out of the sky. He examined the eagle and found the dry skull of a weasel fixed by the jaws to his throat. The supposition is that the eagle had pounced on the weasel and the weasel swiveled and bit as instinct taught him, tooth to neck, and nearly won. I would like to have seen that eagle from the air a few weeks or months before he was shot: was the whole weasel still attached to his feathered throat, a fur pendant? Or did the eagle eat what he could reach, gutting the living weasel with his talons before his breast, bending his beak, cleaning the beautiful airborne bones?

I have been reading about weasels because I saw one last week. I startled a weasel who startled me, and we exchanged a long glance.

Twenty minutes from my house, through the woods by the quarry and across the highway, is Hollins Pond, a remarkable piece of shallowness, where I like to go at sunset and sit on a tree trunk. Hollins Pond is also called Murray's Pond; it covers two acres of bottomland near Tinker Creek with six inches of water and six thousand lily pads. In winter, brown-and-white steers stand in the middle of it, merely dampening their hooves; from the distant shore they look like miracle itself, complete with miracle's nonchalance. Now, in summer, the steers are gone. The water lilies have blossomed and spread to a green horizontal plane that is terra firma to plodding blackbirds, and tremulous ceiling to black leeches, crayfish, and carp.

This is, mind you, suburbia. It is a five-minute walk in three directions to rows of houses, though none is visible here. There's a 55 mph highway at one end of the pond, and a nesting pair of wood ducks at the other. Under every bush is a muskrat hole or a beer can. The far end is an alternating series of fields and woods, fields and woods, threaded everywhere with motorcycle tracks—in whose bare clay wild turtles lay eggs.

So I had crossed the highway, stepped over two low barbed-wire fences, and traced the motorcycle path in all gratitude through the wild rose and poison ivy of the pond's shoreline up into high grassy fields. Then I cut down through the woods to the mossy fallen tree where I sit. This tree is excellent. It makes a dry, upholstered bench at the upper, marshy end of the pond, a plush jetty raised from the thorny shore between a shallow blue body of water and a deep blue body of sky.

The sun had just set. I was relaxed on the tree trunk, ensconced in the lap of lichen, watching the lily pads at my feet tremble and part dreamily over the thrusting path of a carp. A yellow bird appeared to my right and flew behind me. It caught my eye; I swiveled around—and the next instant, inexplicably, I was looking down at a weasel, who was looking up at me.

Weasel! I'd never seen one wild before. He was ten inches long, thin as a curve, a muscled ribbon, brown as fruitwood, soft-furred, alert. His face was fierce, small and pointed as a lizard's; he would have made a good arrowhead. There was just a dot of chin, maybe two brown hairs' worth, and then the pure white fur began that spread down his underside. He had two black eyes I didn't see, any more than you see a window.

The weasel was stunned into stillness as he was emerging from beneath an enormous shaggy wild rose bush four feet away. I was stunned into stillness twisted backward on the tree trunk. Our eyes locked, and someone threw away the key.

Our look was as if two lovers, or deadly enemies, met unexpectedly on an overgrown path when each had been thinking of something else: a clearing blow to the gut. It was also a bright blow to the brain, or a sudden beating of brains, with all the charge and intimate grate of rubbed balloons. It emptied our lungs. It felled the forest, moved the fields, and drained the pond; the world dismantled and tumbled into that black hole of eyes. If you and I looked at each other that way, our skulls would split and drop to our shoulders. But we don't. We keep our skulls. So.

He disappeared. This was only last week, and already I don't remember what shattered the enchantment. I think I blinked, I think I retrieved my brain from the weasel's brain, and tried to memorize what I was seeing, and the weasel felt the yank of separation, the careening splashdown into real life and the urgent current of instinct. He vanished under the wild rose. I waited motionless, my mind suddenly full of data and my spirit with pleadings, but he didn't return.

Please do not tell me about "approach-avoidance conflicts." I tell you I've been in that weasel's brain for sixty seconds, and he was in mine. Brains are private places, muttering through unique and secret tapes—but the weasel and I both plugged into another tape simultaneously, for a sweet and shocking time. Can I help it if it was a blank?

What goes on in his brain the rest of the time? What does a weasel think about? He won't say. His journal is tracks in clay, a spray of feathers, mouse blood and bone: uncollected, unconnected, loose-leaf, and brown.

I would like to learn, or remember, how to live. I come to Hollins Pond not so much to learn how to live as, frankly, to forget about it. That is, I don't think I can learn from a wild animal how to live in particular—shall I suck warm blood, hold my tail high, walk with my

footprints precisely over the prints of my hands?—but I might learn something of mindlessness, something of the purity of living in the physical senses and the dignity of living without bias or motive. The weasel lives in necessity and we live in choice, hating necessity and dying at the last ignobly in its talons. I would like to live as I should, as the weasel lives as he should. And I suspect that for me the way is like the weasel's: open to time and death painlessly, noticing everything, remembering nothing, choosing the given with a fierce and pointed will.

I missed my chance. I should have gone for the throat. I should have lunged for that streak of white under the weasel's chin and held on, held on through mud and into the wild rose, held on for a dearer life. We could live under the wild rose wild as weasels, mute and uncomprehending. I could very calmly go wild. I could live two days in the den, curled, leaning on mouse fur, sniffing bird bones, blinking, licking, breathing musk, my hair tangled in the roots of grasses. Down is a good place to go, where the mind is single. Down is out, out of your ever-loving mind and back to your careless senses. I remember muteness as a prolonged and giddy fast, where every moment is a feast of utterance received. Time and events are merely poured, unremarked, and ingested directly, like blood pulsed into my gut through a jugular vein. Could two live that way? Could two live under the wild rose, and explore by the pond, so that the smooth mind of each is as everywhere present to the other, and as received and as unchallenged, as falling snow?

We could, you know. We can live any way we want. People take vows of poverty, chastity, and obedience—even of silence—by choice. The thing is to stalk your calling in a certain skilled and supple way, to locate the most tender and live spot and plug into that pulse. This is yielding, not fighting. A weasel doesn't "attack" anything; a weasel lives as he's meant to, yielding at every moment to the perfect freedom of single necessity.

I think it would be well, and proper, and obedient, and pure, to grasp your one necessity and not let it go, to dangle from it limp wherever it takes you. Then even death, where you're going no matter how you live, cannot you part. Seize it and let it seize you up aloft even, till your eyes burn out and drop; let your musky flesh fall off in shreds, and let your very bones unhinge and scatter, loosened over fields, over fields and woods, lightly, thoughtless, from any height at all, from as high as eagles.

1983

76.

A Nation at Risk

The year 1983 was notable for not just one but several influential reports on the state of education in the United States. High School: A Report on Secondary Education in America, *by a former Commissioner of Education, Ernest L. Boyer, was critical of the upper half of the public school program. John I. Goodlad's* A Place Called School: Prospects for the Future, *was critical of both ends of the curriculum. Other organizations, among them the College Entrance Board, the National Science Board, the Task Force on Education for Economic Growth, and the Twentieth Century Fund, all issued reports during the year. The most widely discussed and influential of all these criticisms of American education in the '80s appeared under the title* A Nation at Risk. *Prepared by the National Commission on Excellence in Education under the sponsorship of the President himself, it was front-page news, as were its dire predictions about what would happen if the country did not mend its educational ways. A portion of the report is reprinted here.*

Source: *A Nation at Risk: The Imperative for Educational Reform,* Government Printing Office, 1983.

OUR NATION is at risk. Our once unchallenged preeminence in commerce, industry, science, and technological innovation is being overtaken by competitors throughout the world. This report is concerned with only one of the many causes and dimensions of the problem, but it is the one that undergirds American prosperity, security, and civility. We report to the American people that while we can take justifiable pride in what our schools and colleges have historically accomplished and contributed to the United States and the well-being of its people, the educational foundations of our society are presently being eroded by a rising tide of mediocrity that threatens our very future as a Nation and a people. What was unimaginable a generation ago has begun to occur—others are matching and surpassing our educational attainments.

If an unfriendly foreign power had attempted to impose on America the mediocre educational performance that exists today, we might well have viewed it as an act of war. As it stands, we have allowed this to happen to ourselves. We have even squandered the gains in student achievement made in the wake of the Sputnik challenge. Moreover, we have dismantled essential support systems which helped make those gains possible. We have, in effect, been committing an act of unthinking, unilateral educational disarmament.

Our society and its educational institutions seem to have lost sight of the basic purposes of schooling, and of the high expectations and disciplined effort needed to attain them. This report, the result of 18 months of study, seeks to generate reform of our educational system in fundamental ways and to renew the Nation's commitment to schools and colleges of high quality throughout the length and breadth of our land.

That we have compromised this commitment is, upon reflection, hardly surprising, given the multitude of often conflicting demands we have placed on our Nation's schools and colleges. They are routinely called on to provide solutions to personal, social, and political problems that the home and other institutions either will not or cannot resolve. We must understand that these demands on our schools and colleges often exact an educational cost as well as a financial one. . . .

History is not kind to idlers. The time is long past when America's destiny was assured simply by an abundance of national resources and inexhaustible human enthusiasm, and by our relative isolation from the malignant problems of older civilizations. The world is indeed one global village. We live among determined, well-educated, and strongly motivated competitors. We compete with them for international standing and markets, not only with products but also with the ideas of our laboratories and neighborhood workshops. America's position in the world may once have been reasonably secure with only a few exceptionally well-trained men and women. It is no longer.

The risk is not only that the Japanese make automobiles more efficiently than Americans and have government subsidies for development and export. It is not just that the South Koreans recently built the world's most efficient steel mill, or that American machine tools, once the pride of the world, are being displaced by German products. It is also that these developments signify a redistribution of trained capability throughout the globe. Knowledge, learning, information, and skilled intelligence are the new raw materials of international commerce and are today spreading throughout the world as vigorously as miracle drugs, synthetic fertilizers, and blue jeans did earlier. If only to keep and improve on the slim competitive edge we still retain in world markets, we must dedicate ourselves to the reform of our educational system for the benefit of all—old and young alike, affluent and poor, majority and minority. Learning is the indispensable investment required for success in the "information age" we are entering.

Our concern, however, goes well beyond matters such as industry and commerce. It also includes the intellectual, moral, and spiritual strengths of our people which knit together the very fabric of our society. The people of the United States need to know that individuals in our society who do not possess the levels of skill, literacy, and training essential to this new era will be effectively disenfranchised, not simply from the material rewards that accompany competent performance, but also from the chance to participate fully in our national life. A high level of shared education is essential to a free, democratic society and to the fostering of a common culture, especially in a country that prides itself on pluralism and individual freedom.

For our country to function, citizens must be able to reach some common understandings on complex issues, often on short notice and on the basis of conflicting or incomplete evidence. Education helps form these common understandings, a point Thomas Jefferson made long ago in his justly famous dictum:

> I know no safe depository of the ultimate powers of the society but the people themselves; and if we think them not enlightened enough to exercise their control with a wholesome discretion, the remedy is not to take it from them but to inform their discretion.

Part of what is at risk is the promise first made on this continent: All, regardless of race or class or economic status, are entitled to a fair chance and to the tools for developing their individual powers of mind and spirit to the utmost. This promise means that all children by virtue of their own efforts, competently guided, can hope to attain the mature and informed judgment needed to secure gainful employment and to manage their own lives, thereby serving not only their own interests but also the progress of society itself. . . .

This is not the first or only commission on education, and some of our find-ings are surely not new, but old business that now at last must be done. For no one can doubt that the United States is under challenge from many quarters.

Children born today can expect to graduate from high school in the year 2000. We dedicate our report not only to these children, but also to those now in school and others to come. We firmly believe that a movement of America's schools in the direction called for by our recommendations will prepare these children for far more effective lives in a far stronger America.

Our final word, perhaps better characterized as a plea, is that all segments of our population give attention to the implementation of our recommendations. Our present plight did not appear overnight, and the responsibility for our current situation is widespread. Reform of our educational system will take time and unwavering commitment. It will require equally widespread, energetic, and dedicated action. . . . Help should come from students themselves; from parents, teachers, and school boards; from colleges and universities; from local, State, and Federal officials; from teachers and administrators' organizations; from industrial and labor councils; and from other groups with interest in and responsibility for educational reform.

It is their America, and the America of all of us, that is at risk; it is to each of us that this imperative is addressed. It is by our willingness to take up the challenge, and our resolve to see it through, that America's place in the world will be either secured or forfeited. Americans have succeeded before and so we shall again.

77.

Environmental Protection Reagan Style

On March 9, 1983, Anne M. Burford resigned as head of the Environmental Protection Agency (EPA) after a series of confrontations with Congress that, despite denials, had become embarrassing for the President and his administration. (While still Ann Gorsuch she had fenced with Senator Moynihan over the so-called Environmental Superfund; see Selection 58). In a press conference on March 11 President Reagan defended Mrs. Burford and suggested that enemies of the administration had simply been out to get her. But there were more serious and profound objections to the way the administration was protecting, or not protecting, the environment, which are reviewed in the editorial from The New Republic *that is reprinted here, together with excerpts from the press conference.*

Sources: Presidential Documents, week ending March 11, 1983.

The New Republic, March 14, 1983.

A: THE PRESIDENT'S PRESS CONFERENCE

Q. Mr. President, you said that Anne Burford did nothing wrong, that she can leave EPA with her head held high. But there are allegations that she admitted holding up the clean-up of one dump site because it might help California Governor Jerry Brown.

There are also allegations that one of her top aides, James Sanderson, was involved in EPA decisions involving his legal clients. When you say that she did nothing wrong while the investigation of those charges is still outstanding, aren't you in effect saying that those practices are all right with you?

The President. No, I'm not saying anything of the kind. And I heard her last night on television make that statement about the site. And she said that possibly she made some remark to that effect. But it had nothing to do with the decision that was made. . . .

Now, I'm glad that you brought that subject up, because I think that what she did in resigning—I did regret very much. And I never would have asked for her resignation. She was doing a job. And we, this administration, can be very proud of our record in environmental protection. And believe me, it tops what we found when we came here. And the fact that she was able to do it with a reduced budget—well, I've asked everyone in our government to do things with a reduced budget and with fewer employees, if possible. That was what we came in here to do—to make government more efficient, to eliminate waste and extravagance. And she has revealed that she is far more concerned with the national welfare and is a far bigger person than those people who have been sniping at her and who've been going public with unfounded allegations, accusations, and charges. . . .

But I don't think that the people who were attacking her were concerned about the environment. I don't think they were concerned about any possible wrongdoing. As a matter of fact, I think this administration and its policies were their target. And, frankly, I wonder how they manage to look at themselves in the mirror in the morning. . . .

Q. But the Republican polls now show that your policies are perceived by the public, your environmental policies, as being more favorable to polluters than to the public. Are you going to change any of your environmental policies now that Mrs. Burford has gone?

The President. That's all they've heard, but no one has given any evidence that that is true. I'd like to call your attention to the fact that in 8 years as Governor, California not only led every State in the Union, we led the Federal Government in environmental protection. We were the forerunners of the whole movement. And how this idea has come, I sometimes suspect that the lobbyists for the environmental interests feel they have to keep their constituents stirred up or they might not have jobs anymore.

Q. Well, you think the slowness in getting the Superfund into action at a number of sites has contributed to that perception and the fact that you have been quoted in the past as talking about environmental extremism?

The President. Well there is environmental extremism. I don't think they'll be happy until the White House looks like a bird's nest. [*Laughter*]

B: THE FILTHINESS ISSUE

ASKED AT HIS press conference on February 16 about the furor over Anne M. Gorsuch and the Environmental Protection Agency, President Reagan launched into a rambling review of the history and purposes of the Superfund, the program to clean up hazardous wastes that is at the center of the dispute. Mr. Reagan was in his kindly uncle mode, so when he said that "certainly" he retains confidence in E.P.A. and its administrator, and added that they had compiled a "splendid record," his audience must have thought that here was another case in which our affable President has been caught unaware by troubles in some backwater of his empire. Listening citizens could be forgiven for assuming that Mr. Reagan was just giving a pro forma vote of confidence to subordinates while he tries to get to the bottom of all this. The President promised his television audience (or seemed to) that he was ready to cooperate fully with Congressional investigators in the interest of truth and justice, "because I can no longer insist on executive privilege if there's a suspicion in the minds of the people that maybe it is being used to cover some wrongdoing. That we will never stand for."

The next day, after the television cameras were gone, a White House spokesman issued the by-now customary post-press-conference clarification. Executive privilege hadn't been dropped after all; the terms under which Congressional committees may examine E.P.A. documents to determine whether or not the Superfund was being administered politically (and perhaps corruptly) were still to be negotiated. But again, the confused signals left the convenient impression that the President was somehow detached from the E.P.A. issue. He hardly seemed to understand what was coming out of his own mouth, let alone what chemicals might be seeping into the nation's groundwater. If the President only knew, surely he would do something, wouldn't he?

We are all too old for this. Just as Richard Nixon knew that his people were busy with burglaries and cover-ups, Ronald Reagan knows that the environmental laws of this country are being administered by people who are hostile to the intent of those laws. After all, he appointed them. He approved the slashed budgets under which they operate. And he established the climate of bias in favor of polluting industries and the contempt for environmentalism that pervades the Administration.

During the 1980 campaign, Mr. Reagan regularly disparaged "environmental extremists," charging that they would rather "protect rabbit holes and birds' nests" than see industries built and jobs created. Possibly there were occasional cases in which environmental regulators established such restrictive standards as to make it impossible for businesses to operate. Presumably some regulators did overlook costs in their eagerness to achieve benefits. But instead of appointing moderate conservatives to run the environmental agencies, people who would scale back onerous regulatory burdens and weigh costs against benefits while upholding the fundamental goal of environmental protection, Mr. Reagan chose extremists of his own—James G. Watt, head of the notoriously anti-environmentalist Mountain States Legal Foundation, as Secretary of the Interior, and Anne M. Gorsuch, Mr. Watt's frequent ally in the Colorado legislature, as administrator of the Environmental Protection Agency.

Of the two, Mrs. Gorsuch was tendered the more crucial responsibility. Important as public lands, wilderness areas, and mineral rights are to the nation's spirit and economy, E.P.A.'s very purpose is the protection of the lives and health of America's people. It is charged with ensuring the survival not of the snail darter but of human beings who suffer the consequences of poisoned air and tainted water. They suffer by contracting cancer and emphysema, by being unable to work and becoming dependent, by feeling physical and emotional pain because they or their loved ones are made to fall sick.

The kinds of people who tend to be appointed to high government posts in any Administration are unlikely to have shared the experience of people who find themselves and their neighbors ill or dying because they happen to live near a Love Canal or a Times Beach, Missouri. But past Administrations of both parties (E.P.A. was founded, after all, during the Nixon Administration) have cared enough about the lives of such people to see to it that environmental laws were fairly and energetically enforced. The benefits have been tangible—and breathable and drinkable, too.

But a drastic reversal of policy came into effect with the arrival of Mr. Reagan and Mrs. Gorsuch. The Administration tried to have environmental standards lowered by law, but Congress—including the Republican Senate—refused to go along. And so the Administration decided to gut environmental protection by subterfuge—by slashing funds, destroying agency morale, and refusing to enforce the law. Because of new laws to control toxic chemicals, E.P.A.'s workload was scheduled to double during the Reagan years, but the Reagan budgets call for the agency's operating funds to be cut nearly in half from the levels projected by the Carter Administration. Mrs. Gorsuch has claimed that the E.P.A. staff is down by "only" one thousand since the Administration came into office, though environmental groups claim that, using Carter budget projections, nearly three thousand positions have been eliminated. According to President Carter's former deputy E.P.A. administrator, William Drayton, "E.P.A. is losing the cream of its senior civil service—the core of key people with the expertise, wisdom, and respect that are critical to any large institution." According to Russell Train, E.P.A. administrator under Presidents Nixon and Ford, "The budget and personnel cuts, unless reversed, will destroy the agency as an effective institution for many years to come."

Along with budget and personnel levels, E.P.A. enforcement activities have declined dramatically. From 1980 to 1981, the number of cases referred by E.P.A. to the Justice Department dropped from 252 to 78, and Justice filed suit in only 35 cases. One of Mrs. Gorsuch's arguments has been that states could take up the enforcement burden, but last year the Administration proposed a 20 percent cut in funding for state environmental grants, and has announced its intention to "zero-out" such grants completely.

Every day there is mounting evidence that when President Reagan's E.P.A. has moved to enforce the laws, it has done so grudgingly and with bias toward corporate polluters. The legislation setting up the $1.6-billion Superfund provides that the E.P.A. will endeavor to collect cleanup costs from chemical companies responsible for hazardous waste pollution. In the very first Superfund settle-

AP/Wide World

Leaking chemical barrels in a South Carolina storage site. Residents complained that the barrels were moved there from another site after they had begun to leak.

ment, Mrs. Gorsuch's assistant has admitted telling the Inmont Corporation what the government's bottom-line negotiating position was. Congress is currently investigating charges that E.P.A. has pursued a "sweetheart" policy of charging big chemical companies only what it costs to do a superficial cleanup of waste dumps, leaving it to taxpayers (if anyone) to pay for a thorough detoxification.

There is a special kind of horror in the experience of families who live in places like Love Canal or Times Beach, where contamination by the deadly poison dioxin reached three hundred times the level at which danger begins. Their pets fall ill, then their children; they begin to complain, but it is months or even years before anyone listens, let alone acts. And the fear can never be fully assuaged, because the diseases caused by exposure to chemicals like dioxin can take many years to become manifest.

Yet in 1982 Mrs. Gorsuch lifted a ban on dumping liquid chemicals in hazardous waste landfills. That enabled Chemical Waste Management Inc. to unload 1,500 barrels of flammable solvents in a Denver dump. This company is represented by James W. Sanderson, one of Mrs. Gorsuch's close associates, whom she had wanted to make the third-ranking official at E.P.A. In another case, Congressional staffers strongly suspect that Mrs. Gorsuch held up a $6.1 million grant to clean up a California toxic waste dump so that Democratic Governor Jerry Brown could not claim credit for the cleanup in his campaign for the Senate.

In yet another case, when the Thrift-way Company, of Farmington, New Mexico, sought a waiver from laws limiting lead in gasoline, Mrs. Gorsuch is quoted as having said to a Senate aide that she couldn't tell company representatives to break the law, "but she hoped that they got the message." To help administer the Superfund, Mrs. Gorsuch hired Rita M. Lavelle, public affairs specialist for Aero Jet Liquid Rocket, a company that E.P.A. records showed had the third worst pollution record in California. Mrs. Lavelle has been fired in what Congressional investigators suspect was an attempt to calm the furor over the E.P.A.

Now the administration has announced with a flourish that it is willing to spend $33 million in Superfund money to buy out the 2,400 residents of Times Beach. This action comes unconscionably late—the government has known of the danger for a decade—yet it has all the earmarks of political panic. It may not be enough; Mrs. Gorsuch may yet have to be sacrificed. Although President Reagan has declared he retains confidence in her, White House aides know that she is a political liability, symbol of a potentially devastating "filthiness issue" created by tax cuts skewed to the rich and spending cuts skewed to the poor. But Mrs. Gorsuch is only a symbol, and getting rid of her will not change the fact that President Reagan and his environmental policies have been biased toward the same wealthy and powerful groups that were the beneficiaries of his tax policies, and against the same people forced by chance or Reagan economic policy to need food stamps and compensatory education.

Last week, at the height of the controversy, Mrs. Gorsuch got married. This is a traditionalist Administration, so henceforth Anne Gorsuch is to be known as Anne Burford. We wish her well in her personal, if not her professional, life. But what really needs changing is not the name of the environmental protection administrator, but the policies of the man who appointed her.

Scientists consider dioxin to be one of the most toxic substances made by humans—170,000 times more deadly than cyanide. Less than 1 part per billion is enough to kill guinea pigs and rabbits.

U.S. News and World Report, July 4, 1983

78.

Who Will Stop the Acid Rain?

The process that results in the formation of acid rain generally begins with emissions into the atmosphere of sulfur dioxide and nitrogen oxide. These gases are released by automobiles, certain industrial operations, and electric power plants that burn fossil fuels. The gases combine with water vapor in clouds to form sulfuric and nitric acids. When precipitation falls from the clouds it is highly acidic, having a pH value of about 5.6 or lower. (The pH scale ranges from 0 to 14, with lower numbers indicating increased acidity.) At several locations in the eastern United States and in Western Europe, pH values between 2 and 3 have been found. The acidic precipitation, as this article shows, is highly toxic to plants and animals; in fact, it is a deadly peril for the environment. Although the science of acid rain can be described just this matter-of-factly, its elimination was a far more complex matter, as this article indicates.

Source: *Discover,* October 1983.

THE SERENE WATERS of Big Moose Lake, in the western Adirondack Mountains of New York, have the deep, crystalline blue of a watercolor on a fly-fishing calendar. On all sides are woods, the tall trees marching to the lakeside. It is a setting of great beauty and tranquillity.

It is too tranquil. No brook trout break the surface of Big Moose, as they did in great numbers a few years ago. And the lakeside is silent because the voices of chirping tree frogs, of loons and kingfishers, have been hushed by the same insidious poison that killed the trout. The crystalline clarity of the water results from its acidity—ominous evidence that, like hundreds of other lakes in eastern North America, Big Moose is dying, a victim of acid rain.

The effects of acid rain on wilderness, severe as they are, are only part of a phenomenon that has growing ecological, economic, and political implications. Farmers are increasingly concerned about the possibility of serious damage to their crops from acid precipitation. Even man-made structures and monuments have suffered. The corrosive rain is literally dissolving vulnerable building materials such as stone and bronze. Its effect on drinking water may pose a threat to human health. And it has soured relations between Canada and the United States: Canada blames American industry for the acid rain endangering its woodlands.

Now, after two government-sponsored studies confirmed in June that industrial smokestack emissions play the major role in forming acid rain, and suggested that something can—and should—be done about it, the Environmental Protection Agency is taking action. In a major policy shift, the agency this fall will recommend legislation requiring heavy reductions in the air pollution responsible for the problem.

Acid rain is not confined to eastern North America. Some 20,000 lakes in Sweden have been affected. The deadly precipitation has reached such dire proportions in West Germany that the British journal *Nature* recently headlined an acid-rain story: TOO LATE FOR THE BLACK FOREST? In China's industrial city of Chongqing (Chungking), Song dynasty sculptures that survived 800 years of weathering have lost many of their features after only a few years of heavy acid rain. Researchers near Los Angeles have measured fog with a *p*H of 2—more acidic than vinegar.

Although a small amount of acid rain is produced naturally (by, among other things, volcanic eruptions), it results largely from sulphur dioxide and nitrogen oxides created by the burning of fossil fuels. Automobile exhaust fumes are partly to blame, but the worst culprits by far are coal-burning utilities, which are responsible for 86 per cent of the man-made sulphur dioxide in the atmosphere. In the presence of sunlight, which acts as a catalyst, these gases react with water vapor to become dilute sulphuric and nitric acids—acid rain. Scientists believe that acid rain kills trees primarily by soaking into the earth and reacting chemically with clays to release aluminum and potassium. These metals are toxic to the fine root systems of trees. The metals are then carried into lakes and other bodies of water, where they kill aquatic life—especially fish, which are extraordinarily vulnerable to aluminum poisoning.

Scientists have long been aware of the pernicious effects of acid rain, but some questions about the phenomenon remained incompletely answered. Exactly how is it formed? Is there a direct connection between man-made air pollution and acid precipitation? Would industrial controls be effective?

Two reports appearing in June—one issued by the National Academy of Sciences (NAS), the other by a review panel under the auspices of George Keyworth, the White House science adviser—provided some definitive answers and recommendations:

• Acid rain comes from man-made sources.

• Further pollution controls would reduce it.

• Such controls should begin now.

These unequivocal conclusions led the EPA to re-evaluate its acid-rain policy. An internal task force recently reported to the agency's administrator, William Ruckelshaus, on the choices available to him. These range from BAU, bureauspeak for "business as usual," to sweeping reductions in sulphur emissions. Insiders say that the agency staff is recommending annual reductions as high as 12 million tons, or about 50 per cent. Partly because of the approaching presidential primary in New Hampsire, a state hard hit by acid rain, Ruckelshaus is expected to propose late in September an intensive emissions-control program—a radical departure from the EPA's long-standing antiregulatory stance.

The reports and the changing mood at the EPA doomed the Reagan administration's position on acid rain: that the problem was not well enough understood, and that expensive pollution controls might not work and therefore ought not to be rushed into. This policy, supported by industry, had been bolstered by some European air-quality findings indicating that the connection between emissions and precipitation might not be direct. Although some American scientists felt that the European data were faulty, NAS committee chairman Jack Calvert, senior scientist at the National Center for Atmospheric Research in Boulder, Colorado, says that the administration's position was reasonable: "Nature is very complicated. We can't expect to understand every change that takes place in the atmosphere." But the NAS study resolved some of the uncertainty about acid rain. It found that the relationship between emissions and acid depositions in the eastern states, averaged over a year, is linear: a 50 per cent decrease in pollution, for example, would result in a 50 per cent decrease in acid rain. While the report made no recommendation about controls—"That wasn't our mandate," says Calvert—the Keyworth panel urged immediate action to reduce emissions of sulphur compounds into the atmosphere. Although the panel will not publish its full report for several months, members decided to release the summary because they felt a sense of urgency.

"We're persuaded," says William Ackermann, professor of civil engineering at the University of Illinois and vice-chairman of the panel. "The stakes are quite high, because some impacts are only slowly reversible, or perhaps irreversible." One worrisome impact, he says, is that increased acidity may be dangerously disturbing the microorganisms in soil that are responsible for degrading natural wastes. These microbes constitute the bottom of the food chain, turning dead plants and animals into the nitrogen and carbon essential for life.

AP/Wide World

Billowing smokestacks at a Virginia factory.

Many scientists are still puzzled by some aspects of acid rain. For example, they cannot link emissions with acid deposits except in the most general way. Says Calvert, "When it comes to saying 'Smokestack pollution from Power Plant A in Ohio is responsible for acid rain at Point B in the Adirondacks,' we just can't give that kind of specific guidance." The Keyworth report predicted that a "source/receptor model" that might provide such guidance is at least five years away.

Scientists will not be able to develop reliable models until they have more extensive measurements. They can roughly calculate the sources and quantities of smokestack emissions from the fuel-consumption reports of utilities. But measurements of acid rainfall are scanty. The main source is a sophisticated, long-term study conducted since 1963 at the Hubbard Brook Experimental Forest in New Hampshire by ecologist Gene Likens, director of the New York Botanical Garden's Institute for Ecosystem Studies.

Is there any immediate remedy for acid rain? The White House group suggested more intensive use of coal washing. "It's just what it sounds like," says John Miller of the National Oceanic and Atmospheric Administration, a member of the NAS panel. "You wash the coal, and the soluble sulphates come out." Another possibility: seasonal burning of fuels with different sulphur contents. Since acid rain seems to fall most heavily in summer, partly because use of air conditioning makes that the time of greatest electricity consumption, the use of low-sulphur coal might be required in the hot, wet months.

Neither method, however, would have more than a marginal effect on acid rain. Any significant reduction will require the installation of "scrubbers," devices that remove sulphates from gases at the industrial site. The most thorough scrubbing technology is flue-gas desulphurization, which removes as much as 90 per cent of the sulphur dioxide from smokestack emissions. Smokestack gases pass through a chamber containing a slurry of limestone in solution. The slurry absorbs the sulphur dioxide and transforms it into either calcium sulphate—gypsum—which can be safely used as landfill, or calcium sulphite, a gooey substance that is more difficult to dispose of.

A newer control technology, the limestone injection multi-stage burner, is less effective than flue-gas desulphurization but considerably cheaper. Solid limestone is dumped directly into the furnace of the power plant while the coal is burning, and combines with the sulphates (producing calcium sulphate) before they become gases. The process reduces the output of sulphur dioxide by 50 to 60 per cent.

While scrubbers are the best way to clean up acid rain, they are also the most expensive to install—as much as $300 million per plant for flue-gas desulphurization. "Retrofitting is so expensive," says Miller. "It would be nice if we could get the utilities to build new, clean plants, but energy consumption is down, and interest rates are up. It doesn't seem likely."

Hence the many proposals in Congress to clean up existing plants. One of the leading bills, sponsored by Democratic Senator George Mitchell of Maine, would require reduction of sulphur dioxide emissions in the states east of the Mississippi River by 10 million tons, to 56 per cent of the 1980 level. Democratic Congressman Henry Waxman of California has introduced legislation that might resolve who will pay for the clean-up. His bill would require scrubbers on the 50 largest sulphur dioxide-emitting utilities in the 48 contiguous states. Ninety per cent of the money would be raised by a tax of one mill per kilowatt-hour on all non-nuclear-generated electricity; that would increase household utility bills across the country by 50 cents to a dollar a month.

Any comprehensive approach will be expensive, especially for the Midwestern utilities, which claim that an ambitious clean-up will cause consumer rates there to soar. However, emissions-control advocates point out that the necessary rate increases would only bring Midwestern energy bills into line with what consumers in New York and New England are paying already.

Painful or not, new controls seem inevitable now that the EPA has finally begun to move. The only real questions remaining are how stringent the measures will be, and how soon Congress will impose them.

79.

The Challenge of Peace

On May 3, 1983, the National Conference of (Roman) Catholic Bishops, during a meeting in Chicago, approved a 150-page pastoral letter on nuclear weapons. The document, an amended version of a third draft, called for a halt to the development, production, and deployment of nuclear weapons; asserted that nuclear war was essentially immoral; and stressed the bishops' resistance to the idea that a nuclear war could even be survived, much less won. Part of the pastoral letter is reprinted here.

Source: "The Challenge of Peace: God's Promise and Our Response," *Christianity and Crisis,* May 2, 1983.

THE CLASSICAL Christian position [on the morality of war] is confronted with a unique challenge by nuclear warfare. This must be the starting point of any further moral reflection: nuclear weapons, particularly, and nuclear warfare as it is planned today, raise new moral questions. No previously conceived moral position escapes the fundamental confrontation posed by contemporary nuclear strategy. Many have noted the similarity of the statements made by eminent scientists and Vatican II's observation that we are forced today "to undertake a completely fresh reappraisal of war." The task before us is not simply to repeat what we have said before; it is first to consider anew whether and how our religious-moral tradition can assess, direct, contain, and, we hope, help to eliminate the threat posed to the human family by the nuclear arsenals of the world. Pope John Paul II captured the essence of the problem during his pilgrimage to Hiroshima:

In the past it was possible to destroy a village, a town, a region, even a country. Now it is the whole planet that has come under threat.

The Holy Father's observation illustrates why the moral problem is also a religious question of the most profound significance. In the nuclear arsenals of the United States or the Soviet Union alone, there exists a capacity to do something no other age could imagine: we can threaten the entire planet. For people of faith this means we read the Book of Genesis with a new awareness; the moral issue at stake in nuclear war involves the meaning of sin in its most graphic dimensions. Every sinful act is a confrontation of the creature and the Creator. Today the destructive potential of the nuclear powers threatens the human person, the civilization we have slowly constructed, and even the created order itself. In brief, we can threaten the very creative work of God among us.

We live today, therefore, in the midst of a cosmic drama; we possess a power which should never be used, but which might be used if we do not reverse our direction. We live with nuclear weapons on the basis of an extraordinary assumption: We know we cannot afford one serious mistake. This fact dramatizes the precariousness of our position, politically, morally, and spiritually.

A prominent "sign of the times" today is a sharply increased awareness of the danger of the nuclear arms race. Such awareness has produced a public discussion about nuclear policy here and in other countries which is unprecedented in its scope and depth. What has been accepted for years with almost no question is now being subjected to the sharpest criticism. What previously had been defined as a safe and stable system of deterrence is today viewed with political and moral skepticism. Many forces are at work in this new evaluation, and we believe one of the crucial elements is the Gospel vision of peace which guides our work in this pastoral letter. The nuclear age has been the theater of our existence for almost four decades; today it is being evaluated with a new perspective. For many the leaven of the Gospel and the light of the Holy Spirit create the decisive dimension of this new perspective.

At the center of the new evaluation of the nuclear arms race is a recognition of two elements: the destructive potential of nuclear weapons, and the stringent choices which the nuclear age poses for both politics and morals.

The fateful passage into the nuclear age as a military reality began with the bombing of Nagasaki and Hiroshima, events described by Pope Paul VI as a "butchery of untold magnitude." Since then, in spite of efforts at control and plans for disarmament (e.g., the Baruch Plan of 1946), the nuclear arsenals have

escalated, particularly in the two superpowers. The qualitative superiority of these two states, however, should not overshadow the fact that four other countries possess nuclear capacity, and a score of states are only steps away from becoming "nuclear nations."

This nuclear escalation has been opposed sporadically and selectively but never effectively. The race has continued in spite of carefully expressed doubts by analysts and other citizens and in the face of forcefully expressed opposition by public rallies. Today the opposition to the arms race is no longer selective or sporadic, it is widespread and sustained. The danger and destructiveness of nuclear weapons are understood and resisted with new urgency and intensity. There is in the public debate today an endorsement of the position submitted by the Holy See at the United Nations in 1976: The arms race is to be condemned as a danger, an act of aggression against the poor, and a folly which does not provide the security it promises.

Papal teaching has consistently addressed the folly and danger of the arms race; but the new perception of it which is now held by the general public is due in large measure to the work of scientists and physicians who have described for citizens the concrete human consequences of a nuclear war.

In a striking demonstration of his personal and pastoral concern for preventing nuclear war, Pope John Paul II commissioned a study by the Pontifical Academy of Science which reinforced the findings of other scientific bodies. The Holy Father had the study transmitted by personal representative to the leaders of the United States, the Soviet Union, the United Kingdom, and France, and to the President of the

General Assembly of the United Nations. One of its conclusions is especially pertinent to the public debate in the United States:

> Recent talk about winning or even surviving a nuclear war must reflect a failure to appreciate a medical reality: Any nuclear war would inevitably cause death, disease and suffering of pandemonic proportions and without the possibility of effective medical intervention. That reality leads to the same conclusion physicians have reached for life-threatening epidemics throughout history. Prevention is essential for control.

This medical conclusion has a moral corollary. Traditionally, the Church's moral teaching sought first to prevent war and then to limit its consequences if it occurred. Today the possibilities for placing political and moral limits on nuclear war are so minimal that the moral task, like the medical, is prevention: As a people, we must refuse to legitimate the idea of nuclear war. Such a refusal will require not only new ideas and new vision, but what the Gospel calls conversion of the heart.

To say "no" to nuclear war is both a necessary and a complex task. We are moral teachers in a tradition which has always been prepared to relate moral principles to concrete problems. Particularly in this letter we could not be content with simply restating general moral principles or repeating well-known requirements about the ethics of war. . . .

Though certain that the dangerous and delicate nuclear relationship the superpowers now maintain should not exist, we understand how it came to exist. In a world of sovereign states, devoid of central authority, and possessing the knowledge to produce nuclear weapons, many choices were made, some clearly objectionable, others well-intended with mixed results, which brought the world to its present dangerous situation.

We see with clarity the political folly of a system which threatens mutual suicide, the psychological damage this does to ordinary people, especially the young, the economic distortion of priorities—billions readily spent for destructive instruments while pitched battles are waged daily in our legislatures over much smaller amounts for the homeless, the hungry, and the helpless here and abroad. But it is much less clear how we translate a "no" to nuclear war into the personal and public choices which can move us in a new direction, toward a national policy and an international system which more adequately reflect the values and vision of the Kingdom of God.

These tensions in our assessment of the politics and strategy of the nuclear age reflect the conflicting elements of the nuclear dilemma and the balance of terror which it has produced. We have said earlier in this letter that the fact of war reflects the existence of sin in the world. The nuclear threat and the danger it poses to human life and civilization exemplify in a qualitatively new way the perennial struggle of the political community to contain the use of force, particularly among states.

Precisely because of the destructive nature of nuclear weapons, strategies have been developed which previous generations would have found unintelligible. Today military preparations are undertaken on a vast and sophisticated scale, but the declared purpose is not to use the weapons produced. Threats are made which would be suicidal to implement. The key to security is no longer only military secrets, for in many instances security requires informing one's adversary publicly what weapons one has and what plans exist for their use. The presumption of the nation-state system, that sovereignty implies an ability to protect a nation's territory and population, is precisely the presumption denied by the nuclear capacities of both superpowers. In a sense each is at the mercy of the other's perception of what strategy is "rational," what kind of damage is "unacceptable," how "convincing" one side's threat is to the other.

The political paradox of deterrence has also strained our moral conception. May a nation threaten what it may never do? May it possess what it may never use? Who is involved in the threat each superpower makes: government officials? or military personnel? or the citizenry in whose "defense" the threat is made?

In brief, the danger of the situation is clear; but how to prevent the use of nuclear weapons, how to assess deterrence, and how to delineate moral responsibility in the nuclear age are less clearly seen or stated. Reflecting the complexity of the nuclear problem, our arguments in this pastoral must be detailed and nuanced; but our "no" to nuclear war must, in the end, be definitive and decisive.

80.

Hugh Sidey: How to Do Nothing Well

The opposition of the U.S. Catholic bishops to the production and use, under any circumstances, of nuclear weapons (see Selection 79) was highly controversial and brought attacks from many persons in public life, especially in the Reagan administration. In response to such responses there seemed to be a middle position, which might be stated thus: Have nuclear weapons if you wish, but do not use them. Such views were well expressed in the following comment by Hugh Sidey, which appeared in Time *during the summer of 1983.*

Source: "How to Do Nothing Well (The Presidency)," *Time*, August 22, 1983.

In a way, the great power game being played around the globe is made to order for an actor. The object is to do nothing for real.

John Kennedy once pointed that out. He reviewed the Atlantic Fleet in 1962 from behind a huge windscreen on the bow of the heavy cruiser *Northampton* as it steamed between two columns of hulking warships. The crew of each ship lined the deck and fired a salute as it surged by Kennedy.

He was profoundly affected by the event, and he mused about it for weeks. "I felt like Teddy Roosevelt," he joked. But on further reflection, he came to an important realization. "What do you do with all those ships?" he asked himself, then answered his own question: "If you are smart, nothing." Exactly.

Twice in the past four decades we miscalculated, and we had war in Korea and Viet Nam. The worry now is whether Ronald Reagan can perceive the fine line between drama and reality.

Displaying military power, with all its bands and thunder, can become dangerously addictive. And dispatching battle units can begin to look like the cleanest, easiest exercise of power that a President can undertake.

The ships and planes are magnificent machines, the crews totally responsive. Orders are instantly carried out, unlike those given in the glutenous world of Government.

Sometimes the moment of command is unforgettable, its recollection stirring. Lyndon Johnson told and retold the story of standing in the White House situation room and ordering Secretary of Defense Robert McNamara to send the Sixth Fleet toward the warring Middle East in 1967 to protect American interests. During such retellings, Johnson acted as if he could feel the great hulls shudder and begin to wheel around after he spoke a few quiet words. Oh what a lovely war.

But when Johnson played the same part in Viet Nam, he produced a tragedy. Presidential commands produced casualties. The bands were off-key. Bluster was meaningless in that jungle. Theater *vérité*.

Yet those who would opt only for prayer and stickless diplomacy are of just as much concern as Reagan. For instance, Senator Edward Kennedy wants to have Congress order Reagan to keep the fleet from maneuvering in Central American waters: an idea that is probably as unconstitutional as it is bad.

His view of history is very dim. John Kennedy back in 1961 loaded up the Marines and primed the navy's airplanes and sent the Seventh Fleet into the South China Sea to hunker near Laos and impress the Communist Pathet Lao, which was gobbling up the country with Moscow's encouragement. The Marines never got into combat, but the display of force helped bring some allies to our side and finally produce a vague stand-off in the battle.

The same year, after the Berlin Wall went up and the Soviets interfered with access to West Berlin, President Kennedy once more turned to a military display. He ordered 1,500 troops of the U.S. 8th Division to form a battle group and drive in armored trucks 110 miles through East Germany along the Helmstedt-Berlin autobahn. Critics called the move too provocative. Kennedy believed it a crucial symbol of his determination. The battle group made an uninterrupted journey and was effusively greeted in Berlin by Vice President Lyndon Johnson.

There is no sure script written for the leading man in this continuing drama. But when a President begins to fancy the marching bands too much, he had better go to a prayer meeting or two.

Then, about the time he is convinced that meditation in hushed sanctuaries can solve the world's problems, as Jimmy Carter once believed, the President had better get back to the parade ground and relish the martial strains of *The Stars and Stripes Forever*.

81.

JOHN NOBLE WILFORD: Farewell to Pioneer

On June 13, 1983, the unmanned spacecraft Pioneer 10 crossed the orbit of Neptune and thus became the first man-made vehicle ever to travel beyond the solar system. As it began its voyage into interstellar space, it continued to radio information back to Earth. Its journey had already occupied 11 years, but a great future loomed before it. Considering how benign is the environment of outer space, it was possible, even probable, that Pioneer 10 would still be voyaging outward millions or billions of years hence. An account of the spacecraft's journey by a New York Times *reporter is reprinted here.*

Source: *The New York Times*, June 14, 1983.

PIONEER 10 crossed the orbit of Neptune yesterday to become the first spacecraft ever to depart the realm of the known planets and head out toward the stars.

After a voyage of more than 11 years, through the asteroid belt and by Jupiter, across the orbits of Saturn, Uranus and Pluto, the hardy little spacecraft cruised away into the greater unknown at 8 A.M. Eastern daylight time. The 570-pound robot craft was 2.81 billion miles from the Sun and traveling 30,558 miles an hour at the time of the historic crossing.

Pioneer had sped beyond the reaches of Pluto on April 25. Ordinarily Pluto is the outermost planet, but because of its elongated oval orbit Pluto will be nearer the Sun than Neptune for the next 17 years.

Scientists, engineers and flight controllers gathered at the Ames Research Center in Mountain View, Calif., to hail their creation and bid it farewell. They cheered the faraway machine and sipped champagne. "Today, Neptune; yesterday, Pluto, and tomorrow, on to the stars," toasted Jack Dyer, chief of spacecraft operations.

Flight controllers waited four hours and 19 minutes, the time it takes for radio signals traveling at the speed of light to traverse the distance between the spacecraft and Earth, to receive the message that Pioneer 10 had indeed passed its milestone and was continuing to function normally, as it had since the hour it was launched from Cape Canaveral, Fla., March 3, 1972.

Thousands of people also listened in on the departing Pioneer. By dialing a special, extra-long distance telephone number, they heard a recording of the craft's recent radio signals that had been amplified to be made audible. The signals sounded like the rapid, high-pitched tapping of some intergalactic telegraph key.

The spacecraft had earlier transmitted an image of Altair, one of the brighter stars in the heavens. The faint image served as a check of Pioneer's systems as it left the planetary system, and also as a symbol of the incredible journey that lies ahead.

Reflecting the triumphant mood of the occasion, Dr. James A. Van Allen of the University of Iowa, one of the mission's scientists, said, "I consider Pioneer to be one of the greatest of human achievements."

For not only did the craft become the first to fly beyond Mars and make the first close-up reconnaissance of Jupiter, but it surprised its builders by surviving well past its designed 21-month lifetime. Pioneer thus continued to make measurements of interplanetary space beyond Jupiter. The region inhabited by the planets is but the central core of the greater solar system. Pioneer has yet to detect this boundary.

Engineers at the National Aeronautics and Space Administration and the prime contractor, TRW Inc., predict that Pioneer could remain in radio contact with Earth for another decade, until it has ventured out more than 5 billion miles from the Sun. This could be near or beyond the boundary to interstellar space, where the Sun's gravity and radiations cease to dominate.

Over the next few years, scientists will be studying Pioneer's flow of data for clues to such mysteries as whether the solar system has a 10th planet, which has been predicted, where the solar system actually ends and interstellar space begins, and whether gravity waves, a radiation phenomenon predicted by Einstein, can be detected.

Even after the eight-watt radio sends its last message, the craft will cruise on and on where no machine of human design has ever ventured. Pioneer could go on forever, insofar as anything is forever. Interstellar space is "one of the most benign environments one can imagine," explained Dr. John

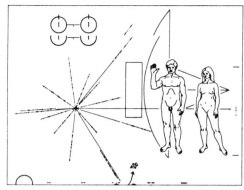

A drawing of the plaque carried by Pioneer 10.

H. Wolfe, the former chief project scientist. "There's absolutely nothing to stop it."

With this in mind, the scientists who celebrated often spoke of matters infinite and eternal.

They calculate, for example, that 10,-507 years from now Pioneer should have its first fairly close encounter with a star. That is when it will pass within 3.8 light years of Barnard's star, a small, cool star. Then it will be on to Ross 248 some 32,000 years from now. Also in the next 862,064 years, by current calculations, Pioneer will approach the vicinities of eight other stars, including Altair, a star bigger and nine times brighter than the Sun.

Somewhere along the way, the derelict craft could come close enough to a star system to be intercepted by intelligent beings, if there are any elsewhere. For this reason Pioneer carries a plaque inscribed with images of a man and a woman, a diagram of the solar system and other symbols that might help others locate the origin of the little craft.

Five billion years from now, the scientists further calculate, Pioneer should be wandering about the outer rim of the Milky Way galaxy, of which the Earth and the Sun are but a tiny part. Or were a part, as the case should be by then. The Sun is expected to burn out and die in 5 billion years, and with it the Earth and the other planets will vanish.

And so the NASA scientists found themselves yesterday raising their glasses and saying farewell to something that will very likely outlast human life on Earth and Earth itself.

82.

Overturn of the Legislative Veto

The U.S. Supreme Court, in a decision handed down on June 23, 1983, in the case of Immigration and Naturalization Service v. Chadha et al, ruled by a vote of seven to two that the one-House legislative veto contained in a section of the Immigration and Nationality Act was unconstitutional. The decision was one of the most important in the history of the Court, for it overturned at one fell swoop more federal laws than had been declared unconstitutional throughout the entire history of the United States. Jagdish Rai Chadha had been born in Kenya of Indian parents and held a British passport. When he tried to return home after six years at Bowling Green State University in Ohio, Kenya refused to take him and Britain told him he would have to wait a year. He asked the Immigration and Naturalization Service for help, but they began deportation proceedings. Chadha then appealed and obtained a favorable ruling from the Justice Department, but Congress vetoed Chadha and five others out of a list of 340 aliens to be granted permanent resident status. The Supreme Court's ruling is highly technical; reprinted below is part of a "syllabus" (headnote) of the decision that was released at the time the opinion was issued.

Source: *The Congressional Digest*, December 1983.

Section 244(c)(2) of the Immigration and Nationality Act (Act) authorizes either House of Congress, by resolution, to invalidate the decision of the Executive Branch pursuant to authority delegated by Congress to the Attorney General, to allow a particular deportable alien to remain in the United States. Appellee-respondent Chadha, an alien who had been lawfully admitted to the United States on a nonimmigrant student visa, remained in the United States after his visa had expired and was ordered by the Immigration and Naturalization Service (INS) to show cause why he should not be deported. He then applied for suspension of the deportation, and, after a hearing, an Immigration Judge, acting pursuant to §244(a)(1) of the Act, which authorizes the Attorney General, in his discretion, to suspend deportation, ordered the suspension, and reported the suspension to Congress as required by §244(c)(1). Thereafter, the

House of Representatives passed a Resolution pursuant to §244(c)(2) vetoing the suspension, and the Immigration Judge reopened the deportation proceedings. Chadha moved to terminate the proceedings on the ground that §244(c)(2) is unconstitutional, but the judge held that he had no authority to rule on its constitutionality and ordered Chadha deported pursuant to the House Resolution. Chadha's appeal to the Board of Immigration Appeals was dismissed, the Board also holding that it had no power to declare §244(c)(2) unconstitutional. Chadha then filed a petition for review of the deportation order in the Court of Appeals, and the INS joined him in arguing that §244(c)(2) is unconstitutional. The Court of Appeals held that §244(c)(2) violates the constitutional doctrine of separation of powers, and accordingly directed the Attorney General to cease taking any steps to deport Chadha based upon the House Resolution.

Held:

1. This Court has jurisdiction to entertain the INS's appeal.

2. Section 244(c)(2) is severable from the remainder of §244. Section 406 of the Act provides that if any particular provision of the Act is held invalid, the remainder of the Act shall not be affected. This gives rise to a presumption that Congress did not intend the validity of the Act as a whole, or any part thereof, to depend upon whether the veto clause of §244(c)(2) was invalid. This presumption is supported by §244's legislative history. Moreover, a provision is further presumed severable if what remains after severance is fully operative as a law. Here, §244 can survive as a "fully operative" and workable administrative mechanism without the one-house veto.

3. Chadha has standing to challenge the constitutionality of §244(c)(2) since he has demonstrated "injury in fact and a substantial likelihood that the judicial relief requested will prevent or redress the claimed injury."

4. The fact that Chadha may have other statutory relief available to him does not preclude him from challenging the constitutionality of §244(c)(2), especially where the other avenues of relief are at most speculative.

5. The Court of Appeals had jurisdiction under §106(a) of the Act, which provides that a petition for review in a court of appeals "shall be the sole and exclusive procedure for the judicial review of all final orders of deportation . . . made against aliens within the United States pursuant to administrative proceedings" under §242(b) of the Act.

6. A case or controversy is presented by these cases.

7. These cases do not present a non-justifiable political question on the asserted ground that Chadha is merely challenging Congress's authority under the Naturalization and Necessary and Proper Clauses of the Constitution. The presence of constitutional issues with significant political overtones does not automatically invoke the political question doctrine. Resolution of litigation challenging the constitutional authority of one of the three branches cannot be evaded by the courts simply because the issues have political implications.

8. The congressional veto provision in §244(c)(2) is unconstitutional.

(a) The prescription for legislative action in Art. I, §1—requiring all legislative powers to be vested in a Congress consisting of a Senate and a House of Representatives—and §7—requiring every bill passed by the House and Senate, before becoming law, to be presented to the President, and, if he disapproves, to be repassed by two-thirds of the Senate and House—represents the Framers' decision that the legislative power of the Federal Government be exercised in accord with a single, finely wrought and exhaustively considered procedure. This procedure is an integral part of the constitutional design for the separation of powers.

(b) Here, the action taken by the House pursuant to §244(c)(2) was essentially legislative in purpose and effect and thus was subject to the procedural requirements of Art. I, §7, for *legislative* action: passage by a majority of both Houses and presentation to the President. The one-House veto operated to overrule the Attorney General and mandate Chadha's deportation. The veto's legislative character is confirmed by the character of the congressional action it supplants; *i.e.,* absent the veto provision of §244(c)(2), neither the House nor the Senate, or both acting together, could effectively require the Attorney General to deport an alien once the Attorney General, in the exercise of legislatively delegated authority, had determined that the alien should remain in the United States. Without the veto provision, this could have been achieved only by legislation requiring deportation. A veto by one House under §244(c)(2) cannot be justified as an attempt at amending the standards set out in §244(a)(1), or as a repeal of §244 as applied to Chadha. The nature of the decision implemented by the one-House veto further manifests its legislative character. Congress must abide by its delegation of authority to the Attorney General until that delegation is legislatively altered or revoked. Finally, the veto's legislative character is confirmed by the fact that when the Framers intended to authorize either House of Congress to act alone and outside of its prescribed bicameral legislative role, they narrowly and precisely defined the procedure for such action in the Constitution.

It's kind of overwhelming.

JAGDISH RAI CHADHA, on being informed that he had won his case and overturned more legislation than in the entire previous history of the United States

83.

LARRY LONG and DIANA DEARE: The Slowing of Urbanization

A number of reports in July 1983—among them this Scientific American *article by two members of the staff of the U.S. Bureau of the Census—revealed that a momentous change had occurred in the relative growth rates of the urban and rural populations of the United States. For the first time, the reports showed, the rural population was growing as fast as the urban population. The age-old tendency for cities to grow ever larger at the expense of the countryside had ended, perhaps forever. At the same time, the geographic expansion and coalescence of urban areas was leading to the appearance of enormous "supercities." Portions of Long's and DeAre's article are reprinted below.*

Source: *Scientific American,* July 1983.

ONE OF THE MOST fundamental features of a modern society is the demographic predominance of the cities over the countryside. Urbanization, along with the industrial growth that has generally accompanied it, has historically distinguished the developed countries from the developing ones. In a country that is undergoing economic development two tendencies usually contribute to the increasing dominance of the urban areas. First, the population of established cities grows faster than the population of the nation as a whole. Second, in some rural areas population growth is rapid enough for the areas to become urban. In the U.S. both of these basic forms of urbanization have been operating almost continuously at least since the decennial census was initiated in 1790.

The detailed results of the census of 1980, however, show that urbanization in this traditional twofold form was strongly modified in the U.S. between 1970 and 1980. The first form of ur-banization ceased during the decade: the population of rural areas grew as fast as that of urban areas. Only the second kind of urbanization is still in progress: between 1970 and 1980 the population of many rural areas grew enough for them to be reclassified as urban. If it had not been for growth in areas that were considered rural in 1970, the fraction of the U.S. population living in urban areas would have decreased for the first time. As the growth of cities was largely attributable to economic factors, so too the decline appears to have economic causes. The available data suggest that the rural areas' attractiveness for industry is responsible for much of their population growth.

Although the deceleration of urban growth is widespread, it is by no means geographically uniform. In the Northeast both kinds of urbanization have ended. In the South and West both kinds are still in progress, but the overall rate of urbanization is lower than it was in the past. Moreover, the current trends have quite different effects on the various geographic components of a city. In the 1950's and 1960's a common pattern was for the city proper to lose population while the suburbs gained. In many instances the city itself continued to lose people in the 1970's and the area subject to population loss expanded to include the inner suburbs. The outer suburbs, however, continued to grow both in population and in area. As a result the urban areas of the U.S. have become larger and less densely populated.

Urban areas that are expanding in area can ultimately run into one another. The coalescence of neighboring cities in the 1970's led to an increase in the number of "supercities": continuously built-up urban areas with a population of a million or more. The growth of the supercities shows that the current trends do not necessarily mean the end of large urban centers. Recent developments do suggest, however, that the economic advantages of locating industry in cities may have been reduced. As a result new and less concentrated forms of human settlement may be in prospect.

Measuring the number of people who live in urban areas requires a definition of what is urban, which would appear to be a straightforward matter. One could, for example, simply count the people who live within the boundaries of cities of a certain size. Such a definition, however, would omit many of the residents of the suburbs, who are certainly part of the urban population. Moreover, the question would naturally arise of how many residents a city must have before it is included in the count.

Because of such ambiguities there are many possible methods of distinguishing the urban population from the rural. The Bureau of the Census has several ways of identifying the urban part of the U.S. The oldest definition includes all incorporated places with a population of 2,500 or more. Such a broad category almost inevitably includes some areas that do not correspond to the ordinary notion of what is urban.

The Census Bureau also employs a narrower category that more closely approximates the usual notion. The second category defines an urbanized area as a city with a population of 50,000 or more together with all the contiguous built-up land that has a population density of at least 1,000 per square mile. The large city included in the urbanized area is termed the central city. In this article we refer to the suburbs that share a boundary line with the city as the inner suburbs; all other parts of the urbanized area are referred to as the outer suburbs.

The concept of the urbanized area was introduced in analyzing the results of the census of 1950. The motivation for its introduction was the rapid growth of the suburbs in the years after World War II. The urbanized area provides a good measure of the demographic limits of a city as opposed to its administrative boundaries, which often do not coincide with the extent of urbanization.

If the urbanized areas are removed from the broad category of all urban places, what remains is the group of nonsuburban cities and towns with a population of more than 2,500 but less than 50,000. In the terminology of the Census Bureau such areas are referred to as "other urban" places; here we shall call them the small cities and towns. Territory that is outside both the urbanized areas and the small cities and towns is considered rural.

We have employed the returns from the census of 1980 to analyze recent trends in the growth of the urban and rural populations. We have examined developments in both the urbanized areas and the small cities and towns, and we shall describe some of the trends in the territory that is urban in the broad sense. We shall concentrate, however, on the urbanized areas. The reason is that included among the small cities and towns are places that in an important sense are more rural than urban. Furthermore, many small cities and towns outgrow that classification to become urbanized areas and others are absorbed in the expansion of the large cities.

The definitions of what is urban employed by the Census Bureau have undergone technical changes since 1970. We have adjusted the data from the census of 1980 to make them comparable with the data from the three preceding censuses. The adjustment has enabled us to make consistent comparisons of trends in population, geographic area and population density in the U.S. from 1950 to 1980. . . .

The most general and significant conclusion that emerges from our work is that the level of urbanization stopped increasing for the first time in the 1970's. The population of the urbanized areas is still growing, but at a rate lower than that of the rural areas. As a result the fraction of the nation's population in urbanized areas is no longer increasing. In 1950, 46 percent of the U.S. population lived in an urbanized area; in 1960, 53 percent did so; in 1970, 58 percent. In 1980 the fraction was still 58 percent. In some parts of the country the fraction is decreasing.

If the urbanized areas are classified according to when they became large enough to be designated as such, the deceleration of the urbanizing process appears even more dramatic. The oldest urbanized areas are the ones designated in 1950. In the 1950's and 1960's these older cities grew substantially faster than the population of the nation. By the 1970's however, the older urbanized areas, with an average annual population growth rate of .8 percent, were growing slower than the national population, which had a rate of 1.1 percent. If it had not been for the faster-than-average growth of the newer urbanized areas, the fraction of the population in the large cities would have declined.

These data imply that one of the two fundamental forms of urbanization— the growth of preexisting urban centers—stopped in the U.S. in the 1970's. The slowing of the growth of the older cities was very rapid. In the 1950's the rate of population growth in the older urbanized areas and those added in 1960 was 23 times the rate of areas outside them. In the 1960's the rate of growth in the older urbanized areas and those that had been added by 1970 was 16 times the rate of the rest of the country. In the 1970's the rate of growth in the urbanized areas was only marginally greater than the rate in other places, and it was higher only because of rapid growth in areas that had been considered rural in 1970. This development is unprecedented in U.S. demographic history.

If the broad concept of what is urban is employed, the level of urbanization did not merely stop increasing in the 1970's but actually declined. If those who live in small cities and towns are included, the fraction of the U.S. population in urban areas was 64 percent in 1950. It increased to 70 percent in 1960 and to 73.5 percent in 1970 before decreasing to 73.3 percent in 1980.

A decline of less than one percentage point is not substantial; its significance is not in its size but in the fact that it comes after a long period of uninterrupted growth. An advantage of the more inclusive definition of urban territory is that it can be applied to census records extending far into the past. The level of urbanization in the broad sense declined only once before: between 1810 and 1820. That decline was the result of population growth in several rural states of the Middle West that had been added by the Louisiana Purchase.

The slowing of the growth of the urban population may be a temporary phenomenon that could be reversed by changes in economic factors such as the price of fuel. It is more probable, however, that we are witnessing a basic demographic reversal. The immediate cause of the reversal is not a decrease in the absolute size of the urban population but a rapid increase in the rate of population growth in rural areas. The rural population declined slightly in the 1950's and 1960's. In the 1970's however, the rural population increased by 12 percent, a rate of growth about equal to that of the urbanized areas and greater than that of the small cities and towns, which increased by 9 percent. Thus the demographic growth outside the large cities took place in the open countryside rather than in the small towns. . . .

The image of a doughnut is often employed to describe an urbanized area with an older central city whose population is decreasing. The image is not new; such population losses have been going on for decades. What is new is the expansion of the region of population loss (the "hole" in the doughnut) to include the inner suburbs. The hole has grown largest in the urbanized areas where the doughnut pattern has prevailed longest.

Moreover, although the doughnut has long been a familiar image in the industrial centers of the Northeast, in the 1970's it spread for the first time to much of the rest of the U.S. About half of all urbanized areas show the pattern, including a fourth of the cities in the South. The city of Atlanta, after growing in the 1950's and 1960's, lost population in the 1970's at a rate greater than that for Newark, N.J.

Population losses in the central cities and inner suburbs have become so great that an increasing number of urbanized areas are losing population. In the 1950's only one area in 20 lost residents; in the 1970's one in six did. Most such urban population declines are invisible to the casual observer. Indeed, in the light of "gentrification" (the movement of young professionals into inner-city neighborhoods) and new housing construction in the outer suburbs many people will find it hard to believe the population of the entire urbanized area around St. Louis declined by 2 percent in the 1970's. . . .

For this reason some of the most significant demographic trends of the past three decades in urban areas have been largely invisible. A count on a large scale, such as the census, is needed to measure them precisely. Our purpose in this article has been to analyze such trends by employing definitions that can be applied consistently over the entire period. The definitions themselves, however, do not remain static. Based on the results of the 1980 census, demographers at the Census Bureau have already begun to redefine the urbanized area. Urban areas are no longer limited to the territory around cities with a population of 50,000 or more. As of 1980 an urbanized area is any group of 50,000 people with an average density of 1,000 per square mile, regardless of the size of the largest city. Thus many people who live in or near a small town have become part of the urbanized-area population.

The change is not particularly surprising. Almost every redefinition of what is urban has expanded the number of people in the category. Indeed, as urbanization reaches its historical peak some uncertainty about who is an urban dweller is almost inevitable. The inability of demographers to agree on what is urban territory may be taken as a sign that urbanization has peaked at a high level.

The uncertainty undoubtedly extends even further than we have proposed here. For some time almost the entire population of the U.S. has been urban in the sense of having access to the amenities of urban life whether or not they live in cities. Perhaps the best model of the population is a continuum in which one end represents the most nearly urban part and the other represents the most nearly rural part. In the 1970's there was an unexpected increase in the demographic growth of the most nearly rural parts of the nation; at the same time the rate of loss increased in the most nearly urban parts. The fundamental cause of the reversal appears to be economic: population has followed jobs. The future distribution of population in the U.S. could well be determined by which regions are able to compete for new jobs both within the U.S. and in international markets.

84.

ROBERT HEILBRONER: Economic Prospects

During the first year of the Reagan administration inflation continued to be a vexing problem for the President and his economic advisors. They had determined to conquer it, and the majority of the population was willing to support their efforts to do so, although the price was high: the worst recession since the Great Depression of the 1930s. As late as the spring of 1983 inflation seemed to hang on, stubbornly resisting the draconian methods that had been adopted to overcome it. Then, in the summer of that year, inflation finally seemed to be yielding. The article by the noted economist Robert Heilbroner that is reprinted here (in part) appeared in The New Yorker *in the late summer of the year.*

Source: "Reflections: Economic Prospects," *The New Yorker*, August 29, 1983.

MOODS CHANGE quickly in economics; problems do not. Only a few months ago, the economics profession was in a state of disarray it had not known since the Great Depression. The disarray had nothing to do with the normal disagreements about when the economic weather would change. Economists dispute about such things just like meteorologists, and for much the same reasons. The confusion among economists was of another kind—comparable, perhaps, to the state of mind that might afflict meteorologists if they perceived that the earth was about to enter a new ice age. Meteorologists, however, are asked only to foretell the weather, not to improve it. Economists are supposed not merely to predict the general shape of things but to suggest ways of coping with what they foresee. If the profession was in a kind of disorder, the reason was both the unwelcome character of what so many saw and an inability to decide what to do about it.

Today, as the economy slowly recovers and the stock market is buoyant, there is more of the normal talk about the chances for rain or sun, and less about whether the climate is changing. Yet I think that, deep down, economists are worried about our prospects. In part, this has to do with the uncertainty about how fully we will emerge from the most arduous economic ordeal since the nineteen-thirties. But the deeper worry, now that the economic news is more reassuring, concerns the problem of inflation. The trouble is that, good news or not, it is becoming ever more difficult to imagine a system that is not *latently* inflation-prone. I can think of no better way to bring home that point than to recall that our parents were happy to lend their money to railroads and utilities and municipalities over spans of thirty and forty years for a fixed-interest return of four or five per cent. It never occurred to them that the money they would get back at the end of their lives would be worth less than when they lent it out in middle age. Such a degree of confidence in the stability of prices is inconceivable today. Different economists may lay the blame on different aspects of today's society—some pointing to big government, some to big business, some to big labor—but all agree, I think, that a world with price horizons as flat as prairies is gone forever. It is enlightening, in this regard, to think back over the two-year ordeal just behind us. The ordeal was the result of an unprecedented effort by the Reagan Administration and the Federal Reserve Board to wring inflation out of the American economy, and the rate of inflation did, in fact, fall from above ten per cent in early 1981 to something between two and three per cent today. Nonetheless, no one believes that the economy has been wrung bone dry. On the contrary, although we are still deeply mired in a depression, with nearly a tenth of the labor force still out of work and a quarter of plant capacity standing idle, voices are already being raised to say that inflation will resurface in a matter of a year, or even less, as we begin to absorb the unemployed, utilize more plant capacity, and avail ourselves of our expanded supplies of credit. We have run a gantlet to rid ourselves of our propensity for inflation, but the propensity is still there. I suspect there is no getting rid of it.

Along with a mounting uneasiness about the inherently inflationary properties of a modern capitalist system has come a changed attitude on the part of the economics profession toward the seriousness of inflation itself. In the early stages of inflation, before we moved into double-digit territory, it was regarded as more of a nuisance than a threat. This was because many studies showed that the well-being of most Americans or Europeans was not noticeably affected by rising prices. The cost of living moved up, but income moved up even faster, so that average "real" income—that is, income adjusted for inflation—continued to rise. Per-capita real income was thirty per cent higher in late 1981 than it had been in 1969, despite a sixty-per-cent fall in the purchasing power of the dollar. At the same time, the distribution of incomes among families had also remained astonishingly stable. The escalator of inflation had neither toppled those at the head of the stairs nor pushed up those at the bottom. In the face of these facts, a good many economists, including myself, tended to view the problem of inflation as more political or psychological than economic. I remember asking my students to imagine that they had been given a cost-of-living increase of a thousand dollars at the beginning of the year and had thereafter been subjected to three hundred and sixty-four encounters with rising prices which collectively ate up nine hundred and eighty dollars of the initial increase. Would they at the end of the year recall that they were still twenty dollars ahead of the game, or would they feel cheated and aggrieved? Operating from this political and psychological perspective, the general economics world (with the exception of a percipient few, mainly in the fields of business and banking) overlooked an aspect of inflation that had nothing to do with "money illusion" or with the wrath stirred up by a generalized feeling of impotence. This was the damage that the inflationary process wreaks upon a nation's structure of credit; that is, upon its ability to borrow and upon the soundness of its banks and other lending institutions. The danger arises because an extended period of mounting prices tempts everyone—businessmen

and householders alike—to borrow. One does not need a Ph.D. in economics to understand that in inflationary times it is better to own things than money. But this crucial insight is not confined to borrowers. Bankers, too, know that the dollars they will receive when their loans are repaid will have a smaller purchasing power than the dollars they originally lent out. Thus, lenders will oblige borrowers only at higher and higher rates of interest, to compensate for the expected loss of purchasing power, and for shorter and shorter periods, to cut down the wait before the loans return. The result is that continued inflation results in the disappearance of a central necessity for a capitalist system—a financial arrangement that will permit companies to borrow for five or ten years for projects requiring that much time in order to pay out. In an inflationary period, such borrowing is out of the question except at horrendous rates of interest. Capital can be raised only by taking on short-term debt, which will have to be repaid long before the enterprise being financed can possibly begin to generate revenues. The trouble with such a state of affairs is that the borrower has no time to turn around, or to exercise foresight or strategy in paying off or refinancing his debt. Borrowers are constantly under pressure to pay off yesterday's loan today, and today's tomorrow. That pressure pushes the system toward what has been called Ponzi finance—named after a famous swindler of the nineteen-twenties who ran a chain-letter-like scheme that promised investors a fifty-per-cent return on their investments in forty-five days. In the corporate world, Ponzi finance results in companies' borrowing money just to pay interest on their existing debts. One reason that Chairman Paul Volcker held the Federal Reserve Board so tenaciously to its tight-money policy was the alarming rate at which the American corporate world was approaching a Ponzi-like condition. In 1960, total corporate indebtedness amounted to less than a hundred billion dollars, only a quarter of which was short-term debt. By 1981, the total had grown to exceed a trillion dollars, of which forty-two per cent was for a term of one year or less. In that same year, interest on corporate indebtedness was equal to a third of total corporate income before taxes. By 1982, interest on corporate indebtedness was over half the total pre-tax income.

The increasing apprehension about the nature of inflation and the difficulties of exorcising it accounts for a good deal of the lurking dismay in my profession. This distress is made more acute by the harsh lesson we have learned from our effort to bring inflation under control through a tight-money policy. Under such a policy, the Federal Reserve Board, by the various means at its disposal, restricts the growth of the supply of money. With this supply increasing more slowly than the demand, the price of money rises. In 1981, the price rose until the prime rate—the rate charged by commercial banks to their best customers—crept over twenty per cent. As a result, millions of consumers were unable to finance cars or homes, and auto dealers and contractors went into bankruptcy by the thousand. Merchants, unable to afford loans, laid off delivery boys; wholesalers laid off stock clerks; manufacturers furloughed factory work forces. By the end of 1982, after fifteen months of tight money, there had been enough layoffs and bankruptcies to raise the unemployment rate from seven and a half per cent to almost eleven per cent,

and enough distress sales, old-fashioned price cutting, and union givebacks to stop the consumer price index from rising altogether.

No one expected the gantlet to last so long, or to cause so much pain. Part of the reason that it did last so long was that inflationary expectations had become so deeply ingrained in everyone's mind. Businessmen, in particular, were certain that, once tight money really started to hurt, the Fed would quickly change its mind and reverse its course, thereby opening the way for more borrowing. By the time business changed its mind, and began to perceive its debts as burdens rather than weightless balloons, the toll in joblessness and business failures had indeed pushed the system into a state of crisis. No less important was the painful effect of the tight-money policy on the international economic scene. As interest rates in the United States reached record heights, tens of billions of dollars' worth of francs and marks and pounds left European banks and portfolios, to be invested in United States bonds and money-market instruments. Rather than risk a disastrous fall in the value of marks and francs as a consequence of this currency flight, European banking authorities sought to counter the suction of high American rates by instituting tight-money policies of their own. In West Germany, interest rates for issues comparable to our Treasury bills rose from four per cent in 1979 to twelve per cent in 1981; in France, interest rates for similar issues went from eight per cent to over nineteen per cent. The consequences were precisely the same there as here: economic activity was brought to a standstill. In Spain and Ireland, two of the hardest-hit countries in Western Europe, unemployment exceeded fifteen per cent; in Belgium, fourteen per cent. Helmut Schmidt, speaking a few days after he was ousted as Chancellor of West Germany, voiced the resentment of many Europeans when he blamed the United States for "weighing the world economy down for all of us with its self-made recession."

The sobering part of our recent experience, then, has been the realization that tight money is a very dangerous instrument for fighting inflation. In Great Britain, the only nation that has tried the monetary cure as relentlessly as we have, industrial production has fallen by twelve per cent since 1979 and unemployment has risen to more than thirteen per cent. Thus, tight money halts inflation, all right, but at the cost of creating a full-scale depression. And, once tight money is relaxed, there we are again, in danger of finding ourselves on the slippery road to inflation. That is why one hears so few economists, in the Administration or out of it, speaking of the hoped-for recovery in other than restrained terms. Once we pass beyond the present environment of high unemployment and unused factory capacity, we will quickly reënter the familiar terrain in which economic growth brings with it the pushes of cost and pulls of demand from which inflation results. If interest rates have declined and inflation resurfaces, the temptation to borrow will become irresistible, because it is rational. Thereafter, the choices will be as before: to allow inflation to run its dangerous course, to keep it half in check by halfhearted measures, or to force the system—and perhaps the Western world—through the gantlet once more.

There are, of course, ways of combatting inflation which avoid the asphyxiation of a monetary contraction: direct wage and price controls; various "incomes policies" that rely on tax incentives or penalties; and yet other schemes, such as knocking out all indexing systems and concerting the nation's wage negotiations at a single time, to avoid the uncoordinated scramble of our present system. The trouble is that none of these policies have gained sufficient political acceptance to enable them to be tried as ruthlessly as was the policy of tight money. For the secret of the "success" of Volcker's effort was not that we finally found the right lever to push but that the monetary policy was pursued until the economy's back was broken. It was not *inflation's* back that was broken, for, as I have said, there is already fear that, with recovery under way, inflation cannot be too far around the corner. Until we can once again sell thirty-year bonds at four or five per cent, that fear is well founded. . . .

These are not, of course, the only problems that haunt economists today. I have passed too lightly over the matter of the still severe depression and its cure, and I have not even glanced in the direction of robotization, or looked at the worldwide slowdown of productivity, or a host of other issues. But I think the problems of international trade and finance account, more than anything else, for the professional disarray of which I have spoken. The reason is that these problems, with their global involvements, bring to many the uneasy suspicion that the basic unit of economic policy—the nation-state—is not appropriate to the problems of late-twentieth-century capitalism. This is all the more remarkable because the nation-state has everywhere assumed such large powers within contemporary capitalism, and the trend of the last two centuries has been unmistakably toward the enlargement of these powers. Modern capitalism is often called "state capitalism," and despite all the efforts of Reagan and Thatcher to the contrary I cannot see the future of capitalism without the national governments' playing a still more prominent role in its propulsion, support, and guidance. What is therefore so confounding about the emergence of an international dimension of finance and production is that it marks the development of a new level of economic life, capable of exerting its independent influence over that of the state. If the rise of state capitalism represents an assertion of political purpose over the blind workings of economic forces, the rise of a supranational realm of finance and production represents a reassertion of economic forces over political purpose. To be sure, there was a very high degree of internationalization of both trade and finance prior to the Great Depression. But things have changed in decisive ways since that forgotten era. One difference is the remarkable opening up of the American economy to foreign trade, which is twice as important now as it was then. A second difference is that today's governments are much more involved in the direct encouragement of exports than they were formerly. A third, and not the least, difference is that the general attitudes of nations, like those of their electorates, are less acquiescent in the face of economic misfortune. Passivity before the currents of international economic life was once regarded as the only possible attitude, however painful it might be. Most nations today are determined to defy international currents to whatever degree they can. It is this modern attitude of national economic self-determination that is threatened by the rise of a supranational realm of finance and production. It is as if capital itself had taken wing—on the one hand, defying the policies of nation-states that are formally capitalist and, on the other, performing its transformational prodigies, for better and for worse, in places that were yesterday ten thousand miles and one thousand years removed from capitalism. And yet all this is taking place at a time when the role of nation-states is greater than it has ever been in the conduct of and the responsibility for economic life. As I see it, this ill-understood confrontation between political power, which is growing at the national level, and economic power, which is growing at the supranational level, is at the root of the perplexity that lies behind the smiles of the social-meteorology profession these days. Whether or not an economic ice age is coming, there is a suspicion that the climate is changing as it has not changed since the traumatic period of the Great Depression a half century ago. As the stock market climbs and the economy slowly regains lost ground, economists, like everyone else, tend to put their worries behind them. But the larger problems are there and will not go away, even in months of sunshine. In the long run, our economic prospects depend very considerably on how we take the measure of the heating up, or cooling down, of the economic planet, and what we determine that we can do about it.

85.

Barbara Honegger and Hans Küng: Women's Challenge

The two rather disparate articles that are reprinted together here reveal the fact that, despite temporary setbacks, women continued throughout the 1980s to seek justice and equality. Barbara Honegger was a Republican delegate who sought to guide the Reagan administration toward a better deal for women in several important posts. Her failure to get done what she wanted is recounted in an article (reprinted in part) that appeared in the Washington Post, *shortly after she had resigned as a Justice Department aide. The second article, by Hans Küng, a controversial Catholic theologian, deals with the relations between women and the Pope. Here, too, women were disappointed by the slow pace of progress toward equality.*

Sources: "The ERA Alternative," *Chicago Sun-Times,* July 1983.

"Will the Pope Win Over Women?", *The New York Times,* November 16, 1983.

A: BARBARA HONEGGER
THE ERA ALTERNATIVE

WASHINGTON—When Ronald Reagan backed off his party's 40-year-long commitment to the broadest constitutional protection for the civil rights of American women—support of the ERA—he gave three reasons.

First, he said, women were already protected by existing constitutional provisions, in particular the 14th Amendment. Second, what was really needed was stronger enforcement of the laws against sex discrimination already on the books. And third, he pledged himself to a "better way"—a two-pronged effort to identify and eliminate or correct remaining individual instances of sex discrimination in federal and states' codes.

All three of these arguments implied certain actions on Reagan's part. But he has not taken them. He has reneged on his commitment.

I know. I have been there from the start—at the Republican National Convention, in the room on the 68th floor of Detroit's Renaissance Center where the platform was hammered out, on the six-man fast-turnaround research team for the president's speechwriters in the campaign, on the transition team after Nov. 4, specializing in outreach to federal departments and agencies that had specific programs relevant to women, and in the West Wing of the White House, at the physical node of the Offices of Policy Development, Public Liaison and Intergovernmental Affairs, personally translating the president's campaign promise for an "ERA alternative" into tangible federal programs.

For the past year and a quarter, I

Barbara Honegger

have been in the Justice Department, as project director of the Attorney General's Gender Discrimination Agency Review, trying to carry out the president's "ERA alternative."

Let's take the president's three reasons one by one. When asked specifically to state which existing constitutional provisions he has in mind that already protect women, the president generally refers to the 14th Amendment—as he did after signing the executive order creating his federal-level "ERA alternative" on Dec. 21, 1981, in the Cabinet Room. But the fact is that women are not today and never have been fully or securely protected under the 14th Amendment against federal sex discrimination, state sex discrimination, or lack of federal enforcement of existing sex-discrimination prohibitions—which, as we shall see, becomes especially important under Reagan.

The 14th Amendment wasn't even used to overturn laws that discriminated against women until just a little more than a decade ago. This wasn't for lack

of women's trying to get the Supreme Court to use it to strike down the vast numbers of laws that discriminated against them purely on the basis of gender. Women brought cases trying to get the Supreme Court to give them the vote under the 14th Amendment and were turned down; and they tried to get permission to work the same hours and the same kinds of jobs as men and were turned down. And to this day the Supreme Court does not rule in sex-discrimination cases based on the same toughest standard of review it uses when considering racial discrimination or religious discrimination cases.

There is, however, one exception to this rule. The one category of gender-specific law the Supreme Court has consistently reviewed under its strictest 14th Amendment standard consists of laws that interfere with a woman's right to choose abortion. But this is the area Reagan is doing everything in his power to remove from the jurisdiction of the court altogether—anti-abortion law.

The second of Reagan's reasons that American women don't need an Equal Rights Amendment is that all America really needs is tougher enforcement of the laws against sex discrimination we already have. But it is the Reagan administration itself that is doing everything in its power to reduce the enforcement and narrow the interpretation of the existing statutes that forbid sex discrimination.

An example is the administration's attempt not to broaden or strengthen but rather to narrow radically the scope of application of Title IX—the federal law that bans discrimination against women in any school, university or educational program receiving federal funds. Most do receive such funds in some form or another.

Earlier administrations, both Democratic and Republican, have interpreted this law against sex discrimination to apply very broadly. [One] Justice Department Title IX brief . . . takes the position that only educational programs or activities that receive federal funds directly should be constrained by existing federal laws that prohibit sex discrimination—not the school, college or university as a whole. If this administration is successful in [that attempt], I believe a precedent will be set to gut enforcement of dozens of federal laws that currently protect Americans against discrimination on the basis of sex, race, color, national origin, religion, creed or handicap in "programs or activities which receive federal funds."

Reagan also undermined the Women's Educational Equity Act Program at the Department of Education. Authorization for the program was slashed to $6 million a year from $80 million. And then, not long ago, the Department of Education testified in a House hearing on its plan to gut the program even further by abolishing jobs that the remaining $6 million would, in part, fund. One of the major reasons women who know give for the absolute necessity of an ERA is precisely the point Ronald Reagan's own administration makes raw: federal statutes can be repealed or, if technically still on the books, be effectively voided by a president who doesn't enforce or who narrows their scope.

The third reason Reagan has given for why women do not require an ERA is that his two-pronged part-federal-law- and part-state-law-oriented ERA alternative will be more efficient in actually eliminating remaining sex-discriminatory federal and state laws and regulations one by one. I believed the president and his men when they said they would do these things. With great expectations I agreed to work to develop and implement these projects in the White House's Office of Policy Development and spent the first year of the administration, from January, 1981, through early 1982, doing just that before I followed the project to the Justice Department.

The president's federal-level "ERA alternative" under his Executive Order 12336 calls for an exhaustive effort to identify and correct or eliminate remaining sex discrimination found in the U.S. Code, the Code of Federal Regulations, and any policy, practice or program of any federal department or agency. As implemented in practice, the order has three stages:

•Identification of the "problems" by a massive computer-assisted search.

•Seeking to change the problem laws and regulations, policies and programs that discriminate against women.

•Implementing these changes in the departments and agencies.

This is an immense project. The identification effort alone took a year to complete just for the laws; our search was more complete and definitive than the previous Civil Rights Commission list in its report of 1977. The results of this effort at identification, which I have directed at the Department of Justice for the past year and a quarter, are forwarded periodically to the president and his Cabinet Council on Legal Policy for decision as to actions. They are to decide what laws to seek to change and what regulations to alter or eliminate through presidentially initiated action— that is the second stage of the process.

The third and last stage—if and when the president decides to make any changes in a regulation, policy or practice of an agency—is the implementation stage. This would be undertaken by another group, called the Task Force on Legal Equity for Women, which has a purely implementary role. This task force is the only feature of the ERA alternative that has received any media attention to date, which is ironic because, so far, it has had nothing to do. The original chairman of the task force, Carol Dinkins—assistant attorney general for land and resources—has left the government, and the White House has not bothered to replace her at the task force.

Now you know what the president's "ERA alternative" is supposed to do. Let's compare that with what has actually happened. The identification effort is known as the Gender Discrimination Agency Review project. Fifteen attorneys and professional staff in the Coordination and Review Section of the Civil Rights Division have been involved in the effort over the past year. To date, three Quarterly Reports of the Attorney General have gone forward to the president, over the signature of William Bradford Reynolds, assistant attorney general for civil rights, but not a single law has been changed. . . .

This summary of the president's federal-level "ERA alternative" would not be complete if I didn't mention an event that happened in the summer of 1982.

Shortly after moving to the Department of Justice to carry out the identification of laws and regulations under the executive order, I was called to the White House. A presidential aide had discovered that our computer review had been programmed to include a search for laws and regulations relating to pregnancy and abortion, and angrily told me that abortion and pregnancy have nothing to do with women's rights and therefore were to have no part in

the identification effort. The final list of laws in the Third Quarterly Report reflects this instruction.

What about the second prong of the president's "ERA alternative," which addresses not federal but state laws and regulations? This is called the "Fifty States Project" and was actually the "brainchild" of myself and Kevin Hopkins, now director of the Office of Policy Information at the White House. After Reagan rescinded his party's longtime commitment to the ERA at the Republican National Convention in 1980 and women were up in arms, the two of us stayed up all night drafting a memo proposing the rock-bottom minimum we thought Reagan might accept as a "compromise" with women. . . .

The project was announced with a sit-down luncheon and all-day briefing for representatives of the 50 governors' offices in October, 1981. All that has resulted from the project to date is a pretty booklet listing what the 50 states had already done without there ever having been a so-called federally directed "ERA alternative."

In a last-ditch effort to salvage something of some lasting value from the president's two-part "ERA alternative," on July 22, after completing the Third Quarterly Report under the federal-law effort, I offered the White House Office of the Assistant to the President for Public Liaison the same exhaustive computer search using the same gender-term keyword program we had just used at Justice to search the federal laws—this time to help the states do the same for their own laws and regulations.

Within a week of my offer, the White House called with its answer. This, I was informed, was "not something that the White House wants to expend any financial or political capital on." I was congratulated for being a "good advocate" and thanked for the generous offer. "Advocate"? Generous offer? Curious. All I was "advocating" was action on something the president promised the American people over a year and a half ago.

When this piece is published, I suppose I shall be characterized as a disappointed job seeker on account of that offer. Well, let me be plain. I *was* seeking to do a job or at least to get someone to do a job to which I thought the White House was committed. But as with the other aspects of the president's so-called "ERA alternative," this, too, turned out to be a sham.

B: HANS KÜNG
WILL THE POPE WIN OVER WOMEN?

AP/Wide World

Reverend Hans Küng

ANN ARBOR, Mich.—What is the No. 1 problem for the Roman Catholic Church in the United States? It is not Christ, not ecumenism, not infallibility, not even celibacy, but—women! This problem is generated by the Vatican. Pope John Paul II has made it absolutely clear that he is determined to keep women in their traditional place: in the pre-Vatican II medieval paradigm.

The symptoms of the emerging conflict are obvious. The great majority of women, especially in questions like birth control, have learned to follow their consciences in opposition to the Pope's teaching. Many, especially religious women, are educated in theology, scripture, church history and law. They outnumber men in most divinity schools and even in the traditional male bastion, the seminary, where they are teachers and spiritual directors as well as students.

Religious women still outnumber priests 2 to 1 in the ministry of the Catholic Church in this country. They are in parishes, hospitals, schools and with the dispossessed and minorities; they often perform functions traditionally reserved to priests. But Rome and many in the official church fear their self-reliance. So they are often pushed to the periphery, and measures are taken to maintain power over them. Ironically, by attempting to muzzle discussion, the Vatican has made the women's ordination issue a major issue even for secular women.

What steps has Rome taken to control women? The Pope, visiting this country in 1979, spoke strongly against birth control, premarital sex, remarriage, optional celibacy, women's ordination—without visible success. Now the Pope, using all his means, tries to convince the American bishops to go against their own faithful, especially in questions of sexual morality: 95 percent of young Catholic adults approve of artificial birth control, 89 percent approve of remarriage after divorce.

Women's religious orders, meanwhile, remain the prime target. Sister Theresa Kane of the Leadership Conference of Religious Women, not a bishop, was the only person who publicly told John Paul the truth about women in the church. She got no response. The Pope, who receives even atheists and Communists, has consistently refused her a private audience. The investigation of women's religious orders, ordered in April, is clearly aimed at regaining control over the sisters.

Bishop John Marshall of Burlington, Vt., recently appointed as an investigator of seminaries, in a letter has directed that women be removed as spiritual directors of priestly students because they do not "reflect manly piety." There is pressure to remove them from teaching jobs and eventually to get rid of all women students—even though women constitute more than half the student body in many seminaries and their presence keeps them open.

Rome is extremely concerned about the issue of women's ordination. Despite the fact that both the United States Catholic Biblical Association and the Pontifical Biblical Commission found nothing in the New Testament against the ordination of women, the Vatican still maintains that women cannot adequately "represent Christ." This, despite the fact that John Paul II says that priests exercise a "fatherhood" and even a certain "motherhood" in their ministry.

Symptomatic of the mentality is the cruel, petty exclusion of girls from serving at the altar. Obviously, it still requires more courage to take an honest stand in "minor" church questions such as altar girls, birth control and infallibility than in major world questions like arms control. One bishop even refused to continue confirmation until the altar girls were removed! Until human rights are granted to all in the church, such foolishness will continue.

But in this papal war, women have much on their side. The first is their emerging worldwide consciousness and growing solidarity. The women's movement is revolutionary in that it challenges sexual taboos and a patriarchy that predates the Christian church. They have political power and are organized. They are already far more involved in the ministry than men. Without them, Catholicism in this country would have to close down much of its work.

John Paul II may win some battles against women, but he will lose the war. If he won it, he would lose the women— as his predecessors lost, in Europe especially, the intellectuals and workers. One could hope that a Pope who has so much devotion to Mary would comprehend the radical feminism of the Magnificat—Mary's prayer in Luke's Gospel. She prays that God "will put down the mighty from their thrones and exalt the lowly." This is probably wishful thinking, for the church has a long way to go to make this prayer a reality in its midst.

86.

Private Violence

In 1983 Time *magazine published a cover story about what it termed "private violence." It examined the violence of husbands, who beat or kill their wives; the violence of parents, both mothers and fathers, who torture and brutalize their children; and the violence of familial rape, by husbands and fathers. Domestic violence toward women—in the form of psychological, verbal, emotional, or physical abuse by a male partner—affects an estimated two to four million women in the United States each year. It remains, in fact, the leading cause of injury among young women from age 15 to 44. Only a portion of the* Time *article is reprinted here.*

Source: *Time,* September 5, 1983.

WHAT MIGHT BE called public violence is as American as assassinations, mob wars and mass murders, the stuff of screaming headlines and periodic national soul searching. What might be called private violence, what people who know each other, even profess to love each other, do to each other, is a nightmarish realm only beginning to be forthrightly explored. Its particular horror stems from its violations of the trust upon which all intimate human relations depend: it is cruelty exercised on those nearest, most vulnerable, least able or inclined to defend themselves from their attackers. For those who commit private violence, who abuse children, beat wives and rape, the usual reasons behind public violence—greed, dementia, vengeance, feral antisocial anger—do not generally apply. How to explain acts of brutality so personal and thus so specially disturbing?

Public violence, at least, can be neatly tallied. The FBI is aware of exactly 22,-516 murders committed in the U.S. in 1981, a fifth of them killings of loved ones, and that is very close to the true total. Even the Government accounting of motor-vehicle thefts, 1,073,998 for 1981, is almost right, since victims cannot get their insurance money unless they file a police report. But when statisticians turn to private violence, the numbers become iffy, approximate in the extreme. Are there 650,000 cases of child abuse annually, or a million? Or 6 million? Bona fide experts, extrapolating and just guessing, variously cite all those figures and others. It is said that every year 2 million women are beaten by their husbands, and it is also said that nearly 6 million are. Pick your figure. A Justice Department survey counted 178,000 rapes during 1981, but for every woman who reported a rape to the police, perhaps nine or maybe 25 did not. It is beyond dispute, however, that

This woman was acquitted of killing her husband after she testified that he had beaten her and her children during seven years of marriage.

extraordinary numbers of women and children are being brutalized by those closest to them.

The uncertainty about the scope of private violence is a function of shame, of hushing up. Such crimes, unlike slashings or shootings on sidewalks and in taverns, often leave a victim more hurt and humiliated than outraged. Historically, beatings by one's husband, like rapes, were bad enough to suffer but more shameful still to reveal publicly. Child-rearing, no matter how harshly executed, was an entirely private matter.

Today, the dirty secrets are no longer being kept. Victims of private violence are talking—to police, prosecutors, counselors, friends, one another—and U.S. society is trying to help. Private violence is becoming less private. Thus, while reports of child abuse in Florida, for example, rose from 35,301

in 1981 to 45,704 last year, such apparent increases may be due mostly to authorities' finding out about more of the violence. Betty Friedan, the feminist author, believes that attacks on women are not necessarily on the rise, just coming out of the shameful murk: "Women don't tolerate it any more because they know it's all right to speak up."

Rape and family violence and incest are still uncomfortable subjects. And the common good is hardly better served by easy statutory fiats—one spouse slapping another is *not* just like any other criminal assault—than by the old silence of misplaced propriety. But the unspeakable must be spoken, in all of its repellent conjugations. Take, for example, the biggest taboo: "As long as incest has that secrecy," says Miriam Ingebritson, a Minneapolis therapist, "it has a potency and power it doesn't deserve. It has to be stripped of that power." There are now all kinds of places to turn to. Rape treatment clinics, shelters for battered wives, and centers for abused children have sprung up across the country. Legal procedures appear to have made prosecution easier. The problems are coming out of the closet in surprising places: in the small Plains city of Salina (pop. 42,600), the Domestic Violence Association of Central Kansas gets around 100 "crisis calls" a month.

There is no place so violent as home. About half of all rapes occur there. It is in the privacy of the home, both in cramped flats and in grand neocolonials, that women are pummeled by husbands and boyfriends. It was in his home in Houston a few years ago, for instance, that Second-Grader Daniel Brownell, whose stepfather's attacks had left him paralyzed and permanently senseless, was found branded with cigarette burns that spelled I CRY. One remarkable Connecticut woman named Carol, 38, who is a volunteer counselor of imprisoned rapists, knows freakishly well that home is not necessarily a haven: it was in her childhood home in the early 1950s that she was the victim of incest, at a friend's home that a half-dozen men gang-raped her, in her very own home that her second husband beat the living daylights out of her again and again.

Out on the street, at least, one's guard is up. Muggers who demand money are, in a sense, just conducting a cutthroat business. Most of the time they do not lay claims on their victims' humanity. Home is meant to be life's one warm, safe place. Violence committed there, especially by somebody understood to be a guardian (husband, father, mother, uncle, babysitter), is a special betrayal. And once brawling becomes routine in a household, or primal taboos are cracked, there is often no stopping the spread of viciousness. Richard Gelles, a sociologist at the University of Rhode Island, describes the grim ecology of a violent family: "The husband will beat the wife. The wife may then learn to beat the children. The bigger siblings learn it's O.K. to hit the little ones, and the family pet may be the ultimate recipient of violence."

The thousands of wife beaters who happen to be in prison (almost all are there for some other, less peculiar crime) regard rapists with contempt, and rapists in turn call the cellblocks' child abusers scum. But in fact the three groups have some rough affinities. The privately violent are often alcoholic or drug-dependent. All three species tend to have low opinions of themselves; they get violent, psychoanalysts say, because it gives them a cheap squirt of power. Like most criminals, they are immature and impulsive. Everything they want they want instantly. And they are uncommonly isolated people, often virtually friendless, cut off from those who lead richer, happier or just plain calmer lives.

The worst thing about family violence is its natural reproduction of itself, like a poisonous plant sending out spores. Most rapists were preyed upon sexually as children, and most violent criminals were raised in violent homes. Children of punched-out women, accustomed to seeing family business transacted with fists, are prone to become battered wives and battering husbands themselves. Worse, battered children grow up predisposed to batter their own offspring. Sexually abused boys often become pedophiles and rapists, while sexually victimized girls, perennial targets, are likelier to become battered wives. Bruce Ritter, a Roman Catholic priest, runs a shelter for teen-age runaways and castoffs in the neon squalor of Manhattan's Times Square. "The girls who walk in off the streets with babies abuse them," Father Ritter says. "If a two-week-old baby is crying, the mother will slap the baby. We try to teach her not to do that."

Yet there are important distinctions between and within the three main genres of private violence. Slapping a spouse is different from shaking a child—an adult can more easily understand, fight back or flee—and both are very unlike rape. Of the three, rape is most unequivocally a statutory crime, and probably every rapist ought to be locked up for some time. They are real criminals. Of course, a parent who willfully scalds a child's arm is a criminal. Of course, a man who stomps his pregnant wife is a criminal. These cases are, ironically, the easiest ones to think about: when the violence is so ugly and utterly inexcusable, you just throw the book at the sick bastards.

But most cases of private violence are closer calls. What to do about a man who rapes his wife? What about the fights between spouses that are not pat, villain-and-victim episodes? What about Darrel Trueblood of Terre Haute, Ind., whose son Travis was taken from him for three months in 1980 because the father had punished with the thwack of a ruler? Greg Dixon, a Baptist minister and head of Indiana's Moral Majority, says Trueblood was "just giving a normal whipping." Says he: "Reasonable people can detect whether it's assault and battery or not."

One problem is that reasonable, well-intentioned people disagree. How should outsiders decide when private violence is a matter for direct public intervention?

Some liberals sound illiberally willing to cut corners when it comes to prosecuting private-violence offenders. In some cities, a man who assaults a woman must be arrested and prosecuted, even if she changes her mind about the whole thing; in Anchorage, Alaska, a woman who declines to testify against her husband may be fined or jailed. It used to be much more difficult to convict rapists, but states are changing their laws so that simply a victim's say-so may be evidence enough. The Washington State legislature, angry over the difficulty of prosecuting a child molester, passed a law last year allowing hearsay testimony in certain criminal trials to corroborate other evidence.

The new zealousness, coming after generations of apathy, is not surprising. It is no wonder that counselors of battered women are inclined to advise a black-and-blue wife to file for divorce and prosecute the brute instead of go-

ing back to him for the third time. When a nuclear family is undergoing a meltdown, about to blow, it is a good idea to evacuate the place. But sometimes the professionals seem eager to denigrate their clients' commitment to marriage. "Women have an incredible amount of hope," says Mary Marecek, a counselor at the oldest women's shelter in Massachusetts. "We want them to get over the hope that the ideal marriage may still come out of it." Yet a hopeful woman, trying to make a go of a not-so-good marriage, is not always a fool. There are those in the field who— like the Ellen Jamesians, the self-mutilating feminists of *The World According to Garp*—seem too quick to find in wife abuse a confirmation and dramatization of sexism, a bloody cartoon of male oppression.

There are more specialized kinds of private violence, of course, only just beginning to be classified as "social problems." Most prominent is "granny bashing," the flip British nickname for the physical mistreatment of old people, usually the victimizers' parents or grandparents. About 5% of dependent elderly Americans may be abused, according to Murray Straus, a University of New Hampshire sociologist. Is a surge of parent bashing possible? It would not be a real surprise: futuristic cabin fever could break out if, on the verge of the 21st century, millions of Americans really are working and living in their hermetic "electronic cottages." Last year in state-of-the-art and otherwise pacific Japan, there were 1,099 reported cases of children assaulting their parents.

In most of the rest of the world, private violence is not considered a high-priority social problem. Not that punch-ups at home are any less prevalent. Rather, as a Thai social worker says, "it's so common that no one thinks it's a problem." If anything, victims abroad are more explicitly shamed into silence, with the legal and medical systems often oblivious. In most countries a man's home is practically his personal free-fire zone, off limits to busybodies. And the U.S. has far and away more shelters and programs where victims can find solace and help. But the vast array of American services is to meet a vast terror: a woman's chances of being raped in the U.S., for instance, are five or ten times as great as in Western Europe.

The U.S. cannot afford to get smug. Not all American victims are getting help, or even sympathy. "As a society," says Sociologist Gelles of private violence, "we laugh at this behavior."

We should not. But indeed, such behavior is not so completely unthinkable that decent folks do not chuckle when Jackie Gleason's Ralph Kramden angrily threatens to sock his ever-loving wife. "I'm gonna send you to the moon," he barks on *The Honeymooners*, his clenched fist waving. "To the *moon*, Alice." But if people on the one hand laugh off private violence, they become raving, sputtering mad about it too. "The pendulum swings to two extremes," says A. Nicholas Groth, a Connecticut prison psychologist. "Either people blame the victim, or see the offender as a fiend who ought to be castrated." The hard duty is to look straight at the problems and, neither laughing nor ranting, figure out what reasonable people can do.

If wolves and bears and birds take meticulous care of their young, why are human beings subjecting theirs to whippings and punches and sexual perversion. Children, with their unrestrained love and unquestioning trust, deserve better . . . . Child abuse is the ultimate crime, the ultimate betrayal.

Time, September 5, 1983

Overflowing storage facilities in north central Washington made it necessary to pile 125,000 bushels of wheat outdoors on the ground until the bumper crop could be sold.

FARMING'S UPS AND DOWNS

The decade from 1977 to 1986 saw some of the highest ups in the history of American agriculture, and some of the lowest downs. At the beginning of the decade, farms were booming and farmers were suddenly richer than they had been in many years. Though farming traditionally was a low-profit business, in the late 1970s, farmers enjoyed an infusion of cash: cash from the sale of their crops and produce, and cash from readily available loans, guaranteed by the government, the proceeds of which could be spent on all kinds of things to improve their lives. On top of that, their land was in-

creasing in value by 10 or 20 percent per year, or even more. And then, almost overnight, the bottom fell out. Interest rates on the loans zoomed to unprecedented levels, the government backed off on its guarantees, and the crops were too abundant, with attendant plummeting prices. In 1986 corn and wheat were selling for about the same price as during the Great Depression, but everything that farmers bought cost 10 times as much or more. And thousands of farmers—some good, some bad, some careful, some improvident—lost their farms.

Photos by AP/Wide World

In the late 1980s, the fruitfulness of the farmland of America had produced a bittersweet harvest. Even with billions of dollars of subsidies paid to farmers to keep them from growing wheat or producing milk, too much was produced even to store—the elevators and refrigerators were full. The problem was compounded by the fact that the whole world was suffering from an over-supply of food, but people were still starving in some countries because of defects in the distribution system. Furthermore, the relatively high cost of producing grains and other staples in the United States priced the country out of the world market; in 1986, for the first time in more than a century, the country imported more food than it exported. An over-abundance existed in spite of the worst drought in 50 years in the southeastern states (see next page). There, farmers had to slaughter their cattle because there was nothing to feed them (although New England and Midwestern farmers generously donated carloads of hay), and more than half a million chickens perished in the 100° heat that lasted for weeks on end. For different reasons, many farmers there also lost their farms.

Photos by AP/Wide World

(Opposite top left) Ripe wheat is fragile, and it must be harvested before it is attacked by rain or hail—or fire; (top right) in a good growing season the corn in Wisconsin sometimes grows more than 10 feet high; (bottom) soybeans, the "wonder crop," are made into oil, which is stored in tank cars. (Top) Mechanical pickers approach the manager of a cotton farm in Mississippi as he checks a cotton boll; (bottom) the owner of these Jersey cattle in southern Florida has moved a large part of his herd northward because of skyrocketing land prices.

Less severe droughts are perennial problems for American farmers, of course, as are insect pests, which arrive from foreign lands in shipments of plants, flowers, and foliage. Customs officials try to intercept the unwelcome immigrants, but the Mediterranean fruit fly (which is supposed to have arrived in a peach), the Formosan termite, the Asian cockroach, and the fire ant (which eats not only crops but also small rodents) have managed to get through. Water shortages also plague farmers. In near-desert areas like Arizona, the aquifers are being drained dry, and so water is being brought in from the Colorado River (lower right).

(Top) This couple had to sell all their cattle because there was no water for them; this pond was normally 15 feet deep; (center) a farmer watches as his truck is loaded with hay at a distribution center; the 1986 drought destroyed the feed for his cattle; (bottom left) herbicide is sprayed by helicopter in Minnesota; (bottom right) the fire ant, a pest that consumes crops. (Opposite top) A group of farmers traveled in 1979 to Washington, D.C., in their tractors to protest low farm prices; (bottom) this vast irrigation canal in Arizona carries vital water to areas of low rainfall.

There are those who say the American family farm is an institution that has had its day. Since the 1980s the vertical integration of agriculture has been profound, with many thousands of family farms consolidated in larger corporate entities. In response, coalitions of family farmers have organized to highlight the benefits of decentralized production, to question the safety of genetically engineered crops, and to seek legislation to stabilize farm prices and income.

(Top) Farmers inspect equipment being auctioned by a neighbor who is deeply in debt; (bottom) a farmer pleads with his fellow farmers not to buy his equipment and thus help the banks put farmers out of business.

87.

The Destruction of Korean Airlines Flight 007

Korean Airlines Flight 007 left Anchorage, Alaska, at 10 am on August 31, 1983, headed for Seoul, with 244 passengers and a crew of 25 aboard. At noon, the Soviets began tracking the plane with radar. For some reason, the Korean pilot began to stray off his regular course, which would have taken him south of Soviet territory, across the main island of Japan, and to Seoul. Shortly after noon Flight 007 crossed the Kamchatka Peninsula, and at 2 pm it was approaching the southern tip of Sakhalin Island, both Soviet territory. A Soviet fighter plane sighted the Boeing 747 at 2:12 pm, and at 2:26 the interceptor shot down the unarmed civilian plane with a missile. All 269 died. The U.S.S.R. did not admit until September 6 that one of its planes had caused the tragedy; on September 12 it vetoed a UN Security Council resolution deploring the destruction of the airliner. On September 21 a Soviet delegate attending a conference in Edinburgh, Scotland, admitted to a BBC interviewer that the Soviet pilot had wrongly identified the airliner as a military reconnaissance plane and made a mistake when he destroyed it. What really happened on that fateful day remains a mystery, and it probably always will. Reprinted here is a resolution adopted by the U.S. House of Representatives on September 14; the U.S. Senate concurred in adopting the measure the next day.

Source: *The New York Times,* September 15, 1983.

WHEREAS the United States joins with the world community in expressing its outrage over the actions of the Soviet Government on Aug. 31, 1983, which caused the destruction of Korean Air Lines Flight 007 with the loss of 269 innocent lives;

WHEREAS on Aug. 31, 1983, Korean Air Lines Flight 007 inadvertently entered Soviet airspace;

WHEREAS Soviet authorities tracked Korean Air Lines Flight 007 for more than two hours but did not adhere to all the internationally recognized procedures necessary to warn the aircraft that it was off course and to protect its passengers;

WHEREAS A Soviet Air Force fighter fired air-to-air missiles at Korean Air Lines Flight 007 and destroyed the unarmed, clearly marked civilian airliner with 269 innocent men, women and children from 14 nations aboard, including 61 of our fellow citizens;

WHEREAS among the victims was a distinguished Member of Congress, the Honorable Larry P. McDonald;

WHEREAS the highest levels of the Soviet Government have lied in an attempt to justify this unconscionable act and have continued to deny access to the area where the airplane went down;

WHEREAS the Soviet Government has publicly proclaimed its intention to repeat its murderous act if another airliner wanders inadvertently into Soviet airspace; and

WHEREAS this cold-blooded barbarous attack on a commercial airliner straying off course is one of the most infamous and reprehensible acts in history: Now, therefore, be it

RESOLVED by the Senate and House of Representatives of the United States of America in Congress assembled, that the United States hereby

1. Condemns the Soviet crime of destroying Korean Air Lines Flight 007 and murdering the 269 innocent people onboard;

2. Calls for a full and frank explanation from the Soviet Union for this brutal massacre;

3. Extends its deepest sympathies to the families who lost loved ones and supports their rights to obtain reparations from the Soviet Union;

4. Calls on the Soviet Union to assist international efforts to recover the remains of the victims;

5. Calls for an international investigation by the International Civil Aviation Organization into this heinous incident;

6. Declares its intention to work with the international community in demanding that the Soviet Union modify its air defense procedures and practices to assure the safe passage of commercial airliners;

7. Finds that this tragic incident, and the Soviet Government's refusal to acknowledge responsibility for its wanton conduct, will make it more difficult for the United States and other nations to accept the Soviet Union as a responsible member of the international community; and

8. Urges our allies and other nations to cooperate with the United States in continuing to demand that the Soviet Government unequivocally apologize for its action, fully compensate the families of the innocent victims and agree to abide by internationally recognized and established procedures which are purposefully designed to prevent the occurrence of such tragedies.

I'm approaching the target. I'm going in closer.... The target's light is blinking.... I have already approached the target to a distance of two kilometers.... I am going around it. I'm already moving in front of the target.... I'm dropping back. Now I will try rockets.... I have executed the launch. The target is destroyed.

Soviet pilot, responding to instructions from the ground, as recorded on tape by U.S. intelligence units

88.

RONALD REAGAN: The Beirut Massacre

On October 23, 1983, a terrorist bent on suicide drove a truckload of high explosives through a series of barricades and into the U.S. Marine Corps headquarters at the Beirut airport in Lebanon. The explosion demolished the four-story building and killed 239 U.S. servicemen immediately; two of the many injured died later. In an almost simultaneous early-morning attack another bomb-laden truck smashed into a building used as a barracks by French paratroopers, killing 58 when the structure collapsed. On October 27 President Reagan delivered an address to the American people, in which he discussed the tragedy that had occurred and gave the reasons why U.S. troops were in Beirut, and why they would have to remain, at least for a while. In fact, the President announced on February 7, 1984, that U.S. troops would be withdrawn from the Beirut airport and "redeployed offshore."

Source: "Lebanon and Granada: The Use of U.S. Armed Forces," *Vital Speeches of the Day,* November 15, 1983.

MY FELLOW AMERICANS, some two months ago we were shocked by the brutal massacre of 269 men, women and children, in the shooting down of a Korean airliner. Now, in these past several days, violence has erupted again, in Lebanon and Grenada.

In Lebanon we have some 1,600 marines, part of a multinational force that's trying to help the people of Lebanon restore order and stability to that troubled land. Our marines are assigned to the south of the city of Beirut near the only airport operating in Lebanon. Just a mile or so to the north is the Italian contingent and not far from them the French and a company of British soldiers.

This past Sunday, at 22 minutes after 6, Beirut time, with dawn just breaking, a truck looking like a lot of other vehicles in the city approached the airport on a busy main road. There was nothing in its appearance to suggest it was any different than the trucks or cars that were normally seen on and around the airport. But this one was different.

At the wheel was a young man on a suicide mission. The truck carried some 2,000 pounds of explosives, but there was no way our marine guards could know this. Their first warning that something was wrong came when the truck crashed through a series of barriers, including a chain link fence and barbed wire entanglements. The guards opened fire but it was too late.

The truck smashed through the doors of the headquarters building in which our marines were sleeping and instantly exploded. The four-story concrete building collapsed in a pile of rubble. More than 200 of the sleeping men were killed in that one hideous insane attack. Many others suffered injury and are hospitalized here or in Europe. This was not the end of the horror.

At almost the same instant another vehicle on a suicide and murder mission crashed into the headquarters of the French peacekeeping force, an eight-story building, destroying and killing more than 50 French soldiers.

Prior to this day of horror there had been several tragedies for our men in the multinational force; attacks by snipers and mortar fire had taken their toll. I called the bereaved parents and/or widows of the victims to express on behalf of all of us our sorrow and sympathy. Sometimes there were questions. And now many of you are asking: Why should our young men be dying in Lebanon? Why is Lebanon important to us?

Well, it's true Lebanon is a small country more than five and a half thousand miles from our shores, on the edge of what we call the Middle East. But every President who has occupied this office in recent years has recognized that peace in the Middle East is of vital concern to our nation and, indeed, to our allies in Western Europe and Japan. We've been concerned because the Middle East is a powder keg. Four times in the last 30 years the Arabs and Israelis have gone to war and each time the world has teetered near the edge of catastrophe. The area is key to the economic and political life of the West. Its strategic importance, its energy resources, the Suez Canal, the well-being of the nearly 200 million people living there; all are vital to us and to world peace.

If that key should fall into the hands of a power or powers hostile to the free world, there would be a direct threat to the United States and to our allies.

We have another reason to be involved. Since 1948, our nation has recognized and accepted a moral obligation to assure the continued existence of Israel as a nation. Israel shares our democratic values and is a formidable force an invader of the Middle East would have to reckon with. For several years, Lebanon has been torn by internal strife. Once a prosperous, peaceful nation, its Government had become ineffective in controlling the militias that warred on each other. . . .

A little over a year ago, hoping to build on the Camp David accords, which have led to peace between Israel and Egypt, I proposed a peace plan for the Middle East to end the wars between the Arab states and Israel. It was based on U.N. Resolutions 242 and 338 and called for a fair and just solution to the Palestinian problem, as well as a fair and just settlement of issues between the Arab states and Israel.

Before the necessary negotiations could begin, it was essential to get all foreign forces out of Lebanon and to end the fighting there. So why are we there? Well, the answer is straightforward: to help bring peace to Lebanon and stability to the vital Middle East. To that end the multinational force was created to help stabilize the situation in Lebanon until a government could be established and the Lebanese Army mobilized to restore Lebanese sovereignty over its own soil as the foreign forces withdrew. . . .

A few weeks ago the Israeli Army pulled back to the Awali River in southern Lebanon. Despite fierce resistance by Syrian-backed forces the Lebanese Army was able to hold the lines and maintain the defensive perimeter around Beirut. In the year that our marines have been there Lebanon has made important steps toward stability and order. The physical presence of the marines lends support to both the Lebanese Government and its army. It allows the hard work of diplomacy to go forward. Indeed without the peace-keepers from the U.S., France, Italy and Britain, the efforts to find a peaceful solution in Lebanon would collapse.

As for that narrower question, what exactly is the operational mission of the marines, the answer is to secure a piece of Beirut; to keep order in their sector and to prevent the area from becoming a battlefield. Our marines are not just sitting in an airport. Part of their task is to guard that airport. Because of their presence the airport has remained operational. In addition they patrol the surrounding area. This is their part— a limited but essential part—in a larger effort that I described.

If our marines must be there, I'm asked, why can't we make them safer? Who committed this latest atrocity against them and why? Well, we'll do everything we can to insure that our men are as safe as possible. We ordered the battleship New Jersey to join our naval forces offshore. Without even firing them, the threat of its 16-inch guns silenced those who once fired down on our marines from the hills. And they're a good part of the reason we suddenly had a cease-fire. We're doing our best to make our forces less vulnerable to those who want to snipe at them or send in future suicide missions. . . .

We have strong circumstantial evidence that the attack on the marines was directed by terrorists who used the same method to destroy our embassy in Beirut. Those who directed this atrocity must be dealt justice, and they will be. The obvious purpose behind the sniping and now this attack was to weaken American will and force the withdrawal of U.S. and French forces from Lebanon.

The clear intent of the terrorists was to limit our support of the Lebanese Government and to destroy the ability of the Lebanese people to determine their own destiny. To answer those who ask if we're serving any purpose in being there, let me answer a question with a question: would the terrorists have launched their suicide attacks against the multinational force if it were not doing its job?

The multinational force was attacked precisely because it is doing the job it was sent to do in Beirut. It is accomplishing its mission.

Now then, where do we go from here?

What can we do now to help Lebanon gain greater stability so that our marines can come home? I believe we can take three steps now that will make a difference.

First, we will accelerate the search for peace and stability in that region. Little attention is being paid to the fact that we have had special envoys there working literally around the clock to bring the warring factions together. . . .

Second, we'll work even more closely with our allies in providing support for the Government of Lebanon and for the rebuilding of a national consensus.

Third, we will insure that the multinational peacekeeping forces, our Marines, are given the greatest possible protection. Our Commandant of the Marine Corps, General Kelley, returned from Lebanon today and will be advising us on steps we can take to improve security.

Beyond our progress in Lebanon let us remember that our main goal and purpose is to achieve a broader peace in all of the Middle East. The factions and bitterness that we see in Lebanon are just a microcosm of the difficulties that are spread across much of that region. A peace initiative for the entire Middle East, consistent with the Camp David accord, and U.N. Resolutions 242 and 338, still offers the best hope for bringing peace to the region.

Let me ask those who say we should get out of Lebanon: If we were to leave Lebanon now, what message would that send to those who foment instability and terrorism? If Americans were to walk away from Lebanon, what chance would there be for a negotiated settlement producing a unified, democratic Lebanon? If we turned our backs on Lebanon now, what would be the future of Israel? At stake is the fate of only the second Arab country to negotiate a major agreement with Israel. That's another accomplishment of this past year, the May 17 accord signed by Lebanon and Israel.

If terrorism and intimidation succeed, it'll be a devastating blow to the peace process and to Israel's search for genuine security. It won't just be Lebanon sentenced to a future of chaos. Can the United States, or the free world, for that matter, stand by and see the Middle East incorporated into the Soviet bloc? What of Western Europe and Japan's dependence on Middle East oil for the energy to fuel their industries? The Middle East is, as I said, vital to our national security and economic well-being.

Brave young men have been taken from us. Many others have been grievously wounded. Are we to tell them their sacrifice was wasted or that they gave their lives in defense of our national security every bit as much as any man who ever died fighting in a war?

We must not strip every ounce of meaning and purpose from their courageous sacrifice. We are a nation with global responsibilities, we're not somewhere else in the world protecting someone else's interest. We're there protecting our own.

I saw a young marine with more tubes going in and out his body than I have ever seen in one body. He couldn't see very well. He reached up and grapped my four stars just to make sure I was who I said I was. He held my hand with a firm grip. He was making signals and we realized he wanted to tell me something. We put a pad of paper in his hand and he wrote: 'semper fi.'

GEN. PAUL KELLEY, Marine Corps commandant,
visiting critically injured marines in an Air Force hospital;
the motto of the Marine Corps is *Semper Fidelis*, "always faithful"

89.

The Long Report

On December 20, 1983, a special commission of investigation of the Pentagon, chaired by retired Admiral Robert L.J. Long, delivered its report on the events before, during, and after the Beirut massacre (see Selection 88). The report, which was not released until December 28, concluded that the marines were not adequately trained to deal with terrorists in an increasingly hostile environment; that the entire chain of command, including the Marine commander in Beirut and the admirals and generals above him, shared blame for the inadequate security at the Beirut headquarters; that the marines lacked the ability to assess the mass of intelligence available to them; that the marines should not have housed so many men in a single building; and that in the weeks following the attack, they reduced their vulnerability, but their precautions were still inadequate. In a hastily called press conference on December 27, the day before the text of the report was released, President Reagan stated that he accepted full blame for the lack of adequate security that obtained in Beirut prior to the massacre and declared that he did not believe any of the Marine commanders should be punished. "They have already suffered quite enough," he said.

Sources: Pentagon Commission Report, *The New York Times,* December 29, 1983.

Presidential Documents, week ending December 31, 1983.

A: THE COMMISSION'S REPORT

TERRORISM

The commission believes that the most important message it can bring to the Secretary of Defense is that the 23 October 1983 attack on the Marine Battalion Landing Team headquarters in Beirut was tantamount to an act of war using the medium of terrorism. Terrorist warfare, sponsored by sovereign states or organized political entities to achieve political objectives, is a threat to the United States that is increasing at an alarming rate. The 23 October catastrophe underscores the fact that terrorist warfare can have significant political impact and demonstrates that the United States, and specifically the Department of Defense, is inadequately prepared to deal with this threat. Much needs to be done, on an urgent basis, to prepare U.S. military forces to defend against and counter terrorist warfare.

SECURITY FOLLOWING THE ATTACK

The security posture of the U.S.M.N.F. subsequent to the 23 October 1983 attack was examined closely by the commission. A series of actions was initiated by the chain of command to enhance the security of the U.S.M.N.F. and reduce the vulnerability of the U.S.M.N.F. to further catastrophic losses. However, the security measures implemented or planned for implementation as of 30 November 1983 were not adequate to prevent continuing significant attrition of U.S.M.N.F. personnel.

INTELLIGENCE SUPPORT

Even the best of intelligence will not guarantee the security of any military position. However, specific data on the terrorist threats to the U.S.M.N.F., data which could best be provided by carefully trained intelligence agents, could have enabled the U.S.M.N.F. commander to better prepare his force and facilities to blunt the effectiveness of a suicidal vehicle attack of great explosive force.

The U.S.M.N.F. commander did not have effective U.S. Human Intelligence (Humint) support. The paucity of U.S. controlled Humint is partly due to U.S. policy decisions to reduce Humint collection worldwide. The U.S. has a Humint capability commensurate with the resources and time that has been spent to acquire it. The lesson of Beirut is that we must have better Humint to support military planning and operations. We see here a critical repetition of a long line of similar lessons learned during crisis situations in many other parts of the world.

CASUALTY HANDLING PROCEDURES

The commission found that, following the initial, understandable confusion, the response of the U.S., Lebanese and Italian personnel in providing immediate on-scene medical care was professional and, indeed, heroic. The

AP/Wide World

Italians and Americans remove a marine's body from the rubble after the bombing that leveled the Marine command center in Beirut, Lebanon.

C.T.F. 61/62 Mass Casualty Plan was quickly implemented: triage and treatment sites were established ashore, and medical support from afloat units was transported to the scene. Evacuation aircraft were requested.

Within 30 minutes of the explosion, the British offered the use of their hospital at the Royal Air Force base in Akrotiri, Cyprus, and this offer was accepted by C.T.F. 61. The additional British offer of medical evacuation aircraft was also accepted. Both offers proved invaluable.

Offers of medical assistance from France and Israel were subsequently received but were deemed unnecessary because the medical capabilities organic to C.T.F. 61 were already operational and functioning adequately, the hospital at Akrotiri was by then mobilized and ready and sufficient U.S. and Royal Air Force medical evacuation aircraft were en route. The commission found no evidence to indicate any considerations but the desire to provide immediate, professional treatment for the wounded influenced decisions regarding these offers of outside assistance.

The commission found no evidence to indicate that deaths among the wounded in action resulted from inadequate or inappropriate care during evacuation to hospitals.

The commission did find several serious problem areas in the evacuation of casualties to U.S. military hospitals in Germany. Actions were taken that resulted in some seriously wounded patients being delayed about four hours in arriving at hospital facilities. The commission believes that these actions warrant further investigation. The commission found no evidence, however, that any patient was adversely affected by these delays.

ACCOUNTABILITY

The commission holds the view that military commanders are responsible for the performance of their subordinates. The commander can delegate some or all of his authority to his subordinates, but he cannot delegate his responsibility for the performance of the forces he commands. In that sense, the responsibility of military command is absolute. This view of command authority and responsibility guided the commission in its analysis of the effectiveness of the exercise of command authority and responsibility of the chain of command charged with the security and performance of the U.S.M.N.F.

The commission found that the combination of a large volume of unfulfilled threat warnings and perceived and real pressure to accomplish a unique and difficult mission contributed significantly to the decisions of the Marine Amphibious Unit (M.A.U.) and Battalion Landing Team (B.L.T.) commanders regarding the security of their force. Nevertheless, the commission found that the security measures in effect in the M.A.U. compound were neither commensurate with the increasing level of threat confronting the U.S.M.N.F. nor sufficient to preclude catastrophic losses such as those that were suffered on the morning of 23 October 1983. The commission further found that while it may have appeared to be an appropriate response to the indirect fire being received, the decision to billet approximately one-quarter of the B.L.T. in a single structure contributed to the catastrophic loss of life.

The commission found that the B.L.T. commander must take responsibility for the concentration of approximately 350 members of his command in the B.L.T. headquarters building, thereby providing a lucrative target for attack. Further, the B.L.T. commander modified prescribed alert procedures, thereby degrading security of the compound.

The commission also found that the M.A.U. commander shares the responsibility for the catastrophic losses in that he condoned the concentration of personnel in the B.L.T. headquarters building, concurred in the relaxation of prescribed alert procedures and emphasized safety over security in directing that sentries on Posts 4, 5, 6 and 7 would not load their weapons.

The commission found further that the Uscinceur operational chain of command shares in the responsibility for the events of 23 October 1983.

Having reached the foregoing conclusions, the commission further notes that although it found the entire Uscinceur chain of command, down to and including the B.L.T. commander, to be at fault, it also found that there was a series of circumstances beyond the control of these commanders that influenced their judgment and their actions relating to the security of the U.S.M.N.F.

B: REMARKS BY THE PRESIDENT

The President. Good morning.

I received the report of the Long Commission last Friday and have reviewed it thoroughly. The report draws a conclusion that the United States and its military institutions are by tradition and training inadequately equipped to deal with the fundamentally new phenomenon of state-supported terrorism. I wholeheartedly agree.

The thrust of the history of this country is that we've recognized a clear distinction between being at peace with other states and being at war. We have never before faced a situation in which others routinely sponsor and facilitate acts of violence against us while hiding behind proxies and surrogates which claim—they claim they do not fully control.

Now, this problem is not unique to Lebanon. We've seen the ugly manifestation in Kuwait, the terrorist bombing in Rangoon, the senseless murder of Turkish diplomats, the attack on the Pope, the bombing of our own Capitol, and on the streets of London.

In the days ahead we need to systematically redevelop our approach to this problem, recognizing that the worst outcome of all is one in which terrorists succeed in transforming an open democracy into a closed fortress. Now, one fact, though, is already obvious:

The problem of terrorism will not disappear if we run from it. This is not to say that we're not working as urgently as possible to create political conditions in Lebanon that will make it possible for us to remove our forces. But we must not delude ourselves into believing that terrorism will vanish on the happy day that our forces come home.

For terrorists to be curbed, civilized countries must begin a new effort to work together, to share intelligence, to improve our training and security and our forces, to deny havens or legal protection for terrorist groups and, most important of all, to hold increasingly accountable those countries which sponsor terrorism and terrorist activity around the world.

The United States intends to be in the forefront of this effort. For the near term, corrective action is being urgently taken to ensure the maximum possible security of our forces. Nearly all the measures that were identified by the distinguished members of the commission have already implemented—or have already been implemented, I should say—and those that have not will be very quickly.

The commission report also notes that the mission of the marines is extremely difficult, and with this, too, there can be no dispute. We recognized the fact at the beginning, and we're painfully mindful of it today. But the point is that our forces have already contributed to achievements that lay the foundation for a future peace, the restoration of a central government, and the establishment of an effective national Lebanese army. We do not expect Utopia, but I believe that we're on the verge of new progress toward national reconciliation and the withdrawal of foreign forces.

And let me finally say that I have

soberly considered the commission's word about accountability and responsibility of authorities up and down the chain of command. And everywhere more should be done to anticipate and prepare for dramatic terrorist assaults. We have to come to grips with the fact that today's terrorists are better armed and financed, they are more sophisticated, they are possessed by a fanatical intensity that individuals of a democratic society can only barely comprehend.

I do not believe, therefore, that the local commanders on the ground, men who have already suffered quite enough, should be punished for not fully comprehending the nature of today's terrorist threat. If there is to be blame, it properly rests here in this Office and with this President. And I accept responsiblity for the bad as well as the good.

90.

JOHN McCLAUGHRY: The Case Against Reverend Moon

In 1981 the Internal Revenue Service charged Sun Myung Moon, founder of the Holy Spirit Association for the Unification of World Christianity, commonly known as the Unification Church, with having failed to pay income tax on large sums received from church members. The Reverend Moon and his "Moonies" were not popular in the United States, owing to accusations that the church kidnapped nice young people, then brainwashed them, and turned them into unthinking robot followers. Whether or not this was true, the case against Moon raised troubling questions about the separation of Church and State, and most of the major American churches objected officially to the legal procedures against the Korean-born religious leader. However, Moon was convicted in 1983 and, after exhausting his legal remedies, began (in 1984) to serve an 18-month prison term. The author of this article was Senior Policy Advisor in the White House in 1982. He has no connection with the Unification Church.

Source: *National Review*, December 23, 1983.

DESPITE THE protests of the Reagan Administration that it supports freedom of religion against government intrusion, the Internal Revenue Service is once again launching an assault on the independence of the nation's churches.

In the 1983 Bob Jones University and Goldsboro Christian Schools cases, the Supreme Court upheld the IRS position by decreeing that church-sponsored schools could not enjoy the benefits of tax exemption and deductibility if they practiced any form of racial discrimination. These cases dealt with schools, not with churches per se. Now, however, there is litigation under way designed to inject the government into the internal workings of bona-fide churches.

The case, brought by the Internal Revenue Service in 1981, is that of Reverend Sun Myung Moon, the Korean founder of the controversial Holy Spirit Association for the Unification of World Christianity, commonly known as the Unification Church, or the "Moonies." The IRS charged Reverend Moon with tax fraud. The District Court of New York convicted him, and he was sentenced to pay a $25,000 fine and serve 18 months in jail. A three-judge panel of the Second Circuit U.S. Court of Appeals recently affirmed the conviction on appeal, by a 2 to 1 vote. (Reverend Moon's lawyers have appealed for an en banc rehearing before the Second Circuit. If that is denied, they will seek review by the Supreme Court.)

It is unfortunate that the defendant in this case is such a controversial figure, for the public's feelings about the Moonies tend to override recognition of the key issue involved in the case. That key issue has nothing to do with Reverend Moon himself, or the theology of his church, or its fundraising and recruitment practices. It is, simply, the extent to which a bona-fide religious body can be penalized for refusing to adopt internal practices acceptable to the government. In addition, the circumstances surrounding the Moon prosecution strongly suggest a government vendetta against a church that politically powerful people find repugnant to their own brand of religion. Roger Williams, trudging south from Massachusetts Bay in 1635, would have understood.

Sun Myung Moon was born in 1920, in a rural part of what is now North Korea. His family converted to Presbyterianism when he was ten years old. When he was 16, he says, Jesus Christ appeared to him on Easter morning, telling him to go forth and complete Jesus's mission of reconciling humanity to God's word and His love. At the end of World War II, Moon, at age 26, founded what became the Unification Church.

He went to Pyongyang, then under Soviet occupation and now the capital of Communist North Korea. For his preaching the Communists had the usual respect. They threw him into a forced labor camp and tortured him to the point of death. American forces arrived at Hungnam in October 1950, and freed the young preacher from captivity. He made his way to Pusan, South Korea, six hundred miles away, pushing a bicycle carrying a comrade with a broken leg. From humble beginnings there the Unification Church took hold in Korea and Japan. By 1971 Reverend Moon, regarded by his followers as the embodiment of the faith and a new world prophet, was ready to go to America.

Now we come to the matter that led to Reverend Moon's prosecution. It is customary for new religions—and, indeed, many well established religions—to view their founders or clergymen as both spiritual and temporal trustees for the faithful. Adherents of the faith make their contributions to the leader of the church, who receives the assets in trust for the support and propagation of the faith.

In March 1972 Japanese church members contributed a substantial amount of money to Reverend Moon in support of the church's new missionary crusade to America. Reverend Moon deposited these funds in an account in his name in the Chase Manhattan Bank. His accountants duly reported funds withdrawn by him for personal living expenses as taxable income to him. But the interest earned on the money in the bank—totaling $106,500 over three years—was not reported as taxable income.

The crux of the matter is whether Reverend Moon accepted the contributions as trustee for the church and used them for traditional religious purposes. If so, the interest was not taxable. If not—*if* Reverend Moon simply pocketed the funds for his personal use— then the interest was indeed taxable, and Reverend Moon committed tax fraud in failing to report it.

Before examining this question further, it is worth noting the circumstances surrounding the prosecution of Reverend Moon, seven years after his failure to report the interest income. (In 1976 the Church incorporated in order to avoid further problems.)

There was in 1981 considerable public resentment against the Moonies. The National Council of Churches refused to accept the Unification Church's doctrines as compatible with traditional Christianity. There was widespread disapproval of the Church's fundraising methods, which included street solicitation. And there were frequent uproars over young people who had allegedly been seduced into Mooniehood by various brainwashing techniques.

In this atmosphere of public hostility the government brought its case for tax fraud. Reverend Moon, who had voluntarily returned from Korea to New York to stand trial, stated publicly his belief that the prosecution was motivated by racial and religious factors. His lawyers asked for a trial without a jury, fearing that no objective jury could be empaneled. Surprisingly, the government, which usually prefers court trials to jury trials, demanded a jury trial. Judge Goettel accepted the government's position.

At first the case seemed simple. It was clear that Reverend Moon had received the funds, put them into the bank, earned interest on them, and ignored the interest on his income-tax form. But Judge Goettel soon recognized that the real question was an intricate one, centering on the elusive nature of an implied trust relationship. At the same time, it became apparent that the jury was out of its depth. Even the judge himself observed, from the bench, that in the effort to secure a relatively unbiased jury it had been necessary to empanel jurors "who don't know much, because they are obviously the persons who start off with the least bias." These were, he said, "the less educated and less intelligent people." To this jury the judge then presented the complicated and subtle question of the implied trust relationship.

The technicalities of this question are better left to the law journals, but the basic issue was this: If the donors intended to give funds to the church for religious purposes, thereby implicitly creating a charitable trust, and if the funds were employed by the trustee (Reverend Moon) for such purposes, then Reverend Moon was not guilty of tax fraud in failing to report the interest on his personal tax return.

Throughout its prosecution, the government insisted on the irrelevance of Reverend Moon's role as the founder of his church, terming him instead "an ordinary high-ranking businessman." When the defense sought to introduce evidence that Reverend Moon was merely a trustee for a religious body, the government objected. Even worse, government counsel openly intimidated the defense by promising to respond to a defense built around Reverend Moon's religious role by introducing "negative things about the church"—whether or

AP/Wide World

Reverend Sun Myung Moon

not related to the financial arrangement in question. (The Christian Legal Society, representing the Christian
evangelical movement, eventually filed
an appellate brief arguing that this trial
behavior by the government "unconstitutionally infringed on the defendant's
free speech, [and] may also have a chilling effect on other individuals freely
discussing and propagating their religions.")

The jury—improperly charged, according to the defense—found Reverend Moon guilty. His appeal was rejected, and at this writing his lawyers
have asked for a rehearing before the
entire appeals court to review what even
the majority of the appeals panel termed
the "troubling issues of religious persecution and abridgement of free speech"
in the Moon case.

That those issues are troubling to
many far beyond the Unification Church
is a fact reflected by the remarkably broad coalition of religious organizations joining in a friend of the
court brief on Reverend Moon's behalf:
the National Council of Churches, the
United Presbyterian Church, the Ameri-

can Baptist Churches, the AME Church,
the Unitarian Universalist Association,
and the National Black Catholic Clergy
Caucus.

In the view of these mainline church
organizations, "when someone's religious beliefs and practices become relevant to refuting the charges against
him, treating him as though religion
had nothing to do with the matter is the
very essence of unfairness and discrimination. . . . Upholding the conviction in
this case," the church groups continued,
"would establish the dangerous principle that courts may simply disregard the
religious reasons for, and the religious
meanings of, someone's conduct.

"The principle that religious notions
and explanations must at least be fully
taken into account . . . is critical to followers of all faiths, not simply those
faiths that are new or small or in dis-
favor," said the brief. "From the tax-
exempt status of a church's parking lot,
to the validity of an unincorporated
church association's assertion of power
to direct the actions of a church corporation, little of what even modern-
day mainstream churches routinely do
would survive intact if squeezed through
a religion-extracting filter.

"Upholding the conviction in this
case," the brief concluded, "would also
establish the proposition that judges and
juries may simply override a religion's
own decisions about how to organize itself, how to allocate responsibility over
church matters, and how to expend
church resources. . . . The judgment in
this case does not simply run roughshod
over religion: It positively penalizes religious fervor and spiritual expression."

At the heart of the government's position seems to be the idea that there
is nothing special about religion. If you
wish to start a church, or contribute

to a church, you must follow practices dictated by the government. Those who do not will be prosecuted vigorously, and the more unorthodox the religious beliefs involved, the more ammunition the government will bring to bear to sway a jury against your cause.

Furthermore—and here is the threat to all organized religions—the government is here assuming the power to penetrate into church affairs. Even a church as established as the Roman Catholic Church observes a doctrine whereby the bishop is the personal manager of church funds. Under the doctrine advanced by the government in its pursuit of Reverend Moon, all decisions of a bishop or other church official would be made under peril of prosecution, if the government was somehow displeased with the result.

One may concede that the government was clever in its choice of victims. Reverend Moon is not a popular figure in the American religious world. He is a non-white, a foreigner who speaks only halting English. His theology is highly unorthodox. In addition, he is outspokenly anti-Communist and sees himself as a rallying force for a great American struggle to roll back the Communist tide in the world. Then there are the allegations concerning the Moonies' fundraising and recruitment practices.

If the government wanted to establish a new doctrine of government supervision of churches, it could hardly have chosen a better target to make its case.

But the case of Reverend Moon is not just his own problem. It should be a matter of grave concern for all those who defend freedom of religion against unwarranted government intrusion. For if Reverend Moon goes to jail—this time not in Communist North Korea, but in the United States of America, the great bastion of religious liberty—something of vital importance to all American religions goes with him.

At this stage, having won on appeal, the government's lawyers can be expected to resist any further review of the case in a higher court. But in view of the momentous issues involved—which the appeals court recognized even as its majority ruled against the defendant— the Reagan Administration should take the unusual step of supporting Reverend Moon's petition for review at the appeals-court level and, if that fails, his petition for review by the Supreme Court.

Such recognition by the Administration that this is more than a simple case of white-collar crime would vastly increase the chances of a definitive consideration of the religious-liberty issue by the highest court in the land.

91.

Chester E. Finn, Jr.: How to Lose the War of Ideas

On December 29, 1983, the U.S. government gave formal notice that it intended to terminate its membership in the United Nations Educational, Scientific, and Cultural Organization (UNESCO) by the end of 1984. A spokesman for the State Department declared: "UNESCO has extraneously politicized virtually every subject it deals with, has exhibited hostility toward the basic institutions of a free society, especially a free market and a free press, and has demonstrated unrestrained budgetary expansion." The United States, which paid 25 percent of UNESCO's budget, had frequently warned that it would quit the organization if it did not respond to U.S. complaints. The following article (reprinted in part) is by an official adviser on the U.S. delegation to the UNESCO conference on education held in Paris in April 1983.

Source: *Commentary,* August 1983.

At the United Nations Educational, Scientific, and Cultural Organization (UNESCO), the United States subsidizes the erosion of intellectual freedom, the degradation of democratic values, the redefinition of human rights, and the manipulation of education into an instrument of political indoctrination by those who wish us ill.

Since returning from Paris a few months ago with these sobering insights, I find that they surprise even worldly people who are accustomed to hearing unpleasant things about the United Nations itself. Surely, they respond, UNESCO has not been wholly politicized. Isn't that the organization that rescued those Egyptian temples from drowning? Doesn't it promote scientific exchange programs? And international education?

In truth, UNESCO was once a fundamentally beneficent undertaking, even a noble one. "Since wars begin in the minds of men," intones the preamble to the UNESCO Constitution of 1945, "it is in the minds of men that the defenses of peace must be constructed." Declaring that "the great and terrible war which has now ended was a war made possible by the denial of the democratic principles of the dignity, equality, and mutual respect of men, and by the propagation, in their place, through ignorance and prejudice, of the doctrine of the inequality of men and races," UNESCO's founders averred that "the peace must therefore be founded, if it is not to fail, upon the intellectual and moral solidarity of mankind."

It was no coincidence that the principles of UNESCO were hammered out in London, that the organization's founders included the likes of Reinhold Niebuhr and Jacques Maritain, that the final editor of its constitution was Archibald MacLeish, that its headquarters were placed in Paris, and that its first Director General was Julian Huxley. Nor is it to be wondered at that the constitution pledged UNESCO and its member states to a belief "in full and equal opportunities for education for all, in the unrestricted pursuit of objective truth, and in the free exchange of ideas and knowledge." For at the outset, UNESCO was a classic expression of Western political, intellectual, and moral values: democratic, rational, optimistic, humane, tolerant, and free. No doubt it was a touch utopian; the founders chose not to deal with the possibility that enhanced knowledge of another nation or culture might cause one to like it less or to fear it more. But nothing about it was incompatible with education, culture, science, and governance as practiced in the liberal democracies.

Thirty-eight years later, however, UNESCO has become, in the main, an instrument of destruction that is wielded to chip away at the idea of freedom and the practice of democracy. Apart from the General Assembly itself, it is perhaps the premier example of Senator Daniel P. Moynihan's 1979 generalization that "The United Nations has become a place where the democracies find themselves under a constant, unremitting, ideological and political attack designed to advance the interests of the totalitarians." Although a handful of worthwhile activities may endure in isolated crannies of the vast UNESCO Secretariat and in scattered paragraphs of the 300-page "medium-term plan" that summarizes UNESCO's current endeavors, they are greatly outnumbered by programs that embody the interests of those who despise or fear the principles enshrined in UNESCO's constitution and in the Universal Declaration

of Human Rights. While the Western democracies have deplored this transformation of UNESCO, they lack the votes to prevail against the combined forces of the Soviet bloc and the Third World nations (the latter known as the "G-77," though there are now many more than seventy-seven of them). And those forces are generally combined, because Moscow takes UNESCO very seriously indeed, recognizing it as an important theater in the war of ideas and in the competition for Third World favor. Accordingly, the Soviets assign to UNESCO duty senior people with great skill at ideological combat. They do their homework with awesome meticulousness. They accumulate gains from one event to the next, turning a phrase adopted at one conference into a full policy statement at the next and into a new UNESCO program (and budget item) at the session after that. UNESCO, for them, is serious enough to warrant inclusion in long-term foreign-policy planning. They have a UNESCO strategy, and in recent years it has been notably successful.

The Western democracies have no such strategy. Their resistance to Soviet gains is fitful and ambivalent. They treat UNESCO conferences as isolated events. Though some of their representatives in Paris are able statesmen, others are weary careerists with no appetite for any kind of combat, and still others are idealistic academics who regard UNESCO as an extended sherry hour in the international common room. Gnawed by doubt about the virtue of their own political, cultural, and economic systems, confident that greater knowledge of other systems will ease world tensions and foster mutual understanding, and predisposed to sympathize with the G-77 delegates who insist that every dollar spent on defense is a dollar subtracted from economic-development programs, they cannot bring themselves to believe that any consensus reached by the well-meaning delegates to a UNESCO conference would be other than beneficial for mankind.

Alas, they are almost entirely wrong. Yet many of their countrymen do not realize this. Save for the one large issue of press freedom, the Western media pay almost no attention to UNESCO, and because our own senior foreign-policy makers nearly always have other matters on their mind, it is not apt to turn up on the evening news, at presidential press conferences, or in constituent mail to Congressmen. Within the intellectual communities, UNESCO is, for obvious reasons, rarely criticized from the Left. Although it is frequently attacked from the Right, the attackers usually take for granted that the United States should withdraw entirely from all UN activities; as a result, they are not obliged to pay serious attention to what actually happens in Paris and tend therefore to depict UNESCO as if it were a primitive society or alien planet with little relevance or consequence for the United States. There is, however, a further explanation for obliviousness among Western elites to the doings of UNESCO, and it is more insidious: the countries that do take UNESCO seriously have figured out how to manipulate the language of liberalism, to exploit the cultural neuroses of the Western democracies, and to take advantage of the West's moral commitment to even-handedness.

Accordingly, UNESCO has become a place where words we value take on strange meanings and where concepts we esteem are turned inside-out. But these days hostile ideas are no longer displayed in the rhetorical garb of Stalinist diatribes or the harangues of the cultural revolution. Besides the now-familiar international euphemisms—terrorist bands that are called liberation movements, and an array of brutal despotisms that style themselves "democratic republics"—UNESCO has a linguistic code of its own. Though written nowhere, it is regularly employed by participants in UNESCO gatherings, often with a wink or grin to signal that the user knows exactly what he is doing. In this code, "peace" is understood to refer to a condition that the Soviet Union favors and that the United States opposes. The "arms race" is actually not a race at all, for only the Western democracies are running in it, and it is well known that their purpose is not to safeguard their own security but to squander resources that would otherwise be transferred to the Third World as part of the "new international economic order." "Interference in the internal affairs of states" is what the United States engages in when it calls attention to human-rights violations in the Soviet Union, not what Moscow is doing in Afghanistan or Cuba in Central America. "Nazism and neo-Nazism" are widespread contemporary Western ideologies that pose imminent threats to peace, human rights, and international understanding. The one concept with some moral force that for a long time could reasonably be said to belong to the West, "human rights and fundamental freedoms," has now been diluted and vitiated by the inclusion of the "rights of peoples," a bit of code that skillfully tranforms individual rights into group interests and makes the state their source and arbiter rather than itself the creature of citizens whose rights are antecedent and inalienable.

Included among the rights of peoples is the "right to development," which confers on nations and groups that have not succeeded at economic development the moral authority to claim the resources of those that have. This sometimes includes the right to a paid vacation, a notion that has attained rough parity with individual liberty in recent UN covenants and pronouncements. . . .

The United States should either take UNESCO seriously or it should get out. We should try the former before considering the latter, but either course of action is preferable to legitimizing and subsidizing the steady erosion of the fundamental principles that undergirded the creation of UNESCO itself—and congratulating ourselves after every conference that the erosion was not even more severe and that we were therefore able to join in the "consensus" that produced it. To be sure, we occasionally vote against specific resolutions—in Paris we demanded the chance in plenary session to vote against aid to terrorism—and we often voice formal "reservations" and informal regrets about various agreements reached through the consensual process. But that is not taking UNESCO seriously; rather, it is the substitution of symbolic protests for serious action, and is widely perceived as such by other delegations.

As a wise and worldly Western ambassador pointed out in Paris, only three kinds of power have direct influence on UNESCO. The first is the ability to command a majority of the votes. This we have not had for many years. The second is the cooperation of the Director General and the Secretariat. This we conspicuously lack. The third is the leverage of money, potentially provided by the 25 percent of UNESCO's budget

that the United States alone contributes, which would be increased to about half if all the industrial democracies acted in concert. . . .

Wielding purse-string power may seem crude and heavy-handed, and it is certainly not the approach favored by most diplomats, but if accompanied by a long-term strategy of asserting democratic values with clarity and conviction, of setting forth the programs we favor and pressing for the policies we respect, of creating situations in which there are costs and consequences associated with repudiating American interests and gutting Western initiatives, the formulation of each biennial American payment to UNESCO could become a major occasion for the defense of human rights and the promotion of freedom.

Of at least equal promise, however, is wider awareness within the United States that UNESCO is a place where sophisticated ideological warfare is constantly being waged for influence over "the minds of men." In recent years, the ideas of freedom, of liberal democracy, of education as a quest for truth, and of inalienable individual human rights have lost nearly all of these battles, such that the values enshrined in the UNESCO constitution are now routinely dishonored by the organization that they created. But if UNESCO's founders were even partly justified in their characteristically Western and enormously hopeful linkage of truth and knowledge to peace and freedom, then the stakes are large enough to justify our close attention to what is said and done on the Place de Fontenoy.

For the defeats suffered by truth and freedom in those corridors and conference rooms have not been administered by a superior ideology or by the force of worldwide public opinion. Rather, they have been the result of lies and distortions successfully perpetrated by regimes that fear truth and despise freedom above all else. But the societies that embody truth and freedom in their own routine arrangements have engaged in something like unilateral disarmament on the very fields of international discourse where these principles undergo the most savage attacks.

Unlike other aspects of our national defense, taking UNESCO seriously does not cost money. It risks no lives. It entails no covert operations. It requires no silos, submarines, or spy satellites. It diverts no funds from social programs.

But taking UNESCO seriously does demand the lavish application of two resources that are in short supply. First, it requires the time and attention of those who make foreign policy for the United States, in both the executive branch and the Congress, for only in that way can we develop a longterm UNESCO strategy that is harmonized with our overall domestic values and international objectives, much as the Soviet Union has long done. We should, for example, have already taken steps to insure that our actions at the UNESCO General Conference in September would be reinforced by positions taken in other international bodies, in our bilateral relations with individual nations, in NATO foreign-minister sessions, and even in "summit" meetings such as the recent Williamsburg gathering. It little avails us to send a capable ambassador to Paris if UNESCO is to be regarded as a remote policy enclave, if its decision-making sessions are treated as isolated episodes, and if the tactics employed in what is essentially a battle of ideas are the products of a bureaucracy that instinctively opts for compromise, invisibility, and damage control. Having a UNESCO strategy means forcefully asserting democratic values and principles, even at the cost of losing votes in Paris, and responding to such losses in ways that encourage other nations—and the UNESCO leadership—to entertain doubts about the wisdom of having inflicted them.

Second, taking UNESCO seriously demands the sustained interest of non-governmental leaders—from business, labor, science, the academy, the media, and the major cultural institutions—in the effective advocacy of the values of liberal democracy in international arenas. Because it deals with intellectual, cultural, and scientific matters, UNESCO is perhaps the least governmental of all the multinational organizations. But so long as UNESCO is ignored, dismissed, idealized, or simply condemned by the heirs and descendants of those who created it, the principles on which it was founded will continue to be eroded, and the United States, which rests on the selfsame principles, will continue to be weakened.

1984

92.

Michael Harrington and W. Warren Wagar: Nineteen Eighty-Four

George Orwell's novel of totalitarian horror, Nineteen Eighty-Four, *was published in 1949. In the years between its date of publication and the date of its title, some ten million copies of the book were sold, and it achieved a quasi-mythical status as a prophecy of things to come. At the beginning of 1984, many comments were published by persons either asserting that the world had become more or less what Orwell had said it would, or denying this vociferously, even indignantly. Still others—for example, Norman Podhoretz in* Reader's Digest—*objected that the furor about the novel masked an attempt to gloss over the real differences between East and West. Reprinted here are two exemplary articles that take opposite sides of the controversy. Michael Harrington is a political scientist and a socialist, the author of a tough book about the poor in America, titled* The Other America. *W. Warren Wagar is a professor of history at the State University of New York at Binghamton; he is a frequent commentator on futurist writings.*

Sources: "That Year Is Here," *Maclean's,* January 9, 1984.

"The Year That Never Came," *The Futurist,* December 1983.

A: MICHAEL HARRINGTON
THAT YEAR IS HERE

The conventional view of George Orwell's *Nineteen Eighty-Four* is that it fictionalized the despotism of an alien and distant police state like the Soviet Union and other Communist countries. For conservatives, it is comforting to read Orwell's novel as an anti-Commu-nist horror story which also proves that socialism, however well intentioned, inevitably leads to the Gulag. But the book is set in England, not the Soviet Union; the totalitarianism it describes is explained as the outcome of a dynamic within Western society itself; and its author lived and died a democratic socialist. In short, Orwell's vision is much more subtle than it might seem.

It is the analysis of Orwell's fictional character Emmanuel Goldstein that, in effect, explains the rise of Big Brother and why the book is about the West as well as the East. There is, that theory suggests, a new form of class society on the horizon, and it is antisocialist as well as anticapitalist. In it the state owns the means of production, and a bureaucratic elite "owns" the state by virtue of a totalitarian monopoly of political power—and it uses that power for its own purposes. Worse, that new bureaucratic collectivism is not the product of Communist invasion or subversion but of tendencies within democracy itself.

Assume that was indeed Orwell's meaning. Does his vision of a totalitarian society apply to the West today? In its literal details, of course not; in its dramatic simplification of trends very much at work today, yes.

In the West democracy persists in 1984, and that is an enormous accomplishment. But at the same time there is a politicization of basic economic decisions which often transfers the crucial choices to corporate and government technocrats, who make them behind closed doors. In fact, those countries are becoming more collectivist even if some of their leaders sing hymns to Adam Smith in the process. Margaret Thatcher spends a higher percentage of the GNP in the public sector than any Labour government ever did; a single year of Ronald Reagan's deficits total more than four years of Jimmy Carter's. And in the United States, when the publicly owned Tennessee Valley Authority followed utterly irresponsible environmental policies in the 1950s and 1960s, the motive was not capitalist profit but bureaucratic and elite power.

But is it not an unpardonable blurring of differences to put Canada and the United States, with their democratic liberties, in the same category as the Soviet Union? In part, it is, and where freedom is concerned there should be no careless equations between flawed democracy and totalitarianism. But in part, there is a sense in which the East and West, for all of the significant differences between them, show certain converging tendencies. The problem is that Orwell the novelist obscured the subtlety of the insight of Orwell the analyst of society. And to correct that error we have to exercise our imaginations as well as our minds.

The totalitarianism of *Nineteen Eighty-Four* is English—but all the details are Russian, right down to details taken from the purge trials in the 1930s. As a result, Orwell fails to exploit the potential of his own daring insight into the totalitarian potential of Western society. During the 1930s, the American fascist Lawrence Dennis said that if fascism ever came to the United States it might call itself antifascism. So too with bureaucratic collectivism. If it did come to North America, it would hardly spell its name in the letters of the Cyrillic alphabet. So one must be prepared to imagine that corporate bureaucrats spouting talk of free enterprise and bespectacled technocrats in the government may be our functional equivalent of the Party in Orwell's *Nineteen Eighty-Four*.

Clearly, it has not come to that yet, but think of just a few of the current trends that make Orwell disturbingly relevant. With the crisis in the world economy—the intersecting transformation of a radically changing world division of labor, the multinationalization of corporate power and technological revolution—every government in the Western world is playing more and more of a directing role in industry. Will that further fuse political and economic power, excluding the people from effective participation in decisions that dominate their lives? That is certainly not inevitable, but it is possible and quite Orwellian.

This notion of a distinctively Western, even seemingly democratic, *Nineteen Eighty-Four* applies to another of Orwell's images. Canadians and Americans are not under the surveillance of official television cameras in their living rooms like the people in the novel. We are, however, increasingly shadowed in other ways, and perhaps more effectively. Consider the social insurance number. It began, innocently enough, as an identification number for the computing of government retirement benefits. It has now become a universal citizen's number, the code that gives access to the enormous data banks about every citizen. It is used by banks, universities, credit card companies, intelligence services, tax and immigration authorities.

There, too, one sees the possibility of a genteel, discreet—"Western"—totalitarianism. A television camera in one's living room is obtrusive, obvious, to be resented; a social insurance number is functional, innocuous *and* the means of a computerized surveillance of the individual.

When one turns from those matters of individual freedom to the fate of the world as portrayed in *Nineteen Eighty-Four*, there are still more disquieting echoes of our present. Orwell's three superpowers—Oceania, Eurasia and Eastasia—are locked in a curiously symbiotic relationship. None of them wants to defeat the other because victory would deprive them of the rationale for internal security that constant war provides. There is much that is dated in that notion—and much that is embarrass-

ingly valuable. Consider the current U.S. commitment to developing the MX missile as a grisly case in point. Back in the 1960s Washington got the brilliant idea to steal a march on the Soviets: the United States would "Mirv" its missiles—that is, fit them out with Multiple Independently targeted Reentry Vehicles. That phrase, with its Orwellian Newspeak and Doublethink, is a delicate way of referring to clusters of city-destroying nuclear bombs. To the surprise and consternation of the U.S. strategists, the unscrupulous Soviets then Mirved *their* missiles, which then required Washington to come up with the MX to protect itself against its own technology. And so on, in a deadly minuet.

There is one more Orwellian anticipation of the present that is an even more complex combination of his being wrong and possibly right than those that have gone before. It has to do with the "Proles," with the docile working class in *Nineteen Eighty-Four*.

The Proles, it will be remembered, are not under the close surveillance of the Party because, as a Party leader tells Orwell's hero, they "will never revolt, not in a thousand years or a million." But Orwell's vision of a passive and unthreatening working class was, we now know, simply wrong. The East German workers in 1953, the Hungarians in 1956, the Czechs in 1968, and the Poles over and over again since 1956 have been anything but passive. And in the West, there have been the tremendous bursts of labor energy like the French general strike of 1973. So Orwell's error was serious and uncharacteristic.

But Orwell could become right if several current trends escalate. There are now attacks throughout the West on historic gains made by working people and even attempts at de-unionization. At the same time, most projections of the future of Western social structure see a society divided between a trained elite and an untrained class doing the dirty work, with little in between. And there is now emerging, in every single Western country, an "underclass" of the marginalized and excluded, many of them members of minority groups. If antiunionism prevails, if technological revolution shapes our social structure without a humane counterresponse, then, in a setting never dreamed of in Orwell's philosophy, his judgment on the Proles could come true. That is, Western genius might succeed in producing a despairing stratum that would be putty in the hands of the managerial elite.

I say "if" these things were to happen, and that gets to the last, and most crucial, point about *Nineteen Eighty-Four*. Orwell was not a fortune-teller of history, and if one reads his book like a deck of tarot cards or the palm of a human hand, the results will be plain silly. Rather, like all the serious prophets of the West, he foretold the present. Like Jeremiah, he said that *if* you persist in these ways, then you will make the future I sadly predict a possibility. But, again like Jeremiah, he spoke precisely, so that his own worst fears would not be realized. He still speaks to those of us who want to challenge the bureaucracies and elites with truly democratic politics. But that is not to ask that we resign ourselves to 1984 as a fate. It is to incite us to act against it.

B: W. WARREN WAGAR
THE YEAR THAT NEVER CAME

GEORGE ORWELL's novel *1984* is easily the most influential fictional scenario of the future published since World War II. Its vocabulary and world view have entered the consciousness of every halfway educated person in Western civilization. Unfortunately, it may have done more harm than good.

The first thing that needs saying about *1984* is that Orwell wrote it not as a venture in scientific forecasting but as one more operation in the war he had declared in 1936 on totalitarianism in general, and on Marxist-Leninist-Stalinist totalitarianism in particular. Almost all the techniques of behavioral control described or mentioned in *1984* already flourished, in some form, in Stalin's Russia in the 1930s and 1940s. Orwell made little effort to extrapolate from dehumanizing trends specific to Anglo-American life: His model for Oceania is unmistakably the USSR under Stalin.

Appearing in 1949, Orwell's novel immediately became what critic Isaac Deutscher once called "an ideological superweapon" in the Cold War. *1984* persuaded many thousands of readers that a Stalinesque regime would eventually arise in the West if the nations of the "Free World" did not maintain ceaseless vigilance against Soviet expansionism abroad and Marxist-Leninist subversion at home. On the assumption that dead was better than red, electorates in the Western countries were easily talked into supporting a broad array of anticommunist policies. Despite fluctuations in temperature, the Cold War is still being fought (on both sides), and *1984* is still doing its bit for the "Free World."

Of course this is not the whole story. *1984* is also a classic parable in defense of privacy and freedom. Most Western civil libertarians, whether neoconservative, liberal-centrist, or social-democratic, have embraced the novel and claimed its author as one of their own.

But the underpinnings of Orwell's fictional edifice are not what these enthusiastic Orwellians usually think. The man who wrote *1984* was a romantic, a Tory anarchist, a bundle of contradictions who had as little faith in the common man as he did in the intellectuals. Because he sought to dissuade his readers from putting their faith in the dominant structures and forces of modern industrial society, the futurists whose vision most nearly approaches Orwell's are those of the decentralist counterculture.

In any event, Orwell's year 1984 never arrived. The real world of 1984 bears little resemblance to it, and in many respects has veered off in the opposite direction. The crude Stalinism of the real 1940s and of Orwell's novel has not spread westward, nor has it survived in the Soviet Union. In the capitalist West, people are kept in line by managed affluence, not managed scarcity. The system continues to tolerate substantial dissent, because it is not fundamentally threatened by dissent. The result is not unlike what political scientist Bertram Gross labels "friendly fascism," spearheaded by the inexorable growth of the big multinational corporations. Such an order is far from utopian, but it is also far from the terrifying one-party superstate of Orwell's Oceania. The Western donkey keeps running because of carrots far more than sticks.

In the Soviet bloc, the totalitarian framework of government and economic life endures. But there is more latitude for the individual, not less, than under Stalin. The existence of a lively intellectual and artistic underground everywhere and the phenomenon of an independent labor movement in Poland bespeak the categorical failure of official Marxism-Leninism to turn human beings into Orwellian zombies.

Only in one respect, perhaps, does *1984* stand up as an anticipation of things to come. Orwell uses James Burnham's theory of a "managerial revolution" to explain the sociohistorical dynamics of the Inner Party in Oceania. O'Brien and his colleagues of the Inner Party were members of a new ruling class of managers and technicians, in the process of forging a new system of global management. I find this part of the novel persuasive, although it is weakly developed. Aldous Huxley had said it all before, and better, in *Brave New World.*

But at least Orwell made an effort. If his Big Brother is only a bogeyman from the 1940s, the myriad little brothers in their gray flannel suits are real, and they're coming our way.

In the main, however, *1984* is an object lesson for contemporary futurists, illuminating the perils of mindless extrapolation. Orwell oversimplified the future, in the service of his obsession with communism. We must take care not to oversimplify Orwell, in the service of liberty.

Big Brother has arrived, and he is your computer!

NORMAN LEAR

I know there's paranoia in the land about computers, but I don't think it's well placed. Far from being a tool of centralized control, I think the computer will become the very symbol of personal liberty.

JOHN NAISBITT

93.

Richard P. Turco, Owen B. Toon, Thomas P. Ackerman, James B. Pollack, and Carl Sagan: The Climatic Effects of Nuclear War

George Orwell's prophecies of the future, as described in his novel Nineteen Eighty-Four *(1949), were horrible, but none was quite so terrifying as the prospect of a nuclear winter described by the authors of this scholarly article from the August 1984 issue of* Scientific American. *The idea of a nuclear winter had been presented by the same writers in a 1983 issue of* Science. *The later version reprinted here (in part) goes into more detail about the possible climatic effects of even a "limited" nuclear war. A "nuclear winter," according to this analysis, would spell the end of global civilization and perhaps of the human species. At the time of the article's publication, Carl Sagan was a well-known interpreter of science for the general public and a professor of astronomy and space sciences at Cornell University. His associates were research scientists at NASA and at R&D Associates, Inc.*

Source: *Scientific American,* August 1984.

SINCE THE BEGINNING of the nuclear arms race four decades ago it has been generally assumed that the most devastating consequence of a major nuclear war between the U.S. and the U.S.S.R. would be a gigantic number of human casualties in the principal target zones of the Northern Hemisphere. Although in the wake of such a war the social and economic structure of the combatant nations would presumably collapse, it has been argued that most of the noncombatant nations—and hence the majority of the human population—would not be endangered, either directly or indirectly. Over the years questions have been raised about the possible global extent of various indirect, long-term effects of nuclear war, such as delayed radioactive fallout, depletion of the pro-

tective ozone layer in the upper atmosphere and adverse changes in the climate. Until recently, however, the few authoritative studies available on these added threats have tended to play down their significance, in some cases emphasizing the uncertainty inherent in any attempt to predict the combined effects of multiple nuclear explosions.

This comparatively optimistic view of the potential global impact of nuclear war may now have to be revised. Recent findings by our group, confirmed by workers in Europe, the U.S. and the U.S.S.R., suggest that the long-term climatic effects of a major nuclear war are likely to be much severer and fartherreaching than had been supposed. In the aftermath of such a war vast areas of the earth could be subjected to prolonged darkness, abnormally low temperatures, violent windstorms, toxic smog and persistent radioactive fallout—in short, the combination of conditions that has come to be known as "nuclear winter." The physical effects of nuclear war would be compounded by the widespread breakdown of transportation systems, power grids, agricultural production, food processing, medical care, sanitation, civil services and central government. Even in regions far from the conflict the survivors would be imperiled by starvation, hypothermia, radiation sickness, weakening of the human immune system, epidemics and other dire consequences. Under some circumstances, a number of biologists and ecologists contend, the extinction of many species of organisms—including the human species—is a real possibility.

Our own involvement in the reassessment of the global effects of nuclear war originated in a confluence of several lines of inquiry. Before joining forces we had separately and collectively been engaged in research on such phenomena as dust storms on Mars and the climatic effects of explosive volcanic eruptions on the earth; more recently we all became interested in the hypothesis that one or more of the mass extinctions of species evident in the geologic record were caused by immense clouds of dust raised by the impact of an asteroid or a comet. In 1982 a committee of the National Academy of Sciences, recognizing the parallels between the dust raised by nuclear explosions and that raised by other cataclysmic events, such as volcanic eruptions and meteorite impacts, asked us to look into the possible climatic effects of the dust likely to result from a nuclear war. We had already been considering the question, and to address it further we had at our dis-

posal sophisticated computer models of both large- and small-scale atmospheric phenomena; the models had been developed over the preceding decade primarily to study the origins, properties and effects of particles in the atmosphere.

At about the same time another important aspect of the question came to our attention. An article in the Swedish environmental journal *Ambio,* coauthored by Paul J. Crutzen of the Max Planck Institute for Chemistry at Mainz in West Germany and John W. Birks of the University of Colorado at Boulder, pointed out that fires ignited by nuclear explosions could generate massive amounts of smoke, severely attenuating the sunlight reaching the ground. Accordingly we added smoke to dust as a likely perturbing influence of nuclear war on the climate.

In brief, our initial results, published in *Science* in December, 1983, showed that "the potential global atmospheric and climatic consequences of nuclear war . . . are serious. Significant hemispherical attenuation of the solar radiation flux and subfreezing land temperatures may be caused by fine dust raised in high-yield nuclear surface bursts and by smoke from city and forest fires ignited by airbursts of all yields." Moreover, we found that long-term exposure to nuclear radiation from the radioactive fallout of a nuclear war in the Northern Hemisphere could be an order of magnitude greater than previous studies had indicated; the radioactivity, like the other nuclear-winter effects, could even extend deep into the Southern Hemisphere. "When combined with the prompt destruction from nuclear blast, fires and fallout and the later enhancement of solar ultraviolet radiation due to ozone depletion," we concluded, "long-term exposure to cold, dark and radioactivity could pose a serious threat to human survivors and to other species." Subsequent studies, based on more powerful models of the general circulation of the earth's atmosphere, have tended to confirm both the validity of our investigative approach and the main thrust of our findings. In what follows we shall review the current state of knowledge on this vital issue.

Before one can understand the climatic effects of nuclear war one must first understand how the Earth's radiation budget is normally balanced. The amount of sunlight absorbed by the atmosphere and the surface of the earth, averaged over time, is equal to the amount of thermal radiation emitted back into space. Because the intensity of the thermal radiation varies as the fourth power of the temperature, both the surface temperature and the atmospheric temperature can adjust fairly quickly to maintain the overall energy balance between the solar energy gained and the thermal energy lost.

If the earth were an airless body like the moon, its surface would radiate the absorbed solar energy directly into space. In this case the globally averaged temperature of the earth would be well below the freezing point of water, and life as we know it could not exist on our planet. Fortunately the earth has an atmosphere, which absorbs and traps some of the heat emitted by the surface, thereby raising the average ground-level temperature to well above freezing and providing a favorable enrionment for forms of life, such as ours, that are based on liquid water.

The thermal insulation of the earth's surface by the atmosphere—the "greenhouse effect"—arises from the fact that sunlight passes through the atmosphere more readily than thermal radiation does. The radiation emitted by the sun is mainly in the visible part of the electromagnetic spectrum, whereas the thermal radiation emitted by the earth's surface is concentrated in the infrared part. The main infrared-absorbing components of the atmosphere are water (in the form of ice crystals, liquid droplets and vapor) and carbon dioxide gas, both of which are essentially transparent to visible light. Hence the atmosphere generally acts as a window for sunlight but as a blanket for heat.

Under normal conditions the temperature of the troposphere, or lower atmosphere, decreases gradually with increasing altitude up to a height of about 12 kilometers, the boundary called the tropopause. Heat from the earth's surface is transferred upward though the atmosphere by several mechanisms: thermal radiation, small-scale turbulence, large-scale convection and the release of latent heat through the condensation of ascending water vapor. In a purely radiative atmosphere (that is, one in which the air does not move vertically and all the energy is transferred by radiation) the lower layers of air, where most of the solar energy is absorbed, would be warmer than the higher layers; in this situation the upward thermal radiation would exceed the downward thermal radiation, allowing the excess heat to escape into space. If the opacity of the atmosphere to infrared radiation were to increase (with no change in the opacity to visible light), the temperature would increase. For example, if carbon dioxide, a good infrared absorber, were added to the atmosphere in sufficient quantities, it would warm the surface.

Conversely, if some component of the atmosphere were to reduce the amount of sunlight reaching the surface without significantly increasing the infrared opacity, the ground temperature would decrease. For example, if all the sunlight were absorbed high in the atmosphere and none reached the ground, and if the surface could radiate energy to space without hindrance, the surface temperature would fall to that of an airless planet. If the absorption of solar energy were to take place above most of the atmosphere, the earth's radiation budget would be balanced without the green-house effect. (Accordingly we refer to this condition as the "anti-green-house effect.") Below the layer where the sunlight was absorbed the temperature of the atmosphere would not vary with altitude: at each lower level the upward infrared flux would equal the downward infrared flux and the net energy transfer would be negligible.

Particles in the atmosphere can affect the earth's radiation balance in several ways: by absorbing sunlight, by reflecting sunlight back into space and by absorbing or emitting infrared radiation. In general a cloud of fine particles—an aerosol—tends to warm the atmospheric layer it occupies, but it can either warm or cool the underlying layers and the surface, depending on whether the particles absorb infrared radiation more readily than they reflect and/or absorb visible light.

The anti-greenhouse effect of an aerosol is maximized for particles that are highly absorbing at visible wavelengths. Thus much less sunlight reaches the surface when an aerosol consists of dark particles such as soot, which strongly absorb visible light, than when an aerosol consists of bright particles such as soil dust, which mainly scatter the light. Consequently in evaluating the possible climatic effects of a nuclear war particular concern should be focused on the soot particles that are generated by fires, since soot is one of the few common particulate materials that absorb visible light much more strongly than they absorb infrared radiation.

How much an aerosol will cool the surface (by blocking sunlight) or warm the surface (by enhancing the greenhouse effect) depends on the size of the particles. If the average diameter of the particles is less than a typical infrared wavelength (about 10 micrometers), the infrared opacity of the aerosol will be less than its visible opacity. Accordingly an aerosol of very fine particles that even weakly absorb sunlight should have a visible effect greater than its infrared effect, giving rise to a significant cooling of the lower atmospheric layers and the surface. In the case of soot this is true even for somewhat larger particles.

The visible and infrared radiation effects associated with particle layers also depend on the thickness and density of the aerosol. The intensity of the sunlight reaching the ground decreases exponentially with the quantity of fine, absorbing particulate matter in the atmosphere. The infrared radiation reaching the ground, however, depends more on the air temperature than it does on the quantity of aerosol. Hence when a large amount of aerosol is present, the dominant climatic consequence tends to be strong surface cooling.

The "optical depth" of an aerosol (a measure of opacity equal to the negative natural logarithm of the attenuation of an incident light beam by absorption and scattering) serves as a convenient indicator of the aerosol's potential climatic effects. For example, a cloud with an optical depth of much less than 1 would cause only minor perturbations, since most of the light would reach the surface, whereas a cloud with an optical depth of 1 or more would cause a major disturbance, since most of the light would be absorbed in the atmosphere and/or scattered away into space. Although volcanic particles happen to have an optimal size for enhancing visible effects over infrared effects, the magnitude of the induced surface cooling is limited by the modest optical depth of volcanic aerosols (less than about .3) and by their very weak intrinsic absorption at visible wavelengths. Nevertheless, the largest volcanic clouds may disturb the earth's radiation balance enough to cause anomalous weather. Much more significant climatic disturbances could result from the huge clouds of dust that would be thrown into the atmosphere by the impact of an asteroid or a comet with a diameter of several kilometers or more. These dust clouds could have a very large optical depth, perhaps initially as high as 1,000.

The radiative effects of an aerosol on the temperature of a planet depend not only on the aerosol's optical depth, its visible absorptivity and the average size of its particles but also on the variation of these properties with time. The longer a significant optical depth can be sustained, the closer the surface temperature and the atmospheric temperature will move toward a new state of equilibrium. Normally it takes the surface of the ocean several years to respond to changes in the global radiation balance, because of the great heat capacity of the mixed uppermost layer of the ocean, which extends to a depth of about 100 meters. In contrast, the air temperature and the continental land temperature approach new equilibrium values in only a few months. In fact, when the atmosphere is strongly cooled, convection above the surface ceases and the

ground temperature falls rapidly by radiative cooling, reaching equilibrium in a few days or weeks. This happens naturally every night, although equilibrium is not reached in such a short period.

Particles are removed from the atmosphere by several processes: falling under the influence of gravity, sticking to the ground and other surfaces and scavenging by water clouds, rain and snow. The lifetime of particles against "wet" removal depends on the frequency of cloud formation and precipitation at various altitudes. In the first few kilometers of altitude in the normal atmosphere particles may in some places be washed out in a matter of days. In the upper troposphere (above five kilometers) the average lifetime of the particles increases to several weeks or more. Still higher, in the stratosphere (above 12 kilometers), water clouds rarely form and so the lifetime of small particles is typically a year or more. Stratospheric removal is primarily by gravitational settling and the large-scale convective transport of the particles. The deposition of particles on surfaces is very inefficient for average-size smoke and dust particles, requiring several months for significant depletion.

Clearly the height at which particles are injected into the atmosphere affects their residence time. In general, the higher the initial altitude, the longer the residence time in the normal atmosphere. Massive injections of soot and dust, however, may profoundly alter both the structure of the atmosphere and the rate of particle removal.

In our analysis of the climatic effects of nuclear war we have adopted a number of specific scenarios, based on what is publicly known about the effects of individual nuclear explosions, the size and deployment of the world's present nuclear arsenals and the nuclear-war-fighting plans of the U.S. and the U.S.S.R. Among the several dozen cases we have analyzed are a 100-megaton "countervalue" attack directed strictly against cities, a 3,000-megaton "counterforce" attack directed strictly against missile silos and a 10,000-megaton "full-scale exchange" directed against an assortment of targets on both sides. Our "base line" case is a 5,000-megaton nuclear exchange, with about 20 percent of the total explosive yield detonated over urban, suburban and industrial areas. All the postulated attack scenarios are well within the present capabilities of the two superpowers.

A nuclear explosion can readily ignite fires in either an urban or a rural setting. The flash of thermal radiation from the nuclear explosion, which has a spectrum similar to that of sunlight, accounts for about a third of the total energy yield of the explosion. The flash is so intense that a variety of combustible materials are ignited spontaneously at ranges of 10 kilometers or more from a one-megaton air burst detonated at a nominal altitude of a kilometer. The blast wave from the explosion would extinguish many of the initial fires, but it would also start numerous secondary fires by disrupting open flames, rupturing gas lines and fuel storage tanks and causing electrical and mechanical sparks. The destruction resulting from the blast wave would also hamper effective fire fighting and so promote the spread of both the primary and the secondary fires. Based on the known incendiary effects of the nuclear explosions over Hiroshima and Nagasaki in 1945 it can be projected that the fires likely to be caused by just one of the far more powerful strategic nuclear weapons available today would extend over an area of from tens to hundreds of square kilometers.

Nuclear explosions over forests and grasslands could also ignite large fires, but this situation is more difficult to evaluate. Among the factors that affect fires in wilderness areas are the humidity, the moisture content of the fuel, the amount of the fuel and the velocity of the wind. Roughly a third of the land area in the North Temperate Zone is covered by forest, and an equal area is covered by brush and grassland. Violent wildfires have been known to spread over tens of thousands of square kilometers from a few ignition points; in the absence of a nuclear war such fires occur about once every decade. Although most wildfires generated by nuclear explosions would probably be confined to the immediate area exposed to the intense thermal flash, it is possible that much larger ones would be started by multiple explosions over scattered military targets such as missile silos.

The total amount of smoke likely to be generated by a nuclear war depends on, among other things, the total yield of the nuclear weapons exploded over each type of target, the efficiency of the explosions in igniting fires, the average area ignited per megaton of yield, the average amount of combustible material in the irradiated region, the fraction of the combustible material consumed by the fires, the ratio of the amount of smoke produced to the amount of fuel burned and the fraction of the smoke that is eventually entrained into the global atmospheric circulation after local rainfall has removed its share. By assigning the most likely values to these parameters for a nuclear war involving less than 40 percent of the strategic arsenals of the two superpowers we were

Smoke from a forest fire like this consists of very fine oily particles that hang in the air and block out sunlight over a small area.

able to calculate that the total smoke emission from a full-scale nuclear exchange could easily exceed 100 million metric tons. In many respects this is a conservative estimate. Crutzen and his co-workers Ian Galbally of the Commonwealth Scientific and Industrial Research Organization (CSIRO) in Australia and Christoph Brühl of the Max Planck Institute at Mainz have recently estimated that the total smoke emission from a full-scale nuclear war would be closer to 300 million tons.

One hundred million tons of smoke, if it were distributed as a uniform cloud over the entire globe, could reduce the intensity of sunlight reaching the ground by as much as 95 percent. The initial clouds would not cover the entire globe, however, and so large areas of the Northern Hemisphere, particularly in the target zones, would be even darker; at noon the light level in these areas could be as low as that of a moonlit night. Daytime darkness in this range, if it persisted for weeks or months, would trigger a climatic catastrophe. Indeed, significant disturbances might be caused by much smaller amounts of smoke.

Wildfires normally inject smoke into the lower atmosphere to an altitude of five or six kilometers. In contrast, large urban fires have been known to inject smoke into the upper troposphere, probably as high as 12 kilometers. The unprecedented scale of the fires likely to be ignited by large nuclear explosions and the complex convective activity generated by multiple explosions might cause some of the smoke to rise even higher. Studies of the dynamics of very large fires suggest that individual smoke plumes might reach as high as 20 kilometers, well into the stratosphere.

During the World War II bombing of Hamburg the center of the city was gutted by an intense firestorm, with heat-generated winds of hurricane force sweeping inward from all directions at ground level. Rapid heat release over a large area can create fire vortexes, heat tornadoes and cyclones with towering convective columns. The sheer intensity of such fires might act to reduce the smoke emission considerably through two processes: the oxidation of carbonaceous smoke particles at the extremely high temperatures generated in the fire zone and the washout of smoke particles by precipitation formed in the convective column. Both effects were taken into account in our estimates of the total smoke emission from a nuclear war.

The climatic impact of smoke depends on its optical properties, which in turn are sensitive to the size, shape and composition of the smoke particles. The most effective light-screening smoke consists of particles with a radius of about .1 micrometer and a very sooty composition rich in graphite. The least effective smoke in attenuating sunlight consists of particles larger than .5 micrometer with a predominantly oily composition. The smoke from a forest fire is typically composed of extremely fine oily particles, whereas the smoke from an urban fire consists of larger agglomerations of sooty particles. Smoke from fierce fires usually contains large particles of ash, char, dust and other debris, which is swept up by the heat-generated winds. The largest of these particles fall out of the smoke clouds just downwind of the fire. Although very intense fires produce less smoke, they lift more fine dust and may burn metals such as aluminum and chromium, which efficiently generate fine aerosols.

The release of toxic compounds in urban fires has not been adequately studied. It is well known that many people who have died in accidental fires have been poisoned by toxic gases. In addition to carbon monoxide, which is produced copiously in many fires, hydrogen cyanide and hydrogen chloride are generated when the synthetic compounds in modern building materials and furnishings burn. If large stores of organic chemicals are released and burned in a nuclear conflict, additional airborne toxins would be generated.

The possibility that vast areas could be contaminated by such pyrotoxins, adsorbed on the surface of smoke, ash and dust particles and carried great distances by winds, needs further investigation.

Nuclear explosions at or near ground level throw up huge amounts of dust. The principal dust-forming mechanisms include the ejection and disaggregation of soil particles from the crater formed by the explosion; the vaporization and subsequent renucleation of soil and rock, and the lifting of surface dust and smoke. A one-megaton explosion on land can excavate a crater hundreds of meters in diameter, eject several million tons of debris, lift between 100,000 and 600,000 tons of soil to a high altitude and inject between 10,000 and 30,000 tons of submicrometer dust particles into the stratosphere. The height at which the dust is injected depends on the yield of the explosion: the dust clouds produced by explosions with a yield of less than about 100 kilotons will generally not penetrate into the stratosphere, whereas those from explosions with a yield of more than about a megaton will stabilize mainly within the stratosphere. Explosions above the ground can also raise large quantities of dust, which is vacuumed off the surface by the rising fireball. The combined effects of multiple explosions could enhance the total amount of dust raised to high altitudes.

The quantity of dust produced in a nuclear war would depend sensitively on the way the weapons were used. Ground bursts would be directed at hard targets, such as missile silos and underground command posts. Soft targets could be attacked by air bursts as well as ground bursts. There are more than 1,000 missile silos in the continental U.S. alone, and at least two Russian warheads are probably committed to each of them. Some 1,400 missile silos in the U.S.S.R. are similarly targeted by U.S. warheads. Air bases and secondary airfields, submarine pens and command and control facilities are among the many other strategic targets to which ground bursts might be assigned. In short, it seems quite possible that at least 4,000 megatons of high-yield weapons might be detonated at or near ground level even in a war in which cities were not targeted, and that roughly 120 million tons of submicrometer soil particles could be injected into the stratosphere in the North Temperate Zone. This is many times greater than all the submicrometer dust lifted into the stratosphere by the eruption of the volcano El Chichón in Mexico in 1982 and is comparable to the global submicrometer dust injections of much larger volcanic eruptions such as that of Tambora in 1815 and Krakatau in 1883.

Analogies between the atmospheric effects of a major volcanic explosion and a nuclear war are often made for convenience. Nevertheless, there is no straightforward way to scale the effects of a volcanic explosion against those of a series of nuclear detonations. The aerosol particles produced by volcanoes are fundamentally different in composition, size and shape from those produced by nuclear explosions. We have therefore based our calculations on the properties of dust measured directly in nuclear-explosion clouds.

The only proper comparison between a volcanic eruption and a nuclear explosion is the optical depth of the long-term aerosols that are produced. In fact, we utilized data on global "dust veils" generated by volcanic explosions to test and calibrate our climate models. In so

doing we have been able to account quantitatively for the hemispheric surface-cooling effect observed after major volcanic eruptions. The present nuclear-dust calculations are entirely consistent with observations of volcanic phenomena. For example, it is now clear that violent eruptions can lead to a significant climatic cooling for a year or more. Even so, in recorded history volcanoes have had only a rather modest climatic role. The fact that volcanoes are localized sources of dust limits their geographic influence; moreover, volcanoes inject comparatively little fine dust (and no soot) into the stratosphere. Nuclear explosions, on the other hand, are a powerful and efficient means of injecting large quantities of fine soot and dust into the atmosphere over large regions.

The atoms produced in the fission reactions of a nuclear explosion are often in unstable isotopic states. Radioactive decay from these states releases alpha, beta and gamma radiation. In most nuclear weapons at least half of the energy yield is generated by fission and the rest by fusion. About 300 distinct radioactive isotopes are produced. Most of them condense onto aerosols and dust formed in (or sucked into) the fireball. Accordingly the dust and the radioactivity generated by nuclear explosions are intimately related.

Of particular interest here are the prompt and the intermediate radioactive fallout. The former is associated with short-lived radioactive isotopes that condense onto large soil particles, which in turn fall to the ground within hours after an explosion. Intermediate fallout is associated with longer-lived radioactive isotopes carried by smaller particles that drift in the wind and are removed by settling and precipitation in the interval from days to months. Prompt fallout is generated by ground bursts, and intermediate fallout is generated by ground bursts and air bursts in the yield range from 10 to 500 kilotons, which deposit their radioactivity in the middle and upper troposphere.

The danger from radioactive fallout is measured in terms of the total dose in rads (a unit of radiation exposure equivalent to 100 ergs of ionizing energy deposited in one gram of tissue), the dose rate in rads per hour and the type of radiation. The most deadly effects are caused by the intense, penetrating gamma radiation from prompt fallout. The widespread intermediate fallout delivers a less potent long-term gamma-ray dose. A whole-body gamma-ray exposure of 450 rads, received over several days, is lethal to half of the healthy adults exposed. Chronic doses of 100 rads or more from intermediate fallout could suppress the immune system even of healthy people and would cause long-term increments in the incidence of cancer, genetic defects and other diseases.

Our most recent studies of the effects of radioactive fallout in our baseline case indicate that the prompt fallout could contaminate millions of square kilometers of land with lethal radioactivity. The intermediate fallout would blanket at least the North Temperate Zone, producing average long-term, whole-body gamma-ray exposures of about 50 rads in unprotected populations. Internal exposures of specific organs to biologically active radioactive isotopes such as strontium 90 and iodine 131, which enter the food chain, could double or triple the total doses. According to Joseph B. Knox of the Lawrence Livermore National Laboratory, if nuclear power plants were targeted directly, the average long-term

gamma-ray dose could be increased to several hundred rads or more.

The computer models we have employed to define the potential magnitude of the long-term global aftereffects of nuclear war are one-dimensional: they treat only the vertical structure of the atmosphere. Obviously the atmosphere is a complex three-dimensional system whose intricate interactions determine its response to perturbations. At present, however, there are no three-dimensional models with the appropriate features to treat the nuclear winter problem with high precision, although several such models are under development. The existing models of the climate and the general circulation of the atmosphere incorporate a number of empirical approaches to physical processes that are not well understood. In the nuclear-winter scenario the climate is so seriously perturbed that such treatments are of dubious applicability.

Our approach has therefore been to estimate the first-order effects through detailed microphysical, chemical and optical calculations in a one-dimensional format. Even this simplified approach had not been attempted before our work, and it was not clear then that more sophisticated three-dimensional work was justified. Based on the predicted first-order one-dimensional effects, the principal three-dimensional meteorological interactions that would have to be treated in more refined studies were deduced. The three-dimensional results generally confirm our one-dimensional results. . . .

There are many additional questions about nuclear winter that remain to be answered. With rapid surface cooling widespread fogs would develop, and they might affect the radiation balance at the surface. The presence of millions of tons of nuclear debris in the atmosphere could modify the properties of cloud droplets and so the removal rate of the debris. The nuclear clouds and modified natural clouds would also affect the overall infrared-radiation balance of the atmosphere, but the implications for surface temperatures remain uncertain. Daily variations, which have not yet been treated in the climate models applied to the nuclear-war problem, could also influence the dynamics and removal of the nuclear debris. Water injected by nuclear explosions and fires might affect atmospheric chemical and radiative processes. All these effects are important second-order refinements of the basic climatic theory of the nuclear winter. On the basis of the existing scientific evidence, however, none of these effects appears to be capable of significantly altering the major climatic impacts now predicted for a nuclear war.

There is also a lack of understanding of the interactions of the atmosphere with the oceans, which may have a major influence on short-term climatic changes. Through what was perhaps a series of coincidences, the eruption of El Chichón in the spring of 1982 was followed by an unusually intense El Niño warming of the South Pacific in the winter of 1982 and spring of 1983, associated with an unexpected calming of the southerly trade winds. These events were followed by unusual weather in North America and Europe in the winter of 1982 and throughout 1983. Most of North America suffered record-breaking cold that winter, and Europe enjoyed a balmy spring in December. Although proof that these events were related is lacking, the evidence suggests a potentially significant coupling of ocean currents, winds and

weather on a comparatively short time scale; such a relation has yet to be defined rigorously.

Our study also considered a number of secondary climatic effects of nuclear war. Changes in the albedo, or reflectivity, of the earth's surface can be caused by widespread fires, by the deposition of soot on snow and ice and by regional modifications of vegetation. Short-term changes in albedo were evaluated and found to be unimportant compared with the screening of sunlight. If significant semipermanent albedo changes were to occur, long-term climatic shifts could ensue. On the other hand, the vast oceanic heat source would act to force the climate toward contemporary norms following any major disturbance. Accordingly we have tentatively concluded that a nuclear war is not likely to be followed by an ice age.

We have also analyzed the climatic effects caused by changes in the gaseous composition of the atmosphere. The maximum hemispheric temperature perturbation associated with the production of oxides of nitrogen and the accompanying depletion of ozone is a cooling of no more than a few degrees C. The concentrations of greenhouse-effect gases would also be modified by a nuclear war; such gases might produce a surface warming of several degrees after the smoke and dust had cleared. These mutually offsetting temperature perturbations are uncertain, however, because the chemical and physical changes in the atmosphere caused by a nuclear war would be coupled through processes that are not adequately treated in existing models. Further analysis is clearly needed on this point.

Of course, the actual consequences of a nuclear war can never be precisely foreseen. Synergistic interactions among individual physical stresses might compound the problem of survival for many organisms. The long-term destruction of the global ecosystem might in the end prove even more devastating for the human species than the awesome short-term destructive effects of nuclear explosions and their radioactive fallout. The strategic policies of both superpowers and their respective military alliances should be reassessed in this new light.

94.

Politics and Bathhouses

In May 1983 the Acquired Immune Deficiency Syndrome (AIDS) was officially declared by the United States government as the country's preeminent medical priority. Certain subgroups within the population who had suffered the most from it had already come to that conclusion. These included homosexuals, Haitians, hemophiliacs, and intravenous drug users. The fact that homosexuals initially were the hardest hit led in the early 1980s to vexing legal, social, religious, and moral problems. An example of the sort of political problems that arose is revealed in this January 1984 article from The San Francisco Chronicle. *San Francisco was one of the few places in the United States where homosexuals wielded significant political power.*

Source: "Politics and Bathhouses: Local Complexities," *San Francisco Chronicle,* January 15, 1984.

RECENT RUMORS that AIDS patients were cavorting in San Francisco's bathhouses presented Dr. Selma Dritz, of the city's Bureau of Communicable Diseases, with one of the most complicated dilemmas she had faced in nearly two decades of work in public health.

"There were questions of civil rights and privacy, up against the problem of protecting the public health," Dritz recalled recently. "We didn't know which way to turn."

A deputy city attorney eventually ruled that the medical uncertainties surrounding AIDS precluded any action by the city: Authorities can't keep AIDS patients out of bathhouses—in effect, quarantine them—because scientists don't know exactly what causes the disorder.

Still, the entire issue demonstrates what enormous complexities a syndrome sexually transmitted among an unconventional minority poses for local health authorities.

The course of policy-making over this uncertain terrain has been rocky. While federal efforts to fight AIDS floundered because gays wield so little clout on the national level, local efforts to deal with the syndrome in San Francisco floundered because gays have so much power that health officials were worried about angering the political Goliath.

The city's confusion about how to deal with gay bathhouses was a prime example. From the start, studies have shown that AIDS victims tend to be the men who engage in frequent anonymous sex at bathhouses. AIDS researchers make little secret of the fact that they consider baths to be breeding grounds of the syndrome. Pragmatic homosexual activists wouldn't mind seeing the baths closed. Gay radicals, however, have loudly maintained that gays have a right to be promiscuous, even if it means contracting AIDS.

Caught between warring gay factions, the Department of Public Health stalled on making any moves that might be controversial. Dr. Mervyn Silverman, the public health director, first said he did not have the authority to require baths to post warnings about AIDS, but changed his mind after Mayor Dianne Feinstein and a majority of the board of supervisors clamored for such warnings.

"The information people listen to is what comes from their own peers," said Silverman when he announced he would require AIDS pamphlets in baths last summer. "We'd have a very hard time getting into the business of telling people how to have sex."

AIDS researchers, who have to confront the dead and dying on a daily basis, insist that officials do need to tackle the sexual issue head-on; sex is clearly the major mode of transmission in a city where more than 95 percent of AIDS victims are gay or bisexual men.

"The baths should be locked up—or at least there should be giant signs in big red letters saying 'This Place Can Kill You,'" says one prominent AIDS researcher, who asked not to be named. "But they won't do it. They're pussy-

footing around this because of politics."

It would be hard to avoid politics with AIDS in San Francisco, the site of the largest and most politically powerful gay community in the country. During the first two years of the epidemic, for example, the health department's AIDS efforts were coordinated by Pat Norman, a lesbian who was then preparing her current campaign for a seat on the board of supervisors. Norman gave AIDS a low profile, she says, because she didn't want to engender hysteria; her detractors say she didn't want to muddy the waters of her own political future. No matter why, the health department did not even put together an AIDS brochure until May 1983, more than two years after AIDS was detected here.

For all the barbs San Francisco officials have faced, a Chronicle survey of other major American cities has found that San Francisco's handling of AIDS is considered the national prototype. Chicago has not allocated any funds at all for public education. Los Angeles got its AIDS program off the ground only last fall. New York City, with about half the nation's AIDS cases, has spent $1 million for its non-hospital health activities relating to AIDS.

San Francisco has also aggressively conducted the best epidemiology on AIDS in the country, work that some scientists say is more comprehensive than that done by the federal Centers for Disease Control. Because relations between public health officials and gay physicians have long been cordial, cooperation has marked efforts by health authorities to monitor information about the spread of AIDS. In New York City, where gay physicians are far more suspicious of health officials, some gay doctors have simply refused to report

AIDS cases, throwing attempts to chart national AIDS trends into disarray.

The headaches for local jurisdictions may only be starting. The costliest aspects of AIDS involve hospital treatment for patients who lack health insurance. Patient services consume most of the $4 million San Francisco is spending on AIDS this year. New York City is spending $30,000 a day to treat patients, and officials expect this sum to soar higher as patients diagnosed within the past year begin needing hospital care. "It's going to be a staggering cost," said Marvin Bogner, assistant health commissioner for New York City. "We're terribly concerned."

Mayor Dianne Feinstein, who heads the U.S. Conference of Mayors AIDS Task Force, has asked the federal government to help cities pay for the immense costs of hospital care. Secretary Margaret Heckler of the U.S. Department of Health and Human Services, however, has maintained that such costs are a local responsibility.

95.

NANCY SHULINS: Not in My Backyard

Some social commentators have described the 1980s as a decade marked by insularity and selfishness. The article reprinted here describes the phenomenon of NIMBY—"not in my backyard." The sentiment was prevalent in debates over the placement of prisons, public housing, and nuclear plants, as well as the storing and transporting of chemical wastes. Nancy Shulins was a feature writer for the Associated Press.

Source: *Chicago Tribune*, February 12, 1984.

THE HIGHEST point of land in South Windsor, Conn., has been home to Frank Niederwerfer for 69 years. "An excellent place," says Niederwerfer. Southern New England Telephone Co. thought so, too.

The phone company chose it as the site for a 100-foot antenna, a link in a new communication system for mobile telephones. Niederwerfer does not dispute the need for the antenna. Nevertheless, he fought it, saying, "You don't have to put it in somebody's yard."

The people of California do not dispute the need for more state prisons. Last June, voters approved Proposition 1, the sale of $495 million in bonds to build more of them.

But not in Pearblossom, the choice of state officials. "We don't need a prison in Pearblossom," says resident Margaret Johnson. "Put it in someone else's backyard."

Columbus, Ohio, has a new tax-funded program to provide shelter for the poor and homeless. At last count, it had been driven out of three sites by area businessmen and residents.

In Last Chance, Colo., it's a hazardous waste dump, in Oak Ridge, Tenn., low-rent housing; in Helena, Mont., an adult group home; in wealthy Darien, Conn., a generational battle over apartment housing.

Across the nation in swelling numbers, Americans are saying no to all kinds of projects, public and private, whose basic usefulness or necessity is generally acknowledged. In the process, they are complicating life for planners, builders, officials and politicians.

Their "no" carries greater clout than in the past. Armed with environmental impact statements, zoning regulations and all manner of weaponry, with names like Save Our Countryside and Keep Towers Out, they organize, they protest, they campaign—and they sue.

Sometimes they succeed in holding up unwelcome enterprises until soaring costs put them out of sight, as the nuclear power industry can attest.

Some people favoring a cleanup of the environment turn prickly when they themselves are asked to pay a price.

"It's a terrible decision to make," says former Arkansas Gov. David Pryor, now a U.S. senator whose home state harbors one new toxic waste dump with another planned. "People are fearful. They want to know, why can't they put all that stuff in Arizona? Frankly, that's my feeling, too."

Swifter punishment of felons and longer prison terms enjoy wide public favor but locating a new penitentiary necessary to accomplish those objectives is something else again.

"There was a time when communities might have lobbied against each other to get a prison," says David Amidon Jr., a lecturer in urban studies at Lehigh University in Bethlehem, Pa. "Now these same communities lobby to fight it."

The nature of prisons hasn't changed. The mood of the country has.

Social scientists, politicians, officials and others say it changed because of Vietnam and Watergate, Three Mile Island and Love Canal, the civil rights and women's movements, skepticism toward government and experts who were often proven wrong, toward unforeseen consequences of development, toward growth as an absolute goal.

Says Harvard University sociologist David Riesman, "There is a curling in to protect. Americans are torn between recognition of nonparochial requirements and a desire to protect their nest, their neighborhood, their parish, their locale, their values."

Niederwerfer, a retired dairy farmer, is not a selfish man. In 1968, he donated 16 acres to South Windsor for a bird sanctuary. He can see it from his house on Niederwerfer Road, named for the five generations of his family who have lived there.

Niederwerfer had never protested anything until that antenna came along. He and his neighbors wanted to protect their quality of life and their property values. They wanted to preserve one of the last stretches of undeveloped land left in South Windsor, transformed over the past 30 years from a rural farm town of 3,000 to a bustling Hartford suburb of 17,000.

"You've got to make an effort to save things," says Niederwerfer. "If we had realized what was coming years ago, homes all over town and so on, maybe we could have saved more."

Whether people dig in their heels against a toxic waste dump or a senior citizens' home, they consider it a defense of their backyard, "their island of security" in the surrounding disorder, as historian Christopher Lasch put it in his book, "The Culture of Narcissism."

Those islands can develop formidable defenses, suggested by the protest movements of a decade and a half ago, by ethnic self-assertion, and the tactics of environmentalists.

Jeffrey Miller, director of the Public Policy Program at Lawrence University in Appleton, Wis., says the activists of the '60s "developed a set of skills, a means of protesting, of taking action, of grass-roots organizing," and neither they nor others who stood by and watched have forgotten.

"Now people are calculated politically," Miller says. "They know how to attract media attention, how to influence legislatures."

Moreover, says Pryor, "the local communites have much more to say and much better vehicles to express opposition: news conferences, legal proceedings, class action suits, environmental impact statements."

Harry Boyte, author of "The Backyard Revolution," agrees. His book chronicles the citizens' movements of the past 20 years. While the movements infused with ideological fervor dwindled, the activist urge "went underground, gathered force and maturity in a great diversity of settings and by the late '70s had begun to achieve a visible national identity."

In fact, he thinks that far more people are active in public life today than in the '60s. "More people are getting a sense of their own power. More people see other people winning things."

They see more of it in part because of media attention. Stories abound about communities battling all sorts of intrusions.

The media used to focus on advocates like Ralph Nader, but now that's less true, he says. "Love Canal was exposed by a housewife. We began paying less attention to the professionals."

In neighborhood organizations, church basements and union halls, in swiftly formed suburban committees and block associations, "people today are starting to believe that if you know what you're doing, you can fight city hall."

Fight they do, over issues that run the gamut.

When Michigan's governor pushed through a 38 percent income tax increase to ease the state's staggering deficit, taxpayers forced recall elections of the two state senators who supported it.

When Atlanta decided on a 2.2-mile extension of a parkway for ready access to Jimmy Carter's proposed presidential library at Emory University, the neighborhoods concerned rose in protest.

In Chicago, Illinois prison officials decided to scrap plans for a minimum security prison in the city and a suburb after protests from community groups.

In Port Washington, on New York's Long Island, federal funds for four senior citizens' apartment houses have gone begging because of zoning restrictions and neighborhood opposition.

In Massachusetts, where factories, laboratories and hospitals generate an estimated 300,000 tons of potent industrial waste each year, legislators passed a law that can, under some circumstances, force communities to negotiate with the developer of a hazardous waste treatment plant. Developers hailed the law as a breakthrough.

Three years later, not a single plant has been built; all have been stymied by local opposition.

Politicians and other citizens in con-

AP/Wide World

A California demonstrator protests restarting a nuclear power plant after a leak was found earlier. The plant is near a residential area.

servative Western states that strongly supported MX missiles in principle proved unreceptive to the idea of basing them on their soil. The permanent disposal of high-level radioactive wastes has been in abeyance for years, less because of technical problems than because of the political difficulty of choosing the site.

The rising prickliness in the grassroots has not been lost on the higher realms of officialdom. Jimmy Carter, at a low point in his presidency, surveyed the scene of naysaying and ascribed it to a national malaise engendered by distrust in government and institutions, an erosion of confidence and, by implication, of public spirit.

Ronald Reagan saw it from another perspective and built his successful campaign on a theme of getting an overbearing government off people's backs.

There has been "a growing revolt against government and what is seen as intrusive control exercised by large organizations that never seem to be responsible to anybody," says historian Lasch.

Norman Mineta, now a congressman from California and who, as a mayor of San Jose, has spent time in the trenches, speaks of a "tendency for a high degree of arrogance, for agencies to do whatever they wanted. Antagonism grows out of cynicism about government."

As Lasch wrote in 1979: "The inadequacy of solutions dictated from above now forces people to invent solutions from below."

Claudine Schneider is a case in point. A U.S. representative from Rhode Island now serving her second term, she launched her political career through a fight with New England Power Co. and the federal government over the proposed siting of a $3 billion nuclear power plant in Charlestown, R.I.

She stepped into the public arena as a founder of Concerned Citizens for Charlestown, a group that filed suit against the siting of the plant. The General Services Administration ultimately decided to deny the power company's bid for 604 acres of abandoned Navy land for the project.

"My original objection was that the audacity of the federal government and the company to change the structure of the community without consulting the residents of the area ran contrary to my idea of democracy," she said recently.

Niederwerfer says he was baffled and angry when telephone company employees appeared mysteriously on the ridge. "I knew something was going to go on. But nobody would tell us what it was about."

He and his neighbors investigated, then mobilized. The telephone company withdrew its application.

Americans are watching their backyards more zealously because, for one reason, the nation's collective backyard is shrinking. "When there was land enough, people could spread out," says Riesman. "There was no overriding power to say no to a steel plant."

Another reason is fear, says Charles Rotman, chairman of the psychology department at Babson College in Wellesley, Mass.

Arguments against a proposed facility on the grounds of endangered property values, he says, are sometimes a smokescreen for other, unexpressed worries.

Among them, he says, is a fear of change. "A big factor is the threat to their own privacy. A fear that somehow, the individual's tranquility or usual routine is going to be disrupted," he says.

"People still want to retain some control, if only over their privacy. People want to determine their own destiny. The home becomes an oasis, a refuge. And in the community itself, there's improved rapport and cohesiveness"— a prompt circling of the wagons against intrusion.

Sometimes a community is painfully split. Darien, Conn., is an affluent town of 18,000 where residents live in one-family homes, an arrangement protected by zoning. Now, with increased maintenance costs and the number of residents 65 and over expected to rise to 15 percent by 1990, many can no longer afford their large homes. But they want to remain in the town where they have lived most of their lives. These older citizens have been pushing for apartment complexes—which they would have opposed in earlier years—and among the young homeowners, there's talk about ghettos and leper colonies.

"What is the responsibility of this community to its own residents?" asks Lewis A. Miller, sponsor of a plan to build 29 apartments for elderly tenants. "Can you be an island in Darien?"

The tendency to place narrow and local interests above wider ones has been spreading. The localism of the '80s, sociologist Riesman says, has its roots in the social movements of one or two decades ago.

"The civil rights movement and the women's movement, both of which were the most powerful movements this country has seen since World War II, both said 'Let's turn our attention to home,' " Riesman says.

He also points to a "cultural backlash" against the idea that America's is a homogenous society.

"We are at once both local and cosmopolitan," he says. "We think of ourselves as a nation of movers, for example, but 20 percent of the people are making 80 percent of the moves. There are a lot more stayers than movers."

Many community battles break down into two sides, he suggests—"locals" vs. "cosmopolitans."

The locals are "community-oriented family people who make friends with people in their parish, their church. The cosmopolitans have friends based on common interests and causes. They tend to be city managers, the county agent, those who do the doctoring and the lawyering. They do not belong to the volunteer fire department."

The outside authorities and experts who create some of the issues and proposals that provoke local residents tend to be cosmopolitans. Arguments between the two sides go back to the fights over fluoridation of water that were widespread in the '50s, Riesman notes.

In recent years, the battles between locals and cosmopolitans have been heating up, he says, not because there are more locals now but because the two sides are more evenly matched.

"The attitudes of the locals were once seen as not wholly legitimate, as lacking compassion. Now, they're legitimized at the highest level.

"The locals have become more affluent and as a result more influential. Locals are more vocal, more powerful, in our society. They now have much more influence, more education, and the courts are more sympathetic to them than they used to be. As a result, it takes less to stop things."

At times, both sides lose sight of the common good. But in a complex society the "common good" is harder to define, as University of Minnesota anthropologist Luther Gerlach noted in examining a dispute between Minnesota farmers and a group of utilities.

For more than a year, the farmers and their sympathizers protested a 400-kilovolt power line to stretch from Underwood, N.D., to Delano, Minn. Between 1978 and 1979, 15 utility towers were toppled and 9,000 to 10,000 insulators were shot out. Arrests were made for obstructing work crews, resisting officers and a nighttime shooting at a supply yard site.

The line, in operation since August 1979, cost the sponsoring utilities $360 million.

"Whose cause is the right one?" asks Gerlach. "Is it that of those who decide to develop coal and lignite as the country's great black hope or of those who say, 'Not over my place'? What do you do when resistance becomes as much a crusade as development? Simply scatter the minority with a whiff of eminent domain?

"But what is the minority? the farmers say they are protecting the basic freedoms and food-producing farmland that we all need. The energy developers say they are protecting the legal processes and the energy-providing system we all need. Government says it is making decisions reflecting study of all the social, economic, technical, political, health and ecological factors. And it says it is facilitating public participation so it can consider all views.

"Maybe what officials expect is that this participation process will achieve consensus. But the participants in this process have emerged flying the banners of their rival holy causes even higher."

Achieving consensus behind a project that one group considers an invasion may be increasingly hard to accomplish, but many officials and decision-makers see greater participation as the best way.

Governments—local, state and national—in the past "have tended to catch citizens by surprise," says Pryor, the senator from Arkansas. "I believe in communication early."

Boyte, who sees much that's positive in backyard activism, puts his faith in building strong, responsible community organizations.

"People are capable of real generosity and intelligent decisions that share the kinds of social costs that need to be shared," Boyte says. "But they're not in a mood to do that when they feel things are imposed on them. When people are feeling defensive, they're going to hunker down and isolate themselves."

It was announced in 1983 that completion of the Marble Hill nuclear power plant in Indiana would be delayed for two years because of cost overruns; spending was to be scaled back and the workforce cut.

TROUBLES AT HOME

"When sorrows come, they come not single spies, but in battalions," said Queen Gertrude in Shakespeare's *Hamlet.* The United States seemed to have more than its share of sorrows during the 1980s. Nuclear accidents and cost overruns in the Defense Department. Toxic waste sites and acid rain. Forest fires and volcanic eruptions. Turmoil in the airline industry and a record year for air crashes. Angry divisions in the body politic. Mass murders—the worst in U.S. history. Decay of the infrastructure, particularly in cities. Bank failures. High energy prices, then low energy prices. A hole in the ozone layer. AIDS. All these troubles filled news reports during this period.

Love Canal: the very name did more to dramatize the problem of polluted dumps than a hundred earnest speeches. Acid rain, another environmental problem, was widely reported. Thousands of acres caught fire on an annual basis in the dry Western states. The greatest fires of all came roaring from the depths of Mount St. Helens in Washington when it erupted in 1980.

(Top left) Weeds grow around boarded-up homes in the Love Canal area near Niagara Falls, N.Y.; (top right) workers open drums of hazardous waste in Ohio to identify the contents; there are 10,000 drums here filled with various chemicals; (bottom left) smoke billows from an open hearth furnace in Birmingham, Alabama; (bottom right) the face of this Chicago statue has been eroded by acid rain.

(Top) A California firefighter runs for his life as flames spurred by high winds and 100-degree heat nearly cut off his escape; (bottom) the Washington volcano, Mt. St. Helens, blasts steam and ash into the air in a second great eruption in 1980, covering everything for miles around with a gray coat of ash.

AP/Wide World

(Top) This crash of a jumbo jet in Dallas was only one of many crashes in 1985; (bottom left) two substitute air traffic controllers work a shift in New York as the air traffic controller's strike continues; (bottom right) steelworkers leave a plant at the end of the day; many were being laid off in 1979.

The year 1985 was the worst year in history to date for air crashes. Nearly 2,000 people died, 520 of them in a single accident in Japan. In December a DC-8 military charter bringing home 248 members of the 101st Airborne Division crashed and burned at Gander, Newfoundland, killing everyone aboard. Accidents aside, the everyday hassles of flying were increasing, with cancelled flights, ever-changing schedules, strikes, mobbed check-in counters, and bad food—all of it ascribable, some said, to the new era of deregulated air travel. And if that wasn't enough, there was the fear of terror-

ist attacks and hijacks, which kept many Americans off trans-Atlantic flights throughout much of 1986. (The previous summer, the strong dollar had attracted more passengers to Europe than ever before.) Some were not flying because of fear, and some because they didn't have the money for any type of travel. The recession that greeted President Ronald Reagan when he took office was the worst since the Great Depression, and layoffs continued in some industries throughout the decade. The country endured a rate of 10 percent unemployment.

UPI/Bettmann

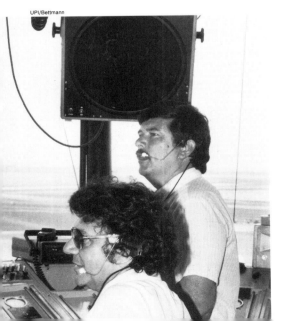

AP/Wide World

(Top) Poor maintenance and bad weather caused the widespread deterioration of roads, such as this one in Pittsburgh; (bottom left) the collapse of I-95 in Connecticut, which killed three people, was attributed to lack of proper inspection; (bottom right) traffic jam caused by accident on rural interstate.

The decay of urban streets was common in the United States during this period. Increasing use of automobiles and trucks, along with diminishing public funds, combined to create hazardous road conditions in many American cities. Although a rise in oil prices slowed the increase of automobiles in the late 1970s, it was only a temporary dip. In fact, in some parts of the country, the motor vehicle fleet grew faster than the human population, as the sum of all miles driven also increased. In overland commercial transport, trucking continued to be emphasized over the delivery of cargo by rail. The end result of this congestion was more wear-and-tear on roadways, longer traffic jams, and rising rates of pollution.

The 1960s and early 1970s introduced Americans to the politics of confrontation: protests about civil rights, the Vietnam War, and women's rights, to name a few. In the late 1970s and through most of the 1980s, confrontation continued. Behind this type of politics lay the conviction that government was not doing enough or that government was wrong. Direct democracy, dealing with the issue in person, seemed to be the answer. Apartheid, disarmament, abortion, gay rights—for their adherents and their opponents, these have become the single issues that determine individual convictions. In espousing the politics of confrontation, all attempts at moderation, conciliation, and compromise are swept aside in the search for quick answers.

(Top) Anti-apartheid protestors march to the South African embassy in Washington in 1985; (center) this was typical of the reactions to the break-up of the Bell System in 1984; (bottom left) 70,000 opponents of abortion march before the Supreme Court building to mark the anniversary of the legalization of abortion; (bottom right) pro-choice demonstrators march at St. Patrick's Cathedral in New York in 1979 to urge the preservation of safe and legal procedures.

96.

Interviews with King Hussein and President Assad

The two interviews, portions of which are reprinted here, took place within a few days of each other in the spring of 1984. King Hussein of Jordan had traditionally been one of America's best friends, and his highly critical remarks about the undependability of the United States as an ally were a shock to readers when the interview was published. One of his main points, that the United States becomes particularly undependable during election years, because Jewish votes are important in certain key states whereas Arab votes are not numerous enough to be important anywhere, was repeated by President Hafez Assad of Syria, speaking to a team of Time *executives in Damascus. Both Hussein and Assad, furthermore, described U.S. policy in the Middle East as unrealistic and based on wishful thinking. These views may or may not be correct; certainly, an interview with a top Israeli official would sound a different note.*

Sources: Interview with King Hussein, *The New York Times*, March 15, 1984.

Interview with President Assad, *Time*, April 2, 1984.

A: INTERVIEW WITH KING HUSSEIN

HUSSEIN: The whole situation is hopeless because it just appears more clearly than before that the United States has forsaken its position as a nation that stands by its word and its commitments. It has chosen to disqualify itself as the sole force in the area that could help us all move towards a just and durable peace. The U.S. is not free to move except within the limits of what Aipac, the Zionists and the State of Israel determine for it.

Q. Was it the American withdrawal from Lebanon that persuaded you that the U.S. was no longer reliable as an honest broker?

A. It is a series of events. Lebanon is part of that series. What it has cost the United States is its credibility. There have been a series of factors in the past, since 1956, really. But if you consider the recent past, first, the President's initiative of Sept. 1: it was destroyed, as was U.S. credibility, by Israel's rejection of it. This was followed by Israel's settlement activity, which was intensified and which was a direct answer to the President's initiative. This was followed by the Lebanese situation, in which they continued, and still continue to be the occupiers of Lebanese territory. This was followed most recently by their attempts to implement a plan to reallocate people in the occupied territories to the Jordan Valley in what appears to be a final step towards pushing them across the river, consistent with their claim that the Palestinian problem is a problem of people, not the land. In addition, there is a plan to implement Israeli land laws on the rest of the occupied territories.

Through all of this and for the last 17 years, Israel has denied Palestinians living under occupation all of their human rights or the rights to express themselves in freedom.

The U.S. looks at us and speaks of direct negotiations being the only way out, while we don't know what the U.S. position is.

We see things in the following way: Israel is on our land. It is there by virtue of American military and economic aid that translates into aid for Israeli settlements. Israel is there by virtue of American moral and political views to the point where the United States is succumbing to Israeli dictates.

It's obvious that this being the case, there is no way by which anyone should imagine it would be possible for Arabs to sit and talk with Israel as long as things are as they are.

As far as the United States is concerned, the question that is posed is: is the United States able to elevate itself to the status of a superpower? To live up to its commitments of being evenhanded? We don't see it happening. We obviously can't deal with the United States as an ally of Israel or as a mediator.

The United States asserts that its present plan is valid, but is it really? Israel has rejected it; Israel has changed conditions on the ground to the point where it almost makes no sense. We have another year of an election campaign in the United States; contenders must appeal for the favors of Aipac and Zionism and Israel. Even this year has seen such drastic changes on the ground that within a year, any fragments of hope left of achieving a peaceful solution to the problem will be destroyed. So that's why I say it's hopeless.

Q. What are the implications of what you're saying?

A. The implications are that as far as I'm concerned, the positions we have adopted over the years, of trying to establish a dialogue with Washington and the United States, of trying to contribute to the creation of a more balanced approach to the problem, which is in the interests of all of the parties to this conflict, have failed.

You obviously have made your choice and your choice is Israel and support of Israel. That being the case, there is no hope of achieving anything.

In point of fact, we have given more than we have taken. We sought peace in the area; we were ready to try to work with the Reagan plan. Israel was the force that rejected it, that did not wish peace, yet we are portrayed as if we are the party that is opposed to peace. Apart from being unjust, it is also incorrect.

Q. Does this mean that you will not participate in any American-sponsored or American-brokered negotiations with Israel?

A. Not the way things look, no. One has to be a realist. It has cost us a lot. U.S. credibility has suffered, but so have those who have believed in the United States. The possibility of having a meaningful policy, of your standing up and defending meaningful principles have also suffered.

We were sincere and honest, and we tried our best. But I can't see anything happening except further deterioration of the situation. We worked for progress in this area, that's all I can say.

Q. What options does this leave you, where does Jordan turn now?

A. Jordan has always been on its own. We have no strategic alliance with the United States; it has no treaty with the Soviet Union. It has a just cause it has been defending and will continue to do so: the Arab identity, the Arab cause. But we face formidable threats that threaten not only oil in this area but world peace. We have stood against all attempts at polarization in this area and will continue to do so, but it seems again that there are two sides that are working for polarization. Israel on one side and some of the Arabs on the other. As I see it, there is more commonality between these two allegedly opposing sides.

Q. Do you mean Syria?

A. I mean those who work for polarization on all sides, including the United States.

Q. So what happens to efforts to put together a so-called moderate Arab coalition?

A. Jordan and the Palestinians will continue to work together to secure our relations on a foundation of trust and common clarity of vision. But as I have said time and time again, it is ridiculous that Israel gives itself the right to question the right of those living under occupation to come and meet with us here, or even meet with the P.L.O. As far as I can understand, when we look at the possibility of a P.N.C. meeting, perhaps very shortly, it is ironic that you have two sides that are preventing the previously silent majority, which isn't silent anymore, from expressing themselves. Israel on one hand and others in Syria who will not participate in the talks— they are preventing the people who really matter from expressing themselves.

Jews in the Soviet Union—the whole world is up in arms that they do not have the right to move, to Israel in particular. Well, they are Soviet citizens and part of the state. The United States has protested vigorously. But people who are not Israeli, who are under occupation, should they not be permitted to

voice an opinion about anything, about what should happen to them? And remember, these are Jordanian citizens, or those for whom Egypt is responsible.

Q. What would have to change to renew the possibility of direct talks with Israel by Jordan and some Palestinians?

A. Jordan and the Palestinians are one team. And we will work together on all fronts. But as for any negotiations, since the United States keeps its current policies, it certainly should not have the right to deny others to be present at any new negotiations. That's why I think the Soviets have the right to be there.

But if both superpowers are taking the position of alliances with some of the belligerents, namely Israel on one hand and Syria on the other, then obviously, they alone probably can't make a contribution to the solution, particularly when they themselves do not have any meaningful relations at this time. Maybe since this is the case, the picture should be broadened. Maybe the five permanent members of the United Nations Security Council should be parties, plus all of the parties to the conflict.

Q. Including the P.L.O.?

A. Yes, of course.

Q. But then is there no one now in a position, neither the U.S. nor the Soviet Union, who can be an honest broker or mediator?

A. No, least of all the United States.

Q. What about the impact of the United States withdrawal from Lebanon on your thinking, especially since you told me the last time I saw you that the Americans should not withdraw without a change on the ground?

A. I would rather not comment. I have a final thought: I am very concerned about the United States and its double standard everywhere. The saddest point for me is that I've always believed values and courageous principles were an area that we shared. I now realize that principles mean nothing to the United States. Short-term issues, especially in election years, prevail. This is the saddest thing that one can experience. I continue to believe that principles matter. If they don't, that's even more disastrous for us all.

B: INTERVIEW WITH PRESIDENT ASSAD

Q. Mr. President, is there a role for the U.S. to play in the Middle East? If so, what should that role be?
A. Certainly there is a role for the U.S. to play in the area. There is also one for the Soviet Union. No reasonable man can ignore the roles of these two superpowers. All that we wish is to see the U.S. play its role in a fair, unbiased and responsible way in accordance with its responsibilities as a superpower. We say this because we always perceive a continued and complete bias by the U.S. toward Israel. This bias, from our point of view, contradicts the interests of American citizens and does not serve the cause of peace.

Needless to say, there are tens, even hundreds of examples to prove this. It is enough to say that the U.S. gives Israel about $3 billion a year. This means that each Israeli gets $1,000 a year from the pockets of American citizens. Now you should know that in 90% of Third World countries, per capita income is much less than this figure. Moreover, we have to take into consideration that a big part of this money is in the form of sophisticated weapons which in turn are used to kill our citizens and to occupy our land.
Q. U.S. aid to Israel is bigger now than

it was in 1975. Have you and other Arab leaders not asked yourselves why this aid increased and why you have not really affected American public opinion?
A. We have asked ourselves this question many times. One of the main reasons is that we do not have voters in the U.S. to elect a President. However, there have been American Presidents who have dealt with Middle East problems in the light of American interests rather than in the light of Israeli interests as imposed by the Zionist lobby in the U.S. Everybody remembers President Eisenhower and credits him with such a stand.

When I say that the main reason is Jewish votes that presidential candidates endeavor to win, this does not mean that I can justify the attitude of American Administrations. Candidates anywhere in the world conduct campaigns on the basis of the interests of the whole country and not just the interests of a certain group, especially when such a group works for the sake of another country and at the expense of the interests of its own. Nobody is unaware of the fact that the Zionist lobby in the U.S. works foremost for Israel and not for the interests of the U.S. Therefore, an American President who heeds the ambitions of such a group is not primarily concerned with the interests of the U.S.
Q. But if you had recognized Israel as a fact, would you not have had a greater influence on American opinion?
A. Why are we asked to give everything? Why not stop the flow of billions of dollars to Israel? Why not stop shipments of American weapons to Israel? Why is it not required to tell the American Jew that he should only be an American Jew, in the same way as an American Christian is only that, an American

Muslim only that? Our view is that the American, whether he is Jewish, Christian or Muslim, should be an American. Only then will the U.S. have an objective view [of the Middle East] and work for genuine peace.

Peace is not mere words. Peace is not wishful thinking. It has a tangible foundation. Had the U.S. really wanted to bring about peace, it would not have given such tremendous aid to Israel, because this has tipped the balance in the area. Do you believe that peace can be achieved while Israel continues to behave like a big power in the region? Any such belief is lacking in logic and objectivity.

Let us look at what happened following the Camp David accords. Egypt represented at least half the Arab force facing Israel. The U.S. always claimed that it supplied Israel with weapons and money in order to strike a balance between Israel and the Arab forces. After the departure of Egypt from the Arab ranks following the Camp David accords, the U.S. was supposed to cut its aid to Israel, and Israeli military forces were supposed to be cut down as well. Instead, the opposite happened. We Arabs lost at least half of our force, and yet American aid to Israel even increased. So, how can we say that this served the purpose of peace?

After the war in Lebanon, I received a delegation from the American Congress, and in discussing aid with them I said, "You offer us only talk about peace, and while you talk to us about peace you will be debating in Congress a few days from now [proposals for] military and economic aid to Israel estimated at billions of dollars. Don't you see that your talk is unbalanced, if on the one hand you offer us nice words about peace but on the other hand you offer the Israelis tanks, artillery, aircraft and dollars? Where is the logic in all this?"

Q. Perhaps you overestimate the power of what you call the Zionist lobby? There is also genuine sympathy for Israel among the general public.

A. I totally disagree. It is not a question of sympathy. The question is one of an organized Jewish force within the Zionist movement that dictates its views through the main centers of the media and through financial institutions. It is not a question of sentiment, but one of material effectiveness. I find it strange that American citizens might sympathize with a state that bombards Beirut indiscriminately, using American aircraft, and yet might not sympathize with millions of displaced persons living in camps. If I am to accept this theory of sympathy, then I will have to change my view of American citizens, which I do not want to do.

Q. Now that the U.S. and Israel have failed in Lebanon, Syria carries a heavy responsibility in that country. Is there a chance for a new start to solve existing problems, particularly between Syria and Israel, the two key countries in the area?

A. We have always sought to achieve peace in the area. We agreed in 1973 to United Nations Security Council Resolution 338 [which asks that negotiations begin in order to establish a "just and durable" peace in the region] and to arrangements adopted by the U.N. that called for an International Peace Conference. However, we found that all this was in conflict with Israel's ambitions.

We want a peace that will restore our rights and put an end to Israeli expansionism. In this context we have supported appeals and proposals calling for an international conference under the auspices of the U.N. We are sorry to say that American attempts made from time to time under the title of "Search for Peace" have not, in most cases, been those of a superpower with special responsibilities in our world. They have, rather, been attempts that in fact were Israeli proposals. We pointed this out frankly to the American officials who conveyed these proposals to us.

Q. Let us suppose that such a conference were convened. How would you envision the Middle East after such a meeting, including the role of Israel?

A. It is difficult to draw a detailed picture. However, we envision the Middle East as a region in which peace prevails, rights are restored to each party in the light of U.N. resolutions and where no feeling of injustice remains with anybody. This is how we envision it.

Q. Can recognition of Israel be a subject of discussion in such a conference?

A. When we talk of a peace conference convened in accordance with U.N. resolutions, then each party puts forward what it thinks is included in these resolutions. You know that the Israelis have always said there should be no preconditions. Your question represents a precondition.

Q. What is the next Syrian move in Lebanon? Can there be a simultaneous withdrawal of Syrian and Israeli troops? Will Syria withdraw from Lebanon if asked to do so by a government of national reconciliation?

A. Lebanese reconciliation is the only way. This has remained true despite continued fighting for many years and despite Israel's invasion. We emphasized this in 1976. We re-emphasize it now and are endeavoring to bring it about. Our attitude recently in Lausanne is quite clear. It is true that the Lausanne conference did not succeed to the extent that we or the Lebanese parties

hoped, but there was maximum cooperation on our part. We cooperated fully with the Lebanese President, and the Syrian representative made hectic efforts at the bilateral and trilateral level. We will continue to work for reconciliation, especially as the Lebanese parties are now convinced that there is no alternative.

Our position with regard to a government of national unity is one of full support. When such a government is formed, we will respond to its requests because it will be representative of the Lebanese people. Such a government will stand side by side with Syria to expel Israel from Lebanon unconditionally.

The Syrians and the Lebanese are one people, their past is one and the same, their history is one and their future is one and the same. At the same time we are two independent states. What is there in common between Israel and Lebanon? Israel is an invading force in Lebanon, while we defended Lebanon against Israel. So where is the logic in any attempt to link the Syrian presence to the Israeli presence or to link Syrian withdrawal to Israeli withdrawal? That is why we say our position is clear. We will never accept any linkage between Syrian and Israeli withdrawal. But when a government of national unity is formed as a result of the desire of the Lebanese government, we will meet its request to withdraw unreluctantly, and this could be within a month or within days or months.

Q. The differences in Lebanon are deep and bitter. Have you not perhaps bitten off more than you can chew?

A. No. The people of Lebanon are our people. The U.S. may have bitten off more than it could chew, even if it is a superpower. The reason is that the U.S.

and Lebanon do not form one people. The Arabs can solve their own problems because of their common history. More than anyone else, we want to see Lebanon united, stable and strong.

Q. There is concern in the U.S. and other countries about state-supported terrorism, such as the attack on the U.S. Marine headquarters in Beirut. It is said that this attack would not have been possible without Syrian negligence or even Syrian approval. What is your comment?

A. Are there no terrorist acts that take place in the U.S.? If we accept your logic, then we have to conclude that somehow these acts were arranged or condoned by the U.S. government. If foreign missions [in the U.S.] are attacked, are we to hold the U.S. responsible? We have had terrorist acts committed in recent years in Syria. Are we to say that the Syrian government was behind them? Why are we to be held responsible for an act that took place in Beirut when we have no presence in Beirut? Some American officials have made such accusations, but I doubt that they believe what they say. I told one of them that if we failed to prevent such acts in areas under our control, why did the Lebanese Army then fail to prevent those who carried out these acts from passing through areas under its control? And why did the other Lebanese forces also fail to prevent them from crossing their areas? Why did the American forces fail? In other words, all those who failed are not responsible except for Syria. There is no logic in this.

Q. Did King Hussein learn from you when he made his recent remarks about the U.S.?

A. [He laughs] I wish he did learn. We are facing a very serious situation. Israel wants our land, wants Jordan and wants Saudi Arabia. Facing such a situation we are bound to learn, and that guarantees that King Hussein as well as others will also learn.

Rome, Antwerp, Copenhagen, Paris, Vienna, and now Istanbul: will there ever be an end to the shedding of Jewish blood? Will insane fanatics forever continue to murder Jews in Jewish places of worship? Are Jews destined to be in danger, always?

ELIE WIESEL, after massacre of Jews in Istanbul
synagogue, by Arab terrorists 1986

97.

Beauty Pageants

The following article from Forbes *magazine detailed the nuts-and-bolts business that underlay beauty pageants. Their wide appeal to television viewers boosted profits in the form of broadcast advertising and apparel licensing. The article appeared in June 1984; only a short time later the Miss America pageant suffered a blow when it was revealed that erotic nude photos of Vanessa Williams, the first black Miss America, had been published in a men's magazine. Williams resigned as Miss America in August, though her career as a singer and actress eventually rebounded.*

Source: *Forbes,* June 18, 1984.

THIS YEAR, it's easy to remember that Lorraine Downes is Miss Universe and that Vanessa Williams is Miss America, the first black Miss America. But for the people who do business over lunch at "21" and the Four Seasons, Vanessa Williams' race means nothing. It's her measurements that count. And Miss Universe's—not Miss America's—are now the best in the land.

Best bust? Waist? Hips? Remember which magazine you are reading this in. The measurements we are talking about are Nielsens and advertising efficiencies, audience sizes and demographics. And Miss Universe leads in all categories. More than 1.7 million more households tuned in to the Miss Universe pageant from St. Louis in July of last year than watched that old standby of Americana, the Miss America pageant, in Atlantic City in September. Moreover, Miss Universe's audience was the kind that Madison Avenue loves: 53% are women of the prime 18-to-49 buying age, compared with only 48% in the same group for Miss America.

What is even better for the people at Miss Universe, Inc., the Paramount Pictures subsidiary of Gulf & Western, is that the tide is clearly running in their favor. Miss Universe's TV audience has remained relatively constant: in 1974, 24.7% of all television households, compared with 22.6% today. Miss America, meanwhile, has shown a precipitous decline: in 1974, 30.3% of viewing households; in 1983, a mere 20.5%.

Does the decline of Miss America bother Albert A. Marks Jr., 71, chairman and CEO of the nonprofit Miss America Pageant, Inc., for the past 20 years? "You bet it bothers us," says Marks. "We put on a very good show that has a loyal following. It's one of the few things that little girls are allowed to stay up late and watch."

Unfortunately, that may be the nub

of the problem. Beauty pageants are great fun, but sponsors invest money in them because they are a terrific merchandising vehicle, and little girls just don't have much purchasing power. Nor do old ladies, also among Miss America's most loyal viewers.

Miss America still has its loyal supporters. Listen to Thomas Ryan, vice president of advertising services at Gillette, which has sponsored Miss America continuously for 26 years: "The show delivers a huge audience at a very modest cost." A single 30-second unit of advertising on, say, a popular network series, would normally cost $75,000, Ryan points out. But Gillette and this year's three co-sponsors—American Greetings, Pillsbury and Beatrice Foods—pay NBC on average a little over $21,000 per spot for each of 28 spots of 30 seconds. Compare it with the $450,000 that sponsors now pay for 30 seconds on the Superbowl and you understand why they love beauty pageants.

NBC gets away with paying the Miss America Pageant a mere $250,000 for the rights to broadcast a highly watched, strongly commercial show. Why such a bargain? In part, Miss America is a nonprofit operation whose surplus goes to provide $3 million in college scholarships for participants; there is no real pressure for maximizing returns. Says the idealistic Albert Marks: "Why should we raise rates? We budget this operation very tightly. More money for us wouldn't be the answer."

Does that sound like misplaced philanthropy? It did to Harold L. Glasser, an ex-corporate lawyer (who, like some beauty pageant contestants, won't reveal his age). Glasser has transformed Miss Universe, started 33 years ago by a bathing suit maker with a grudge

AP/Wide World

Miss Universe flanked by two runners-up.

against the Miss America pageant, into a textbook case of realized market potential.

Not that Glasser wants to stir up the meat-market criticism, either. He changes the subject when you ask him how profitable a beauty pageant can be when properly run. "Profit isn't the point," he says. "It's the vehicle we create for the sponsors that you should keep your eye on. As long as we're doing our job and keeping everybody happy, it doesn't matter how much money we make."

A fair guess: about $1 million. Glasser refuses to confirm or deny.

Miss Universe was created as a protest to Miss America by Pacific Knitting Mills in 1951 after Miss America refused to provide it with photos of contestants who were wearing Pacific's Catalina bathing suits in the pageant. Idealistic even then, Miss America's sponsors were worried about commercialization. But the owners of Pacific Knitting knew that beauty pageants were a good advertising vehicle, and rightly reasoned that the point of the advertising was to show off beautiful women in bathing suits. People would pay to see that, and didn't much care what name was on the crown or the banner across the winner's chest. Pacific Knitting was able to sell that idea to the city fathers of Long Beach, Calif., who were then—and still are—looking for ways to get out from under the shadow of Los Angeles. Miss Universe was born.

Glasser, then general counsel to a firm that acquired Pacific Knitting in 1955, while looking over the assets, found that his firm, Kayser-Roth, owned a beauty pageant. As Glasser tells it, "All the people at Kayser-Roth wanted to keep their names clean with Wall Street, so they decided to put the company's lawyer in charge."

Glasser threw himself into the task of making Miss Universe valuable to sponsors. Would mighty Procter & Gamble, the nation's biggest advertiser, be interested in sponsoring? Only if the pageant were moved East, so that it could be shown live in major market prime time. Glasser brought Miss Universe to Miami the following year and P&G became sole sponsor and remains so to this day.

Enter Gulf & Western, which acquired Paramount in 1966 and Kayser-Roth in 1976. With Charlie Bluhdorn's lawyers in the picture, Glasser was left with few duties other than Miss Universe, which he felt was lost in Kayser-Roth. In 1981 Paramount took over Miss Universe. "Our ratings were improving steadily, and we provided good entertainment," Glasser says. "The whole point of the exercise had changed from selling swimsuits to providing the sponsor with a good platform."

In addition to the seven-figure fees it receives each year from sole sponsor Procter & Gamble (neither party will give an exact figure), Miss Universe, Inc. gets a fee from the host city: Last year the Convention & Visitors Bureau of Greater St. Louis paid the pageant $500,000. Then there are the fees that Miss Universe and Miss USA, another of Glasser's pageants, command for promotional appearances—$2,000 and $1,500 per day, respectively. All these proceeds go to Miss Universe, Inc. Then there are fees from license arrangements such as J.C. Penney, which sells Miss USA swimwear (still made by Catalina).

The preliminary competitions are the source of other lucrative promotional fees. Miss USA alone is a culmination of hundreds of local pageants and 50 state pageants plus one in the District of Columbia. And of course, Glasser does not have Marks' $3 million scholarship to cover.

All in all, Miss Universe has convinced Paramount that beauty pageants are good showbiz: In addition to the Miss Universe and Miss USA, Glasser's company also produces Miss Teen USA for TV. Says Glasser, "Series are expensive to create, and they have a high rate of failure. Specials like Miss Universe don't cost as much to bring on air, and they present, apart from the marketing, a good image for any parent company."

Albert Marks and Harold Glasser make no secret of the fact that they don't like each other, and it probably doesn't help that Glasser tends to give Marks gratuitous advice. "Albert likes to pretend he is a nonprofit," says Glasser, "but he has to pay his bills, and that means he has to generate income." Replies Marks: "Harold should mind his own business. He runs a very commercial operation, one that spends as much time promoting the host city as it does the pageant."

The decline of Miss America and the rise of Miss Universe make Glasser's point well enough. So even though Marks pooh-poohs the commercial aspects of his pageant, Vanessa Williams was recently paid $25,000 by Coca-Cola for a brief appearance in a Diet Coke commercial. That's something new for Miss America, which has eschewed endorsements. "But," Marks says, "it was an internal error never to be repeated."

Miss America needs a larger cash flow in order to remain viable over the long haul. For one thing, the winner of the Miss America pageant is poorly paid. She gets only $25,000 for winning, a drop in the bucket compared with Miss Universe's $175,000, and her personal appearances go for only $500 to $1,000, half the going rate for Miss Universe and Miss USA. Will Marks take the necessary steps to capitalize on his potential assets? He firmly denies he will move away from the traditional Miss America format. "Unlike some pageants," he says pointedly, "we don't depend on having a lot of stars to draw audience. This show belongs to the girls."

A noble sentiment, perhaps, but not one likely to keep Miss America America's Miss over the long haul. In the end even Albert Marks might decide a little marketing is not such a dangerous thing.

98.

Mark Helprin: Liberty Enlightening the World

The Statue of Liberty, a gift from France, was installed on its harbor pedestal in New York City in 1886. By the 1970s it was evident that the 305-foot statue was in serious need of repair, prompting a 65-million-dollar renovation. In the early 1980s, when the statue was covered in scaffolding, with its electric-powered torch turned off, people began to think about its symbolic power as a national icon. This lyrical article by Mark Helprin, author of the novel Winter's Tale *(1983), appeared midway through 1984.*

Source: *Art & Antiques*, June 1984.

OFTEN WHEN I HAVE been abroad I have found myself longing for America and bewildered by the intensity of my emotions in this regard, though, when I explain them, the reasons underlying them invariably come clear and seem easily self-evident. The longings to which I confess are as easily directed toward the emblematic and representational as they are toward the American landscape itself. They derive not only from my own recollections, but from the work of visionary painters, writers, and composers. Winslow Homer, Walt Whitman, and Aaron Copland have been as much responsible for my frantic changes of plans and travel arrangements (I think I have never not come home early) as the girl on the coast of Maine during the Vietnam War (I lost her to a technical sergeant); an irresistible image of San Francisco, suspended in pure light; and the idea I had, which brought me back from England, of solving my financial problems by living off the land in the Everglades, even though I have always been desperately afraid of alligators.

I love this country as if it were a woman with whom I had been infatuated all my life. An undeniably American face, a regional dialect, the flag, a resonant place name can move me deeply or entrance me. And yet I must admit that I have never, not even during my most patriotic hypnopiasis, given a thought to the Statue of Liberty.

Perhaps this is because I am a New Yorker, and it is too familiar. And, yet, familiar things set me off on raptures better than almost anything else. I can see the statue without obstruction from every window in my apartment, and have only recently learned that when out-of-state visitors exclaim "There she is!" or "There's the Lady!" I must not respond with "Who?" or "What lady?" Where I was brought up, we called it the "Sta-chew-a-liberty," and this Lady in the Harbor business makes me very uneasy.

My further discomfort comes not from the fact that, like the Liberty Bell, the Statue of Liberty is a prime national symbol that is made of hollow metal—something which might be of interest, perhaps, to an anti-American semioticist—but from my view that Liberty Enlightening the World (the statue's original name) is far from aesthetically perfect, is rather new as a symbol, and has been bested on her home ground.

The statue's stocky proportions originate not in the nineteenth century's preference for women of considerable substance. But in the need to satisfy requirements for structural stability and wind-loading—*Sic transit ars gratia artis.* It was erected in New York Harbor in 1886—110 years after the Declaration of Independence, 279 years after the first settlement at Jamestown. Washington, Franklin, Jefferson, and Lincoln lived and died before the statue was conceived by its creator, Frederic Auguste Bartholdi, an Alsatian who had previously tried to interest the Egyptian government in placing by the Suez Canal a colossal metal representation of a woman holding a lamp.

It may be unfair to cite the statue's late arrival, since it became an indelible symbol of America nonetheless, especially during the two world wars, when its image was intermingled in a hundred ways with the war efforts (bonds, stamps, the name of a division, et al.) and during the period of immigration, when it assumed its real power.

Save for some low hills, dunes, a lighthouse, and a skiff or two, it was the first thing a new immigrant saw of America, and to its contrived grandiosity must have been added enough genuine and justifiable deep emotion to turn its copper skin, so to speak, into pure gold. This, I believe, is the reason it has become a powerful and enduring symbol, far more than its commemoration of Gallic-American friendship (if that were the case, we should have as well statues of Garibaldi, John Bull, Simon Bolivar, Herzl, Gandhi, and many others, so that New York Harbor would look like a chess board or the top of the Duomo), and far more than the frequent attempts to cast it without reason or association into a mystical symbol of the abstract ideals of liberty. Its green goldenness comes only partially from what its creators had intended, and mostly from what they could not have foreseen. It comes as a result of the immigrants, the returning soldiers, and the tourists coming home, who associated with it and invested in it part of the momentous and complicated feelings they had when arriving in America.

Thus, despite its imperfection, it must be judged a tremendous success as a symbol, although the passing of those generations that gave to it its meaning by their shipboard arrivals may well lessen its power and strengthen the unthinking acceptance of it, much as when, in the Middle Ages, a saint could be long forgotten and his statue venerated as if by animists.

Though too rich a diet of national symbols can in some ways diminish the impact of each one (as in Washington, D.C.), in other ways it can synergistically enhance them. This is a piece of good luck for Liberty, because neither New York nor America has stood as still as she has since 1886, and much has been added in the way of local color.

It is true that by the time the statue arrived the Brooklyn Bridge was a familiar sight, but the other spans, "the wind-polished bridges standing in the summer sun," followed soon after and became symbols of America far more potent and enduring than the Statue of Liberty itself because they are part of the lifeblood and purpose of the country, they are simpler (even mystical), and they are symbols not by declaration but by example. Though the buildings of Manhattan may have dwarfed the statue, the bridges are what challenge it as a symbol.

Yet because the statue derived from the same age and largely from the same impulses as the bridges themselves, it is in many ways a complement to them. It was constructed in a smoky and astoundingly disordered workshop in Paris that was typical of the nineteenth-century forges and ateliers in which structures and machinery were crafted by artisans rather than built solely according to principles. Its nearly pure copper skin was hammered into shape against the contours of 300 different exploded sections, in a process known as *repoussé,* because casting would have been too expensive and the advantage in detail imperceptible from the ideal distances at which the statue, 302 feet high including the pedestal, would be viewed. The copper sections were attached to a pylon designed and built by Gustav Eiffel, whose tower infuriated many Parisians because it was supposed to be temporary and yet it did not go away. Nor was the statue surrounding his pylon entirely well appreciated in New York. For example, *The New York Times,* perhaps confusing skepticism with wisdom, hinted at the beginning that the whole project might be some sort of a French scam. But both Eiffel's tower and his structure under the copper sheeting of the statue are relatives of the graceful railway bridges he built, and represent in a somewhat ungainly manner the same principles and dreams that led to the building of the bridges themselves, and to the mechanical world as we know it.

A statue probably should not be hollow. Or at least if it is hollow it should give the illusion of being solid, as is presumably that which it was sculpted to represent. One way to forfeit a hollow statue's illusion of solidity is to go inside it and climb up into its head, as millions have done in Liberty herself. But the statue has succeeded here, too, in confounding expectations, for the fact that one can go inside it is certainly one of the best things about it. And making the climb on the extraordinary spiral stairway is the best part of going inside, especially for children. Once within Liberty, you see that she is not perfect, and you may feel, as *The New York Times* did, that there is something illusory and illicit about her. But, when inside, you see a demonstration of the principles that hold her up, and you see that behind the beauty there is reason.

Time is the statue's ally in overcoming its inherent weaknesses and contradictions. Traditions build around it, giving it substance, protecting it, compensating. For example, schoolchildren and the general public contributed en masse, at the instigation mainly of *The New York World,* to build the pedestal. A hundred years later a banking company has decided to contribute for the restoration of the statue a small portion of the company's considerable revenue in travelers' checks, with the idea, justified or not, that millions of people will again be drawn into the process of raising funds for the Statue of Liberty. History brought to the statue the immigrants, the soldiers, and the companion bridges. And history will undoubtedly bring other gifts and other conditions of light in which to view it. As the light varies, so will the views, for the face of Liberty Enlightening the World, like that of a real woman, can appear to be faulted and imperfect, or beautiful beyond measure. It depends upon the time, the view, and the light. And if the past is any indication, time is on Liberty's side.

99.

Ads For Prescription Drugs

One of the enduring issues in American life revolves around the question of how much information laymen can, or should, have about the things that doctors know. This article focuses on the subject of advertising for prescription drugs. It is decidedly unpleasant for many patients to feel that their doctor is not interested in informing them what medication he is prescribing for their ills. On the other hand, is any lay patient qualified to make an informed choice between different medications?

Source: *Consumer Reports,* July 1984.

IN LATE 1981, readers of Reader's Digest, Modern Maturity, and eight newspapers saw an ad for *Pneumovax,* a prescription vaccine made by Merck, Sharpe & Dohme designed to prevent pneumococcal pneumonia. Addressed to elderly readers, the ad promoted the product's benefits, noted that Medicare would repay its cost, and advised readers to ask their doctors about it.

At about the same time, arthritis sufferers were invited, in print ads and drugstore displays, to switch their prescriptions from Upjohn's *Motrin* to Boots Pharmaceuticals' *Rufen,* which is chemically identical. The inducement was a rebate of $1.50 on a 100-tablet bottle of *Rufen.* Soon after, the Washington Post carried a full-page ad by Peoples Drug Stores for Burroughs Wellcome's

Zovirax, a prescription ointment for initial infection with herpes simplex virus.

Traditionally, prescription drugs have been advertised only to physicians, usually through professional journals and medical trade magazines. The law requires such ads to carry a "brief summary," approved by the U.S. Food and Drug Administration, of the drug's side effects, contraindications, warnings, and precautions—all meant to provide prescribing physicians with balanced information about the drug.

The same requirement applies to the advertising of prescription drugs directly to consumers. Such ads must carry the FDA-approved summary information. In fact, the FDA complained to Boots that just such information was absent in some of the ads for *Rufen,* and they were subsequently changed.

The possibility that a high-pressure advertising campaign might pit an uninformed consumer's demand against a physician's depth of knowledge led the FDA's then-Commissioner, Arthur Hull Hayes Jr., to call for a voluntary moratorium on such advertising in 1983. The aim was to give the FDA time to research its effect on consumers and to formulate appropriate regulations. Since Hayes' announcement, the moratorium has been broken only by TV and print ads for *Rufen* in the Tampa, Fla., area.

While the Federal Trade Commission also has jurisdiction over most prescription-drug ads, its consideration of the issues lags far behind the FDA's. The FTC is likely to await FDA action before deciding whether to get involved.

WHO'S FOR THE ADS?

Years ago, an effective new prescription drug could anticipate a long, profitable run without rivals. Patents on a new drug give a manufacturer a monopoly on its production for 17 years. That is, during the patent period, competing manufacturers may not produce and sell drugs that are chemically identical to the patented drug. These days, however, the debut of a new drug may soon be followed by the introduction of drugs designed to achieve the same result. Some may be chemically similar but not identical; some may not be at all similar. But all are competing against the original for the same market, and all are advertising to health professionals. Some manufacturers hope that advertising directly to consumers will give them an edge.

The media that would carry the advertising are also, presumably, in favor of prescription-drug advertising to consumers. At least one communications company found a deft way to support the proposal. Earlier this year, the CBS television network said that, according to a survey it had taken, consumers want more drug information—especially in such areas as safety, efficacy, and proper use. In a press release about the study, CBS said that "health care communications can be improved through direct-to-consumer advertising of prescription drugs which meets high standards of education and information."

But nothing in the CBS survey itself indicated that consumers wanted—or would trust—advertising as a source of prescription-drug information. A recent FDA report cited an independent study showing that only 9 percent of surveyed consumers considered advertising an appropriate way to disseminate information about prescription drugs.

WHO'S AGAINST THE ADS?

Consumers who have spoken at FDA-sponsored meetings around the country have generally opposed such advertising. So have the majority of physicians, pharmacists, and consumer groups who have taken a stand on the issue.

"It is disgraceful for the industry to try to pass off direct-to-consumer prescription-drug advertising as consumer information. Advertising is promotional," contends Fred Wegner, a pharmaceutical specialist for the American Association of Retired Persons, which operates pharmacies for its members.

He points to the present competitive advertising for many over-the-counter drugs as an indication that the pharmaceutical industry does not use advertising as a vehicle for information.

"It's a terrible thing," says Dr. Sidney M. Wolfe, Director of the Health Research Group. Wolfe says that the proper sources of drug information are books, educational courses in schools, and appropriately written brochures inserted in drug packages dispensed to consumers. "Madison Avenue will not provide information to consumers," he asserts.

Needless to say, industry representatives disagree. David Taylor, public policy director for Ciba-Geigy, a major drug manufacturer, claims that prescription-drug ads won't be modeled after other consumer-product advertising—simply because that approach won't work. Early in its research, Ciba developed a test TV commercial for an antihypertension product. Set on a beach, the ads equated the "good life" with freedom from high blood pressure achieved by using Ciba's product. That prototypical advertising approach apparently failed with consumer-test-audiences.

To be effective, Taylor says, drug ads will have to balance promotion with information. They'll also have to offer a fair balance of positive and negative information about a product.

IS BALANCE POSSIBLE?

Advertisers have not had problems giving physicians balanced drug information in ads. The phrasing can be highly technical, since it's aimed at those who understand the technicalities. And in the journals involved, advertisers can usually afford to buy space for all the "brief summary" information about risk and benefits that the law requires.

Consumer ads are something else again. For one thing, some "brief" summaries aren't really brief; they can spread over several pages of small print. Radio and TV ads, however, are brief— typically, they last only 30 or 60 seconds. Many of the summaries couldn't be presented understandably in so short a time even by themselves, let alone in conjunction with the sales pitch that would be the point of the exercise.

Then there's the language problem. Even in a print ad, where space might be available, the information that present law requires might not be comprehensible to consumers. The FDA could hardly demand that an ad satisfy the legal requirements for balance by presenting warnings couched in unexplained medical terms such as "nephrotoxicity" and "trophic ulceration."

The American Medical Association supports the FDA's current moratorium, but the organization has taken no formal position on drug advertising to consumers. The AMA's official policy statement does point out that physicians are generally opposed to the ads and are concerned about their effects on the doctor-patient relationship.

The opposition is not surprising. Ad campaigns can build powerful expectations for particular products. Patients may then be confused by a doctor's choice of some other course of treatment. Ads may also induce consumers to pressure doctors to prescribe inappropriate products. At the least, doctors would be concerned about the time they may have to spend answering ad-prompted inquiries on products that aren't relevant to a patient's treatment.

POCKETBOOK EFFECTS?

The push for direct-to-consumer advertising has raised another question: Would the ads lead to higher drug prices? There's no clear answer.

Prescription-drug makers are already spending some $2-billion a year to advertise in just the limited media available to them. A drug firm might decide to shift some of its promotional budget from doctor-directed to consumer-directed promotions, rather than increase the total spent in advertising. Increased sales resulting from consumer-directed advertising might also absorb some or all of the advertising costs.

In general, however, there is a clear relationship between the cost of drug promotions and the price of the drug products. Study after study has shown that, once a new drug's patent has expired, identical drugs sold under generic names cost much less than the advertised brand-name.

In all 50 states, a consumer can ask a pharmacist to substitute a generic for a prescribed brand-name drug, unless the prescribing physician indicates otherwise. Some critics see consumer advertising as potentially discouraging the choice of cheaper generics.

William Haddad, the author of New York's generic-substitution law, says that undermining confidence in generic products is the sole reason behind direct-to-consumer ads. Haddad, who is now president of the Generic Pharmaceutical Industry Association, predicts that brand-name drug makers will "push an artificial difference" between identical branded and generic products, based on the shapes and colors of the branded products. Haddad foresees heavy brand-name promotion at the time a product is about to lose its patent protection and become fair game for generic rivals. The effect could be to stamp out competition before it begins.

THE FDA'S OPTIONS

While the FDA has broad powers over drug advertising, there's some question about how far those powers reach. Some critics want all consumer advertising banished from the prescription-drug field. But a flat ban on *all* ads to consumers may not be legally possible—or even desirable. For example, consumer advocates long ago successfully fought for the legal right of pharmacies to publish price comparisons of prescription drugs. But the FDA can and, in CU's opinion, should ban certain kinds of drug ads:

• Ads for products on the market less than three years—products that have not been in general use long enough to establish a safety record.

• Ads for psychoactive drugs, and for drugs that create dependence, that are apt to be abused, or that are known to be overused.

Other approaches are, of course, possible. Without actually establishing a ban, the FDA could effectively keep most drug ads off radio and TV by insisting on an unabbreviated disclosure of a given drug's "brief summary." In addition (or instead), the agency could insist that the package of any advertised prescription drug contain an FDA-approved insert of information for patients.

It remains to be seen whether any set of regulations can assure prescription-drug advertising with useful and balanced information for consumers.

100.

MARIO CUOMO: Keynote Address

The Democratic National Convention kicked off in San Francisco on July 17, 1984, and was keynoted by this address by New York Governor Mario Cuomo. Apart from its brilliance of rhetoric, the speech was also notable for its liberal thrust: the keynoter, as it turned out, was probably a good deal to the left of the candidate the convention chose, ex-Vice President Walter Mondale of Minnesota. But the speech brought Governor Cuomo a kind of national attention he had not received before, and he began to be spoken of as a possible candidate in 1988.

Source: *Vital Speeches of the Day*, August 15, 1984.

ON BEHALF OF THE Empire State and the family of New York, I thank you for the great privilege of being allowed to address this convention.

Please allow me to skip the stories and the poetry and the temptation to deal in nice but vague rhetoric.

Let me instead use this valuable opportunity to deal with the questions that should determine this election and that are vital to the American people.

Ten days ago, President Reagan admitted that although some people in this country seemed to be doing well nowadays, others were unhappy, and even worried, about themselves, their families and their futures.

The President said he didn't understand that fear. He said, "Why, this country is a shining city on a hill."

The President is right. In many ways we are "a shining city on a hill."

But the hard truth is that not everyone is sharing in this city's splendor and glory.

A shining city is perhaps all the President sees from the portico of the White House and the veranda of his ranch, where everyone seems to be doing well.

But there's another part of the city, the part where some people can't pay their mortgages and most young people can't afford one, where students can't afford the education they need and middle-class parents watch the dreams they hold for their children evaporate.

In this part of the city there are more poor than ever, more families in trouble. More and more people who need help but can't find it.

Even worse: There are elderly people who tremble in the basements of the houses there.

There are people who sleep in the

city's streets, in the gutter, where the glitter doesn't show.

There are ghettos where thousands of young people, without an education or a job, give their lives away to drug dealers every day.

There is despair, Mr. President, in faces you never see, in the places you never visit in your shining city.

In fact, Mr. President, this nation is more a "Tale of Two Cities" than it is a "Shining City on a Hill."

Maybe if you went to Appalachia where some people still live in sheds and to Lackawanna where thousands of unemployed steel workers wonder why we subsidized foreign steel while we surrender their dignity to unemployment and to welfare checks; maybe if you stepped into a shelter in Chicago and talked with some of the homeless there; maybe, Mr. President, if you asked a woman who'd been denied the help she needs to feed her children because you say we need the money to give a tax break to a millionaire or to build a missile we can't even afford to use—maybe then you'd understand.

Maybe, Mr. President.

But I'm afraid not.

Because, the truth is, this is how we were warned it would be.

President Reagan told us from the beginning that he believed in a kind of social Darwinism. Survival of the fittest. "Government can't do everything," we were told. "So it should settle for taking care of the strong and hope that economic ambition and charity will do the rest. Make the rich richer and what falls from their table will be enough for the middle-class and those trying to make it into the middle-class."

The Republicans called it trickle-down when Hoover tried it. Now they call it supply side. It is the same shin-

ing city for those relative few who are lucky enough to live in its good neighborhoods.

But for the people who are excluded—locked out—all they can do is to stare from a distance at that city's glimmering towers.

It's an old story. As old as our history.

The difference between Democrats and Republicans has always been measured in courage and confidence. The Republicans believe the wagon train will not make it to the frontier unless some of our old, some of our young and some of our weak are left behind by the side of the trail.

The strong will inherit the land!

We Democrats believe that we can make it all the way with the whole family intact.

We have. More than once.

Ever since Franklin Roosevelt lifted himself from the wheelchair to lift this nation from its knees. Wagon train after wagon train. To new frontiers of education, housing, peace. The whole family aboard. Constantly reaching out to extend and enlarge that family. Lifting them up into the wagon on the way. Blacks and Hispanics, people of every ethnic group, and Native Americans—all those struggling for their families claim to some small share of America.

For nearly 50 years we carried them to new levels of comfort, security, dignity, even affluence.

Some of us are in this room today only because this nation had that confidence.

It would be wrong to forget that.

So, we are at this convention to remind ourselves where we come from and to claim the future for ourselves and for our children.

Today, our great Democratic Party, which has saved this nation from de-

New York Governor Mario Cuomo

pression, from fascism, from racism, from corruption, is called upon to do it again—this time to save the nation from confusion and division, most of all from a fear of a nuclear holocaust.

In order to succeed, we must answer our opponent's polished and appealing rhetoric with a more telling reasonableness and rationality.

We must win this case on the merits.

We must get the American public to look past the glitter, beyond the showmanship—to reality, to the hard substance of things. And we will do that not so much with speeches that sound good as with speeches that are good and sound.

Not so much with speeches that bring people to their feet as with speeches that bring people to their senses.

We must make the American people hear our "tale of two cities."

We must convince them that we don't have to settle for two cities, that we can have one city, indivisible, shining for all its people.

We will have no chance to do that if what comes out of this convention, what is heard throughout the campaign, is a babel of arguing voices.

To succeed we will have to surrender small parts of our individual interests, to build a platform we can all stand on, at once, comfortably, proudly singing out the truth for the nation to hear, in chorus, its logic so clear and commanding that no slick commercial, no amount of geniality, no martial music will be able to muffle it.

We Democrats must unite so that the entire nation can. Surely the Republicans won't bring the country together. Their policies divide the nation: into the lucky and the left-out, the royalty and the rabble.

The Republicans are willing to treat that division as victory. They would cut this nation in half, into those temporarily better off and those worse off than before, and call it recovery.

We should not be embarassed or dismayed if the process of unifying is difficult, even at times wrenching.

Unlike any other party, we embrace men and women of every color, every creed, every orientation, every economic class. In our family are gathered everyone from the abject poor of Essex County in New York to the enlightened affluent of the gold coasts of both ends of our nation. And in between is the heart of our constituency. The middle class, the people not rich enough to be worry-free but not poor enough to be on welfare, those who work for a living because they have to. White collar and blue collar. Young professionals. Men and women in small business desperate for the capital and contracts they need to prove their worth.

We speak for the minorities who have not yet entered the mainstream.

For ethnics who want to add their culture to the mosaic that is America.

For women indignant that we refuse to etch into our governmental commandments the simple rule "thou shalt not sin against equality," a commandment so obvious it can be spelled in three letters: E.R.A.!

For young people demanding an education and a future.

For senior citizens terrorized by the idea that their only security, their Social Security, is being threatened.

For millions of reasoning people fighting to preserve our environment from greed and stupidity. And fighting to preserve our very existence from a macho intransigence that refuses to make intelligent attempts to discuss the possibility of nuclear holocaust with our enemy. Refusing because they believe we can pile missiles so high that they will pierce the clouds and the sight of them will frighten our enemies into submission.

We're proud of this diversity. Grateful we don't have to manufacture its appearance the way the Republicans will next month in Dallas, by propping up mannequin delegates on the convention floor. But we pay a price for it.

The different people we represent have many points of view. Sometimes they compete and then we have debates, even arguments. That's what our primaries were.

But now the primaries are over, and it is time to lock arms and move into this campaign together.

If we need any inspiration to make the effort to put aside our small differences, all we need to do is to reflect on the Republican policy of divide and cajole and how it has injured our land since 1980.

The President has asked us to judge him on whether or not he's fulfilled the promises he made four years ago. I accept that. Just consider what he said and what he's done.

Inflation is down since 1980. But not because of the supply-side miracle promised by the President. Inflation was reduced the old-fashioned way, with a recession, the worst since 1932. More than 55,000 bankruptcies. Two years of massive unemployment. Two hundred thousand farmers and ranchers forced off the land. More homeless than at any time since the Great Depression. More hungry, more poor—mostly women— and a nearly $200 billion deficit threatening our future.

The President's deficit is a direct and dramatic repudiation of his promise to balance our budget by 1983.

That deficit is the largest in the history of this universe; more than three times larger than the deficit in President Carter's last year.

It is a deficit that, according to the President's own fiscal advisor, could grow as high as $300 billion a year, stretching "as far as the eye can see."

It is a debt so large that as much as one-half of our revenue from the income tax goes to pay the interest on it each year.

It is a mortgage on our children's futures that can only be paid in pain and that could eventually bring this nation to its knees.

Don't take my word for it—I'm a Democrat.

Ask the Republican investment bankers on Wall Street what they think the chances are this recovery will be permanent. If they're not too embarassed to tell you the truth, they'll say they are appalled and frightened by the President's deficit. Ask them what they think of our economy, now that it has been driven by the distorted value of the dollar back to its colonial condition, exporting agricultural products and importing manufactured ones.

Ask those Republican investment bankers what they expect the interest rate to be a year from now. And ask them what they predict for the inflation rate then.

How important is this question of the deficit?

Think about it: What chance would the Republican candidate have had in 1980 if he had told the American people that he intended to pay for his so-called economic recovery with bankruptcies, unemployment and the largest Government debt known to humankind? Would American voters have signed the loan certificate for him on Election Day? Of course not! It was an election won with smoke and mirrors, with illusions. It is a recovery made of the same stuff.

And what about foreign policy?

They said they would make us and the whole world safer. They say they have.

By creating the largest defense budget in history, one even they now admit is excessive, failed to discuss peace with our enemies. By the loss of 279 young Americans in Lebanon in pursuit of a plan and a policy no one can find or describe.

We give monies to Latin American governments that murder nuns, and then lie about it.

We have been less than zealous in our support of the only real friend we have in the Middle East, the one democracy there, our flesh and blood ally, the state of Israel.

Our policy drifts with no real direction, other than an hysterical commitment to an arms race that leads nowhere, if we're lucky. If we're not— could lead us to bankruptcy or war.

Of course we must have a strong defense!

Of course Democrats believe that there are times when we must stand and fight. And we have. Thousands of us have paid for freedom with our lives. But always, when we've been at our best, our purposes were clear.

Now they're not. Now our allies are as confused as our enemies.

Now we have no real commitment to our friends or our ideals of human rights, to the refuseniks, to Sakharov, to Bishop Tutu and the others struggling for freedom in South Africa.

We have spent more than we can afford. We have pounded our chest and made bold speeches. But we lost 279 young Americans in Lebanon and we are forced to live behind sand bags in Washington.

How can anyone believe that we are stronger, safer or better?

That's the Republican record.

That its disastrous quality is not more fully understood by the American people is attributable, I think, to the President's amiability and the failure by some to separate the salesman from the product.

It's now up to us to make the case to America.

And to remind Americans that if they are not happy with all the President has done so far, they should consider how much worse it will be if he is left to his radical proclivities for another four years unrestrained by the need once again to come before the American people.

If July brings back Anne Gorsuch Buford, what can we expect of December?

Where would another four years take us?

How much larger will the deficit be?

How much deeper the cuts in programs for the struggling middle class and the poor to limit that deficit? How high the interest rates? How much more acid rain killing our forests and fouling our lakes?

What kind of Supreme Court? What kind of court and country will be fashioned by the man who believes in having government mandate people's religion and morality?

The man who believes that trees pollute the environment, that the laws against discrimination go too far. The man who threatens Social Security and Medicaid and help for the disabled.

How high will we pile the missles?

How much deeper will be the gulf between us and our enemies?

Will we make meaner the spirit of our people?

This election will measure the record of the past four years. But more than that, it will answer the question of what kind of people we want to be.

We Democrats still have a dream. We still believe in this nation's future.

And this is our answer—our credo:

We believe in only the government we need, but we insist on all the government we need.

We believe in a government characterized by fairness and reasonableness, a reasonableness that goes beyond labels, that doesn't distort or promise to do what it knows it can't do.

A government strong enough to use the words "love" and "compassion" and smart enough to convert our noblest aspirations.

We believe in encouraging the talented, but we believe that while survival of the fittest may be a good working description of the process of evolution, a government of humans should elevate itself to a higher order, one which fills the gaps left by chance or a wisdom we don't understand.

We would rather have laws written by the patron of this great city, the man

called the "world's most sincere Democrat," St. Francis of Assisi, than laws written by Darwin.

We believe, as Democrats, that a society as blessed as ours, the most affluent democracy in the world's history, that can spend trillions on instruments of destruction, ought to be able to help the middle class in its struggle, ought to be able to find work for all who can do it, room at the table, shelter for the homeless, care for the elderly and infirm, hope for the destitute.

We proclaim as loudly as we can the utter insanity of nuclear proliferation and the need for a nuclear freeze, if only to affirm the simple truth that peace is better than war because life is better than death.

We believe in firm but fair law and order, in the union movement, in privacy for people, openness by government, civil rights, and human rights.

We believe in a single fundamental idea that describes better than most textbooks and any speech what a proper government shoud be. The idea of family. Mutuality. The sharing of benefits and burdens for the good of all. Feeling one another's pain. Sharing one another's blessings. Reasonably, honestly, fairly, without respect to race, or sex, or geography or political affiliation.

We believe we must be the family of America, recognizing that at the heart of the matter we are bound one to another, that the problems of a retired school teacher in Duluth are our problems. That the future of the child in Buffalo is our future. The struggle of a disabled man in Boston to survive, to live decently is our struggle. The hunger of a woman in Little Rock, our hunger. The failure anywhere to provide what reasonably we might, to avoid pain, is our failure.

For 50 years we Democrats created a better future for our children, using traditional democratic principles as a fixed beacon, giving us direction and purpose, but constantly innovating, adapting to new realities; Roosevelt's alphabet programs; Truman's NATO and the GI Bill of Rights; Kennedy's intelligent tax incentives and the Alliance For Progress; Johnson's civil rights; Carter's human rights and the nearly miraculous Camp David peace accord.

Democrats did it—and Democrats can do it again.

We can build a future that deals with our deficit.

Remember, 50 years of progress never cost us what the last four years of stagnation have. We can deal with that deficit intelligently, by shared sacrifice, with all parts of the nation's family contributing, building partnerships with the private sector, providing a sound defense without depriving ourselves of what we need to feed our children and care for our people.

We can have a future that provides for all the young of the present by marrying common sense and compassion.

We know we can, because we did it for nearly 50 years before 1980.

We can do it again. If we do not forget. Forget that this entire nation has profited by these progressive principles. That they helped lift up generations to the middle class and higher: gave us a chance to work, to go to college, to raise a family, to own a house, to be secure in our old age and, before that, to reach heights that our own parents would not have dared dream of.

That struggle to live with dignity is the real story of the shining city. It's a story I didn't read in a book, or learn in a classroom. I saw it, and lived it. Like many of you.

I watched a small man with thick calluses on both hands work 14 and 16 hours a day. I saw him once literally bleed from the bottoms of his feet, a man who came here uneducated, alone, unable to speak the language, who taught me all I needed to know about faith and hard work by the simple eloquence of his example. I learned about our kind of democracy from my father. I learned about our obligation to each other from him and from my mother. They asked only for a chance to work and to make the world better for their children and to be protected in those moments when they would not be able to protect themselves. This nation and its government did that for them.

And that they were able to build a family and live in dignity and see one of their children go from behind their little grocery store on the other side of the tracks in south Jamaica where he was born, to occupy the highest seat in the greatest state of the greatest nation in the only world we know, is an ineffably beautiful tribute to the democratic process.

And on Jan. 20, 1985, it will happen again. Only on a much grander scale. We will have a new President of the United States, a Democrat born not to the blood of kings but to the blood of immigrants and pioneers.

We will have America's first woman Vice President, the child of immigrants, a New Yorker, opening with one magnificent stroke a whole new frontier for the United States.

It will happen, if we make it happen.

I ask you, ladies and gentlemen, brothers and sisters—for the good of all of us, for the love of this great nation, for the family of America, for the love of God. Please make this nation remember how futures are built.

101.

JESSE JACKSON: Campaign Speech

The 1984 presidential campaign was not noted for its fine speeches. The Republican incumbent, Ronald Reagan, seemed almost certain to win, and so he did not have to say much. The Democrat, Walter Mondale, seemed almost sure to lose, so his speeches often seemed rather strident. Perhaps the only really fresh note in the campaign was the presence of Jesse Jackson as a serious, or quasi-serious, candidate for the Democratic nomination. Jackson, the first black politician to make a genuine run for the presidency, ran on what he called a "rainbow coalition" of blacks, whites, reds, yellows, and other more or less disadvantaged groups. His standard speech, which he gave in many places and on many occasions, is reprinted here.

Source: *The New York Times*, February 27, 1984.

AMERICA IS NOT a blanket of one piece of unbroken cloth, one color, one texture. America is a quilt of many patches, many pieces, many colors, various textures. But everybody fits somewhere. That's what makes America great. Give me your tired, your poor, your huddled masses; in this nation we will make room for you.

America is not always right, but we have the right to protest for the right. That's what makes America a great nation.

It's not enough to have the ingredients—you must have leadership. Leadership will not just follow opinion polls—leadership molds opinion. Leadership will not just find out where there is a tailwind and jump in front—leadership will face a headwind and make a difference.

The rainbow coalition is winning. When I see young Americans standing up, we're winning. Last time around,

Reagan won by default. It was our fault: We did not register and vote as we should have voted. We were not aware of the dangers.

But under his Administration, the misery index is on the rise, the danger index is on the rise; five million more people in poverty, three million more children in poverty, schools closing while jails are being built, jail wardens getting tenure while teachers with master's degrees lose their jobs. The No. 1 agricultural system in the history of the world, and yet there are 20 million Americans malnourished tonight, a half-billion people in the world malnourished. Farm prices going down, consumer prices going up—something has gone wrong.

A 52-cent box of Wheaties, only 2 cents of wheat in the box. Something has gone wrong!

We need leadership, we need leadership. Our leadership has become mean and punitive. We say we will relate to Russia and we will not be afraid. It's not enough to not be afraid—we must affirm life. We cannot just remain with Russia on a nuclear threat confrontation. It's not enough to know that Russia can kill us tonight and we can kill them tonight. Mutual annihilation capacity is not great human achievement!

We must use our agriculture, our training, our technology. There is a law called the divine law of reciprocity: You cannot hurt somebody without hurting yourself; you cannot help somebody without helping yourself. We imposed the grain embargo on the Russians in 1979. Since that time, we've lost $22 billion in agribusiness, starving Russian cattle and American farmers. Let's be civilized and go another way.

We're so vain as to destroy the human race and our planet. These nuclear weapons are now on automatic; they are beyond human verifiability. We could have a nuclear war based on the margin of human error, computer malfunction, unauthorized agent or zealot. We must freeze these weapons and eliminate them and save the human race.

We must use our agriculture, our great natural gift. We must feed the world, not fight the world. We must use our minds to become more civilized and not just use our trigger finger. We must go another way. We must make judgments.

You have the power to be more than what you are. Three million high school seniors will graduate this May and June. You should come across that stage with a diploma in one hand symbolizing knowledge and wisdom, and a voter card in the other hand symbolizing power and responsibility. You can make a difference.

There are 11 million college stu-dents—11 million can choose jobs over jails. There are 28 million young Americans between 18 and 24, 17 million unregistered. You don't have the right to do less than your best. We have the power to choose a new course, a new coalition and leadership. Boys have lost their lives in Central America, the Caribbean, Lebanon, a nuclear stand-off in Europe. America deserves better leadership.

We must be the hope of the free world, not the threat to planet Earth. We can be. But our nation tries to overthrow a Government in Nicaragua; they have no patience with their transition and development. We're wrong. When our nation will cut off aid to American education and increase aid to El Salvador, we're wrong.

When the nation of democracy becomes South Africa's No. 1 trading partner, we're wrong, this is wrong. When in Lebanon we pull back the boys and send the bombs and destroy Lebanese villages and churches and temples and men and women and children, when I think that God is a just God, like Jefferson I shudder for my country. That is wrong, we must choose to save the children, give peace a chance. We must give peace a chance. We must give peace a chance. We must, we must!

I come here today to ask you to join me in seeking a new course for America, a new course that requires hard work, great effort, great sacrifice on the part of each of us, but effort worth the price.

I ask you to help me set this new course because I believe this country is wasting its most precious resources, our economy, our environment, the best minds of your and my generation. The future of the world itself is at stake as this country devotes more and more of its resources to its military budget.

AP/Wide World

Reverend Jesse Jackson

More and more of the resources of the entire globe are being spent on arms and armaments while the people suffer. Every minute 30 children die for want of food and inexpensive vaccines, and every minute the world's military budget absorbs $1.3 million of the public treasure. We must go another way.

The people of this country have it in their power to set the whole world on a new course. We set the pace. We developed the first atom bomb; we used the first atom bomb. Under President Reagan we have set a pace of increasing military spending in this country and around the world. The Reagan Administration has asked for $1.6 trillion in military expenditures over five years with a projected $750 billion in cost overruns.

These numbers rocket the mind until you begin to think about them a little bit, what they could mean if we spent this money on meeting human needs— $750 billion is enough money to pro-

vide every state with $15 billion over five years. It could put you to work solving the problems that exist around you instead of adding to them.

That is the nightmare of science in the world today, that with all our knowledge, all our resources, all our technology, we are creating problems rather than solving them.

What have been our achievements as a people since World War II? We've put our best minds to work developing the atom bomb. We hailed the dawn of the nuclear age and nuclear power that was clean, safe and too cheap to meter. We developed thousands of new chemicals.

What are the results of these great scientific achievements? The horror of Hiroshima. Nuclear waste that must be stored for generation after generation. The tremendous rise in the rate of cancer among our people as they are exposed to more and more carcinogens. Twenty thousand hazardous waste sites by E.P.A. estimates throughout the United States. Whole communities where children are sickening, where people can no longer sell their homes, because the world now knows those homes are poisoned.

I do not believe that any of you want a future where you add to the world's problems. That is the great hope of America, the fundamental values of our people. There are so many of us who want the same thing: jobs that will allow us to contribute to society; jobs that will allow us to support our families; the chance to use our minds and hearts to improve the world around us; the chance to raise our children in decent neighborhoods, to send them to schools where they will learn to read and write, not take drugs and drop out; the chance to endure the world around us; clean air to breathe; clean water to drink.

Every poll shows that Americans want the same thing: peace abroad and justice at home. That has been the message of our rainbow coalition, that surely, surely the people of this country, black and white and Hispanic, men and women, old and young, inner-city dweller and farmer, teacher and factory worker, want the same thing.

The leadership of this country has strayed far from the best and most fundamental values of the people. Under Ronald Reagan we have a Government that has put might before right. Under Ronald Reagan we have encouraged the corporations to put profits before people. We need new leadership. We need leadership willing to be the conscience of the nation, not leadership that will close the country's eyes to the hungry, to the sick, to the old and the poor.

That is why I need your help. There's so much that we could do. You could be learning to use all your skills and abilities to feed the hungry, to clean up the toxic waste sites, to develop mass transportation systems that would stop the waste in our energy resources, to rebuild our cities, to rid our world of poisons rather than add to them. We must change direction.

We must begin now. We must set a new course for this nation. You can send a clear message that you want to stop the arms race. That is the first step. It is imperative that we stop throwing our money and our resources into this black hole, the arms race. It is only if we stop this horrible waste that we can begin to solve our problems here at home.

We must look at what the Reagan Administration has done to see how severe these problems are. We have gone backwards as a society in the last four years.

In the 60's we discovered hunger in America. John F. Kennedy held an Appalachian baby in his arms, hungry, crying, sick, and we resolved as a nation to do something about the problem of hunger: food stamp programs, school lunch and breakfast programs, hot-lunch programs and meals on wheels for the elderly, supplemental food programs for pregnant women and their children. We did something as a nation. And for more than a decade, every study showed that there was less hunger in this nation. But what have we seen in the last four years?

We have seen cuts in domestic spending. Sixty-seven percent of the cuts are in human resources programs. One million people lost eligibility for food stamps since 1981: 3.2 million children no longer get free lunches, 475,000 children no longer get breakfast at school.

In the last four years, with the Reagan cutbacks we have seen more and more people fall from poverty into destitution. We have seen more and more people in bread lines and soup kitchens. We have seen rising infant mortality rates, most clearly related to inadequate nutrition, and inadequate prenatal care.

Feed the hungry. Save the children. These are the first messages of my campaign. We must restore the conscience of this nation. I am speaking to you here today because I believe we can do much more than that. We can do so much more than provide our people with the barest necessities of life. Once we begin to take our money out of the defense budget and into our economy, into meeting human needs, we can do far more than feed the hungry.

We can take every problem that we face as a people and start to solve it from the point of view of meeting human needs. The tasks before us—a new foreign policy, a new domestic policy, decent schools, a clean environment, a safe and inexpensive energy program—look impossible if we face them one at a time, if we face them alone. But together we can change the agenda of this country.

We can call this country to a new hope and a new belief in itself. Each problem that we face as a nation is related to every other problem. It is our task to define that relationship, to set a new agenda that solves the problems.

Our campaign, our rainbow coalition, has come together around this new agenda, a new foreign policy.

We can begin to make cuts in our defense budget on the day that we begin to deal with our neighbors around the world in a just, fair and equal fashion.

We can begin to cut our defense budget on the day that we pull our troops out of Honduras and stop bombing Lebanon. We can begin to cut our defense budget on the day that we decide we want to sit down with the Russians, on the day that we decide negotiations are preferable to deployment.

And the day that we start to cut our defense budget, we start to solve our problems here at home. Every billion dollars spent on guided missiles creates only 14,000 jobs. That money invested in our economy would create 65,000 jobs in retail trades, 62,000 jobs in education, 48,000 jobs in hospitals. When we put more money in this economy, when we change our priorities as a nation, U.S. science students can put your skills and knowledge to work cleaning up toxic wastes, developing alternative energy resources, advancing the health of this country and its people.

I offer you this challenge. I ask for your help. I cannot undertake this enterprise alone, but I believe our nation is capable of new direction and new vision. The people of this country want to change direction, want to move to a higher ground, to move from racial battleground to new economic common ground. I'm asking you to join me now and in the months ahead to build the rainbow coalition, to set a new agenda: justice at home, peace abroad.

If you have any doubts at all, you should not campaign for public office. The physical, emotional, and financial costs are too high to entertain any reservations.
EDWARD SCHWARTZMAN, "Political Campaign Craftmanship"

Watching this [1984] campaign has made me a born-again monarchist.
PRINCE BANDAR BIN SULTAN,
Saudi Arabian ambassador to the U.S.

102.

The 1984 Olympics

The summer games of the XXIII Olympiad of the modern era opened in Los Angeles on July 28. President Reagan formally initiated the Games after some 7,800 athletes from a record 140 nations paraded into the Los Angeles Memorial Coliseum. Nearly 100,000 spectators and millions more on TV then watched a program of spectacular entertainment that lasted more than three hours. The United States dominated the Games, but the Soviet Union, East Germany, and a few other athletic powerhouses of the Eastern bloc stayed away. Reprinted here are three comments on the political problems of the Olympics. First, an article by Christopher Brasher, a British gold medal winner in 1956, suggests that the disease affecting the Olympics is now terminal and predicts that the Games may not survive even until their centenary in 1996. Second, an editorial in the Jesuit publication America *calls for a rethinking of the Olympics and proposes a suspension of the Games for a few years. Finally, Vladimir Siminov, a Soviet spokesman, attempts to explain Moscow's refusal to participate in Los Angeles and expresses the hope that the Games will flourish in the future.*

Sources: *The Observer* (London), May 13, 1984.

   America, May 26, 1984.

   Novisti (Soviet News Agency), Moscow, July 1984.

A: CHRISTOPHER BRASHER
THE OLYMPICS MUST CHANGE

No, THE Russians are not boycotting the 1984 Olympics in Los Angeles: they are just staying at home because they believe that there are fringe groups in California who would delight in putting a bullet through the back of an athlete wearing a Soviet tracksuit.

No, the Olympics are not dead: they are just suffering from a terminal disease which lodged in the body of an idealistic movement in 1964 and then broke out in a violent form in 1968 and again in 1972. Four years later, in 1976, the violence was contained by stringent se-

curity measures so the disease changed course and erupted as blackmail.

Now the situation is different. I do not believe that the Russians and some of their satellites are refusing the invitation to go to the Los Angeles Games in the spirit of tit-for-tat; the real reason is that they are genuinely concerned about the security of their sports men and women. It is not defections that they are worried about: their track and field teams have travelled the world and so have their gymnasts and ice hockey players, without any defections so far as any of us in sport know. It is simply a concern for the personal safety of their team.

I have been to the States three times already this year and each time I have become more alarmed at a nationalistic fervour that is being built up. People whom I thought were genuine lovers of sport have said farewell with the words: 'See you next in Los Angeles and then watch our guys beat the hell out of them damned Russkies.'

When that is said in the context of a nation which has witnessed the assassination of Jack and Robert Kennedy, of Martin Luther King and the shooting of President Reagan, it is no surprise to learn that some extremist groups are now distributing lapel badges which say 'Kill a Russkie.'

Once, many years ago, when I was working for the BBC, the switchboard received a call from an individual threatening my life. And this in England. I will always remember my utter disbelief, and then the warning from a senior official that it was apparently serious. It is the only time in my life when I have known the true meaning of that phrase: 'A shiver down my spine.'

There is a connection between that incident long ago and the troubles that now beset the Olympic Games, and the connection is called television, the most powerful form of communication in the world. Television is the disease from which the Olympics is suffering.

My first full Olympics—1952 and 1956 as an athlete, 1960 and 1964 as a journalist—were, for me, proof that all the peoples of the world could live together and strive together in peace and friendship. Then, in 1968, an oppressive Mexican Government obliterated a rally of protest by turning machine guns on to the crowd in the 'Place of the Three Cultures' in Mexico City. Over 200 people died because the Mexican Government did not wish the world,

which was going to see the Olympic Games the following week, to see on the television screens in their homes that there was a huge body of opinion vehemently opposed to that Government.

That is a horror often forgotten when people talk of the troubled Olympics: 1968, the Black Power protest by the American athletes Carlos and Smith in Mexico City; 1972, the Black September gang's assault on the Israeli team and the carnage which followed in Munich; 1976 and the African nations' boycott in Montreal because the New Zealanders had played rugby against the South Africans; 1980 and the boycott of Moscow, led by the Americans as a feeble attempt to protest against the invasion of Afghanistan.

All these have been visited on the Olympics since 1964, the year of Tokyo—the first games to be televised 'live' to the world by satellites. That was when the disease was implanted in the body of the Olympic movement. It was then that those people who wished to make a statement to the world realised the Olympics were the ideal vehicle. The games occurred regularly, once every four years, with an exact timetable published widely throughout the world and with a worldwide audience of ordinary people—an audience of a size which no other happening in the world could match.

And so that audience has been used: sometimes by athletes; often by commerce; once by terrorists; and, in 1980, even by responsible politicians like President Carter and Prime Minister Thatcher. What a very strange mix!

As long as the Olympic Games stay in their present form, then there is no cure for the disease: the Games will die before their centenary in 1996, unless.

Unless nationalism is muted: that

means that national teams and national flags and national anthems must be done away with. Instead the individuals eligible to take part in the Games and vie for the medals would be chosen through regional championships in each sport.

And unless the Games find a permanent home—and that home should be Greece.

Two important objectives of the present Olympic movement would be lost. First, the right of every nation in the world to enter at least one competitor, of whatever standard, in every event in the showpiece of the Games, athletics or, as the Americans call it, Track and Field. This right is designed to encourage sport all over the world but, alas, it involves nations and it involves national teams which breeds nationalism, which leads some nations to use the Olympic arena as a substitute for the battlefield.

Second, the right of every city in the world to bid for the Games. Baron de Coubertin, the idealist who founded the modern Games, believed in the city principle. Now his successors on the International Olympic Committee are proud of the fact that when they award the Games to a particular city, that city is able to attract money, from governments and sponsors and television, to build facilities for the use of its peoples for many years after the Games. However, such facilities are sometimes not appreciated because they are far too grandiose and far too expensive— as the citizens of Montreal know to their cost. They are still paying for the 1976 Games and the Olympic stadium itself is still without its roof.

So I would amputate those two limbs of the Olympic ideal in the hope that surgery would save the body of the movement. And then I would move that body permanently to Greece.

My favourite place is Delphi, which was once known as the centre of the world. There, on a hill, is a stadium built many thousands of years ago.

That stadium could still be used, symbolically for some events—such as the 100 metres. Just below the stadium is an ancient Greek threatre, an ideal place for the best ballet dancers and best musicians of the world to entertain the best athletes of the world during the Olympic Festival. Ballet and music and sport are the three universal languages of the world and the language in each of them could be transmitted to the world by television. And far below the theatre, beyond the temple of Apollo, there is a plain on which the modern stadium and an Olympic village could be built. And beyond that is the sea which gives the world access to the site, the site which would have to be owned not by any particular person, nor by the Greek Government, but by the world itself.

I wrote about this dream of Delphi in these columns eight years ago, I spoke out against nationalism and flags and anthems at a press conference 28 years ago after I won an Olympic medal in the Melbourne Games. There are now only 12 years to go before we celebrate the centenary of the first Games of the modern era, the Games of Athens in 1896. Can the surgery be done in time?

B: EDITORIAL
RETHINKING THE OLYMPICS

"CHARIOTS OF FIRE" did its best to present a squeaky clean image of the 1924 Olympics, but even in this instance something was wrong. All in the interests of Britannia, the Prince of Wales casually but persistently tried to persuade Eric Liddell to compromise his religious principles by competing on the sabbath.

For the Prince, the glory of England superseded Mr. Liddell's quaint religiosity and personal integrity. A clever compromise allowed Mr. Liddell to compete on another day and thus save his integrity, but the Prince had already revealed his.

The film had a happy ending, but the real-world Olympics are not likely to resolve their ongoing internal tensions so easily. The Soviet decision to withdraw from the 1984 summer Olympics in Los Angeles and the speculation that has followed it point out the key flaw in the present Olympic structure: The games have become a competition not of athletes but of nations and even of competing ways of life. From their founding in 1896 until 1952, the United States won every single Olympiad with the exception of 1936, which Nazi Germany won for the glory of the Führer. From 1956 to the present, the United States has won two, and the Soviet Union five. It has become a two-way competition between superpowers.

The Soviets are convinced they must demonstrate the debilitating decadence of the West. Furthermore, the danger that one of their athletes would defect to the West during the Los Angeles games became for them an intolerable risk. By withdrawing from the games, the Soviet Union eliminates the possibility of either defeat or defection.

There will be demonstrations and protests, as the Soviets charge, and the United States is neither willing nor able to prevent them without suspending the Constitution and holding the games in an isolated garrison. Sadly, too, Soviet fear that some protest groups could actually threaten the safety of its athletes is not groundless, as was demonstrated in Munich in 1972, when 11 Israelis were murdered. By its action the Soviet Union is calling the world's attention to what it considers a weakness in a free society. Just four years ago, President Carter made a similar gesture when he withdrew the American team from the games to protest the Soviet invasion of Afghanistan. Revenge was undoubtedly a part of the Soviet's present motivation.

Whatever they are, the Olympics as presently conceived are not amateur athletic contests. They are too important to be left to amateurs. The Soviets and other Communist nations carefully nurture and generously subsidize their representatives. In the United States, the subsidies come from private enterprise, which pays handsomely to have the Olympic seal emblazoned on various products. The American Broadcasting Company paid the International Olympic Committee $225 million for broadcast rights, and it has sold $428 million of advertising to be shown during 187 hours of air time.

With political and commercial interest so high, the line between professionalism and amateurism becomes exceedingly fine. In the present climate, it would be no great tragedy if the Olympics were suspended for a few years, perhaps eventually to be refounded under new auspices and with a different format that would lend itself less easily to superpower politics. Athletics are too important to be left to politicians.

C: VLADIMIR SIMINOV
NOVOSTI, MOSCOW

THE U.S. HAS invented some incredible reasons for the Soviet non-participation and ignores the reason stated by the Soviet National Olympic Committee: that American authorities did not make adequate security provisions for the Soviet athletes. Many people say that this is the Soviet's revenge for the American boycott of the 1980 Games. I want to point out that the U.S.S.R. paid about $3 million—nonrefundable—for television coverage of the Los Angeles Olympics, so clearly we were preparing to participate. Can you imagine any U.S. enterprise paying such an amount knowing that it was being spent in vain?

I also heard statements that the U.S.S.R. is afraid its Olympic team will not get enough medals and will do poorly in the competition. May I remind you that at the world championships and world cup performances last year the Soviet Union took sixty-two first places and the U.S. twenty-eight?

It is also said that we were afraid our athletes would defect. Each year we send either a basketball team or a hockey team to the U.S., and there has not been a single defection.

Under the influence of the anti-Soviet policies of the Reagan administration, the U.S. press and general population have lost their sense of reality. I listen to Mayor Koch in New York, and he says that my country is monstrous.

As for the Olympics, it is clear to the organizers, the athletes, and the general public that the quality of this Olympics is greatly reduced because of the non-participation of my country and other countries. You have lost the best opportunity for good sportsmanship and competition. Your athletes are greatly disappointed. They would like to have less of the tarnished Los Angeles gold and more competition with Soviet athletes.

My country's decision will have a positive influence on future Olympic Games. Our decision is directed against the distortion of the Olympic ideals as we and the international community understand them.

What you call politicization of the Olympics is closely connected to the international policies of various American administrations. To avoid the politicization of future Games, there should be steps to ease international tensions and normalize international relations.

There will be no changes in the current anti-Soviet trend if President Reagan is reelected. He will continue this confrontational policy toward the U.S.S.R. I hope the world will survive, and I hope the Games will survive.

After Los Angeles, any city in the world should be able to survive an Olympics.

PETER UEBERROTH, president of the Los Angeles
Olympic Organizing Committee, after announcing that
the 1984 Games had turned a profit of $150 million

103.

LOWELL P. WEICKER, JR.: Religion in Politics

On August 22, 1984, in Dallas, the Republican National Convention broke tradition by simultaneously nominating Ronald Reagan and George Bush to run again for President and Vice-President. The next day, during a speech delivered at an ecumenical prayer breakfast, also in Dallas, President Reagan remarked: "The truth is, politics and morality are inseparable, and as morality's foundation is religion, religion and politics are necessarily related." These and similar statements kindled a national debate on the separation of church and state, a fundamental tenet of the Constitution. The discussions, often heated, persisted throughout the campaign, with the President usually getting the better of the many arguments. The following speech, by Senator Lowell Weicker of Connecticut, reflects the views of a member of the President's party—albeit a notably liberal member, who did not always agree with his leader.

Source: Office of Senator Weicker.

THANK YOU FOR THE opportunity to be here with you in Chicago today. The writer Nelson Algren once likened this city to a woman with a broken nose. "There may well be lovelier lovelies," he said, "but never a lovely so real." If you've spent some time here, you know what he meant by that remark. This is not a city apt to put on a false face. People are what they are and proud of it—whatever their race, religion, or ancestry. And when it comes to opinions or beliefs, they don't mince words.

Now, whether or not Chicago is your kind of town you have to admit that it is a quintessentially American one. The drive and diversity which characterize it are a direct result of our democratic system of government. This system not only drew people here in the first place—from famine-stricken Ireland, from the war-ravaged European mainland and from all parts of the globe—but once they were here it enabled them to work at what they chose and worship as they saw fit.

The freedoms of speech and religion secured by the First Amendment to the Constitution laid the foundation for a nation where no one ideology or theology would dominate to the exclusion of others. And for more than 200 years, that foundation has spared us the sectarian violence visited on so many other countries. Whether we look at Lebanon, Northern Ireland, Iran or India, the lesson is the same—don't mix government and religion.

The world has just witnessed the tragic assassination of Prime Minister Indira Gandhi. Her death was greeted by some of her countrymen with the cheer: "Long live the Sikh religion." Now it is not my place to take sides in that nation's religious strife, nor do I mean to assume a holier-than-thou attitude. But I believe we must realize that there but for the grace of our Constitution go you and I. Senator Sam Ervin used to quote from the opinion of Chief Justice Walter P. Stacy of the North Carolina Supreme Court in *State* v. *Beal.* "For some reason, too deep to fathom," wrote Stacy, "men contend more furiously over the road to heaven, which they cannot see, than over their visible walks on earth. It would be almost unbelievable if history did not record the tragic fact, that men have gone to war and cut each other's throats because they could not agree as to what was to become of them after their throats were cut."

History records it, and current events confirm it. Yet here in the United States some people still aren't convinced. The new fusion of Christian fundamentalism with a so-called political conservatism has been branded the most potent political force in the nation today. Potent it is. Conservative it is not. For if the goal of this movement is to Christianize America, then it must be seen for what it is—a form of radical extremism which we all—liberal and conservative, Christian and Jew alike—must resist.

Now don't get me wrong. I don't fault the fundamentalists on what they choose to believe or how they interpret the Bible. I fault them for attempting to foist that interpretation off on the rest of us via our public schools.

People who practice fundamentalist politics and have school prayer at the top of their legislative agenda talk of a return to "traditional values." I say to them that here in the United States there is no value more traditional, more central to our way of life, than that of separation of church and state. It is our great gift to the history of the world.

Senator Lowell P. Weicker, Jr.

For as Theodore White put it, "Never in civilization, since the earliest ziggurats and temples went up in the mud-walled villages of prehistoric Mesopotamia, had there been any state that left each individual to find his way to God without the guidance of the state."

During the 97th and 98th Congresses, there were repeated attempts to dilute—and in some cases outright destroy—this quality which has distinguished our society from all others. There have been bills to strip the federal courts of jurisdiction over school prayer. During floor consideration of the Fiscal Year 1985 Appropriations bill for the Departments of Labor, Health and Human Services, and Education, Senator Helms offered an amendment which would have in effect provided for organized school prayer. We were able to change the language to read "individual" and not "group" prayer— which is, in fact, the law of the land. Nowhere does it say an individual cannot pray. The amendment was dropped in its entirety in conference on the bill.

A similar scenario took place on the House side when a "voluntary school prayer" amendment was added to the Education Act Amendments. After I objected the House/Senate Conference on H.R. 11 deleted the reference and sent the bill to the President free of school prayer language.

I very much resent these back door raids on the Constitution. At least one thing good can be said for the proposed Constitutional amendment on school prayer that was defeated last March: for once the correct procedure was being used. But since that effort came up 13 votes shy of a two-thirds majority, the school prayer proponents have had to resort to highly questionable tactics that threaten to undermine not just the First Amendment but the separation of powers as well.

What is worse is that these radical rewrites of our Constitution have been put forward as good, old-fashioned morality. How can a little prayer hurt? we are asked. For one answer, I will defer to eight-year-old Justin Ross, who earlier this year wrote to the White House about his experiences at a school in Canada. "In my school," writes Justin, "we had to say a prayer. Some of the children stood in the hall instead of saying the prayer. Everybody thought they were bad. One boy told me that I was going to Hell. Please don't make people hate me because I am Jewish. I do not hate you because you are not Jewish. It made me feel terrible to say the prayer."

The child speaks with the voice of authority. I can remember when I was growing up and Protestantism was de facto the official religion in the United States. So that to be a Roman Catholic or a Jew or anything but some main line Protestant denomination meant you were different, and by the definition of the times, discriminated against. I can remember feeling uncomfortable myself when, as an Episcopalian, I was made to recite a Presbyterian prayer as part of my schooling. Those among my classmates who refused to participate were made to stand outside in the park. You can be sure we looked upon them as different. Mine was a private school where attendance was voluntary. The dilemma is even greater for a child compelled to attend a public school.

In his opinion on *McCollum* v. *Board of Education* in 1948, Justice Hugo Black discussed the special role public schools play in our society. "Designed to serve as perhaps the most powerful agency for promoting cohesion among a heterogeneous democratic people, the public school must keep scrupulously free from entanglement in the strife of sects," wrote Justice Black. "The preservation of the community from divisive conflicts, of Government from irreconcilable pressures by religious groups, of religion from censorship and coercion however subtly exercised, requires strict confinement of the State to instruction other than religious, leaving to the individual's church and home, indoctrination in the faith of his choice."

In other words, it is not up to me as a Member of Congress or to a public school teacher to take up on Monday where the minister left off on Sunday or the rabbi on Saturday. This is why I ultimately opposed legislation that passed the 98th Congress allowing the use of public school facilities for religious purposes. I say "ultimately" because up until the 11th hour I was involved in negotiations to modify the language. We were able to restrict such meetings to before and after school only. But because it was still a bad bill, I voted against it.

In just four more days, the American people will decide who will lead them during the next four years. The voter registration drives are over. The door-to-door canvassing is done. The last of the ads are being aired. The campaigning is coming to a close.

As leaders in your communities, you can not ignore the significance of November 6. But at the same time, you know full well that the business of democratic government is not an every-four-years affair. You may help get your candidate elected, you may see your political party prevail, but that does not mean that come November 7th you can afford to sit back and relax. For democracy means much more than pulling a lever. It means pulling together, whatever our party, to achieve progress and to preserve our political heritage.

The Constitution is not a self-enforcing document. Each succeeding generation must shore up the wall of separation between church and state or else it will come tumbling down. The decisions of the courts did much to strengthen that wall in the early 60s. Now it is up to us to see that those decisions are not undone by a simple legislative majority.

One thing is certain: we will have our work cut out for us in the 99th Congress. This will be the case no matter who wins the White House and whatever the composition of the Congress. The attack on the First Amendment has been bipartisan in nature. So must its defense be bipartisan.

And not simply bipartisan but composed of people of all faiths and no faith at all. What we are all fighting for is the freedom to interpret life and the world around us as we choose. Our purpose in banding together as a nation is not to promote Catholicism or Judaism or Buddhism or the faith of Islam but to ensure that as individuals we are free to find our own way to God. The Statue of Liberty holds up for all the world to see a lamp—not a cross but a lamp. And it is by the light of religious liberty that we must continue to make our journey.

The politicians, who once stated that war was too important to be left to the generals, now act as though peace were too complex to be left to themselves.

The decision to destroy the brilliant accomplishments of seven millennia of poets and architects, to destroy all God's handiwork, to place in jeopardy the lives of almost five billion people—that decision lies essentially in the hands of two men, one in Washington, the other in Moscow.

PIERRE TRUDEAU, ex-Prime Minister of Canada, 1984

Reggie Jackson hits three home runs in the New York Yankees' sixth-game 1977 World Series victory, beating the Los Angeles Dodgers four to two.

SPORTS AND THE OLYMPICS

During the decade 1977–1986 professional sports, heavily influenced by the demands of television, became an enormously big business. Not only were athletes paid increasingly higher salaries but the opportunities for sports celebrity product endorsements and personal appearances multiplied wildly. Gone forever was the day of the professional football player who sold cars or insurance in the off-season. As a result the temptations of sudden wealth facing young athletes were numerous. Unknown numbers of beefy athletes pumped up their bodies with steroids in order to gain a competitive edge. Other athletes received press coverage for using such drugs as cocaine. Nevertheless, measured advances in training regimens and coaching techniques, in addition to the infusion of new funding from lucrative television contracts, resulted in a high level of athletic competition and performance.

Three of the greatest sports stars of this period are pictured on this page. Kareem Abdul-Jabbar, born Lew Alcindor, lost only two basketball games throughout his entire high school and college career. When he moved into the NBA, playing first for the Milwaukee Bucks and then for the Los Angeles Lakers, he continued his graceful dominance of the game. By 1986 he was the oldest starting player in the league, and still one of the best. The 1986 season was Pete Rose's last as a baseball player, but he had capped off his career in 1985 by beating Ty Cobb's lifetime hitting record—one of the all-time great accomplishments in sports. In 1984 Walter Payton of the Chicago Bears surpassed Jim Brown's career rushing record in football—another remarkable feat. Pele, the brilliant soccer player who brought three World Cup titles to Brazil in 12 years, may have been the greatest star of all, although most American sports fans did not follow soccer, the world game. Despite soccer's gain in popularity in the United States in the 1970s, when Pele played for the New York Cosmos and drew large crowds, by the mid-1980s American soccer leagues were failing, nearly lost among the far more popular perennial attractions of baseball, football, and basketball.

(Top) Pete Rose gets his 4,192nd hit; (center) Kareem Abdul-Jabbar scores two of his 28 points to help the Lakers defeat Dallas 130–116; (bottom) Walter Payton evades tacklers from the New York Jets. (Opposite, top) Brazil's star, Pele, of the Cosmos, takes the ball downfield in a game against the L.A. Aztecs; (bottom) Giorgio Chinaglia battles for the ball during Soccer Bowl '80.

The 1980 Olympic Summer Games were scheduled for Moscow, and both American and Soviet athletes looked forward to a showdown in many sports. Then the U.S.S.R. invaded Afghanistan in December 1979. Soon after, President Jimmy Carter announced that the United States would not attend the games. They went on anyway, and the Soviets won most of the medals; but it wasn't much of a show for most Americans. The Winter Games that year, in Lake Placid, had been another matter. There, in one of the most surprising Olympic upsets of all time, the young U.S. hockey team took the gold medal, winning from the perennial Soviet champions. The 1984 Winter Games were held in Sarajevo, Yugoslavia. Phil Mahre won the first gold medal ever taken by an American in alpine skiing, beating his brother Steve by a split second in the slalom, and Bill Johnson shocked the Austrians, perennial champions in the downhill, by taking that gold as well. The 1984 Summer Games were scheduled for Los Angeles, but the Russians—together with several other athletic powers, including East Germany—didn't come. The absence of the Russian team, and especially of the

(Top) U.S. hockey team members and fans rejoice over their 4–2 victory against Finland in the 1980 Olympics; (bottom left) Phil Mahre of the U.S. takes a gold medal in the 1984 Olympics; (bottom right) Mary Lou Retton is the first American to win a gold medal in women's gymnastics.

superb Russian women and of the East German swimmers, ensured that the United States would win the Games; Americans also took the largest number of gold medals. A notable facet of the Games in Los Angeles was a national outpouring of patriotic emotion. It didn't matter that, in the absence of the Eastern bloc, there wasn't much competition in some events. The crowds swayed back and forth in ecstasy repeating "USA, USA, USA!" Some of the best known American winners are shown here—Mary Lou Retton, Edwin Moses, Joan Benoit, and Carl Lewis (who equalled Jesse Owens' 50-year-old record of four golds in men's track and field events). Olympic organizer Peter Ueberroth was able at the end to announce that the Games had made millions of dollars in profits.

(Top left) Edwin Moses, U.S. hurdler at the 1984 Olympics, was undefeated for nearly a decade; (top right) Joan Benoit wins a gold medal in the first Olympic marathon for women; (bottom) Carl Lewis celebrates after capturing his fourth gold medal, in a world record relay.

During the summer of 1986 a new athletic competition took place: the Goodwill Games in Moscow between American and Soviet athletes. They served, in a sense, as a substitute for the Soviet-American matchups that did not occur at the 1984 Olympic Games. Ted Turner, organizer of the Goodwill Games, lost as much as $25,000,000 by sponsoring them, but he fulfilled his aim to demonstrate that the Goodwill Games could play a role in reducing international tensions. This section began with a picture of Reggie Jackson of the New York Yankees who hit three homers in the last game of the 1977 World Series, and it ends here with a picture of the New York Mets celebrating their dramatic come-from-behind victory over the Boston Red Sox in the 1986 World Series. Baseball was long viewed as the quintessential American game.

(Top) N.Y. Mets catcher Gary Carter is hoisted into the air by pitcher Jesse Orosco after the Mets' 8–5 World Series victory over the Boston Red Sox in 1986; (bottom) the opening of the Goodwill Games in Moscow in 1986; (inset) Ted Turner, who originated and financed the games.

104.

American Ignorance

Over the years commentators have bemoaned the alleged lack of learning, literacy, and culture of the "average" American. The first of two such complaints is by Kalev Pehme, executive editor of a community weekly in New York City; it was adapted by Publishers Weekly, *and that version is reprinted here. Pehme considers the declining influences of the classics, or the "great books" of international literature, while the second article, by* Chicago Tribune *columnist Bill Granger, focuses particularly on American literature and the young.*

Sources: "My Say," *Publishers Weekly,* September 21, 1984.

"Ignorance—Our Cultural Blight," *Chicago Tribune,* November 14, 1984.

A: KALEV PEHME
WHO READS GREAT BOOKS?

IT USED TO BE that there was a canon of books students read that were meant to develop not mere literacy, but to affect the individual's taste and critical abilities as well—to open a vista to understanding the world. Often these books were used to reinforce a particular view of the world, but the content of these books was of such a caliber that they would help anyone who read to attain a high degree of mental refinement. For years, for example, people read the King James version of the Bible because it was part of their cultural and religious heritage; but the very language and importance of the issues involved helped to develop an individual's mind on an elevated plane.

One example comes readily: Abraham Lincoln. When one reads his speeches, one is struck by the influence of the King James version of the Bible. The Gettysburg Address has the rhythmic and tonal character of the Bible that Lincoln always read. Obviously, what we read influences what we think to the extent that we even speak or write in the language we are accustomed to reading. Compare a speech written by Lincoln to anything uttered by Reagan, Nixon, or one of today's politicians.

But a canon of classics as the basis of education is no longer a standard in this country. American students do not feel compelled to read Shakespeare, Dante, Cervantes or even 20th century writers such as Kafka. The problem is even more acute when one considers the grim statistics regarding basic literacy. According to Barbara Fenton, national director of the literacy initiative taken by B. Dalton (the chain has spent $3 million to raise the level of literacy in this country), 23 million adult Americans are functionally illiterate, and 46 million more Americans are only marginally literate.

The implication of this staggering inability to read on the part of the American public is manifest every Sunday in the *New York Times* bestseller lists. Current bestsellers are manifestly inferior, both in content and in the use of language. Few people read books of any kind; fewer people read good books. Thus, the American public is bereft of poetry, philosophy and the real joys of literature.

It's not like this everywhere. While I was in rural France, I overheard an argument between two itinerant truck drivers in a cafe. They were not arguing the relative merits of a sports team; instead, one driver asserted that Shelley was a better poet than Keats. The comment ignited a recital of long passages from various poems in support of each side's position. Neither driver had gone to Oxford or Cambridge; yet both knew their poets with the same familiarity an American worker has with ad jingles. I have never encountered a similar conversation between truck drivers at an oasis on Route 80 in Ohio or at a bar in New York City, nor is it likely that the strains of "Hyperion" will be heard in too many public places when even privileged college students no longer read even "Ode to Autumn."

The books that are being sold at B. Dalton and elsewhere and the books that are read even at college level are ephemeral appeals to sentimentality and self-improvement, with language and images formulated for television and movies. Soap opera emotions have dulled the sensibility of millions of people to Lear's suffering, and sitcom humor has robbed millions of people of the ability to laugh at the comedy of *Lysistrata*. Education is a lifelong pro-

cess, while schooling generally is not. The books we read are the foundation of our education, both in school and afterwards. Great literature teaches us about ourselves and how we live with others. Most of all, it refines our emotions and intellect. The complexities of love, for example, pervade all our lives. However, with no access to the great examinations of love found, for example, in great books from Proust's pessimistic *Recherche* to the interracial conflict of *Othello*, people are mentally unequipped to deal with love. Instead, they turn to Phil Donahue's experts or how-to books or measure the weight of their emotions against fantasy pseudo-romances that limit the reader's emotional response to and intellectual understanding of love.

We cannot expect the so-called "quality of life," that nonsensical bastard phrase, to improve in the U.S. until people not merely become functionally literate, but learn to read books that do not shirk the complexities of human life, but come to grips with them. The great books are great because their writers have reflected on the most essential human problems and have exhibited that thought in the most powerful rhetorical expressions that language allows. The greatest writers also find expression for that which language fails to articulate. Not to read great books means to be deprived of beauty, goodness and truth. It means to be consigned to oblivion.

B: BILL GRANGER

IGNORANCE—OUR CULTURAL BLIGHT

A FEW READERS let me know what a racist dope I was to suggest in a Sunday column that removing "Huckleberry Finn" from the required reading list in Waukegan schools was dumb. The letters were sad because, with one exception, it was obvious from the tone of them that the writers had never read the book. Ignorance has become a prerequisite for the exercise of free speech.

I wasn't going to write again about "Huckleberry Finn" and Mark Twain's savage stripping of the hypocrisy and pretense of American society justifying itself by justifying the institution of slavery—and that is just part of what "Huck Finn" is about.

But then, over the weekend, I reread a long essay by Edmund Wilson concerning Harriet Beecher Stowe and her remarkable novel, "Uncle Tom's Cabin."

In mentioning Wilson, I probably have lost most of the teaching profession, not to mention a quorum of book-hating aldermen like the fellow who banned "Huck" in Waukegan. But they probably wouldn't be interested anyway.

About 25 years ago, Wilson wrote a book called "Patriotic Gore," which examined the Civil War with a reporter's cold eye and a commentator's warm heart. He saw in the letters, biographies and lives of the war's participants a clear sympathetic portrait of America transformed. It is a great book, one of the best ever written about the Civil War era. One of the essays in the book examined the life of Harriet Beecher Stowe and her great work that electrified a nation and probably contributed as much to the doom of slavery in the States as any other single act.

I was stretched out on a couch, reading the marvelous words and sentences, finding my picture of that remarkable lady filled in again in mind and . . . suddenly, I realized what a crime intentional illiteracy has become.

"Uncle Tom" is a pejorative for blacks without black pride. Everyone, even an alderman, knows that. But is there one person in 50 who has heard

that term who has ever read the book that helped begin a civil war? One in a hundred? A thousand?

I bet not. Kids—black and white, suburban and city, rich and poor— are slouching to adulthood without the faintest notion of what preceded them, what shapes their institutions, their ways of thought. Intentional illiteracy is the rule of thumb in too many schools, among too many teachers—it is easier to read a text of what a book is about than to read the book itself. That is intentional illiteracy.

Forget Wilson, forget Mencken, forget the essayists of times past or obscure but worthy second-rate writers. Who reads the best anymore? Is there one English teacher in 10 in secondary schools who has read "Moby Dick," another candidate for our greatest American novel? Or who has the faintest idea what it is about? One in a hundred who has read the seminal work on slavery by Mrs. Stowe? One in a thousand who has read all the words of "Leaves of Grass," our great national heroic song?

The commercials for the United Negro College Fund say, poignantly, "A mind is a terrible thing to waste." But we waste it as we waste water, as casually as we pollute the air. Not black minds, not just white minds, all minds.

Our heritage is not white or black, it is American; it is also in our native language, English; it is also from the great languages whose complexities, evolved over centuries, finally permitted inarticulate men to speak great thoughts or, at least, ask great questions.

It is normal for kids to be arrogantly ignorant. But it is sacrilege for a well fed, well housed, well clothed civilization to neglect to show its children some ways of the past that created the road we travel on now.

The Chicago public schools have recently opted to drop geography as a required subject worthy of the attention of its captive audience. Drop geography. Incredible, isn't it?

We don't know where we have been and we don't know where we are going. We stride the country like new-day dinosaurs, massive and belligerent but with the brains of peas.

I was once a slum kid on the South Side, sitting on a gray-painted back porch step one summer day, and Joey from upstairs came down and showed me a book and said, "This is all about the colored and how they got here."

"What?"

"This is about the colored, about Uncle Tom's Cabin, remember when we heard that?"

I vaguely remembered something about slaves and a bad man named Simon Legree but I couldn't remember where I had heard about it. Joey gave me the book. I was 8 maybe, or 9. It was easy to read because the type was large. Fell into the trance of the words then a century old. About Uncle Tom and Eliza and Topsy. Tears in my eyes at the cruelty of the white world. Finished the book.

And then another. And another. And another. And another.

Books. Sad that rhetoric comes so easily to those with nothing to say. Sad that those wasted minds will never be transformed. Sad that the music of the soul is never heard because of the drumbeat insistence of the ignorant to remain well and truly ignorant and to insist that ignorance continues to be the right of every man.

105.

GLENN DOMAN: Function Determines Structure

This selection highlights the accomplishments of brain-injured children at Philadelphia's Institutes for the Achievement of Human Potential. Often unable to see, hear, or walk, these children were taught by founder Glenn Doman and his associates to become more capable human beings. Reprinted here is an article from the Institutes' In Report; *it is taken from Doman's book,* What to Do About Your Brain-Injured Child.

Source: *In Report,* October/December 1984.

THERE IS A LAW in nature that is of vital importance to all children and of overwhelming importance to brain-injured children. We have known this law for many years but we have managed somehow to ignore its staggering implications.

At The Institutes it was what we were seeing happening daily to our brain-injured children that forced us to consider this law and what it meant to them.

We were seeing severely brain-injured children arrive with bodies that were almost invariably tiny and sometimes twisted, with shoulders, eyes, mouths and feet that were frequently extremely abnormal, with heads so tiny as to be microcephalic and chests so shallow as to barely supply a breathing apparatus.

When we failed those children, their bodies remained tiny or twisted and so did their backs, hips, eyes, mouths and heads.

But when we succeeded, their bodies became in every way normal.

What is the law that explains this staggering fact? That law states simply that "function determines structure." That law explains why life on earth developed as it did from single-celled life in the primordial tide pools, to fishes, amphibians, mammals and man (phylogeny). That law also explains how human life develops from embryo, to foetus, to newborn (ontogeny).

It is the law that states that weight lifters have huge muscles because they lift weights. It is not that they lift weights because they have big muscles. Function determines structure.

Architects must first know what a building is to be used for before they can draw plans for it because its function will determine the structure.

A baby who is raised for the first year of life in near darkness (as is the case with certain beautiful but pre-Stone Age Xingu tribes with whom we have lived in the interior of Brazil's Mato Grosso) will not develop visually and will retain the visual pathways and competence of a newborn until brought out of the dark hut into light. His lack of visual function will have prevented earlier maturation of his visual pathway.

A child chained since infancy to a bedpost in an isolated attic by a psychotic adult will not develop normal hip sockets since no child is born with true hip sockets but instead actually cuts hip sockets by wearing them into the bone as a result of crawling, creeping, and walking. It is not that we walk because we have hip sockets (as we once insisted on believing) but rather that we have hip sockets because we crawl, creep, and walk. It is *not* that structure determines function but rather that function (moving) creates structure (hip sockets).

The brain-injured child who cannot move (due to his brain injury) does not develop hip sockets either. Sooner or later someone who does not believe that brain injury is in the brain but instead believes that brain injury is in the legs will send him for hip X rays and will find that he does not have normal hip sockets. The child will then have orthopedic surgery to create artificial hip sockets. This of course will not work since the child will still not walk for the precise same reason that he did not walk in the first place (brain injury). Not only is it true that function determines structure, but it is equally true that lack of function results in an immature or abnormal structure.

The vast majority of severely brain-injured children are quite tiny in physical size when they are first seen at The Institutes. That is to say, in height, in chest, in head size, in weight, they are, in about 75 per cent of the cases, significantly below average, and 50 per cent are below the smallest 10 per cent of the population, sometimes far, far below. Yet at birth (except for the premature ones) they tended to be at or very near average size.

As they get older they become smaller and smaller as compared to children their own age since the lack of physical functioning results in a lack of physical structure. This is exactly the opposite of what happens to the weight lifter. Yet once we start such a child on a program of neurological organization, his rate of growth will change, and often change dramatically. Quite often, in fact, a child who had been growing far slower than normal will suddenly start to grow far faster than normal for his age. Even where he began the program smaller in height, in head and chest circumference, and in weight than 90 per cent of other children in his age bracket, it is commonplace to find him suddenly growing at 250 per cent of the norm for his age.

While this phenomenon appears to be virtually unknown to those who deal with brain-injured children, it is well known to anthropologists and even has a name.

It is called the *catch-up phenomenon.*

This rule says that if a child is seriously ill for any reason, his physical growth will slow down or virtually stop, depending on the illness and its severity. The rule further states that if the child becomes normal, he will then grow faster than his peers to catch up. This, of course, is why it is called the *catch-up phenomenon.*

We see this occurring every day of our lives at The Institutes.

We see also, and it is hardly surprising, that there seems to be a high correspondence between the rate of success and the rate of growth as well as between the ultimate degree of growth and the ultimate degree of success.

That is to say, children who fail to make progress also fail to change in growth rate, children who succeed markedly but not completely, grow markedly but not completely, and children who succeed entirely, grow entire. While this rule, like all other rules I know, is not invariable, it is almost always so.

This is simply another way of saying that lack of function creates an immature or abnormal structure and function determines structure.

At The Institutes in Philadelphia, all brain-injured children above the age of eighteen months, except those who are completely blind, are started on a program of reading, using extra-large letters that can be discerned by the immature visual pathways of all except children who are terribly blind or who are unable to discern outlines. (With blind children reading is delayed until they are made able to see outlines.) As a result of this exposure to reading, two things happen.

First: There are many hundreds of brain-injured children two, three, or four years old, who can read with total understanding from a few words for some to many, many books for others. I know a few three-year-olds who can read in several languages with complete understanding. The size of the words is reduced as they progress.

Second: Although the world at large believes that children under five are unable to read because their visual pathways are too immature and because their brains are not sufficiently developed, there are hundreds of two-, three- and four-year-olds who are in *fact* reading. What is more, they are brain-injured and what is more, their visual pathways are now *more* highly developed than are the visual pathways of older children who are not brain-injured and who do not read. How can this possibly be explained?

It certainly can *not* be explained on the basis of age, since they are younger, not older, than the children who do not read (normal five-year-olds).

It certainly can *not* be explained on the grounds of some natural superiority. Far from being superior, these children are brain-injured and have often previously been diagnosed as being "mentally retarded." I don't know any one who believes it is an advantage to be brain-injured.

It can only be explained on the grounds that these children have simply had an *opportunity* to read that other children have not had. That opportunity permitted function, and function in turn created more mature visual pathways since function determines structure.

Very few facts are more important in the treatment of brain-injured children.

The lack of this realization is what has been wrong with the world of brain-injured children in the past. The awareness that function determines structure is one of the important things that is right about the world of brain-injured children today.

106.

DANIEL J. BOORSTIN: Myths of a Scientific Society

The great discoveries, inventions, and insights that change our lives, are made not by the average man or woman but by the extraordinary individual who, often to our astonishment, sees things in an utterly new way. This point is eloquently made by Daniel Boorstin, Pulitzer Prize-winning historian and Librarian of Congress, in this article from Science Digest.

Source: *Science Digest,* December 1984.

THE PAST and the future have much in common. Nearly all the past was a time when we were not there, and nearly all the future is a time when we will not be there. Therefore both have the appeal of mystery and romance. And—most important for our purpose—both have their mythologies. Primitive peoples have myths to frame their past; we have myths to frame our future.

In recent years we have learned a great deal about the myths of primitive peoples. Scholars of comparative religion are now generally agreed that for primitive peoples of the past and of the present, myths are not mere fanciful tales and random flights of the imagination. Quite the contrary. For primitive peoples, the brilliant historian of mythology Mircea Eliade explains, "Myth is always an account of a creation; it relates how something was produced, began to *be*. Myths tell only of that which *really* happened."

Since myths tell of all beginnings, they are the framework and the vocabulary of all primitive reality. They provide the archetypes governing present and future. For primitives, the unique is the *un*real. "The primitive, at bottom, finds meaning and interest in human actions (in farm labor, for instance, or social customs, sexual life, or culture) insofar as they repeat actions revealed by his gods, culture heroes, or ancestors," writes Eliade. The traditional stories of how the Earth and the seas and the plants and animals and man and woman came into being explain the presence and the nature of everything that surrounds man. Myths become the easiest, most vivid, most persuasive ways of generalizing about the world.

Our modern scientific mythology takes a quite different form, so we may not recognize it as a mythology. But it performs a similar function. It also limits our thinking and our imagination. While the myths of primitive peoples are about their past, ours are about our future. While theirs occurred in a distant sacred time, and their actors are supernatural human beings cast in the familiar heroic mold, ours occur in the scientific time to come. But the actors in our myths are also forces and entities cast in the mold of our recent past and our present, and our myths also dominate our ways of talking about the present and the future.

Our myths of the future, instead of being dominated by a sky-god and an Earth-god, are governed by large generalizing abstractions inherited from the science of the past two centuries. One comes from the biological sciences, and its name is Evolution. The other comes from mathematics and the physical and social sciences, and its name is Extrapolation. Just as primitive peoples can imagine no reality unless it is encompassed in the mythical origins of everything, so we find it hard to imagine a future that is not encompassed in these ways of extending experience into the scientific future.

The primitive myths of origin and creation were personal dramas of the gods—the Babylonian Marduk in battle with Tiamat, the Greeks Cronos and Zeus, Prometheus and Pandora. But our scientific myths of destiny and futurity are a drama of impersonal forces—natural selection, struggle for survival, adaptation, acceleration, deceleration. This crucial distinction grows naturally out of the differences between hindsight and foresight. The Euhemerist school of historians still insists that each ancient god is a deification of some hero who really lived. But the future heroes of Evolution and Extrapolation are still to come. "Truths," Descartes observed, "are more likely to have been discovered by one man than by a nation."

The myths of primitive peoples are emphatically retail. They deal in individual gods who can be dramatized and propitiated by ritual and sacrifice. But the myths of a scientific society are just as emphatically wholesale. Evolution is a dogma about groups of plants and animals, and the key word here is *species*. Extrapolation, the elementary technique of modern statistics, is nothing but the process of estimating or predicting a value or a quantity on the basis of a known quantity. It is concerned with trends—of population, prices, interest rates, diseases, etc.—estimated from what is already known of that category of facts. And extrapolation is assumed to be reliable in proportion to the size and representative character of the sample. In Evolution and Extrapolation there are no heroes and no villains, no Zeuses or Prometheuses. But still, in the grand arena of the future, potent forces compete, conflict and advance, true to their characters.

In ancient days, too, there were prophets of wholesale destiny. Job and Jeremiah foretold the future of whole peoples—the people of Israel, with whom God had made a covenant, or the people of Sodom and Gomorrah, on whom he would visit his retribution. The Prophet, as etymology attested, was one who spoke for God. He was a moralist first and a forecaster as a consequence. While such moralistic prophecies were wholesale, the myths were still retail, providing the community with vividly recognizable, familiar heroic figures. The modern scientist-forecaster, too, has built his myths in the wholesale mode. He speaks of the future of groups and quantities—of endangered species, of exploding populations, of "developing" economies, of declining birthrates and of increasing GNP. At the same time, the advances of science, always remarkably collaborative among unseen collaborators, have themselves become more obviously and more visibly collaborative. This is due not only to the high cost of experimental equipment but to the elaborated communications that make it easier to share incremental advances of science.

Still, we would do well, before betting on the predictions to which our mythology commits us, to remind ourselves of how our wholesale view may have boxed in our vision, imprisoning us in our past and our present. The ancient Greeks did finally escape from their mythology—their way of explaining the creation and the origins of things— into a universe of abstractions, into a world of forces and elements. By doing this they made possible the beginnings of modern Western philosophy and science. We seem now to have come full circle, for we have boxed ourselves into a world of abstractions and forces, and so committed ourselves to a mythology of destiny and futurity.

Perhaps we then overlook or underestimate the greatest force for change in human experience. Which is, of course, the individual discoverer, creator, artist, thinker or inventor. We can be misled here, too, by the fact that a number of crucial scientific discoveries have been made nearly simultaneously by widely separated individuals. The familiar examples are the calculus (Newton and Leibniz) and natural selection (Darwin and Wallace). But the fact remains that, in every case, the grand new insight was made by individuals. If they were unknown to each other as they developed their ideas, and if they were people of diverse heredity, temperament and environment, this confirms rather than contradicts the unpredictable creative power of the thinking individual. Coincidence is not collaboration.

Applying our mythology—the doctrines of Evolution or the techniques of Extrapolation—to our future must not be mistaken for forecasting the crucial grand advances of scientific discovery and technological innovation. The more wholesale our prophecies become, the more unprepared we will be for the unexpected.

If there is any lesson of scientific discovery from the past it is that its course is meandering and unpredictable: from the vagrant claims of a Paracelsus to the insights of a Newton to the inventions of a Thomas Edison or an Edwin Land.

While, of course, we can always chronicle the march of thought down the highways (or the ruts) of scientific research, we cannnot predict the grand innovations by men and women who wander off the safe, well-marked path. These rovers have been the great Discoverers. Once they have been sanctified by later generations as the high priests of scientific orthodoxy, we are misled by our historical hindsight. We can find predecessors for Newton's revolution in optics or for Darwin's view of emergent species. But these are far more conspicuous to us than they were to their respectable, doubting and sometimes outraged contemporaries.

We are also confused by the increasingly intimate interrelation of science and technology. The costly commitment of scientific enterprises to equipment that must be managed by large groups and can be justified only for use by teams of scientists misleads us. We feel that the surprises, the discoveries themselves, are somehow the work not of the men and women but of the machines. Some of our best recent historians of science have given the credit for crucial advances in thought to advances in the apparatus. "The scientific revolution, as we call it," the late Derek de Solla Price suggested, "was largely the improvement and invention and use of a series of instruments of revelation that expanded the reach of science in innumerable directions." Obvious examples are the telescope and the microscope, which helped spell the death of ancient stereotypes about the heavenly bodies, diseases and spontaneous generation.

But we must not mistake the properties and the sets for the drama. True enough, Galileo could not have caused the stir that he did without the telescope, which had been invented for military uses. But Galileo's triumph and his tragedy came not from what he saw but from what he made of what he— and now everybody else—could see. A telescope without a Galileo (and without a Copernicus before him) would be an atom without a Thomson or a Rutherford, an Einstein or a Fermi. Our computer enthusiasms tempt the uninitiated to take our hopes and our laurels away from the human discoverer. We are too eager to make the machine a collabo-

rator, when it really remains only our tool, a source of data, not of ideas. The most important apparatus for the greatest discoveries of the future will probably continue to be pencil and paper.

We are misled, too, by our very language for describing the progress of technology. We speak glibly of the first and second "generation" of computers, and we have not been too far off in predicting the next stages of technological advance. But we forget that only a century ago the computer itself was not in the respectable popular scheme of things. It was imagined only by a few erratic, inglorious Babbages. The British government refused to buy Babbage's grand calculating machine, the triumph of his life and his imagination. Not surprisingly, when he then invented an ophthalmoscope he would not reveal what he had done, but he did produce a cowcatcher for use on locomotives and a speedometer.

The course of technological progress, governed as it is by the available machinery, seems to be somewhat predictable—but only in terms borrowed from the inflexible language of Evolution and of "species." We have had some recent success in predicting *what* will be done—but very little in predicting *who* will do it. And why should this surprise us? We complacently predict the next "generation" of computers or of space vehicles. But who could ever have predicted an Einstein, a Von Kármán, a Von Neumann or a Goddard— much less the "generations" that follow from them? In preparing for our future we must not allow the high cost and collaborative uses of the machinery of experiment to tempt us to mistake the machine for the man.

The inevitability, the sense of fate and of destiny, revealed by our language of

Evolution and Extrapolation is only another clue to the mythological character of our thinking—and the mythological ruts in which we have got stuck. It is too much to hope that we will liberate ourselves from our confident mythology. The Greeks never fully succeeded in doing so, and Greek mythology has become part of our own. But self-awareness is itself a kind of liberation. To know the prison of our thoughts may help us leap over the walls—or at least remind us that there is a greater, freer world outside, and so prepare us for unpredicted generations of Darwins, Freuds and Einsteins to come.

107.

GERALD W. McENTREE: Labor Strategy Next Time

The election of 1984 was notably lacking in drama. Ronald Reagan, who was expected to win, did so with a record victory. His Democratic challenger, Walter Mondale, who had been Vice-President under Jimmy Carter, struggled valiantly to catch up in pre-election polls but never did. Mondale's main supporters were most of the country's labor leaders, and after the election it was commonly remarked that their strategy had been misguided. Gerald W. McEntree, president of the American Federation of State, County and Municipal Employees, did not agree with that judgment of Democratic election strategy, as this article makes clear.

Source: *The New York Times*, November 30, 1984.

WASHINGTON—The pundits have been telling us that organized labor's election strategy—to back a candidate early and stay the course—was a terrible flop, as if the "union bosses" formed up shoulder-to-shoulder and, on the count of three, shot themselves in the foot. And eight of 10 columnists go on to say that these "bosses" have lost touch with the rank-and-file.

The American Federation of State, County and Municipal Employees is probably the most diverse union in the country. Its decision to support the Mondale-Ferraro ticket didn't take place in a locked room; it was the outcome of extensive checking with the membership at all levels. This took several months and involved almost all of A.F.S.C.M.E.'s 3,000 local unions. The upshot was that we put our money and marbles on Walter F. Mondale, support that included an estimated 25,000 rank-and-file volunteers. They weren't at it because I was out there with whip and gun; they were there because they were committed.

If the race were to be replayed tomorrow, we'd all do the same thing, only harder. And President Reagan's re-election does nothing to change labor's purpose or commitment. Our domestic

AP/Wide World

Walter Mondale waves to a crowd of union members during his campaign. AFL-CIO's Lane Kirkland is at Mondale's left.

priorities are different from his, particularly on questions of tax reform, defense spending and social spending. We don't feel that the election was a referendum on these issues. Quite the contrary, scores of successful Senate and House candidates stressed the same bread-and-butter issues as the labor movement did.

The first purpose of a labor union is to protect the job-related rights of its members: fair wages and decent conditions of employment. But these basic rights depend on more than collective bargaining or management's good will; they are profoundly influenced by the condition of the nation's economic and social health. Therefore, A.F.S.C.M.E. worked for a candidate who favored fair taxation, equitable trade relationships, enforcement of laws that protect life and health on the job and in our communities, equality for women and minorities, and decent treatment for the old, the sick and the luckless.

Pie in the sky? Polling data throughout this election year demonstrated the effectiveness of the union vote. Exit

polling during the Democratic Party's nominating process showed that labor made a difference for Mr. Mondale in key states like New York, Pennsylvania, Illinois and Wisconsin. In the election, A.F.L.-C.I.O. members voted for the Democratic ticket by a 60-40 percent margin, and played a key role in the Democratic Party's effort to stem conservative control of the Congress and various statehouses.

But while organized labor has enjoyed its moments of victory, we've been unable—at least since 1968—to make a decisive impact on those big, overriding issues that shape the lives of working people. Historically, labor has done much to reduce the distinctions and tensions between classes. It won the 40-hour week, the minimum wage, disability pay and collective bargaining. And over the years it has fought for fairness and compassion in many other areas of public policy.

Yet labor must find ways of expanding its message. And to do so it must go back to the ABC's of organizing, bargaining and political action. If the trade union movement is to rebuild itself, it is going to require something more than passing out leaflets and boasting of the victories of a past age. Labor must build something that no other major institution in the country has—a membership of millions of people in every city, town and state. Whether this resource is strengthened or weakened over the next several years is up to us.

Service industries and service-related industries like financial institutions, high-tech manufacturers, telecommunications as well as state and local government offer labor its biggest organizing targets. Recently, A.F.S.C.M.E won the right to represent 6,000 clericals working for Iowa's state government and the

University of Iowa system.

The labor movement has to reach back to its roots. We have to carry labor's basic message to a new generation of workers: you're somebody; you have dignity; you have a voice. That's our challenge during the next four years.

108.

Pastoral Letter on the U.S. Economy

On November 11, 1984, in Washington, a long-awaited first draft of a report by a committee of Roman Catholic bishops was issued. When it appeared, it was immediately seen as highly controversial, for it did not merely complain that the economy, with all its record achievements of affluence, had allowed some to remain in relative poverty. Instead, it condemned the "massive and ugly" failures of the system, citing in particular a "morally unjustified" rate of unemployment and "gross inequalities" of wealth and income. "The fact that more than fifteen percent of our nation's population live below the official poverty level," the authors of the pastoral letter asserted, "is a social and moral scandal." Furthermore, the letter called for a radical attack, led by the government, on economic problems, and it ended by proclaiming that these problems had to be addressed in other parts of the world as well. Portions of the document are reprinted here.

Source: *The New York Times*, November 12, 1984.

THE POOR HAVE a special claim on our concern because they are vulnerable and needy. We believe that all Christians, Jews, those of other faiths or no faith at all—must measure their actions and choices by what they do *for* and *to* the poor. As pastors and as citizens we are convinced of one fundamental criterion for economic decisions, policies and institutions: They must all be at the service of human beings. The economy was made for people, *all* people, and not the other way around.

Everyone knows the significance of economic policy, economic organizations and economic relationships, a significance that goes beyond purely secular or technical questions to profoundly human, and therefore moral, matters. It touches our very faith in God and what we hope and believe about the destiny of humanity. The signs of our time direct the pastoral concern of the church to these moral aspects of economic activity. Interpreting this activity in the light of the Gospel—at the local, national and international levels—is the task we have set for ourselves in this pastoral letter.

In this effort to discern the signs of the times in U.S. economic life we have listened to many ways of analyzing the problems and many proposed solutions. In our discussion, study and reflection one thing has become evident. There is no clear consensus about the nature of the problems facing the country or about the best ways to address these problems effectively. The nation wonders whether it faces fundamentally new economic challenges that call for major changes in its way of doing business or whether adjustments within the framework of existing institutions will suffice. . . .

We are well aware of the difficulties involved in relating moral and religious values to economic life. Modern society has become so complex and fragmented that people have difficulty sensing the relationship among the different dimensions of their lives, such as the economic, the moral and the religious. During the preparation of this letter we have often been asked what possible connection there could be between Christian morality and the technical questions of economic policy. We acknowledge the problem of discovering these links, and we also fully accept the fact that social and economic affairs "enjoy their own laws and values which must be gradually deciphered, put to use and regulated by human beings." Religious and moral conviction cannot, simply by itself, produce solutions to economic dilemmas. We are confident, however, that the Christian moral tradition can make an important contribution to finding the right path. In the words of the Second Vatican Council:

"This split between the faith which many profess and their daily lives deserves to be counted among the more serious errors of our age. Long since, the prophets of the Old Testament fought vehemently against this scandal, and even more did Jesus Christ himself in the New Testament threaten it with grave consequences."

In many areas of Church life, to be a follower of Christ demands suffering and renunciation. Questions of family life, sexual morality, and war and peace face Catholics of the United States with challenges that summon them to the deepest commitment of faith. This is no less true in the area of economics and social justice. We live in one of the most affluent cultures in history where many of the values of an increasingly materialistic society stand in direct conflict with the gospel vision. We have been exhorted by John Paul II to break with "the frenzy of consumerism" and to adopt a "simple way of living." Our contemporary prosperity exists alongside the poverty of many both at home and abroad, and the image of disciples who "left all" to follow Jesus is difficult to reconcile with a contemporary ethos that encourages amassing as much as possible.

If the economy is to function in a way that respects the dignity of persons, these qualities should be present: It should enable persons to find a significant measure of self-realization in their labor; it should permit persons to fulfill their material needs through adequate remuneration, and it should make possible the enhancement of unity and solidarity within the family, the nation and the world community. . . .

While the United States can be rightfully proud of its achievements as a society, we know full well that there have been failures, some of them massive and ugly. Hunger persists in our country, as our church-sponsored soup kitchens testify. Far too many people are homeless and must seek refuge from the cold in our church basements. As pastors we know the despair that can devastate individuals, families and whole communities when the plague of unemployment strikes. Inadequate funding for education puts a high mortgage on our economic future. Racial discrimination has devastating effects on the economic well-being of minorities. Inequality in employment opportunity, low wages for women and lack of sufficient child care services can undermine family life. . . .

The citizenry of the United States needs a new and stronger will to pursue this task in a sustained way in the years ahead. It will be an undertaking which involves struggle: a struggle for greater understanding, a struggle with our own selfishness and a struggle to develop institutions that support active participation in economic life for all.

The effort to guarantee the economic rights of all will face resistance until the fullness of the kingdom of God has been established by God's gracious initiative. Until that day arrives Christ calls us to the conversion of heart which will enable us to engage in this struggle with courage and hope. . . .

To restructure the international order along lines of greater equity and participation will require a far more stringent application of the principles of affirmative action than we have seen in the United States itself. Like the struggle for political democracy at home, it will entail sacrifices. But that is what the recognition and acceptance of re-

sponsibility means. As a nation founded on Judeo-Christian religious principles, we are called to make those sacrifices in order to bring justice and peace to the world, as well as for our own long-term self-interest. The times call for the kinds of leadership and vision that have characterized our nation in the past when the choices were clear. Now we need to call upon these qualities again. . . .

We hope that this letter has begun to clarify how Catholic social teaching applies to the situations we are describing, so that our country can move in the direction the Pope indicated. We share his conviction that many of these issues generally called economic are, at root, moral and therefore require the application of moral principles derived from the Gospels and from the evolving social teaching of the church.

There are indeed different paths to holiness in the church and vocations to different forms of sharing in the effort to achieve the goals presented in this letter. These reflections on worship and liturgy, however, make vividly clear that none of us can afford to live a spiritually schizophrenic existence in which our private lives are oriented toward Christian discipleship while our economic activities are devoid of these same values.

1985

109.

Small Caps: James Cook: Nuclear Follies

In the 1980s the U.S. nuclear power industry found itself in deep trouble. In other parts of the world, the industry was thriving: in France, in Belgium, in Japan, even in the Soviet Union, despite the disaster at the Chernobyl nuclear power station. But the building of new plants in the United States was at an end. Why? Was it the fault of outsiders—for example, environmentalists—whose interference had made things more difficult? Or was it the fault of the industry itself? This article, written by James Cook, the executive editor of Forbes, *points the finger at the industry, not at the industry's enemies.*

Source: *Forbes*, February 11, 1985.

The failure of the U.S. nuclear power program ranks as the largest managerial disaster in business history, a disaster on a monumental scale. The utility industry has already invested $125 billion in nuclear power, with an additional $140 billion to come before the decade is out, and only the blind, or the biased, can now think that most of the money has been well spent. It is a defeat for the U.S. consumer and for the competitiveness of U.S. industry, for the utilities that undertook the program and for the private enterprise system that made it possible. Without even recognizing the risks, the U.S. electric power industry undertook a commitment bigger than the space program ($100 billion) or the Vietnam War ($111 billion) and, in little more than a decade, transformed what elsewhere in the world is a low-cost, reliable, environmentally impeccable form of energy into a power source that is not only high in cost and unreliable, but perhaps not even safe.

The scale of the U.S. nuclear power program's collapse is appalling: 75 plants canceled since 1978, including 28 already under construction, with another half-dozen or so cancelations in prospect. Even in its death throes, the U.S. nuclear program looks ambitious: 16 new stations put into commercial operation since 1979, another 3 this past year, and 40 more units by the end of the decade. By that time nuclear power will account for something like 20% of the U.S.' total generating capacity, up from 14% today. Altogether, these stations will be producing 129,725 megawatts, more than the nuclear capacity of France, West Germany, Japan and the Soviet Union put together. But that's it. Once these plants are completed, the U.S. nuclear power program is at an end.

Elsewhere in the world, some 148 nuclear power plants are under construction, 9 more are on order and 157 are in the planning stage. By 1990 the Japanese should be getting close to 20% of their electricity production from nuclear power, the Taiwanese 30%, the Belgians 40%, the French 55%. That's low-cost energy, all of it, and, according to one study, 30% to 50% lower in cost than coal. The newest French nuclear plant, at Cruas in the south of the country, produces power for under 4 cents a kilowatt-hour, and that's cheap by almost any standard.

In the U.S., however, nuclear power makes less and less economic sense. Production costs of existing coal and nuclear plants run neck and neck, but as the new nuclear plants go into service, coal should gain ground decisively. In upstate New York, New York State Electric & Gas' newest coal-fired station at Somerset began producing power last August at a cost of 7.5 cents per kwh. A hundred miles away, Niagara Mohawk's $5.1 billion Nine Mile Point nuclear plant will produce power two years from now for 18 cents per kwh.

At such levels, nuclear power can't compete with oil, much less with coal. That's why, for the U.S., nuclear power is dead—dead in the near term as a hedge against rising oil prices and dead

in the long run as a source of future energy. Nobody really disputes that. Not the Nuclear Regulatory Commission (NRC) or the Office of Technology Assessment. Not even the Atomic Industrial Forum (AIF), the trade organization that represents the nuclear power industry. And certainly not the 200 or so executives who head the U.S.' investor-owned electric companies. Nuclear power is an option nobody in his right mind would now seriously consider . . . .

What destroyed the nuclear option in the U.S.? How could U.S. nuclear power costs run so outrageously out of control? And why didn't the NRC or the state regulators, never mind the utility managements, do something abut them? Most important of all, why did the U.S. fail where the French, Germans and Japanese succeeded? The answers to such questions are important, and they suggest a good deal about where the U.S. is going to go—or perhaps ought to go—in the future. Without an understanding of what caused the nuclear debacle, the U.S. will lack any clear sense of what it must do not only to restore nuclear energy as a viable energy option but also to assure that history does not repeat itself.

1: THE INCREDIBLE PRICE

It wasn't technology that doomed nuclear power in the U.S. As experience everywhere demonstrates, the technology is as sound and productive as its promoters always have claimed it would be.

Nor was it the dedicated and imaginative obstructionist tactics of the antinuclear forces, effective though they were. The opponents of nuclear power have hampered and harassed it, inflated its costs and stretched out construction times to unconscionable lengths, but they could not, unassisted by events, have prevailed.

The truth is that nuclear power was killed, not by its enemies, but by its friends.

• The federal government and the Nuclear Regulatory Commision, which not only botched the day-to-day management of the program but also failed to consider the economic cost of the regulations it imposed.

• The equipment manufacturers, who maintained that nuclear power was just another way of boiling water.

• The contractors and subcontractors, the designers, engineers and construction managers who, insulated by their own cost-plus contracts had little incentive to question the cost-effectiveness of the NRC's dictates.

• The utility executives, who believed that no matter what happened to cost and construction schedules, the rate commissions would somehow provide the revenues to bail them out.

• And the state regulatory commissions themselves, whose grossly inadequate oversight of the schemes, ambitions and monstrous expenditures for nuclear projects made it easier for all of the above to betray consumers and investors alike.

These collective failures are reflected in the . . . 35 nuclear power projects that had not yet gone into commercial operation at the beginning of 1984. These new plants cost six to eight times more than originally projected, three to four times more on average than nuclear plants already operating. As a result, more than half the plants on the list are no longer competitive with coal nor, some of them, even with oil.

These plants, some conceived as early as the late Sixties, were subjected to all the problems that afflicted the industry over the past decade. All suffered the delays and cost overruns that doubled the average construction time from 6 to 12 years. Yet for all their common technical, social and political environment, the costs of these plants differ widely, ranging from a commendable $932 a kilowatt for Duke Power's McGuire 2 station to a grotesque $5,192 a kilowatt for Long Island Lighting's Shoreham plant. The pressures of regulation and anti-nuclear interveners created more problems for some plants than for others, but they are not enough to explain so wide a range of differences. Labor costs are not appreciably lower in Chicago than they are in New York. Opposition to nuclear power is no more intense on Long Island than it is in northern California.

The disparities in cost are so great as to make a prima facie case for mismanagement in the first degree. At least a dozen projects still going forward—more than one in four—are problem plants by any measure, suffering from quality, construction and design problems as well as cost overruns.

The mismanagement extends beyond design and construction to financial management. At least half a dozen utilities have abandoned plants already well on their way to completion—Marble Hill and Midland among them—because they simply did not have the financial resources to complete them. Other projects still alive—Shoreham, Seabrook and second units everywhere—are similarly imperiled. The financial pressures have been so extreme that at least six major utilities—including Lilco, Public Service of New Hampshire, Consumers Power in Michigan, Public Service of Indiana—are in serious danger of going into bankruptcy.

ADDED COST
PER DAY
$2 million

TOTAL TO
DATE
$5.4 billion

1973 ESTIMATE
$1.2 billion

This nuclear plant was proposed as a $1.2 billion project in 1973. The chart made from a photo shows that the cost had reached $5.4 billion 11 years later and was costing the builders $2 million a day until completion.

But for legal reasons—never mind pride—managements can admit no wrong. Any admission of mismanagement is tantamount to an admission of "imprudence," and some state regulatory commissions, growing increasingly worried about the effect these plants will have on the cost of electricity, have begun disallowing at least part of their costs on just such ground . . . .

Bankruptcy would not put the companies out of business. They are certain to survive as operating, if not corporate, entities. But a price will have to be paid—indeed, already is being paid—in the form of higher rates . . . .

What is so heartbreaking is that if things had been different—if the times were not what they were, if the regulators had been more responsible, if the utility managements and nuclear con-

tractors had been more competent, and, of course, if the antinuclear obstructionists had not been so imaginative and successful—none of it need have happened. But it did. And the U.S. will pay the price for decades to come.

2: THE SETUP

The electric utilities burst into the nuclear age with an enormous and far from unjustified confidence in their own technical abilities and those of the experts they committed their fortunes to, an unshakable optimism about their growth prospects and a conviction that they and the commissions that regulated them had a community of interest. They would soon learn otherwise.

The first commercial reactors in the U.S. were turnkey plants, built at fixed prices and turned over, ready to go, to their owners. In the Fifties and Sixties, General Electric and Westinghouse built 21 of them. The first plants cost more than their sponsors intended—as much as $800 million, according to one estimate—but they did their job well enough to persuade the utilities that nuclear power would be cost-effective. Nuclear power was not an unmixed blessing. It involved capital costs higher than for oil or coal, but its fuel costs were low, so low that promoters claimed it could practically be given away.

Impelled by evangelism, optimism and seemingly irresistible economics, the nuclear bandwagon began to roll, and in the late Sixties and again in the early Seventies the orders began flooding in. But the suppliers had learned their lesson. The new generation of plants would be built under reimbursable-cost-plus-fixed-fee contracts. Without that, the nuclear power program would probably have sputtered out in the mid-Seventies, when costs lurched out of control.

At the time, these new plants seemed priced reasonably enough, costing maybe $200 million to $300 million apiece, a sizable but hardly insupportable commitment for a utility to take on. And the technology seemed not all that exotic. As reactor manufacturers explained it, a power plant was a power plant, and nuclear fission was just another way of heating water.

Well, even in the late Sixties it should have been clear that heating water with nuclear fuel was infinitely more complex and sophisticated than doing it with coal, and complexity meant cost. Perhaps the clearest signal was that coal remained competitive, so competitive that, as the nuclear program gathered momentum, most of the new plants had to be scaled up—to maybe 1.2 million kilowatts—to retain their cost advantage. In scaling up, however, the utilities were moving into unexplored territory. Nobody knew what the design problems were or, worse, what they were going to become. Says J. Christopher Young, senior vice president of Donaldson, Lufkin & Jenrette, "The assumption was you had a mature technology when in fact it was still evolving." . . .

The industry, however, had little doubt about its ability to meet any challenge presented to it. As the Sixties ended, after all, electric utilities had closed out the most prosperous decade in their 100-year history. Year after year, the scale economies of power production enabled them to reduce the costs of producing power, and those economies were so accessible that even mediocre managements could partially achieve them.

Thanks to their declining costs, the utilities came to be thought of as a growth business, showing a return on equity, despite regulation, pretty much in line with the rest of U.S. industry. And with consumers getting the benefit of steadily declining power costs, most utilities succeeded in establishing a long-term community of interest with the politically sensitive state commissions that regulated them. Until the late Sixties at least, the commissions had little to do other than step in from time to time and order a rate reduction when returns got unconscionably high.

As these cost reductions began to tail off and reverse themselves in the late Sixties, the utilities and commissions were able to work out a series of accounting accommodations—deferred-tax and flow-through accounting, for example—that enabled the utilities to keep their rates low (taking the political heat off the commissions) and their reported earnings high (protecting the utilities in the stock market). Later on, in the early Seventies, when energy costs first began rising rapidly, the commissions turned more and more to fuel adjustment clauses to enable higher fuel costs to be quickly passed along in higher rates. Later still, when rising construction costs began posing financial problems, a number of commissions even permitted the utilities to include a portion of their construction work in progress—CWIP, as it became known—in the rate base, on which they could earn a cash return. Consumerist pressures to hold rates down were rising, but the community of interest between the utilities and the commissions endured.

This genial climate was to play a considerable part in the miscalculations that followed . . . .

The utilities, after all, were a cost-recovery industry, whose executives did not think about cost the way executives in other industries did. When accused of committing $50 million of stockholders' money to a nuclear project the government was prepared to finance, the chairman of Consolidated Edison once shrugged and said, "Hell, it's only $50 milllion." And what was $50 million to a $3 billion company? But shrug often enough, and the cost begins to add up.

But why worry even then? Few utility managers thought demand growth would stay low. Electrical demand had been growing at 7% a year for over 40 years, and despite some fits and starts in the early Seventies, there was no reason to think that anything fundamental had changed. The energy crisis, in fact, made nuclear power more vital than ever . . . .

In a program geared to a 7% annual growth pattern, however, the mathematics of miscalculating the market was awesome. At 7% annual growth, you needed to double your capacity every 10 years. At 3%, every 24 years. At 1%, every 70 years. After the second runup in oil prices, in 1978, utility executives had to accept the fact that something basic might be happening to demand, that all the nuclear capacity they were planning might not be needed until a decade or more later than they thought. The Tennessee Valley Authority canceled 8 out of 17 nuclear projects, Public Service Electric & Gas 5 out of 8, Duke Power 6 out of 13, Detroit Edison 3 out of 4. The cancelations continue.

Of all the woes that descended on the U.S. nuclear industry beginning in 1978—high inflation, high interest rates, slackening demand—none was to prove more traumatic than the accident at Three Mile Island on Mar. 28, 1979. On that day, a stuck valve and inadequately trained operating personnel caused the nuclear reactor to overheat dangerously. Though the reactor core was damaged, no one was hurt or even seriously endangered, but the accident demonstrated the fallibility of the utilities, the NRC and the manufacturers, and produced a public relations disaster from which nuclear power has not yet recovered.

After Three Mile Island—TMI, as everyone in the industry antiseptically calls it—safety became an obsession. The NRC promulgated hundreds of new safety regulations between 1978 and 1983 to cope with contingencies ranging from earthquakes to missile strikes . . . . The utilities had no choice but to adjust, in some instances tearing apart nearly completed plants to conform to the changes, or redesigning plants just under way. The process seemed unending . . . .

Some utilities had risked starting construction with designs only 20% complete, rather than the 40% considered minimal, only to discover, with the NRC changes, that they were not even that far along. Florida Power & Light's much admired St. Lucie 2, which started out with a design 70% complete, wound up with a design only 30% complete. The logistical and morale problems were overwhelming . . . .

There was another cost consequence of TMI, more subtle than delays as such but scarcely less profound. "After TMI," as AIF's Carl Walske sums it up, "the balance of decision-making power shifted sharply from the utilities to the regulators." The NRC itself didn't worry about the cost impact of the regulations it imposed; it wasn't supposed to. And under cost-plus contracts, of course, suppliers and contractors had virtually no incentive to be efficient; they were reimbursed for the costs of retrofitting NRC-dictated changes as they were for any others. The industry itself was on the ropes, and most companies were prepared to do whatever was asked of them, never mind the cost . . . .

Many utilities were totally unprepared for projects requiring management skills of such a high order . . . . The bungling the industry was capable of boggles the mind. In the Zimmer control room, according to a study for the Ohio PUC, the control panel would catch fire when the alarm nodule lights went on close together, so that in an emergency the panel would have knocked itself out and the staff would have been unable to control the plant. But nobody worried about that. Many of the lights had burned out, and the staff had unplugged others to decrease the risk of fire.

The ineptitude had no pattern, and virtually anything could go wrong, and did. How could an experienced contractor like Bechtel have prepared the Midland plant site so poorly that the diesel generator building began settling excessively? How could Bechtel have installed the reactor backwards at San Onofre? How could Brown & Root have got the reactor supports 45 degrees out of whack at Comanche Peak? How could experienced operators pour defective concrete at Marble Hill and the South Texas project? How could the NRC itself approve designs for the Mark II reactor when what Grand Gulf was building was a Mark III? How could design control have been so lax that PG&E used the wrong drawings in calculating seismic response for the steel in the Diablo Canyon containment building?

The NRC has a partial answer. "In some cases," an NRC study concluded, "no one was managing the project, the project had inertia, but no guidance and direction." The NRC's diagnosis may seem self-serving, but an Office of Technology Assessment study last spring came to the same conclusion: "Inadequate management has been one of the major causes of construction cost overruns and erratic operation." . . .

Most disheartening of all, perhaps, are the instances of mendacity and worse in U.S. nuclear projects. A number of major contractors allegedly rigged bids at the Washington Nuclear, Diablo Canyon and Marble Hill projects, and some have gone to jail for it. Quality control inspectors have been intimidated, documents have been forged, operator training records have been falsified. Metropolitan Edison pleaded guilty to using faulty test procedures at TMI. Wolf Creek even managed to document as inspected a weld that didn't exist.

One conclusion seems inescapable: Any utility that failed to involve itself directly in every aspect of the project was likely to end up with a mismanaged project. And as Lilco and PSI made clear, even that may not be enough . . . . So it's a catch 22 dilemma. Lacking knowhow, utilities hired experts to manage nuclear projects. But the experts themselves all too often bungled the job.

Apologists argue that most of the nuclear industry's troubles were simply beyond the industry's control. Can't keep your costs under control? Can't meet your construction schedules? Blame the NRC, blame the antinuclear forces, blame inflation, blame interest costs. Don't blame the fact that you haven't the slightest idea of how to control costs or schedule production. " 'Regulatory problems' is a kind of a catchall for all the cost overruns," says one consultant who understandably wishes not to be named. "They made mistakes and could have done a better job. The construction mentality is to build the plant and don't let paperwork slow you up."

But the NRC's requirements, while burdensome and sometimes outrageous, were not insupportable, and some utilities and construction firms had considerable success in coping with them. Arizona Public Service even anticipated many of the design changes the NRC imposed after TMI—simply because it had committed itself to building the best plant it could. And Duke Power has consistently brought in the lowest-cost and most efficient plants in the industry.

The project that serves as a model—and a reproach—to almost everyone is Florida Power & Light's St. Lucie 2 project. Despite post-TMI design changes and a brutal hurricane, St. Lucie 2 was built in six years at a cost of only $1,795 per kw. FP&L had nuclear experience, and much of the design was complete when construction began. But management made the difference. "They expected the NRC to respond to the schedule," says Russell J. Christensen, president of Ebasco Services, the engineering firm that designed and built the plant, "and whatever the NRC had to do, the company made happen. Current regulatory procedures need not necessarily preclude meeting construction schedules and budgets."

3: POINTS OF NO RETURN

What the utilities, the contractors and the suppliers began, the state regulatory commissions finished. High inflation and higher interest rates exploded the costs of the nuclear program and ultimately dissolved the community of interest between the regulators and the utilities.

Even before TMI, the costs of the industry's nuclear program had been rising faster than prices in the economy at large, faster even than costs in the construction industry as a whole. The effect of everything that went wrong after TMI—every schedule that was missed, every design that was reworked, every pipe hanger that had to be ripped out and reinstalled, every quality problem, every stretch-out, every postponement, every legal or antinuclear delay—served to double and triple these costs. Cincinnati Gas & Electric's Zimmer plant, for instance, started out in 1969 costing $240 million, was budgeted at $500 million by 1975, $1 billion by 1980 and $1.7 billion in 1982, with an additional $1.4 billion yet to be spent when construction was abandoned in 1984.

NRC regulation was responsible for at least part of these cost increases. But the accounting practices prescribed by the state regulatory commissions were responsible for even more.

If an industrial company builds a plant, the interest cost of any debt it incurs traditionally went into the profit-and-loss statement as a charge against income. Not in utility accounting. Today's customers, the regulators' argument runs, shouldn't be required to pay even the interest cost of tomorrow's power. A power plant usually has to be "used and usable" before the investment can go into the rate base and earn a return.

Instead of charging off interest costs, the utility imputes an interest charge to the money it has invested in a project based on its average cost of capital, capitalizes the amount (that is, adds it to the total investment) and reports it as a noncash credit in its income statement. The credit is called AFUDC, Allowance for Funds Used During Construction. AFUDC increases reported net income, but it also increases the cost of the project. Impute a 10% or 15% return to a

$2 billion investment and then capitalize it, and the cost increases by $200 million, $300 million a year. Worse, the capitalized amount is then imputed a return of its own. And so the costs of an unfinished plant expand and compound, and the longer a project takes, the more the cost compounds . . . .

In such circumstances, poor management is not simply failing to develop a construction project properly. It is also failing to recognize that you lack the financial resources to fund a project or, having recognized it only belatedly, failing to shut the project down. Some utility managers accepted their financial limitations and acted accordingly—Boston Edison and Dominion Resources, for example. Many more did not. "In terms of its financial viability, Public Service of New Hampshire should never have built Seabrook," DLJ Vice President Mariel Clemensen says bluntly about one case in point. "It simply could not support close to 80% of its capital in a construction project. We can't blame regulatory reluctance for the problems the companies got themselves into." . . .

Perhaps so. Yet the commissions do manage to a degree, and so they are not completely off the hook. Many commissions, after all, can approve or disapprove the financing for utility construction programs. Just as a good many companies were derelict in failing to monitor what their contractors were doing, a good many commissions were equally derelict in failing to monitor what the utilities were up to. If completion of a project was in the best interest of the ratepayers, even the normally difficult Massachusetts commission has had to concede, a utility was entitled to expect regulatory support. But all too often, it failed to get it.

The commissions are now in a box no matter what they do. With interest capitalized rather than written off, rates have to rise sharply when a new and very much higher-cost plant representing a major proportion of assets enters the rate base. It's not the cost of the plant as such that makes the difference, but the cost of the plant in relation to the rate base. Thus Niagara Mohawk may need only a 19% rate increase to account for its $5.1 billion Nine Mile Point plant, whereas Union Electric may need 42% and more to offset Callaway, which cost only half as much. Big comapnies like PG&E or Duquesne Light can absorb such increases with ease. But for smaller companies, the projected impact is chilling . . . .

And so for the first time the threat of bankruptcy has become a reality for at least a handful of major electric companies. A bankrupt utility is obviously not going to suspend operations, but established procedures for utility bankruptcies, unlike the railroad industry, don't exist. Nobody is eager to deal with such questions as who—a utility regulator or a bankruptcy court—has primary jurisdiction over utility property, who has the authority to dispose of assets, repudiate power or fuel contracts or even, conceivably, set rates.

Nobody knows either what will happen to a utility's costs in bankruptcy. "While the lights may stay on in bankruptcy," according to Jay Worenklein and Glenn Gerstell, utility and bankruptcy experts at Milbank Tweed, the New York law firm, "the costs may be higher, the service less reliable and the economic environment less attractive to new business." With inordinately high-cost plants such as Shoreham and Seabrook, it's not inconceivable that in the short run the consumer would be better off if bankruptcy forced a drastic scaling down of all the companies' debts. Their debt burdens aside, after all, both Lilco and PSNH are demonstrably viable companies.

Nobody wants to see the utilities go bankrupt. The states would lose tax revenue and probably jobs. A Consumers Power bankruptcy would even jeopardize the $108 million in pension fund money that the state of Michigan has invested in CP bonds. Even the tough-minded New York PSC ordered a rate increase to keep Lilco from bankruptcy. Large industrial customers have been paying their utility bills early. Suppliers have been letting utilities pay their bills late. And last December a group of industrial customers even supported Consumers Power's petition for a rate increase to avert bankruptcy. So chances are the utilities in trouble will somehow be kept afloat.

The repercussions of even a single bankruptcy could be fairly widespread, undermining the integrity of utilities everywhere and demonstrating that the unthinkable needed to be thought about after all . . . .

One way or another, then, the utilities are likely to come through. Indeed, once the current construction program is at an end, they should recover their traditional earning power, if not necessarily their traditional growth. In the very long run—how's this for irony?—their biggest problem may turn out to be finding an outlet for their rising cash flow.

But there still will be a price to be paid for the nuclear industry's miscalculations, inefficiencies and mismanagement over the years. When the last nuclear plants go into operation, by one authoritative reckoning, power costs in the U.S. will be 5% higher on average than they might have been otherwise. That's hardly any burden in itself, perhaps, but in many parts of the country the price increases should be powerful enough to reshape the economic patterns of the region, weakening regions where power costs will go sharply higher and strengthening those where they will not. Lilco worries that high-cost nuclear power will drive industry away from Long Island, while Commonwealth Edison is counting on low-cost nuclear power to make northern Illinois increasingly attractive to industry. And there you have it: both the penalty and the promise of the U.S. nuclear program. The penalties will remain. The promise expires with the program itself.

4: TOMORROW

Can the U.S. afford to let the nuclear option die? Sooner or later—in the mid-Nineties, in the late Eighties even—the U.S. will almost certainly need to begin planning large central power stations again. As the Atomic Industrial Forum points out, assuming a 3% annual growth in electrical demand, the U.S. will need 300,000 megawatts of additional capacity by 2000. Only 100,-000 megawatts—implying a 1% annual growth expectation—is currently being planned. Given the long lead times involved in building new capacity, someone must get moving in a timely way. If no one does, as Harvard utility expert Peter Navarro points out, "A shortage of electricity generation could become the binding restraint on GNP growth."

There are ways to temporize, of course, between now and the end of the century even if demand does grow by as much as 3% annually. Since any shortages are likely to be regional, the utilities could strengthen their interconnections with companies and regions with surpluses. Then, too, there's plenty of excess power in Canada. And the utilities could even use their existing capacity more efficiently through various load management schemes. Finally, various small power sources—small dams, geothermal or solar energy—may prove more effective in providing capacity than most utility men expect.

But there's little likelihood of much of this happening, as matters now stand. Protective of their own territories, many utilities are reluctant to wheel power from one interconnection to another, while the U.S. itself may be reluctant to become overdependent on Canadian power supplies, even if the Canadians are willing to sell their surplus at reasonable prices.

So, after the temporizing, what kind of generation will we choose? Hardly anyone believes oil and gas prices will be low enough or supplies abundant and secure enough for oil to be a real possibility. There's coal, of course, but nobody willingly uses coal unless there is no alternative. And conceivably the acid rain problem could one day limit coal usage considerably. But if not coal, and if not oil and gas, then what?

Everywhere else in the world the answer is nuclear. Could it not be so for the U.S. if only its cost, regulatory and management problems could be solved? As Commonwealth Edison's Chairman James O'Connor points out, "American engineering, American equipment, American constructors are building plants all over the world and bringing them in at roughly one-quarter to one-third the cost of plants in the U.S. We can do it technically. We have to learn to do it institutionally, rationalizing the process to eliminate the adversarial system that we have presently.

And if we learn how to do it institutionally, I think the nuclear option is very much alive."

The federal—NRC—regulatory problem that has produced open-ended costs, rework and delay may be on the way to solving itself. The torrent of NRC regulations since TMI suggests that the NRC believes the present generation of plants is not really safe. But that may be changing. Recent research into what would happen in an accident involving a reactor core indicates that the radiation hazards are so much less than previously thought that the risk to the public is virtually nil. The China Syndrome is, like the movie that popularized the phrase, just a fiction after all.

Even without any new assessment of nuclear risk, NRC Chairman Nunzio Palladino recently urged the industry to develop one standardized design, get a site approved and demonstrate just how quickly and cheaply a standard plant can be built. Booz, Allen & Hamilton, the management consultants, have taken up the challenge and proposed an industry consortium to do just that.

Standardization has its own drawbacks, in any case. It tends to discourage innovation, and it freezes design defects as well as solutions. As the French themselves are uncomfortably aware, their nuclear program could one day be in real trouble if they have mistakenly standardized on the current equivalent of TMI or General Electric's troubled Mark II containment structure.

And standarization is not enough in itself to solve all cost problems. Union Electric's Callaway and Kansas Gas & Electric's Wolf Creek are twins, but for all that, both are fairly high-cost twins. Indiana Public Service's Marble Hill and Commonwealth Edison's Byron were twinned plants as well, but what made Byron a success and Marble Hill a failure was not the standardized design but the managerial talents of the companies that undertook them. Management talent, or the lack of it, is what has made most of the difference in virtually every other nuclear project as well. It would be unfortunate if the technocrats forgot the central lesson of the nuclear follies . . . .

Such are the possibilities and the problems. The means of reviving the nuclear option are available, but they cannot be implemented without sacrificing consumer interests to those of the community at large, corporate interests to those of the states, state interests to those of the federal government. Is the U.S. really so inflexible?

In the end the problem may boil down simply to this: Can a technology as rigorous and demanding and, for all that, as useful as nuclear power find a place in a society as open as the U.S.?

110.

Myra and David Sadker: Sexism in the Classroom

The age-old question of whether women are intellectually equal to men is debated today as fiercely as it was a century ago. Some commentators argue that simply comparing standardized test results between the sexes is inaccurate. Boys have higher SAT scores than girls in reading and basic computation; does this mean boys are smarter? According to the authors of the article below—professors of education at American University in Washington, D.C.—girls are systematically discriminated against throughout their schooling, such as in standardized testing. Intellectual sexism, in other words, is made, not born.

Source: *Psychology Today,* March 1985.

If a boy calls out in class, he gets teacher attention, especially intellectual attention. If a girl calls out in class, she is told to raise her hand before speaking. Teachers praise boys more than girls, give boys more academic help and are more likely to accept boys' comments during classroom discussions. These are only a few examples of how teachers favor boys. Through this advantage boys increase their chances for better education and possibly higher pay and quicker promotions. Although many believe that classroom sexism disappeared in the early '70s, it hasn't.

Education is not a spectator sport. Numerous researchers, most recently John Goodlad, former dean of education at the University of California at Los Angeles and author of *A Place Called School,* have shown that when students participate in classroom discussion they hold more positive attitudes toward school, and that positive attitudes enhance learning. It is no coincidence that girls are more passive in the classroom and score lower than boys on SAT's.

Most teachers claim that girls partic-

Secretary of Education William Bennett teaches a third grade class.

ipate and are called on in class as often as boys. But a three-year study we recently completed found that this is not true; vocally, boys clearly dominate the classroom. When we showed teachers and administrators a film of a classroom discussion and asked who was talking more, the teachers overwhelmingly said the girls were. But in reality, the boys in the film were outtalking the girls at a ratio of three to one. Even educators who are active in feminist issues were unable to spot the sex bias until they counted and coded who was talking and who was just watching. Stereotypes of garrulous and gossipy women are so strong that teachers fail to see this communications gender gap even when it is right before their eyes.

Field researchers in our study observed students in more than a hundred fourth-, sixth- and eighth-grade classes in four states and the District of Columbia. The teachers and students were male and female, black and white, from urban, suburban and rural communities. Half of the classrooms covered language arts and English—subjects in which girls traditionally have excelled; the other half covered math and science—traditionally male domains.

We found that at all grade levels, in all communities and in all subject areas, boys dominated classroom communication. They participated in more interactions than girls did and their participation became greater as the year went on.

Our research contradicted the traditional assumption that girls dominate classroom discussion in reading while boys are dominant in math. We found that whether the subject was language arts and English or math and science, boys got more than their fair share of teacher attention.

Some critics claim that if teachers talk more to male students, it is simply because boys are more assertive in grabbing their attention—a classic case of the squeaky wheel getting the educational oil. In fact, our research shows that boys are more assertive in the classroom. While girls sit patiently with their hands raised, boys literally grab teacher attention. They are eight times more likely than girls to call out answers. However, male assertiveness is not the whole answer.

Teachers behave differently, depending on whether boys or girls call out answers during discussions. When boys call out comments without raising their hands, teachers accept their answers. However, when girls call out, teachers reprimand this "inappropriate" behavior with messages such as, "In this class we don't shout out answers, we raise our hands." The message is subtle but powerful: Boys should be academically assertive and grab teacher attention; girls should act like ladies and keep quiet.

Teachers in our study revealed an interaction pattern that we called a "mind sex." After calling on a student, they tended to keep calling on students of the same sex. While this pattern applied to both sexes, it was far more pronounced among boys and allowed them more than their fair share of airtime.

It may be that when teachers call on someone, they continue thinking of that sex. Another explanation may be found in the seating patterns of elementary, secondary and even postsecondary classrooms. In approximately half of the classrooms in our study, male and female students sat in separate parts of the room. Sometimes the teacher created this segregation, but more often, the students segregated themselves. A teacher's tendency to interact with same-sex students may be a simple matter of where each sex sits. For example, a teacher calls on a female student, looks around the same area and then continues questioning the students around this girl, all of whom are female. When the teacher refocuses to a section of the classroom where boys are seated, boys receive the series of questions. And because boys are more assertive, the teacher may interact with their section longer.

Girls are often shortchanged in quality as well as in quantity of teacher attention. In 1975 psychologists Lisa Serbin and K. Daniel O'Leary, then at the State University of New York at Stony Brook, studied classroom interaction at the preschool level and found that teachers gave boys more attention, praised them more often and were at least twice as likely to have extended conversations with them. Serbin and O'Leary also found that teachers were twice as likely to give male students detailed instructions on how to do things for themselves. With female students, teachers were more likely to do it for them instead. The result was that boys learned to become independent, girls learned to become dependent.

Instructors at the other end of the educational spectrum also exhibit this same "let me do it for you" behavior toward female students. Constantina Safilios-Rothschild, a sociologist with the Population Council in New York, studied sex desegregation at the Coast Guard Academy and found that the instructors were giving detailed instructions on how to accomplish tasks to male students, but were doing the jobs and operating the equipment for the female students. Years of experience have shown that the best way to learn something is to do it yourself; classroom chivalry is not only misplaced, it is detrimental. It is also important to give students specific and direct feedback about the quality of their work and answers. During classroom discussion, teachers in our study reacted to boys' answers with dynamic, precise and effective responses, while they often gave girls bland and diffuse reactions.

Teachers' reactions were classified in four categories: praise ("Good answer"); criticism ("That answer is wrong"); help and remediation ("Try again—but check your long division"); or acceptance without any evaluation or assistance ("OK"; "Uh-huh").

Despite caricatures of school as a harsh and punitive place, fewer than 5 percent of the teachers' reactions were criticisms, even of the mildest sort. But praise didn't happen often either; it made up slightly more than 10 percent of teachers' reactions. More than 50 percent of teachers' responses fell into the "OK" category.

Teachers distributed these four reactions differently among boys than among girls. Here are some of the typical patterns.

Teacher: "What's the capital of Maryland? Joel?"

Joel: "Baltimore."

Teacher: "What's the largest city in Maryland, Joel?"

Joel: "Baltimore."

Teacher: "That's good. But Baltimore isn't the capital. The capital is also the location of the U.S. Naval Academy. Joel, do you want to try again?"

Joel: "Annapolis."

Teacher: "Excellent. Anne, what's the capital of Maine?"

Anne: "Portland."

Teacher: "Judy, do you want to try?"

Judy: "Augusta."

Teacher: "OK."

In this snapshot of a classroom discussion, Joel was told when his answer was wrong (criticism); was helped to discover the correct answer (remediation); and was praised when he offered the correct response. When Anne was wrong, the teacher, rather than staying with her, moved to Judy, who received only simple acceptance for her correct answer. Joel received the more specific teacher reaction and benefited from a longer, more precise and intense educational interaction.

Too often, girls remain in the dark about the quality of their answers. Teachers rarely tell them if their answers are excellent, need to be improved or are just plain wrong. Unfortunately, acceptance, the imprecise response packing the least educational punch, gets the most equitable sex distribution in classrooms. Active students receiving precise feedback are more likely to achieve academically. And they are more likely to be boys. Consider the following:

• Although girls start school ahead of boys in reading and basic computation, by the time they graduate from high school, boys have higher SAT scores in both areas.

• By high school, some girls become less committed to careers, although their grades and achievement-test scores may be as good as boys'. Many girls' interests turn to marriage or stereotypically female jobs. Part of the reason may be that some women feel that men disapprove of their using their intelligence.

• Girls are less likely to take math and science courses and to participate in special or gifted programs in these subjects, even if they have a talent for them. They are also more likely to believe that they are incapable of pursuing math and science in college and to avoid the subjects.

• Girls are more likely to attribute failure to internal factors, such as ability, rather than to external factors, such as luck.

The sexist communication game is played at work, as well as at school. As reported in numerous studies it goes like this:

• Men speak more often and frequently interrupt women.

• Listeners recall more from male speakers than from female speakers, even when both use a similar speaking style and cover identical content.

• Women participate less actively in conversation. They do more smiling and gazing; they are more often the passive bystanders in professional and social conversations among peers.

• Women often transform declarative statements into tentative comments. This is accomplished by using qualifiers ("kind of" or "I guess") and by adding tag questions ("This is a good movie, isn't it?"). These tentative patterns weaken impact and signal a lack of power and influence.

Sexist treatment in the classroom encourages formation of patterns such as these, which give men more dominance and power than women in the working world. But there is a light at the end of the educational tunnel. Classroom biases are not etched in stone, and training can eliminate these patterns. Sixty teachers in our study received four days of training to establish equity in classroom interactions. These trained teachers succeeded in eliminating classroom bias.

Although our training focused on equality, it improved overall teaching effectiveness as well. Classes taught by these trained teachers had a higher level of intellectual discussion and contained more effective and precise teacher responses for all students.

There is an urgent need to remove sexism from the classroom and give women the same educational encouragement and support that men receive. When women are treated equally in the classroom, they will be more likely to achieve equality in the workplace.

I thought the women were going to come along and save us with new humane values. And what do they do? They adopt the worst values of the young male and go off to law school.
CHARLES A. PETERS, editor, *Washington Monthly*, October 1985

111.

Visit to Bitburg

President Reagan completed an eventful trip to Europe early in May 1985. An economic summit conference of seven major industrial democracies began in Bonn on May 2. On May 5 the President inaugurated a series of ceremonies commemorating the 40th anniversary of the end of the war in Europe in 1945. On that day he laid a wreath from "The People of the United States of America" at an obelisk at the Bergen-Belsen concentration camp in West Germany, where thousands of Jews perished in the gas ovens at the end of World War II. Later that day Reagan and West German Chancellor Helmut Kohl stood side by side at Kolmeshoehe Cementery at Bitburg in a symbolic demonstration of reconciliation between the German and American people. Reagan's visit to Bitburg had touched off an uproar, since among the 2,000 German soldiers buried there were 49 members of the Nazi/Waffen SS, the elite corps that had been largely responsible for the torture and murder of more than 6,000,000 Jews during the war. Israeli political leaders denounced the President's visit to Bitburg, as did many Americans, both Jewish and not. Reagan's speeches at Bergen-Belsen and Bitburg expressed his loathing for the acts of the SS during the war, and his wreath at Bitburg said simply "From the President of the United States." Despite pressure to cancel the appearance at Bitburg, he had kept the date with Chancellor Kohl out of gratitude to Germans for their staunch loyalty to U.S. foreign policy during the postwar years. Reprinted here is an open letter that appeared in the Chicago Sun-Times *on the day of the President's visit to Bitburg. It was paid for by the United German-American Societies of Greater Chicago.*

Source: *Chicago Sun-Times*, May 5, 1985.

Dear Mr. President: We are German-Americans. According to the 1980 census approximately 70 million Americans are of German descent of which over 2 million have come to this country since the second world war.

It is obvious that the real meaning of your participation in a ceremony honoring German war dead has been distorted. This ceremony has been held at Bitburg for the past twenty-five years with a representative of the United States participating (a fact little reported, unfortunately). Never before has it been deemed an abomination or tribute to murderers.

Unfortunately, the symbolism of your visit as interpreted by victims of the Holocaust and some American veterans overshadows its reality as a reconciliatory gesture toward a former adversary who is now a strong ally and friend. Surely no one can say that you intend any honor whatsoever to those two percent of Hitler's SS who are buried among 2000 soldiers.

We have heard the fervent pleas that you stay away from this cemetery, which those who suffered under the SS see as a place of evil. The presence of those few SS graves, in their perception, has tainted the earth you will stand on. Let us not be misunderstood: we do not and can not dismiss such reactions as unfounded simply because we do not ourselves see such a symbolism in that place. While we reject a collective guilt for what happened in Nazi Germany, we can hardly reject a special responsibility to be sensitive to the feelings of survivors of the Holocaust.

What response shall we make then— we who wish to have our fathers and brothers and uncles remembered for sacrificing their lives as soldiers—we who wish to have our former country reconciled and bonded to our new homeland. What can we tell you, Mr. President, to confirm that your decision is the right one?

That which troubles us most is this: If Bitburg is some unholy and evil place, no one should go there. If those ceremonies are seen as paying homage to an organization which ran death camps, then Chancellor Kohl, and other European representatives have no business there either. For that matter, no one of German heritage who has any respect for the sufferings of Hitler victims should go there. Should then the gates at Bitburg be locked and a sign posted: "Tainted ground, keep out"?

We obviously do not accept this proposition. Though the Germans of today may bear burdens of blame and shame, either willingly, or unwillingly, we are not prepared to accept as punishment the idea that 2000 of those soldiers at Bitburg are buried in unholy

AP/Wide World

President Reagan lays a wreath at Bitburg Cemetery in West Germany. With him is Gen. Matthew B. Ridgeway, veteran of World War II.

ground. They did not choose their final resting place. Did any of the many young conscripts have any choice about going to war? Was there some nearby neutral country that they could have gone to for asylum or to flee the draft?

To come to terms with the past, it is important for Germans to grieve for what the victims of Nazis have lost. But it is also important, and the Germans' right, to grieve for what they themselves have lost. There were not only flames in the concentration camps, but firestorms from incendiary bombs which consumed whole German cities, annihilating civilians as well as soldiers, churches as well as cannons and the innocent with the guilty until their ashes were indistinguishable.

We have a message for those who are so terribly troubled by the presence of the spirits of their persecutors at that cemetery: For some of you reconciliation with the post-war and future German generations will be possible, for others it will not. But there will come a fiftieth and a sixtieth and a one hundredth anniversary of the end of that War and the end of that Holocaust. Germany, we can hope, will still exist as a free and democratic nation. The tombstones of the soldiers and the memorials to the concentration camp victims will still be there. The scattered individuals still alive today who bear some personal responsibility for what happened will be long dead. Your children's children and ours will conduct their ceremonies of remembrance.

Will there then be true reconciliation? Or is it better that German soil forever be regarded as profane, as a kind of taboo resting place for ancestral spirits who can never find peace because of the terrible way in which they died? If you will have it so, it will be so.

There are 10 millions of German war dead, both military and civilians. You agreed to extend honor to them, Mr. President, and it is no longer possible to withdraw it without telling those dead men and their survivors that they must be shunned because of an evil which once occurred.

So then, in all this turmoil, what are you to do. Mr. President? You should still go to Bitburg. But since the symbolism of your being in that place has assumed such awesome significance you should not in your remarks pay tribute to soldiers in general lest it be misinterpreted as some forgiveness of KZ cruelties in general. Instead, we suggest, go to an individual grave. A grave of one of those teenage conscripts who

was thrown into a last mad battle of an already lost war.

A grave, surely, of a victim of Nazism. Lay a wreath there. Then turn to his surviving relatives and friends and speak some words of consolation (as you will have done with the survivors and relatives at Bergen-Belsen). As you depart the cemetery there is an iron gate. Leave it open. It will be a symbol that for those who see their persecutors there, a tragic chapter in German history can never be closed off and forgotten. And it will also be a symbol that the Germans of today will not shut out the memories of their own dead and their own suffering.

We also have a message for our former countrymen in Bitburg and in all of Germany: If our President would not go to your cemetery or does not pay his respects in as full a measure as originally intended, please forgive him. Please do not consider it a lack of respect for German-American friendship by him or the American people. Please do not blame those in the US who have been so vociferously opposed to this visit. This whole controversy is somehow another 40-year old debt you must pay. And pay it you will, surely with sadness that the innocent are being judged with the guilty, but hopefully not with anger or malice.

Let all of us who are somehow tied to that wrenching conflict which ended forty years ago pray for the repose of each other's dead. And remembering the past—ah, how can its agony ever be forgotten—pray for peace and reconciliation among all enemies of yesterday and today.

112.

RONALD REAGAN: A Tax System That Is Unwise, Unwanted, and Unfair

On May 28, 1985, President Reagan delivered an impassioned TV speech in which he strongly criticized the U.S. tax system, which he declared was "unwise, unwanted, and unfair," and proposed that the Congress adopt a new system, which he described in detail. Presidents before him had made similar proposals, but despite widespread agreement that the tax code was a veritable grab bag of special interest legislations, with more loopholes than anyone but an expert could count, nothing really significant had ever been done. And the cynics even now predicted that nothing would be done. But, astonishingly, something was done, although not immediately. Congress struggled throughout the remainder of 1985 to come up with a workable plan. The work proceeded quickly after the turn of the year, and by the end of May 1986 tax bills had been reported by both the Senate and the House. They were different from the President's proposals, and different from each other. But a new tax system was agreed on by both houses of Congress and signed into law by the President before the 1986 congressional elections. It was a signal achievement, and everyone deserved praise. Reprinted here is most of the President's May 28, 1985, speech.

Source: Presidential Documents, week ending May 28, 1985.

MY FELLOW CITIZENS, I'd like to speak to you tonight about our future, about a great historic effort to give the words freedom, fairness and hope new meaning and power for every man and woman in America.

Specifically, I want to talk about taxes; about what we must do as a nation this year to transform a system that's become an endless source of confusion and resentment into one that is clear, simple and fair for all; a tax code that no longer runs roughshod over Main Street America, but insures your families and firms incentives and rewards for hard work and risk-taking in an American future of strong economic growth.

No other issue goes so directly to the heart of our economic life; no other issue will have more lasting impact on the well-being of your families and your future.

In 1981 our critics charged that letting you keep more of your earnings would trigger an inflationary explosion, send interest rates soaring and destroy our economy. Well, we cut your tax rates anyway by nearly 25 percent. And what that helped trigger was falling inflation, falling interest rates and the strongest economic expansion in 30 years.

We have made one great dramatic step together. We owe it to ourselves now to take another. For the sake of fairness, simplicity and growth we must radically change the structure of a tax system that still treats our earnings as the personal property of the I.R.S.; radically change a system that still treats people earning similar incomes much differently regarding the tax they pay and, yes, radically change a system that still causes some to invest their money, not to make a better mousetrap but simply to avoid a tax trap.

Over the course of this century our tax system has been modified dozens of times and in hundreds of ways. Yet most of those changes didn't improve the system, they made it more like Washington itself: complicated, unfair, cluttered with gobbledygook and loopholes designed for those with the power and influence to hire high-priced legal and tax advisors.

But there is more to it than that.

Some years ago someone—a historian I believe—said that every time in the past when a Government began taxing above a certain level of the people's earnings trust in Government began to erode. He said it would begin with efforts to avoid paying the full tax. This would become outright cheating, and eventually a distrust and contempt of Government itself until there would be a breakdown in law and order.

Well, how many times have we heard people brag about clever schemes to avoid paying taxes, or watched luxuries casually written off to be paid for by somebody else—that somebody being you. I believe that in both spirit and substance our tax system has come to be un-American.

Death and taxes may be inevitable, but unjust taxes are not. The first American Revolution was sparked by an unshakable conviction: Taxation without representation is tyranny. Two centuries later a second American Revolution for hope and opportunity is gathering force again, a peaceful revolution but born of popular resentment against a tax system that is unwise, unwanted and unfair.

I've spoken with and received letters from thousands of you, Republicans, Democrats and Independents. I know how hungry you are for change. Make no mistake, we, the sons and daughters of those first brave souls who came to this land to give birth to a new life in liberty, we can change America again; we can change America forever. So let's get started, let's change the tax code to make it fairer, and change tax rates so they are lower.

The proposal I am putting forth tonight for America's future will free us from the grip of special interests and create a binding commitment to the only special interest that counts, you, the people who pay America's bills. It will create millions of new jobs for working people and it will replace the politics of envy with a spirit of partnership, the opportunity for everyone to hitch their wagon to a star and set out to reach the American dream.

I'll start by answering one question on your minds — will our proposal help you? You bet it will. We call it America's tax plan because it will reduce tax burdens on the working people of this country, close loopholes that benefit a privileged few, simplify a code so complex even Albert Einstein reportedly needed help on his 1040 form, and lead us into a future of greater growth and opportunity for all. . . .

How would the proposal work? The present tax system has 14 different brackets of tax rates ranging from 11 to 50 percent. We would take a giant step toward an ideal system by replacing all that with a simple three-bracket system, with tax rates of 15, 25 and 35 percent. . . . By lowering everyone's tax rates all the way up the income scale, each of us will have a greater incentive to climb higher, to excel, to help America grow.

I believe the worth of any economic policy must be measured by the strength of its commitment to American families, the bedrock of our society. There is no instrument of hard work, savings and job creation as effective as the family. There is no cultural institution as ennobling as family life. And there is no superior, indeed, no equal means to rear the young, protect the weak or attend the elderly. None.

Yet past Government policies betrayed families and family values. They permitted inflation to push families relentlessly into higher and higher tax brackets. And not only did the personal exemption fail to keep pace with inflation, in real dollars its actual value dropped dramatically over the last 30 years.

The power to tax is the power to destroy. For three decades, families have paid the freight for the special interests. Now families are in trouble. As one man from Memphis, Tennessee, recently wrote: "The taxes that are taken out of my check, is money that I need, not extra play money. Please do all that you can to make the tax system more equitable toward the family."

Well, sir, that's just what we intend to do, to pass the strongest profamily initiative in postwar history. In addition to lowering your tax rates further we will virtually double the personal exemption, raising it by next year to $2,000 for every taxpayer and every dependent. And that $2,000 exemption will be indexed to protect against inflation.

Further, we propose to increase the standard deduction, raising it to $4,000 for joint returns.

Beyond this we intend to strengthen families' incentives to save through individual retirement accounts, I.R.A.'s, by nearly doubling—to $4,000—the amount all couples can deduct from their taxable income. From now on each spouse could put up to $2,000 a year into his or her I.R.A. and invest the money however they want. And the value of the I.R.A. would not be taxable until they approach retirement.

Some families could save more, others less, but whether it's $400 or $4,000, every dollar saved up to $4,000 each year would be fully deductible from taxable earnings. Let me add that we would also raise, by nearly a full third, the special tax credit for low-income working Americans. That special incentive, a credit to reduce the tax they owe, would be raised from the present $550 to a maximum level of over $700. . . .

The power of these incentives would send one simple, straightforward message to an entire nation: America, go for it.

We are reducing tax rates by simplifying the complex system of special provisions that favor some at the expense of others. Restoring confidence in our tax system means restoring, and respecting, the principle of fairness for all. This means curtailing some business deductions now being written off; it means ending several personal deductions, including the state and local tax deduction, which actually provides a special subsidy for high-income individuals, especially in a few high-tax states.

Two-thirds of Americans don't even itemize, so they receive no benefit from the state and local tax deduction. But they're being forced to subsidize the high-tax policies of a handful of states.

This is truly taxation without representation.

But other deductions widely used, deductions central to American values, will be maintained. The mortgage interest deduction on your home would be fully retained. And on top of that no less than $5,000 in other interest expenses would still be deductible. The itemized deductions for your charitable contributions will remain intact. The deductions for your medical expenses will be protected and preserved. Deductions for casualty losses would be continued; so too would the current preferential treatment of Social Security. Military allowances will not be taxed. And veteran's disability payments will remain totally exempt from Federal taxation. These American veterans have already paid their dues.

The number of taxpayers who need to itemize would be reduced to one in four. We envision a system where more than half of us would not even have to fill out a return. We call it the return-free system and it would be totally voluntary. If you decided to participate you would automatically receive your refund or a letter explaining any additional tax you owe. Should you disagree with this figure you would be free to fill out your taxes using the regular form. We believe most Americans would go from the long form or the short form to no form. Comparing the distance between the present system and our proposal is like comparing the distance between a Model T and the space shuttle. I should know; I've seen both.

I have spoken of our proposed changes to help individuals and families. Let me explain how we would complement them with proposals for business, proposals to ensure fairness by eliminating or modifying special privileges that are economically unjustifiable, and to strengthen growth by preserving incentives for investment, research and development.

We begin with a basic recognition: The greatest innovations for new jobs, technologies, and economic vigor today come from a small but growing circle of heroes, the small-business people, American entrepreneurs, the men and women of faith, intellect, and daring who take great risks to invest in and invent our future. The majority of the 8 million new jobs created over the last two and a half years were created by small enterprises, enterprises often born in the dream of one human heart.

To young Americans wondering tonight, where will I go, what will I do with my future, I have a suggestion: Why not set out with your friends on the path of adventure and try to start up your own business. Follow in the footsteps of those two college students who launched one of America's great computer firms from the garage behind their house. You, too, can help us unlock the doors to a golden future. You, too, can become leaders in this great new era of progress, the age of the entrepreneur.

My goal is an America bursting with opportunity, an America that celebrates freedom every day by giving every citizen an equal chance, an America that is once again the youngest nation on earth, her spirit unleashed and breaking free. For starters, lowering personal tax rates will give a hefty boost to the nearly 15 million small businesses which are individual proprietorships or partnerships.

To further promote business formation we propose to reduce the maximum corporate tax rate, now 46 percent, to 33 percent. And most small corporations would pay even lower rates. So with lower rates small business can lead the way in creating jobs for all who want to work.

To these incentives we would add another, a reduction in the tax on capital gains. Since the capital gains tax rates were cut in 1978 and 1981, capital raised for new ventures has increased by over one-hundredfold. That old, tired economy wheezing from neglect in the 1970's has been swept aside by a young, powerful locomotive of progress carrying a trainload of new jobs, higher incomes and opportunities for more and more Americans of average means.

So to marshal more venture capital for more new industries, the kind of efforts that begin with a couple of partners setting out to create and develop a new product, we intend to lower the maximum capital gains tax rate to $17\frac{1}{2}$ percent.

Under our new tax proposal, the oil and gas industry will be asked to pick up a larger share of the national tax burden. The old oil depletion allowance will be dropped from the tax code, except for wells producing less than 10 barrels a day. By eliminating this special preference we will go a long way toward insuring that those who earn their wealth in the oil industry will be subject to the same taxes as the rest of us. This is only fair. To continue our drive for energy independence, the current treatment of the costs of exploring and drilling for new oil will be maintained.

We are determined to cut back on special preferences that have too long favored some industries at the expense of others. We would repeal the investment tax credit and reform the depreciation system. Incentives for research and experimentation, however, would be preserved.

There is one group of losers in our tax plan, those individuals and corporations who are not paying their fair share or, for that matter, any share. These abuses cannot be tolerated. From now on they shall pay a minimum tax. The free rides are over.

This, then, is our plan, America's plan: a revolutionary first for fairness in our future; a long-overdue commitment to help working Americans and their families, and a challenge to our entire nation to excel, a challenge to give the U.S.A. the lowest overall marginal rates of taxation of any major industrial democracy. And, yes, a challenge to lift us into a future of unlimited promise, an endless horizon lit by the star of freedom guiding America to supremacy in jobs, productivity, growth and human progress.

The tax system is crucial not just to our personal, material well-being and our nation's economic well being, it must also reflect and support our deeper values and highest aspirations. It must promote opportunity, lift up the weak, strengthen the family and, perhaps most importantly, it must be rooted in that unique American quality, our special commitment to fairness. It must be an expression of both America's eternal frontier spirit, and all the virtues from the heart and soul of a good and decent people—those virtues held high by the Statue of Liberty standing proudly in New York Harbor.

A great national debate now begins. It should not be a partisan debate, for the authors of tax reform come from both parties and all of us want greater fairness, incentives and simplicity in taxation. I am heartened by the cooperation and serious interest already shown by key Congressional leaders, including the chairman of the Senate Finance

Committee, Republican Bob Packwood, and the chairman of the House Ways and Means Committee, Democrat Dan Rostenkowski.

The pessimists will give a hundred reasons why this historic proposal won't pass and can't work. Well, they've been opposing progress and predicting disaster for four years now. Yet here we are tonight, a stronger, more united, more confident nation than at any time in recent memory.

Remember, there are no limits to growth and human progress when men and women are free to follow their dreams. The American dream belongs to you; it lives in millions of different hearts; it can be fulfilled in millions of different ways: And with you by our side we're not going to stop moving and shaking this town until that dream is real, for every American, from the sidewalks of Harlem to the mountaintops of Hawaii.

My fellow citizens, let's not let this magnificent moment slip away. Tax relief is in sight. Let's make it a reality. Let's not let prisoners of mediocrity wear us down. Let's not let the special interest raids of the few rob us all of our dreams.

In these last years we've made a fresh start together. In these next four we can begin a new chapter in our history, freedom's finest hour. We can do it. If you help we will do it this year.

113.

NANCY JOHNSON and GEORGE KITTLE: Aid to the Contras

On June 12, 1985, the House of Representatives voted 248–184 to allocate $27 million in nonmilitary aid to Nicaraguan Contras fighting to overcome the country's Sandinista government. The bill stated that neither the Pentagon nor the C.I.A. could distribute the money. The House had voted against aid to the Contras in April, but Nicaraguan President Daniel Ortega had gone to Moscow shortly thereafter to seek Soviet assistance, and this action apparently changed a lot of House votes. Nancy Johnson was the Representative of the 6th District of Connecticut; the statement that appears below was published shortly after her Yes vote on aid. The letter from George Kittle, a frequent visitor to Central America, appeared in the same newspaper the next week. The conflict between their two views of the Nicaraguan situation accurately reflects the differences between the two sides in the Congress vote.

Source: *The Lakeville* (Connecticut) *Journal,* June 20 and 27, 1985.

A: REP. JOHNSON
AID TO THE CONTRAS

THE HOUSE OF REPRESENTATIVES last week approved by a large majority a plan to renew aid to the rebels seeking democracy in Nicaragua and voted to provide $27 million in humanitarian aid to these so-called Contras over two years. You will recall that in April, the

House narrowly voted down all forms of aid to the Contras, though even at that time it was clear that a majority of my colleagues favored some new American investment in the region, though consensus had not jelled on the form the aid should take.

The humanitarian aid package was adopted after the White House agreed to send aid to the Contras through agencies other than the Central Intelligence Agency and the Department of Defense, to provide detailed reports on its use before release of each new segment of aid, and to include $2 million to implement the Contadora agreements when verification procedures are agreed upon.

I supported the effort to provide humanitarian aid to the Contras—as I did in April—because while military solutions or the overthrow of the Sandinistas will not bring peace or stability to the region, neither will abandonment of the Contras. We must have the patience and constancy to persevere with our assistance so that the legitimacy of moderate political groups will be acknowledged and their right to participate in the peaceful democratic process of elections in Nicaragua be granted. As I have previously stated following the April vote, by continuing to acknowledge the existence and exclusion of these political groups from the process, we can eventually gain their inclusion and assure that over time the process of reconciliation so essential to peace in Nicaragua and the region will take place and the government in Nicaragua will become the democracy the revolution sought.

With the support of the Congress, the President can now move forward with his plans to seek an extension of the ceasefire and resume direct negotiations with the Sandinistas, among other things. The goals of negotiations should be setting up regular elections (which no law now requires), assurance of the right of Contra groups to organize into political parties and peaceably assemble, and access to the press.

In addition, we should encourage all Central American nations, including Nicaragua, to negotiate the means of verifying compliance with the Contadora principles and thereby guarantee the security of all Central American nations, and the withdrawal of all foreign military advisors.

The measure passed by the House ratchets down our support from covert military assistance to overt humanitarian aid while offering incentives to negotiations and renewing diplomatic efforts. The President has promised to seek resumption of bilateral negotiations with Nicaragua and renew regional diplomatic efforts with the Contadora process.

As I stated earlier, the bill includes $2 million to help the Contadora process. The legislation also requires the President to report on human rights violations against civilians by both the Sandinistas and the Contras every 90 days, and the steps being taken to end such atrocities.

Such a combination of policies has created an opportunity for the establishment of democracy in El Salvador and for reconciliation with that nation's guerrillas. Nicaragua deserves no less.

B: GEORGE KITTLE
WHAT THE CONTRA AID VOTE MEANS

FIRST LET ME SAY that I wish all elected officials were as conscientious and energetic as U.S. Rep. Nancy Johnson is in maintaining a dialogue with her constituency. Having said that, I have to take issue with her on her report in

This is all that is left of a Nicaraguan health post demolished by Contras. U.S. doctors returning from Nicaragua say that the Contras deliberately attack rural health centers.

last week's issue, explaining why she voted to renew aid to the U.S.-backed forces attacking Nicaragua from protected bases in Honduras.

In her first sentence she says these "so-called Contras" are "rebels seeking democracy in Nicaragua." There are at least three groups of Contras: the band of Miskito Indians in Northeastern Honduras, Eden ("Commander Zero") Pastora's small army in Costa Rica, and the 15,000-member FDN in Honduras. It is this last that will receive the $27 million voted by Congress.

Of this group, all but one of the 47 military leaders are former members of Somoza's National Guard. (In fact, in Northern Nicaragua, where most of the attacks occur, the Contras are known as "La Guardia.") Established by the CIA in 1981, this band of mercenaries has as its avowed aim the overthrow of the Sandinista government. It hopes to do this by destroying the infrastructure of

the country, focusing on achievements of the revolution.

Sometimes they raid small settlements or farm cooperatives, burning everything and killing indiscriminately. At other times they are more selective, blowing up tobacco barns, granaries, power stations, bridges, trucks, schools, day-care centers, clinics. Or they target key individuals for murder or kidnaping: teachers, doctors, nurses, agronomists, coffee pickers, lay preachers, cooperative leaders, mayors. The women are often raped, the men sometimes made an example of by having their eyes gouged out or their genitals cut off before they are hacked to death.

The Contras mainly go after civilian targets. They never seek an encounter with the Nicaraguan army. In the last four years the Contras forced the closing of 359 schools and 840 adult education centers, and in 1984 alone they kidnaped 171 teachers and murdered

98. Since the Triumph in July, 1979, they have killed roughly 10,000 people, mostly civilians, of whom 3,000 were children or teenagers. This is how the Contras go about "seeking democracy" in Nicaragua.

Mrs. Johnson says we must not abandon these Contras, but instead persevere in our assistance to them "so that the legitimacy of the moderate groups will be acknowledged, and their rights to participate in the peaceful democratic process of elections in Nicaragua be granted." This right has never been denied them.

In last November's elections there were six opposition parties, which garnered a third of the seats in the Assembly. This, it seems to me, is the "democratic" way to seek a voice in the government, not by raping and pillaging. (It's worth noting that 70 per cent of the voting-age population participated in these elections, as opposed to 52 per cent in the U.S. elections, and that the Sandinistas got support from 44 per cent of this population, as opposed to 31 per cent for Reagan).

Several parties, members of the so-called Democratic Coordinator—a coalition of political parties, labor unions, and a business group (COSEP)—boycotted the elections, despite the fact that the Sandinistas, to accommodate the last-minute entry into the race of Coordinator-member Arturo Cruz, offered to postpone them until Jan. 13 if the Contras would agree to a cease fire by Oct. 25. Cruz, probably under pressure from COSEP, failed to register by the Oct. 1 deadline. Thus, there was no "exclusion of these groups from the political process"—they excluded themselves.

When I was in Nicaragua in April I talked with the leader of one of these boycotting parties, the Christian Social Party, and while he had very few good words for the Sandinistas (he did acknowledge their achievements in health and education), he had no good words at all for the Reagan Administration's military and economic aggression against his country. In fact, I know of no party in Nicaragua which supports our war.

Who, then, are these people Mrs. Johnson says have been excluded from the political process? Only those whose avowed aim is to bring down the government. This now includes Cruz, who was once a respected political figure, but who has lost his political base in Nicaragua by living in Washington for the past 20 years, and who has recently made himself *persona non grata* in Nicaragua by coming out in support of the Contras.

Prodded by the Reagan Administration, he has formed something called the Unified Nicaraguan Opposition to try to sanitize the Contras. This of course is just for U.S. consumption; it will be terrorism as usual under Col. Enrique Bermudez and his crew.

One who knows the nature of the Contras far better than Cruz does is Edgar Chamorro, who said in *The New York Times* of June 24: "My experience as a former rebel leader convinced me that the Nicaraguan Democratic Force (FDN) cannot contribute to the democratization of Nicaragua. The rebels are in the hands of former National Guardsmen who control the Contra army, stifle internal dissent and intimidate or murder those who oppose them. The rebels have been subject to manipulation by the Central Intelligence Agency which has reduced it to a front organization." Later on he says that "the funds voted by Congress are simply another vehicle to prolong this war."

Mrs. Johnson goes on to suggest that we seek "an extension of the ceasefire" (what ceasefire?), resume "direct negotiations with the Sandinistas" (fine), one aim of which would be to set up regular elections (does Mrs. Johnson know that it was seven years after our own revolution before we had provisions for regular elections?), encourage the Contadora process (which Reagan walked away from), and create the opportunity for democracy in Nicaragua the way we have in El Salvador (God forbid!)

Does she really believe that we are spending all those millions of dollars, turning Honduras into a fortress that threatens the stability of the whole region, in order to bring "democracy" to Nicaragua? Since when have we ever cared about democracy in Latin America? Our history there has been one of unwavering support for right-wing military dictatorships dedicated to the preservation of feudal societies in which all the wealth is in the hands of the few, while the rest are kept poor, ill-fed, ill-housed and illiterate.

We have opposed every attempt to alleviate this miserable condition, orchestrating the overthrow of elected governments committed to change in Guatemala (1954), Brazil (1964), Chile (1972) and now Nicaragua. We supported the infamous National Guard under Somoza, and we support them now. We haven't changed and neither have they.

So why are we using military and economic force to overthrow a sovereign government that has neither attacked nor threatened us? It is to stem the tide of communism? But Nicaragua has a freely-elected, multi-party government,

a mixed economy (60 per cent in private hands) and a nonaligned foreign policy (though we're doing our damndest to align them).

Minister of Education Fernando Cardinal, when asked if Nicaragua was Communist, said, "For all their faults the Sandinistas have put above everything the interests of the poor. If this is communism, then we have communism." The achievements of the Sandinistas in the fields of health, education, and land reform are well-known.

Equally important are the intangible achievements: They have given the people back their dignity; they have freed them from a condition of serfdom (Somoza called them his "oxen"); they have given them a voice in their government, and hope for the future of their children. And now we are taking all these things away from them again, destroying their revolution and plunging them back into darkness, where terror, hunger, and hopelessness will reign once again.

Why are we doing this? I'm pretty sure it has nothing to do with "democracy." I'm not even sure it has much to do with communism. I suspect it has a lot to do with colonialism and our attitude toward our "backyard," with imperialism and keeping things safe for the multinationals, and with making people down there "say uncle."

P.S. The bill passed by the House calls for the $27 million to be applied over a period of *nine months,* not two years as Mrs. Johnson states. That's quite a difference. It means the Contras will now be funded at the highest rate since the CIA set them up in 1981.

114.

The Taking of TWA Flight 847

On June 14, 1985, two Shi'ite Muslims, said to be members of Islamic Jihad ("Islamic Holy War"), hijacked a Trans World airliner after it had left Athens airport on the way to Rome. Of the 153 passengers and crew aboard, 104 were Americans. The pilot was forced to fly to Beirut, where a U.S. navy diver was brutally beaten and shot to death. A dozen other Shi'ite Muslims then joined the first two and concurred in a demand that Israel release more than 700 prisoners it had captured in Lebanon. Finally, after a two-week ordeal, the 39 hostages who had not been among those released in stages were driven to Damascus and put on a flight to West Germany. Israel released 31 of its prisoners on June 24, although insisting that the decision was not connected to the hijackers' demands. The hijacking, which altogether lasted for 17 days, was a media event of enormous proportions in the United States as well as the rest of the world. In a sense, it was widely felt, the affair was a joint creation of the hijackers and the media, notably television; that led to severe criticism of the press handling of the event. Reprinted here is a statement by the President, on June 18; an article on the significance of the hijacking by an Israeli author; and an editorial from Time *magazine about the relevance of the affair to the role of the media in American life.*

Sources: Presidential Documents, week ending June 21, 1985.

The New York Times, July 2, 1985.

Time, July 5, 1985.

A: THE PRESIDENT'S PRESS CONFERENCE

PLEASE BE SEATED. I have a statement.

One hour ago, the body of a young American hero, Navy diver Robert Dean Stethem, was returned to his native soil in a coffin after being beaten and shot at point-blank range.

His murder and the fate of the other American hostages still being held in Beirut underscore an inescapable fact: the United States is tonight a nation being attacked by international terrorists who want only to kill and who seize our innocent citizens as their prisoners.

In response to this situation, I am directing that the following steps be taken:

I have directed the Secretary of Transportation, in cooperation with the Secretary of State, to explore immediately an expansion of our armed sky marshal program aboard international flights of U.S. air carriers for better protection of passengers.

I have directed the Secretary of State to issue an immediate travel advisory for U.S. citizens traveling through the

Athens International Airport, warning them of dangers.

This warning shall remain in effect until the Greek Government has improved the security situation there. And until it has demonstrated a willingness to comply with the security provisions of the U.S.-Greek civil aviation agreement and the Tokyo, Montreal and Hague Conventions regarding prosecution and punishment of air pirates.

I've asked for a full explanation of the events surrounding the takeover of the aircraft in Athens. I have appealed through the Department of Transportation and the Federal Aviation Administration for all U.S. air carriers to review the wisdom of continuing any flights into Athens until the security situation there improves.

And further, I have asked Secretaries Shultz and Dole to report to me on whether we should terminate the service of foreign air carriers whose governments do not honor appropriate international conventions or provide adequate security at their airports.

I'm calling upon all allied and friendly governments to redouble their efforts to improve airport security and take other measures to prevent the hijacking of aircraft.

I will also be asking them to take steps to prevent travel to places where lawlessness is rampant and innocent passengers are unprotected.

And I'm urging that no American enter any Middle Eastern country that does not publicly condemn and disassociate itself from this atrocity and call for the immediate safe release of our citizens.

Let me further make it plain to the assassins in Beirut and their accomplices wherever they may be that America will never make concessions to terrorists. To do so would only invite more terrorism.

Nor will we ask nor pressure any other government to do so. Once we head down that path, there'll be no end to it. No end to the suffering of innocent people; no end to the bloody ransom all civilized nations must pay.

This act of terrorism is a stain on Lebanon and particularly on those Lebanese in whose name it has been done. Those in Lebanon who commit these acts damage their country and their cause, and we hold them accountable.

I call upon those holding our people to release them without condition. I call upon the leaders of Lebanon, political and religious, to meet their responsibilities and to do all that is necessary to end this crime now in the name of the God they worship.

And I call on other governments to speak out and use their influence as well.

This attack is an attack on all citizens of the world who seek to live free from the fear and scourge of terrorism.

My thoughts and prayers are, as are those of all of Americans, with the prisoners now being held in Lebanon and with their families.

Let me conclude by stating the obvious: We're in the midst of a dangerous and volatile situation. Before taking your questions I must stress that speculation tonight over what steps we might or might not take in hypothetical circumstances can only lead terrorists to work harder.

Consequently, there are many questions to which I should not and cannot respond. I think I have in this statement covered virtually all the points that I can safely discuss, and I'm sure that you would understand the reason for that.

And so that said, Mike Putzel, Associated Press, ask the first question.

B: ZE'EV CHAFETS
WHY THE U.S. WAS A TARGET

THE HIJACKING of Trans World Airlines Flight 847 has once again raised the question of whether the United States' close association with Israel is a detriment to American interests in the Arab world. That, certainly, is what the hijackers were trying to impress upon us at the point of their rifles. In fact, nothing could be further from the truth. America is a target not because of who its friends are but because of what it is and what it represents.

A recent poll published in the United States, and widely quoted here, shows that 42 percent of the American public favors reducing ties with Israel in order to protect the United States from terrorism. The result is not surprising— in last week's climate, 42 percent of the American public would probably have favored painting the White House green to protect the hostages—and, given the United States' basic support for Israel, it is almost certainly a temporary reaction. Still, the poll reflected the success of the hijackers and their American supporters in portraying Washington's support for Israel as the underlying cause of anti-American terror in the Arab world.

In the Arab lobby, "underlying cause" has become a code phrase, like "even-handed" (which means pro-Arab) and "moderate" (the term for extremists friendly to the United States). In this contest, the "underlying cause" of Arab terrorism is always Israel. The basic premise is simple—that it is Israel's policies that force otherwise reasonable and peace-loving people into acts of violent desperation. The reasoning echoes what the [Jets] once told Officer Krupke in "West Side Story," "We're depraved on account of we're deprived."

That was precisely the argument made last week in defense of the hijacking of TWA Flight 847. The event posed a thorny problem for Arab apologists in the United States, who were understandably reluctant to actually applaud kidnapping, blackmail and murder. That is where "underlying causes" came to the rescue. The hijackers, so the story went, were Shi'ite militiamen roused into action by Israel's policies in southern Lebanon. Motivated by patriotism and grievance, they staged a kind of Lebanese Boston Tea Party—and if dozens of American civilians were terrorized, a Marine murdered and Jewish passengers separated from the others Auschwitz-style, it was the regrettable but justifiable reaction to Israeli provocation.

The "underlying cause" theory is not new—it has been used to blame Israel for virtually every Arab outrage, from the assassination of President Anwar el-Sadat to Palestine Liberation Organization attacks on innocent civilians—and its corollary is equally well-known. If Israel is the cause of Arab terror, then support for Israel puts America on the wrong side of the terrorists. After all, the old Arab proverb states that "The friend of my enemy is my enemy."

This argument would make sense if it weren't for the fact that terrorism is the hallmark of many of the Islamic Middle East's most prestigious governments and organizations: They routinely use mindless violence as an instrument of policy, without reference to Israel, in international conflicts, domestic politics and disputes with other Islamic countries and groups. In recent years, Iran has seized and tortured American citizens; Iraq has used poison gas against Iran; Colonel Muammar el-Qaddafi's gunmen have shot British passersby in the center of London; the Syrian Government has carried out political mass murders against its own people; rival factions of the P.L.O. have massacred each other in Tripoli; and a wild and uncontrolled civil war has turned Lebanon into perhaps the most violent, irrational and uncivilized place on earth.

Israel is not even remotely responsible for any of these developments. They flow naturally out of the fanaticism and despotism that characterizes regimes led by the Ayatollah Ruhollah Khomeini, Colonel Qaddafi, the Iraqi President, Saddam Hussein, the Syrian President, Hafez el-Assad, Yassir Arafat and the heads of the various factions in Lebanon. No one with any dealings in the region, including America, can be immune from violent, often irrational, outbreaks for the simple reason that they are so widespread (not to say applauded) in the Islamic Middle East. And if America is a special target, a "great Satan" in the Ayatollah Khomeini's words, it is not because the United States has an alliance with Israel but because it represents values—liberalism, personal freedom, secular government, Western democracy—that seem threatening and abhorrent to many Middle Eastern radicals and religious fanatics.

Israel was right to do whatever it could to cooperate with the United States in achieving the release of the American hostages. Having done so, the two countries, along with other civilized nations, ought to look for ways to fight back against terrorists and their accomplices. This will require patience, steadfastness and the capacity to recognize what the "underlying causes" of the problem really are. The terrorists and their supporters notwithstanding, Israel and the United States will remain targets (and allies) in the Middle East not because of what they do but because of what they are—good countries in a bad neighborhood.

C: CHARLES KRAUTHAMMER
LOOKING EVIL DEAD IN THE EYE

THE PROBLEM OF EVIL has long been the province of philosophy. Philosophy is not particularly interested in that question anymore. (Nor is the world much interested in philosophy, but that is another matter.) Journalism has taken up the slack. Unfortunately, journalism is not terribly well equipped to handle it, principally because journalism is a medium of display and demonstration. When evil is the subject, the urge to display leads to dark places indeed.

Last month, for example, it led to Osaka, Japan, where reporters and photographers stood around while two men broke into the apartment of an accused swindler, murdered him with 13 bayonet stabs, then emerged blood splattered to a press corps stunned, but not too stunned to keep the TV camaras rolling. It led to West Germany, where a couple of magazines, *Bunte Illustrierte* and *Stern,* tried to auction off to other media bits of Mengele, photographs, letters and other memorabilia. Finally, it led to Beirut, where during 17 days of astonishing symbiosis, television and terrorists co-produced—there is no better word—a hostage drama.

For journalism, as for other performing arts, evil is a fascinating and indispensable subject. The question is how to fix on the subject without merging with it. For many arts, the solution is to interpose time: their reflections on evil are, for the most part, recollections in tranquility. On television news, that protective distance disappears.

No event has demonstrated the

AP/Wide World

TV crews and reporters cover the hijacking of TWA Flight 847 parked at Beirut International Airport, sometimes ducking hijackers' bullets.

bizarre consequences of that fact quite as dramatically as the TWA hijacking. There, under laboratory conditions, journalism met terror, in a pure culture, uncontaminated by civilization. The results are not encouraging. Terror needed a partner in crime to give the event life. The media, television above all, obliged.

Driven not by malevolence but by those two journalistic imperatives, technology and competition, journalism will go where it can go. When it has the technology, it shoots first and asks questions later. For the correspondent bargaining for access to hostages, the important questions are Can I get the story/show? and Will anyone else? The question What am I doing? comes up after the tape has been relayed from Damascus, if at all.

As a result, others ask the question and produce a depressingly familiar list of findings: insensitivity to the families; exploitation of the hostages; absurd, degrading deference to jailers; interfer-ence with diplomacy; appropriation of the role of negotiatior. (David Hartman to Nabih Berri: "Any final words to President Reagan this morning?") And finally, giving over the airwaves to people whose claim to airtime is based entirely on the fact that they are forcibly holding innocent Americans.

The principal defense against these charges is perhaps best called the cult of objectivity. Journalists are led to believe, and some may actually believe, that they only hold a mirror to life. And mirrors can hardly be accused of bad faith. After all, the idea of neutrality inheres in the very word medium. There is a story out there to be got, and as Sam Donaldson, prominent preacher of this doctrine, puts it, "It's our job to cover the story . . . we bring information."

Not even physicists, practitioners of a somewhat more exact science, have so arrogant a belief in the out there. For 60 years, physics has learned to live with its Uncertainty Principle: that the act of observing an event alters its nature.

Journalism continues to resist the idea.

And journalism, which shines lights at people, not electrons, does more than alter. It creates. First, out of the infinite flotsam of "events" out there, it makes "stories." Then, by exposing them (and their attached people, ideas, crimes), it puts them on the map. "As seen on TV" gives substance to murder as surely as it does to Ginzu knives. The parade of artifacts is varied, but the effect is the same: coverage makes them real.

No one knows this better than terrorists. No one is more grudging in acknowledging this than television journalists. Their self-criticism takes place generally at the periphery. For example, the TV anchors were much embarrassed that reporters' unruliness caused the first hostage press conference to be temporarily called off (by terrorists, mind you). But that misses the point. The real point is what they were doing when not unruly: blanketing American airwaves with shows choreographed by the captors, with the hostages, under constant but concealed threat, acting as their spokesmen.

Another fine point was whether to run live pictures. Dan Rather said no, averring that his network would not be handed over the terrorists. This was in contrast to ABC, which had broadcast live interviews. But what purpose does it serve to broadcast these interviews at all? If the purpose is to show that the hostages are alive and well, the tools of the print media—a still picture and a summary of what had happened—are perfectly adequate. But that would be bad television. And that is exactly the point: the play's the thing. These terrorist productions are coveted for their dramatic, not their news value.

That realization might open the way to some solution, or at least some approach to the problem of reducing terrorist control of the airwaves. If much of the coverage is indeed not news but entertainment—bizarre guerrilla theater that outdoes *Network*—then television might place voluntary limits on it, as it does on other entertainments.

Broadcast television imposes limits, strict but self-enforced limits, on explicit sex. Why not on explicit terror? There is no reason why all the news of a terrorist event, like news of a rape, cannot be transmitted in some form. But in the interest of decency, diplomacy and our own self-respect, it need not be live melodrama.

A few years ago, when some publicity seekers started dashing onto baseball fields during televised games, TV producers decided to discourage the practice by averting the camera's eye. So now, the crowd roars at the commotion, and the viewer strains to see what it is all about, but cannot. Yet he accepts this restraint, this self-censorship, if you will, without complaint because it serves to avoid delays at ball games. Yet we won't do the same when the end is reducing the payoff for political murder.

If we did the same, the drama we would miss would no doubt be riveting. Evil is riveting. From watching Hitchcock we know of the perverse, and fully human, enjoyment that comes from looking evil dead in the eye. But when the evil is real and the suffering actual, that enjoyment is tinged with shame, the kind of shame one experiences when exposed to pornography.

And like pornography, terrorist television, the graphic unfolding of evil on camera, sells. During the hostage crisis, network news ratings rose markedly. But this fascination has its price. Lot's wife fixed her gaze on evil and turned to salt.

115.

Robert MacNeil: The Mass Media and Public Trust

The First Amendment endured many challenges during the 1980s, often in attacks on the media. As this speech at the Gannett Center for Media Studies at Columbia University contends, the attacks seemed to become more bitter as the 1980s wore on. This might have been because the media were becoming more irresponsible, or it might have been because its targets were becoming more sensitive. Robert MacNeil, cohost of the MacNeil/Lehrer News Hour on Public Broadcasting, wrote the following selection.

Source: *Columbia* Magazine, June 1985.

MEDIA RELATIONS with the public are perplexing. To some in our ranks it feels like a crisis, and unless something feels like a crisis, most journalists can't be bothered with it. So, we're bothered. To others it is just another chapter in the tension-packed story that began a few miles north of here with the tribulations of John Peter Zenger, a story we hope will never end, because it is the story of society struggling to live with the prickly reality of a free press.

Determining just how grave the situation is—and what, if anything, should be done about it—is a major task for the Center. There is plenty of evidence that the public trust is an ebbing tide.

There is the large number of libel suits, growing trend for juries to find against journalist defendants and to award huge damages to the plaintiffs. These are not always upheld on appeal, but they reveal an attitude. Eugene Patterson, editor of the *St. Petersburg Times,* says, "Juries are the American people. They want to punish us."

Then there are the megaton libel suits, like Westmoreland's, Ariel Sharon's, and Senator Paul Laxalt's, brought, the media defendants believe, with punitive or intimidatory intent.

There are the opinion surveys that can be read to indicate some decline in public confidence, or can be read the other way. The glass can often seem two-thirds full and one-third empty. The findings are inconsistent and sometimes contradictory. They all show distressing assumptions about what government could or should do to the press and amazing ignorance of the First Amendment—all coupled with general applause for the abstract idea of a free press.

There is a proliferation of groups of aroused citizens wanting to discipline or curb or regulate journalists. One of them, Fairness in Media, is trying to buy equity control of CBS to become Dan Rather's boss.

There is an unquantifiable but, to all of us working in the media, evident

Yelena Bonner, wife of Soviet dissident Andrei Sakharov, is nearly crushed by reporters as she tries to reach her Italian eye doctor's office for an examination.

spirit of rancor abroad in the land. When the Reagan Administration initially excluded the press from Grenada, and the public applauded. *Time* Magazine reported that its letters ran eight to one against the press and that the opposition "was expressed in gleeful, even vengeful terms."

David Gergen, then White House communications director, commented: "Unfortunately, kicking the press is a sure-fire-applause line with almost any audience."

So why, the editors began to ask, do they hate us?

Survey after survey shows specific irritants turning up consistently. Significant parts of the public—minorities, true, but large minorities—think the media are often inaccurate, unfair, biased, intrusive of privacy, unethical, arrogant, and preoccupied with bad news.

It is a verdict pretty well summed up in a pop song, "Dirty Linen," sung by Don Henley:

Dirty little secrets,
Dirty little lies,
We got our dirty little fingers

In everybody's pies.
We love to cut you down to size.
And the refrain:
Kick'em when they're up,
Kick'em when they're down.
And there is the Anne Murray song:
There's a local paper rolled up
in a rubber band.
One more sad story's one more
than I can stand.
Just once I'd like to see the
headlines say:
"Not much to print today,
Couldn't find nothin' bad to say."

And the bulletin of the American Society of Newspaper Editors, which printed those songs, also pointed out that in novels, plays, movies and television shows recently, the public sees journalists in a very unfavorable light.

Why do they hate us?

Daniel Schorr, chief correspondent of Cable News Network, said last year: "The words 'power of the press' always carried a white-hat connotation of power exercised for good. But 'power of the media' has a black-hat sound of power exercised against people."

According to opinion surveys, many Americans resented the behavior of some television crews intruding on the grief of bereaved families after the marine barracks were blown up in Lebanon. The public seems to discount the defense of journalists that some such families find release and catharsis in exposing their grief.

I remember being very hesitant about approaching the father of a boy killed in Vietnam to ask permission to film his son's funeral. He gave it gladly. "It will give Ron's death some meaning," he said.

People felt like that after Lebanon. But the public remembers the crews that staked out houses and filmed as Marine officers delivered the news of a loved one's death. The public remembers the shrieks. The public may even want to hear them, and then feel ashamed of its voyeurism.

When the *Washington Post* returned a Pulitzer Prize because Janet Cooke, its young reporter, confessed to inventing an eight-year-old heroin addict, 61 percent of Americans in a Gallup sampling said they believed "very little" or "only some" of the news we print or broadcast. Only 33 percent said they believed most news reports.

Why do they hate us?

Some thoughtful journalists suggest we may have been wearing the First Amendment too brazenly, not as a shield but as a challenge.

Michael O'Neill, former editor of the New York *Daily News,* said two years ago, "We have to be careful not to claim more than we have a right to claim in the public interest. After all, it is the public's interest, not ours."

Lou Boccardi, president of the Associated Press and a member of the advisory board of this center, points out that the media occupy a different place in this society than they used to. He wonders, "Have we reached a point where we must recognize an obligation not to do some of the things the First Amendment gives us the right to do?" Others dispute this, but clearly there is a lot of soul-searching going on, and soon passersby will notice the scorched odor of souls being searched in this new center. Perhaps it will replace the odor of sanctity, or sanctimoniousness, that some detect around the media.

Many other explanations are offered—for example, that we are the purveyors of bad news. After Reuven Frank of NBC, I think it was, first recalled that the Persian kings executed messengers bearing bad news, it became a handy cliché to grasp at. Many think it is still apt.

Some think that the media companies have become just like other large corporations Americans suspect of wielding too much power. Interestingly, the surveys often show that people love their local paper or news show but hate newspapers or television in general.

Obviously there is something in all this, and it will be good to have objective and disciplined minds analyzing the phenomena, not just in one survey hastily taken to test the impact of one event—like the Janet Cooke affair—but regularly, to permit some rational assessment of what is going on.

But none of us would be journalists if we were content to wait for the results of several years of academic research. We are paid to plunge in and describe, as best we can, on deadline, the here and now as we see it. Recognizing that this center's research may blow my ideas full of holes, let me discuss two aspects of the reality I see.

The first occurred to me at the time of the Janet Cooke business. It is the changing media context in which news is made, reported, and perceived—in other words, how the attitudes of journalists and the public may have been changed by the changing structure and purpose of the communications media themselves. There are many pieces to this, but let me explore one: the respect for facts.

It used to be that the media for news, for popular entertainment, for ideas, for advertising, for politicking were fairly distinct. But they have been converging, especially since radio and television arrived. Today the lines are very blurred. Journalists have to share the media of communications with the most powerful vehicles for mass entertainment, politicking, advertising, and marketing ever devised. One of the most difficult tasks of journalists today is to keep our piece of the media spectrum dedicated to the facts and the truth.

Yet we also have to compete for the attention of the public with all the rest of these uses, where facts and truth are not sacred, where—to greater or lesser extent—the facts are something to be played with, manipulated, shaded, improved, distorted, colored, exaggerated, even ignored if they are inconvenient, to make a better docudrama, movie, play, pop song, commercial, or political speech. Or sermon. . . .

Freedom to play with the facts often makes the product very compelling, capable of attracting bigger audiences than the often prosaic business we are in. In a recent *New York Times* article, a producer at WNET, Michael Rosenblum, suggested this as the reason for presenting the new argument in the case of the Atlanta child murders as a television docudrama, not a documentary.

Rosenblum says, "Dramatic television is more exciting than real life, easier to produce, gets vastly higher ratings, and is far simpler to defend from a 'journalistic perspective.' " He adds, "You can be sure that if 'The uncounted enemy: a Vietnam deception' had been a docudrama, there would have been no multimillion-dollar lawsuit."

I'm fascinated by this blurred media context, where fact and fiction coexist so intimately, where news fact cohabits with ad fact, journalistic truth with political truth. It must produce in some minds a blurring of the distinction, perhaps an indifference to the distinction, perhaps a contempt for the real facts and the boring people who survey them.

Dressed-up facts, entertainment facts, facts with makeup and false eyelashes on are so satisfying. There are always solutions to difficult problems. Angry people get results. Protestors get satisfaction. The insolence of office, the law's delays, the pangs of despiséd love—all the rest of it—are dealt with before the last commercial. There are solutions to difficult problems, with warm bodies personifying them.

Messy, unresolved facts, like budget deficits, Middle East hostilities, and poverty on the real news, keep droning on night after night, newspaper headline after newspaper headline—untidy, unresolved, negative. What does that foster? Contempt in the mind of the public? Envy in the breast of some journalists who would like to make the raw materials they deal with neat, their quotes pithy, their characters dynamic? So sometimes they do, and—like Janet Cooke—they get caught.

It is hard to be young, ambitious, and hungry to star in a media world where everyone else can adjust the truth and you can't. Take the current campaign for Newport cigarettes: sexy young people, bursting with health, cavorting in bright sports clothes, with the word "Alive" the biggest message—clearly a very limited reality in view of all that is known about cigarette smoking, yet a message perhaps as powerful to the young as any news story.

My other observation concerns fairness. I believe that there is a rising public expectation of fairness, that a higher standard of fairness is demanded of our profession than in the old days when journalism was local, pointed, and hot. The rise of a national journalism has long ago cooled off the partisanship. The days have gone when a paper like the *Los Angeles Times* could deny access to political opponents; the trend today is to open up access, to broaden the range of views printed.

From the beginning, broadcasters, using limited public airways, could not be sharply partisan, first out of practicality, later by regulation. Some feel that broadcasters, who have influenced print in so many other ways, thus created expectations of fairness among readers and that that made newspapers more objective, as did declining competition and probably a better-educated public.

Still, fairness—even-handedness, balance, objectivity—is the demand I hear more consistently from the public than anything else, and the greatest complaint I hear is the lack of it. The public defines fairness very broadly and is spurred on by people with axes to grind who want to define fairness their own way.

I see a danger that unless our profession redefines fairness and its importance to us, others will increasingly try to define it for us—and perhaps succeed. . . .

I think there is, frankly, scorn for fairness in some journalistic quarters. It may be left over from the new journalism, which died because it excused mediocre practitioners from the drudgery of gathering facts and because people got tired of reality filtered through perceptions no more interesting than their own. In some quarters it is clearly a yearning for straight advocacy journalism, which regards fairness as effete and unmanly and thinks telling both sides of a story and letting the public decide the merits is wimpy and even irresponsible.

There is an attitude common in the media that any good journalist can apply common sense and quickly fathom what is right and what is wrong in any complicated issue, and that professional pride demands that he say so. The targets of this often facile journalism—the company, the school, the military, the hospital—see the superficiality, the shallowness, of the story and consider it unfair.

Coupled with this attitude is one in which a reporter or a camera crew acts as though their presence, their action in covering a story, is more important than the event they are covering.

Then there is the more cynical belief that the American public loves the myths of good guys and bad guys and wants the real world fitted into such molds, so someone always has to be the bad guy.

I also see what the public may perceive as unfairness in the aggressive negativism, sometimes of a rather theatrical, posturing kind, that has pervaded much reporting, especially from Washington, since Vietnam and Watergate. It is as though the media had not yet digested these events but still felt obliged to deal with ghosts.

There is a difference between skepticism and disbelief. It is true that all the icons of our beliefs trembled on the walls in the decade from 1965 to 1975. Scarcely an institution went untouched. Most of them have been rehabilitated in the public mind, including the presidency. Even university administrators are not the great satans they were once considered, except perhaps by the new secretary of education.

Yet in Washington I feel that some media representatives are continuing to act out a ritual hostility learned when they thought government was lying to them every day about virtually everything. It may have started as a collective professional attitude of "Boy, they're never going to pull the wool over our eyes again." It may be the influence of television exposure, which feeds on adversarial confrontation. Never ignore how the values fashionable in entertainment programs inform the journalistic end of the medium. All television gravitates toward drama, and what passes for drama is often belligerence, people barking at each other, like soap opera actors, sounding vehement to make up for cardboard characters or too little rehearsal time.

So we have the media sounding vehement, belligerent, barking at President Reagan, who responds by grinning ruefully. Who is going to win that kind of contest? Perhaps reporters feel that the climate of the time requires them to sound hostile so that they will appear to be tough. But what if that merely feeds a perception that shows up in the surveys: that the press is simply being rude, that it is being, in the words of a Citizens Choice study, "too hard" on government, in this case the president? What if the effect is to substitute in the public mind, and perhaps the press's own, this rather theatrical toughness for the real thing?

Few people in the business think the news media are tougher on this president than on his recent predecessors. Yet the public thinks we are picking on him. So we may be reinforcing public perception of unfairness without any corresponding trenchancy to back it up.

But another effect of the news media's pseudo-toughness could be to strengthen the hand of government—any administration—in manipulating the media to make the public think that we are unfair to government.

It must be puzzling to the public, then, to see the increasing use of unnamed sources, which implies some complicity with government. Does it strain credibility to have us barking at the administration like a watchdog outside while licking hands and eating scraps from every stray official inside?

But broaden the definition of fairness even further: It is very difficult to be fair when you have to squeeze reality into too small a space or time. It is a criticism made more often of television than print, but not exclusively. Time and space are arbitrarily parceled out by assumptions about the importance of a story and the degree of public interest. But if the slot is too small, all but the newest opinions or facts get left out—the context, the qualifications, the contrary views, the explanations, extenuations—all the things that tend to make the treatment fair, or make it seem unfair if they are left out. By a still wider conception of fairness, some might argue that it is unfair to present to the public a story so truncated that it gives a too simple or lopsided view of reality. . . .

Of course, the reason all this is so much in our minds right now is because the macho arm of American journalism—the commandos of the Fourth Estate, the investigative reporters—have recently been on trial in the most spectacular way.

There has been a lot of media relief that *Time* magazine was found guilty only of inaccuracy, not libel, and that General Westmoreland withdrew his case against CBS. Clearly, that relief is justified in the sense that neither case advanced or encouraged the use of the court system by public officials for punitive revenge on journalists who have attacked their reputations. They may have even served the purpose of clarifying the need for some restraint in damage awards.

That is looking at it from the press point of view, the press anxious to preserve its clear and necessary right to criticize public officials.

But look at it from the public point of view, and take the CBS-Westmoreland case because it was an American official involved, a man many admired for his long and distinguished career of service to this country.

The trial judge and the CBS lawyer said early on to the jury and to the public that the issue was not fairness. The general had to prove not that CBS was unfair but that it had knowingly, maliciously, and recklessly broadcast a false report. And yet, outside the confines of the courtroom, for most of the American people, I strongly suspect that the issue was fairness.

By its own admission, CBS did not treat General Westmoreland by its own standards of fairness. Since the aborted trial, CBS says the documentary was fair and accurate, but that is not quite what CBS said in the internal investigation conducted by Burton Benjamin.

Benjamin said the issue of whether General Westmoreland cooked the books of enemy troop strength in Viet-

nam for political reasons was "obviously and historically controversial," and that there was an imbalance in presenting the two sides. General Westmoreland and his one defender got a total of five minutes and fifty-nine seconds. Sam Adams, the former CIA official who was his chief accuser, and his eight supporting witnesses got nineteen minutes and nineteen seconds. Sympathetic witnesses were coddled, one was interviewed twice to improve his testimony, and there were other violations of CBS news standards.

Benjamin also pointed out that the documentary had not included portions of an interview in which President Johnson said that he was fully aware of the size of the enemy force that confronted the United States in the Tet Offensive.

To its credit, CBS acknowledged the Benjamin report and finally released it in full. The network said it would have been better if the word "conspiracy" had not been used, if more people who disagreed with the premise had been interviewed, and if there had been strict compliance with CBS news standards. Those are pretty big *ifs*.

If those *ifs* had been followed, the documentary would have been perceived as a fair, objective inquiry, charges made and charges denied, not a trial on television with CBS in full control of the evidence, playing prosecutor, judge, and jury. Perceived as a fair inquiry, it would have been much harder for General Westmoreland to dismiss as a hatchet job. More to the point, it seems very unlikely that there would have been a libel suit at all.

Perhaps CBS's conclusions about General Westmoreland's conduct were completely correct. The network says so, and late testimony in the trial was clearly pointing in that direction. Perhaps the reality was a good deal more complicated than they made it seem. It was certainly a legitimate, if not a very new, piece of Vietnam history to subject to this dramatic inquiry. It can be argued that it was a public service. The war was tragically expensive for the United States, and the judgments good and bad that prosecuted the war deserve the fullest airing.

But why is it necessary in a piece of journalism to treat a distinguished American less fairly than he would be treated in a court of law if charged with a criminal offense?

It makes ordinary people ask, What was the motive? What was the *animus*? Was it intended to be a serious effort to contribute to the nation's knowledge of the war while some principal characters were still around? Or was it the jungle motive—to get him?

I single out CBS because they are a great news organization and they had the courage to single themselves out in this case by insisting that this hot piece of journalism be tested against CBS traditions and experience. . . .

In one of the *Federalist Papers,* Alexander Hamilton asks, "What is the liberty of the free press? Its security, whatever fine declarations may be inserted in any constitution respecting it, must altogether depend on public opinion, and on the general spirit of the people and the government."

And so the liberty of the American press had depended for two centuries. Journalistic carelessness that ignores basic fairness—a decent respect for the opinions of mankind—will invite attacks on that liberty, and turn the general spirit of the people more hostile.

One survey found majorities of 70 to 80 percent of the American people in favor of laws requiring newspapers and television to give political opponents of major parties and opponents on controversial issues equal time.

Until now, American journalists have ignored or laughed off such views, confident that the right-thinking majority would protect them, and that when their enemies had them surrounded, the First Amendment cavalry would gallop up just in time. Perhaps it always will. And perhaps not. I am confident that the work done at this center will help us understand what the threat really is.

He wanted to live in the greatest country in the world and take advantage of all its freedoms, but he didn't want to be loyal to it. He wanted to sell it.
LAURA WALKER SNYDER, daughter of convicted spy
John A. Walker, June 1985

Egyptian President Anwar Sadat, center, watched a military display from a reviewing stand moments before he was assassinated by gunmen in a speeding car.

TROUBLES ABROAD CONTINUED

The troubles that had beset the Carter administration in the field of foreign policy continued under Ronald Reagan. Alexander Haig started out as Secretary of State but resigned the post when he found some foreign policy initiatives taken out of his hands. He was replaced by George P. Shultz. The so-called Reagan Doctrine began to emerge as time went on: support freedom fighters everywhere in their efforts to overthrow Marxist regimes. On the other hand, there seemed to be little enthusiasm about overthrowing the government of Chile's Augusto Pinochet Ugarte, Paraguay's Al-

fredo Stroessner, or other right-wing dictatorships. Nicaragua became the focal point in the Western Hemisphere: the freedom fighters in this case, called Contras, were heavily backed by administration rhetoric and, later, money and arms. Congress, sometimes reluctantly, went along with support for the Contras, although there was strong evidence that many of these so-called freedom fighters were little more than terrorists. Another major problem for Reagan was international terrorism, which the administration found hard to deal with, especially when it involved the taking of hostages.

AP/Wide World

(Top) In the wreckage of the U.S. Marine operations center at Beirut Airport rescue attempts continue for the second day; cranes and bulldozers had worked all night under floodlights trying to find bodies of Marines trapped in the rubble; (bottom) on November 25, 1983, a few days after the disaster in Beirut, the U.S. invaded Grenada; this sign was erected by the 82nd Airborne by the runway of the airport.

UPI/Bettmann

October 1983 was both a bad and a good month for the Reagan administration. On the 23rd of the month a truck bomb driven by a suicidal terrorist exploded inside Marine Corps headquarters at the Beirut Airport and killed 239 U.S. servicemen; many others were wounded, and two died later. Simultaneously a truck bomb exploded in a French paratrooper barracks, killing 58. An investigation concluded that the Marines had been inadequately prepared for such an attack, which led, three months later, to Reagan's withdrawal of U.S. forces from Lebanon. Two days after the attack a seven-nation assault force, headed by U.S. Marines and Army Rangers, invaded the tiny Caribbean nation of Grenada in order to avert what the administration stated was a strong likelihood that the country would become "a Soviet-Cuban colony." It was a very small war but a successful one, in fact the first really successful U.S. military operation in years. As such, it won widespread popular approval. In October 1985 four Palestinian terrorists hijacked the cruise ship *Achille Lauro* and then surrendered in Egypt after murdering an American passenger. The hijackers were flown to Tunisia in an Egyptian aircraft that was intercepted by U.S. F-14 fighters and forced to land in Italy. The affair ended in a standoff, but Egypt, Italy, and Tunisia were all offended by what Egypt called U.S. "air piracy." The disaster at Bhopal, India, in December 1984 was not a failure of U.S. foreign policy, but it nevertheless was a severe problem for America's image abroad. A leak of toxic gas at a Union Carbide plant killed over 2,000 and hurt many thousands more, blinding many for life. Suits and countersuits were filed, and the Union Carbide company reeled under the impact. Throughout the third world politicians denounced the U.S., claiming that it was heedless of the health and safety of nonwhite peoples.

(Top) Egyptian military police guard the Italian ship *Achille Lauro* after the four Palestinian hijackers surrendered; (bottom) in Bhopal, India, friends and relatives bury victims of a massive pesticide leak from the Union Carbide plant in the background.

UPI/Bettmann

AP/Wide World

(Top) Bodies lie on the floor of the lounge of Rome's Leonardo da Vinci Airport; on the same day in December 1985 the Vienna Airport was attacked by a Palestinian group headed by Abu Nidal; (bottom) the Greenpeace ship *Rainbow Warrior* lies partly submerged at the dock in Auckland, New Zealand.

Terrorism was a continuing problem for the United States during the Reagan years. Bombings, kidnappings, and hijackings were frequent occurrences in 1984 and 1985, reaching a crescendo of violence in the latter year when extremists hijacked a TWA plane and held many of its passengers hostage for days. Each evening on the news there was another frantic report, including interviews with the hostages. In December 1985 terrorists struck simultaneously at airports near Rome and Vienna. In Rome, the terrorists started shooting into crowds of passengers checking in for El Al and TWA flights and rolled armed grenades across the floor in their direction. Further bombings and threats of terror in the spring of 1986 enraged President Reagan and many other Americans, and he ordered an air strike against Muammar Qaddafi's Libya in April, despite the fact that there was some doubt whether Libya

Photos by AP/Wide World

(Top) When the U.S. bombed Libya in 1986, Col. Muammar Qaddafi's home was almost destroyed in retaliation for Libya's support of terrorism; Qaddafi's adopted daughter was killed and others of his family were injured; (bottom) freed hostage David Jacobsen greets his father in California.

had been involved in some of the terrorist acts. Beginning in 1984, American citizens were kidnapped and held in Beirut by various extremist groups. There was suspicion that most of the kidnappings were masterminded by the Iranians or by groups sympathetic to Iran's revolution. Nevertheless, covert negotiations with certain factions, thought to be politically moderate, within the Iranian government were initiated by U.S. officials in 1985. One hostage who may or may not have been freed as a result was David Jacobsen. Others were Benjamin Weir and Martin Lewis Jenco, a priest. There was a further occasion for outrage when the tactics of terrorist groups were mirrored by French security agents, who sank the Greenpeace vessel *Rainbow Warrior* to prevent it from sailing to the South Pacific to protest French nuclear tests; one person was killed in the explosions that sank the ship.

AP/Wide World

AP/Wide World

UPI/Bettmann

(Top) Former Philippine President Ferdinand Marcos arrives in Honolulu; (center) President Corazon Aquino addresses a joint session of Congress, applauded by Speaker Thomas "Tip" O'Neill and Rep. Strom Thurmond; (bottom) thousands of Filipinos surround tanks to prevent them from reaching Aquino aides in Camp Crame military complex.

The government of Ferdinand Marcos of the Philippines was in serious trouble by the fall of 1985. When President Ronald Reagan sent an envoy, Senator Paul Laxalt of Nevada, to confer with Marcos, a Filipino government newspaper greeted Laxalt with the headline "Another Meddler from the U.S." When Laxalt left, the paper trumpeted "Good Riddance!" But the writing was on the wall for Marcos. He announced in November that he would be willing to have an election early the next year. Corazon Aquino, widow of murdered anti-Marcos leader Ninoy Aquino, entered the contest for the presidency. The election took place in February, and the Marcos forces attempted to steal victory; however, a mass uprising in support of Aquino by thousands wearing yellow, her signature color, drove Marcos out of the country. Aquino was installed as the new president of the Philippines, but many serious political and economic problems remained to be solved. In September 1986, she impressed many in Washington with the speech she delivered to a joint session of Congress. Closer to the United States, Central America, a region that had long been a focus of American economic and political interest, again was brought to the forefront of U.S. foreign policy. According to the Reagan administration, the region required American military assistance. The president was vocal in his belief that it was in the interest of both the United States and Central America that the United States provide the help necessary to counteract the Marxist-oriented Sandinista govern-

(Above) Most of a fishing boat lies below the surface after it struck a mine planted by CIA-backed rebels in a Nicaraguan port; (top right) Contras after a raid in Nicaragua in 1985; (center) Salvadoran troops in Honduras; (bottom) Eugene Hasenfus was taken prisoner by the Nicaraguan army when his plane, carrying arms to the Contras, was shot down.

ment of Nicaragua. Congress, remembering the early days of the Vietnam conflict, was reluctant to commit major resources and tried to place tight restrictions on what the President could do. In the fall of 1986 it was revealed that for months, at least, members of the administration had been secretly supplying the Contras, U.S.-backed rebels, with arms paid for by sales of arms to Iran. In early December 1986 Reagan was said to have conferred with ex-President Richard Nixon about how to deal with matters of this sort—hence the cartoon below. In any event, aid to the Contras seemed doomed.

THE DANCING LESSON

Learning The "Side Step"

Marc Simont

During the second week of October 1986 President Reagan met the leader of the Soviet Union, Mikhail Gorbachev, in a hastily called summit at Reykjavik, Iceland. Gorbachev had a briefcase full of specific proposals, which included a plan for the elimination of long-range missiles by the end of the century. Since the price of such an agreement was the reduction of the Star Wars defense program to the level of "laboratory research," Reagan would not accept the Soviet proposal. The threat of nuclear weapons aside, there remained the dangers of accidents like the nuclear meltdown at the Chernobyl power plant in the Soviet Union in 1986.

(Top) Soviet leader Mikhail Gorbachev and President Reagan shake hands in Geneva before the 1985 summit; (center) a Soviet medical technician checks a baby for radiation after the Chernobyl meltdown; the family was evacuated to a state farm near Kiev; (bottom) President Reagan and Soviet leader Gorbachev have some final words at the close of the summit in Reykjavik, Iceland, in 1986.

116.

What Will the Bank Dicks Do Now?

The first half of the decade of the 1980s saw more bank failures than the total of the previous 40 years—that is, since the Great Depression. The following selection from Forbes *examines the crisis.*

Source: *Forbes*, July 1, 1985.

IN AN ERA that frowned on public profanity, W.C. Fields was a profane man. The censors wouldn't stand for casual references to the Diety. So, in his performances, Fields would often respond to a patent absurdity by exclaiming: "Godfrey Daniels!" The audience got the point and laughed. . . . We suspect that "Godfrey Daniels!" is the appropriate response to anyone who says our banking system is fundamentally healthy and that the recent failures and near failures are just aberrations.

The fact is that the savings and loan system is busted and the commercial banks as a whole are stuffed with questionable paper, both domestic and foreign. So, are we on the verge of a 1930s-type banking panic? No way. Behind the banking system now stands the Federal Treasury. But just because depositors are safe does not mean there is no problem. Deposit insurance simply sweeps the real problem under the rug. So we have a basically green-eyeshade and greenback banking system unable to cope with a situation in which money is simply a blip on a computer screen.

Untold billions of dollars' worth of uncollectible loans to countries are still carried on banks' books as assets. Manufacturers Hanover, to name one, has $3.7 billion—112% of its net worth—tied up in loans to Brazil and Argentina. Chase Manhattan also has $3.6 billion—92% of its net worth—in loans to the same two countries. Falling prices of oil, farm commodities and commercial real estate have dug scores of institutions into holes they will never climb out of. Some go-go S&Ls are loaded with bad investments that have wiped out their net worth. Bank of America obviously has serious, long-term problems.

Godfrey Daniels!

Federal Reserve Chairman Paul Volcker complains, and rightly so, about the massive diversion of bank credit to such speculative purposes as takeovers. But Volcker isn't telling the whole story—as a public official he probably can't. He neglects to say that the authorities, including the Fed, helped to create the present situation by allowing their deposit guarantees to cover deposits used to fund loans made for speculative purposes. Not merely allowed—but actually made it necessary.

Because we have deregulated the rates banks and S&Ls can pay for deposits, these institutions must pay high interest rates for once-cheap money—which means reaching for loans and stretching their capital. Citicorp set up "orphan subsidiaries" to move loans off its books, thus increasing its capital as a percent of assets. "Orphans" are merely one aspect of banks' staggering amount of off-balance-sheet activity, such as engaging in interest-rate swaps and issuing guarantees that borrowers will make interest and principal payments on time. This generates fee income that doesn't tie up assets and need not be backed by capital.

To cite just one example, Crocker National Bank has guaranteed that the Alaska Housing Finance Corp. will have the money to redeem $75 million of bonds if holders ask for early redemption. For this it gets a fee without having to commit capital, but it also incurs a potential liability whose timing it cannot control.

But the history of banking has shown that when you go out gunning for big fees, you have profit today, problems tomorrow. Financial Corp. of America's tortured bookkeeping was a classic example, and Fincorp is not alone.

As Rutgers University banking Professor Paul Nadler puts it, "I've got a 5-ton truck with 10 tons of canaries in it. I have to keep 5 tons of canaries in the air at all times."

But how long can you keep canaries in the air? In the past three years, 3 of the nation's 25 largest banks—Continental Illinois, Crocker and Seattle-First National—have needed bailouts; two others—Chase Manhattan and Bank of America—suffered big losses; and the biggest S&L company in the country, Fincorp, failed in all but name. Count-

ing the 52 failures so far this year, more than 400 banks and S&Ls have gone under in the 1980s, exceeding the total of the previous 40 years. There's more where this came from.

Fifty years ago, with the banking system near collapse, the Glass-Steagall Act turned banking into a heavily regulated industry, almost a public utility. Bankers didn't like it, but they had no choice. The federal government guaranteed that most depositors would not lose their money if their bank failed. In return, the banks were forced to give up much of their freedom to wheel and to deal. A key part of the new straitjacket was giving the Federal Reserve Board power to issue what became known as Regulation Q, which set maximum rates banks could pay.

But times have changed drastically. Regulation Q is gone and so are many of the other restrictions. But the insurance guarantees remain. It is as if the federal government continued to keep its share of the bargain but the bankers were no longer obligated to keep theirs.

Today's mess is not the inevitable result of deregulation but of the brand of deregulation being practiced, under which savers get the highest possible interest rates with perfect safety of their principal, but banks and S&Ls aren't supposed to fail.

Following 1980 legislation, the rates institutions could pay were virtually deregulated in 1982. This permitted banks and S&Ls to slug it out for deposits with money market mutual funds, which had grown to over $200 billion in less than a decade.

But in economics, as in life, there's no free lunch. If bank and S&L depositors could earn market rates on their money instead of, say, $6^3/_4$ under a Reg Q ceiling, someone has to pay for it.

The only way to pay the higher costs is to reach for higher-yielding assets. The market is brutal. Every form of deregulation has its dark side: death.

When an industry is deregulated, some companies prosper, others die. Failure is the way the market enforces discipline. Before airlines were deregulated, no major line had gone broke. Now airlines go under all the time. So do trucking companies. And so do banks and S&Ls.

But airlines and trucking companies are different from financial institutions. Banks and S&Ls are the economic underpinning of our financial system, and they are intermeshed with one another. You can't let a really big institution go under without risking having entire pieces of the system fail. Braniff Airways and Continental Airlines went into Chapter 11 without anything else going down. The not unreasonable rationale for saving Continental Illinois was to protect foreign financial institutions.

And as the recent panics in Maryland and Ohio show, once people lose confidence in the system, the infection spreads, with even sound institutions having to close because depositors all want their money at once and there's no way to pay them.

Anyone who wants to see what total financial freedom for banks can become need look only as far back as March 1933, when Franklin Delano Roosevelt began his presidency. The U.S. financial system had all but collapsed. There were bank holidays in 31 of the then 48 states.

The reaction to the crisis was the Banking Act of 1933, a.k.a. Glass-Steagall. Senator Carter Glass and Representative Henry Steagall, with Federal Reserve Chairman Mariner Eccles in the background, wrought better than they knew. They realized that bankers, left to their own devices, would succumb to folly and greed, and bad banking would drive out good banking.

Banking became a regulated quasi-monopoly in which it was tough to fail unless you were an incompetent or a crook. Money was cheap for the banks. Your average person settled for a passbook savings rate and your average corporation left on deposit large amounts of interest-free demand deposits as a kind of payment for services the banks rendered. It was a stuffy world, perfect for Egbert Sousé, W.C. Fields' bank dick, to parody. It was almost impossible to make a lot of money or to have earnings consistently grow faster than the economy as a whole. Banks could thus operate safely with capital of only 5% or so of assets, 3% for S&Ls. Bank stocks? Oh, they were for the proverbial widows and orphans, or for old folks too unimaginative to buy anything else.

The system worked well enough for more than 30 years. But the world changed, as nonbanks began poaching and inflation and interest rates began rising. There were no longer enough widows and orphans who wanted to buy bank stocks. Nor could the industry pay from its regulated profits the kinds of salaries needed to attract the bright young people. In the late 1960s Walter Wriston of Citibank publicly propounded the astounding theory that bank companies could increase profits 15% a year forever. In the world of Reg Q, which effectively barred banks from outbidding each other for funds, this couldn't be done. So Wriston et al. formed bank holding companies to get around the rules. The go-go bankers began playing with Eurodollars, which were virtually unregulated, and using other devices—peddling bank holding company commercial paper, selling loans with a commitment to repurchase them—to evade Reg Q.

Sure enough, bank stocks started to act like growth stocks, and banking salaries went way up. Walter Wriston's aggressive policies seemed to make sense.

Bank deregulation took a quantum leap in 1970, after the Penn Central bankruptcy, when the Fed suspended Reg Q ceilings on short-term certificates of deposit of $100,000 and up, to make sure banks could buy enough deposits to forestall liquidity problems. Ceilings on longer-term, $100,000 and up CDs were lifted in 1973. These big-CD ceilings were never reimposed.

This move in turn opened the door wide for money market funds. These allowed small savers, whose deposits were subject to Reg Q, to pool their funds and buy unregulated-rate big CDs. The first money market fund, Reserve Fund, began operating in 1972 and had little impact. But when interest rates rose into the teens in 1980 and Reg Q rates were still in single digits, money funds caught on with a vengeance.

"The banks can't accuse us of stealing their money," says Henry Brown, a Reserve cofounder. "Hell, we just recirculated it in bigger bunches. They had tremendous margins to play with, they were getting money at $5^{1}/_{4}\%$ and they could lend it out at 10% or better. With the average banker, the doorknob would hit him in the tail at 3 p.m. and then the only place you could find him was the golf course."

With money pouring out of banks and S&Ls into money funds, Congress in 1980 deregulated interest rates in a frenzy. Unwilling to rein in money funds, which by then had a large constituency, Congress set banks and S&Ls free to compete with them.

But most bankers had grown up in a protected, Glass-Steagall world. With rate deregulation, banking got to be as competitive as other businesses, only more risky. Today's profitable loan can be tomorrow's disaster. It's easy to manipulate earnings for a while, which explains why it took a few years for the effects of deregulation to produce corpses en masse.

"Once banks started competing for deposits," says House Banking Committee member Charles Schumer (D-N.Y.), "there were people who had been trained for 50 years to walk on land who were now thrown into the water, and they really don't know how to swim."

Savings and loan executives were even worse off. They had been even more protected than banks. With constantly rising house values, how could you make a bad mortgage loan? About the only way S&Ls could go broke was if the rates they paid for deposits rose above the rates they were getting on existing mortgage loans.

When S&Ls began dying from interest spread problems—74, a record number, failed in 1982—the reaction was the Garn–St. Germain bill, which vastly expanded the borrowing powers of federally chartered S&Ls and modestly expanded their investment powers. But many states—primarily California and Texas—totally deregulated not only what S&Ls could pay for their money but also what they could do with it. Naturally, if they did something really stupid and the institution failed, federal insurance picked up the tab, up to $100,000 per account.

That's not what Glass and Steagall had in mind when they invented the FDIC. "Deposit insurance was designed to cover individuals who put their life savings into banks, not to finance speculative activities," observes William Isaac, FDIC chairman.

The combination of deposit insurance, unregulated interest rates and unlimited investment authority in effect licensed go-go S&Ls to raise money in vast quantities nationally by bidding high rates, and to do with it as they pleased. Columbia Savings & Loan of Beverly Hills has raised some $2.6 billion of such money, putting it mostly into junk bonds and GNMA securities. The defunct Beverly Hills Savings & Loan, the second-largest S&L ever to fail, sold some $500 million of CDs through stockbrokers. Shades of the 1920s, except that the money was federally insured.

No one, least of all the Federal Home Loan Bank Board, was ready for the explosion as sharpies ran rings around the regulators. Richard Pratt, the former FHLBB chief who was a proponent of total S&L deregulation, says he intended to fix the system so S&L owners couldn't speculate wildly on the basis of "heads I win, tails the FSLIC picks up the pieces," but left the government before he had a chance to do it.

His successor, Edwin Gray, seems a bit bemused by a world in which S&Ls invest in what interests them—takeovers, junk bonds, fast food franchises, speculative real estate, windmills—and pay only lip service, if that, to housing finance, their ostensible public purpose.

"There's not much you can do to enforce discipline other than to close them," Gray says. Gray has imposed capital limits and other growth constraints on the industry, but the cow is long gone from the barn.

Both Gray and the FDIC's Isaac talk about the need to have risk-related premiums for deposit insurance. A worthy idea, to be sure, but not so easy to implement.

Beelzebub! What's a bank dick to do?

There are two ways to go. One is to strap on the straitjacket again, but that runs against the tenor of the times. Reregulating interest rates is out of the question—the general public wouldn't, and shouldn't, stand for it. Why should the saver subsidize the borrower?

The other is to permit the banks and S&Ls the freedom they want, but make them assume responsibilities to match. These would include:

• Boosting capital requirements in stages, maybe to 10% of assets.

• Making sure that if a crucial bank or S&L must be bailed out by the government, shareholders' investments are wiped out completely.

• Holding directors publicly accountable for their stewardship. (Bill Isaac made a worthy start by publicly humiliating, then firing, Continental Illinois' board.)

• Forcing institutions that want to raise deposits from outside their primary market area to get privately underwritten insurance to supplement federal deposit insurance on a portion, say 10%, of that money. (A private insurer will force a bank or S&L to stop horsing around much more quickly than any regulator can.)

We cannot and should not try going back to the dear, dead days of Glass-Steagall. The cure for the problem that is caused by today's brand of one-sided deregulation is to deregulate all the way, with risks to match. If it is left to function freely, the market can take care of irresponsible madmen long before regulators can stop them.

117.

PHOEBE ELLSWORTH: Juries on Trial

In May 1986 the Supreme Court upheld the right of the prosecution to eliminate known opponents of the death penalty from serving on a jury in a capital case. The New York Times, *in a subsequent editorial, objected to the ruling, stating that "Jurors who harbor doubts about capital punishment tend to be more sympathetic to the defense. Jurors who favor executions tend to sympathize with the prosecution." The* Times's *position was widely attacked as being based merely on opinion, not fact. The article reprinted here from* Psychology Today *was published a year before the Supreme Court ruling and the* Times *editorial. The research on which it is based supports the* Time's *view of the matter. Phoebe Ellsworth is a professor of psychology at Stanford University.*

Source: *Psychology Today*, July 1985.

IN AN ILLINOIS courtroom, one day in 1960, William C. Witherspoon, his life at stake, waited for his capital murder trial to begin. The judge, prosecutor and defense attorney were winnowing 100 prospective jurors down to the 12 who would decide his guilt or innocence and whether he would live or die. "Let's get these conscientious objectors out of the way without wasting any time on them," the judge commented, and quickly dismissed 47 people as unqualified for jury duty because they said they were opposed to capital punishment. Witherspoon's jury consisted of 12 people who favored the death penalty. That jury found him guilty and sentenced him to death.

Witherspoon appealed his case, which finally reached the Supreme Court in 1968. He argued that in a fair jury, all points of view are presented in deciding a person's guilt or innocence; a jury made up only of people willing to sentence a person to death is also likely to find the person guilty in the first place.

Basically, Witherspoon was posing an empirical question: Compared with people who oppose the death penalty, are people who favor it more likely to favor the prosecution, ignore the presumption of innocence and vote guilty? Witherspoon's lawyers presented a few reports of studies by sociologist Hans Zeisel and others suggesting that there was, indeed, a correlation between death-penalty attitudes and guilty votes.

The Supreme Court reviewed the reports but found their results "too tentative and fragmentary" to conclude that a "death-qualified" jury (one that excluded people with conscientious scruples against capital punishment) was more like to return a guilty verdict than one including all points of view on the death penalty. However, the court clearly recognized that new research might provide more conclusive evidence and invited such studies.

The court allowed the Witherspoon verdict to stand but reversed his death sentence, holding that in deciding on the penalty, a jury made up solely of supporters of capital punishment was alarmingly prejudiced against the defendant, "a tribunal organized to return a verdict of death." In the future, the court held, criteria used to exclude jurors should be more stringent, applying only to those who say they could never consider imposing the death penalty in any case or who say that their opposition to the death penalty would prevent them from fairly determining the defendant's guilt or innocence. Since 1968, these "Witherspoon" standards have guided most capital trials in the United States.

During the 17 years since the Witherspoon decision, thousands of people have been tried and found guilty of capital crimes. More than 2,500 have been sentenced to death, more than 41 have been executed and the number of executions increases each month. In almost all of these cases, the decision was made by a death-qualified jury. Compared with juries that try all other cases, do these juries favor a guilty verdict?

In 1968 this question was left open by the Supreme Court, pending further research. During the next decade, the answer became increasingly clear. Numerous studies showed that people's attitudes toward the death penalty are correlated with a number of other attitudes about the criminal-justice system: Those who, by any standard, favor the death penalty are most likely to favor a swift and efficient criminal-justice system that maximizes convictions. They are also more likely to feel that the courts coddle criminals, to oppose ba-

sic constitutional due-process guarantees protecting the rights of defendants and to sympathize with the prosecution.

The studies also revealed that those who oppose the death penalty are more likely to endorse the presumption of innocence and other procedural guarantees protecting the rights of defendants, to feel that the courts are necessary to protect those unfairly accused of wrongdoing and to sympathize with the defense. In the late Herbert Packer's terms, those who favor the death penalty are more oriented toward "crime control," while those who oppose it are more concerned with the "due process of law."

None of these studies, however, identified and excluded people barred from jury service because of their ability to reach an impartial verdict. And none provided reliable estimates of the size of the Witherspoon-excludable group or its demographic composition. Therefore, in 1978, sociologist Robert Fitzgerald and I designed a survey that would provide such data and would allow attitudinal comparisons between those excluded and death-qualified using the Witherspoon criteria. First, we asked our respondents, drawn from a random sample of eligible jurors, whether their death-penalty attitudes would prevent them from being fair and impartial in determining the accused person's guilt. The 9 percent of our sample who said that this was so were eliminated from our sample, as they would be eliminated from all jury trials. This left 717 would-be jurors who reported that they could judge guilt fairly. Of these, 17.2 percent would still be excluded from judging guilt under Witherspoon standards because they said they would not be able to consider voting for death if later called on to decide the penalty.

Our interviews with the 717 jurors revealed that those who would be death-qualified were significantly more likely to favor the prosecution position than were those who would be excluded. The death-qualified jurors were also more punitive and more likely to reject basic due-process guarantees such as the protection against self-incrimination and the insanity defense. Excluded jurors were equally skeptical of defense and prosecution attorneys, but death-qualified jurors trusted the prosecution much more than the defense. (Also in line with a great deal of previous work, our survey found blacks more likely to be excluded on the basis of their death-penalty attitudes than members of other groups and women more likely to be excluded than men.)

The Supreme Court's bottom-line question, of course, is whether these attitudinal differences actually translate into verdicts. Using the same careful methods for differentiating those who would be death-qualified or excluded, lawyer Claudia Cowan, psychologist William Thompson and I showed another group of potential jurors a 2$^1/_2$-hour videotape of a homicide trial and asked for their verdict. The death-qualified jurors were much more likely than those excluded to find the defendant guilty: A guilty verdict was reached by 78 percent of the death-qualified jurors, compared with 53 percent of those excluded. We then allowed our participants to deliberate in 12-person juries for an hour and found that exposure to other points of view did not appreciably lessen the difference between the groups.

Five other studies, some of which were presented before the Supreme Court in 1968, have also compared the votes of death-qualified and -excluded jurors in real or simulated criminal tri-

als. In studies of jurors in actual trials in Brooklyn and Chicago, of black and white student jurors in Georgia and of industrial workers in New York, the results have indicated the same thing as ours: Death-qualified jurors are more likely to vote guilty than are those who are excluded.

Numerous other studies have shown differences in willingness to believe prosecution and defense witnesses, willingness to convict defendants who plead insanity and in thresholds of reasonable doubt.

Furthermore, psychologist Craig Haney found that the standard practice of questioning potential jurors at length about their attitudes toward capital punishment suggests to them that the defendant is probably guilty. Essentially, they think: "If the judge and lawyers didn't think the defendant was guilty, why would they spend so much time asking about the appropriate punishment?"

By 1979, the research evidence consistently attested to the biased nature of death-qualified juries in both their attitudes and verdicts. But in a number of trials since then, the courts have taken quite inconsistent positions regarding both the adequacy and relevance of such findings. All the research described here was first presented in its entirety in a California court in 1979 and was addressed by the California Supreme Court in 1980. The state supreme court agreed that the data did demonstrate a bias toward conviction in juries death-qualified by the Witherspoon standard. However, it added, California excludes both people opposed to the death penalty and those who would automatically vote in favor of the death penalty when it is an option. Since none of the studies examined the effect of excluding "automatic-death-penalty" jurors, their results might not be relevant to California.

In response to this ruling, a question to identify this group was included in a 1981 nationwide Harris poll. As it turned out, only 1 percent of the national sample said that they would never be able to consider any penalty except death when that penalty was allowed. As statistician Joseph B. Kadane showed, excluding automatic-death-penalty jurors would not significantly lessen the overall bias toward conviction in death-qualified juries.

In a new hearing in Arkansas in 1981, all of the studies considered in the California case were presented again, as well as extensive new evidence demonstrating that excluding automatic-death-penalty jurors could not conceivably move capital juries back to neutrality. The court held that the practice of death qualification is unconstitutional, first, because it biases capital juries against the defendant in determining guilt and innocence and, second, because it denies the defendant a "representative jury drawn from a fair cross-section of the community." This opinion was recently upheld on appeal by the Eighth Circuit.

When the same evidence was presented in a 1984 North Carolina case, the District Court judge reached the same conclusion. However, the Fourth Circuit then reversed the decision and held that death-qualification was constitutional. It did not address the validity of the psychological evidence; rather, it declined to consider that evidence at all. Death-qualified juries may be more likely to convict than all other juries, it ruled, but that fact has no implications for their constitutionality.

Because of these conflicting rulings, the Supreme Court may once again assess the fairness of death-qualified juries and the relevance and adequacy of behavioral research bearing on this constitutional issue: The North Carolina case may well be considered in the next session.

By now, more than a dozen investigators have studied the Supreme Court's 1968 question, using different methods and subject samples. The research record, no longer "tentative and fragmentary," is unified and unequivocal: On average, compared to all other people accused of crimes, defendants in capital-punishment cases do assume the extra handicap of juries predisposed to find them guilty.

If the Supreme Court chooses to consider the North Carolina case, it will face an issue framed more sharply by the empirical evidence it solicited many years ago: When a person's life is at stake, does the Constitution permit us to choose juries that are uncommonly willing to convict?

The real tragedy in Central America these days is that whichever faction in whatever country prevails, we will eventually wish the other side had won.
SIDNEY J. HARRIS, 1985

118.

A World Without Insurance?

By the early 1980s a full-blown crisis existed in the U.S. insurance industry. Whether or not it was really "open season" on insurance companies, as this Forbes *article suggests, it was a fact that jury awards for damages in civil suits seemed to be growing almost without limit, and according to their own figures, the insurers were paying out substantially more each year than they were collecting in premiums for liability insurance. Two of the hardest-hit consumer groups were doctors, for whom malpractice insurance began to cost many times what it had only a few years before, and municipalities. In some cases, no insurance could be obtained by the latter at all, which meant the closing of many municipal activities and services. The article reprinted here reviews the situation primarily from an industry point of view. Some lawyers, who admittedly gained most from large jury awards, claimed that although some awards were high, the average was not much higher than in previous decades, when inflation was taken into account.*

Source: *Forbes*, July 15, 1985.

A 41-YEAR-OLD body-builder entered a footrace with a refrigerator strapped to his back to prove his prowess. During the race, he alleged, one of the straps came loose and the man was hurt. He sued everyone in sight, including the maker of the strap. Jury award: $1 million.

Two Maryland men decided to dry their hot-air balloon in a commercial laundry dryer. The dryer exploded, injuring them. They won $885,000 in damages from American Laundry Machinery, which manufactured the dryer.

An overweight man with a history of coronary disease suffered a heart attack while trying to start a Sears lawnmower. He sued Sears, charging that too much force was required to yank the mower's pull rope. A jury in Pennsylvania awarded him $1.2 million, plus dam-ages of $550,000 for delays in settling the claim. (Sears appealed but eventually settled out of court.)

Isolated cases of absurdly generous awards? Far from it. Last year the average product liability award in the U.S. was $1.07 million—up from $345,000 ten years earlier—and the average medical malpractice award was $950,000. In 1983 alone 360 personal-injury cases were settled with million-dollar awards or more, an incredible 13 times the number in 1975.

Americans now seem to look on a civil suit against a corporation or munic-ipality as a kind of lottery—a lottery to be played whenever they can. Last year there was 1 private civil lawsuit filed for every 15 Americans. An estimated 16.6 million private civil suits were tried in state courts last year. Another 150,000 private civil suits were tried in federal courts, which is nearly twice the number ten years ago.

Just handling the paperwork probably cost taxpayers over $360 million on all these actions last year. It cost insurance companies far more. In 1984 the property and casualty insurance industry as a whole paid out $116.10 for every $100 received in premiums—the worst numbers since the San Francisco earthquake and fire. Reinsurers, who take the brunt of the unpredictable risks, paid out nearly $141 for every $100 in premium income.

No industry can keep that up for long. "It's impossible for insurance companies to price liability products when they have no idea what the settlements and risks are going to be," says David O'Leary, a Hartford-based insurance analyst with the London brokerage firm of Fox-Pitt, Kelton. "Courts have expanded the definitions of liabilities for accountants and other industries to such an extent that insurers have started saying, we don't need the business."

For example, obstetricians can now be sued for "wrongful birth" if, for instance, a sterilized woman conceives. Accountants can be sued under "third party liability" by anyone who might reasonably have relied upon numbers they audited. The list goes on and on, and why not? Insurers have been picking up the tab and covering costs in part through their investment income for so long that the system has taken on the look of natural law.

But insurers are not in the business of losing money. Their losses have become so appalling that at this pont they are either raising their rates out of sight or getting out of the business. In April Utica Mutual Insurance informed some 229 New York State municipalites that it would not renew their policies. Transit Casualty, a large carrier for restaurants in Connecticut, canceled most of that group's liability coverage. Mutual Fire, Marine & Inland Insurance announced it would not renew the malpractice policies of about 1,300 midwives as of July 3.

"I can't get any kind of coverage for sand-and-gravel and cement companies," says David Brennan, president of the Insurance Management Center, a Manchester, Conn., agency. "I've got one client who is a distributor of frozen chickens. Last year he paid $25,000 for coverage. This year I can't get anyone to even give me a quote. It's the same thing with an insulated-wire manufacturer, a fish distributor and even a group of nuns who own real estate as investment properties."

If they are willing to pound pavements, most business people can still find insurance. But they are paying vastly more for much lower coverage. One supermarket chain, for example, saw its average rates go from $8,000 per store a year and a half ago to $40,000 per store. Florida Power & Light's premiums for general liability coverage doubled in 1984 over 1983. The coverage provided was halved, $200 million instead of $400.

Pricey, but at least it got protection. For industries that have been especially hard hit by lawsuits, prospects have gotten much worse. Consider Acmat Corp., a $50 million (sales) asbestos-removal firm based in East Hartford. According to the firm, Cigna notified Acmat last December that all its coverage was being canceled because of its asbestos exposure. When Acmat protested, Cigna agreed to renew—so long as Acmat pulled out of the asbestos-removal business entirely. Acmat agreed, even though it meant "cutting our revenues in half overnight," says Henry Nozko Jr., executive vice president. But even that drastic measure failed to satisfy Cigna, which canceled the company's account on Apr. 1.

Nozko approached over 30 carriers, including Lloyd's of London. All turned him down. Finally, he convinced Great American Surplus Lines and three other firms to give him coverage. The price, assuming last year's volume of business: $6 million to buy $6 million of general liability coverage, including only $1 million of asbestos protection. That compares with $300,000 last year for $10 million of coverage. Why didn't he just bank that $6 million instead? "The policy gives us a worthless amount of protection, but we couldn't bid on public jobs without it," says Nozko.

A note on retributive justice: Now that legal-malpractice suits are becoming trendy, even lawyers are having a tough time finding coverage. Reuben & Proctor, an 80-member Chicago law firm, lost its coverage on July 1 from Crum & Forster's International Insurance.

The flight of insurers and reinsurers is most visible where the risks of winding up in a courtroom are great—both gradual and sudden-and-accidental pollution, directors' liability, municipal liability, medical malpractice and accountants' malpractice. "Our agent notified us a couple of months ago that everybody in our business was being canceled," says Irwin Singer, president of Atlas Oil Co., a fuel distributor. "They didn't care how good our safety record was. In fact, the very company that canceled our coverage complimented us on it."

In some cases, the retreat can be gradual. "Our normal general liability policy used to exclude all pollution, unless it was sudden and accidental," says Chuck Henry, a second vice president at Travelers. "Then the courts started saying in some cases that if the insured did not intend to cause damage, it was 'sudden and accidental'—even if it took years for the stuff to seep out." Now Travelers completely excludes pollution coverage on its general liability policy and will underwrite environmental hazard coverage only at restricted levels and only for customers who also buy Travelers' general liability policy.

Even such restrictions aren't enough for some insurers. Since the beginning of the year frightened insurers have been pulling out of property and casualty lines like the British army at Dunkirk.

Property and casualty insurance has always been a boom and bust business, but the bust has never been this bad. Blame part of it on greed. After five years of cash-flow underwriting—that is, pricing products at a loss in underwriting terms in order to bring in extra dollars to invest at once-tempting interest rates—the industry has hit rock bottom. Last year it recorded a pretax loss of $3.8 billion.

Face it: There's no way that the insurance industry can fully recover from its current downswing until Congress—or state legislatures—step in and impose order on our self-destructive legal system. Pennsylvania has already made a start with legislation that curbs pain and suffering awards from municipalities. but it's only a start. Remedies in law will not become effective overnight.

In the meantime, property and casualty insurance is going to become much tougher to get, at any price. For example, insurance agent David Brennan expects that by September none of 13 insurers he does business with will be willing to write new commercial policies for anyone.

Companies will have to scramble for any type of coverage they can find. By far the most common strategy is to accept limits on coverage—higher deductibles, lower protection levels and, increasingly, exclusions for items such as legal defense costs and pollution liability. "We're paying more than double what we used to pay and we still haven't been able to replace all the coverage we lost," says Singer of Atlas Oil Co.

Insurers have also started pushing "claims-made" policies, which pay off only those claims filed during the policy term. Supporters of these insurance straitjackets argue that they will help insurers define their legal risks better and thus enable them to keep selling their products. But many are dubious. "Claims-made policies just postpone the problem," says Jon Harkavy, director of governmental affairs at the Risk and Insurance Management Society.

The last resort, of course, is self-insurance, either setting up a reserve fund to cover uninsured costs or, more commonly, paying them out of operating expenses. "Corporations of our size can afford to self-insure up to certain levels," says General Foods' risk manager Peter McDonough. "But that's not going to solve any of the major problems with the system."

Some companies are again setting up insurance captives, as they did in the mid-1970s. But captives are not very attractive from a tax standpoint and they are risky to boot. Says O'Leary of Fox-Pitt, Kelton: "Many companies that set up captives ended up losing so much money that they have for the most part withdrawn."

But some see self-insurance as a curb

on litigation. "I hope we're moving to the age of self-insurance," says Irving S. Shapiro, former chairman of E.I. Du Pont and now a partner at Skadden, Arps. "Once lawyers realize they're suing a defendant who doesn't have an insurance firm with deep pockets beyond them, they'll sue somebody else." Unless, perhaps, the company is as big as Du Pont.

For companies that aren't as big as Du Pont—and even for some that are—self-insurance today carries the risk of being pushed into Chapter 11 tomorrow. Shapiro's solution: a federal disaster-insurance fund for corporations, similar to the federal flood-insurance program. But wouldn't such a pot of gold be even jucier bait for plaintiffs' lawyers?

Marsh & McLennan is testing its own version of disaster relief—a stock insurance company for big firms known as ACE, for American Casualty Excess Insurance. ACE will provide the final $100 million in coverage—excess of at least $100 million in self-insurance or policies. Eleven firms have jumped at the opportunity to join up—but that's out of the reach of many companies.

Industry insurance pools are popular with utilities, lawyers, accountants, fuel distributors and others. Of course, the exposure for any insurer of a single high-risk industry is enormous, even when only claims-made policies are sold. So some companies, instead, try to spread their risk by setting up multi-industry insurance pools. Result: High-risk companies, again, are out of luck.

The fact is, the problem cannot be dealt with solely from the insurance side of the equation. It must be approached from the legal side. So long as judges keep expanding the definition of liability and juries keep handing out astronomically high awards, the chilling prospect of a world without insurance draws ever closer.

One simple but unpopular solution would be to prohibit—or at least severely limit—the contingency fee system that encourages lawyers to seek the highest possible damages. "You don't see any other country having the kind of insurance problems that we have, because none of them have the kind of jury awards or contingency system we've got," says James Corcoran, New York State's superintendent for insurance.

But there are problems with such a move. "We may be the only country that really has a contingency fee system," says F. Lee Bailey, a member of the three-lawyer consortium representing the Bhopal victims. "On the other hand, in most of the world, poor people go without any relief."

In the long run, maybe the only practical solution is legislative action to define liabilities and cap them at a fair and reasonable level. In New York, where obstetricians and neurosurgeons are turning away patients because of high malpractice insurance rates and where municipalities are scrambling for coverage, legislators have debated bills that attempt to cap liabilities for doctors and municipalities. Congress has contemplated a proposal by Senator Robert Kasten (R-Wis.) that would put a limit on corporate liabilities.

No longer do we have the luxury of pretending that the monster we have created will just go away.

It won't.

119.

STUART M. BUTLER: The Privatization of the Postal Service

In February 1985 the cost of a first class letter rose from 20 cents to 22 cents, a ten percent increase. But the increased revenues led neither to improved service nor to a more secure financial situation for the Post Office; in August 1985 it let it be known that it was losing a million dollars a day. The rise in costs and the disappointing result repeated a pattern that had seemed endemic. The article reprinted here suggested one thing to do about it. Stuart Butler was the author of Privatizing Federal Spending.

Source: *The New York Times,* August 9, 1985.

WASHINGTON—The United States Postal Service is at it again. Created out of the old Post Office Department in 1971 as a Federal corporation, it was given a clear mandate: Operate like a business and end the need for taxpayer subsidies. Well, it hasn't quite worked out that way. Postmaster General Paul Carlin just announced that the Service is losing $1 million a day—despite a 10 percent hike this February in the price of a first-class stamp.

The response of Postal Service officials to the financial crisis has been typical of the management of nationalized industries the world over. They have announced token sacrifices by top executives and cut costs in a way that will guarantee further deterioration of service quality—while hiding behind the corporation's monopoly status to avoid real reforms. So Mr. Carlin's newly purchased private airplane will be rented out, staff training will be cut back, paper clips will be reused and, no doubt, lines will grow at the counter.

In fairness to Mr. Carlin and his senior staff, it's doubtful anyone could have prevented the current financial mess. When a large corporation owned and operated by the Government is given the exclusive right to "serve" customers, it will never act like a private business.

Management decisions are always influenced by the need to satisfy the constituency demands of politicians, and everyone in the organization knows that the Government "corporation" is insulated from another pressure that concentrates the minds of private managers—the threat of a takeover on the stock exchange by tough, new owners. No private company could survive the Postal Service's history of extravagance, which includes a 185 percent increase in stamp prices since 1971 and the addition, in the last nine months alone, of 40,000 new employees to an already bloated payroll. Rather than applaud cosmetic cost-cutting, we should demand the ultimate cold shower for the Postal Service: privatization.

Opponents of privatization claim all manner of disasters will ensue if the Postal Service is transferred to the private sector. Rural deliveries will end, costs will skyrocket with the end of subsidies—all the usual spurious claims of a monopoly under fire.

In fact, costs would be brought down dramatically if normal private-sector cost management were put in place. An example: the General Accounting Office found in 1982 that $90 million a year could be lopped off postal costs simply by using non-Postal Service janitors. Another $150 million could be saved annually, the G.A.O. found in 1981, by replacing 7,000 limited-service post offices with extended rural routes or community post offices operated by private contractors. Postal rate commissioner John Crutcher proposed in 1983 that the entire rural service be put out for private bidders. The savings from this, Mr. Crutcher said, could reach $6 billion a year.

With a new director, James Miller, replacing David A. Stockman at the Office of Management and Budget, the Administration should take a fresh look at the Service and draw up plans for privatizing it. To maintain the principle of a nationwide system with a single pricing schedule for first class mail, the changeover would require several steps.

In phase one, bids should be taken for delivering rural mail. Successful contractors should also be permitted to deliver certain other items, such as newspapers. In this way, commercial pressure would encourage innovative cost-cutting and service improvement—each contractor would know that he could lose the franchise if a competitor became more efficient. Contracting out in this way would be nothing new. Almost 5,000 delivery routes have already been signed over to private carriers, saving up to two-thirds of normal costs. At the same time, chains of local supermarkets and convenience stores, such as Safeway or 7-11, or even gas stations, could be allowed to take over the functions of smaller post offices.

In the second phase, the Postal Service should be broken up into a group of private companies quoted on the stock exchange, much like the newly created regional telephone companies. These companies would be responsible for intercity and interregional mail distribution, and would contract with local delivery companies and post offices. Clearly some regions would be more attractive private ventures than others. That would be reflected in the initial stock price. Once in the private sector, and subject to the obligation to serve all citizens at a standard price, the open buying and selling of stock would make sure that management was on its toes.

Privatizing in this way would not threaten the national postal network. But it would enable private competition to make the kind of productivity gains the Government-owned Postal Service is plainly incapable of achieving, leading to better service at lower cost. And by letting the Government sell stock in a privatized company to entrepreneurial Americans, $500 million a year in red ink could be converted into a cash inflow of billions of dollars to help reduce the deficit.

120.

The Hands of Anger, Frustration, Humiliation

On Monday, December 9, 1985, Dale Burr, a 63-year-old farmer in Hills, Iowa, shot and killed his wife, a bank president, and a neighbor before turning the gun on himself and committing suicide on a lonely road near his farm. Burr had been troubled by financial difficulties that threatened to take his land, livestock, machinery, and even his stored grain; all he owned had been put up as collateral for a government loan. Burr's tragic rampage of violence focused the nation's attention on the desperate plight of thousands of farmers, in every state of the Union. The following editorial appeared in the Iowa City Press-Citizen *the day after Burr's death.*

Source: *Iowa City Press-Citizen*, December 10, 1985.

IMAGINE FOR A MINUTE that tomorrow, your boss tells you that for the next 12 months, you're going to earn only two-thirds of your salary. You can't quit your job.

What would you do? Quick.

The mortgage payment is already a week overdue. The kids need boots, and it's snowing. Quick.

The last two checks you wrote bounced, and the bank wouldn't pay them. The pediatrician's bill is overdue. The corner grocery store won't let you put anything on your charge account. Quick.

Your spouse is angry; you're not holding up your end of the deal. What are you going to do? Quick.

Your father and grandfather have done the same job as you're doing now.

They went through the Depression. They lived on pork and potatoes, and they made it. You are the third generation. You're blowing it. Think fast. You don't have much time. Weeks, maybe months.

The pressure builds, the stress is stronger. You keep going to work, hanging on. It doesn't matter. Nothing you do matters. You are powerless.

This is the kind of thing Dale Burr probably felt. And it is the kind of thing many other Iowa farmers feel every day.

There are accounts of bank transactions and economic explanations and other hypotheses as the murder and suicide story unravels. But that's not what it is really all about. It's about people—alone, desperate and powerless, with nowhere to turn.

Once the Burrs were one of the wealthier families in the county. They were well-thought-of people. Salt of the earth. Churchgoers. A family of farmers carrying on a tradition. That was a year or two ago. That's how fast things crumble.

Target prices, price supports, ceilings, sealing crops. The terminology doesn't matter. It's welfare. Farmers know it. And farmers are proud people. Nobody really wants to live that way. But for now, there is no choice.

Many Iowa farmers already have taken deep pay cuts. They've scaled down operations. They've swallowed their pride—gone to stress clinics,

sought therapy, stood in line at the market with food stamps in their pockets.

Some of it was bad judgment. The mid-1970s was a boom time for Iowa agriculture, but everyone else caught on. Physicians' fees rose, hospital costs rose, the cost of cars and homes and tractors and loans and mortgages and a college education rose. Then the bottom fell out—for farmers. Now things are so out of kilter that people who once were pillars of their communities are falling into poverty, depression, and disrepute.

This is the farm crisis—the people who are alive and hanging on, and those who have died at the hands of anger, frustration, humiliation. And they are here.

Politicians tell us it is only a matter of balancing the books. That if we can reduce the deficit, deflate the value of the dollar, increase exports and give the free market reign—then, everything will be all right.

But if there's one thing that is clear from Monday's tragic series of murder and suicide, it is that the farm crisis is *not* numbers and deficits and bushels of corn. It is people and pride and tears and blood.

The time has come for the state and country to reach out to farmers who are suffering—not because they are failed businessmen and women, but because they are human beings whose lives are falling apart—fast.

1986

121.

For and Against a One-Term Presidency

The argument has been going on for nearly two centuries—whether the President of the United States should serve for a single (six-year) term or be required to stand for re-election to a second four-year term. The opposing views on this perennial issue are presented here by eloquent apologists. Arguing for a one-term, six-year presidency are Griffin R. Bell, Attorney General from 1977 to 1979; Herbert Brownell, Attorney General, 1953 to 1957; William E. Simon, Secretary of the Treasury, 1974 to 1977; and Cyrus R. Vance, Secretary of State, 1977 to 1980. The four serve as national co-chairmen of the Committee for a Single Six-Year Presidential Term. Opposing them and arguing for maintenance of the status quo is Arthur Schlesinger, Jr., professor of the humanities at the City University of New York and a noted American historian.

Sources: *The New York Times,* December 31, 1985.

The New York Times, January 10, 1986.

A: MESSRS. BELL, BROWNELL, SIMON, AND VANCE. FOR

ONCE AGAIN, thanks to President Reagan's observations about the 22d Amendment, the nation is turning its attention to the Presidential term. How long can—or should—a chief executive run the country? Does reelection enhance or diminish a President's ability to govern effectively?

Mr. Reagan has advocated repeal of the 22d Amendment so that Presidents may again run for an unlimited number of four-year terms. We agree that it *is* time to repeal the 22d Amendment: However, we believe a new amendment should replace it. It is our belief—a belief shared by many Americans—that the national interest would be better served by a Constitutional amendment providing for a single six-year term.

The idea of a single term is older than the Republic. The length and number of Presidential terms was debated at the Constitutional convention, and the decision was left to the discretion of George Washington. Once in office, he ran for a second term—but reluctantly—because he believed that service in official capacities should be limited. Sixteen Presidents since Washington, beginning with Andrew Jackson and continuing through Jimmy Carter, have endorsed a single six-year term as a preferable alternative to multiple terms. The six-year term proposal was a part of the Democratic platform in 1913 and passed the Senate that year.

The single six-year term has received renewed attention in recent years because of widespread bipartisan concern that, under the two-term system, re-election pressures lie at the heart of our inability to manage complex, long-term national problems, domestic and foreign. Opponents of the idea declare that the potential hazards facing "lame duck" Presidents under a single term outweigh the damage now caused by delays in decision-making during a re-election campaign. Historical evidence contradicts that view.

According to Kenneth P. O'Donnell, President John F. Kennedy's appointments secretary, in early 1963 Mr. Kennedy told Senator Mike Mansfield that although he knew there was no future for us in Vietnam, he could not expect to be re-elected, given the mood of the country, if he withdrew American forces before the election.

Richard M. Nixon acknowledged in his book "The Real War" that he exaggerated the potential of détente in 1972 because he wanted "political credit" in the coming election. The break-in at the Watergate Hotel and subsequent upheaval were directly attributable to the Nixon Administration's obsession with re-election.

Gerald R. Ford did not press to

a conclusion the strategic arms agreements reached at the Vladivostok summit meeting when those agreements were opposed by his challenger in the Presidential primaries, Ronald Reagan.

In 1980, the Middle East autonomy negotiations were not pushed by President Jimmy Carter as vigorously as they might have been in a non-election year.

In the 1984 election, if President Reagan did not have to face the Federal deficit as a campaign issue, he would likely have acknowledged its importance earlier and begun addressing it as early as 1982 and 1983, rather than now.

These examples indicate that important policy decisions are often deferred because of the enormous pressures a re-election campaign places on Presidents. The result is that long-term foreign and domestic policies often lack steadiness, continuity and predictability.

Regardless of party affiliation or popularity, all Presidents have delayed some of the hardest and most important decisions until a second term. Lyndon B. Johnson summed it up when he said, after leaving office: "If a fellow knew from the beginning that he had a definite limitation and the bell is going to ring at a certain time, he might be able to tackle some of the problems he's inclined to postpone."

What of being a "lame duck" President? That factor is largely a myth. If it now appears more difficult for Presidents to get the job done at the beginning of the second term, it is because there is a strong temptation built into the two-term system to defer the hard, unpopular decisions until the second term.

Dwight D. Eisenhower, as the only President to have served two full terms under the 22d Amendment, provides a test case of the "lame duck" theory.

Despite Democratic control of Congress in both terms, he won passage of more constructive legislation in his second term than in his first. The time spent on re-election activity was minimized, permitting the President to function more effectively as a political leader. In 1959, he declared he would veto major spending bills and, if overridden, would increase taxes. That decision would have been very unpopular in a first-term election period but it helped contribute to low inflation and unemployment in his second term.

Ronald Reagan now has the opportunity to dispel the "lame duck" notion that clouds perceptions of his second term. We're already talking about who will be the next President. Yet the responsibility for managing this nation is in the hands of today's, not tomorrow's, chief executive. That responsibility begins the moment a President takes office and remains until the moment his term ends.

President Eisenhower entered his second term opposing the 22d Amendment for the same reason as President Reagan. He left office a vigorous proponent of a single six-year term because of his strong belief that he was able to function more effectively once the pressures of re-election were removed. Perhaps experience will also lead Mr. Reagan to his view.

As the nation approaches 1987, the 200th anniversary of the drafting of the Constitution, it is appropriate to respond to Thomas Jefferson's plea that each generation re-examine it in light of contemporary needs. Dr. Milton Eisenhower, founder of the current national movement for the single six-year Presidential term, spoke for many Americans when he wrote that he favored a single six-year term so that a President would "have no incentive to propose and fight for measures conceived mainly to enhance his chances for re-election or merely to confound the opposition."

Rather than relegate Mr. Reagan prematurely to a "lame duck" status, we would more profitably spend our time determining how we can manage government more effectively during his whole term. The single six-year term is the right place to start, and Congressional hearings are the first essential step to put the issue squarely before the American people.

B: MR. SCHLESINGER. AGAINST

THE PROPOSAL of a single six-year Presidential term has been around for a long time. High-minded men have argued it from the beginning of the Republic. The Constitutional Convention turned it down in 1787, and recurrent efforts to put it in the Constitution have regularly failed in the two centuries since. Quite right: It is a terrible idea for a number of reasons, among them that it is at war with the philosophy of democracy.

The basic argument for the one-term, six-year Presidency is that the quest for re-election is at the heart of our problems with self-government. The desire for re-election, it is claimed, drives Presidents to do things they would not otherwise do. It leads them to make easy promises and to postpone hard decisions. A single-six-year term would liberate Presidents from the pressures and temptations of politics. Instead of worrying about re-election, they would be free to do only what was best for the country.

The argument is superficially attractive. But when you think about it, it is profoundly anti-democratic in its implications. It assumes Presidents know better than anyone else what is best for the country and that the people are so wrongheaded and ignorant that Presidents should be encouraged to disregard their wishes. It assumes that the less responsive a President is to popular desires and needs, the better President he will be. It assumes that the democratic process is the obstacle to wise decisions.

The theory of American democracy is quite the opposite. It is that the give-and-take of the democratic process is the best source of wise decisions. It is that the President's duty is not to ignore and override popular concerns but to acknowledge and heed them. It is that the President's accountability to the popular will is the best guarantee that he will do a good job.

The one-term limitation, as Gouverneur Morris, final draftsman of the Constitution, persuaded the convention, would "destroy the great motive to good behavior," which is the hope of re-election.

A President, said Oliver Ellsworth, another Founding Father, "should be re-elected if his conduct prove worthy of it. And he will be more likely to render himself worthy of it if he be rewardable with it."

Few things have a more tonic effect on a President's sensitivity to public needs and hopes than the desire for re-election. "A President immunized from political considerations," Clark Clifford told the Senate Judiciary Committee when it was considering the proposal some years ago, "is a President who need not listen to the people, respond to majority sentiment or pay attention to views that may be diverse, intense and perhaps at variance with his own. . . . Concern for one's own politi-

cal future can be a powerful stimulus to responsible and responsive performance in office."

We all saw the tempering effect of the desire for re-election on Ronald Reagan in 1984. He dropped his earlier talk about the "evil empire," announced a concealed passion for arms control, slowed down the movement toward intervention in Central America, affirmed his loyalty to Social Security and the "safety net" and in other ways moderated his hard ideological positions. A single six-year term would have given Reaganite ideology full, uninhibited sway.

The ban on re-election has other perverse consequences. Forbidding a President to run again, Gouverneur Morris said, is "as much as to say that we should give him the benefit of experience, and then deprive ourselves of the use of it." George Washington stoutly opposed the idea. "I can see no propriety," he wrote, "in precluding ourselves from the service of any man, who on some great emergency shall be deemed universally most capable of serving the public."

Jefferson, after initially favoring a single seven-year term, thought more carefully and changed his mind. Seven years, he concluded, were "too long to be irremovable"; "service for eight years with a power to remove at the end of the first four" was the way to do it. Woodrow Wilson agreed, observing that a six-year term is too long for a poor President and too short for a good one and that the decision belongs to the people. "By seeking to determine by fixed constitutional provision what the people are perfectly competent to determine by themselves," Wilson said in 1913, "we cast a doubt upon the whole theory of popular government."

A single six-year term would release Presidents from the test of sub-
mitting their records to the voters. It
would enshrine the "President-knows-
best" myth, which has already got us
into sufficient trouble as a nation.

It would be a mighty blow against
Presidential accountability. It would be
a mighty reinforcement of the imperial
Presidency. It would be an impeach-
ment of the democratic process itself.

The Founding Fathers were everlast-
ingly right when they turned down this
well-intentioned but ill-considered proposal 200 years ago.

122.

The End of *Challenger*

*At 11:39 in the morning of January 28, 1986, there occurred the worst disaster
in the history of U.S. space exploration and a devastating blow to America's
self-esteem. The space shuttle* Challenger *rose majestically from its launching
platform at Cape Canaveral, Florida, and then, in full view of thousands
watching from the ground and millions more watching on television, a minute
or so after launch, exploded in a ball of orange fire. Unnumbered millions of
Americans, including the President himself, asked when they heard the news:
"Was that the one with the teacher on board?" It was; the teacher was Christa
McAuliffe, of Concord (New Hampshire) High School, who was scheduled to teach
a lesson on space flight from* Challenger, *via satellite transmission, later that
day. As a consequence her own students were among the many who watched the
seven crew members perish. Reprinted here are a piece by John Noble Wilford,*
New York Times *reporter, written the day of the accident; excerpts from the
report on the disaster presented on June 9 by the Rogers Commission, set up by
President Reagan to investigate the explosion of* Challenger; *and a comment
from* Scientific American.

Sources: *The New York Times,* January 29, 1986.

    National Aeronautics and Space Agency.

    Scientific American, "Science and The Citizen," August 1986.

A: JOHN NOBLE WILFORD

PASADENA, Calif., Jan. 28—In almost
three decades, American astronauts and
those who had watched them soar so
often into space had grown used to success.

Indeed, modern society has come to
live by the technology of its own creation and, over the years, the space
shuttle program seemed to epitomize
the very notion of technical imagination
and excellence.

Yes, there had been disaster in the

United States' space program: Three Apollo 1 astronauts died in a spacecraft fire on the launching pad in January 1967.

The shuttle program itself had setbacks. There were mishaps, delays, interruptions. Launchings were put off. Hardware malfunctioned.

But no Americans had died in flight, and in 24 missions going back to April 1981, the United States space shuttles had made their way to and from orbit without one serious brush with disaster. It almost seemed that only time stood between space technology and its unfulfilled promises of the future.

REALIZATION OF VULNERABILITY

Today the almost casual acceptance of technology exploded in a fireball.

And suddenly, as a result, people are jolted into realizing once again the extreme vulnerabilities that all humans must inevitably subject themselves to when they attempt exploration, or even when they are simply willing to place their fates in the hands of technology.

The recent space flights were beginning to seem so matter-of-fact that the television networks ceased their live coverage of launchings and landings. Newspaper accounts were often relegated to the inside pages. The shuttles went up, and life went on with hardly a passing glance.

This was the way it was supposed to be. In promoting the shuttle project, the National Aeronautics and Space Administration promised that these reusable vehicles, combining the most advanced technologies of aviation and space flight, would eventually replace the conventional expendable rockets and make space travel more economical and relatively routine.

To underscore the increasingly routine nature of space flight NASA had moved to include non-astronauts on some missions, a senator, a congressman and now a schoolteacher.

Yet one needs no reminder now that those who take off for space in a shuttle are riding atop 2,000 tons of explosive fuel, the power needed to break the bonds of earth gravity and lift them above their world.

"What is it," Tom Wolfe wrote in "The Right Stuff" about earlier, preshuttle flights, "that makes a man willing to sit up on top of an enormous Roman candle, such as a Redstone, Atlas, Titan or Saturn rocket, and wait for someone to light the fuse?"

The answer is, of course, individual. But what is universal is the danger that all must accept when they climb aboard and put their trust in this technology.

"This is a day we have managed to avoid for a quarter of a century," said Senator John Glenn, who was the first American to orbit the earth. "We've talked about it before and speculated about it, and it finally has occurred. We hoped we could push this day back forever."

ASSESSING BARGAIN WITH TECHNOLOGY

At times like these, the nation is shaken into a reappraisal of the bargain modern society makes in relying so much on advanced technologies.

It has known these moments before. Nuclear power plants operate quietly and efficiently for years, generating electricity that runs our technological society, and then, at Three Mile Island in Pennsylvania, the system collapses and brings attention to the perils in our midst. Chemical factories go along processing the materials that have come to be expected in making lives easier, and then, at Bhopal in India, the system runs amok and brings death and injury instead of the better life. Airplane crashes, oil spills, pesticide contamination and other tragedies add to our feeling of vulnerability.

Still, there is no going back. The world's dependence on technology makes that impossible, and, it seems in the end, there is an enduring optimism that technology's benefits generally outweigh its ill effects and the disastrous moments that seem to make it undesirable.

The shuttles will no doubt fly again. There are three others in the fleet, Columbia, Discovery and Atlantis. But it could be months before space agency engineers can diagnose the cause of the catastrophe, devise and test the necessary corrections and feel confident enough to give the "go" for another countdown.

When the three Apollo astronauts died in the 1967 fire, it was 20 months before American astronauts ventured again into orbit, and then it was on to the first moon landings without further interruption. When an oxygen-tank explosion rocked Apollo 13 on its way to the moon in April 1970, it was nine months before another Apollo crew was dispatched on a mission.

Whenever shuttles are again prepared for launching, the nation will probably follow the countdown with a hushed dread.

Reporters watching dozens of spaceships lift off in a burst of controlled energy follow the trail of smoke and fire and know that something catastrophic could happen at any second. But with the run of dazzling successes the dark thoughts have receded in our minds, as they seemed to do for all people.

AP/Wide World

Space Shuttle Mission 51-L explodes just after liftoff from Kennedy Space Center.

But the nation has now seen that space travel, whatever the future may hold, is not yet routine. The risks are real.

As John Glenn said, NASA has known this all along and has taken the probability of failures into account in designing its spaceships and planning the missions.

Most systems in the shuttles, the computers, fuel lines, power generators and such, are built with the knowledge that malfunctions do occur. The systems come in pairs, one backing up another should it fail.

CONTINGENCY PLANNING

The moment at liftoff, and the following minutes of ascent to orbit, have long been recognized as potentially the most hazardous time of a space mission. Accordingly, flight controllers plan ways to "abort" the mission early, bringing the craft back quickly to landings at Cape Canaveral or at a number of "contingency landing sites" around the world.

Nothing could save the crew of the Challenger this time. The odds had finally caught up with NASA. It was, given the imperfections of all things technological, even the most finely wrought systems of the shuttle, just a matter of time.

Astronauts rarely speak of the risks they know they take. It is part of the test-pilot tradition to put "your hide on the line" with a nonchalance belying the knowledge and expertise they bring to the task. This attitude and the safe journeys of so many astronauts over the years made the risks seem somehow unreal.

Seeing the Challenger, with its crew of seven on board, blow up in the sky in the full view of everyone at Cape Canaveral and all the others watching on television will leave an indelible impression in the national memory, like the moment of a Presidential assassination or the attack on Pearl Harbor.

Americans will again put their trust in this bold new technology. Astronauts will fly the shuttles again because it is their calling, and they believe in what they are doing. Others, including journalists, will probably venture into space, too, no doubt approaching the adventure with a new respect, and some dread, with the image of the Challenger fireball in mind forever.

B: FROM THE ROGERS COMMISSION REPORT

PREFACE

The accident of space shuttle Challenger, mission 51-L, interrupting for a time one of the most productive engineering, scientific and exploratory programs in history, evoked a wide range of deeply felt public responses. There

was grief and sadness for the loss of seven brave members of the crew; firm national resolve that those men and women be forever enshrined in the annals of American heroes and a determination, based on that resolve and in their memory, to strengthen the space shuttle program so that this tragic event will become a milestone on the way to achieving the full potential that space offers to mankind. . . .

THE CAUSE OF THE ACCIDENT

The consensus of the commission and participating investigative agencies is that the loss of the space shuttle Challenger was caused by a failure in the joint between the lower segments of the right solid rocket motor. The specific failure was the destruction of the seals that are intended to prevent hot gases from leaking through the joint during the propellant burn of the rocket motor. The evidence assembled by the commission indicates that no other element of the space shuttle system contributed to this failure. . . . The failure was due to a faulty design unacceptably sensitive to a number of factors. These factors were the effects of temperature, physical dimensions, the character of materials, the effects of reusability, processing and the reaction of the joint to dynamic loading.

THE CONTRIBUTING CAUSE OF THE ACCIDENT

The decision to launch the Challenger was flawed. Those who made that decision were unaware of the recent history of problems concerning the O rings and the joint and were unaware of the initial written recommendation of the contractor advising against the launch at temperatures below 53 degrees Fahrenheit and the continuing opposition of the engineers at (Morton) Thiokol after the management reversed its position. They did not have a clear understanding of Rockwell's concern that it was not safe to launch because of ice on the pad. If the decision-makers had known all of the facts, it is highly unlikely that they would have decided to launch 51-L on Jan. 28, 1986.

Findings

1. The commission concluded that there was a serious flaw in the decision-making process leading up to the launch of Flight 51-L. A well-structured and managed system emphasizing safety would have flagged the rising doubts about the solid rocket booster joint seal. Had these matters been clearly stated and emphasized in the flight readiness process in terms reflecting the views of most of the Thiokol engineers and at least some of the Marshall (Space Flight Center in Huntsville, Ala.) engineers, it seems likely that the launch of 51-L might not have occurred when it did.

2. The waiving of launch constraints appears to have been at the expense of flight safety. There was no system which made it imperative that launch constraints and waivers of launch constraints be considered by all levels of management.

3. The commission is troubled by what appears to be a propensity of management at Marshall to contain potentially serious problems and to attempt to resolve them internally rather than communicate them forward. This tendency is altogether at odds with the need for Marshall to function as part of a system working toward successful flight missons, interfacing and commu-

nicating with the other parts of the system that work to the same end.

4. The commission concluded that the Thiokol management reversed its position and recommended the launch of 51-L, at the urging of Marshall and contrary to the views of its engineers in order to accommodate a major customer.

AN ACCIDENT ROOTED IN HISTORY

Early Design

The space shuttle's solid rocket booster problem began with the faulty design of its joint and increased as both NASA and contractor management first failed to recognize it as a problem, then failed to fix it and finally treated it as an acceptable flight risk.

Morton Thiokol Inc., the contractor, did not accept the implication of tests early in the program that the design had a serious and unanticipated flaw. NASA did not accept the judgment of its engineers that the design was unacceptable, and as the joint problems grew in number and severity, NASA minimized them in management briefings and reports. Thiokol's stated position was that, "The condition is not desirable but is acceptable."

Neither Thiokol nor NASA expected the rubber O rings sealing the joints to be touched by hot gases of motor ignition, much less to be partially burned. However, as tests and then flights confirmed damage to the sealing rings, the reaction by both NASA and Thiokol was to increase the amount of damage considered "acceptable." At no time did management either recommend a redesign of the joint or call for the shuttle's grounding until the problem was solved.

Findings

The genesis of the Challenger accident—the failure of the joint of the right solid rocket motor—began with decisions made in the design of the joint and in the failure by both Thiokol and NASA's solid rocket booster project office to understand and respond to facts obtained during testing.

Specifically, the commission has found that:

1. The joint test and certification program was inadequate. There was no requirement to configure the qualifications test motor as it would be in flight, and the motors were static tested in a horizontal position, not in the vertical flight position.

2. Prior to the accident, neither NASA nor Thiokol fully understood the mechanism by which the joint sealing action took place.

3. NASA and Thiokol accepted escalating risk apparently because they "got away with it last time." As commissioner Feynman observed, the decision-making was:

"a kind of Russian roulette. . . .(The shuttle) flies (with O-ring erosion) and nothing happens. Then it is suggested, therefore, that the risk is no longer so high for the next flights. We can lower our standards a little bit because we got away with it last time. . . .You got away with it, but it shouldn't be done over and over again like that.". . .

THE SILENT SAFETY PROGRAM

The commission was surprised to realize after many hours of testimony that NASA's safety staff was never mentioned. No witness related the approval or disapproval of the reliability engineers and none expressed the satisfaction or dissatisfaction of the quality assurance staff. No one thought to invite a safety representative or a reliability and quality assurance engineer to the Jan. 27, 1986, teleconference between Marshall and Thiokol. Similarly, there was no representative of safety on the mission management team that made key decisions during the countdown on Jan. 28, 1986. The commission is concerned about the symptoms that it sees.

The unrelenting pressure to meet the demands of an accelerating flight schedule might have been adequately handled by NASA if it had insisted upon the exactingly thorough procedures that were its hallmark during the Apollo program. An extensive and redundant safety program comprising interdependent safety, reliability and quality assurance functions existed during and after the lunar program to discover any potential safety problems. Between that period and 1986, however, the program became ineffective. This loss of effectiveness seriously degraded the checks and balances essential for maintaining flight safety. . . .

Concluding Thought

The commission urges that NASA continue to receive the support of the Administration and the nation. The agency constitutes a national resource that plays a critical role in space exploration and development. It also provides a symbol of national pride and technological leadership.

The commission applauds NASA's spectacular achievements of the past and anticipates impressive achievements to come. The findings and recommendations presented in this report are intended to contribute to the future NASA successes that the nation both expects and requires as the 21st century approaches.

C: FROM *SCIENTIFIC AMERICAN*

IN ITS FINAL REPORT the presidential commission charged with examining the explosion of the space shuttle *Challenger* identifies the design flaw that caused the accident and describes in detail the events leading up to the tragedy. It does not describe the underlying causes, within the organization of the National Aeronautics and Space Administration, that made it possible for serious dangers to be ignored. One of the commissioners, Richard P. Feynman of the California Institute of Technology, has addressed this question in a separate document, in which he treats the errors in judgment and execution discovered by the commission as symptoms by which to diagnose larger problems within the space agency. He concludes that NASA's effectiveness in selling its projects to Congress has interfered with its effectiveness as a science and engineering agency.

It is well known by now that the immediate cause of the accident was found to be a faulty seal in one of the joints between sections of the shuttle's right-hand solid-rocket booster. Hot gases eroded a rubber O-ring in the seal and "blew by" it, creating a leak that eventually allowed a plume of flame to escape through the joint and pierce the shuttle's external fuel tank.

The finding came as no surprise. Testimony before the Rogers commission (named for its chairman, William P. Rogers, a former secretary of state) revealed that O-rings in the solid-rocket boosters had been a matter of concern for nearly a decade. Seals are an essential part of the boosters because, like all large solid rockets, they are built in sections. There are several reasons for such a design. One is that the fuel is first cast as a liquid, and it might not dry and cure correctly if it were deposited in a single container as large as the shuttle booster. Another reason is that an intact booster rocket would be too large to be transported by rail from the manufacturer to the launch site; because the boosters were made in landlocked Utah, no other means of transportation was available. The particular method of jointing the sections that was proposed by the manufacturer, Morton Thiokol, Inc., had been criticized by NASA, however. That was in 1977, when tests first indicated that Thiokol's method of sealing the joints between sections might lead to erosion and leaks.

During the second flight of the space shuttle, in November, 1981, one O-ring in the right-hand solid-rocket booster was eroded, although no gases blew by it. O-rings were eroded during 11 subsequent flights—often in more than one joint—and in nine flights hot gases blew by the "primary" O-ring in at least one joint but did not pass completely through the rest of the seal.

Engineers at Thiokol were alarmed by the unexpected frailty of the seals. In July, 1985, Roger M. Boisjoly, a Thiokol engineer, wrote a memorandum to Robert K. Lund, the vice-president of engineering, "to insure that management is fully aware of the seriousness of the current O-ring erosion problem. . . . It is my honest and very real fear that if we do not take immediate action to dedicate a team to solve the problem . . . we stand in jeopardy of losing a flight along with all the launch pad facilities." A later memorandum, written in October, 1985, by the head of the task force eventually created to solve the problem, begins with the word "HELP!" and ends with "This is a red flag." The engineers' concern came to a head the night before the *Challenger* launch, when, in a teleconference, they tried to convince both the NASA and Thiokol managements not to launch because of the extremely cold temperatures at the launch pad.

Why were shuttles allowed to fly when critical parts were being damaged in unexpected ways? According to Feynman, managers at NASA and at Thiokol came to regard O-ring erosion as an acceptable risk because O-rings had eroded on previous flights without causing the boosters to fail. Officials noted that in the earlier flights the rings had been eroded by no more than one-third of their radius. Experiments had indicated that an O-ring would have to be eroded by one full radius before it would fail, and so the officials asserted that there was "a safety factor of three." Feynman observes, "This is a strange use of the engineer's term 'safety factor.' . . . Erosion was a clue that something was wrong. Erosion was not something from which safety can be inferred."

Officials tried to understand the erosion by making a mathematical model, based on data from flights on which the O-rings eroded, to predict the amount of damage to be expected under various conditions. Feynman discusses the way the model was developed and the final form it took and then adds: "There is nothing much so wrong with this as believing the answer! Uncertainties appear everywhere. . . . The empirical formula was known to be uncertain, for it did not go through the very data points by which it was determined." NASA used this mathematical model to rationalize flying with ever greater risks. Feynman also discusses the design, testing and

certification of the shuttle's main liquid-fuel engine and concludes that here too there was a "slow shift toward decreasing safety factor." In these and other cases, "subtly, and often with apparently logical arguments, the criteria are altered so that flights may still be certified in time."

To estimate the chances of a space shuttle's failing, NASA managers substituted what they termed "engineering judgment" for the standard methods of probability. They set the probability of failure at about one chance in 100,000. Working engineers thought the chances were closer to one in 100. "If we are to replace standard numerical probability usage with engineering judgment," Feynman asks, "Why do we find such an enormous disparity between the management estimate and the judgment of the engineers?"

Feynman hypothesizes that the fundamental cause of NASA's systemic overconfidence was that a major role of NASA management was to get funding from Congress. To do so, he says, they painted too rosy a picture of what could be accomplished with current technology. At a press conference held when he released his independent remarks, Feynman speculated that "by exaggerating what they said they could do, they got in a position where they didn't want to hear too much about the truth. . . . The *Challenger* mission was the final accident of a sequence of things in which there was warning after warning after warning that something was wrong. . . . For 10 years they discussed this problem and didn't do anything about it. . . because it was hard for information to come up. But we know the information was there at the lowest levels. Why the engineers are at the lowest levels I have no idea, but the guys who know something about what the world is really like are at the lowest levels of these organizations and the ones who know how to influence other people by telling them how the world would be nice. . . they're at the top.''

Although Feynman judges NASA management more harshly than the official report, the latter does suggest that NASA's original plans for the shuttle were overambitious: the commitment to provide routine and economical access to space locked the agency into a schedule too tight to be met with the available resources. For example, the inventory of spare parts was not large enough to accommodate the launch schedule, and so each orbiter was made ready for launch by cannibalizing parts from other orbiters. The commission suggests that NASA's desire to make the shuttle the only major U.S. launch system put too much pressure on the program to meet tight schedules and to be able to handle any payload. NASA's can-do attitude, its willingness to undertake challenging tasks at the last minute, also strained the resources of the ground crews and forced NASA officials to focus on the near term at the expense of long-term safety and economy.

Yet the report does not recommend any major changes in the overall structure of the space program, nor does it hold the highest levels of management responsible for the accident; it reserves its strongest criticism for management at Thiokol and at NASA's Marshall Space Flight Center, the division of NASA responsible for the boosters. The report concludes by urging the Administration and the country to continue supporting NASA.

Feynman's report goes on to draw the connection betweeen the overoptimistic attitude of top management and the accident. He concludes by admonishing NASA to be realistic in estimating costs and setting schedules. "If in this way the Government would not support them, then so be it. NASA owes it to the citizens from whom it asks support to be frank, honest and communicative, so that these citizens can make the wisest decisions for the use of their limited resources." His final remark is that of a physicist who is galled to see what he calls "fantasy" enter the realm of science and engineering: "For a successful technology, reality must take precedence over public relations, for nature cannot be fooled."

Preliminary analysis of the tape shows the crew was unaware of the events associated with the tragedy and the internal communications were being maintained as would be expected during a normal ascent.
                    NASA report on analysis of tape of last words
                    of shuttle crew, released July 17, 1986

123.

Oriana Fallaci: The Europeans' Qaddafi Cowardice

President Ronald Reagan and his advisers blamed Colonel Muammar Qaddafi, dictator of Libya, for many of the terrorist acts directed against American servicemen and civilians in the early 1980s—acts that were either committed by Libyans or by others who were financed, trained, and supported by the Libyan government. In retaliation, during the week of April 14, 1986, American F-111 bombers took off from the United Kingdom, flew south along the coast of France (because France would not allow overflights of its territory) and through the Strait of Gibraltar, across the Mediterranean and to the coast to Libya, where they dropped a hail of bombs on Bengazi, the Libyan capital. The majority of Europeans, especially Italians, who bought most of their oil from Libya and did much business with Qaddafi, expressed outrage at this American act of "international terrorism," and protests were mounted widely, even in Great Britain, where many Britons disagreed with Prime Minister Margaret Thatcher's decision to allow the American planes to launch from and land on British soil. Television broadcasts of children claimed to have been killed in the raid further provoked anti-American feeling in Europe. But not all Europeans shared those feelings. Some, like the author of this article, Italian journalist Oriana Fallaci, remembered a time in the past when Europeans willingly received America's help. Fallaci's article was the introduction to the text of an interview she conducted with Qaddafi; it was first published in Italy, then translated by her for
The Washington Post.

Source: *The Washington Post*, April 20, 1986.

THE ITALIANS have not understood Qaddafi. Or they pretend to have not understood him. The French and the Spanish and the Germans and the Swedish and some English have not understood him, either. Or they pretend to have not understood him. The same must be said of anyone else who sheds tears for Qaddafi these days. That is, anyone who turns the tables and sees him as a victim of the evil Americans who are always attacking someone and who now attack this poor innocent and defenseless man.

It is the fault of the Americans if Qaddafi flings his missiles against the Italian island of Lampedusa. It is the fault of the Americans if he shoots Italian fishermen when they go to fish in waters that are everybody's waters, but he says: not everybody's, mine. It is the fault of the Americans if he kidnaps

Italian citizens in Libya and if he orders the murder of Libyan exiles in Rome or in London or in Paris. It is the fault of the Americans if—exploiting the sorrow of others and taking advantage of their misfortunes, especially those of the Palestinians—he finances and trains and instructs those who hijack TWA planes and kill their passengers. And it is the fault of the Americans if terrorists bring death in their luggage, so that death bursts in flight and mothers with their infant children are spit out the hole made by the explosion and smash themselves God knows where, two miles below. It is the fault of the Americans if an army sergeant blows up at a Berlin discotheque where 200 others are mutilated or wounded. It is the fault of the Americans if 399 American and French soldiers are massacred in Beirut in 1983 by the kamikazes from the Bekaa Valley, the place where Qaddafi and Khomeini keep their Sons of God. (Qaddafi feeds them the money, Khomeini the faith that one needs to disintegrate himself with a truck.) It is the fault of the Americans if, in the last slaughters at the Rome and Vienna airports, 19 people get killed, including a twelve-year-old girl. It is the fault of the Americans if on the *Achille Lauro,* an old man is assassinated in his wheelchair.

So my fellow Europeans, let us shout it loud and clear in our marches and demonstrations: What has Qaddafi to do with the Shi'ite or Palestinian escapades, or with the crimes of Abu Abbas, the killer whom the Italian government helped to escape, even protecting him as he boarded the Yugoslav plane? Poor Mr. Qaddafi only thinks of his oil. "Holy Oil who art in Heaven. . . pardon me, in the deserts of Libya. . . give us today our daily gasoline and protect the Colonel, if you please. Pay attention

that he does not catch even a cold, that none of his officers or students not yet executed at Benghazi organize a revolt or a putsch against him. Mind that nobody hangs him by the feet as we did to Mussolini. Let him finance and train and instruct those who persecute us. Amen." And any man or woman who thinks in a different way is a fascist, a reactionary, a traitor, a servant of the Americans. Who cares if the Americans die? Let them die. (Except for calling them each time there is an earthquake or a Mussolini to chase away.)

All right. Americans are far from being saints, we know that. America is an elephant—often clumsy and arrogant, at times rather vindictive, too often forgetful of his ancestors, and in any event incapable of making people love him. Besides, he sleeps easily in spite of the hate and the jealousy of the other animals because his skin is so hard that it takes a blowtorch to get to his heart. But when he wakes up and gets angry, he sweeps away all the forests, he crashes everything he finds in his way: squirrels and tigers, poisonous trees and innocent orchids. (If it were not so, this elephant would not have won the Second World War and we would now speak German. Something that someone might like. I do not. Or we would speak Russian. Something that someone else might like as much. I do not). However, if America is that kind of elephant, Qaddafi is a hyena that feeds herself on the dead: the new Mussolini of the Mediterranean.

Here is what the Italians have not understood, or pretend to have not understood. And the French, the Spanish, the Germans, the Swedish, some English and anyone who sheds tears for Qaddafi these days. Or anyone who does business with him, anyone who sells him workers and weapons, anyone who keeps open his embassies—which are stores of ammunition and explosives, nests of terrorism in many languages, Kalashnikovs ready to shoot as they did in London where a bullet shot from a window of their embassy killed a young unarmed policewoman. When these Europeans criticize Qaddafi, at most they smile and say that yes, he is a clown, a little scamp, yet also a guy with whom you can talk. (They talk with Khomeini too, they sell workers and weapons to him, too.) Well, in 1938 the Europeans who were not Italian or German said the same about Mussolini and Hitler. They tolerated them in the same way, they believed that they could talk with them. (The Americans too). They went on deluding themselves until Hitler invaded Poland, until Mussolini stabbed France in the back. History teaches us nothing. Again, if it is true that history does not repeat itself, it is also true that it does not help us to understand the similarities or sad lessons.

Pricking and piercing and boring and digging, the blowtorch has burned a hole in the skin of the elephant. The flame has penetrated to his heart. And now the elephant has woken up. He has trumpeted for awhile, he has remained for awhile to mourn his dead children, then he has asked for help from the other animals of the forest. Deluding themselves that they can have immunity and a cheaper price for the Holy Oil, the other animals have answered No. Except in one case, the English case. (Nobody can deny that Margaret Thatcher has guts.) Then the elephant has remembered to be what he is, and he has thrown himself on the hyena that tormented him and killed or helped to kill his children. Doing that, he has crashed squirrels and tigers, poisonous trees and innocent orchids. (Faintly reminiscent, is it not, of the time when he bombed Hitler's Germany and Mussolini's Italy, I mean, us.)

Wars disgust me. As a war correspondent, I have seen almost all the wars of our time. I was in Vietnam for years. When it comes to spitting on wars, I don't need lessons from anyone. I hate any object that bursts and kills, from the explosives of the Shi'ite or the Palestinian or the Iranian or the Libyan, to the bombs of the F-111. I have seen much death in my life, too much, but I never got accustomed to death in war. When I see a child killed by war, I cry. Always. Even if I see him or her on TV. So, of course I cried when I saw on TV those dead Libyan children. But just as I don't cry when I see the photos of Mussolini dead, I would not have cried if I had seen Qaddafi dead. I would simply have said: Pity that the Libyans could not do justice by themselves and hang him by his feet as we did to Mussolini. Justice has nothing to do with war. And there are times when in order to do justice, we have to hang the guilty by his feet. In this case such a right belongs to the Libyans. Unless the only innocent ones left there are the children.

I know that threats will come to me after publishing this. I know that Qaddafi's followers and servants will say that I must pay for this, that they will kill me, that they know how to find me and how to wait. I know that music. I have heard it sung to me by others, in the past. My answer to them is the recommendation I make to the Italians, to the French, to the Spanish, to the Germans, to the Swedish, to some English, to anyone who has not understood Qaddafi or pretends to have not understood him. Do not be afraid to understand him and to say it out loud. Beware the man or woman who is afraid of the Qaddafis. I am not.

124.

JOHN HALFORD: Cultural Terrorism

The weapons of modern terrorism, according to this article, are not confined to bombs, machine guns, and grenades. The author claims that another kind of terrorism manifests itself in "graphic and sonic violence" through violence and eroticism in rock music, among other forms of entertainment. This religious message is reprinted from The Plain Truth, *a periodical published by the Worldwide Church of God, in Pasadena, California.*

Source: *The Plain Truth,* February 1986.

IN THE LAST five years the American entertainment industry—which has never been saintly—has taken a particularly nasty turn.

Instead of being merely suggestive, films and pop songs—with a few exceptions—now openly wallow in themes such as rape, drug abuse, satanism and perverted sex.

No subject is off limits. Nothing is too outrageous, revolting or disgusting for a lyric or a screenplay, and half of all movies now produced in the U.S.A. are for a "mature audience." The greatest tragedy is that most of this appalling material is aimed to appeal to the young. The damage that has been done—and is being done—to the morals of a whole generation is incalculable.

But it doesn't just affect the United States. American media provide the most persuasive cultural influences the world has ever seen. This flood of violence, pornography and perversion is seeping into nearly every country on earth. It is playing havoc with the some-times fragile cultures of the developing countries. Educators and intellectuals have criticized this invasion, calling it "cultural colonialism." Well, maybe. Sometimes it seems more like cultural *terrorism!*

A terrorist who hijacks an airplane or plants a bomb in a crowded airport lounge apparently doesn't care who gets hurt, as long as he achieves his aim. That innocent people are blown to pieces or maimed for life is not his concern. Is the cultural terrorist any different? His aim is to make money. His weapons are anything that makes him money—a movie, a video tape or a new song. And he is apparently little concerned how violent, how perverted, how degenerate, how much his material appeals to the very lowest of emotions, or how much it twists and pollutes fresh young minds and further warps those already in trouble. If it makes money it achieves the cultural terrorist's aim and he will use it.

Thankfully, not all producers, songwriters and artists have become cultural terrorists.

But developing nations are often helpless in the face of cultural terrorism. They need the contact, even at the risk of exposing themselves to a contagious subculture that threatens their societies as surely as it is subverting the younger generation of "advanced" countries.

DEATH OF TRADITION

Any modernization can pose a threat, but sometimes the trauma is worth it, when it brings a genuine improvement to human minds and in the standard of living. But when poorer nations must confront the *worst* aspects of Western culture, they stand to lose more than they gain.

Typical is this story from India. A village elder was lamenting the passing of a form of dance that had long been performed in his district. He complained that young people were now able to afford tape players and radios, which opened to them the world of canned culture. Now they were no longer interested in learning the old dances. The intricate movements and slow rhythm could not compete with the unchallenging beat of the latest pop songs. The older people felt thwarted and hurt because of the youngsters' lack of interest in preserving the cultural heritage. The traditional dances were about to die out, which was indeed sad.

But they would lose more than their dances. When this alien culture and technology tore into the village it opened up a generation gap that had not existed before. The young had always looked to the old to teach them, and they had valued what the old people knew. They eagerly anticipated the time when they too could be trusted

with the traditions of the elders. They may have been poor, but there was a decency and stability in their way of life.

They lost a link with centuries of tradition with its emphasis on respect for the elderly, charity, close family ties and other "old fashioned" ideals. Almost overnight all that was swept away as the youngsters became addicted to an instant, no-thought-required, counterfeit culture. Parents found they were unable to pass anything on, for they had no point of reference with the new set of values that their children were absorbing. And of course, these children will have nothing to pass on to *their* children when the time comes, for in the ever-changing world of pop culture, nothing lasts long enough to become a heritage.

This story is repeated many times over throughout Asia, Africa, South America and the islands of the South Pacific. Some countries, like Burma, have tried to protect themselves by hiding their faces from the 20th century. Iran opened up the floodgates for a while, then made a desperate leap backward into the 12th century.

HELPING WITHOUT HURTING

The Chinese are opening their door more cautiously. At first, some purists worried that the country was going too far down the "capitalist" road, but so far the economic experiments have met with success.

"Who cares what color the cat is as long as it catches mice?" China's pragmatic leader Deng Xiaoping has said. But even a good mouse catcher can have fleas, and the Chinese realize that they must be very careful, if the open-door policy is not also to let in the less desirable traits of the Western world. China is learning that its people can still

AP/Wide World

Young listeners enjoy the music at an Amnesty International benefit concert. The all-day rock festival drew thousands of people.

be infected by the "capitalist sins" of greed, dishonesty and exploitation, and that their youths are not immune from the erosion of decent values.

Last year, for example, the Chinese agreed to allow a tour by a British rock group. To the utter astonishment of officials and audience alike, the performers incited the concertgoers to disobey the instructions of the police. The Chinese tolerated the misbehavior of the touring group, but breathed a collective sigh of relief when the musicians finally left the country. A similar tour by an Australian group has been "postponed."

STEMMING THE TIDE?

Third World readers may derive some comfort from knowing that there *is* a debate going on in the United States over whether the government should step in to legislate against the swelling tide of explicit violence and perversion. "I don't believe that our founding fathers ever intended . . . the rights of pornographers [to] take precedence over the rights of parents, and the violent and malevolent be given free rein to prey upon our children," President Ronald Reagan has said.

It isn't quite as easy as that, though.

In a country that prides itself on its respect for freedom, any legislation can be labeled unconstitutional if it looks like it might infringe on the "rights" of an individual—even when what that individual is doing is undermining society.

Certainly the United States and Britain are not the only culprits. Scandinavia, West Germany and other European countries must share the guilt. But it is *American* culture that is the dominant influence in the world today. From Copenhagen to Cape Town, Caracas to Calcutta, people watch American television and movies, listen to American music, read American magazines, covet American goods and follow American fashions. No other nation ever wielded this kind of cultural clout.

A DAY OF RECKONING

It is no accident that the Anglo-Saxon people have held a preeminent position in the world. Many have realized that America and once-great Britain have been unusually favored. The chorus of the robust old anthem "America the Beautiful" trumpets "God shed His grace on thee." He certainly did, on America and Britain both.

But with that blessing should have come a sense of responsibility. The third verse continues, "Confirm thy soul in self-control, thy liberty in law." Today the outpourings of some American and British souls are not tempered with self-control, and the much vaunted "liberty" is permitting the production of spiritual pollutants, the like of which may not have been seen since the days of Sodom or Imperial Rome.

How can these great nations, which have so much *good* to offer, allow themselves to be represented so badly?

We may place elaborate safeguards at airports to separate would-be hijackers from their weapons. But *cultural* terrorists are free to distribute their soul-destroying weapons without fear of prosecution!

If ever a people are asking for it, it is the United States and Britain, when far too many of their actors and actresses portray fornication, murder and rape across the screens of the world, and their entertainers scream in song obscenities from countless millions of radios and cassette players.

They are compounding the national sins of a people who are already in very deep trouble with God.

125.

ROGER MORRIS: Reclaiming the Reclamation Beat

The U.S. Bureau of Reclamation is one of the more powerful U.S. agencies, but its power and effects are little known outside of the West, the site of most of the dams it has built and now administers. This article by a newspaperman who lives in Santa Fe, New Mexico, reveals why the Bureau is not better known, and also why it should be.

Source: *Columbia Journalism Review*, March-April 1986.

FROM A SMALL band of government engineers who pioneered the dam-building boom of the 1930s, thus making it possible for the Great American Desert to literally bloom with cities and farms, the U.S. Bureau of Reclamation has evolved into the overlord of a vast water empire stretching from the Great Plains to California. Its controlled rivers provide the irrigation for 15 percent of the nation's agriculture and the same proportion of its livestock; its reservoirs, in addition to serving as recreational lakes, provide drinking water for more than fifteen million dwellers in the Los Angeles basin. Meanwhile, the bureau's generators provide the energy that lights the homes and offices of millions more Americans in the Rocky Mountain states, as well as the far west—power that, in recent years, has produced as much as $600 million in annual revenues to the federal government. Thus, when politicians in a dozen statehouses throughout the Midwest and the West talk about "the bureau," in all likelihood they are referring not to the FBI or some other Potomac bureaucracy but to Reclamation, whose main offices are in Salt Lake City and Denver.

Yet, despite its enormous power and importance for so much of the nation, the Bureau of Reclamation remains one of the worst reported and least understood of all federal offices. Media coverage of its decisions and doings tends to be fitful and shallow, a tendency that became strikingly apparent in June 1983, when heavy spring rains and a late and large snowmelt created a torrent of high water on the upper Colorado River— and what ought to have been the water story of the decade.

Eating away at the emergency spillways on either side of the 710-foot-high Glen Canyon Dam, the northeastern bulwark of the reservoir system, the swollen river threatened to carve out a deep new channel circumventing the dam, which would have released the raging waters with full force against lesser dams downstream. Had these smaller dams been toppled, the result would have been an immense disaster. As it was, the Colorado River flood of 1983 caused millions of dollars in property damage downstream, mainly in Arizona, California, and Mexico, not to mention the costs in human suffering and damage to the environment.

This was a huge story, and it was covered in some detail by papers throughout the region—notably, Phoenix's *Republic* and *Gazette,* the *Los Angeles Times, The Denver Post,* and the *Deseret News* of Salt Lake City. Each told parts of the story well. One of the best accounts to appear after the flood had abated was an August 1 *Los Angeles Times* piece, by staff writer Richard E. Meyer, which explained how the overlapping state and federal agencies downstream in Arizona and California had, on the one hand, warned elderly retirees and others off the Colorado's flood plain while, on the other hand, encouraging settlement for the sake of the resulting tax and landlease revenues.

Unfortunately, neither the *Times* nor the other papers published comparably detailed and thoughtful analyses of policies *upstream,* where, as the *Times* itself observed editorially, the Bureau of Reclamation had adopted a policy of "hoarding [water], keeping reservoirs filled almost to the brim," thus virtually assuring that an unusually heavy snowmelt would cause damaging floods downstream.

This, of course, was a crucial point which, had it been borne in mind by editors and reporters, might have led them to question the bureau's assertion (unchallenged in most news accounts and parroted by a June 30 *Deseret News* editorial) that, if any human agency could be blamed for the flood, it was not Reclamation but the National Weather Service for failing to provide accurate snowmelt predictions. One paper, to its credit, did question the bureau's self-serving statements. This was *High Country News,* a biweekly devoted to conservation and environmental news put out in Paonia, Colorado. On December 12, 1983, it ran a remarkable story by freelancer T.J. Wolf, the son of a bureau engineer. Based on bureau documents and expert sources no other reporter had managed to unearth or contact, Wolf's account was both a compelling chronicle of the heroism displayed by bureau engineers during the critical days at Glen Canyon and a scathing critique of the bureau's full-reservoir policy—a policy reflecting the high priority placed on keeping the government's profitable hydroelectric generators running at top capacity.

The bureau itself has acknowledged the accuracy of Wolf's reporting. But reporters at larger papers seem slow to draw lessons from Wolf's work. The performance of papers closest to where the bureau makes its decisions has been particularly cryptic. . . .

Conceivably, digging into the Reclamation story requires more persistence—and skepticism—than most reporters are urged to bring to it. The persistence of Paul Krza, a veteran reporter and chief of the Casper, Wyoming, *Star-Tribune*'s Green River bureau, is as commendable as it is rare. Last spring when Krza turned up government documents that spoke of "serious distress" in the Fontenelle Dam— one of the bureau's newer structures, the dam is situated forty-five miles upstream from Green River—he found that bureau officials were anything but eager to cooperate with a reporter in his pursuit of this story. As Krza knew from his reading of the documents, the bureau's own engineers had already recommended a quick drain of the Fontenelle reservoir, but, Krza recalls, "They were telling us it was all routine and, at the same time, were quietly warning Green River Emergency Service to take the necessary precautions. I had to pull teeth to get information

on the dam. To get timely and straight information [from the bureau], even in a potential disaster, is very difficult."

Krza's early May 1985 dispatches, which were based on bureau memorandums and sources within the bureau, together with a *Star-Tribune* editorial, angered officials. "They accused me of causing panic and even tried to get me called on the carpet with my editor for alleged bias," Krza says. "But the story was right." (Asked for comment, a bureau spokesman did not dispute Krza's claim, acknowledging that "Mr. Krza is a well-informed reporter who clearly does his homework.")

"The bureau's trying to be more accessible in the wake of the eighty-three flood," observes James Udall, a freelance reporter who has written about the agency for *Audubon, High Country News,* and other publications, "but it's still hard to report the real story. They immediately route you to public relations, where they put on a gloss and don't have the stuff you want anyway. You have to get through to the people who know something."

Kathy Wood Loveless, a spokesperson in the bureau's Salt Lake City headquarters, says that, while she will occasionally pass inquiring reporters along to bureau experts, "technical explanations usually confuse lay journalists." Besides, she says of the bureau's engineers, "They're not hired to talk to reporters."

"They don't ever really lie," Deborah Frazier of the *Rocky Mountain News* says of the bureau's public relations people. "But you have to know how to get the incredible wealth of information that's there inside and not being offered to you. There's no lack of information if you end-run the press office."

Frazier demonstrated her point when,

together with fellow *News* staff member Steve Chawkins, she produced an eight-part series on water policy and problems that ran in June 1984. Containing detailed reporting on the bureau, on the growing demands on the Colorado's yearly flow by the seven basin states and Mexico, on the salinity problem, and on Indian water rights and interstate feuding, the series was a model of its kind.

The Frazier-Chawkins series was memorable for another reason: it touched on one of the great unmentionables of the bureau beat—namely, the prominent role played in the U.S. Bureau of Reclamation by the Mormons, "who to this day dominate the agency," in the words of the series. "It's such an underlying truth it's never talked about," Frazier says of the agency's theocracy. "You may not even realize it until you're sitting in the bureau cafeteria and notice that no one is drinking coffee."

From almost any approach, the subject is rich in potential. One could, for example, consider the effect on a vital government office and on national policy of such singular influence by one religious group, or use the bureau to exemplify the growing Mormon political and bureaucratic influence throughout the West. But few papers seem ready to explore the story, least of all Salt Lake City's own *Tribune* or *Deseret News*.

The problems plaguing newsrooms are plain enough in part. There is obviously old-fashioned lethargy, reinforced perhaps by company-town cooption in places like Salt Lake City and even Denver. Also, there is the problem of acquiring a good working knowledge of the complex water-power system and of Reclamation's bureaucracy, although neither is any more arcane than issues and bureaucracies in myriad other energy and environmental subjects journalists must tackle. And then there's the turnover problem: "By the time you learn the ropes," observes Deborah Frazier, "you may be gone." The high turnover rate on this beat affects coverage not only of the smaller papers but also that of *The New York Times,* the *Los Angeles Times,* and *The Wall Street Journal,* where a Denver or flood-coverage assignment may be only a brief stopover for a reporter on the way to what seem to be bigger stories.

In the end, though, the press's poor showing may be as much the result of the defensive and offensive tactics of the bureau as of indolence, ignorance, and a high turnover rate in the newsroom. Still the darling of many editors and publishers as the result of its glorious past and present-day clout, the bureau is not accustomed to being treated with anything but respect. Its attitude toward the press, meanwhile, is anything but respectful. "The press has not been fair and, more damaging, it has not been accurate," bureau spokesperson Loveless says, "I question the mental capacity of writers," she adds. "If it's not incompetence, then it's stupidity."

This disdain and distrust were evident in an official directive, issued during the 1983 flood, declaring that only public information officers were to speak to the press—and then only if both person-to-person and telephone interviews were taped. Loveless says that she did not personally tape telephone interviews; a number of other bureau press officers reportedly simply ignored the directive. (Several journalists who covered the flood say they were unaware of the taping practice.)

Ever since 1983, relations between the bureau and the media have been strained. "The press doesn't understand the bureau, absolutely not," Loveless insists. But J. Hunter Holloway, a veteran of The Associated Press who served as a bureau spokesperson in Denver in 1983 and 1984, offers a different perspective.

"There are some people in the bureau," says Holloway, "who don't understand the importance of being frank with the press constituency. If few journalists know how the bureau operates, stonewalling doesn't help either side. Too many press officers bow before their bosses."

Holloway, whom many reporters credit with trying to make the agency more open, left Reclamation in the spring of 1985 for private publishing— a move these journalists fear will make coverage more difficult than before. (Loveless, too, has now left the bureau and is an investment banker specializing in the financing of water and power projects.) "They see the media as the enemy," says *High Country News* publisher Ed Marston of the bureau's press officers, "and getting the story can be a battle."

Whether or not the press decides to rouse itself from its lethargy and cover Reclamation in a manner befitting the bureau's importance, one fact of the story is clear: Mother Nature has her own deadline. Her story begins in the autumn, high in some mountain amphitheater, with the first flakes of snow, and it builds to a climax when the winter snow melts. The Colorado will rise again, pounding down into the bureau's reservoirs in its ancient trial of strength with engineering pride and bureaucratic policy and politics. Reported or not, it is a story that will determine much of the future of the American West.

During a recent visit to the Soviet Union, I was asked by several political and scientific leaders to define nuclear parity. I replied that parity exists when each side is deterred from initiating a strategic strike by the recognition that such an attack would be followed by a retaliatory strike that would inflict unacceptable damage on the attacker. I went on to say: "I will surprise you by stating that I believe parity existed in October 1962, at the time of the Cuban missile crisis. The U.S. then had approximately 5,000 strategic warheads, compared with the Soviets' 300. Despite an advantage of 17 to 1 in our favor, President Kennedy and I were deterred from even considering a nuclear attack on the U.S.S.R. by the knowledge that although such a strike would destroy the Soviet Union, tens of their weapons would survive to be launched against the U.S. These would kill millions of Americans. No responsible political leader would expose his nation to such a catastrophe."

ROBERT S. McNAMARA, *Time*, October 20, 1986

126.

Desmond M. Tutu: Sanctions *v.* Apartheid

*The question of whether or not to impose economic sanctions against South Africa
agitated American public opinion, and the American Congress, throughout 1985
and 1986. The President's position was well known; as he stated in a speech
broadcast on July 22, 1986, he did not believe in sanctions, but preferred instead
"quiet diplomacy," which he hoped would influence the South African government
to treat its black subjects—the great majority—better. Others felt that nothing
short of economic sanctions with real teeth in them would get the government
to act differently than it always had, and to dismantle the system of apartheid
that reduced most South African blacks to virtual economic slavery. Among
the best known of the South African leaders who opposed—but nonviolently—
the white minority government was Desmond Tutu, Anglican Archbishop-elect of
Cape Town. This article is adapted from a commencement speech that he gave at
Hunter College, New York City, in June 1986.*

Source: *The New York Times,* June 16, 1986.

A CLEAR MESSAGE resounds in recent surveys in South Africa in which more than 70 percent of blacks supported sanctions against the Government. Blacks are saying: "We are suffering already. To end it, we will support sanctions, even if we have to take on additional suffering."

Our people have shown they mean business by their use of consumer boycotts. Last year, organizations representing more than 12 million South Africans called for sanctions and economic pressure. These are not insignificant actions or irresponsible bodies or individuals.

I must ask, To whom is the international community willing to listen? To the victims and their spokesmen or to the perpetrators of apartheid and those who benefit from it?

I would be more impressed with those who made no bones about the reason they remain in South Africa and said, honestly, "We are concerned for our profits," instead of the baloney that the businesses are there for our benefit. We don't want you there. Please do us a favor: get out and come back when we have a democratic and just South Africa.

It is true that many foreign corporations in South Africa have introduced improvements for their black staff. They now have a better chance of promotion. They get better salaries. But these improvements have come about largely through the pressures of the disinvestment campaign. American companies, especially, have begun to speak out more forthrightly against apartheid than has been their wont, and they would be the first to admit that they got a considerable jog to their consciences from the disinvestment campaign.

Reuters/Bettman

Bishop Desmond Tutu in a funeral procession.

There has been progress, but we do not want apartheid ameliorated or improved. We do not want apartheid made comfortable. We want it dismantled.

You hear people say sanctions don't work. That may be so. But if they don't work, why oppose them so vehemently? If they don't work, why did Margaret Thatcher apply them to Argentina during the Falkland war? Why did the United States apply them to Poland and to Nicaragua? Why was President Reagan so annoyed that his European allies did not want to impose sanctions against Libya? If sanctions are so ineffective, why does the United States still maintain a blockade of Cuba? Yet we have all this wonderful sophistry when it comes to South Africa.

I am unaware of anything that has changed in South Africa without pressure. Changes in the sports policy were due to pressure from the sports boycott and not because there had been a change of heart on the part of white sports administrators.

We hear some say that sanctions will destroy the South Africa economy and leave us with a financial morass. My response is that the ball is surely in the South African Government's court. Its decisions about the future of the country will determine whether sanctions should be invoked or not. I certainly do not want to destroy a land I love passionately. But if the South African Government remains intransigent and obstinate, then sanctions or no sanctions the economy will be destroyed in the wake of the violence, bloodshed and chaos that will ensue if a full-scale civil war breaks out.

There is no guarantee that sanctions will topple apartheid, but it is the last nonviolent option left, and it is a risk with a chance. President Reagan's policy of constructive engagement, and similar efforts to persuade white South Africans who support apartheid to change, have failed dismally. Let's try another strategy.

There are those who are not ashamed to argue that if they pull out others will come in to exploit black South Africa. The moral turpitude of that argument is quite breathtaking. We are not asking people to make economic or political decisions. We are asking for a moral decision.

There is no room for neutrality. When you say you are neutral in a situation of injustice and oppression, you have decided to support the unjust status quo. Are you on the side of injustice? Are you on the side of oppression or liberation? Are you on the side of death or of life? Are you on the side of goodness or of evil?

127.

Ben Sharp and Dan Sharp: What Soccer Means

The most watched event in human history—viewed by some 120,000 spectators at the stadium in Mexico City and by an estimated three billion persons worldwide (more than half the human race)—was the finals of the 1986 World Cup competition in soccer won by Argentina over West Germany by the score of 3–2. Americans who cared about soccer could not help noticing that an American team was not among the 24 finalists that convened in Mexico in May; in fact, the U.S. entry had been knocked out by a team from Costa Rica many months before. Why do Americans, who love sports so much and play most sports so well, do so badly at soccer, the world's most popular game? Is the answer to be found in the American character? Or in the character of soccer itself? Ben Sharp, an athlete, was a senior at King High School, in Stamford, Connecticut; his father, Dan Sharp, was director of international relations for the Xerox Corporation, and as such familiar with the passions that soccer raises in other countries.

Source: *The New York Times,* June 29, 1986.

WHILE WATCHING SOCCER'S World Cup this past week with friends in Europe and the United States, we reflected on why the world's most popular sport is only of minor interest in the United States, and why this particular championship did not include an American team. In most countires, the Cup commands major interest, filling the newspapers and dominating conversation. Normal commerce seems to come to a halt, and, particularly in Latin America, a visitor finds it almost impossible to do business with some government ministries.

Yet here at home, the results of the matches cannot easily be found in many newspapers. Most of the games have been shown on subsidiary television channels. When a major network does broadcast a match, as happened with the quarter-final game between England and Argentina, the announcers dutifully described the World Cup as "the world's greatest sporting tournament." But that acknowledgement was not reflected in most of our programming, perhaps because other soccer matches didn't have the same political aura: England and Argentina are still legally at war over the Falkland or Malvinas Islands. And professional soccer failed in the United States a few years ago despite large-scale investments in many of the world's greatest players.

There may be cultural and philosophical reasons for this. The most popular team sports in the United States are football and baseball, and in both there are many aspects of American culture. Both involve a series of encounters in which one team wins and one loses, and it all happens very quickly. Even in base-

In World Cup soccer Argentina's Maradona gives West Germany's Briegel a little push.

A coed game of soccer in Illinois, but soccer is not every kid's game in the U.S.

ses by talkative announcers.

By contrast, soccer games are long, with few scores and a large number of very small incidents in which somebody gains a temporary advantage but whose consequences seldom show up on the scoreboard.

Unlike football and baseball, whose tactical possibilities fascinate the American spectator (it's third down and six— run or pass?), soccer reflects not a transactional view of life but rather a continuous flowing in which neither side achieves measurable gains and play continues virtually without interruption. And can you imagine an American sponsor patiently waiting for the half-time break, and being content with five-second ads flashed at the bottom of the screen, as happens in most countries?

But how then does one account for the immense popularity of basketball, which, like soccer, is a continuously flowing game? Well, there's a big difference. Basketball involves frequent scoring, with more than 100 scoring opportunities in a professional basketball game as against an average of three or four in a soccer match. And here again, the action is faster and more explosive.

What does this teach us about differences in culture? Perhaps nothing; perhaps it reflects little more than the fact that soccer was introduced to this country when the market for televised sports had become saturated. But it may also suggest differences in how we think and act; and maybe by understanding these differences we might understand our allies and adversaries a bit better and find a basis for accommodating our more important differences.

Researchers have been able to track quantitative correlations between the values expressed in a society's nursery rhymes and its gross national product

ball, the action is frequently explosive, and in football it is sometimes violent. The rules are complex and require considerable understanding, appealing to our legalistic tradition. Detailed statistics are kept on the most minute aspects of each player and team, which appeals to our desire to quantify everything. Frequent breaks in the action allow us to indulge in conversation with fellow viewers, as well as endure lengthy analy-

some years later. Might we also learn something by comparing the values implicit in our favorite spectator sports with those of our allies and competitors? Perhaps we might find a way to increase our long-term economic competitiveness, even a way to avoid war. Wild thoughts, surely, but are we accomplishing those objectives with our present analyses?

128.

Byron R. White and Harry A. Blackmun: Crime in the Bedroom

On June 30, 1986, the Supreme Court handed down its decision in a case involving the right of the state of Georgia to declare sodomy a crime. In 1982, Michael Hardwick, a homosexual bartender from Atlanta, was arrested in his bedroom and charged with sodomy, a crime in Georgia. Hardwick was not prosecuted, but he sued nevertheless on the grounds that the right to conduct intimate relations with a consenting adult in the privacy of one's own home was absolute. The Court, by a bitterly divided vote of 5-4, disagreed, with Justice Byron White writing the opinion. Justice Harry Blackmun, in an impassioned dissent, declared that the Court was wrong to reverse a 50-year trend toward support of the right of privacy and asserted the hope that the Court would soon reverse its opinion in this case. The Court's decision was applauded by religious fundamentalist groups. Reprinted here are portions of Justice White's opinion and Justice Blackmun's dissent.

Source: *Bowers v. Hardwick,* __ U.S. __, 106 S. Ct. 2841, 92 L. Ed. 2d 140 (1986).

A: JUSTICE WHITE
OPINION OF THE COURT

THIS CASE DOES NOT require a judgment on whether laws against sodomy between consenting adults in general, or between homosexuals in particular, are wise or desirable. It raises no question about the right or propriety of state legislative decisions to repeal their laws that criminalize homosexual sodomy, or of state court decisions invalidating those laws on state constitutional grounds.

The issue presented is whether the Federal Constitution confers a fundamental right upon homosexuals to engage in sodomy and hence invalidates the laws of the many states that still make such conduct illegal and have done so for a very long time. The case also calls for some judgment about the limits of the court's role in carrying out its constitutional mandate.

We first register our disagreement with the Court of Appeals and with respondent that the Court's prior cases have construed the Constitution to confer a right of privacy that extends to homosexual sodomy and for all intents and purposes have decided this case. . . . Three cases were interpreted as construing the Due Process Clause of the Fourteenth Amendment to confer a fundamental individual right to decide whether or not to beget or bear a child.

Accepting the decisions in these cases and the above description of them, we think it evident that none of the rights announced in those cases bears any resemblance to the claimed constitutional right of homosexuals to engage in acts of sodomy that is asserted in this case. No connection between family, marriage, or procreation on the one hand and homosexual activity on the other has been demonstrated, either by the Court of Appeals or by respondent. Moreover, any claim that these cases nevertheless stand for the proposition that any kind of private sexual conduct between consenting adults is constitutionally insulated from state prescription is unsupportable. . . .

Precedent aside, however, respondent would have us announce, as the Court of Appeals did, a fundamental right to engage in homosexual sodomy. This we are quite unwilling to do. It is true that despite the language of the Due Process Clauses of the Fifth and Fourteenth Amendments, which appears to focus only on the processes by which life, liberty, or property is taken, the cases are legion in which those clauses have been interpreted to have substantive content, subsuming rights that to a great extent are immune from Federal or state regulation or proscription. Among such cases are those recognizing rights that have little or no textual support in the constitutional language. . . .

It is obvious to us that neither of these formulations would extend a fundamental right to homosexuals to engage in acts of consensual sodomy. Proscriptions against that conduct have ancient roots. Sodomy was a criminal offense at common law and was forbidden by the laws of the original thirteen states when they ratified the Bill of Rights. In 1868, when the Fourteenth Amendment was ratified, all but 5 of the 37 states in the Union had criminal sodomy laws. In fact, until 1961, all 50 states outlawed sodomy, and today, 24 states and the District of Columbia continue to provide criminal penalties for sodomy performed in private and between consenting adults. Against this background, to claim that a right to engage in such conduct is "deeply rooted in this nation's history and tradition" or "implicit in the concept of ordered liberty" is, at best, facetious.

Nor are we inclined to take a more expansive view of our authority to discover new fundamental rights imbedded in the Due Process Clause. The Court is most vulnerable and comes nearest to illegitimacy when it deals with judge-made constitutional law having little or no cognizable roots in the language or design of the Constitution. That this is so was painfully demonstrated by the face-off between the Executive and the Court in the 1930's, which resulted in the repudiation of much of the substantive gloss that the Court had placed on the Due Process Clause of the Fifth and Fourteenth Amendments. There should be, therefore, great resistance to expand the substantive reach of those Clauses, particularly if it requires redefining the category of rights deemed to be fundamental. Otherwise, the Judiciary necessarily takes to itself further authority to govern the country without express constitutional authority. The claimed right pressed on us today falls far short of overcoming this resistance.

Respondent, however, asserts that the result should be different where the homosexual conduct occurs in the privacy of the home. He relies on *Stanley v. Georgia* (1969), where the Court held that the First Amendment prevents conviction for possessing and reading obscene material in the privacy of his home: "If the First Amendment means anything, it means that a state has no business telling a man, sitting alone in his house, what books he may read or what films he may watch."

Stanley did protect conduct that would not have been protected outside the home, and it partially prevented the enforcement of state obscenity laws; but the decision was firmly grounded in the First Amendment. The right pressed upon us here has no similar support in the text of the Constitution, and it does not qualify for recognition under the prevailing principles for construing the Fourteenth Amendment. Its limits are also difficult to discern. Plainly enough, otherwise illegal conduct is not always immunized whenever it occurs in the home. Victimless crimes, such as the possession and use of illegal drugs do not escape the law where they are committed at home. *Stanley* itself recognized that its holding offered no protection for the possession in the home of drugs, firearms, or stolen goods. And if respondent's submission is limited to the voluntary sexual conduct between consenting adults, it would be difficult, except by fiat, to limit the claimed right to homosexual conduct while leaving exposed to prosecution adultery, incest, and other sexual crimes even though they are committed in the home. We are unwilling to start down that road.

Even if the conduct at issue here is not a fundamental right, respondent asserts that there must be a rational basis for the law and that there is none in this case other than the presumed belief of a majority of the electorate in Georgia that homosexual sodomy is immoral and unacceptable. This is said to be an inadequate rationale to support the law. The law, however, is constantly based on notions of morality, and if all laws representing essentially moral choices are to be invalidated under the Due Process Clause, the courts will be very busy indeed. Even respondent makes no such claim, but insists that majority sentiments about the morality of homosexuality should be declared inadequate. We do not agree, and are unpersuaded that the sodomy laws of some 25 states should be invalidated on this basis.

Accordingly, the judgment of the Court of Appeals is reversed.

B: JUSTICE BLACKMUN
DISSENT

THIS CASE IS NO more about "a fundamental right to engage in homosexual sodomy," as the court purports to declare, than *Stanley v. Georgia* (1969) was about a fundamental right to watch obscene movies, or *Katz v. United States* (1967) was about a fundamental right to place interstate bets from a telephone booth. Rather, this case is about "the most comprehensive of rights and the right most valued by civilized men," namely "the right to be let alone." *Olmstead v. United States* (1928) (Brandeis, J., dissenting).

The statute at issue, Ga. Code Ann. section 16–6–2, denies individuals the right to engage in particular forms of private, consensual sexual activity. The Court concludes that section 16–6–2 is valid essentially because "the laws of many states still make such conduct illegal and have done so for a very long time." But the fact that the moral judgments expressed by statutes like section 16–6–2 may be "natural and familiar ought not to conclude our judgment upon the question whether statutes embodying them conflict with the Constitution of the United States." *Roe v. Wade* (1973).

Like Justice Holmes, I believe that "(i)t is revolting to have no better reason for a rule of law than that so it was laid down in the time of Henry IV. It is still more revolting if the grounds upon which it was laid down have vanished long since, and the rule simply persists from blind imitation of the past." Holmes, The Path of the Law (1897). I believe we must analyze respondent's claim in the light of the values that underlie the constitutional right to privacy. If that right means anything, it means that, before Georgia can prosecute its citizens for making choices about the most intimate aspects of their lives, it must do more than assert that the choice they have made is an "abominable crime not fit to be named among Christians." *Herring v. State* 119 Ga. 709, (1904).

In its haste to reverse the Court of Appeals and hold that the Constitution does not "confe(r) a fundamental right upon homosexuals to engage in sodomy," the Court relegates the actual statute being challenged to a footnote and ignores the procedural posture of the case before it. A fair reading of the statute and of the complaint clearly reveals that the majority has distorted the question this case presents.

First, the Court's almost obsessive focus on homosexual activity is particularly hard to justify in light of the broad language Georgia has used. Unlike the court, the Georgia Legislature has not proceeded on the assumption that homosexuals are so different from other citizens that their lives may be controlled in a way that would not be tolerated if it limited the choices of those other citizens. Rather, Georgia has provided that "(a) person commits the offense of sodomy when he performs or submits to any sexual act involving the sex organs of one person and the mouth or anus of another." Ga. Code Ann. section 16–6–2(a).

The sex or status of the persons who engage in the act is irrelevant as a matter of state law. In fact, to the extent I can discern a legislative purpose for Georgia's 1968 enactment of section 16–6–2, that purpose seems to have been to broaden the coverage of the law to reach heterosexual as well as homosexual activity. I therefore see no basis for the Court's decision to treat this case as an "as applied" challenge to section 16–6–2, or for Georgia's attempt, both in its brief and at oral argument, to defend section 16–6–2 solely on the grounds that it prohibits homosexual activity. Michael Hardwick's standing may rest in significant part on Georgia's apparent willingness to enforce against homosexuals a law it seems not to have any desire to enforce against heterosexuals. But his claim that section 16–6–2 involves an unconstitutional intrusion into his privacy and his right of intimate association does not depend in any way on his sexual orientation.

Second, I disagree with the Court's refusal to consider whether section 16–6–2 runs afoul of the Eighth or Ninth Amendments or the Equal Protection Clause of the Fourteenth Amendment. . . . I need not reach either the Eighth Amendment or the Equal Protection Clause issues because I believe that Hardwick has stated a cognizable claim that section 16–6–2 interferes with constitutionally protected interests in privacy and freedom of intimate association. But neither the Eighth Amendment nor the Equal Protection Clause is so clearly irrelevant that a claim resting on either provision should be peremptorily dismissed. The Court's cramped reading of the issue before it makes for a short opinion, but it does little to make for a persuasive one.

"Our cases long have recognized that the Constitution embodies a promise that a certain private sphere of individual liberty will be kept largely beyond the reach of government." *Thornburgh v. American Coll. of Obst. & Gyn.*, (1986). In construing the right to privacy, the Court has proceeded along two somewhat distinct, albeit complementary, lines. First, it has recognized a privacy interest with reference to certain *decisions* that are properly for the individual to make. Second, it has recognized a privacy interest with reference to certain *places* without regard for the particular activities in which the individuals who occupy them are engaged. The case before us implicates both the decisional and the spatial aspects of the right of privacy.

The Court concludes today that none of our prior cases dealing with various decisions that individuals are entitled to make free of governmental interference "bears any resemblance to the claimed constitutional right of homosexuals to engage in acts of sodomy that is asserted in this case." While it is true that these cases may be characterized by their connection to protection of the family, the Court's conclusion that they extend no further than this boundary ignores the warning in *Moore v. East Cleveland*, (1977) (plurality opinion), against "clos(ing) our eyes to the basic reasons why

certain rights associated with the family have been accorded shelter under the Fourteenth Amendment's Due Process Clause."

We protect those rights not because they contribute, in some direct and material way, to the general public welfare, but because they form so central a part of an individual life. . . . We protect the decision whether to marry precisely because marriage "is an association that promotes a way of life, not causes; a harmony in living, not political faiths; a bilateral loyalty, not commercial or social projects." *Griswold v. Connecticut.* We protect the decision whether to have a child because parenthood alters so dramatically an individual's self-definition, not because of demographic considerations or the Bible's command to be fruitful and multiply. And we protect the family because it contributes so powerfully to the happiness of individuals, not because of a preference for stereotypical households.

Only the most willful blindness could obscure the fact that sexual intimacy is "a sensitive, key relationship of human existence, central to family life, community welfare, and the development of human personality," *Paris Adult Theatre I v. Slayton,* (1973). The fact that individuals define themselves in a significant way through their intimate sexual relationships with others suggests, in a nation as diverse as ours, that there may be many "right" ways of conducting those relationships, and that much of the richness of a relationship will come from the freedom an individual has to choose the form and nature of these intensely personal bonds.

In a variety of circumstances we have recognized that a necessary corollary of giving individuals freedom to choose how to conduct their lives is acceptance of the fact that different individuals will make different choices. For example, in holding that the clearly important state interest in public education should give way to a competing claim by the Amish to the effect that extended formal schooling threatened their way of life, the Court declared: "There can be no assumption that today's majority is 'right' and the Amish and others like them are 'wrong.' A way of life that is odd or even erratic but interferes with no rights or interests of others is not to be condemned because it is different." *Wisconsin v. Yoder* (1972). The Court claims that its decision today merely refuses to recognize a fundamental right to engage in homosexual sodomy; what the Court really has refused to recognize is the fundamental interest all individuals have in controlling the nature of their intimate associations with others.

The behavior for which Hardwick faces prosecution occurred in his own home, a place to which the Fourth Amendment attaches special significance. The Court's treatment of this aspect of the case is symptomatic of its overall refusal to consider the broad principles that have informed our treatment of privacy in specific cases. Just as the right to privacy is more than the mere aggregation of a number of entitlements to engage in specific behavior, so too, protecting the physical integrity of the home is more than merely a means of protecting specific activities that often take place there. . . .

The Court's interpretation of the pivotal case of *Stanley v. Georgia* (1969), is entirely unconvincing. *Stanley* held that Georgia's undoubted power to punish the public distribution of constitutionally unprotected, obscene material did not permit the state to punish the private possession of such material. Ac-

cording to the majority here, *Stanley* relied entirely on the First Amendment, and thus, it is claimed, sheds no light on cases not involving printed materials. But that is not what *Stanley* said. Rather, the *Stanley* Court anchored its holding in the Fourth Amendment's special protection for the individual in his home. . . . The right of an individual to conduct intimate relationships in the intimacy of his or her own home seems to me to be the heart of the Constitution's protection of privacy. . . .

First, petitioner asserts that the acts made criminal by the statute may have serious adverse consequences for "the general public health and welfare," such as spreading communicable diseases or fostering other criminal activity. . . . Nothing in the record before the Court provides any justification for finding the activity forbidden by section 16–6–2 to be physically dangerous, either to the persons engaged in it or to others.

The core of petitioner's defense of section 16–6–2, however, is that respondent and others who engage in the conduct prohibited by section 16-6-2 interfere with Georgia's exercise of the "right of the nation and of the states to maintain a decent society." Essentially, petitioner argues, and the Court agrees, that the fact that the acts described in section 16–6–2 "for hundreds of years, if not thousands, have been uniformly condemned as immoral" is a sufficient reason to permit a state to ban them today.

I cannot agree that either the length of time a majority has held its convictions or the passions with which it defends them can withdraw legislation from this Court's scrutiny. As Justice Jackson wrote so eloquently for the Court in *West Virginia Board of Education v. Barnette* (1943), "we apply the limitations of the Constitution with no fear that freedom to be intellectually and spiritually diverse or even contrary will disintegrate the social organization. (F)reedom to differ is not limited to things that do not matter much. That would be a mere shadow of freedom. The test of its substance is the right to differ as to things that touch the heart of the existing order." It is precisely because the issue raised by this case touches the heart of what makes individuals what they are that we should be especially sensitive to the rights of those whose choices upset the majority.

The assertion that "traditional Judeo-Christian values proscribe" the conduct involved, cannot provide an adequate justification for section 16–6–2. That certain, but by no means at all, religious groups condemn the behavior at issue gives the State no license to impose their judgments on the entire citizenry. The legitimacy of secular legislation depends instead on whether the State can advance some justification for its law beyond its conformity to religious doctrine. Thus, far from buttressing his case, petitioner's invocation of Leviticus, Romans, St. Thomas Aquinas, and sodomy's heretical status during the Middle Ages undermines his suggestion that section 16–6–2 represents a legitimate use of secular coercive power. A State can no more punish private behavior because of religious intolerance than it can punish such behavior because of racial animus. . . .

Nor can section 16–6–2 be justified as a "morally neutral" exercise of Georgia's power to "protect the public environment," *Paris Adult Theatre I*. Certainly, some private behavior can affect the fabric of society as a whole. Reasonable people may differ about whether

particular sexual acts are moral or immoral, but "we have ample evidence for believing that people will not abandon morality, will not think any better of murder, cruelty and dishonesty, merely because some private sexual practice which they abominate is not punished by the law." Petitioner and the Court fail to see the difference between laws that protect public sensibilities and those that enforce private morality.

Statutes banning public sexual activity are entirely consistent with protecting the individual's liberty interest in decisions concerning sexual relations; the same recognition that those decisions are intensely private which justifies protecting them from governmental interference can justify protecting individuals from unwilling exposure to the sexual activities of others. But the mere fact that intimate behavior may be punished when it takes place in public cannot dictate how States can regulate intimate behavior that occurs in intimate places.

This case involves no real interference with the rights of others, for the mere knowledge that other individuals do not adhere to one's value system cannot be a legally cognizable interest, let alone an interest that can justify invading the houses, hearts, and minds of citizens who choose to live their lives differently. . . .

I can only hope that the Court soon will reconsider its analysis and conclude that depriving individuals of the right to choose for themselves how to conduct their intimate relationships poses a far greater threat to the values most deeply rooted in our Nation's history than tolerance of nonconformity could ever do. Because I think the Court today betrays those values, I dissent.

Auguste Bartholdi (second from right), designer of the Statue of Liberty, watches in a Paris workshop in 1882 as workers prepare the left arm and book for casting. Plaster will be formed over the wooden frame, then a copper skin will be crafted from the plaster.

STILL YEARNING
TO BE FREE

The United States exists as a beacon of freedom and a call to opportunity for millions throughout the world. Immigrants from all parts of the globe have responded by coming to America's shores, both east and west, in untold numbers. The great mass of immigrants began their trek about 1820. Most of these arrived at New York City, the chief port of entry. By the end of the 20th century the busiest port of entry was mainly along the border with Mexico or at Los Angeles. The early arrivals were from Europe. In the late 20th century, the places of origin were different, with large numbers from Latin America—especially Mexico, Cuba, and Puerto Rico—but also from East Asia. Nearly every group, when it first arrived, was faced with some resentment or even outright hostility. There was always fear that newcomers would take jobs and other opportunities away from those who got there first. Somehow, the later arrivals do establish themselves. Their children grow up, attend schools, and make for themselves a better life than their immigrant parents had. New immigration legislation was passed in the fall of 1986.

Photos by AP/Wide World

(Top) Immigrants from many countries crowd the rail of their ship as it enters New York Harbor, within sight of the Statue of Liberty; (bottom) a group has arrived at Ellis Island to be processed.

The Statue of Liberty was raised in New York Harbor to symbolize liberty enlightening the world. Soon, however, it became a sign of welcome for the millions of immigrants who were arriving from Europe. The statue was given to the United States by France and erected in 1886. It underwent a massive restoration effort in the early 1980s. To celebrate the restoration a large, national party was held in New York City over the Fourth of July weekend in 1986. The President rededicated the Statue of Liberty before an audience of millions who had gathered to witness the event. Added to these were more millions who watched the three-day event on television around the world. The tall ships, which had not appeared in the United States since the Bicentennial in 1976, returned to parade up the Hudson River. Some of America's best-known entertainers appeared on a specially constructed stage opposite the statue. Other public events were held at the Meadowlands in New Jersey. The first evening's festivities were capped with a brilliant display of fireworks.

(Top left) After two years of renovation, the Statue of Liberty is surrounded by scaffolding; the torch is being repaired separately; (top right) the renovation is almost finished, but the stains from air pollution cannot be removed; (bottom) at the rededication in 1986 fireworks light up the statue.

Far fewer immigrants encountered the Statue of Liberty when they arrived in the United States in the 1970s and 1980s than those of earlier decades. Ellis Island, the main entry point for immigrants in the early 20th century, was completely decommissioned by mid-century. In 1950 about half of the foreign-born resided in the Northeast, but by 1980, only one-third lived there, with an equal number residing in the West. Many immigrants in 1980 crossed the Mexican border, arrived by boat from Cuba or Haiti, or entered through airports and harbors in Los Angeles and San Francisco, as non-Europeans comprised the

(Top) Immigrants tend to gather together in ethnic enclaves in the city neighborhoods where they have settled, as on this crowded street in New York's Chinatown; (bottom) immigrants from Cuba have created a neighborhood known as Little Havana in Union City, New Jersey.

new majority of immigrants. Like their predecessors, the new wave of immigrants shared similar economic and political motives for relocating and tended to repeat patterns of settlement, often first congregating in ethnic enclaves of major cities, despite the fact that they may have lived in rural areas in their homeland. Overall, the foreign-born population rose from 9.6 million in 1970 to 14.1 million in 1980. Immigration was liberalized in the 1980s as new legislation granted amnesty to illegal aliens, raised admission limits, and created a system for validating refugees.

(Top) Vietnamese families who have escaped from Vietnam to the Philippines harbor hopes of eventually immigrating to the U.S.; (bottom) a shortage of children in the U.S. available for adoption has resulted in many mixed-race and international adoptions; a father plays with his adopted son from Mexico.

(Top) A group of Mexican immigrants is turned back after entering the U.S. illegally; (center) the renowned architect I.M. Pei came to the U.S. to study at M.I.T. and never returned to China as he had planned to after World War II; (bottom) Salvador Edward Luria, a Nobel Prize winner in medicine, is an Italian Jew who fled fascism in Italy in 1938, resettling in the U.S.

In February 1980 a Congressional committee announced that there were six million illegal aliens in the United States. The United States has a vast and easily penetrable coastline. And it shares a border nearly 2,000 miles long with Mexico. Such borders are difficult to close against illegal entrants. Mexicans cross the border in uncounted numbers, while Haitians, Cubans, and others arrive on the shores of Florida. Not all immigrants, of course, fit the description of "your tired, your poor," as described in the Emma Lazarus poem inscribed on the base of the Statue of Liberty. Some, albeit a minority, are well educated if not necessarily wealthy when they arrive. Many, called the "intellectual migration," came to America as a consequence of the Nazi takeover of Germany in the 1930s.

129.

THEODORE H. WHITE: The American Idea

"When the best city in the world," crowed New York City Mayor Ed Koch, "throws the best party in the world, the entire world is invited." The occasion was the 100th anniversary of the Statue of Liberty, the American icon that had graced New York's harbor for a century and had presided over the arrival of millions of immigrants through nearby Ellis Island. A gift from France, the 305-foot statue was erected on Bedloe's Island (later Liberty Island) in October 1886. In the mid-1980s the sculpture was repaired by American and French workers. On July 4, 1986, the 210th birthday of America, President Ronald Reagan relit the torch of Liberty after three years of costly repairs. The 29-foot torch, which was converted to electric power in 1916, was redesigned during the restoration process. According to The New York Times *the celebration was marked by a parade of tall ships and exemplary speeches from Reagan and his guest, President François Mitterrand of France. Reprinted here is a portion of an article that author Theodore H. White was working on when he died, seven weeks before the event.*

Source: *The New York Times Magazine,* July 6, 1986.

THE IDEA WAS there at the very beginning, well before Thomas Jefferson put it into words—and the idea rang the call.

Jefferson himself could not have imagined the reach of his call across the world in time to come when he wrote:

"We hold these truths to be self-evident, that all men are created equal, that they are endowed by their Creator with certain unalienable rights, that among these are life, liberty and the pursuit of happiness."

But over the next two centuries the call would reach the potato patches of Ireland, the ghettoes of Europe, the paddyfields of China, stirring farmers to leave their lands and townsmen their trades and thus unsettling all traditional civilizations.

It is the call from Thomas Jefferson, embodied in the great statue that looks down the Narrows of New York Harbor, and in the immigrants who answered the call, that we now celebrate.

Some of the first European Americans had come to the new continent to worship God in their own way, others to seek their fortunes. But, over a century-and-a-half, the new world changed those Europeans, above all the Englishmen who had come to North America. Neither King nor Court nor Church could stretch over the ocean to the wild continent. To survive, the first emigrants had to learn to govern them-

Immigrants arrive at Ellis Island in 1920.

selves. But the freedom of the wilderness whetted their appetites for more freedoms. By the time Jefferson drafted his call, men were in the field fighting for those new-learned freedoms, killing and being killed by English soldiers, the best-trained troops in the world, supplied by the world's greatest navy. Only something worth dying for could unite American volunteers and keep them in the field—a stated cause, a flag, a nation they could call their own.

When, on the Fourth of July, 1776, the colonial leaders who had been meeting as a Continental Congress in Philadelphia voted to approve Jefferson's Declaration of Independence, it was not puffed-up rhetoric for them to pledge to each other "our lives, our fortunes and our sacred honor." Unless their new "United States of America" won the war, the Congressmen would be judged traitors as relentlessly as would the irregulars-under-arms in the field. And all knew what English law allowed in the case of a traitor. The

victim could be partly strangled; drawn, or disemboweled, while still alive, his entrails then burned and his body quartered.

The new Americans were tough men fighting for a very tough idea. How they won their battles is a story for the schoolbooks, studied by scholars, wrapped in myths by historians and poets.

But what is most important is the story of the idea that made them into a nation, the idea that had an explosive power undreamed of in 1776.

All other nations had come into being among people whose families had lived for time out of mind on the same land where they were born. Englishmen are English, Frenchmen are French, Chinese are Chinese, while their governments come and go; their national states can be torn apart and remade without losing their nationhood. But Americans are a nation born of an idea; not the place, but the idea, created the United States Government.

The story we celebrate this weekend

is the story of how this idea worked it-self out, how it stretched and changed and how the call for "life, liberty and the pursuit of happiness" does still, as it did in the beginning, mean different things to different people.

130.

STEVEN GREENHOUSE: The Average Guy Takes It on the Chin

This article by a New York Times *business reporter in July 1986 reported that young people of the time had a slim chance of obtaining the kind of financial success that their parents did a generation earlier. Adjusted for inflation, the average 30-year-old in the United States in 1986 made substantially less than the average 30-year-old did in 1976, and only a few dollars more than did the average 30-year-old in 1959. (Adjusted to year 2000 dollars, the median income of those between the ages of 25 and 34 fell almost ten percent between 1976 and 1986. To make matters worse, the median income for young people would not recover to the level of the mid-1970s until the end of the twentieth century.) The reason, according to some analysts, was that American productivity had failed to keep pace with inflation or with productivity in most of the other industrial nations of the world.*

Source: *The New York Times*, July 13, 1986.

FOR MILLIONS of breadwinners, the American dream is becoming the impossible dream.

The prospect of owning the prover-bial split-level with a two-car garage is receding. The cheerful expectation of being better off than one's parents has died among many baby boomers. Even the most basic tenet of the dream—that a young family will be more prosperous in its middle age—has grown more elu-sive.

The statistics tell the harsh story of Americans struggling just to stay in place economically:

•Average hourly earnings, adjusted for inflation, boomed in the 1950's and 1960's, but fell in the 1970's and stum-bled along with no real growth in the first half of the 1980's.

•Average weekly earnings, held down slightly by a shorter work week, have de-clined an astonishing 14.3 percent since 1973, after accounting for inflation.

•Median household income, which was $26,433 in1984, has dipped about 6 percent since 1973.

"From the end of World War II to 1973, everybody was getting better off, but from 1973 through now that has stopped," said Frank S. Levy, a profes-sor of public policy at the University of Maryland.

Americans are struggling in many

The Squeeze on Income: Symptoms and a Possible Cause

Grim Prospects for 30-Year-Old Men . . .

Earnings data in 1984 dollars

Age 30 In:	Average Earnings Age 30	Average Earnings Age 40	Change
1949	$11,924	$19,475	+63%
1959	17,188	25,627	+49
1973	23,580	23,395	− 1
1983	17,520	—	—

Sources: Bureau of Labor Statistics, Commerce Department

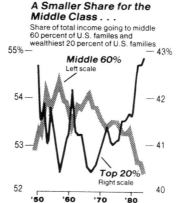

A Smaller Share for the Middle Class . . .

Share of total income going to middle 60 percent of U.S. familes and wealthiest 20 percent of U.S. families

Middle 60% Left scale

Top 20% Right scale

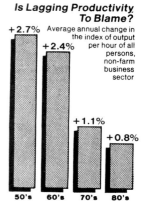

Is Lagging Productivity To Blame?

Average annual change in the index of output per hour of all persons, non-farm business sector

ways to fight off downward mobility. Moonlighting at extra jobs is popular. More married women with young children are working than ever before. With their incomes failing to keep pace with their desires, Americans are putting their credit cards to work hard too, even at stubbornly high interest rates.

Their troubles continue to mount. Business, reeling from toughening competition abroad, is keeping a tight rein on wages and on hiring. Many union workers have lost the cost-of-living adjustment clauses they won during the high-inflation years. And the boom that dazzled Wall Street has left many average folks behind, since they hold no stock except in their pension plans. Even the tax bills passed by the House and Senate do not look like they will give the average American family much relief—under either plan, families with the median household income of $26,-433 would receive tax cuts of only $200.

Economists generally agree that the only way workers can manage to make substantial strides in real earnings during the years ahead is through steady and strong productivity growth—which very few economists are predicting now.

In the short run, this means that unless consumers continue piling up debt to fuel the economy, the nation's economic growth might slow during the rest of 1986 below the predicted 3 percent growth rate—and perhaps even below a paltry 2 percent.

"In the first half, the economy was kept afloat by housing and consumer spending," said Sandra Shaber, an economist with Chase Econometrics. "But the job market has been very slack, and wages and salaries have been extremely weak in the past few months. Unless we get some improvement, there is very little hope for consumer spending and without that the economy could be weaker in the second half."

In the longer run—and more important—a failure to grow could profoundly transform the American standard of living and the nation's economy. Many economists point out that other countries such as Japan and West Germany have achieved higher growth in productivity. Some even suggest that the United States may be starting to undergo the same wrenching economic decline that the British have experienced in recent decades.

"What's been happening in Britain," said Sar Levitan, an economics professor at George Washington University, "is a slow deterioration, so that by now it has the lowest income per capita in the European Community, except for Spain and Portugal. We're starting in that direction."

One stark measure of the change under way is offered by the University of Maryland's Professor Levy. A man who was 30 in 1949 saw his earnings, corrected for inflation, rise by 63 percent by the time he turned 40. But a man who was 30 in 1973 saw his real average earnings decline by 1 percent by the time he hit 40.

"Unlike their parents, who enjoyed a real increase of earnings of 3 percent a year in the 1950's, these young people know they can't expect that now," said Professor Levitan.

Nonetheless, households are stubbornly refusing to change their spending habits. And spirits—despite the grim income statistics—remain high. According to the University of Michigan Survey Research Center, consumer confidence is far higher now than it was during the recent times of double-digit inflation, interest rates and unemployment.

"Consumers are saying that this rather stable economic environment, even if it is not at high rates of growth, is a rather pleasant alternative to the volatile times they've come through," siad Richard T. Curtin, director of consumer surveys at the University of Michigan.

Consumers are often spending more than they can afford, many economists say. The ratio of consumer debt to income has climbed to record heights—and not coincidentally, delinquencies on consumer loans are on the rise.

"A lot of forecasters were saying debt-to-income levels would come down as people retrenched and started pulling down debt," said Jay Schmiedeskamp, director of economic surveys for The Gallup Organization. "But that's not happening." Despite the stagnation in income, he says, consumers are maintaining a "not to worry" attitude.

"People don't want to throw in the towel on the American dream," said A. Gary Shilling, president of an economics consulting firm. "Most Americans seem to regard as their birthright their belief that they will live higher on the hog than their parents. They don't want to admit that what they thought was happening economically no longer is. When they are finally forced to bite the bullet, there could be a tough situation with potential social and political overtones."

Indeed, during the late 1970s, towering inflation rates appeared to be the chief obstacle to achieving the American dream. Growth in real income started its long slide in 1973, the year of the Arab oil embargo. The decade's oil shocks helped produce a wave of price increases that rose faster than people's incomes.

But now that inflation has receded, other problems plague workers. The pressure from foreign competition—along with deregulation of industry—pushed American business to take a tough new attitude about wage passalongs.

"Right now, what is driving down real income is cost control," said Mr. Shilling. He points out that real weekly manufacturing earnings have declined 5 percent since 1978, while construction wages are down 15 percent.

The cost-cutting trend seems to be hitting baby boomers hardest. When companies with seniority rules pare their payrolls, the young get axed first. Two-tier union contracts pay new workers less than experienced ones. Industry is pushing to hire part-time and temporary workers, who are usually young and paid less than full-time workers.

As young workers enter the job market, many can find only low-paid jobs in the service sector.

"For every 25-year-old I read about making $300,000 on Wall Street, there are hundreds of 25-year-olds working as fast-food people or hospital orderlies earning $3.50 an hour," said Ms. Shaber of Chase Econometrics. "It's very skewed. I see this as a big problem. It denies young people the opportunity to earn the middle class income that their parents had."

The rate of home ownership among people under 35 has fallen to 39.7 percent from 43.3 percent in 1981. Many young households have two breadwinners. Among couples aged 25 to 34, the proportion of women working outside the home has soared to 62 percent, more than twice the percentage in 1961. Although this filed certainly raises household income, Joel E. Popkin, a Washington-based economics consultant, said, "A lot of people are asking whether this means that families are necessarily better off."

When asked the reason for lagging income growth, economists speak with rare unanimity: Slow productivity growth is Public Enemy No. 1. "In the long term," said Audrey Freedman, executive director of the Conference Board, "the only way to get wages to increase without inflation is to increase productivity, but we haven't been doing very well in that department."

Productivity gains—defined as increases in output per hour—averaged about 3 percent a year in the 1950's and 1960's, but slowed to under 1 per-

cent a year from 1973 to 1980. In the last five years, the figure has edged up to slightly more than 1 percent a year.

"If productivity continues to grow at the puny rate that it has the last few years, you can't expect that we'll get real raises in income," said Professor Levitan. "You can't get water or money out of a stone."

The productivity slowdown was triggered by the oil shocks and the high inflation of the 1970's. Persistent stagflation discouraged companies from investing in new equipment that would raise productivity. The 1981 tax reduction act was designed to spur productivity by pumping up the savings rate, which presumably would lead to increased investment in plant and equipment. Ironically, the savings rate has fallen—partly because income growth has been so elusive for so many Americans.

As the nation's economy moves from manufacturing to services, the productivity problem compounds. It is generally easier to turn out more widgets per hour than to squeeze more hourly output from lawyers, travel agents or hamburger flippers.

A further obstacle is that pressure from imports has held down industry's capacity utilization rate, thus reducing operating efficiencies. Indeed, high real interest rates have combined with worldwide overcapacity in many industries, such as appliances and chemicals, to discourage many American companies from making major investments in equipment that would hike productivity.

The experts are not optimistic about the outlook for productivity growth. "I really don't see productivity growth coming back to the 3 percent levels that we had in the 1950's," said Douglas P. Handler, a productivity specialist with Wharton Econometrics.

DRI/McGraw Hill forecasts that productivity will grow by four-tenths of 1 percent this year and by slightly under 1.5 percent a year for the remainder of the decade. This is better than in the late 1970's—but half the rate of the 1950's and 1960's.

"There is very little on the horizon that would cause us to be optimistic about productivity improvements over the remainder of this decade," said Robert A. Gough, a senior vice president at DRI.

To spur productivity gains, Professor Levitan urges major government efforts to bolster the savings rate and to encourage research and development. An increased emphasis on worker training and improved labor-management relations would also be helpful.

"The eroding standard of living for much of the population has not surfaced as a public issue," said Professor Levitan. "If and when it does, then there might be more concern about increasing productivity."

131.

ALICE HUGHEY: The Changing Face of Star Wars

President Reagan's "Star Wars" speech on March 23, 1983, inaugurated a new era in the arms race. His proposal that the United States begin research on a Strategic Defense Initiative (SDI) that would in effect provide an impermeable missile shield and thus end forever the fear of a nuclear attack began a process, and a controversy, that was still heating up more than three years later when this article appeared. The author was director of international relations for the League of Women Voters Education Fund.

Source: *The National Voter*, September/October 1986.

THE CHALLENGES OF ballistic missile defense—that is, defending against a Soviet missile attack—are daunting. Theoretically such a system would involve a "layered" defense, in which missiles could be destroyed in all four phases of flight: the boost-phase ($2\frac{1}{2}$-5 minutes), when missile engines are burning and producing noticeable emissions; the post-boost phase (5-8 minutes), when reentry vehicles containing warheads and penetration aids are dispersed; the midcourse phase (25 minutes), when reentry vehicles and thousands of decoys float through space; and the terminal phase (20-50 seconds), when reentry vehicles descend through the atmosphere and head toward their targets.

To accomplish these tasks, a variety of "directed-energy" (lasers and particle beams) and "kinetic-energy" (high-speed rockets and bullets) technologies are being explored. As described by its proponents, an SDI defense might include hundreds of orbiting battle stations equipped with rockets or lasers to attack Soviet missiles as they are fired. Other missiles might be launched from many sites on earth upon warning of an attack. The Fletcher panel, appointed by President Reagan following his March 1983 speech, formulated an SDI plan that envisioned a system of four to five layers containing a number of space-based elements, each layer having a "leakage" or failure rate of about 20 percent.

But new studies by Pentagon contractors of potential SDI "architectures" (the configuration of weapons in a defensive shield) completed in 1985 instead proposed a system of up to seven layers, each with an average leakage rate of as much as 40 percent. In contrast to the Fletcher plan's design for space-based elements, the options laid out in these new studies contained few or no space-based components.

This design shift reflects disappointing results in developing key SDI technologies. A March 1986 staff study conducted at the request of Senators Proxmire (D WI), Johnston (D LA) and Chiles (D FL) reported that the Administration has downgraded, reoriented or given new missions to almost one-half of SDI's weapons projects because of technological difficulties. For example, the space-based chemical laser, which was being considered for the task of boost-phase attack, has been downgraded in importance because, according to the Senate report, "there was too much evidence indicating that space-based chemical laser weapons had serious operational limitations that would make them militarily ineffective."

The neutral-particle beam effort has changed from research as a potential defensive *weapon* to use in discriminating between decoys and warheads in flight. The same fate has befallen the x-ray laser, which is now only being considered in the near-term for discrimination

purposes. Overall, the report concludes, there is a change in emphasis in the directed-energy program from *weapons* to *discrimination* functions.

The free-electron laser, on the other hand, has been upgraded as a potential weapon for boost-phase defense, but serious problems remain, including building the laser beam, projecting it through the atmosphere and constructing the elaborate space-based mirrors off which to reflect the beam.

Contributing to the technical problems is the fact that the Administration has committed itself (and its successor) to a decision by the early 1990s on whether to proceed with full-scale development and deployment of an SDI system. Because of this self-imposed deadline, experiments and research are being driven by the schedule rather than by technological progress, according to the Senate staff report. This means it is likely that "a development decision in the early 1990s would be made not only with significant risks, but also with significant gaps of information."

One of the stiffest technological challenges is making SDI weapons effective against missiles in the boost-phase of flight. Most scientists agree that boost-phase defense is critical. This first line of defense would have two to five minutes to shoot down enemy missiles before they split into separate warheads and decoys. If the Soviets developed "fast-burn" boosters, which burned their fuel within two minutes, the defense would have even less time to react. And if the defense is ineffective in the boost-phase, the problems of defense in the midcourse phase, when missiles have multiplied into warheads, become even more difficult.

In addition, the Soviets are likely to develop countermeasures to a U.S. defensive system such as hardening rocket boosters against attack or spinning them to evade laser beams, developing lasers of their own to attack the U.S. defense and creating decoys and disguises for missiles.

Even presuming that SDI weapons worked, scientists would have to determine how to put the defense in place and maintain it. The Senate staff report concluded that "the transportation-support-logistics system for a comprehensive strategic defense may well be as complex and unprecedented as the defense itself." The most recent studies of potential SDI architectures predicted that 20 to 200 million pounds of SDI material would have to be put into space, a feat requiring from 600 to 5,000 space shuttle flights. The baseline (minimal) architecture reportedly calls for lifting 58 million pounds into orbit at a cost in today's dollars of $87 to $174 billion for transportation alone.

With the recent failures of the *Challenger* space shuttle and the Titan and Delta rockets, the United States now has almost no launch capacity. But even if this capacity is developed, the time involved is staggering. SDI officials have estimated that it could take as long as eight years just to physically deploy the system.

Added to these difficulties is the challenge of designing the computer software to coordinate and operate such an elaborate defense system. A December 1985 report by a Department of Defense panel of computer experts (nicknamed the "Eastport Study Group") singled out this issue as the paramount strategic defense problem. Asked to examine the computer design requirement for an SDI system, the panel concluded that a space-based defense is theoretically feasible but that existing designs are likely to fail because too much emphasis has been placed on weapons and hardware and not enough on the computer software needed to make the system work. According to the authors of the report, "These architectures are not likely to be implemented successfully because they demand excessively sophisticated software and can not be adequately tested."

As significant as these problems are, perhaps the most important set of issues facing U.S. policymakers is the role of SDI in U.S. strategic policy and in arms control.

Behind the existing limits on missile defenses embodied by the 1972 SALT I Anti-Ballistic Missile (ABM) Treaty are the assumptions: (1) that because of the enormous firepower of nuclear warheads, offensive weapons have an insurmountable advantage over defensive systems; (2) that the large-scale deployment of missile defenses would be inherently destabilizing and dangerous, as each side increased its offensive nuclear forces to penetrate or overwhelm the other's defenses; and (3) that an arms race in offensive and defensive weapons would be prohibitively expensive for both sides.

Within the Administration, tough lines already are being drawn over the role of SDI in shaping future U.S. policy. Secretary of Defense Caspar Weinberger and Assistant Secretary Richard Perle have waged a battle within the Administration to reinterpret the 1972 ABM Treaty to permit development and testing of space-based defensive weapons and to reject the SALT II limits on offensive weapons. Others, including Secretary of State George Shultz, have advocated a more restrictive interpretation of the ABM Treaty, at least for the time being, and believe that potential limits on SDI should be discussed with the Soviets in exchange for reductions in offensive weapons.

The Soviet Union recently proposed that both nations continue adhering to the ABM Treaty for 15 to 20 years in exchange for deep reductions in strategic nuclear weapons. Statements made by Soviet officials, including Soviet leader Gorbachev, outside the formal negotiating arena have indicated a willingness to permit laboratory *research* on missile defense programs.

President Reagan has stated in the past that SDI will create incentives for the Soviet Union to negotiate reductions in offensive weapons, particularly Soviet land-based ICBMs (intercontinental ballistic missiles). Implicit in the President's statement is a belief that SDI has some value as an arms control bargaining chip. Yet press reports containing details of the United States' July 25 response to the latest Soviet offer indicate that President Reagan does not want to bargain and that his long-term goal is that of securing Moscow's agreement to *deploy* space-based missile defenses, not to ban or limit them on either side.

New York Times correspondent Leslie Gelb wrote in a July 27, 1986 article, "[Reagan] is giving Moscow a choice: Either stay with the 1972 Anti-Ballistic Missile Treaty, which permits withdrawal from observance and deployment of new systems on six month's notice, or sign a new treaty that would delay the deployments as much as seven years, after which the two sides could deploy jointly or the United States would go ahead alone." In other words, the U.S. position appears to have shifted from describing SDI as a research effort to explore the *feasibility* of deploying defenses to discussing actual *deployment* of defenses.

According to the *New York Times* ar-

ticle, Reagan's letter is also said to state that, while the deployment of a space-based defense is delayed, he intends to proceed with development and testing of related ballistic missile defense technologies. If carried out, these plans will result in the ultimate abandonment of the ABM Treaty in favor of a nationwide defense system.

The recent U.S. decision no longer to be bound by the provisions of the unratified but until-now-observed SALT II limits on offensive weapons also has raised important issues for SDI. If existing limits on offensive weapons are removed, SDI's task becomes even more difficult. Some experts argue that the Soviet Union, because of its existing strategic weapons development programs, is in a much better position to "break out" of the SALT II limits than the United States. Thus, reneging on the SALT limits now may result in a much larger Soviet offensive threat . . . .

Three years after the President's introduction of Star Wars, the United States by its actions has moved sharply away from the SALT I ABM Treaty and SALT II arms control framework. In so doing, it has rejected the fundamental assumptions behind the ABM Treaty's limits on missile defenses—that offense always beats defense, that missile defenses are destabilizing and that arms races in both offensive and defensive weapons are prohibitively expensive.

While discarding and dismantling the existing arms control framework in order to pursue SDI, the Administration appears to be be trying to persuade the Soviets to deploy nationwide defenses along with the United States. The most recent U.S. proposal suggests that any future arms control agreements should be based on some mix of offensive and defensive weapons.

But if the original assumptions behind the SALT agreements remain valid—and there is no historical or current evidence to suggest otherwise—the dramatic shift away from the existing arms control framework that is reflected in the Strategic Defense Initiative may signal the onset of an uncontrollable escalation of the nuclear arms race and the end of arms control.

132.

STEPHEN M. WALT: Reagan Has Fooled Us Again

The meeting in Reykjavik, Iceland, between President Ronald Reagan and Soviet leader Mikhail S. Gorbachev over the weekend of October 10–12, 1986, roused high hopes but then flattened them when it was announced that the two leaders had been unable to agree on anything, most notably on real arms cuts the likes of which had not been proposed for years. After the meeting Gorbachev blamed Reagan and Reagan blamed Gorbachev, and it was hard to tell who was right, if either was. There was more than a sneaking suspicion among many Americans, however, that Reagan had not been so disappointed by the impasse as he claimed. Such at least was the opinion of author Walt, a professor of politics and international affairs at Princeton University.

Source: *Chicago Tribune*, October 23, 1986.

WE HAVE BEEN HAD. Not by the Russians, but by our own President. More than anything else, the summit meeting at Reykjavik reveals how successfully the Reagan administration has duped the American people, their congressional representatives and the Democratic opposition. Time and time again, the President has tricked his opponents into believing that he was just waiting for the right moment to make a deal. But when that moment came—when Mikhail Gorbachev offered us something for virtually nothing—Ronald Reagan's true colors showed: He got up and left the room.

The debacle in Iceland—and the propaganda blitz that has been marshaled to explain it away—is not unique. It should be seen as one more episode in the administration's long campaign to avoid an arms control agreement. During its first two years, the administration responded to public pressure by making a series of one-sided proposals that obviously were calculated to ensure Soviet rejection. Meanwhile, it added several thousand strategic warheads to the American inventory, claiming that the Soviets would not negotiate seriously unless we built up. In 1983, the administration overcame congressional opposition to the MX missile by promising to begin a new, sincere approach to negotiations, and by allowing Congress to send "observers" to the Geneva talks. Congressmen who arranged this deal were suckered along with the rest of us: The administration got the MX and then did nothing.

This happened again before the recent summit. Fed up with lame administration excuses, the House passed a series of restrictions on nuclear testing and other strategic programs. But when it came time to go to Reykjavik, the Democrats in Congress quickly caved in so as not to "tie the President's hands." Once again, Reagan got what he wanted. And we saw how much he did with the "free hands" they gave him.

What is most revealing about the Iceland episode is that the administration refused an offer that would have vindicated its entire approach to arms control. Since taking office in 1981, the administration has maintained that real progress in arms reduction required a tough negotiating position and a major American build-up. Suddenly, this seemed to have worked: Gorbachev offered Reagan a deal that was far better than anything Jimmy Carter or Richard Nixon ever imagined. In exchange for substantial reductions, all Gorbachev wanted was an American pledge that we would abide by the ABM treaty for 10 more years. Remember: We have already signed and ratified this agreement, which is intended to be of unlimited duration. Although important details remained unresolved, this was a remarkable breakthrough and an historic opportunity.

Had the President accepted Gorbachev's offer, just imagine what hardliners could have said. You can just hear Richard Perle gloating: "I told you how to negotiate with the Russians. You build up, and you hang tough and eventually they'll cave in." And he would have been right. But when the Soviets finally caved, suddenly it wasn't good enough. By rejecting these Soviet concessions, Reagan and Co. showed that their entire line of argument—that an arms build-up eventually would make reductions easier—was nothing but propaganda to justify a sustained arms race.

Since returning home, of course, the President has sought to blame this fiasco on the Soviet Union. While the Democrats sat and watched, the administration began an all-out campaign to defend the President's "principled" conduct in Reykjavik. According to the polls, it's working: More than twice as many Americans blame Gorbachev for the failure as blame the President.

As in the past, the administration's public relations campaign rests on a web of distortions and errors. Reagan says he rejected the deal because "Star Wars" offers better protection for the American people, but not even the administration's own experts believe it can ever protect our cities. Even if it could, we still would be vulnerable to other delivery systems such as cruise missiles and bombers. The President tells us that the Soviets are way ahead in research on strategic defenses, but most experts believe they are at least five years behind. He asks us to ponder why the USSR wants to keep us "vulnerable." The answer is obvious: Because both sides' security is based on preventing the opponent from attacking by threatening unacceptable retaliation. The President must realize this, or why is his administration spending millions each year on offensive improvements to keep the USSR "vulnerable"? Finally, the President refuses to explain how America's security interests in Europe, the Middle East and elsewhere will be protected from Soviet conventional attack, if the deterrent effect of nuclear weapons is eliminated. Either he hasn't thought this through, or he knows that his dream is a fiction.

Americans should reject this attempt to camouflage the President's blunder. Those who realize the enduring folly of Star Wars must redouble their efforts to expose its weaknesses. And the Democratic Party must regain the courage to challenge the President.

It is obvious that Reagan will never abandon his impossible vision, because Star Wars is primarily a way to avoid arms control rather than a way to achieve it. That is not news, of course, so it is not surprising that he and his associates have accomplished absolutely nothing, or that he walked away in Reykjavik. What is surprising is how well he has fooled us, and especially those in Congress who have given him whatever he wanted. After six years of deceit, we ought to have learned.

133.

DON MCLEOD: Democrats on the Budget Bandwagon

Despite their loss in the 1986 mid-term elections of several state houses, the Democrats emerged from the election with a sense that things were finally turning their way again, after six years of Republican dominance of American politics as a result of the presidency of Ronald Reagan. The Democrats held both the House and the Senate and believed they had a chance for the White House, too. Some Democrats felt that they had a good chance to take over the powerful political center, with the Republicans hedged in on the right. Their maneuvers are described in the following article.

Source: *Insight*, November 10, 1986.

UNLIKELY AS IT MAY seem for a party that was successfully tagged as irresponsible with the nation's coffers by Ronald Reagan, the national economy has become the No. 1 issue for those Democrats who are trying to find new directions for a party that has lost four of the last five presidential elections.

Most parts of the economy are doing well under the Reagan administration, and the president's personal popularity provides support for his economic policy. Still, the Democrats are betting that the popularity of the president outweighs the popularity of his policies. "There is this nagging concern," says Democratic National Committee Chairman Paul Kirk. "I'm clear that the one thing that people have is a nagging concern that this is a uniquely popular president who has left uniquely large problems in terms of debts and deficits and the real security of the country, and they're going to ask, 'What's next?' "

The first toehold for climbing Democrats is the huge federal budget deficit, which has been running at about $200 billion a year. Even under the knife of the Gramm-Rudman-Hollings balanced budget law, this fiscal year's deficit target is $144 billion.

So far, however, the deficit has

not played well as an issue for the Democrats. After all, the House is ultimately in charge of the nation's purse strings, and it has been dominated by the Democrats. But with the end of the Reagan presidency in sight, they think concerns about the deficit will gain currency. The public still trusts Reagan, they feel, but it is not so sure about what will happen when he is no longer president and the deficit remains. . . .

After the rhetoric, however, Democrats are a little short on solutions other than the tax reform and budget balancing laws already adopted. They have successfully made Pentagon waste a catchy topic, and the House caucus pledges "a balance in spending cuts between guns and butter." However, other Democrats have been calling for a drastic improvement in U.S. conventional defenses, a hugely expensive project that would result in a Pentagon budget increase, not a diminution.

Former Virginia Gov. Charles S. Robb is among the few who will bite the real bullet and say taxes are going to have to be raised sooner or later. Since a pledge to raise taxes was deadly to 1984 presidential nominee Walter F. Mondale, most Democrats are treading softly around this one.

Robb alone has said the sacrosanct entitlements, chief among which is Social Security, will have to be contained. The Democratic Policy Commission, an official party body chaired by former Utah Gov. Scott M. Matheson, sidestepped this issue.

The Democrats think their hottest issue is foreign trade and protectionism. . . . The Democratic approach to trade begins with demands that the United States do more to promote world economic growth, beginning with relief for the debt-ridden Third World. That relief will help defuse Third World debt problems and get debtor nations to buy U.S. goods again.

The rest of the program is contained largely in the 1986 Trade Expansion Act cosponsored by Sen. Lawton Chiles and Rep. Daniel A. Mica. It stalled in the busy 99th Congress, but it is providing talking points and ammunition for Democrats anxious to show both local and national constituencies that they are trying to do something to improve the economic picture.

The Floridians' bill would require the U.S. trade representative to take vigorous action against competing nations that deal unfairly with U.S. products and would provide various forms of support for domestic manufacturers having a difficult time trading in the world market.

The Reagan administration is firmly opposed to this approach, in the name of the free trade that is central to its overall economic philosophy. But in pockets of the nation where the loss of overseas sales and the encroachment of foreign products have caused business and plant closings and the loss of jobs, Democrats are finding receptive ears for their proposals. The difficulty for them at this stage is that the problem is localized and has not yet become a national issue in the minds of most voters.

The economic area in which the party sees the most promise for its own future is in the rapidly and radically changing nature of the country's whole economic order: the increase in two wage-earner families, the swap of high-paying industrial jobs for lower-paying service sector jobs, the constant displacement of workers, the permanent loss of traditional standby industries.

"Ours is a world of change," says the Matheson report. "People leave as jobs dry up, and new people move in as new industries are born. Housing developments, new schools, new business facilities are going up in some cities and regions, while in others, homes are sold at fire-sale prices, factories are abandoned, schools close. In some places, a spirit of optimism prevails as new possibilities are unleashed. In others, fear takes over as people struggle to maintain communities that have been home since they were born."

The real problem is not that pervasive yet, but such things are happening in localized areas. The question is whether it will spread and get worse. The Republican response to this situation is that Reaganomics has the country in a bounding recovery and that in time free market entrepreneurs, spurred by friendly government and lower taxes, will produce enough growth to offset the problems of a changing economy.

The Democrats have remedies of their own, and most involve some government intervention to help people in need—although there is an unusually large element (for Democrats) of private sector approaches in their program.

"For an increasing number of families, now approaching 50 percent, the second income has become a necessity," the Matheson report says.

The Democrats propose a variety of approaches to provide care for latchkey children. They also favor flexible hours in the workplace to allow families more time together, tax breaks for families and more moderate interest rates for families seeking homes—though how such policies would be implemented is a bit vague.

They hope to capitalize on the instability felt by many in the modern economy by proposing measures to allay their fears and prepare them better for future challenges. The Matheson report concludes: "People entering the work force today can expect to have as many as three careers and six or seven jobs."

This, say the Democrats, will be too much for individuals—no matter how conscientious and determined they may be—to handle alone. Even if the supply-side Republicans do produce the string of new jobs they promise, the worker must be prepared for them, the Democrats say. Doing this not only will require retraining but also continuing lifelong education.

Their other suggestions include portable pension funds that allow workers changing jobs to retain their retirement security.

The touchiest issue is one that Robb first broached in a speech at Hofstra University in April: what to do about those still left in the economic cellar despite the war on poverty and the Reagan Revolution.

"America faces a new social dilemma," Robb said. "It is the rise of a dependent, demoralized and self-perpetuating underclass in our cities—several million Americans who are drifting farther and farther from the economic and social mainstream of our nation. For the first time in our history, the bottom segment of our society has become immobile." . . .

Robb called for a new form of assistance built on self-discipline and hard work on the part of recipients but promising opportunity and upward mobility. While this sounds too much like workfare for some libertarian-minded Democrats, others have hailed it as an alternative to past failure.

134.

Adam Platt: The Japanese Look Is Here to Stay

In the late twentieth century Japanese products—autos, cameras, electronic gear—flooded the American market, and the United States struggled to find the solution for a trade deficit with Japan in the tens of billions of dollars annually. But Japan not only exported manufactured goods and technological expertise to America but had a strong cultural resonance with the West as well. In addition to Japanese microelectronics, the author notes that Americans began cultivating a taste for sushi, kabuki theater, and Japanese fashion designers.

Source: *Insight*, November 3, 1986.

Oblivious to the power chatter and tony suits at the Taro sushi bar on Madison Avenue in Midtown Manhattan, Eleanor hunkers down to her noonday meal. Raised in the Borough Park area of Brooklyn on pasta and scungili, she has, in the past three years, acquired a taste for raw fish. "Isn't it sushi that the yuppies are supposed to go for?" she asks. "I hear it is supposed to be healthful. I am not into it from that aspect, but that's what I understand."

Eleanor is no yuppie. Nor does she spend much of her time in health clubs. Heavyset, ebullient, she comes downtown because her job as a conference organizer brings her there. *Toro* (tuna belly) and *hamachi* (yellowtail), octopus and salmon skin—Eleanor knows and loves them all. "It's pretty, it's interesting and it's better than a burger or fried chicken for lunch." So busy is she eyeing the *sushiya* (sushi chef) at work preparing her tuna that she forgets to remove her blue raincoat. "I'm hooked," says Eleanor. "Yes, definitely."

Bernard Portelli is hooked in a more elemental way. He requires the staff of Okyo, his hair salon in Washington's trendy Georgetown, to wear black. He has had his hair in a ponytail since 1983, "the beginning," he says, "of my Japanese mind." The store's walls are washed white, the clean, open layout modeled along sparse Japanese lines. Patrons can watch Tokyo fashion shows on Sony monitors while having their hair colored or permed. During facials they can stare at the shoji ceiling, made from rice paper and plywood. "The Japanese look is not trendy; it is here to stay," he says. . . . If anything, the influence will be stronger in the years to come." Portelli holds up a tapered calligraphy brush, which he uses to remove hair from his customers' shoulders. "It is both simple and handsome to look at." He holds up a bulky Western hairbrush. "Which would you rather use? In Europe they make things attractive. In the United States they make them useful. Only in Japan do they do both."

Portelli says he abandoned his native France three years ago, selling his three shops in Paris. "French style—it's over. There's nothing new, nothing in food, nothing in clothes. They're following the Japanese; that's all they can do." He presents his booming business as evidence of this. "In the beginning [the customers] thought it was a bit empty, but now they like it," he says. "It's not crowded, the colors are soft. They come in uptight and leave peaceful and relaxed."

He has even visited Japan. "Once," he says with a smile. "Too crowded."

William Watts calls the phenomenon "food, fashion and crossword puzzles." His company, Potomac Associates, has been tracking U.S. attitudes toward Japan and the rest of Asia for the past decade. While popular perceptions of the country still hinge largely on economic production and policy, there is what he calls "the softer side" shaping local attitudes. "Every crossword puzzle I do . . . contains some Japan-related clue. 'Japanese sash'—obi. 'Japanese school of meditation'—Zen. What that says is that American people are now supposed to know these things."

Japanese products, long present in garages and game rooms throughout the United States, have begun making further inroads into the American psyche. California rolls, Kikkoman soy sauce, teriyaki marinade and the flip-flop sandal have taken their place beside minibikes, meditation and the sliding door. They have transcended import status, becoming part of the everyday pattern of American life.

Cultural infatuation with Japan, long a coastal phenomenon, has begun creeping toward the heartland. According to food writer Barbara Kafka, some of the best yellowtail tuna in the country can be had in Aspen, Colo. Lesser samples can be found as far afield as Columbus, Ohio.

In the past 10 years, Japan societies have sprouted up in St. Louis and Atlanta. According to the Modern Language Association, college enrollment in Japanese language classes has risen some 40 percent since the beginning of this decade, making it one of the fastest-rising languages of study in the country.

"Japan is a national issue," says Watts. "It's fed into our culture now." Booming trade relations, continued domestic economic penetration by Japanese firms and the ease of trans-Pacific travel and communications have facilitated this process. In polls conducted for Potomac Associates by The Gallup Organization, Japan's "dependability" now rates, in the American mind, with that of many European countries. "Japan is perceived by most Americans as having improved their lives," says Watts. "It has brought them cars, food, fashions and all the rest, and there is a lot of respect."

To some, none of this is news. On both coasts, fashionable folk for several years have been wandering the East Village and Los Angeles's Melrose Avenue in spare, voluminous costume either purchased from or inspired by Japanese designers. Most months they will take in a film by Ozu or Kurosawa, or possibly a Japanese-related production at La Mama in New York. In the evening many will return to their spare, floor-lit apartments. They may mix some tea or browse through a volume of Basho. And when at last their day is done, they will lay their heads to rest on *futons*, mattresses that have been made in the U.S.A.

Much of Japan's high cultural profile, particularly in areas of design, food and fashion, is generated in Tokyo.

Large Japanese corporations are sanitizing their moves into U.S. markets by sponsoring cultural extravaganzas such as the recent "Focus on Japan" in Los Angeles. "It's a pretty harmless way of getting mileage," says a Los Angeles businessman. "They think that once Americans grasp the Japanese point of view, not just culturally but across the board, we will come around to agreeing with Japan's [economic] policy."

On a different plane, Tokyo designers have been pursuing import strategies with as much fervor as their industrial counterparts. "They are very curious about the Western aesthetic," says Julian Tomschin, fashion director of home furnishings for Bloomingdale's department stores. "They are very curious about what it is we want and why we want it." This curiosity, he says, is the product of economic strategies as sophisticated as those pursued by the great Japanese trading houses. "It is almost as if they held a conference, sometime in the 1960s, and said, 'We will become international design leaders.' " . . .

Cultural events have had more success. Two summers ago, Japanese sumo wrestlers sold out Madison Square Garden in New York three days straight, something the Knicks basketball team has rarely been able to do. Kabuki theater, which for decades played to small elite audiences in this country, now regularly plays to packed houses.

"It's being treated like real theater," says Peter M. Grilli of the Japan Society in New York. "The audiences read the notes. They cry at the right moments. They are clearly being moved." . . .

Across town, on Seventh Avenue, Japan has had a more fundamental impact. "Japanese fashion has had an enormous effect in this country," says Diane Benson, proprietor of the Diane B. fashion boutiques. "Ten years ago Issey Miyake [fashion] was an alien idea in every way, shape or form. Today even the French designers will be the first to give credit to the Japanese for a kind of breakthrough in freedom. It has happened in the minds of editors and buyers over the last five years. It was a pioneering idea, and it came from Japan." Tinges of the Japanese sensibility show up in the loose flannel trousers of television's Don Johnson, the clothes of Giorgio Armani and Calvin Klein—the latter's material is made in Japan—and in the more extreme designs of hot U.S. designers such as Donna Karan.

"Of all the people it has affected, I suppose the person who has used it best is Karan," reports Dianne Benson, who also runs designer Rei Kawakubo's Comme des Garcons boutique in SoHo. "The clothes don't have any structure. They can be twisted and draped; there is a general absence of color, a tendency toward black or gray or navy blue."

"They are not just clothes," insists choreographer Lucinda Childs. "Potentially, they dictate a whole style of life." She thinks the impact of Japanese fashions is "absolutely extraordinary" and is not confined to aesthetics. "They affect how people move, how they feel about their bodies."

Japanese food, some Americans will swear, has become just as pervasive. "Over the last 20 years," says Elizabeth Andoh, author of "An American Taste of Japan," "I have seen a tremendous change from people who could not define general Oriental food to Americans who probably during a week eat one or more Japanese meals. In terms of those who, years ago, maybe once a year had a Japanese meal, now a large number of their meals at home are going to be Japanese-based." . . .

Japanese food is still, Andoh says, predominantly a restaurant phenomenon in the United States. Fashion and design are equally upscale. Portelli admits that there is no distinctly Japanese way of cutting hair. The substance of his business remains European; only the style is Japanese. Nor is it likely that Eleanor will ever take raw tuna home to her friends in Borough Park.

"I like the Japanese culture; I like their gardens," says interior designer Jay Specter, "but I don't understand their head, and I don't know any white man who does."

135.

ARMS TO IRAN, MONEY TO THE CONTRAS

On November 3, 1986, a Lebanese magazine disclosed that the United States had sent arms to Iran in clear contravention of the Reagan administration's stated policy. After several further disclosures and repeated denials by the President it was admitted that arms had been delivered to Iran with the hope of obtaining Iranian help in freeing American hostages in Lebanon. The action had apparently been taken without the knowledge of Secretary of State Shultz, who said he disapproved of it. On November 25 Reagan announced that he had just discovered that funds obtained from the sale of arms to Iran had been transferred, through a Swiss bank account, to the contras in Nicaragua. There ensued an outcry against the administration and even against the President, who had previously been for the most part immune to criticism. Reprinted here are an article by columnist Jon Carroll that appeared the day after Reagan's TV speech in which he blamed the media for spoiling his plan to free the hostages, and the text of the President's statement of November 26, conceding that improprieties had occurred.

Sources: *San Francisco Chronicle,* November 14, 1986.

Presidential Documents, Week Ending November 29, 1986.

JON CARROLL:
A. REMEMBER THE PLUMBERS?

REMEMBER THE PLUMBERS? They plugged the leaks in the Nixon White House. They were both secret and secretive. They planted the bug that led to the burglary that led to the arrests that led to the payoffs that led to the coverup that led to the hearings that led to the firings that led to the resignation that toppled the house that Dick built.

Cultural fallout from that event included events as diverse as the acting debut of G. Gordon Liddy and the founding of the Betty Ford Center.

So now we have the New Improved Plumbers. They don't have a cute name anymore; they have a nice bureaucratic title: the National Security Council.

But, like the Plumbers, they deal in paranoia. They don't trust anyone but a few presidential aides. They don't trust Congress; they don't trust the CIA; they don't trust the Defense Department; they don't trust the State Department.

They lie; they sneak; they deny.

Most of all, they don't trust the Constitution. The system of checks and balances central to the American government is perceived as a nuisance. They'd rather make policy by themselves; so much easier, so much more . . . efficient.

And when they get in trouble, they blame the press. Just like the original Plumbers.

So here's what the New Plumbers did. They shipped arms to Iran, despite our policy of not dealing with terrorists, despite our support of Iraq in its war with Iran, despite everything.

Then they got found out. So Larry Speakes, designated mouthpiece, announced that "speculative" press reports "dashed our hopes" of freeing more hostages.

Why? Surely not because the government of Iran was upset. The publicity for them was golden. The revelations proved that the American government was duplicitous; that it lied to its own people.

Not only that, it proved that terrorism does in fact work; that kidnaping Americans is a great way to get weapons and money. And it strengthened Iran's position within the Moslem world as a heroic nation capable of bending the mighty American Satan to its will.

No, the only folks hurt by the press revelations were the New Plumbers. Their ability to arrange secret deals was reduced; their accountability was increased. No wonder they were upset.

The Nixon plumbers, it turned out, were a bunch of insecure, brainless creeps. The New Plumbers are the same, except more powerful and more dangerous.

They might have gotten their own way. They could have discussed the options with members of their own administration and with leading Republicans on Capitol Hill. They might even have carried the day; releasing hostages is a popular political stance.

But they were afraid of debate, afraid of dissent. Like their opposite numbers in the Kremlin, they prefer unilateral decisions and secret negotiations.

So once again, Americans are in the position of being ashamed of their own government. Once again, Americans have been betrayed by closet monarchists supported by the president.

Once again, the White House stands in voluntary isolation from its own citizens. Even as it did during the Nixon years, the presidency straddles the line between farce and tragedy. Sad but true; true but sad; either; both.

B. THE PRESIDENT'S PRESS CONFERENCE, NOVEMBER 25

LAST FRIDAY, after becoming concerned whether my national security apparatus had provided me with a security, or a complete factual record with respect to the implementation of my policy toward Iran, I directed the Attorney General to undertake a review of this matter over the weekend and report to me on Monday.

And yesterday, Secretary Meese provided me and the White House chief of staff with a report on his preliminary findings. And this report led me to conclude that I was not fully informed on the nature of one of the activities undertaken in connection with this initiative. This action raises serious questions of propriety.

I've just met with my national security advisers and Congressional leaders to inform them of the actions that I'm taking today. Determination of the full details of this action will require further review and investigation by the Department of Justice.

Looking to the future, I will appoint a special review board to conduct a comprehensive review of the role and procedures of the National Security Council staff in the conduct of foreign and national security policy.

I anticipate receiving the reports from the Attorney General and the special review board at the earliest possible date. Upon the completion of these reports, I will share their findings and conclusions with the Congress and the American people.

Although not directly involved, Vice Adm. John Poindexter has asked to be relieved of his assignment as assistant to the President for national security affairs and to return to another assignment in the Navy. Lieut. Col. Oliver North has been relieved of his duties on the National Security Council staff.

I am deeply troubled that the implementation of a policy aimed at resolving a truly tragic situation in the Middle East has resulted in such controversy. As I've stated previously, I believe our policy goals toward Iran were well founded. However, the information brought to my attention yesterday convinced me that in one aspect, implementation of that policy was seriously flawed.

While I cannot reverse what has happened, I am initiating steps, including those I've announced today, to assure that the implementation of all future, foreign and national security policy initiatives will proceed only in accordance with my authorization.

Over the past six years, we've realized many foreign policy goals. I believe we can yet achieve, and I intend to pursue, the objectives on which we all agree—a safer, more secure and stable world.

INDEX

Note: An asterisk (*) following a proper name indicates that the person is the author of one or more selections in this volume. In the case of multiple references, the more important ones are listed first.